Psychology
Concepts and Connections

Seventh Edition

Spencer A. Rathus
New York University

THOMSON

WADSWORTH

Australia · Canada · Mexico · Singapore · Spain · United Kingdom · United States

Psychology
Spencer A. Rathus

Executive Editors:
Michele Baird, Maureen Staudt &
Michael Stranz

Project Development Manager:
Linda de Stefano

Marketing Coordinators:
Lindsay Annett and Sara Mercurio

Production/Manufacturing Supervisor:
Donna M. Brown

Pre-Media Services Supervisor:
Dan Plofchan

Kalina Hintz and Bahman Naraghi

Cover Image
Getty Images*

The Adaptable Courseware Program
consists of products and additions to
existing Thomson products that are
produced from camera-ready copy.
Peer review, class testing, and
accuracy are primarily the responsibility
of the author(s).

Psychology / Spencer A. Rathus –
Seventh Edition

ISBN 0-495-15864-X

International Divisions List

Asia (Including India):
Thomson Learning
(a division of Thomson Asia Pte Ltd)
5 Shenton Way #01-01
UIC Building
Singapore 068808
Tel: (65) 6410-1200
Fax: (65) 6410-1208

Australia/New Zealand:
Thomson Learning Australia
102 Dodds Street
Southbank, Victoria 3006
Australia

Latin America:
Thomson Learning
Seneca 53
Colonia Polano
11560 Mexico, D.F., Mexico
Tel (525) 281-2906
Fax (525) 281-2656

Canada:
Thomson Nelson
1120 Birchmount Road
Toronto, Ontario
Canada M1K 5G4
Tel (416) 752-9100
Fax (416) 752-8102

UK/Europe/Middle East/Africa:
Thomson Learning
High Holborn House
50-51 Bedford Row
London, WC1R 4L$
United Kingdom
Tel 44 (020) 7067-2500
Fax 44 (020) 7067-2600

Spain (Includes Portugal):
Thomson Paraninfo
Calle Magallanes 25
28015 Madrid
España
Tel 34 (0)91 446-3350
Fax 34 (0)91 445-6218

Custom Contents

Chapter Outlines

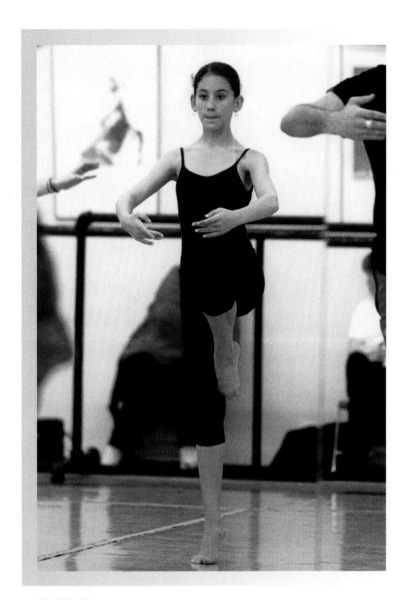

TO TAYLOR,

The youngest of the Rathi

Brief Contents

Contents

9 *Motivation and Emotion* 334

11 *Personality: Theory and Measurement* 412

12 *Psychological Disorders* 452

Features

Controversy in Psychology

A Closer Look

Self-Assessment

In Review Charts

Preface

My favorite psychology professor told the class, "You probably judge how well you did in the course by your grade. I judge how well *I* did in the course in terms of how many additional psychology courses you sign up for."

It's my turn. Users of this textbook will judge what they have obtained from it in various ways. I will consider myself to have been successful if it inspires students to take additional courses in psychology.

I had several goals in writing this introductory textbook: They include painting psychology as the rigorous science it is, teaching students how to think critically, and introducing students to the various fields of psychology and the concepts they investigate. I wanted to present this material in a concise, yet thorough fashion. It was also essential to me to inspire students with the subject matter. Thus I used a warm, engaging writing style, including humor and personal anecdotes to help draw readers into the material. I've made sure that the text is closely linked to all the accompanying resources available online and on CD-ROM that enrich and enhance the learning experience in this technological age.

PSYCHOLOGY: CONCEPTS AND CONNECTIONS—MORE THAN JUST A TITLE

All academic disciplines have their own concepts, and psychology is no exception. One of the key tasks of any introductory course is to acquaint students with the basic concepts of the discipline. At the same time, an important goal of an introductory psychology course is to clarify how these concepts apply to students' lives.

Making Learning Connections

Students of introductory psychology are unlikely to be surprised that concepts such as *intelligence, personality, stress, psychological disorder,* and *psychotherapy* are important to the discipline. They may be surprised to learn that psychologists debate whether some familiar concepts, such as *psychoanalysis,* have a place—other than a historic place—in psychology as a science. Students are unlikely to be surprised that the concepts of *personality* and *learning* and *memory* are found in psychology, but they may find that these concepts—as defined and used by psychologists—are not quite what they thought they were. Students may also be somewhat surprised that the very concept they had of the field of psychology—of what psychology *is*—probably makes up less than half of what they will find in this textbook.

All this is very good. Psychology consists of things that are familiar and things that are new. One of the purposes of this course is to set the record straight, to show students what does and what does not belong within the science of psychology.

Making Life Connections

I also believe that it is important to show students how psychology connects with important issues in their own lives. Psychology is not just "out there"; its many concepts provide information and ideas that all students can apply for the benefit of those they care about and themselves. These connections are a major theme throughout the book and are highlighted, as well, in a special "Life Connections" section at the end of every chapter.

Given that the first chapter is about psychology as a science, it should come as no surprise that the "Life Connections" section focuses on distinguishing between true sciences such as psychology, chemistry, and physics, and false sciences (called *pseudo-sciences*) like clairvoyance and astrology.

Consider two more examples of "Life Connections." Chapter 4 is about "Sensation and Perception"—how people make sense of the world in which they dwell. The "Life Connections" section in that chapter is about a fortunate and unfortunate aspect of sensation and perception: pain—how and why we experience pain (it serves a positive function as well as being a, well, pain), and what we can do to alleviate pain. After reading this section, you will see that you may go to the psychology cabinet as well as the medicine cabinet for relief.

Chapter 9 is about the closely related topics of "Motivation and Emotion." The chapter discusses one of our most pressing motives—the hunger drive. The chapter's "Life Connections" section discusses problems connected with what—for too many people—is a perpetual battle with the hunger drive. It explores reasons why too many people in the United States overeat and why a significant minority eat too little. Either extreme carries significant health risks, and the section also offers concrete advice as to what to do about these problems.

Thinking Critically About Controversies in Psychology—And in Life

Another goal of this course is to show that psychologists, like other scientists, are open minded. They thrive on debate. They do not even necessarily agree on the definitions of the topics they discuss.

As we look more deeply into the field of psychology, we will see that it is rife with controversy. For example, psychologists do not even universally agree on the definition of *psychology*. When we approach the topic of learning, we will similarly see that experts in that field disagree as to how to define *learning*. Later we will see that psychologists disagree as to what *intelligence* is and as to whether there is one kind of general intelligence or there are several "intelligences." As if this were not enough, we will see that there is also major controversy over the origins of intelligence.

Again, all of this is very good. Scientific debate is not to be confused with pointless arguments. Honest debate helps psychologists—and you—come ever closer to the truth. You may come away from this course having memorized some standard definitions of concepts such as *psychology, learning,* and *intelligence;* however, it is more important that you come away from this course with an understanding of the true scientific nature of psychology and of the controversies in psychology. What is most important is that you be able to think about these controversies—and about controversies in other areas of your life—*critically.* In a world where too many individuals blindly follow the demands of authority figures, the value of critical thinking cannot be stressed too highly.

Come into this course as you will. Leave this course as a skeptic. Believe nothing until you have had an opportunity to see and evaluate the evidence—for yourself.

Three Ways to Make the "Connections": Book, CD-ROM, and Web Site

Clearly, learning is not a passive process—the more ways students can get involved, the more they're likely to learn and remember. I've emphasized throughout this book ways to get students involved, by encouraging them to go the accompanying *Connections* CD-ROM for animations, videos, tutorials, and interactive self-assessments, to go to the Web site for interactive versions of the pedagogical tools in the book as well as links out to the greater world of the discipline; and to approach the subject through the active learning system that informs the entire text.

PQ4R—A COMPLETE PEDAGOGICAL SYSTEM FOR MAKING LEARNING CONNECTIONS

The active learning system that is integral to this textbook—PQ4R—is intended to create "learning connections"—that is, connections between the text and the student that facilitate learning and retention. The acronym PQ4R refers to Preview, Question, Read, Reflect, Review, and Recite—a method related to the work of educational psychologist Francis P. Robinson. This pedagogical system discourages students from believing that they are learning sponges. After all, sponges need merely passively sit in a pool of water to soak it up. The PQ4R method stimulates students to *actively* engage the subject matter. Students are encouraged to become *proactive* rather than *reactive*.

PQ4R is more than the standard built-in study guide. It goes well beyond a few pages of questions and exercises that are found at the ends of the chapters of many textbooks. It is an integral part of every chapter. It flows throughout every chapter. It begins and ends every chapter, and it accompanies the student page by page, and out to the book-specific Web site and accompanying *Connections* CD-ROM.

PowerPreview®

Previewing the material helps shape students' expectations. It enables them to create mental templates or "advance organizers" into which they categorize the subject matter. Each chapter of *Psychology: Concepts and Connections, Brief Version* previews the subject matter with PowerPreviews that outline the sections in each chapter but also do much more. They are made up of provocative statements and questions that give students a sense of what each section covers, often in an entertaining manner. They also speak directly to students in personal ways.

Here are some items from three PowerPreview chapter openers:

Chapter 2: Biology and Behavior

- Charles Darwin was nearly excluded from the voyage that led to the development of his theory of evolution because the captain did not like the shape of his nose.
- A single brain cell can send out hundreds of messages each second—and manage to catch some rest in between.
- If a surgeon were to stimulate a certain part of your brain electrically, you might swear in court that someone had stroked your leg.

Chapter 7: Memory: Remembrance of Things Past—and Future

- What does a penny look like? Are you sure?
- A woman who could not remember who she was automatically dialed her mother's phone number when the police gave her a telephone.
- You may always recall where you were and what you were doing on the morning of September 11, 2001.

Chapter 14: Social Psychology

- Do "opposites attract" or do "birds of a feather flock together"?
- Most people tend to obey authority figures. (Are you one of them?)
- Nearly 40 people stood by and did nothing while a woman was being stabbed to death.

Question

Devising questions about the subject matter, before reading it in detail, is another feature of the PQ4R method. Writing questions gives students goals: They attend class or read the text *in order to answer the questions.* Questions are placed in all primary sections of the text to help students use the PQ4R method most effectively. They are printed in **blue.** When students see a question, they can read the following material in order to answer that question. If they wish, they can also write the questions and answers in their notebooks, as recommended by Robinson.

Read

Reading is the first R in the PQ4R method. Although students will have to read for themselves, they are not alone. The text helps them by providing lively and motivating PowerPreviews that help them organize the material and by presenting the subject matter in clear, stimulating prose. A running glossary defines key terms in the margin, near where the terms appear in the text. Concepts are developed in an orderly fashion and built one upon the other.

The writing style is "personal" in that it speaks directly to the student and employs humor and personal anecdotes as ways of motivating and stimulating students. All in all, *Psychology: Concepts and Connections, Brief Version* aims to be as alive and as relevant as possible, to leave the reader interested and refreshed.

Reflect

Students learn more effectively when they *reflect* (the second "R" in PQ4R) on what they are learning. Psychologists who study learning and memory refer to reflection on subject matter as *elaborative rehearsal.* One way of reflecting on a subject is to relate it to things students already know about, whether it be academic material or events in their own lives (Willoughby et al., 1994[1]). Reflecting makes the material meaningful and easier to remember (Woloshyn et al., 1994[2]). It also makes it more likely that students will be able to *apply* the information to their own lives (Kintsch, 1994[3]). Through effective reflection, students can embed material firmly in their memory so that rote repetition is unnecessary.

Because of the value of reflection, "Reflect" boxes are placed within or adjacent to the main narrative. Some of them ask students to compare what they are reading with the ideas they had before they took the course. Students can also use the Web site bulletin board to post their reflections for class discussion.

Review

Review sections (the third "R" in PQ4R) follow major sections in the text and are provided in interactive form on the book's Web site, with answers listed in Appendix C. They include two types of items that foster active learning and retention. The first type of item is in a fill-in-the-blank format. Students are asked to *produce,* not simply *recognize,* the answer. For example, the review on "The Endocrine System" in the chapter on "Biology and Behavior" reads as follows:

(34) The _____ secretes hormones that regulate the pituitary gland. (35) The pituitary hormone _____ regulates maternal behavior in lower animals and stimulates production of milk in women. (36) The thyroid hormone _____

---

[1]Willoughby, T., Wood, E., & Khan, M. (1994). Isolating variables that impact on or detract from the effectiveness of elaboration strategies. *Journal of Educational Research, 86,* 279–289.

[2]Woloshyn, V. E., Paivio, A., & Pressley, M. (1994). Use of elaborative interrogation to help students acquire information consistent with prior knowledge and information inconsistent with prior knowledge. *Journal of Educational Psychology, 86,* 79–89.

[3]Kintsch, W. (1994). Text comprehension, memory, and learning. *American Psychologist, 49,* 294–303.

affects the metabolism. (37) Corticosteroids are secreted by the adrenal _____ and promote development of muscle mass and increase resistance to stress. (38) Epinephrine is secreted by the adrenal _____ and is involved in emotional arousal.

The second type of item, "Critical Thinking," includes questions that encourage students to think critically about the subject matter and relate it to the bigger picture. The "Critical Thinking" item in the first review in the chapter on "Consciousness" reads:

Critical Thinking: Is it possible to study the consciousness of another person?

Recite

The PQ4R method recommends that students regularly recite the answers to the questions aloud. Reciting answers aloud helps students remember them by means of repetition, by stimulating students to produce concepts and ideas they have learned, and by associating them with spoken words and gestures (Dodson & Schacter, 2001).[4]

Recite sections are found at the end of each chapter and in an interactive form on the book's Web site. They help students summarize the material, but they are active summaries. They are written in question-and-answer format. To provide a sense of closure, the summaries repeat the questions found within the chapters, and are again printed in **blue** in the book. The answers are concise but include most of the key terms found in the text.

The "Recite" sections in the book are designed in two columns so that students can cover the second column (the answers) as they read the questions. Students can recite the answers as they remember or reconstruct them and then check what they have recited against the answers they had covered in the text. Or they can go to the Web site to get interactive flash cards of the questions and answers. Students should not feel that they are incorrect if they have not exactly produced the answer provided; their individual approach might be slightly different, even more inclusive. The answers provided in the second column are intended to be a guide, to provide a check on students' learning. They are not carved in stone.

FEATURES

Psychology: Concepts and Connections, Brief Version includes a number of features that are intended to enhance learning and foster critical thinking.

"Controversy in Psychology" Feature

The field of psychology does not shy away from controversy, and neither does *Psychology: Concepts and Connections, Brief Version.* Psychologists welcome controversy as a vehicle for enhancing knowledge and stimulating critical thinking.

Some of the controversies exist between psychologists from various schools of psychology. For example, a "Controversy in Psychology" feature in the chapter on learning is titled "How should we define learning?" We see at the outset of the chapter that behaviorists and cognitive psychologists define learning in different ways and that their definitions affect their entire view of the subject matter of learning. We continue the theme with another controversy feature in the same chapter: "Should children be punished for misbehavior?" We see that punishment has many consequences, some of them unintended, and that the issue is more complex than most readers might expect.

Other controversy features address historic issues in psychology. For example, the chapter on psychological disorders contains "Are somatoform disorders the special province of women?" We confront issues surrounding the concept of "hysteria" and the results of research evidence in attempting to arrive at some closure on the matter.

[4]Dodson, C. S., & Schacter, D. L. (2001). "If I had said it I would have remembered it": Reducing false memories with a distinctiveness heuristic. *Psychonomic Bulletin & Review, 8*(1), 155–161.

The controversy feature in the chapter on methods of therapy is "Should health professionals use electroconvulsive therapy?" When we view people receiving electroconvulsive therapy, it looks somewhat barbaric. There are also unanswered questions as to why it works—when it does. But what else should we consider in attempting to solve the controversy?

Still other "Controversy in Psychology" features address the application of psychology in life. For example, in the chapter on motivation and emotion, we address "Is aggression natural?" The discussion addresses political and social issues as well as psychological issues. All in all, this feature and the rest of the text stimulate students to understand that many issues in psychology—and in society at large—are complex and require careful thought. Students can also use the Web site bulletin board to post their responses to the controversies for class discussion.

Emphasis on the Evolutionary Perspective

The importance of various schools of psychology has changed over the generations. In Chapter 1 we see that we can trace psychology's roots to the Golden Age of Greece and beyond. In the early part of the 20th century, there were multiple schools and emphases, including behaviorism (brought to prominence by John B. Watson and others), psychoanalysis (based mainly on the theory of Sigmund Freud), Gestalt psychology (which focused on perception and cognitive processes). In the second half of the 20th century, learning theory broadened to include behaviorism and cognitive views, cognitive–developmental theory (as propounded by theorists such as Jean Piaget and Lawrence Kohlberg) gained importance and humanistic–existential psychology developed (to some degree, as an answer to feelings of alienation following the horrors of World War II). Also, work in cognitive psychology mushroomed in the laboratory and the clinic, and the overlaps of biology and psychology exploded in the forms of neuroscience (the study of the nervous system) and endocrinology (the study of hormones).

By now you will not be surprised to learn that few psychologists would agree as to the relative importance of these various perspectives. But perhaps most would agree that there is a current surge of interest in evolutionary psychology. Psychology today recognizes the influence of evolution not only on physical traits but also on behavior and mental processes. As humans and their ancestors evolved over millions of years, their fitness for survival gained prominence in terms of intelligence and the ability to acquire various skills, as well as in terms of traits such as sharpness of eye, fleetness of foot, and brawn. *Psychology: Concepts and Connections, Brief Version* addresses the impact of the evolutionary perspective in several ways, as suggested, in part, by the chart on the facing page.

"A Closer Look" Features

"A Closer Look" features highlight certain topics, allowing students to pursue them in greater depth. These features can be grouped according to certain themes.

A number of "A Closer Look" features underscore the indispensability of human diversity within the field of psychology. For example, Chapter 1's feature, "Gender, Ethnicity, and Psychology: Real People in the Real World," speaks of the contributions of women and people of color to the development of psychology. Chapter 3's "Aging, Gender, and Ethnicity: Different Patterns of Aging" discusses why women tend to outlive men and why people from certain ethnic groups tend to outlive people from other ethnic groups. Chapter 8's "Socioeconomic and Ethnic Differences in Intelligence" discusses group differences in intelligence and sets the stage for a comprehensive discussion of the genetic and environmental determinants of intelligence. Chapter 12's "The Case of Women and Depression" explores research findings that tend to show that women, as a group, tend to be more depressed than men—and why.

Other "A Closer Look" features stimulate critical thinking. For example, Chapter 6's feature "Contingency Theory" compares and contrasts the behaviorist view of conditioning with a cognitive perspective. Chapter 9's "Just What Do Lie Detectors Detect?" examines what lie detectors actually measure and how these measurements are (or are not) related to lying.

The Evolutionary Perspective in *Psychology: Concepts and Connections, Brief Version*

Chapter 2: Begins with section "Evolution and Evolutionary Psychology: 'Survivor' Is More Than Just a Game"

Chapter 4: The evolutionary perspective on how pain and the location of taste buds are adaptive and promote survival

Chapter 6: Discussion of the evolutionary value of taste aversions, spontaneous recovery, generalization and discrimination, and cognitive learning

Chapter 9: Discussion of evolution and instinct, stimulus motives, aggression, and universal recognition of facial expressions

Chapter 10: Discussion of gender differences in response to threats—such as the (predominantly male?) tendency for "fight or flight" as compared with the (predominantly female?) tendency to "tend and befriend"

Chapter 11: Discussion of the possible roles of evolution in gender typing, gender differences in mate selection, gender differences in pursuit of casual sexual relationships, and sexual aggression

Chapter 12: Discussion of how evolutionary forces might have favored the survival of individuals who were predisposed toward acquiring fears of large animals, spiders, snakes, heights, entrapment, sharp objects, and strangers

Chapter 14: Discussion of the evolutionary benefits of altruism

Still other "A Closer Look" features focus on topics of high interest such as Chapter 2's "Steroids, Behavior, and Mental Processes," Chapter 8's "*Wired*—The Awesome Future of Artificial Intelligence," and Chapter 12's "The Insanity Plea."

Some "A Closer Look" features serve other functions. For example, Chapter 3's "How Child Abuse May Set the Stage for Psychological Disorders in Adulthood" follows the methodology of a key research study in detail. Chapter 4's "Advances in Science? The Case of the Aromatic T-Shirts" is a light-hearted tale of a research study that may sound absurd but that has important implications for evolutionary psychology. Other "A Closer Look" features highlight other topics of interest.

Self-Assessments

Self-assessment features stimulate student interest by helping them satisfy their curiosities about themselves and enhance the relevance of the text to students' lives. These features include:

Chapter 5: Sleep Quiz: Are You Getting Your Z's?
Chapter 8: The Remote Associates Test (a self-test of creativity)
Chapter 11: Do You Strive to Be All That You Can Be? (a self-test of whether or not one tends to be a self-actualizer)
Chapter 13: Do You Speak Your Mind or Do You Wimp Out? The Assertiveness Schedule

All the self-assessments in the text—as well as additional self-assessments—are provided in an interactive format on the *Connections* CD-ROM.

ANCILLARIES

Psychology: Concepts and Connections, Brief Version is accompanied by a wide array of supplements prepared for both the instructor and student. Many are available free to professors or students. Others can be packaged with this text at a discount. For more information on any of the listed resources, please call the Thomson Learning™ Academic Resource Center at 800-423-0563.

For the Instructor

Instructor's Resource Manual Notebook

Written by Cameron John of Utah Valley State College, this manual contains a wealth of instructional aids and resources. Available for the first time in a three-ring binder format, it provides chapter-specific lecture outlines; concept charts; annotated lists of suggested readings, films, and Web sites; and student learning objectives. The manual has a special emphasis on active learning with suggested student activities and projects for each chapter. These activities include ideas for in and out of class, for large lecture classes, and small discussion sections, journal assignments for student reflection. The *Instructor's Resource Manual* includes general teaching strategies, references, ideas for lecture and class discussion, and other helpful materials, such as handout masters. All of these activities and ideas for instruction are organized by major chapter headings to guarantee that the instructor can draw on rich materials for each major section of a given chapter. The manual's *Resource Integration Guide* will help you coordinate the many teaching and learning supplements available for this text. This is available in a three-ring binder or loose-leaf format.

Test Bank

Written by Ann M. Cooper of St. Petersburg Junior College, the test bank consists of 2,000 multiple-choice questions and 280 fill-in questions. Each item is labeled with question type (factual, application, or conceptual), level of difficulty, and page reference.

ExamView® Computerized Testing

Create, deliver, and customize printed and online tests and study guides in minutes with this easy-to-use assessment and tutorial system. ExamView includes a Quick Test Wizard and an Online Test Wizard to guide instructors step by step through the process of creating tests. The test appears on screen exactly as it will print or display online. Using ExamView's complete word processing capabilities, instructors can enter an unlimited number of new questions or edit questions included with ExamView.

Instructor's Edition

Each *Instructor's Edition* of *Psychology: Concepts and Connections, Brief Version* includes a "Resource Integration Guide" to help you seamlessly integrate all of the online, CD-ROM, and print resources offered with this text.

Wadsworth Media Guide for Introductory Psychology

This booklet lists hundreds of video and feature film recommendations for all major topics for the Introductory Psychology course. Each entry has a clear description of the content and length of the video, and select feature film entries also provide discussion questions and specific scene analyses.

Classroom Presentation Tools for the Instructor

Transparency Acetates

Many acetates featuring full-color figures from the text to enhance lecture presentations.

Multimedia Manager for Rathus's *Psychology: Concepts and Connections, Brief Version, 7e:* A Microsoft® PowerPoint® Link Tool

With the one-stop digital library and presentation tool, instructors can assemble, edit, and present custom lectures with ease. The Multimedia Manager contains a selection of digital media from Wadsworth's latest titles in introductory psychology, including figures and tables. Also included are animations, CNN video clips, and preassembled Microsoft PowerPoint lecture slides based on each specific text. Instructors can use the material or add their own material for a truly customized lecture presentation.

CNN Today Videos for Introductory Psychology

Illustrate the relevance of psychology to everyday life with this exclusive series of videos for the introductory psychology course. Jointly created by Wadsworth and CNN, each video consists of approximately 45 minutes of footage originally broadcast on CNN and specifically selected to illustrate important introductory psychology concepts. The videos are divided into short two- to seven-minute segments, perfect for use as lecture launchers or as illustrations of key concepts. Special adoption conditions apply.

CNN Today: Introductory Psychology, Volume I
   (ISBN: 0-534-36634-1)
CNN Today: Introductory Psychology, Volume II
   (ISBN: 0-534-50420-5)
CNN Today: Introductory Psychology, Volume III
   (ISBN: 0-534-50749-2)
CNN Today: Introductory Psychology, Volume IV
   (ISBN: 0-534-50751-4)
CNN Today: Introductory Psychology, Volume V
   (ISBN: 0-534-54905-5)

Psychology Digital Video Library CD-ROM

This CD-ROM provides access to over 100 video clips that feature a broad range of materials, such as classic footage of prominent psychologists, demonstrations and simulations of important experiments, and selections from the *CNN Today* videos.

Wadsworth Psychology Film and Video Library

This large selection of thought-provoking films is available to instructors based on adoption size. Contact your Thomson/Wadsworth representative or Wadsworth Academic Resource Center for a more detailed video list, more information on the video policy, and more information on ordering products from the Wadsworth Film and Video Library.

For the Student

Study Guide

Written by M. Lisa Valentino of Seminole County Community College, the Study Guide is designed to promote active learning through a guided review of the important principles and concepts in the text. The Study Guide is closely aligned with the PQ4R learning model found in the text and is offered free to students with each new book. The materials for each chapter include fill-in-the-blank summaries of every chapter section, reflection "break" matching exercises, key concepts, review multiple-choice and essay questions, and practical Internet and hands-on activities.

Connections CD-ROM

Free with every book, this CD-ROM is customized to support *Psychology: Concepts and Connections, Brief Version.* By using the CD icons in the margin of the text, students can easily navigate to the "Learning" and "Life" connections. "Learning Connections" help students more fully explore key psychological concepts and theories with the aid of tutorials accompanied by videos and animations. The CD features 48 tutorials that provide written and oral narration accompanied by outstanding animations and videos that bring concepts to life. In each chapter of the book, icons in the margins indicate that the topic can be "seen" and "heard" on the CD. For example, in Chapter 2, Biology and Behavior, students are directed to topics such as "The Action Potential," which shows the intricacies of the firing of a neuron through animations, and the "Cerebral Cortex," which helps them better understand the structure and functions of this part of the brain. They also are directed to experiments, such as the classic "Processing of Inverted Visual Stimuli in the Brain" in Chapter 4, Sensation and Perception, which shows a video of a woman who adapts to glasses that turn her visual world upside down. When reading Chapter 12, Psychological Disorders, students are directed to an interview on the CD that features a person suffering from schizophrenia, along with his doctor's discussion of his symptoms. Other topics include "Anatomy of the Eye," "The Ames Room," "Stages of Sleep," "The Basics of Classical Conditioning," "Antipsychotic Drugs and Schizophrenia," and many more.

In addition, students will find a "Life Connections" icon in the book next to each Self-Assessment so they can access the interactive form of these valuable tests. Once they are viewing the CD, they also will see a list of additional Self-Assessments to try. There are 18 Self-Assessments that help students answer questions such as "Why do you smoke?," "Are you blue? The Self-Rating Depression Scale," "Are You Making Yourself Miserable? The Irrational Beliefs Questionnaire," and "The Rathus Assertiveness Scale."

Finally, when the student has completed a particular tutorial, he or she can move directly to the Companion Book Web Site from a link on the CD. There, they will find a wealth of interactive quizzing, audio flash cards, glossary, games, narrated animations, and learning simulations.

Psyk.trek™ for Introductory Psychology: A Multimedia Introduction to Psychology 2.0

Psych.trek's visual learning environment delivers course content in a brand new way that reinforces key concepts. This CD-ROM includes 62 interactive learning modules that present the core content of psychology with real-time video, animated graphics, and hundreds of photos and illustrations. Students using *Psyk.trek* will take part in experiments using simulations and then quiz themselves on the content. *Psyk.trek* also includes interactive concept checks and a multimedia glossary with an audio pronunciation guide.

PsychNow! Interactive Experiences in Psychology 2.0

PsychNow! provides a dynamic, multimedia experience that goes beyond the boundaries of the classroom. Graphics and animations, interesting video clips, interactive exercises, and Web links bring psychology to life. This CD-ROM also allows students to conduct 15 different interactive research experiments in areas such as neurocognition, perception, and memory.

Internet-Based Supplements Resources

InfoTrac® College Edition

With *InfoTrac College Edition,* instructors can stimulate discussion and supplement lectures with the latest developments in introductory psychology. Available as a free option with newly purchased texts, *InfoTrac College Edition* gives instructors and students four months of free access to an extensive database of reliable, full-length articles (not just abstracts) from hundred of top academic journals and popular periodicals. In-text exercises suggest search terms to make the most of this resource.

Wadsworth Psychology Resource Center   http://psychology.wadsworth.com

At Wadsworth's psychology home site, students and instructors have access to a rich array of discipline-specific teaching and learning resources. Learn more about Wadsworth's media offerings through *Teaching and Learning with Technology;* engage in on line Web activities, animations, and simulations at *Cool Stuff;* visit *Careers in Psychology;* hear Wadsworth authors discuss their texts at *Author Insight;* and access the *Connections* book companion site.

Book Companion Web Site for Psychology: Concepts and Connections, Brief Version

The "Connections" book companion site continues the text's primary themes of Life Connections and Learning Connections through features that support the active learning system, PQ4R (Preview, Question, Read, Reflect, Review, Recite):

- *"Review" boxes online:* Students can fill in the review questions in the review boxes throughout each chapter online and get instant feedback.

- *"Reflect" questions online:* The thought-provoking "Reflect" questions that encourage students to apply the concepts they're learning to their own lives are linked to the interactive bulletin board. This allows for class and individual discussion.
- *"Recite" feature online:* Students can check their understanding of each chapter through the interactive version of the chapter summary that is presented through audio flash cards.
- *Interactive quizzing:* These chapter-by-chapter interactive quizzes include multiple-choice, true/false, fill-in-the-blank, matching, essay, and critical thinking questions with a direct-to-professor e-mail function.
- *MediaWorks:* Interactive demonstrations and simulations allow students to directly experience some of the phenomena they are studying.
- *Power Visuals:* Figures from the text are presented in an interactive, drag-and-drop mode for study and drill of key concepts and terms.

WebTutor™ Advantage on WebCT and Blackboard

This Web-based software for students and instructors takes a course beyond the classroom to an anywhere, anytime environment. Students gain access to a full array of study tools, including chapter outlines, chapter-specific quizzing material, interactive games, and videos. With WebTutor Advantage, instructors can provide virtual office hours, post syllabi, track student progress with the quizzing material, and even customize content to meet their needs. Instructors can also use the communication tools to set up threaded discussions and conduct real-time chats. "Out of the box" or customized, WebTutor Advantage provides a powerful tool for instructors and students alike. Also, WebTutor is now available on eCollege. For details about WebTutor, visit http://webtutor.thomsonlearning.com. Click on eCollege to learn more about that option.

NewsEdge

This online news service is moderated by expert editors and allows instructors to scan articles as they arrive or set up a customized news feed that draws the most relevant articles from a wide range of local, national, and international sources. NewsEdge can be customized to deliver the types of articles individual instructors prefer.

MyCourse 2.0

This free online course builder can greatly enhance course administration. With *MyCourse* 2.0, you can easily create a custom course Web site that allows you to assign, track, and report on student progress, load your syllabus, and more. Contact your Thomson/Wadsworth sales representative for details or visit http://mycourse.thomsonlearning.com for more information.

Supplementary Books

There are several other supplementary books that offer help to students.

Challenging Your Preconceptions: Thinking Critically About Psychology, second edition

This paperbound book (ISBN: 0-534-26739-4), written by Randolph Smith, helps students strengthen their critical thinking skills. Psychological issues such as hypnosis and repressed memory, statistical seduction, the validity of pop psychology, and other topics are used to illustrate the principles of critical thinking.

Writing Papers in Psychology: A Student Guide, fifth edition

The fifth edition of *Writing Papers in Psychology* (ISBN: 0-534-52975-5), by Ralph L. Rosnow and Mimi Rosnow, is a valuable "how-to" manual for writing term papers and research reports. This new edition has been updated to reflect the latest APA guidelines. The book covers each task with examples, hints, and two complete writing samples. Citation ethics, how to locate information, and new research technologies are also covered.

College Survival Guide: Hints and References to Aid College Students, fourth edition

This fourth edition of Bruce Rowe's *College Survival Guide* (ISBN: 0-534-35569-2) is designed to help students succeed. Rowe provides valuable tips on how to finance an education, how to manage time, how to study for and take exams, and more. Other sections focus on maintaining concentration, credit by examination, use of the credit/no credit option, cooperative education programs, and the importance of a liberal arts education.

Cross-Cultural Perspectives in Psychology, fourth edition

How well do the concepts of psychology apply to various cultures? What can we learn about human behavior from cultures different from our own? These questions lie behind a collection of original articles written by William F. Price and Rich Crapo. The fourth edition of *Cross-Cultural Perspectives in Psychology* (ISBN: 0-534-54653-6) contains articles on North American ethnic groups as well as cultures from around the world.

Culture and Psychology: People Around the World, second edition

David Matsumoto's unique book (ISBN: 0-534-35436-X) discusses similarities and differences in research findings in the United States and other cultures. By doing so, it helps students see psychology and their own behavior from a broader, more culturally aware perspective.

Psychology Resources on the World Wide Web

This handy guide is designed to serve as a directory for students who may be conducting research via the Internet. The author, Edward P. Kardas, presents an up-to-date, comprehensive book that is organized topically (similar to that of a typical introductory psychology text) and includes a chapter on how to perform research on the Web (ISBN: 0-534-35941-8).

Psychology/Careers for the Twenty-First Century

This 30-page pamphlet describes the field of psychology, as well as how to prepare for a career in psychology. This is available through an agreement with the American Psychological Association and includes a discussion of career options and resources.

ACKNOWLEDGMENTS

It is sometimes thought that writing is lonely work. It is true that writing a textbook such as this requires day upon day of concentration, but I was hardly alone. To begin with, I enjoyed and profited from the advice of my peers, who read painstakingly through earlier drafts of this book and helped me hone it to the work you now hold in your hands. These professors include: Christian D. Amundsen, North Lake College; Beth Arrigo, Central Piedmont Community College; Jeffrey Bartel, Kansas State University; David E. Baskind, Delta College; Julia A. Bishop, Maple Woods Community College; Susan R. Burns, Kansas State University; Saundra K. Ciccarelli, Gulf Coast Community College; Mary Webber Coplen, Hutchinson Community College; Joseph Culkin, Queensborough Community College–The City University of New York; Teddi S. Deka, Missouri Western State College; Susan R. Edwards, Mott Community College; B. J. Hart, Glendale Community College; Mark Kelland, Lansing Community College; Gloria J. Lawrence, Wayne State College; Vicki Lucey, Las Positas College; Laura Madson, New Mexico State University; Joseph Manganello, Gloucester County College; Horace Marchant, Westfield State College; Marnie Moist, St. Francis University; Alinde J. Moore, Ashland University; Russell Ohta, Phoenix College; Brian J. Oppy, California State University–Chico; Debra Parish, Tomball College–North Harris Montgomery Community College District; Michelle L. Pilati, Rio Hondo College; Laura Reichel, Front Range Community College; Theresa Rufrano-Ruffner, Indiana University of Pennsylvania; H. R. Schiffman, Rutgers University; Debra Schwiesow, Creighton University; Carolyn E. Tasa, Erie Community College; Sheralee Tershner, Western New England College; Rhonda G. Trollinger, Guilford Technical Community College; Karen M. Wolford, State University of New York College at Oswego.

Also involved in the text at every step of the process was a fine group of publishing professionals, many "in-house" at Wadsworth/Thomson Learning, and some freelance. These individuals include many who have become old (although most youthful!) friends: Sean Wakely, senior vice president/editorial director; Susan Badger, president/CEO; Eve Howard, vice president/editor-in-chief, social sciences; Sherry Symington, senior development editor; and Michelle Vardeman, technology project manager. I have also enjoyed the opportunity to develop new relationships with individuals at Wadsworth/Thomson Learning: Michele Sordi, senior acquisitions editor; Chris Caldeira, marketing manager; Dan Moneypenny, assistant editor; Laurel Anderson, marketing assistant; Kari Hopperstead, editorial assistant; Stephan Rapley, creative director; and Kirk Bomont, senior production project manager. Others involved in the text include Elizabeth Zuber, permissions editor; Ben Schroeter, composition buyer; Karen Hunt, senior print/media buyer; Roy Neuhaus, interior designer, Roy Neuhaus Design; Lisa Torri, art editor; Margaret Pinette, copyeditor; Sarah Evertson, photo researcher, Image Quest; Precision Graphics and Lori Heckelman, artists; Leoni McVey, indexer; Bill Heckman, proofreader; and Parkwood Composition.

Finally, I would like to acknowledge the support of my family, who, over the years, have refined the arts of knowing when to be there for me and when to leave me to my own devices. They include my wife, Lois Fichner-Rathus, and my daughters, Jill, Allyn, Jordan, and Taylor. Phoebe, my cream-colored standard poodle (don't ask why) has sort of been there for me, always ready to wag her tail and bark for a biscuit. And now and then she forces me to remain healthy by insisting that I take her for a walk.

PowerPreview®

Psychology as a Science

- WHAT IS psychology? And what else?

What Psychologists Do: Fields of Psychology

- IT ISN'T JUST the couch. Psychologists are involved in every aspect of life, from conception through death, from your behavior as an individual to your behavior in a group.

Where Psychology Comes From: A History

- MORE THAN 2,000 years ago, Aristotle wrote a book on psychology, with contents similar to the book you are now holding.

- THE ANCIENT GREEK philosopher Socrates suggested a research method that is still used in psychology.

- AS WILHELM WUNDT lay on his deathbed, his main concern was to analyze the experience of dying.

- JOHN B. WATSON was annoyed when he was asked to explain what a rat thinks while it is navigating a maze.

- IN PSYCHOLOGY, the whole can equal *more* than the sum of its parts.

How Today's Psychologists View Behavior and Mental Processes

- IN THE AGE-OLD STRUGGLE for survival, only the "fittest" (most adaptive) organisms manage to reach maturity and reproduce.

- YOUR THOUGHTS, fantasies, and dreams are made possible by your nervous system.

- COGNITIVE PSYCHOLOGISTS believe that you keep them "in mind."

- HOW MUCH OF HUMAN behavior is built in, and how much is learned?

How Psychologists Study Behavior and Mental Processes

- YOU COULD SURVEY 20 million voters and still not predict the outcome of a presidential election.

- IN MANY EXPERIMENTS, neither the subjects nor the researchers know who is receiving the real treatment and who is not.

Ethical Issues in Psychological Research and Practice

- PSYCHOLOGISTS WOULD NOT be able to carry out many kinds of studies without keeping subjects in the dark about the purposes and methods of the studies.

- IS IT ETHICAL to use animals in experiments for the benefit of people?

Life Connections: Critical Thinking, Science, and Pseudoscience

- A PSYCHOLOGIST COULD write a believable personality report about you without interviewing you, testing you, or even knowing who you are.

Mirror, mirror on the wall,

Who is the fairest of them all?

The answer to this fabled question depends on how you define *fair*. If by *fair* one means beautiful, then one can be talking of the human form in motion, or perhaps of the "face that launched a thousand ships" in the Greek epic.

But if by *fair* one means fair-minded, we voyage into another realm. The fair-minded among us include the critical thinkers and the scientists—those who are willing to challenge an argument, no matter who makes that argument. They are skeptical. They can peer into human nature without needing to support any one theory of human behavior and mental processes. They are willing to say "I don't know."

Among them are the psychologists.

Psychologists observe creativity and destruction and want to know how and why. They observe generosity and selfishness and want to know how and why. Psychologists observe newborns as they develop into creatures who are as large, clever, and talented as we, and they want to know how it all happens and why. Many people, not just psychologists, are intrigued by the mysteries of behavior, but psychologists make the scientific study of behavior their life's work. **Question: What is psychology?**

PSYCHOLOGY AS A SCIENCE

Psychology is the scientific study of behavior and mental processes. Topics of interest to psychologists include the nervous system, sensation and perception, learning and memory, intelligence, language, thought, growth and development, personality, stress and health, psychological disorders, ways of treating those disorders, sexual behavior, and the behavior of people in social settings such as groups and organizations.

Sciences have certain goals. **Question: What are the goals of psychology?** Psychology, like other sciences, seeks to describe, explain, predict, and control the events it studies. Psychology thus seeks to describe, explain, predict, and control behavior and mental processes.

When possible, descriptive terms and concepts are interwoven into **theories.** Theories are formulations of apparent relationships among observed events. They allow us to derive explanations and predictions. Many psychological theories combine statements about behavior (such as eating or aggression), mental processes (such as attitudes and mental images), and biological processes. For instance, many of our responses to drugs such as alcohol and marijuana can be measured as overt behavior, and they are presumed to reflect the biochemical actions of these drugs and our (mental) expectations about their effects.

A satisfactory psychological theory allows us to predict behavior. For instance, a theory of hunger should allow us to predict when people will or will not eat. If our observations cannot be adequately explained by, or predicted from, a given theory, we should consider revising or replacing it.

REFLECT

How would you have defined psychology before you began this course or opened your book? How does the true scientific nature of psychology differ from your expectations?

► CONTROVERSY IN PSYCHOLOGY ◄

What do psychologists mean by "controlling" behavior and mental processes?

"Controlling" behavior and mental processes doesn't mean to psychologists what it may sound like to most people. Some erroneously think that psychologists seek ways to make people do their bidding, like puppets on strings. This is not so. Psychologists are committed to a belief in the dignity of human beings, and human dignity demands that people be free to make their own decisions and choose their own behavior. Psychologists are learning more about the influences on human behavior all the time, but they use this knowledge only on request and in order to help people clarify and meet their own goals.

Psychology
The science that studies behavior and mental processes.

Theory
A formulation of relationships underlying observed events.

The remainder of this chapter presents an overview of psychology as a science. You will see that psychologists have diverse interests and fields of specialization. We discuss the history of psychology and the major perspectives from which today's psychologists view behavior. Finally, we consider the research methods psychologists use to study behavior and mental processes.

R E V I E W

(1) Psychology is defined as the study of _behavior_ and mental processes. (2) Psychology seeks to describe, explain, _____, and control behavior. (3) Behavior is explained through psychological _____, which are sets of statements that involve assumptions about behavior.

Critical Thinking: What is the difference between the way that psychologists and other scientists view the world and laypeople view the world?

Learning Connections
See Web site for an interactive version of these review questions.

WHAT PSYCHOLOGISTS DO: FIELDS OF PSYCHOLOGY

Psychologists share a keen interest in behavior, but in other ways they may differ markedly. ***Question: Just what do psychologists do?*** Psychologists engage in research, practice, and teaching. Some researchers engage primarily in basic, or **pure, research.** Pure research has no immediate application to personal or social problems and therefore has been characterized as research for its own sake. Others engage in **applied research,** which is designed to find solutions to specific personal or social problems. Although pure research is sparked by curiosity and the desire to know and understand, today's pure research frequently enhances tomorrow's way of life (Leibowitz, 1996; Miller, 1995). For example, pure research on learning and motivation in pigeons, rats, and monkeys done early in the 20th century has actually found widespread applications in today's school systems. Pure research into the workings of the nervous system has enhanced knowledge of disorders such as epilepsy, Parkinson's disease, and Alzheimer's disease.

Many psychologists do not conduct research. Instead, they *practice* psychology by applying psychological knowledge to help individuals change their behavior so that they can meet their own goals more effectively. Still other psychologists engage primarily in teaching. They share psychological knowledge in classrooms, seminars, and workshops. Some psychologists engage in all three: research, practice, and teaching.

Psychologists are found in a number of different specialties. Although some psychologists wear more than one hat, most of them carry out their functions in the following fields.

Clinical psychologists help people with psychological disorders adjust to the demands of life. People's problems may range from anxiety and depression to sexual dysfunctions to loss of goals. Clinical psychologists evaluate these problems through interviews and psychological tests. They help their clients resolve their problems and change self-defeating behavior. Clinical psychologists are the largest subgroup of psychologists (Kyle & Williams, 2000; see Figure 1.1). These psychologists differ from psychiatrists in that *psychiatrists* are *medical* doctors who specialize in the study and treatment of psychological disorders.

Counseling psychologists, like clinical psychologists, use interviews and tests to define their clients' problems. Their clients typically have adjustment problems but not serious psychological disorders. For example, clients may have trouble making academic or vocational decisions or making friends in college. They may experience marital or family conflicts, have physical disabilities, or have adjustment problems such as those encountered by people who lose their jobs because of mergers or downsizing. Counseling psychologists help clients clarify their goals and overcome obstacles and are

Pure Research
Research conducted without concern for immediate applications.

Applied Research
Research conducted in an effort to find solutions to particular problems.

R E F L E C T
If a friend had a problem, would you advise him or her to see a psychologist? What kind of psychologist?

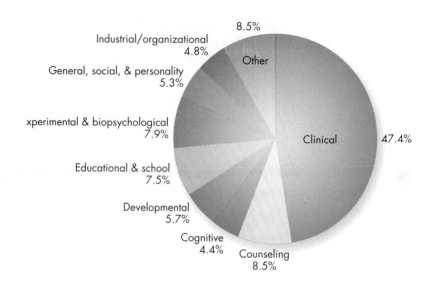

■ **Figure 1.1**
Students Enrolled in Doctoral Programs in Fields of Psychology

Nearly half (47%) of the doctoral students who enrolled in doctoral programs in psychology in 1998–1999 enrolled in clinical programs. (Current enrollments were used because they are the best indicator of the current directions of psychology.) The next most popular field was counseling psychology. The figure combines students enrolled in public and private institutions.

Source: Kyle, T. M., & Williams, S. (2000, May). Results of the 1998–1999 APA survey of graduate departments of psychology, Tables 13A & 13B. APA Research Office. Washington, D.C.: American Psychological Association.

often employed in college and university counseling and testing centers. As suggested by Figure 1.1, more than half of doctoral students in psychology are enrolled in clinical or counseling psychology programs.

School psychologists are employed by school systems to identify and assist students who have problems that interfere with learning. Such problems range from social and family problems to emotional disturbances and learning disorders. They help schools make decisions about the placement of students in special classes.

Educational psychologists, like school psychologists, attempt to facilitate learning. But they usually focus on course planning and instructional methods for a school system rather than on individual children. Educational psychologists research theoretical issues related to learning, measurement, and child development. For example, they study how learning is affected by psychological factors such as motivation and intelligence, sociocultural factors such as poverty and acculturation, and teacher behavior. Some educational psychologists prepare standardized tests such as the Scholastic Assessment Tests (SATs).

Developmental psychologists study the changes—physical, cognitive, social, and personality—that occur throughout the life span. They attempt to sort out the influences of heredity and the environment on development. Developmental psychologists conduct research on issues such as the effects of maternal use of drugs on an embryo, the outcomes of various patterns of child rearing, children's concepts of space and time, conflicts during adolescence, and problems of adjustment among older people.

Personality psychologists focus on goals such as identifying and measuring human traits; determining influences on human thought processes, feelings, and behavior; and explaining psychological disorders. They are particularly concerned with issues such as anxiety, aggression, and gender roles.

Social psychologists are primarily concerned with the nature and causes of individuals' thoughts, feelings, and behavior in social situations. Whereas personality psychologists tend to look within the person for explanations of behavior, social psychologists tend to focus on external or social influences.

Psychologists in all specialties may conduct experiments. However, those called *experimental psychologists* specialize in basic processes such as the nervous system, sensation and perception, learning and memory, thought, motivation, and emotion. For example, experimental psychologists have studied what areas of the brain are involved in processing math problems or listening to music. They have used animals such as pigeons and rats to study processes of learning in the laboratory.

Industrial psychology and organizational psychology are closely related fields. *Industrial psychologists* focus on the relationships between people and work. *Organizational psychologists* study the behavior of people in organizations such as businesses. *Human factors psychologists* make technical systems such as automobile dashboards

© Jeff Greenberg/ The Image Works

■ Developmental Psychology

Developmental psychologists study the changes that occur throughout the life span. They attempt to sort out the influences of heredity and the environment. Their concerns range from the effects of day care on infants to the adjustment issues of older people.

and computer keyboards more user friendly. *Consumer psychologists* study the behavior of shoppers in an effort to predict and influence their behavior. They advise store managers how to lay out the aisles of a supermarket in ways that boost impulse buying, how to arrange window displays to attract customers, and how to make newspaper ads and TV commercials more persuasive.

Health psychologists examine the ways in which behavior and mental processes such as attitudes are related to physical health. They study the effects of stress on health problems such as headaches, cardiovascular disease, and cancer. Health psychologists also guide clients toward healthier behavior patterns—such as exercising and quitting smoking—and diets.

Sport psychologists help people improve their performance in sports. They help athletes concentrate on their performance and not on the crowd, use cognitive strategies such as positive visualization (imagining themselves making the right moves) to enhance performance, and avoid choking under pressure (Van Raalte & Brewer, 2002).

Psychologists continue to apply their knowledge and skills in new areas.

REFLECT

Which fields of psychology are most in keeping with your own interests? Why?

Learning Connections
See Web site for an interactive version of these review questions.

REVIEW

(4) Some psychologists engage in basic, or _____, research, which has no immediate applications. (5) Other psychologists engage in _____ research, which seeks solutions to specific problems. (6) Clinical psychologists help people resolve problems through _____. (7) _____ psychologists work with individuals who have adjustment problems but do not show seriously abnormal behavior. (8) _____ psychologists assist students with problems that interfere with learning. (9) _____ psychologists are more concerned with theoretical issues concerning human learning. (10) _____ psychologists study the changes that occur throughout the life span. (11) _____ psychologists study the nature and causes of our thoughts, feelings, and behavior in social situations. (12) _____ psychologists conduct research into basic psychological processes, such as sensation and perception, learning and memory, and motivation and emotion. (13) _____ psychologists focus on the relationships between people and work.

Critical Thinking: What unites all the various fields of psychology?

WHERE PSYCHOLOGY COMES FROM: A HISTORY

Know then thyself, presume not God to scan,
The proper study of mankind is man . . .
Created half to rise, and half to fall,
Great lord of all things, and yet a prey to all;
Sole judge of truth, in endless error hurled;
The glory, jest, and riddle of the world!

From "An Essay on Man," Alexander Pope

The English poet Alexander Pope advised "Know then thyself" in the 1700s. He was not the first. The ancient Greek philosopher Socrates, more than 2,000 years earlier, also advised "Know thyself." Psychology, which is in large part the endeavor to know ourselves, is as old as history and as modern as today. Knowledge of the history of psychology allows us to appreciate its theoretical conflicts, its place among the sciences, the evolution of its methods, and its social and political roles.

Question: Who were some of the ancient contributors to psychology? One of them is the ancient Greek philosopher Aristotle (384–322 BCE). In fact, the outline for this textbook could have been written by Aristotle. One of Aristotle's works, *Peri Psyches*, translates as "About the Psyche." Like this book, *Peri Psyches* begins with a history of psychological thought and historical perspectives on the nature of the mind and behavior. Aristotle argued that human behavior, like the movements of the stars and the seas, is subject to rules and laws. Then he delved into his subject matter topic by topic: personality, sensation and perception, thought, intelligence, needs and motives, feelings and emotion, and memory. This book presents these topics in a different order, but each is here.

What were Aristotle's contributions to psychology? He was a proponent of *empiricism*—the view that science could rationally treat only information gathered by the senses. He numbered the so-called five senses of vision, hearing, smell, taste, and touch. (In Chapter 5, you will see that we actually have more than five senses—no peeking!) Aristotle explored the nature of cause and effect. He pointed out that people differ from other living things in their capacity for rational thought. He explained how the imagination and dreaming contained images that represented the sensory stimulation that caused them. And he outlined laws of *associationism*—how experience leads to expectations and how thought to leads to thought—which have lain at the heart of learning theory for more than 2,000 years.

Aristotle also declared that people are motivated to seek pleasure and avoid pain. This view remains as current today as it was in ancient Greece.

■ **Aristotle**

How do we number the ancient Greek philosopher's contributions to psychology and scientific thought? He was among the first to argue that people could only deal rationally with information obtained through the senses. He explored the nature of cause and effect and noted that people differ from other organisms in the capacity for rational thought.

Brown Brothers

REFLECT

Do you think it is useful for this book to talk about topics like the history of psychology? Would you prefer it if the book just listed the 100 or 200 "facts" you need to know for the final exam? Why or why not?

Other ancient Greek philosophers also contributed to psychology. Around 400 BCE, Democritus suggested that we could think of behavior in terms of a body and a mind. (Contemporary psychologists still talk about the interaction of biological and mental processes.) He pointed out that our behavior is influenced by external stimulation. Democritus was one of the first to raise the question of whether there is free will or choice. Putting it another way, where do the influences of others end and our "real selves" begin?

Plato (ca. 427–347 BCE) was a disciple of the great philosopher Socrates. He recorded Socrates' advice to "Know thyself," which has remained a motto of psychology ever since. Socrates claimed that we could not attain reliable self-knowledge through our senses because the senses do not mirror reality exactly. Because the senses provide imperfect knowledge, Socrates suggested that we should rely on processes such as rational thought and **introspection**—careful examination of one's own thoughts and

Introspection

Deliberate looking into one's own cognitive processes to examine one's thoughts and feelings.

emotions—to achieve self-knowledge. He also pointed out that people are social creatures who influence one another.

Had we room enough and time, we could trace psychology's roots to thinkers even farther back in time than the ancient Greeks, and we could trace its development through the great thinkers of the Renaissance. As it is, we must move on to the development of psychology as a laboratory science during the second half of the 19th century. Some historians set the marker date at 1860. It was then that Gustav Theodor Fechner (1801–1887) published his landmark book *Elements of Psychophysics,* which showed how physical events (such as lights and sounds) are related to psychological sensation and perception. Fechner also showed how we can scientifically measure the effect of these events. Most historians set the debut of modern psychology as a laboratory science in the year 1879, when Wilhelm Wundt established the first psychological laboratory in Leipzig, Germany.

Structuralism: The Elements of Experience

The German psychologist Wilhelm Wundt (1832–1920) looked as if he were going to be another problem child. He did poorly in elementary school—his mind would wander—and he had to repeat a year. Eventually he attended medical school because he wanted to earn a good living. But he did not like working with patients and dedicated himself to philosophy and psychology. He became such a workaholic that his wife and family received only one paragraph in his autobiography. During a serious illness, his main preoccupation lay in analyzing the experience of dying. He went on to live a long life, nonetheless.

Wundt also analyzed the experience of living. Like Aristotle, he saw the mind as a natural event that could be studied scientifically, like light, heat, and the flow of blood. He used introspection to try to discover the basic elements of experience. When presented with various sights and sounds, he and his colleagues tried to look inward as objectively as possible to describe their sensations and feelings.

Wundt and his students founded the school of psychology called **structuralism.** ***Question: What is structuralism?*** Structuralism attempted to break conscious experience down into *objective* sensations, such as sight or taste, and *subjective* feelings, such as emotional responses, will, and mental images like memories or dreams. Structuralists believed that the mind functions by combining objective and subjective elements of experience.

Functionalism: Making Psychology a Habit

I wished, by treating Psychology like a natural science, to help her become one.

—William James

William James (1842–1910), brother of the novelist Henry James, has been called the first true American psychologist. He came from a wealthy family, and his home was visited regularly by the likes of Ralph Waldo Emerson; Henry David Thoreau; Nathaniel Hawthorne; Alfred, Lord Tennyson; and John Stuart Mill. James received an MD degree from Harvard University but never practiced medicine. He made his career teaching at Harvard—first in physiology, then in philosophy, and finally in psychology. He described his views in the first modern psychology textbook, *The Principles of Psychology,* a huge two-volume work that was published in 1890. Two years later he came out with a brief edition, which students affectionately called the "Jimmy." He was often seen strolling across Harvard Yard, talking animatedly with students, in an era when most professors were more formal. James was also fascinated by religious experience and occult phenomena such as extrasensory perception. He once brought the young Helen Keller an ostrich feather—a gift he believed the blind and deaf girl could appreciate.

James was a major figure in the development of psychology in the United States. He focused on the relation between conscious experience and behavior. He argued, for example, that the stream of consciousness is fluid and continuous. Introspection

■ **Wilhelm Wundt**

On one occasion, Wundt, the founder of structuralism, believed he lay dying. Rather than despair, he analyzed the structure of his experience—breaking it down into sensations, feelings, and thoughts.

Structuralism

The school of psychology that argues that the mind consists of three basic elements—sensations, feelings, and images—that combine to form experience.

■ **William James**

In his youth, 19th-century "glitterati" like Ralph Waldo Emerson, Nathaniel Hawthorne, and Alfred, Lord Tennyson visited the family home. James received an MD degree but never practiced medicine. He was a pioneer in psychology in the United States and founded the school of functionalism.

■ John B. Watson

Watson, the founder of behaviorism in the United States, argued that psychologists could treat only observable behavior if psychology were to be a natural science like biology, chemistry, or physics. When his career in the academic world was foreshortened by the revelation of an affair with a student, Watson went on to a second successful career in an advertising agency. He was one of the originators of the idea of associating an attractive woman with a product, such as an automobile.

R E F L E C T

Why do behaviorists object to schools of psychology that use introspection? Do you agree with the behaviorist point of view? Why or why not?

Functionalism

The school of psychology that emphasizes the uses or functions of the mind rather than the elements of experience.

Behaviorism

The school of psychology that defines psychology as the study of observable behavior and studies relationships between stimuli and responses.

convinced him that experience cannot be broken down into objective sensations and subjective feelings as the structuralists maintained.

R E F L E C T

William James visited Helen Keller when she was a child and brought a gift of an ostrich feather. Why do you think he did that?

James was a founder of the school of **functionalism.** *Question: What is functionalism?* The school of functionalism focused on behavior in addition to the mind or consciousness. Functionalists looked at how our experience helps us function more adaptively in our environments—for example, how habits help us cope with common situations. They also turned to the laboratory for direct observations as a way to supplement introspection. The structuralists tended to ask, "What are the pieces that make up thinking and experience?" In contrast, the functionalists tended to ask, "How do behavior and mental processes help people adapt to the requirements of their lives?"

James was also influenced by Charles Darwin's (1809–1882) theory of evolution. Earlier in the 19th century, the British naturalist Darwin had argued that organisms with adaptive features—that is, the "fittest"—survive and reproduce. Functionalists adapted Darwin's theory and proposed that adaptive behavior patterns are learned and maintained. Maladaptive behavior patterns tend to drop out, and only the "fittest" behavior patterns survive. These adaptive actions tend to be repeated and become habits. James wrote that "habit is the enormous flywheel of society." Habit keeps the engine of civilization running.

Habits include such deceptively simple acts as how we lift a spoon to our mouth or turn a doorknob. At first, these acts require our full attention. If you are in doubt, stand by with paper towels and watch a baby's first efforts at eating oatmeal by himself. Through repetition, the movements that make up self-feeding become automatic, or habitual. The multiple acts involved in learning to drive a car also become routine through repetition, so we can focus on other matters such as telling a joke to our passenger or changing the CD. This idea of learning by repetition is also basic to the behavioral tradition in psychology.

Behaviorism: Practicing Psychology in Public

Imagine you have placed a hungry rat in a maze. It meanders down a pathway that ends in a T. It can then turn left or right. If you consistently reward the rat with food for turning right at this choice point, it will learn to turn right when it arrives there, at least when it is hungry. But what does the rat *think* when it is learning to turn right? "Hmm, last time I was in this situation and turned to the right, I was given some Purina rat chow. Think I'll try that again"?

Does it seem absurd to try to place yourself in the "mind" of a rat? So it seemed to John Broadus Watson (1878–1958), the founder of American behaviorism. *Question: What is behaviorism?* We will talk more about behaviorism shortly, but first let us note that Watson was asked to consider the contents of a rat's "mind" as one of the requirements for his doctoral degree, which he received from the University of Chicago in 1903. Functionalism was the dominant view of psychology at the University of Chicago, and functionalists were concerned with the stream of consciousness as well as observable behavior. But Watson (1913) believed that if psychology was to be a natural science, like physics or chemistry, it must limit itself to observable, measurable events—that is, to behavior alone—hence, **behaviorism.** Observable behavior includes activities such as pressing a lever; turning left or right; eating and mating; even involuntary body functions such as heart rate, dilation of the pupils of the eyes, blood pressure, and emission of brain waves. These behaviors are *public.* They can be measured by simple observation or by laboratory instruments, and different observers would readily agree about their existence and features. Behaviorists, by the way, define psychology as the scientific study of *behavior,* not of *behavior and mental processes.*

Who was Watson? He was the son of a Southern farmer and tended to get into fights in his youth. Later—much later—he taught rats to find their way through a miniature maze that was modeled on the maze at King Henry VIII's retreat in the London suburbs.

Watson's aim was to show how most human behavior and emotional reactions—other than a few inborn reflexes—resulted from conditioning. Perhaps his most renowned experiment was with "Little Albert," an infant who was conditioned by Watson and his student Rosalie Rayner to develop a fear of furry white animals (see Chapter 7). Watson later was forced to resign by the president of Johns Hopkins University when it was discovered that he and Rayner were having an affair. He left the academic world for New York, where he worked as a psychologist for the J. Walter Thompson advertising agency. He grew wealthy through successful ad campaigns for products such as Camel cigarettes, Johnson & Johnson Baby Powder, and Maxwell House Coffee—in which he introduced the idea of the "coffee break."

He married Rosalie Rayner, and the couple had two sons. Tragically, his wife died from dysentery in her thirties, and Watson, 58, never married again. He lived to be 80, and a year before he died, the APA awarded him a gold medal for his contributions to psychology.

Another major modern contributor to behaviorism was Harvard University psychologist B. F. Skinner (1904–1990). He believed that organisms learn to behave in certain ways because they have been **reinforced** for doing so—that is, their behavior has a positive outcome. He demonstrated that laboratory animals can be trained to carry out behaviors through strategic use of reinforcers, such as food. He trained rats to turn in circles, climb ladders, and push toys across the floor. Many psychologists adopted the view that, in principle, one could explain complex human behavior in terms of thousands of instances of learning through reinforcement.

Gestalt Psychology: Making Psychology Whole

In the 1920s, another school of psychology—**Gestalt psychology**—was prominent in Germany. In the 1930s, the three founders of the school—Max Wertheimer (1880–1943), Kurt Koffka (1886–1941), and Wolfgang Köhler (1887–1967)—left Europe to escape the Nazi threat. They carried on their work in the United States, giving further impetus to the growing American ascendance in psychology.

Question: What is Gestalt psychology? Gestalt psychologists focused on perception and on how perception influences thinking and problem solving. In contrast to the behaviorists, Gestalt psychologists argued that we cannot hope to understand

Reinforcement
A stimulus that follows a response and increases the frequency of the response.

Gestalt Psychology
The school of psychology that emphasizes the tendency to organize perceptions into wholes and to integrate separate stimuli into meaningful patterns.

■ **The Power of Reinforcement**

In the photo on the left, we see how our feathered friends have earned their keep in experiments on reinforcement. Here, the parrot places the star in the correct hole because this behavior has been followed (reinforced) with food. In the photo on the right, "Air Raccoon" shoots a basket. Behaviorists teach animals complex behaviors such as shooting baskets by first reinforcing approximations to the goal (or target behavior). As time progresses, closer approximations are demanded before reinforcement is given.

Insight
In Gestalt psychology, the sudden reorganization of perceptions, allowing the sudden solution of a problem.

Psychoanalysis
The school of psychology that emphasizes the importance of unconscious motives and conflicts as determinants of human behavior.

human nature by focusing only on overt behavior. In contrast to the structuralists, they claimed that we cannot explain human perceptions, emotions, or thought processes in terms of basic units. Perceptions are *more* than the sums of their parts: Gestalt psychologists saw our perceptions as wholes that give meaning to parts. The German word *Gestalt* translates roughly to "pattern" or "organized whole."

Gestalt psychologists illustrated how we tend to perceive separate pieces of information as integrated wholes, depending on the contexts in which they occur. Consider Figure 1.2. The dots in the centers of the configurations at the left are the same size, yet we may perceive them as being of different sizes because of what surrounds them. The inner squares in the central figure are equally bright, but they do not appear so because of their contrasting backgrounds. The second symbol in each line at the right is identical, but in the top row we may perceive it as a B and in the bottom row as the number 13. The symbol has not changed, but the context in which it appears has. There are many examples of this in literature and everyday life. In *The Prince and the Pauper,* Mark Twain dressed a peasant boy as a prince, and the kingdom bowed to him. Do clothes sometimes make the man or woman? Try wearing cutoffs for a job interview!

Gestalt psychologists believed that learning could be active and purposeful, not merely responsive and mechanical as in Watson and Skinner's experiments. They demonstrated that much learning, especially in problem solving, is accomplished by **insight,** not by mechanical repetition.

Wolfgang Köhler was marooned during World War I on one of the Canary Islands, where the Prussian Academy of Science kept a colony of apes, and his research while there gave him, well, insight into the process of learning by insight. Have you ever pondered a problem for quite a while and then, suddenly, seen the solution? Did the solution seem to come out of nowhere? In a "flash"? Consider the chimpanzee in Figure 1.3. At first, it is unsuccessful in reaching for bananas suspended from the ceiling. Then it suddenly stacks the boxes and climbs up to reach the bananas. It seems the chimp has experienced a sudden reorganization of the mental elements of the problem—that is, it has had a "flash of insight." Köhler's findings suggest that we often manipulate the elements of problems until we group them in such a way that we believe we will be able to reach a goal. The manipulations may take quite some time as mental trial and error proceeds. Once the proper grouping has been found, however, we seem to perceive it all at once as a clear pattern or whole.

Psychoanalysis: Digging Beneath the Surface

Psychoanalysis, the school of psychology founded by Sigmund Freud, differs from the other schools in both background and approach. Freud's theory has invaded popular culture, and you may be familiar with a number of its concepts. For example, perhaps a friend has tried to "interpret" a slip of the tongue you made or has asked you what you thought might be the meaning of an especially vivid dream.

■ **Figure 1.2**
The Importance of Context

Gestalt psychologists have shown that our perceptions depend not only on our sensory impressions but also on the context of our impressions. You will interpret a man running toward you very differently depending on whether you are on a deserted street at night or at a track in the morning.

A. Are the dots in the center of the configurations the same size? Why not take a ruler and measure them?

B. Is the second symbol in each line the letter B or the number 13?

C. Which one of the gray squares is brighter?

■ Figure 1.3
Some Insight into Insight
At first, the chimpanzee cannot reach the bananas hanging from the ceiling. After some time has passed, it has an apparent "flash of insight" and piles the boxes to reach the fruit.

Question: What is psychoanalysis? The notions that verbal errors and dreams represent unconscious wishes lie at the heart of the school of psychology known as psychoanalysis. These ideas largely reflect the influence of Freud (1856–1939), a Viennese physician who fled to England in the 1930s to escape the Nazis. While academic psychologists of the early 1900s were conducting their research in the laboratory, Freud gained his understanding of people by working with patients. He was astounded at how little insight his patients seemed to have into their motives. Some patients justified, or rationalized, the most abominable behavior with absurd explanations. Others seized the opportunity to blame themselves for nearly every misfortune that had befallen the human species.

Freud came to believe that unconscious processes, especially sexual and aggressive impulses, are more influential than conscious thought in determining human behavior. He thought that most of the mind is unconscious—a seething cauldron of conflicting impulses, urges, and wishes. People are motivated to gratify these impulses, ugly as some of them are. But at the same time, people are motivated to see themselves as decent and hence may delude themselves about their true motives. Because Freud proposed that the motion of underlying forces of personality determines our thoughts, feelings, and behavior, his theory is referred to as **psychodynamic.**

Freud devised a method of psychotherapy called psychoanalysis. Psychoanalysis aims to help patients gain insight into many of their deep-seated conflicts and find socially acceptable ways of expressing wishes and gratifying needs. It can extend for years. Psychoanalysis is discussed in more detail in Chapters 11 and 13.

R E F L E C T

Had you heard of Sigmund Freud before you began this course? What had you heard? Were your impressions accurate? Why or why not?

Psychodynamic
Referring to Freud's theory, which proposes that the motion of underlying forces of personality determines our thoughts, feelings, and behavior.

 Learning Connections
See Web site for an interactive version of these review questions.

R E V I E W

The Greek philosopher (14) _____ was among the first to argue that human behavior is subject to rules and laws. (15) _____ proclaimed "Know thyself" and suggested the use of introspection to gain self-knowledge. (16) Wilhelm _____ founded the school of structuralism. (17) William James founded the school of _____, which dealt with behavior as well as conscious experience. (18) John B. _____ founded the school of behaviorism. (19) _____ psychologists saw our perceptions as wholes that give meaning to parts. (20) Sigmund _____ founded the school of psychoanalysis.

Critical Thinking: Do you believe that the richness and complexity of human behavior can be explained as the summation of so many instances of learning? Explain.

HOW TODAY'S PSYCHOLOGISTS VIEW BEHAVIOR AND MENTAL PROCESSES

Today we no longer find psychologists who describe themselves as structuralists or functionalists. Although the school of Gestalt psychology gave birth to current research approaches in perception and problem solving, few would consider themselves Gestalt psychologists. The numbers of orthodox behaviorists and psychoanalysts have also been declining (Robins et al., 1999). Many contemporary psychologists in the behaviorist tradition look on themselves as social–cognitive theorists,[1] and many psychoanalysts consider themselves neoanalysts rather than traditional Freudians.

The history of psychological thought has taken many turns, and contemporary psychologists differ in their approaches. Today there are several broad, influential perspectives in psychology: the biological, cognitive, humanistic-existential, psychodynamic, learning, and sociocultural perspectives. Each emphasizes different topics of investigation. Each approaches its topics in its own ways.

The Evolutionary and Biological Perspectives

Psychologists are interested in the roles of evolution and heredity in behavior and mental processes such as psychological disorders, criminal behavior, and thinking. Generally speaking, our heredity provides a broad range of behavioral and mental possibilities. Environmental factors interact with inherited factors to determine specific behavior and mental processes.   *Question: What are the evolutionary and biological perspectives?*

Modern evolutionary psychologists focus on the evolution of behavior and mental processes. Charles Darwin argued that in the age-old struggle for existence, only the "fittest" (most adaptive) organisms manage to reach maturity and reproduce. For example, fish that swim faster or people who are naturally immune to certain diseases are more likely to survive and transmit their **genes** to future generations. Individuals die, but species tend to evolve in adaptive directions. Evolutionary psychologists suggest that much human social behavior, such as aggressive behavior and mate selection, has a hereditary basis. People may be influenced by social rules, cultural factors, even personal choice, but evolutionary psychologists believe that inherited tendencies sort of whisper in people's ears and tend to move them in certain directions.

Psychologists assume that our thoughts, fantasies, and dreams are made possible by the nervous system and especially by the brain. Psychologists with a biological perspective seek the links between the electrical and chemical activity of the brain, the chemical activity of hormones, and heredity, on the one hand, and behavior and mental processes on the other. They use techniques such as CAT scans and PET scans to show what parts of the brain are involved in activities like language, mathematical problem solving, and music. We have learned how natural chemical substances in the brain are involved in the formation of memories. Experiments have shown that among some animals, electrical stimulation of parts of the brain prompts the expression of "prewired," or inborn, sexual and aggressive behaviors.

Biological psychologists are also concerned with the influences of the endocrine system on behavior and mental processes. The endocrine system consists of glands that secrete hormones and release them into the bloodstream. In people, for instance, the hormone prolactin stimulates production of milk. In rats, however, prolactin also gives rise to maternal behavior. In many animals, sex hormones determine whether mating behavior will follow stereotypical masculine or feminine behavior patterns. In humans, sex hormones regulate the menstrual cycle and are also connected with feelings of psychological well-being.

The biological perspective tends to focus on events that occur below the level of consciousness. The cognitive perspective is the essence of consciousness.   *Question: What is the cognitive perspective?*

Genes
The basic building blocks of heredity.

[1] Formerly termed *social-learning theorists.*

The Cognitive Perspective: Keeping Psychology "In Mind"

Psychologists with a **cognitive** perspective venture into the realm of mental processes to understand human nature (Sperry, 1998). They investigate the ways in which we perceive and mentally represent the world, how we learn, remember the past, plan for the future, solve problems, form judgments, make decisions, and use language (Basic Behavioral Science Task Force, 1996a). Cognitive psychologists, in short, study those things we refer to as the *mind.*

The cognitive tradition has roots in Socrates' advice to "Know thyself" and in his suggested method of introspection. We also find cognitive psychology's roots in structuralism, functionalism, and Gestalt psychology, each of which, in its own way, addressed issues that are of interest to cognitive psychologists. In general, cognitive science has experienced a rapid expansion in the past couple of decades and continues to attract interest and inspire research.

R E F L E C T
How would you define the mind?
Why do some psychologists argue that it is fruitless to talk about people's minds?

The Humanistic–Existential Perspective

The humanistic–existential perspective is cognitive in flavor, yet it emphasizes more the role of subjective (personal) experience. *Question: What is the humanistic–existential perspective?* Let us consider each of the parts of this perspective: *humanism* and *existentialism*. **Humanism** stresses the human capacity for self-fulfillment and the central roles of consciousness, self-awareness, and decision making. Humanistic psychology considers personal, or subjective, experience to be the most important event in psychology. Humanists believe that self-awareness, experience, and choice permit us, to a large extent, to "invent ourselves" and our ways of relating to the world as we progress through life. Humanistic–existential psychologists stress the importance of subjective experience and assert that people have the freedom to make choices. Consciousness—our sense of being in the world—is seen as the force that unifies our personalities. **Existentialism** views people as free to choose and be responsible for choosing ethical conduct.

Humanistic–existential psychologists stress the importance of subjective experience and assert that people have the freedom to make real choices. Grounded in the work of Carl Rogers (1951) and Abraham Maslow (1970), the humanistic perspective continues to find many contemporary adherents (Moss, 2002; Schneider et al., 2001).

The Psychodynamic Perspective

There are still modern psychologists who continue to embrace the diverse theories descended from Freud. In fact, in the 1940s and 1950s, psychodynamic theory dominated the practice of psychotherapy and was influential in scientific psychology and the arts. Most psychotherapists were psychodynamically oriented. Many renowned artists and writers consulted psychodynamic therapists as a way to liberate the expression of their unconscious ideas. Today, Freud's influence continues to be felt, although it no longer dominates methods of psychotherapy.

Question: What is the role of psychoanalysis today? Contemporary psychologists who follow theories derived from Freud are likely to call themselves *neo-analysts.* Famous neoanalysts such as Karen Horney (1885–1952) and Erik Erikson (1902–1994) focused less on unconscious processes and more on conscious choice and self-direction. The same is true of modern neoanalysts today, such as former APA president Dorothy Cantor.

Many Freudian ideas are retained in some form by the population at large. For example, sometimes we have ideas or desires that seem unusual for us. We may even say that it sometimes seems as if some unconscious idea or impulse is trying to get the better of us. In the Middle Ages, such thoughts and impulses were usually attributed to the devil or to demons. Dreams, likewise, were thought to enter us magically from the spirit world. Followers of Sigmund Freud tend to attribute dreams and unusual ideas or desires to unconscious processes, and dreams are commonly viewed this way in popular culture.

Cognitive
Having to do with mental processes such as sensation and perception, memory, intelligence, language, thought, and problem solving.

Humanism
The philosophy and school of psychology that asserts that people are conscious, self-aware, and capable of free choice, self-fulfillment, and ethical behavior.

Existentialism
The view that people are free and responsible for their own behavior.

Perspectives on Learning

Many contemporary psychologists study the effects of experience on behavior. Learning, to them, is the essential factor in describing, explaining, predicting, and controlling behavior. The term *learning* has different meanings to psychologists of different persuasions, however. Some students of learning find roles for consciousness and insight. Others do not. This distinction is found today among those who adhere to the behavioral and social-cognitive perspectives. *Question: What are the two major perspectives on learning?*

For the founder of American behaviorism, John B. Watson, behaviorism was an approach to life as well as a broad guideline for psychological research. Not only did Watson despair of measuring consciousness and mental processes in the laboratory, he also applied behavioral analysis to virtually all situations in his daily life. He viewed people as doing things because of their learning histories, their situations, and rewards rather than because of conscious choice.

Like Watson, contemporary behaviorists emphasize environmental influences and the learning of habits through repetition and reinforcement. Modern **social–cognitive theorists** (previously termed *social-learning theorists*), in contrast, suggest that people can modify or even create their environments. They also grant cognition a key role. They note that people engage in intentional learning by observing others. Since the 1960s, social–cognitive theorists have gained influence in the areas of personality development, psychological disorders, and methods of therapy.

The Sociocultural Perspective

The profession of psychology focuses mainly on the individual and is committed to the dignity of the individual. However, many psychologists today believe we cannot understand people's behavior and mental processes without reference to their diversity (Basic Behavioral Science Task Force, 1996b). Studying perspectives other than their own helps psychologists understand the role of a culture's beliefs, values, and attitudes in behavior and mental processes. It helps them perceive why people from diverse cultures behave and think in different ways and how the science of psychology is enriched by addressing those differences (Denmark, 1998; Reid, 1994).

Question: What is the sociocultural perspective? The **sociocultural perspective** addresses many of the ways in which people differ from one another. It studies the influences of ethnicity, gender, culture, and socioeconomic status on behavior and mental processes (Allen, 1993; Lewis-Fernández & Kleinman, 1994). For example, what is often seen as healthful, self-assertive, outspoken behavior by most U.S. women may be interpreted as brazen behavior in Latino and Latina American or Asian American communities.

Ethnicity

One kind of diversity involves people's ethnicity. Members of an **ethnic group** are united by their cultural heritage, race, language, and common history. The experiences of various ethnic groups in the United States highlight the impact of social, political, and economic factors on human behavior and development (Basic Behavioral Science Task Force, 1996b; Phinney, 1996).

The probing of human diversity enables students to appreciate the cultural heritages and historical problems of various ethnic groups. This textbook considers many psychological issues related to ethnicity, such as the representation of ethnic minority groups in psychological research studies, substance abuse among adolescents from various ethnic minority groups, bilingualism, ethnic differences in intelligence test scores, the prevalence of suicide among members of different ethnic groups, ethnic dif-

---

REFLECT

Do you learn by observing others? Is your learning intentional? How would you know?

REFLECT

How does the sociocultural perspective help us understand behavior and mental processes? Why is knowledge of human diversity important to the dignity of the individual?

Social–Cognitive Theory
A school of psychology in the behaviorist tradition that includes cognitive factors in the explanation and prediction of behavior. Formerly termed *social-learning theory.*

Sociocultural Perspective
The view that focuses on the roles of ethnicity, gender, culture, and socioeconomic status in behavior and mental processes.

Ethnic Group
A group characterized by common features such as cultural heritage, history, race, and language.

The Sociocultural Perspective

The United States is a mosaic of people from various ethnic backgrounds. The sociocultural perspective teaches that we cannot understand the hopes and problems of people from a particular ethnic group without understanding that group's history and cultural heritage. The sociocultural perspective helps us understand and appreciate the scope of behavior and mental processes.

ferences in vulnerability to physical problems and disorders ranging from obesity to hypertension and cancer, multicultural issues in the practice of psychotherapy, and prejudice.

Gender

Gender refers to the culturally defined concepts of *masculinity* and *femininity*. Gender is not simply a matter of anatomic sex. It involves a complex web of cultural expectations and social roles that affect people's self-concepts and hopes and dreams as well as their behavior. How can sciences such as psychology and medicine hope to understand the particular viewpoints, qualities, and problems of women if most research is conducted with men and by men (Matthews et al., 1997)?

Just as members of ethnic minority groups have experienced prejudice, so too have women. Even much of the scientific research on gender roles and gender differences assumes that male behavior represents the norm (Ader & Johnson, 1994).

Our discussion of the sociocultural perspective naturally leads us to reflect on the roles of women and people from various racial and ethnic backgrounds in psychology.

Gender
The culturally defined concepts of *masculinity* and *femininity*.

Learning Connections
See Web site for an interactive version of these review questions.

REVIEW

(21) _____ oriented psychologists study the links between behavior, the brain, hormones, and heredity. (22) _____ psychologists note that only the fittest organisms reach maturity and reproduce, thereby transmitting their genes to future generations and causing species to evolve in adaptive directions. (23) _____ psychologists study the ways in which we perceive and mentally represent the world. (24) Humanistic–_____ psychologists stress the importance of self-awareness and people's freedom to make choices. Many contemporary psychoanalysts—neoanalysts—generally follow Freud but focus less on unconscious processes and more on people's capacity to make conscious choices. (25) _____–cognitive theorists are in the behaviorist tradition but also find roles for intentional learning and note that people can create or modify their environments. (26) The _____ per-

A Closer Look

Gender, Ethnicity, and Psychology: Real People in the Real World

Although the overwhelming majority of psychologists in the 1800s and early 1900s were European American males, women and people from various racial and ethnic backgrounds have made key contributions to the science of psychology in the past century. Let's consider some of the women.

Women in Psychology: Opening the Floodgates

She just said no. Mary Whiton Calkins (1863–1930) had completed all the requirements for the PhD, but accepting the degree would endorse prejudice against women. So she turned it down. Calkins studied psychology at Harvard University. However, she had to attend Harvard as a "guest student," because Harvard was not yet admitting women. It did not matter that William James considered Calkins to be his brightest student. When she completed her degree requirements, Harvard would not award her the degree because of her gender. Instead, Harvard offered to grant her a doctorate from its sister school, Radcliffe. She declined the offer.

Even without a doctorate, Calkins went on to pioneer research in memory at Wellesley College, where she founded a psychology laboratory in 1891. She introduced the method of paired associates and discovered the primacy and recency effects. In 1905 she became the first female president of the American Psychological Association—doctorate or no.

Despite the fact that women have traditionally been excluded from the world outside the home, Mary Whiton Calkins is just one of the thousands of women who have made indispensable contributions to psychology.   **Question: What contributions have women made to psychology?** Consider Christine Ladd-Franklin (1847–1930). She, like Calkins, was born during an era in American history in which women were expected to remain in the home and were excluded from careers in science (Minton, 2000). She nevertheless pursued a career in psychology, taught at Johns Hopkins and Columbia Universities, and formulated a theory of color vision.

Margaret Floy Washburn (1871–1939) was the first woman to receive a PhD in psychology. Washburn wrote *The Animal Mind,*

■ Mary Whiton Calkins

She just said no—to the doctorate from Radcliffe that was offered her, that is. She had completed her graduate work at Harvard, but Harvard was not admitting women as matriculated students at the time. Despite her academic "deficiency," Calkins went on to pioneer research in memory at Wellesley College.

Archives of the History of American Psychology

a work containing many ideas that would later become part of behaviorism.

Helen Bradford Thompson (1874–1947) was the first psychologist to study psychological gender differences. Her 1903 book *The Mental Traits of Sex* analyzed the performance of 25 women and 25 men on tests of intellect, emotional response, and sensation and perception (Milar, 2000). Thompson was ahead of her time in her conclusion that gender differences in these areas appeared to be strongly influenced by the social environment from infancy through adulthood.

Let us note that it was not until relatively modern times that women were generally considered suitable for higher education. (In many parts of the world, women are still denied an education.) Women have attended college in the United States only since 1833, when Oberlin College opened its doors to women. Today, however, more than half of American college students are women. Women today receive nearly three-quarters of the undergraduate degrees in psychology and two-thirds of the doctoral degrees (Kohout & Williams, 1999).

Ethnicity and Psychology

Question: What contributions to psychology have been made by people from various racial and ethnic groups? Numerous early psychologists came from different ethnic backgrounds. Back in 1901, Gilbert Haven Jones, an African Amerispective fosters the consideration of matters of ethnicity, gender, culture, and socio-economic status in psychology.

Critical Thinking: How does the biological perspective differ from other perspectives in psychology? What is the value of the sociocultural perspective?

By now we have a sense of the various fields of psychology, the history of psychology, and the ways in which today's psychologists look at behavior and mental processes. Basically, psychology has sought to be the scientific study of behavior and mental processes. Like other scientists, psychologists rely on research to find answers to the questions that interest them. The next section addresses some questions of interest to psychologists to demonstrate how research is conducted.

can, received his PhD in psychology in Germany. J. Henry Alston engaged in research on perception of heat and cold and was the first African American psychologist to be published in a major psychology journal (the year was 1920).

Kenneth Bancroft Clark was born in 1914, the son of West Indian parents. He earned his bachelor's degree from Howard University in Washington, DC, where he also met and married Mamie Phipps. The couple then earned their doctorates in psychology at Columbia University.

The couple were committed to children's welfare (Lal, 2002). In the 1940s, the Clarks founded the Northside Center for Child Development and conducted research that showed the negative effects of school segregation on African American children. In one such study, African American children were shown white and brown dolls and asked to "Give me the pretty doll," or "Give me the doll that looks bad." Most children's choices showed that they preferred the white dolls over the brown ones. The Clarks concluded that the children had swallowed the larger society's prejudiced views that favored European Americans.

The Clarks were activists as well as psychologists (Keppel, 2002; Lal, 2002). In the 1950s, Kenneth Clark began working with the NAACP to end school segregation. Clark's research was cited by the Supreme Court in 1954 when it overturned the "separate but equal" schools doctrine that had actually allowed inequalities in school services for various ethnic groups. Clark went on to study the quality of education and juvenile delinquency. He was among the first to recommend education for preschoolers, after-school programs, and community participation in educational decision making.

Today African Americans continue to have a powerful impact on the profession of psychology. For example, psychologist Robert Williams—sometimes referred to as the "father of Ebonics"—has offered us insight into language differences that are often found between European Americans and African Americans. Psychologist Claude Steele has shown that many African Americans sabotage their own performance on intelligence tests because of *stereotype threat*. That is, rather than focus on the test items, they worry about the stereotype, or widespread belief, that African Americans are not as bright as European Ameri-

Library of Congress

■ **Mamie Phipps Clark and Kenneth B. Clark**

The Clarks earned their doctorates in psychology at Columbia University, promoted the welfare of children, and undertook research that was cited in the Supreme Court's decision to overturn the doctrine of "separate but equal" schools for African American and European American children.

cans, and thereby hurt their own performance. According to Steele, this phenomenon can apply to any negatively stereotyped group as well—to women in mathematics, for example.

Latino and Latina American and Asian American psychologists have also made their mark. Jorge Sanchez was among the first to show how intelligence tests are culturally biased—to the disadvantage of Mexican American children. Asian American psychologist Stanley Sue has shown that discrimination may be connected with racial differences in intelligence and achievement.

Today two-thirds of the PhDs in psychology are awarded to women (Kohout & Williams, 1999). African Americans make up 6–7% of first-year students in doctoral departments in psychology; 6% are Asian American; 5% are Latino and Latina Americans; and about 1% are Native American (American Psychological Association Research Office, 2000). Even though these percentages do not yet reflect these groups' numbers in the general population, psychology is being increasingly enriched as it increasingly attracts a diverse population (Kite, 2001).

HOW PSYCHOLOGISTS STUDY BEHAVIOR AND MENTAL PROCESSES

His parents named him Francis. I call him Mr. Measurement.

The Englishman Sir Francis Galton (1822–1911) was reading and writing by the age of two and a half. He read Shakespeare for pleasure at the age of seven. He invented weather maps and coined the terms *high, low,* and *front.* He innovated the use of fingerprinting for purposes of identification. He was also Charles Darwin's cousin. Independently wealthy, young Galton attended medical school for a while and then dropped out. He traveled in the Middle East and Africa and mapped out previously uncharted territories. He assumed that intelligence could be measured by means of sensory sharpness (it cannot) and constructed devices to measure the keenness of the senses. He also believed that intelligence was inherited and founded the *eugenics* movement, which proposed that only bright people should mate. In fact, he wanted the British government to pay people who shared desirable traits to marry and bear children. These misguided views have since branded him as exclusionary and racist.

But Galton's fascination with measurement led to many positive innovations in the field of psychology, such as the use of questionnaires and twin studies. He invented the use of the **correlational method** so that there would be a mathematical way to see what goes with what—that is, the relationship between variables, as discussed on p. 24. For example, he sought ways to measure the amount of boredom in the audience at scientific lectures—an undertaking that probably did not heighten his popularity with his fellow scientists. He also sought to measure the effectiveness of prayers (he concluded that they were ineffective) and to determine which nation had the world's most attractive women. He chose his native England, mistakenly assuming that the local standards for beauty were universal.

Despite Galton's missteps, observation and the measurement of observations are keys to the scientific method. Much of what Galton taught, such as the use of questionnaires and the correlational method, remains in use today. These are important for answering the kinds of questions of interest to psychologists: Does alcohol cause aggression? Why do some people hardly ever think of food, whereas others are obsessed with it and snack all day long? Why do some unhappy people attempt suicide, whereas others seek ways of coping with their problems? Does having people of different ethnic backgrounds collaborate in their work serve to decrease or increase feelings of prejudice?

Many of us have expressed opinions—maybe even some strong opinions—on questions like these. Various psychological theories also suggest possible answers. Modern psychology aims to be an *empirical* science, however. In an empirical science, we cannot test assumptions about the behavior of cosmic rays, chemical compounds, cells, or people unless we observe and measure that behavior. Assumptions must be supported by evidence. Strong arguments, reference to authority figures, even tightly knit theories are not adequate as scientific evidence. The guiding principle behind this kind of skepticism is the scientific method.

Correlational Method
A mathematical method of determining whether one variable increases or decreases as another variable increases or decreases. For example, there is a correlation between intelligence test scores and grades in school.

R E F L E C T

Do you believe that it is possible to understand people from a scientific perspective? Why or why not?

The Scientific Method: Putting Ideas to the Test

Question: What is the scientific method? The scientific method is an organized way of using experience and testing ideas in order to expand and refine knowledge. Psychologists do not necessarily follow the steps of the scientific method as we might follow a recipe in a cookbook. However, modern research ideally is guided by certain principles.

Psychologists usually begin by *formulating a research question.* Research questions can have many sources. Our daily experiences, psychological theory, even folklore all help generate questions for research. Consider some questions that may arise from daily experience. Daily experience in using day care centers may motivate us to conduct research on whether day care affects the development of social skills or the bonds of attachment between children and mothers.

Or consider questions that might arise from psychological theory (see Figure 1.4). Social–cognitive principles of observational learning may prompt research on the effects of TV violence.

Research questions may also arise from common knowledge. Consider familiar adages such as "Misery loves company," "Opposites attract," and "Seeing is believing." Psychologists may ask, *Does* misery love company? *Do* opposites attract? *Can* people believe what they see?

A research question may be studied as a question or reworded as a hypothesis (see Figure 1.4). A **hypothesis** is a specific statement about behavior or mental processes that is tested through research. One hypothesis about day care might be that preschoolers who are placed in day care will acquire greater social skills in relating to peers than preschoolers who are cared for in the home. A hypothesis about TV violence might be that elementary school children who watch more violent TV shows tend to behave more aggressively toward their peers.

Psychologists next examine the research question or *test the hypothesis* through controlled methods such as the experiment. For example, we could take a group of preschoolers who attend day care and another group who do not and introduce each preschoolder to a new child in a controlled setting such as a child research center. We could then observe how children in each group interact with the new acquaintance.

R E F L E C T

Have you heard the expressions "Misery loves company," "Opposites attract," or "Seeing is believing"? Is there evidence for them? Is the evidence scientific? Why or why not?

Psychologists draw conclusions about their research questions or the accuracy of their hypotheses on the basis of their observations or findings. When their observations do not bear out their hypotheses, they may modify the theories from which the hypotheses were derived. Research findings often suggest refinements to psychological theories and, consequently, new avenues of research.

In our research on day care, we would probably find that children in day care show greater social skills than children who are cared for in the home (Belsky et al., 2001). We would probably also find that more aggressive children spend more time watching TV violence.

As psychologists draw conclusions from research evidence, they are guided by principles of critical thinking. For example, they try not to confuse correlations—or associations—between findings with cause and effect. Although more aggressive children apparently spend more time watching violent TV shows, it may be erroneous to conclude from this kind of evidence that TV violence *causes* aggressive behavior. Perhaps a **selection factor** is at work—because the children studied choose (select) for themselves what they will watch. Perhaps more aggressive children are more likely than less aggressive children to tune in to violent TV shows.

R E F L E C T

People who exercise are generally healthier than people who do not. Does this fact show that exercise is a causal factor in good health? Why or why not?

To better understand the effects of the selection factor, consider a study on the relationship between exercise and health. Imagine that we were to compare a group of people who exercised regularly with a group of people who did not. We might find that the exercisers were physically healthier than the couch potatoes. But could we conclude without doubt that exercise is a causal factor in good health? Perhaps not. The selection factor—the fact that one group chose to exercise and the other did not—could also explain the results. Perhaps healthy people are more likely to *choose* to exercise.

Some psychologists include publication of research reports in professional journals as a crucial part of the scientific method. Researchers are obligated to provide enough details of their work so that others will be able to repeat or **replicate** it to see whether the findings hold up over time and with different subjects. Publication of research also permits the scientific community at large to evaluate the methods and conclusions of other scientists.

Power Visual
See Web site for an interactive version of this figure.

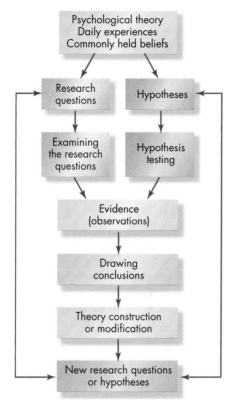

Figure 1.4
The Scientific Method

The scientific method is a systematic way of organizing and expanding scientific knowledge. Daily experiences, common beliefs, and scientific observations all contribute to the development of theories. Psychological theories explain observations and lead to hypotheses about behavior and mental processes. Observations can confirm the theory or lead to its refinement or abandonment.

Hypothesis

In psychology, a specific statement about behavior or mental processes that is tested through research.

Selection Factor

A source of bias that may occur in research findings when subjects are allowed to choose for themselves a certain treatment in a scientific study.

Replicate

Repeat, reproduce, copy.

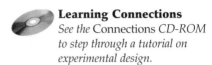

Learning Connections
See the Connections *CD-ROM to step through a tutorial on experimental design.*

Samples and Populations: Hitting the Target Population

Consider a piece of history that never quite happened: The Republican candidate Alf Landon defeated the incumbent president, Franklin D. Roosevelt, in 1936. Or at least Landon did so in a poll conducted by a popular magazine of the day, the *Literary Digest.* In the actual election, however, Roosevelt routed Landon by a landslide of 11 million votes. How, then, could the *Digest* predict a Landon victory? How was so great a discrepancy possible?

The *Digest,* you see, had surveyed voters by phone. Today telephone sampling is a widely practiced and reasonably legitimate polling technique. But the *Digest* poll was taken during the Great Depression, when people who had telephones were much wealthier than those who did not. People at higher income levels are also more likely to vote Republican. No surprise, then, that the overwhelming majority of those sampled said they would vote for Landon.

Question: How do psychologists use samples to represent populations? The *Digest* poll failed because of its method of sampling. Samples must be drawn so that they accurately *represent* the population they are intended to reflect. Only representative samples allow us to **generalize**—or *extend*—our findings from research samples to populations.

In surveys such as that conducted by the *Literary Digest,* and in other research methods, the individuals who are studied are referred to as a **sample.** A sample is a segment of a **population** (the group that is targeted for study). Psychologists and other scientists need to ensure that the people they observe *represent* their target population, such as U.S. voters, and not subgroups such as southern Californians or European American members of the middle class.

Problems in Generalizing from Psychological Research

All generalizations are dangerous, even this one.

—Alexandre Dumas

Many factors must be considered in interpreting the accuracy of the results of scientific research. One is the nature of the research sample.

Later in the chapter we consider research in which the subjects were drawn from a population of college men who were social drinkers. That is, they tended to drink at social gatherings but not when alone. Who do college men represent, other than themselves? To whom can we extend, or generalize, the results? For one thing, the results may not extend to women, not even to college women. In the chapter on consciousness, for example, we will learn that alcohol affects women more quickly than men.

Also, compared to the general adult male population, college men tend to be younger and score higher on intelligence tests. We cannot be certain that the findings extend to older men or to those with lower intelligence test scores, although it seems reasonable to assume they do. Social drinkers may also differ biologically and psychologically from alcoholics, who have difficulty controlling their drinking. Nor can we be certain that male college social drinkers represent people who do not drink at all.

By and large, we must also question whether findings of research with men can be generalized to women and whether research with European American men can be extended to members of ethnic minority groups. For example, personality tests completed by European Americans and by African Americans may need to be interpreted in diverse ways if accurate conclusions are to be drawn. The well-known Kinsey studies on sexual behavior (Kinsey et al., 1948, 1953) did not adequately represent African Americans, low-income people, older people, and numerous other groups.

Random and Stratified Sampling

One way to achieve a representative sample is by means of **random sampling.** In a random sample, each member of a population has an equal chance of being selected to participate. Researchers can also use a **stratified sample,** which is selected so that identified subgroups in the population are represented proportionately in the sample. For instance, 13% of the American population is African American. A stratified sample would thus be 13% African American. As a practical matter, a large randomly selected

Generalize
To extend from the particular to the general; to apply observations based on a sample to a population.

Sample
Part of a population.

Population
A complete group of organisms or events.

Random Sample
A sample drawn so that each member of a population has an equal chance of being selected to participate.

Stratified Sample
A sample drawn so that identified subgroups in the population are represented proportionately in the sample. How can stratified sampling be carried out to ensure that a sample represents the ethnic diversity we find in the population at large?

sample will show reasonably accurate stratification. A random sample of 1,500 people will represent the broad American population reasonably well. A haphazardly drawn sample of 20 million, however, might not.

Large-scale magazine surveys of sexual behavior have asked readers to fill out and return questionnaires. Although many thousands of readers completed the questionnaires and sent them in, did the survey respondents represent the American population? Probably not. These studies and similar ones may have been influenced by **volunteer bias.** People who offer or volunteer to participate in research studies differ systematically from people who do not. In the case of research on sexual behavior, volunteers may represent subgroups of the population—or of readers of the magazines in question—who are willing to disclose intimate information and therefore may also be likely to be more liberal in their sexual behavior (Rathus et al., 2002). Volunteers may also be more interested in research than other people, as well as have more spare time. How might such volunteers differ from the population at large? How might such differences slant or bias the research outcomes?

Methods of Observation: The Better to See You

Many people consider themselves experts on behavior and mental processes. How many times, for example, have you or someone else been eager to share a life experience that proves some point about human nature?

Indeed, we see much during our lifetimes. However, our personal observations tend to be fleeting and unsystematic. We sift through experience for the things that interest us. We often ignore the obvious because it does not fit our assumptions about the way things ought to be. Scientists, however, have devised more controlled ways of observing others.   *Question: What methods of observation are used by psychologists?*   In this section we consider three methods of observation widely used by psychologists and other behavioral scientists: the case study, survey, and naturalistic observation methods.

Case Study

We begin with the case study method because our own informal ideas about human nature tend to be based on **case studies,** or information we collect about individuals and small groups. But most of us gather our information haphazardly. We often see only what we want to see. Unscientific accounts of people's behavior are referred to as *anecdotes.* Ideally, psychologists attempt to gather information about individuals more carefully.

The Swiss biologist and psychologist Jean Piaget (1896–1980) developed much of his theory of cognitive development on the basis of extensive research with his own children. We will discuss his views in depth in Chapter 3.

Case studies are sometimes used to investigate rare occurrences, as in the case of "Eve," immortalized in the film *The Three Faces of Eve.* Eve was an example of a person with multiple personalities (technically termed *dissociative identity disorder*). "Eve White" was a mousy, well-intentioned woman who had two other "personalities" living inside her. One of them was "Eve Black," a promiscuous personality who emerged now and then to take control of her behavior. The third personality, "Jane," was a well-adjusted woman who integrated parts of Eve White and Eve Black.

Case studies can provide compelling portraits of individuals, but they also have some sources of inaccuracy. For example, there are gaps and factual inaccuracies in people's memories (Azar, 1997a; Brewin et al., 1993). People may also distort their pasts to please the interviewer or because they want to remember things in certain ways. Interviewers may also have certain expectations and may subtly encourage subjects to fill in gaps in ways that are consistent with these expectations. Psychoanalysts, for example, have been criticized for guiding people who seek their help into viewing their own lives from the psychodynamic perspective (Hergenhahn, 2001). No wonder, then, that many people provide "evidence" that is consistent with psychodynamic theory—such as, "My parents' inept handling of my toilet training is the source of my compulsive neatness." However, interviewers and other kinds of researchers who hold *any* theoretical viewpoint run the risk of indirectly prodding people into saying what they want to hear.

REFLECT

Would a random sample of students from your own college or university represent the general American population? Why or why not?

REFLECT

What methods of observation do you use when you try to "figure out" other people? Are your methods scientific? Why or why not?

Volunteer Bias
A source of bias or error in research reflecting the prospect that people who offer to participate in research studies differ systematically from people who do not.

Case Study
A carefully drawn biography that may be obtained through interviews, questionnaires, and psychological tests.

The Survey

Just as computers and pollsters predict election results and report national opinion on the basis of scientifically selected samples, psychologists conduct **surveys** to learn about behavior and mental processes that cannot be observed in the natural setting or studied experimentally. Psychologists conducting surveys may employ questionnaires and interviews or examine public records. One of the advantages of the survey is that by distributing questionnaires and analyzing answers with a computer, psychologists can study many thousands of people at a time.

Alfred Kinsey of Indiana University and his colleagues published two surveys of sexual behavior, based on interviews, that shocked the nation. These were *Sexual Behavior in the Human Male* (1948) and *Sexual Behavior in the Human Female* (1953). Kinsey reported that masturbation was virtually universal in his sample of men at a time when masturbation was still widely thought to impair health. He also reported that about 1 woman in 3 who was still single at age 25 had engaged in premarital intercourse.

Surveys, like case studies, have various sources of inaccuracy. People may recall their behavior inaccurately or purposely misrepresent it. Some people try to ingratiate themselves with their interviewers by answering in what they perceive to be the socially desirable direction. The Kinsey studies all relied on male interviewers, for example. It has been speculated that female interviewees might have been more open and honest with female interviewers. Similar problems may occur when interviewers and the people surveyed are from different ethnic or socioeconomic backgrounds. Other people may falsify their attitudes and exaggerate their problems in order to draw attention to themselves or intentionally foul up the results.

Consider some examples of survey measurement errors caused by inaccurate self-reports of behavior (Barringer, 1993). If people brushed their teeth as often as they claimed, and used the amount of toothpaste they indicated, three times as much toothpaste would be sold in the United States as is actually sold. People also appear to over-report church attendance and to underreport abortions (Barringer, 1993). Why do you think this is so?

Naturalistic Observation

You use **naturalistic observation**—that is, you observe people in their natural habitats—every day. So do psychologists. The next time you opt for a fast-food burger lunch, look around. Pick out slender people and overweight people and observe whether they eat their burgers and fries differently. Do the overweight people eat more rapidly? Chew less frequently? Leave less food on their plates? Psychologists have used this method to study the eating habits of normal-weight and overweight people.

Naturalistic observation has the advantage of allowing psychologists and other scientists to observe behavior where it happens, or "in the field." In doing so, researchers use *unobtrusive* measures to avoid interfering with the behaviors they are observing. For example, Jane Goodall has observed the behavior of chimpanzees in their natural environment to learn about their social behavior, sexual behavior, use of tools, and other facts of chimp life. Her observations have shown us that (1) we were incorrect to think that only humans use tools; and (2) kissing on the lips, as a greeting, is apparently used by chimpanzees as well as by humans (Goodall, 2000).

Correlation: On How Things Go Together—Or Not

Are people with higher intelligence more likely to do well in school? Are people with a stronger need for achievement likely to climb higher up the corporate ladder? What is the relationship between stress and health?

Such questions are often answered by means of the correlational method. ***Question: What is the correlational method?*** Correlation follows observation. By using the correlational method, psychologists investigate whether observed behavior or a measured trait is related to, or correlated with, another. Consider the variables of intelligence and academic performance. These variables are assigned numbers such as intelligence test scores and academic averages. Then the numbers are mathematically related and expressed as a **correlation coefficient.** A correlation coefficient is a number that varies between +1.00 and −1.00.

REFLECT

Have you read the results of a survey or a poll in a popular magazine or online? Were they representative of the general population? Why or why not?

Survey

A method of scientific investigation in which a large sample of people answer questions about their attitudes or behavior.

Naturalistic Observation

A scientific method in which organisms are observed in their natural environments.

Correlation Coefficient

A number between +1.00 and −1.00 that expresses the strength and direction (positive or negative) of the relationship between two variables.

■ The Naturalistic-Observation Method

Jane Goodall has observed the behavior of chimpanzees—our closest genetic relatives—in the field, "where it happens." She has found that chimps use sticks to grub for food and that they apparently kiss each other as a social greeting. Scientists who use this method try not to interfere with the animals or people they observe, even though this sometimes means allowing an animal to be mistreated by other animals or to die from a curable illness.

Studies report **positive correlations** between intelligence test scores and academic achievement, as measured, for example, by grade point averages. Generally speaking, the higher people score on intelligence tests, the better their academic performance is likely to be. The scores attained on intelligence tests tend to be positively correlated (about +0.60 to +0.70) with academic achievement (see Figure 1.5). But factors *other* than performance on intelligence tests also contribute to academic success. These include achievement motivation, adjustment, and common sense (Collier, 1994; Sternberg et al., 1995).

Positive Correlation
A relationship between variables in which one variable increases as the other also increases.

Negative Correlation
A relationship between two variables in which one variable increases as the other decreases.

REFLECT

What kinds of correlations (positive or negative) would you expect to find among behavior patterns such as the following: Churchgoing and crime? Language ability and musical ability? Level of education and incidence of teenage pregnancy? Grades in school and delinquency? Why?

There is a **negative correlation** between stress and health. As the amount of stress affecting us increases, the functioning of our immune system decreases. Under high levels of stress, many people show poorer health.

Correlational research may suggest but does not prove cause and effect. For instance, it may seem logical to assume that high intelligence makes it possible for children to profit from education. Research has also shown, however, that education contributes to higher scores on

■ Figure 1.5
Positive and Negative Correlations

When there is a positive correlation between variables, as there is between intelligence and achievement, one increases as the other increases. By and large, the higher people score on intelligence tests, the better their academic performance is likely to be, as in the diagram to the left. (Each dot represents an individual's intelligence test score and grade point average.) But there is a negative correlation between stress and health. As the amount of stress we experience increases, the functioning of our immune system tends to decrease. Correlational research may suggest but does not demonstrate cause and effect.

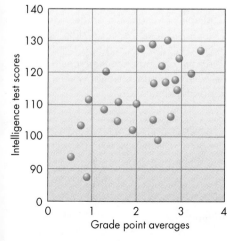

Positive correlation, as found between intelligence and academic achievement

Negative correlation, as found between stress and functioning of the immune system

Experiment
A scientific method that seeks to confirm cause-and-effect relationships by introducing independent variables and observing their effects on dependent variables.

Treatment
In experiments, a condition received by subjects so that its effects may be observed.

Independent Variable
A condition in a scientific study that is manipulated so that its effects may be observed.

Dependent Variable
A measure of an assumed effect of an independent variable.

intelligence tests. Preschoolers who are placed in stimulating Head Start programs later attain higher scores on intelligence tests than age-mates who did not have this experience. The relationship between intelligence and academic performance may not be as simple as we might think. What of the link between stress and health? Does stress impair health, or is it possible that people in poorer health encounter more stress? (See Figure 1.6.)

The Experimental Method: Trying Things Out

Question: What is the experimental method?   Most psychologists agree that the preferred method for answering questions about cause and effect is the experiment. In an **experiment,** a group of subjects obtains a **treatment,** such as a dose of alcohol, a change in room temperature, perhaps an injection of a drug. The subjects are then observed carefully to determine whether the treatment makes a difference in their behavior. Does alcohol alter the ability to take tests, for example? What about differences in room temperatures and level of background noise?

Experiments are used whenever possible because they allow psychologists to control the experiences of subjects and draw conclusions about cause and effect. A psychologist may theorize that alcohol leads to aggression because it reduces fear of consequences or because it energizes the activity levels of drinkers. She or he may then hypothesize that a treatment in which subjects receive a specified dosage of alcohol will lead to increases in aggression. Let us follow the example of the effects of alcohol on aggression to further our understanding of the experimental method.

Independent and Dependent Variables

In an experiment to determine whether alcohol causes aggression, subjects would be given an amount of alcohol and its effects would be measured. In this case, alcohol is an **independent variable.** The presence of an independent variable is manipulated by the experimenters so that its effects may be determined. The independent variable of alcohol may be administered at different levels, or doses, from none or very little to enough to cause intoxication or drunkenness.

The measured results, or outcomes, in an experiment are called **dependent variables.** The presence of dependent variables presumably depends on the independent variables. In an experiment to determine whether alcohol influences aggression, aggressive behavior would be a dependent variable. Other dependent variables of interest might include sexual arousal, visual–motor coordination, and performance on intellectual tasks such as defining words or doing numerical computations.

■ **Figure 1.6**
Correlational Relationships, Cause, and Effect
Correlational relationships may suggest but do not demonstrate cause and effect. In part A, there is a correlation between variables X and Y. Does this mean that either variable X causes variable Y or that variable Y causes variable X? Not necessarily. Other factors could affect both variables X and Y. Consider the examples of academic grades (variable X) and juvenile delinquency (variable Y) in part B. There is a negative correlation between the two. Does this mean that poor grades contribute to delinquency? Perhaps. Does it mean that delinquency contributes to poor grades? Again, perhaps. But there could also be other variables—such as a broken home, lack of faith in the educational system, or peer influences—that contribute to both poor grades and delinquency.

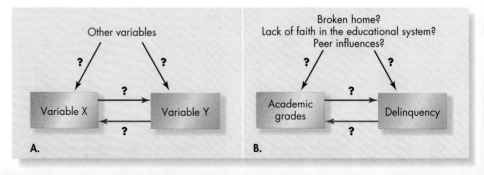

In an experiment on the relationships between temperature and aggression, temperature would be an independent variable and aggressive behavior would be a dependent variable. We could set temperatures from below freezing to blistering hot and study their effects on aggression. We could also use a second independent variable such as social provocation. That is, we could insult some subjects but not others and see whether insults affect their level of aggression. This method would allow us to study the ways in which two independent variables—temperature and social provocation—affect aggression, singly and/or together.

Experimental and Control Groups

Ideal experiments use "experimental groups" and "control groups." Subjects in **experimental groups** obtain the treatment. Members of **control groups** do not. Every effort is made to ensure that all other conditions are held constant for both groups. This method enhances the researchers' ability to draw conclusions about cause and effect. The researchers can be more confident that outcomes of the experiment are caused by the treatments and not by chance factors or chance fluctuations in behavior.

For example, in an experiment on the effects of alcohol on aggression, members of the experimental group would ingest alcohol and members of the control group would not. The researcher would then measure how much aggression was expressed by each group. In a complex version of this experiment, different experimental groups might ingest different dosages of alcohol and be exposed to different types of social provocations as well.

Blinds and Double Blinds

One experiment on the effects of alcohol on aggression (Boyatzis, 1974) reported that men at parties where beer and liquor were served acted more aggressively than men at parties where only soft drinks were served. But subjects in the experimental group *knew* they had drunk alcohol, and those in the control group *knew* they had not. Aggression that appeared to result from alcohol might not have reflected drinking per se. Instead, it might have reflected the subjects' *expectations* about the effects of alcohol. People tend to act in stereotypical ways when they believe they have been drinking alcohol. For instance, men tend to become less anxious in social situations, more aggressive, and more sexually aroused.

A **placebo,** or "sugar pill," often results in the kind of behavior that people expect. Physicians sometimes give placebos to healthy patients who insist on treatment. Many of these people then report feeling better. When subjects in psychological experiments are given placebos—such as tonic water—but think they have drunk alcohol, we can

Experimental Groups
In experiments, groups whose members obtain the treatment.

Control Groups
In experiments, groups whose members do not obtain the treatment, while other conditions are held constant.

Placebo
A bogus treatment that has the appearance of being genuine.

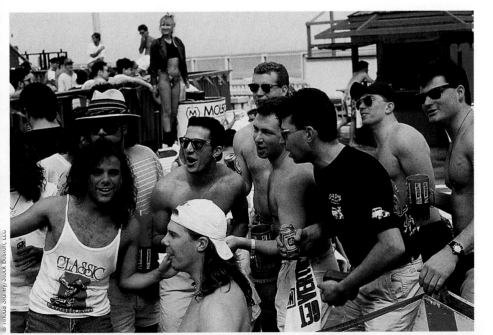

■ **What Are the Effects of Alcohol?**

Psychologists have conducted numerous studies to determine the effects of alcohol. Questions have been raised about the soundness of research in which people *know* that they have drunk alcohol. Why would such research be questioned, and how can we keep people blind to the fact that they have drunk alcohol?

Blind

In experimental terminology, unaware of whether or not one has received a treatment.

Double-Blind Study

A study in which neither the subjects nor the observers know who has received the treatment.

conclude that changes in their behavior stem from their beliefs about alcohol, not from the alcohol itself.

Well-designed experiments control for the effects of expectations by creating conditions under which subjects are unaware of, or **blind** to, the treatment (Day & Altman, 2000). Yet researchers may also have expectations. They may, in effect, be "rooting for" a certain treatment. For instance, tobacco company executives may wish to show that cigarette smoking is harmless. In such cases, it is useful if the people measuring the experimental outcomes are unaware of which subjects have received the treatment. Studies in which neither the subjects nor the experimenters know who has obtained the treatment are called **double-blind studies.**

The Food and Drug Administration requires double-blind studies before it allows the marketing of new drugs. The drug and the placebo look and taste alike. Experimenters assign the drug or placebo to subjects at random. Neither the subjects nor the observers know who is taking the drug and who is taking the placebo. After the final measurements have been made, a neutral panel (a group of people who have no personal stake in the outcome of the study) judges whether the effects of the drug differed from those of the placebo.

In one double-blind study on the effects of alcohol, Alan Lang and his colleagues (1975) pretested a highball of vodka and tonic water to determine that it could not be discriminated by taste from tonic water alone. They recruited college men who described themselves as social drinkers to participate in the study. Some of the men drank vodka and tonic water. Others drank tonic water only. Of the men who drank vodka, half were misled into believing they had drunk tonic water only (Figure 1.7). Of those who drank tonic water only, half were misled into believing their drink contained vodka. Thus, half the subjects were blind to their treatment. Experimenters who measured the men's aggressive responses were also blind concerning which subjects had drunk vodka.

The research team found that men who believed that they had drunk vodka responded more aggressively to a provocation than men who believed that they had drunk tonic water only. The actual content of the drink was immaterial. That is, the men's *belief* about what they drank affected their aggressive behavior more than what they actually consumed. The results of the Lang study differ dramatically from those reported by Boyatzis, perhaps because the Boyatzis study did not control for the effects of expectations or beliefs about alcohol. Table 1.1 reviews research methods.

Learning Connections
See Web site for an interactive version of these review questions.

R E V I E W

The scientific method is an organized way of expanding and refining knowledge. (27) Scientists often test a specific statement, or _____, about behavior or mental processes. (28) Samples must accurately represent the target _____. (29) In a _____ sample, each member of a population has an equal chance of being selected to participate. (30) A _____ sample is drawn so that identified subgroups in the population are represented proportionately in the sample. (31) A _____ study is a carefully drawn biography. (32) In the _____, a large sample of people answer questions about their attitudes or behavior. (33) The _____-observation method observes individuals in their natural habitats. (34) The _____ method investigates whether behaviors or traits are related to

■ **Figure 1.7**
The Experimental Conditions in the Lang Study
The taste of vodka cannot be discerned when vodka is mixed with tonic water. For this reason, it was possible for subjects in the Lang study on the effects of alcohol to be kept "blind" as to whether or not they had actually drunk alcohol. Blind studies allow psychologists to control for the effects of subjects' expectations.

TABLE 1.1 Research Methods

Method	What Happens	About . . .
Case Study *Freud's method*	The researcher uses interviews and records to gather in-depth information about an individual or a small group.	The accuracy of case studies is compromised by gaps and mistakes in memory and by subjects' tendency to present themselves in a socially desirable manner.
Survey	The researcher uses interviews, questionnaires, or public records to gather information about large numbers of people.	Surveys can include thousands of people but are subject to the same limitations as case studies. People who volunteer to participate in surveys may also differ from people who do not. There may thus be problems in generalization of results to people who do not participate.
Naturalistic Observation	The researcher observes behavior where it happens—"in the field."	Researchers try to avoid interfering with the behaviors they are observing by using *unobtrusive* measures.
Correlation	The researcher uses statistical (mathematical) methods to reveal positive and negative relationships between variables.	The correlational method does not show cause and effect. Correlation coefficients vary between +1.00 (a perfect positive correlation) and −1.00 (a perfect negative correlation).
Experiment	The researcher manipulates independent variables and observes their effects on dependent variables.	Experimental groups obtain the treatment; control groups do not. Researchers use *blinds* to control for the effect of expectations. With *double blinds*, neither the subjects nor the observers know which subject has received which treatment. The experimental method allows researchers to draw conclusions about cause and effect.

others. (35) Correlational research does not reveal _____ and effect. (36) An _____ is conducted in an effort to determine cause and effect. (37) The _____ variable is manipulated by the experimenters so that its effects may be determined. (38) Ideal experiments use experimental and _____ groups. (39) Well-designed experiments control for the effects of expectations by creating conditions under which subjects are unaware of, or _____ to, the treatment they have received.

Critical Thinking: Couples who live together before marriage are more likely to get divorced once they are married than couples who did not. Does this research finding mean that living together before getting married *causes* marital instability? Why or why not? Can you think of alternative explanations for the relationship?

ETHICAL ISSUES IN PSYCHOLOGICAL RESEARCH AND PRACTICE

The researchers in the Lang study gave some participants alcohol to drink and deceived the entire group about the purposes and methods of the study. Was their method **ethical**? We'll return to this question, but let's first address a broader one. *Question: What are the ethical issues that concern psychological research and practice with humans?*

Psychologists adhere to a number of ethical standards that are intended to promote individual dignity, human welfare, and scientific integrity. The standards are also intended to ensure that psychologists do not undertake research methods or treatments that are harmful.

Ethical
Moral; referring to one's system of deriving standards for determining what is moral.

Research with Humans

Ethics Review Committee
A group found in an institutional setting that helps researchers consider the potential harm of their methods and reviews proposed studies according to ethical guidelines.

Informed Consent
A subject's agreement to participate in research after receiving information about the purposes of the study and the nature of the treatments.

Debrief
To provide information about a completed procedure.

If the Lang group were running their experiment today rather than in the 1970s, they might have been denied permission to do so by a university ethics review committee. Why? Because in virtually all institutional settings, including colleges, hospitals, and research foundations, **ethics review committees** help researchers consider the potential harm of their methods and review proposed studies according to ethical guidelines. When such committees find that proposed research might be unacceptably harmful to subjects, they may withhold approval until the proposal has been modified. Ethics review committees also weigh the potential benefits of research against the potential harm.

Today individuals must provide **informed consent** before they participate in research. Having a general overview of the research and the opportunity to choose not to participate apparently gives them a sense of control and decreases the stress of participating (Dill et al., 1982). Is there a way in which subjects in the Lang study could have provided informed consent? What do you think?

Psychologists treat the records of research subjects and clients as confidential. This is because they respect people's privacy and also because people are more likely to express their true thoughts and feelings when researchers or therapists keep their disclosures confidential. Sometimes conflicts of interest arise, however—for example, when a client threatens to harm someone and the psychologist feels an obligation to warn that person (Follingstad & McCormick, 2002).

Ethics also limit the types of research that psychologists may conduct. For example, how can we determine whether early separation from one's mother impairs social development? One way would be to observe the development of children who were separated from their mothers at an early age for reasons such as the death of the mother or court-ordered protective custody. It is difficult to draw conclusions from such research, however, because of the selection factor. That is, the same factors that led to the separation—such as family tragedy or irresponsible parents—and *not* the separation itself may have led to the outcome. Scientifically, it would be more sound to run experiments in which researchers separate children from their mothers at an early age and compare their development with that of other children. But psychologists would not undertake such research because of the ethical issues they pose. Yet, they run experiments in which infant animals are separated from their mothers, which has brought criticism from animal-rights groups.

Many psychological experiments cannot be run without deceiving the people who participate. However, the use of deception also raises important ethical issues.

▶ CONTROVERSY IN PSYCHOLOGY ◀

Should psychologists ever break confidences?

Psychologists are expected to keep things that clients tell them confidential. However, if a client in therapy were to tell his psychologist that he was thinking of hurting you, should the psychologist tell you about it? Why or why not?

▶ CONTROVERSY IN PSYCHOLOGY ◀

Is it ethical for psychologists to deceive research participants about the methods and objectives of their research?

Some studies could not be done if subjects knew what the researchers were trying to find out, or which treatment they had received (e.g., a new medicine or a "sugar pill"). As you can imagine, psychologists have long debated the ethics of deceiving subjects. According to the American Psychological Association's (1992a) *Ethical Principles of Psychologists and Code of Conduct,* psychologists may use deception only when they believe the benefits of the research outweigh its potential harm, they believe the individuals might have been willing to participate if they had understood the benefits of the research, and subjects are **debriefed.** Debriefing means that the purposes and methods of the research are explained afterward.

Return to the Lang (Lang et al., 1975) study on alcohol and aggression. In this study, the researchers (1) misinformed subjects about the beverage they were drinking and (2) misled them into believing they were giving other subjects electric shocks when they were actually only pressing switches on a dead control board. (*Aggression* was defined as pressing these switches in the study.) In the Lang study, students who believed they had drunk vodka were "more aggressive"—that is, selected higher levels of shock—than students who believed they had not. The actual content of the beverages was immaterial.

Research with Nonhuman Animals

Psychologists and other scientists frequently use animals to conduct research that cannot be carried out with humans (Carroll & Overmier, 2001). For example, experiments on the effects of early separation from the mother have been done with monkeys and other animals. Such research has helped psychologists investigate the formation of attachment bonds between parent and child.

► CONTROVERSY IN PSYCHOLOGY ◄

Is it ethical to harm aniamls in conducting research when the results may be beneficial to humans?

Researchers often use animals to conduct research that they could not carry out with people. Do you agree with the practice? Why or why not?

Question: What are the ethical issues that concern research with animals? Experiments with infant monkeys highlight some of the ethical issues faced by psychologists and other scientists who contemplate potentially harmful research. Psychologists and biologists who study the workings of the brain destroy sections of the brains of laboratory animals to learn how they influence behavior. For instance, a lesion in one part of a brain structure causes a rat to overeat. A lesion elsewhere causes the rat to go on a crash diet. Psychologists generalize to humans from experiments such as these in the hope of finding solutions to problems such as eating disorders. Proponents of the use of animals in research argue that major advances in medicine and psychology could not have taken place without them (Bekoff, 2002).

The majority of psychologists disapprove of research in which animals are exposed to pain or killed (Plous, 1996). According to the ethical guidelines of the American Psychological Association (1992b), animals may be harmed only when there is no alternative and when researchers believe that the benefits of the research justify the harm.

■ The Ethics of Using Animals in Research

Is it ethical for researchers to harm animals in order to obtain knowledge that may benefit humans?

© Michael Rosenfeld/Getty Images/Stone

Learning Connections
See Web site for an interactive version of these review questions.

R E V I E W

(40) Psychologists adhere to _____ standards that help promote the dignity of the individual, maintain scientific integrity, and protect subjects or clients from harm. (41) In order to help avoid harm, human subjects must provide _____ consent. Psychologists treat the records of research subjects and clients as confidential. Many experiments cannot be run without deceiving people. (42) Ethics require that subjects who are deceived be _____ afterward to help eliminate misconceptions and anxieties about the research. (43) Researchers use _____ to conduct research that cannot be carried out with humans. Psychologists follow the principle that animals should be harmed only when there is no alternative and the benefits of the research justify the harm.

Critical Thinking: Under what circumstances do researchers deceive subjects? What does your own belief system say about the ethical treatment of animals?

Critical Thinking, Science, and Pseudoscience

Nonsense and pseudoscience (false science) beckon us from the tabloids at supermarket checkout counters. Each week, there are ten new sightings of Elvis and ten new encounters with extraterrestrials. There are ten new "absolutely proven effective" ways to take off weight and ten new ways to beat stress and depression. There are ten new ways to tell if your partner has been cheating and, of course, ten new predictions by astrologers and psychics. For example, 1997 was the year when Mick Jagger was supposed to be elected to Parliament and Hillary Clinton was supposed to get pregnant again.

He wasn't. She didn't—at least, not that we know of. But will those facts dissuade people who believe in psychics and astrologers? Clairvoyance and astrology are pseudosciences, not true sciences. Unfortunately, a survey of 1,574 adults by the National Science Foundation (2002) found that 70% of Americans do not understand the scientific process.

Let us look at the world through the eyes of the psychologist. Psychologists are guided by scientific principles, and one hallmark of science is *critical thinking.* **Question: What is critical thinking?** Critical thinking has many meanings. On one level, it means taking nothing for granted. It means not believing things just because they are in print or on the Web or because they were uttered by authority figures or celebrities. It means not necessarily believing that it is healthful to express all of your feelings just because a friend in "therapy" urges you to do so. On another level, critical thinking refers to a process of thoughtfully analyzing and probing the questions, statements, and arguments of others. It means examining definitions of terms, examining the premises or assumptions behind arguments, and then scrutinizing the logic with which arguments are developed.

A group of psychologists (McGovern, 1989) defined the goals of critical thinking as fostering the following thinking skills:

- Development of skepticism about explanations and conclusions.
- The ability to inquire about causes and effects.
- Increased curiosity about behavior.
- Knowledge of research methods.
- The ability to analyze arguments critically.

Principles of Critical Thinking

Let us consider some principles of critical thinking that can be of help to you in college and beyond:

- *Be skeptical.* Keep an open mind. Politicians and advertisers try to persuade you. Even research reported in the media or in textbooks may take a certain slant. Extend this principle to yourself. Are some of your own attitudes and beliefs superficial or unfounded? Accept nothing as the truth until you have examined the evidence.
- *Examine definitions of terms.* Some statements are true when a term is defined in one way but not when it is defined in another way. Consider the statement "Head Start programs have raised children's IQs." The correctness of the statement depends on the definition of "IQ." (You will see later in the text that *IQ* has a specific meaning and is not exactly the same as *intelligence.*)
- *Examine the assumptions or premises of arguments.* Consider the statement that one cannot learn about human beings by engaging in research with animals. One premise in the statement

seems to be that human beings are not animals. We are, of course. (Would you rather be a plant?)

- *Be cautious in drawing conclusions from evidence.* For many years studies had shown that most clients who receive psychotherapy improve. It was therefore generally assumed that psychotherapy worked. Some 40 years ago, however, a psychologist named Hans Eysenck pointed out that most psychologically troubled people who did *not* receive psychotherapy also improved. The question thus becomes whether people receiving psychotherapy are *more* likely to improve than those who do not. Current research on the effectiveness of psychotherapy therefore carefully compares the benefits of therapy techniques to the benefits of other techniques or of no treatment at all. Be especially skeptical of anecdotes. When you hear "I know someone who—," ask yourself whether this one person's reported experience is satisfactory as evidence.
- *Consider alternative interpretations of research evidence.* Does alcohol cause aggression? We reported evidence that there is a clear *connection,* or "correlation," between alcohol and aggression. For example, many people who commit violent crimes have been drinking. But what of the experiment by Lang and his colleagues? Does the evidence show that drinking causes aggression? Might other factors, such as gender, age, or willingness to take risks, account for both drinking and aggressive behavior?
- *Do not oversimplify.* Most human behavior involves complex interactions of genetic and environmental influences. Also consider the issue of whether psychotherapy helps people with psychological problems. A broad answer to this question—a simple yes or no—might be oversimplifying. It is more worthwhile to ask, What *type* of psychotherapy, practiced by *whom,* is most helpful for *what kind of problem?*
- *Do not overgeneralize.* Consider the statement that one cannot learn about human beings by engaging in research with non-human animals. Is the truth of the matter an all-or-nothing issue? Are there certain kinds of information we can obtain about people from research with animals? What kinds of things are you likely to be able to learn only through research with people?
- *Apply critical thinking to all areas of life.* A skeptical attitude and a demand for evidence are not only useful in college, but are of value in all areas of life. Be skeptical when you are bombarded by TV commercials, when political causes try to sweep you up, when you see the latest cover stories about Elvis and UFO sightings in supermarket tabloids. How many times have you heard the claim "Studies have shown that . . ."? Perhaps such claims sound convincing, but ask yourself: Who ran the studies? Were the researchers neutral scientists, or were they biased toward obtaining certain results?

These are the kinds of principles that guide psychologists' thinking as they observe behavior, engage in research, or advise clients as to how to improve the quality of their lives. Perhaps these principles will help you improve the quality of your own life.

Critical Thinking and Astrology

Let's apply principles of critical thinking to one pseudoscience—astrology. But first read this personality report. I wrote it about you:

You have your strengths and your weaknesses; but, much of the time, you do not give yourself enough credit for your strengths. You are one of those people who has the inner potential for change, but you need to pay more attention to your own feelings so that you can determine the right direction for yourself.

You have many times found yourself to be in conflict as your inner impulses have run up against the limits of social rules and moral codes. Most of the time you manage to resolve conflict in a way that makes sense to you, but now and then you have doubts and wonder whether you have done the right thing. You would often like to be doing two or more things at the same time, and you occasionally resent the fact that you cannot.

There is an inner you known to you alone, and you often present a face to the world that does not quite reflect your genuine thoughts and feelings. And now and then you look at the things you have done and the path that you have taken, and you have some doubt as to whether it is all worth it.

That's you to a *T*, isn't it? It probably sounds familiar enough. The tendency to believe a generalized (but phony) personality report is called the *Barnum effect,* after circus magnate P. T. Barnum, who once declared that a good circus had a "little something for everybody." The Barnum effect—the tendency for general personality reports to have a "little something for everybody"—also allows fortune-tellers to make a living. That is, most of us have enough in common so that a fortune-teller's "revelations" about us may ring true.

Most of us have personality traits in common. But what do tea leaves, bird droppings, palms (of your hands, not on the tropical sands), and the stars have in common? Let us see.

P. T. Barnum also once declared, "There's a sucker born every minute." The tendency to believe generalized personality reports has made people vulnerable to phonies throughout history. It enriches the pocketbooks of astrologists who offer to "read your personality" and predict your future based on the movements of the stars and planets (Browne, 1995). Astrology has been popular for centuries. Gallup and Newport (1991) report that one person out of four in the United States believes in astrology. Another one in four to five is not sure. Even in an age in which science has proved itself capable of making significant contributions to people's daily lives and health, more people are likely to check their horoscope than seek scientific information when they have to make a decision.

Astrology is based on the notion that the positions of the sun, the moon, and the stars affect human temperament and human affairs. For example, people born under the sign of Jupiter are believed to be jovial, or full of playful good humor. People born under the sign of Saturn are thought to be gloomy and morose (saturnine). And people born under the sign of Mars are believed to be warlike (martial). One supposedly can also foretell the future by studying the positions of these bodies.

Astrologers maintain that the positions of the heavenly bodies at the time of our birth determine our personality and destiny. They prepare forecasts called *horoscopes* that are based on our birthdates and indicate what it is safe for us to do. If you get involved with someone who asks for your "sign" (for example, Aquarius or Taurus), he or she is inquiring about your birthdate in astrological terms. Astrologers claim that your sign, which reflects the month during which you were born, indicates whom you will be compatible with. You may have been wondering

© Gregg Mancuso/Stock Boston LLC

■ The Lure of Astrology

Astrology has been shown to be a pseudoscience, not a real science. How, then, do we account for its allure to so many millions of people?

whether you should date someone of another religion. If you start to follow astrology, you may also be wondering whether it is safe for a Sagittarius to be dating a Pisces or a Gemini.

Although psychologists and other scientists consider astrology to be a pseudoscience, it has millions of followers. The National Science Foundation (2002) found that astrology is rejected by 60% of Americans, but 43% still check their horoscopes from time to time. How do we account for astrology's allure? What can we tell people who believe in it?

The allure of astrology is understandable in that people generally want to know about themselves and about the world. One could argue that understanding one's abilities and limits and the nature of the world foster the survival of the individual. Evolutionary forces would thus favor the survival of individuals who are curious. It is not much of a stretch to speculate that curiosity is embedded in our genes and transmitted from generation to generation. Research and theory do suggest that people are drawn to astrology and other pseudosciences as a way of understanding the self and the world—especially unexpected events (Lillqvist & Lindeman, 1998; Lindeman, 1998). But it becomes a bit self-serving, because people are most likely to believe in astrology when the descriptions they hear about their personalities are favorable (Hamilton, 2001). It seems to go like this: The "validity" of astrology is confirmed when the astrologer—or palm reader, or reader of tea leaves, or reader of Tarot cards, or even the reader of bird droppings—says something positive about the individual. If the message is bad, there goes the validity of the messenger!

Believers in of astrology also tend to provide arguments such as the following:

- Astrology has been practiced for many centuries and is a time-honored aspect of human history, tradition, and culture.
- Astrology seems to provide a path to the core meaning in the universe for people who are uneducated and, for a fortunate few with limited means, a road to riches.
- People in high positions in government have followed the advice of astrologers. (Nancy Reagan, wife of former president Ronald Reagan, is reported to have consulted an astrologer in arranging her husband's schedule.)
- One heavenly body (the moon) is powerful enough to sway the tides of the seas. The pulls of heavenly bodies are therefore easily capable of affecting people's destinies.
- Astrology is a special art and not a science. Therefore, we shouldn't subject astrology to the rigors of scientific testing.
- Astrology has been shown to work.

Think critically about the claims of astrologers. Does the fact that there may be a long-standing tradition in astrology affect its scientific credibility? Does Nancy Reagan's (or anyone else's) belief in astrology affect its scientific credibility? Psychology is an *empirical* science. In an empirical science, beliefs about the behavior of cosmic rays, chemical compounds, cells, people—or the meaning of bird droppings or the movements of the stars—must be supported by evidence. Persuasive arguments and reference to authority figures are *not* scientific evidence. Pseudoscientists have made specific forecasts of events, and their accuracy—or lack of it—provides a means of evaluation. Mick Jagger was *not* elected to Parliament and Hillary Clinton did *not* get pregnant in 1997. Astrological predictions are no more likely to come true than predictions based on chance (Crowe, 1990; Munro & Munro, 2000). That is fact, but does it matter?

Maybe not. Magical predictions tend to keep their allure. For one thing, scientists make predictions about groups, not individuals. They may say that obesity heightens the risk of heart disease but may not be able to predict with certainly whether a given individual will develop heart disease. Individuals may turn to "psychics" to find out—even if they are fed false knowledge. In addition, many people just want some magic in their lives (Munro & Munro, 2000). Sad to say, even in our age of scientific enlightenment, many people are more comfortable with fanciful stories and leaps of faith than they are with objective evidence and statistical probabilities.

But what about you? Will you be more skeptical in the future?

Recite Recite Recite

Learning Connections
See Web site for an interactive version of this chapter summary

1. What is psychology?

Psychology is the scientific study of behavior and mental processes.

2. What are the goals of psychology?

Psychology seeks to describe, explain, predict, and control behavior and mental processes. Behavior and mental processes are explained through psychological theories, which are sets of statements that involve assumptions about behavior. Explanations and predictions are derived from theories. Theories are revised, as needed, to accommodate new observations.

3. What do psychologists do?

Psychologists engage in research and practice. Research can be pure or applied. Basic or pure research has no immediate applications. Applied research seeks solutions to specific problems. Psychologists also specialize in various fields. Clinical psychologists help people with psychological disorders adjust to the demands of life. Counseling psychologists work with people with adjustment problems. School psychologists assist students with problems that interfere with learning. Developmental psychologists study the changes that occur throughout the life span. Personality psychologists study influences on our thought processes, feelings, and behavior. Social psychologists focus on the nature and causes of behavior in social situations. Experimental psychologists conduct research into basic psychological processes such as sensation and perception, learning and memory, and motivation and emotion. Industrial psychologists focus on the relationships between people and work. Health psychologists study the ways in which behavior and mental processes such as attitudes are related to physical health.

4. Who were some of the ancient contributors to psychology?

The ancient Greek philosopher Aristotle declared that people are motivated to seek pleasure and avoid pain. Another Greek, Democritus, suggested that we could think of behavior in terms of a body and a mind and raised the question of whether there is free will or choice. Plato recorded Socrates' advice to "Know thyself," primarily by means of introspection.

5. What is structuralism?

Structuralism, founded by Wilhelm Wundt, used introspection to study the objective and subjective elements of experience. Wundt also established the first psychological laboratory in Leipzig, Germany, in 1879.

6. What is functionalism?

Functionalism is the school founded by William James. It dealt with observable behavior as well as conscious experience and focused on the importance of habit.

7. What is behaviorism?

Behaviorism, founded by John B. Watson, argues that psychology must limit itself to observable behavior and not attempt to deal with subjective consciousness. Behaviorism focuses on learning by conditioning, and B. F. Skinner introduced the concept of reinforcement as an explanation of how learning occurs.

8. What is Gestalt psychology?

Gestalt psychology is the school of psychology founded by Wertheimer, Koffka, and Köhler. It is concerned with perception and argues that the wholeness of human experience is more than the sum of its parts.

9. What is psychoanalysis?

Psychoanalysis was founded by Sigmund Freud. The school asserts that people are driven by hidden impulses and that they distort reality to protect themselves from anxiety.

10. What are the evolutionary and biological perspectives?

The biological perspective views the links between behavior and mental processes, on the one hand, and evolution, heredity, the nervous system, and the endocrine system on the other. Evolutionary psychology is based on the work of Charles Darwin, who argued that in the age-old struggle for survival, only the "fittest" organisms reach maturity and reproduce, thereby transmitting the traits that enable them to survive to their offspring. The endocrine system releases hormones into the bloodstream.

Recite   Recite   Recite

11. **What is the cognitive perspective?**

The cognitive perspective is concerned with the ways in which we mentally represent the world and process information. Cognitive psychologists study how we learn, remember the past, plan for the future, solve problems, form judgments, make decisions, and use language.

12. **What is the humanistic–existential perspective?**

Humanistic–existential psychologists stress the importance of subjective experience and assert that people have the freedom to make choices.

13. **What is the role of psychoanalysis today?**

Contemporary psychoanalysts often call themselves neoanalysts because they focus less on unconscious processes and more on conscious choice and self-direction. Psychoanalysis remains popular in the culture at large.

14. **What are the two major perspectives on learning?**

The two key perspectives on learning are the behavioral perspective and the social–cognitive perspective. Behaviorism focuses on environmental influences on learning. Social–cognitive theory argues that psychologists can address thought processes, that people engage in intentional learning, and that people are free to modify and create environments.

15. **What is the sociocultural perspective?**

The sociocultural perspective focuses on the roles of ethnicity, gender, culture, and socioeconomic status in behavior and mental processes.

16. **What contributions have women made to psychology?**

Women have made major contributions to psychology in the United States for more than a century, despite the fact that many entered the field when it was still widely believed that "a woman's place" was in the home. Calkins studied memory and heightened awareness of prejudice against women. Ladd-Franklin formulated a theory of color vision. Washburn's views presaged behaviorism.

17. **What contributions to psychology have been made by people from various ethnic groups?**

People from ethnic minority groups have contributed to all areas of psychology, but some, like Kenneth Clark and Robert Williams, have heightened awareness of issues concerning their groups, such as prejudice and Ebonics.

18. **What is the scientific method?**

The scientific method is an organized way of expanding and refining knowledge. Psychologists reach conclusions about their research questions or the accuracy of their hypotheses on the basis of their research observations or findings.

19. **How do psychologists use samples to represent populations?**

The individuals who participate in research are referred to as a sample. A sample is a segment of a population. Samples must accurately represent the population they are intended to reflect. In a *random sample,* each member of a population has an equal chance of being selected to participate. Researchers can also use a *stratified sample,* which is selected so that identified subgroups in the population are represented proportionately in the sample.

20. **What methods of observation are used by psychologists?**

The methods used include the case study, the survey, and naturalistic observation. Case studies gather information about the lives of individuals or small groups. The survey method uses interviews, questionnaires, or public records to gather information about behavior that cannot be observed directly. The naturalistic-observation method observes behavior where it happens—"in the field."

21. **What is the correlational method?**

The correlational method reveals relationships between variables but does not determine cause and effect. In a positive correlation, variables increase simultaneously. In a negative correlation, one variable increases while the other decreases.

Recite Recite Recite

22. **What is the experimental method?**

Experiments are used to discover cause and effect—that is, the effects of independent variables on dependent variables. Experimental groups receive a specific treatment, whereas control groups do not. Blinds and double blinds may be used to control for the effects of the expectations of the subjects and the researchers. Results can be generalized only to populations that have been adequately represented in the research samples.

23. **What are the ethical issues that concern psychological research and practice with humans?**

The ethical standards of psychologists are intended to protect subjects in research and clients in practice from harm. Records of human behavior are kept confidential. Ethics review committees judge the harmfulness of proposed research and help make it less harmful. Human subjects are required to give informed consent prior to participating in research and are debriefed afterward.

24. **What are the ethical issues that concern research with animals?**

Some research can be conducted only with animals. Ethical standards require that animals may be harmed only if there is no alternative and the benefits justify the harm.

25. **What is critical thinking?**

Critical thinking is a hallmark of psychologists and of scientists in general. Critical thinking is associated with skepticism. It involves thoughtfully analyzing the questions, statements, and arguments of others. It means examining the definitions of terms, examining the premises or assumptions behind arguments, and scrutinizing the logic with which arguments are developed. Critical thinking also refers to the ability to inquire about causes and effects, as well as knowledge of research methods. Critical thinkers are cautious in drawing conclusions from evidence. They do not oversimplify or overgeneralize.

Active Learning Resources

Search Online with InfoTrac® College Edition

For additional information on the topics in this chapter, explore InfoTrac College Edition, your online library. Go to **http://www.infotrac.thomsonlearning.com** and use the passcode that came on the card with your book. Try these search terms: critical thinking, experimental psychologists, introspection, behaviorism in psychology, cognitive psychology, sociocultural perspective, volunteer bias, and placebo.

Visit Our Web Site

Go to **http://www.wadsworth.com/psychology**, where you will find online resources directly linked to your book, including interactive exercises related to PQ4R and Power Visuals for mastering and reviewing key concepts. In addition, you will find hints on using InfoTrac College Edition to answer the Critical Thinking questions throughout the text. Start with the **Self Study Assessment** for a customized **Study Plan** generated by taking the **Pre-Test** and **Post-Test.**

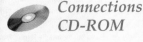

Connections CD-ROM

Go to the Wadsworth *Connections* CD-ROM for further study of the concepts in this chapter. The CD-ROM includes videos, animations, quizzes, and additional activities to expand your learning experience, plus interactive self-assessments to help connect the material to your own life.

Psyk.trek™ CD-ROM

The Wadsworth *Psyk.trek* CD-ROM offers tutorials, simulations, videos, multimedia glossary, and quizzing to help you master the material.

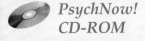

PsychNow! CD-ROM

The Wadsworth *PsychNow!* CD-ROM includes interactive exercises, videos, and animations to enhance your learning.

PowerPreview®

Evolution and Evolutionary Psychology: "Survivor" Is More Than Just a Game

- CHARLES DARWIN WAS nearly excluded from the voyage that led to the development of his theory of evolution because the captain did not like the shape of his nose.

- BIRDS WHO HAVE BEEN reared without ever seeing another bird or a nest will still build nests during the mating season. How do they do it?

- WAS THE UNIVERSE and all the life therein created in six days?

Heredity: The Nature of Nature

- 99.9% OF YOUR genetic code overlaps with that of other people.

- ARE NEANDERTHALS lurking in your genes?

- WHY ARE SCIENTISTS so interested in the similarities and differences between twins?

The Nervous System: On Being Wired

- ALTHOUGH CELLS ARE microscopic, a cell can stretch all the way from your spine to your toe.

- A SINGLE BRAIN CELL can send out hundreds of messages each second— and manage to catch some rest in between.

- YOUR NERVOUS SYSTEM, like a computer, has peripheral devices and a central processing unit.

- PERHAPS YOU'VE KNOWN that fear can give you indigestion. Now you'll learn why.

The Brain: The Star of the Human Nervous System

- MEN'S BRAINS ARE larger on average than women's brains. Women might point out that in this case, size doesn't matter.

The Cerebral Cortex

- IF A SURGEON WERE TO stimulate a certain part of your brain electrically, you might swear in court that someone had stroked your leg.

- THE EXECUTIVE CENTER of your brain retrieves information from files in storage and manipulates it in memory.

- ARE YOU "LEFT-BRAINED" or "right-brained"? (Or *both*?)

The Endocrine System: Chemicals in the Blood

- A HORMONE TURNS a disinterested male rodent into a doting father. (Female readers may wonder where they can buy some of it.)

- WHEN THEY ARE OVULATING, women are more attracted to men with highly masculine faces.

Life Connections: "Raging Hormones" ("More, Please"?)

- SOME WOMEN ELIMINATE PMS by eliminating their periods. Period.

- *MANOPAUSE, ANDROPAUSE, VIROPAUSE*— the results of a decline in sex hormones by any other name can be just as troublesome.

He almost missed the boat. Literally. The British naturalist Charles Darwin had volunteered to serve as the scientist for an expeditionary voyage by HMS *Beagle,* but the captain, Robert Fitz-Roy, objected to Darwin because of the shape of his nose. Fitz-Roy believed that you could judge a person's character by the outline of his facial features, and Darwin's nose didn't fit the . . . bill. But Fitz-Roy relented, and in the 1830s, Darwin undertook the historic voyage that led to the development of his theory of evolution.

Questions: Who was Charles Darwin? What did he do?   Darwin was a dabbler who, in one of history's coincidences, was born on the same day as Abraham Lincoln (February 12, 1809). Darwin's father was a well-known physician and his mother was Susannah Wedgwood, of the chinaware family. His cousin was Sir Francis Galton, who made many innovations in psychological measurement. Unlike Galton, Darwin gave no early signs of genius. He did so poorly in school that his father feared that he would disgrace himself and the family. Nevertheless, Darwin went on to change the face of modern thought.

Darwin enjoyed collecting and classifying plants, minerals, and animals. In school he dabbled. He tried medical school, entered Cambridge University to become an Anglican priest, and eventually graduated with a degree in science. Because he was independently wealthy, Darwin undertook the five-year volunteer position aboard *Beagle.* The ship stopped at the Galápagos Islands, where Darwin observed how species of lizards, tortoises, and plants varied from island to island. Although Darwin undertook his voyage as a believer in the Book of Genesis account of creation, his observations convinced him that the organisms he observed shared common ancestors but had *evolved* in different directions.

In midlife Darwin almost missed the boat again. From his observations of sea lions and tortoises and insects and plants, he was ready to formulate his theory of evolution upon his return from his voyage. Reading Thomas Malthus's *Essay on the Principle of Population,* which had been written back in 1798, also helped. Malthus pointed out that the earth's food supply was increasingly mathematically (1, 2, 3, 4, 5, 6, etc.) while population was increasing geometrically (1, 2, 4, 8, 16, 32, etc.). Therefore, the world's population would outstrip the world's ability to feed it, except for tragic events such as war, famine, and plague. Darwin applied Malthus's ideas to all species:

> In October 1838 . . . I happened to read for amusement Malthus on *Population,* and being well prepared to appreciate the struggle for existence which everywhere goes on from long-continued observation of the habits of animals and plants, it at once struck me that under these circumstances favourable variations would tend to be preserved and unfavourable ones to be destroyed. The result of this would be the formation of new species. Here, then, I had at last got a theory by which to work; but I was so anxious to avoid prejudice, that I determined not for some time to write even the briefest sketch of it. (C. Darwin, 1892/1958, pp. 42–43)

Because he was "anxious to avoid prejudice," Darwin did not want his theory of evolution to be published until after his death. He feared it would be immensely unpopu-

■ **Charles Darwin**

The British naturalist developed his theory of evolution after an expedition to the Galápagos Islands aboard HMS *Beagle.* He began the voyage believing in the biblical account of creation but changed his mind when he observed how species evolved over the generations as they adapted to the demands of their environments.

lar because it contradicted religious views and that it would bring scorn on his family. He shared his ideas with a few fellow scientists, but he finally published his ideas more broadly 20 years later because he learned that other scientists, including Alfred Russel Wallace, were about to present similar ideas on evolution. Wallace, a scientist who had worked in the Amazon, was about to publish his own views, which were very similar to Darwin's. Papers by both theorists were read at the Linnaean Society, and Darwin's *On the Origin of Species by Natural Selection* (1859) was published shortly thereafter. The public's interest in evolutionary theory had been aroused, and the first printing of Darwin's book sold out on the first day. Needless to say, Darwin's views became better known than those of Wallace. (Have you ever heard of Wallace's theory of evolution?)

R E F L E C T

Why was Darwin reluctant to publish his theory of evolution? Do you believe that this textbook, and other textbooks, should present the theory of evolution? Why or why not?

EVOLUTION AND EVOLUTIONARY PSYCHOLOGY: "SURVIVOR" IS MORE THAN JUST A GAME

In 1871 Darwin published *The Descent of Man,* which made the case that humans, like other species, were a product of evolution. He argued that the great apes (chimpanzees, gorillas, and so on) and humans shared a common primate ancestor (see Figure 2.1). Many ridiculed Darwin's views because they were displeased with the notion that they might share ancestry with apes. Darwin's theory also contradicted

◼ **Figure 2.1**
Humans and Some "Relatives"

The idea that humans were genetically related to apes and other animals was so distant from 19th-century views of the species that Darwin was initially reluctant to disclose his theory of evolution. *The Descent of Man,* published in 1871, made the case that humans, like other species, were a product of evolution. Darwin believed that the great apes (chimpanzees, gorillas, and so on) and humans shared a common primate ancestor.

■ **Dinosaurs**
Long ago and right here on planet Earth, dinosaurs once ruled the day. However, they—along with 99.99% of all species who ever existed—are now extinct. Evidence that they existed, and when they existed, is found in the fossil record.

Natural Selection
A core concept of the theory of evolution that holds that adaptive genetic variations among members of a species enable individuals with those variations to survive and reproduce. As a result, such variations tend to be preserved, whereas nonadaptive variations tend to drop out.

Mutation
A sudden variation in an inheritable characteristic, as distinguished from a variation that results from generations of gradual selection.

the Book of Genesis, which stated that humans had been created in one day in the image of God.

At the Galápagos Islands, Darwin found himself immersed in the unfolding of a huge game of "Survivor." But here the game was for real, and the rewards had nothing to do with fame or fortune. The rewards were reaching sexual maturity and transmitting one's genes into subsequent generations.

Question: What are some of the basic concepts in the theory of evolution? The concept of a *struggle for existence* lies at the core of the theory of evolution. The universe is no bed of roses. Since the beginning of time, the universe has been changing. For billions of years, microscopic particles have been forming immense gas clouds in space. Galaxies and solar systems have been condensing from the clouds, sparkling for some eons, then winking out. Change has brought life and death and countless challenges to survival. As described by evolutionary theory, some creatures have adapted successfully to these challenges, and their numbers have increased. Others have not met the challenges and have fallen back into the distant mists of time. The species that prosper and those that fade away are thus determined by **natural selection.**

When we humans first appeared on earth, our survival required a different sort of struggle than it does today. We fought or fled predators such as leopards. We foraged across parched lands for food. We might have warred with humanoid creatures very much like ourselves—creatures who have since become extinct. But because of the evolution of our intellect, not fangs nor wings nor claws, we prevailed. Our numbers have increased. We continue to transmit the traits that led to our selection down through the generations by means of genetic material whose chemical codes are only now being cracked.

Just what is handed down through the generations? The answer is biological, or physiological, structures and processes. Our biology serves as the material base for our behaviors, emotions, and cognitions (our thoughts, images, and plans). Biology somehow gives rise to specific behavioral tendencies in some organisms, such as the chick's instinctive fear of the shadow of the hawk. But the behavior of higher species, especially humans, is flexible and affected by environmental factors and choice, as well as by heredity.

"Doing What Comes Naturally"

According to the theory of evolution, there is a struggle for survival as various species and individuals compete for the same resources. There are small variations—random genetic variations called **mutations**—that lead to differences among individuals in physical traits. Those individuals whose traits are better adapted to their environments are more likely to survive (that is, to be "naturally selected").

Survival permits them to reach sexual maturity, to reproduce, and to transmit their features or traits to the next generation. What began as chance variation becomes embedded in more and more individuals over the generations—if it fosters survival. Chance variations that hinder survival are likely to disappear from the gene pool.

Evolutionary Psychology

These same concepts of *adaptation* and *natural selection* have also been applied to psychological traits and are key concepts in **evolutionary psychology.**   *Question: What is evolutionary psychology?*   Evolutionary psychology studies the ways in which adaptation and natural selection are connected with mental processes and behavior (Buss, 2000; Buss et al., 1998). Over the eons evolution has provided organisms with advantages such as stronger fins and wings, sharper claws, and camouflage. Human evolution has given rise to various physical traits and also to such diverse activities as language, art, committed relationships, and warfare.

One of the concepts of evolutionary psychologists is that not only physical traits but also patterns of behavior, including social behavior, evolve and are transmitted genetically from generation to generation. In other words, behavior patterns that help an organism to survive and reproduce are likely to be transmitted to the next generation (Fisher, 2000). Such behaviors are believed to include aggression, strategies of mate selection, even altruism (that is, self-sacrifice of the individual to help perpetuate the family grouping) (Archer, 1996). The behavior patterns are termed *instinctive* or *species-specific* because they evolved within certain **species.**

Question: What is meant by the concept "instinct"?   An **instinct** is a stereotyped pattern of behavior that is triggered in a specific situation. Instinctive behavior is nearly identical among the members of the species in which it appears. It tends to resist modification, even when it serves no purpose (as in the interminable barking of some breeds of dogs) or results in punishment. Instinctive behavior also appears when the individual is reared in isolation from others of its kind and thus cannot learn the behavior from experience.

Consider some examples of instinctive behavior. If you place an egg from the nest of a goose a few inches in front of her, she will roll it back to the nest with her beak. However, she won't retrieve it if it's farther away—in the "not my egg" zone. If you rear a white-crowned sparrow in isolation from other sparrows, it will still sing a recognizable species-specific song when it matures. The male stickleback fish instinctively attacks fish (or pieces of painted wood) with the kinds of red bellies that are characteristic of other male sticklebacks. Many psychologists consider language to be "instinctive" among humans. Psychologists are trying to determine what other kinds of human behavior may be instinctive. However, even instinctive behavior can be modified to some degree by learning, and most psychologists agree that the richness and complexity of human behavior are made possible by human learning ability.

© David Thompson/OSF/Animals, Animals

■ **Instinctive Behavior**
The male stickleback instinctively attacks fish (or pieces of painted wood) with the kinds of red bellies that are characteristic of other male sticklebacks. Sticklebacks will show the stereotyped instinctive behavior even when they are reared in isolation from other members of their species. Rearing an organism in isolation prevents it from learning from another member of its species.

R E F L E C T

Have you known family pets that have engaged in instinctive behavior? What was the behavior? Why do you believe it was instinctive?

Evolutionary Psychology
The branch of psychology that studies the ways in which adaptation and natural selection are connected with mental processes and behavior.

Species
A category of biological classification consisting of related organisms who are capable of interbreeding. *Homo sapiens*—humans—make up one species.

Instinct
A stereotyped pattern of behavior that is triggered by a particular stimulus and nearly identical among members of a species, even when they are reared in isolation.

R E V I E W

(1) Darwin's first book on evolution was titled *On the Origin of Species by Natural* _____. (2) The concept of a struggle for _____ lies at the core of the theory of evolution. (3) Mutations are believed to occur at _____ but to be subject to natural selection. (4) Individuals whose traits are better _____ to their environments are more likely to survive and reproduce. (5) _____ psychology studies the ways in which adaptation and natural selection are connected with mental processes and behavior. (6) Stereotypical behavior patterns that have evolved within certain species are called _____.

Critical Thinking: Need science and scripture be in conflict over the origins of the species?

Learning Connections
See Web site for an interactive version of these review questions.

HEREDITY: THE NATURE OF NATURE

Heredity

The transmission of traits from parent to offspring by means of genes.

Genetics

The area of biology that focuses on heredity.

Behavioral Genetics

The area of biology and psychology that focuses on the transmission of traits that give rise to behavior. Behavioral genetics also addresses individual differences in behavior.

Molecular Genetics

The area of genetics that focuses on the identification of specific genes that are connected with the development of traits, behavior, and mental processes.

Gene

A basic unit of heredity, which is found at a specific point on a chromosome.

Chromosome

A microscopic rod-shaped body in the cell nucleus that carries genes that transmit hereditary traits from generation to generation. Humans normally have 46 chromosomes.

Deoxyribonucleic Acid (DNA)

A substance that forms the basic material of chromosomes, takes the form of a double helix, and contains the genetic code.

R E F L E C T

Which family members seem to be like you physically or psychologically? Which seem to be very different? How do you explain the similarities and differences?

Consider some facts of life:

- People cannot breathe underwater (without special equipment).
- People cannot fly (again, without rather special equipment).
- Fish cannot learn to speak French or do an Irish jig even if you rear them in enriched environments and send them to finishing school.
- Chimpanzees and gorillas can use sign language but cannot speak.

People cannot breathe underwater or fly (without oxygen tanks, airplanes, or other devices) because of their **heredity.** *Question: What is meant by the concept of "heredity"?* Heredity defines one's *nature*—which is based on one's biological structures and processes. Heredity refers to the biological transmission of traits that have evolved from generation to generation. Fish are limited in other ways by their natural traits. Chimpanzees and gorillas can understand many spoken words and express some concepts through nonverbal symbol systems such as American Sign Language. However, apes cannot speak. They have probably failed to inherit humanlike speech areas of the brain. Their nature differs from ours. Our speech mechanisms have evolved differently.

Genetics and Behavioral Genetics

Heredity both makes behaviors possible and places limits on them. *Question: What is meant by the concepts "genetics," "behavioral genetics," and "molecular genetics"?* The subfield of biology that studies heredity is called **genetics.** **Behavioral genetics** bridges the sciences of psychology and biology. It is concerned with the genetic transmission of traits that give rise to patterns of behavior.

The field of genetics looks at both species-specific behavior patterns (instincts) and individual differences among the members of a species. Behavioral genetics focuses on individual differences (Plomin & Crabbe, 2000). Psychologists consider behavioral genetics when they ask why individuals differ in their behavior and mental processes—for example, why do children acquire language at different rates? One answer may be found in the individual's genetic code, but children also differ in their exposure to language at early ages.

Our genetic code (discussed in the next section) is made up of molecules. So-called **molecular genetics** attempts to identify specific genes that are connected with behavior and mental processes. For example, researchers are attempting to identify genes that are connected with various psychological disorders. Some day it may be possible to cure these disorders by modifying the genetic code of affected individuals.

Heredity is involved in almost all aspects of human behavior, personality, and mental processes (Bouchard & Loehlin, 2001; Rutter, 1997). Examples include sociability, shyness, social dominance, aggressiveness, leadership, thrill seeking, effectiveness as a parent or a therapist, even interest in arts and crafts (Carey & DiLalla, 1994; Lykken et al., 1992).

Genetic influences are also involved in psychological health and illness, including anxiety and depression, schizophrenia, bipolar disorder, alcoholism, even criminal behavior (Kendler et al., 2000a, 2000b; Plomin, 2000; E. V. Sullivan et al., 2000). In one study, for example, Kenneth Kendler and his colleagues (2000a) studied 794 pairs of female twins and found that six aspects of psychological health were connected with genetic factors: one's sense of physical well-being, one's social relationships, symptoms of anxiety and depression, substance abuse, the availability of social support, and self-esteem. However, the Kendler group also found that the family environment contributed strongly to social relationships, substance abuse, and social support. Although psychological health is clearly influenced by environmental factors, our understanding of the role of heredity continues to expand. Unlocking these mysteries depends on how well we understand genes and chromosomes. *Question: What are the roles of genes and chromosomes in heredity?*

Genes and Chromosomes: The Building Blocks of Heredity

Genes are the most basic building blocks of heredity. They are the biochemical materials that regulate the development of specific traits. Some traits, such as blood type, are controlled by a single pair of genes. (One gene is derived from each parent.) Other traits are determined by combinations of genes. The inherited component of complex psychological traits, such as intelligence, is believed to be determined by combinations of genes. It is estimated that within every cell of your body, there are 30,000 to 40,000 genes (International Human Genome Sequencing Consortium, 2001).

Genes are segments of **chromosomes.** That is, chromosomes are made up of strings of genes. Each cell in the body contains 46 chromosomes arranged in 23 pairs. Chromosomes are large complex molecules of **deoxyribonucleic acid,** which has several chemical components. (You can breathe a sigh of relief, for this acid is usually referred to simply as DNA.) The tightly wound structure of DNA was first demonstrated in the 1950s by James Watson and Francis Crick. It takes the form of a double helix—a twisting ladder (see Figure 2.2). In all living things, the sides of the ladder consist of alternating segments of phosphate (P) and a kind of sugar (S). The "rungs" of the ladder are attached to the sugars and consist of one of two pairs of bases, either *adenine* with *thymine* (A with T) or *cytosine* with *guanine* (C with G). A single gene can contain hundreds of thousands of base pairs. Altogether, the Human Genome Project has learned that the sequencing of your DNA consists of about 3 billion DNA sequences (Plomin & Crabbe, 2000). These sequences make up the *genetic code* that caused you to grow arms and not wings, and skin rather than scales.

The Amazing 0.1% of Difference

Here are a couple of facts for your next conversation at Starbucks. First, the sequence of your DNA overlaps about 99.9% with that of other humans (Plomin & Crabbe, 2000). But even with that overlap, people differ greatly in their skin coloration, their body shape, and their psychological makeup, including their individual talents and skills. Some compose symphonies, and others are tone-deaf. Some tackle differential equations, and others cannot add or subtract. Some figure skate in the Olympics, and others trip over their own feet. As noted by Robert Plomin and John Crabbe (2000), "Identifying the 0.1% of the DNA sequences that differ is one

■ **That 0.1% of Difference Can Be Quite a Difference**

The genetic codes of humans overlap by 99.9%. However, the remaining 0.1% makes quite a differences, as in the cases of cellist Yo Yo Ma (left) and professional wrestler "The Rock" (right).

■ **Figure 2.2**
The Double Helix of DNA

Segments of DNA are made up of genes that determine physical traits such as height, eye color, and whether pigs have wings (no, because of their genetic makeup, they don't). The overlap of DNA from person to person is 99.9%! Yet the difference of 0.1% accounts for the differences between Mozart and Nelson Mandela, and between Michelle Kwan and Oprah Winfrey. Psychologists debate the extent to which genes influence psychological traits such as intelligence, aggressiveness, and happiness, and the appearance of psychological disorders such as schizophrenia.

Female   Male

■ **Figure 2.3**
The 23 Pairs of Human Chromosomes
People normally have 23 pairs of chromosomes. Whether one is female or male is determined by the 23rd pair of chromosomes. Females have two X sex chromosomes, whereas males have an X and a Y sex chromosome.

of the next goals of the Human Genome Project because these 3 million DNA sequences are responsible for the genetic differences among human beings behaviorally as well as biologically." Even though we differ but 0.1% in genetic code from our fellows, it often seems easier to focus on how much we differ rather than on how much we have in common.

Are We Part Neanderthal?

The second fact is that Neanderthals and other ancient humanoids may not be quite as extinct as has been believed. They may be lurking in your own genetic code. Recent analysis of DNA suggests that modern humans—that's us—probably interbred with other humanoids for hundreds of thousands of years rather than simply replaced them (Cann, 2002). When you misbehave, you can now say it's the Neanderthal in you—although the truth could be quite the reverse.

REFLECT
So, there's evidence that you are likely to share genes with Neanderthals. If you do, do those genes make you less human or exactly as human as you are?

We normally receive 23 chromosomes from our father's sperm cell and 23 chromosomes from our mother's egg cell (ovum). When a sperm cell fertilizes an ovum, the chromosomes form 23 pairs (Figure 2.3). The 23rd pair consists of **sex chromosomes,** which determine whether we are female or male. We all receive an X sex chromosome (so called because of the X shape) from our mother. If we also receive an X sex chromosome from our father, we develop into a female. If we receive a Y sex chromosome (named after the Y shape) from our father, we develop into a male.

Down Syndrome

When people do not have the normal number of 46 chromosomes (23 pairs), physical and behavioral abnormalities may result. The risk of these abnormalities rises with the age of the parents. Most persons with **Down syndrome,** for example, have an extra, or third,

REFLECT
Do you know anyone with Down syndrome? What is the person like?

chromosome on the 21st pair. The extra chromosome is usually contributed by the mother, and the condition becomes increasingly likely as the mother's age at the time of pregnancy increases. Persons with Down syndrome have a downward-sloping fold of skin at the inner corners of the eyes, a round face, a protruding tongue, and a

Sex Chromosomes
The 23rd pair of chromosomes, whose genetic material determines the sex of the individual.

Down Syndrome
A condition caused by an extra chromosome on the 21st pair and characterized by cognitive impairment, a broad face, and slanting eyes.

broad, flat nose. They are cognitively disabled and usually have physical problems that cause death by middle age (Schupf, 2000).

Down syndrome is a result of the **nature** of the individual. Behavioral geneticists are attempting to sort out the relative importance of nature (heredity) and **nurture** (environmental influences) in the origins of behavior. Psychologists are especially interested in the roles of nature and nurture in intelligence and psychological disorders. Organisms inherit physical features that set the stage for certain behaviors. But none of us is the result of heredity alone. Environmental factors such as nutrition, learning opportunities, cultural influences, exercise, and (unfortunately) accident and illness also determine whether genetically possible behaviors will be displayed. Behavior thus represents the interaction of nature and nurture. A potential Shakespeare who is reared in poverty and never taught to read or write will not create a *Hamlet*.

Kinship Studies: Is the Behavior of Relatives Related?

The more *closely* people are related, the more *genes* they have in common. Parents and children have 50% of their genes in common, as do siblings (brothers and sisters). Aunts and uncles related by blood have a 25% overlap with nieces and nephews. First cousins share 12.5% of their genes. If genes are involved in a trait or behavior pattern, people who are more closely related should be more likely to show similar traits or behavior.

Question: What are kinship studies?   Kinship studies are ways in which psychologists compare the presence of traits and behavior patterns in people who are biologically related or unrelated to help determine the role of genetic factors in their occurrence. Psychologists and behavioral geneticists are especially interested in running kinship studies with twins and adopted individuals (Plomin et al., 2001).

Twin Studies: Looking into the Genetic Mirror

The fertilized egg cell (ovum) that carries genetic messages from both parents is called a *zygote*. Now and then, a zygote divides into two cells that separate, so that instead of developing into a single person, it develops into two people with the same genetic

REFLECT

Do you know sets of twins? Are they monozygotic or dizygotic? How are they alike? How do they differ?

makeup. Such people are identical, or **monozygotic (MZ), twins.** If the woman releases two ova in the same month and they are both fertilized, they develop into fraternal, or **dizygotic (DZ), twins.** DZ twins, like other siblings, share 50% of their genes. MZ twins are important in the study of the relative influences of nature (heredity) and nurture (the environment) because differences between MZ twins are the result of nurture. (They do not differ in their heredity—that is, their nature—because their genetic makeup is the same.)

Twin studies compare the presence of traits and behavior patterns in MZ twins, DZ twins, and other people to help determine the role of genetic factors in their occurrence. If MZ twins show greater similarity on a trait or behavior pattern than DZ twins, a genetic basis for the trait or behavior is suggested.

Twin studies show that genetic factors have a strong influence on physical features. MZ twins are more likely to look alike and to be similar in height, even to have more similar cholesterol levels than DZ twins (Heller et al., 1993). This finding holds even when the identical twins are reared apart and the fraternal twins are reared together (Stunkard et al., 1990).

Other physical similarities between pairs of MZ twins may be more subtle, but they are also strong. For example, research shows that MZ twin sisters begin to menstruate about one to two months apart, whereas DZ twins begin to menstruate about a year apart. MZ twins are more alike than DZ twins in their blood pressure, brain wave patterns, even in their speech patterns, gestures, and mannerisms (Hansell et al., 2001; Lensvelt-Mulders & Hettema, 2001; Lykken et al., 1992).

MZ twins resemble one another more strongly than DZ twins in intelligence and in personality traits such as sociability, anxiety, friendliness, and conformity, even

© Michael Greenlar/The Image Works

■ A Couple with Down Syndrome

Down syndrome is caused by an extra chromosome on the 21st pair and becomes more likely to occur as the mother's age at the time of pregnancy increases. Persons with Down syndrome have characteristic facial features, including downward-sloping folds of skin at the inner corners of the eyes, are mentally retarded, and usually have health problems that lead to death by middle age.

Nature
The inborn, innate character of an organism.

Nurture
The sum total of the environmental factors that affect an organism from conception onward. (In another usage, *nurture* refers to the act of nourishing and otherwise promoting the development of youngsters.)

Monozygotic (MZ) Twins
Twins that develop from a single fertilized ovum that divides in two early in prenatal development. MZ twins thus share the same genetic code. Also called *identical twins.*

Dizygotic (DZ) Twins
Twins that develop from two fertilized ova and who are thus as closely related as brothers and sisters in general. Also called *fraternal twins.*

happiness (McCourt et al., 1999; McCrae et al., 2000). David Lykken and Auke Tellegen (1996) suggest that we inherit a tendency toward a certain level of happiness. Despite the ups and downs of life, we tend to drift back to our usual levels of cheerfulness (or irritability). It seems that our bank accounts, our levels of education, and our marital status are less influential than genes as contributors to happiness. Heredity is also a key contributor to developmental factors such as cognitive functioning, autism, and early signs of attachment such as smiling, cuddling, and expression of fear of strangers (DiLalla et al., 1996; Scarr & Kidd, 1983).

MZ twins are more likely than DZ twins to share psychological disorders such as autism, depression, schizophrenia, and even vulnerability to alcoholism (McGue et al., 1992; Plomin, 2000). In one study on autism, the concordance rate for MZ twins was 96%. (That is, if one member of a pair of MZ twins was autistic, the other member had a 96% chance of being so.) The concordance rate for DZ twins was only 24% (Ritvo et al., 1985).

Of course, twin studies are not perfect. MZ twins may resemble each other more closely than DZ twins partly because they are treated more similarly. MZ twins frequently are dressed identically, and parents sometimes have difficulty telling them apart (Vandell & Corasaniti, 1990).

One way to get around this difficulty is to find and compare MZ twins who were reared in different homes. Any similarities between MZ twins reared apart cannot be explained by a shared home environment and would appear to be largely a result of heredity. In the fascinating Minnesota Study of Twins Reared Apart (Bouchard et al., 1990; DiLalla et al., 1999; Lykken et al., 1992), researchers have been measuring the physiological and psychological characteristics of 56 sets of MZ adult twins who were separated in infancy and reared in different homes. Constance Holden (1980) wrote a progress report on the study at the time when it had processed 9 pairs of MZ twins and was about to study 11 other pairs. A team of psychologists, psychiatrists, and other professionals analyzed the twins' life histories, including their interests, medical problems, abilities, and intelligence. All in all, there were some uncanny similarities between the pairs, except when there were extreme differences in their environment. Consider one pair of twins, both of whom were named Jim. Both were married and divorced. Both had been trained to become police. They each named their first sons James Allan. They drove the same kind of car and vacationed at the same beach. They each mentioned carpentry as a hobby; each had constructed a bench around a tree in the yard. There are certainly coincidences in their histories, and they were chosen for this lengthy description because of them. However, the interests in police work and carpentry are probably more than coincidental.

In sum, MZ twins reared apart are about as similar as MZ twins reared together on a variety of measures of intelligence, personality, temperament, occupational and leisure-time interests, and social attitudes. These traits thus would appear to have a genetic underpinning.

Adoption Studies

The interpretation of kinship studies can be confused when relatives share similar environments as well as genes. This is especially true of identical twins, who may be dressed identically and encouraged to follow similar interests. Adoptee studies that compare children who have been separated from their parents at an early age (or in which identical twins are separated at an early age) and reared in different environments provide special opportunities for sorting out nature and nurture. Psychologists look for similarities between children and their adoptive and natural parents. When children reared by adoptive parents are more similar to their natural parents in a particular trait, strong evidence exists for a genetic role in the appearance of that trait.

Later in the text we will see that children are more like their natural parents than their adoptive parents in intelligence and in the psychological disorder of schizophrenia. Even so, we will see that environmental factors also influence the development of intelligence and schizophrenia.

■ Identical Twins

The study of identical twins is important to psychologists because they fully share their genetic heritage. Therefore, any differences in appearance, traits, and behavior are presumed to reflect environmental influences. Why have psychologists been particularly interested in identical twins who have been separated near birth and reared in different families?

© Norbert Schaefer/CORBIS

Parent-generation rats

A. Total blind alley entrances in 19 trials

Fourth-generation rats

B₄ (Bright)   D₄ (Dull)

C. Total blind alley entrances in 19 trials

Second-generation rats

B₂ (Bright)   D₂ (Dull)

B. Total blind alley entrances in 19 trials

Seventh-generation rats

B₇ (Bright)   D₇ (Dull)

D. Total blind alley entrances in 19 trials

■ Figure 2.4
Selective Breeding for Maze-Learning Ability in Rats

Humans selectively breed animals and plants to achieve desired physical traits. However, in the case of animals, it is also possible to selectively breed for psychological traits and behaviors such as aggressiveness and trainability (in dogs) and maze-learning ability (in rats). In the classic Tryon (1940) study, "maze-bright" and "maze-dull" rats were selectively bred over several generations, until the distributions of their maze-learning ability barely overlapped.

Selective Breeding: The Nurture of Nature

Under natural selection, traits that enable animals and plants to adapt better to their environments are likely to be—in Darwin's wording—"preserved." But then there is another kind of selection: selection not by nature, but by humans; and we call it *selective breeding*.   ***Question: What is selective breeding?***

We selectively breed plants and animals to enhance desired physical and—in the case of animals—behavioral traits. We breed cattle and chickens to be bigger and fatter so that they provide more food calories for less feed.

Dogs have been selectively bred for size, gentleness, tendencies to protect their territory (serve as watchdogs), and for ease of training, including housebreaking. We haven't tried to housebreak rats (although some rats break into houses), but we have selectively bred rats for maze-learning ability. In classic research, an initial group of rats was tested for maze-learning ability, as measured by the number of errors they make in repeated trials to reach a food goal (Tryon, 1940). Rats making the fewest mistakes are labeled B_1, indicating high maze-learning ability. Those making the most errors are labeled D_1. The distribution of errors for the first or parent generation is shown in Figure 2.4A, which shows the number of blind-alley entrances (errors) over a series of 19 runs through the maze. Note that the distribution of errors for the parent generation (part A) is rather even, ranging from very few to about 200. Rats with high maze-learning ability are then bred with other rats with high maze-learning ability; rats with low maze-learning ability are similarly bred with other "maze-dull" rats. Their offspring, the second generation (part B), begins to show dramatic differences in maze-learning ability. The offspring of the maze-bright rats (B_2) are beginning to form a group that differs distinctly from the offspring of the maze-dull rats (D_2). Parts C and D show that if we selectively breed subsequent generations of

■ An A-Maze-ing Rat?

Rats have been selectively bred for maze-learning ability, as measured by the number of errors they make in repeated trials to reach a food goal.

maze-bright and maze-dull rats, we begin to arrive at a point where the distributions of the brightest and the dullest hardly overlap at all. By the seventh generation, the maze-bright (B_7) rats are making about one error per trial, whereas the maze-dull (D_7) rats are making nine to ten errors per trial.

Maze-learning ability could be considered reflective of animal intelligence. It certainly requires some visual-motor skills and the ability to profit from experience. A key issue in psychology is the role of genetic factors in the behaviors and mental processes that make up intelligence in humans. We look more closely at that issue in Chapter 8.

Learning Connections
See Web site for an interactive version of these review questions.

REVIEW

(7) The field of _____ genetics deals with the genetic transmission of traits that give rise to patterns of behavior. (8) _____ genetics attempts to identify specific genes that are connected with behavior and mental processes. (9) _____ are the most basic building blocks of heredity. (10) People with _____ syndrome have an extra chromosome on the 21st pair. (11) The behavior of _____ twins is of special interest because their genetic endowment is the same. (12) Rats have been selectively bred for _____-learning ability.

Critical Thinking: What ethical, social, and political issues would be involved in attempting to selectively breed humans for desired traits?

THE NERVOUS SYSTEM: ON BEING WIRED

"Gage is no longer Gage," said those who had known him before the accident.

There are many key characters in the history of psychology, and some of them did not arrive there intentionally. One of these was a promising railroad worker who was helping our young nation stretch from coast to coast. His name was Phineas Gage. Gage was highly admired by his friends and his coworkers. But all that changed one day in 1848. While he was tamping down the blasting powder for a dynamite charge, Gage accidentally set the powder off. The inch-thick metal tamping rod shot upward through his cheek and brain and out the top of his head.

If the trajectory of the rod had been slightly different, Gage would have died. Although Gage fell back in a heap, he was miraculously alive. His coworkers watched

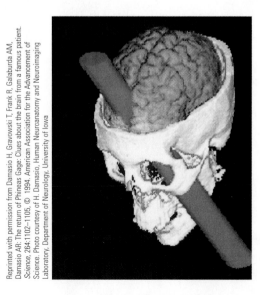

Reprinted with permission from Damasio H, Gravowski T, Frank R, Galaburda AM, Damasio AR: The return of Phineas Gage: Clues about the brain from a famous patient. *Science.* 264:1102–1105. © 1994. American Association for the Advancement of Science. Photo courtesy of H. Damasio, Human Neurcanatomy and Neuroimaging Laboratory, Department of Neurology, University of Iowa

■ **Phineas Gage**

The young railroad worker survived a horrendous accident in which a metal tamping rod was shot through his head. But the brain damage appears to have markedly changed his personality.

in shock as he stood up a few moments later and spoke. While the local doctor marveled at the hole through Gage's head, Gage asked when he'd be able to return to work. Two months later, Gage's external wounds had healed, but the psychological aspects of the wound were now obvious. Gage had become undependable, foul-mouthed, and ill-mannered.

Generations of researchers—psychologists, physicians, biologists, neuroscientists—have wondered how the changes in Gage's personality might have been caused by the damage to his brain. Perhaps the trajectory of the rod spared parts of the frontal lobes that are involved in language and movement but damaged areas connected with personality and emotional response (Damasio, 2000).

In this section we continue the voyage of these scientists and explore the ways in which our brains and other aspects of our nervous systems serve as the material base for our behaviors, emotions, and cognitions (our thoughts, images, and plans). The nervous system is composed of cells, most of which are neurons. That is where we begin.

Neurons: Into the Fabulous Forest

Within the brain of Phineas Gage lay a fabulous forest of nerve cells, or neurons. Even after his accident, billions upon billions of neurons in his brain and elsewhere in his body continued to function. *Question: What are neurons?* **Neurons** are cells that can be visualized as having branches, trunks, and roots—something like trees. As we voyage through this forest, we see that many nerve cells lie alongside one another like a thicket of trees. But neurons can also lie end to end, with their "roots" intertwined with the "branches" of the neurons that lie below. Trees receive sunlight, water, and nutrients from the soil. Neurons receive "messages" from a number of sources such as light, other neurons, and pressure on the skin, and they can pass these messages along in a complex biological dance. As described in detail later in this chapter, the electrical signal jumps between neurons via chemical **neurotransmitters.**

We are born with more than 100 billion neurons. Most of them are found in the brain. The nervous system also contains **glial cells.** Glial cells remove dead neurons and waste products from the nervous system, nourish and insulate neurons, and direct their growth. But neurons occupy center stage in the nervous system. The messages transmitted by neurons somehow account for phenomena ranging from the perception of an itch from a mosquito bite to the coordination of a skier's vision and muscles to the composition of a concerto to the solution of an algebraic equation. These messages also enabled Phineas Gage to pick himself up and think about getting back to work.

Neurons vary according to their functions and their location. Neurons in the brain may be only a fraction of an inch in length, whereas others in the legs are several feet long. A neuron is a nerve cell. Most neurons include a cell body, dendrites, and an axon (see Figure 2.5). The cell body contains the core or *nucleus* of the cell. The nucleus uses oxygen and nutrients to generate the energy needed to carry out the work of the cell. Anywhere from a few to several hundred short fibers, or **dendrites,** extend like roots from the cell body to receive incoming messages from thousands of adjoining neurons. Each neuron has an **axon** that extends like a trunk from the cell body. Axons are very thin, but those that carry messages from the toes to the spinal cord extend several feet.

Like tree trunks, axons can branch off in different directions. Axons end in small bulb-shaped structures called *terminals* or *terminal buttons.* Neurons carry messages in one direction only: from the dendrites or cell body through the axon to the axon terminals. The messages are then transmitted from the terminal buttons to other neurons, muscles, or glands.

As a child matures, the axons of neurons become longer, and the dendrites and terminals proliferate, creating vast interconnected networks for the transmission of complex messages. The number of glial cells also increases as the nervous system develops, contributing to its dense appearance.

Neuron
A nerve cell.

Neurotransmitters
Chemical substances involved in the transmission of neural impulses from one neuron to another.

Glial Cells
Cells that nourish and insulate neurons, direct their growth, and remove waste products from the nervous system.

Dendrites
Rootlike structures, attached to the cell body of a neuron, that receive impulses from other neurons.

Axon
A long, thin part of a neuron that transmits impulses to other neurons from branching structures called *terminal buttons.*

SENDING NEURON   RECEIVING NEURON

Neural impulse

Axon

Axon terminals

Dendrites

Nucleus

Cell body
(soma)

Myelin sheath

Closeup of axon terminal
button and synapse

Neurotransmitters

Synaptic cleft   Receptor sites

Power Visual
*See Web site for an interactive
version of this figure.*

■ Figure 2.5
The Anatomy of a Neuron

"Messages" enter neurons through dendrites, are transmitted along the trunklike
axon, and then are sent from axon terminal buttons to muscles, glands, and other
neurons. Axon terminal buttons contain sacs of chemicals called *neurotransmitters.*
Neurotransmitters are released into the synaptic cleft, where many of them bind to
receptor sites on the dendrites of the receiving neuron. Dozens of neurotransmitters
have been identified.

Myelin: Miniature Bratwurst?

The axons of many neurons are wrapped tightly with white, fatty **myelin** that makes
them look like strings of sausages under the microscope (bratwurst, actually). The fat
insulates the axon from electrically charged atoms, or ions, found in the fluids that surround the nervous system. The myelin sheath minimizes leakage of the electrical current being carried along the axon, thereby allowing messages to be conducted more
efficiently.

Myelination is part of the maturation process that leads to the child's ability to
crawl and walk during the first year. Infants are not physiologically "ready" to engage
in visual–motor coordination and other activities until the coating process reaches certain levels. In people with the disease multiple sclerosis, myelin is replaced with a hard
fibrous tissue that throws off the timing of nerve impulses and disrupts muscular control. Affliction of the neurons that control breathing can result in suffocation.

Afferent and Efferent Neurons

If someone steps on your toes, the sensation is registered by receptors or sensory
neurons near the surface of your skin. Then it is transmitted to the spinal cord and
brain through **afferent neurons,** which are perhaps two to three feet long. In the

Myelin
A fatty substance that encases and
insulates axons, facilitating transmission of neural impulses.

Afferent Neurons
Neurons that transmit messages from
sensory receptors to the spinal cord
and brain. Also called *sensory neurons.*

brain, subsequent messages might be conveyed by associative neurons that are only a few thousandths of an inch long. You experience the pain through this process and perhaps entertain some rather nasty thoughts about the perpetrator, who is now apologizing and begging for understanding. Long before you arrive at any logical conclusions, however, motor neurons (**efferent neurons**) send messages to your foot so that you withdraw it and begin an impressive hopping routine. Other efferent neurons stimulate glands so that your heart is beating more rapidly, you are sweating, and the hair on the back of your arms has become erect! Being a good sport, you say, "Oh, it's nothing." But considering all the neurons involved, it really is something, isn't it?

In case you think that afferent and efferent neurons will be hard to distinguish because they sound pretty much the SAME to you, remember that they *are the* "SAME." That is, *Sensory = Afferent*, and *Motor = Efferent*. But don't tell your professor I let you in on this secret.

The Neural Impulse: Let Us "Sing the Body Electric"[1]

In the 18th century, the Italian physiologist Luigi Galvani (1737–1798) conducted a shocking experiment in a rainstorm. While his neighbors had the sense to remain indoors, Galvani and his wife were out on the porch connecting lightning rods to the heads of dissected frogs whose legs were connected by wires to a well of water. When lightning blazed above, the frogs' muscles contracted. This is not a recommended way to prepare frogs' legs. Galvani was demonstrating that the messages (**neural impulses**) that travel along neurons are electrochemical in nature.

Question: What are neural impulses? Neural impulses are messages that voyage within neurons at somewhere between 2 (in nonmyelinated neurons) and 225 miles an hour (in myelinated neurons). This speed is not impressive when compared with that of an electrical current in a toaster oven or a lamp, which can travel at close to the speed of light—over 186,000 miles per second. Distances in the body are short, however, and a message will travel from a toe to the brain in perhaps 1/50th of a second.

An Electrochemical Voyage (No Tickets Needed, Just "Charges")

The process by which neural impulses travel is electrochemical. Chemical changes take place within neurons that cause an electrical charge to be transmitted along their lengths. Neurons and body fluids contain ions—positively or negatively charged atoms. In a resting state—that is, when a neuron is not being stimulated by its neighbors—negatively charged chloride (Cl^-) ions are plentiful within the neuron, contributing to an overall negative charge in relation to the outside. The difference in electrical charge **polarizes** the neuron with a negative **resting potential** of about -70 millivolts in relation to the body fluid outside the cell membrane.

When an area on the surface of the resting neuron is adequately stimulated by other neurons, the cell membrane in the area changes its permeability to allow positively charged sodium ions to enter. Thus the area of entry becomes positively charged, or **depolarized** with respect to the outside (Figure 2.6). The permeability of the cell membrane then changes again, allowing no more sodium ions to enter.

The inside of the cell axon at the disturbed area has an **action potential** of 110 millivolts. This action potential, added to the -70 millivolts that characterize the resting potential, brings the membrane voltage to a positive charge of about $+30$ to $+40$ millivolts (Figure 2.7). This inner change causes the next section of the cell to become permeable to sodium ions. At the same time, other positively charged (potassium) ions are being pumped out of the area of the cell that was previously affected, which returns the area to its resting potential. In this way, the neural impulse is transmitted continuously along an axon. Because the impulse is created anew as it progresses, its strength does not change (Figure 2.7).

[1]From Walt Whitman's *Leaves of Grass*.

 Learning Connections
See the Connections *CD-ROM for an animation on the structure of the neuron.*

 Learning Connections
See the Connections *CD-ROM for an animation on the action potential.*

 Learning Connections
See the Connections *CD-ROM for an animation on the interference of the action potential.*

Efferent Neurons
Neurons that transmit messages from the brain or spinal cord to muscles and glands. Also called *motor neurons.*

Neural Impulse
The electrochemical discharge of a nerve cell, or neuron.

Polarize
To ready a neuron for firing by creating an internal negative charge in relation to the body fluid outside the cell membrane.

Resting Potential
The electrical potential across the neural membrane when it is not responding to other neurons.

Depolarize
To reduce the resting potential of a cell membrane from about -70 millivolts toward zero.

Action Potential
The electrical impulse that provides the basis for the conduction of a neural impulse along an axon of a neuron.

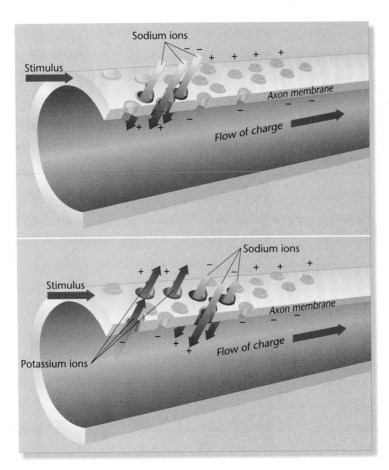

A. During an action potential, sodium gates in the neuron membrane open and sodium ions enter the axon, bringing a positive charge with them.

B. After an action potential occurs, the sodium gates close at that point, and open at the next point along the axon. When the sodium gates close, potassium gates open and potassium ions flow out of the axon, carrying a positive charge with them.

■ Figure 2.6
The Neural Impulse
When a section of a neuron is stimulated by other neurons, the cell membrane becomes permeable to the sodium ions so that an action potential (A) of about 30 millivolts is induced. This action potential is transmitted along the axon (A, B). The neuron fires according to the all-or-none principle.

REFLECT
Had you heard that the brain runs on electricity? If so, what did you imagine? How are messages actually transmitted in the nervous system?

All-or-None Principle
The fact that a neuron fires an impulse of the same strength whenever its action potential is triggered.

Refractory Period
A phase following firing during which a neuron is less sensitive to messages from other neurons and will not fire.

Firing: How Messages Voyage from Neuron to Neuron

The conduction of the neural impulse along the length of a neuron is what is meant by "firing." When a rifle fires, it sends a bullet speeding through its barrel and discharges it at more than 1,000 feet per second. ***Question: What happens when a neuron fires?*** Neurons also fire, but instead of a barrel, a neuron has an axon. Instead of discharging a bullet, it releases neurotransmitters.

Some neurons fire in less than 1/1,000 of a second. In firing, neurons attempt to transmit messages to other neurons, muscles, or glands. However, other neurons will not fire unless the incoming messages combine to reach an adequate *threshold*. A weak message may cause a temporary shift in electrical charge at some point along a neuron's cell membrane, but this charge will dissipate if the neuron is not stimulated to its threshold.

A neuron may transmit several hundred messages in a second. Yet, in accordance with the **all-or-none principle,** each time a neuron fires, it transmits an impulse of the same strength. Neurons fire more frequently when they have been stimulated by larger numbers of other neurons. Stronger stimuli cause more frequent firing.

For a few thousandths of a second after firing, a neuron is insensitive to messages from other neurons and will not fire. It is said to be in a **refractory period.** This period is a time of recovery during which sodium is prevented from passing through the neuronal membrane. When we realize that such periods of recovery might take place hundreds of times per second, it seems a rapid recovery and a short rest indeed.

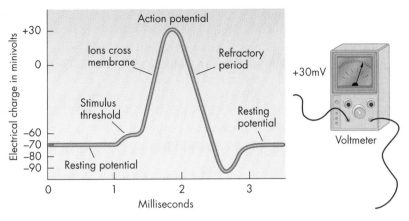

■ Figure 2.7
Changes in Electrical Charges as a Neural Impulse Is Transmitted Across an Axon
The resting potential of a segment of a cell axon is about −70 millivolts. But the inside of the cell axon at the disturbed area has an action potential of about 110 millivolts. When we add this figure to the −70 millivolts that characterize the resting potential, we bring the membrane voltage to a positive charge of about +30 to +40 millivolts. This inner change causes the next section of the cell to become permeable to sodium ions. In this way, the neural impulse is transmitted continuously along an axon.

The Synapse: On Being Well Connected

A neuron relays its message to another neuron across a junction called a **synapse.** *Question: What is a synapse?* A synapse consists of an axon terminal button from the transmitting neuron, a dendrite or the body of a receiving neuron, and a fluid-filled gap between the two that is called the *synaptic cleft* (see Figure 2.5). Although the neural impulse is electrical, it does not jump across the synaptic cleft like a spark. Instead, when a nerve impulse reaches a synapse, axon terminals release chemicals into the synaptic cleft like myriad ships being cast into the sea.

Neurotransmitters: The Chemical Keys to Communication

Sacs called synaptic vesicles in the axon terminals contain neurotransmitters. When a neural impulse (action potential) reaches the axon terminal, the vesicles release varying amounts of neurotransmitters—the chemical keys to communication—into the synaptic cleft. From there, they influence the receiving neuron. *Questions: Which neurotransmitters are of interest to psychologists? What do they do?*

Dozens of neurotransmitters have been identified. Each has its own chemical structure, and each can fit into a specifically tailored harbor, or **receptor site,** on the receiving cell. The analogy of a key fitting into a lock is often used to describe this process. Once released, not all molecules of a neurotransmitter find their way into receptor sites of other neurons. "Loose" neurotransmitters are usually either broken down or reabsorbed by the axon terminal (a process called *reuptake*).

Some neurotransmitters act to *excite* other neurons—that is, to cause other neurons to fire. Other neurotransmitters act to *inhibit* receiving neurons. That is, they prevent them from firing. The sum of the stimulation—excitatory and inhibitory—determines whether a neuron will fire and, if so, when neurotransmitters will be released.

Neurotransmitters are involved in physical processes such as muscle contraction and psychological processes such as thoughts and emotions. Excesses or deficiencies of neurotransmitters have been linked to psychological disorders such as depression and schizophrenia. Let us consider the effects of some neurotransmitters of interest to psychologists: acetylcholine (ACh), dopamine, norepinephrine, serotonin, and endorphins.

Learning Connections
See the Connections *CD-ROM for an animation on synaptic transmission.*

Life Connections
See the Connections *CD-ROM for an animation on the interference of synaptic transmission.*

Synapse
A junction between the axon terminals of one neuron and the dendrites or cell body of another neuron.

Receptor Site
A location on a dendrite of a receiving neuron tailored to receive a neurotransmitter.

Acetylcholine (ACh)
A neurotransmitter that controls muscle contractions.

Hippocampus
A part of the limbic system of the brain that is involved in memory formation.

Dopamine
A neurotransmitter that is involved in Parkinson's disease and that appears to play a role in schizophrenia.

Acetylcholine (ACh) controls muscle contractions. It is excitatory at synapses between nerves and muscles that involve voluntary movement but inhibitory at the heart and some other locations. The effects of curare highlight the functioning of ACh. Curare is a poison that is extracted from plants by native South Americans and used in hunting. If an arrow tipped with curare pierces the skin and the poison enters the body, it prevents ACh from binding to the receptor sites on neurons. Because ACh helps muscles move, curare causes paralysis. The victim is prevented from contracting the muscles used in breathing and therefore dies from suffocation. Botulism, a disease that stems from food poisoning, prevents the release of ACh and has the same effect as curare.

ACh is also normally prevalent in a part of the brain called the **hippocampus,** a structure involved in the formation of memories. When the amount of ACh available to the brain decreases, memory formation is impaired, as in Alzheimer's disease (de Toledo-Morrell, 2000).

Dopamine is involved at the level of the brain and affects voluntary movements, learning and memory, and emotional arousal. Deficiencies of dopamine are linked to Parkinson's disease, in which people progressively lose control over their muscles (Olanow, 2000). They develop muscle tremors and jerky, uncoordinated movements. The boxer Muhammad Ali and actor Michael J. Fox are two of the better-known individuals who are afflicted with Parkinson's disease. The drug L-dopa, a substance that enters the brain where it is converted to dopamine, helps slow the progress of Parkinson's disease.

The psychological disorder *schizophrenia* is characterized by confusion and false perceptions, and it has been linked to dopamine. People with schizophrenia may have more receptor sites for dopamine in an area of the brain that is involved in emotional responding. For this reason, they may *overutilize* the dopamine available in the brain

■ **Former Heavyweight Champion Muhammad Ali and Actor Michael J. Fox—Two of the Many Afflicted with Parkinson's Disease**
Parkinson's disease is connected with deficiencies in the neurotransmitter dopamine and is characterized by tremors, loss of coordination, and jerky movement. In this photo, Ali and Fox meet with two senators in the effort to secure more funding for research on the disease.

(Butcher, 2000). This leads to hallucinations and disturbances of thought and emotion. The phenothiazines, a group of drugs used in the treatment of schizophrenia, inhibit the action of dopamine by blocking some dopamine receptor sites (Lidow et al., 2001). Because of their action, phenothiazines may have Parkinson-like side effects, which are usually treated by lowering the dose, prescribing additional drugs, or switching to another drug.

Norepinephrine is produced largely by neurons in the brain stem. It acts both as a neurotransmitter and as a hormone. It is an excitatory neurotransmitter that speeds up the heartbeat and other body processes and is involved in general arousal, learning and memory, and eating. Excesses and deficiencies of norepinephrine have been linked to mood disorders.

The stimulants cocaine and amphetamines ("speed") create excesses of norepinephrine (as well as dopamine) in the nervous system, increasing the firing of neurons and leading to persistent arousal. Amphetamines act by facilitating the release of these neurotransmitters and also prevent their reabsorption by the releasing synaptic vesicles—that is, their reuptake. Cocaine also blocks reuptake.

Serotonin is involved in emotional arousal and sleep. Deficiencies of serotonin have been linked to eating disorders, alcoholism, depression, aggression, and insomnia (Azar, 1997b; Leyton et al., 2000). The drug LSD decreases the action of serotonin and may also influence the utilization of dopamine. With LSD, "two no's make a yes." By inhibiting an inhibitor, it increases brain activity, in this case frequently producing hallucinations.

Gamma-aminobutyric acid (GABA) is an inhibitory neurotransmitter that may help calm anxiety reactions (Stroele et al., 2002). Tranquilizers and alcohol may quell anxiety by binding with GABA receptors and amplifying its effects. One class of antianxiety drug may also increase the sensitivity of receptor sites to GABA.

Endorphins are inhibitory neurotransmitters. The word *endorphin* is the contraction of *endogenous morphine. Endogenous* means "developing from within." Endorphins occur naturally in the brain and in the bloodstream and are similar to the narcotic morphine in their functions and effects. They lock into receptor sites for chemicals that transmit pain messages to the brain. Once the endorphin "key" is in the "lock," the pain-causing chemicals are locked out. Endorphins may also increase our sense of competence, enhance the functioning of the immune system, and be connected with the pleasurable "runner's high" reported by many long-distance runners (Jonsdottir et al., 2000; Oktedalen et al., 2001). Table 2.1 reviews much of the information on neurotransmitters.

There you have it—a fabulous forest of neurons in which billions upon billions of vesicles are pouring neurotransmitters into synaptic clefts at any given time: when you are involved in strenuous activity, now as you are reading this page, even as you are passively watching television. This microscopic picture is repeated several hundred times every second. The combined activity of all these neurotransmitters determines which messages will be transmitted and which ones will not. You experience your sensations, your thoughts, and your control over your body as psychological events, but the psychological events somehow result from many billions of electrochemical events.

The Parts of the Nervous System

As a child, I did not think it was a good thing to have a "nervous" system. After all, if your system were not jittery, you might be less likely to jump at strange noises.

REFLECT

Before taking this course, had you heard of "nerves"? How do the definitions of neurons *and* nerves *agree with your earlier ideas?*

Question: What are the parts of the nervous system? Later I learned that a nervous system is not a system that is nervous. It is a system of nerves involved in thought processes, heartbeat, visual–motor coordination, and so on. (A **nerve** is a bundle of axons.) I also learned that the human nervous system is more complex than that of any other animal and that our brains are larger than those of any other animal. Now, this last piece of business is not quite true. A human brain weighs about three pounds, but

Norepinephrine
A neurotransmitter whose action is similar to that of the hormone epinephrine and that may play a role in depression.

Serotonin
A neurotransmitter, deficiencies of which have been linked to affective disorders, anxiety, and insomnia.

Gamma-aminobutyric Acid (GABA)
An inhibitory neurotransmitter that apparently helps calm anxiety.

Endorphins
Neurotransmitters that are composed of amino acids and that are functionally similar to morphine.

Nerve
A bundle of axons from many neurons.

■ **Runner's High?**

Why have thousands of people taken up long-distance running? Running promotes cardiovascular conditioning, muscle strength, and weight control. But many long-distance runners also experience a "runner's high" that appears to be connected with the release of endorphins. Endorphins are naturally occurring substances that are similar in function to the narcotic morphine.

TABLE 2.1 Key Neurotransmitters and Their Functions

Neurotransmitter	Functions	About . . .
Acetylcholine (ACh)	Causes muscle contractions and is involved in formation of memories	Found at synapses between motor neurons and muscles. Deficiencies are linked with paralysis and Alzheimer's disease.
Dopamine	Plays a role in movement, learning, attention, memory, and emotional response	Tremors of Parkinson's disease are linked with low levels of dopamine. People with schizophrenia may *overutilize* dopamine.
Norepinephrine	Accelerates the heart rate, affects eating, and is linked with activity levels, learning, and remembering	Imbalances are linked with mood disorders such as depression and bipolar disorder.
Serotonin	Is involved in behavior patterns and psychological problems, including obesity, depression, and insomnia, alcoholism, and aggression	Drugs that block the re-uptake of serotonin are helpful in the treatment of depression.
Gamma-aminobutyric acid (GABA)	An inhibitory neurotransmitter that may lessen anxiety	Tranquilizers and alcohol may counter anxiety by binding with GABA receptors or increasing the sensitivity of receptor sites to GABA.
Endorphins	Inhibit pain by locking pain-causing chemicals out of their receptor sites	Endorphins may be connected with some people's indifference to pain, the painkilling effects of acupuncture, and the "runner's high" experienced by many long-distance runners.

the brains of elephants and whales may be four times as heavy. Still, our brains account for a greater part of our body weight than do those of elephants or whales. Our brains weigh about 1/60 of our body weight. Elephant brains weigh about 1/1,000 of their total weight, and whale brains are a paltry 1/10,000 of their weight. So, humans win the brain-as-a-percentage-of-body-weight contest.

The brain is only one part of the nervous system. The nervous system consists of the brain, the spinal cord, and the nerves linking them to the sensory organs, muscles, and glands. As shown in Figure 2.8, the brain and spinal cord make up the **central nervous system.** If you compare your nervous system to a computer, your central nervous system would be your central processing unit (CPU).

The sensory (afferent) neurons, which receive and transmit messages to the brain and spinal cord, and the motor (efferent) neurons, which transmit messages from the brain or spinal cord to the muscles and glands, make up the **peripheral nervous system.** In the comparison of the nervous system to a computer, the peripheral nervous system makes up the nervous system's peripheral devices—keyboard, mouse, diskettes, and so on. You would not be able to feed information to your computer's central processing unit without these *peripheral* devices. Other peripheral devices, such as your monitor and printer, allow you to follow what is happening inside your CPU and to see what it has accomplished.

The Peripheral Nervous System: The Body's Peripheral Devices

Question: What are the divisions and functions of the peripheral nervous system? The peripheral nervous system consists of sensory and motor neurons that transmit messages to and from the central nervous system. Without the peripheral nervous system, our brains would be like isolated CPUs. There would be no keyboards, mouses, diskettes, or other ways of inputting information. There would be no monitors, printers, modems, or other ways of displaying or transmitting information. We would be detached from the world: We would not be able to perceive it; we would not be able to act on it. The two main divisions of the peripheral nervous system are the *somatic nervous system* and the *autonomic nervous system.*

The **somatic nervous system** contains sensory (afferent) and motor (efferent) neurons. It transmits messages about sights, sounds, smells, temperature, body positions, and so on, to the central nervous system. As a result, we can experience the beauties and the horrors of the world, its physical ecstasies and agonies. Messages transmitted

Central Nervous System
The brain and spinal cord.

Peripheral Nervous System
The part of the nervous system consisting of the somatic nervous system and the autonomic nervous system.

Somatic Nervous System
The division of the peripheral nervous system that connects the central nervous system with sensory receptors, skeletal muscles, and the surface of the body.

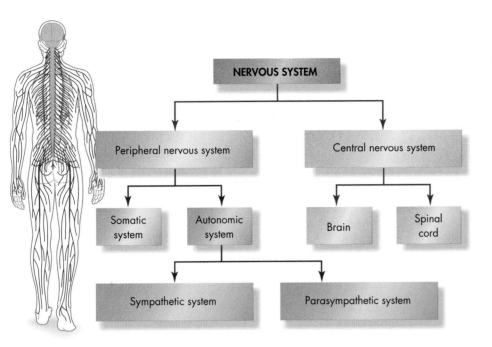

Figure 2.8
The Divisions of the Nervous System

The nervous system contains two main divisions: the central nervous system and the peripheral nervous system. The central nervous system consists of the brain and spinal cord. The peripheral nervous system contains the somatic and autonomic systems. In turn, the autonomic nervous system has sympathetic and parasympathetic divisions.

Power Visual
See Web site for an interactive version of this figure.

from the brain and spinal cord to the somatic nervous system control purposeful body movements such as raising a hand, winking, or running, as well as the tiny, almost imperceptible movements that maintain our balance and posture.

Autonomic means "automatic." The **autonomic nervous system (ANS)** regulates the glands and the muscles of internal organs. Thus, the ANS controls activities such as heartbeat, respiration, digestion, and dilation of the pupils of the eyes. These activities can occur automatically, while we are asleep. But some of them can be overridden by conscious control. You can breathe at a purposeful pace, for example. Methods like biofeedback and yoga also help people gain voluntary control of functions such as heart rate and blood pressure.

The ANS also has two branches, or divisions: **sympathetic** and **parasympathetic.** These branches have largely opposing effects. Many organs and glands are stimulated by both branches of the ANS (Figure 2.9). When organs and glands are simultaneously stimulated by both divisions, their effects can average out to some degree. In general, the sympathetic division is most active during processes that involve spending body energy from stored reserves, such as a fight-or-flight response to a predator or when you find out that your rent is going to be raised. The parasympathetic division is most active during processes that replenish reserves of energy, such as eating. When we are afraid, the sympathetic division of the ANS accelerates the heart rate. When we relax, the parasympathetic division decelerates the heart rate. The parasympathetic division stimulates digestive processes, but the sympathetic branch inhibits digestion. Because the sympathetic division predominates when we feel fear or anxiety, these feelings can cause indigestion.

The ANS is of particular interest to psychologists because its activities are linked to various emotions such as anxiety and love. Some people seem to have overly reactive sympathetic nervous systems. In the absence of external threats, their bodies still respond as though they were faced with danger. Psychologists often help them learn to relax.

REFLECT

Is breathing voluntary or involuntary (autonomic, automatic)? Could it be both? Explain.

Autonomic Nervous System (ANS)
The division of the peripheral nervous system that regulates glands and activities such as heartbeat, respiration, digestion, and dilation of the pupils.

Sympathetic
The branch of the ANS that is most active during emotional responses, such as fear and anxiety, that spend the body's reserves of energy.

Parasympathetic
The branch of the ANS that is most active during processes such as digestion that restore the body's reserves of energy.

REFLECT

Have you ever lost your appetite or thrown up because of anxiety or fear? What biological processes caused fear to produce indigestion?

The Central Nervous System: The Body's Central Processing Unit

It is your central nervous system that makes you so special. Other species see more sharply, smell more keenly, and hear more acutely. Other species run faster, or fly through the air, or swim underwater—without the benefit of artificial devices such as airplanes and submarines. But it is your central nervous system that enables you to use symbols and language, the abilities that allow people not only to adapt to their

■ **Figure 2.9**
The Branches of the Autonomic Nervous System (ANS)
The parasympathetic branch of the ANS generally acts to replenish stores of energy in the body. The sympathetic branch is most active during activities that expend energy. The two branches of the ANS frequently have antagonistic effects on the organs they service.

Power Visual
See Web site for an interactive version of this figure.

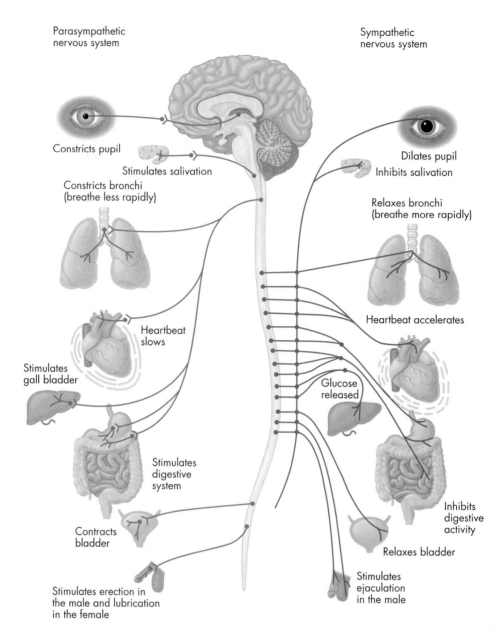

Parasympathetic nervous system

Sympathetic nervous system

Constricts pupil

Dilates pupil
Inhibits salivation

Stimulates salivation

Constricts bronchi (breathe less rapidly)

Relaxes bronchi (breathe more rapidly)

Heartbeat slows

Heartbeat accelerates

Stimulates gall bladder

Glucose released

Stimulates digestive system

Inhibits digestive activity

Contracts bladder

Relaxes bladder

Stimulates erection in the male and lubrication in the female

Stimulates ejaculation in the male

Spinal Cord
A column of nerves within the spine that transmits messages from sensory receptors to the brain and from the brain to muscles and glands throughout the body.

Spinal Reflex
A simple, unlearned response to a stimulus that may involve only two neurons.

Interneuron
A neuron that transmits a neural impulse from a sensory neuron to a motor neuron.

R E F L E C T

Does it seem possible that sexual responses like erection and orgasm are reflexive? Why or why not?

environment but to create new environments and give them names (Bandura, 1999). *Question: What are the divisions and functions of the central nervous system?* The central nervous system consists of the spinal cord and the brain.

The **spinal cord** is a true "information superhighway"—a column of nerves about as thick as a thumb. It transmits messages from sensory receptors to the brain and from the brain to muscles and glands throughout the body. The spinal cord is also capable of some "local government." That is, it controls some responses to external stimulation through **spinal reflexes.** A spinal reflex is an unlearned response to a stimulus that may involve only two neurons—a sensory (afferent) neuron and a motor (efferent) neuron (Figure 2.10). In some reflexes, a third neuron, called an **interneuron,** transmits the neural impulse from the sensory neuron through the spinal cord to the motor neuron.

We have many reflexes. We blink in response to a puff of air in our faces. We swallow when food accumulates in the mouth. A physician may tap the leg below the knee to elicit the knee-jerk reflex, a sign that the nervous system is operating adequately. Urinating and defecating are reflexes that occur in response to pressure in the bladder and the rectum. Parents typically spend weeks or months toilet-training infants—in other words, teaching them to involve their brains in the process of elimination. Learning to inhibit these reflexes makes civilization possible.

Sexual response also involves many reflexes. Stimulation of the genital organs leads to erection in the male, vaginal lubrication in the female (both are reflexes that make

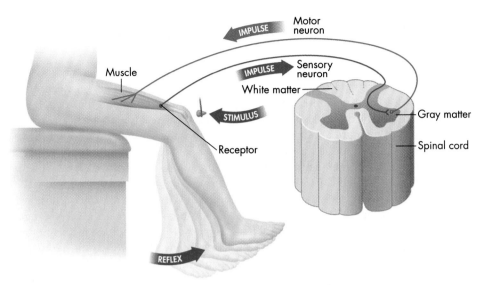

■ Figure 2.10
The Reflex Arc

Reflexes are inborn, stereotyped behavior patterns that have apparently evolved because they help individuals adapt to the environment even before they can understand and purposefully manipulate the environment. Here we see a cross section of the spinal cord, highlighting a sensory neuron and a motor neuron, which are involved in the knee-jerk reflex. In some reflexes, interneurons link sensory and motor neurons.

sexual intercourse possible), and the involuntary muscle contractions of orgasm. As reflexes, these processes need not involve the brain, but most often they do. Feelings of passion, memories of an enjoyable sexual encounter, and sexual fantasies usually contribute to sexual response by transmitting messages from the brain to the genitals through the spinal cord.

The spinal cord (and the brain) consists of gray matter and white matter. The **gray matter** is composed of nonmyelinated neurons. Some of these are involved in spinal reflexes. Others send their axons to the brain. The **white matter** is composed of bundles of longer, myelinated (and thus whitish) axons that carry messages to and from the brain. As you can see in Figure 2.10, a cross section of the spinal cord shows that the gray matter, which includes cell bodies, is distributed in a butterfly pattern.

Gray Matter

In the spinal cord, the grayish neurons and neural segments that are involved in spinal reflexes.

White Matter

In the spinal cord, axon bundles that carry messages from and to the brain.

R E V I E W

(13) Neurons transmit messages to other neurons by means of chemical substances called _____. (14) Neurons have a cell body, or soma; _____, which receive "messages"; and an axon, which extends from the cell body. (15) The axons of many neurons have a fatty insulating sheath called _____. (16) _____ neurons conduct messages from the central nervous system that stimulate glands or cause muscles to contract. (17) The conduction of the neural impulse along the length of the neuron is called _____. (18) A _____ consists of an axon terminal, a dendrite, and a fluid-filled gap between them. (19) ACh is normally prevalent in a brain structure essential to the formation of memories: the _____. (20) It is theorized that people with _____ overutilize dopamine. (21) Deficiencies of _____ are linked to anxiety, depression, and insomnia. (22) The nervous system is made up of the _____ and central nervous systems. (23) The _____ nervous system (ANS) regulates the glands and involuntary activities such as heartbeat and digestion.

Learning Connections
See Web site for an interactive version of these review questions.

Critical Thinking: Psychology is the study of behavior and mental processes. Why, then, are psychologists interested in the nervous system?

THE BRAIN: THE STAR OF THE HUMAN NERVOUS SYSTEM

Every show has a star, and the brain is the undisputed star of the human nervous system. The size and shape of your brain are responsible for your large, delightfully rounded head. In all the animal kingdom, you (and about 6 billion other people) are unique because of the capacities for learning and thinking residing in the human brain.

The brains of men are about 15% larger than those of women on average (Blum, 1997), which is related to the difference in body size. Of course, feminists might argue that this proves that bigger is not necessarily better. In the human brain it may be that how well-connected one is (in terms of synapses) is more important than size. After all, Albert Einstein's brain was only average in size (Witelson et al., 1999). Moreover, women's brains "run hotter" than men's. Women metabolize more glucose (sugar) and appear to use more of their brains on a given task (Blum, 1997). In fact, columnist Maureen Dowd (1997) suggests that men squander many of their neurons in preoccupation with things like seduction techniques, sexual fantasies, thinning hair, stock tips, Web sites, and better gear (like cross-training socks). (Your author's wife could have told you that all along.)

Scientists who have engaged in brain research generally agree that the mind is a function of the brain (Bogen, 1998; Voneida, 1998) *Question: How do researchers learn about the functions of the brain?*

Seeing the Brain Through the Eyes of the Psychologist

One of French surgeon Paul Broca's (1824–1880) hobbies was *craniometry,* or measurement of the skull. He believed that the size of the brain was related to intelligence. (Generally speaking, it isn't.) He argued that the brains of mature people were larger than those of older people, in "superior" races than in "inferior" ones, in men than in women, and in accomplished men than in run-of-the-mill men. Broca was well aware of evidence that contradicted his views. He knew that the brains of Asians were generally smaller than those of Europeans, although Asians were at least as bright. He knew of extremely intelligent women and of criminals with large brains. Nevertheless, he and his fellow craniometrists touted their views. Upon his death, it was discovered that Broca's own brain was but a bit above average in size—nothing to brag about.

Despite his only slightly-above-average-sized brain, Broca was the first to observe a behavior problem and then locate the area of the brain that caused it. In 1861, Leborgne, a 51-year-old patient at La Bicêtre, the Paris asylum, came down with gangrene in the leg and was admitted to the surgical ward. Leborgne could understand what was said to him but could only utter the meaningless sound "tan" and sometimes blurt out "Sacred name of God!" in frustration. Leborgne had entered the asylum 21 years earlier, when he had lost the ability to speak.

Leborgne died six days later, and Broca performed an autopsy. He discovered that an egg-sized area just in front of the region of the motor cortex that regulates movement of the face on the left side of the brain had deteriorated. Broca concluded that this part of the brain was the seat of speech, and we now refer to it as *Broca's area.*

As in the cases of Phineas Gage and Leborgne, people have noticed the effects of various kinds of damage to the brain throughout history. It has been known for about two centuries that damage to the left side of the brain is connected with loss of sensation or movement on the right side of the body, and vice versa. Thus it has been assumed that the brain's control mechanisms must cross over from right to left, and vice versa, as they descend into the body.

Let's look at the brain through the eyes of the psychologist. Let's explore the various ways in which researchers have learned about the functioning of the brain.

Accidents

Many accidents have taught us about the brain. From injuries to the head—some of them minimal, some horrendous—we have learned that brain damage can impair con-

■ Paul Broca

The French surgeon was the first to locate the specific area of the brain that is involved in production of language. Although he was a renowned scientist, he believed—as did many of his era—that the size of the brain was related to intelligence. But upon his death, his own brain was revealed to be only average in size.

Culver Pictures

sciousness and awareness. Brain damage can result in loss of vision and hearing, confusion, or loss of memory. In some cases, the loss of large portions of the brain may result in little loss of function. Ironically, the loss of smaller portions in particularly sensitive locations can result in language problems, memory loss, or death.

Accidents provide unplanned and uncontrolled opportunities of studying the brain. Scientists have learned more about the brain, however, through methods like experimentation, use of the electroencephalograph, and brain scans.

Experimenting with the Brain

The results of disease (as in the case of Leborgne) and accidents (as in the case of Phineas Gage) have shown us that brain injuries can be connected with changes in behavior and mental processes. Scientists have also purposefully experimented with the brain to observe the results. For example, **lesioning** (damaging) part of the brain region called the hypothalamus causes rats to overeat. Damaging another part of the hypothalamus causes them to stop eating. It is as if parts of the brain contain on–off switches for certain kinds of behavior, at least in lower animals.

Surgeon Wilder Penfield (1969) stimulated parts of the brain with electrical probes, and as a result his patients reported the occurrence of certain kinds of memories. Similar experiments in electrical stimulation of the brain have found that parts of the brain are connected with specific kinds of sensations (as of light or sound) or motor activities (such as movement of an arm or leg).

The Electroencephalograph

Penfield stimulated parts of the brain with an electrical current and asked people to report what they experienced as a result. Researchers have also used the electroencephalograph (EEG) to record the natural electrical activity of the brain.

When I was an undergraduate psychology student, I first heard that psychologists studied sleep by "connecting" people to the EEG. I had a gruesome image of people somehow being plugged in. Not so. Electrodes are simply attached to the scalp with tape or paste. Once the brain activity under study has been recorded, the electrodes are removed. A bit of soap and water, and you're as good as new.

The EEG detects minute amounts of electrical activity—called brain waves—that pass between the electrodes. Certain brain waves are associated with feelings of relaxation and with various stages of sleep.

Brain-Imaging Techniques

When Phineas Gage had his fabled accident, and when Leborgne came under the scrutiny of Paul Broca, the only ways to look into the brain were to drill holes in the skull or crack it open, neither of which would have contributed to the well-being of the subject. But in the latter years of the 20th century, researchers tapped the computer's capacity to generate images of the parts of the brain from sources of radiation to develop imaging techniques that have been useful to researchers and physicians.

The CAT (computerized axial tomograph) scan passes a narrow X-ray beam through the head and measures the structures that reflect the X-rays from various angles, generating a three-dimensional image of the brain. The CAT scan reveals deformities in shape and structure that are connected with blood clots, tumors, and other health problems.

A second method, positron emission tomography (PET scan), forms a computer-generated image of the activity of parts of the brain by tracing the amount of glucose used (or metabolized) by these parts. More glucose is metabolized in more active parts of the brain. To trace the metabolism of glucose, a harmless amount of a radioactive compound, called a *tracer,* is mixed with glucose and injected into the bloodstream. When the glucose reaches the brain, the patterns of activity are revealed by measurement of the positrons—positively charged particles—that are given off by the tracer. The PET scan has been used by researchers to see which parts of the brain are most active when we

---

Lesion

(LEE-shun). An injury that results in impaired behavior or loss of a function.

REFLECT

Would you be upset if it happened that certain types of behavior could be switched on or off by use of electrodes attached to your brain? Why or why not?

■ **The Computerized Axial Tomograph (CAT) Scan**

In the CAT scan, an X-ray is passed through the head and the amount of radiation that passes through is measured from various angles. The computer integrates the measurements into a view of the brain.

REFLECT

Do you know of anyone who has had a "brain scan"? What kind of scan? For what purpose? What was the outcome?

Prefrontal
cortex

■ **Figure 2.11**
The Prefrontal Cortex of the Brain

The prefrontal cortex comes in pairs. One is found in each hemisphere, a bit above the outer edge of the eyebrow. The prefrontal cortex is highly active during visual and spatial problem solving. Your sense of self—your continuous sense of being in and operating on the world—may also reside largely in the prefrontal cortex.

Medulla
An oblong area of the hindbrain involved in regulation of heartbeat and respiration.

are, for example, listening to music, working out a math problem, using language, or playing chess. Research with the PET scan suggests that the prefrontal cortex of the brain may be where we process much of the information involved in verbal and spatial problem solving (Duncan et al., 2000). Figure 2.11 shows the prefrontal cortex. One prefrontal region is found in each hemisphere, a bit above the outer edge of the eyebrow.

A third imaging technique is magnetic resonance imaging (MRI). In MRI, the person lies in a powerful magnetic field and is exposed to radio waves that cause parts of the brain to emit signals, which are measured from multiple angles. MRI relies on subtle shifts in blood flow. (More blood flows to more active parts of the brain, supplying them with oxygen.) So-called "fast MRI" (fMRI) can be used to show which parts of the brain are active when we are, say, solving math problems (Rickard et al., 2000) or speaking (Dogil et al., 2002). MRI has shown that people with schizophrenia have smaller prefrontal regions of the cortex than other people (Flashman et al., 2000) but larger ventricles (hollow spaces) in the brain (Wright et al., 2000).

A Voyage Through the Brain

Your brain is a fascinating archaeological site. It reveals much of what is so special about you. It also holds a record of your connectedness with other animals that have walked, swum, and flown the earth for hundreds of millions of years. In fact, some parts of your brain—those that we meet first on our tour—are not all that different from the corresponding parts of the brains of rats, cats, and monkeys. They even bear some resemblance to the brains of birds and fish (Figure 2.12). The "older" parts of your brain, evolutionarily speaking—those that are found beneath your rounded skull—also have functions very similar to those of these other species. They are involved in basic survival functions such as breathing, feeding, and the regulation of cycles of sleeping and waking. *Question: What are the structures and functions of the brain?*

Let us now begin our tour of the brain (Figure 2.13). We begin with the oldest part of our "archaeological dig"—the hindbrain, where the spinal cord rises to meet the brain. The hindbrain consists of three major structures: the medulla, the pons, and the cerebellum. Many pathways that connect the spinal cord to higher levels of the brain pass through the **medulla.** The medulla regulates vital functions such as heart rate, blood pressure, and respiration. (In fact, Gage survived his accident because his medulla escaped injury.) The medulla also plays a role in sleeping, sneezing, and

R E F L E C T

What is meant by the "old" versus the "new" parts of your brain? (After all, your brain was all born at the same time, wasn't it?)

■ **Figure 2.12**
Comparison of the Human Brain to the Brains of Other Species
Some parts of the human brain, especially the older parts, are quite similar to the corresponding parts of the brains of other mammals. They are even somewhat similar to those of birds and fish and are involved in survival functions such as breathing, feeding, and the regulation of the sleeping–waking cycle. However, the cerebrums, which are involved in cognitive processes, are quite different.

Power Visual
See Web site for an interactive version of this figure.

Bass   Pigeon   Cat   Chimpanzee   Human

coughing. The **pons** is a bulge in the hindbrain that lies forward of the medulla. *Pons* is the Latin word for "bridge." The pons is so named because of the bundles of nerves that pass through it. The pons transmits information about body movement and is involved in functions related to attention, sleep and alertness, and respiration.

Behind the pons lies the **cerebellum** ("little brain" in Latin). The cerebellum has two hemispheres that are involved in maintaining balance and in controlling motor (muscle) behavior. Injury to the cerebellum may lead to lack of motor coordination, stumbling, and loss of muscle tone.

The **reticular activating system (RAS)** begins in the hindbrain and ascends through the midbrain into the lower part of the forebrain. It is vital in the functions of attention, sleep, and arousal. Injury to the RAS may result in a coma. Stimulation of the RAS causes it to send messages to the cerebral cortex (the large wrinkled mass that you think of as your brain), making us more alert to sensory information. In classic neurological research, Guiseppe Moruzzi and Horace Magoun (1949) discovered that electrical stimulation of the reticular formation of a sleeping cat caused it to awaken at once. But when the reticular formation was severed from higher parts of the brain, the animal fell

Pons

A structure of the hindbrain involved in respiration, attention, and sleep and dreaming.

Cerebellum

A part of the hindbrain involved in muscle coordination and balance.

Reticular Activating System (RAS)

A part of the brain involved in attention, sleep, and arousal.

■ **Figure 2.13**
The Parts of the Human Brain

This view of the brain, split top to bottom, shows some of the most important structures. Note how close the hypothalamus is to the pituitary gland. The proximity allows the hypothalamus to readily influence the pituitary gland. The "valleys" in the cerebrum are called fissures.

Corpus callosum
Thick bundle of axons that serves as a bridge between the two cerebral hemispheres

Cerebrum
Center of thinking and language; prefrontal area contains "executive center" of brain

Thalamus
Relay station for sensory information

Hypothalamus
Secretes hormones that stimulate secretion of hormones by the pituitary gland; involved in basic drives such as hunger, sex, and aggression

Cerebellum
Essential to balance and coordination

Pituitary gland
Secretes hormones that regulate many body functions, including secretion of hormones from other glands; sometimes referred to as the "master gland"

Reticular activating system
Involved in regulation of sleep and waking; stimulation of RAS increases arousal

Pons
Involved in reulation of movement, sleep and arousal, respiration

Medulla
Involved in reulation of heart rate, blood pressure, respiration, circulation

Power Visual
See Web site for an interactive version of this figure.

Thalamus

An area near the center of the brain involved in the relay of sensory information to the cortex and in the functions of sleep and attention.

Hypothalamus

A bundle of nuclei below the thalamus involved in body temperature, motivation, and emotion.

Limbic System

A group of structures involved in memory, motivation, and emotion that forms a fringe along the inner edge of the cerebrum.

Amygdala

A part of the limbic system that apparently facilitates stereotypical aggressive responses.

R E F L E C T

If your brain had a pleasure center, would you like to have your finger on the switch that turns it on or off? Might religious leaders be concerned? Why or why not?

into a coma from which it would not awaken. Drugs known as central nervous system depressants, such as alcohol, are thought to work, in part, by lowering RAS activity.

Sudden loud noises stimulate the RAS and awaken a sleeping animal or person. But the RAS may become selective through learning. That is, it comes to play a filtering role. It may allow some messages to filter through to higher brain levels and awareness while screening others out. For example, the parent who has primary responsibility for child care may be awakened by the stirring sounds of an infant, while the sounds of traffic or street noise are filtered out, even though they are louder. The other parent, in contrast, may sleep through loud crying by the infant. If the first parent must be away for several days, however, the second parent's RAS may quickly become sensitive to noises produced by the child. This sensitivity may rapidly fade again when the first parent returns.

Also located in the midbrain are areas involved in vision and hearing. These include the area that controls eye reflexes such as dilation of the pupils and eye movements.

Key areas of the forwardmost part of the brain, or forebrain, are the thalamus, the hypothalamus, the limbic system, and the cerebrum (see Figure 2.13). The **thalamus** is located near the center of the brain. It consists of two joined egg- or football-shaped structures. The thalamus serves as a relay station for sensory stimulation. Nerve fibers from the sensory systems enter from below; the information carried by them is then transmitted to the cerebral cortex by way of fibers that exit from above. For instance, the thalamus relays sensory input from the eyes to the visual areas of the cerebral cortex. The thalamus is also involved in controlling sleep and attention in coordination with other brain structures, including the RAS.

The **hypothalamus** lies beneath the thalamus and above the pituitary gland. It weighs only 4 grams, yet it is vital in the regulation of body temperature, concentration of fluids, storage of nutrients, and various aspects of motivation and emotion. Experimenters learn many of the functions of the hypothalamus by implanting electrodes in parts of it and observing the effects of an electrical current. They have found that the hypothalamus is involved in hunger, thirst, sexual behavior, caring for offspring, and aggression. Among lower animals, stimulation of various areas of the hypothalamus can trigger instinctual behaviors such as fighting, mating, or even nest building.

Canadian psychologists James Olds and Peter Milner (1954) made a wonderful mistake in the 1950s. They were attempting to implant an electrode in a rat's reticular formation to see how stimulation of the area might affect learning. Olds, however, was primarily a social psychologist and not a biological psychologist. He missed his target and found a part of the animal's hypothalamus instead. Olds and Milner dubbed this area the "pleasure center" because the animal would repeat whatever it was doing when it was stimulated. The term *pleasure center* is not used too frequently, because it appears to attribute human emotions to rats. Yet the "pleasure centers" must be doing something right, because rats stimulate themselves in these centers by pressing a pedal several thousand times an hour, until they are exhausted (Olds, 1969).

The hypothalamus is just as important to humans as it is to lower animals. Unfortunately (or fortunately), our "pleasure centers" are not as clearly defined as those of the rat. Then, too, our responses to messages from the hypothalamus are less automatic and relatively more influenced by higher brain functions—that is, cognitive factors such as thought, choice, and value systems. It is all a part of being human.

The **limbic system** is made up of several structures, including the amygdala, hippocampus, and parts of the hypothalamus (Figure 2.14). The limbic system lies along the inner edge of the cerebrum and is fully evolved only in mammals. It is involved in memory and emotion and in the drives of hunger, sex, and aggression. People in whom surgical operations have damaged the hippocampus can retrieve old memories but cannot permanently store new information. As a result, they may reread the same newspaper day in and day out without recalling that they read it before. Or they may have to be perpetually reintroduced to people they have met just hours earlier (Squire, 1993, 1996).

The **amygdala** looks like two little almonds. Studies using lesioning and electrical stimulation show that the amygdala is connected with aggressive behavior in monkeys, cats, and other animals. Early in the 20th century, Heinrich Klüver and Paul Bucy (1939) lesioned part of the amygdala of a rhesus monkey. Rhesus monkeys are normally a scrappy lot and try to bite or grab at intruders, but destruction of this animal's amygdala made it docile. No longer did it react aggressively to people. It even allowed people to poke and pinch it. Electrical stimulation of the part of the amygdala that Klüver and Bucy had destroyed, however, triggers a "rage response." For example, it causes a cat to hiss and arch its back in preparation to attack. The amygdala is also connected with a fear response (LeDoux, 1998). If you electrically stimulate another part of the amygdala, the cat cringes in fear when you cage it with a mouse—not very tigerlike.

The amygdala is also connected with vigilance. It is involved in emotions, learning, and memory, and it sort of behaves like a spotlight, focusing attention on matters that are novel and important to know more about. In studies reported in 2000, researchers used fMRI to scan the amygdala while subjects were shown faces of European Americans and African Americans. One study flashed the photos by four men and four women, half European American and half African American (Hart et al., 2000). The subjects showed less activity in the amygdala when they viewed faces belonging to people of their own ethnic group, suggesting that they were more comfortable with "familiar" faces.

Other studies attempted to connect the "lighting up" of the amygdala with other racially oriented responses. In one, European American subjects were shown photos of young European Americans and African Americans (Phelps et al., 2000). Days later, the subjects were given tests to measure their responses to African Americans. For example, one test involved sitting at a computer and classifying the photos by race at the same time they were classifying words flashing on the screen as "good" or "bad." Most of the European American subjects tend to associate positive words like joy, love, and peace with European Americans and negative words like cancer, bomb, and devil with African Americans. It turned out that subjects who were more likely to associate African Americans with negative words also showed greater activity in the amygdala when presented with faces of African Americans. The researchers do not suggest that the amygdala activity—or even the word-association test—is a sign of conscious prejudice. They offer the alternative hypothesis that European Americans may simply be less familiar with faces of African Americans and that the relative lack of familiarity could trigger activity in the amygdala and negative feelings (fear of the unknown). The researchers find evidence for this interpretation in the fact that European Americans did *not* show the heightened activity of the amygdala when photos of familiar African Americans—Michael Jordan and Denzel Washington—flashed by.

The **cerebrum** is the crowning glory of the brain. Only in humans does the cerebrum make up such a large part of the brain (Figure 2.15). The cerebrum is responsible for thinking and language. The surface of the cerebrum—the **cerebral cortex**—is wrinkled, or convoluted, with ridges and valleys. The convolutions allow a great deal of surface area to be packed into the brain—and surface area is apparently connected with cognitive ability.

Valleys in the cortex are called *fissures*. A key fissure almost divides the cerebrum in half, creating two hemispheres with something of the shape of a walnut. The hemispheres are connected by the **corpus callosum** (Latin for "thick body" or "hard body"), a bundle of some 200 million nerve fibers.

Power Visual
See Web site for an interactive version of this figure.

■ **Figure 2.14**
The Limbic System

The limbic system is made up of structures that include the amygdala, the hippocampus, and parts of the hypothalamus. It is evolved fully only in mammals and forms a fringe along the inner edge of the cerebrum. The limbic system is involved in memory and emotion and in the drives of hunger, sex, and aggression.

THE CEREBRAL CORTEX

The cerebral cortex is the part of the brain that you usually think of as your brain. *Cortex* is a Latin word meaning "bark," as in the bark of a tree. Just as the bark is the outer coating of a tree, the cerebral cortex is the outer coating of the cerebrum. It is only about one-eighth of an inch thick.

The cerebral cortex is involved in almost every bodily activity, including most sensations and most responses. It is also the part of the brain that frees people from the

Cerebrum
The large mass of the forebrain, which consists of two hemispheres.

Cerebral Cortex
The wrinkled surface area (gray matter) of the cerebrum.

Corpus Callosum
A thick fiber bundle that connects the hemispheres of the cortex.

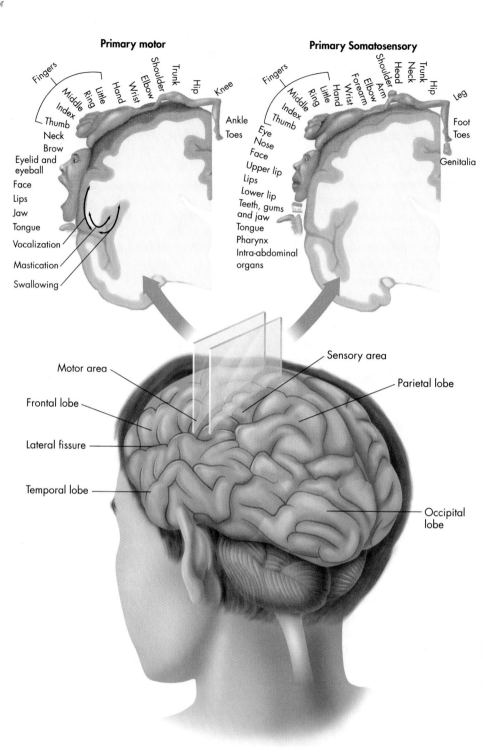

Learning Connections
See the Connections *CD-ROM to manipulate a virtual brain.*

■ **Figure 2.15**
The Geography of the Cerebral Cortex
The cortex is divided into four lobes: frontal, parietal, temporal, and occipital. The visual area of the cortex is located in the occipital lobe. The hearing or auditory cortex lies in the temporal lobe. The sensory and motor areas face each other across the central fissure. What happens when a surgeon stimulates areas of the sensory or motor cortex during an operation?

tyranny of genetic dictates and instinct. It is the seat of thinking and language, and it enables humans to think deeply about the world outside and to make decisions. Other organisms run faster than we do, are stronger, or bite more sharply. Yet humans think faster, are intellectually "stronger," and, we might add, have a "biting" wit—all of which is made possible by the cerebral cortex. *Question: What are the parts of the cerebral cortex?*

The cerebral cortex has two hemispheres, left and right. Each of the hemispheres is divided into four lobes, as shown in Figure 2.15. The **frontal lobe** lies in front of the central fissure, and the **parietal lobe** behind it. The **temporal lobe** lies below the side, or lateral, fissure—across from the frontal and parietal lobes. The **occipital lobe** lies behind the temporal lobe and behind and below the parietal lobe.

When light strikes the eyes, neurons in the occipital lobe fire, and as a result, we "see" (that is, the image is projected in the brain). Direct artificial stimulation of the occipital lobe also produces visual sensations. If neurons in the occipital region of the cortex were stimulated with electricity, you would "see" flashes of light even if it were pitch black or your eyes were covered. The hearing or auditory area of the cortex lies in the temporal lobe along the lateral fissure. Sounds cause structures in the ear to vibrate. Messages are relayed from those structures to the auditory area of the cortex; and, when you hear a noise, neurons in this area are firing.

Just behind the central fissure in the parietal lobe lies an area called the **somatosensory cortex,** which receives messages from skin senses all over the body. These sensations include warmth and cold, touch, pain, and movement. Neurons in different parts of the sensory cortex fire, depending on whether you wiggle your finger or raise your leg. If a brain surgeon were to stimulate the proper area of your somatosensory cortex with an electrical probe, it might seem as if someone were touching your arm or leg. A Swedish MRI study found that just the expectation of being tickled in a certain part of the body activates the corresponding area of the somatosensory cortex (Carlsson et al., 2000).

Figure 2.15 suggests that our face and head are overrepresented (too big) on the cortex compared with, say, our trunk and legs. This overrepresentation is one of the reasons that our face and head are more sensitive to touch than other parts of the body.

Many years ago it was discovered that patients with injuries to one hemisphere of the brain would show sensory or motor deficits on the opposite side of the body below the head. This led to the recognition that sensory and motor nerves cross in the brain and elsewhere. The left hemisphere controls, acts on, and receives inputs from the right side of the body. The right hemisphere controls, acts on, and receives inputs from the left side of the body.

How do you make a monkey smile? One way is by inserting an electrical probe in its motor cortex and giving it a burst of electricity. Let us see what we mean by this.

The **motor cortex** lies in the frontal lobe, just across the valley of the central fissure from the somatosensory cortex. Neurons firing in the motor cortex cause parts of our body to move. More than 100 years ago, German scientists electrically stimulated the motor cortex in dogs and observed that muscles contracted in response (Fritsch & Hitzig, 1870/1960). Since then, neuroscientists have mapped the motor cortex in people and lower animals by inserting electrical probes and seeing which muscles contract. For example, José Delgado (1969) caused one patient to make a fist even though he tried to prevent his hand from closing. The patient said, "I guess, doctor, that your electricity is stronger than my will" (Delgado, 1969, p. 114). Delgado also made a monkey smile in this manner, many thousands of times in a row. If a surgeon were to stimulate a certain area of the right hemisphere of the motor cortex with an electrical probe, you would raise your left leg. This action would be sensed in the somatosensory cortex, and you might have a devil of a time trying to figure out whether you had intended to raise that leg!

Thinking, Language, and the Cortex

Areas of the cerebral cortex that are not primarily involved in sensation or motor activity are called *association areas*. They make possible the breadth and depth of human learning, thought, memory, and language. *Question: What parts of the cerebral cortex are involved in thinking and language?* The association areas in the *prefrontal* region of the brain—that is, in the frontal lobes, near the forehead—could be called the brain's executive center. It appears to be where we solve problems and make plans and decisions (Chafee & Goldman-Rakic, 2000; Constantinidis et al., 2001; Duncan et al., 2000).

Frontal Lobe
The lobe of the cerebral cortex that lies to the front of the central fissure.

Parietal Lobe
The lobe that lies just behind the central fissure.

Temporal Lobe
The lobe that lies below the lateral fissure, near the temples of the head.

Occipital Lobe
The lobe that lies behind and below the parietal lobe and behind the temporal lobe.

Somatosensory Cortex
The section of cortex in which sensory stimulation is projected. It lies just behind the central fissure in the parietal lobe.

Motor Cortex
The section of cortex that lies in the frontal lobe, just across the central fissure from the sensory cortex. Neural impulses in the motor cortex are linked to muscular responses throughout the body.

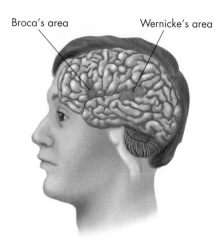

■ **Figure 2.16**

Broca's and Wernicke's Areas of the Cerebral Cortex

The areas that are most involved in speech are Broca's area and Wernicke's area. Damage to either area can produce an *aphasia*—a disruption of the ability to understand or produce language.

R E F L E C T

As you read the words on this page, neurons in your brain are firing. Where are the neurons whose firing results in your seeing the words? If you "hear" the words inside your head, what neurons are making that possible?

Epilepsy
Temporary disturbances of brain functions that involve sudden neural discharges.

Aphasia
A disruption in the ability to understand or produce language.

Wernicke's Aphasia
A language disorder characterized by difficulty comprehending the meaning of spoken language.

Broca's Aphasia
A language disorder characterized by slow, laborious speech.

Executive functions like problem solving also require memory, like the memory in your computer. These areas also provide the core of your working memory (Chafee & Goldman-Rakic, 2000; Constantinidis et al., 2001). They are connected with various sensory areas in the brain and can tap whatever kind of sensory information is needed or desired. The prefrontal region of the brain thus retrieves visual, auditory, and other kinds of memories and manipulates them—similar to the way in which a computer retrieves information from files in storage and manipulates it in working memory.

Certain neurons in the visual area of the occipital lobe fire in response to the visual presentation of vertical lines. Others fire in response to presentation of horizontal lines. Although one group of cells may respond to one aspect of the visual field and another group of cells may respond to another, association areas put it all together. As a result, we see a box or an automobile or a road map and not a confusing array of verticals and horizontals.

Language Functions

In some ways, the left and right hemispheres of the brain duplicate each other's functions. In other ways, they differ. The left hemisphere contains language functions for nearly all right-handed people and for two out of three left-handed people (Pinker, 1994a). However, the brain remains "plastic," or changeable, through about the age of 13. As a result, children who lose the left hemisphere of the brain because of surgery to control **epilepsy** usually transfer speech functions to the right hemisphere (Zuger, 1997).

Two key language areas lie within the hemisphere of the cortex that contains language functions (usually the left hemisphere): Broca's area and Wernicke's area (see Figure 2.16). Damage to either area is likely to cause an **aphasia**—that is, a disruption of the ability to understand or produce language.

Wernicke's area lies in the temporal lobe near the auditory cortex. It responds mainly to auditory information. As you are reading this page, however, the visual information is registered in the visual cortex of your occipital lobe. It is then recoded as auditory information as it travels to Wernicke's area. Broca's area is located in the frontal lobe, near the section of the motor cortex that controls the muscles of the tongue, throat, and other areas of the face used when speaking (Pinker, 1994a; Raichle, 1994). Broca's area processes the information and relays it to the motor cortex. The motor cortex sends the signals that cause muscles in your throat and mouth to contract. If you are "subvocalizing"—saying what you are reading "under your breath"—that is because Wernicke's area transmits information to Broca's area via nerve fibers.

People with damage to Wernicke's area may show **Wernicke's aphasia,** which impairs their abilities to comprehend speech and to think of the proper words to express their own thoughts. Ironically, they usually speak freely and with proper syntax. Wernicke's area is essential to understanding the relationships between words and their meanings. When Broca's area is damaged, people usually understand language well enough but speak slowly and laboriously, in simple sentences. This pattern is termed **Broca's aphasia.**

A part of the brain called the *angular gyrus* lies between the visual cortex and Wernicke's area. The angular gyrus "translates" visual information, as in perceiving written words, into auditory information (sounds) and sends it on to Wernicke's area. It appears that problems in the angular gyrus can give rise to *dyslexia,* or serious impairment in reading, because it becomes difficult for the reader to segment words into sounds (Pugh et al., 2000).

Left Brain, Right Brain?

We often hear of being "left-brained" or "right-brained." *Question: What would it mean to be "left-brained" or "right-brained"?* The notion is that the hemispheres of the brain are involved in very different kinds of intellectual and emotional functions and responses. According to this view, left-brained people would be primarily logical and intellectual. Right-brained people would be intuitive, creative, and emotional. Those of us who are fortunate enough to have our brains "in balance" would presumably have the best of it—the capacity for logic combined with emotional richness.

Like so many other popular ideas, the left-brain–right-brain notion is at best exaggerated. Research does suggest that in right-handed individuals, the left hemisphere is relatively more involved in intellectual undertakings that require logical analysis and problem solving, language, and mathematical computation (Gazzaniga, 1995). The other hemisphere (usually the right hemisphere) is usually superior in visual–spatial functions (it's better at putting puzzles together), recognition of faces, discrimination of colors, aesthetic and emotional responses, understanding metaphors, and creative mathematical reasoning.

Despite these differences, it would be erroneous to think that the hemispheres of the brain act independently—that some people are truly left-brained and others right-brained (Gazzaniga, 1995). The functions of the left and right hemispheres overlap to some degree, and the hemispheres tend to respond simultaneously as we focus our attention on one thing or another. The hemispheres are aided in their "cooperation" by the corpus callosum, the bundle of 200 million axons that connects them.

Now let us consider another issue involving sidedness: left-handedness. People who are left-handed are different from people who are right-handed in terms of the way they write, throw a ball, and so on. But there are interesting questions as to whether people who are left-handed are psychologically different from "righties."

CONTROVERSY IN PSYCHOLOGY

Are some people left-brained and others right-brained?

What aspects of behavior and mental processes are considered left-brained? Which are considered right-brained? Does research evidence support a sharp distinction between left-brain and right-brain functions?

Handedness: Is It Gauche or Sinister to Be Left-Handed?

What do Michelangelo, Leonardo da Vinci, and Steve Young all have in common? No, they are not all artists. Only one is a football player. But they are all left-handed. Some other well-known lefties are shown in Figure 2.17. *Questions: Does it matter whether one is left-handed? Why are people right-handed or left-handed?*

Being a "lefty" is often regarded as a deficiency. The language swarms with slurs on lefties. We speak of "left-handed compliments," of having "two left feet," of strange events as "coming out of left field." The word *sinister* means "left-hand or unlucky side" in Latin. *Gauche* is a French word that literally means "left," though in English it is used to mean awkward or ill-mannered. The English word *adroit*, meaning "skillful," derives from the French *à droit*, literally translated as "to the right." Also consider positive usages such as "being righteous" or "being on one's right side."

Yet, 8% to 10% of us are lefties. Left-handedness is more common in boys than girls (Rosenbaum, 2000). We are usually labeled right-handed or left-handed on the basis of our handwriting preferences, yet some people write with one hand and pass a football with the other. Some people even swing a tennis racket and pitch a baseball with different hands. President Ronald Reagan wrote and ate with his right hand, but shot pistols and waved with his left hand (Rosenbaum, 2000).

Being left-handed may not be gauche or sinister, but it may matter in that it appears to be connected with language problems such as dyslexia and stuttering and health problems such as migraine headaches and allergies (Geschwind & Galaburda, 1987). Left-handedness is also apparently connected with psychological disorders like schizophrenia (Rosenbaum, 2000). On the other hand, there may be advantages to being left-handed. According to a British study, left-handed people are twice as likely as right-handed people to be numbered among the ranks of artists, musicians, and mathematicians (Kilshaw & Annett, 1983). Figure 2.17 shows that some of the greatest artists were lefties.

Handedness is also apparently connected—although weakly—with sexual orientation. A meta-analysis of 20 studies found that gay males and lesbians are 39% more likely than people with a heterosexual orientation to be left-handed (Lalumière et al., 2000). Even so, we should note that the majority of gay males and lesbians are right-handed.

The origins of handedness are likely to have a genetic component. Left-handedness runs in families. In the English royal family, the Queen Mother, Queen Elizabeth II, and Princes Charles and William are all left-handed (Rosenbaum, 2000). If

REFLECT

Do you know anyone who was changed from a lefty to a righty? Why was the change made? How was it done? Was it successful? Explain.

From Napoleon to Oprah—Famous Lefties

Historical figures:
Alexander the Great,
Charlemagne,
Julius Caesar,
Napoleon Bonaparte,
Albert Schweitzer

Napoleon Bonaparte—
Soldier, emperor, and leftie

Entertainers (present):
Oprah Winfrey,
Whoopi Goldberg,
Jay Leno, Jerry Seinfeld,
Robert Redford

Oprah Winfrey—Talk show
host, actor, author, and leftie

People in the news: Colin L. Powell,
H. Norman Schwarzkopf, Fidel Castro,
Steve Forbes, Ross Perot

Entertainers (past): Marilyn Monroe, Greta
Garbo, Judy Garland, W. C. Fields, Charlie
Chaplin

Authors: Mark Twain, Lewis Carroll, Eudora
Welty, James Baldwin, Peter Benchley

Athletes: Ben Hogan (golf), Mark Spitz (swimming), Pelé (soccer), Bill Russell (basketball),
Bruce Jenner (track)

Artists: Leonardo da Vinci, Michelangelo,
Raphael, Albrecht Dürer

Music: Ludwig van Beethoven, Ringo Starr,
Paul McCartney, Cole Porter, Jimi Hendrix

Law: Ruth Bader Ginsberg, Anthony M. Kennedy,
Marcia Clark, Clarence Darrow, F. Lee Bailey

Criminals: John Dillinger, Billy the Kid, Boston
Strangler, Jack the Ripper, John Wesley Hardin

■ Figure 2.17
Some Well-Known Left-Handed People

Being left-handed is connected with language problems such as dyslexia and stuttering, physical health problems such as migraine headaches and allergies, and psychological disorders like schizophrenia. However, left-handed people are also twice as likely as right-handed people to be artists, musicians, and mathematicians.

Source: Rosenbaum, D. E. (2000, May 16). On left-handedness, its causes and costs. *The New York Times,* p. F6.

both of your parents are right-handed, your chances of being right-handed are about 92%. If one of your parents is left-handed, your chances of being right-handed drop to about 80%. And if both of your parents are left-handed, your chances of also being left-handed are about 1 in 2 (Rosenbaum, 2000). In any event, handedness comes early. A study employing ultrasound found that about 95% of fetuses suck their right thumbs rather than their left (Hepper et al., 1990). Geneticist Amar J. S. Klar believes that about 80% of people have a dominant gene that makes them right-handed. The other 20% lack this gene and have a 50–50 chance of becoming right-handed or left-handed. This view explains why about 10% of us are left-handed and why about 18% of identical twins have different handedness (Rosenbaum, 2000). UCLA neurologist Daniel H. Geschwind (2000) agrees that handedness involves genetics, but he doubts that a single gene is responsible and finds a role for developmental factors.

Whether we are talking about language functions, being "left-brained" or "right-brained," or handedness, we are talking about people whose hemispheres of the cerebral cortex communicate back and forth. Now let us see what happens when the major avenue of communication between the hemispheres shuts down.

Split-Brain Experiments: How Many Brains Do You Have?

A number of people with severe cases of epilepsy have split-brain operations in which much of the corpus callosum is severed (Engel, 1996). The purpose of the operation is to confine seizures to one hemisphere of the cerebral cortex rather than allowing a neural tempest to reverberate. Split-brain operations do seem to help people with epilepsy. ***Question: What happens when the brain is split in two?***

People who have undergone split-brain operations can be thought of as winding up with two brains, yet under most circumstances their behavior remains ordinary enough. Still, some aspects of hemispheres that have stopped talking to each other are intriguing.

As reported by pioneering brain surgeon Joseph Bogen (1969, 2000), each hemisphere may have a "mind of its own." One split-brain patient reported that her hemispheres frequently disagreed on what she should be wearing. What she meant was that one hand might undo her blouse as rapidly as the other was buttoning it. A man reported that one hemisphere (the left hemisphere, which contained language functions) liked reading but the other one did not. If he shifted a book from his right hand to his left hand, his left hand would put it down. The left hand is connected with the right hemisphere of the cerebral cortex, which in most people—including this patient—does not contain language functions.

Another pioneer of split-brain research, Roger Wolcott Sperry (Bogen, 1998; Corballis, 1998), found that people with split brains whose eyes are closed may be able to orally describe an object such as a key when they hold it in one hand, but not when they hold it in the other hand. As shown in Figure 2.18, if a person with a split brain handles a key with his left hand behind a screen, tactile impressions of the key are projected into the right hemisphere, which has little or no language ability. Thus, he will not be able to describe the key. If he holds it in his right hand, he will have no trouble describing it because sensory impressions are projected into the left hemisphere of the cortex, which contains language functions. To further confound matters, if the word *ring* is projected into the left hemisphere while the person is asked what he is handling, he will say "ring," not "key."

However, this discrepancy between what is felt and what is said occurs only in people with split brains. Most of the time the two hemispheres work together, even when we are playing the piano or solving math problems.

 Learning Connections
See Web site for an interactive version of these review questions.

R E V I E W

(24) The _____ records the electrical activity of the brain. (25) In magnetic _____ imaging, radio waves cause parts of the brain to emit signals. (26) The _____ is involved in balance and coordination. (27) The _____ is involved in body temperature, motivation, and emotion. (28) The hemispheres of the cerebrum are connected by the corpus _____. (29) The visual cortex is in found in the _____ lobe of the cortex. (30) The executive center of the brain is found in the _____ lobe. (31) Language areas are usually found in the (left or right?)

■ **Figure 2.18**
A Divided-Brain Experiment

In the drawing on the left, we see that visual sensations in the left visual field are projected in the occipital cortex of the right hemisphere. Visual sensations from the right visual field are projected in the occipital cortex in the left hemisphere. In the divided-brain experiment diagramed on the right, a person with a severed corpus callosum handles a key with his left hand and perceives the written word *key* in his left visual field. The word *key* is projected in the right hemisphere. Speech, however, is usually a function of the left hemisphere. The written word *ring*, perceived by the right visual field, is projected in the left hemisphere. So, when asked what he is handling, the divided-brain subject reports "ring," not "key."

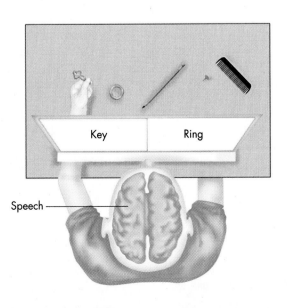

hemisphere. (32) Left-handed people are (more or less?) likely than right-handed people to be artists, musicians, and mathematicians. (33) Split-brain operations sever much of the corpus callosum in order to control —————————.

Critical Thinking: Does the research evidence reported in this section demonstrate that the mind is a function of the brain? Why or why not?

Gland
An organ that secretes one or more chemical substances such as hormones, saliva, or milk.

Endocrine System
The body's system of ductless glands that secrete hormones and release them directly into the bloodstream.

Hormone
A substance secreted by an endocrine gland that regulates various body functions.

Pituitary Gland
The gland that secretes growth hormone, prolactin, antidiuretic hormone, and other hormones.

THE ENDOCRINE SYSTEM: CHEMICALS IN THE BLOOD

The body contains two types of **glands:** glands with ducts and glands without ducts. A *duct* is a passageway that carries substances to specific locations. Saliva, sweat, tears, and breast milk all reach their destinations through ducts. Psychologists are interested in the substances secreted by ductless glands because of their behavioral effects. ***Question: What is the endocrine system?*** The ductless glands constitute the **endocrine system,** and they secrete **hormones** (from the Greek *horman,* meaning "to stimulate" or "to excite").

Hormones are released into the bloodstream and circulate through the body. Like neurotransmitters, hormones have specific receptor sites. That is, they act only on receptors in certain locations. Some hormones that are released by the hypothalamus influence only the **pituitary gland.** Other hormones released by the pituitary influence the adrenal cortex; still others influence the testes and ovaries, and so on (see Table 2.2).

Much hormonal action helps the body maintain steady states, as in fluid levels, blood sugar levels, and so on. Bodily mechanisms measure current levels, and when these levels deviate from optimal, they signal glands to release hormones. The maintenance of steady states requires feedback of bodily information to glands. This type of system is referred to as a *negative feedback loop.* That is, when enough of a hormone has been secreted, the gland is signaled to stop.

The hypothalamus secretes a number of releasing hormones, or factors, that influence the pituitary gland—also called the master gland—to secrete related hormones. For example, growth-hormone releasing factor (hGRF) causes the pituitary to produce growth hormone. A dense network of blood vessels between the hypothalamus and the pituitary gland provides a direct route of influence for these factors.

◼ **Figure 2.19**
Major Glands of the Endocrine System

The endocrine system consists of ductless glands that form and release hormones directly into the bloodstream, but hormones are taken up only by parts of the body that have appropriate receptor sites.

 Power Visual
See Web site for an interactive version of this figure.

TABLE 2.2 The Endocrine System

Gland	Hormone	About . . .
Hypothalamus	Releasing hormones or factors (e.g., growth-hormone releasing factor, corticotrophin-releasing hormone)	Influence the pituitary gland to secrete corresponding hormones (e.g., growth hormone, adrenocorticotrophic hormone)
Pituitary	Growth hormone	Causes growth of muscles, bones, and glands
	Adrenocorticotrophic hormone (ACTH)	Regulates adrenal cortex
	Thyrotrophin	Causes thyroid gland to secrete thyroxin
	Follicle-stimulating hormone	Causes formation of sperm and egg cells
	Luteinizing hormone	Causes ovulation, maturation of sperm and egg cells
	Prolactin	Stimulates production of milk
	Antidiuretic hormone (ADH)	Inhibits production of urine
	Oxytocin	Stimulates uterine contractions during delivery and ejection of milk during nursing
Pineal	Melatonin	Involved in regulation of sleep–wake cycle; possibly connected with aging
Pancreas	Insulin	Enables body to metabolize sugar; regulates storage of fats
Thyroid	Thyroxin	Increases metabolic rate
Adrenal	Corticosteroids	Increase resistance to stress; regulate carbohydrate metabolism
	Epinephrine (adrenaline)	Increases metabolic activity (heart and respiration rates, blood sugar level, etc.)
	Norepinephrine (noradrenaline)	Raises blood pressure; acts as neurotransmitter
Testes	Testosterone	Promotes development of male sex characteristics; involved in sex drive and aggressiveness
Ovaries	Estrogen	Regulates menstrual cycle; promotes development of female sex characteristics; connected with feelings of well-being

The pituitary gland lies below the hypothalamus (see Figure 2.19). Although it is only about the size of a pea, it is so central to the body's functioning that it has been referred to as the "master gland." Despite this designation, today we know that the hypothalamus regulates much pituitary activity. (The hypothalamus could be called the "master of the master gland.") The anterior (front) and posterior (back) lobes of the pituitary gland secrete many hormones. **Growth hormone** regulates the growth of muscles, bones, and glands. Children whose growth patterns are abnormally slow may catch up to their age-mates when they obtain growth hormone. **Prolactin** largely regulates maternal behavior in lower mammals such as rats and stimulates production of milk in women. As a water conservation measure, **antidiuretic hormone** (ADH) inhibits production of urine when fluid levels in the body are low. ADH is also connected with stereotypical paternal behavior patterns in some mammals. For example, it transforms an unconcerned male meadow vole (a mouselike rodent) into an affectionate and protective mate and father (Parker et al., 2001). The hormone is not known to have such a powerful effect with humans, however. (Sorry, female readers.) **Oxytocin** stimulates labor in pregnant women and is connected with maternal behavior (cuddling and caring for young) in some mammals (Insel, 2000; Taylor et al., 2000). Obstetricians may induce labor by injecting pregnant women with oxytocin. During nursing, stimulation of nerve endings in and around the nipples sends messages to the brain that cause the secretion of oxytocin. Oxytocin then causes the breasts to eject milk.

Growth Hormone
A pituitary hormone that regulates growth.

Prolactin
A pituitary hormone that regulates production of milk and, in lower animals, maternal behavior.

Antidiuretic Hormone
A pituitary hormone that conserves body fluids by increasing reabsorption of urine and is connected with paternal behavior in some mammals. Also called *vasopressin*.

Oxytocin
A pituitary hormone that stimulates labor and lactation.

The pineal gland secretes the hormone **melatonin,** which helps regulate the sleep–wake cycle and may affect the onset of puberty. Some researchers speculate that melatonin is also connected with aging. However, it appears that melatonin fosters sleep, and some people use it as a "sleeping pill" (Arendt, 2000; Nagtegaal et al., 2000).

The thyroid gland could be considered the body's accelerator. It produces **thyroxin,** which affects the body's *metabolism*—the rate at which the body uses oxygen and produces energy. Some people are overweight because of *hypothyroidism,* a condition that results from too little thyroxin. Thyroxin deficiency in children can lead to *cretinism,* a condition characterized by stunted growth and mental retardation. Adults who secrete too little thyroxin may feel tired and sluggish and may put on weight. People who produce too much thyroxin may develop *hyperthyroidism,* which is characterized by excitability, insomnia, and weight loss.

The adrenal glands, located above the kidneys, have an outer layer, or cortex, and an inner core, or medulla. The adrenal cortex is regulated by pituitary ACTH. It secretes hormones known as **corticosteroids,** or cortical steroids. These hormones increase resistance to stress; promote muscle development; and cause the liver to release stored sugar, making more energy available in emergencies, as when you see another car veering toward your own. Epinephrine and norepinephrine are secreted by the adrenal medulla. **Epinephrine,** also known as adrenaline, is manufactured exclusively by the adrenal glands, but norepinephrine (noradrenaline) is also produced elsewhere in the body. The sympathetic branch of the autonomic nervous system causes the adrenal medulla to release a mixture of epinephrine and norepinephrine that helps arouse the body to cope with threats and stress. Epinephrine is of interest to psychologists because it has emotional as well as physical effects. It intensifies most emotions and is crucial to the experience of fear and anxiety. Norepinephrine raises blood pressure and acts as a neurotransmitter in the nervous system.

The testes and ovaries also produce steroids, among them testosterone and estrogen. If it were not for the secretion of the male sex hormone **testosterone** about six weeks after conception, we would all develop the external genital organs of females. Testosterone is produced not only by the testes but in smaller amounts by the ovaries and adrenal glands. A few weeks after conception, testosterone causes the male sex organs to develop. During puberty, testosterone stokes the growth of muscle and bone and the development of primary and secondary sex characteristics. *Primary sex characteristics* such as the increased size of the penis and the sperm-producing ability of the testes are directly involved in reproduction. *Secondary sex characteristics* such as presence of a beard and a deeper voice differentiate males from females but are not directly involved in reproduction.

The ovaries produce **estrogen** and **progesterone.** Estrogen is also produced in smaller amounts by the testes. Estrogen fosters female reproductive capacity and secondary sex characteristics such as accumulation of fat in the breasts and hips. Progesterone stimulates growth of the female reproductive organs and prepares the uterus to maintain pregnancy.

Testosterone levels remain fairly stable, but estrogen and progesterone levels vary and regulate the woman's menstrual cycle. Following menstruation—the monthly sloughing off of the lining of the uterus—estrogen levels increase, leading to the ripening of an ovum (egg cell) and the growth of the lining of the uterus. Ovulation (release of the ovum by an ovary) occurs when estrogens reach peak blood levels. Then the lining of the uterus thickens in response to the secretion of progesterone, gaining the capacity to support an embryo if fertilization should occur. If the ovum is not fertilized, estrogen and progesterone levels drop suddenly, triggering menstruation once more.

This chapter's "Life Connections" feature dwells more deeply on hormones, menstruation, and menstrual problems. It also delves into hormone-related issues that affect men.

There are thus important links between biological factors, behavior, and mental processes. Thoughts and mental images may seem like intangible pictures that float in our heads, but they have "substance." They involve billions of brain cells (neurons) and the transmission of thousands of chemicals from one neuron to another—repeated hundreds of times per second. These countless bits of microscopic activity give rise to feelings, plans, computation, art and music, and all the cognitive activities that make us

Melatonin

A pineal hormone that helps regulate the sleep–wake cycle and may affect the onset of puberty.

Thyroxin

The thyroid hormone that increases metabolic rate.

Corticosteroids

Steroids produced by the adrenal cortex that regulate carbohydrate metabolism and increase resistance to stress by fighting inflammation and allergic reactions. Also called *cortical steroids.*

Epinephrine

A hormone produced by the adrenal medulla that stimulates sympathetic ANS activity. Also called *adrenaline.*

Testosterone

A male sex hormone produced by the testes that promotes growth of male sexual characteristics and sperm.

Estrogen

A generic term for several female sex hormones that promote growth of female sex characteristics and regulate the menstrual cycle.

Progesterone

A female sex hormone that promotes growth of the sex organs and helps maintain pregnancy.

human. We pour chemicals called hormones into our own bloodstreams, and they affect our activity levels, our anxiety levels, even our sex drives. We inherit traits that make us human, that enable us to think more deeply and act more cleverly than any other organism (after all, we write the textbooks). An understanding of biology helps us grasp many psychological events that might otherwise seem elusive and without substance.

REVIEW

Learning Connections
See Web site for an interactive version of these review questions.

(34) The _____ secretes hormones that regulate the pituitary gland. (35) The pituitary hormone _____ regulates maternal behavior in lower animals and stimulates production of milk in women. (36) The thyroid hormone _____ affects the metabolism. (37) Corticosteroids are secreted by the adrenal _____ and promote development of muscle mass and increase resistance to stress. (38) Epinephrine is secreted by the adrenal _____ and is involved in emotional arousal.

Critical Thinking: If so many behaviors and mental processes are affected by "glands," do people have free will?

A Closer Look

Steroids, Behavior, and Mental Processes

Anabolic steroids (synthetic versions of the male sex hormone testosterone) have been used, sometimes in tandem with growth hormone, to enhance athletic prowess. Steroids increase muscle mass, heighten resistance to stress, and increase the body's energy supply by signaling the liver to release sugar into the bloodstream. The steroid testosterone is connected with the sex drive in both males and females (females secrete some testosterone in the adrenal glands) (Davis, 2000). Testosterone is also connected with self-confidence, aggressiveness, even memory functioning in males (Janowsky et al., 2000).

Anabolic steroids are generally outlawed in amateur and professional sports. The lure of steroids is understandable. Sometimes the difference between an acceptable athletic performance and a great one is rather small. Thousands of athletes try to make it in the big leagues, and the "edge" offered by steroids—even if minor—can spell the difference between a fumbling attempt and a smashing success. If steroids help, why the fuss? Some of it is related to the ethics of competition—the idea that athletes should "play fair." But steroid use is also linked to liver damage and other health problems.

Estrogen, like testosterone, has psychological effects as well as biological effects. For one thing, higher levels of estrogen seem to be connected with optimal cognitive functioning and feelings of well-being among women (Ross et al., 2000; Yaffe et al., 2000). Women are also more interested in sexual activity when estrogen levels are high—particularly during ovulation, when they are fertile (see Figure 2.20).

Estrogen even affects women's perceptions of who is attractive. (Really.) Research shows that women in Britain and Japan prefer feminized male faces, as shown in Figure 2.20B, during most phases of the menstrual cycle (Penton-Voak & Perrett, 2000). Women apparently associate such facial fea-

tures with personality traits like warmth and honesty. However, they prefer the masculinized faces, as shown in Figure 2.20A, when they are ovulating. Perhaps they unconsciously interpret such features as indicative of reproductive capacity—that is, they instinctively see these men as likely to father children.

■ Figure 2.20
Which One Is Mr. Right?

The answer may depend on the phase of the woman's menstrual cycle. Women are apparently more attracted to men with masculinized features when they are capable of conceiving (part A), and men with more feminized features (part B) when they are not.

A.   B.

Science Photo Library/Photo Researchers, Inc.

"Raging Hormones" ("More, Please"?)

Most of us are familiar enough with the phrase "raging hormones" when it comes to the alleged irritability shown by some women prior to menstruation and apparently related to the fluctuations of sex hormones during the menstrual cycle. Yet men, too, could be said to be prey to "raging hormones." The male sex hormone testosterone is related to tendencies to dominate other people. There is research evidence that aggressive boys and college students have higher testosterone levels than their peers (Chance et al., 2000; Dabbs et al., 1996). For this reason, social commentator Anna Quindlen once wrote an article titled "Is Testosterone Toxic?"

In this Life Connections feature, we explore a number of issues related to sex hormones. These include premenstrual syndrome (PMS) and menopause in women and "manopause" ("andropause" or "viropause") in men (pick a name.) Andropause is a cluster of psychological problems that is apparently connected with the normal age-related male decline in testosterone. But some researchers now say that there is another issue, termed *irritable male syndrome*, that suggests that the decline in male sex hormones does not necessarily mean that older men are more content to bask in the sun. The actuality, in many cases, could be quite the reverse. In any event, we will see that the answer to Anna Quindlen's question might be yes—that is, testosterone might well be toxic—for reasons that she was not writing about. Sad to say, hormone replacement therapy for menopausal women may also be toxic. As the years have gone by and research findings have accumulated, the obvious has become less obvious, and the simple has grown quite complex. Yet there are millions of women and men who might profit from hormone replacement therapy, if . . .

Let's begin with an overview of PMS. Then we'll move on to menopause and to what is almost but not quite its male counterpart—andropause.

Premenstrual Syndrome (PMS)

Psychologists study the effects of menstruation because of stereotypes about menstruating women and because of the discomfort many women experience. For several days prior to and during menstruation, according to the outmoded stereotype, raging hormones doom women to irritability and poor judgment—two traits alleged to be part of PMS.

Women have historically been assumed to be more likely to commit suicide or crimes, call in sick at work, or develop physical and emotional problems during the eight-day period prior to and during menstruation. Moreover, the ability of college women to focus on academic tasks during this period has been called into question. Three out of four women report *some* psychological and physical problems, such as depression, anxiety, and headaches, during the four to six days that precede menstruation (Brody, 1996). However, fewer than one woman in ten has symptoms severe enough to impair her academic, occupational, or social functioning (Brody, 1996). Symptoms of PMS are shown in Table 2.3.

Causes of PMS

The causes of PMS are not fully understood. It was once believed that psychological factors such as negative attitudes toward men-

struation played a crucial role. Now the prevailing view is that attitudes toward menstruation—for example, conceptualizing the menstrual flow as unclean—can worsen menstrual problems, but that PMS has a biological basis. Researchers are searching out relationships between menstrual problems, including PMS, and chemical imbalances in the body. They have found that peak estrogen levels are connected with optimal cognitive functioning and psychological well-being in women (Ross et al., 2000; Yaffe et al., 2000). If peaks in female sex hormones are connected with psychological well-being, then perhaps the precipitous drop-off in hormones that precedes and accompanies menstruation is connected with discomfort. But PMS is also linked with imbalances in neurotransmitters such as serotonin and beta-endorphins (Condon, 2001; Lin & Thompson, 2001). Serotonin imbalances are also linked to changes in appetite, so women with PMS tend to be hungrier during part of the cycle than other women. Sensitivity to menstrual pain may be heightened by low levels of endorphins, the body's natural painkillers (Straneva et al., 2002). PMS may reflect a complex interaction between ovarian hormones and neurotransmitters.

A generation ago, PMS was seen as something a woman must tolerate. No longer. Today there are many treatment options. These include exercise, diet (for example, eating several small meals a day rather than two or three large meals; limiting salt and sugar; and vitamin supplements), hormone treatments (usually progesterone), and medications that affect levels of neurotransmitters in the nervous system. PMS is connected with drops in serotonin levels, and drugs called selective serotonin reuptake inhibitors (SSRIs) have helped many women with PMS (Condon, 2001; Steiner & Pearlstein, 2000). SSRIs are also known as "antidepressants" because depression is also connected with low serotonin levels. The fact that these drugs help many women with PMS does not mean that the women are suffering from underlying depression, but only that serotonin is involved in both. Women who use SSRIs to help with PMS do not take them continuously, as people do to fight depression, but rather for about two weeks each month.

TABLE 2.3 Symptoms of PMS*

Depression	Insomnia or too much sleeping
Anxiety	
Mood swings	Feelings of being out of control or overwhelmed
Anger and irritability	
Loss of interest in usual activities	Physical problems such as headaches, tenderness in the breasts, joint or muscle pain, weight gain or feeling bloated
Difficulty concentrating	
Lack of energy	
Overeating or cravings for certain foods	

*Most women experience only a few of these symptoms, if any at all.

How to Handle Menstrual Discomfort

Most women experience some degree of menstrual discomfort. Women with persistent menstrual distress may profit from the suggestions listed below. Why not adopt the techniques that sound right for you? (All of them, if you wish.)

1. First of all, don't blame yourself. Menstrual problems were once erroneously attributed to women's "hysterical" nature. This is nonsense. Menstrual problems appear to largely reflect supersensitivity to fluctuations in levels of hormones and neurotransmitters. Researchers have not yet have fully pinpointed the causal elements and patterns, but there is no evidence that women with PMS are "hysterical."

2. Keep track of your menstrual symptoms to help you (and your doctor) identify patterns.

3. Develop strategies for dealing with days on which you experience the most distress—strategies that will enhance pleasure and minimize stress. Try things that will distract you. Go to a film or get into that novel you've been meaning to read.

4. Ask yourself whether you harbor self-defeating attitudes that might be compounding distress. Do close relatives or friends see menstruation as an illness, a time of "pollution," a "dirty thing"? Have you adopted any of these attitudes—if not verbally, then in ways that affect your behavior, as by restricting social activities during your period?

5. See a doctor about your symptoms. Severe discomfort can be caused or worsened by health problems such as endometriosis and pelvic inflammatory disease (PID). Check it out.

6. Develop nutritious eating habits—and continue them throughout the entire cycle (that means *always*). Consider limiting intake of alcohol, caffeine, fats, salt, and sweets, especially during the days preceding menstruation.

7. If you feel bloated, eat smaller meals (or nutritious snacks) throughout the day, rather than a couple of highly filling meals.

8. Vigorous exercise—jogging, swimming, bicycling, fast walking, dancing, skating, jumping rope—helps relieve premenstrual and menstrual discomfort in some women. Try it out. But why limit exercise to days prior to and during your period? Weave it into your lifestyle.

9. Check with your doctor about herbal, vitamin, and mineral supplements (chaste berry, calcium, evening primrose, magnesium, vitamin E, wild yams, and so on) (Chavez & Spitzer, 2002). Vitamin B$_6$ seems to have helped some women. But *check* before using.

10. Ibuprofen (brand names: Medipren, Advil, Motrin, etc.) and other medicines available over the counter may be helpful for cramping. Prescription drugs such as tranquilizers (e.g., alprazolam) and SSRIs may be of help (Condon, 2001; Lin & Thompson, 2001). Ask your doctor for a recommendation. *In these cases, you are not taking the tranquilizer to treat anxiety or the SSRI to treat depression. You are taking the drugs to treat imbalances in neurotransmitters that can also give rise to anxiety and depression.*

© Bob Daemmrich/Stock Boston

■ Exploring Ways of Fighting PMS

Women today have many options available for fighting premenstrual syndrome. Some women find that vigorous exercise and eating smaller portions of food help. Still others appear to have profited from herbal or vitamin supplements (check with your gynecologist). Various medicines, including ibuprofen and SSRIs, may also be of help. Above all, women should not blame themselves for discomfort and should feel free to consult a physician who is sensitive to their concerns and ready to try various methods of helping.

11. Speaking of medicines, remember that menstruation is triggered by a sharp drop-off in sex hormones. Some gynecologists prescribe estrogen replacement as a method of relieving symptoms of PMS, although this approach is not hazard free. One method is simply to continue certain oral contraceptives for 28 days rather than 21 days and thus to forego menstruation altogether (Freeman et al., 2001; Sommerfeld, 2000). However, the pills chosen for this approach are not the same as those used for 21 days. Check with your gynecologist.

12. Remind yourself that menstrual problems are time limited. Don't worry about getting through life or a career. Just get through the next couple of days.

Menopause: When the Decline in Sex Hormones Becomes Permanent

Menopause, like PMS, is caused by a drop-off in female sex hormones. But with menopause, the drop-off becomes permanent. Menopause is the cessation of menstruation. Menopause is a misnomer: It's not a *pause*, it's an *end*.

Menopause usually occurs during the late 40s or early 50s, although there are wide variations in the age at which it occurs. Menopause is the final stage of a broader female experience, the *climacteric*, which is caused by a falling off in the secretion of the hormones estrogen and progesterone and during which many changes occur that are related to the gradual loss of reproductive ability (Morley & van den Berg, 2000). At this time ovulation also draws to an end. There is some loss of breast tissue and of elasticity in the skin. There can also be a loss of bone density that leads to osteoporosis (a condition in which the bones break easily) in late adulthood.

During the climacteric, many women encounter symptoms such as hot flashes (uncomfortable sensations characterized by heat and perspiration) and loss of sleep. Loss of estrogen can be accompanied by feelings of anxiety and depression. Ironically, however, many women are more likely to experience serious depression *prior* to menopause, when they are buffeted about by the conflicting demands of the workplace, child rearing, and homemaking (*Depression research*, 2000).

Although menopause is a highly meaningful life change for most women, most women get through the mood changes that can accompany menopause without great difficulty. According to psychologist Karen Matthews, who followed a sample of hundreds of women through menopause, "The vast majority [of women] have no problem at all getting through the menopausal transition" (Matthews, 1994, p. 25). But many women *do* experience physical and emotional problems during the climacteric. To ignore these problems can create as many difficulties as exaggerating them.

Hormone Replacement Therapy (HRT)

Some women who experience physical distress during the climacteric have been helped by hormone replacement therapy (HRT). HRT typically consists of synthetic (humanmade) estrogen and progesterone. The hormones are used to offset the effects of declines in their naturally occurring counterparts. HRT may help reduce hot flashes and other symptoms brought about by hormonal declines during menopause (den Tonkelaar & Oddens, 2000). There are other apparent benefits. Estrogen replacement appears to lower women's risk of osteoporosis (Davidson, 1995), colon cancer (Newcomb & Storer, 1995), and, perhaps, age-related cognitive declines (Henderson et al., 2000; Mulnard et al., 2000). Other research suggests that HRT raises levels of HDL ("good cholesterol") and lowers levels of LDL ("bad cholesterol") (Herrington et al., 2000; Nieto et al., 2000; Shlipak et al., 2000). Since high levels of LDL are connected with cardiovascular disease, it has been thought that HRT might reduce the risk of heart disease in women (Varas-Lorenzo et al., 2000). A survey by the Centers for Disease Control and Prevention and the National Institutes of Health of more than 9,200 women aged 35 to 64 also found no connection between usage of oral contraceptives, which contain estrogen and/or progesterone, and the incidence of breast cancer (Marchbanks et al., 2002).

But not all findings are positive. Some research has suggested that HRT does increase the risk of some kinds of cancer, including breast cancer and endometrial cancer, among postmenopausal women (Wenger et al., 2002; Writing Group for the Women's Health Initiative Investigators, 2002). One study followed nearly 2,700 women for an average of 6.8 years and found no cardiac benefits for HRT (Grady et al., 2002). In 2002, the National Institutes of Health stopped a five-year test of HRT after three years because of increased risk of stroke, heart attacks, and breast cancer among participants (Kolata, 2002). Check with your gynecologist for the latest information on the benefits and risks of the drugs that are available to help cope with menopausal problems, such as hot flashes.

■ Figure 2.21
Age of Onset of Andropause

According to one study, andropause is most likely to initially affect men in the 50–60-year-old age range.

Source: Tan, R. S. (Accessed March 23, 2002). Managing the andropause in aging men. *Clinical Geriatrics.* http://www.mmhc.com/cg/articles/CG9907/Tan.html

Andropause (or Viropause, or Manopause)— What's in a Name?

Historically speaking, more research has been done with men's health problems than women's. Yet the problems related to low levels of sex hormones in men do not yet even have an agreed-upon name. *Andropause* suggests a fall-off in androgens—male sex hormones. *Viropause* suggests a decline in virility, which is not a scientific term and suggests a general loss of ability. *Manopause* is a widely used but unscientific knockoff of the scientific term *menopause.*

For women, menopause is a time of relatively distinct age-related declines in sex hormones and fertility. In men, the decline in the production of male sex hormones and fertility is more gradual (Morley & van den Berg, 2000). It therefore is not surprising to find a man in his 70s or older fathering a child. However, many men in their 50s and 60s experience problems in achieving and maintaining erections (Laumann et al., 1994), which may reflect circulatory problems or have to do with hormone production. Figure 2.21 indicates the ages at which one group of researchers found symptoms of andropause to begin.

But sexual performance is only one part of the story. Table 2.4 lists a number of symptoms of andropause. Between the ages of 40 and 70, the typical American male loses 12 to 20 pounds of muscle, about 2 inches in height, and 15% of his bone mass. (Men as well as women are at risk for osteoporosis [Tan, 2001, 2002].) The percent of fat in the body nearly doubles. The eardrums thicken, as do the lenses of the eyes, resulting in some loss of hearing and vision. There is loss of endurance as the cardiovascular system and lungs become less capable of adapting to exertion.

Some of these changes can be slowed or even reversed. Exercise helps maintain muscle tone, keeps the growth of fatty tissue in check, and helps combat osteoporosis (Tan, 2002). A diet rich in

TABLE 2.4 Symptoms of Andropause

Loss of sexual desire	Joint problems
Difficulty maintaining an erection	Changes in hair and skin
Ejaculatory problems	Mood swings
Sleep problems	Reduced fertility
Decreased energy	Urinary problems, e.g., increased frequency, incontinence, difficulty starting
Hot flashes	

Source: http://womenshealth.about.com/library/blandropause.htm. Andropause—Male "Menopause." Accessed March 22, 2002.

calcium and vitamin D can help ward off bone loss in later life in both sexes. Hormone replacement may also help, but we will see that it is controversial.

Irritable Male Syndrome (?)

If the terms *manopause, andropause,* and *viropause* raise an eyebrow, the term *irritable male syndrome* is likely to raise eyebrows, hackles, and arguments. This term has come into recent and—for the moment—spotty usage as a result of observations of animal behavior by English researcher Gerald Lincoln (2001) and some others. Lincoln suggests that drops in testosterone may lead to anxiety, depression, or irritability in men, parallel to what he has observed in animals.

Testosterone levels decline with stress as well as age. Testosterone is a steroid; so is cortisol, a steroid produced by the adrenal glands. Under stress, large amounts of cortisol can be secreted, enhancing resistance to stress. However, the endocrine system works by means of a negative feedback loop. When there is enough of a hormone in the bloodstream, the gland is signaled to cut production. When high amounts of cortisol—the steroid—are detected, the endocrine system may be signaled to cut output of another steroid—testosterone.

Lincoln first observed irritable male syndrome among sheep. In winter, with the mating season over, the sheep's interest in sex declines along with their testosterone levels. Thus they will not contest other males to create a harem. Even so, ironically, low-testosterone sheep were more likely to be injured than those with high levels. Members of a group of eight rams no longer passed one another with calm "respect"; instead, nervousness led to unpredictable, injurious attacks. Lincoln observed similar behavior among red deer, reindeer, and Indian elephants when their breeding seasons drew to a close. They became grumps. Lincoln admits that the link between the behavior of these animals and that of humans remains unclear, but a decline in testosterone might affect men in similar ways.

David Abbott, a hormone specialist, agrees with Lincoln. When a man "gets grumpy and irritable, [health professionals] explain it only in terms of cortisol levels and depression," he says. "They ignore the fact that testosterone levels are probably falling too. Instead of putting stressed men on [antidepressants], a little testosterone may do the job" (Male PMT, 2002).

But will testosterone replacement therapy do the job? And what are the risks?

Hormone Replacement Therapy (HRT) in Men

Physicians in the United States write more than one million prescriptions for testosterone and related drugs for men each year, but the benefits are not fully proven, and the risks should make the caution lights blink.

The history of HRT with men goes back more than 100 years and involves some experiments with highly questionable ethics. In 1889 a 72-year-old French physiologist injected himself with an extract from the testes of dogs and guinea pigs. He reported an increase in strength and intellectual energy, even improvements with his constipation (Hoberman, 2002). Some 30 years later, the prison doctor at San Quentin was transplanting the testicles of executed criminals into other prisoners and claimed that the surgery increased their sexual potency and general health. Later the same doctor used testicles from goats, rams, and deer and claimed that they worked as well. By 1935 the hormone testosterone was isolated. In 1939 the prestigious *Journal of the American Medical Association* recommended use of testosterone to treat "the male climacteric." The idea of a male menopause was born.

Research suggests that testosterone replacement sometimes boosts strength, energy, and the sex drive as advertised, but it is connected with increased risks of prostate cancer and cardiovascular disease (Morley & van den Berg, 2000; Tan, 2002). In fact, in 2002, the government decided not to proceed with a study of the effects of testosterone on aging men precisely because of these concerns (Kolata, 2002). Dr. Richard Hodis (2002), director of the National Institute on Aging, comments, "In understanding the role of testosterone replacement, we are in many ways where we were decades ago with estrogen replacement with women. It is clear that we do not know enough to inform men and their doctors on the potential advantages or risks of hormone replacement."

Men who wish to try testosterone therapy will probably have little difficulty finding a physician who will prescribe it. For those who are reluctant because of the risks, diet and exercise may be of help, as noted. Effective treatments for erectile problems are also on the market and under development. Erection occurs because blood flows into caverns within the penis (vasocongestion), causing the penis to stiffen like a balloon when air is pumped in. The drug Viagra facilitates erection by relaxing the muscles that surround the caverns, enabling blood to flow in. Other drugs that will help facilitate erection in this and other ways—such as by stimulating the erection center in the spine—are under development.

Recite Recite Recite

1. **Who was Charles Darwin? What did he do?**

Darwin was a 19th-century British naturalist who voyaged to the Galápagos Islands, where he observed how species varied from island to island. He noted that "favourable variations" were preserved and unfavorable ones were not. From his observations, he founded his theory of evolution.

2. **What are some of the basic concepts of the theory of evolution?**

The struggle for existence refers to the competition among species and among members within a species to survive and reproduce. Small random variations called mutations change organisms' ability to adapt. Mutations that enhance survival are likely to be preserved. Natural selection refers to the finding that organisms who are better adapted to their environments tend to survive and transmit their genes to subsequent generations.

3. **What is evolutionary psychology?**

Evolutionary psychology studies the ways in which adaptation and natural selection are connected with mental processes and behavior. Evolutionary psychologists suggest that not only physical traits but also patterns of behavior, including social behavior, evolve and are transmitted from generation to generation.

4. **What is meant by the concept "instinct"?**

An instinct is a stereotypical behavior pattern that is nearly identical among the members of a species. It occurs even when the individual is reared in isolation from others of its kind.

5. **What is meant by the concept of "heredity"?**

Heredity involves the biological transmission of traits from generation to generation.

6. **What is meant by the concepts "genetics," "behavioral genetics," and "molecular genetics"?**

Genetics is the area of biology that studies heredity. Behavioral genetics is concerned with the genetic transmission of traits that give rise to behavior and focuses on individual differences. Molecular genetics attempts to identify specific genes that are connected with behavior and mental processes.

7. **What are the roles of genes and chromosomes in heredity?**

Genes are the biochemical materials that regulate the development of traits. Genes are segments of chromosomes. Humans have 46 chromosomes arranged in 23 pairs. Chromosomes are molecules of DNA, which takes the form of a twisting ladder. We normally receive 23 chromosomes from each parent. Sex chromosomes and specific genes—e.g., SRY—determine the sex of the child. SRY is also connected with aggressive behavior. People with Down syndrome have an extra chromosome on the 21st pair.

8. **What are kinship studies?**

Psychologists conduct kinship studies to help determine the influences of genetic and environmental factors on behavior and mental processes. Twin studies are useful because identical (monozygotic) twins share the same genetic code; therefore, differences reflect environmental factors. When children reared by adoptive parents are more similar to their natural parents in a particular trait, evidence exists for a genetic role in the expression of that trait.

9. **What is selective breeding?**

In selective breeding, one breeds offspring that are closest to a desired trait and continues to breed their offspring that are yet closer to the goal. Humans have been selectively breeding many animals, including dogs, for both physical and behavioral traits.

10. **What are neurons?**

Neurons are cells that transmit information through neural impulses and glial cells, which mainly serve support functions. Neurons have a cell body; dendrites, which receive messages; and trunklike axons, which conduct and then transmit messages to other cells by means of chemicals called neurotransmitters. Many neurons have a myelin coating that insulates their axons, allowing for more efficient conduction of messages. Afferent neurons transmit sensory messages to the central nervous system. Efferent neurons conduct messages from the central nervous system that stimulate glands or cause muscles to contract.

Recite Recite Recite

11. What are neural impulses?

Neural transmission is electrochemical. An electrical charge is conducted along an axon through a process that allows sodium ions to enter the cell and then pumps them out. The neuron has a resting potential of −70 millivolts and an action potential of about +40 millivolts.

12. What happens when a neuron fires?

Neurons fire (transmit messages to other neurons, muscles, or glands) by releasing neurotransmitters. They fire according to an all-or-none principle, up to hundreds of times per second. Each firing is followed by a refractory period, during which neurons are insensitive to messages from other neurons.

13. What is a synapse?

Neurons fire across synapses, which consist of an axon terminal from the transmitting neuron; a dendrite, or the body of a receiving neuron; and a fluid-filled synaptic cleft between the two.

14. Which neurotransmitters are of interest to psychologists? What do they do?

These include acetylcholine, which is involved in muscle contractions and memory; dopamine, imbalances of which have been linked to Parkinson's disease and schizophrenia; norepinephrine, which accelerates the heartbeat and other body processes; serotonin, which is involved in eating, sleep, and emotional arousal; GABA, which inhibits anxiety; and endorphins, which are naturally occurring painkillers.

15. What are the parts of the nervous system?

A nerve is a bundle of axons and dendrites. The nervous system is one of the systems that regulates the body. It is involved in thought processes, emotional responses, heartbeat, motor activity, and so on.

16. What are the divisions and functions of the peripheral nervous system?

The peripheral nervous system has two main divisions: somatic and autonomic. The somatic nervous system transmits sensory information about skeletal muscles, skin, and joints to the central nervous system. It also controls skeletal muscular activity. The autonomic nervous system (ANS) regulates the glands and activities such as heartbeat, digestion, and dilation of the pupils. The sympathetic division of the ANS helps expend the body's resources, such as when fleeing from a predator, and the parasympathetic division helps build the body's reserves.

17. What are the divisions and functions of the central nervous system?

The central nervous system consists of the brain and spinal cord. Reflexes involve the spinal cord but not the brain. The central nervous system has gray matter, which is composed of nonmyelinated neurons, and white matter, which is composed of bundles of myelinated (and thus whitish) axons.

18. How do researchers learn about the functions of the brain?

Researchers historically learned about the brain by studying the effects of accidents. They have also studied the effects of purposeful damage to the brain, made by lesions. They have seen how animals and people respond to electrical stimulations of certain parts of the brain. They have studied the waves emitted by the brain with the electroencephalograph. With CAT scans, PET scans, and MRIs, computer-generated images are made by passing radiation of some sort through the brain.

19. What are the structures and functions of the brain?

The hindbrain includes the medulla, which regulates the heart rate, blood pressure, and respiration; the pons, which is involved in movement, attention, and respiration; and the cerebellum, which is involved in balance and coordination. The reticular activating system, which is involved in wakefulness and sleep, begins in the hindbrain and continues through the midbrain into the forebrain. Important structures of the forebrain include the thalamus, which serves as a relay station for sensory stimulation; the hypothalamus, which regulates body temperature and various aspects of motivation and emotion, such as eating and sexual behavior; the limbic system, which is involved in memory, emotion, and motivation; and the cerebrum, which is the brain's center of thinking and language.

Recite Recite Recite

20. What are the parts of the cerebral cortex?

The outer fringe of the cerebrum is the cerebral cortex, which is divided into two hemispheres and four lobes: frontal, parietal, temporal, and occipital. The visual cortex is in the occipital lobe, and the auditory cortex is in the temporal lobe. The somatosensory cortex lies behind the central fissure in the parietal lobe, and the motor cortex lies in the frontal lobe, across the central fissure from the somatosensory cortex. The prefrontal cortex may be the executive center of the brain—making plans, solving problems, and drawing upon sensory information from other areas of the cortex as needed.

21. What parts of the cerebral cortex are involved in thinking and language?

Language areas of the cortex usually lie in the left hemisphere, near the intersection of the frontal, temporal, and parietal lobes. Wernicke's area in the temporal lobe responds mainly to auditory information. Broca's area is located in the frontal lobe and is mainly responsible for speech. Damage to either area can result in an aphasia—a problem in understanding (Wernicke's aphasia) or producing (Broca's aphasia) language.

22. What would it mean to be "left-brained" or "right-brained"?

The left hemisphere is usually relatively more involved in cognitive functions involving logical analysis and problem solving, whereas the right hemisphere is usually superior in visual–spatial functions, aesthetic and emotional responses, and creative mathematical reasoning. But the notion that some people are "left-brained" (that is, only logical and lacking completely in functions involving visual–spatial responses, etc.) and others are "right-brained" is exaggerated.

23. Does it matter whether one is left-handed? Why are people right-handed or left-handed?

About one person in ten is left-handed. Learning disabilities are somewhat more common among left-handed people, but so is creativity, as shown in the arts. Handedness appears to have a genetic component.

24. What happens when the brain is split in two?

For the most part, the behavior of people who have had split-brain operations (which sever most of the corpus callosum) is perfectly normal. However, although they may orally be able to describe a screened-off object such as a pencil held in the hand connected to the hemisphere that contains language functions, they cannot do so when the object is held in the other hand.

25. What is the endocrine system?

The endocrine system consists of ductless glands that secrete hormones. The pituitary gland secretes growth hormone; prolactin, which regulates maternal behavior in lower animals and stimulates production of milk in women; and oxytocin, which stimulates labor in pregnant women. The pineal hormone melatonin is connected with the sleep–wake cycle and the onset of puberty. Thyroxin affects the body's metabolism, and deficiency in childhood is connected with mental retardation. The adrenal cortex produces steroids, which promote the development of muscle mass and increase activity level. The adrenal medulla secretes epinephrine (adrenaline), which increases the metabolic rate and is involved in general emotional arousal. The sex hormones are responsible for prenatal sexual differentiation. Female sex hormones regulate the menstrual cycle.

Active Learning Resources

Search Online with InfoTrac® College Edition

For additional information on the topics in this chapter, explore InfoTrac College Edition, your online library. Go to **http://www.infotrac.thomsonlearning.com** and use the passcode that came on the card with your book. Try these search terms: Charles Darwin, natural selection, behavior genetics, nature and nurture, neuroscience and psychology, neurotransmitters, brain abnormalities, aphasia, and left- and right-handedness.

Visit Our Web Site

Go to **http://www.wadsworth.com/psychology**, where you will find online resources directly linked to your book, including interactive exercises related to PQ4R and Power Visuals for mastering and reviewing key concepts. In addition, you will find hints on using InfoTrac College Edition to answer the Critical Thinking questions throughout the text. Start with the **Self Study Assessment** for a customized **Study Plan** generated by taking the **Pre-Test** and **Post-Test.**

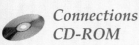

Connections CD-ROM

Go to the Wadsworth *Connections* CD-ROM for further study of the concepts in this chapter. The CD-ROM includes videos and animations, as well as additional activities to expand your learning experience, plus interactive self-assessments to help connect the material to your own life.

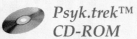

Psyk.trek™ CD-ROM

The Wadsworth *Psyk.trek* CD-ROM offers tutorials, simulations, videos, multimedia glossary, and quizzing to help you master the material.

PsychNow! CD-ROM

The Wadsworth *PsychNow!* CD-ROM includes interactive exercises, videos, and animations to enhance your learning.

■ **Prenatal Development: The Beginning of Our Life Story**

- ■ IF IT WERE NOT for the secretion of male sex hormones a few weeks after conception, we would all develop into females.

- ■ YOUR HEART STARTED beating when you were only one-fifth of an inch long and weighed a fraction of an ounce.

■ **Childhood: Physical, Cognitive, and Social Developments**

- ■ PRIOR TO 6 MONTHS or so of age, "out of sight" is literally "out of mind."

- ■ FORGET ABOUT "Yes, but . . ." To a young child, if you did it, you're guilty.

- ■ NEWLY HATCHED GEESE live by the motto, "If it moves, it must be Mother."

- ■ DOES THE PATH to a baby's heart lie through its stomach or its skin? Do babies become attached to those who feed them or to those who cuddle them?

- ■ SHOULD PARENTS BE strict or lax if they wish to foster self-esteem, achievement motivation, and independence in their children?

■ **Adolescence: Physical, Cognitive, and Social Developments**

- ■ ADOLESCENTS ARE NEITHER fish nor fowl—they are like adults physically but often treated like children.

- ■ MANY ADOLESCENTS think they are Superboy or Supergirl—invulnerable.

- ■ ADOLESCENTS MAY STRIVE for independence, but their views of the world are much like their parents'.

■ **Adulthood: Physical, Cognitive, and Social Developments**

- ■ WOMEN OUTLIVE MEN and European Americans outlive African Americans. Why?

- ■ THE ARCHITECT Frank Lloyd Wright designed New York's innovative spiral-shaped Guggenheim Museum when he was 89 years old.

- ■ DO MOST MOTHERS suffer from the "empty-nest syndrome" when the youngest child leaves home, or do they shout "Free at last"?

- ■ WHAT IS THE SECRET of successful aging—avoiding new challenges or taking on new challenges?

■ **On Death and Dying**

- ■ WHAT DOES PSYCHOLOGY teach us about death and dying?

■ *Life Connections: Day Care—Blessing, Headache, or Both?*

- ■ DAY CARE TODAY is a necessity for most families, not a luxury.

- ■ SO, HOW CAN WE find you high-quality day care? There are no guarantees, but we have a checklist for you to consider.

There is no cure for birth or death save to enjoy the interval.

—George Santayana

We have a story to tell. An important story. A fascinating story. It is your story. It is about the remarkable voyage you have already taken through childhood and adolescence. It is about the unfolding of your adult life. Billions have made this voyage before. You have much in common with them. Yet you are unique, and things will happen to you, and because of you, that have never happened before.

Let us watch as Ling and Patrick Chang begin such a story by conceiving a child. On a summerlike day in October, Ling and Patrick rush to their jobs as usual. While Ling, a trial attorney, is preparing a case to present in court, a very different drama is unfolding in her body. Hormones are causing a follicle (egg container) in one of her ovaries to ovulate—that is, to rupture and release an egg cell, or ovum. Ling, like other women, possessed from birth all the egg cells she will ever have. How this particular ovum was selected to ripen and be released this month is unknown. But in any case, Ling will be capable of becoming pregnant for only a couple of days following ovulation.

When it is released, the ovum begins a slow voyage down a 4-inch-long fallopian tube to the uterus. It is within this tube that one of Patrick's sperm cells will unite with the egg. The fertilized ovum, or zygote, is 1/175 of an inch across—a tiny stage for the drama that is about to unfold.

Developmental psychologists are interested in studying Patrick and Ling's new child's voyage through the lifespan for several reasons. The discovery of early influences and developmental sequences helps psychologists understand adults. Psychologists are also interested in the effects of genetic factors, early interactions with parents and siblings (brothers and sisters), and the school and community on traits such as aggressiveness and intelligence.

Developmental psychologists seek to learn the causes of developmental abnormalities. For instance, should pregnant women abstain from smoking and drinking? (Yes.) Is it safe for a pregnant woman to take aspirin for a headache or tetracycline to ward off a bacterial invasion? (Perhaps not. Ask your obstetrician.) What factors contribute to child abuse? Some developmental psychologists focus on adult development. For example, what conflicts and disillusionments can we expect as we voyage through our 30s, 40s, and 50s? The information acquired by developmental psychologists can help us make decisions about how we rear our children and lead our own lives.

Let us now turn to prenatal developments—the changes that occur between conception and birth. They are spectacular, but they occur "out of sight."

PRENATAL DEVELOPMENT: THE BEGINNING OF OUR LIFE STORY

The most dramatic gains in height and weight occur during prenatal development. *Question: What developments occur from conception through birth?* Within 9 months the newly conceived organism develops from a nearly microscopic cell to a **neonate** (newborn) about 20 inches long. Its weight increases a billionfold.

During the months following conception, the single cell formed by the union of sperm and egg—the **zygote**—multiplies, becoming two cells, then four, then eight, and so on. By the time the infant is ready to be born, it contains trillions of cells.

The zygote divides repeatedly as it proceeds on its 3- to 4-day voyage to the uterus. The ball-like mass of multiplying cells wanders about the uterus for another 3 to 4 days before beginning to implant in the uterine wall. Implantation takes another week or so. The period from conception to implantation is called the **germinal stage,** or the **period of the ovum.**

The **embryonic stage** lasts from implantation until about the eighth week of development. During this stage, the major body organ systems take form. As you can see from Figure 3.1, the growth of the head precedes that of other parts of the body. The

Neonate
A newly born child.

Zygote
A fertilized ovum (egg cell).

Germinal Stage
The first stage of prenatal development, during which the dividing mass of cells has not become implanted in the uterine wall.

Period of the Ovum
Another term for the *germinal stage.*

Embryonic Stage
The baby from the third through the eighth weeks following conception, during which time the major organ systems undergo rapid differentiation.

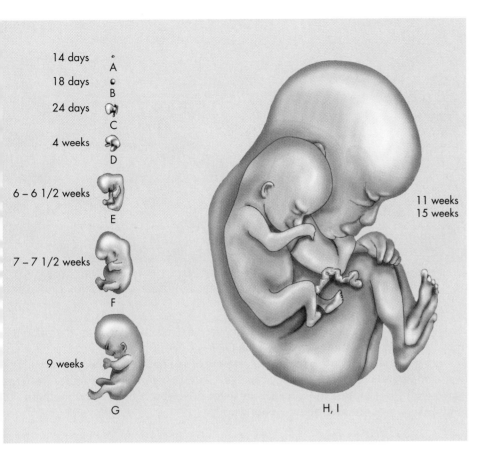

14 days
18 days
24 days
4 weeks
6 – 6 1/2 weeks
7 – 7 1/2 weeks
9 weeks

A
B
C
D
E
F
G

11 weeks
15 weeks

H, I

■ **Figure 3.1**

Embryos and Fetuses at Various Intervals of Prenatal Development

Development of the head (and brain) precedes that of other parts of the body. The development of the organs— heart, lungs, and so on—also precedes the development of the limbs. The relatively early maturation of the brain and the organ systems allows them to participate in the nourishment and further development of the embryo.

growth of the organs—heart, lungs, and so on—also precedes the growth of the extremities. The relatively early **maturation** of the brain and the organ systems allows them to participate in the nourishment and further development of the embryo. During the fourth week, a primitive heart begins to beat and pump blood—in an organism that is one-fifth of an inch long. The heart will continue to beat without rest every minute of every day for the better part of a century, perhaps longer.

By the end of the second month, the head has become rounded and the facial features distinct—all in an embryo that is about 1 inch long and weighs 1/30 of an ounce. During the second month, the nervous system begins to transmit messages. By 5 to 6 weeks, the embryo is only a quarter to half an inch long, yet nondescript sex organs have formed. By about the seventh week, the genetic code (XY or XX) begins to assert itself, causing the sex organs to differentiate. If a Y sex chromosome is present, testes form and begin to produce **androgens** (male sex hormones), which further masculinize the sex organs. In the absence of these hormones, the embryo develops female sex organs.

As it develops, the embryo is suspended within a protective **amniotic sac** in the mother's uterus. The sac is surrounded by a clear membrane and contains amniotic fluid. The fluid is a sort of natural air bag, allowing the child to move or even jerk around without injury. It also helps maintain an even temperature.

From now until birth, the embryo exchanges nutrients and wastes with the mother through the **placenta.** The embryo is connected to the placenta by the **umbilical cord.** The placenta is connected to the mother by blood vessels in the uterine wall.

The **fetal stage** lasts from the beginning of the third month until birth. By the end of the third month, the major organ systems and the fingers and toes have formed. In the middle of the fourth month, the mother usually detects the first fetal movements. By the end of the sixth month, the fetus moves its limbs so vigorously that mothers often feel that they are being kicked. The fetus opens and shuts its eyes, sucks its thumb, alternates between periods of being awake and sleeping, and responds to light. It also turns somersaults, which can be perceived clearly by the mother. The umbilical

Maturation
The process of development as guided by the unfolding of the genetic code.

Androgens
Male sex hormones.

Amniotic Sac
A sac within the uterus that contains the embryo or fetus.

Placenta
A membrane that permits the exchange of nutrients and waste products between the mother and her developing child but does not allow the maternal and fetal bloodstreams to mix.

Umbilical Cord
A tube between the mother and her developing child through which nutrients and waste products are conducted.

Fetal Stage
The baby from the third month following conception through childbirth, during which time there is maturation of organ systems and dramatic gains in length and weight.

■ An Exercise Class for Pregnant Women

Years ago pregnant women were not expected to exert themselves. Today, it is recognized that exercise is healthful for pregnant women because it promotes fitness, which is beneficial during childbirth as well as at other times.

© Robert McElroy/Woodfin Camp & Associates

cord is composed so that it will not break or become dangerously wrapped around the fetus, no matter how many acrobatic feats the fetus performs.

During the last 3 months, the organ systems of the fetus continue to mature. The heart and lungs become increasingly capable of sustaining independent life. The fetus gains about 5½ pounds and doubles in length. Newborn boys average about 7½ pounds and newborn girls about 7 pounds.

Learning Connections
See Web site for an interactive version of these review questions.

R E V I E W

(1) It is possible to become pregnant for a day or so after _____. (2) A sperm cell combines with an ovum to form a _____. (3) The zygote implants in the wall of the _____. (4) Prenatal development is divided into the germinal stage, the _____ stage, and the fetal stage.

Critical Thinking: Many researchers use terms like *zygote, embryo,* and *fetus* to refer to the human organism as it undergoes prenatal development. How do these terms differ in meaning from commonly used terms such as *baby* and *unborn child*?

CHILDHOOD: PHYSICAL, COGNITIVE, AND SOCIAL DEVELOPMENTS

Childhood begins with birth. When my children are enjoying themselves, I kid them and say "Stop having fun. You're a child, and childhood is the worst time of life." I get a laugh because they know that childhood is supposed to be the best time of life—a time for play and learning and endless possibilities. For many children it is that, but other children suffer from problems such as malnutrition, low self-esteem, and child abuse.

Let us chronicle the events of childhood. The most obvious aspects of child development are physical. Let us therefore begin with physical development. Then we turn our attention to cognitive and social and emotional developments.

Physical Development

Physical development includes gains in height and weight; maturation of the nervous system; and development of bones, muscles, and organs. *Question: What physical developments occur during childhood?*

During infancy—the first two years of childhood—dramatic gains in height and weight continue. Babies usually double their birth weight in about 5 months and triple it by their first birthday (Kuczmarski, 2000). Their height increases by about 10 inches in the first year. Children grow another 4 to 6 inches during the second year and gain some 4 to 7 pounds. After that, they gain about 2 to 3 inches a year until they reach the adolescent growth spurt. Weight gains also remain fairly even at about 4 to 6 pounds per year until the spurt begins. Other aspects of physical development in childhood include reflexes and perceptual development.

Reflexes—Entering the World Prewired

Soon after you were born, a doctor or nurse probably pressed her fingers against the palms of your hands. Although you would have had no idea what to do in response, most likely you grasped the fingers firmly—so firmly that you could have been lifted from your cradle!

Grasping at birth is inborn, an example of the importance of nature in human development. Grasping is one of the neonate's many reflexes. **Reflexes** are simple, unlearned, stereotypical responses elicited by specific stimuli. Reflexes are essential to survival and do not involve higher brain functions. They occur automatically—that is, without thinking about them.

Newborn children do not know that it is necessary to eat to survive. Fortunately, they have rooting and sucking reflexes that cause them to eat. They turn their head toward stimuli that prod or stroke the cheek, chin, or corner of the mouth. This is termed **rooting.** They suck objects that touch their lips.

Neonates have numerous other reflexes that aid in survival. They withdraw from painful stimuli. This is known as the withdrawal reflex. They draw up their legs and arch their backs in response to sudden noises, bumps, or loss of support while being held. This is the startle, or Moro, reflex. They grasp objects that press against the palms of their hands (the grasp, or palmar, reflex). They fan their toes when the soles of their feet are stimulated (the Babinski reflex). Pediatricians assess babies' neural functioning by testing these reflexes.

Babies also breathe, sneeze, cough, yawn, and blink reflexively. And it is guaranteed that you will learn about the sphincter (anal muscle) reflex if you put on your best clothes and hold an undiapered neonate on your lap for a while.

Perceptual Development: On *Not* Going Off the Deep End

Newborn children spend about 16 hours a day sleeping and do not have much opportunity to learn about the world. Yet they are capable of perceiving the world reasonably well soon after birth.

Within a couple of days, infants can follow, or track, a moving light with their eyes (Kellman & von Hofsten, 1992). By the age of 3 months, they can discriminate most colors (Banks & Shannon, 1993; Teller, 1998). Neonates are nearsighted; but, by about the age of 4 months, infants seem able to focus on distant objects about as well as adults can.

The visual preferences of infants are measured by the amount of time, termed **fixation time,** they spend looking at one stimulus instead of another. In classic research by Robert Fantz (1961), 2-month-old infants preferred visual stimuli that resembled the human face to newsprint, a bull's-eye, and featureless red, white, and yellow disks. At this age the complexity of facelike patterns may be more important than their content. For example, babies have been shown facelike patterns that differ either in the number of elements they contain or the degree to which they are organized to match the human face. Five- to 10-week-old babies fixate longer on patterns with high numbers of elements. The organization of the elements—that is, the degree to which they resemble the face—is less important. By 15 to 20 weeks, the organization of the pattern also matters. At that age babies dwell longer on facelike patterns (e.g., Haaf et al., 1983).

Infants thus seem to have an inborn preference for complex visual stimuli. However, preference for faces as opposed to other equally complex stimuli may not emerge until infants have had experience with people.

Classic research has shown that infants tend to respond to cues for depth by the time they are able to crawl (at about 6 to 8 months). Most also have the good sense to

R E F L E C T

How would you explain the fact that babies are born with reflexes?

Reflex
A simple unlearned response to a stimulus.

Rooting
The turning of an infant's head toward a touch, such as by the mother's nipple.

Fixation Time
The amount of time spent looking at a visual stimulus.

R E F L E C T

Why do you think developmental psychologists are interested in when and how babies develop an interest in human faces?

A Closer Look

Motor Development—Laboratory for the Nature–Nurture Controversy

The motor development of the child—that is, the progression from simple acts like lifting the head to running around—offer psychologists a wondrous laboratory for sorting out genetic and environmental influences on development. In the field of developmental psychology, genetic factors are generally discussed in terms of the concept of maturation, that is, the unfolding of traits and behavior, as determined by the genetic code. The American psychologist Arnold Gesell (1880–1961) emphasized the importance of maturation in human development and argued that all areas of development are self-regulated by the unfolding of natural plans and processes. The essential role of maturation in areas such as physical development (for example, gains in height and weight and the effects of puberty), language development, and motor development is clear. But even in these areas, environmental factors cannot be ignored. Individuals may have certain genetic potentials for body size and growth rates, but these potentials are not reached unless environmental factors such as nutrition, exposure to relatively clean air, and so on are also available. In terms of language development, we can assert that organisms do not comprehend or produce language unless their genetic codes spark the development of structures and processes in the brain that enable the use of language. But let us not downplay environmental factors: Children learn to speak the languages used in their homes, communities, and in the media that are available to them. They do not speak tongues used in foreign parts of the world without being exposed to them. Moreover, children obtain different levels of facility with their languages—again, an apparent reflection of the interaction of genetic factors and environmental opportunities. Let us focus on motor development as a key example of the interaction of nature and nurture.

■ **Figure 3.2**
Motor Development in Infancy

Motor development proceeds in an orderly sequence, which suggests that there is a strong maturational or genetic component in motor development. However, there is considerable variation in the timing of the marker events shown in this figure. An infant who is a bit behind will most likely develop without problems, and a precocious infant will not necessarily become a rocket scientist (or gymnast).

Research with humans and other species leaves little doubt that maturation and experience (environmental influences) both play indispensable roles in motor development (Muir, 2000; Pryce et al., 2001; Roncesvalles et al., 2001). Humans show automatic responses called reflexes at birth. These include the sucking reflex and the swallowing reflex. (You don't have to teach a newborn baby how to eat!) As time goes on, many reflexes drop out. (Sucking becomes voluntary, for example.)

Motor development provides some of the most fascinating changes in infants, in part because so much seems to happen so quickly—and so much of it during the first year. Children gain the capacity to move about through a sequence of activities that includes rolling over, sitting up, crawling, creeping, walking, and running. The ages at which infants first engage in these activities vary, but the sequence generally remains the same (see Figure 3.2). Some children skip a step. For example, an infant may creep without ever having crawled. But by and large, the sequence remains intact. Invariant sequences are usually interpreted as reflecting the unfolding of the genetic code (maturation). Maturation of the brain is a key element in motor development.

Infants also need some motor experience before they engage in milestones such as sitting up and walking. But although it may take them several months to sit up and more months to take their first steps, most of this time can apparently be attributed to maturation. In a classic study, Wayne and Marsena Dennis (1940) reported on the motor development of Native American Hopi children who spent their first year strapped to a cradleboard. Although denied a year of experience in locomotion, the Hopi infants gained the capacity to walk early in their second year, at about the same time as children reared in other cultures.

On the other hand, evidence is mixed as to whether training can accelerate the appearance of motor skills. For example, in a classic study with identical twins, Arnold Gesell (1929) gave one twin extensive training in hand coordination, block building, and stair climbing from early infancy. The other was allowed to develop on his or her own. But as time passed, the untrained twin became as skilled in these activities as the other.

More recent research suggests that the appearance and development of motor skills can be accelerated by training (Zelazo et al., 1993; Zelazo, 1998). Yet the effects of training mostly remain slight; guided practice in the absence of neural maturation apparently has limited results. There is also little evidence that this sort of training eventually leads to superior motor skills.

Genetic factors provide the reaction range for the expression of the behaviors that are possible for the individual and the species. Environmental factors can determine whether the child will develop in accord with the upper limits of the range. There may be little purpose to training children in motor skills before they are ready. Once they are ready, however, teaching and practice do make a difference. One does not become an Olympic athlete without "good genes." But one also usually does not become an Olympic athlete without high-quality training as well.

© Mike Greenlar/The Image Works

■ **A Native American Infant Strapped to a Cradleboard**
Researchers have studied children who are strapped to cradleboards during the first year to see if their motor development is delayed significantly. Once released from their boards, these children make rapid advances in motor development, suggesting the importance of maturation in motor development.

■ **Figure 3.3**
The Classic Visual Cliff Experiment
This young explorer has the good sense not to crawl out onto an apparently unsupported surface, even when Mother beckons from the other side. Rats, pups, kittens, and chicks also will not try to walk across to the other side. (So don't bother asking why the chicken crossed the visual cliff.)

avoid crawling off ledges and table tops into open space (Campos et al., 1978). Note the setup (Figure 3.3) in the classic "visual cliff" experiment run by Walk and Gibson (1961). An 8-month-old infant crawls freely above the portion of the glass with a checkerboard pattern immediately beneath it, but hesitates to crawl over the portion of the glass beneath which the checkerboard has been dropped a few feet. Because the glass would support the infant, this is a "visual cliff," not an actual cliff.

Normal neonates hear well unless their middle ears are clogged with amniotic fluid. In such cases, hearing improves rapidly after the ears are opened up. Most neonates reflexively turn their heads toward unusual sounds, suspending other activities as they do so. This finding, along with findings about visual tracking, suggests that infants are preprogrammed to survey their environments. Speaking or singing softly in a low-pitched tone soothes infants. This is why some parents use lullabies to get infants to fall asleep.

Three-day-old babies prefer their mother's voice to those of other women, but they do not show a similar preference for their father's voice (DeCasper & Prescott, 1984; Freeman et al., 1993). By birth, of course, babies have had many months of "experience" in the uterus. For at least 2 or 3 months before birth, babies have been capable of hearing sounds. Because they are predominantly exposed to sounds produced by their mother, learning may contribute to neonatal preferences.

The odors preferred by babies are similar to those preferred by adults. Newborn infants spit, stick out their tongue, and literally wrinkle their nose at the odor of rotten eggs. They smile and make licking motions in response to chocolate, strawberry, vanilla, and honey. The sense of smell, like the sense of hearing, may provide a vehicle for mother–infant recognition. Within the first week, nursing infants prefer to turn to look at their mother's nursing pads (which can be discriminated only by smell) rather than those of strange women (Macfarlane, 1975). By 15 days, nursing infants prefer their mother's underarm odor to those of other women (Porter et al., 1992). Bottle-fed babies do not show this preference.

Shortly after birth, infants can discriminate tastes. They eagerly suck liquid solutions of sugar and milk but grimace and refuse to suck salty or bitter solutions (Petrov et al., 2001; Rosenstein & Oster, 1988).

Newborn babies are sensitive to touch. Many reflexes (including rooting and sucking) are activated by pressure against the skin. The sense of touch is an extremely important avenue of learning and communication for babies. Sensations of skin against skin appear to provide feelings of comfort and security that may contribute to the formation of affectionate bonds between infants and their caregivers.

▶ CONTROVERSY IN PSYCHOLOGY ◀

Is development continuous or discontinuous?

Do developmental changes tend to occur gradually (continuously)? Or do they tend to occur in major leaps (discontinuously) that dramatically alter our bodies and behavior? *Question: Does development occur gradually or in stages?*

Watson and other behaviorists viewed development as a mainly continuous process in which the effects of learning mount gradually, with no major sudden changes. Maturational theorists, however, argue that people are prewired or preset to change dramatically at certain times of life. Rapid qualitative changes can be ushered in during new stages of development. They point out that the environment, even when enriched, profits us little until we are ready, or mature enough, to develop in a certain direction. For example, newborn babies do not imitate their parents' speech, even when the parents speak clearly and deliberately. Nor does aided practice in "walking" during the first few months after birth significantly accelerate the date at which the child can walk on her own.

Stage theorists, such as Jean Piaget—whose theory of cognitive development we discuss next—and Sigmund Freud saw development as discontinuous. Both theorists saw biological changes as providing the potential for psychological changes. Piaget's research centered on the ways in which maturation of the nervous system permits cognitive advances. Freud focused on the ways in which sexual development might provide the basis for personality development.

Certain aspects of physical development do occur in stages. For example, many of the changes that occur during prenatal development are discontinuous. For several days the dividing mass of cells that becomes the baby travels through the fallopian tube and the uterus—literally unattached to the mother. Then it becomes implanted in the uterine wall and a whole new way of obtaining nourishment begins. Similarly, organs develop so rapidly that the fetus is clearly human-looking before the end of the first trimester. The changes from the age of 2 to the onset of puberty (the period of development during which reproduction becomes possible) are continuous, with children gradually growing larger. Then a new stage of development begins with the adolescent growth spurt. The spurt is triggered by hormones and characterized by rapid changes in structure and function (as in the development of the sex organs) as well as size.

Psychologists disagree more strongly on whether aspects of development such as cognitive development, attachment, and gender typing occur in stages. But as we see next, Jean Piaget believed that cognitive development was discontinuous and consisted of four stages of development. In this chapter we will also see that Lawrence Kohlberg's theory of moral development consists of three levels and two stages within each level. Erik Erikson's theory of psychosocial development consists of eight stages.

Cognitive Development

The ways in which children mentally represent and think about the world—that is, their *cognitive development*—are explored in this section. Because cognitive functioning develops over many years, young children have ideas about the world that differ considerably from those of adults. Many of these ideas are charming but illogical—at least to adults.   *Question: What are Jean Piaget's views of cognitive development?*

Jean Piaget's Cognitive-Developmental Theory

Jean Piaget (1896–1980) was offered the curatorship of a museum in Geneva, but he had to turn it down. After all, he was only 11 at the time. Piaget's first intellectual love was biology, and he published his first scientific article at the age of 10. He then became a laboratory assistant to the director of a museum of natural history and engaged in research on mollusks (oysters, clams, snails, and such). The director soon died, and Piaget published the research findings himself. On the basis of these papers, he was offered the curatorship.

During adolescence Piaget studied philosophy, logic, and mathematics, but he earned his PhD in biology. In 1920 he obtained a job at the Binet Institute in Paris, where work on intelligence tests was being conducted. His first task was to adapt English verbal reasoning items for use with French children. To do so, he had to try out the items on children in various age groups and see whether they could arrive at correct answers. The task was boring until Piaget became intrigued by the children's *wrong* answers. Another investigator might have shrugged them off, but Piaget found meaningful patterns in the children's "mistakes." The wrong answers reflected consistent, if illogical, cognitive processes. Piaget's observations led to his influential theory of cognitive development.

Piaget's original texts are difficult to read—even when translated into English. In fact, Piaget once remarked that he had the advantage of not having to read Piaget!

Piaget hypothesized that children's cognitive processes develop in an orderly sequence of stages. Although some children may be more advanced than others at

■ **Jean Piaget**
The Swiss biologist-psychologist worked for a while at the Binet Institute in Paris. His fascination with cognitive development was sparked by his observation of children's *wrong* answers to questions on intelligence tests. Others might simply have checked these answers off as wrong; Piaget wanted to know *how* children arrived at them.

Assimilation
According to Piaget, the inclusion of a new event into an existing scheme.

Scheme
According to Piaget, a hypothetical mental structure that permits the classification and organization of new information.

Accommodation
According to Piaget, the modification of schemes so that information inconsistent with existing schemes can be integrated or understood.

particular ages, the developmental sequence remains the same. Piaget (1963) identified four major stages of cognitive development: sensorimotor, preoperational, concrete operational, and formal operational (see Table 3.1).

Assimilation and Accommodation

Piaget described human thought, or intelligence, in terms of two basic concepts: assimilation and accommodation. **Assimilation** means responding to a new stimulus through a reflex or existing habit. Infants, for example, usually try to place new objects in their mouth to suck, feel, or explore. Piaget would say that the child is assimilating a new toy to the sucking scheme. A **scheme** is a pattern of action or a mental structure involved in acquiring or organizing knowledge.

Piaget regarded children as natural physicists who seek to learn about and control their world. In the Piagetian view, children who squish their food and laugh enthusiastically are often acting as budding scientists. In addition to enjoying the responses of their parents, they are studying the texture and consistency of their food. (Parents, of course, often wish their children would practice these experiments in the laboratory, not the dining room.)

Accommodation is the creation of new ways of responding to objects or looking at the world. In accommodation, children transform existing schemes—action patterns or ways of organizing knowledge—to incorporate new events. Children (and adults) accommodate to objects and situations that cannot be integrated into existing schemes. (For example, children who study biology learn that whales cannot be assimilated into the "fish" scheme. They accommodate by constructing new schemes, such as "mammals without legs that live in the sea.") The ability to accommodate to novel stimuli advances as a result of maturation and experience.

Most of the time, newborn children assimilate environmental stimuli according to reflexive schemes, although adjusting the mouth to contain the nipple is a primitive kind of accommodation. Reflexive behavior, to Piaget, is not "true" intelligence. True intelligence involves adapting to the world through a smooth, fluid balancing of the processes of assimilation and accommodation. Let us now apply these concepts to the stages of cognitive development.

The Sensorimotor Stage

The newborn infant is capable of assimilating novel stimuli only to existing reflexes (or ready-made schemes) such as the rooting and sucking reflexes. But by the time an infant reaches the age of 1 month, he or she already shows purposeful behavior by repeating behavior patterns that are pleasurable, such as sucking his or her hand. Dur-

TABLE 3.1 Piaget's Stages of Cognitive Development

Stage	Approximate Age	About . . .
Sensorimotor	Birth–2 years	At first, the child lacks language and does not use symbols or mental representations of objects. In time, reflexive responding ends and intentional behavior begins. The child develops the object concept and acquires the basics of language.
Preoperational	2–7 years	The child begins to represent the world mentally, but thought is egocentric. The child does not focus on two aspects of a situation at once and therefore lacks conservation. The child shows animism, artificialism, and objective responsibility for wrongdoing.
Concrete operational	7–12 years	The child develops conservation concepts, can adopt the viewpoint of others, can classify objects in series, and shows comprehension of basic relational concepts (such as one object being larger or heavier than another).
Formal operational	12 years and above	Mature, adult thought emerges. Thinking is characterized by deductive logic, consideration of various possibilities (mental trial and error), abstract thought, and the formation and testing of hypotheses.

ing the first month or so, an infant apparently does not connect stimuli perceived through different senses. Reflexive turning toward sources of auditory and olfactory stimulation cannot be considered purposeful searching. But within the first few months the infant begins to coordinate vision with grasping to look at the object being held or touched.

A 3- or 4-month-old infant may be fascinated by his or her own hands and legs. The infant may become absorbed in watching him- or herself open and close the fists. The infant becomes increasingly interested in acting on the environment to make interesting results (such as the sound of a rattle) last longer or occur again. Behavior becomes increasingly intentional and purposeful. Between 4 and 8 months of age, the infant explores cause-and-effect relationships such as the thump that can be made by tossing an object or the way kicking can cause a hanging toy to bounce.

Prior to the age of 6 months or so, out of sight is literally out of mind. Objects are not yet represented mentally. For this reason, as you can see in Figure 3.4, a child makes no effort to search for an object that has been removed or placed behind a

Learning Connections
See the Connections *CD-ROM for an animation on the absence of object permanence.*

■ **Figure 3.4**
Object Permanence

To the infant at the top, who is in the early part of the sensorimotor stage, out of sight is truly out of mind. Once a sheet of paper is placed between the infant and the toy elephant, the infant loses all interest in it. The toy is apparently not yet mentally represented. The photos on the bottom shows a child later in the sensorimotor stage. This child does mentally represent objects and pushes through a towel to reach one that has been screened from sight.

© Doug Goodman/Photo Researchers, Inc.

© George Zimbel

Learning Connections
See the Connections *CD-ROM for an animation on the presence of object permanence.*

Object Permanence
Recognition that objects removed from sight still exist, as demonstrated in young children by continued pursuit.

Sensorimotor Stage
The first of Piaget's stages of cognitive development, characterized by coordination of sensory information and motor activity, early exploration of the environment, and lack of language.

Preoperational Stage
The second of Piaget's stages, characterized by illogical use of words and symbols, spotty logic, and egocentrism.

Egocentrism
According to Piaget, the assumption that others view the world as one does oneself.

Animism
The belief that inanimate objects move because of will or spirit.

Artificialism
The belief that natural objects have been created by human beings.

Conservation
According to Piaget, recognition that basic properties of substances such as weight and mass remain the same when superficial features change.

R E F L E C T

Can you think of examples of adults using egocentrism, animism, or artificialism in their own thinking? Why do you imagine that they do?

screen. By the age of 8 to 12 months, however, infants realize that objects removed from sight still exist and attempt to find them. In this way, they show what is known as **object permanence,** thereby making it possible to play peek-a-boo.

By the way, comparative psychologists have also studied the development of object permanence in nonhuman species, including dogs and cats . . . and magpies. Magpies are notorious thieves in the bird world, and they also hide their food to keep it safe from other animals—especially other magpies. Bettina Pollock and her colleagues (2000) found that magpies develop object permanence before they begin to hide food. Magpies would not profit from secreting away their food if out of sight meant the same thing as "out of existence."

Between 1 and 2 years of age, children begin to show interest in how things are constructed. It may be for this reason that they persistently touch and finger their parents' faces and their own. Toward the end of the second year, children begin to engage in mental trial and error before they try out overt behaviors. For instance, when they look for an object you have removed, they will no longer begin their search in the last place they saw it. Rather, they may follow you, assuming you are carrying the object even though it is not visible. It is as though they are anticipating failure in searching for the object in the place where they last saw it.

Because the first stage of development is dominated by learning to coordinate perception of the self and of the environment with motor (muscular) activity, Piaget termed it the **sensorimotor stage.** This stage comes to a close with the acquisition of the basics of language at about age 2.

The Preoperational Stage

The **preoperational stage** is characterized by the use of words and symbols to represent objects and relationships among them. But be warned—any resemblance between the logic of children between the ages of 2 and 7 and your own logic very often is purely coincidental. Children may use the same words that adults do, but this does not mean their views of the world are similar to adults'. Preoperational children tend to think one-dimensionally—to focus on one aspect of a problem or situation at a time.

One consequence of one-dimensional thinking is **egocentrism.** Preoperational children cannot understand that other people do not see things the same way they do. When Allyn was 2½, I asked her to tell me about a trip to the store with her mother. "You tell me," she replied. Upon questioning, it seemed she did not understand that I could not see the world through her eyes.

To egocentric preoperational children, all the world's a stage that has been erected to meet their needs and amuse them. When asked, "Why does the sun shine?" they may say, "To keep me warm." If asked, "Why is the sky blue?" they may respond, "'Cause blue's my favorite color." Preoperational children also show **animism.** They attribute life and consciousness to physical objects like the sun and the moon. They also show **artificialism.** They believe that environmental events like rain and thunder are human inventions. Asked why the sky is blue, 4-year-olds may answer, "'Cause Mommy painted it." Examples of egocentrism, animism, and artificialism are shown in Table 3.2.

To gain further insight into preoperational thinking, consider these problems:

- Imagine that you pour water from a tall, thin glass into a low, wide glass. Now, does the low, wide glass contain more, less, or the same amount of water that was in the tall, thin glass? I won't keep you in suspense. If you said the same amount of water (with possible minor exceptions for spillage and evaporation), you were correct. Now that you're on a roll, go on to the next problem.
- If you flatten a ball of clay into a pancake, do you wind up with more, less, or the same amount of clay? If you said the same amount of clay, you are correct once more.

To arrive at the correct answers to these questions, you must understand the law of **conservation.** This law holds that basic properties of substances such as mass, weight, and volume remain the same—that is, are *conserved*—when you change superficial properties such as their shape or arrangement.

TABLE 3.2 Examples of Preoperational Thought

Type of Thought	Sample Questions	Typical Answers
Egocentrism	Why does it get dark out? Why does the sun shine? Why is there snow? Why is grass green? What are TV sets for?	So I can go to sleep. To keep me warm. For me to play in. Because that's my favorite color. To watch my favorite shows and cartoons.
Animism (attributing life and consciousness to physical objects)	Why do trees have leaves? Why do stars twinkle? Why does the sun move in the sky? Where do boats go at night?	To keep them warm. Because they're happy and cheerful. To follow children and hear what they say. They sleep like we do.
Artificialism (assuming that environmental events are human inventions)	What makes it rain? Why is the sky blue? What is the wind? What causes thunder? How does a baby get in Mommy's tummy?	Someone emptying a watering can. Somebody painted it. A man blowing. A man grumbling. Just make it first. (How?) You put some eyes on it, then put on the head.

Conservation requires the ability to think about, or **center** on, two aspects of a situation at once, such as height and width. Conserving the mass, weight, or volume of a substance requires the recognition that a change in one dimension can compensate for a change in another. But the preoperational boy in Figure 3.5 focuses on only one dimension at a time. First he is shown two tall, thin glasses of juice and agrees that they contain the same amount of juice. Then, while he watches, juice is poured from a tall glass into a squat glass. Now he is asked which glass contains more juice. After mulling over the problem, he points to the tall glass. Why? Because when he looks at the glasses he is "overwhelmed" by the fact that the thinner glass is taller. The preoperational child focuses on the most apparent dimension of the situation—in this case, the greater height of the thinner glass. He does not realize that the increased width of the squat glass compensates for the decreased height. By the way, if you ask him whether any juice has been added or taken away in the pouring process, he readily says no. But if you then repeat the question about which glass contains *more* juice, he again points to the taller glass. If all this sounds rather illogical, that is because it is illogical—or, in Piaget's terms, preoperational.

Center
According to Piaget, to focus one's attention.

Learning Connections
See the Connections *CD-ROM for an animation on the preoperational stage.*

■ Figure 3.5
Conservation
The boy in drawing A agreed that the amount of water in two identical containers is equal. As shown in drawing B, he then watched as water from one container was poured into a tall, thin container. In drawing C, he is examining one of the original containers and the new container. When asked whether he thinks the amounts of water in the two containers are now the same, he says no. Apparently, he is impressed by the height of the new container, and, prior to the development of conservation, he focuses on only one dimension of the situation at a time—in this case, the height of the new container.

After you have tried the experiment with the juice, try the following. Make two rows of five pennies each. In the first row, place the pennies about half an inch apart. In the second row, place the pennies 2 to 3 inches apart. Ask a 4- to 5-year-old child which row has more pennies. What do you think the child will say? Why?

Piaget (1997) found that the moral judgment of preoperational children is also one-dimensional. The five-year-olds he observed tended to be slaves to rules and authority. When you ask them why something should be done in a certain way, they may insist "Because that's the way to do it!" or "Because my Mommy says so!" Right is right and wrong is wrong. Why? "Because!"—that's why.

According to most older children and adults, an act is a crime only when there is criminal intent. Accidents may be hurtful, but the perpetrators are usually seen as blameless. But in the court of the one-dimensional, preoperational child, there is **objective responsibility.** People are sentenced (and harshly!) on the basis of the amount of damage they have done, not their motives or intentions.

To demonstrate objective responsibility, Piaget would tell children stories and ask them which character was naughtier and why. John, for instance, accidentally breaks 15 cups when he opens a door. Henry breaks 1 cup when he sneaks into a kitchen cabinet to find forbidden jam. The preoperational child usually judges John to be naughtier. Why? Because he broke more cups.

The Concrete-Operational Stage

By about age 7, the typical child is entering the stage of **concrete operations.** In this stage, which lasts until about age 12, children show the beginnings of the capacity for adult logic. However, their logical thoughts, or *operations*, generally involve tangible objects rather than abstract ideas. Concrete operational children are capable of **decentration;** they can center on two dimensions of a problem at once. This attainment has implications for moral judgments, conservation, and other intellectual undertakings.

Children now become **subjective** in their moral judgments. When assigning guilt, they center on the motives of wrongdoers as well as on the amount of damage done. Concrete-operational children judge Henry more harshly than John because John's misdeed was an accident.

Concrete-operational children understand the laws of conservation. The boy in Figure 3.5, now a few years older, would say that the squat glass still contains the same amount of juice. If asked why, he might reply, "Because you can pour it back into the other one." Such an answer also suggests awareness of the concept of **reversibility**—the recognition that many processes can be reversed or undone so that things are restored to their previous condition. Centering simultaneously on the height and the width of the glasses, the boy recognizes that the loss in height compensates for the gain in width.

Concrete-operational children can conserve *number* as well as weight and mass. They recognize that the number of pennies in each of the rows described earlier is the same, even though one row may be spread out to look longer than the other.

Children in this stage are less egocentric. They are able to take on the roles of others and to view the world, and themselves, from other people's perspectives. They recognize that people see things in different ways because of different situations and different sets of values.

During the concrete-operational stage, children's own sets of values begin to emerge and acquire stability. Children come to understand that feelings of love between them and their parents can endure even when someone feels angry or disappointed at a particular moment. We continue our discussion of Piaget's theory—his stage of formal operations—in the section on adolescence. A critique of his theory begins on page 111.

Lawrence Kohlberg's Theory of Moral Development

His car was found parked beside Boston Harbor. Three months later his body washed up onto the shore. He had discussed the moral dilemma posed by suicide with a friend, and perhaps Lawrence Kohlberg (1927–1987) had taken his own life. He was

---

REFLECT

Is reliance on objective responsibility limited to children? Can you think of situations in which adults you know have shown objective responsibility in their thinking?

Learning Connections
See the Connections *CD-ROM for an animation on the concrete-operational stage.*

Learning Connections
See the Connections *CD-ROM for an animation on the concrete-operational stage and the absence of abstract reasoning.*

Objective Responsibility
According to Piaget, the assignment of blame according to the amount of damage done rather than the motives of the actor.

Concrete-Operational Stage
Piaget's third stage, characterized by logical thought concerning tangible objects, conservation, and subjective morality.

Decentration
Simultaneous focusing on more than one dimension of a problem, so that flexible, reversible thought becomes possible.

Subjective Moral Judgment
According to Piaget, moral judgments that are based on the motives of the perpetrator.

Reversibility
According to Piaget, recognition that processes can be undone, that things can be made as they were.

suffering from a painful parasitic intestinal disease that he had acquired 40 years earlier while smuggling Jewish refugees from Europe past the British blockade into Israel. There had also been recent disappointments in his work.

Kohlberg was born into a wealthy family in suburban New York. He graduated from Phillips Academy as World War II came to an end. Rather than go on immediately to college, he became a merchant mariner and helped save people who had been displaced by the war. He was captured and imprisoned on the Mediterranean island of Cyprus. He soon escaped, but not before acquiring the disease that would bring him a lifetime of pain. Between high school and college, Kohlberg had already decided that one must attend more to one's own conscience than to law and authority figures in determining what was right and wrong.

Kohlberg believed that a key aspect of cognitive development has to do with the ways in which people arrive at judgments of right or wrong.   ***Question: How do children reason about right and wrong?***   Kohlberg (1981) used the following tale in his research into children's moral reasoning:

> In Europe a woman was near death from a special kind of cancer. There was one drug that the doctors thought might save her. It was a form of radium that a druggist in the same town had recently discovered. The drug was expensive to make, but the druggist was charging ten times what the drug cost him to make. He paid $200 for the radium and charged $2,000 for a small dose of the drug. The sick woman's husband, Heinz, went to everyone he knew to borrow the money, but he could only get together about $1,000, which was half of what it cost. He told the druggist that his wife was dying and asked him to sell it cheaper or let him pay later. But the druggist said: "No, I discovered the drug and I'm going to make money from it." So Heinz got desperate and broke into the man's store to steal the drug for his wife. (Kohlberg, 1969)

Heinz is caught in a moral dilemma. In such dilemmas, a legal or social rule (in this case, the law forbidding stealing) is pitted against a strong human need (his desire to save his wife). Children and adults arrive at yes or no answers for different reasons. According to Kohlberg, the reasons can be classified according to the level of moral development they reflect.

As a stage theorist, Kohlberg argues that the stages of moral reasoning follow a specific sequence (see Table 3.3). Children progress at different rates, and not all children (or adults) reach the highest stage. But the sequence is always the same: Children must go through stage 1 before they enter stage 2, and so on. According to Kohlberg, there are three levels of moral development and two stages within each level.

When it comes to the dilemma of Heinz, Kohlberg believed that people could justify Heinz's stealing of the drug or his decision not to steal it by the reasoning of any level or stage of moral development. In other words, Kohlberg was not as interested in the eventual "yes" or "no" as he was in *how a person reasoned* to arrive at yes or no.

The Preconventional Level

The **preconventional level** applies to most children through about the age of 9. Children at this level base their moral judgments on the consequences of behavior. For instance, stage 1 is oriented toward obedience and punishment. Good behavior is obedient and allows one to avoid punishment. However, a child in stage 1 can decide that Heinz should or should not steal the drug, as shown in Table 3.3.

In stage 2, good behavior allows people to satisfy their needs and those of others. (Heinz's wife needs the drug; therefore, stealing the drug—the only way of obtaining it—is not wrong.)

The Conventional Level

In the **conventional level** of moral reasoning, right and wrong are judged by conformity to conventional (familial, religious, societal) standards of right and wrong. According to the stage 3 "good-boy orientation," moral behavior is that which meets the needs and expectations of others. Moral behavior is what is "normal"—what the majority does. (Heinz should steal the drug because that is what a "good husband" would do. It is "natural" or "normal" to try to help one's wife. *Or*, Heinz should *not* steal the drug because "good people do not steal.")

Harvard University Archives

■ Lawrence Kohlberg

Even though she disagreed with many of Kohlberg's views, Carol Gilligan wrote that he "almost singlehanded established moral development as a central concern of developmental psychology" (Hunt, 1993, p. 381).

REFLECT

What do you think? Should Heinz have tried to steal the drug? Was he right or wrong? Is the answer more complicated than a simple yes or no?

Preconventional Level

According to Kohlberg, a period during which moral judgments are based largely on expectation of rewards or punishments.

Conventional Level

According to Kohlberg, a period during which moral judgments largely reflect social conventions. A "law and order" approach to morality.

TABLE 3.3 Kohlberg's Levels and Stages of Moral Development

	Stage of Development	Examples of Moral Reasoning That Support Heinz's Stealing the Drug	Examples of Moral Reasoning That Oppose Heinz's Stealing the Drug
Level I: Preconventional	*Stage 1:* Judgments guided by obedience and the prospect of punishment (the consequences of the behavior)	It isn't wrong to take the drug. Heinz did try to pay the druggist for it, and it's only worth $200, not $2,000.	Taking things without paying is wrong because it's against the law. Heinz will get caught and go to jail.
	Stage 2: Naively egoistic, instrumental orientation (Things are right when they satisfy people's needs.)	Heinz ought to take the drug because his wife really needs it. He can always pay the druggist back.	Heinz shouldn't take the drug. If he gets caught and winds up in jail, it won't do his wife any good.
Level II: Conventional	*Stage 3:* Good-boy orientation (Moral behavior helps others and is socially approved.)	Stealing is a crime, so it's bad, but Heinz should take the drug to save his wife or else people would blame him for letting her die.	Stealing is a crime. Heinz shouldn't just take the drug because his family will be dishonored and they will blame him.
	Stage 4: Law-and-order orientation (Moral behavior is doing one's duty and showing respect for authority.)	Heinz must take the drug to do his duty to save his wife. Eventually, he has to pay the druggist for it, however.	If everyone took the law into their own hands, civilization would fall apart, so Heinz shouldn't steal the drug.
Level III: Postconventional	*Stage 5:* Contractual, legalistic orientation (One must weigh pressing human needs against society's need to maintain social order.)	This thing is complicated because society has a right to maintain law and order, but Heinz has to take the drug to save his wife.	I can see why Heinz feels he has to take the drug, but laws exist for the benefit of society as a whole and can't simply be cast aside.
	Stage 6: Universal ethical principles orientation (People must follow universal ethical principles and their own conscience, even if it means breaking the law.)	In this case, the law comes into conflict with the principle of the sanctity of human life. Heinz must take the drug because his wife's life is more important than the law.	If Heinz truly believes that stealing the drug is worse than letting his wife die, he should not take it. People have to make sacrifices to do what they think is right.

In stage 4, moral judgments are based on rules that maintain the social order. Showing respect for authority and doing one's duty are valued highly. (Heinz *must* steal the drug; it would be his fault if he let his wife die. He would pay the druggist later, when he had the money.) Many people do not mature beyond the conventional level.

The Postconventional Level

Postconventional moral reasoning is more complex and focuses on dilemmas in which individual needs are pitted against the need to maintain the social order and on personal conscience. We discuss the postconventional level in the section on adolescence. A critique of Kohlberg's theory is provided on page 114.

Social and Emotional Development

Social relationships are crucial to us as children. When we are infants, our very survival depends on them. Later in life, they contribute to our feelings of happiness and satisfaction. In this section we discuss many aspects of social development, including Erikson's theory of psychosocial development, attachment, styles of parenting, and child abuse.

Erik Erikson's Stages of Psychosocial Development

Trust Versus Mistrust
Erikson's first stage of psychosexual development, during which children do—or do not—come to trust that primary caregivers and the environment will meet their needs.

According to Erik Erikson, we undergo several stages of psychosocial development (see Table 3.4). ***Question: What are Erikson's stages of psychosocial development?*** During Erikson's first stage, **trust versus mistrust,** we depend on our primary caregivers (usually our parents) and come to expect that our environments will—or will not—meet our needs. During early childhood and the preschool years, we begin

TABLE 3.4 Erikson's Stages of Psychosocial Development

Time Period	Life Crisis	The Developmental Task
Infancy (0–1)	Trust versus mistrust	Coming to trust the mother and the environment—to associate surroundings with feelings of inner goodness
Early childhood (1–3)	Autonomy versus shame and doubt	Developing the wish to make choices and the self-control to exercise choice
Preschool years (4–5)	Initiative versus guilt	Adding planning and "attacking" to choice, becoming active and on the move
Elementary school years (6–12)	Industry versus inferiority	Becoming eagerly absorbed in skills, tasks, and productivity; mastering the fundamentals of technology
Adolescence	Identity versus role diffusion	Connecting skills and social roles to formation of career objectives; developing a sense of who one is and what one stands for
Young adulthood	Intimacy versus isolation	Committing the self to another; engaging in sexual love
Middle adulthood	Generativity versus stagnation	Needing to be needed; guiding and encouraging the younger generation; being creative
Late adulthood	Integrity versus despair	Accepting the time and place of one's life cycle; achieving wisdom and dignity

From: Erikson, 1963, pp. 247–269.

to explore the environment more actively and try new things. At this time, our relationships with our parents and friends can encourage us to develop **autonomy** (self-direction) and initiative, or feelings of shame and guilt. During the elementary school years, friends and teachers take on more importance, encouraging us to become industrious or to develop feelings of inferiority.

As you see in Table 3.4, Erikson's theory includes eight stages that straddle the life-span. We revisit his theory with the stage of *ego identity versus role diffusion* in the section on adolescence. We will then come across his views again in the sections on adult development.

Attachment: Ties That Bind

At the age of 2, my daughter Allyn almost succeeded in preventing me from finishing a book. When I locked myself into my study, she positioned herself outside the door and called, "Daddy, oh Daddy." At other times, she would bang on the door or cry outside. When I would give in (several times a day) and open the door, she would run in and say, "I want you to pick up me" and hold out her arms or climb into my lap. Although we were separate human beings, it was as though she were very much *attached* to me.   ***Questions: How do feelings of attachment develop? What kinds of experiences affect attachment?***

Psychologist Mary D. Salter Ainsworth (1913–1999) defined **attachment** as an emotional tie that is formed between one animal or person and another specific individual. Attachment keeps organisms together—it is vital to the survival of the infant—and it tends to endure.

The behaviors that define attachment include (1) attempts to maintain contact or nearness and (2) shows of anxiety when separated. Babies and children try to maintain contact with caregivers to whom they are attached. They engage in eye contact, pull and tug at them, ask to be picked up, and may even jump in front of them in such a way that they will be "run over" if they are not picked up!

The Strange Situation and Patterns of Attachment

The ways in which infants behave in strange situations are connected with their bonds of attachment with their caregivers. Given this fact, Ainsworth and her colleagues (1978) innovated the *strange situation method* to learn how infants respond to separations

Autonomy
Self-direction.

Attachment
The enduring affectional tie that binds one person to another.

■ Allyn

At the age of 2, the author's daughter Allyn nearly succeeded in preventing the publication of a book by continually pulling him away from the computer when he was at work. Because of their mutual attachment, separation was painful.

© Marvin S. Roberts

Mary D. Salter Ainsworth

Ainsworth's cross-cultural studies and her innovation of the strange situation method have made her a key figure in the development of theories of the formation of bonds of attachment between children and their caregivers.

Indiscriminate Attachment
Showing attachment behaviors toward any person.

and reunions with a caregiver (usually the mother) and a stranger. Using this method, Ainsworth and her colleagues identified three major types of attachment: secure attachment and two types of insecure attachment:

1. *Secure attachment.* Securely attached infants mildly protest their mother's departure, seek interaction upon reunion, and are readily comforted by her.
2. *Avoidant attachment.* Infants who show avoidant attachment are least distressed by their mother's departure. They play by themselves without fuss and ignore their mothers when they return.
3. *Ambivalent/resistant attachment.* Infants with ambivalent/resistant attachment are the most emotional. They show severe signs of distress when their mother leaves and show ambivalence upon reunion by alternately clinging to and pushing their mother away when she returns.

Attachment is connected with the quality of care that infants receive. The parents of securely attached children are more likely to be affectionate and reliable caregivers (Isabella, 1998; Posada et al., 2002). A wealth of research literature speaks of the benefits of secure attachment. For example, securely attached children are happier, more sociable, and more cooperative than insecurely attached children (Bohlin et al., 2000). Securely attached preschoolers have longer attention spans, are less impulsive, and are better at solving problems (Frankel & Bates, 1990). At ages 5 and 6, securely attached children are liked better by their peers and teachers, are more competent, and have fewer behavior problems than insecurely attached children (Granot & Mayseless, 2001; Moss & St-Laurent, 2001). In this vein, we can also note that having mother present during stressful situations, such as pediatric exams, helps children cope with these situations (Ybarra et al., 2000).

The majority of children in all societies tend to be securely attached. However, as noted in Table 3.5, different patterns of insecure attachment predominate in various cultures and appear to be connected with parental child-rearing practices and attitudes.

Stages of Attachment

Ainsworth also studied phases in the development of attachment. She and her colleagues observed infants in many societies, including the African country of Uganda. She noted the efforts of infants to maintain contact with the mother, their protests when separated from her, and their use of her as a base for exploring their environment. At first, infants show **indiscriminate attachment.** That is, they prefer being held or being with someone to being alone, but they show no preferences for particular people. Specific attachment to the mother begins to develop at about 4 months of age and

TABLE 3.5   Some Patterns of Insecure Attachment and Child-Rearing Practices Found in Other Countries

Country	Predominant Patterns of Insecure Attachment	Child-Rearing Practices and Attitudes (compared with other European and Asian countries and with the United States)
Germany	Avoidant	• Parents are less likely to pick up a crying infant. • Parents are more likely to leave the infant alone in bed.
Japan	Ambivalent/Resistant	• Parents are less likely to leave an infant with strangers. • Parents are more likely to emphasize continuous, close contact with the mother.
Israel	Ambivalent/Resistant	• Parents are less likely to leave an infant with strangers. • Parents are more likely to emphasize continuous, close contact with primary caregivers.

Source: Rathus, S. A. (2003). *Voyages: Childhood and adolescence.* Belmont, CA: Wadsworth Publishing.

becomes intense by about 7 months of age. Fear of strangers, which develops in some but not all children, follows 1 or 2 months later.

From studies such as these, Ainsworth identified three stages of attachment:

1. The **initial-preattachment phase,** which lasts from birth to about 3 months and is characterized by indiscriminate attachment.
2. The **attachment-in-the-making phase,** which occurs at about 3 or 4 months and is characterized by preference for familiar figures.
3. The **clear-cut-attachment phase,** which occurs at about 6 or 7 months and is characterized by intensified dependence on the primary caregiver.

John Bowlby (1988), a colleague of Mary Ainsworth, believed that attachment is also characterized by fear of strangers ("stranger anxiety"). That is, at about 8 to 10 months of age, children may cry and cling to their parents when strangers try to befriend them. But not all children develop fear of strangers. It therefore does not seem necessary to include fear of strangers as an essential part of the process of attachment.

Theoretical Views of Attachment

Early in the century, behaviorists argued that attachment behaviors are learned through experience. Caregivers feed their infants and tend to their other physiological needs. Thus, infants associate their caregivers with gratification of needs and learn to approach them to meet their needs. The feelings of gratification associated with the meeting of basic needs generalize into feelings of security when the caregiver is present.

Classic research by psychologist Harry F. Harlow suggests that skin contact may be more important than learning experiences. Harlow noted that infant rhesus monkeys reared without mothers or companions became attached to pieces of cloth in their cages. They maintained contact with them and showed distress when separated from them. Harlow conducted a series of experiments to find out why (Harlow, 1959).

In one study, Harlow placed infant rhesus monkeys in cages with two surrogate mothers, as shown in Figure 3.6. One "mother" was made of wire mesh from which a baby bottle was extended. The other surrogate mother was made of soft, cuddly terry cloth. The infant monkeys spent most of their time clinging to the cloth mother, even though "she" did not gratify their need for food. Harlow concluded that monkeys—and perhaps humans—have an inborn need for **contact comfort** that is as basic as the need for food. Gratification of the need for contact comfort, rather than food, might be why infant monkeys (and humans) cling to their mothers.

Harlow and Zimmerman (1959) found that a surrogate mother made of terry cloth could also serve as a comforting base from which an infant monkey could explore its environment (Figure 3.7). Toys such as stuffed bears and oversized wooden insects

Initial-Preattachment Phase
The first phase in forming bonds of attachment, characterized by indiscriminate attachment.

Attachment-in-the-Making Phase
The second phase in forming bonds of attachment, characterized by preference for familiar figures.

Clear-Cut-Attachment Phase
The third phase in forming bonds of attachment, characterized by intensified dependence on the primary caregiver.

Contact Comfort
A hypothesized primary drive to seek physical comfort through contact with another.

REFLECT

Do you know children (or adults) who seem to be quite independent of their parents? Do you know others who find it difficult to separate from their parents? Can you account for the difference? Have you had experience with a child who showed fear of strangers? How did he or she act in their presence?

■ Figure 3.6
Attachment in Infant Monkeys

Although this rhesus monkey infant is fed by the wire "mother," it spends most of its time clinging to the soft, cuddly terry-cloth "mother." It knows where to get a meal, but contact comfort is apparently more important than food in the development of attachment in infant monkeys (and infant humans?).

Harlow Primate Lab, University of Wisconsin

Harlow Primate Lab, University of Wisconsin

■ **Figure 3.7**
Security

With its terry-cloth surrogate mother nearby, this infant rhesus monkey apparently feels secure enough to explore the "bear monster" placed in its cage. But infants with wire surrogate mothers or no mothers at all cower in a corner when such "monsters" are introduced.

Ethologist
A scientist who studies the characteristic behavior patterns of species of animals.

Critical Period
A period of time when an instinctive response can be elicited by a particular stimulus.

Imprinting
A process occurring during a critical period in the development of an organism, in which that organism responds to a stimulus in a manner that will afterward be difficult to modify.

Instrumental Competence
Ability to manipulate one's environment to achieve one's goals.

Authoritative Parents
Parents who are strict and warm. Authoritative parents demand mature behavior but use reason rather than force in discipline.

Authoritarian Parents
Parents who are rigid in their rules and who demand obedience for the sake of obedience.

were placed in cages with infant rhesus monkeys and their surrogate mothers. When the infants were alone or had wire surrogate mothers for companions, they cowered in fear as long as the "bear monster" or "insect monster" was present. But when the terry-cloth mothers were present, the infants clung to them for a while and then explored the intruding "monster." With human infants, too, the bonds of mother–infant attachment appear to provide a secure base from which infants feel encouraged to express their curiosity.

Other researchers, such as **ethologist** Konrad Lorenz, note that for many animals, attachment is an instinct—inborn. (Ethologists study the behavioral characteristics of various species of animals.) Attachment, like other instincts, is theorized to occur in the presence of a specific stimulus and during a **critical period** of life—that is, a period during which the animal is sensitive to the stimulus.

Some animals become attached to the first moving object they encounter. The unwritten rule seems to be, "If it moves, it must be Mother." It is as if the image of the moving object becomes "imprinted" on the young animal. The formation of an attachment in this manner is therefore called **imprinting.**

Lorenz (1981) became well known when pictures of his "family" of goslings were made public (Figure 3.8). How did Lorenz acquire his following? He was present when the goslings hatched and during their critical period, and he allowed them to follow him. The critical period for geese and some other animals is bounded, at the younger end, by the age at which they first walk and, at the older end, by the age at which they develop fear of strangers. The goslings followed Lorenz persistently, ran to him when they were frightened, honked with distress at his departure, and tried to overcome barriers between them. If you substitute crying for honking, it all sounds rather human.

Ainsworth and Bowlby (1991) consider attachment to be instinctive in humans. However, the process would not be quite the same as with ducks and geese. The upper limit for waterbirds is the age at which they develop fear of strangers, but not all children develop this fear. When children do develop fear of strangers, they do so at about 6 to 8 months of age—*prior to* independent locomotion, or crawling, which usually occurs 1 or 2 months later. Moreover, the critical period with humans would be quite extended.

Another issue in social and emotional development is parenting styles. Parental behavior not only contributes to the development of attachment, but also to the development of self-esteem, self-reliance, achievement motivation, and competence.

Parenting Styles

Many psychologists have been concerned about the relationships between parenting styles and the personality development of the child. ***Question: What types of parental behavior are connected with variables such as self-esteem, achievement motivation, and independence in children?*** Diana Baumrind (1973) and her colleagues (Lamb & Baumrind, 1978) have been particularly interested in the connections between parental behavior and the development of **instrumental competence** in their children. (*Instrumental competence* refers to the ability to manipulate the environment to achieve ones goals.) Baumrind has largely focused on four aspects of parental behavior: (1) strictness; (2) demands for the child to achieve intellectual, emotional, and social maturity; (3) communication ability; and (4) warmth and involvement. She labeled the three most important parenting styles the *authoritative, authoritarian,* and *permissive* styles. Other researchers have identified and studied the *uninvolved* style.

1. *Authoritative parents.* The parents of the most competent children rate high in all four areas of behavior (see Table 3.6). They are strict (restrictive) and demand mature behavior. However, they temper their strictness and demands with willingness to reason with their children and with love and support. They expect a lot, but they explain why and offer help. Baumrind labeled these parents **authoritative parents** to suggest that they know what they want but are also loving and respectful of their children.

2. *Authoritarian parents.* **Authoritarian parents** view obedience as a virtue to be pursued for its own sake. They have strict guidelines about what is right and wrong, and they demand that their children adhere to those guidelines. Both authoritative and authoritarian parents adhere to strict standards of conduct. However, authori-

tative parents explain their demands and are supportive, whereas authoritarian parents rely on force and communicate poorly with their children. Authoritarian parents do not respect their children's points of view, and they may be cold and rejecting. When their children ask them why they should behave in a certain way, authoritarian parents often answer, "Because I say so!"

3. *Permissive parents.* **Permissive parents** are generally easygoing with their children. As a result, the children do pretty much whatever they wish. Permissive parents are warm and supportive, but poor at communicating.

4. *Uninvolved parents.* **Uninvolved parents** tend to leave their children on their own. They make few demands and show little warmth or encouragement.

© Thomas McAvoy/Time Life Pictures/Getty Images

■ **Figure 3.8**
Imprinting

Quite a following? Konrad Lorenz may not look like Mommy to you, but these goslings became attached to him because he was the first moving object they perceived and followed. This type of attachment process is referred to as *imprinting.* Imprinting among goslings is an instinctive pattern of behavior that is triggered by a specific stimulus (a moving object) and which occurs during a critical period of development.

R E F L E C T

Were your parents warm or cold, restrictive or permissive? How did their parenting style affect your feelings and behavior?

Research evidence shows that the children of warm parents are more likely to be socially and emotionally well-adjusted. They are also more likely to internalize moral standards— that is, to develop a conscience (MacDonald, 1992; Miller et al., 1993).

Strictness appears to pay off, provided it is tempered with reason and warmth. Children of authori*tative* parents have greater self-reliance, self-esteem, social competence, and achievement motivation than other children (Baumrind, 1991a; Kim & Rohner, 2002). Children of authori*tarian* parents are often withdrawn or aggressive, and they usually do not do as well in school as children of authoritative parents (Kim & Rohner, 2002; Steinberg, 2001). Children of permissive parents seem to be the least mature. They are frequently impulsive, moody, and aggressive. In adolescence, lack of parental monitoring is often linked to delinquency and poor academic performance. Children of uninvolved parents tend to obtain poorer grades than children whose parents make demands on them (Ginsburg & Bronstein, 1993). The children of uninvolved parents also tend to be more likely to "hang out" with crowds who "party" a good deal and use drugs (Durbin et al., 1993). The message? Simple enough: Children appear to profit when their parents make reasonable demands, show warmth and encouragement, and spend time with them.

Child Abuse

The incidence of child abuse is underreported, but it is estimated that nearly 3 million children in the United States are neglected or abused by parents or other caregivers each year (Herman-Giddens et al., 1999). More than half a million suffer serious injuries; thousands die.

Many factors contribute to child abuse: stress, a history of child abuse in at least one of the parents' families of origin, acceptance of violence as a way of coping with stress, failure to become attached to the children, substance abuse, and rigid attitudes toward child rearing (Belsky, 1993; Burgess & Drais, 2001). Unemployment and low socioeconomic status are common stressors that lead to abuse (Lewin, 1995).

TABLE 3.6 Parenting Styles

Style of Parenting	Parental Behavior			
	Restrictiveness	Demands for Mature Behavior	Communication Ability	Warmth and Support
Authoritative	High (use of reasoning)	High	High	High
Authoritarian	High (use of force)	Moderate	Low	Low
Permissive	Low (easygoing)	Low	Low	High
Uninvolved	Low (uninvolved)	Low	Low	Low

Note: Research suggests that the children of authoritative parents develop as the most competent.

Permissive Parents
Parents who impose few, if any, rules and who do not supervise their children closely.

Uninvolved Parents
Parents who generally leave their children to themselves.

Children who are abused are quite likely to develop personal and social problems and psychological disorders. They are less likely than other children to venture out to explore the world (Aber & Allen, 1987). They are more likely to have psychological problems such as anxiety, depression, and low self-esteem (Wagner, 1997). They are less likely to be intimate with their peers and more likely to be aggressive (Benda & Corwyn, 2002; Parker & Herrera, 1996; Rothbart & Ahadi, 1994). As adults, they are more likely to be violent toward their dates and spouses (Benda & Corwyn, 2002).

Many children are also victims of sexual abuse. The effects of child sexual abuse are variable, and it does not appear that there is a single, identifiable syndrome that results from such abuse (Saywitz et al., 2000). Nevertheless, the research literature shows that sexually abused children are more likely to develop physical and psychological health problems than unabused children (Saywitz et al., 2000). Child sexual abuse can also have lasting effects on children's relationships once they become adults.

Child abuse runs in families to some degree (Ertem et al., 2000). Child abusers are more likely to have been abused than is true for the general population. Even so, *most children who are abused do* not *abuse their own children as adults* (Kaufman & Zigler, 1989).

Why does abuse run in families? There are several hypotheses (Belsky, 1993). One is that parents serve as role models. According to Murray Straus (1995), "Spanking teaches kids that when someone is doing something you don't like and they won't stop doing it, you hit them." Another is that children adopt parents' strict philosophies about discipline. Exposure to violence in their own home leads some children to view abuse as normal. A third is that being abused can create feelings of hostility that are then expressed against others, including one's own children.

Learning Connections
See Web site for an interactive version of these review questions.

R E V I E W

(5) Infants double their birth weight in about (how many?) —————— months and triple it by the first birthday. (6) Piaget saw intelligence as including —————— (responding to events according to existing schemes) and accommodation. (7) Object

---

A Closer Look 👁

How Child Abuse May Set the Stage for Psychological Disorders in Adulthood

One way in which child abuse may set the stage for psychological disorders in adulthood is by increasing people's bodily responses to stress. Responses to stress are typically measured in terms of the reactivity of the endocrine system (particularly stress hormones such as ACTH and cortisol) and the autonomic nervous system (e.g., heart rate). A study by Christine Heim and her colleagues (2000, 2002) recruited 49 generally healthy women with an average age of 35. Twenty-seven of the women reported childhood physical and/or sexual abuse in interviews; 22 did not. Twenty-three of the women were currently diagnosed with major depression; 26 were not. All 49 women were exposed to a stressor that has been shown to induce endocrine and autonomic reactions in a number of studies: The women anticipated and presented a public speech that included some mental arithmetic. Meanwhile, their levels of stress hormones and heart rates were being assessed. As shown in Table 3.7, the presence of depression alone did not distinguish women who were depressed (group B) from women who were not (group A). However, women who reported a history of child abuse (groups C and D) were significantly more likely to show higher blood levels of ACTH and cortisol in response to the stressor

than women who did not report a history of child abuse (groups A and B). Group D, consisting of women who reported a history of abuse and who were also diagnosed with major depression, showed significantly higher levels of stress hormones and heart rate than all other groups. Therefore, the combination of early abuse and current depression apparently makes the body most sensitive to stress. But even among women who were not depressed, the history of abuse was connected with greater reactivity of the endocrine system and autonomic nervous system.

The Heim study has its shortcomings: For example, it categorized women according to self-reported history of child abuse. Not all women in the study could provide independent confirmation of abuse, such as court records. Also, it is unclear how well the stressor used in the experiment represents the types of stress people are actually exposed to in their lives. Nevertheless, the experiment suggests that child abuse may well affect bodily reactivity to stress that endures well into adulthood, and further research along these lines is certainly warranted.

permanence develops during the _____ period of cognitive development. (8) The _____-operational period is characterized by conservation and reversibility. (9) Kohlberg hypothesizes that moral reasoning develops through (how many?) _____ "levels" and two stages within each level. (10) Erikson presents a theory of _____ development. (11) Ainsworth identified three stages of attachment: The _____-_____ phase, which is characterized by indiscriminate attachment, the attachment-in-the-making phase, and the clear-cut-attachment phase. (12) The Harlow studies with monkeys suggest that _____ comfort is more important than conditioning in the development of attachment. (13) Ethologists argue that attachment is an _____ that occurs during a critical period. (14) Baumrind labeled the three most important parenting styles _____, authoritarian, and permissive.

Critical Thinking: Which aspects of child development provide evidence for the concept of stages of development? How does the study by Christine Heim and her colleagues illustrate the ongoing interaction of nature and nurture?

ADOLESCENCE: PHYSICAL, COGNITIVE, AND SOCIAL DEVELOPMENTS

Perhaps no other period of life is as exciting—and as bewildering—as adolescence. Except for infancy, more changes occur during adolescence than during any other time of life.

In our society, adolescents are "neither fish nor fowl," as the saying goes—neither children nor adults. Adolescents may be old enough to reproduce and are as large as their parents, yet they are required to remain in school through age 16, they may not

TABLE 3.7 Responses of Women With or Without a History of Child Abuse to a Stressor

	Women Who Are Not Experiencing a Major Depressive Episode	Women Who Are Experiencing a Major Depressive Episode
Women with No History of Child Abuse	GROUP A—12 WOMEN Endocrine System: ACTH peak: 4.7 parts/liter Cortisol peak: 339 parts/liter Autonomic Nervous System: Heart rate: 78.4/minute	GROUP B—10 WOMEN Endocrine System: ACTH peak: 5.3 parts/liter Cortisol peak: 337 parts/liter Autonomic Nervous System: Heart rate: 83.8/minute
Women with a History of Child Abuse	GROUP C—14 WOMEN Endocrine System: ACTH peak: 9.3 parts/liter Cortisol peak: 359 parts/liter Autonomic Nervous System: Heart rate: 82.2/minute	GROUP D—13 WOMEN Endocrine System: ACTH peak: 12.1 parts/liter Cortisol peak: 527 parts/liter Autonomic Nervous System: Heart rate: 89.7/minute

■ Adolescents

In our culture, adolescents are "neither fish nor fowl." Although they may be old enough to reproduce and may be as large as their parents, they are often treated like children.

be allowed to get drivers' licenses until they are 16 or 17, and they cannot attend R-rated films unless accompanied by an adult. Given the restrictions placed on adolescents, their growing yearning for independence, and a sex drive heightened by high levels of sex hormones, it is not surprising that adolescents occasionally are in conflict with their parents.

This section further chronicles human development with the changes of adolescence. **Adolescence** is a time of transition from childhood to adulthood. Like childhood, adolescence entails physical, cognitive, and social and emotional changes. Let us begin with physical changes.

Physical Development

Following infancy, children grow about 2 to 3 inches a year. Weight gains also remain fairly even at about 4 to 6 pounds per year. *Question: What physical developments occur during adolescence?* One of the most noticeable physical developments of adolescence is a growth spurt. The adolescent growth spurt lasts for 2 to 3 years and ends the stable patterns of growth in height and weight that characterize most of childhood. Within this short span of years, adolescents grow some 8 to 12 inches. Most boys wind up taller and heavier than most girls.

In boys, the weight of the muscle mass increases notably. The width of the shoulders and circumference of the chest also increase. Adolescents may eat enormous quantities of food to fuel their growth spurt. Adults fighting the "battle of the bulge" stare at them in wonder as they wolf down french fries and shakes at the fast-food counter and later go out for pizza.

Puberty: More Than "Just a Phase"?

Puberty is the period during which the body becomes sexually mature. It heralds the onset of adolescence. Puberty begins with the appearance of **secondary sex characteristics** such as body hair, deepening of the voice in males, and rounding of the breasts and hips in females. In boys, pituitary hormones stimulate the testes to increase the output of testosterone, which in turn causes enlargement of the penis and testes and the appearance of body hair. By the early teens, erections become common, and boys may ejaculate. Ejaculatory ability usually precedes the presence of mature sperm by at least a year. Ejaculation thus is not evidence of reproductive capacity.

In girls, a critical body weight in the neighborhood of 100 pounds is thought to trigger a cascade of hormonal secretions in the brain that cause the ovaries to secrete higher levels of the female sex hormone, estrogen (Frisch, 1997). Estrogen stimulates

Adolescence
The period of life bounded by puberty and the assumption of adult responsibilities.

Puberty
The period of physical development during which sexual reproduction first becomes possible.

Secondary Sex Characteristics
Characteristics that distinguish the sexes, such as distribution of body hair and depth of voice, but that are not directly involved in reproduction.

the growth of breast tissue and fatty and supportive tissue in the hips and buttocks. Thus the pelvis widens, rounding the hips. Small amounts of androgens produced by the adrenal glands, along with estrogen, spur the growth of pubic and underarm hair. Estrogen and androgens together stimulate the development of female sex organs. Estrogen production becomes cyclical during puberty and regulates the menstrual cycle. The beginning of menstruation, or **menarche,** usually occurs between the ages of 11 and 14. Girls cannot become pregnant until they begin to ovulate, however, and ovulation may begin as much as two years after menarche.

Cognitive Development

I am a college student of extremely modest means. Some crazy psychologist interested in something called "formal operational thought" has just promised to pay me $20 if I can make a coherent logical argument for the proposition that the federal government should under no circumstances ever give or lend more to needy college students. Now what could people who believe that possibly say by way of supporting argument? Well, I suppose they could offer this line of reasoning . . .

(Adapted from Flavell et al., 2002)

The adolescent thinker approaches problems very differently from the elementary school child. *Question: What cognitive developments occur during adolescence?* Let us begin to answer this question by comparing the child's thought processes to that of the adolescent. The child sticks to the facts, to concrete reality. Speculating about abstract possibilities and what might be is very difficult. The adolescent, on the other hand, is able to deal with the abstract and the hypothetical. As shown in the above example, adolescents realize that one does not have to believe in the truth or justice of something in order to argue for it (Flavell et al., 2002). In this section we explore some of the cognitive developments of adolescence by referring to the theories of Jean Piaget and Lawrence Kohlberg.

The Stage of Formal Operations

According to Piaget, children typically undergo three stages of cognitive development prior to adolescence: sensorimotor, preoperational, and concrete operational. They develop from infants who respond automatically to their environment to older children who can focus on various aspects of a situation at once and solve complex problems. The stage of **formal operations** is the final stage in Jean Piaget's theory of cognitive development, and it represents cognitive maturity. For many children in Western societies, formal operational thought begins at about the beginning of adolescence—the age of 11 or 12. However, not all individuals enter this stage at this time, and some individuals never reach it.

The major achievements of the stage of formal operations involve classification, logical thought, and the ability to hypothesize. Central features are the ability to think about ideas as well as objects and to group and classify ideas—symbols, statements, entire theories. The flexibility and reversibility of operations, when applied to statements and theories, allow adolescents to follow arguments from premises to conclusions and back again.

Several features of formal operational thought give the adolescent a generally greater capacity to manipulate and appreciate the outer environment and the world of the imagination: hypothetical thinking, the ability to use symbols to stand for symbols, and deductive reasoning.

Formal-operational adolescents (and adults) think abstractly. They become capable of solving geometric problems about circles and squares without reference to what the circles and squares may represent in the real world. Adolescents in this stage derive rules for behavior from general principles and can focus, or center, on many aspects of a situation at once in arriving at judgments and solving problems.

In a sense, it is during the stage of formal operations that adolescents tend to emerge as theoretical scientists—even though they may see themselves as having little

R E F L E C T
Did you go through a phase of adolescence during which you thought you "knew it all"? Why do you think that happened?

 Learning Connections
See the Connections *CD-ROM for an animation on the formal-operational stage.*

Menarche
The beginning of menstruation.

Formal-Operational Stage
Piaget's fourth stage, characterized by abstract logical thought; deduction from principles.

Imaginary Audience
An aspect of adolescent egocentrism; the belief that other people are as concerned with our thoughts and behaviors as we are.

or no interest in science. They become capable of dealing with hypothetical situations. They realize that situations can have different outcomes, and they think ahead, experimenting with different possibilities. Adolescents also conduct experiments to determine whether their hypotheses are correct. These experiments are not conducted in the laboratory. Rather, adolescents may try out different tones of voice, ways of carrying themselves, and of treating others to see what works best for them.

Adolescent Egocentrism: "You Just Don't Understand!"

Adolescents in the formal operational stage can reason deductively, or draw conclusions about specific objects or people once they have been classified accurately. Adolescents can be somewhat proud of their new logical abilities, and so a new sort of egocentrism can develop in which adolescents emotionally press for acceptance of their logic without recognizing the exceptions or practical problems that are often considered by adults. Consider this example: "It is wrong to hurt people. Company A occasionally hurts people" (perhaps through pollution or economic pressures). "Therefore, Company A must be severely punished or shut down." This thinking is logical. By impatiently pressing for immediate major changes or severe penalties, however, one may not fully consider various practical problems such as the thousands of workers who would be laid off if the company were shut down. Adults frequently have undergone life experiences that lead them to see shades of gray in situations, rather than just black or white.

The thought of preschoolers is characterized by egocentrism in which they cannot take another's point of view. Adolescent thought is marked by another sort of egocentrism, in which they can understand the thoughts of others but still have trouble separating things that are of concern to others and those that are of concern only to themselves (Elkind, 1967, 1985). Adolescent egocentrism gives rise to two interesting cognitive developments: *the imaginary audience* and the *personal fable*.

The concept of the **imaginary audience** refers to the belief that other people are as concerned with our thoughts and behavior as we are. As a result, adolescents see themselves as the center of attention and assume that other people are about as preoccupied with their appearance and behavior as they are (Milstead et al., 1993). Adolescents may feel they are on stage and all eyes are focused on them.

The concept of the imaginary audience may fuel the intense adolescent desire for privacy. It helps explain why adolescents are so self-conscious about their appearance, why they worry about every facial blemish and spend long hours grooming. Self-consciousness seems to peak at about the age of 13 and then decline. Girls tend to be more self-conscious than boys (Elkind & Bowen, 1979).

REFLECT

Did you have an intense need for privacy as an adolescent? How do you explain that need in terms of Piaget's theory?

■ **Adolescent Self-Consciousness**
The concept of the imaginary audience may help explain why adolescents are self-conscious about their appearance, why they worry about minor facial imperfections, and why they devote so much time to grooming.

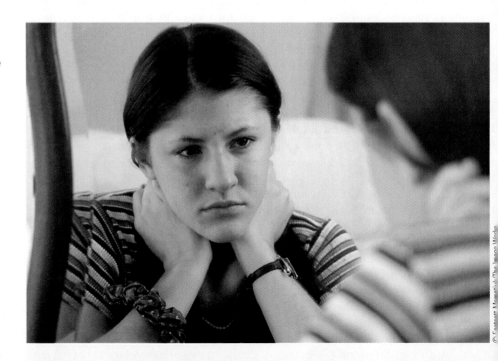

The **personal fable** is the belief that our feelings and ideas are special, even unique, and that we are invulnerable. The personal fable seems to underlie adolescent behavior patterns such as showing off and taking risks (Cohn et al., 1995; Milstead et al., 1993). Some adolescents adopt an "It can't happen to me" attitude; they assume they can smoke without risk of cancer or engage in sexual activity without risk of sexually transmitted infections (STIs) or pregnancy. "All youth—rich, poor, black, white—have this sense of invincibility, invulnerability," says Ronald King (2000) of the HIV Community Coalition of Washington, DC, explaining why many teens who apparently know the risks still expose themselves to HIV. Another aspect of the personal fable is the idea that no one else has experienced or can understand one's "unique" feelings such as needing independence or being in love. The personal fable may underlie the common teenage lament, "You just don't understand me!"

R E F L E C T

Do you know adolescents who act as if they believe that they will live forever? Why do adolescents think like this?

Evaluation of Piaget's Theory

A number of questions have been raised concerning the accuracy of Piaget's views. (For a quick review of his theory of cognitive development, see Table 3.1 on page 96.) Among them are these:

- *Was Piaget's timing accurate?* Some critics argue that Piaget's methods led him to underestimate children's abilities (Bjorklund, 2000; Meltzoff & Gopnik, 1997). Other researchers using different methods have found, for example, that preschoolers are less egocentric and that children are capable of conservation at earlier ages than Piaget thought.
- *Does cognitive development occur in stages?* Cognitive events such as egocentrism and conservation appear to develop more continuously than Piaget thought—that is, they may not occur in stages (Bjorklund, 2000; Flavell, 2000). Although cognitive developments appear to build on previous cognitive developments, the process may be more gradual than stagelike.
- *Are developmental sequences always the same?* Here, Piaget's views have fared better. It seems there is no variation in the sequence in which cognitive developments occur.

In sum, Piaget's theoretical edifice has been rocked, but it has not been reduced to rubble. Psychologist Andrew Meltzoff believes that "Piaget's theories were critical for getting the field of [cognitive development] off the ground, . . . but it's time to move on" (1997, p. 9). Some psychologists are moving on to *information processing*. That is, they view children (and adults) as akin to computer systems. Children, like computers, obtain information (receive "input") from their environment, store it, retrieve, manipulate it (think about it), and then respond to it overtly in terms of their behavior (produce "output") (Bjorklund, 2000). One goal of the information-processing approach is to learn just how children do these things, how their "mental programs" develop. Critical issues involve children's capacity for memory and their use of cognitive strategies, such as the ways in which they focus their attention (Bjorklund, 2000; Case, 1992; Kail, 2000). The future of cognitive development remains to be written.

The Postconventional Level of Moral Reasoning

Kohlberg's theory of moral reasoning involves three levels: preconventional, conventional, and postconventional (see Table 3.3 on page 102). Individuals can arrive at the same decision—for example, as to whether or not Heinz should save his wife by taking the drug without paying for it—but they would be doing so for a different kind of reason. (Deciding not to take the drug for fear of punishment is cognitively less complex than not taking the drug because of the belief that doing so could have negative consequences for the social order.)

None of Kohlberg's levels is tied precisely to a person's age. Although postconventional reasoning is the highest level, for example, most adolescents and adults reason conventionally. However, when postconventional reasoning does emerge, it usually does so in adolescence. Kohlberg's (1969) research showed that postconventional moral judgments were clearly absent among the 7- to 10-year-olds. But by age 16, stage 5 reasoning is shown by about 20% of adolescents, and stage 6 reasoning is shown by about 5% of adolescents.

R E F L E C T

Can you think of situations—historic or current—in which people have had to break the law in order to do the right thing? Can you think of situations in which people have done the wrong thing by following the law?

Postconventional Level

Postconventional Level
According to Kohlberg, a period during which moral judgments are derived from moral principles and people look to themselves to set moral standards.

At the **postconventional level,** moral reasoning is based on the person's own moral standards. In each instance, moral judgments are derived from personal values, not from conventional standards or authority figures. In the contractual, legalistic orientation characteristic of stage 5, it is recognized that laws stem from agreed-upon procedures and that the rule of law is in general good for society; therefore, laws should not be violated. But under exceptional circumstances laws cannot bind the individual. (Although it is illegal for Heinz to steal the drug, in this case it is the right thing to do.)

Stage 6 moral reasoning demands adherence to supposed universal ethical principles such as the sanctity of human life, individual dignity, justice, and the Golden Rule ("Do unto others as you would have them do unto you"). If a law is unjust or contradicts the rights of the individual, it is wrong to obey it.

People at the postconventional level look to their conscience as the highest moral authority. This point has created confusion. To some it suggests that it is right to break the law when it is convenient. But this interpretation is incorrect. Kohlberg means that people at this level of moral reasoning must do what they believe is right even if this action runs counter to social rules or laws or requires personal sacrifice.

Evaluation of Kohlberg's Theory

For a quick review of Kohlberg's theory, see Table 3.3 on page 102. Consistent with Kohlberg's theory, research suggests that moral reasoning does follow a developmental sequence (Dawson, 2002), even though most people do not reach the level of postconventional thought. Postconventional thought, when found, first occurs during adolescence. It also seems that Piaget's stage of formal operations is a prerequisite for postconventional reasoning, which requires the capacities to understand abstract moral principles and to empathize with the attitudes and emotional responses of other people (Flavell et al., 2002).

Also consistent with Kohlberg's theory, children do not appear to skip stages as they progress (Flavell et al., 2002). Classic research shows that when children are exposed to adult models who exhibit a lower stage of moral reasoning, they can be enticed to follow along (Bandura & McDonald, 1963). Children who are exposed to examples of moral reasoning above and below their own stage generally prefer the higher stage, however (Rest, 1983). The thrust of moral development would therefore appear to be from lower to higher in terms of Kohlberg's levels and stages, even if children can be influenced by the opinions of others.

▶ CONTROVERSY IN PSYCHOLOGY ◀

Are there gender differences in moral development?

A number of studies using Heinz's dilemma found that boys show higher levels of moral reasoning than girls. But Carol Gilligan (1982; Gilligan et al., 1989) argues that this gender difference reflects different patterns of socialization for boys and girls—not differences in morality. Gilligan points to 11-year-old Jake. Jake weighs the scales of justice like a math problem. He shows that life is worth more than property and concludes that it is Heinz's duty to steal the drug (stage 4 reasoning). Gilligan also points to 11-year-old Amy. Amy vacillates. Amy says that stealing the drug and letting Heinz's wife die are both wrong. So Amy looks for alternatives, such as getting a loan, because it wouldn't help Heinz's wife if he went to jail.

Gilligan finds Amy's reasoning to be as sophisticated as Jake's, yet Amy would be rated as showing a lower level of moral development in Kohlberg's scheme. Gilligan asserts that Amy and other girls are socialized to focus on the needs of others and forgo simplistic judgments of right and wrong. Amy is therefore more likely to show stage 3 reasoning, which focuses in part on empathy—on caring for others. Jake has been socialized to make judgments based on logic. To him, clear-cut conclusions are derived from premises.

We could argue endlessly about which form of moral reasoning—Jake's or Amy's—is "higher." Instead, let us point to a meta-analysis of the research in the area that shows that there is only a slight tendency for boys to favor Jake's "justice" approach, and a slight tendency for girls to favor Amy's "caring" approach (Jaffee & Hyde, 2000). We cannot say that the justice orientation is used predominantly by boys, or the care orientation predominantly by girls.

Social and Emotional Development

Adolescents also differ markedly from children in their social and emotional development. *Question: What social and emotional developments occur during adolescence?* In terms of social and emotional development, adolescence has been associated with turbulence. In the 19th century, psychologist G. Stanley Hall described adolescence as a time of *Sturm und Drang*—storm and stress. More current views challenge the assumption that "storm and stress" is normal for adolescents (Griffin, 2001). Jeffrey Arnett (1999) argues that that we need to take individual differences and cultural variations into consideration. He notes that not all adolescents experience storm and stress but admits that, for those who do, it is most likely to occur during adolescence.

Certainly, many American teenagers abuse drugs, get pregnant, contract STIs, become involved in violence, fail in school, even attempt suicide (CDC, 2000b). The U.S. Centers for Disease Control and Prevention regularly survey the behavior of young people in an effort to uncover risks to health. The CDC (2000b) reported that 72% of all deaths among people aged 10 to 24 years result from only four causes: motor-vehicle crashes (31%), other unintentional injuries (11%), homicide (18%), and suicide (12%). Numerous high school students engage in behaviors that increase their likelihood of death from these four causes:

- 16% rarely or never wear seat belts.
- 33% ride with drivers who have been drinking alcohol.
- 17% carry weapons.
- 50% drank alcohol during the 30 days preceding the survey.
- 27% used marijuana during the 30 days preceding the survey.
- 8% attempted suicide during the 12 months preceding the survey.

Statistics collected on the behavior of high school students revealed that:

- 50% had engaged in sexual intercourse.
- 42% of the sexually active students did not use a condom during their last sexual encounter.
- 2% had injected an illegal drug.

Two-thirds of all deaths among people aged 25 and above result from two causes: cardiovascular disease and cancer. The majority of risk behaviors associated with these two causes of death are initiated during adolescence. For example, 35% of high school students had smoked cigarettes within the past 30 days; 76% did not eat enough fruits and vegetables; 16% were at risk for becoming overweight; and 71% did not exercise regularly.

Hall attributed the conflicts and distress of adolescence to biological changes. Research evidence suggests that hormonal changes affect the activity levels, mood swings, and aggressive tendencies of many adolescents, but that sociocultural influences have a relatively greater impact (Buchanan et al., 1992).

Striving for Independence

Adolescents do try to become more independent from their parents, which often leads to some bickering (Smetana & Gaines, 1999). They usually bicker about issues such as homework, chores, money, appearance, curfews, and dating (Galambos & Turner, 1999). Arguments are common when adolescents want to make their own choices about matters such as clothes and friends.

The striving for independence is also characterized by withdrawal from family life, at least relative to prior involvement. In one study, children ranging in age from 9 to 15 carried electronic pagers for a week so that they could report what they were doing and whom they were with when signaled (Larson & Richards, 1991). The amount of time spent with family members decreased dramatically with greater age. The 15-year-

■ **Adolescent Relationships with Parents**

Adolescents strive for some independence from their parents, including some distancing. But most adolescents continue to feel love, respect, and loyalty toward their parents. Adolescents and parents also tend to share social, political, religious, and economic views.

Ego Identity

Erikson's term for a firm sense of who one is and what one stands for.

Role Diffusion

Erikson's term for lack of clarity in one's life roles (due to failure to develop ego identity).

R E F L E C T

Have you yet formed your own ego identity? If so, what was the process like? If not, are you concerned? Why or why not?

olds spent only half as much time with their families as the 9-year-olds. Yet this change does not mean that most adolescents spend their time on the streets. For 15-year-old boys in the study, time with the family tended to be replaced by time spent alone. For older girls, this time was divided between friends and solitude.

Adolescents and parents are often in conflict because adolescents experiment with many things that can be harmful to their health. Yet—apparently because of the personal fable—adolescents often do not perceive such activities to be as risky as their parents see them as being. Lawrence Cohn and his colleagues (1995) found, for example, that parents perceived drinking, smoking, failure to use seat belts, drag racing, and a number of other activities to be riskier than did their teenagers (see Table 3.8).

Some distancing from parents is beneficial for adolescents (Galambos & Turner, 1999). After all, they do have to form relationships outside the family. But greater independence does not necessarily mean that adolescents become emotionally detached from their parents or fall completely under the influence of their peers. Most adolescents continue to feel love, respect, and loyalty toward their parents (Eberly & Montemayor, 1999). Adolescents who feel close to their parents actually show greater self-reliance and independence than do those who are distant from their parents. Adolescents who retain close ties with their parents also fare better in school and have fewer adjustment problems (Steinberg, 1996).

Despite parent–adolescent conflict over issues of control, parents and adolescents tend to share social, political, religious, and economic views (Sagrestano et al., 1999). In sum, there are frequent differences between parents and adolescents on issues of personal control. However, there apparently is no "generation gap" on broader matters.

Ego Identity Versus Role Diffusion: "Who Am I?"

According to Erik Erikson, individuals undergo eight stages of psychosocial development, each of which is characterized by a certain kind of "crisis." (See Table 3.4 on page 103.) Four of these stages, beginning with the stage of trust versus mistrust, occur during the years of childhood. The fifth stage, that of *ego identity versus role diffusion*, occurs during adolescence. The major challenge of adolescence is the creation of an adult identity. Identity is achieved mainly by committing oneself to a particular occupation or a role in life. But identity also extends to sexual, political, and religious beliefs and commitments.

Erikson (1963) theorized that adolescents experience a life crisis of ego identity versus role diffusion. **Ego identity** is a firm sense of who one is and what one stands for. It can carry one through difficult times and give meaning to one's achievements. Adolescents who do not develop ego identity may experience **role diffusion.** They spread

TABLE 3.8 Mean Ratings of Perceived Harmfulness of Various Activities

Activity	Experimental Involvement (doing activity once or twice to see what it is like)		Frequent Involvement	
	Teenager	Teenager's Parents	Teenager	Teenager's Parents
Drinking alcohol	2.6	3.5	4.4	4.8
Smoking cigarettes	3.0	3.6	4.4	4.8
Using diet pills	2.8	3.8	4.1	4.7
Not using seat belts	3.0	4.3	4.0	4.8
Getting drunk	3.2	4.2	4.4	4.8
Sniffing glue	3.6	4.6	4.6	4.9
Driving home after drinking a few beers	3.8	4.5	4.6	4.8
Drag racing	3.8	4.6	4.5	4.8
Using steroids	3.8	4.4	4.7	4.9

themselves too thin, running down one blind alley after another and placing themselves at the mercy of leaders who promise to give them the sense of identity that they cannot find for themselves.

Adolescent Sexuality—When? What? (How?) Who? Where? and Why?—Not to Mention "Should I?"

My first sexual experience occurred in a car after the high school junior prom. We were both virgins, very uncertain but very much in love. We had been going together since eighth grade. The experience was somewhat painful. I remember wondering if I would look different to my mother the next day. I guess I didn't because nothing was said.

(Adapted from Morrison et al., 1980, p. 108)

Although adolescents may not form enduring romantic relationships or be able to support themselves, the changes of puberty ready their bodies for sexual activity. High hormone levels also stir interest in sex. Adolescents therefore wrestle with issues of how and when to express their awakening sexuality. To complicate matters, Western culture sends mixed messages about sex. Teenagers may be advised to wait until they have married or at least entered into meaningful relationships, but they are also bombarded by sexual messages in films, TV and radio commercials, print advertising, and virtually every other medium. All in all, about half of U.S. high school students have engaged in sexual intercourse (CDC, 2000b).

Adolescent girls and boys usually obtain little advice at home or in school about how to handle their emerging sexuality. Fewer than half of sexually active adolescents use contraceptives reliably (CDC, 2000b). As a result, about 800,000 teenage girls get pregnant each year, resulting in 500,000 births (CDC, 2000d). Nearly 3 million American teenage boys and girls contract a sexually transmitted infection (STI) each year (CDC, 2000b).

Why is teenage pregnancy so common? Most girls become pregnant because they and their partner misunderstand reproduction and contraception or miscalculate the odds of conception. Even those who are well-informed about contraception often do not use it consistently. Peers also play an important role in determining the sexual behavior of adolescents. When teenagers are asked why they do not wait to have sexual intercourse until they are older, the top reason cited is usually peer pressure (Dickson et al., 1998).

The medical, social, and economic costs of unplanned teenage pregnancies are enormous to teenage parents and their children. Teenage mothers are more likely to have medical complications during pregnancy and to have prolonged labor. Their babies are more likely to be born prematurely and to have low birth weight. It appears that these medical problems are largely due not to the young age of the mother but to the inadequate prenatal care and poor nutrition obtained by teenage mothers living in poverty (Fraser et al., 1995).

Teenage parents are also less likely to graduate from high school or attend college (CDC, 2000b). Their lack of educational achievement leads to a lower standard of living and a greater need for public assistance. Few receive consistent financial or emotional help from the babies' fathers, who generally are unable to support themselves, let alone a family.

Still, there is encouraging news. The final decade of the 20th century saw a decline in the teenage pregnancy rate because of increased use of contraception and a leveling off of sexual activity among teenagers (CDC, 2000b). The teenage pregnancy rate was falling (CDC, 2000b). CDC researchers attribute the decrease in risky sexual behavior to educational campaigns in the schools, the media, churches, and communities.

REFLECT

How important a part of your adolescence (or that of your peers) was sexuality? Did any of your peers experience problems related to their sexuality during adolescence? Did they resolve these problems? If so, how?

REVIEW

(15) Puberty begins with the appearance of _____ sex characteristics, such as the growth of body hair, deepening of the voice in males, and rounding of the breasts and hips in females. (16) The changes of puberty are stimulated by _____ in the male and by estrogen and androgens in the female. (17) _____ operational

Learning Connections
See Web site for an interactive version of these review questions.

thought is characterized by hypothetical thinking and deductive logic. (18) Adolescent egocentrism gives rise to the _____ audience and the personal fable. (19) In stage 6 moral reasoning, people consider behavior that is consistent with _____ ethical standards as right. (20) G. Stanley Hall described adolescence as a time of *Sturm und Drang*—storm and _____. (21) Erik Erikson considers the life crisis of adolescence to be ego identity versus role _____.

Critical Thinking: Can you make the case that adolescence is a distinct stage of life? Explain.

ADULTHOOD: PHYSICAL, COGNITIVE, AND SOCIAL DEVELOPMENTS

Development continues throughout the lifespan. Many theorists believe that adult concerns and involvements follow observable patterns, so that we can speak of "stages" of adult development. Others argue that there may no longer be a standard life cycle with predictable stages or phases. Age now has an "elastic quality" (Butler, 1998). People are living longer than ever before and are freer than ever to choose their own destiny.

Physical Development

The most obvious aspects of development during adulthood are physical. *Question: What physical developments occur during adulthood?* Let us consider the physical developments that take place in young, or early, adulthood, which covers the period between the ages of 20 and 40; middle adulthood, which spans the ages of about 45 to 65; and late adulthood, which begins at 65.

Young Adulthood

Physical development peaks in young adulthood. Most people are at their height of sensory sharpness, strength, reaction time, and cardiovascular fitness. Women gymnasts find themselves going downhill in their early 20s because they accumulate body fat and lose suppleness and flexibility. Other athletes are more likely to experience a decline in their 30s. Most athletes retire before they reach 40.

Sexually speaking, most people in early adulthood become readily aroused. They tend to attain and maintain erections as desired and to lubricate readily. A man in his 20s is more likely to be concerned about ejaculating too quickly than about whether or not he will be able to obtain an erection.

Middle Adulthood

As we enter our middle years, we are unlikely to possess the strength, coordination, and stamina that we had during our 20s and 30s. The decline is most obvious in the professional sports ranks, where peak performance is at a premium. Gordie Howe still played hockey at 50 and George Blanda was still kicking field goals at that age, but most professionals at those ages can no longer keep up with the "kids."

But the years between 40 and 60 are reasonably stable. There is gradual physical decline, but it is minor and only likely to be of concern if we insist on competing with young adults—or with idealized memories of ourselves (Morley & van den Berg, 2000). And many of us first make time to develop our physical potentials during middle adulthood. The 20-year-old couch potato occasionally becomes the 50-year-old marathoner. By any reasonable standard, we can maintain excellent cardiorespiratory condition throughout middle adulthood.

Because the physical decline in middle adulthood is gradual, people who begin to eat more nutritious diets (e.g., decrease intake of fats and increase intake of fruits and vegetables) and to exercise during this stage of life may find themselves looking and feeling better than they did in young adulthood. Sedentary people in young adulthood may gasp for air if they rush half a block to catch a bus, whereas fit people in middle adulthood—even in late adulthood—may run for miles before they feel fatigued.

Menopause usually occurs during the late 40s or early 50s (see Chapter 2's "Life Connections" section). It is the final phase of the *climacteric*, which is caused by a decline in the secretion of female sex hormones. Ovulation also comes to an end. There is some loss of breast tissue and of elasticity in the skin. Loss of bone density can lead to osteoporosis (brittle bones). During the climacteric, many women experience hot flashes, loss of sleep, and some anxiety and depression. By and large, a woman's adjustment to menopause reflects the intensity of the physical symptoms and the extent to which her self-concept was wrapped up with her reproductive capacity. But, as noted in Chapter 2, most women have little or no problem getting through this transition.

Late Adulthood

Did you know that an *agequake* is coming? With improved health care and knowledge of the importance of diet and exercise, more Americans than ever before are 65 or older (Abeles, 1997). In 1900, only 1 American in 30 was over 65, compared with 1 in 9 in 1970. By 2030, 1 American in 5 will be 65 or older ("Longer, healthier, better," 1997; see Figure 3.9).

Various changes—some of them troublesome—do occur during the later years (Figure 3.10). Changes in calcium metabolism lead to increased brittleness in the bones and heightened risk of breaks due to accidents such as falls. The skin becomes less elastic and subject to wrinkles and folds. Older people see and hear less acutely. Because of a decline in the sense of smell, they may use more spice to flavor their food. Older people need more time (called **reaction time**) to respond to stimuli. Older drivers, for example, need more time to respond to traffic lights, other vehicles, and changing road conditions. As we grow older, our immune system also functions less effectively, leaving us more vulnerable to disease. These changes ultimately result in death.

Age-related changes in the nervous system increase reaction time—the amount of time it takes to respond to a stimulus. Older people cannot catch rapidly moving baseballs or footballs or dodge other cars as easily when driving.

Age-related changes affect sexual functioning as well as other areas of functioning. Yet people are capable of enjoying sexual experience for a lifetime, if they remain generally healthy and adjust their expectations.

Theories of Aging

Although it may be hard to believe it will happen to us, every person who has walked the earth so far has aged—which may not be a bad fate, considering the alternative. *Question: Why do we age?* Various factors, some of which are theoretical, apparently contribute to aging.

The theory of **programmed senescence** sees aging as determined by a biological clock that ticks at a rate governed by instructions in the genes. Just as genes program children to grow and reach sexual maturation, they program people to deteriorate and die. There is evidence to support a role for genes in aging. Longevity runs in families. People whose parents and grandparents lived into their 80s and 90s have a better chance of reaching these ages themselves.

Breaks in the strands of genetic material—DNA—that guide our development and help maintain our well-being are common enough throughout our lifetime, but they are repaired better when we are young (Roth & Gellert, 2000). As we age, our genetic codes tend to stray from their original design, permitting the development of cancer and other health problems.

■ **Figure 3.9**
Living Longer

In the third millennium, more people than ever in the United States are living to be age 65 or above. The increased effects of the presence of older people on financial and cultural institutions has been referred to as an "agequake."

Percentage of the U.S. population 65 or older

Percentage of the U.S. population under 65

Menopause
The cessation of menstruation.

Reaction Time
The amount of time required to respond to a stimulus.

Programmed Senescence
The view that aging is determined by a biological clock that ticks at a rate governed by genes.

■ **Figure 3.10**
The Relentless March of Time

A number of physical changes occur during the later years. However, the reasons for aging are not yet completely understood. People can also affect the pace of their aging by eating properly, exercising, maintaining a positive outlook, and finding and meeting challenges that are consistent with their abilities.

Power Visual
See Web site for an interactive version of this figure.

Hair and nails
Hair often turns gray and thins out. Men may go bald. Fingernails can thicken.

Brain
The brain shrinks, but it is not known if that affects mental functions.

The senses
The sensitivity of hearing, sight, taste, and smell can all decline with age.

Skin
Wrinkles occur as the skin thins and the underlying fat shrinks, and age spots often crop up.

Glands and hormones
Levels of many hormones drop, or the body becomes less responsive to them.

Immune system
The body becomes less able to resist some pathogens.

Lungs
It doesn't just seem harder to climb those stairs; lung capacity drops.

Heart and blood vessels
Cardiovascular problems become more common.

Muscles
Strength usually peaks in the 20s, then declines.

Kidneys and urinary tract
The kidneys become less efficient. The bladder can't hold as much, so urination is more frequent.

Digestive system
Digestion slows down as the secretion of digestive enzymes decreases.

Reproductive system
Women go through menopause, and testosterone levels drop for men.

Bones and joints
Wear and tear can lead to arthritic joints, and osteoporosis is common, especially in women.

Wear-and-Tear Theory
The view that factors such as pollution, disease, and ultraviolet light contribute to wear and tear on the body, so that the body loses the ability to repair itself.

The **wear-and-tear theory** does not suggest that people are programmed to self-destruct. Instead, environmental factors such as pollution, disease, and ultraviolet light are assumed to contribute to wear and tear on the body over time. The body is like a machine whose parts wear out through use. Wear and tear saps cells of the ability to regenerate themselves, and vital organs are worn down.

Research with roundworms can be said to support both the programmed senescence and wear-and-tear theories (Wolkow et al., 2000). Genetically determined messages from the brain may determine the timing of growth and development. However, the brain cells become damaged in part because of damaging effects of by-products of metabolism ("free radicals"). Then the body begins to decay.

Behavior also influences aging. Smoking, overeating, stress, and risky behavior can contribute to an early death. Fortunately, we can control some of these factors.

Americans are living longer than ever. Part of the reason is that many of them are taking charge of their own lives, influencing not only how long they live, but how well they live (Clay, 2000). Regular medical evaluations, proper diet (for example, consuming less fat), and exercise all help people live longer.

Exercise helps older people maintain flexibility and cardiovascular condition. The exercise need not be of the type that pounds the body and produces rivers of sweat. Because older people tend to have more brittle bones and more rigid joints, fast or prolonged walking is an excellent aerobic choice.

Amy Hakim of the University of Virginia School of Medicine and her colleagues (1998) provided dramatic evidence of the value of exercise—in this case, walking—for older people. They reviewed 12 years of data on 707 retired men from the Honolulu Heart Program and found that 43.1% of the men who walked less than a mile per day died during that period, as compared with 27.7% of those who walked from 1 to 2 miles a day and 21.5% of those who walked at least 2 miles daily. Additional findings: 6.6% of the men who walked less than a mile a day died from coronary heart disease or strokes, as compared with only 2.1% of those who walked upwards of 2 miles (see Figure 3.11). Moreover, 13.4% of the men who walked less than a mile died from cancer, as compared with 5.3% of men who walked more than 2 miles a day. Because the study was not experimental, one can ask whether those who walked less died sooner because they were hobbled by health problems that made them less able or willing to walk. Hakim and her colleagues recognized this problem and got around it partly by using data only on nonsmokers who were physically able to walk a few miles. Older people can also continue to fight heart disease and cancer by eating diets low in cholesterol and saturated fats (Wolk et al., 1998).

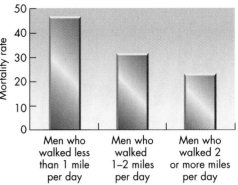

■ **Figure 3.11**
Causes of Death and Distance Walked in Miles Per Day Among Participants in the Honolulu Heart Program

Men who walked more than 2 miles a day had a lower mortality rate than men who walked between 1 and 2 miles a day and men who walked less than a mile a day. Men who took long walks were less likely to die from cancer and heart disease (Hakim et al., 1998).

Cognitive Development

Question: What cognitive developments occur during adulthood? As is the case with physical development, people are also at the height of their cognitive powers during early adulthood. Many professionals show the broadest knowledge of their

A Closer Look ◉

Aging, Gender, and Ethnicity: Different Patterns of Aging

Although Americans in general are living longer, there are gender and ethnic differences in life expectancy. *Question: What are the gender and ethnic differences in life expectancy?* For example, women in our society tend to outlive men by about six years (Health, United States, 2002). European Americans live longer on the average than do Latino and Latina Americans, African Americans, and Native Americans (Health, United States, 2002). Life expectancy for Latino and Latina Americans falls somewhere between the figures for African Americans and European Americans. The longevity of Asian Americans falls closer to that of European Americans than to that of African Americans. Native Americans have the lowest average longevity of the major racial/ethnic groups in the United States.

Why do women in the United States outlive men? For one thing, heart disease, the nation's leading killer, typically develops later in women than in men. Men are also more likely to die because of accidents, cirrhosis of the liver, strokes, suicide, homicide, AIDS, and cancer (Health, United States, 2002).

Many such deaths reflect excessive drinking and reckless behavior.

Many men are also reluctant to have regular physical exams or to talk to their doctors about their health problems. "In their 20s, [men are] too strong to need a doctor; in their 30s, they're too busy, and in their 40s, too scared" (Courtenay, 2000). Women are much more likely to examine themselves for signs of breast cancer than men are even to recognize the early signs of prostate cancer.

Socioeconomic differences play a role in ethnic differences in life expectancy. Members of ethnic minority groups in our society are more likely to be poor, and poor people tend to eat less nutritious diets, encounter more stress, and have less access to health care. There is a seven-year difference in life expectancy between people in the highest income brackets and those in the lowest. Yet other factors, such as cultural differences in diet and lifestyle, the stress of coping with discrimination, and genetic differences, may partly account for ethnic group differences in life expectancy.

fields at about the time they are graduating from college or graduate school. At this time their course work is freshest. They may have just recently studied for comprehensive examinations. Once they enter their fields, they often specialize. As a result, knowledge deepens in certain areas, but understanding of related areas may grow relatively superficial.

Cognitive development in adulthood has many aspects—creativity, memory functioning, and intelligence. People can be creative for a lifetime. At the age of 80, Merce Cunningham choreographed a dance that made use of computer-generated digital images (Teachout, 2000). Hans Hofmann created some of his most vibrant paintings at 85, and Pablo Picasso was painting in his 90s. Grandma Moses did not even begin painting until she was 78 years old. Giuseppe Verdi wrote his joyous opera *Falstaff* at the age of 79. The architect Frank Lloyd Wright designed New York's innovative spiral-shaped Guggenheim Museum when he was 89 years old.

Memory functioning declines with age. It is common enough for older people to have trouble recalling the names of common objects or people they know. Memory lapses can be embarrassing, and older people sometimes lose confidence in their memories, which then lowers their motivation to remember things (Cavanaugh & Green, 1990). But declines in memory are not usually as large as people assume and are often reversible (Villa & Abeles, 2000). Memory tests usually measure ability to recall meaningless information. Older people show better memory functioning in areas in which they can apply their experience, especially their specialties, to new challenges (Graf, 1990). For example, who would do a better job of learning and remembering how to solve problems in chemistry—a college history major or a retired professor of chemistry?

People also obtain the highest intelligence test scores in young adulthood (Baltes, 1997). Yet people tend to retain their verbal skills, as demonstrated by their vocabularies and general knowledge, into advanced old age. It is their performance on tasks that require speed and visual–spatial skills, such as putting puzzles together, that tends to fall off (Schaie, 1994).

Crystallized Versus Fluid Intelligence

Consider the difference between *crystallized intelligence and fluid intelligence.* **Crystallized intelligence** represents one's lifetime of intellectual attainments, as shown by vocabulary and accumulated facts about world affairs. Therefore, crystallized intelligence generally increases over the decades. **Fluid intelligence** is defined as mental flexibility, demonstrated by the ability to process information rapidly, as in learning and solving problems in new areas of endeavor.

In terms of people's worth to their employers, familiarity in solving the kinds of problems found on the job (their crystallized intelligence) may be more important than their fluid intelligence. Experience on the job enhances people's specialized vocabularies and their knowledge of the area. People draw on fluid intelligence when the usual solutions no longer work, but experience is often more valuable than fluid intelligence.

The Seattle Longitudinal Study

Psychologist Walter Schaie and his colleagues (Schaie, 1994) have been studying the cognitive development of adults for four decades and discovered factors that contribute to intellectual functioning across the lifespan:

- *General health.* People in good health tend to retain higher levels of intellectual functioning into late adulthood. Therefore, paying attention to one's diet, exercising, and having regular medical checkups contribute to intellectual functioning as well as physical health.
- *Socioeconomic status (SES).* People with high SES tend to maintain intellectual functioning more adequately than people with low SES. High SES is also connected with above-average income and levels of education, a history of stimulating occupational pursuits, maintenance of intact families, and better health.
- *Stimulating activities.* Cultural events, travel, participation in professional organizations, and extensive reading contribute to intellectual functioning.
- *Marriage to a spouse with a high level of intellectual functioning.* The spouse whose level of intellectual functioning is lower at the beginning of a marriage tends to increase

Crystallized Intelligence
One's lifetime of intellectual achievement, as shown largely through vocabulary and knowledge of world affairs.

Fluid Intelligence
Mental flexibility as shown in learning rapidly to solve new kinds of problems.

in intellectual functioning as time goes by. Perhaps that partner is continually challenged by the other.

- *Openness to new experience.* Being open to new challenges of life apparently helps keep us young—at any age.

Alzheimer's Disease

Questions: What is Alzheimer's disease? What are its origins? **Alzheimer's disease** is a progressive form of mental deterioration that affects about 10% of people over the age of 65 and nearly half of those over the age of 85 (Katzman, 2000). Although Alzheimer's is connected with aging, it is a disease and not a normal part of aging (Haan, 2000).

Alzheimer's disease is characterized by general, gradual deterioration in cognitive processes such as memory, language, and problem solving. As the disease progresses, people may fail to recognize familiar faces or forget their names. At the most severe stage, people with Alzheimer's disease become helpless. They become unable to communicate or walk and require help in toileting and feeding. More isolated memory losses (for example, forgetting where one put one's glasses) may be a normal feature of aging (Abeles, 1997). Alzheimer's, in contrast, seriously impairs vocational and social functioning.

Alzheimer's disease is characterized by reduced levels of the neurotransmitter acetylcholine (ACh) and by the buildup of a sticky plaque in the brain. One form of drug therapy has aimed at boosting ACh levels by slowing its breakdown. This approach achieves modest benefits with many people. The plaque is formed from fragments of a body protein (beta amyloid) (Cotman, 2000; Frangione, 2000). Normally, the immune system prevents the buildup of plaque, but not effectively in the case of people with Alzheimer's disease. Thus another approach to the treatment of Alzheimer's is the development of a vaccine made from beta amyloid that will stimulate the immune system to recognize and attack the plaque more vigorously (Janus et al., 2000; Morgan et al., 2000; Schenk, 2000).

Alzheimer's, as noted, is a disease and does not reflect the normal aging process. However, there are normal, more gradual declines in intellectual functioning and memory among older people (Butler, 1998; Villa & Abeles, 2000). But we understand very little about *why* these declines occur. Depression and losses of sensory acuity and motivation may contribute to lower cognitive test scores. B. F. Skinner (1983) argued that much of the fall-off is due to an "aging environment" rather than an aging person. That is, the behavior of older people often goes unreinforced. This idea is substantiated by a classic study of nursing-home residents who were rewarded for remembering recent events and showed improved scores on tests of memory (Langer et al., 1979).

Social and Emotional Development

Changes in social and emotional development during adulthood are probably the most "elastic" or fluid. These changes are clearly affected by cultural expectations and individual behavior patterns. As a result, there is so much variety that it can be misleading to expect that any individual will follow a particular pattern. Nevertheless, many developmental theorists suggest that there are enough commonalities that we can speak of trends. One trend that will become obvious, however, is that the outlook for older people has become much more optimistic over the past generation—not only because of medical advances but also because the behavior and mental processes of many older people are remaining younger than at any other time in history.

There is more good news. Research evidence suggests that people tend to grow psychologically healthier as they advance from adolescence through middle adulthood. Psychologists Constance Jones and William Meredith (2000) studied information on 236 participants in California growth studies who had been followed from early adolescence for about 50 years and found that they generally became more productive and had better interpersonal relationships as the years went on. Certainly there are individual differences, but many individuals, even some with a turbulent adolescence,

Alzheimer's Disease
(AHLTS-high-mers). A progressive form of mental deterioration characterized by loss of memory, language, problem solving, and other cognitive functions.

Dream

In this usage, Levinson's term for the overriding drive of youth to become someone important, to leave one's mark on history.

Intimacy Versus Isolation

Erikson's life crisis of young adulthood, which is characterized by the task of developing abiding intimate relationships.

Age-30 Transition

Levinson's term for the ages from 28 to 33, which are characterized by reassessment of the goals and values of the 20s.

R E F L E C T

Where do you fit into the chronicle of the adult years? Do events in your own life fit with any of the research findings or theories presented in this chapter?

■ **Establishing Intimate Relationships**

According to Erik Erikson, establishing intimate relationships is a central task of young adulthood.

showed dramatically better psychological health at age 62 than they had half a century earlier.

Young Adulthood

Question: What social and emotional developments occur during young adulthood? Many theorists suggest that young adulthood is the period of life during which people tend to establish themselves as independent members of society.

At some point during the 20s, many people become fueled by ambition. Many strive to advance in their careers. Those who seek professional careers may spend much of their 20s acquiring the skills that will enable them to succeed in them (Levinson et al., 1978; Levinson, 1996). It is largely during the 20s that people become generally responsible for their own support, make their own choices, and are free from parental influences. Many young adults adopt what theorist Daniel Levinson and his colleagues (1978) call the **dream**—the drive to "become" someone, to leave their mark on history—which serves as a tentative blueprint for their life.

During young adulthood, people tend to leave their families of origin and to create families of their own. Erik Erikson (1963) characterized young adulthood as the stage of **intimacy versus isolation.** (For a summary of Erikson's stages, see Table 3.4 on page 103.) Erikson saw the establishment of intimate relationships as central to young adulthood. Young adults who have evolved a firm sense of identity during adolescence are ready to "fuse" their identities with those of other people through marriage and abiding friendships. People who do not reach out to develop intimate relationships risk retreating into isolation and loneliness.

Erikson warned that we may not be able to commit ourselves to others until we have achieved ego identity—that is, established stable life roles. Achieving ego identity is the central task of adolescence. Lack of personal stability is connected with the high divorce rate for teenage marriages.

Levinson labeled the ages of 28 to 33 the **age-30 transition.** For men and women, the late 20s and early 30s are commonly characterized by reassessment: "Where is my life going?" "Why am I doing this?" During our 30s, we often find that the lifestyles we adopted during our 20s do not fit as comfortably as we had expected.

Many psychologists find that the later 30s are characterized by settling down or planting roots. Many young adults feel a need to make a financial and emotional

© Richard Lord

investment in their home. Their concerns become more focused on promotion or tenure, career advancement, and long-term mortgages.

Middle Adulthood

There are also a number of key changes in social and emotional development that tend to occur during middle adulthood.   *Question: What social and emotional developments occur during middle adulthood?*   Consider Erikson's views on the middle years.

Erikson (1963) labeled the life crisis of the middle years **generativity versus stagnation.** Generativity involves doing things that we believe are worthwhile, such as rearing children or producing on the job. Generativity enhances and maintains self-esteem. Generativity also involves helping to shape the new generation. This shaping may involve rearing our own children or making the world a better place, for example, through joining church or civic groups. Stagnation means treading water, as in keeping the same job at the same pay for 30 years, or even moving backward, as in moving into a less responsible and poorer-paying job or removing oneself from rearing one's children. Stagnation has powerful destructive effects on self-esteem.

According to Levinson and colleagues (1978), whose research involved case studies of 40 men, there is a **midlife transition** at about age 40 to 45 characterized by a shift in psychological perspective. Previously, men had thought of their age in terms of the number of years that had elapsed since birth. Now they begin to think of their age in terms of the number of years they have left. Men in their 30s still think of themselves as older brothers to "kids" in their 20s. At about age 40 to 45, however, some marker event—illness, a change of job, the death of a friend or parent, or being beaten at tennis by their son—leads men to realize that they are a full generation older. Suddenly there seems to be more to look back on than forward to. It dawns on men that they will never be president or chairperson of the board. They will never play shortstop for the Dodgers. They mourn the passing of their own youth and begin to adjust to the specter of old age and the finality of death.

There are gender differences. Research suggests that women may undergo a midlife transition a number of years earlier than men do (Stewart & Ostrove, 1998). Why? Much of it has to do with the winding down of the "biological clock"—that is, the abilities to conceive and bear children. For example, once they turn 35, women are usually advised to have their fetuses routinely tested for Down syndrome and other chromosomal disorders. At age 35, women also enter higher risk categories for side effects from birth control pills. Yet many women today are having children in their 40s and, now and then, beyond.

According to Levinson, the midlife transition may trigger a crisis—the **midlife crisis.** The middle-level, middle-aged businessperson looking ahead to another 10 to 20 years of grinding out accounts in a Wall Street cubbyhole may encounter severe depression. The housewife with two teenagers, an empty house from 8:00 AM to 4:00 PM, and a 40th birthday on the way may feel that she is coming apart at the seams. Both feel a sense of entrapment and loss of purpose. Some people are propelled into extramarital affairs by the desire to prove to themselves that they are still attractive.

Yet many Americans find that these years present opportunities for new direction and fulfillment. Many people are at the height of their productive powers during this period. Many or most of today's robust 45- to 55-year-olds can look forward to another 30 to 40 healthy years. Yet some people in this age group experience what Stewart and Ostrove (1998) refer to as a midcourse correction. And why not? Many decades remain for self-fulfillment.

Women frequently experience a renewed sense of self in their 40s and 50s. Women in their early 40s are more likely than women in their early 30s to feel confident; to exert an influence on their community; to feel secure and committed; to feel productive, effective, and powerful; and to extend their interests beyond their family (Helson et al., 1995; Stewart & Ostrove, 1998).

Generativity Versus Stagnation
Erikson's term for the crisis of middle adulthood, characterized by the task of being productive and contributing to younger generations.

Midlife Transition
Levinson's term for the ages from 40 to 45, which are characterized by a shift in psychological perspective from viewing ourselves in terms of years lived to viewing ourselves in terms of the years we have left.

Midlife Crisis
A crisis experienced by many people during the midlife transition when they realize that life may be more than halfway over and reassess their achievements in terms of their dreams.

■ Midlife Crisis or Midcourse Correction?

Many middle-aged people undergo a second quest for identity (the first occurs during adolescence). They are trying to decide what they will do with the three to four healthy decades they may have left.

© Tom McCarthy/PhotoEdit

CONTROVERSY IN PSYCHOLOGY

Do women experience an "empty-nest syndrome" when the youngest child leaves home?

In earlier decades, psychologists placed great emphasis on a concept referred to as the **empty-nest syndrome.** This concept was applied most often to women. It was assumed that women experience a profound sense of loss when their youngest child goes off to college, gets married, or moves out of the home. The sense of loss was assumed to be greatest among women who had remained in the home (Stewart & Ostrove, 1998).

Research findings paint a more optimistic picture, however. Certainly there can be a sense of loss when the children have left home, and the loss applies to both parents. Parents may find it difficult to let go of the children after so many years of mutual dependence. However, many mothers report increased marital satisfaction and personal changes such as greater mellowness, self-confidence, and stability once the children have left home (Stewart & Ostrove, 1998).

Stewart and her colleagues (1998) developed scales to assess four personality variables in women of various ages: identity certainty, generativity, confident power, and awareness of aging. **Identity certainty** is the feeling having a strong and clear identity. *Generativity* is Erikson's sense of an enlarged vision of one's role in the world and increased feelings of responsibility and commitment to society. **Confident power** is the same as feelings of self-efficacy. Awareness of aging is self-explanatory (and all too familiar to your author!). The researchers assessed these variables among college women in their 40s and 50s, and retrospectively for the 30s. The evidence revealed that all of these variables grew to be more prominent in the 40s than in the 30s, and then again in the 50s than in the 40s. Yes, the older women were more aware of their aging both because of physical changes (e.g., menopause) and psychosocial markers (e.g., the maturation of the children). However, they were also more certain as to who they were and what they stood for. They had assumed more responsibility for society at large (e.g., occupational, civic, and political activities), and were more achievement-oriented, self-confident, dominant, and self-assertive. It is as if middle age frees many women—at least educated women—from traditional gender-related shackles.

Empty-Nest Syndrome
A sense of depression and loss of purpose felt by some parents when the youngest child leaves home.

Identity Certainty
A strong and clear sense of who one is and what one stands for.

Confident Power
Feelings of self-confidence, self-efficacy.

Ego Integrity Versus Despair
Erikson's term for the crisis of late adulthood, characterized by the task of maintaining one's sense of identity despite physical deterioration.

Wisdom
Expert knowledge concerning the meaning of life, concern for people's welfare, and a push toward excellence.

Late Adulthood

Question: What social and emotional developments occur during late adulthood? According to Erikson, late adulthood is the stage of **ego integrity versus despair.** The basic challenge is to maintain the belief that life is meaningful and worthwhile in the face of the inevitability of death. Ego integrity derives from **wisdom,** which can be defined as expert knowledge about the meaning of life, balancing one's own needs and those of others, and pushing toward excellence in one's behavior and achievements (Baltes & Staudinger, 2000; Sternberg, 2000). Erikson also believed that wisdom enabled people to accept their lifespan as occurring at a certain point in the sweep of history and as being limited. We spend most of our lives accumulating objects and relationships. Erikson also argues that adjustment in the later years requires the ability to let go. Other views of late adulthood stress the importance of creating new challenges; however, biological and social realities may require older people to become more selective in their pursuits.

Successful Aging

The later years were once seen mainly as a prelude to dying. Older people were viewed as crotchety and irritable. It was assumed that they reaped little pleasure from life. *No more.* Many stereotypes about aging are becoming less prevalent. *Question: How do people in the United States age today?* Despite the changes that accompany aging, most people in their 70s report being generally satisfied with their lives

Volz, 2000). Americans are eating more wisely and exercising at later ages, so many older people are robust. According to a national poll of nearly 1,600 adults by the *Los Angeles Times*, 75% of older people feel younger than their age—19 years on average (Stewart & Armet, 2000). People in their 70s and 80s felt as though they were in their 60s. People in their 60s reported feeling as though they were in their early 50s.

One aspect of successful aging is subjective well-being. A sense of well-being in late adulthood is linked to more than physical health and feeling younger than one's years. A meta-analysis of 286 studies noted three factors that are connected with subjective well-being: socioeconomic status, social network, and competence (Pinquart & Sörensen, 2000). One's level of income is more important to subjective well-being than is his or her level of education. Having social contacts with friends and one's own adult children are both related to subjective well-being. Competence enables one to take charge of one's life to fill one's days with meaningful activities and handle the problems that can arise at any age.

Developmental psychologists are using the term *successful aging* (Volz, 2000) in their study of characteristics that enable older people to lead more enjoyable and productive lives. There are three components of successful aging:

1. *Reshaping one's life to concentrate on what one finds to be important and meaningful.* Laura Carstensen's (1997) research on people aged 70 and above reveals that successful agers form emotional goals that bring them satisfaction. For example, rather than cast about in multiple directions, they may focus on their family and friends. Successful agers may have less time left than younger people, but they tend to spend it more wisely (Garfinkel, 1995).

   Researchers (Baltes, 1997; Schulz & Heckhausen, 1996) use terms such as "selective optimization and compensation" to describe the manner in which successful agers lead their lives. That is, successful agers no longer seek to compete in arenas best left to younger people—such as certain kinds of athletic or business activities. Rather, they focus on matters that allow them to maintain a sense of control over their own actions. Moreover, they use available resources to make up for losses. If their memory is not quite what it once was, they make notes or other reminders. For example, if their senses are no longer as acute, they use devices such as hearing aids or allow themselves more time to take in information. There are also some ingenious individual strategies. The great pianist Arthur Rubinstein performed into his 80s, even after he had lost much of his pianistic speed. In his later years, he would slow down before playing faster passages in order to enhance the impression of speed during those passages.

■ "Successful Aging"?
The later years were once seen mainly as a prelude to dying. In the third millennium, however, many older people—termed "successful agers"—are seeking new challenges.

2. *A positive outlook.* For example, some older people attribute occasional health problems such as aches and pains to *specific* and *unstable* factors like a cold or jogging too long. Others attribute aches and pains to *global* and *stable* factors such as aging itself. Not surprisingly, those who attribute these problems to specific, unstable factors are more optimistic about surmounting them. They thus have a more positive outlook or attitude. Of particular interest here is research conducted by William Rakowski (1995). Rakowski followed 1,400 people aged 70 or older with nonlethal health problems such as aches and pains. He found that those who blamed the problems on aging itself were significantly more likely to die in the near future than those who blamed the problems on specific, unstable factors.

3. *Self-challenge.* Many people look forward to late adulthood as a time when they can rest from life's challenges. But sitting back and allowing the world to pass by is a prescription for vegetating, not for living life to its fullest. Consider an experiment conducted by Curt Sandman and Francis Crinella (1995) with 175 people whose average age was 72. They randomly assigned subjects either to a foster grandparent program with neurologically impaired children or to a control group and followed both groups for 10 years. The foster grandparents carried out various physical challenges, such as walking a few miles each day, and also engaged in new kinds of social interactions. Those in the control group did not engage in these activities. When they were assessed by the experimenters, the foster grandparents showed improved overall cognitive functioning, including memory functioning, and better sleep patterns. Moreover, the foster grandparents showed superior functioning in these areas compared with people assigned to the control group.

The *Los Angeles Times* poll found that 25% of people who had retired believed that they had done so too soon (Stewart & Armet, 2000). Many older adults today are in what they call their "third age" (following their second or middle age). They are returning to school in record numbers, becoming entrepreneurs, volunteering, and, in many cases, continuing to work. According to retirement specialist Helen Dennis (2000),

> Work is a tremendous social environment. Generally, people spend more time at work with colleagues and friends than they do with their families. Those people who are currently retiring have had long-term experiences with an employer. They've lived through marriages, births, deaths, Christmases and Thanksgivings.

Nearly half (45%) of those polled by the *Los Angeles Times* agreed with the statement, "When you give up your job, you give up a large part of who you are" (Stewart & Armet, 2000).

Learning Connections
See Web site for an interactive version of these review questions.

R E V I E W

(22) In _____ adulthood, most people are at their height in sensory acuteness, reaction time, and cardiovascular fitness. (23) According to the _____-_____ theory of aging, aging is determined by a genetic biological clock. (24) According to _____-and-tear theory, cells lose the ability to regenerate because of environmental factors such as pollution, disease, and ultraviolet light. (25) _____ intelligence refers to one's lifetime of intellectual achievement, as shown by vocabulary and general knowledge. (26) _____ intelligence is mental flexibility, as shown by the ability to solve new kinds of problems. (27) Alzheimer's disease (is or is not?) _____ a normal feature of the aging process. (28) Erikson labeled the life crisis of the middle years _____ versus stagnation. (29) Research shows that most middle-aged U.S. women (do or do not?) _____ suffer from the empty-nest syndrome. (30) Erikson labeled late adulthood the stage of ego _____ versus despair.

Critical Thinking: How do the factors that contribute to longevity demonstrate the essential nature of both heredity and environmental factors?

ON DEATH AND DYING

Death is the last great taboo. Psychiatrist Elisabeth Kübler-Ross commented on our denial of death in her landmark book *On Death and Dying:*

> We use euphemisms, we make the dead look as if they were asleep, we ship the children off to protect them from the anxiety and turmoil around the house if the [person] is fortunate enough to die at home, [and] we don't allow children to visit their dying parents in the hospital. (1969, p. 8)

Question: What are psychological perspectives on death and dying?

In her work with terminally ill patients, Kübler-Ross found some common responses to news of impending death. She identified five stages of dying through which many patients pass, and she suggested that older people who suspect that death is approaching may undergo similar stages:

1. *Denial.* In the denial stage, people feel that "It can't be happening to me. The diagnosis must be wrong."
2. *Anger.* Denial usually gives way to anger and resentment toward the young and healthy and, sometimes, toward the medical establishment—"It's unfair. Why me?"
3. *Bargaining.* Next, people may try to bargain with God to postpone their death, promising, for example, to do good deeds if they are given another six months, another year to live.
4. *Depression.* With depression come feelings of loss and hopelessness—grief at the inevitability of leaving loved ones and life itself.
5. *Final acceptance.* Ultimately, an inner peace may come, a quiet acceptance of the inevitable. Such "peace" does not resemble contentment. It is nearly devoid of feeling.

Psychologist Edwin Shneidman, who has specialized in the concerns of suicidal and dying individuals, acknowledges the presence of feelings such as those identified by Kübler-Ross, but he does not perceive them to be linked in a sequence like the one just described. Instead, he suggests that dying people show a variety of emotional and cognitive responses that tend to be fleeting or relatively stable, to ebb and flow, and to reflect pain and bewilderment. He also points out that the kinds of responses shown by individuals reflect their personality traits and their philosophies of life.

"Lying Down to Pleasant Dreams . . ."

The American poet William Cullen Bryant is best known for his poem "Thanatopsis," which he composed at the age of 18. "Thanatopsis" expresses Erik Erikson's goal of ego integrity—optimism that we can maintain a sense of trust through life. By meeting squarely the challenges of our adult lives, perhaps we can take our leave with dignity. When our time comes to "join the innumerable caravan"—the billions who have died before us—perhaps we can depart life with integrity.

"Live," wrote the poet, so that

> *. . . when thy summons comes to join*
> *The innumerable caravan that moves*
> *To that mysterious realm, where each shall take*
> *His chamber in the silent halls of death,*
> *Thou go not, like the quarry-slave at night,*
> *Scourged to his dungeon, but, sustained and soothed*
> *By an unfaltering trust, approach thy grave*
> *Like one that wraps the drapery of his couch*
> *About him, and lies down to pleasant dreams.*

Bryant, of course, wrote "Thanatopsis" at age 18, not at 85, the age at which he died. At that advanced age, his feelings—and his verse—might have differed. But literature and poetry, unlike science, need not reflect reality. They can serve to inspire and warm us.

REFLECT

Erik Erikson wrote that one aspect of wisdom is the ability to visualize one's role in the march of history and to accept one's own death. Do you believe that acceptance of death is a sign of wisdom? Why or why not?

Day Care—Blessing, Headache, or Both?

Looking for a phrase that can strike fear in the hearts of millions of American parents? Try "day care." Only a relatively small percentage of American families still fits the conventional model that places the husband at the head of the table as the breadwinner and the wife as the, well, "housewife." We may no longer use the oppressive term *housewife,* but we do speak of full-time *homemakers.* Nowadays the great majority of mothers, including the majority of mothers of infants, are in the workforce (Erel et al., 2000; U.S. Bureau of the Census, 2002). As a result, millions of American parents are obsessed with trying to find proper day care.

When both parents spend the day on the job, the children—at least young children—must be taken care of by others. What happens to them? Does day care affect children's bonds of attachment with their parents? Does it affect their social and cognitive development?

How Does Day Care Affect Bonds of Attachment?

Many parents wonder whether day care will affect their children's attachment to them. Are such concerns valid? The issue has been hotly debated. Some studies have found that infants who are in day care full-time (more than 20 hours a week) are somewhat more likely than children without day-care experience to show insecure attachment (Baydar & Brooks-Gunn, 1991). Some psychologists have concluded from these studies that a mother who works full-time puts her infant at risk for developing emotional insecurity (Belsky, 1990a, 1990b). Others note that infants whose mothers work may be less distressed by her departure in the Strange Situation and less likely to seek her out when she returns. Also keep in mind that the likelihood of insecure attachment is not much greater in infants placed in day care than in those cared for in the home; most infants in both groups are securely attached (Clarke-Stewart, 1989; Lamb et al., 1992).

How Does Day Care Influence Social and Cognitive Development?

Day care has mixed effects on children's social and cognitive development. Infants with day-care experience are more peer oriented and play at higher developmental levels than do home-reared babies. Day-care children are also more likely to share their toys. They are more independent, self-confident, outgoing, and affectionate as well as more helpful and cooperative with

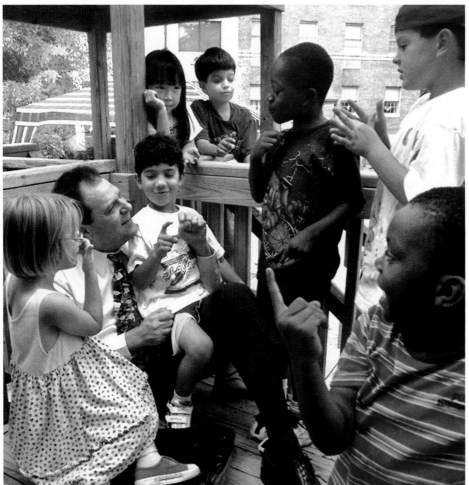

■ **Day Care**
Because most parents in the United States are in the workforce, day care is not a luxury—it's a necessity. Day care has become a major influence on the lives of millions of children, and parents are concerned about the effects of day care on their bonds of attachment with their children and on their children's cognitive and social development.

peers and adults (Clarke-Stewart, 1991; Field, 1991). Participation in day care also is associated with better school performance during the elementary school years, especially for children from poor families (Caughy et al., 1994).

A study funded by the National Institute of Child Health and Human Development compared the development of children in "high-quality" day care with that of children in low-quality day care, and with that of children reared in the home by their mothers. The quality of the day care was defined in terms of the richness of the learning environment (availability of toys, books, and other materials), the ratio of caregivers to children (high quality meant more caregivers), the amount of individual attention received by the child (more was better), and the extent to which caregivers talked to the children and asked them questions (again: more was considered better). The researchers found high-quality day care resulted in scores on tests of language and cognitive skills that rivaled those of the children reared in the home by their mothers (Belsky et al., 2001). A study carried out in Sweden found that children placed in high-quality day care actually fared better on tests of language skills and math than children who were reared in the home by their mothers (Broberg et al., 1997). It thus appears that high-quality day care enhances the development of social and cognitive skills, although low-quality day care may be problematic.

Yet some studies find that children placed in day care are less cooperative and more aggressive toward peers and adults than children who are reared in the home by their mothers. Consider findings of the the National Institute of Child Health and Human Development study that went off like an H-bomb among parents in 2001.

The Child Care H-Bomb of 2001

One of the findings of the study from the National Institute of Child Health and Human Development was that the more time preschoolers spent in child care, the more likely they were to display behavioral problems in kindergarten (Belsky et al., 2001). The more time spent away from their mothers, the more likely the children were to be rated as defiant, aggressive, and disobedient once they got to kindergarten. Seventeen percent of children who were in child care for more than 30 hours a week received higher scores on rating items like "gets in lots of fights," "cruelty," "talking too much," and "explosive behavior," "argues a lot," and "demands a lot of attention." Only 6% of children who were in child care for less than 10 hours a week had these problems. The finding held regardless of the background of the child or the quality or type of child care the children received. It held for African American and European American children, for boys and for girls, for children whose parents were affluent or poor. Children who were cared for in traditional day-care settings, by a grandmother, by a nanny, even by their fathers received the troublesome ratings. Could it be that Mom was the only answer?

The research findings sent shudders through millions of American homes. Nevertheless, the study also held good news for working parents. For example, it found that children who are enrolled in high-quality child care show cognitive benefits as compared with children who are in lower-quality day care or who spend more time in the home with their mothers. For example, they perform better on tests of memory, language, and knowledge.

Although the study found a positive correlation between time spent away from mothers and aggression, disobedience, and defiance in kindergarten, the reason for the behavioral problems was not clear. For example, was it actually the time spent away from mothers that brought on the problems, or did the problems stem from other factors such as the stresses encountered by families who need to get by on two incomes? The researchers also had to admit that they did not know whether the problem behavior would continue as the children moved into higher grades. Most of them cautioned against reading too much into the study, not in the least because most of the children's behavior fell within the normal range; even most of the aggressive behavior was not out of bounds.

Still, the findings of the National Institute of Child Health and Human Development study sent many parents into a tizzy. Many working mothers worried about their choices or emotionally defended them, while stay-at-home mothers seized on the findings as vindication. But a number of the researchers on the team said that if other information yielded by the study—or *not* yielded by the study—had been emphasized to the public, the reaction might have been different. Note the following:

- Although 17% of kindergartners who had been in child care acted more assertively and aggressively, that percentage is actually the norm for the general population of children. (And it remains true that 9% of the children who spent most of their time with their mothers were also rated by teachers as showing the more troubling behaviors.)
- The nature of family–child interactions had a greater impact on children's behavior than the number of hours spent in child care.
- Cruelty is never acceptable, but some other aspects of aggressiveness—and the fact that infants in day care may demand more attention as kindergartners—may in many ways be adaptive social responses to being placed in a situation in which multiple children may be competing for limited physical and human resources.
- In addition, the researchers admitted that the statistics are very modest: Yes, 17% acted aggressively and assertively, but only a few of them exhibited above-average behavior problems. Moreover, the problems were not that serious.

In any event, millions of parents have to make decisions not about *whether* to place their children in day care, but *where* to place their children in day care. The following suggestions may be of help.

Finding Child Care You (and Your Child) Can Live With

It's normal to be anxious. You are thinking about selecting a day-care center or a private home for your precious child, and there are risks. So be a little anxious, but it may not be necessary to be overwhelmed. You can go about the task with a checklist that can guide your considerations. Above all: Don't be afraid to open your mouth and ask questions, even pointed, challenging questions. If the day-care provider doesn't like questions, or if the provider does not answer them satisfactorily, *you want your child someplace else*. So much for the preamble. Here's the checklist.

1. Does the day-care center have a license? Who issued the license? What did the day-care center have to do to acquire

the license? (You can also call the licensing agency to obtain the answer to the last question.)

2. How many children are cared for by the center? How many caregivers are there? Remember this nursery rhyme:

There was an old woman who lived in a shoe.

She had so many children she didn't know what to do.

All right, the rhyme is sexist and ageist and maybe even shoe-ist. But it suggests that it is important for caregivers not to be overburdened by too many children, especially infants. It is desirable to have at least one caregiver for every four infants, although fewer workers are required for older children.

3. How were the caregivers hired? How were they trained? Did the center check references? What were the minimum educational credentials? Did the center check them out? Do the caregivers have any education or training in the behavior and needs of children? Do the caregivers seem to be proactive and attempt to engage the children in activities and educational experiences? Or are they inactive unless a child cries or screams? Sometimes it is impossible to find qualified day-care workers, because they tend to be paid poorly—often the minimum wage, and sometimes less.

4. Is the environment child-proofed and secure? Can children stick their fingers in electric sockets? Are toys and outdoor equipment in good condition? Are sharp objects within children's reach? Can anybody walk in off the street? What is the history of children being injured or otherwise victimized in this day-care center? Is the day-care provider hesitant about answering any of these questions?

5. When are meals served? Snacks? What do they consist of? Will your child find them appetizing or go hungry? Some babies are placed in day care at 6 months or younger, and parents will need to know what formulas are used.

6. Is it possible for you to meet the caregivers who will be taking care of your child? If not, why not?

7. With what children will your child interact and play?

8. Does the center seem to have an enriching environment? Do you see books, toys, games, and educational objects strewn about?

9. Are there facilities and objects like swings and tricycles that will enhance your child's physical and motor development? Are children supervised when they play with these things, or are they pretty much left on their own?

10. Does the center's schedule coincide with your needs?

11. Is the center located conveniently for you? Does it appear to be in a safe location or else to have adequate security arrangements? (Let me emphasize that you have a right to ask whether neighborhood or other people can walk in unannounced to where the children are. It's a fair question. You can also ask what they would do if a stranger broke into the place.)

12. Are parents permitted to visit unannounced?

13. Do you like the overall environment and feel of the center or home? Listen to your "gut."

There may be no perfect solution, but some are better than others.

Recite Recite Recite

Learning Connections
See Web site for an interactive version of this chapter summary

---

1. **What developments occur from conception through birth?**

Prenatal development occurs in stages: the germinal, embryonic, and fetal stages. During the germinal stage, the zygote divides as it travels through the fallopian tube and becomes implanted in the uterine wall. The major organ systems are formed during the embryonic stage, and the fetal stage is characterized by maturation and gains in size.

2. **What physical developments occur during childhood?**

Reflexes are inborn responses to stimuli that in many cases are essential to the survival of the infant. Examples include sucking and swallowing. The motor development of the child involves the interaction of maturation and experience. Children whose experience is restricted often catch up. Early physical training does not necessarily provide important advantages. Newborn babies can see quite well and show greater interest in complex visual stimuli than in simple ones. Infants are capable of depth perception by the time they can crawl. Newborns can normally hear and show a preference for their mother's voice. Newborns show preferences for pleasant odors and sweet foods.

3. **Does development occur gradually or in stages?**

Stage theorists like Freud and Piaget view development as discontinuous. According to them, people go through distinct periods of development that differ in quality and follow an orderly sequence. Learning theorists, in contrast, tend to view psychological development as a more continuous process. Some aspects of development, such as the adolescent growth spurt, are discontinuous. There is controversy as to whether cognitive development is continuous or discontinuous.

4. **What are Jean Piaget's views of cognitive development?**

Piaget saw children as budding scientists who actively strive to make sense of the perceptual world. He defined intelligence as involving the processes of assimilation and accommodation. Piaget's view of cognitive development includes four stages: sensorimotor (prior to the use of symbols and language); preoperational (characterized by egocentric thought, animism, artificialism, and inability to center on more than one aspect of a situation); concrete operational (characterized by conservation, less egocentrism, reversibility, and subjective moral judgments); and formal operational (characterized by abstract logic).

5. **How do children reason about right and wrong?**

Lawrence Kohlberg hypothesized that children's moral reasoning develops through three levels, each of which consists of two stages. Moral decisions develop from being based on pain and pleasure ("preconventional"), through necessity to maintain the social order ("conventional"), to reliance on one's own conscience ("postconventional"). Not all individuals reach the postconventional level.

6. **What are Erikson's stages of psychosocial development?**

Erikson hypothesizes that there are eight stages of psychosocial development. Each represents a life crisis. The first of these is "trust versus mistrust," during which the crisis centers on the child's learning that the world is a good place that can meet his or her needs.

7. **How do feelings of attachment develop? What kinds of experiences affect attachment?**

According to Ainsworth, there are three stages of attachment: the initial-preattachment phase, the attachment-in-the-making phase, and the clear-cut-attachment phase. Bowlby adds fear of strangers as a factor in attachment. Behaviorists have argued that children become attached to their mothers through conditioning because their mothers feed them and attend to their other needs. Harlow's studies with rhesus monkeys suggest that an innate motive, contact comfort, may be more important than conditioning in the development of attachment. There are critical developmental periods during which animals such as geese and ducks become attached instinctively to (or imprinted on) an object that they follow.

8. **What types of parental behavior are connected with variables such as self-esteem, achievement motivation, and independence in children?**

Styles of parental behavior include the authoritative, authoritarian, and permissive styles. The children of authoritative parents are the most achievement-oriented and well-adjusted.

Recite Recite Recite

9. What physical developments occur during adolescence?

Adolescence begins at puberty and ends with assumption of adult responsibilities. Changes that lead to reproductive capacity and secondary sex characteristics are stimulated by increased levels of testosterone in the male and of estrogen and androgens in the female. During the adolescent growth spurt, young people may grow 6 or more inches in a year.

10. What cognitive developments occur during adolescence?

Formal operational thinking appears in adolescence, but not everyone reaches it. Two consequences of adolescent egocentrism are the imaginary audience and the personal fable. The imaginary audience refers to the adolescent beliefs that they are the center of attention and that other people are as concerned with their appearance and behavior as they are. The personal fable refers to the adolescent belief that one's feelings and ideas are special, even unique, and that one is invulnerable.

11. What social and emotional developments occur during adolescence?

Adolescents and parents are often in conflict because adolescents desire more independence and may experiment with things that can jeopardize their health. Despite bickering, most adolescents continue to love and respect their parents. According to Erikson, adolescents strive to forge an ego identity—a sense of who they are and what they stand for. High hormone levels stir interest in sex. Most sexually active adolescents do not use contraceptives reliably. Thus about 1 teenage girl in 10 gets pregnant each year.

12. What physical developments occur during adulthood?

People are usually at the height of their physical powers during young adulthood. Middle adulthood is characterized by a gradual decline in strength. Research suggests that most women go through menopause without great difficulty. Older people show less sensory acuity, and their reaction time lengthens. The immune system weakens.

13. What are the gender and ethnic differences in life expectancy?

Women outlive men by nearly seven years, and European and Asian Americans tend to outlive other ethnic groups in the United States. By and large, the groups who live longer are more likely to seek and make use of health care.

14. Why do we age?

Heredity plays a role in longevity. One theory (programmed senescence) suggests that aging and death are determined by our genes. Another theory (wear-and-tear theory) holds that factors such as pollution, disease, and ultraviolet light weaken the body so that it loses the ability to repair itself. Exercise, proper diet, and *not* smoking all contribute to longevity.

15. What cognitive developments occur during adulthood?

People are usually at the height of their cognitive powers during early adulthood, but people can be creative for a lifetime. Memory functioning declines with age. People tend to retain verbal ability, as shown by vocabulary and general knowledge, into advanced old age. Crystallized intelligence—one's vocabulary and accumulated knowledge—generally increases with age. Fluid intelligence—the ability to process information rapidly—declines.

16. What is Alzheimer's disease? What are its origins?

Alzheimer's disease is characterized by cognitive deterioration in memory, language, and problem solving. On a biological level, it is connected with reduced levels of acetylcholine in the brain and with the buildup of plaque in the brain.

17. What social and emotional developments occur during young adulthood?

Young adulthood is generally characterized by efforts to advance in the business world and the development of intimate ties. Many young adults reassess the directions of their lives during the "age-30 transition."

Recite Recite Recite

18. **What social and emotional developments occur during middle adulthood?**

Many theorists view middle adulthood as a time of crisis (the "midlife crisis") and further reassessment. Many adults try to come to terms with the discrepancies between their achievements and the dreams of their youth during middle adulthood. Some middle-aged adults become depressed when their youngest child leaves home (the so-called empty-nest syndrome), but many report increased satisfaction, stability, and self-confidence.

19. **What social and emotional developments occur during late adulthood?**

Erikson characterizes late adulthood as the stage of ego integrity versus despair. He saw the basic challenge as maintaining the belief that life is worthwhile in the face of physical deterioration.

20. **How do people in the United States age today?**

Most older Americans report being generally satisfied with their lives. "Successful agers" reshape their lives to focus on what they find important, maintain a positive outlook, and find new challenges.

21. **What are psychological perspectives on death and dying?**

Kübler-Ross has identified five stages of dying among people who are terminally ill: denial, anger, bargaining, depression, and final acceptance. However, other investigators find that psychological reactions to approaching death are more varied than Kübler-Ross suggests.

Active Learning Resources

 Search Online with InfoTrac® College Edition

For additional information on the topics in this chapter, explore InfoTrac College Edition, your online library. Go to **http://www.infotrac.thomsonlearning.com** and use the passcode that came on the card with your book. Try these search terms: newborn development, Jean Piaget, Lawrence Kohlberg, psychosocial development, attachment behavior in children, authoritative parenting, psychological aspects of adolescence, adolescent sexuality, and Alzheimer's disease.

 Visit Our Web Site

Go to **http://www.wadsworth.com/psychology**, where you will find online resources directly linked to your book, including interactive exercises related to PQ4R and Power Visuals for mastering and reviewing key concepts. In addition, you will find hints on using InfoTrac College Edition to answer the Critical Thinking questions throughout the text. Start with the **Self Study Assessment** for a customized **Study Plan** generated by taking the **Pre-Test** and **Post-Test.**

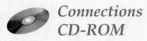 ***Connections CD-ROM***

Go to the Wadsworth *Connections* CD-ROM for further study of the concepts in this chapter. The CD-ROM includes videos, animations, quizzes, and additional activities to expand your learning experience, plus interactive self-assessments to help connect the material to your own life.

 Psyk.trek™ CD-ROM

The Wadsworth *Psyk.trek* CD-ROM offers tutorials, simulations, videos, multimedia glossary, and quizzing to help you master the material.

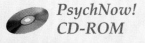 ***PsychNow! CD-ROM***

The Wadsworth *PsychNow!* CD-ROM includes interactive exercises, videos, and animations to enhance your learning.

Sensation and Perception: Your Tickets of Admission to the World Outside

■ PEOPLE HAVE FIVE senses, right? Wrong.

■ ON A CLEAR, DARK NIGHT you could probably see the light from a candle burning 30 miles away.

■ IF WE COULD SEE waves of light with slightly longer wavelengths, warm-blooded animals would glow in the dark.

■ SOMETIMES WE HEAR what we want to hear.

Vision: Letting the Sun Shine In

■ "WHITE" SUNLIGHT IS actually composed of all the wavelengths that we perceive as colors of the rainbow.

■ A PARTLY COLOR-BLIND person might put on one red sock and one green sock but would not mix red and blue socks.

Visual Perception: How Perceptive?

■ HOW DO YOU JUDGE the distance of a car heading in your direction? (How do you know it's heading in your direction?)

■ YOU PERCEIVE A DOOR to be a rectangle even when it is a trapezoid (when seen ajar) or a thick line (when seen on end).

■ VISUAL ILLUSIONS TRICK the eye—even your sophisticated eye.

Hearing: Making Sense of Sound

■ WHY IS IT THAT "In space, no one can hear you scream"?

■ LIKE YOUR STEREO, your ears have amplifiers.

The Chemical Senses: Smell and Taste

■ YOU ARE A NATURAL chemist: Your senses of smell and taste sample molecules.

■ CATFISH HAVE TASTE BUDS all over their bodies. Nevertheless, most people are more concerned with how *good* catfish taste than with how *well* they taste.

The Skin Senses (Yes, It Does)

■ THE SKIN IS A sensory organ as well as a protective coating for the body.

Kinesthesis and the Vestibular Sense

■ YOU CAN TOUCH YOUR finger to your nose even when your eyes are closed. How do you do it?

■ WHICH SENSE KEEPS you an upright person?

Extrasensory Perception: Is There Perception Without Sensation?

■ CAN SOME PEOPLE read other people's minds?

Life Connections: Pain, Pain, Go Away— Don't Come Again Another Day

■ SONG TITLE: "The pain 'in' the brain is mainly outside the cranium." In English: Although people can have fierce headaches, there are no nerve endings for pain in the brain.

■ MANY PEOPLE EXPERIENCE pain "in" limbs that have been amputated.

■ RUBBING OR SCRATCHING a sore toe often relieves pain.

Five thousand years ago in China, so the story goes, a soldier shot an arrow high into the air. Where did it land? In the outstretched hand of a fierce warrior and master of the martial arts. According to legend, the warrior had grown fierce because of a chronic toothache. Incessant pain had ruined his disposition.

On that fateful day, our hero watched as invading hordes assembled on surrounding hills. His troops were trembling in the face of the enemy's great numbers, and he raised his arms to boost their morale. Just at that moment, the arrow shot from beyond sliced into the warrior's palm. Although he saw the arrow pass through his palm, he did not scream. He did not run. He did not even complain. He was astounded. His toothache had vanished. In fact, his whole jaw was numb.

Meanwhile the invaders looked on, horrified. What sort of warrior could watch an arrow pierce his hand with such indifference? Even with a smile? If this was the caliber of the local warriors, the invaders would be better off traveling west and looking for a brawl in Sumer or in Egypt. They sounded the retreat and withdrew.

Back in town, our warrior received a hero's welcome. A physician offered to remove the arrow for free—a tribute to bravery. But the wounded man would have none of it. The arrow had worked wonders for his toothache, and he would brook no meddling. He had already discovered that if his tooth started to throb, he need only twirl the arrow and the pain receded.

But all was not well on the home front. His wife was thrilled to find him jovial once more, but the arrow put a crimp in their romance. When he put his arms around her, she was in danger of being stabbed. Finally, she gave him an ultimatum: The arrow must go, or she would.

Placed in deep conflict, our warrior consulted a psychologist, who then huddled with the physician and the village elders. After much to-do, they asked the warrior to participate in an experiment. They would remove the arrow and replace it with a metal pin that the warrior could twirl as needed.

To the warrior's wife's relief, the pin worked. And here, in ancient China, lay the origins of the art of **acupuncture**—the use of needles to relieve pain and treat assorted ills.

I confess that this tale is not entirely accurate. Like other historic breakthroughs, acupuncture has been the subject of legend and lore. To my knowledge, there were no psychologists in ancient China (their loss). Moreover, the part about the warrior's wife is fictitious. It is claimed, however, that acupuncture as a means of dealing with pain originated in ancient China when a soldier was, in fact, wounded in the hand by an arrow and discovered that a chronic toothache disappeared. Historians say the Chinese then set out to map the body by sticking pins into various parts of it to learn how the pins would influence the perception of pain.

Control of pain is just one of the many issues that interest psychologists who study the closely related concepts of sensation and perception. *Question: What are sensation and perception?* **Sensation** is the stimulation of sensory receptors and the transmission of sensory information to the central nervous system (the spinal cord or brain). Sensory receptors are located in sensory organs such as the eyes and ears, the skin, and elsewhere in the body. Stimulation of the senses is an automatic process. It results from sources of energy like light and sound or from the presence of chemicals, as in smell and taste.

Perception is not automatic. Perception is an active process in which sensations are organized and interpreted to form an inner representation of the world. Perception may begin with sensation, but it also reflects our experiences and expectations as it makes sense of sensory stimuli. A person standing 15 feet away and a 12-inch-tall doll may cast similar-sized images on the back of your eye, but whether you interpret the shape to be a foot-long doll or a full-grown person 15 feet away is a matter of perception that depends on your experience with dolls, people, and distance.

In this chapter you will see that your personal map of reality—your ticket of admission to a world of changing sights, sounds, and other sources of sensory input—depends largely on the so-called five senses: vision, hearing, smell, taste, and touch. We will see, however, that touch is just one of several "skin senses," which also include pressure, warmth, cold, and pain. There are also senses that alert you to your own body position without your having to watch every step you take. As we explore the

Acupuncture
The ancient Chinese practice of piercing parts of the body with needles to deaden pain and treat illness.

Sensation
The stimulation of sensory receptors and the transmission of sensory information to the central nervous system.

Perception
The process by which sensations are organized into an inner representation of the world.

nature of each of these senses, we will find that similar sensations may lead to different perceptions in different people—or within the same person in different situations.

SENSATION AND PERCEPTION: YOUR TICKETS OF ADMISSION TO THE WORLD OUTSIDE

Before we begin our voyage through the senses, let us consider a number of concepts that apply to all of them: absolute threshold, difference threshold, signal-detection theory, and sensory adaptation. In doing so, we will learn why we can dim the lights gradually to near darkness without anyone noticing. (Sneaky?) We will also learn why we might become indifferent to the savory aromas of delightful dinners. (Disappointing?) *Questions: How do we know when something is there? How do we know when it has changed?*

Absolute Threshold: So, Is It There or Not?

Gustav Theodor Fechner (1801–1887) was interested in the occult and reported attending seances in which a bed, a table, and he himself moved in response to strange forces. He was interested in spiritual phenomena and wrote a bereaved friend that death is but a transition to another state of existence, in which one's soul merges with others to join the Supreme Spirit. Yet he advocated scientific rigor in all other matters and contributed to the precise measurement of the senses. Under the pen name of "Dr. Mises," he ridiculed unscientific thought by a tongue-in-cheek argument: (a) Insects have six legs; (b) mammals have four; and (c) birds, who ascend closest to heaven, only two. (d) Therefore, angels, higher yet, must have none. In contrast to his humorous treatise on legless angels, Fechner insisted on actually measuring things rather than just arguing about them.

Fechner obtained a degree in medicine at the University of Leipzig, but his interests turned to physics and math. He founded the discipline known as *psychophysics*, which deals with the ways in which we translate physical events such as lights and sounds into psychological experiences. Light and sound are types of physical energy. It may surprise you that we do not sense them directly, powerful as they may seem to us. Instead, these sources of energy are converted into neural impulses by our sensory receptors—our eyes and ears and so on. The process of transforming physical energy (in the cases of light, sound, and touch) or chemicals (in the cases of odors and tastes) into neural impulses is called **transduction.** Many of Fechner's laboratory methods remain in use today.

Transduction
The process by which we transform physical energy (in the cases of light, sound, and touch) or chemicals (in the cases of odors and tastes) into neural impulses.

Absolute Threshold
The minimal amount of energy that can produce a sensation.

Psychophysicist
A person who studies the relationships between physical stimuli (such as light or sound) and their perception.

REFLECT

What is the dimmest light you can see? The softest sound you can hear? How do psychophysicists answer such questions?

Fechner used the term **absolute threshold** to refer to the weakest amount of a stimulus that a person can distinguish from no stimulus at all. For example, the absolute threshold for light would be the minimum brightness (physical energy) required to activate the visual sensory system.

Psychophysicists look for the absolute thresholds of the senses by exposing individuals to progressively stronger stimuli until they find the minimum stimuli that the person can detect no more (and no less) than 50 percent of the time. However, it has been discovered that these absolute thresholds are not really absolute. That is, some people are more sensitive than others, and even the same person might have a slightly different response from one occasion to another.

Nevertheless, under ideal conditions, our ability to detect stimuli are amazingly sensitive. The following are measures of the absolute thresholds for the senses of vision, hearing, taste, smell, and touch:

- Vision: a candle flame viewed from about 30 miles on a clear, dark night
- Hearing: a watch ticking from about 20 feet away in a quiet room
- Taste: 1 teaspoon of sugar dissolved in 2 gallons of water

■ Gustav Theodor Fechner

Fechner was a complex person. He attended seances as well as fathering the budding area of psychology we call *psychophysics*. Some historians of psychology date the beginning of psychology as a science to 1860, when Fechner published *Elements of Psychophysics*.

The Granger Collection, New York

■ Ernst Heinrich Weber

Weber was one of 13 children, and three of them became renowned scientists.

Pitch

The highness or lowness of a sound, as determined by the frequency of the sound waves.

Difference Threshold

The minimal difference in intensity required between two sources of energy so that they will be perceived as being different.

Weber's Constant

The fraction of the intensity by which a source of physical energy must be increased or decreased so that a difference in intensity will be perceived.

Just Noticeable Difference (jnd)

The minimal amount by which a source of energy must be increased or decreased so that a difference in intensity will be perceived.

Signal-Detection Theory

The view that the perception of sensory stimuli involves the interaction of physical, biological, and psychological factors.

- Smell: about one drop of perfume diffused throughout a small house (1 part in 500 million)
- Touch: the pressure of the wing of a fly falling on a cheek from a distance of about 0.4 inch

It's interesting to imagine how our lives would be different if the absolute thresholds for the human senses differed substantially. For example, if your ears were more sensitive to sounds that are low in **pitch,** you might hear the collisions among molecules of air. If you could see light with slightly longer wavelengths, you would see infrared light waves. Your world would be transformed because heat generates infrared light. Warm-blooded creatures such as your pet canary or mate would glow in the dark. Also, the worlds of those who are blind, deaf, or have other variations in their sensory capabilities can be substantially different. These different experiences of reality may not be viewed as losses, either. For example, some deaf people have advocated against artificial restoration of hearing through surgical means because of the beauty and value of a world of silence and sign language. (For more on deafness, see page 164.)

Difference Threshold: Is It the Same or Is It Different?

How much of a difference in intensity between two lights is required before you will detect one as being brighter than the other? The minimum difference in magnitude of two stimuli required to tell them apart is their **difference threshold.** As with the absolute threshold, psychologists have agreed to the criterion of a difference in magnitudes that can be detected 50% of the time.

R E F L E C T

Can you think of a personal example of a just noticeable difference? How much weight do you have to gain or lose to notice a difference? How much harder would you have to work to make a noticeable difference in your grades?

Psychophysicist Ernst Weber (1795–1878) discovered through laboratory research that the threshold for perceiving differences in the intensity of light is about 2% (actually closer to 1/60th) of their intensity. This fraction, 1/60th, is known as **Weber's constant** for light. A closely related concept is the **just noticeable difference (jnd),** the minimum difference in stimuli that a person can detect. For example, at least 50 percent of the time, most people can tell if a light gets just 1/60th brighter or dimmer. Weber's constant for light holds whether we are comparing two quite bright lights or two moderately dull lights. However, it becomes inaccurate when we compare extremely bright or extremely dull lights.

Weber, by the way, was born in Wittenberg, Germany. He was the third of thirteen children and one of three sons who became distinguished scientists. If the times had been different, one wonders what his sisters might have achieved.

Weber's constant for noticing differences in lifted weight is 1/53rd. (Round it off to 1/50th.) That means if you are strong enough to heft a 100-pound barbell, you would not notice that it was heavier until about 2 pounds were added. Yet if you are a runner who carries 1-pound dumbbells, you would definitely notice if someone slipped you dumbbells even a pound heavier because the increase would be 100 percent, not a small fraction.

What about sound? People are most sensitive to changes in the pitch (frequency) of sounds. The Weber constant for pitch is 1/333, meaning that on average, people can tell when a tone rises or falls in pitch by an extremely small one-third of 1%. (Singers have to be right on pitch. The smallest error makes them sound sharp or flat.) Remember this when friends criticize your singing—you may not be "tone deaf" but just slightly off. The sense of taste is much less sensitive. On average, people cannot detect differences in saltiness of less than 20 percent. That is why those low-salt chips that have 15 percent less salt than your favorite do not taste so bad.

Signal-Detection Theory: Is Being Bright Enough?

From the discussion so far it might seem as if people are simply switched on by certain amounts of stimulation. This is not quite so. People are influenced by psychological factors as well as by external changes. **Signal-detection theory** considers the human aspects of sensation and perception. *Question: What is signal-detection theory?*

According to signal-detection theory, the relationship between a physical stimulus and a sensory response is not just mechanical. People's ability to detect stimuli such as meaningful blips on a radar screen depends not only on the intensity of the blips but also on their training (learning), motivation (desire to perceive meaningful blips), and psychological states such as fatigue or alertness.

The intensity of the signal is just one factor that determines whether people will perceive sensory stimuli (signals) or a difference between signals. Another is the degree to which the signal can be distinguished from background noise. It is easier to hear a friend in a quiet room than in a room in which people are talking loudly and clinking glasses. The sharpness or acuteness of a person's biological sensory system is still another factor. Is sensory capacity fully developed? Is it diminished by advanced age?

Signal-detection theory also considers psychological factors such as motivation, expectations, and learning. For example, the place in which you are reading this book may be abuzz with signals. If you are outside, perhaps a breeze is blowing against your face. Perhaps the shadows of passing clouds darken the scene now and then. If you are inside, perhaps there are the occasional clanks and hums emitted by a heating system. Perhaps the aromas of dinner are hanging in the air, or the voices from a TV set suggest a crowd in another room. Yet, you are focusing your attention on this page (I hope). Thus, the other signals recede into the background of your consciousness. One psychological factor in signal detection is the focusing or narrowing of attention to signals that the person deems important.

Feature Detectors in the Brain: Firing on Cue

Imagine that you are standing by the curb of a busy street as a bus approaches. When neurons in your sensory organs—in this case, your eyes—are stimulated by the approach of the bus, they relay information to the sensory cortex in the brain. Nobel prize winners David Hubel and Torsten Wiesel (1979) discovered that various neurons in the visual cortex of the brain fire in response to particular features of the visual input. *Question: What are feature detectors?* Many cells in the brain detect (fire in response to) lines presented at various angles—vertical, horizontal, and in between. Other cells fire in response to specific colors.

Because they respond to different aspects or features of a scene, these brain cells are termed **feature detectors.** In the example of the bus, visual feature detectors respond to the bus's edges, depth, contours, textures, shadows, speed, and kinds of motion (up, down, forward, and back). There are also feature detectors for other senses. Auditory feature detectors, for example, respond to the pitch, loudness, and other aspects of the sounds of the bus.

Sensory Adaptation: Where Did It Go?

Our sensory systems are admirably suited to a changing environment. *Question: How do our sensory systems adapt to a changing environment?* We become more sensitive to stimuli of low magnitude and less sensitive to stimuli that remain the same (such as the background noises outside the window). **Sensory adaptation** refers to these processes of adjustment.

Consider how the visual sense adapts to lower intensities of light. When we first walk into a darkened movie theater, we see little but the images on the screen. As we search for our seats, however, we become increasingly sensitive to the faces around us and to the features of the theater. The process of becoming more sensitive to stimulation is referred to as **sensitization,** or positive adaptation.

But we become less sensitive to constant stimulation. Sources of light appear to grow dimmer as we adapt to them. In fact, if you could keep an image completely stable on the retinas of your eyes—which is virtually impossible to accomplish without a motionless image and stabilizing equipment—the image would fade within a few seconds and be very difficult to see. Similarly, at the beach we soon become less aware of

Feature Detectors
Neurons in the sensory cortex that fire in response to specific features of sensory information such as lines or edges of objects.

Sensory Adaptation
The processes by which organisms become more sensitive to stimuli that are low in magnitude and less sensitive to stimuli that are constant or ongoing in magnitude.

Sensitization
The type of sensory adaptation in which we become more sensitive to stimuli that are low in magnitude. Also called *positive adaptation.*

■ **Signal Detection**
The detection of signals is determined not only by the physical characteristics of the signals but also by psychological factors such as motivation and attention. The people in this photo are tuned in to their newspapers for the moment and not to each other.

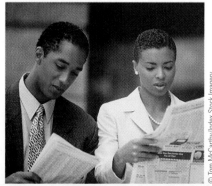

Desensitization
The type of sensory adaptation in which we become less sensitive to constant stimuli. Also called *negative adaptation.*

Visible Light
The part of the electromagnetic spectrum that stimulates the eye and produces visual sensations.

Hue
The color of light, as determined by its wavelength.

the lapping of the waves. When we live in a city, we become desensitized to traffic sounds except for the occasional backfire or siren. And as you may have noticed from experiences with freshly painted rooms, sensitivity to disagreeable odors fades quite rapidly. The process of becoming less sensitive to stimulation is referred to as **desensitization,** or negative adaptation.

Learning Connections
See Web site for an interactive version of these review questions.

R E V I E W

(1) _____ is a mechanical process that involves the stimulation of sensory receptors and the transmission of sensory information to the central nervous system. (2) _____ is the organization of sensations into an inner representation of the world; it reflects learning and expectations, as well as sensations. (3) The _____ threshold for a stimulus, such as light, is the lowest intensity at which it can be detected. (4) The minimum difference in intensity that can be discriminated is the _____ threshold. (5) According to _____-detection theory, many factors determine perception of a stimulus: the sensory stimuli, the biological sensory system of the person, and psychological factors, such as motivation and attention.

Critical Thinking: Which factors in sensation and perception reflect our nature? Which reflect nurture?

VISION: LETTING THE SUN SHINE IN

Our eyes are literally our "windows on the world." More than half of our brain's cerebral cortex is devoted to visual functions (Basic Behavioral Science Task Force, 1996b). Because vision is our dominant sense, blindness is considered by many to be the most debilitating type of sensory loss. To understand vision, let us first consider the nature of light.

Light: How Dazzling?

Light is fascinating stuff. It radiates. It illuminates. It dazzles. It glows. It beckons like a beacon. We speak of the "light of reason." We speak of genius as "brilliance." In almost all cultures, light is a symbol of goodness and knowledge. People who aren't in the know are said to be "in the dark." *Question: Just what is light?*

It is **visible light** that triggers visual sensations. Yet visible light is just one small part of a spectrum of electromagnetic energy that surrounds us (see Figure 4.1). All forms of electromagnetic energy move in waves, and different kinds of electromagnetic energy have signature wavelengths, as follows:

- Cosmic rays: wavelengths are only a few *trillionths* of an inch long.
- Radio waves: Some radio signals extend for miles.
- Visible light: Different colors have different wavelengths, with violet the shortest at about 400 *billionths* of a meter in length and red the longest at 700 billionths of a meter.

R E F L E C T
Have you ever seen a rainbow? How do you account for the colors in it?

Have you seen rainbows or light that has been broken down into several colors as it filtered through your windows? Sir Isaac Newton, the British scientist, discovered that sunlight could be broken down into different colors by means of a triangular solid of glass called a *prism* (Figure 4.1). When I took introductory psychology, I was taught to remember the colors of the spectrum, from longest to shortest wavelengths, by using the mnemonic device *Roy G. Biv* (red, orange, yellow, green, blue, indigo, violet). I must have been a backward student because I found it easier to recall them in reverse order, using the meaningless acronym *vibgyor.*

The wavelength of visible light determines its color, or **hue.** The wavelength for red is longer than the wavelength for orange, and so on through the spectrum.

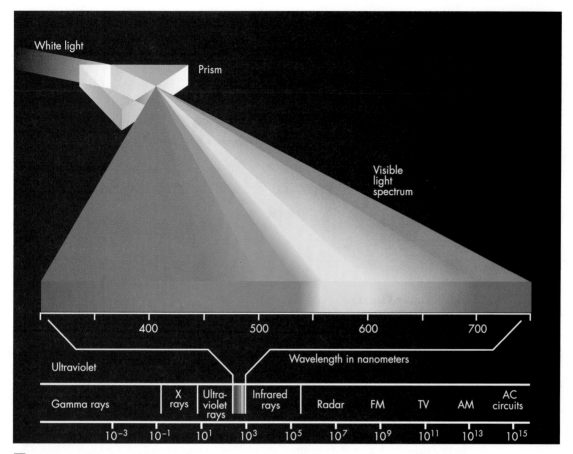

■ **Figure 4.1**
The Visible Spectrum
By passing a source of white light, such as sunlight, through a prism, we break it down into the colors of the visible spectrum. The visible spectrum is just a narrow segment of the electromagnetic spectrum. The electromagnetic spectrum also includes radio waves, microwaves, X-rays, cosmic rays, and many others. Different forms of electromagnetic energy have wavelengths which vary from a few trillionths of a meter to thousands of miles. Visible light varies in wavelength from about 400 to 700 *billionths* of a meter. (A meter = 39.37 inches.)

The Eye: The Better to See You With

Consider that magnificent invention called the camera, which records visual experiences. In traditional cameras, light enters an opening and is focused onto a sensitive surface, or film. Chemicals on film create a lasting impression of the image that entered the camera.

Question: How does the eye work? The eye—our living camera—is no less remarkable. Look at its major parts, as shown in Figure 4.2. As with a film or TV camera, light enters through a narrow opening and is projected onto a sensitive surface. Light first passes through the transparent **cornea,** which covers the front of the eye's surface. (The "white" of the eye, or *sclera,* is composed of hard protective tissue.) The amount of light that passes through the cornea is determined by the size of the opening of the muscle called the **iris,** which is the colored part of the eye. The opening in the iris is the **pupil.** The size of the pupil adjusts automatically to the amount of light present. You do not have to try purposefully to open your eyes further to see better in low lighting conditions. The more intense the light, the smaller the opening. In a similar fashion, we adjust the amount of light allowed into a camera according to its brightness. Pupil size is also sensitive to emotional response: We can literally be "wide-eyed with fear."

Once light passes through the iris, it encounters the **lens.** The lens adjusts or accommodates to the image by changing its thickness. Changes in thickness permit a clear image of the object to be projected onto the retina. These changes focus the light

Learning Connections
See the Connections *CD-ROM to manipulate a virtual eye.*

Cornea
Transparent tissue forming the outer surface of the eyeball.

Iris
A muscular membrane whose dilation regulates the amount of light that enters the eye.

Pupil
The apparently black opening in the center of the iris, through which light enters the eye.

Lens
A transparent body behind the iris that focuses an image on the retina.

■ Figure 4.2
The Human Eye

In both the eye and a camera, light enters through a narrow opening and is projected onto a sensitive surface. In the eye, the photosensitive surface is called the retina, and information concerning the changing images on the retina is transmitted to the brain. The retina contains photoreceptors called rods and cones. Rods and cones transmit sensory input back through the bipolar neurons to the ganglion neurons. The axons of the ganglion neurons form the optic nerve, which transmits sensory stimulation through the brain to the visual cortex of the occipital lobe.

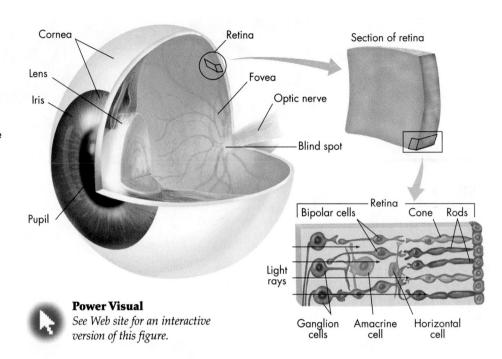

Power Visual
See Web site for an interactive version of this figure.

Retina
The area of the inner surface of the eye that contains rods and cones.

Photoreceptors
Cells that respond to light.

Bipolar Cells
Neurons that conduct neural impulses from rods and cones to ganglion cells.

Ganglion Cells
Neurons whose axons form the optic nerve.

Optic Nerve
The nerve that transmits sensory information from the eye to the brain.

Rods
Rod-shaped photoreceptors that are sensitive only to the intensity of light.

Cones
Cone-shaped photoreceptors that transmit sensations of color.

Fovea
An area near the center of the retina that is dense with cones and where vision is consequently most acute.

Blind Spot
The area of the retina where axons from ganglion cells meet to form the optic nerve.

Visual Acuity
Sharpness of vision.

according to the distance of the object from the viewer. If you hold a finger at arm's length and slowly bring it toward your nose, you will feel tension in the eye as the thickness of the lens accommodates to keep the retinal image in focus. When people squint to bring an object into focus, they are adjusting the thickness of the lens. The lens in a camera does not accommodate to the distance of objects. Instead, to focus the light that is projected onto the film, the camera lens is moved farther from the film or closer to it, as in a zoom lens.

The **retina** is like the film or image surface of the camera. However, the retina consists of cells called **photoreceptors** that are sensitive to light (photosensitive). There are two types of photoreceptors: *rods* and *cones*. The retina (see Figure 4.2) contains several layers of cells: the rods and cones, **bipolar cells,** and **ganglion cells.** All of these cells are neurons. The rods and cones respond to light with chemical changes that create neural impulses that are picked up by the bipolar cells. These then activate the ganglion cells. The axons of the million or so ganglion cells in our retina ultimately converge to form the **optic nerve.** The optic nerve conducts sensory input to the brain, where it is relayed to the visual area of the occipital lobe. As if this were not enough, the eye has additional neurons to enhance this process. Amacrine cells and horizontal cells make sideways connections at a level near the rods and cones and at another level near the ganglion cells. As a result, single bipolar cells can pick up signals from many rods and cones, and, in turn, a single ganglion cell is able to funnel information from multiple bipolar cells. In fact, rods and cones outnumber ganglion cells by more than 100 to 1.

Rods and Cones

As mentioned, **rods** and **cones** are the photoreceptors in the retina (see Figure 4.3). About 125 million rods and 6.4 million cones are distributed across the retina. The cones are most densely packed in a small spot at the center of the retina called the **fovea** (Fig. 4.2). Visual acuity (sharpness and detail) is greatest at this spot. The fovea is composed almost exclusively of cones. Rods are most dense just outside the fovea and thin out toward the periphery of the retina.

Rods allow us to see in black and white. Cones provide color vision. In low lighting, it is possible to photograph a clearer image with black-and-white film than with color film. Similarly, rods are more sensitive to dim light than cones. Therefore, as the illumination grows dim, as during the evening and nighttime hours, objects appear to lose their color well before their outlines fade completely from view.

Rod   Cone

A.

B. Each human retina contains two types of photoreceptor cells: rods and cones. As shown in this color-enhanced photo, the rods are rod-shaped in appearance and the cones are cone-shaped.

■ **Figure 4.3**
A Schematic Drawing and a Photograph of Rods and a Cone

You have about 125 million rods and 6.4 million cones distributed across the retina of each eye. Only cones provide sensations of color. The fovea of the eye is almost exclusively populated by cones, which are then distributed more sparsely as you work toward the periphery of the retina.

Learning Connections
See the Connections *CD-ROM for an animation on transmission of light through the eye.*

In contrast to the visual acuity of the fovea is the **blind spot,** which is insensitive to visual stimulation. It is the part of the retina where the axons of the ganglion cells converge to form the optic nerve (see Figures 4.2 and 4.4).

Visual acuity (sharpness of vision) is connected with the shape of the eye. People who have to be unusually close to an object to discriminate its details are *nearsighted.* People who see distant objects unusually clearly but have difficulty focusing on nearby objects are *farsighted.* Nearsightedness can result when the eyeball is elongated so that the images of distant objects are focused in front of the retina. When the eyeball is too short, the images of nearby objects are focused behind the retina, causing farsightedness. Eyeglasses or contact lenses can be used to help nearsighted people focus distant objects on their retinas. Farsighted people usually see well enough without eyeglasses until they reach their middle years, when they may need glasses for reading.

Beginning in the late 30s to the mid-40s, the lenses start to grow brittle, making it more difficult to accommodate to, or focus on, objects. This condition is called *presbyopia,* from the Greek words for "old man" and "eyes," but presbyopia occurs by middle adulthood, not late adulthood. Presbyopia makes it difficult to perceive nearby visual stimuli. People who had normal visual acuity in their youth often require corrective lenses to read in middle adulthood and beyond.

R E F L E C T

Are you or someone you know nearsighted or farsighted? Have you or someone you know yet experienced presbyopia? How do you or the other person cope with the visual problem?

■ **Figure 4.4**
The Blind Spot

To try a "disappearing act," close your left eye, hold the book close to your face, and look at the boy with your right eye. Slowly move the book away until the pie disappears. The pie disappears because it is being projected onto the blind spot of your retina, the point at which the axons of ganglion neurons collect to form the optic nerve. Note that when the pie disappears, your brain "fills in" the missing checkerboard pattern, which is one reason that you're not usually aware that you have blind spots.

■ Figure 4.5
Dark Adaptation

This illustration shows the amount of light necessary for detection as a function of the amount of time spent in the dark. Cones and rods adapt at different rates. Cones, which permit perception of color, reach maximum dark adaptation in about ten minutes. Rods, which permit perception of dark and light only, are more sensitive than cones. Rods continue to adapt for up to about 45 minutes.

Power Visual
See Web site for an interactive version of this figure.

R E F L E C T

Have you entered a dark theater and gradually seen more and more of your surroundings as time goes on? What processes account for the adjustment?

Light Adaptation

When we walk out onto a dark street, we may at first not be able to see people, trees, and cars clearly. But as time goes on, we are better able to discriminate the features of people and objects. The process of adjusting to lower lighting conditions is called **dark adaptation.**

Figure 4.5 shows the amount of light needed for detection as a function of the amount of time spent in the dark. The cones and rods adapt at different rates. The cones, which permit perception of color, reach their maximum adaptation to darkness in about 10 minutes. The rods, which allow perception of light and dark only, are more sensitive to dim light and continue to adapt to darkness for up to about 45 minutes.

Adaptation to brighter lighting conditions takes place much more rapidly. When you emerge from the theater into the brilliance of the afternoon, you may at first be painfully surprised by the featureless blaze around you. The visual experience is not unlike turning the brightness of the TV set to its maximum setting, at which the edges of objects seem to dissolve into light. Within a minute or so of entering the street, however, the brightness of the scene dims and objects regain their edges.

Color Vision: Creating an Inner World of Color

For most of us, the world is a place of brilliant colors—the blue-greens of the ocean, the red-oranges of the setting sun, the deepened greens of June, the glories of the purple rhododendron and red hibiscus. Color is an emotional and aesthetic part of our everyday lives. In this section we explore some of the dimensions of color and then examine theories about how we manage to convert different wavelengths of light into perceptions of color. ***Question: What are some perceptual dimensions of color?*** These include hue, value, and saturation.

The wavelength of light determines its color, or *hue*. The value of a color is its degree of lightness or darkness. The saturation refers to how intense a color appears to us. A fire-engine red will appear more saturated than a pale pinkish red.

Colors can also have psychological associations within various cultural settings. For example, in the United States a bride may be dressed in white as a sign of purity. In traditional India, the guests would be shocked since white is the color for funerals. Here we mourn in black.

Warm and Cool Colors

If we bend the colors of the spectrum into a circle, we create a color wheel, as shown in Figure 4.6. Psychologically, the colors on the green-blue side of the color wheel are considered to be cool in temperature. Those colors on the yellow-orange-red side are considered to be warm. Perhaps greens and blues suggest the coolness of the ocean and the sky, whereas things that are burning tend to be red or orange. A room decorated in green or blue may seem more appealing on a hot July day than a room decorated in red or orange.

Dark Adaptation
The process of adjusting to conditions of lower lighting by increasing the sensitivity of rods and cones.

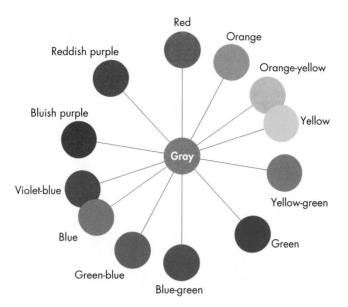

■ Figure 4.6
The Color Wheel
A color wheel can be formed by bending the colors of the spectrum into a circle and placing complementary colors across from one another. (A few colors between violet and red are not found in the spectrum and must be added to complete the circle.) When lights of complementary colors such as yellow and violet-blue are mixed, they dissolve into neutral gray. The afterimage of a color is its complement.

Complementary Colors

The colors across from one another on the color wheel are labeled **complementary**. Red–green and blue–yellow are the major complementary pairs. If we mix complementary colors together, they dissolve into gray.

"But wait!" you say. "Blue and yellow cannot be complementary because by mixing pigments of blue and yellow we create green, not gray." True enough, but we have been talking about mixing *lights,* not *pigments.* Light is the source of all color. Pigments reflect and absorb different wavelengths of light selectively. The mixture of lights is an *additive* process. The mixture of pigments is *subtractive.* Figure 4.7 shows mixtures of lights and pigments of various colors.

Pigments gain their colors by absorbing light from certain segments of the spectrum and reflecting the rest. For example, we see most plant life as green because the pigment in chlorophyll absorbs most of the red, blue, and violet wavelengths of light. The remaining green is reflected. A red pigment absorbs most of the spectrum but reflects red. White pigments reflect all colors equally. Black pigments reflect very little light.

In *Place des Lices* (Figure 4.8), French painter Paul Signac molded his figures and forms from dabs of color. Instead of mixing his pigments, he placed points of pure color next to one another. When the painting is viewed from very close, the sensations are of pure color. But from a distance the juxtaposition of pure colors creates the impression of mixtures of color.

Complementary
Descriptive of colors of the spectrum that when combined produce white or nearly white light.

■ Figure 4.7
Additive and Subtractive Color Mixtures Produced by Lights and Pigments
Thomas Young discovered that white light and all the colors of the spectrum could be produced by adding combinations of lights of red, green, and violet-blue and varying their intensities (see Part A). Part B shows subtractive color mixtures, which are formed by mixing pigments, not light.

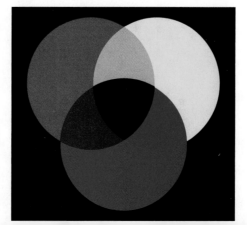

■ **Figure 4.8**
Place des Lices

The French painter Paul Signac molded his figures and forms from dabs of color. Instead of mixing his pigments, he placed points of pure color next to one another. When the viewer is close to the canvas, the points of color are apparent. But from a distance they create the impression of color mixtures.

Afterimages

Before reading on, why don't you try a brief experiment? Look at the strangely colored American flag in Figure 4.9 for at least half a minute. Then look at a sheet of white or gray paper. What has happened to the flag? If your color vision is working properly, and if you looked at the miscolored flag long enough, you should see a flag composed of the familiar red, white, and blue. The flag you perceive on the white sheet of paper is an **afterimage** of the first. (If you didn't look at the green, black, and yellow flag long enough the first time, try it again.) In afterimages, persistent sensations of color are followed by perception of the complementary color when the first color is removed. The same holds true for black and white. Staring at one will create an afterimage of the other. The phenomenon of afterimages has contributed to one of the theories of color vision, as we will see.

Afterimage

The lingering visual impression made by a stimulus that has been removed.

Theories of Color Vision

Adults with normal color vision can discriminate many thousands of colors across the visible spectrum. Different colors have different wavelengths. Although we can vary the physical wavelengths of light in a continuous manner from shorter to longer, many changes in color are discontinuous. For example, our perception of a color shifts suddenly from blue to green, even though the change in wavelength may be smaller than that between two blues.

■ **Figure 4.9**
Three Cheers for the . . . Green, Black, and Yellow?

Don't be concerned. We can readily restore Old Glory to its familiar hues. Place a sheet of white paper beneath the book and stare at the black dot in the center of the flag for at least 30 seconds. Then remove the book. The afterimage on the paper beneath will look familiar.

Question: How do we perceive color? Our ability to perceive color depends on the eye's transmission of different messages to the brain when lights with different wavelengths stimulate the cones in the retina.

▶ CONTROVERSY IN PSYCHOLOGY ◀

What happens in the eye and in the brain when lights with different wavelengths stimulate the retina? How many kinds of color receptors are there?

In this section we explore this controversy by discussing two theories of color vision: the *trichromatic theory* and the *opponent-process theory*.

Trichromatic theory is based on an experiment conducted by the British scientist Thomas Young in the early 1800s. As in Figure 4.7, Young projected three lights of different colors onto a screen so that they partly overlapped. He found that he could create any color from the visible spectrum by simply varying the intensities of the lights. When all three lights fell on the same spot, they created white light, or the appearance of no color at all. The three lights manipulated by Young were red, green, and blue-violet.

The German physiologist Hermann von Helmholtz saw in Young's discovery an explanation of color vision. Von Helmholtz suggested that the retina in the eye must have three different types of color photoreceptors or cones. Some cones must be sensitive to red light, some to green, and some to blue. We see other colors when two different types of color receptors are stimulated. The perception of yellow, for example, would result from the simultaneous stimulation of receptors for red and green. The trichromatic theory is also known as the Young–Helmholtz theory.

In 1870, another German physiologist, Ewald Hering, proposed the **opponent-process theory** of color vision: There are three types of color receptors; however, they are not sensitive just to the simple hues of red, green, and blue as Helmholtz claimed. Hering suggested instead that afterimages (such as that of the American flag shown in Figure 4.9) are made possible by three types of color receptors: red–green, blue–yellow, and a type that perceives differences in brightness. According to Hering, since a red–green cone could not transmit messages for red and green at the same time, if you stare at the green, black, and yellow flag for 30 seconds, that would disturb the balance of neural activity. The afterimage of red, white, and blue would represent the eye's attempt to reestablish a balance.

Research suggests that each theory of color vision is partially correct—in fact, this might simply be a two-stage process in which the cones are as von Helmhotz says, and the transmission signals to the brain are as Hering proposes. For example, research shows that some cones are sensitive to blue, some to green, and some to red (Solomon et al., 2002). But studies of the bipolar and ganglion neurons suggest that messages from cones are transmitted to the brain and relayed by the thalamus to the occipital lobe in an opponent-process fashion (DeValois & Jacobs, 1984). Some opponent-process cells that transmit messages to the visual centers in the brain are excited ("turned on") by green light but inhibited ("turned off") by red light. Others can be excited by red light but are inhibited by green light. A second set of opponent-process cells responds in an opposite manner to blue and yellow. A third set responds in an opposite manner to light and dark.

A neural rebound effect apparently helps explain the occurrence of afterimages. That is, a green-sensitive ganglion that had been excited by green light for half a minute or so might switch briefly to inhibitory activity when the light is shut off. The effect would be to perceive red even though no red light is present.

These theoretical updates allow for the afterimage effects with the green, black, and yellow flag and are also consistent with Young's experiments in mixing lights of different colors.

Color Blindness: What Kind of "Chromat" Are You?

If you can discriminate among the colors of the visible spectrum, you have normal color vision and are labeled a **trichromat.** This means that you are sensitive to red–green, blue–yellow, and light–dark. *Questions: What is color blindness? Why*

Trichromatic Theory
The theory that color vision is made possible by three types of cones, some of which respond to red light, some to green, and some to blue. (From the Greek roots *treis*, meaning "three," and *chroma*, meaning "color.")

Opponent-Process Theory
The theory that color vision is made possible by three types of cones, some of which respond to red or green light, some to blue or yellow, and some only to the intensity of light.

Trichromat
A person with normal color vision.

REFLECT
How do you imagine that color-blind people know when to stop at a traffic light and when to proceed?

■ Figure 4.10
Plates from a Test for Color Blindness

Can you see the numbers in these plates from a test for color blindness? A person with red–green color blindness would not be able to see the 6, and a person with blue–yellow color blindness would probably not discern the 12. (Caution: These reproductions cannot be used for actual testing of color blindness.)

Monochromat
A person who is sensitive to black and white only and hence color-blind.

Dichromat
A person who is sensitive to black–white and either red–green or blue–yellow and hence partially color-blind.

Closure
The tendency to perceive a broken figure as being complete or whole.

Perceptual Organization
The tendency to integrate perceptual elements into meaningful patterns.

are some people color-blind? People who are totally color-blind, called **monochromats,** are sensitive only to lightness and darkness. Total color blindness is rare. Fully color-blind individuals see the world as trichromats would on a black-and-white TV set or in a black-and-white movie.

Partial color blindness is a sex-linked trait that affects mostly males. Partially color-blind people are called **dichromats.** They can discriminate only between two colors—red and green or blue and yellow—and the colors that are derived from mixing these colors. Figure 4.10 shows the types of tests that are used to diagnose color-blindness.

A dichromat might put on one red sock and one green sock, but would not mix red and blue socks. Monochromats might put on socks of any color. They would not notice a difference as long as the socks' colors did not differ in intensity—that is, brightness.

REVIEW

Learning Connections
See Web site for an interactive version of these review questions.

(6) Visible light is part of a spectrum of _____ energy. (7) The color of visible light is determined by its _____. (8) Light enters the eye through the _____. (9) The muscle called the _____ determines the amount of light that is let in. (10) The _____ accommodates to an image by changing thickness and focusing light onto the retina. (11) The retina is made up of photoreceptors called rods and _____. (12) The axons of ganglion cells make up the _____ nerve, which conducts visual information to the brain. (13) Rods transmit sensations of light and dark, and cones permit perception of _____.

Critical Thinking: What is the evidence for the different theories of color vision?

VISUAL PERCEPTION: HOW PERCEPTIVE?

What do you see in Figure 4.11? Do you see meaningless splotches of ink or a rider on horseback? If you perceive a horse and rider, it is not just because of the visual sensations provided by the drawing. Each of the blobs is meaningless in and of itself, and the pattern is vague. Despite the lack of clarity, however, you may still perceive a horse and rider.

Visual perception is the process by which we organize or make sense of the sensory impressions caused by the light that strikes our eyes. Visual perception involves our knowledge, expectations, and motivations. Whereas sensation may be thought of as a mechanical process (e.g., light stimulating the rods and cones of our retina), perception is an active process through which we interpret the world around us. *Question: How do we organize bits of visual information into meaningful wholes?* The answer has something to do with your general knowledge and your desire to fit incoming bits and pieces of information into familiar patterns.

In the case of the horse and rider, your integration of disconnected pieces of information into a meaningful whole also reflects what Gestalt psychologists (see Chapter 1) refer to as the principle of **closure,** or the tendency to perceive a complete or whole figure even when there are gaps in the sensory input. Put another way, in perception the whole can be very much more than the mere sum of the parts. A collection of parts can be meaningless. It is their configuration that matters.

Perceptual Organization: Getting It Together

Early in the 20th century, Gestalt psychologists noted certain consistencies in the way we integrate bits and pieces of sensory stimulation into meaningful wholes. They attempted to identify the rules that govern these processes. Max Wertheimer, in particular, discovered many such rules. As a group, these rules are referred to as the laws of **perceptual organization.** We examine several of them, beginning with those concerning figure–ground perception. Then we consider top-down and bottom-up processing.

Figure–Ground Perception

If you look out your window, you may see people, buildings, cars, and streets, or perhaps grass, trees, birds, and clouds. All these objects tend to be perceived as figures against backgrounds. Individual cars seen against the background of the street are easier to pick out than cars piled on top of one another in a junkyard. Birds seen against the sky are more likely to be perceived than birds seen "in the bush."

When figure–ground relationships are ambiguous, or capable of being interpreted in various ways, our perceptions tend to be unstable, shifting back and forth. As an example, look for a while at Figure 4.12. How many people, objects, and animals can you find? If your eye is drawn back and forth, so that sometimes you are perceiving light figures on a dark background and at other time dark figures on a light background, you are experiencing figure–ground reversals. In other words, a shift is occurring in your perception of what is figure and what is ground, or background. The artist was able to have some fun with us because of our tendency to try to isolate geometric patterns or figures from a background. However, in this case the "background" is as meaningful and detailed as the "figure." Therefore, our perceptions shift back and forth.

Figure 4.13 shows a Rubin vase, one of psychologists' favorite illustrations of figure–ground relationships. The figure–ground relationship in part A of the figure is ambiguous. There are no cues that suggest which area must be the figure. For this reason, our perception may shift from seeing the vase to seeing two profiles. There is no such problem in part B. Since it seems that a white vase has been brought forward against a colored ground, we are more likely to perceive the vase than the profiles. In part C, we are more likely to perceive the profiles than the vase because the profiles are whole and the vase is broken against the background. Of course, if we wish to, we can still perceive the vase in part C, because experience has shown us where it is. Why not have some fun with friends by covering up parts B and C and asking them what they see? (They'll catch on quickly if they can see all three drawings at once.)

■ Figure 4.11
Closure

Meaningless splotches of ink or a horse and rider? This figure illustrates the Gestalt principle of closure.

REFLECT

Why is it easier to spot a friend walking alone than in a crowd?

■ Figure 4.12
Figure and Ground

How many animals and demons can you find in this Escher print? Do we have white figures on a black background or black figures on a white background? Figure–ground perception is the tendency to perceive geometric forms against a background.

Figure 4.13
The Rubin Vase

A favorite drawing used by psychologists to demonstrate figure–ground perception. Part A is ambiguous, with neither the vase nor the profiles clearly the figure or the ground. In part B, the vase is the figure; in part C, the profiles are.

Power Visual
See Web site for an interactive version of this figure.

A.   B.   C.

The Necker cube (Figure 4.14) is another ambiguous drawing that can lead to perceptual shifts. Hold this page at arm's length and stare at the center of the figure for 30 seconds or so. Try to allow your eye muscles to relax. (The feeling is of your eyes "glazing over.") After a while you will notice a dramatic shift in your perception of the box. What was once a front edge is now a back edge, and vice versa. The perceptual shift is made possible by the fact that the outline of the drawing permits two interpretations.

Other Gestalt Rules for Organization

In addition to the law of closure, Gestalt psychologists have noted that our perceptions are guided by rules or laws of *proximity, similarity, continuity,* and *common fate.*

Without reading further, describe part A of Figure 4.15. Did you say it consists of six lines or of three groups of two parallel lines? If you said three sets of lines, you were influenced by the **proximity,** or nearness, of some of the lines. There is no other reason for perceiving them in pairs or subgroups: All of the lines are parallel and of equal length.

Now describe part B of the figure. Did you perceive the figure as a 6 × 6 grid, or as three columns of *x*'s and three columns of *o*'s? According to the law of **similarity,** we perceive similar objects as belonging together. For this reason, you may have been more likely to describe part B in terms of columns than in terms of rows or a grid.

What about part C? Is it a circle with two lines stemming from it, or is it a (broken) line that goes through a circle? If you saw it as a single (broken) line, you were probably organizing your perceptions according to the rule of **continuity.** That is, we perceive a series of points or a broken line as having unity.

According to the law of **common fate,** elements seen moving together are perceived as belonging together. A group of people running in the same direction appears unified in purpose. Birds that flock together seem to be of a feather. (Did I get that right?)

Proximity
Nearness. The perceptual tendency to group together objects that are near one another.

Similarity
The perceptual tendency to group together objects that are similar in appearance.

Continuity
The tendency to perceive a series of points or lines as having unity.

Common Fate
The tendency to perceive elements that move together as belonging together.

Figure 4.14
The Necker Cube

Ambiguity in the drawing of the cube makes perceptual shifts possible. Therefore, the darker tinted surface can become either the front or back of the cube.

Power Visual
See Web site for an interactive version of this figure.

R E F L E C T

Have you ever seen two people walking next to each other and then been surprised to see them split up without saying anything? Why did you assume that they knew each other?

Figure 4.15
Some Gestalt Laws of Perceptual Organization

These drawings illustrate the Gestalt laws of proximity, similarity, continuity, and closure.

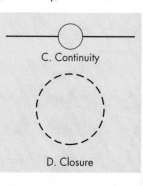

A. Proximity   B. Similarity   C. Continuity   D. Closure

Part D of Figure 4.15 provides another example of the law of closure. The arcs tend to be perceived as a circle (or circle with gaps) rather than as just a series of arcs.

Top-Down Versus Bottom-Up Processing

Imagine that you are trying to put together a 1,000-piece jigsaw puzzle—a task I usually avoid, despite the cajoling of my children. Now imagine that you are trying to accomplish it after someone has walked off with the box showing the picture formed by the completed puzzle.

When you have the box—when you know what the "big picture" or pattern looks like—cognitive psychologists refer to the task of assembling the pieces as **top-down processing.** The "top" of the visual system refers to the image of the pattern in the brain, and the top-down strategy for putting the puzzle together implies that you use the larger pattern to guide subordinate perceptual motor tasks such as hunting for particular pieces. Without knowledge of the pattern (without the box), the assembly process is referred to as **bottom-up processing.** You begin with bits and pieces of information and become aware of the pattern formed only after you have worked at it for a while.

Top-down and bottom-up processing can be applied to many cognitive matters, even politics. If you consider yourself to be a liberal or a conservative, you can "fill in" your attitude toward many specific issues by applying the liberal or conservative position. That is top-down processing. But many people do not label themselves liberal or conservative. They look at issues and form positions on an issue-by-issue basis. Eventually they may discover an overall pattern that places them more or less in the liberal or conservative camp. That is bottom-up processing.

Life on the Move—Perception of Motion

Moving objects—people, animals, cars, or boulders plummeting down a hillside—are vital sources of sensory information. Moving objects even capture the attention of newborn infants. *Question: How do we perceive movement?*

To understand how we perceive movement, recall what it is like to be on a train that has begun to pull out of the station while the train on the adjacent track remains stationary. If your own train does not lurch as it accelerates, you might think at first that the other train is moving. Or you might not be certain whether your train is moving forward or the other train is moving backward.

The visual perception of movement is based on change of position relative to other objects. To early scientists, whose only tool for visual observation was the naked eye, it seemed logical that the sun circled the earth. You have to be able to imagine the movement of the earth around the sun as seen from a theoretical point in outer space—you cannot observe it directly.

How, then, do you determine which train is moving when your train is pulling out of the station (or the other train is pulling in)? One way is to look for objects that you know are stable, such as platform columns, houses, signs, or trees. If you are stationary in relation to them, your train is not moving. Observing people walking on the station platform may not provide the answer, however, because they are also changing their position relative to stationary objects. You might also try to sense the motion of the train in your body. You know from experience how to do these things quite well, although it may be difficult to phrase explanations for them.

We have been considering the perception of real movement. Psychologists have also studied several types of apparent movement, or **illusions** of movement. These include the *autokinetic effect, stroboscopic motion,* and the *phi phenomenon.*

The Autokinetic Effect

If you were to sit quietly in a dark room and stare at a point of light projected onto the far wall, after a while it might appear that the light had begun to move, even if it actually remained quite still. The tendency to perceive a stationary point of light as moving in a dark room is called the **autokinetic effect.**

Over the years, psychologists have conducted interesting experiments in which they have asked people, for example, what the light is "spelling out." The light has

Top-Down Processing
The use of contextual information or knowledge of a pattern in order to organize parts of the pattern.

Bottom-Up Processing
The organization of the parts of a pattern to recognize, or form an image of, the pattern they compose.

Illusions
Sensations that give rise to misperceptions.

Autokinetic Effect
The tendency to perceive a stationary point of light in a dark room as moving.

Stroboscopic Motion

A visual illusion in which the perception of motion is generated by a series of stationary images that are presented in rapid succession.

Phi Phenomenon

The perception of movement as a result of sequential presentation of visual stimuli.

Monocular Cues

Stimuli suggestive of depth that can be perceived with only one eye.

spelled out nothing, of course, and the words perceived by subjects reflect their own cognitive processes, not external sensations.

Stroboscopic Motion

Stroboscopic motion makes motion pictures possible. In **stroboscopic motion,** the illusion of movement is provided by the presentation of a rapid progression of images of stationary objects. So-called motion pictures do not really consist of images that move. Rather, the audience is shown 16 to 22 pictures, or *frames,* per second. Each frame differs slightly from the preceding one. Showing the frames in rapid succession provides the illusion of movement.

At the rate of at least 16 frames per second, the "motion" in a film seems smooth and natural. With fewer than 16 or so frames per second, the movement looks jumpy and unnatural. That is why slow motion is achieved by filming perhaps 100 or more frames per second. When they are played back at about 22 frames per second, the movement seems slowed down, yet still smooth and natural.

The Phi Phenomenon

Have you seen news headlines spelled out in lights that rapidly wrap around a building? Have you seen an electronic scoreboard in a baseball or football stadium? When the home team scores, some scoreboards suggest explosions of fireworks. What actually happens is that a row of lights is switched on and then off. As the first row is switched off, a second row is switched on, and so on for dozens, perhaps hundreds of rows. When the switching occurs rapidly, the **phi phenomenon occurs:** the on–off process is perceived as movement.

Like stroboscopic motion, the phi phenomenon is an example of apparent motion. Both appear to occur because of the law of continuity. We tend to perceive a series of points as having unity, so each series of lights (points) is perceived as a moving line.

Depth Perception: How Far Is Far?

Think of the problems you might have if you could not judge depth or distance. You might bump into other people, believing them to be farther away. An outfielder might not be able to judge whether to run toward the infield or the fence to catch a fly ball. You might give your front bumper a workout in stop-and-go traffic. *Question: How do we perceive depth?* It happens that *monocular* and *binocular cues* both help us perceive the depth of objects—that is, their distance from us.

Monocular Cues

Now that you have considered how difficult it would be to navigate through life without depth perception, ponder the problems of the artist who attempts to portray three-dimensional objects on a two-dimensional surface. Artists use a type of **monocular cue**—pictorial cues—to create an illusion of depth. These are cues that can be perceived by one eye (*mono-* means "one"). They include perspective, relative size, clearness, interposition, shadows, and texture gradient, and they cause certain objects to appear more distant from the viewer than others.

■ **Stroboscopic Motion**
In a motion picture, viewing a series of stationary images at the rate of about 16 to 22 frames per second provides an illusion of movement termed *stroboscopic motion*. The actual movement that is occurring is the rapid switching of stationary images.

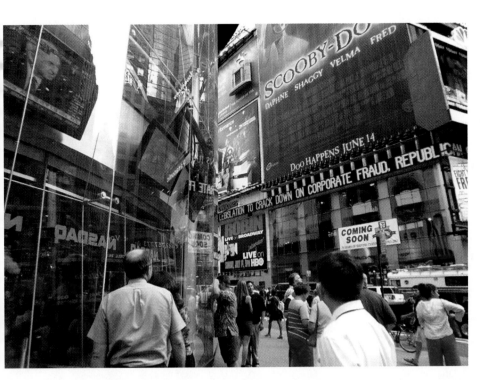

■ The Phi Phenomenon
The phi phenomenon is an illusion of movement that is produced by lights blinking on and off in sequence, as with New York Stock Exchange electronic "tickers," electronic scoreboards, and news "flowing" around a building in Times Square.

Distant objects stimulate smaller areas on the retina than nearby ones. The amount of sensory input from them is smaller, even though they may be the same size. The distances between far-off objects also appear to be smaller than equivalent distances between nearby objects. For this reason, the phenomenon known as **perspective** occurs. That is, we tend to perceive parallel lines as coming closer together, or converging, as they recede from us. However, as we will see when we discuss *size constancy*, experience teaches us that distant objects that look small are larger when they are close. In this way, their relative size also becomes a cue to their distance.

The two engravings in Figure 4.16 represent impossible scenes in which the artists use principles of perspective to fool the viewer. In the one on the left, *Waterfall*, note that the water appears to be flowing away from the viewer in a zigzag because the stream gradually becomes narrower (that is, lines we assume to be parallel are shown to be converging) and the stone sides of the aqueduct appear to be stepping down. However, given that the water arrives at the top of the fall, it must actually be flowing upward somehow. However, the spot from which it falls is no farther from the viewer than the collection point from which it appears to (but does not) begin its flow backward.

Artists normally use *relative size*—the fact that distant objects look smaller than nearby objects of the same size—to suggest depth in their works. The paradoxes in the engraving on the right, *False Perspective*, are made possible because more distant objects are *not* necessarily depicted as smaller than nearby objects. Thus, what at first seems to be background suddenly becomes foreground, and vice versa.

The *clearness* of an object also suggests its distance. Experience teaches us that we sense more details of nearby objects. For this reason, artists can suggest that objects are closer to the viewer by depicting them in greater detail. Note that the "distant" hill in the Hogarth engraving (Figure 4.16) is given less detail than the nearby plants at the bottom of the picture. Our perceptions are mocked when a man "on" the distant hill in the background is shown conversing with a woman leaning out a window in the middle ground.

We also learn that nearby objects can block our view of more-distant objects. Overlapping, or *interposition*, is the placing of one object in front of another. Experience teaches us that partly covered objects are farther away than the objects that obscure them (Figure 4.17). In the Hogarth engraving (Figure 4.16), which looks closer: the group of trees in the background (background?) or the moon sign hanging from the building (or is it buildings?) to the right? How does the artist use interposition to confuse the viewer?

Perspective

A monocular cue for depth based on the convergence (coming together) of parallel lines as they recede into the distance.

FRONTISPIECE TO KERBY.

■ Figure 4.16
What Is Wrong with These Pictures?

In *Waterfall*, to the left, how does Dutch artist M. C. Escher suggest that fallen water flows back upward, only to fall again? In *False Perspective*, to the right, how does English artist William Hogarth use monocular cues for depth perception to deceive the viewer?

■ Figure 4.17
The Effects of Interposition

The four circles are all the same size. Which circles seem closer? The complete circles or the circles with chunks bitten out of them?

■ Figure 4.18
Shadowing as a Cue for Depth

Shadowing makes the circle on the right look three-dimensional.

Additional information about depth is provided by *shadowing* and is based on the fact that opaque objects block light and produce shadows. Shadows and highlights give us information about an object's three-dimensional shape and its relationship to the source of light. For example, the left part of Figure 4.18 is perceived as a two-dimensional circle, but the right part tends to be perceived as a three-dimensional sphere because of the highlight on its surface and the shadow underneath. In the "sphere," the highlighted central area is perceived as closest to us, with the surface receding to the edges.

Another monocular cue is *texture gradient*. (A gradient is a progressive change.) Closer objects are perceived as having rougher textures. In the Hogarth engraving (Figure 4.16), the building just behind the large fisherman's head has a rougher texture and therefore seems to be closer than the building with the window from which the woman is leaning. Our surprise is heightened when the moon sign is seen as hanging from both buildings.

REFLECT

Have you ever driven in the country and perceived the stars or distant hills to be moving along with you? How do you explain the phenomenon?

Motion cues are another kind of monocular cue. If you have ever driven in the country, you have probably noticed that distant objects such as mountains and stars appear to move along with you. Objects at an intermediate distance seem to be stationary, but nearby objects such as roadside markers, rocks, and trees seem to go by quite rapidly. The tendency of objects to seem to move backward or forward as a function of their distance is known as *motion parallax*. We learn to perceive objects that appear to move with us as being at greater distances.

Earlier we noted that nearby objects cause the lens of the eye to accommodate or bend more in order to bring them into focus. The sensations of tension in the eye muscles also provide a monocular cue to depth, especially when we are within about 4 feet of the objects.

Binocular Cues

Binocular cues, or cues that involve both eyes, also help us perceive depth. Two binocular cues are *retinal disparity* and *convergence.*

Try an experiment. Hold your right index finger at arm's length. Now hold your left index finger about a foot closer, but in a direct line. If you keep your eyes relaxed as you do so, you will see first one finger and then the other. An image of each finger will be projected onto the retina of each eye, and each image will be slightly different because the finger will be seen from different angles. The difference between the projected images is referred to as *retinal disparity* and serves as a binocular cue for depth perception. Note that in the case of the closer finger, the "two fingers" appear to be farther apart. Closer objects have greater retinal disparity.

If we try to maintain a single image of the closer finger, our eyes must turn inward, or converge on it, making us cross-eyed. *Convergence* causes feelings of tension in the eye muscles and provides another binocular cue for depth. (After convergence occurs, try looking at the finger first with one eye closed, then the other. You will readily see how different the images are in each eye.) The binocular cues of retinal disparity and convergence are strongest when objects are close. Table 4.1 summarizes monocular and binocular cues for depth perception.

Perceptual Constancies: Keeping the World a Stable Place

The world is a constantly shifting display of visual sensations. Think how confusing it would be if you believed that a door was a trapezoid and not a rectangle because it is ajar. Or what if we perceived a doorway to be a different doorway when seen from 6 feet away as compared to 4 feet? As we neared it, we might think it was larger than the door we were seeking and become lost. Or consider the problems of the pet owner who recognizes his dog from the side but not from above because its shape is different when seen from above. Fortunately, these problems tend not to occur—at least with familiar objects—because perceptual constancies enable us to recognize objects even when their apparent shape or size differs. ***Questions: What are perceptual constancies? Why do we perceive a door to be a rectangle even when it is partly open?***

© David Dempster/Offshoot

■ **Retinal Disparity and Convergence as Cues for Depth**

As an object nears your eyes, you begin to see two images of it because of retinal disparity. To maintain perception of a single image, your eyes must converge on the object.

TABLE 4.1 Cues for Depth Perception

Monocular Cues		
Pictorial Cues*	Perspective	Perceiving parallel lines as coming closer together, or converging, as they recede from us
	Relative Size	Perceiving larger objects as being closer to us
	Clearness	Perceiving objects with greater detail as being closer to us
	Interposition	Perceiving objects that block our view of other objects as being closer to us (also called *overlapping*)
	Shadowing	Perceiving shadows and highlights as giving depth to two-dimensional objects
	Texture Gradient	Perceiving objects with rougher textures as being closer
Motion Cues	Motion Parallax	Perceiving objects that seem to move forward with us as distant and objects that seem to move backward as nearby
Binocular Cues		
Retinal Disparity		Perceiving objects that cast more greatly differing images on the retinas of the eyes as being closer
Convergence		Perceiving objects for whom focusing requires greater inward movement of the eyes (and therefore greater feelings of tension in the eyes) as being closer

*These cues are commonly used by artists to create the impression of depth (a third dimension) in two-dimensional works such as drawings and paintings.

■ Figure 4.19
Brightness Constancy

The orange squares within the blue squares are the same hue, yet the orange within the dark blue square is perceived as brighter. Why?

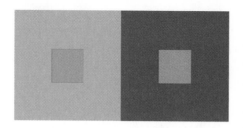

Size Constancy

The tendency to perceive an object as being the same size even as the size of its retinal image changes according to the object's distance.

Color Constancy

The tendency to perceive an object as being the same color even though lighting conditions change its appearance.

Brightness Constancy

The tendency to perceive an object as being just as bright even though lighting conditions change its intensity.

Shape Constancy

The tendency to perceive an object as being the same shape although the retinal image varies in shape as it rotates.

■ Figure 4.20
Shape and Size Constancy

A. We perceive the three doors to be rectangles, although the images projected onto the retina can be a wide line when the door is fully open, a trapezoid when the door is partly open, and a rectangle only when it is closed and we stand directly in front of it. B. We perceive the woman's hand to remain the same size, although the images projected onto the retina grow larger as the hand comes closer to us.

A.

B.

There are a number of perceptual constancies, including that of **size constancy.** We may say that people "look like ants" when viewed from the top of a tall building, but because of size constancy, we know they remain full-sized people even if the details of their forms are lost in the distance. We can thus say that we *perceive* people to be the same size, even when viewed from different distances.

The image of a dog seen from 20 feet away occupies about the same amount of space on your retina as an inch-long insect crawling on your hand. Yet you do not perceive the dog to be as small as the insect. Through your visual experiences you have acquired size constancy—that is, the tendency to perceive an object as the same size even though the size of its image on your retina varies as a function of its distance. Experience teaches us about perspective—that the same object seen at a distance appears to be smaller than when it is nearby.

Color constancy is the tendency to perceive objects as retaining their color even though lighting conditions may alter their appearance. Your bright yellow car may edge toward gray as the hours wend their way through twilight. But when you finally locate the car in the parking lot, you may still think of it as yellow. You expect to find a yellow car and still judge it to be "more yellow" than the (twilight-faded) red and green cars on either side of it.

Brightness constancy is similar to color constancy. Consider Figure 4.19. The orange squares within the blue squares are equally bright, yet the one within the dark blue square is perceived as brighter. Why? Again, consider the role of experience. If it were nighttime, we would expect orange to fade to gray. The fact that the orange within the dark square stimulates the eye with equal intensity suggests that it must be much brighter than the orange within the lighter square.

Shape constancy is the tendency to perceive objects as maintaining their shape, even if we look at them from different angles so that the shape of their image on the retina changes dramatically. You perceive the top of a coffee cup or a glass to be a circle even though it is a circle only when seen from above. When seen from an angle, it is an ellipse. When the cup or glass is seen on edge, its retinal image is the same as that of a straight line. So why do you still describe the rim of the cup or glass as a circle? Perhaps for two reasons: First, experience has taught you that the cup will look circular when seen from above. Second, you may have labeled the cup as circular or round. Experience and labels help make the world a stable place. Can you imagine the chaos that would prevail if we described objects as they appear as they stimulate our sensory organs with each changing moment?

Let us return to the door that "changes shape" when it is ajar. The door is a rectangle only when viewed straight on (Figure 4.20). When we move to the side or open it, the left or right edge comes closer and appears to be larger, changing the retinal image to a trapezoid. Yet we continue to think of doors as rectangles. Also, we would not assume that someone's hand is growing as it gets closer to us (Figure 4.20).

Learning Connections
See Web site for an interactive version of these review questions.

R E V I E W

(14) Perceptual organization concerns the grouping of bits of sensory stimulation into a meaningful _____. (15) Gestalt rules of perceptual organization refer to _____-ground relationships, proximity, similarity, continuity, common fate, and closure. (16) When we are putting puzzle pieces together, a picture of the result enables us to engage in _____-_____ processing;

A Closer Look

Visual Illusions: Is Seeing Believing?

The principles of perceptual organization make it possible for our eyes to "play tricks" on us. Psychologists, like magicians, enjoy pulling a rabbit out of a hat now and then. Let me demonstrate how the perceptual constancies trick the eye through *visual illusions*.

The Hering–Helmholtz and Müller–Lyer illusions (Figure 4.21, parts A and B) are named after the people who devised them. In the Hering–Helmholtz illusion, the horizontal lines are straight and parallel. However, the radiating lines cause them to appear to be bent outward near the center. The two lines in the Müller–Lyer illusion are the same length, but the line on the left, with its reversed arrowheads, looks longer.

Let us try to explain these illusions. Because of our experience and lifelong use of perceptual cues, we tend to perceive the Hering–Helmholtz drawing as three-dimensional. Because of our tendency to perceive bits of sensory information as figures against grounds, we perceive the white area in the center as a circle in front of a series of radiating lines, all of which lie in front of a white ground. Next, because of our experience with perspective, we perceive the radiating lines as parallel. We perceive the two horizontal lines as intersecting the "receding" lines, and we know that they would have to appear bent out at the center if they were to be equidistant at all points from the center of the circle.

Experience probably compels us to perceive the vertical lines in the Müller–Lyer illusion as the corners of a building (see Figure 4.21, part B). We interpret the length of the lines based on our experience with corners of buildings.

Figure 4.22 is known as the Ponzo illusion. In this illusion, the two monsters are the same size. However, do you perceive the top monster as being bigger? The rule of size constancy may give us some insight into this illusion as well. Perhaps the converging lines again strike us as being lines receding into the distance. Again, the rule of size constancy tells us that if two objects appear to be the same size and one is farther away, the object that looks farther away must be larger. So we perceive the top monster as being larger.

■ **Figure 4.22**
A Monstrous Illusion

The two monsters in this drawing are exactly the same height and width. Yet the top one appears to be much larger. Can you use the principle of size constancy to explain why?

Learning Connections
See the Connections *CD-ROM for animations on size constancy and visual illusions and on the Ames Room.*

■ **Figure 4.21**
The Hering–Helmholtz and Müller–Lyer Illusions

In the Hering–Helmholtz illusion, are the horizontal lines straight or curved? In the Müller–Lyer illusion, are the vertical lines equal in length?

The Hering-Helmholtz Illusion

The Müller-Lyer Illusion

A.

Power Visual
See Web site for an interactive

B.

Life Connections
See the Connections *CD-ROM for an animation on the moon illusion.*

otherwise we must solve the puzzle by bottom-up processing. (17) We perceive movement by sensing motion across the _____ and change of position in relation to other objects. (18) _____ motion, used in films, is an illusion of motion caused by the rapid presentation of a series of still images.

Critical Thinking: How do creators of visual illusions use laws of perception to trick the eye?

HEARING: MAKING SENSE OF SOUND

Consider the advertising slogan for the old science fiction film *Alien:* "In space, no one can hear you scream." It's true. Space is an almost perfect vacuum. Hearing requires a medium through which sound can travel, such as air or water. ***Question: What is sound?***

Sound, or **auditory** stimulation, travels through the air as waves. If you could see them, they would look something like the ripples in a pond when you toss in a pebble. You hear the splash even if you can't see the sound of it. The sound of the splash is caused by changes in air pressure. The air is alternately compressed and expanded like the movements of an accordion. If you were listening under water, you would also hear the splash because of changes in the pressure of the water. In either case, the changes in pressure are vibrations that approach your ears in waves. These vibrations—sound waves—can also be created by a ringing bell (Figure 4.23), your vocal cords, guitar strings, or the slam of a book thrown down on a desk. A single cycle of compression and expansion is one wave of sound. Sound waves can occur many (many!) times in 1 second. The human ear is sensitive to sound waves with frequencies of from 20 to 20,000 cycles per second.

Auditory
Having to do with hearing.

Hertz (Hz)
A unit expressing the frequency of sound waves. One hertz equals one cycle per second.

Decibel (dB)
A unit expressing the loudness of a sound.

Pitch and Loudness—All Sorts of Vibes

Pitch and loudness are two psychological dimensions of sound. The pitch of a sound is determined by its frequency, or the number of cycles per second as expressed in the unit **hertz (Hz).** One cycle per second is 1 Hz. The greater the number of cycles per second (Hz), the higher the pitch of the sound. The pitch of women's voices is usually higher than that of men's voices because women's vocal cords are usually shorter and therefore vibrate at a greater frequency. The strings of a violin are shorter than those of a viola or bass viol. They vibrate at greater frequencies, and we perceive them as higher in pitch. Pitch detectors in the brain allow us to tell the difference.

The loudness of a sound roughly corresponds to the height, or amplitude, of sound waves. Figure 4.24 shows records of sound waves that vary in frequency and amplitude. Frequency and amplitude are independent. Both high- and low-pitched sounds can be either high or low in loudness.

REFLECT

Are you familiar with the violin, viola, cello, and bass fiddle? How do their sounds differ? How do you account for the differences?

The loudness of a sound is expressed in **decibels (dB).** Zero dB is equivalent to the threshold of hearing—the lowest sound that the typical person can hear. How loud is that? It's about as loud as the ticking of a watch 20 feet away in a very quiet room.

The decibel equivalents of many familiar sounds are shown in

■ **Figure 4.23**
Creation of Sound Waves

The ringing of a bell compresses and expands (rarifies) air molecules, sending forth vibrations that stimulate the sense of hearing and are called sound waves.

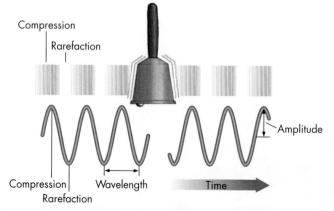

Figure 4.25. Twenty-five dB is equivalent in loudness to a whisper at 5 feet. Thirty dB is roughly the limit of loudness at which your librarian would like to keep your college library. You may suffer hearing damage if you are exposed to sounds of 85 to 90 dB for very long periods.

Now let us turn our attention to the human ear—the marvelous instrument that senses all these different "vibes."

The Ear: The Better to Hear You With

The human ear is good for lots of things—including catching dust, combing your hair around, hanging jewelry from, and nibbling. It is also well-suited to sensing sounds. *Question: How does the ear work?* The ear is shaped and structured to capture sound waves, vibrate in sympathy with them, and transmit them to centers in the brain. In this way, you not only hear something, you can also figure out what it is. The ear has three parts: the outer ear, middle ear, and inner ear (see Figure 4.26).

The outer ear is shaped to funnel sound waves to the **eardrum**, a thin membrane that vibrates in response to sound waves and thereby transmits them to the middle and inner ears. The middle ear contains the eardrum and three small bones—the hammer, the anvil, and the stirrup—which also transmit sound by vibrating. These bones were given their names (actually the Latin *malleus, incus,* and *stapes* [pronounced STAY-peas], which translate as hammer, anvil, and stirrup) because of their shapes. The middle ear functions as an amplifier: It increases the pressure of the air entering the ear.

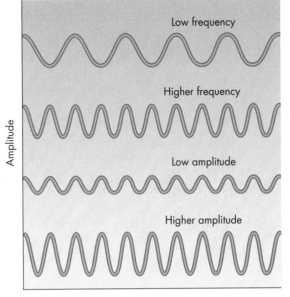

■ **Figure 4.24**
Sound Waves of Various Frequencies and Amplitudes
Which sounds have the highest pitch? Which are loudest?

Eardrum
A thin membrane that vibrates in response to sound waves, transmitting the waves to the middle and inner ears.

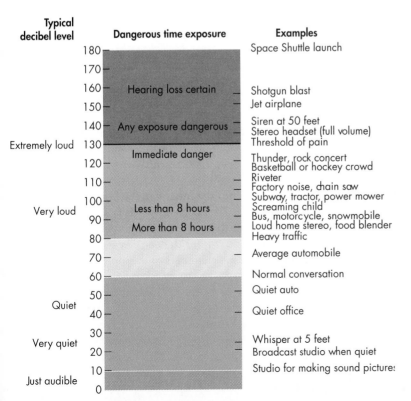

■ **Figure 4.25**
Decibel Ratings of Familiar Sounds
Zero dB is the threshold of hearing. You may suffer hearing loss if you incur prolonged exposure to sounds of 85 to 90 dB.

Power Visual
See Web site for an interactive version of this figure.

Organ of Corti

Basilar membrane

Tectorial membrane

Hair cells

Section through cochlea

Hammer (malleus)

Anvil (incus)

Stirrup (stapes)

Semicircular canals

Auditory nerve

Oval window

Cochlea

Auditory nerve

Round window

Outer ear (auditory canal)

Eardrum

Middle ear

Eustachian tube

■ Figure 4.26
The Human Ear

The outer ear funnels sound to the eardrum. Inside the eardrum, vibrations of the hammer, anvil, and stirrup transmit sound to the inner ear. Vibrations in the cochlea transmit the sound to the auditory nerve by way of the basilar membrane and the organ of Corti.

Cochlea
The inner ear; the bony tube that contains the basilar membrane and the organ of Corti.

Basilar Membrane
A membrane that lies coiled within the cochlea.

Organ of Corti
The receptor for hearing that lies on the basilar membrane in the cochlea.

Auditory Nerve
The axon bundle that transmits neural impulses from the organ of Corti to the brain.

The stirrup is attached to another vibrating membrane, the *oval window*. The *round window* shown in Figure 4.26 balances the pressure in the inner ear. It pushes outward when the oval window pushes in, and it is pulled inward when the oval window vibrates outward.

The oval window transmits vibrations into the inner ear, the bony tube called the **cochlea** (from the Greek word for "snail"). The cochlea, which is shaped like a snail shell, contains two longitudinal membranes that divide it into three fluid-filled chambers. One of the membranes that lies coiled within the cochlea is called the **basilar membrane.** Vibrations in the fluids within the chambers of the inner ear press against the basilar membrane.

The **organ of Corti,** sometimes referred to as the "command post" of hearing, is attached to the basilar membrane. There are some 16,000 receptor cells—called hair cells because they project like hair from the organ of Corti—in each ear (Larkin, 2000). Hair cells "dance" in response to the vibrations of the basilar membrane. Their up-and-down movements generate neural impulses, which are transmitted to the brain via the **auditory nerve.** Auditory input is then projected onto the hearing areas of the temporal lobes of the cerebral cortex.

Locating Sounds—Up, Down, and Around

R E F L E C T
Have you ever been unsure where a sound was coming from? How did you locate the source of the sound?

How do you balance the loudness of a stereo set? You sit between the speakers and adjust the volume until the sound seems to be equally loud in each ear. If the sound to the right is louder, the musical instruments are perceived as being to the right rather than in front.

Question: How do we locate sounds? There is a resemblance between balancing a stereo set and locating sounds. A sound that is louder in the right ear is perceived as coming from the right. A sound coming from the right also reaches the right ear first. Both loudness and the sequence in which the sounds reach the ears provide directional cues.

But it may not be easy to locate a sound coming from directly in front or in back of you or overhead. Such sounds are equally distant from each ear and equally loud. So what do we do? Simple—usually we turn our head slightly to determine in which ear the sound increases. If you turn your head a few degrees to the right and the loudness increases in your left ear, the sound must be coming from in front of you. Of course, we also use vision and general knowledge in locating the source of sounds. If you hear the roar of jet engines, most of the time you can bet that the airplane is overhead.

Perception of Loudness and Pitch

Sounds are heard because they cause vibration in parts of the ear and information about these vibrations is transmitted to the brain. *Question: How do we perceive loudness and pitch?*

The loudness and pitch of sounds appear to be related to the number of receptor neurons on the organ of Corti that fire and how often they fire. Psychologists generally agree that sounds are perceived as louder when more of these sensory neurons fire.

► CONTROVERSY IN PSYCHOLOGY ◄

How do we explain pitch perception? What happens when the basilar membrane runs out of places to vibrate? What happens when it cannot vibrate fast enough?

It takes two processes to explain perception of color: *trichromatic theory* and *opponent-process theory*. Similarly, it takes at least two processes to explain pitch perception—that is, perception of sound waves with frequencies that vary from 20 to 20,000 cycles per second: *place theory* and *frequency theory*.

Hermann von Helmholtz helped develop the place theory of pitch discrimination as well as the Young–Helmholtz (trichromatic) theory of color vision. **Place theory** holds that the pitch of a sound is sensed according to the place along the basilar membrane that vibrates in response to it. In classic research with guinea pigs and cadavers that led to the award of a Nobel prize, Georg von Békésy (1957) found evidence for place theory. He determined that receptors at different sites along the membrane fire in response to tones of differing frequencies. Receptor neurons appear to be lined up along the basilar membrane like piano keys. The higher the pitch of a sound, the closer the responsive neurons lie to the oval window (Larkin, 2000). However, place theory appears to apply only to pitches that are at least as high as 4,000 Hz. But what about lower pitches? That's where frequency theory comes in.

Frequency theory notes that for us to perceive these lower pitches, we need the stimulation of neural impulses that match the frequency of the sound waves. That is, in response to low pitches—pitches of about 20 to 1,000 cycles per second—hair cells on the basilar membrane fire at the same frequencies as the sound waves. However, neurons cannot fire more than 1,000 times per second. Therefore, frequency theory can account only for perception of pitches between 20 and 1,000 cycles per second. In actuality, frequency theory appears to account only for pitch perception between 20 and a few hundred cycles per second.

Place Theory
The theory that the pitch of a sound is determined by the section of the basilar membrane that vibrates in response to the sound.

Frequency Theory
The theory that the pitch of a sound is reflected in the frequency of the neural impulses that are generated in response to the sound.

I noted that it takes *at least two processes* to explain how people perceive pitch. The *volley principle* is the third, and it accounts for pitch discrimination between a few hundred and 4,000 cycles per second (Matlin & Foley, 1995). In response to sound waves of these frequencies, groups of neurons take turns firing, in the way that one row of soldiers used to fire rifles while another row knelt to reload. Alternating firing—that is, volleying—appears to transmit sensory information about pitches in the intermediate range.

Deafness

REFLECT

Do you know anyone with hearing problems? What is the source of the impairment? How does the person cope with the impairment?

More than 1 in 10 Americans has a hearing impairment, and 1 in 100 cannot hear at all (Canalis & Lambert, 2000). Deaf people are deprived of a key source of information about the world around them. In recent years, however, society has made greater efforts to bring them into the mainstream of sensory experience. People are usually on hand to convert political and other speeches into hand signs (such as those of American Sign Language) for hearing-impaired members of the audience. Many TV shows are "closed captioned" so that they can be understood by people with hearing problems. Special decoders render the captions visible. Also, as mentioned earlier, advocates for deaf people have emphasized the positive aspects of dwelling in a world of silence.   *Questions: What is deafness? What can we do about it?*

The two major types of deafness are conductive deafness and sensorineural deafness. **Conductive deafness** stems from damage to the structures of the middle ear—either to the eardrum or to the three bones that conduct (and amplify) sound waves from the outer ear to the inner ear (Canalis & Lambert, 2000). This is the hearing impairment often found among older people. People with conductive deafness often profit from hearing aids, which provide the amplification that the middle ear does not. Surgical treatment can be successful as well.

Sensorineural deafness usually stems from damage to the structures of the inner ear, most often the loss of hair cells, which normally do not regenerate. (However, researchers are attempting to stimulate production of new hair cells by means of gene therapy and other measures; see Larkin, 2000.) Sensorineural deafness can also stem from damage to the auditory nerve, caused by such factors as disease or acoustic trauma (prolonged exposure to very loud sounds). In sensorineural deafness, people tend to be more sensitive to some pitches than to others. In the hearing impairment called Hunter's notch, the loss is limited to particular frequencies—in this case, the frequencies of the sound waves generated by a gun firing. Prolonged exposure to 85 dB can cause hearing loss. People who attend rock concerts, where sounds may reach 140 dB, risk permanently damaging their ears, as do workers who run pneumatic drills or drive noisy vehicles. The ringing sensation that often follows exposure to loud sounds probably means that hair cells in the inner ear have been damaged. If you find yourself suddenly exposed to loud sounds, remember that your fingertips serve as good emergency ear protectors.

Cochlear implants, or "artificial ears," contain microphones that sense sounds and electronic equipment that transmits sounds past damaged hair cells to stimulate the auditory nerve directly. Such implants have helped many people with sensorineural deafness (Geers et al., 2002). However, they cannot assume the functions of damaged auditory nerves.

Conductive Deafness
The forms of deafness in which there is loss of conduction of sound through the middle ear.

Sensorineural Deafness
The forms of deafness that result from damage to hair cells or the auditory nerve.

Learning Connections
See Web site for an interactive version of these review questions.

REVIEW

(19) Sound waves alternately _____ and expand molecules of a medium like air. (20) The human ear can hear sounds varying in frequency from 20 to _____ cycles per second (Hz). (21) The frequency of sound waves determines their _____. (22) Loudness is measured in _____ (dB). (23) The middle ear contains three bones—the "hammer," " _____," and "stirrup." (24) The cochlea contains fluids that vibrate against the _____ membrane. (25) The "command post" of hearing—called the organ of _____—is attached to the basilar mem-

brane. (26) Sound waves travel from the organ of Corti to the brain by the _____ nerve.

Critical Thinking: What is the evidence for the different theories of pitch perception?

THE CHEMICAL SENSES: SMELL AND TASTE

Smell and taste are the chemical senses. In the cases of vision and hearing, physical energy strikes our sensory receptors. With smell and taste, we sample molecules of the substances being sensed.

Smell: Sampling Molecules in the Air

People are underprivileged when it comes to the sense of smell. Dogs, for instance, devote about seven times as much of the cerebral cortex as we do to the sense of smell. Male dogs sniff in order to determine where the boundaries of other dogs' territories leave off and whether female dogs are sexually receptive. Dogs have been selectively bred to enhance their sense of smell. Some now earn a living by sniffing out explosive devices or illegal drugs in suitcases.

Smell also has an important role in human behavior. It makes a crucial contribution to the flavor of foods, for example. If you did not have a sense of smell, an onion and an apple would taste the same to you! People's sense of smell may be deficient when we compare them to those of a dog, but we can detect the odor of 1 one-millionth of a milligram of vanilla in a liter of air.

Question: How does the sense of smell work?   Smell is the sense that senses odors. An *odor* is a sample of the substance being sensed. Odors are detected by sites on receptor neurons in the **olfactory** membrane high in each nostril. Receptor neurons fire when a few molecules of the substance in gaseous form come into contact with them. Their firing transmits information about odors to the brain via the **olfactory nerve.** That is how the substance is smelled.

It is unclear how many basic kinds of odors there are. In any event, olfactory receptors may respond to more than one kind of odor. Mixtures of smell sensations also help produce the broad range of odors that we can perceive.

The sense of smell adapts rapidly to odors, such that you lose awareness of them, even obnoxious ones. This might be fortunate if you are in a locker room or an outhouse. It might not be so fortunate if you are exposed to paint fumes or secondhand smoke, because you may lose awareness of them while danger remains. One odor can mask another, which is how air fresheners work.

In many species, odors trigger instinctive responses. One experiment reveals how readers might be able to earn tongue flicks (sexual advances) from one species of lizard. Sex recognition in various species of lizards relies either on color or odor. This particular research group (López et al., 2002) aimed to determine whether color or odor, or a combination of the two, stimulated aggressive responses or sexual advances from males of the Spanish lizard, *P. hispanicus.* They experimentally manipulated the color and odor of male lizards, creating groups with all combinations of color and odor of males and females. They found that males reacted significantly more aggressively to intruders with male odors regardless of their color, whereas intruders with female odors were courted, regardless of their actual sex and coloring. Intruders with female odors also elicited more tongue flicks than those with male odor.

Taste: Yes, You've Got Taste

Your cocker spaniel may jump at the chance to finish off your bowl of sherbet, but your Siamese cat may turn up her nose at the opportunity. Why? Dogs can perceive the taste quality of sweetness, as can pigs, but cats cannot.

R E F L E C T
Has food ever seemed to lose its flavor when you had a cold or an allergy attack? Why?

R E F L E C T
Have you had the experience of growing accustomed to a noxious odor so that you have lost awareness of it?

Olfactory
Having to do with the sense of smell.

Olfactory Nerve
The nerve that transmits information concerning odors from olfactory receptors to the brain.

■ **Sensational?**

The flavors of foods are determined not only by their taste, but also by their odor, texture, and temperature.

Taste Cells

Receptor cells that are sensitive to taste.

Taste Buds

The sensory organs for taste. They contain taste cells and are located on the tongue.

Question: How does the sense of taste work?   There are four primary taste qualities: sweet, sour, salty, and bitter. The *flavor* of a food involves its taste but is more complex. Although apples and onions are similar in taste, their flavors differ greatly. After all, you wouldn't chomp into a nice cold onion on a warm day, would you? The flavor of a food depends on its odor, texture, and temperature as well as on its taste. If it were not for odor, heated tenderized shoe leather might pass for steak.

Taste is sensed through **taste cells**—receptor neurons located on **taste buds.** You have about 10,000 taste buds, most of which are located near the edges and back of your tongue. Taste buds tend to specialize a bit. Some, for example, are more responsive to sweetness, whereas others react to several tastes. Other taste receptors are found in the roof, sides, and back of the mouth, and in the throat. Some taste buds are even found in the stomach, although we only perceive tastes in the mouth and top of the throat. Buds deep in the mouth are evolutionarily adaptive because they can warn of poisonous food as it is about to be swallowed (Brand, 2000).

According to Joseph Brand (2000) of the Monell Chemical Senses Center in Philadelphia, catfish are "swimming tongues." They can detect food through murky water and across long distances because their bodies are studded with nearly 150,000 taste buds.

People live in different taste worlds. Those of us with low sensitivity for the sweet taste may require twice the sugar to sweeten our food as others who are more sensitive to sweetness. Those of us who claim to enjoy very bitter foods may actually be taste-blind to them. Sensitivities to different tastes apparently have a strong genetic component (Bartoshuk, 2000).

By eating hot foods and scraping your tongue, you regularly kill off many taste cells. But you need not be alarmed at this inadvertent oral aggression. Taste cells are the rabbits of the sense receptors. They reproduce rapidly enough to completely renew themselves about once a week.

REFLECT

Why do older people tend to spice their food heavily?

Although older people often complain that their food has little or no "taste," they are more likely to experience a decline in the sense of smell. Because the flavor of a food represents both its tastes and its odors or aromas,

---

A Closer Look 👁

Advances in Science? The Case of the Aromatic T-Shirts

Readers may be familiar with perfume and cologne as aids to sexual attraction, but how about body odor? Body odor? Yes, body odor.

A group of researchers (Jacob et al., 2002) had a variety of men wear T-shirts for two days. Throughout that period they kept their aromas "pure" by avoiding deodorants, spicy foods (no garlic, please), pets, and sex. They then placed the T-shirts in boxes where they could not be seen but could clearly be smelled. Women in the study then made a sacrifice for science that may have been greater than the men's. They were asked to smell each of the boxes and choose the one they would be most willing to live with—that is, the one they would choose "if they had to smell it all the time."

Now, the women were kept blind as to the purpose of the study and also blind to the fact that they were smelling "ripe" T-shirts. Despite the source of the odor, the women generally found them to be mildly pleasant. It also happens that the women had no difficulty differentiating the "boxes" from one another and that they could select a favorite.

The T-shirt study apparently has something to do with evolution and genes. By and large, the shirts selected as favorites had been worn by men who were similar in genetic makeup to the women's fathers. The particular genes that seem to do the trick are called M.H.C. genes, and they produce proteins that identify cells within one's body as "self," not foreign. The cells that reap the stamp of approval are not attacked by the body's immune system. But why the father? Here the researchers become speculative. Perhaps by finding odors that are suggestive of genetic similarity to the father, but not the mother, women are enticed to mate with men who are similar but not overly similar to themselves.

This is not to suggest that the major factor in modern mate selection is, well, nasal inspiration. Physical attractiveness, education, interests, and financial security all have something to do with it, and may be more prominent factors. But it could be that the nose also knows something about what it takes for a woman to live comfortably in a home with a man for year after year.

older people experience loss in the *flavor* of their food. Older people often spice their food heavily to enhance its flavor.

REVIEW

An odor is a sample of molecules of the substance being smelled. (27) Odors are detected by the —————— membrane in each nostril. (28) There are four primary taste qualities: sweet, sour, salty, and ——————. (29) The receptor neurons for taste are called —————— cells, which are located in taste buds on the tongue.

Critical Thinking: Critical thinkers pay close attention to definitions. What is the difference between the *taste* and the *flavor* of food?

THE SKIN SENSES (YES, IT DOES)

The skin is much more than a protective coating for your body. As you may know from lying on the sand beneath a broiling sun, and perhaps from touching the person lying next to you, the skin also discriminates among many kinds of sensations. ***Questions: What are the skin senses? How do they work?*** The skin senses include touch, pressure, warmth, cold, and pain. We have distinct sensory receptors for pressure, temperature, and pain, but some nerve endings may receive more than one type of sensory input. Here let's focus on touch, pressure, and temperature. We consider pain—and what to do about it—in this chapter's "Life Connections" feature.

Touch and Pressure: How Touching

Sensory receptors located around the roots of hair cells appear to fire when the surface of the skin is touched. You may have noticed that if you are trying to "get the feel of" a fabric or the texture of a friend's hair, you must move your hand over it. Otherwise the sensations quickly fade. If you pass your hand over the fabric or hair and then hold it still, again the sensations of touching will fade. This sort of "active touching"

■ **Active Touching**
Sometimes we need to move our hands to continue sensing what we are touching.

Two-Point Threshold
The least distance by which two rods touching the skin must be separated before the person will report that there are two rods, not one, on 50% of occasions.

Kinesthesis
The sense that informs us about the positions and motion of parts of our bodies.

REFLECT

How can a drink that is 70°F be either warming or cooling, depending on the weather?

■ Kinesthesis
This young acrobat receives information about the position and movement of the parts of his body through the sense of kinesthesis. Information is fed to his brain from sensory organs in the joints, tendons, and muscles. This allows him to follow his own movements without looking at himself.

© 1990 Andy Levin/Photo Researchers, Inc.

involves reception of information concerning not only touch per se but also pressure, temperature, and feedback from the muscles involved in movements of our hands.

Other structures beneath the skin are sensitive to pressure. Different parts of the body are more sensitive to touch and pressure than others. Psychophysicists use methods such as the **two-point threshold** to assess sensitivity to pressure. This method determines the smallest distance by which two rods touching the skin must be separated before the (blindfolded) individual reports that there are two rods rather than one. With this method, psychophysicists have found that our fingertips, lips, noses, and cheeks are more sensitive than our shoulders, thighs, and calves. That is, the rods can be closer together but perceived as distinct when they touch the lips more than when they touch the shoulders. Why the difference in sensitivity? First, nerve endings are more densely packed in the fingertips and face than in other locations. Second, more sensory cortex is devoted to the perception of sensations in the fingertips and face (see Figure 2.15 on page 68).

The sense of pressure, like the sense of touch, undergoes rapid adaptation. For example, you may have undertaken several minutes of strategic movements to wind up with your hand on the arm or leg of your date, only to discover that adaptation to this delightful source of pressure reduces the sensation.

Temperature: Sometimes Everything Is Relative

The receptors for temperature are neurons located just beneath the skin. When skin temperature increases, the receptors for warmth fire. Decreases in skin temperature cause receptors for cold to fire.

Sensations of temperature are relative. When we are at normal body temperature, we might perceive another person's skin as warm. When we are feverish, though, the other person's skin might seem cool. We also adapt to differences in temperature. When we walk out of an air-conditioned house into the July sun, we feel intense heat at first. Then the sensations of heat tend to fade (although we may still be uncomfortable because of high humidity). Similarly, when we first enter a swimming pool, the water may seem cool or cold because it is below our body temperature. Yet after a few moments an 80°F pool may seem quite warm. In fact, we may chide a newcomer for not diving right in.

Learning Connections
See Web site for an interactive version of these review questions.

REVIEW

(30) The _____-_____ threshold method allows psychophysicists to assess sensitivity to pressure by determining the distance by which two rods touching the skin must be separated before a person will report that there are two rods, not one. (31) When the skin is touched, sensory receptors around the _____ of hair cells fire.

Critical Thinking: Does it seem strange to think of the skin as a sensory organ? If it does, be my guest and check out the discussion of "functional fixedness" in Chapter 9.

KINESTHESIS AND THE VESTIBULAR SENSE

Try this experiment. Close your eyes, and then touch your nose with your finger. If you weren't right on target, I'm sure you came close. But how? You didn't see your hand moving, and you didn't hear your arm swishing through the air.

Kinesthesis: How Moving?

Question: What is kinesthesis? **Kinesthesis** is the sense that informs you about the position and motion of parts of the body. The term is derived from the ancient Greek words for "motion" (*kinesis*) and "perception" (*aisthesis*). In kinesthesis, sensory information is fed back to the brain from sensory organs in the joints, tendons, and muscles. You were able to bring your finger to your nose easily by employing your kinesthetic sense. When you make a muscle in your arm, the sensations of tightness and hardness are also provided by kinesthesis.

Imagine going for a walk without kinesthesis. You would have to watch the forward motion of each leg to be certain you had raised it high enough to clear the curb. And if you had tried the nose-to-finger brief experiment without the kinesthetic sense, you would have had no sensory feedback until you felt the pressure of your finger against your nose (or cheek, or eye, or forehead), and you probably would have missed dozens of times.

Are you in the mood for another experiment? Close your eyes again. Then "make a muscle" in your right arm. Could you sense the muscle without looking at it or feeling it with your left hand? Of course you could. Kinesthesis also provides information about muscle contractions.

The Vestibular Sense: How Upright?

Your **vestibular sense** tells you whether you are upright (physically, not morally). *Question: How does the vestibular sense work?* Sensory organs located in the **semicircular canals** and elsewhere in the ears monitor your body's motion and position in relation to gravity. They tell you whether you are falling and provide cues to whether your body is changing speed, such as when you are in an accelerating airplane or automobile. It is thus the vestibular sense that keeps us physically upright.

Table 4.2 summarizes key points about the senses.

Vestibular Sense
The sense of equilibrium that informs us about our bodies' positions relative to gravity.

Semicircular Canals
Structures of the inner ear that monitor body movement and position.

Learning Connections
See Web site for an interactive version of these review questions.

R E V I E W

(32) Kinesthesis is the sensing of bodily _____ and movement. (33) Kinesthesis relies on sensory organs in the joints, tendons, and _____. (34) The vestibular sense informs us as to whether we are in an _____ position or changing speeds.

TABLE 4.2 The Senses

Sense	What We Sense	Receptor Organs	Nature of Sensory Receptors
Vision	Visible light (part of the spectrum of electromagnetic energy; different colors have different wavelengths)	Eyes	Photoreceptors in the retinas (*rods*, which are sensitive to the intensity of light; and *cones*, which are sensitive to color)
Hearing	Changes in air pressure (or in another medium, such as water) that result from vibrations called *sound waves*	Ears	"Hair cells" in the organ of Corti, which is attached to a membrane (the *basilar membrane*) within the inner ear (the *cochlea*)
Smell	Molecules of the substance	Nose	Receptor neurons in the olfactory membrane high in each nostril
Taste	Molecules of the substance	Tongue	Taste cells located on taste buds on the tongue
Touch, Pressure	Pushing or pulling of the surface of the body	Skin	Nerve endings in the skin, some of which are located around the hair follicles
Kinesthesis	Muscle contractions	Sensory organs in joints, tendons, and muscles	Receptor cells in joints, tendons, and muscles
The Vestibular Sense	Movement and position in relation to gravity	Sensory organs in the ears (e.g., in the *semicircular canals*)	Receptor cells in the ears

(35) The vestibular sense is housed mainly in the _____ _____ of the ears.

Critical Thinking: Why are some people "natural athletes"? What genetic factors may contribute to their performance?

EXTRASENSORY PERCEPTION: IS THERE PERCEPTION WITHOUT SENSATION?

Using our familiar computer analogy, sensation is the peripheral device that feeds information into our central processing unit—the brain. A topic on the edge of psychology asks the question: What if there were such as thing as extrasensory perception (ESP)? What if sensation were bypassed, and we directly perceived things in the world outside? Make no mistake: The hard research evidence comes down pretty hard against perception in the absence of sensation. Nevertheless, 60% of the American public believes that some people have psychic powers or ESP (National Science Foundation, 2002). Therefore, the topic is worth at least a sideways glance.

Precognition, Psychokinesis, Telepathy, and Clairvoyance

Imagine the wealth you could amass if you had *precognition,* that is, if you were able to perceive future events in advance. Perhaps you would check the next week's stock market reports and know what to buy or sell. Or you could bet with confidence on who would win the next Super Bowl or World Series. Or think of the power you would have if you were capable of *psychokinesis,* that is, of mentally manipulating or moving objects. You may have gotten a glimpse of the possibilities in films like *The Matrix, The Sixth Sense,* and *Star Wars.* Precognition and psychokinesis are two concepts associated with ESP. Two other theoretical forms of ESP are *telepathy,* or direct transmission of thoughts or ideas from one person to another, and *clairvoyance,* or the perception of objects that do not stimulate the sensory organs. An example of clairvoyance is "seeing" what card will be dealt next, even though it is still in the deck and unseen even by the dealer.

Extrasensory perception (ESP)—also referred to as psi communication—refers to the perception of objects or events through means other than sensory organs. Psi communication refers to the transfer of information through an irregular or unusual process—not through the usual senses. Many psychologists do not believe that ESP is an appropriate area for scientific inquiry. Scientists study natural events, but ESP smacks of the supernatural, even the occult. ESP also has the flavor of a nightclub act in which a blindfolded "clairvoyant" calls out the contents of an audience member's pocketbook. Other psychologists, however, believe that there is nothing wrong with investigating ESP. The issue for them is not whether ESP is sensationalistic but whether its existence can be demonstrated in the laboratory. *Question: Is there really such a thing as extrasensory perception (ESP)?*

Perhaps the best known of the ESP researchers was Joseph Banks Rhine of Duke University. Rhine studied ESP for several decades, beginning in the late 1920s. In a typical experiment in clairvoyance, Rhine would use a pack of 25 cards, which contained 5 sets of the cards shown in Figure 4.27. Pigeons pecking patterns at random to indicate which one was about to be turned up would be "correct" 20% of the time. Rhine found that some people guessed correctly significantly more often than the 20% chance rate. He concluded that these individuals might have some degree of ESP.

A more current method for studying telepathy is the *ganzfeld procedure* (Parker, 2000). In this method, one person acts as a "sender" and the other as a "receiver." The sender views randomly selected visual stimuli such as photographs or videotapes, while the receiver, who is in another room and whose eyes are covered and ears are

REFLECT

Do you believe in ESP? Why or why not?

■ **Figure 4.27**
Zener Cards

Joseph Banks Rhine used these Zener cards in research on clairvoyance. Participants are asked to predict which card will be turned up.

blocked, tries to mentally tune in to the sender. After a session, the receiver is shown four visual stimuli and asked to select the one transmitted by the sender. A person guessing which stimulus was "transmitted" would be correct 25% of the time (1 time in 4) by chance alone. An analysis of 28 experiments using the ganzfeld procedure, however, found that receivers correctly identified the visual stimulus 38% of the time (Honorton, 1985), a percentage unlikely to be due to chance. A series of 11 more studies with the ganzfeld procedure obtained similar results (Bem & Honorton, 1994; Honorton et al., 1990).

Overall, however, there are many reasons for skepticism of ESP. One is the *file-drawer* problem. Buyers of supermarket magazines tend to forget "psychics'" predictions when they fail to come true (that is, they have "filed" them away). Similarly, ESP researchers are less likely to report research results that show failure. Therefore, we would expect unusual findings (for example, a subject with a high success rate at psi-communication tasks over a period of several days) to appear in the research literature. In other words, if you flip a coin indefinitely, eventually you will flip 10 heads in a row. The odds against this are high, but if you report your eventual success and do not report the weeks of failure, you give the impression that you have unique coin-flipping ability. (You may even fool yourself.)

Then, too, it has not been easy to replicate experiments in ESP. People who have "demonstrated" ESP with one researcher have failed to do so with another researcher or have refused to participate in other studies. Also, the findings in one study are usually noticeably absent in follow-ups or under careful analysis. For example, Julie Milton and Richard Wiseman (1999) reviewed the research reported by Bem and Honorton (1994). They weighed the results of 30 ganzfeld ESP studies from 7 laboratories. They found no evidence—zero—that subjects in these studies scored above chance levels on the ESP task. But a follow-up to the Milton and Wiseman (1999) review once more argues that results of the Honorton ganzfeld studies are not due to chance fluctuation (Bem et al., 2001).

Let's make one point clearly: From all of these studies, *not one person has emerged who can reliably show psi communication from one occasion to another and from one researcher to another.* Research has not identified one single indisputable telepath or clairvoyant. In sum, most psychologists do not grant ESP research much credibility. They prefer to study perception that involves sensation. After all, what is life without sensation?

REVIEW

(36) _____ refers to perception of objects or events through means other than sensory organs. (37) Rhine used _____ cards to study clairvoyance. The ganzfeld procedure is currently used to study telepathy. (38) One reason for skepticism about ESP is the _____-drawer problem; that is, researchers are less likely to report research results that show failure.

Critical Thinking: What kind of evidence is required to support the existence of ESP? Why will many readers continue to believe in ESP despite the lack of scientific evidence?

REFLECT

Do you believe that some people are "psychics"? What is the evidence for their supposed abilities? Is it scientific? Explain.

Learning Connections
See Web site for an interactive version of these review questions.

LIFE CONNECTIONS

Pain, Pain, Go Away—Don't Come Again Another Day

For most people in the United States, pain is a frequent visitor. Headaches, backaches, toothaches—these are only a few of the types of pain that most of us encounter from time to time. According to a national Gallup survey of 2,002 adults in the United States (Arthritis Foundation, 2000), 89% experience pain at least once a month. More than half (55%) of people aged 65 and above say they experience pain daily. Sad to say, people aged 65 and above are most likely to attribute pain to getting older (88%), with a sense that they can do nothing about disabilities such as arthritis. By contrast, people aged 18 to 34 are more likely to attribute pain to tension or stress (73%), to overwork, (64%), or to their lifestyle (51%). When we assume that there is nothing we can do about pain, we are less likely to try. Yet 43% of Americans say that pain curtails their activities, and 50% say that pain puts them in a bad mood. There are also a number of gender differences in the experiencing of, and response to, pain, as shown in Table 4.3. What is pain? What can we do about it?

Pain means something is wrong in the body. Evolutionary psychologists would point out that pain is adaptive, if unpleasant, because it motivates us to do something about it. For some of us, however, chronic pain—pain that lasts once injuries or illnesses have cleared—saps our vitality and interferes with the pleasures of everyday life (Turk & Okifuji, 2002).

We can sense pain throughout most of the body, but pain is usually sharpest where nerve endings are densely packed, as in the fingers and face. Pain can also be felt deep within the body, as in the cases of abdominal pain and back pain. Even though headaches may seem to originate deep inside the head, there are no nerve endings for pain in the brain. Brain surgery can be done with a local anesthetic that prevents the patient from feeling the drilling of a small hole through the skull.

Pain usually originates at the point of contact, as when you bang a knee (see Figure 4.28). But its reverberations throughout the nervous system are extensive. The pain message to the brain is initiated by the release of chemicals, including prostaglandins, bradykinin, and a chemical called P (yes, P stands for "pain"). Prostaglandins facilitate transmission of the pain message to the brain and heighten circulation to the injured area, causing the redness and swelling that we call inflammation. Inflammation serves the biological function of attracting infection-fighting blood cells to the affected area to protect it against invading germs. Pain-relieving drugs such as aspirin and ibuprofen work by inhibiting the production of prostaglandins.

The pain message is relayed from the spinal cord to the thalamus and then projected to the cerebral cortex, making us aware of the location and intensity of the damage. Ronald Melzack (1999) speaks of a "neuromatrix" that includes these chemical reactions but involves

■ The Toll of Pain

Nearly half of Americans report that pain curbs their activities, and half say that pain puts them in a bad mood. There are a number of medical methods for dealing with pain. Psychologists are also developing many methods for eradicating or coping with pain.

TABLE 4.3 Gender Differences in Experiencing and Responding to Pain

Percent Who Report . . .	Women	Men
Experiencing daily pain	46	37
Feeling they have a great deal of control over their pain	39	48
Feeling that tension and stress are their leading causes of pain	72	56
Going to see the doctor about pain only when other people urge them to do it	27	38
Balancing the demands of work and family life to be the key cause of their pain	35	24
Frequent headaches	17	8
Frequent backaches	24	19
Arthritis	20	15
Sore feet	25	17

Why do you think that women are more likely than men to experience pain? What is the gender difference in willingness to see the doctor about pain? How would you explain the gender difference in willingness to see the doctor?

Source of data: Arthritis Foundation (2000, April 6). Pain in America: Highlights from a Gallup survey. http://www.arthritis.org

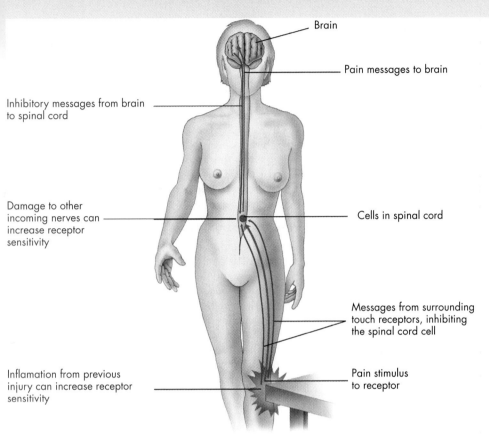

Brain

Pain messages to brain

Inhibitory messages from brain to spinal cord

Damage to other incoming nerves can increase receptor sensitivity

Cells in spinal cord

Messages from surrounding touch receptors, inhibiting the spinal cord cell

Inflamation from previous injury can increase receptor sensitivity

Pain stimulus to receptor

■ **Figure 4.28**
Perception of Pain

Pain originates at the point of contact, and the pain message to the brain is initiated by the release of prostaglandins, bradykinin, and substance *P*.

other aspects of our physiology and psychology in our reaction to pain. For example, visual and other sensory inputs tell us what is happening and influence the cognitive interpretation of the situation. Our emotional response affects the degree of pain, and so do the ways in which we respond to stress. For example, if the pain derives from an object we fear, perhaps a knife or needle, we may experience more pain. If we perceive that there is nothing we can do to change the situation, perception of pain may increase. If we have self-confidence and a history of successful responding to stress, the perception of pain may diminish.

Phantom Limb Pain

One of the more fascinating phenomena of psychology is the fact that many people experience pain in limbs that are no longer there. About 2 out of 3 combat veterans with amputated limbs report feeling pain in missing, or "phantom," limbs (Kooijman et al., 2000). In such cases, the pain occurs in the absence of the limb, but the pain itself is real enough. It sometimes involves activation of nerves in the stump of the missing limb, but local anesthesia does not always eliminate the pain. Researchers have found that many people who experience phantom limb pain have also undergone reorganization of the motor and somatosensory cortex that is consistent with the reported pain (Karl et al., 2001).

Gate Theory

Simple remedies like rubbing a banged knee frequently help relieve pain. Why? One possible answer lies in the *gate theory* of pain originated by Melzack (1999). From this perspective, the nervous system can process only a limited amount of stimulation at a time. Rubbing the knee transmits sensations to the brain that, in a sense, compete for the attention of neurons. Many nerves are thus prevented from transmitting pain messages to the brain. The mechanism is analogous to shutting down a "gate" in the spinal cord. It is like a switchboard being flooded with calls. The flooding prevents any of the calls from getting through.

Acupuncture

Back to our ancient Chinese warrior . . .

Thousands of years ago, the Chinese began mapping the body to learn where pins might be placed to deaden pain. Acupuncture remained largely unknown in the West, even though Western powers occupied much of China during the 1800s. But the practice got some wider attention in the 1970s when *New York Times* columnist James Reston wrote about his appendectomy in China. He reported no discomfort although acupuncture was his primary anesthetic. More recently, TV journalist Bill Moyers's report (1993) on current usage of acupuncture in China received much attention. For example, one woman underwent brain surgery to remove a tumor after receiving anesthesia that consisted of a mild sedative, a small dose of narcotics, and six needles placed in her forehead, calves, and ankles. The surgery itself and the use of a guiding CAT scan were consistent with contemporary American practices.

Traditional acupuncturists believe that the practice balances the body's flow of energy, but research has shown that it stimulates nerves that reach the hypothalamus and may also result in the release of *endorphins* (Reaney, 1998). Endorphins are naturally occurring chemical messengers that are similar to the narcotic morphine in their chemical structure and effects. The drug *naloxone* blocks both the painkilling effects of morphine and of acupuncture. Therefore, the analgesic effects of acupuncture may be due to the morphinelike endorphins.

Modern Psychological Methods for Coping with Pain

Coping with that age-old enemy—pain—has traditionally been a medical issue. The primary treatment has been chemical, as in the use of painkilling drugs. However, psychology has dramatically expanded our arsenal of weapons for fighting pain.

Accurate Information

One irony of pain management is that giving people accurate and thorough information about their condition often helps them manage pain (Jacox et al., 1994; Ross & Berger, 1996). Most people in pain try *not* to think about why things hurt during the early phases of an illness (Moyers, 1993). Physicians, too, often neglect the human aspects of relating to their patients. That is, they focus on diagnosing and treating the causes of pain, but they often fail to discuss with patients the meaning of the pain and what the patient can expect.

Yet when uncomfortable treatment methods are used, such as cardiac catheterization or chemotherapy for cancer, knowledge of the details of the treatment, including how long it will last and how much pain there will be, can help people cope with the pain (Ludwick-Rosenthal & Neufeld, 1993). Knowledge of medical procedures reduces stress by helping people maintain control over their situation. Some people, on the other hand, do not *want* information about painful medical procedures. Their attitude is "Do what you have to do and get it over with." It may be most helpful to match the amount of information provided with the amount desired (Ludwick-Rosenthal & Neufeld, 1993).

Distraction and Fantasy: The Nintendo Approach to Coping with Pain?

Diverting attention from pain helps many people cope with it (Cohen, 2002). Psychologists frequently recommend that people use distraction or fantasy as ways of coping with pain. For example, imagine that you've injured your leg and you're waiting to see the doctor in an emergency room. You can distract yourself by focusing on details of your environment. You can count ceiling tiles or the hairs on the back of a finger. You can describe (or criticize) the clothes of medical personnel or passers-by. Playing video games also distracts people from the pain and discomfort of medical procedures (Kolko & Rickard-Figueroa, 1985; Redd et al., 1987; Robbins, 2000). For example, child cancer patients can become wrapped up in video games while they receive injections of nausea-producing chemicals. Other distraction methods that

help children deal with pain include combing one's hair and blowing on a noisemaker (Adler, 1990).

Hypnosis

In 1842 London physician W. S. Ward amputated a man's leg after using a rather strange anesthetic: hypnosis. According to reports, the man experienced no discomfort. Several years later, operations were being performed routinely under hypnosis at his infirmary. Today hypnosis is often used to reduce chronic pain (Patterson & Ptacek, 1997) and as an anesthetic in dentistry, childbirth, even in some forms of surgery (Montgomery et al., 2000).

In using hypnosis to manage pain, the hypnotist usually instructs the person that he or she feels nothing or that the pain is distant and slight. Hypnosis can also aid in the use of distraction and fantasy. For example, the hypnotist can instruct the person to imagine that he or she is relaxing on a warm, exotic shore.

Relaxation Training and Biofeedback

When we are in pain, we often tense up. Tensing muscles is uncomfortable in itself, arouses the sympathetic nervous system, and focuses our attention on the pain. Relaxation counteracts these self-defeating behavior patterns (Ross & Berger, 1996). Some psychological methods of relaxation focus on relaxing muscle groups. Some involve breathing exercises. Others use relaxing imagery: The imagery distracts the person and deepens feelings of relaxation. Biofeedback is also used to help people relax targeted muscle groups. Relaxation training with biofeedback seems to be at least as effective as most medications for migraine headaches (Martin, 2002) and for chronic pain in the lower back and jaw (Flor & Birbaumer, 1993).

Coping with Irrational Beliefs

Irrational beliefs can heighten pain (Turk & Okifuji, 2002.) For example, telling oneself that the pain is unbearable and that it will never cease increases discomfort (Turk & Okifuji, 2002). Some people seem to feel obligated to focus on things that distress them. They may be unwilling to allow themselves to be distracted from pain and discomfort. Thus, cognitive methods aimed at changing irrational beliefs hold some promise (Jensen et al., 1994; Stroud et al., 2000).

Other Methods

Pain is a source of stress, and psychologists have uncovered many factors that seem to moderate the effects of stress. One is a sense of commitment. For example, if we are undergoing a painful medical procedure to diagnose or treat an illness, it might help if we recall that we *chose* to participate, rather than see ourselves as helpless victims. Thus, we are in control of the situation, and a sense of control enhances the ability to cope with pain (Turk & Okifuji, 2002).

Supportive social networks help as well. The benefits of having friends visit us—or visiting friends who are unwell—are as consistent with psychological findings as they are with folklore.

And don't forget gate theory. When you feel pain in a toe, squeeze all your toes. When you feel pain in your calf, rub your thighs. People around you may wonder what you're doing, but you're entitled to try to "flood the switchboard" so that some pain messages don't get through.

Recite Recite Recite

Learning Connections
See Web site for an interactive version of this chapter summary

1. What are sensation and perception?

Sensation is a mechanical process that involves the stimulation of sensory receptors (neurons) and the transmission of sensory information to the central nervous system. Perception is not mechanical. Perception is the active organization of sensations into a representation of the outside world, and it reflects learning and expectations.

2. How do we know when something is there? How do we know when it has changed?

We know something is there when the intensity of the stimulus, such as a light, exceeds the absolute threshold for that stimulus. The absolute threshold is the lowest intensity at which the stimulus can be detected. We know that something has changed when the change in intensity exceeds the difference threshold. The difference threshold is the minimum difference in intensity that can be discriminated. Difference thresholds are expressed in Weber's constants.

3. What is signal-detection theory?

Signal-detection theory explains the ways in which stimulus characteristics and psychological factors—for example, motivation, familiarity with a stimulus, and attention—interact to influence whether a stimulus will be detected.

4. What are feature detectors?

Feature detectors are neurons that fire in response to specific features of sensed stimuli. For example, detectors in the visual cortex fire in response to particular features of visual input, such as lines sensed at various angles or specific colors.

5. How do our sensory systems adapt to a changing environment?

We become more sensitive to stimuli of low magnitude and less sensitive to stimuli that remain the same (such as the background noises outside the window). Growing more sensitive to stimulation is termed sensitization, or positive adaptation. Growing less sensitive to continuous stimulation is called desensitization, or negative adaptation.

6. What is light?

Visible light is the part of the range of electromagnetic energy that triggers visual sensations. Light is made up of waves of energy; the color violet has the shortest wavelength, and red has the longest. White sunlight can be broken down into the colors of the rainbow by means of a prism.

7. How does the eye work?

The eye senses and transmits visual stimulation to the occipital lobe of the cerebral cortex. After light passes through the cornea, the size of the pupil determines the amount that can pass through the lens. The lens focuses light onto the retina, which is composed of photoreceptors (neurons) called rods and cones. Cones permit perception of color. Rods transmit sensations of light and dark only. Light is transmitted from the retina to the brain via the optic nerve.

8. What are some perceptual dimensions of color?

These include hue, value, and saturation. The wavelength of light determines its hue. Yellow–orange–red colors are considered to be warm. Greens and blues are considered to be cool. Colors across from one another on the color wheel are complementary. In afterimages, persistent sensations of color are followed by perception of the complementary color when the first color is removed.

9. How do we perceive color?

There are two theories as to how we perceive color. According to the trichromatic theory, there are three types of cones—some sensitive to red, others to green, and still others to blue–violet. The opponent-process theory proposes three types of color receptors: red–green, blue–yellow, and light–dark. Opponent-process theory is supported by the appearance of afterimages. These two theories may actually reflect a two-step process.

10. What is color blindness? Why are some people color-blind?

People with normal color vision are called trichromats. Monochromats see no color, and dichromats are blind to some parts of the spectrum. Partial color blindness is a sex-linked trait that impairs the working of cones sensitive to red–green.

Recite Recite Recite

11. **How do we organize bits of visual information into meaningful wholes?**

Perceptual organization involves recognizing patterns and processing information about relationships between parts and the whole. Gestalt rules of perceptual organization involve figure–ground relationships, proximity, similarity, continuity, common fate, and closure. Perception of a whole followed by perception of parts is termed top-down processing. Perception of the parts that leads to perception of a whole is termed bottom-up processing.

12. **How do we perceive movement?**

We visually perceive movement when the light reflected by moving objects moves across the retina and also when objects shift in relation to one another. Distant objects appear to move more slowly than nearby objects, and objects in the middle ground may give the illusion of moving backward. Stroboscopic motion, responsible for the illusion of motion pictures, occurs through the presentation of a rapid progression of images of stationary objects (frames).

13. **How do we perceive depth?**

Depth perception involves monocular and binocular cues. Monocular cues include pictorial cues such as perspective, clearness, interposition, shadows, and texture gradient, and motion cues such as motion parallax. Binocular cues include retinal disparity and convergence.

14. **What are perceptual constancies? Why do we perceive a door to be a rectangle even when it is partly open?**

Perceptual constancies are acquired through experience and make the world a stable place. For example, we learn to assume that objects retain their size, shape, brightness, and color despite their distance from us, their position, or changes in lighting conditions.

15. **What is sound?**

Sound waves require a medium such as air or water in order to be transmitted. Sound waves alternately compress and expand molecules of the medium, creating vibrations. The human ear can hear sounds varying in frequency from 20 to 20,000 cycles per second (Hz). The greater the frequency, the higher the sound's pitch. The loudness of a sound roughly corresponds to the amplitude of sound waves measured in decibels (dB).

16. **How does the ear work?**

The ear captures sound waves, vibrates in sympathy with them, and transmits auditory information to the brain. The outer ear funnels sound waves to the eardrum, which vibrates in sympathy with them and transmits the auditory information through the bones of the middle ear to the cochlea of the inner ear. The basilar membrane of the cochlea transmits those stimuli to the organ of Corti. From there, sound travels to the brain via the auditory nerve.

17. **How do we locate sounds?**

We locate sounds by determining in which ear they are louder. We may turn our heads to pin down that information.

18. **How do we perceive loudness and pitch?**

Sounds are perceived as louder when more sensory neurons fire. The place theory of pitch perception holds that the pitch of a sound is sensed according to the place along the basilar membrane that vibrates in response to it; it accounts for sounds whose frequencies exceed 4,000 Hz. Frequency theory states that pitch perception depends on the stimulation of neural impulses that match the frequency of the sound waves and accounts for frequencies of 20 to 1,000 Hz. The volley principle accounts for pitch discrimination between a few hundred and 4,000 cycles per second.

19. **What is deafness? What can we do about it?**

Conductive deafness—common among older people—is caused by damage to the middle ear and is often ameliorated by hearing aids, which amplify sounds. Sensorineural deafness is usually caused by damage to neurons in the inner ear and can sometimes be corrected by cochlear implants.

Recite Recite Recite

20. **How does the sense of smell work?**

The sense of smell is chemical. It samples molecules of substances called odors through the olfactory membrane in each nostril. Smell makes a key contribution to the flavor of foods.

21. **How does the sense of taste work?**

There are four primary taste qualities: sweet, sour, salty, and bitter. Flavor involves the odor, texture, and temperature of food, as well as its taste. Taste is sensed through taste cells, which are located in taste buds on the tongue.

22. **What are the skin senses? How do they work?**

The skin senses include touch, pressure, warmth, cold, and pain. Touches and pressure are sensed by receptors located around the roots of hair cells below the surface of the skin. We have separate receptors for warmth and cold beneath the skin.

23. **What is kinesthesis?**

Kinesthesis is the sensation of body position and movement. It relies on sensory organs in the joints, tendons, and muscles.

24. **How does the vestibular sense work?**

The vestibular sense is mostly housed in the semicircular canals of the ears and tells us whether we are in an upright position.

25. **Is there really such a thing as extrasensory perception (ESP)?**

ESP, or psi communication, refers to the perception of objects or events through means other than sensory organs. Because of the file-drawer problem and lack of replication of positive results, there is no reliable evidence for the existence of ESP.

Active Learning Resources

 Search Online with InfoTrac® College Edition

For additional information on the topics in this chapter, explore InfoTrac College Edition, your online library. Go to **http://infotrac.thomsonlearning.com** and use the passcode that came on the card with your book. Try these search terms: psychophysics, color vision research, Gestalt psychology, depth cues, pitch perception, and extrasensory perception.

 Visit Our Web Site

Go to **http://www.wadsworth.com/psychology**, where you will find online resources directly linked to your book, including interactive exercises related to PQ4R, and Power Visuals for mastering and reviewing key concepts. In addition, you will find hints on using InfoTrac College Edition to answer the Critical Thinking questions throughout the text. Start with the **Self Study Assessment** for a customized **Study Plan** generated by taking the **Pre-Test** and **Post-Test.**

 Connections CD-ROM

Go to the Wadsworth *Connections* CD-ROM for further study of the concepts in this chapter. The CD-ROM includes videos and animations, as well as additional activities to expand your learning experience, plus interactive self-assessments to help connect the material to your own life.

 Psyk.trek™ CD-ROM

The Wadsworth *Psyk.trek* CD-ROM offers tutorials, simulations, videos, multimedia glossary, and quizzing to help you master the material.

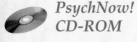 *PsychNow! CD-ROM*

The Wadsworth *PsychNow!* CD-ROM includes interactive exercises, videos, and animations to enhance your learning.

PowerPreview®

Just What *Is* Consciousness?

- **ARE YOU CONSCIOUS?** (How do you know?)

Sleep and Dreams

- **IF THERE WERE** no clocks and you did not see the sun rise and set, would you awaken at the same time each day?
- **DO DREAMS** have meanings?
- **MANY PEOPLE** have insomnia because they try too hard to fall asleep at night.
- **IS IT DANGEROUS** to awaken a sleepwalker?

Altering Consciousness Through Hypnosis: On Being Entranced

- **COULD SOMEONE** hypnotize you? (And just what is hypnosis?)
- **YOU MUST KNOW** what is expected of you in order to be hypnotized.

Altering Consciousness Through Meditation: Letting the World Fade Away

- **IS MEDITATION** a spiritual or psychological event?
- **MEDITATION CAN** be good for your blood pressure.

Altering Consciousness Through Biofeedback: Getting in Touch with the Untouchable

- **RATS WILL LEARN** to do whatever they can, such as pressing a lever, to obtain a burst of electricity in the brain.

- **YOU CAN LEARN** how to emit a specific brain wave.

Altering Consciousness Through Drugs

- **WHY CAN SOME** people try drugs and walk away from them, while other people become dependent on them?
- **DOES ALCOHOL** "go to the heads" of women more quickly than to men's?
- **HEROIN WAS ONCE** used as a cure for addiction to morphine.
- **THE NUMBER OF** people who die from smoking-related causes is greater than the number lost to motor vehicle accidents, abuse of alcohol and all other drugs, suicide, homicide, and AIDS *combined*.
- **A STIMULANT IS** commonly used to treat children who are already too highly stimulated.
- **COCAINE BOOSTS** your self-confidence but also the burden on your heart.
- **IS MARIJUANA HARMFUL?** What does the research evidence reveal?

Life Connections: Getting to Sleep—and Elsewhere—Without Drugs

- **YOU MAY BE ABLE** to beat insomnia by using your bed only as a place for sleeping—no more studying, eating snacks, or discussing Proust in bed!
- **YOU CAN'T SMOKE** the cigarettes or drink the beer you left on the shelf at the supermarket.

JUST WHAT *IS* CONSCIOUSNESS?

When you talk to yourself, who talks, and who listens? This is the type of question posed by philosophers and scientists who study consciousness. ***Question: What is consciousness?***

Consciousness cannot be directly seen or touched, yet it is real enough to most people. Consciousness, like anxiety or aggressiveness, is a psychological *construct* (pronounced CON-struct)—that is, a concept that is devised to help us understand our observations of behavior. The construct of consciousness has several meanings.

Consciousness as Sensory Awareness

One meaning of consciousness is *sensory awareness* of the environment. The sense of vision enables us to see, or be *conscious* of, the sun gleaming on the snow. The sense of hearing allows us to hear, or be conscious of, a concert.

Consciousness as the Selective Aspect of Attention

Sometimes we are not aware of sensory stimulation. We may be unaware, or unconscious, of sensory stimulation when we do not pay attention to it. The world is abuzz with signals, yet you are conscious of, or focusing on, only the words on this page (I hope).

Focusing one's consciousness on a particular stimulus is referred to as *selective attention.* The concept of selective attention is important to self-control. To pay attention in class, you must screen out the pleasant aroma of the cologne or perfume wafting toward you from the person in the next seat. To keep your car on the road, you must pay more attention to driving conditions than to your hunger pangs or your feelings about an argument with a friend. If you are out in the woods at night, attending to rustling sounds in the brush nearby may be crucial to your survival.

Adaptation to our environment involves learning which stimuli must be attended to and which ones can be safely ignored. Selective attention makes our senses keener (Basic Behavioral Science Task Force, 1996b). This is why we can pick out the speech of a single person across a room at a cocktail party, a phenomenon suitably termed the *cocktail party effect.*

Although we can decide where and when we will focus our attention, various kinds of stimuli also tend to capture attention. Among them are these:

- Sudden changes, as when a cool breeze enters a sweltering room or we receive a particularly high or low grade on an exam;
- Novel stimuli, as when a dog enters the classroom or a person shows up with an unusual hairdo;
- Intense stimuli, such as bright colors, loud noises, or sharp pain; and
- Repetitive stimuli, as when the same TV commercial is played a dozen times throughout the course of a football game.

How do advertisers of Nike, Microsoft, or cologne use these facts to get "into" our consciousness and, they hope, into our pocketbooks?

▶ CONTROVERSY IN PSYCHOLOGY ◀

Is consciousness a proper area for psychological study?

Although it might seem that psychologists, who study the brain, are also equipped to look into consciousness, consciousness has not always been an acceptable topic in psychology (Crick & Koch, 1997). In 1904, William James wrote an article with the intriguing title "Does Consciousness Exist?" James did not think that consciousness was a proper area of study for psychologists because no scientific method could directly observe or measure another person's consciousness.

John Watson, the "father of modern behaviorism," agreed. Watson insisted that only observable, measurable behavior is the province of psychology: "The time seems to have come when psychology must discard all references to consciousness" (1913, p. 163). In 1914, Watson was elected president of the American Psychological Association. This honor further cemented his ideas in the minds of many psychologists.

Today, however, many psychologists believe that we cannot capture the richness of the human experience without referring to consciousness. Such psychological constructs as consciousness acquire scientific status from being tied to behavior, and studies connecting consciousness with behavior have turned from a stream into a flood. Psychologists, neuroscientists, philosophers, physicists, even computer scientists are searching for the elusive marvel of consciousness. Most assume that the biological basis for consciousness dwells within the brain (e.g., Chafee & Goldman-Rakic, 2000; Duncan et al., 2000).

Consciousness as Direct Inner Awareness

Close your eyes and imagine spilling a can of bright red paint across a black tabletop. Watch it spread across the black, shiny surface and then spill onto the floor. Although this image may be vivid, you did not "see" it literally. Neither your eyes nor any other sensory organs were involved. You were *conscious* of the image through **direct inner awareness.**

We are conscious of—or have direct inner awareness of—thoughts, images, emotions, and memories. We may not be able to measure direct inner awareness scientifically. Nevertheless, many psychologists argue "It is detectable to anyone that has it" (Miller, 1992, p. 180). These psychological processes are connected with the firings of myriads of neurons. We do not consciously experience the firing of individual neurons, but consciousness reflects the total of millions or billions of neural events.

Sigmund Freud, the founder of psychoanalysis, differentiated between the thoughts and feelings we are conscious, or aware, of and those that are preconscious and unconscious. **Preconscious** material is not currently in awareness but is readily available. For example, if you answer the following questions, you will summon up "preconscious" information: What did you eat for dinner yesterday? About what time did you wake up this morning? What is your phone number? You can make these preconscious bits of information conscious by directing your inner awareness, or attention, to them.

According to Freud, still other mental events are **unconscious.** This means that they are unavailable to awareness under most circumstances. Freud believed that some painful memories and sexual and aggressive impulses are unacceptable to us, so we *automatically* (unconsciously) eject them from our awareness. In other words, we *repress* them. **Repression** of these memories and impulses allows us to avoid feelings of anxiety, guilt, or shame.

People can also *choose* to stop thinking about unacceptable ideas or distractions. When we consciously eject unwanted mental events from awareness, we are engaging in **suppression.** We may, for example, suppress thoughts of a date when we need to study for a test. We may also try to suppress thoughts of a test while we are on a date!

Some bodily processes, such as the firings of neurons, are **nonconscious.** They cannot be experienced through sensory awareness or direct inner awareness. The growing of hair and the carrying of oxygen in the blood are nonconscious. We can see that our hair has grown, but we have no sense receptors that give us sensations of growing. We can feel the need to breathe but do not directly experience the exchange of carbon dioxide and oxygen.

Consciousness as Personal Unity: The Sense of Self

As we develop, we differentiate ourselves from that which is not us. We develop a sense of being persons, individuals. There is a totality to our impressions, thoughts, and feelings that makes up our conscious existence—our continuing sense of self in a changing world. That self forms intentions and guides its own behavior. In this usage of the word, consciousness *is* self.

Consciousness as the Waking State

The word *conscious* also refers to the waking state as opposed, for example, to sleep. From this perspective, sleep, meditation, the hypnotic "trance," and the distorted perceptions that can accompany use of consciousness-altering drugs are considered *altered states of consciousness.*

In the remainder of this chapter, we explore various types of altered states of consciousness. They include sleep and dreams, hypnosis, meditation, biofeedback, and finally, the effects of psychoactive drugs.

Direct Inner Awareness
Knowledge of one's own thoughts, feelings, and memories without use of sensory organs.

Preconscious
In psychodynamic theory, descriptive of material that is not in awareness but can be brought into awareness by focusing one's attention.

Unconscious
In psychodynamic theory, descriptive of ideas and feelings that are not available to awareness.

R E F L E C T
Do you think people have an "unconscious" mind? If so, what do you think happens within it?

Repression
In psychodynamic theory, the automatic (unconscious) ejection of anxiety-evoking ideas, impulses, or images from awareness.

Suppression
The deliberate, or conscious, placing of certain ideas, impulses, or images out of awareness.

Nonconscious
Descriptive of bodily processes such as the growing of hair, of which we cannot become conscious. We may "recognize" that our hair is growing but cannot directly experience the biological process.

■ **Consciousness as the Sense of Self**

The concept of consciousness has many meanings in psychology and in general usage. One is the sense of self, as we see here. The concept of consciousness also refers to sensory awareness, the selective aspect of attention, direct inner awareness, and the waking state.

 Learning Connections
See Web site for an interactive version of these review questions.

R E V I E W

(1) John B. Watson argued that only observable _____ should be studied by psychologists. (2) *Consciousness* has several meanings, including sensory awareness, the selective aspect of attention, direct inner _____, personal unity, and the waking state. (3) Sigmund _____ differentiated among ideas that are conscious, preconscious, and unconscious.

Critical Thinking: Is it possible to study the consciousness of another person?

Circadian Rhythm

Referring to cycles that are connected with the 24-hour period of the earth's rotation.

 Learning Connections
See the Connections *CD-ROM for an animation on brain wave patterns while awake.*

Learning Connections
See the Connections *CD-ROM for an animation on brain wave patterns during sleep stage 1.*

SLEEP AND DREAMS

Sleep is a fascinating topic. After all, we spend about one-third of our adult lives asleep. Sleep experts recommend that adults get eight hours of sleep a night, but according to the National Sleep Foundation (2000b), adults in the United States typically get a bit less than seven. About one-third get six hours or less of sleep a night during the work week. One-third admit that lack of sleep impairs their ability to function during the day, and nearly one in five admits to falling asleep at the wheel at some time within the past year.

Our alternating periods of wakefulness and sleep provide an example of an internally generated **circadian rhythm.** *Question: What is a circadian rhythm?* A circadian rhythm is a cycle that is connected with the 24-hour period of the earth's rotation. A cycle of wakefulness and sleep is normally 24 hours long. However, when people are removed from cues that signal day or night, a cycle tends to become extended to about 25 hours, and people sleep nearly 10 of them (National Sleep Foundation, 2000b). Why? We do not know.

Why do we sleep? Why do we dream? Next we explore the nature of sleep, dreams, and sleep disorders.

The Stages of Sleep

A major tool of sleep researchers is the electroencephalograph, or EEG. The EEG measures the electrical activity of the brain, or brain waves. Figure 5.1 shows EEG patterns that reflect the frequency and strength of brain waves that occur during the waking state, when we are relaxed, and when we are in the various stages of sleep. *Question: What occurs during sleep?*

Awake

Awake — beta waves
(low amplitude, high frequency)

Drowsy — alpha waves
(higher amplitude, slower frequency)

NREM
Sleep

Stage 1 sleep — theta waves
(low frequency, low amplitude)

Sleep spindle   K complex

Stage 2 sleep — sleep spindles
and the K complex

Stage 3 sleep — beginning of
delta waves (low frequency,
high amplitude)

Stage 4 sleep — delta waves
continue to increase
in amplitude

REM Sleep
(occurs when we re-enter
Stage 1, about 90 minutes
after falling asleep
— frequently called
"paradoxical sleep")

REM sleep — brain-wave
patterns are very similar
to those of initial
NREM Stage 1

Power Visual
*See Web site for an interactive
version of this figure.*

■ **Figure 5.1
The Stages of Sleep**

This figure illustrates typical EEG patterns for the stages of sleep. During REM sleep, EEG patterns resemble those of the lightest stage of sleep, stage 1 sleep. For this reason, REM sleep is often termed *paradoxical sleep.* As sleep progresses from stage 1 to stage 4, brain waves become slower, and their amplitude increases. Dreams, including normal nightmares, are most vivid during REM sleep. More disturbing sleep terrors tend to occur during deep stage 4 sleep.

Learning Connections
See the Connections *CD-ROM for animations on brain wave patterns during sleep stages 2, 3, and 4.*

Brain waves, like other waves, are cyclical. During the various stages of sleep, the brain emits waves with different *frequencies* (numbers of waves per second) and *amplitudes* (heights—an index of strength). The printouts in Figure 5.1 show what happens during a period of 15 seconds or so. Brain waves that are high in frequency are associated with wakefulness. The amplitude of brain waves reflects their strength. The strength or energy of brain waves is expressed in volts (an electrical unit).

Figure 5.1 shows five stages of sleep: four stages of **non-rapid-eye-movement (NREM)** sleep and one stage of **rapid-eye-movement (REM)** sleep. When we close our eyes and begin to relax before going to sleep, our brains emit many **alpha waves.** Alpha waves are low-amplitude brain waves of about 8 to 13 cycles per second.

As we enter stage 1 sleep, our brain waves slow down from the alpha rhythm and enter a pattern of **theta waves.** Theta waves, with a frequency of about 6 to 8 cycles per second, are accompanied by slow, rolling eye movements. The transition from alpha waves to theta waves may be accompanied by a **hypnagogic state** during which we may experience brief dreamlike images that resemble vivid photographs. Stage 1 sleep is the lightest stage of sleep. If we are awakened from stage 1 sleep, we may feel that we have not slept at all.

After 30 to 40 minutes of stage 1 sleep, we undergo a rather steep descent into stages 2, 3, and 4 (see Figure 5.2). During stage 2, brain waves are medium in amplitude with a frequency of about 4 to 7 cycles per second, but these are punctuated by *sleep spindles.* Sleep spindles have a frequency of 12 to 16 cycles per second and represent brief bursts of rapid brain activity.

During deep sleep stages 3 and 4, our brains produce slower **delta waves.** During stage 3, the delta waves have a frequency of 1 to 3 cycles per second. Delta waves reach relatively great amplitude compared with other brain waves. Stage 4 is the deepest stage of sleep, from which it is the most difficult to be awakened. During stage 4 sleep, the delta waves slow to about 0.5 to 2 cycles per second, and their amplitude is greatest.

After perhaps half an hour of deep stage 4 sleep, we begin a relatively rapid journey back upward through the stages until we enter REM sleep (Figure 5.2). REM sleep derives its name from the *rapid eye movements,* observable beneath the closed eyelids, that characterize this stage. During REM sleep we produce relatively rapid, low-amplitude brain waves that resemble those of light stage 1 sleep. REM sleep is also called *paradoxical sleep* because the EEG patterns observed suggest a level of arousal

Non-Rapid-Eye-Movement (NREM) Sleep
Stages of sleep 1 through 4.

Rapid-Eye-Movement (REM) Sleep
A stage of sleep characterized by rapid eye movements, which have been linked to dreaming.

Alpha Waves
Rapid low-amplitude brain waves that have been linked to feelings of relaxation.

Theta Waves
Slow brain waves produced during the hypnagogic state.

Hypnagogic State
The drowsy interval between waking and sleeping, characterized by brief, hallucinatory, dreamlike experiences.

Delta Waves
Strong, slow brain waves usually emitted during stage 4 sleep.

■ **Figure 5.2**
Sleep Cycles
This figure illustrates the alternation of REM and non-REM sleep for the typical sleeper. There are about five periods of REM sleep during an eight-hour night. Sleep is deeper earlier in the night, and REM sleep tends to become prolonged toward morning.

Learning Connections
See the Connections CD-ROM for an animation on brain wave patterns during REM sleep.

similar to that of the waking state (Figure 5.1). However, it is difficult to awaken a person during REM sleep. When people are awakened during REM sleep, as is the practice in sleep research, about 80% of the time they report that they have been dreaming. (We also dream during NREM sleep, but less frequently. People report dreaming only about 20% of the time when awakened during NREM sleep.)

Each night we tend to undergo five trips through the stages of sleep (see Figure 5.2). These trips include about five periods of REM sleep. Our first journey through stage 4 sleep is usually longest. Sleep tends to become lighter as the night wears on. Our periods of REM sleep tend to become longer, and toward morning our last period of REM sleep may last close to half an hour.

Now that we have some idea of what sleep is like, let us consider *why* we sleep.

Functions of Sleep

Question: Why do we sleep?   Researchers do not have all the answers as to why we sleep. One hypothesis is that sleep helps rejuvenate a tired body. Most of us have had the experience of going without sleep for a night and feeling "wrecked" or "out of it" the following day. Perhaps the next evening we went to bed early in order to "catch up on our sleep." What happens to you if you do not sleep for one night? For several nights?

Compare people who are highly sleep deprived with people who have been drinking heavily. Sleepless people's abilities to concentrate and perform may be seriously impaired, but they may be the last ones to recognize their limitations.

Most students can pull successful "all-nighters" (Webb, 1993). They can cram for a test through the night and then perform reasonably well the following day. When we are deprived of sleep for several nights, however, aspects of psychological functioning such as attention, learning, and memory deteriorate notably (Maas, 1998). The National Sleep Foundation (2000b) estimates that sleep deprivation is connected with 100,000 vehicular crashes and 1,500 deaths each year. Many people sleep late or nap on their days off (National Sleep Foundation, 2000b). Perhaps they suffer from mild sleep deprivation during the week and catch up on the weekend.

R E F L E C T

How much sleep do you need? (How do you know?) Did you ever "pull an all-nighter"? What were the effects?

Why Do You Need the Amount of Sleep You Need?

The amount of sleep we need seems to be in part genetically determined (Webb, 1993). People also tend to need more sleep during periods of stress, such as a change of job, an increase in workload, or an episode of depression (Maas, 1998). Sleep seems to help us recover from stress.

Newborn babies may sleep 16 hours a day, and teenagers often sleep around the clock. It is widely believed that older people need less sleep than younger adults do. However, sleep in older people is often interrupted by physical discomfort or the need to go to the bathroom. Older people often sleep more during the day to make up for sleep lost at night.

Figure 5.3 shows that different animals need different amounts of sleep.

REM   1   2   3 2 A 1   REM   A 1 A   2   REM

4 A.M.   5 A.M.   6 A.M.   7 A.M.

Sleep, Learning, and Memory

REM sleep and deep sleep are both connected with the consolidation of learning and memory (Maquet, 2001; Poe et al., 2000; Stickgold et al., 2000). In some studies, animals or people have been deprived of REM sleep. Under these conditions animals and people learn more slowly and forget what they have learned more rapidly (Kennedy, 2002; Le Marec et al., 2001). Fetuses have periods of waking and sleeping, and REM sleep may foster the development of the brain before birth (McCarley, 1992). REM sleep may also help maintain neurons in adults by "exercising" them at night. Deprivation of REM sleep is accomplished by monitoring EEG records and eye movements and waking the person during REM sleep. There is too much individual variation to conclude that people who are deprived of REM sleep learn more poorly than they otherwise would. It does seem, though, that such deprivation interferes with memory—that is, retrieval of information that has been learned previously. In any event, people and other animals that are deprived of REM sleep tend to show *REM rebound*. They spend more time in REM sleep during subsequent sleep periods. In other words, they catch up. It is mostly during REM sleep that we dream. Let us now consider dreams, a mystery about which philosophers, poets, and scientists have theorized for centuries.

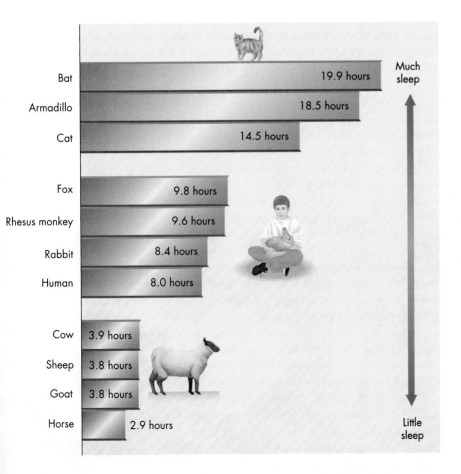

Bat	19.9 hours
Armadillo	18.5 hours
Cat	14.5 hours
Fox	9.8 hours
Rhesus monkey	9.6 hours
Rabbit	8.4 hours
Human	8.0 hours
Cow	3.9 hours
Sheep	3.8 hours
Goat	3.8 hours
Horse	2.9 hours

Much sleep

Little sleep

■ Figure 5.3
Typical Amounts of Time Animals Spend Sleeping

You may need about eight hours of sleep to feel well rested, but some animals require a good deal more sleep, and some much less. Evolutionary psychologists note that, by and large, animals in greater danger of attack from predators tend to sleep less, which increases their chance of survival.

(Based on data from Zepelin & Rechtschaffen, 1974.)

Dreams: What Is the "Stuff" of Dreams?

To quote from Shakespeare's *The Tempest,* just what is the "stuff" of dreams? What are they "made on"? ***Questions: What are dreams? Why do we dream what we dream?*** Like memories and fantasies, dreams involve imagery in the absence of external stimulation. Some dreams seem very real. In college I often had "anxiety dreams" the night before a test. I dreamed repeatedly that I had taken the test and it was all over. (Imagine the disappointment when I awakened and realized that the test still lay before me!)

Dreams are most likely to have vivid imagery during REM sleep. Images are vaguer and more fleeting during NREM sleep. You may dream every time you are in REM sleep. So if you sleep for eight hours and undergo five sleep cycles, you may have five dreams. Upon waking, you may think that time seemed to expand or contract during your dream, so that during 10 or 15 minutes of actual time, the content of your dream ranged over days or weeks. But dreams actually tend to take place in "real time." Fifteen minutes of events fills about 15 minutes of dreaming. Your dream theater is quite flexible. You can dream in black and white or in full color.

Theories of the Content of Dreams

You may recall dreams involving fantastic adventures, but most dreams involve memories of the activities and problems of the day (Domhoff, 2001). If we are preoccupied with illness or death, sexual or aggressive urges, or moral dilemmas, we are likely to dream about them. The characters in our dreams are more likely to be friends and neighbors than spies, monsters, and princes.

"A dream is a wish your heart makes," is a song lyric from the Disney film *Cinderella.* Freud theorized that dreams reflect unconscious wishes and urges. He argued that through dreams we can express impulses we would censor during the day. Moreover, he said that the content of dreams is symbolic of unconscious fantasized objects such as the genitals (see Table 5.1). A key part of Freud's method of psychoanalysis involved interpretation of his clients' dreams. Freud also believed that dreams "protect sleep" by providing imagery that helps keep disturbing, repressed thoughts out of awareness.

The theory that dreams protect sleep has been challenged by the observation that disturbing events tend to be followed by disturbing dreams on the same theme—not by protective imagery (Reiser, 2001). Our behavior in dreams is also generally consistent with our waking behavior. Most dreams, then, are unlikely candidates for the expression of repressed urges (even disguised). A person who leads a moral life tends to dream moral dreams.

REFLECT

What do you dream about? Has anyone tried to interpret your dreams? Is the interpretation consistent with any of the theories of dreams discussed in the chapter?

■ **Dream Images?**
In *The Persistence of Memory,* Salvador Dali seems to depict images born in dreams. What is "such stuff as dreams are made on"? Where do dreams come from? Why do they contain what they contain? Are most dreams exciting adventures or dull recurrences of the events of the day?

TABLE 5.1 Dream Symbols in Psychodynamic Theory*

Symbols for the Male Genital Organs

airplanes	fish	neckties	tools	weapons
bullets	hands	poles	trains	
feet	hoses	snakes	trees	
fire	knives	sticks	umbrellas	

Symbols for the Female Sexual Organs

bottles	caves	doors	ovens	ships
boxes	chests	hats	pockets	tunnels
cases	closets	jars	pots	

Symbols for Sexual Intercourse

climbing a ladder	entering a room
climbing a staircase	flying in an airplane
crossing a bridge	riding a horse
driving an automobile	riding a roller coaster
riding an elevator	walking into a tunnel or down a hall

Symbols for the Breasts

apples	peaches

*Freud theorized that the content of dreams symbolizes urges, wishes, and objects of fantasy that we would censor if we were awake.

There are also biological views of the "meanings" of dreams. According to the **activation-synthesis model,** acetylcholine (a neurotransmitter) and the pons (a structure in the lower part of the brain) stimulate responses that lead to dreaming (Hobson, 1999, 2003). One is *activation* of the reticular activating system (RAS), which arouses us, but not to waking. During the waking state, firing of these cells in the reticular formation is linked to movement, particularly the movements involved in walking, running, and other physical acts. During REM sleep, however, neurotransmitters generally inhibit activity so we usually do not thrash about as we dream (Bassetti et al., 2000). In this way, we save ourselves (and our bed partners) some wear and tear. The eye muscles are stimulated and thus show the rapid eye movement associated with dreaming. The RAS also stimulates neural activity in the parts of the cortex involved in memory. The cortex then *synthesizes,* or puts together, these sources of stimulation to some degree to yield the stuff of dreams. Yet research with the PET scan shows that the frontal lobes of the brain, which seem to be where we make sense of experience, are pretty much shut down during sleep (Wade, 1998). Dreams are therefore more likely to be emotionally gripping than coherent in plot.

Another view of dreams is that with the brain cut off from the world outside, memories are replayed and consolidated during sleep (Wade, 1998). Still another possibility is that REM activity is a way of testing whether the individual has benefitted from the restorative functions of sleep (Wade, 1998). When restoration is adequate, the brain awakens. According to this view, dreams are just the by-products of the testing.

Activation-Synthesis Model
The view that dreams reflect activation of cognitive activity by the reticular activating system and synthesis of this activity into a pattern by the cerebral cortex.

Nightmares

Have you ever dreamed that something heavy was sitting on your chest and watching you as you breathed? Or that you were trying to run away from a terrible threat but couldn't gain your footing or coordinate your leg muscles?

Nightmares, like most pleasant dreams, are generally products of REM sleep. College students report an average of two nightmares a month in dream logs (Wood & Bootzin, 1990). Traumatic events can spawn nightmares, as reported in studies of the aftermath of the terrorist attacks on the World Trade Center and Pentagon in 2001 (Gorman, 2001). People who suffer frequent nightmares are more likely than other people to also suffer from anxieties, depression, and other kinds of psychological discomfort (Berquier & Ashton, 1992).

Sleep Disorders

There are a number of sleep disorders. Some, like insomnia, are all too familiar. *Question: What kinds of sleep disorders are there?* In this section we discuss insomnia, narcolepsy, apnea, and the deep-sleep disorders—sleep terrors, bedwetting, and sleepwalking.

Insomnia

According to the National Sleep Foundation (2000b), more than half of American adults (58%) are affected by insomnia in any given year. Women complain of insomnia more often than men do, by 61% to 53% (National Sleep Foundation, 2000b). Table 5.2 shows a number of factors that contribute to insomnia.

People with insomnia tend to compound their sleep problems when they try to force themselves to fall asleep. Their concern heightens autonomic activity and muscle tension (Edinger et al., 2001). You cannot force or will yourself to go to sleep. You can only set the stage for sleep by lying down and relaxing when you are tired. If you focus on sleep too closely, it will elude you.

You will find strategies for tackling insomnia—and winning—in this chapter's "Life Connections" feature.

Narcolepsy

A person with **narcolepsy** falls asleep suddenly and irresistibly. Narcolepsy afflicts as many as 100,000 people in the United States and seems to run in families. The "sleep attack" may last about 15 minutes, after which the person awakens feeling refreshed. Nevertheless, these sleep episodes are dangerous and frightening. They can occur while a person is driving or working with sharp tools. They also may be accompanied by the sudden collapse of muscle groups or even of the entire body—a condition called *sleep paralysis.* In sleep paralysis, the person cannot move during the transition from the waking state to sleep, and hallucinations (such as of a person or object sitting on the chest) occur.

Although the causes are unknown, narcolepsy is thought to be a disorder of REM–sleep functioning. Stimulants and antidepressant drugs have helped many people with narcolepsy (Littner et al., 2001).

Apnea

Apnea is a dangerous sleep disorder in which the air passages are obstructed. People with apnea stop breathing periodically, upwards of ten times an hour (National Sleep Foundation, 2000b). Obstruction may cause the sleeper to suddenly sit up and gasp for air, before falling back asleep. People with apnea are stimulated nearly, but not quite, to waking by the buildup of carbon dioxide. Some 10 million Americans have apnea, and it is associated with obesity and chronic loud snoring. Apnea is more than a sleep problem. It can lead to high blood pressure, heart attacks, and strokes (Flemons, 2002).

Narcolepsy
A "sleep attack" in which a person falls asleep suddenly and irresistibly.

Apnea
Temporary absence or cessation of breathing. (From Greek and Latin roots meaning "without" and "breathing.")

TABLE 5.2 Gender Differences in Factors That Disrupt Sleep

Factor	Percent of women reporting factor	Percent of men reporting factor
Stress (e.g., restlessness, muscle tension): 22% of adults overall	26	20
Pain: 20% of adults overall	25	13
Children: 17% of adults overall	21	12
Partner's snoring: 16% of adults overall	22	7
Pauses in partner's breathing: 8% of adults overall	11	2

Based on data reported by the National Sleep Foundation, 2000b.

■ **Narcolepsy**
In an experiment on narcolepsy, the dog barks, nods it head, and then falls suddenly asleep.

Causes of apnea include anatomical deformities that clog the air passageways, such as a thick palate, and problems in the breathing centers in the brain. Apnea is treated by such measures as weight loss, surgery, and *continuous positive airway pressure.* Airway pressure through the nose keeps the airway open during sleep.

Deep-Sleep Disorders: Sleep Terrors, Bed-Wetting, and Sleepwalking

Sleep terrors, bed-wetting, and sleepwalking all occur during deep (stage 3 or 4) sleep, are more common among children, and may reflect immaturity of the nervous system (Vgontzas & Kales, 1999).

Sleep terrors are similar to, but more severe than, nightmares. They usually occur during deep sleep, whereas nightmares take place during REM sleep. Sleep terrors occur during the first couple of sleep cycles; nightmares are more likely to occur later on. Experiencing a surge in the heart and respiration rates, the dreamer may suddenly sit up, talk incoherently, and move about wildly. The dreamer is never fully awake, returns to sleep, and may recall a vague image as of someone pressing on his or her chest. (Memories of nightmares tend to be more vivid.) Sleep terrors are often decreased by taking a minor tranquilizer at bedtime. The drug reduces the amount of time spent in stage 4 sleep.

Bed-wetting is often seen as a stigma that reflects parental harshness or the child's attempt to punish the parents, but this disorder, too, may stem from immaturity of the nervous system. In most cases it resolves itself before adolescence, often by age 8. Behavior-therapy methods that condition children to awaken when they are about to urinate have been helpful. The drug imipramine often helps, although the reason is not fully known. Sometimes all that is needed is reassurance that no one is to blame for bed-wetting and that most children "outgrow" it.

Perhaps half of all children occasionally talk in their sleep. Nearly 15% walk in their sleep (Mindell, 1993). Only about 2% of a random sample of nearly 5,000 people aged 15 to 100 did so (Ohayon et al., 1999). Sleepwalkers may roam about almost nightly while their parents fret about the accidents that could befall them. Sleepwalkers typically do not remember their excursions, although they may respond to questions while they are up and about. Contrary to myth, there is no evidence that sleepwalkers become violent if they are awakened, although they may be confused and upset. Mild tranquilizers and maturity typically put an end to sleepwalking.

The Greek word for "sleep" is *hypnos,* which raises the question as to whether there are connections between the state of consciousness we call sleep and another one we call hypnosis. Although many people are hypnotized by being told that they are "going to sleep," we now see many differences between sleep and hypnosis.

Sleep Terrors
Frightening dreamlike experiences that occur during the deepest stage of NREM sleep. Nightmares, in contrast, occur during REM sleep.

Learning Connections
See Web site for an interactive version of these review questions.

REVIEW

(4) EEG research shows that different stages of sleep are characterized by different _____ waves. (5) Because EEG patterns during REM sleep resemble those of the waking state, REM sleep is also called _____ sleep. (6) During a typical eight-hour night, we undergo about _____ trips through the different stages of sleep. (7) Dreams are most vivid during (REM or NREM?) sleep. (8) According to the _____-synthesis model, dreams reflect neural activity. (9) Sleep terrors, bed-wetting, and sleepwalking all occur during _____ sleep.

Critical Thinking: Why are so many people fascinated by what their dreams might "mean"?

ALTERING CONSCIOUSNESS THROUGH HYPNOSIS: ON BEING ENTRANCED

Hypnosis

A condition in which people appear to be highly suggestible and behave as though they are in a trance.

Perhaps you have seen films in which Count Dracula hypnotized resistant victims into a stupor. Then he could give them a bite in the neck with no further nonsense. Perhaps you have watched a fellow student try to place a friend in a "trance" after reading a book on hypnosis. Or perhaps you have seen an audience member hypnotized in a nightclub act. If so, chances are the person acted as if he or she had returned to childhood, imagined that a snake was about to have a nip, or lay rigid between two chairs for a while. *Question: What is hypnosis?*

Hypnosis, a term derived from the Greek word for sleep, is an altered state of consciousness in which people appear to be highly suggestible and behave as though they are in a trance. Hypnosis has only recently become a respectable subject for psychological inquiry. Modern hypnosis seems to have begun with the ideas of Franz Mesmer in the 18th century. Mesmer asserted that everything in the universe was connected by forms of magnetism—which actually may not be far from the mark. He claimed that people, too, could be drawn to one another by "animal magnetism." (No bull's-eye here.) Mesmer used bizarre props to bring people under his "spell." He did manage a respectable cure rate for minor ailments. However, scientists attribute his successes to the placebo effect, not to animal magnetism.

Today hypnotism retains its popularity in nightclubs, but it is also used as an anesthetic in dentistry, childbirth, even surgery (Montgomery et al., 2000). Some psychologists use hypnosis to teach clients how to reduce anxiety or overcome fears (Pinnell & Covino, 2000). A study with 241 surgery patients in a Boston hospital shows how hypnosis can help people deal with pain and anxiety. The patients underwent procedures in which only local anesthetics were used (Lang et al., 2000). They could use as much pain medication as they desired by means of an intravenous tube. Patients who were hypnotized during these procedures needed less additional medication for pain and experienced less anxiety as measured by blood pressure and heart rate. The hypnotized patients focused on pleasant imagery rather than the details of the surgery. Hypnosis as an aid in relaxation training also helps people cope with stress and enhance the functioning of their immune systems (Kiecolt-Glaser et al., 2001). Research also shows that hypnosis is a useful supplement to other forms of therapy, especially in helping obese people lose weight (Kirsch et al., 1995). Police also use hypnosis to prompt the memories of witnesses.

The state of consciousness called the *hypnotic trance* has traditionally been induced by asking people to narrow their attention to a small light, a spot on the wall, an object held by the hypnotist, or the hypnotist's voice. The hypnotist usually suggests that the person's limbs are becoming warm, heavy, and relaxed. People may also be told that they are becoming sleepy or falling asleep. Hypnosis is *not* sleep, however. This is shown by differences between EEG recordings for the hypnotic trance and the stages of sleep. But the word *sleep* is understood by subjects to suggest a hypnotic trance.

■ **Hypnosis**

Hypnotized people become passive and follow the suggestions of the hypnotist. Only recently has hypnosis become a respectable subject for psychological inquiry.

It is also possible to induce hypnosis through instructions that direct subjects to remain active and alert (Alarcon et al., 1999; Winter, 2001). So the effects of hypnosis probably cannot be attributed to relaxation.

People who are readily hypnotized are said to have *hypnotic suggestibility.* Part of "suggestibility" is knowledge of what is expected during the "trance state." Generally speaking, suggestible people are prone to fantasy, can compartmentalize unwanted memories, and want to cooperate with the hypnotist (Barber, 2000). As a result, they pay close attention to the hypnotist's instructions. It is therefore extremely unlikely that someone could be hypnotized against his or her will.

Question: What changes in consciousness are induced by hypnosis?   Hypnotists and people who have been hypnotized report that hypnosis can bring about the changes shown in Table 5.3.

R E F L E C T

Do you believe it's true that you can be hypnotized only if you want to be hypnotized? Why or why not?

▶ CONTROVERSY IN PSYCHOLOGY ◀

How do psychologists explain hypnosis?

Hypnotism is no longer explained in terms of animal magnetism, but psychodynamic and learning theorists have offered explanations. According to Freud, hypnotized adults permit themselves to return to childish modes of responding that emphasize fantasy and impulse rather than fact and logic. Modern views of hypnosis are quite different.   **Question: How do modern psychologists explain the effects of hypnosis?**

Role Theory

Theodore Sarbin offers a **role theory** view of hypnosis (Sarbin & Coe, 1972). He points out that the changes in behavior attributed to the hypnotic trance can be successfully imitated when people are instructed to behave *as though* they were hypnotized. For example, people can lie rigid between two chairs whether they are hypnotized or not. Also, people cannot be hypnotized unless they are familiar with the hypnotic "role"—

Role Theory
A theory that explains hypnotic events in terms of the person's ability to act *as though* he or she were hypnotized. Role theory differs from faking in that subjects cooperate and focus on hypnotic suggestions instead of pretending to be hypnotized.

TABLE 5.3 Changes in Consciousness Attributed to Hypnosis*

Change	Comments
Passivity	Awaiting instructions and suspending planning.
Narrowed attention	Focusing on the hypnotist's voice or a spot of light and not attending to background noise or intruding thoughts.
Pseudomemories and hypermnesia	Reporting pseudomemories (false memories) or highly detailed memories (hypermnesia). Police hypnotists attempt to heighten witnesses' memories by instructing them to focus on details of a crime and reconstruct the scene. Some studies challenge the accuracy of such memories.
Suggestibility	Responding to suggestions that an arm is becoming lighter and will rise or that the eyelids are becoming heavier and must close.
Playing unusual roles	Playing roles calling for increased strength or alertness, such as riding a bicycle with less fatigue than usual. In *age regression*, people may play themselves as infants or children. A person may speak a language forgotten since childhood.
Perceptual distortions	Acting as though hypnotically induced hallucinations and delusions are real. Behaving as though one cannot hear loud noises, smell odors, or feel pain.
Posthypnotic amnesia	Acting as though one cannot recall events that take place under hypnosis.
Posthypnotic suggestion	Following commands given "under" hypnosis after one "awakens," such as falling quickly into a deep trance when given the command "Sleep!" or—in the case of a would-be quitter of smoking—finding cigarette smoke aversive.

*Research evidence in support of these changes in consciousness is mixed.

Sources: Barber, 2000; Bowers & Woody, 1996; Green & Lynn, 2000; Lancaster et al., 2000; Loftus, 1994; Miller & Bowers, 1993; Weekes et al., 1992; Woody & Szechtman, 2000.

Response Set Theory

The view that response expectancies play a key role in the production of the experiences suggested by the hypnotist.

Neodissociation Theory

A theory of hypnotic events as the splitting of consciousness.

the behavior that constitutes the trance. Sarbin is not saying that subjects *fake* the hypnotic role. Research evidence suggests that most people who are hypnotized are not faking (Kinnunen et al., 1994). Instead, Sarbin is suggesting that people *allow* themselves to enact this role under the hypnotist's directions.

Response Set Theory

The **response set theory** of hypnosis is closely related to role theory. It suggests that response expectancies (the things we know we are expected to do) play a key role in the production of personal experiences and also in experiences suggested by the hypnotist (Kirsch, 2000).

Role theory and response set theory appear to be supported by research evidence that "suggestible" people want to be hypnotized, are good role players, have vivid and absorbing imaginations, and also know what is expected of them (Barber, 2000; Kirsch, 2000). The fact that the behaviors shown by hypnotized people can be mimicked by people who know what is expected of them means that we need not resort to the concept of the "hypnotic trance"—an unusual and mystifying altered state of awareness—to explain hypnotic events.

Neodissociation Theory

Runners frequently get through the pain and tedium of long-distance races by *dissociating*—by imagining themselves elsewhere, doing other things. (My students inform me that they manage the pain and tedium of *other* instructors' classes in the same way.) Ernest Hilgard (1904–2001) similarly explained hypnotic phenomena through **neodissociation theory** (Hilgard, 1994). This is the view that we can selectively focus our attention on one thing (like hypnotic suggestions) and dissociate ourselves from the things going on around us—just as the surgery patients in the Boston study focused on pleasant thoughts and not on the surgery itself (Lang et al., 2000).

Subjects in one study of neodissociation theory were hypnotized and instructed to submerge their arms in ice water—causing "cold pressor pain" (Miller et al., 1991). Subjects were given suggestions to the effect that they were not in pain, however. Highly hypnotizable people reported dissociative experiences that allowed them to avoid the perception of pain, such as imagining that they were at the beach or that their limbs were floating in air above the ice water.

Although hypnotized people may be focusing on the hypnotist's suggestions and perhaps imagining themselves to be somewhere else, they still tend to perceive their actual surroundings peripherally. In a sense, we do this all the time. We are not fully conscious, or aware, of everything going on about us. Rather, at any given moment we selectively focus on events such as tests, dates, or television shows that seem important or relevant. Yet, while taking a test we may be peripherally aware of the color of the wall or the sound of rain.

Role theory and neodissociation theory do not suggest that the phenomena of hypnosis are phony. Instead, they suggest that we do not need to explain these events through an altered state of awareness called a trance. Hypnosis may not be special at all. Rather, it is *we* who are special—through our imagination, our role-playing ability, and our capacity to divide our consciousness—concentrating now on one event that we deem important, and concentrating on another event later.

Let us now consider two other states of consciousness that involve different ways of focusing our attention: meditation and biofeedback.

Learning Connections
See Web site for an interactive version of these review questions.

R E V I E W

(10) Franz Mesmer explained the hypnotic "trance" through his concept of animal _____. (11) Hypnosis typically brings about the following changes in consciousness: passivity, narrowed attention, _____ (heightened memory), suggestibility, assumption of unusual roles, perceptual distortions, posthypnotic amnesia, and posthypnotic suggestion. (12) According to _____ set theory, knowledge of what one is expected to do is a key component of being hypnotized.

Critical Thinking: Is it possible to explain hypnosis without referring to a special "trance" state?

ALTERING CONSCIOUSNESS THROUGH MEDITATION: LETTING THE WORLD FADE AWAY

Question: What is meditation?   The dictionary defines *meditation* as the act or process of thinking. But the concept usually suggests thinking deeply about the universe or about one's place in the world, often within a spiritual context. As the term is commonly used by psychologists, however, meditation refers to various ways of focusing one's consciousness to alter one's relationship to the world. As used by psychologists, ironically, *meditation* can also refer to a process in which people seem to suspend thinking and allow the world to fade away.

The kinds of meditation that psychologists and other kinds of helping professionals speak of are *not* the first definition you find in the dictionary. Rather, they tend to refer to rituals, exercises, and even passive observation—activities that alter the normal relationship between the person and her or his environment. They are various methods of suspending problem solving, planning, worries, and awareness of the events of the day. These methods alter consciousness—that is, the normal focus of attention—and help people cope with stress by inducing feelings of relaxation.

R E F L E C T

Do you know anyone who has tried meditation? What was the purpose? Were the effects consistent with what is reported in this text? Why or why not?

Let us consider one common form of meditation in more detail. **Transcendental meditation (TM)** is a simplified form of Far Eastern meditation that was brought to the United States by the Maharishi Mahesh Yogi in 1959. Hundreds of thousands of Americans practice TM by repeating and concentrating on *mantras*—words or sounds that are claimed to help the person achieve an altered state of consciousness. TM has a number of spiritual goals, such as expanding consciousness so that it encompasses spiritual kinds of experiences, but there are also more worldly goals, such as reducing anxiety and normalizing blood pressure.

Question: What are the effects of meditation?   In early research, Herbert Benson (1975) found no scientific evidence that TM expands consciousness (how do you measure spiritual experience with earthly instruments?), despite the claims of many of its practitioners. However, TM lowered the heart and respiration rates—changes that can be measured through commonly used medical instruments—and also produced what Benson labeled a *relaxation response.* The blood pressure of people with hypertension—a risk factor in cardiovascular disease—decreased. In fact, people who meditated twice daily tended to show more normal blood pressure through the day. Meditators produced more frequent alpha waves—brain waves associated with feelings of relaxation. Meditation also increases nighttime concentrations of the hormone melatonin, which is relaxing and helps people get to sleep (Tooley et al., 2000).

In more recent years, an apparently careful research program has been conducted at the College of Maharishi Vedic Medicine in Fairfield, Iowa (Ready, 2000). It has focused on older African Americans because African Americans are more prone to hypertension than European Americans. Two studies compared the effects of TM, progressive relaxation (a muscle relaxation technique), and a "health education" placebo on high blood pressure (Alexander et al., 1996; Schneider et al., 1995). They both found that TM was significantly more effective at reducing high blood pressure than progressive relaxation or the placebo. A third study reported that TM practiced by African Americans aged 20 and above for 6 to 9 months was significantly more likely than the health education placebo to reduce the progression of atherosclerosis (hardening of the arteries) (Castillo-Richmond et al., 2000).

© 1987 Joel Gordon

■ **Meditation**

People use many forms of meditation to try to expand their inner awareness and experience inner harmony. Although practitioners of some forms of meditation claim that it has spiritual effects, research does suggest that meditation can have healthful effects on the blood pressure and other health-related bodily functions.

Transcendental Meditation (TM)

The simplified form of meditation brought to the United States by the Maharishi Mahesh Yogi and used as a method for coping with stress.

Learning Connections
See Web site for an interactive version of these review questions.

(13) In meditation, one focuses "passively" on a _____ in order to alter the normal person–environment relationship. (14) Investigators have shown that meditation can reduce high _____ pressure.

Critical Thinking: Does the research show that meditation is a spiritual experience?

ALTERING CONSCIOUSNESS THROUGH BIOFEEDBACK: GETTING IN TOUCH WITH THE UNTOUCHABLE

Let us begin our discussion of biofeedback by recounting some remarkable experiments in which psychologist Neal E. Miller (1909–2002) trained laboratory rats to increase or decrease their heart rates. His procedure was simple but ingenious. As discovered by psychologists James Olds and Peter Milner (1954), there is a "pleasure center" in the rat's hypothalamus. A small burst of electricity in this center is strongly reinforcing: Rats learn to do what they can, such as pressing a lever, to obtain this stimulus.

Miller (1969) implanted electrodes in the rats' pleasure centers. Then some rats were given a burst of electricity in their brain's pleasure center whenever their heart rate happened to increase. Other rats received the stimulus when their heart rate went lower. In other words, one group of rats was consistently "rewarded" (that is, their pleasure center stimulated) when their heart rate showed an increase. The other group was consistently rewarded for a decrease in heart rate. After a single 90-minute training session, the rats learned to alter their heart rates by as much as 20% in the direction for which they had been rewarded.

Miller's research was an early example of **biofeedback training (BFT)**. *Question: What is biofeedback training?* Biofeedback is a system that provides, or "feeds back," information about a bodily function. Miller used electrical stimulation of the brain to feed back information to rats when they had engaged in a targeted bodily response (in this case, raised or lowered their heart rates). Somehow the rats then used this information to raise or lower their heart rates voluntarily.

REFLECT

How do you think that a rat manages to elevate or decrease its heart rate? Does it seem pointless to speculate on an answer? Why or why not?

Biofeedback Training (BFT)
The systematic feeding back to an organism of information about a bodily function so that the organism can gain control of that function.

■ **Biofeedback**
Biofeedback is a system that provides, or "feeds back," information about a bodily function to an organism. Through biofeedback training, people have learned to gain voluntary control over a number of functions that are normally automatic, such as heart rate and blood pressure.

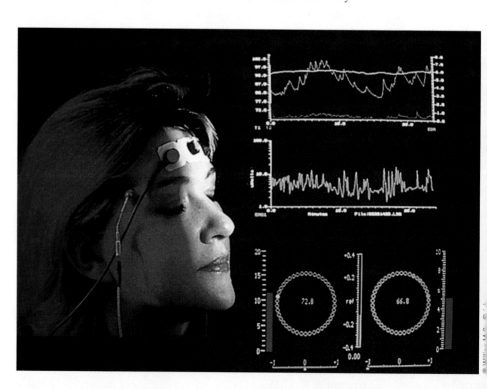

Similarly, people have learned to change various bodily functions voluntarily, including heart rate, that were once considered to be beyond their control. However, electrodes are not implanted in people's brains. Rather, people hear a "blip" or observe some other signal that informs them when the targeted response is being displayed.

Question: How is biofeedback training used? BFT has been used in many ways, including helping people combat stress, tension, and anxiety. For example, people can learn to emit alpha waves (and feel somewhat more relaxed) through feedback from an EEG. A blip may increase in frequency whenever alpha waves are being emitted. The psychologist's instructions are simply to "make the blip go faster." An **electromyograph (EMG),** which monitors muscle tension, is commonly used to help people become more aware of muscle tension in the forehead, fingers, and elsewhere and to learn to lower the tension (Martin, 2002). Through the use of other instruments, people have learned to lower their heart rate, their blood pressure, and the amount of sweat in the palm of the hand (Nagourney, 2002). All of these changes are relaxing. Biofeedback is widely used by sports psychologists to teach athletes how to relax muscle groups that are unessential to the task at hand so that they can control anxiety and tension.

Sleep, hypnosis, meditation, and biofeedback training all involve "natural" ways of deploying our attention or consciousness. Some altered states depend on the ingestion of psychoactive chemical substances we call "drugs." Let us now deploy our attention to the effects of alcohol and other drugs.

Electromyograph (EMG)
An instrument that measures muscle tension.

Psychoactive Substances
Drugs that have psychological effects such as stimulation or distortion of perceptions.

Depressant
A drug that lowers the rate of activity of the nervous system.

Stimulant
A drug that increases activity of the nervous system.

REVIEW

(15) Neal Miller taught rats to increase or decrease their _____ rates by giving them an electric shock in their "pleasure centers" when they performed the targeted response. (16) Through biofeedback training, people and lower animals have learned to control _____ functions like the heart rate.

Critical Thinking: Is it possible to explain what the rats in Miller's research were "thinking" when they learned to increase or decrease their heart rates?

Learning Connections
See Web site for an interactive version of these review questions.

ALTERING CONSCIOUSNESS THROUGH DRUGS

The world is a supermarket of **psychoactive substances,** or drugs. The United States is flooded with drugs that distort perceptions and change mood—drugs that take you up, let you down, and move you across town. Some people use drugs because their friends do or because their parents tell them not to. Some are seeking pleasure; others are seeking inner truth or escape.

For better or worse, drugs are part of American life. Young people often become involved with drugs that impair their ability to learn at school and are connected with reckless behavior (Wills et al., 2002). Alcohol is the most popular drug on high school and college campuses (Johnston et al., 2001). More than 40% of college students have tried marijuana, and 1 in 6 or 7 smokes it regularly (Johnston et al., 2001). Many Americans take **depressants** to get to sleep at night and **stimulants** to get going in the morning. Karl Marx charged that "religion . . . is the opium of the people," but heroin is the real "opium of the people." Cocaine was, until recently, a toy of the well-to-do, but price breaks have brought it into the lockers of high-school students.

Table 5.4 shows the lifetime and 30-day prevalence of use of various drugs by twelfth graders in the United States. Note that the majority have at least experimented with an illicit substance, and that about half have tried marijuana. Among twelfth graders, European Americans are more likely to smoke cigarettes than African Americans or Latino and Latina Americans.

© Larry Kolvoord/The Image Works

■ **The Deluge of Drugs**
The lives of many Americans are flooded with drugs—licit and illicit. People use drugs to get going in the morning, to get to sleep at night, and to feel better about themselves and other people in between. When does substance use become substance abuse? When does substance abuse become substance dependence? Why do so many deceive themselves about the nature of their use of drugs?

TABLE 5.4 Ethnic Comparisons of Lifetime and 30-Day Prevalence of Use of Various Drugs Among Twelfth Graders (Percents)

Drug	Ever Use Drug?			Use Drug in Past 30 Days?		
	European American	African American	Latino/Latina American	European American	African American	Latino/Latina American
Any illicit drug	54.8%	48.7%	60.0%	25.9%	20.3%	27.4%
Marijuana	49.4	45.7	55.5	22.7	19.0	24.6
Inhalants	16.7	4.6	15.4	2.1	1.3	3.1
LSD	13.2	1.7	13.1	2.3	0.8	2.4
MDMA (Ecstasy)	10.5	1.6	13.3	3.3	0.9	4.5
Cocaine	9.9	1.9	13.3	2.5	0.8	3.6
Crack	4.4	0.8	6.3	1.0	0.4	2.1
Heroin	0.9	0.4	2.6	0.5	0.2	1.2
Amphetamines	18.2	4.9	15.1	5.3	1.2	4.5
Barbiturates	10.3	2.4	8.1	3.2	0.8	2.2
Methaqualone	1.1	0.3	0.4	0.2	0.1	0.0
Alcohol	82.0	70.3	84.3	55.1	30.0	51.2
Cigarettes	67.2	45.5	66.1	37.9	14.3	27.7
Steroids	2.8	1.3	3.4	0.8	0.4	1.5

Source of data: Johnston et al., 2001.

Substance Abuse and Dependence: Crossing the Line

Where does drug use end and abuse begin? *Question: What are substance abuse and dependence?* The American Psychiatric Association (2000) defines **substance abuse** as repeated use of a substance despite the fact that it is causing or compounding social, occupational, psychological, or physical problems. If you are missing school or work because you are drunk or "sleeping it off," you are abusing alcohol. The amount you drink is not as crucial as the fact that your pattern of use disrupts your life.

Dependence is more severe than abuse. Dependence has both behavioral and biological aspects (American Psychiatric Association, 2000). Behaviorally, dependence is often characterized by loss of control over one's use of the substance. Dependent people may organize their lives around getting and using a substance. Biological or physiological dependence is typified by tolerance, withdrawal symptoms, or both. **Tolerance** is the body's habituation to a substance so that, with regular usage, higher doses are required to achieve similar effects. There are characteristic withdrawal symptoms, or an **abstinence syndrome,** when the level of usage suddenly drops off. The abstinence syndrome for alcohol includes anxiety, tremors, restlessness, weakness, rapid pulse, and high blood pressure.

When doing without a drug, people who are *psychologically* dependent show signs of anxiety (such as shakiness, rapid pulse, and sweating) that may be similar to abstinence syndromes. Because of these signs, they may believe that they are physiologically dependent on—or addicted to—a drug when they are actually psychologically dependent. But symptoms of abstinence from some drugs are unmistakably physiological. One is **delirium tremens** ("the DTs"), experienced by some chronic alcoholics when they suddenly lower their intake of alcohol. The DTs are characterized by heavy sweating, restlessness, general disorientation, and terrifying hallucinations—often of crawling animals.

Substance Abuse

Persistent use of a substance even though it is causing or compounding problems in meeting the demands of life.

Tolerance

Habituation to a drug, with the result that increasingly higher doses of the drug are needed to achieve similar effects.

Abstinence Syndrome

A characteristic cluster of symptoms that results from sudden decrease in an addictive drug's level of usage.

Delirium Tremens

A condition characterized by sweating, restlessness, disorientation, and hallucinations. The DTs occur in some chronic alcohol users when there is a sudden decrease in usage.

Causal Factors in Substance Abuse and Dependence

Question: What are the causes of substance abuse and dependence?   Substance abuse and dependence usually begin with experimental use in adolescence (Chassin et al., 2000; Lewinsohn et al., 2000a). Why do people experiment with drugs? Reasons include curiosity, conformity to peer pressure, parental use, rebelliousness, escape from boredom or pressure, and the seeking of excitement or pleasure (Andrews et al., 2002; Chassin et al., 2001; Finn et al., 2000; Wills et al., 2002; Unger et al., 2001a). There are even some parents who introduce their children to illicit drugs (Leinwand, 2000).

A CDC survey of more than 15,000 teenagers across the United States found that use of drugs and cigarettes has increased over the past decade, despite public-education campaigns about the risks (CDC, 2000b). Cigarette smoking was up slightly, with 35% of teenagers reporting lighting up in the previous month. The number of teens who reported smoking marijuana in the previous month nearly doubled from about 15% in 1991 to 27% at the turn of the millennium. Self-reported cocaine use also doubled in the same period, from about 2% to 4%. Alcohol use (within the past month) remained steady at about 50%. However, drinking in early adolescence is a risk factor for alcohol abuse later on (De Wit et al., 2000). Let us have a look at some theories of substance abuse.

Psychological Views

Social-cognitive theorists suggest that people commonly try tranquilizing agents such as Valium (the generic name is diazepam) and alcohol on the basis of a recommendation or observation of others. Expectations about the effects of a substance are powerful predictors of its use (Cumsille et al., 2000). In one study, researchers studied a diary of stress, expectations about alcohol, and drinking (Armeli et al., 2000). They found that men who expected that alcohol would lessen feelings of stress were more likely to drink on stressful days. But men who expected that alcohol would impair their coping ability drank *less* on stressful days.

Use of a substance may be reinforced by peers or by the drug's positive effects on mood and its reduction of unpleasant sensations such as anxiety, fear, and stress (Unger et al., 2001b; Wills et al., 2002). Many people use drugs as a form of self-medication for anxiety and depression, even for feelings of low self-esteem (Beitchman et al., 2001; Dierker et al., 2001). Substance abuse is also often found in the same people who have problems such as eating disorders and impulsiveness, but it is difficult to tease out cause and effect in these cases (Moeller et al., 2001; Stice & Bearman, 2001).

For people who are physiologically dependent, avoidance of withdrawal symptoms is also reinforcing. Carrying a supply of the substance is reinforcing because one need not worry about doing without it. Some people, for example, do not leave home without it—Valium, that is.

Parents who use drugs may increase their children's knowledge of drugs. They also, in effect, show their children when to use them—for example, when drinking alcohol to reduce tension or to "lubricate" social interactions (Stacy & Newcomb, 1999).

Biological Views

Certain people may have a genetic predisposition toward physiological dependence on various substances, including alcohol, opioids, cocaine, and nicotine (Ellenbroek et al., 2000; Finn et al., 2000; Kendler et al., 2000a, 2000d). For example, the biological children of alcoholics who are reared by adoptive parents seem more likely to develop alcohol-related problems than the natural children of the adoptive parents. An inherited tendency toward alcoholism may involve greater sensitivity to alcohol (that is, greater enjoyment of it) and greater tolerance of it (Pihl et al., 1990; Schuckit et al., 2001). College students with alcoholic parents exhibit better muscular control and visual–motor coordination when they drink than do college students whose parents are not alcoholics. They also feel less intoxicated when they drink (Pihl et al., 1990).

There are many kinds of psychoactive drugs. Some are depressants, others stimulants, and still others hallucinogenics. Let us consider the effects of these drugs on consciousness.

R E F L E C T

Do you know anyone who has a problem with substance abuse or dependence? Does he or she admit to the problem or deny it? What can be done about the problem?

Depressants

Depressant drugs generally act by slowing the activity of the central nervous system. There are also effects that are specific to each depressant drug. In this section we consider the effects of alcohol, opiates, barbiturates, and methaqualone.

Alcohol—The Swiss Army Knife of Psychoactive Substances

No drug has meant so much to so many as alcohol. Alcohol is our dinnertime relaxant, our bedtime sedative, our cocktail-party social facilitator. We use alcohol to celebrate holy days, applaud our accomplishments, and express joyous wishes. The young assert their maturity with alcohol. Alcohol is used at least occasionally by the majority of high school and college students (Johnston et al., 2001; Wilgoren, 2000). Alcohol even kills germs on surface wounds.

People use alcohol like a Swiss Army knife. It does it all. Alcohol is the all-purpose medicine you can buy without prescription. It is the relief from anxiety, depression, or loneliness that you can swallow in public without criticism or stigma (Bonin et al., 2000; Swendsen et al., 2000). A man who takes a Valium tablet may look weak. A man who downs a bottle of beer may be perceived as "macho."

But the army knife also has a sharp blade. No drug has been so abused as alcohol. Ten million to 20 million Americans are alcoholics. In contrast, 750,000 to 1 million use heroin regularly and about 800,000 use cocaine regularly (O'Brien, 1996). Excessive drinking has been linked to lower productivity, loss of employment, and downward movement in social status. Yet, half of all Americans use alcohol regularly. Experiments with rats (Feola et al., 2000) and humans (de Wit et al., 2000) show that alcohol lowers inhibitions.

What of alcohol on campus? A study by the National Institute of Alcohol and Alcoholism (Hingson et al., 2002) found that about four college students die each day due to alcohol-related causes, another 1,300 to 1,400 have alcohol-related injuries, and nearly 200 are raped by their dates after drinking. Binge drinking (having five or more drinks in a row for a male, or four or more for a female) is connected with aggressive behavior, poor grades, sexual promiscuity, and serious accidents (Abbey et al., 2001; MacDonald et al., 2000; Vik et al., 2000). Nevertheless, 44% of college students binge at least twice a month, and half this number binge three or more times every two weeks (Hingson et al., 2002). The media seem to pay more attention to deaths due to heroin and cocaine overdoses, but many more college students die each year from causes related to drinking, including accidents and alcohol overdoses (Hingson et al., 2002; Li et al., 2001). (Yes, a person can die from drinking too much at one sitting.) Despite widespread marijuana use, alcohol remains the drug of choice among adolescents.

Question: What are the effects of alcohol? The effects of alcohol vary with the dose and the duration of use. Low doses of alcohol may be stimulating because alcohol dilates blood vessels, which ferry sugars through the body. But higher doses of alcohol have a clear sedative effect, which is why alcohol is classified as a depressant. Alcohol relaxes people and deadens minor aches and pains. Alcohol also intoxicates: It impairs cognitive functioning, slurs the speech, and reduces motor coordination. Alcohol is involved in about half of the fatal automobile accidents in the United States.

Because alcohol lessens inhibitions, drinkers may do things they would not do if they were sober, such as engage in sexual activity on the first date or engage in unprotected sex (MacDonald et al., 2000; Vik et al., 2000). Why? Perhaps alcohol impairs the thought processes needed to inhibit impulses (Steele & Josephs, 1990). When drunk, people may be less able to foresee the consequences of their behavior. They may also be less likely to summon up their moral beliefs. Then, too, alcohol induces feelings of elation and euphoria that may wash away doubts. Alcohol is also associated with a liberated social role in our culture. Drinkers may place the blame on alcohol ("It's the alcohol, not me"), even though they choose to drink.

Adolescent involvement with alcohol has repeatedly been linked to poor school grades and other stressors (Wills et al., 2002). Drinking can, of course, contribute to poor grades and other problems, but adolescents may drink to reduce academic and other stresses.

Regardless of how or why one starts drinking, regular drinking can lead to physiological dependence. People are then motivated to drink to avoid withdrawal symptoms. Still, even when alcoholics have "dried out"—withdrawn from alcohol—many

R E F L E C T

Do you believe that people can be held responsible for their behavior when they have been drinking? Why or why not?

return to drinking (Schuckit, 1996). Perhaps they still want to use alcohol as a way of coping with stress or as an excuse for failure.

▶ CONTROVERSY IN PSYCHOLOGY ◀

Is a drink a day good for you?

What are the physical and cognitive effects of drinking? The effects of alcohol on health are complex. Light drinking can be beneficial. One effect of having a drink or two a day is to increase levels of high-density lipoprotein (HDL, or "good" cholesterol) in the bloodstream and thus decrease the risk of cardiovascular disorders (Mukamal et al., 2001). Another positive effect is cognitive: A study of 400 older adults by researchers at the Institute of Psychiatry in London found that those who had been having a drink a day from before the age of 60 were less likely to see their cognitive abilities decline with age (Cervilla et al., 2000). A drink or two a day may even cut the risk of Alzheimer's disease (Norton, 2000). According to the London researchers (Cervilla et al., 2000), the path to positive cognitive results from alcohol may be through the heart: Small doses of alcohol may help maintain a healthful flow of oxygen-laden blood to the brain. On the other hand, the positive effects of alcohol tend to disappear among people who drink heavily (Cervilla et al., 2000; Xin et al., 2001). Also, there is the danger that people who drink lightly to achieve positive effects may run into problems with self-control.

Now, for the negative. As a food, alcohol is fattening. Even so, chronic drinkers may be malnourished. Although it is high in calories, alcohol does not contain nutrients such as vitamins and proteins. Moreover, it can interfere with the body's absorption of vitamins, particularly thiamine, a B vitamin. Thus chronic drinking can lead to a number of disorders such as **cirrhosis of the liver,** which has been linked to protein deficiency, and **Wernicke-Korsakoff syndrome,** which has been linked to vitamin B deficiency. Chronic heavy drinking has been linked to cardiovascular disorders and cancer. In particular, heavy drinking places women at risk for breast cancer (Singletary & Gapstur, 2001). Drinking by a pregnant woman may also harm the embryo.

So, is a drink a day good for you? Apparently, yes. However, most health professionals are reluctant to advise that people drink regularly, though lightly. One cause for concern is that regular drinkers may lose control of the quantity of alcohol they ingest, become physiologically dependent, and then suffer the effects of heavy drinking.

Alcoholics Anonymous (AA) is the most widely used program to treat alcoholism, yet research suggests that other approaches work as well for most people (Ouimette et al., 1997; "Tailoring treatments," 1997). The National Institute on Alcohol Abuse and Alcoholism funded an eight-year study in which more than 1,700 problem drinkers were randomly assigned to AA's 12-step program, cognitive–behavioral therapy, or "motivational-enhancement therapy." The cognitive–behavioral treatment taught problem drinkers how to cope with temptations and how to refuse offers of drinks. Motivational enhancement was designed to enhance drinkers' desires to help themselves. The treatments worked equally well for most people with some exceptions. For example, people with psychological problems fared somewhat better with cognitive–behavioral therapy.

Research is also under way on the use of medicines in treating problem drinking. Disulfiram (Antabuse), for example, cannot be mixed with alcohol. People who take disulfiram experience symptoms such as nausea and vomiting if they drink (Schuckit, 1996).

Opiates

Opiates are a group of **narcotics** that are derived from the opium poppy, from which they obtain their name. **Opioids** are similar in chemical structure but are synthesized in a laboratory. The ancient Sumerians gave the opium poppy its name: It means "plant of joy." Opiates include morphine, heroin, codeine, Demerol, and similar drugs. *Question: What are the effects of opiates?* The major medical application of this group of drugs is relief from pain.

Cirrhosis of the Liver
A disease caused by protein deficiency in which connective fibers replace active liver cells, impeding circulation of the blood. Alcohol does not contain protein; therefore, persons who drink excessively may be prone to this disease.

Wernicke-Korsakoff Syndrome
A cluster of symptoms associated with chronic alcohol abuse and characterized by confusion, memory impairment, and filling in gaps in memory with false information (confabulation).

Opiates
A group of narcotics derived from the opium poppy that provide a euphoric rush and depress the nervous system.

Narcotics
Drugs used to relieve pain and induce sleep. The term is usually reserved for opiates.

Opioids
Chemicals that act on opiate receptors but are not derived from the opium poppy.

Life Connections
See the Connections *CD-ROM
for an animation on the
interaction of endorphins and
opiates.*

Morphine was introduced in the United States in the 1860s, at about the time of the Civil War, and in Europe during the Franco-Prussian War. It was used liberally to deaden pain from wounds. Physiological dependence on morphine therefore became known as the "soldier's disease." Little stigma was attached to dependence before morphine became a legally restricted substance.

Heroin was so named because it made people feel "heroic." It was also hailed as the "hero" that would cure physiological dependence on morphine.

Heroin can provide a strong euphoric "rush." Users claim that it is so pleasurable it can eradicate any thought of food or sex. Although regular users develop tolerance for heroin, high doses can cause drowsiness and stupor, alter time perception, and impair judgment.

Heroin is illegal. Because the penalties for possession or sale are high, it is also expensive. For this reason, many physiologically dependent people support their habit through dealing (selling heroin), prostitution, or selling stolen goods.

Methadone is a synthetic opioid. It has been used to treat physiological dependence on heroin in the same way that heroin was once used to treat physiological dependence on morphine. Methadone is slower acting than heroin and does not provide the thrilling rush. Some people must be maintained on methadone for many years before they can be gradually withdrawn from it (Fiellin et al., 2001). Some must be maintained on methadone indefinitely because they are unwilling to undergo any withdrawal symptoms.

A Closer Look ◎

Alcoholism, Gender, and Ethnicity

Men are more likely than women to become alcoholics. Why? A cultural explanation is that tighter social constraints are usually placed on women. A biological explanation is that alcohol hits women harder. If, for example, you have the impression that alcohol "goes to women's heads" more quickly than to men's, you are probably correct. Women seem to be more affected by alcohol because they metabolize very little of it in the stomach. Women have less of an enzyme that metabolizes alcohol in the stomach than men do (Lieber, 1990). Thus alcohol reaches women's bloodstream and brain relatively intact. Women metabolize alcohol mainly in the liver. According to one health professional, for women "drinking alcohol has the same effect as injecting it intravenously" (Lieber, 1990). Strong stuff indeed.

Ethnicity is connected with alcohol abuse. Native Americans and Irish Americans have the highest rates of alcoholism in the United States. Jewish Americans have relatively low rates of alcoholism, a fact for which a cultural explanation is usually offered. Jewish Americans tend to expose children to alcohol (wine) early in life, but they do so within a strong family or religious context. Wine is offered in small quantities, with consequent low blood alcohol levels. Alcohol therefore is not connected with rebellion, aggression, or failure in Jewish culture.

There are also biological explanations for low levels of drinking among some ethnic groups (e.g., Asian Americans). Asians are more likely than Europeans and European Americans to show a "flushing response" to alcohol, as evidenced by redness of the face, rapid heart rate, dizziness, and headaches (Ellickson et al., 1992). Such sensitivity to alcohol may inhibit immoderate drinking among Asian Americans as it may among women.

© Jeff Greenberg/PhotoEdit

■ **Why Does Alcohol Affect Women More Quickly Than Men?**
Alcohol "goes to women's heads" more quickly, even when we control for body weight.

Narcotics can have distressing withdrawal syndromes, especially when used in high doses. Such syndromes may begin with flu-like symptoms and progress through tremors, cramps, chills alternating with sweating, rapid pulse, high blood pressure, insomnia, vomiting, and diarrhea. However, these syndromes are variable from one person to another.

Many people who obtain prescriptions for opiates for pain relief neither experience a euphoric rush nor become psychologically dependent on them (Joranson et al., 2000). If they no longer need opiates for pain but have become physiologically dependent on them, they can usually quit with few, if any, side effects by gradually decreasing their dosage (Joranson et al., 2000). Thus difficulty or ease of withdrawal may be connected with one's motives for using psychoactive drugs. Those who are seeking habitual relief from psychological pain seem to become more dependent on them than people who are seeking time-limited relief from physical pain.

Barbiturates and Methaqualone

Question: What are the effects of barbiturates and methaqualone? **Barbiturates** are depressants with several medical uses, including relief of anxiety and tension, relief from pain, and treatment of epilepsy, high blood pressure, and insomnia. Barbiturates lead rapidly to physiological and psychological dependence. The effects of the depressant **methaqualone** are similar to those of barbiturates. Methaqualone also leads to physiological dependence.

Barbiturates and methaqualone are popular as street drugs because they are relaxing and produce mild euphoria. High doses of barbiturates result in drowsiness, motor impairment, slurred speech, irritability, and poor judgment. A physiologically dependent person who is withdrawn abruptly from barbiturates may experience severe convulsions and die. Because of additive effects, it is dangerous to mix alcohol and other depressants.

Stimulants

All stimulants increase the activity of the nervous system. Their other effects vary somewhat, and some contribute to feelings of euphoria and self-confidence.

Amphetamines

Question: What are the effects of amphetamines? **Amphetamines** are a group of stimulants that were first used by soldiers during World War II to help them remain alert through the night. Truck drivers have used them to stay awake all night. Amphetamines have become perhaps more widely known through students, who have used them for all-night cram sessions, and through dieters, who use them because they reduce hunger. Because amphetamines stimulate cognitive activity, they apparently help rats (Feola et al., 2000) and humans (de Wit et al., 2000) control impulses.

Called speed, uppers, bennies (for Benzedrine), and dexies (for Dexedrine), these drugs are often abused for the euphoric rush they can produce in high doses. Some people swallow amphetamines in pill form or inject liquid methedrine, the strongest form, into their veins. They may stay awake and high for days on end. Such highs must end. People who have been on prolonged highs sometimes "crash," or fall into a deep sleep or depression. Some people commit suicide when crashing.

A related stimulant, methylphenidate (Ritalin), is widely used to treat **attention-deficit/hyperactivity disorder** in children. Although critics believe that Ritalin is prescribed too freely (Pear, 2000), Ritalin has been shown to increase attention span, decrease aggressive and disruptive behavior, and lead to academic gains (Evans et al., 2001). Why should Ritalin, a stimulant, calm children? Hyperactivity may be connected with immaturity of the cerebral cortex, and Ritalin may stimulate the cortex to exercise control over more primitive centers in the brain.

Tolerance for amphetamines develops rapidly, and users can become dependent on them, especially when they use them to self-medicate themselves for depression. Regular use of the powerful amphetamine called methamphetamine may well be physically addictive (Volkow et al., 2001a, 2001b), but the extent to which amphetamines

REFLECT
Do you think that cocaine and narcotics such as heroin are the most dangerous psychoactive drugs? Why or why not?

Learning Connections
See the Connections *CD-ROM for an animation on normal synaptic transmission of dopamine.*

Learning Connections
See the Connections *CD-ROM for an animation on the interaction of dopamine and amphetamines.*

Barbiturate
An addictive depressant used to relieve anxiety or induce sleep.

Methaqualone
An addictive depressant. Often called "ludes."

Amphetamines
Stimulants derived from *a*-*m*ethyl-beta-*p*henyl-*et*hyl-*amine*, a colorless liquid consisting of carbon, hydrogen, and nitrogen.

Attention-Deficit/Hyperactivity Disorder
A disorder that begins in childhood and is characterized by a persistent pattern of lack of attention, with or without hyperactivity and impulsive behavior.

cause physical addiction has been a subject of controversy. It is widely accepted, however, that high doses of amphetamines may cause restlessness, insomnia, loss of appetite, hallucinations, paranoid delusions (e.g., false ideas that others are eavesdropping or intend to harm them), and irritability.

Cocaine

Do you recall the commercials claiming that "Coke adds life"? Given its caffeine and sugar content, "Coke"—Coca-Cola, that is—should provide quite a lift. But Coca-Cola hasn't been "the real thing" since 1906, when the company discontinued the use of cocaine in its formula. Cocaine is derived from coca leaves—the plant from which the soft drink took its name.

Question: What are the effects of cocaine? Cocaine is a stimulant that produces euphoria, reduces hunger, deadens pain, and bolsters self-confidence. Only about 4% of adolescents aged 15 to 19 have used cocaine within the past month (CDC, 2000b). Most high school students believe that use of cocaine is harmful (Johnston et al., 2001).

Cocaine may be brewed from coca leaves as a "tea," "snorted" in powder form, or injected in liquid form. Repeated snorting constricts blood vessels in the nose, drying the skin and sometimes exposing cartilage and perforating the nasal septum. These problems require cosmetic surgery. The potent cocaine derivatives known as "crack" and "bazooka" are inexpensive because they are unrefined.

Biologically speaking, cocaine stimulates sudden rises in blood pressure, constricts the coronary arteries and thickens the blood (both of which decrease the oxygen supply to the heart), and quickens the heart rate (Kollins & Rush, 2002). These events occasionally result in respiratory and cardiovascular collapse (Moliterno et al., 1994). The sudden deaths of a number of athletes have been caused in this way. Overdoses can lead to restlessness and insomnia, tremors, headaches, nausea, convulsions, hallucinations, and delusions. Use of crack has been connected with strokes.

Cocaine—also called *snow* and *coke,* like the nickname for the soft drink—has been used as a local anesthetic since the early 1800s. In 1884 it came to the attention of a young Viennese neurologist named Sigmund Freud, who used it to fight his own depression and published an article about it titled "Song of Praise." Freud's early ardor was tempered when he learned that cocaine is habit-forming and can cause hallucinations and delusions. Cocaine causes physiological as well as psychological dependence.

Nicotine

Smoking: A "custome lothesome to the Eye, hatefull to the Nose, harmefull to the Braine, dangerous to the Lungs."

—King James I, 1604

Nicotine is the stimulant found in cigarettes and cigars. *Question: What are the effects of nicotine?* Nicotine stimulates discharge of the hormone adrenaline and the release of many neurotransmitters, including dopamine and acetylcholine. Adrenaline creates a burst of autonomic activity that disrupts normal heart rhythms (Wang et al., 2000), accelerates the heart rate, and pours sugar into the blood. Acetylcholine is vital in memory formation, and nicotine appears to enhance memory and attention; improve performance on simple, repetitive tasks; and enhance the mood (Gentry et al., 2000; Rezvani & Levin, 2001). Despite its stimulative properties, it also appears to relax people and reduce stress (O'Brien, 1996).

Nicotine depresses the appetite and raises the metabolic rate. Thus some people smoke cigarettes in order to control their weight (Jeffery et al., 2000). People also tend to eat more when they stop smoking (Jeffery et al., 2000), causing some to return to the habit.

Nicotine is the agent that creates physiological dependence on tobacco products (F. Baker et al., 2000; American Lung Association, 2000). Nicotine may be as addictive as heroin or cocaine (MacKenzie et al., 1994). Regular smokers adjust their smoking to maintain fairly even levels of nicotine in their bloodstream (Shiffman et al., 1997).

© Roy Morsch/CORBIS

■ **Snorting Cocaine**

Cocaine is a powerful stimulant that boosts self-confidence. However, health professionals have become concerned about its physical effects, including sudden rises in blood pressure, constriction of blood vessels, and acceleration of heart rate. Several athletes have died from cocaine overdoses.

Learning Connections

See the Connections *CD-ROM for an animation on the interaction of dopamine and cocaine.*

Symptoms of withdrawal from nicotine include nervousness, drowsiness, loss of energy, headaches, irregular bowel movements, lightheadedness, insomnia, dizziness, cramps, palpitations, tremors, and sweating. Because many of these symptoms resemble those of anxiety, it was once thought that they might reflect the anxiety of attempting to quit smoking, rather than addiction.

It's no secret. Cigarette packs sold in the United States carry messages like "Warning: The Surgeon General Has Determined That Cigarette Smoking Is Dangerous to Your Health." Cigarette advertising has been banned on radio and television. Nearly 430,000 Americans die from smoking-related illnesses each year (American Lung Association, 2000). This is the equivalent of two jumbo jets colliding in midair each day with all passengers lost. It is higher than the number of people who die from motor vehicle accidents, alcohol and drug abuse, suicide, homicide, and AIDS *combined.*

The percentage of American adults who smoke cigarettes declined from more than 40% in the mid-1960s to about 25% in recent years, but there have been increases among women, African Americans, and 8th to 12th graders (American Lung Association, 2000). The incidence of smoking is connected with gender and level of education (see Table 5.5) (American Lung Association, 2000). Better-educated people are less likely to smoke (Cavelaars et al., 2000). They are also more likely to quit smoking (Rose et al., 1996).

Nancy Rigotti and her colleagues (2000) polled more than 14,000 students from 119 nationally representative four-year colleges and universities. Sixty percent of students polled responded to the survey. Among college students, European Americans were most likely to smoke cigarettes, and African Americans were least likely to smoke (corresponding to the findings in Table 5.4). In addition to smoking cigarettes, many men reported using cigars, pipes, and smokeless tobacco, all of which are also associated with health risks. Athletes and more achievement-oriented students were less likely to smoke than students whose priorities were more social. Thus many students experiment with tobacco in college, and many become dependent on nicotine—a dependence that can haunt them for a lifetime.

Every cigarette smoked steals about seven minutes of a person's life. The carbon monoxide in cigarette smoke impairs the blood's ability to carry oxygen, causing shortness of breath. It is apparently the hydrocarbons ("tars") in cigarette and cigar smoke that lead to lung cancer (American Lung Association, 2000). Smoking is responsible for about 87% of cases of lung cancer (American Lung Association, 2000). Cigarette smoking is also linked to death from heart disease, chronic lung and respiratory diseases, and other health problems. Women who smoke show reduced bone density, increasing the risk of fracture of the hip and back (Hopper & Seeman, 1994). Pregnant women who smoke have a higher risk of miscarriage, preterm births, low-birth-weight babies, and stillborn babies (American Lung Association, 2000).

Cigar smokers are less likely to inhale than cigarette smokers, so it had been assumed that cigar smoking was relatively safe. However, researchers at the American Cancer Society and the Centers for Disease Control and Prevention have found that cigar smokers are five times as likely as nonsmokers to develop lung cancer, even

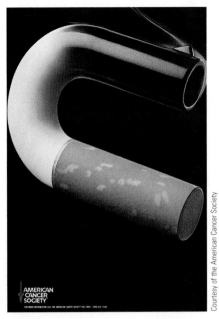

Courtesy of the American Cancer Society

■ **Cigarettes: Smoking Guns?**

The perils of cigarette smoking are widely known today. One Surgeon General declared that cigarette smoking is the chief preventable cause of death in the United States. The numbers of Americans who die from smoking are comparable to the number of lives that would be lost if two jumbo jets crashed *every day.* If flying were that unsafe, would the government ground all flights? Would the public continue to make airline reservations?

R E F L E C T

Do you think that researchers have exaggerated the dangers of smoking? Why or why not?

TABLE 5.5 Snapshot, U.S.A.: Gender, Level of Education, and Smoking

Factor	Group	Percent Who Smoke
Gender	Women	22
	Men	27
Level of Education	Fewer than 12 years	38
	16 years and above	14

Source: American Heart Association (2000). 2000 Heart and Stroke Statistical Update, http://www.americanheart.org; American Lung Association (2000). Smoking Fact Sheet, http://www.lungusa.org.

when they do not inhale ("Cigars increase lung cancer risk," 2000). When they do inhale, cigar smokers run 11 times the risk of lung cancer as nonsmokers. Cigar smokers also run increased risks of cancers of the mouth, throat, and esophagus (F. Baker et al., 2000).

Passive smoking is also connected with respiratory illnesses, asthma, and other health problems. Prolonged exposure to household tobacco smoke during childhood is a risk factor for lung cancer (Janerich et al., 1990). Because of the noxious effects of secondhand smoke, smoking has been banished from many public places such as airplanes, restaurants, and elevators.

Why, then, do people smoke? For many reasons—such as the desire to look sophisticated (although these days smokers may be more likely to be judged foolish than sophisticated), to have something to do with their hands, and—of course—to take in nicotine.

Hallucinogenics

Hallucinogenic drugs are so named because they produce hallucinations—that is, sensations and perceptions in the absence of external stimulation. But hallucinogenic drugs may also have additional effects such as relaxation, euphoria, or, in some cases, panic.

Marijuana

Marijuana is a substance that is produced from the *Cannabis sativa* plant, which grows wild in many parts of the world.   *Question: What are the effects of marijuana?* Marijuana helps some people relax and can elevate their mood. It also sometimes produces mild hallucinations, which is why we discuss it in the section on **psychedelic,** or hallucinogenic, drugs. The major psychedelic substance in marijuana is delta-9-tetrahydrocannabinol, or THC. THC is found in the branches and leaves of the plant, but it is highly concentrated in the sticky resin. **Hashish,** or "hash," is derived from the resin. Hashish is more potent than marijuana.

In the 19th century, marijuana was used much as aspirin is used today for headaches and minor aches and pains. It could be bought without a prescription in any drugstore. Today marijuana use and possession are illegal in most states. Marijuana also carries a number of health risks. For example, it impairs the perceptual–motor coordination used in driving and operating machines. It impairs short-term memory and slows learning (Ashton, 2001). Although it causes positive mood changes in many people, there are also disturbing instances of anxiety and confusion and occasional reports of psychotic reactions (Johns, 2001).

Some people report that marijuana helps them socialize at parties. Moderate to strong intoxication is linked to reports of heightened perceptions and increases in self-insight, creative thinking, and empathy for the feelings of others. Time seems to pass more slowly for people who are strongly intoxicated. A song might seem to last an hour rather than a few minutes. There is increased awareness of bodily sensations such as heartbeat. Marijuana smokers also report that strong intoxication heightens sexual sensations. Visual hallucinations are not uncommon. Strong intoxication may cause smokers to experience disorientation. If the smoker's mood is euphoric, loss of a sense of personal identity may be interpreted as being in harmony with the universe.

Some marijuana smokers have negative experiences. An accelerated heart rate and heightened awareness of bodily sensations leads some smokers to fear that their heart will "run away" with them. Some smokers find disorientation threatening and are afraid that they will not regain their identity. Strong intoxication sometimes causes nausea and vomiting.

People can become psychologically dependent on marijuana, but use of marijuana had not been thought to lead to physiological dependence. Recent research, however, suggests that regular users of marijuana may experience tolerance and withdrawal symptoms (American Psychiatric Association, 2000; Johns, 2001).

Learning Connections
See the Connections *CD-ROM for an animation on the interaction of anandamide and marijuana.*

Passive Smoking
Inhaling of smoke from the tobacco products and exhalations of other people; also called *secondhand smoking.*

Hallucinogenic
Giving rise to hallucinations.

Marijuana
The dried vegetable matter of the *Cannabis sativa* plant.

Psychedelic
Causing hallucinations, delusions, or heightened perceptions.

Hashish
A drug derived from the resin of *Cannabis sativa.* Often called "hash."

▶ CONTROVERSY IN PSYCHOLOGY ◀

Is marijuana harmful? Should it be available as a medicine?

There are many controversies concerning marijuana. One is the issue as to whether marijuana should be made available as a medicine to those who could benefit from it. Marijuana has been used to treat health problems, including glaucoma and the nausea experienced by cancer patients undergoing chemotherapy (Robson, 2001). Psychiatrist Lester Grinspoon (2000), a long-time supporter of marijuana for medical uses, refers to it as an inexpensive, versatile, and reasonably safe medicine. Other medical researchers agree that marijuana has some positive effects, but the action of THC also has its negatives (Nahas et al., 2000). THC binds to a membrane receptor, 7TM, which is found in every cell. THC displaces the natural substance that would bind with the receptor and disrupts the receptor's signaling. As a result, the functioning of the brain, the immune system, and the cardiovascular and reproductive systems (e.g., it interferes with development of sperm and conception) are all impaired. Moreover, in some cases, alternate drugs achieve similar benefits (Watson et al., 2000).

Marijuana smoke also contains more hydrocarbons than tobacco smoke—a risk factor in cancer. Smokers of marijuana often admit that they know that marijuana smoke can be harmful, but they counter that compared with cigarette smokers, they smoke very few "joints" per day. Yet, as noted, marijuana elevates the heart rate and, in some people, the blood pressure. This higher demand on the heart and circulation poses a threat to people with hypertension and cardiovascular disorders. One study found that middle-aged men were five times more likely to have a heart attack within an hour of smoking marijuana (Middleman, 2000).

Another issue is whether researchers and public figures exaggerate the dangers of marijuana to discourage people from using it. Does the information about marijuana in this textbook seem to be biased? Why or why not?

■ Smoking Marijuana

Marijuana is highly popular among high school and college students and adults. For many years, it was widely assumed that authority figures warned youngsters about the hazards of marijuana smoking for moralistic reasons. However, recent research reveals some findings about the effects of marijuana on learning, memory, and attention—even on the structure of the brain—that readers should evaluate when they make decisions as to whether or not to use marijuana.

LSD
Lysergic acid diethylamide. A hallucinogenic drug.

Flashbacks
Distorted perceptions or hallucinations that occur days or weeks after LSD usage but mimic the LSD experience.

Marijuana has been with us for decades, but new research on its effects continues—with more sophisticated methods. For example, it has been known that marijuana usage impairs learning, memory, and attention (Solowij et al., 2002), but it was assumed by many that marijuana distracted people from learning tasks. Now, however, laboratory research suggests that marijuana also reduces the release of neurotransmitters involved in the consolidation of learning (J. M. Sullivan, 2000). MRI and PET scan studies suggest that marijuana may have little or no effect on the size or makeup of the brain of adults (Block et al., 2000). However, males who began using marijuana before the age of 17 may have smaller brains and less gray matter than other males (Wilson et al., 2000). Both males and females who started using marijuana early may be generally smaller in height and weight than other people. William Wilson and his colleagues (2000) suggest that these differences may reflect the effect of marijuana on pituitary and sex hormones.

More research is needed on the effects of marijuana. While some of the horror stories of the 1960s and 1970s may have been exaggerated, marijuana could be quite harmful in a number of ways, especially when used by adolescents. More evidence—not more speculation—is needed.

LSD and Other Hallucinogenics

LSD is the abbreviation for lysergic acid diethylamide, a synthetic hallucinogenic drug. ***Question: What are the effects of LSD and other kinds of hallucinogenic drugs?*** Users of "acid" claim that it "expands consciousness" and opens up new worlds to them. Sometimes people believe they have achieved great insights while using LSD, but when it wears off they often cannot apply or recall these discoveries. As a powerful hallucinogenic, LSD produces vivid and colorful hallucinations.

Some LSD users have **flashbacks**—distorted perceptions or hallucinations that mimic the LSD "trip" but occur days, weeks, or longer after usage. The experiencing of flashbacks is more technically termed *hallucinogen persisting perception disorder* (HPPD) by the American Psychiatric Association (2000), although some writers distinguish between the two (Smith & Seymour, 1994). Over the years, both psychological and physiological explanations of HPPD have appeared. The psychological explanation, in a nutshell, is that people who would use LSD regularly are also more

■ **An LSD Trip?**
This hallucinogenic drug can give rise to a vivid parade of colors and visual distortions. Some users claim to have achieved great insights while "tripping," but typically they have been unable to recall or apply them afterward.

likely to allow flights of fancy. Yet research with 38 people with HPPD suggests that following extensive use of LSD, the brain may fail to inhibit certain internal sources of visionlike experiences, especially when the eyes are closed (Abraham & Duffy, 2001). Such visionlike experiences are also apparently more likely to occur in the presence of excessive sympathetic nervous system activity—that is, anxiety (Lerner et al., 2000).

Other hallucinogenic drugs include **mescaline** (derived from the peyote cactus) and **phencyclidine (PCP)**. Phencyclidine (PCP) was developed as an anesthetic and goes by the street names "angel dust," "ozone," "wack," and "rocket fuel." The street terms "killer joints" and "crystal supergrass" refer to PCP that is combined with marijuana.

"Ecstasy," or MDMA (the abbreviation of 3,4-Methylenedioxymethamphetamine) is a synthetic drug that possesses the properties of stimulant and hallucinogenic drugs (Concar, 2002). MDMA possesses chemical variations of the stimulant amphetamine or methamphetamine and a hallucinogen, most often mescaline.

Regular use of hallucinogenics may lead to tolerance and psychological dependence. But hallucinogenics are not known to lead to physiological dependence. High doses may induce frightening hallucinations, impaired coordination, poor judgment, mood changes, and paranoid delusions.

Table 5.6 summarizes information about drugs.

Mescaline
A hallucinogenic drug derived from the mescal (peyote) cactus.

Phencyclidine (PCP)
Another hallucinogenic drug whose name is an acronym for its chemical structure.

"Ecstasy"
A synthetic drug that possesses the properties of stimulant and hallucinogenic drugs. Also referred to as *MDMA* (the acronym for 3, 4-Methylenedioxymethamphetamine).

TABLE 5.6 Psychoactive Drugs and Their Effects

Drug	Type	How Taken	Desired Effects	Tolerance	Abstinence Syndrome	Side Effects
Alcohol	Depressant	By mouth	Relaxation, euphoria, lowered inhibitions	Yes	Yes	Impaired coordination, poor judgment, hangover
Opiates	Depressants	Injected, smoked, by mouth	Relaxation, euphoria, relief from anxiety and pain	Yes	Yes	Impaired coordination and mental functioning, drowsiness, lethargy
Barbiturates and Methaqualone	Depressants	By mouth, injected	Relaxation, sleep, euphoria, lowered inhibitions	Yes	Yes	Impaired coordination and mental functioning, drowsiness, lethargy
Amphetamines	Stimulants	By mouth, injected	Alertness, euphoria	Yes	?	Restlessness, loss of appetite, psychotic symptoms
Cocaine	Stimulant	By mouth, snorted, injected	Euphoria, self-confidence	Yes	Yes	Restlessness, loss of appetite, convulsions, strokes, psychotic symptoms
Nicotine	Stimulant	By tobacco (smoked, chewed, or sniffed)	Relaxation, stimulation, weight control	Yes	Yes	Cancer, heart disease, lung and respiratory diseases
Marijuana	Hallucinogenic	Smoked, by mouth	Relaxation, perceptual distortions, enhancement of experience	?	?	Impaired coordination, learning, respiratory problems, panic
LSD, Mescaline, PCP	Hallucinogenics	By mouth	Perceptual distortions, vivid hallucinations	Yes	No	Impaired coordination, psychotic symptoms, panic

Learning Connections
See Web site for an interactive version of these review questions.

R E V I E W

(17) Substance _____ is characterized by loss of control over the substance. (18) Physiological dependence is evidenced by tolerance or by an _____ syndrome when one discontinues use of the substance. (19) Women seem to be (more or less?) affected by alcohol than men. (20) Opiates are used in medicine to reduce _____, but they are bought "on the street" because of the euphoric rush they provide. (21) Barbiturates are used medically to treat _____. (22) Ritalin is used to treat _____-deficit/hyperactivity disorder in children. (23) _____ is a stimulant that boosts self-confidence but also triggers rises in blood pressure and constricts the coronary arteries. (24) Tobacco contains the stimulant _____. (25) _____ substances distort perceptions. (26) _____ often produces feelings of relaxation and empathy, the feeling that time is slowing down, and reports of new insights. (27) LSD produces vivid _____

Critical Thinking: Does the textbook's presentation of information about the effects of drugs seem to be straightforward or biased? What is the evidence for your view?

Getting to Sleep—and Elsewhere—Without Drugs

Where do you want to go? Do you want to go to sleep? Do you want to go on a psychological trip searching for inner truth? Do you want to go on a stimulating trip that will drench your bloodstream with adrenaline? There are ways to do all these things—ways that rely on you rather than on drugs.

Check it out. There are ideas here for getting to sleep without sleeping pills. There are suggestions for thinking helpful thoughts rather than blowing the situation out of proportion. There are ways of relaxing that let you do your own mellowing out—again, drug-free. These methods are largely cognitive–behavioral (Edinger et al., 2001).

Getting to Sleep Without Drugs

Do you have a problem with insomnia? The questionnaire below, "Are You Getting Your Z's?", may offer some insight. If you decide that you do, what can you do about it?

No question about it: The most common medical method for getting to sleep in the United States is taking pills (Edinger et al., 2001). Sleeping pills may work—for a while. So may tranquilizers. They generally work by reducing arousal and also distract you from trying to *get* to sleep. Expectations of success may also help.

But there are problems with sleeping pills. First, many may attribute success to the pill and not to themselves, and come to depend on the pill. Second, a person may develop tolerance for many kinds of sleeping pills and, with regular use, need higher doses to achieve the same effects. Third, high doses of these chemicals can be dangerous, especially if mixed with alcohol. Fourth, sleeping pills do not enhance your skills at handling insomnia. Thus, when you stop taking them, insomnia is likely to return (Morin et al., 1999).

There are excellent psychological methods for coping with insomnia, which can be effective alternatives for many. Some methods, like muscle relaxation exercises, reduce tension directly. Psychological methods also divert us from the "task" of trying somehow to *get* to sleep, which, of course, is one of the ways in which we keep ourselves awake (Mimeault & Morin, 1999). You can try any or all of the following psychological methods:

- *Relax.* Take a hot bath at bedtime or try meditating. Releasing muscle tension has been shown to reduce the amount of time needed to fall asleep and the incidence of waking up during the night (Murtagh & Greenwood, 1995).
- *Challenge exaggerated fears.* You need not be a sleep expert to realize that convincing yourself that the day will be ruined unless you get to sleep *right now* may increase, rather than decrease, bedtime tension. However, cognitive–behavioral psychologists note that we often exaggerate the problems that will befall us if we do not sleep (Edinger et al., 2001; Morin et al., 1999). Table 5.7 shows some beliefs that increase bedtime tension and some alternatives.
- *Don't ruminate in bed.* Don't plan or worry about tomorrow while in bed (National Sleep Foundation, 2000a). When you lie down for sleep, you may organize your thoughts for the next day for a few minutes, but then allow yourself to relax or engage in a soothing fantasy. If an important idea comes to you, jot it down on a handy pad so that you won't worry about forgetting it. If thoughts or inspirations persist, however, get up and think about them elsewhere. Let your bed be a place for relaxation and sleep—not your second office. A bed—even a waterbed—should not be a think tank.
- *Establish a regular routine.* Sleeping late can end up causing problems falling asleep (sleep-onset insomnia). Set your alarm for the same time each morning and get up, regardless of how long you have slept (Mimeault & Morin, 1999; National Sleep Foundation, 2000a). By rising at a regular time, you'll encourage yourself to fall asleep at a regular time.

Self-Assessment ☑

Life Connections
See the Connections *CD-ROM for an interactive version of this Self-Assessment and for other Self-Assessments*

Sleep Quiz: Are You Getting Your Z's?

This questionnaire can help you learn whether you are getting enough sleep. Circle the *T* if an item is true or mostly true, or the *F* if an item is false or mostly false for you. Then check the meaning of your answers in Appendix B.

T	F	
___	___	1. I need an alarm clock in order to wake up at the appropriate time.
___	___	2. It's a struggle for me to get out of bed in the morning.
___	___	3. Weekday mornings I hit the snooze button several times to get more sleep.
___	___	4. I feel tired, irritable, and stressed out during the week.
___	___	5. I have trouble concentrating and remembering.
___	___	6. I feel slow with critical thinking, problem solving, and being creative.

T	F	
___	___	7. I often fall asleep watching television.
___	___	8. I often fall asleep after heavy meals or after a low dose of alcohol.
___	___	9. I often fall asleep while relaxing after dinner.
___	___	10. I often fall asleep within five minutes of getting into bed.
___	___	11. I often feel dowsy while driving.
___	___	12. I often sleep extra hours on weekend mornings.
___	___	13. I often need a nap to get through the day.
___	___	14. I have dark circles around my eyes.

Source: James Maas (1998). *Power Sleep.* New York: HarperCollins.

- *Try fantasy.* Fantasies or daydreams are almost universal and may occur naturally as we fall asleep. You can allow yourself to "go with" soothing, relaxing fantasies that occur at bedtime, or purposefully use pleasant fantasies to get to sleep. You may be able to ease yourself to sleep, for example, by focusing on a sun-drenched beach with waves lapping on the shore or on a walk through a mountain meadow on a summer day. You can construct your own "mind trips" and paint in the details.

Above all: Accept the idea that it really doesn't matter if you don't get to sleep early *this night*. You will survive. In fact, you'll do just fine.

Strategies for Gaining and Maintaining Self-Control

I can resist everything except temptation.

—Oscar Wilde *(Lady Windermere's Fan)*

■ Insomnia

"You know I can't sleep at night" goes the 1960s song by the Mamas and the Papas. Why are women more likely than men to have insomnia? What can people do about insomnia?

With a little bit of help, you probably *can* resist temptation. There are physiological and psychological aspects to coping with the temptation of drugs. People who regularly use many of the substances discussed in this chapter can become dependent on them. In the cases of alcohol, nicotine, cocaine, opiates, and sedatives, serious physiological dependence can develop. In some cases, as with nicotine, users can stop using the substance on their own despite the discomforts of doing so. Going "cold turkey" is safe enough. This may not be so with other substances, particularly alcohol. Going cold turkey can be dangerous. So-called alcohol "detoxification" is a complex procedure that takes a week or so and is best carried out under medical supervision, often in a hospital.

Even when someone is no longer physiologically dependent, the battle is not over. Avoiding temptation can mean maintaining a deep personal commitment to changing one's lifestyle, sometimes including choosing a different set of friends or different leisure activities.

Cognitive–behavioral approaches to substance abuse and dependence focus on modifying abusive and dependent ideas and behavior patterns (Niaura & Abrams, 2002; Waldron et al., 2001). They teach abusers either to avoid temptation or to change their behavior when they are faced with temptation. For example, people can learn to avoid socializing with others with substance abuse problems (Latimer et al., 2000). They can avoid situations linked to abuse—bars, the street, bowling alleys, and so on. They can learn to frequent substance-free environments such as gyms, museums, evening classes. They can learn to use competing responses when they are tempted—taking a bath or shower, walking the dog, walking around the block, taking a

---

TABLE 5.7 Beliefs That Increase Tension and Alternatives

Beliefs That Increase Tension	Alternatives
If I don't get to sleep, I'll feel wrecked tomorrow.	Not necessarily. If I'm tired, I can go to bed early tomorrow night.
It's unhealthy for me not to get more sleep.	Not necessarily. Some people do very well on only a few hours of sleep.
I'll wreck my sleeping schedule for the whole week if I don't get to sleep very soon.	Not at all. If I'm tired, I'll just go to bed a bit earlier. I'll get up about the same time with no problem.
If I don't get to sleep, I won't be able to concentrate on that big test/conference tomorrow.	Possibly, but my fears may be exaggerated. I may just as well relax or get up and do something enjoyable for a while.

drive, calling a friend, or exercising. The cognitive behavioral method of social skills training helps people develop effective social behavior in situations that are connected with substance abuse (Blake et al., 2001). They may teach individuals how to fend off social pressures to drink or have a cigarette. Many people learn how to say "no, thanks," without getting into an argument or having to leave the situation.

The cognitive–behavioral strategies outlined in Table 5.8 can help readers maintain commitment to do without drugs and deal with temptations. In the case of smoking cigarettes, some suggestions are of use in cutting down, others in going cold turkey (Niaura & Abrams, 2002). In the case of alcohol, the suggestions largely have to do with controlling the amount being used. However, many health professionals believe that it is wisest for people who have been physiologically dependent on alcohol to avoid drinking altogether.

Cognitive–behavioral psychologists note that much of the "cure" for substance abuse lies in what we tell ourselves and other people about our behavior. For example, if you're going to quit smoking, why not tell your family and friends that you're quitting? By making a public commitment to do so, you shore up your resolve. Also plan a target date for quitting, perhaps a date when you will be on vacation or away from the usual settings in which you smoke (see Table 5.8). You can use a nicotine substitute like a skin patch to help cut down before the target date and to prove to yourself that you can survive on fewer cigarettes (and, ultimately, on no cigarettes). You can plan specific things to tell yourself when you feel the urge to smoke: how you'll be stronger, free of fear of cancer, ready for the marathon, and so on, and so on. Once you have stopped, you can remind yourself repeatedly that the first few days are the hardest. After that, withdrawal symptoms weaken dramatically. And don't forget to pat yourself on the back by reminding yourself that you are accomplishing something that many millions of others find to be out of reach.

The suggestions in Table 5.8 can be generalized to nearly any substance. The following suggestions involve alternatives to substance abuse.

Getting There Without Drugs: Don't Just Say No, Do *Something Else*

All of us feel depressed, tense, or just plain bored from time to time. Many are intrigued by the possibility of exploring the still dark reaches of their inner selves. Many feel inadequate to face the challenges of college life now and then. Some of us see our futures as bleak and unrewarding. A vast wilderness or desert seems to lie before us.

So we all have feelings like these now and then. Then what? If you are wavering on whether or not to get involved with drugs, here are some drug-free alternatives to consider.

If you are . . .

- Feeling tense or anxious, try practicing self-relaxation or meditation, or exercise, or listen to relaxing music.
- Feeling bored, find a new activity or interest. Start an exercise program or get involved in athletics. Take up a hobby. Become involved in a political campaign or social cause.
- Feeling angry, write down your feelings or channel your anger into constructive pursuits aimed at solving what has angered you or pursuits that allow you time to cool off.
- Feeling worthless, hopeless, or depressed, or putting yourself down, seek assistance from a friend or loved one. Focus on your abilities and accomplishments, not on your deficits. If that doesn't help, visit the college counseling center or health center. You may be suffering from a treatable case of depression.
- Wanting to probe the inner depths of your consciousness, try meditation or yoga. Or seek the advice of a counselor or minister, priest, or rabbi.
- Pressured into using drugs by friends, learn how to say "no" politely but firmly. If you need help saying no, read a self-help book on self-assertion or go to the college counseling center for advice. If necessary, get new friends. (A real friend will not push you into doing anything that makes you feel uncomfortable, including using drugs.)
- Seeking to heighten your sensations, try dancing, jogging, parachuting, snow-boarding, roller-blading, or mountain climbing. There are many ways to get your adrenaline flowing that do not involve chemical stimulants.
- Feeling stressed out to the point where you can't take it anymore, sit down to figure out the pressures acting upon you. List your priorities. What must be done *right now?* What can wait? If this approach fails, see your academic advisor or visit the college counseling center or health center. If you can afford the time, you may choose to take a day or two off. Sometimes the key is to establish more reasonable expectations of yourself. No drug will help you do that.
- Wanting to discover new insights on the human condition, take classes or workshops on philosophy and theology. Attend lectures by prominent thinkers. Read great works of literature. Ponder great works of art. Attend the symphony. Visit a museum. Let your mind connect with the great minds of the past and present.
- Searching for deeper personal meaning in life, become more involved in spiritual activity in your church or synagogue. Do volunteer work in hospitals or charitable organizations. Get involved in a cause you believe in. Or seek personal counseling to get in touch with your inner self.

TABLE 5.8 Getting There Without Drugs—Cognitive–Behavioral Strategies for Putting an End to Substance Abuse

	Strategy	Examples of Use of the Strategy
Strategies Aimed at the Stimuli That Trigger Substance Abuse	Restriction of the stimulus field	Gradually exclude the problem behavior from more environments. At first, make smoking off limits in the car; then make it off limits in the home.
	Avoidance of powerful stimuli that trigger habits	Avoid obvious sources of temptation. (People who go window-shopping often wind up buying more than windows.) Walk briskly through the market; don't linger by the packs of cigarettes or the alcohol section. Sit in nonsmokers' sections of restaurants and trains. Go on a smoke-ending vacation to get away from places and situations in which you're used to smoking. Don't go to the bar with "the guys" where you keep pace by chug-a-lugging the beer.
	Stimulus control	Place yourself in an environment in which desirable behavior is likely to occur. Fill your days with novel activities—things that won't remind you of smoking or having that extra beer. Beat insomnia by using your bed only as a place for sleeping—no more studying or eating snacks in bed. In that way your bed will come to "mean" sleep to you.
Strategies Aimed at the Abusive Behavior Itself	Response prevention	Make unwanted behavior difficult or impossible. You cannot smoke the cigarettes or drink the beer you left on the shelf at the corner store.
	Competing responses	Engage in behaviors that are incompatible with the problem behavior. Stuff your mouth with sugar-free mints, not cigarettes. Consider nicotine replacement therapy in the form of a nicotine gum or skin patch. The use of nicotine replacements helps to avert withdrawal symptoms when dependent smokers discontinue cigarettes. Or use sugar-free mints or gum as substitutes for cigarettes. (Don't light them!)
	Chain breaking	Interfere with unwanted habitual behavior by complicating the process of engaging in it. Break the chain of reaching for a readily available cigarette and placing it in your mouth by wrapping the pack in aluminum foil and placing it on the top shelf of a closet. Rewrap the pack after taking one cigarette. Hold your cigarettes with your nondominant hand only. Put the cigarette out before you reach the end. (No more eating the filter.) Put your cigarette in the ashtray between puffs.
	Successive approximations	Gradually approach targets through a series of relatively painless steps. Decrease smoking by pausing for a minute when the cigarette is smoked halfway, or by putting it out a minute before you would wind up eating the filter.
Strategies Aimed at the Reinforcers That Maintain Abusive Behavior	Reinforcement of desired behavior	Why give yourself something for nothing? Make pleasant activities such as going to films, walking on the beach, or reading a new novel contingent on meeting reasonable daily behavioral goals. Each day you remain abstinent from cigarettes or limit your alcohol intake to one drink, sock away a dollar toward that camera or vacation trip you have been dreaming of.
	Response cost	Heighten awareness of the long-term reasons for dieting or cutting down on smoking by punishing yourself for not meeting a daily goal or for engaging in a bad habit. For example, if you light up, make out a check to a cause you oppose and mail it at once.
	"Grandma's method"	How did Grandma persuade children to eat their vegetables? Simple: No veggies, no dessert. In this method, desired behaviors such as quitting smoking can be encouraged by insisting that you read cards such as the following before leaving the house or the apartment: "Every day it becomes a little easier," and "Your lungs will turn pink again."
	Covert sensitization*	Create imaginary horror stories about problem behavior. Psychologists have successfully reduced overeating and smoking by having clients imagine that a cigarette is made from vomit. Some horror stories are not "imaginary." Deliberately focusing on heart strain and diseased lungs every time you overeat or smoke, rather than ignoring these long-term consequences, might also promote self-control.
	Covert reinforcement**	Create rewarding imagery for desired behavior. Interpret withdrawal symptoms from stopping smoking or going without that beer as a sign that you're winning and getting healthier. After all, you wouldn't have withdrawal symptoms if you were smoking or drinking.

*Imagining punishing consequences for engaging in undesirable behavior. *Covert* means "hidden," and you use this strategy by imagining scenarios. Because you imagine them, they are hidden from the outside world and perceptible to you alone.
**Imagining rewarding consequences for engaging in desirable behavior. This strategy, like covert sensitization, is used by imagining various scenarios.

Recite Recite Recite

Learning Connections
See Web site for an interactive version of this chapter summary

1. **What is consciousness?**

The term *consciousness* has several meanings, including sensory awareness, direct inner awareness of cognitive processes, the selective aspect of attention, the sense of self, and the waking state.

2. **What is a circadian rhythm?**

A circadian rhythm is a cycle that is connected with the 24-hour period of the earth's rotation, such as the sleep–wake cycle.

3. **What occurs during sleep?**

We undergo several stages of sleep. According to electroencephalograph (EEG) records, each stage of sleep is characterized by a different type of brain wave. There are four stages of non-rapid-eye-movement (NREM) sleep and one stage of REM sleep. Stage 1 sleep is the lightest, and stage 4 is the deepest.

4. **Why do we sleep?**

Sleep apparently serves a restorative function, but we do not know exactly how sleep restores us or how much sleep we need. Animals and people who have been deprived of REM sleep learn more slowly and forget what they have learned more rapidly.

5. **What are dreams? Why do we dream what we dream?**

Dreams are a form of cognitive activity that occurs mostly while we are sleeping. Most dreaming occurs during REM sleep. Freud believed that dreams reflected unconscious wishes and "protected sleep" by keeping unacceptable ideas out of awareness. The activation-synthesis hypothesis suggests that dreams largely reflect automatic biological activity by the pons and the synthesis of subsequent sensory stimulation by the frontal part of the brain. The content of most dreams is an extension of the events of the previous day. Nightmares are also dreams that occur during REM sleep.

6. **What kinds of sleep disorders are there?**

A common sleep disorder is insomnia, which is most often encountered by people who are anxious and tense. Deep sleep disorders include sleep terrors, bed-wetting, and sleepwalking.

7. **What is hypnosis?**

Hypnosis is an altered state of consciousness in which people are suggestible and behave as though they are in a trance.

8. **What changes in consciousness are induced by hypnosis?**

People who are hypnotized may show passivity, narrowed attention, hypermnesia (heightened memory), suggestibility, assumption of unusual roles, perceptual distortions, posthypnotic amnesia, and posthypnotic suggestion.

9. **How do modern psychologists explain the effects of hypnosis?**

Current theories of hypnosis deny the existence of a special trance state. Rather, they emphasize people's ability to role-play the "trance" (role theory), to do what is expected of them (response set theory), and to divide their consciousness (neodissociation theory) as directed by the hypnotist.

10. **What is meditation?**

In meditation, one focuses "passively" on an object or a mantra in order to alter the normal relationship between oneself and the environment. In this way, consciousness (that is, the normal focuses of attention) is altered.

11. **What are the effects of meditation?**

Meditation often has the effect of inducing relaxation. TM appears to reduce the blood pressure of hypertensive individuals.

12. **What is biofeedback training?**

Biofeedback is a method for increasing consciousness of bodily functions. In biofeedback, the organism is continuously provided with information about a targeted biological response such as heart rate or emission of alpha waves.

13. **How is biofeedback training used?**

People and lower animals can learn to control involuntary functions such as heart rate, blood pressure, even the emission of certain brain waves through biofeedback training.

Recite Recite Recite

14. What are substance abuse and dependence?	Substance abuse is use of a substance that persists even though it impairs one's functioning. Dependence has behavioral and physiological aspects. It may be characterized by organizing one's life around getting and using the substance and by the development of tolerance, withdrawal symptoms, or both.
15. What are the causes of substance abuse and dependence?	People usually try drugs out of curiosity, but usage can be reinforced by anxiety reduction, feelings of euphoria, and other positive sensations. People are also motivated to avoid withdrawal symptoms once they become physiologically dependent on a drug. People may have genetic predispositions to become physiologically dependent on certain substances.
16. What are the effects of alcohol?	Alcohol, the most widely used drug, is a depressant. It belongs to the group of substances that act by slowing the activity of the central nervous system. Alcohol is also intoxicating and can lead to physiological dependence. It provides an excuse for failure or for antisocial behavior, but it has not been shown to induce such behavior directly.
17. What are the effects of opiates?	The opiates morphine and heroin are depressants that reduce pain, but they are also bought on the street because of the euphoric "rush" they provide. Opiate use can lead to physiological dependence.
18. What are the effects of barbiturates and methaqualone?	Barbiturates and a similar drug, methaqualone, are depressants. Barbiturates have medical uses, including relaxation, pain management, and treatment of epilepsy, high blood pressure, and insomnia. Barbiturates lead rapidly to physiological and psychological dependence.
19. What are the effects of amphetamines?	Stimulants are substances that act by increasing the activity of the nervous system. Amphetamines are stimulants that produce feelings of euphoria when taken in high doses. But high doses may also cause restlessness, insomnia, psychotic symptoms, and a "crash" upon withdrawal. Amphetamines and a related stimulant, Ritalin, are commonly used to treat hyperactive children.
20. What are the effects of cocaine?	The stimulant cocaine provides feelings of euphoria and bolsters self-confidence. Physically, it causes spikes in blood pressure and constricts blood vessels. Overdoses can lead to restlessness, insomnia, psychotic reactions, and cardiorespiratory collapse.
21. What are the effects of nicotine?	Nicotine is the addictive stimulant in cigarettes that can paradoxically help people relax. Cigarette smoke also contains carbon monoxide and hydrocarbons. Smoking has been linked to death from heart disease and cancer and to other health problems.
22. What are the effects of marijuana?	Marijuana is a hallucinogenic substance whose active ingredients, including THC, may produce relaxation, heightened and distorted perceptions, feelings of empathy, and reports of new insights. Marijuana elevates the heart rate and the smoke is harmful. Although it has some medical uses, it impairs learning and memory and may affect the growth of adolescents.
23. What are the effects of LSD and other kinds of hallucinogenic drugs?	LSD and other hallucinogenic drugs produce hallucinations. Some LSD users have "flashbacks" to earlier experiences. "Ecstasy" often combines a stimulant with a hallucinogenic drug.

Active Learning Resources

Search Online with InfoTrac® College Edition

For additional information on the topics in this chapter, explore InfoTrac College Edition, your online library. Go to **http://www.infotrac.thomsonlearning.com** and use the passcode that came on the card with your book. Try these search terms: unconscious mind, circadian rhythms, REM sleep, sleep disorders, hypnotism, transcendental meditation, biofeedback training, and psychotropic drugs.

Visit Our Web Site

Go to **http://www.wadsworth.com/psychology**, where you will find online resources directly linked to your book, including interactive exercises related to PQ4R and Power Visuals for mastering and reviewing key concepts. In addition, you will find hints on using InfoTrac College Edition to answer the Critical Thinking questions throughout the text. Start with the **Self Study Assessment** for a customized **Study Plan** generated by taking the **Pre-Test** and **Post-Test.**

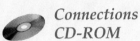

Connections CD-ROM

Go to the Wadsworth *Connections* CD-ROM for further study of the concepts in this chapter. The CD-ROM includes videos and animations, as well as additional activities to expand your learning experience, plus interactive self-assessments to help connect the material to your own life.

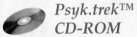

Psyk.trek™ CD-ROM

The Wadsworth *Psyk.trek* CD-ROM offers tutorials, simulations, videos, multimedia glossary, and quizzing to help you master the material.

PsychNow! CD-ROM

The Wadsworth *PsychNow!* CD-ROM includes interactive exercises, videos, and animations to enhance your learning.

Learning: Experience, Change, Adaptation, and . . .

- HERE'S A SURPRISE: Psychologists do not agree on how to define learning.

Classical Conditioning: Learning What Comes After What

- IVAN PAVLOV STUMBLED upon classical conditioning by chance, when he was studying salivation in dogs.

- A SINGLE NAUSEATING meal can give rise to a taste aversion that lasts for years.

Factors in Classical Conditioning

- WHEN SPECIES ARE extinct, they're gone forever. But when responses are extinguished, they can be recovered.

- PSYCHOLOGISTS HELPED a young boy overcome his fear of rabbits by having him eat cookies while a rabbit was brought closer and closer.

- HOW DO YOU TEACH a sleeping child? (Stay tuned, and we'll show you how.)

Operant Conditioning: Learning What Does What to What

- DURING WORLD WAR II, B. F. Skinner created a guided missile. But this missile was to be guided by pigeons.

- PIGEONS WILL LEARN to do whatever they are doing when a food pellet drops in from pigeon heaven.

Factors in Operant Conditioning

- WHAT'S THE DIFFERENCE between a reinforcer and a reward?

- IF PUNISHMENT USUALLY works, why do many psychologists advise against using it?

- YOU CAN TRAIN A RAT to climb a ramp, cross a bridge, climb a ladder, pedal a toy car, and do several other tasks— all in proper sequence.

- WHY DO PEOPLE keep pouring coins into slot machines when they haven't won in ages?

- MUST WE MAKE mistakes in order to learn?

Cognitive Factors in Learning: Is It Natural to Mentally Represent the Environment?

- HOW DO YOU DESIGN an experiment to demonstrate that rats have cognitive maps of their environment?

- PEOPLE LEARN BY observing other people. Does this mean "People see, people do"?

Life Connections: Violence in the Media and Aggression

- VIOLENCE IN THE MEDIA teaches aggressive skills and decreases sensitivity to real violence. Do we have a problem with that?

was teaching my new dog, Phoebe, to fetch. I bought a soft yellow ball for her that squeaked when she bit into it. She enjoyed playing with it, and I assumed she would want to run after it. (Wrong!) I waved it under her nose. She sniffed at it, barked, and wagged her tail excitedly.

I tossed the ball about 20 feet away. "Fetch!" I said as the ball bounced invitingly in the grass.

Phoebe just stared.

I ran after the ball, picked it up, and waved it under Phoebe's nose again. She barked and wagged her tail rapidly like a reed in a brisk wind.

"Fetch!" I said and tossed the ball again.

Again Phoebe refused to run. She barked and snapped at my legs again. "This is ridiculous," I muttered, and I went to get the ball. As I brought it back to Phoebe, my daughter Allyn said, "Don't you see what's happening?"

"What?"

"Phoebe's teaching you to fetch."

LEARNING: EXPERIENCE, CHANGE, ADAPTATION, AND . . .

One could say that Phoebe was teaching me what to do by showing excitement when I did the "right" thing by fetching the ball. I was learning. Learning is a key area in psychology. *Question: What is learning?*

Learning as defined by psychology is more than what we traditionally associate with learning—such as listening to teachers in classrooms, honing skateboard jumps, or mastering a complex cake recipe. In fact, behaviorists define learning one way and cognitive psychologists another.

From the behaviorist perspective, **learning** is a relatively permanent change in behavior that arises from practice or experience. But what about changes in behavior that are associated with physical changes like growth? No, those do not reflect learning. For example, tadpoles start out life swimming; but, after they develop legs, they hop on land in appropriate frog fashion—without any hopping lessons. From the behaviorist perspective, I learned to fetch the ball (a change in behavior) not because of any physical changes but because Phoebe reinforced me for doing so.

Cognitive psychologists define learning as a mental change that may not be associated with changes in behavior. These mentals changes may affect, but do not directly cause, changes in behavior. They argue that learning is *demonstrated* by changes in behavior, but learning itself is a mental process. From the cognitive perspective, my dog's excitement when I retrieved that ball gave me information. It showed me that Phoebe wanted me to repeat the act. But my continued fetching was not mechanical or automatic.

In many animals, much behavior is instinctive, or inborn—rather than learned. Fish (and tadpoles) are born "knowing" how to swim. Salmon instinctively use the sense of smell to find and return to spawn in the stream where they were hatched after they have spent years roaming the seas. Robins instinctively know how to sing the song of their species and to build nests. Among humans, however, the variety and complexity of behavior patterns are largely products of experience. We learn to read, to compute numbers, and to surf the Internet. We learn to seek out the foods that are valued in our culture when we are hungry. We learn which behavior patterns are deemed socially acceptable and which are considered wrong. We also unfortunately learn prejudices and stereotypes and negative behaviors such as using violence to deal with conflict. Our families and communities use verbal guidance, set examples, and apply rewards and punishments to aid our learning and perpetuate cultural values.

▶ CONTROVERSY IN PSYCHOLOGY ◀

How should we define learning?

Psychologists disagree on the definition of learning. Behaviorists define learning as a relatively permanent change in behavior that arises from experience. Cognitive psychologists define learning as a matter of experience changing the way in which an organism represents the environment. Why do they have these different approaches?

Learning
(1) According to behaviorists, a relatively permanent change in behavior that results from experience. (2) According to cognitive theorists, the process by which organisms make relatively permanent changes in the way they represent the environment because of experience. These changes influence the organism's behavior but do not fully determine it.

Sometimes our learning experiences are direct, as when my dog trained me to fetch. But we can also learn from the experiences of others. From books and visual media, we learn about the past, about other peoples, and about how to put things together. And we learn as we invent ways of doing things that have never been done before.

In this chapter we will consider various kinds of learning. These include the simple forms of learning called classical and operant conditioning and kinds of learning in which cognition plays a more central role. We will see that learning is crucial to the adaptation and survival of organisms and that we humans engage in many different kinds of learning, which makes us adaptive and also sets the stage for social ills.

Learning Connections
See Web site for an interactive version of these review questions.

REVIEW

(1) Behaviorists define learning in terms of a change in _____ . (2) Cognitive psychologists define learning in terms of a change in the way organisms mentally _____ the environment.

Critical Thinking: Critical thinkers pay attention to the definitions of terms. What does it mean to say that fish "know" how to swim when they are born? What type of "knowledge" can this be?

Getty Images/Image Bank

■ **Instinct**
The bird builds a nest on the basis of its genetic code. It is an example of instinctive behavior, which is not learned through experience.

CLASSICAL CONDITIONING: LEARNING WHAT COMES AFTER WHAT

Classical conditioning involves some of the ways in which we learn to associate events with other events. Consider this: We have a distinct preference for a grade of A rather than F. We are also (usually) more likely to stop for a red light than for a green light. Why? We are not born with instinctive attitudes toward the letters *A* and *F*. Nor are we born knowing that red means stop and green means go. We learn the meanings of these symbols because they are associated with other events. A's are associated with instructor approval and the likelihood of getting into graduate school. Stopping at red lights is associated with avoiding accidents and traffic citations.

    Question: What is classical conditioning? **Classical conditioning** is a simple form of associative learning that enables organisms to anticipate events.

Ivan Pavlov Rings a Bell

One severe Russian winter, when he was too poor to heat his home adequately, biologist Ivan Pavlov (1849–1936) was dismayed to see all his butterflies die. At the time, Pavlov was studying the life cycle of butterflies, and he was crushed by the loss. Fortunately, he persisted in biology despite this setback.

    If the name Ivan Pavlov rings a bell with us, it is most likely because of his research in learning with dogs. *Question: What is the contribution of Ivan Pavlov to the psychology of learning?* Ivan Pavlov (1927) made his great contribution to the psychology of learning by accident. Pavlov was actually attempting to identify neural receptors in the mouth that triggered a response from the salivary glands. But his efforts were hampered by the dogs' annoying tendency to salivate at undesired times, such as when a laboratory assistant was clumsy and banged the metal food trays.

    Just as you salivate after you've taken a big bite of cake, a dog salivates if meat powder is placed on its tongue. Pavlov was dosing his dogs with meat powder for his research because he knew that salivation in response to meat powder is a **reflex**. Reflexes are simple automatic responses to stimuli. These "unlearned" responses are evoked by stimuli. A **stimulus** is an environmental condition that evokes a response from an organism, such as when your leg jerks forward after the doctor taps just below the knee. Ivan Pavlov made the surprising discovery that reflexes

Classical Conditioning
A simple form of learning in which an organism comes to associate or anticipate events. A neutral stimulus comes to evoke the response usually evoked by another stimulus by being paired repeatedly with the other stimulus. (Cognitive theorists view classical conditioning as the learning of relationships among events so as to allow an organism to represent its environment.) Also referred to as *respondent conditioning* or *Pavlovian conditioning.*

Reflex
A simple unlearned response to a stimulus.

Stimulus
An environmental condition that elicits a response.

■ **Ivan Pavlov and His Associates—Including a Professional Furry Salivator**

Pavlov was working to identify neural receptors in the mouth that triggered salivation but found that his laboratory animals salivated at undesired times, as when a food tray clinked. He thus set about to study why the animals salivated in response to the clinking of the food tray.

(involuntary responses) can also be learned, or *conditioned,* through association. His dogs began salivating in response to clanging food trays because in the past this noise had repeatedly been paired with the arrival of food. The dogs would also salivate when an assistant entered the laboratory. Why? In the past, the assistant had brought food.

Pavlov at first viewed the extra salivation of his dogs as an annoyance, a hindrance to his research. But in 1901 it finally dawned on him that perhaps this "problem" was worth looking into. He found out that he could actually train, or condition, his dogs to salivate when he wished and in response to any stimulus he chose. Pavlov was excited by this because it gave him new insights into how we learn on a most basic level.

Pavlov termed these trained salivary responses "conditional reflexes." They were *conditional* upon the repeated pairing of a previously neutral stimulus (such as the clanging of a food tray) and a stimulus (in this case, food) that predictably elicited the target response (in this case, salivation). Today, conditional reflexes are more generally referred to as **conditioned responses (CRs).** They are responses to previously neutral stimuli that now have a definite association that has been learned, or conditioned.

Pavlov demonstrated conditioned responses by strapping a dog into a harness like the one shown in Figure 6.1. When meat powder was placed on the dog's tongue, the dog salivated. Pavlov repeated the process several times, with one difference. He preceded the meat powder by half a second or so with the sounding of a bell on each occasion. After several pairings of meat powder and bell, Pavlov sounded the bell but did *not* follow the bell with the meat powder. Still the dog salivated. It had learned to salivate in response to the bell.

REFLECT

Had you heard the expression "That rings a bell"? If so, did you know what it referred to?

Conditioned Response (CR)

In classical conditioning, a learned response to a conditioned stimulus.

■ **Figure 6.1**
Pavlov's Demonstration of Conditioned Reflexes in Laboratory Dogs

From behind a one-way mirror, a laboratory assistant rings a bell and then places meat on the dog's tongue. After several pairings, the dog salivates in response to the bell alone. A tube collects saliva and passes it to a vial. The quantity of saliva is taken as a measure of the strength of the animal's response.

▶ CONTROVERSY IN PSYCHOLOGY ◀

Why did Pavlov's dogs learn to salivate in response to the bell?

Behaviorists and cognitive psychologists explain the learning process in very different ways. Behaviorists explain the outcome of this process, termed *classical conditioning,* in terms of the publicly observable conditions of learning. They define classical conditioning as a simple form of learning in which one stimulus comes to evoke the response usually evoked by a second stimulus by being paired repeatedly with the second stimulus. In Pavlov's demonstration, the dog learned to salivate in response to the bell *because* the sounding of the bell had been paired with meat powder. That is, in classical conditioning, the organism forms associations between stimuli because the stimuli are *contiguous*—that is, they occur at about the same time. Behaviorists do *not* say that the dog "knew" food was on the way. They argue that we cannot speak meaningfully about what a dog "knows." We can only outline the conditions under which targeted behaviors reliably occur.

Cognitive psychologists view classical conditioning as the learning of relationships among events. The relationships allow organisms to mentally represent their environments and make predictions (Rescorla, 1988). In Pavlov's demonstration, the dog salivated in response to the bell because the bell—from the cognitive perspective—became mentally connected with the meat. The cognitive focus is on *the information gained by the organism*. Organisms are seen as seekers of information that generate and test rules about relationships among events.

Living outside New York City, I was used to seeing the World Trade Center and other tall buildings. When I now see "Ground Zero" from a distance, visions of airplanes driving into the towers and exploding fill my head. When I look at the other tall buildings in the city, or visit Chicago and see its own wondrous towers, visions of them exploding also enter my mind. Why? Did the repeated TV broadcasting of the attack on the World Trade Center mechanically "condition" me to mentally envision such explosions, or did they provide information which changed the way in which I mentally represent skyscrapers? Did it do both? Experience somehow mixed their majesty with their potential as magnets for future attacks.

Stimuli and Responses in Classical Conditioning

In Pavlov's experiment, the meat powder is an unlearned or **unconditioned stimulus (US)**. Salivation in response to the meat powder is an unlearned or **unconditioned response (UR)**. The bell was at first a meaningless or neutral stimulus. It might have produced an *orienting reflex* in the dog because of its distinctness. That is, the animal might have oriented itself toward the bell by turning toward it. But the bell was not yet associated with food. Then, through repeated association with the meat powder, the bell became a learned or **conditioned stimulus (CS)** for the salivation response. Salivation in response to the bell (or CS) is a learned or conditioned response (CR). A conditioned response is a response similar to an unconditioned response, but the response evoked by the conditioned stimulus is defined as a conditioned response, not an unconditioned response (see Figure 6.2).

Taste Aversion: Are All Stimuli Created Equal?

When I was a child in The Bronx, my friends and I would go to the movies on Saturday mornings. One day my friends dared me to eat two huge containers of buttered popcorn by myself. I had no problem with the first enormous basket of buttered popcorn. More slowly—much more slowly—I forced down the second basket. I felt bloated and nauseated. The taste of the butter, corn, and salt lingered in my mouth and nose, and my head spun. It was obvious to me that no one could talk me into even another handful of popcorn that day. But I was surprised that I couldn't face buttered popcorn again for a year.

Years later I learned that psychologists refer to my response to buttered popcorn as a *taste aversion*. ***Questions: What are taste aversions? Why are they of special interest to psychologists?*** Many decades have now passed, and the distinctive odor of buttered popcorn still turns my stomach. Such is the power of taste aversions.

Taste aversions are fascinating examples of classical conditioning. Taste aversions are adaptive because they motivate organisms to avoid potentially harmful foods. Although taste aversions are acquired by association, they are of special interest because they differ from other kinds of classical conditioning in a couple of ways. First, only one association may be required. A single overdose of popcorn left me with a lifetime aversion. Second, whereas most kinds of classical conditioning require that the unconditioned stimulus (US) and conditioned stimulus (CS) be close together in time (contiguous), in taste aversion the unconditioned stimulus (in this case, nausea) can occur hours after the conditioned stimulus (in this case, the flavor of food).

REFLECT

Would behaviorists say that after a few pairings of bell and food a dog "knows" that the bell "means" food is on its way? Why or why not?

Unconditioned Stimulus (US)
A stimulus that elicits a response from an organism prior to conditioning.

Unconditioned Response (UR)
An unlearned response to an unconditioned stimulus.

Conditioned Stimulus (CS)
A previously neutral stimulus that elicits a conditioned response because it has been paired repeatedly with a stimulus that already elicited that response.

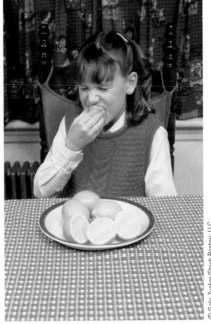

© Gale Zucker/Stock Boston, LLC

■ **Formation of a Taste Aversion?**

Taste aversions can be acquired by means of a single pairing of the US and the CS. Evolutionary psychologists point out that the rapid acquisition of a taste aversion would make it more likely that an animal would survive and reproduce.

■ **Figure 6.2**
A Schematic Representation of Classical Conditioning
Prior to conditioning, food elicits salivation. The bell, a neutral stimulus, elicits either no response or an orienting response. During conditioning, the bell is rung just before meat is placed on the dog's tongue. After several repetitions, the bell, now a CS, elicits salivation, the CR.

Power Visual
See Web site for an interactive version of this figure.

Learning Connections
See the Connections *CD-ROM for an animation on the basics of classical conditioning.*

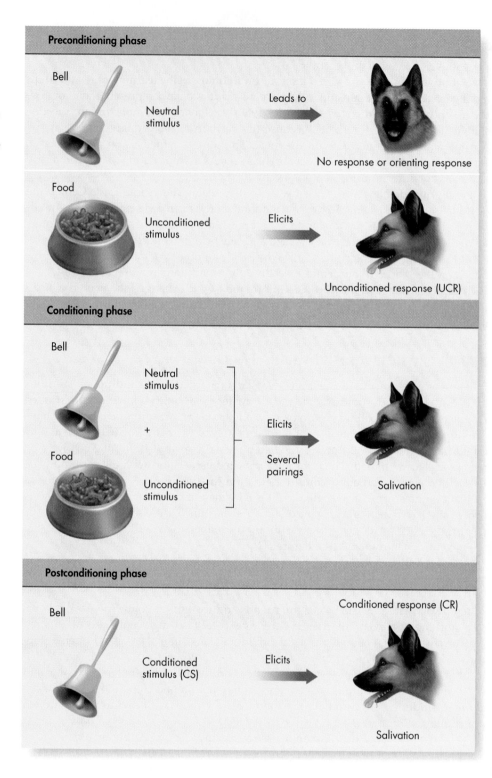

The Evolution of Taste Aversion

Research on taste aversion also challenges the behaviorist view that organisms learn to associate any stimuli that are linked in time. In reality, not all stimuli are created equal. The evolutionary perspective suggests that animals (and humans) would be biologically predisposed to develop aversions that are adaptive in their environmental settings (Garcia et al., 1989). That is, those of us who develop taste aversions quickly are less likely to feast on poisonous food, more likely to survive, and thus more likely to contribute our genes to future generations.

In a classic study, Garcia and Koelling (1966) conditioned two groups of rats. Each group was exposed to the same three-part conditioned stimulus (CS): a taste of sweetened water, a light, and a clicker. Afterward, one group was presented with an unconditioned stimulus (US) of nausea (induced by poison or radiation), and the other group was presented with an unconditioned stimulus (US) of electric shock.

After conditioning, the rats who had been nauseated showed an aversion for sweetened water but not to the light or clicker. Although all three stimuli had been presented at the same time, *the rats had acquired only the taste aversion.* After conditioning, the rats that had been shocked avoided both the light and the clicker, *but they did not show a taste aversion to the sweetened water.* For each group of rats, the conditioning that took place was adaptive. In the natural scheme of things, nausea is more likely to stem from poisoned food than from lights or sounds. So, for nauseated rats, acquiring the taste aversion was appropriate. Sharp pain, in contrast, is more likely to stem from natural events involving lights (fire, lightning) and sharp sounds (twigs snapping, things falling). Therefore, it was more appropriate for the shocked animals to develop an aversion to the light and the clicker than to the sweetened water.

Let us now consider various factors in classical conditioning.

R E V I E W

(3) A _____ is an environmental condition that evokes a response from an organism. (4) A response to an unconditioned stimulus (US) is called an _____ response (UR). (5) A response to a conditioned stimulus (CS) is termed a _____ response (CR). (6) In conditioning a taste aversion, (only one or several?) association (s) is/are usually required.

Critical Thinking: Agree or disagree with the following statement and support your answer: The existence of taste aversions provides support for the evolutionary perspective.

Learning Connections
See Web site for an interactive version of these review questions.

FACTORS IN CLASSICAL CONDITIONING

In classical conditioning organisms learn to connect stimuli, such as a bell with food. In the following section we consider various factors in classical conditioning, beginning with what happens when the connection between stimuli is severed. This is of great interest to psychologists because, as we will see, psychologists have used extinction to help people overcome fears.

Learning Connections
See the Connections *CD-ROM for an animation on features and phases of classical conditioning.*

Extinction and Spontaneous Recovery

Question: What are the roles of extinction and spontaneous recovery in classical conditioning? Extinction and spontaneous recovery are aspects of conditioning that help us adapt by updating our expectations or revising our thinking about (representations of) the changing environment. For example, a dog may learn to associate a new scent (a conditioned stimulus, or CS) with the appearance of a dangerous animal. It can then take evasive action when it catches a whiff of that scent. A child may learn to connect hearing a car pull into the driveway (a conditioned stimulus, or CS) with the arrival of his or her parents (an unconditioned stimulus, or US). Thus, the child may begin to squeal with delight (squealing is a conditioned response, or CR) when the car is heard.

But times can change. The once-dangerous animal may no longer be a threat. (What a puppy perceives to be a threat may lose its fearsomeness once the dog matures.) After moving to a new house, the child's parents may commute by means of public transportation. The sound of a car in a nearby driveway may signal a neighbor's, not a parent's, homecoming. When conditioned stimuli (such as the scent of a dog or the sound of a car) are no longer followed by unconditioned stimuli (a dangerous animal, a parent's homecoming), they lose their ability to elicit conditioned responses. In this way the organism adapts to a changing environment.

Extinction

In classical conditioning, **extinction** is the process by which conditioned stimuli (CSs) lose the ability to elicit conditioned responses (CRs), because the conditioned stimuli (CSs) are no longer associated with unconditioned stimuli (USs). That is, the puppy loses its fear of the scent of the neighbor's dog, or the toddler is no longer gleeful at the sounds of the car in the driveway. From the cognitive perspective, extinction changes the animals mental representation of its environment, because the learned or conditioned stimulus (CS) no longer allows it to make the same prediction.

In experiments on the extinction of conditioned responses (CRs), Pavlov found that repeated presentations of the conditioned stimulus (in this case, the bell) without the unconditioned stimulus (in this case, meat powder) led to extinction of the conditioned response (salivation in response to the bell). That is, the dog stopped salivating at the sound of the bell. Figure 6.3 shows that a dog that had been conditioned began to salivate (show a conditioned response, or CR) in response to a bell (the conditioned stimulus) after only a couple of pairings—referred to as *acquisition trials*—of the bell with meat powder. Continued pairings of the stimuli led to increased salivation (measured in number of drops of saliva). After seven or eight trials, salivation leveled off at 11 to 12 drops.

In the next series of experiments, salivation in response to the bell was extinguished through several trials—referred to as *extinction trials*—in which the bell was presented without the meat powder. After about ten extinction trials, the animal no longer salivated. That is, it no longer showed the learned or conditioned response (salivation in response to the bell) when the bell was rung (the bell is the learned or conditioned stimulus).

Extinction

An experimental procedure in which stimuli lose their ability to evoke learned responses because the events that had followed the stimuli no longer occur. (The learned responses are said to be *extinguished*.)

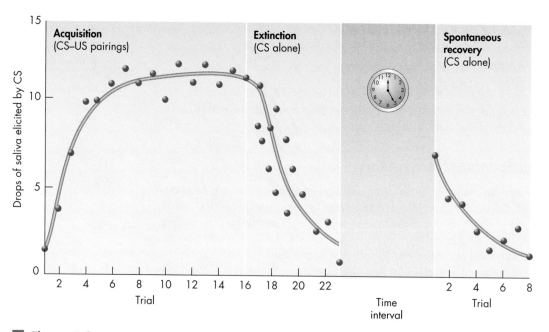

■ Figure 6.3
Learning and Extinction Curves

Actual data from Pavlov (1927) compose the jagged line, and the curved lines are idealized. In the acquisition phase, a dog salivates (shows a CR) in response to a bell (CS) after a few trials in which the bell is paired with meat powder (the US). Afterward, the CR is extinguished in about ten trials during which the CS is not followed by the US. After a rest period, the CR recovers spontaneously. A second series of extinction trials leads to more rapid extinction of the CR.

Spontaneous Recovery

What would happen if we were to allow a day or two to pass after we had extinguished salivation (the CR) in Pavlov's dog and then again rang the bell (the CS)? Where would you place your bet? Would the dog salivate or not?

If you bet that the dog would again show the conditioned response (in this case, salivation in response to the bell), you were correct. Organisms tend to show **spontaneous recovery** of extinguished conditioned responses (CRs) merely as a function of the passage of time. For this reason, the term *extinction* may be a bit misleading. When a species of animal becomes extinct, all the members of that species capable of reproducing have died. The species vanishes. But the experimental extinction of conditioned responses (CRs) does not lead to their permanent eradication. Rather, it seems that they *inhibit* the response. The response remains available for future performance under the "right" conditions.

Evolutionary psychologists note that spontaneous recovery, like extinction, is adaptive. What would happen if the child heard no car in the driveway for several months? It could be that the next time a car entered the driveway, the child would associate the sounds with a parent's homecoming (rather than with the arrival of a neighbor). This expectation could be appropriate. After all, *something* had changed when no car entered the nearby driveway for so long. In the wild, a water hole may contain water for only a couple of months during the year. But evolution would favor the survival of animals that associate the water hole with the thirst drive from time to time so that they will return to it when it again holds water.

As time passes and the seasons change, things sometimes follow circular paths and arrive where they were before. Spontaneous recovery seems to function as a mechanism whereby organisms can adapt successfully to situations that recur from time to time.

Generalization and Discrimination

No two things are exactly alike. Traffic lights are hung at slightly different heights, and shades of red and green differ a little. The barking of two dogs differs, and the sound of the same animal differs slightly from one bark to the next. Rustling sounds in the undergrowth differ, but evolution would favor the survival of rabbits and deer that flee when they perceive any one of many possible rustling sounds. Adaptation requires us to respond similarly (or *generalize*) to stimuli that are equivalent in function and to respond differently to (or *discriminate* between) stimuli that are not. *Question: What are the roles of generalization and discrimination in classical conditioning?*

REFLECT
What is the difference between extinction and forgetting?

Spontaneous Recovery
The recurrence of an extinguished response as a function of the passage of time.

■ **Spontaneous Recovery of the Tendency to Visit a Water Hole After Time Has Passed**
If a water hole dries up, animals' tendencies to go to the water hole in a given season may be extinguished. However, when another season rolls around, the tendency to visit the water hole may spontaneously recover. Evolution would favor the survival of animals that associate the water hole with reduction of the thirst drive from time to time so that they are likely to return to it when it again holds water.

Generalization

In conditioning, the tendency for a conditioned response to be evoked by stimuli that are similar to the stimulus to which the response was conditioned.

Discrimination

In conditioning, the tendency for an organism to distinguish between a conditioned stimulus and similar stimuli that do not forecast an unconditioned stimulus.

Higher-Order Conditioning

(1) According to behaviorists, a classical conditioning procedure in which a previously neutral stimulus comes to elicit the response brought forth by a *conditioned* stimulus by being paired repeatedly with that conditioned stimulus. (2) According to cognitive psychologists, the learning of relationships among events, none of which evokes an unlearned response.

■ **Generalization at the Crossroads**

Chances are that you have never seen this particular traffic light in this particular setting. Because of generalization, however, we can safely bet that you would know what to do—stop or go—if you were to drive up to it.

Generalization

Pavlov noted that responding to different stimuli as though they are functionally equivalent—*generalizing*—is adaptive for animals. **Generalization** is the tendency for a conditioned response to be evoked by stimuli that are similar to the stimulus to which the response was conditioned. Pavlov demonstrated generalization by getting his dog to salivate when it was shown a circle. Then later the dog salivated in response to being shown closed geometric figures—even squares! The more closely the figure resembled a circle, however, the greater the *strength* of the response (as measured by drops of saliva).

Discrimination

Organisms must also learn that (1) many stimuli perceived as being similar are functionally different and (2) they must respond adaptively to each. During the first couple of months of life, for example, babies can discriminate their mother's voice from those of other women. They often stop crying when they hear their mother but not when they hear a stranger.

Pavlov showed that a dog conditioned to salivate in response to circles could be trained *not* to salivate in response to ellipses. After a while, the dog no longer salivated in response to the ellipses. Instead, it showed **discrimination:** It salivated only in response to circles.

Pavlov found that increasing the difficulty of the discrimination task apparently tormented the dog. After the dog was trained to salivate in response to circles but not ellipses, Pavlov showed it a series of progressively rounder ellipses. Eventually the dog could no longer distinguish the ellipses from circles. The animal was so stressed that it urinated, defecated, barked profusely, and snapped at laboratory personnel.

How do we explain the dog's belligerent behavior? In a classic work written more than 65 years ago, titled *Frustration and Aggression,* a group of behaviorally oriented psychologists suggested that frustration induces aggression (Dollard et al., 1939). Why is failure to discriminate circles from ellipses frustrating? For one thing, in such experiments, rewards—such as food—are usually contingent on correct discrimination. That is, if the dog errs, it doesn't get fed. Cognitive theorists, however, disagree (Rescorla, 1988). They would say that in Pavlov's experiment, the dog lost the ability to adjust its mental map of the environment as the ellipses grew more circular. Thus it was frustrated.

Daily living requires appropriate generalization and discrimination. No two hotels are alike, but when we travel from one city to another it is adaptive to expect to stay in a hotel. It is encouraging that a green light in Washington has the same meaning as a green light in Paris. But returning home in the evening requires the ability to discriminate between our home and those of others. And if we could not readily discriminate our spouse from others, we might land in divorce court.

REFLECT

Can you think of examples of generalization and discrimination in your own life?

Higher-Order Conditioning

Consider a boy who burns himself by touching a hot stove. After this experience, the sight of the stove may evoke fear. And because hearing the word *stove* may evoke a mental image of the stove, just hearing the word may evoke fear. This is an example of higher-order conditioning. ***Question: What is higher-order conditioning?***

In **higher-order conditioning,** a previously neutral stimulus comes to serve as a learned or conditioned stimulus (CS) after being paired repeatedly with a stimulus that has already become a learned or conditioned stimulus (CS). Pavlov demonstrated higher-order conditioning by first conditioning a dog to salivate in response to a bell (a CS). He then repeatedly paired the shining of a light with the sounding of a bell. After several pairings, shining the light (the higher-order conditioned stimulus) came to evoke the response (salivation) that had been elicited by the bell (the first-order conditioned stimulus).

REVIEW

(7) Repeated presentation of a CS (e.g., a bell) without the US (e.g., meat) will _____ the CR (salivation). (8) Extinguished responses often show _____ recovery as a function of the passage of time. (9) In stimulus _____, organisms show a CR in response to a range of stimuli similar to the CS. (10) In stimulus _____, organisms learn to show a CR in response to a more limited range of stimuli. (11) In _____-order conditioning, a previously neutral stimulus comes to serve as a CS after being paired repeatedly with another CS.

Critical Thinking: Consider this question as if you were an evolutionary psychologist. Why are organisms that are capable of extinction and spontaneous recovery of conditioned responses more likely to survive and transmit their genes to subsequent generations?

Learning Connections
See Web site for an interactive version of these review questions.

Life Connections
See the Connections *CD-ROM for an animation on classical conditioning of emotional responses.*

OPERANT CONDITIONING: LEARNING WHAT DOES WHAT TO WHAT

Through classical conditioning, we learn to associate stimuli so that a simple, usually passive, response made to one stimulus is then made in response to the other. In 1920 the behaviorist John B. Watson and his future wife, Rosalie Rayner, published a report of their demonstration that emotional reactions can be acquired through classical conditioning. The subject of their demonstration was a lad later known as "Little Albert." At the age of 11 months, Albert was a calm child, not given to ready displays of emotion. But he did enjoy playing with a fuzzy white laboratory rat. Using a method that many psychologists have since criticized as unethical, Watson startled Little Albert by clanging steel bars behind his head whenever the infant played with the rat. After repeated pairings, Albert showed fear of the rat even when the clanging was halted. Albert's fear also generalized to objects that were similar in appearance to the rat, such as a rabbit and the fur collar on a woman's coat.

However, classical conditioning is only one kind of learning that occurs in these situations. After Little Albert acquired his fear of the rat, his voluntary behavior changed. He avoided the rat as a way of reducing his fear. Thus, Little Albert engaged in another kind of learning—*operant conditioning.* In operant conditioning, organisms learn to do things—or *not* to do things—because of the consequences of their behavior. I avoided buttered popcorn in order to prevent nausea. But we also seek fluids when we are thirsty, sex when we are aroused, and an ambient temperature of 68° to 70° F when we feel too hot or too cold. *Classical conditioning focuses on how organisms form anticipations about their environments. Operant conditioning focuses on what they do about them.*

We begin this section with the historic work of psychologist Edward L. Thorndike. Then we examine the more recent work of B. F. Skinner.

Edward L. Thorndike and the Law of Effect

In the 1890s stray cats were mysteriously disappearing from the streets and alleyways of Harlem. Some of them, it turned out, were being brought to the quarters of Columbia University doctoral student Edward Thorndike. Thorndike was using the cats as subjects in experiments on the effects of rewards and punishments on learning.

Thorndike placed the cats in so-called puzzle boxes. If the animal managed to pull a dangling string, a latch would be released, allowing it to jump out and reach a bowl of food.

When first placed in a puzzle box, a cat would try to squeeze through any opening and would claw and bite at the confining bars and wire. It would claw at anything it could reach. Through such random behavior, it might take 3 to 4 minutes for the cat to

Archives of the History of American Psychology

■ **"Little Albert" with Rosalie Rayner and John B. Watson**

Little Albert was classically conditioned to fear a laboratory rat. Little Albert then did what he could to avoid the rat in order to reduce his fear.

chance upon the response of pulling the string. Pulling the string would open the cage and allow the cat to reach the food. When placed back in the cage, it might again take several minutes for the animal to pull the string. But with repetition, it took progressively less time for the cat to pull the string. After seven or eight repetitions, the cat might pull the string immediately when placed back in the box.

A Closer Look 👁

Applications of Classical Conditioning: Are Cookies Psychological Health Food?

If you happen across a gentleman nearly 80 years old who cringes at the sight of a fur coat, he may not be concerned about animal rights. Perhaps he is "Little Albert," who was conditioned to fear furry objects before he reached his first birthday.

Watson has been criticized for not attempting to *countercondition* Albert's fear. But a few years later Mary Cover Jones did so with another boy—under Watson's supervision. Let us consider counterconditioning and other applications of classical conditioning.

Counterconditioning

Early in the 20th century, John Watson's protégé Mary Cover Jones (1924) reasoned that if fears could be conditioned by painful experiences, she could *countercondition* them by substituting pleasant experiences. In *counterconditioning*, a pleasant stimulus is repeatedly paired with a fear-evoking object, thereby counteracting the fear response.

Two-year-old Peter had an intense fear of rabbits. Jones arranged for a rabbit to be gradually brought closer to Peter while he engaged in some of his favorite activities, such as munching on candy and cookies. She did not simply plop the rabbit in Peter's lap, as in flooding. Had she done so, the cookies on the plate, not to mention those already eaten, might have decorated the walls. Instead, she first placed the rabbit in a far corner of the room while Peter munched and crunched. Peter, to be sure, cast a wary eye, but he continued to consume the treat. Gradually the animal was brought closer until eventually Peter ate treats and touched the rabbit at the same time. Jones theorized that the joy of eating was incompatible with fear and thus counterconditioned it.

Flooding and Systematic Desensitization

Counterconditioning is a behavior therapy method for reducing fears. Two others are flooding and systematic desensitization, and they are based on the classical conditioning principle of extinction (Wolpe & Plaud, 1997). In one, *flooding*, the client is exposed to the fear-evoking stimulus until the fear response is extinguished. Little Albert, for example, might have been placed in close contact with a rat until his fear had become fully extinguished. In extinction, the CS (in this case, the rat) is pre-

sented repeatedly in the absence of the US (the clanging of the steel bars) until the CR (fear) is no longer evoked.

A German study of 416 people evaluated the effectiveness of a flooding-type treatment for agoraphobia (fear of being out in busy, open areas). Agoraphobic participants were exposed persistently— for two to three weeks, all day long— to densely populated, open places.

Can Chocolate Chip Cookies Countercondition Fears?

In the 1920s Mary Cover Jones helped a boy overcome his fear of rabbits by having him munch on cookies as the animal was brought closer.

Six weeks after therapy and at a one-year follow-up, the participants showed significant reductions in anxiety and in avoidance of busy, open places.

Although flooding is usually effective, it is unpleasant. (When you are fearful of rats, being placed in a small room with one is no picnic.) For this reason, behavior therapists frequently prefer to use *systematic desensitization*, in which the client is gradually exposed to fear-evoking stimuli under circumstances in which he or she remains relaxed. For example, while feeling relaxed, Little Albert might have been given an opportunity to look at photos of rats or to see live rats from a distance before they were brought closer to him. Systematic desensitization takes longer than flooding but is not as unpleasant.

The Bell-and-Pad Treatment for Bed-Wetting

By the age of 5 or 6, children normally awaken in response to the sensation of a full bladder. They inhibit the urge to urinate, which is an automatic or reflexive response to bladder tension, and instead go to the bathroom. But bed-wetters tend not to respond to bladder tension while asleep. They remain asleep and frequently wet their beds.

The Law of Effect

Thorndike explained the cat's learning to pull the string in terms of his **law of effect.** According to this law, a response (such as string pulling) is "stamped in" or strengthened in a particular situation (such as being inside a puzzle box) by a reward (escaping from the box and eating). Rewards, that is, stamp in S–R (stimulus–response) connections. Punishments, in contrast, "stamp out" stimulus–response

Law of Effect

Thorndike's principle that responses are "stamped in" by rewards and "stamped out" by punishments.

■ **Will Fear of Busy, Open Places Be Extinguished by Persistent Exposure?**
Research results are encouraging. It seems that persistent exposure of agoraphobic individuals to busy, open areas reduces their anxiety and their avoidance of such places.

By means of the bell-and-pad method, children are taught to wake up in response to bladder tension. They sleep on a special sheet or pad that has been placed on the bed. When the child starts to urinate, the water content of the urine causes an electrical circuit in the pad to close. The closing of the circuit triggers a bell or buzzer, and the child is awakened. (Similar buzzer circuits have been built into training pants as an aid to toilet training.) In terms of classical conditioning, the bell is a US that wakes the child (waking up is the UR). By means of repeated pairings, a stimulus that precedes the bell becomes associated with the bell and also gains the capacity to awaken the child. What is that stimulus? The sensation of a full bladder. In this way, bladder tension (the CS) gains the capacity to awaken the child *even though the child is asleep during the classical conditioning procedure.*

The bell-and-pad method is a superb example of why behaviorists prefer to explain the effects of classical conditioning in terms of the pairing of stimuli and not in terms of what the learner knows. The behaviorist may argue that we cannot assume a sleeping child "knows" that wetting the bed will cause the bell to ring. We can only note that by repeatedly pairing bladder tension with the bell, the child eventually *learns* to wake up in response to bladder tension alone. *Learning* is demonstrated by the change in the child's behavior. One can only speculate on what the child *knows* about the learning process.

In any event, it appears that humans are capable of learning by means of simple association. In terms of the evolutionary perspective, it would appear that organisms that can learn by means of several routes—including conditioning and conscious reflection—would have a greater chance of survival than organisms whose learning is limited to a single route.

connections. Organisms would learn *not* to engage in behavior that brings on punishment. Later we shall see that the effects of punishment on learning are not so certain.

Burrhus Frederic Skinner

During his first TV appearance, the psychologist B. F. Skinner (1904–1990) was asked, "Would you, if you had to choose, burn your children or your books?" He said with a wry smile that he would have chosen to burn his children, because his contribution to the future lay more in his writings than in his genes. Skinner delighted in controversy and enjoyed shocking TV viewers with his irreverent wit.

Skinner was born into a middle-class Pennsylvania family. As a youth he was always building things—scooters, sleds, wagons, rafts, slides, and merry-go-rounds. Later he would become famous for building the so-called Skinner box, which improved on Thorndike's puzzle box, as a way of studying operant behavior. He earned an undergraduate degree in English and turned to psychology only after failing to make his mark as a writer in New York's Greenwich Village.

A great popularizer of his own views, Skinner used reinforcement to teach pigeons to play basketball and the piano—sort of. On a visit to his daughter's grammar school class, it occurred to him that similar techniques might work with children. Thus he developed *programmed learning.* Although he had earlier failed at writing, he gathered a cultish following when he published *Walden Two,* a novel in which children are socialized to *want* to behave prosocially.

Skinner and his followers have applied his principles not only to programmed learning but also to behavior modification programs for helping people with disorders ranging from substance abuse to phobias to sexual dysfunctions. He died in 1990 eight days after receiving an unprecedented Lifetime Contribution to Psychology award from the American Psychological Association.

The Concept of Reinforcement

When it comes to unusual war stories, few will top that of B. F. Skinner. One of Skinner's wartime efforts was "Project Pigeon."   *Question: What is the contribution of B. F. Skinner to the psychology of learning?*

During World War II Skinner proposed that pigeons be trained to guide missiles to their targets. In their training, the pigeons would be **reinforced** with food pellets for pecking at targets projected onto a screen (see Figure 6.4). Once trained, the pigeons would be placed in missiles. Their pecking at similar targets displayed on a screen would correct the missile's flight path, resulting in a "hit" and a sacrificed pigeon. However, plans for building the necessary missile—for some reason called the *Pelican* and not the *Pigeon*—were scrapped. The pigeon equipment was too bulky and, Skinner lamented, his suggestion was not taken seriously. Apparently the Defense Department concluded that Project Pigeon was for the birds.

Project Pigeon may have been scrapped, but the principles of learning that Skinner applied to the project have found wide application. Project Pigeon also affords insight into the inventiveness of B. F. Skinner. Not only did Skinner make contributions to the understanding of learning, we will see that he also made technological innovations such as the Skinner box and the cumulative recorder. In operant conditioning, an animal learns to *do* something because of the effects or consequences of that behavior.

Skinner taught pigeons and other animals to engage in **operant behavior,** behavior that operates on, or manipulates, the environment. In classical conditioning, involuntary responses such as salivation or eye-blinks are often conditioned. In operant conditioning, *voluntary* responses such as pecking at a target, pressing a lever, or many of the skills required for playing tennis are acquired, or conditioned.   *Question: What is operant conditioning?*

Reinforce
To follow a response with a stimulus that increases the frequency of the response.

Operant Behavior
Voluntary responses that are reinforced.

■ Figure 6.4
Project Pigeon

During World War II, B. F. Skinner suggested using operant conditioning to train pigeons to guide missiles to their targets. The pigeons would first be reinforced for pecking targets projected on a screen. Afterward, in combat, pecking the on-screen target would keep the missile on course.

Operant conditioning is defined as a simple form of learning in which an organism learns to engage in certain behavior because of the effects of that behavior. In operant conditioning, we learn to engage in operant behaviors, also known simply as **operants,** that result in presumably desirable consequences such as food, a hug, an A on a test, attention, or social approval. Some children learn to conform their behavior to social rules to earn the attention and approval of their parents and teachers. Other children, ironically, may learn to "misbehave," because misbehavior also gets attention from other people. In particular, children may learn to be "bad" when their "good" behavior is routinely ignored. On the other hand, children who do not do well in school may also turn to a gang, in which their behavior is more likely to be reinforced by their peers.

Operant Conditioning
A simple form of learning in which an organism learns to engage in behavior because it is reinforced.

Operant
The same as an operant behavior.

■ B. F. Skinner

Skinner was a great popularizer of his ideas about operant conditioning and the ways in which societies control individuals. In his day, he became something of a cult figure.

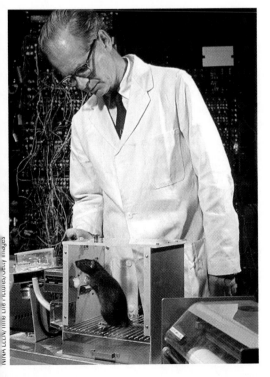

Methods of Operant Conditioning

In his most influential work, *The Behavior of Organisms,* Skinner (1938) made many theoretical and technological innovations. Among them was his focus on discrete behaviors such as lever pressing as the *unit,* or type, of behavior to be studied (Glenn et al., 1992). Other psychologists might focus on how organisms think or "feel." Skinner focused on measurable things that they do. Many psychologists have found these kinds of behavior inconsequential, especially when it comes to explaining and predicting human behavior. But Skinner's supporters point out that focusing on discrete behavior creates the potential for helpful changes. For example, in helping people combat depression, one psychologist might focus on their "feelings." A Skinnerian psychologist would focus on cataloguing (and modifying) the types of things that depressed people actually *do.* Directly modifying depressive behavior might also brighten clients' self-reports about their "feelings of depression." The Life Connections section in the chapter on Methods of Therapy (Chapter 13) explains how people can use this principle in their own lives.

To study operant behavior efficiently, Skinner devised an animal cage (or "operant chamber") that was dubbed the *Skinner box* by psychologist Clark Hull, whose theory of drive-reductionism is discussed in Chapter 9. (Skinner himself repeatedly requested that his operant chamber *not* be called a Skinner box. History has thus far failed to honor his wishes, however.) Such a box is shown in Figure 6.5. The cage is ideal for laboratory experimentation because experimental conditions (treatments) can be carefully introduced and removed, and the effects on laboratory animals (defined as changes in rates of lever pressing) can be carefully observed. The operant chamber (or Skinner box) is also energy-efficient—in terms of the energy of the experimenter. In contrast to Thorndike's puzzle box, a "correct" response does not allow the animal to escape and have to be recaptured and placed back in the box. According to psychologist John Garcia, Skinner's "great contribution to the study of behavior was the marvelously efficient operant methodology" (1993, p. 1158).

The rat in Figure 6.5 was deprived of food and placed in a Skinner box with a lever at one end. At first it sniffed its way around the cage and engaged in random behavior. When an animal behaves in a random manner, responses that have favorable consequences tend to occur more frequently. Responses that do not have favorable consequences are performed less frequently.

The rat's first pressing of the lever was inadvertent. However, because of this action, a food pellet dropped into the cage. The arrival of the food pellet increased the probability that the rat would press the lever again. The pellet is thus said to have *reinforced* lever pressing.

Skinner further mechanized his laboratory procedure by making use of a turning drum, or *cumulative recorder,* a tool that had previously been used by physiologists. The cumulative recorder provides a precise measure of operant behavior. The experimenter need not even be present to record the number of correct responses.

The First "Correct" Response

In operant conditioning, it matters little how the first response that is reinforced comes to be made. The animal can happen on it by chance, as in random learning. The animal can also be physically guided to make the response. You may command your dog to "Sit!" and then press its backside down until it is in a sitting position. Finally you reinforce sitting with food or a pat on the head and a kind word.

Animal trainers use physical guiding or coaxing to bring about the first "correct" response. Can you imagine how long it would take to train your dog if you waited for it to sit or roll over and then seized the opportunity to command it to sit or roll over? Both of you would age significantly in the process.

People, of course, can be verbally guided into desired responses when they are learning tasks such as spelling, adding numbers, or operating a machine. But they need to be informed when they have made the correct response. Knowledge of results often is all the reinforcement people need to learn new skills.

Types of Reinforcers

Any stimulus which increases the probability that responses preceding it will be repeated serves as a reinforcer. *Question: What are the various kinds of reinforcers?* Reinforcers include food pellets when an animal has been deprived of food, water when it has been deprived of liquid, the opportunity to mate, and the sound of a bell that has previously been associated with eating. Skinner distinguished between positive and negative reinforcers.

Water Light Screen

Food pellet dispenser

Food tray Lever

■ **Figure 6.5**
The Effects of Reinforcement

One of the celebrities of modern psychology, a laboratory rat, earns its keep in a Skinner box. The animal presses a lever because of reinforcement—in the form of food pellets—delivered through the feeder. The habit strength of this operant is the frequency of lever pressing.

Positive and Negative Reinforcers

Positive reinforcers increase the probability that a behavior will occur when they are applied. Food and approval usually serve as positive reinforcers. **Negative reinforcers** increase the probability that a behavior will occur when the reinforcers are *removed* (see Figure 6.6). People often learn to plan ahead so that they need not fear that things will go wrong. In such cases fear acts as a negative reinforcer, because *removal* of fear increases the probability that the behaviors preceding it (such as planning ahead or fleeing a predator) will be repeated.

Some reinforcers have more impact than others. For example, pigeons who learn that one food well has more food than another choose the well with more food (Olthof & Roberts, 2000). (Size matters.) Similarly, you would probably choose a job that paid $1,000 over a similar job that paid $10. (If not, get in touch with me—I have some chores for you.) With sufficient reinforcement, operants become *habits*. They have a high probability of recurrence in certain situations.

Immediate Versus Delayed Reinforcers

Immediate reinforcers are more effective than delayed reinforcers. Therefore, the short-term consequences of behavior often provide more of an incentive than the long-term consequences. Some students socialize when they should be studying because the pleasure of socializing is immediate. Studying may not pay off until the final exam or graduation. (This is why younger students do better with frequent tests.) It is difficult to quit smoking cigarettes because the reinforcement of nicotine is immediate and the health hazards of smoking more distant. Focusing on short-term reinforcement is also connected with careless sexual behavior.

Primary and Secondary Reinforcers

We can also distinguish between primary and secondary, or conditioned, reinforcers. **Primary reinforcers** are effective because of an organism's biological makeup. Food, water, adequate warmth (positive reinforcers), and pain (a negative reinforcer) all serve as primary reinforcers. **Secondary reinforcers** acquire their value through being associated with established reinforcers. For this reason they are also termed **conditioned reinforcers.** We may seek money because we have learned that it may be exchanged for primary reinforcers. Money, attention, social approval—all are

Positive Reinforcer
A reinforcer that when *presented* increases the frequency of an operant.

Negative Reinforcer
A reinforcer that when *removed* increases the frequency of an operant.

Primary Reinforcer
An unlearned reinforcer.

Secondary Reinforcer
A stimulus that gains reinforcement value through association with established reinforcers.

Conditioned Reinforcer
Another term for a secondary reinforcer.

Procedure	Behavior	Consequence	Change in behavior
Use of positive reinforcement	Behavior (Studying)	Positive reinforcer (Teacher approval) is *presented* when student studies	Frequency of behavior *increases* (Student studies more)
Use of negative reinforcement	Behavior (Studying)	Negative reinforcer (Teacher disapproval) is *removed* when student studies	Frequency of behavior *increases* (Student studies more)

Power Visual
See Web site for an interactive version of this figure.

■ **Figure 6.6**
Positive Versus Negative Reinforcers

All reinforcers *increase* the frequency of behavior. However, negative reinforcers are aversive stimuli that increase the frequency of behavior when they are *removed*. In these examples, teacher approval functions as a positive reinforcer when students study harder because of it. Teacher *disapproval* functions as a negative reinforcer when its *removal* increases the frequency of studying. Can you think of situations in which teacher approval might function as a negative reinforcer?

conditioned reinforcers in our culture. We may be suspicious of, or not "understand," people who are not interested in money or the approval of others. Part of understanding others lies in being able to predict what they will find reinforcing.

Reinforcers are a key factor in operant conditioning. Let us consider others.

Learning Connections
See Web site for an interactive version of these review questions.

REVIEW

(12) Thorndike originated the law of _____ in learning. (13) He believed that _____ stamp in behavior and punishments stamp it out. (14) Skinner developed the concept of _____ as an alternative to the concepts of reward and punishment. (15) _____ reinforcers increase the probability that operants will occur when they are applied. (16) _____ reinforcers increase the probability that operants will occur when they are removed. (17) _____ reinforcers such as food have their value because of the biological makeup of the organism. (18) _____ reinforcers, such as money, acquire their value through association with established reinforcers.

Critical Thinking: Is Skinner's concept of *reinforcement* more scientific than that of *reward*? Explain.

FACTORS IN OPERANT CONDITIONING

Keisha's teacher writes "Good" on all of her homework assignments before returning them. One day, her teacher no longer writes anything on the assignments. The reinforcement ends. Reinforcers are used to strengthen responses. What happens when reinforcement stops? *Question: What are the roles of extinction and spontaneous recovery in operant conditioning?* In the following sections we consider this question and others.

Extinction and Spontaneous Recovery in Operant Conditioning

In Pavlov's experiment, the meat powder was the event that followed and confirmed the appropriateness of salivation. In operant conditioning, the ensuing events are reinforcers. In operant conditioning the extinction of learned responses results from the repeated performance of operant behavior without reinforcement. If you go for a month without mail, you may stop checking the mailbox because the mail served as reinforcement.

Spontaneous recovery of learned responses occurs in operant conditioning as well as in classical conditioning. That is, finding a few letters in the mailbox one week may again encourage you to check the mailbox regularly.

Reinforcers Versus Rewards and Punishments

Reinforcers are defined as stimuli that increase the frequency of behavior. *Question: Why did Skinner make a point of distinguishing between reinforcers on the one hand and rewards and punishments on the other?* Reinforcers are known by their effects, whereas rewards and punishments are known by how they feel. It may be that most reinforcers—food, hugs, having the other person admit to starting the argument, and so on—feel good, or are pleasant events. Yet things that we might assume would feel bad, such as a slap on the hand or disapproval from a teacher, may be reinforcing to some—perhaps because such experiences confirm negative feelings toward teachers.

Rewards, like reinforcers, tend to increase the frequency of behavior, but rewards are defined as pleasant events, things that tend to feel good. Skinner preferred the concept of reinforcement to that of reward because reinforcement does not suggest trying to "get inside the head" of an organism (whether a human or lower animal) to guess what it would find pleasant or unpleasant. A list of reinforcers is arrived at scientifically, *empirically*—that is, by observing what sorts of stimuli increase the frequency of the behavior. However, we should note that some psychologists use the term *reward* synonymously with *positive reinforcement*.

Punishments are defined as aversive events that suppress or decrease the frequency of the behavior they follow (see Figure 6.7). Punishment can rapidly suppress undesirable behavior (Gershoff, 2002) and may be warranted in "emergencies," such as when a child tries to run into the street.

Question: Why do many psychologists disapprove of punishment?   However, many psychologists argue that punishment—especially corporal punishment—often fails to achieve the goals of parents, teachers, and others. Psychologist Elizabeth Gershoff (2002) analyzed 88 studies of more than 36,000 children and found connections between physical punishment (e.g., spanking) and 11 results in childhood and adulthood. For example:

- Children who are physically punished are less likely to develop internal moral standards.
- Physical punishment is connected with poorer parent–child relationships.
- Physically punished children are more likely to be aggressive toward other children and to engage in criminal behavior later on.
- Physically punished children are more likely to abuse their spouses or their own children as adults.

Gershoff (2002) adds that punishment tends to suppress undesirable behavior only under circumstances in which its delivery is guaranteed. It does not take children long to learn that they can "get away with murder" with one parent or teacher but not with another. Moreover, punishment does not in itself suggest an alternative acceptable form of behavior.

CONTROVERSY IN PSYCHOLOGY

Should children be punished for misbehavior?

Every time I tell my classes that many psychologists frown on the use of punishment, many students chide me for being unrealistic and "goody-goody." Let's try some critical thinking: What are the effects of punishment? Does it work? If so, when? Are there other ways of encouraging desirable behavior? Which is preferable? How can we judge?

Punishment
An unpleasant stimulus that suppresses the behavior it follows.

Power Visual
See Web site for an interactive version of this figure.

■ **Figure 6.7**
Negative Reinforcers Versus Punishments

Negative reinforcers and punishments both tend to be aversive stimuli. However, reinforcers *increase* the frequency of behavior. Punishments *decrease* the frequency of behavior. Negative reinforcers increase the frequency of behavior when they are *removed*. Punishments decrease or suppress the frequency of behavior when they are *applied*. Can you think of situations in which punishing students might have effects other than those desired by the teacher?

There are some other reasons for not using physical punishment:

- It hurts.
- Punished individuals may withdraw from the situation. Severely punished children may run away, cut class, or drop out of school.
- Children also *learn* responses that are punished. Whether or not children choose to perform punished responses, punishment rivets their attention on them.

Gershoff's research findings have not gone unchallenged. Diana Baumrind and her colleagues (2002) point out, for example, that most of the studies examined by Gershoff were correlational, not experimental. Therefore, we cannot be certain about cause and effect. Consider the connection between parental punishment and childhood aggression. Does parental punishment contribute to childhood aggression, or are more aggressive children likely to frustrate their parents, leading their parents to use physical punishment?

In any event, most psychologists tend to prefer rewarding children for desirable behavior to punishing them for unwanted behavior. By ignoring misbehavior, or by using **time out** from positive reinforcement, one can avoid reinforcing misbehavior.

To reward or positively reinforce children for desired behavior takes time and care. Avoiding the use of punishment is not enough. First, we must pay attention to children when they are behaving well. If we take their desirable behavior for granted and respond to them only when they misbehave, we may be encouraging misbehavior. Second, we must be certain that children are aware of, and capable of performing, desired behavior. It is harmful and fruitless merely to punish children for unwanted behavior. We must also carefully guide them, either physically or verbally, into making the desired responses, and then reward them. We cannot teach children table manners by waiting for them to exhibit proper responses at random and then reinforcing them for their responses. Try holding a reward of ice cream behind your back and waiting for a child to exhibit proper manners. You will have a slippery dining room floor long before the child develops good table manners.

Discriminative Stimuli: Do You Step on the Accelerator When the Light Is Green or Red?

B. F. Skinner might not have been able to get his pigeons into the drivers' seats of missiles, but he had no problem training them to respond to traffic lights. Imagine yourself trying the following experiment.

You find a pigeon. Or you sit on a park bench, close your eyes, and one finds you. You place it in a Skinner box with a button on the wall. You drop a food pellet into the cage whenever the pigeon pecks the button. (Soon it will learn to peck the button whenever it has not eaten for a while.) Now you place a small green light in the cage and turn it on and off intermittently throughout the day. Reinforce button pecking with food whenever the green light is on, but not when the light is off. It will not take long for this clever city pigeon to learn that it will gain as much by grooming itself or cooing and flapping around as it will by pecking the button when the light is off.

The green light has become a discriminative stimulus.   ***Question: What are discriminative stimuli?***   **Discriminative stimuli** such as green or red lights act as cues. They provide information about when an operant (in the case of the pigeon, pecking a button) will be reinforced (by a food pellet being dropped into the cage).

Operants that are not reinforced tend to be extinguished. For the pigeon in our experiment, the behavior of pecking the button *when the light is off* is extinguished.

A moment's reflection will suggest many ways in which discriminative stimuli influence our behavior. Isn't it more efficient to answer the telephone when it is ringing? Do you think it is wise to try to kiss your date when she or he is blowing smoke in your face or chewing antacid tablets?

We noted that a pigeon learns to peck a button if food drops into its cage when it does so. What if you want the pigeon to continue to peck the button, but you're running out of food? Do not despair. (Worse things have happened.) As we see in the fol-

Time Out
Removal of an organism from a situation in which reinforcement is available when unwanted behavior is shown.

Discriminative Stimulus
In operant conditioning, a stimulus that indicates that reinforcement is available.

■ **A Discriminative Stimulus**
You might not think that pigeons are very discriminating, yet they readily learn that pecking will not bring food in the presence of a discriminative stimulus such as a red light.

lowing section, you can keep that bird pecking away indefinitely, even as you hold up on most of the food.

Schedules of Reinforcement: How Often? Under What Conditions?

In operant conditioning, some responses are maintained by means of **continuous reinforcement.** You probably become warmer every time you put on heavy clothing. You probably become less thirsty every time you drink water. Yet if you have ever watched people toss their money down the maws of slot machines, you know that behavior can also be maintained by means of **partial reinforcement.** *Questions: What are the various schedules of reinforcement? How do they affect behavior?*

Folklore about gambling is based on solid learning theory. You can get a person "hooked" on gambling by fixing the game so as to allow heavy winnings at first. Then you gradually space out the winnings (reinforcements) until gambling is maintained by infrequent winning—or even no winning at all. Partial reinforcement schedules can maintain gambling, like other behavior, for a great deal of time, even though it goes unreinforced (Pulley, 1998).

New operants or behaviors are acquired most rapidly through continuous reinforcement or, in some cases, through "one-trial learning" that meets with great reinforcement. People who cannot control their gambling often had big wins at the racetrack or casino or in the lottery in their late teens or early twenties (Blanco et al., 2000). But once the operant has been acquired, it can be maintained by tapering off to a schedule of partial reinforcement.

Responses that have been maintained by partial reinforcement are more resistant to extinction than responses that have been maintained by continuous reinforcement (Rescorla, 1999). From the cognitive perspective, we could suggest that organisms that have experienced partial reinforcement do not expect reinforcement every time they engage in a response. Therefore, they are more likely to persist in the absence of reinforcement.

There are four basic types of reinforcement schedules. They are determined by changing either the *interval* of time that must elapse between correct responses before reinforcement occurs or the *ratio* (number) of responses that must occur before reinforcement is provided. If reinforcement of responses is immediate (zero seconds), the reinforcement schedule is continuous. A larger interval of time, such as 1 or 30 seconds, is one kind of partial-reinforcement schedule. A one-to-one (1:1) ratio of correct responses to reinforcements is also a continuous-reinforcement schedule. A higher ratio such as 2:1 or 5:1 creates another kind of partial-reinforcement schedule.

More specifically, the four basic reinforcement schedules are *fixed-interval, variable-interval, fixed-ratio,* and *variable-ratio* schedules.

Interval Schedules

In a **fixed-interval schedule,** a fixed amount of time—say, a minute—must elapse between the previous and subsequent times when reinforcement for correct responses occurs. With a fixed-interval schedule, an organism's response rate falls off after each reinforcement and then picks up again as the time when reinforcement will occur approaches. For example, in a 1-minute fixed-interval schedule, a rat is reinforced with, say, a food pellet for the first operant—for example, the first pressing of a lever— that occurs after a minute has elapsed. After each reinforcement, the rat's rate of lever pressing slows down, but as the end of the 1-minute interval draws near, lever pressing increases in frequency, as suggested in Figure 6.8. It is as if the rat has learned that it must wait a while before it is reinforced. The resultant record on the cumulative recorder shows a series of characteristic upward-moving waves, or scallops, which are referred to as *fixed-interval scallops.*

Car dealers use fixed-interval reinforcement schedules when they offer incentives for buying up the remainder of the year's line every summer and fall. In a sense, they are suppressing buying at other times, except for consumers whose current cars are in their death throes or those with little self-control. Similarly, you learn to check your e-mail only at a certain time of day if your correspondent writes at that time each day.

Continuous Reinforcement
A schedule of reinforcement in which every correct response is reinforced.

Partial Reinforcement
One of several reinforcement schedules in which not every correct response is reinforced.

Fixed-Interval Schedule
A schedule in which a fixed amount of time must elapse between the previous and subsequent times that reinforcement is available.

REFLECT

How do you think a behaviorist and a cognitive psychologist might each explain the effects of a partial-reinforcement schedule on gamblers?

■ **Figure 6.8**
The "Fixed-Interval Scallop"

Organisms who are reinforced on a fixed-interval schedule tend to slack off responding after each reinforcement. The rate of response picks up as they near the time when reinforcement will become available. The results on the cumulative recorder look like upward-moving waves, or scallops.

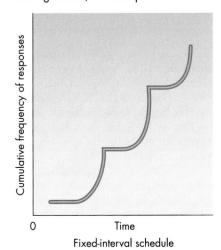

Variable-Interval Schedule

A schedule in which a variable amount of time must elapse between the previous and subsequent times that reinforcement is available.

Fixed-Ratio Schedule

A schedule in which reinforcement is provided after a fixed number of correct responses.

Variable-Ratio Schedule

A schedule in which reinforcement is provided after a variable number of correct responses.

Reinforcement is more unpredictable in a **variable-interval schedule.** Therefore, the response rate is steadier but lower. If the boss calls us in for a weekly report, we probably work hard to pull things together just before the report is to be given, just as we might cram the night before a weekly quiz. But if we know that the boss might call us in for a report on the progress of a certain project at any time (variable-interval schedule), we are likely to keep things in a state of reasonable readiness at all times. However, our efforts are unlikely to have the intensity they would in a fixed-interval schedule (for example, a weekly report). Similarly, we are less likely to cram for unpredictable pop quizzes than we are to study for regularly scheduled quizzes. But we are likely to do at least some studying on a regular basis. If you receive e-mail from your correspondent irregularly, you are likely to check your e-mail regularly, but with less eagerness.

Ratio Schedules

In a **fixed-ratio schedule,** reinforcement is provided after a fixed number of correct responses have been made. In a **variable-ratio schedule,** reinforcement is provided after a variable number of correct responses have been made. In a 10:1 variable-ratio schedule, the mean number of correct responses that would have to be made before a subsequent correct response would be reinforced is 10, but the ratio of correct responses to reinforcements might be allowed to vary from, say, 1:1 to 20:1 on a random basis.

A Closer Look

Applications of Operant Conditioning: Bleeps, Behavior Mod, and Programmed Learning

Operant conditioning, like classical conditioning, is not just an exotic laboratory procedure. We use it every day in our efforts to influence other people. Parents and peers induce children to acquire so-called gender-appropriate behavior patterns through rewards and punishments. Parents also tend to praise their children for sharing their toys and to punish them for being too aggressive. Peers participate in the socialization process by playing with children who are generous and nonaggressive and, often, by avoiding those who are not (Warman & Cohen, 2000).

Operant conditioning also plays a role in attitude formation. Adults often reward children for expressing attitudes that coincide with their own and punish or ignore them for expressing contradictory attitudes. Let us now consider some specific applications of operant conditioning.

Biofeedback Training: Gaining "Bleep" Control?

Biofeedback training (BFT) is based on principles of operant conditioning. BFT has enabled people and lower animals to learn to control autonomic responses in order to attain reinforcement (Miller, 1969). BFT has been an important innovation in the treatment of health-related problems during the past few decades.

Through BFT, organisms can gain control of autonomic functions such as the flow of blood in a finger. They can also learn to improve their control over functions that can be manipulated voluntarily, such as muscle tension. When people receive BFT, reinforcement is given in the form of *information*. Perhaps a sound changes in pitch or frequency of occurrence to signal that they have modified the autonomic function in the desired direction. For example, we can learn to emit alpha waves—the kind of brain wave associated with feelings of relaxation—through feedback from an electroencephalograph (an instrument that

measures brain waves). Through the use of other instruments, people have learned to lower their muscle tension, their heart rates, and even their blood pressure.

BFT is also used with people who have lost neuromuscular control of parts of their body as a result of an accident. A "bleep" sound informs them when they have contracted a muscle or sent an impulse down a neural pathway. By concentrating on changing the bleeps, they also gradually regain voluntary control over the damaged function.

Principles of operant conditioning have also enabled psychologists and educators to develop many beneficial innovations, such as behavior modification in the classroom and programmed learning.

Behavior Modification in the Classroom: Accentuating the Positive

Remember that reinforcers are defined as stimuli that increase the frequency of behavior—not as pleasant events. Ironically, adults frequently reinforce undesirable behavior in children by paying attention to them, or punishing them, when they misbehave but ignoring them when they behave in desirable ways. Similarly, teachers who raise their voices when children misbehave may be unintentionally conferring hero status on those pupils in the eyes of their peers. To the teacher's surprise, some children may go out of their way to earn disapproval.

Teacher preparation and in-service programs show teachers how to use behavior modification to reverse these response patterns. Teachers are taught to pay attention to children when they are behaving appropriately and, when possible, to ignore (that is, avoid reinforcing) misbehavior. The younger the child, the more powerful the teacher's attention and approval seem to be.

Fixed- and variable-ratio schedules maintain a high response rate. With a fixed-ratio schedule, it is as if the organism learns that it must make several responses before being reinforced. It then "gets them out of the way" as rapidly as possible. Consider the example of piecework. If a worker must sew five shirts to receive $10, he or she is on a fixed-ratio (5:1) schedule and is likely to sew at a uniformly high rate, although there might be a brief pause after each reinforcement. With a variable-ratio schedule, reinforcement can come at any time. This unpredictability also maintains a high response rate. Slot machines tend to pay off on variable-ratio schedules, and players can be seen popping coins into them and yanking their "arms" with barely a pause. I have seen players who do not even stop to pick up their winnings. Instead, they continue to pop in the coins, whether from their original stack or from the winnings tray.

Shaping

If you are teaching hip-hop to people who have never danced, do not wait until they have performed it precisely before telling them they're on the right track. The foxtrot will be back in style before they have learned a thing.

We can teach complex behaviors by **shaping.** *Question: How can we use shaping to teach complex behavior patterns?* Shaping reinforces progressive steps toward the behavioral goal. At first, for example, it may be wise to smile and say

Shaping

A procedure for teaching complex behaviors that at first reinforces approximations of the target behavior.

Among older children and adolescents, peer approval is often a more powerful reinforcer than teacher approval. Peer approval may maintain misbehavior, and ignoring misbehavior may only allow peers to become more disruptive. In such cases it may be necessary to separate troublesome children from less-disruptive peers.

Teachers also frequently use time out from positive reinforcement to discourage misbehavior. In this method, children are placed in a drab, restrictive environment for a specified period, usually about 10 minutes, when they behave disruptively. While they are isolated, they cannot earn the attention of peers or teachers, and no reinforcers are present.

Programmed Learning: Step by Step

B. F. Skinner developed an educational method called *programmed learning* that is based on operant conditioning. This method assumes that any complex task involving conceptual learning as well as motor skills can be broken down into a number of small steps. These steps can be shaped individually and then combined in sequence to form the correct behavioral chain.

Programmed learning does not punish errors. Instead, correct responses are reinforced. Every child earns "100," but at her or his own pace. Programmed learning also assumes it is the task of the teacher (or program) to structure the learning experience in such a way that errors will not be made.

Some argue that behaviorism is too mechanical to be applied to humans. But the bell-and-pad method, behaviorist methods of fear reduction, use of avoidance learning to prevent the baby from vomiting, and other methods suggest that some useful methods would not have been derived from any other psychological theory. Because of applications like these, some psychologists argue that the full promise of behaviorism has not yet been realized (DeGrandpre, 2000).

■ Praise

Praise from the teacher reinforces desirable behavior in most children. Behavior modification in the classroom applies principles of operant conditioning.

■ Slot Machines Pay Off on Unpredictable Variable-Ratio Schedules

Because "one-armed bandits" make unpredictable payoffs, people tend to maintain a high response rate—that is, to drop coins into them in rapid succession.

REFLECT

A pianist's fingers fly over the keys faster than the player can read notes or even think notes. What kinds of learning are at work in learning to play the piano?

Successive Approximations
Behaviors that are progressively closer to a target behavior.

Learning Connections
See Web site for an interactive version of these review questions.

"Good" when a reluctant newcomer gathers the courage to get out on the dance floor, even if your feet are flattened by his initial clumsiness. If you are teaching someone to drive a car with a standard shift, at first generously reinforce the learner simply for shifting gears without stalling.

But as training proceeds, we come to expect more before we are willing to provide reinforcement. We reinforce **successive approximations** of the goal. If you want to train a rat to climb a ladder, first reinforce it with a food pellet when it turns toward the ladder. Then wait until it approaches the ladder before giving it a pellet. Then do not drop a pellet into the cage until the rat touches the ladder. In this way, the rat will reach the top of the ladder more quickly than if you had waited for the target behavior to occur at random.

Learning to drive a new standard-shift automobile to a new job also involves a complex sequence of operant behaviors. At first we actively seek out all the discriminative stimuli or landmarks that give us cues for when to turn—signs, buildings, hills, valleys. We also focus on shifting to a lower gear as we slow so the car won't stall. After many repetitions, these responses, or chains of behavior chains, become habitual and we need to pay very little attention to them.

Have you ever driven home and suddenly realized that you couldn't recall exactly how you got there? Your entire trip may seem "lost." Were you in great danger? How could you allow such a thing to happen? Actually, your driving and your responses to the demands of the route may have become so habitual that you did not have to focus on them. As you drove, you were able to think about dinner, work, or the weekend. But if something unusual had occurred on the way, such as an engine problem or a rainstorm, you would have devoted as much attention to your driving as was needed to arrive home. Your trip was probably quite safe after all.

REVIEW

(19) In operant conditioning, repeated performance of a learned response in the absence of reinforcement leads to _____ of that response. (20) _____ are aversive stimuli that suppress the frequency of behavior. (21) A _____ stimulus indicates when an operant will be reinforced. (22) In a _____-_____ schedule, a specific amount of time must elapse since a previous correct response before reinforcement again becomes available. (23) In a _____

_____ schedule, the number of correct responses that must be performed before reinforcement becomes available is allowed to vary. (24) In shaping, we reinforce _____ approximations to the goal.

Critical Thinking: Agree or disagree with the following statement and support your answer: We should not punish children.

COGNITIVE FACTORS IN LEARNING: IS IT NATURAL TO MENTALLY REPRESENT THE ENVIRONMENT?

Classical and operant conditioning were originally conceived of as relatively simple forms of learning. Much of conditioning's appeal is that it can be said to meet the behaviorist objective of explaining behavior in terms of observable events—in this case, laboratory conditions. Building on this theoretical base, some psychologists have suggested that the most complex human behavior involves the summation of a series of instances of conditioning. However, many psychologists believe that conditioning is too mechanical a process to explain all instances of learned behavior, even in laboratory rats (Weiner, 1991). They turn to cognitive factors to describe and explain additional findings in the psychology of learning. *Question: How do we explain what happens during classical conditioning from a cognitive perspective?*

A Closer Look ◉

Contingency Theory

We have noted that behaviorists and cognitive psychologists interpret the conditioning process in different ways. Behaviorists explain it in terms of the pairing of stimuli. Cognitive psychologists explain classical conditioning in terms of the ways in which stimuli provide information that allows organisms to form and revise mental representations of their environment (Basic Behavioral Science Task Force, 1996b). Robert Rescorla conducted research in an effort to demonstrate which view is more accurate. His viewpoint, *contingency theory,* suggests that learning occurs only when the conditioned stimulus provides *information* about the unconditioned stimulus.

In classical conditioning experiments with dogs, Rescorla (1988) obtained some results that are difficult to explain without reference to cognitive concepts. Each phase of his work paired a tone (a learned or conditioned stimulus, or CS) with an electric shock (an unlearned or unconditioned stimulus, or US), but in different ways. With one group of animals, the shock was consistently presented after the tone. That is, the unconditioned stimulus followed on the heels of the conditioned stimulus, as in Pavlov's studies. The dogs in this group learned to show a fear response when the tone was presented.

A second group of dogs heard an equal number of tones and received an equal number of electric shocks, but the shock never immediately followed the tone. In other words, the tone and the shock were not paired. Now, from the behaviorist perspective, the dogs should not have learned to associate the tone and the shock because one did not predict the other. Actually, the dogs learned quite a lot: They learned that they had nothing to fear when the tone was sounded! They showed vigilance and

fear when the laboratory was quiet—for the shock could apparently come at any time—but they were calm in the presence of the tone.

The third group of dogs also received equal numbers of tones and shocks, but the stimuli were presented at purely random intervals. Occasionally they were paired, but most often they were not. According to Rescorla, behaviorists might argue that intermittent pairing of the tones and shocks should have brought about some learning. Yet it did not. The animals showed no fear in response to the tone. Rescorla suggests that the animals in this group learned nothing because the tones did not allow them to make predictions about electric shock.

Rescorla concluded that contiguity—that is, the co-appearance of two events (the unconditioned stimulus and the conditioned stimulus)—cannot in itself explain classical conditioning. Instead, learning occurs only when the conditioned stimulus (in this case, the tone) provides information about the unconditioned stimulus (in this case, the shock). According to contingency theory, learning occurs because a conditioned stimulus indicates that the unconditioned stimulus is likely to follow.

Behaviorists might counter, of course, that for the second group of dogs the *absence* of the tone became the signal for the shock. Shock may be a powerful enough event that the fear response becomes conditioned to the laboratory environment. For the third group of dogs, the shock was as likely to occur in the presence of the neutral stimulus as in its absence. Therefore, many behaviorists would expect no learning to occur.

In addition to concepts such as *association* and *reinforcement,* cognitive psychologists use concepts such as *mental structures, schemas, templates,* and *information processing.* Cognitive psychologists see people as searching for information, weighing evidence, and making decisions. Let us consider some classic research that points to cognitive factors in learning, as opposed to mechanical associations. These cognitive factors are not necessarily limited to humans—although, of course, people are the only species that can talk about them.

Latent Learning: Forming Cognitive Maps

I'm all grown up. I know the whole mall.

—The author's daughter Jordan at age 7

Many behaviorists argue that organisms acquire only responses, or operants, for which they are reinforced. E. C. Tolman, however, showed that rats also learn about their environment in the absence of reinforcement. In doing so, he demonstrated that rats must form cognitive maps of their surroundings. **Question: What is the evidence that people and lower organisms form cognitive maps of their environments?**

Tolman trained some rats to run through mazes for standard food goals. Other rats were permitted to explore the same mazes for several days without food goals or other rewards. After the unrewarded rats had been allowed to explore the mazes for ten days, food rewards were placed in a box at the far end of the maze. The previously unrewarded rats reached the food box as quickly as the rewarded rats after only one or two reinforced trials (Tolman & Honzik, 1930).

REFLECT

Have you ever studied an atlas, a road map, a cookbook, or a computer manual for the pleasure of doing so? What kind of learning were you engaging in?

Tolman concluded that rats learned about mazes in which they roamed even when they were unrewarded for doing so. He distinguished between *learning* and *performance.* Rats would acquire a cognitive map of a maze; and, even though they would not be motivated to follow an efficient route to the far end, they would learn rapid routes from one end to the other just by roaming about within the maze. Yet this learning might remain hidden, or **latent,** until they were motivated to follow the rapid routes to obtain food goals.

Latent
Hidden or concealed.

■ How Do They Learn Their Way Around the Mall?
Have these shoppers simply been conditioned to turn left or right at various choice points like so many rats in a maze, or have they learned to mentally represent the mall? (And do rats also learn to mentally represent mazes?)

Observational Learning: Monkey See, Monkey *May* Choose to Do?

How many things have you learned from watching other people in real life, in films, and on television? From films and television, you may have gathered vague ideas about how to sky-dive, ride a surfboard, climb sheer cliffs, run a pattern to catch a touchdown pass in the Super Bowl, and dust for fingerprints, even if you have never tried these activities yourself. *Question: How do people learn by observing others?*

In their studies of social learning, Albert Bandura and his colleagues conducted experiments (e.g., Bandura et al., 1963) that show that we can acquire operants by observing the behavior of others. We may need some practice to refine the operants, but we can learn them through observation alone. We may also allow these operants or skills to remain latent. For example, we may not imitate aggressive behavior unless we are provoked and believe that we are more likely to be rewarded than punished for it.

Observational learning may account for most human learning. It occurs when, as children, we watch our parents cook, clean, or repair a broken appliance. Observational learning takes place when we watch teachers solve problems on the blackboard or hear them speak in a foreign language. Observational learning is not mechanically acquired through reinforcement. We can learn through observation without engaging in overt responses at all. It appears sufficient to pay attention to the behavior of others.

In the terminology of observational learning, a person who engages in a response to be imitated is a **model.** When observers see a model being reinforced for displaying an operant, the observers are said to be *vicariously* reinforced. Display of the operant thus becomes more likely for the observer as well as for the model. Table 6.1 reviews various kinds of learning.

It would be of little use to discuss how we learn if we were not capable of remembering what we learn from second to second, from day to day, or in many cases for a lifetime. In the next chapter we turn our attention to the subject of memory. In Chapter 8 we will see how learning is intertwined with thinking, language, and intelligence.

Observational Learning
The acquisition of knowledge and skills through the observation of others (who are called *models*) rather than by means of direct experience.

Model
An organism that engages in a response that is then imitated by another organism.

■ Observational Learning
Cognitive psychologists note that people usually do not learn complex skills on the basis of the summation of so many instances of conditioning. Rather, we can intend to learn, focus on models, and imitate or adapt the behaviors we observe.

TABLE 6.1 Kinds of Learning

Kind of Learning	What Is Learned	How It Is Learned
Classical conditioning	Association of events; anticipations, signs, expectations; automatic responses to new stimuli	A neutral stimulus (CS) is repeatedly paired with a stimulus (US) that elicits a response (UR) until the neutral stimulus produces a response (CR) that anticipates and prepares for the US.
Operant conditioning	Behavior that operates on, or affects, the environment to produce consequences	A response is rewarded or reinforced so that it occurs with greater frequency in similar situations.
Observational learning	Expectations (if–then relationships), knowledge, and skills	A person observes the behavior of another person (live or through media such as films, television, or books) and its effects.

Learning Connections
See Web site for an interactive version of these review questions.

REVIEW

(25) According to _____ theory, learning occurs when the CS provides information about the US. (26) Tolman's work with rats suggests that they develop _____ maps of the environment. (27) Tolman refers to learning without performing as _____ learning.

Critical Thinking: How do the results of research into cognitive factors in learning challenge behaviorist principles? Refer to contingency theory, latent learning, and observational learning in your answer.

LIFE CONNECTIONS

Violence in the Media and Aggression

Much human learning occurs through observation. We learn by observing parents and peers, attending school, reading books, and watching media such as television and films. Nearly all of us have been exposed to television, videotapes, and films in the classroom. Children in day care centers often watch *Sesame Street.* There are filmed and electronic versions of great works of literature such as Orson Welles's *Macbeth* or Laurence Olivier's *Hamlet.* Nearly every school shows films of laboratory experiments. Sometimes we view "canned lectures" by master teachers.

But what of our exposure to these media *outside* the classroom? Television is one of our major sources of informal observational learning. Children are routinely exposed to scenes of murder, beating, and sexual assault—just by turning on the TV set (Huesmann & Miller, 1994; Wilson, 1997). If a child watches two to four hours of TV a day, she or he will have seen 8,000 murders and another 100,000 acts of violence *by the time she or he has finished elementary school* (Eron, 1993). Are kids less likely to be exposed to violence by going to the movies? No. One study found that virtually all G-rated animated films have scenes of violence, with a mean duration of 9 to 10 minutes per film (Yokota & Thompson, 2000). Other media that contain violence include movies, rock music and music videos, advertising, video games, and the Internet (Villani, 2001).

A classic study by Bandura, Ross, and Ross (1963) suggests the powerful influence of televised models on children's aggressive behavior.

■ What Are the Effects of Media Violence?

Preschool children in the United States watch TV an average of four hours a day. Schoolchildren spend more hours at the TV set than in the classroom. Is it any wonder that psychologists, educators, and parents express concern about the effects of media violence?

One group of preschool children observed a film of an adult model hitting and kicking an inflated Bobo doll, while a control group saw an aggression-free film. The experimental and control children were then left alone in a room with the same doll, as hidden observers recorded their behavior. The children who had observed the aggressive model showed significantly more aggressive behavior toward the doll themselves (see Figure 6.9). Many children imitated bizarre attack behaviors devised for the model in this experiment—behaviors that they would not have thought up themselves.

The children exposed to the aggressive model also showed aggressive behavior patterns that had not been modeled. Observing the model, therefore, not only led to imitation of modeled behavior patterns, but also apparently disinhibited previously learned aggressive responses. The results were similar whether children observed human or cartoon models on film.

Violence tends to be glamorized in the media. For example, in one cartoon show, superheroes battle villains who are trying to destroy or take over the world. Violence is often shown to have only temporary or minimal effects. (How often has Wile E. Coyote fallen from a cliff and been pounded into the ground by a boulder, only to bounce back and pursue the Road Runner once more?) In the great majority of violent TV shows, there is no remorse, criticism, or penalty for violent behavior (Cantor, 1997). Few TV programs depict harmful long-term consequences of aggressive behavior. Seeing the perpetrator of the violence go unpunished increases the chances that the child will act aggressively (Krcmar & Cooke,

■ Figure 6.9
Classic Research on the Imitation of Aggressive Models

Albert Bandura and his colleagues found evidence that children frequently imitate the aggressive behavior that they observe. In the top row, an adult model strikes a clown doll. The lower rows show a boy and a girl imitating the aggressive behavior.

2001). Children may not even view death as much of a problem. How many times do video-game characters "die"—only to be reborn to fight again because the children have won multiple lives?

Why all this violence? Simple: Violence sells. But does violence do more than sell? That is, does media violence *cause* real violence? If so, what can parents and educators do to prevent the fictional from spilling over into the real world?

In any event, most organizations of health professionals agree that media violence does contribute to aggression (Holland, 2000;

Villani, 2001). This relationship has been found for girls and boys of different ages, social classes, ethnic groups, and cultures. Consider a number of ways in which depictions of violence make such a contribution:

- *Observational learning.* Children learn from observation (Holland, 2000). TV violence supplies *models* of aggressive "skills," which children may acquire. In fact, children are more likely to imitate what their parents do than to heed what they say. If adults say that they disapprove of aggression but smash furniture or slap each other when frustrated, children are likely to develop the notion that aggression is the way to handle frustration. Classic experiments show that children tend to imitate the aggressive behavior they see in the media (Bandura et al., 1963). Media violence also provides viewers with aggressive *scripts*—that is, ideas about how to behave in situations like those they have observed (Huesmann & Miller, 1994).
- *Disinhibition.* Punishment inhibits behavior. Conversely, media violence may disinhibit aggressive behavior, especially when media characters "get away" with violence or are rewarded for it.
- *Increased emotional arousal.* Media violence and aggressive video games increase viewers' level of emotional arousal. That is, television "works them up." We are more likely to be aggressive when we are highly aroused
- *Priming of aggressive thoughts and memories.* Media violence "primes" or arouses aggressive ideas and memories (Bushman, 1998).
- *Habituation.* We become "habituated to," or used to, repeated stimuli. Repeated exposure to TV violence may decrease viewers' sensitivity to real violence. If children come to perceive violence as the norm, they may become more tolerant of it and place less value on restraining aggressive urges (Holland, 2000).

A joint statement issued by the American Medical Association, the American Academy of Pediatrics, the American Psychological Association, and the American Academy of Child and Adolescent Psychiatry (Holland, 2000) made some additional points:

- Children who see a lot of violence are more likely to view violence as an effective way of settling conflicts. Children exposed to violence are more likely to assume that violence is acceptable.
- Viewing violence can decrease the likelihood that one will take action on behalf of a victim when violence occurs.
- Viewing violence may lead to real-life violence. Children exposed to violent programming at a young age are more likely to be violent themselves later on in life.

There seems to be a circular relationship between exposure to media violence and aggressive behavior (Anderson & Dill, 2000; Eron, 1982; Funk et al., 2000). Yes, TV violence and violent video games contribute to aggressive behavior, but aggressive youngsters are also more likely to seek out this kind of "entertainment." Figure 6.10 explores the possible connections between TV violence and aggressive behavior among viewers.

Aggressive children are frequently rejected by agemates who are not aggressive—at least in middle-class culture (Eron, 1982; Warman & Cohen, 2000). Aggressive children may watch more television because their peer relationships are less fulfilling and because the high incidence of TV violence tends to confirm their view that aggressive behavior is normal (Eron, 1982). Media violence interacts with other contributors to violence. The family constellation also affects the likelihood that children will imitate the violence they see on TV. Studies find that parental substance abuse, paternal physical punishments, and single motherhood contribute to the likelihood of aggression in early childhood (Brook et al., 2001; Gupta et al., 2001). Parental rejection and use of physical punishment further increase the likelihood of aggression in children (Eron, 1982). These family factors suggest that the parents of aggressive children are absent or unlikely to help young children understand that the kinds of socially inappropriate behaviors they see in the media are not for them. A harsh home life may also confirm the TV viewer's vision of the world as a violent place and further encourage reliance on television for companionship.

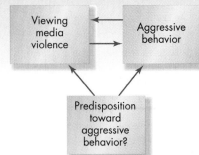

■ Figure 6.10
What Are the Connections Between Media Violence and Aggressive Behavior?

Does media violence cause aggressive behavior? Do aggressive children prefer to tune in to violent shows? Or do third factors, such as personality traits that create a disposition toward aggression, contribute both to aggressive behavior and the observation of violent shows?

Teaching Children Not to Imitate Media Violence

Children are going to be exposed to media violence—if not in Saturday morning cartoon shows, then in evening dramas and in the news. Or they'll hear about violence from friends, watch other children get into fights, or read about violence in the newspapers. If all those sources of violence were somehow hidden from view, they would learn about violence in *Hamlet, Macbeth,* and even the Bible. The notion of preventing children from being exposed to violent models may be impractical.

What, then, should be done? Parents and educators can do many things to tone down the impact of media violence (Broder, 2000; Huesmann et al., 1983). Children who watch violent shows act less aggressively when they are informed that:

- The violent behavior they observe in the media does *not* represent the behavior of most people.
- The apparently aggressive behaviors they watch are not real. They reflect camera tricks, special effects, and stunts.
- Most people resolve conflicts by nonviolent means.
- The real-life consequences of violence are harmful to the victim and, often, the aggressor.

Despite our history of evolutionary forces, and despite the fact that in most species, successful aggression usually wins individuals the right to transmit their genes to future generations, humans are thinking beings. If children consider violence to be inappropriate for them, they will be less likely to act aggressively, even when they have acquired aggressive skills from exposure to the media or other sources.

Recite Recite Recite

Learning Connections
See Web site for an interactive version of this chapter summary

1. **What is learning?**

Learning is the process by which experience leads to modified representations of the environment (the cognitive perspective) and relatively permanent changes in behavior (the behavioral perspective).

2. **What is classical conditioning?**

Classical conditioning is a simple form of associative learning in which a previously neutral stimulus (the conditioned stimulus, or CS) comes to elicit the response evoked by a second stimulus (the unconditioned stimulus, or US) as a result of repeatedly being paired with the second stimulus.

3. **What is the contribution of Ivan Pavlov to the psychology of learning?**

The Russian physiologist Ivan Pavlov happened upon conditioning by chance, as he was studying salivation in laboratory dogs. Pavlov discovered that reflexes can be learned, or *conditioned*, through association.

4. **What are taste aversions? Why are they of special interest to psychologists?**

Taste aversions are examples of classical conditioning in which organisms learn that a food is noxious on the basis of a nauseating experience. Taste aversions are of special interest because learning may occur on the basis of a single association and because the unconditioned stimulus (in this case, nausea) can occur hours after the conditioned stimulus (in this case, the flavor of food). Taste aversions apparently provide organisms with an evolutionary advantage.

5. **What are the roles of extinction and spontaneous recovery in classical conditioning?**

Extinction and spontaneous recovery help organisms adapt to environmental changes. After a US–CS association has been learned, for example, repeated presentation of the CS (for example, a bell) without the US (meat powder) extinguishes the CR (salivation). Extinguished responses may show spontaneous recovery as a function of the time that has elapsed since extinction occurred.

6. **What are the roles of generalization and discrimination in classical conditioning?**

Generalization and discrimination are also adaptive. Generalization helps organisms adapt to new events by responding to a range of stimuli similar to the CS. In discrimination, organisms learn to show a CR in response to a more limited range of stimuli by pairing only the limited stimulus with the US.

7. **What is higher-order conditioning?**

In higher-order conditioning, a previously neutral stimulus comes to serve as a CS after being paired repeatedly with a stimulus that has already become a CS.

8. **What is the contribution of B. F. Skinner to the psychology of learning?**

Skinner developed the concept of reinforcement, encouraged the study of discrete behaviors such as lever pressing by rats, and innovated many techniques for studying operant conditioning such as the "Skinner box" and the cumulative recorder. He was also involved in the development of behavior modification and programmed learning.

9. **What is operant conditioning?**

Operant conditioning is a simple form of learning in which organisms learn to engage in behavior that is reinforced. Reinforced responses occur with greater frequency.

10. **What are the various kinds of reinforcers?**

These include positive, negative, primary, and secondary reinforcers. Positive reinforcers increase the probability that operants will occur when they are applied. Negative reinforcers increase the probability that operants will occur when they are removed. Primary reinforcers have their value because of the organism's biological makeup. Secondary reinforcers such as money and approval acquire their value through association with established reinforcers.

11. **What are the roles of extinction and spontaneous recovery in operant conditioning?**

Extinction and spontaneous recovery are also adaptive in operant conditioning. In operant conditioning, learned responses are extinguished as a result of repeated performance in the absence of reinforcement. (Why continue to engage in a response that goes unreinforced?) And as in classical conditioning, spontaneous recovery occurs as a function of the passage of time, which is adaptive because things may return to the way they were.

Recite   Recite   Recite

12. **Why did Skinner make a point of distinguishing between reinforcers on the one hand and rewards and punishments on the other?**

Rewards and punishments are defined, respectively, as pleasant and aversive events that affect behavior. Skinner preferred the concept of *reinforcement* because its definition does not rely on getting inside the head of the organism. Instead, lists of reinforcers are obtained empirically, by observing their effects on behavior.

13. **Why do many psychologists disapprove of punishment?**

Many psychologists recommend not using punishment because it hurts, it does not suggest acceptable behavior, it may create feelings of hostility, it may only suppress behavior in the specific situation in which it is used, it may generalize to the suppression of wide varieties of behavior, and it may suggest that recipients punish others as a way of coping with stress.

14. **What are discriminative stimuli?**

Discriminative stimuli (such as green lights) indicate when operants (such as pecking a button) will be reinforced (as with food).

15. **What are the various schedules of reinforcement? How do they affect behavior?**

Continuous reinforcement leads to the most rapid acquisition of new responses, but operants are maintained most economically through partial reinforcement. There are four basic schedules of reinforcement. In a fixed-interval schedule, a specific amount of time must elapse after a previous correct response before reinforcement again becomes available. In a variable-interval schedule, the amount of time is allowed to vary. In a fixed-ratio schedule, a fixed number of correct responses must be performed before one is reinforced. In a variable-ratio schedule, this number is allowed to vary. Ratio schedules maintain high response rates.

16. **How can we use shaping to teach complex behavior patterns?**

In shaping, successive approximations of the target response are reinforced, leading to the performance of a complex sequence of behaviors.

17. **How do we explain what happens during classical conditioning from a cognitive perspective?**

According to contingency theory, organisms learn associations between stimuli only when stimuli provide new information about each other. From this perspective, classical conditioning does not occur mechanically but because it provides information.

18. **What is the evidence that people and lower organisms form cognitive maps of their environments?**

Some evidence is derived from Tolman's research on latent learning. He demonstrated that rats can learn—that is, they can modify their cognitive map of the environment—in the absence of reinforcement.

19. **How do people learn by observing others?**

Bandura has shown that people can learn to do things simply by observing others; it is not necessary that they emit responses that are reinforced in order to learn. Learners may then choose to perform the behaviors they have observed "when the time is ripe"—that is, when they believe that the learned behavior is appropriate or is likely to be rewarded.

Active Learning Resources

 Search Online with InfoTrac® College Edition

For additional information on the topics in this chapter, explore InfoTrac College Edition, your online library. Go to **http://www.infotrac.thomsonlearning.com** and use the passcode that came on the card with your book. Try these search terms: behaviorism in psychology, classical conditioning, conditioned taste aversion, operant conditioning, B. F. Skinner, reinforcement, cognitive map, and violence in the media.

 Visit Our Web Site

Go to **http://www.wadsworth.com/psychology**, where you will find online resources directly linked to your book, including interactive exercises related to PQ4R and Power Visuals for mastering and reviewing key concepts. In addition, you will find hints on using InfoTrac College Edition to answer the Critical Thinking questions throughout the text. Start with the **Self Study Assessment** for a customized **Study Plan** generated by taking the **Pre-Test** and **Post-Test.**

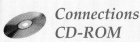 *Connections CD-ROM*

Go to the Wadsworth *Connections* CD-ROM for further study of the concepts in this chapter. The CD-ROM includes videos and animations as well as additional activities to expand your learning experience, plus interactive self-assessments to help connect the material to your own life.

 Psyk.trek™ CD-ROM

The Wadsworth *Psyk.trek* CD-ROM offers tutorials, simulations, videos, multimedia glossary, and quizzing to help you master the material.

 PsychNow! CD-ROM

The Wadsworth *PsychNow!* CD-ROM includes interactive exercises, videos, and animations to enhance your learning.

7 Memory: Remembrance of Things Past—and Future

Five Challenges to Memory

- **WHAT DOES A PENNY** look like? Are you sure?

Kinds of Memory: Looking Back, Looking Forward

- **A WOMAN WHO COULD** not remember who she was automatically dialed her mother's phone number when the police gave her a telephone.

- **OH SAY, CAN YOU SEE?** If the answer is yes, you have a photographic memory.

Processes of Memory: Processing Information in Our Most Personal Computers

- **YOUR MEMORY HAS** "Save" and "Find" functions.

- **AS WITH A COMPUTER,** you usually need to know the names of the files in your memory if you expect to retrieve them.

Stages of Memory: Making *Sense* of the *Short* and the *Long* of It

- **SEVEN IS A** "magic number"—sort of.

- **YOU HAVE A BIOCHEMICAL** hard drive with no known limits on the gigabytes of information it can store.

- **YOU MAY ALWAYS RECALL** exactly where you were and what you were doing on the morning of September 11, 2001.

- **IF YOU STUDY WITH** the stereo on, you would probably do better to take the test with the stereo on. (This doesn't mean that your professor will allow you to bring the stereo.)

Forgetting: Will You Remember How We Forget?

- **LEARNING SPANISH CAN** make it harder to remember French—and vice versa.

- **CAN CHILDREN REMEMBER** the things that happen to them during the first couple of years of life?

- **WHY CAN'T THE QUARTERBACK** remember the play in which he was knocked unconscious?

The Biology of Memory: The Brain as a Living Time Machine

- **YOUR MEMORY USES** "better living through chemistry"—chemicals in the brain are connected with memory.

Life Connections: Using the Psychology of Memory to Enhance Your Memory

- **HERE'S HOW YOU CAN** do better at remembering the names of people you meet at a party and the material that's going to be on the test.

- **WANT TO REMEMBER** your shopping list? Think of the meat loaf in your navel.

My oldest daughter Jill was talking about how she had run into a friend fro elementary school and they had had a splendid time recalling the goo things they did during their school years. Her sister Allyn, age 6 at the tim was not to be outdone. "I can remember when I was born," she put in.

The family's ears perked up. Being a psychologist, I knew exactly what to say. "Yc can remember when you were born?" I said.

"Oh, yes," she insisted. "Mommy was there."

So far she could not be faulted. I cheered her on, and she related a remarkabl detailed account of how it had been snowing in the wee hours of a bitter Decembe morning when Mommy had to go to the hospital. You see, she said, her memory wa so good that she could also summon up what it had been like *before* she was born. Sh wove a wonderful patchwork quilt, integrating details we had given her with her ow recollections of the events surrounding the delivery of her younger sister, Jordan. A in all, she seemed quite satisfied that she had pieced together a faithful portrait of he arrival on the world stage.

Later in the chapter, we will see that children usually do not recall events tha occurred in their first two years, much less those of their first hours. But Allyn's tal dramatized the way we "remember" many of the things that have happened to us When it comes to long-term memories, truth can take a back seat to drama and embel lishment. Very often, our memories are like the bride's apparel—there's somethin old, something new, something borrowed, and from time to time something blue.

Memory is what this chapter is about. Without memory, there is no past. Withou memory, experience is trivial and learning is lost. Shortly we will see what psycholo gists have learned about the ways in which we remember things. First, try to meet th following challenges to your memory.

FIVE CHALLENGES TO MEMORY

Before we go further, let's test your memory. If you want to participate, find four sheets of blank paper and number them 1 through 4. Then follow these directions:

1. Following are ten letters. Look at them for 15 seconds. Later in the chapter, I will ask you if you can write them on sheet number 1. (No cheating! Don't do it now.)

THUNSTOFAM

2. Look at these nine figures for 30 seconds. Then try to draw them in the proper sequence on sheet number 2. (Yes, right after you've finished looking at them. We'll talk about your drawings later.)

⌐∪∟ ⊒□⊏ ˥∩˩

3. Okay, here's another list of letters, 17 this time. Look at the list for 60 seconds and then see whether you can reproduce it on sheet number 3. (I'm being generous this time—a full minute.)

GMC-BSI-BMA-TTC-IAF-BI

4. Which of these pennies is an accurate reproduction of the Lincoln penny you see every day? This time there's nothing to draw on another sheet; just circle or put a check mark by the penny that you think resembles the ones you throw in the back of the drawer.

A   B   C   D   E   F

5. Examine the following drawings for 1 minute. Then copy the names of the figures on sheet number 4. When you're finished, just keep reading. Soon I'll be asking you to draw those figures.

eyeglasses

hourglass

seven

gun

KINDS OF MEMORY: LOOKING BACK, LOOKING FORWARD

There are various kinds of memories. Allyn remembered some things she had personally done, for example, such as what she had for breakfast on the morning of Jill's visit. Remembering what you had for breakfast is an example of an *episodic memory*—an episode in your life. But Allyn claimed to remember when she was born, which was clearly an invented memory based on her general knowledge of the process, not of that particular episode in her life. While she was talking about all this, she was "remembering" how to talk and prance about the room. And while all this was happening, I was trying to remind myself over and over again not to forget to jot down notes about it and write it up as soon as I could. All of these are different kinds of memories, and psychologists debate whether they represent different systems of memory or are just different examples of the same system of memory (Schacter, 1992). Let us consider each type of memory identified by psychologists today.

Explicit Versus Implicit Memories

Question: What is meant by explicit memory?   **Explicit memory**—also referred to as *declarative memory*—is memory for specific information. Things that are *explicit* are clear, or clearly stated or explained. The use of the term *declarative* indicates that these memories state or reveal (i.e., *declare*) specific information. The information may be autobiographical or refer to general knowledge. ("Well, I declare!")

Implicit memory—also referred to as *nondeclarative memory*—is memory of how to perform a task, how to *do* something (Witt et al., 2002). First let us talk more about two kinds of explicit memories described by psychologist Endel Tulving (1985; Tulving & Markowitsch, 1998): episodic and semantic. They are identified according to the type of information they hold.

Episodic Memory

Question: What is meant by episodic memory?   **Episodic memories** are kinds of explicit memories. They are memories of the things that happen to us or take place in our presence (Wheeler et al., 1997). Episodic memory is also referred to as *autobiographical memory*. Your memories of what you ate for breakfast and of what your professor said in class this afternoon are examples of episodic memory.

REFLECT

What are the earliest episodes you can remember? Is your memory of them accurate? Can you be sure?

Return to Allyn's "recollection." Of course Allyn could not really remember her own birth. That is, she could not recall the particular event or *episode* in which she had participated. What Allyn did recount is more accurately characterized as generalized knowledge than as an episodic or autobiographical memory of her birth. From listening to her parents and from her experience with the events of her sister Jordan's birth, she had learned much about what happens during childbirth. She erroneously thought that this knowledge represented her own birth.

Explicit Memory
Memory that clearly and distinctly expresses (explicates) specific information.

Implicit Memory
Memory that is suggested (implied) but not plainly expressed, as illustrated in the things that people *do* but do not state clearly.

Episodic Memory
Memories of events experienced by a person or that take place in the person's presence.

© Yves De Braine/Black Star

■ **An Example of an Implicit Memory**

Memories of how to ride a bicycle, how to type, how to turn the lights on and off, and how to drive a car are implicit memories. Implicit memories tend to persist even when we do not use them for many years. This photo of the older Jean Piaget, the cognitive-developmental theorist discussed in Chapter 4, suggests that we may ne forget how to ride a bicycle.

It is common for us to build or "reconstruct" inaccurate memories that have a bit of this and that—something that might reflect autobiographical experience, things we hear about from family members and others, the stuff we read about or see in the media, and even things that other people suggest might have happened to us. These memories are fiction, as we see in novels, but we may believe that they are truly autobiographical (Clancy et al., 2000).

Semantic Memory: On *Not* Getting Personal

Question: What is meant by semantic memory?   General knowledge is referred to as **semantic memory.** *Semantics* concerns meanings. Allyn was reporting her understanding of the meaning of childbirth rather than an episode in her own life. You can "remember" that the United States has 50 states without visiting them and personally adding them up. You "remember" who authored *Hamlet,* although you were not looking over Shakespeare's shoulder as he did so. These, too, are examples of semantic memory.

Your future recollection that there are several kinds of memory is more likely to be semantic than episodic. In other words, you are more likely to "know" that there are several types of memory than to recall the date on which you learned about them, where you were, how you were sitting, and whether you were also thinking about dinner at the time. We tend to use the phrase "I remember . . ." when we are referring to episodic memories, as in "I *remember* the blizzard of 2002." But we are more likely to say "I know . . ." in reference to semantic memories, as in "I *know* about—" (or, "I heard about—") "—the blizzard of 1898." Put it another way: You may *remember* that you wrote your mother, but you *know* that Shakespeare wrote *Hamlet.*

Implicit Memory: When Remembering Is Doing

Now let us think more about implicit memory. *Question: What is meant by implicit memory?*   As the term *implicit* implies (should I start this sentence again?), implicit memories are suggested (or implied) but not plainly stated or expressed (not declared). Implicit memories are illustrated by the things that people *do* but not by the things they state clearly. Implicit memories involve skills, both cognitive and physical; they reveal habits; and they involve the effects of conditioning. My taste aversion to buttered popcorn is an implicit memory. Because I was once nauseated by buttered popcorn, I feel queasy when I smell it. It's a conditioned response. I don't have to think about it. (And I don't want to think about it, to tell you the truth. I wrote about it here because of my deep commitment to you.)

Here are some other examples of implicit memories: You have learned and now remember how to speak at least one language, how to ride a bicycle, how to swim or swing a bat, how to type, how to turn on the lights, and how to drive a car. It is said that you never "forget" how to ride a bicycle. This is because implicit memories can persist even when we have not used them for many years. Getting to class "by habit"—without paying attention to landmarks or directions—is another instance of implicit memory. If someone asked you what 2 times 2 is, the number 4 would probably "jump" into your mind without much thinking about it or conscious calculation. After going over the alphabet or multiplication tables hundreds of times, our memory of them becomes automatic or implicit. We don't have to pay conscious attention to them in order to remember them.

Your memory of the alphabet or the multiplication tables is the result of a great deal of repetition that makes associations automatic, a phenomenon which psychologists refer to as *priming.* Studies involving brain imaging reveal that priming makes it possible for people to carry out a mental task with less neural activity (Savage et al., 2001; Schacter & Badgaiyan, 2001). Years of priming helps people make complete words out of the word fragments (Roediger et al., 1992; Schacter et al., 1999). Even though the perceptual cues in the following word fragments are limited, you may very well make them into words:

PYGY   NVSY   MRCA   TXT   BUFL

Let us jump ahead to the next chapter ("Thinking, Language, and Intelligence") to mention a couple of factors that will be involved in how many words you can make out of these fragments. One is your expertise with the English language. If English is

Semantic Memory
General knowledge, as opposed to episodic memory.

your second language, you will probably make fewer associations to these fragments than if English is your first language. In fact, you might not perceive any complete words. Another factor could be creativity. Can you think of other factors?

Daniel Schacter (1992) also illustrates implicit memory with the story of the woman with amnesia who was wandering the streets. The police picked her up and discovered that she could not remember who she was, or any other fact about her life, and that she had no identification. After extensive fruitless interviewing, the police hit on the idea of asking her to dial phone numbers—just any number at all. Even though the woman did not "know" what she was doing, she dialed her mother's number. When asked for the phone numbers of people she knew, she had had no answer. She could not *declare* her mother's phone number. She could not make the number *explicit*. She could not even remember her mother's name, or whether she had a mother. All this explicit information was gone. But dialing her mother's phone number was apparently a habit, and she did it "on automatic pilot." We can assume that she had been *primed* for this task by dialing the number hundreds of times, perhaps many thousands of times. Implicit memory reveals the effects of experience when we are not specifically trying to recall information.

Retrospective Memory Versus Prospective Memory

Retrospective memory is the recalling of information that has been previously learned. *Episodic, semantic,* and *implicit memories* all involve remembering things that were learned previously. ***Question: What is the difference between restrospective memory and prospective memory?***

Prospective memory involves remembering to do things in the future. Tasks that depend on prospective memory include remembering to brush your teeth before going out, to pay your bills (yuck), to take out some cash, and to make the list of things to do so that you won't forget what to do! And if one does make a list of things to do, one must remember to use it. Most of us have had failures of prospective memory in which we have the feeling that we were supposed to do something, but we can't remember what. Prospective memory tends to fail when we are preoccupied (caught up in surfing the Net or fantasizing about you-know-who), distracted (we get a phone call just as we are about to get going on something), or feeling the stress of time pressure (Schacter, 1999).

There are various kinds of prospective memory tasks. For example, *habitual tasks* such as getting to class on time are easier to remember than occasional tasks such as meeting someone for coffee at an arbitrary time (d'Ydewalle et al., 1999). But motivation also plays a role. You are more likely to remember the coffee date if the person you are meeting is the local Justin Timberlake or Christina Aguilera look-alike. Psychologists also distinguish between event-based and time-based prospective memory tasks (McDonald-Miszczak et al., 1999). *Event-based tasks* are triggered by events, such as remembering to take one's medicine at breakfast or to brush one's teeth after eating. *Time-based tasks* are to be performed at a certain time or after a certain amount of time has elapsed between occurrences, such as tuning in to a favorite news program at 7:30 PM or taking a pill every four hours (d'Ydewalle et al., 1999).

There is an age-related decline in both retrospective and prospective memory (Einstein et al., 1998; West & Craik, 1999). In the case of prospective memory, older adults appear to be about as aware of specific cues or reminders as young adults; however, it takes them longer to respond to the cues or reminders (West & Craik, 1999). That is, if they meet with a friend, they are likely to remember that they were supposed to ask something, but it may take longer for them to remember the particular question. Divided attention (distraction) plays a role and older people are especially vulnerable (Einstein et al., 1998). However, older adults with greater verbal ability and occupational status are better able to keep their intentions in mind (Cherry & LeCompte, 1999).

Moods and attitudes have an effect on prospective memory (Villa & Abeles, 2000). For example, negative emotional states such as depression also impair prospective memory. Depressed people are less likely to push to remind themselves to do what they intend to do (Rude et al., 1999). On the other hand, older people who are confident in their ability to remember to carry out tasks are more likely to actually remember to do them (McDonald-Miszczak et al., 1999). Yet the same confidence in one's memory does

Retrospective Memory
Memory for past events, activities, and learning experiences, as shown by explicit (episodic and semantic) and implicit memories.

Prospective Memory
Memory to perform an act in the future, as at a certain time or when a certain event occurs.

not appear to be associated with better performance at *retrospective* memory tasks (recalling the past) (McDonald-Miszczak et al., 1999). The various kinds of memory are summarized in Figure 7.1.

Before proceeding to the next section, why don't you turn to the piece of paper on which you wrote the names of the four figures—that is, sheet number 4—and draw them from memory as exactly as you can. Hold on to the drawings. We'll talk about them a bit later.

Learning Connections
See Web site for an interactive version of these review questions.

R E V I E W

(1) _____ memories are memories of specific information. (2) Memories of the events that happen to a person are _____ memories. (3) _____ memories concern generalized knowledge.

Critical Thinking: Definitions matter. Should this chapter be called *Memory* or *Memories?* Think of the many different kinds of memories you have: retrospective versus

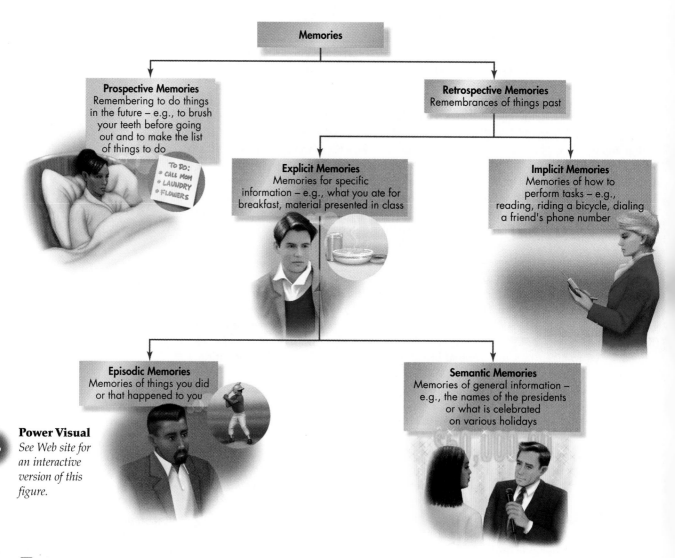

Power Visual
See Web site for an interactive version of this figure.

■ **Figure 7.1**
The Relationships Among the Various Kinds of Memories
Memories can address past events (*retrospective memories*) or future events (*prospective memories*). Memories of the past can be *explicit* (declarative) or *implicit* (nondeclarative). Explicit memories include memories of personal episodes (which are called *episodic* or *autobiographical memories*) or of general information (*semantic memories*).

prospective, implicit versus explicit, and so on. Do these different kinds of memories represent different *systems* of memory, or are they just different examples of memories?

PROCESSES OF MEMORY: PROCESSING INFORMATION IN OUR MOST PERSONAL COMPUTERS

Both psychologists and computer scientists speak of processing information. Think of using a computer to write a term paper. Once the system is up and operating, you begin to enter information. You can enter information into the computer's memory by, for example, typing letters on a keyboard or—in the case of voice recognition technology—speaking. If you were to do some major surgery on your computer (which I am often tempted to do) and open up its memory, however, you wouldn't find these letters or sounds inside it. This is because the computer is programmed to change the letters or sounds—that is, the information you have entered—into a form that can be placed in its electronic memory. Similarly, when we perceive information, we must convert it into a form that can be remembered if we are to place it in our memory.

Encoding: The Memory's "Transformer"

Information about the outside world reaches our senses in the form of physical and chemical stimuli. The first stage of information processing is changing information so that we can place it in memory: **encoding.**   *Question: What is the role of encoding in memory?*   When we encode information, we transform it into psychological formats that can be represented mentally. To do so, we commonly use visual, auditory, and semantic codes.

Let us illustrate the uses of coding by referring to the list of letters you first saw in the section on challenges to memory. Try to write the letters on sheet number 1. Go on, take a minute and then come back.

Okay, now: If you had used a **visual code** to try to remember the list, you would have mentally represented it as a picture. That is, you would have maintained—or attempted to maintain—a mental image of the letters. Some artists and art historians seem to maintain marvelous visual mental representations of works of art. This enables them to quickly recognize whether a work is authentic.

You may also have decided to read the list of letters to yourself—that is, to silently say them in sequence: "t," "h," "u," and so on. By so doing, you would have been using an **acoustic code,** or representing the stimuli as a sequence of sounds. You may also have read the list as a three-syllable word, "thun-sto-fam." This is an acoustic code, but it also involves the "meaning" of the letters, in the sense that you are interpreting the list as a word. This approach has elements of a semantic code.

Semantic codes represent stimuli in terms of their meaning. Our ten letters were meaningless in and of themselves. However, they can also serve as an acronym—a term made up of the first letters of a phrase—for the familiar phrase "THe UNited STates OF AMerica." This observation lends them meaning.

Storage: The Memory's "Save" Function

The second memory process is **storage.**   *Question: What is the role of storage in memory?*   Storage means maintaining information over time. If you were given the task of storing the list of letters—that is, told to remember it—how would you attempt to place it in storage? One way would be by **maintenance rehearsal**—by mentally repeating the list, or saying it to yourself. Our awareness of the functioning of our memory, referred to by psychologists as **metamemory,** becomes more sophisticated as we develop.

Encoding
Modifying information so that it can be placed in memory. The first stage of information processing.

Visual Code
Mental representation of information as a picture.

Acoustic Code
Mental representation of information as a sequence of sounds.

Semantic Code
Mental representation of information according to its meaning.

Storage
The maintenance of information over time. The second stage of information processing.

Maintenance Rehearsal
Mental repetition of information in order to keep it in memory.

Metamemory
Self-awareness of the ways in which memory functions, allowing the person to encode, store, and retrieve information effectively.

R E F L E C T
As you read this page, are you transforming the sensory stimulation by means of an acoustic code? Are you surprised that you know how to do this?

You could also have condensed the amount of information you were rehearsing by reading the list as a three-syllable word; that is, you could have rehearsed three syllables (said "thun-sto-fam" over and over again) rather than ten letters. In either case, repetition would have been the key to memory. (We talk more about such condensing, or "chunking," very soon.)

However, you could also encode the list of letters by relating it to something that you already know. This coding is called **elaborative rehearsal.** That is, you are "elaborating" or extending the semantic meaning of the letters you are trying to remember. For example, did you recognize that the list of ten letters is an acronym for "The United States of America"? (That is, you take the first two letters of each of the words in the phrase and string them together to make up the 10 letters of THUNSTOFAM.) If you had recognized this, storage of the list of letters might have been almost instantaneous, and it would probably have been permanent.

Retrieval: The Memory's "Find" Function

The third memory process is **retrieval.** *Question: What is the role of retrieval in memory?* The retrieval of stored information means locating it and returning it to consciousness. With well-known information such as our names and occupations, retrieval is effortless and, for all practical purposes, immediate. But when we are trying to remember massive quantities of information, or information that is not perfectly understood, retrieval can be tedious and not always successful. It is easiest to retrieve information stored in a computer by using the name of the file. Similarly, retrieval of information from our memories requires knowledge of the proper cues.

If you had encoded THUNSTOFAM as a three-syllable word, your retrieval strategy would involve recollection of the word and rules for decoding. In other words, you would say the "word" *thun-sto-fam* and then decode it by spelling it out. You might err in that "thun" sounds like "thumb" and "sto" could also be spelled "stow." However, using the semantic code, or recognition of the acronym for "The United States of America," could lead to flawless recollection.

I stuck my neck out by predicting that you would immediately and permanently store the list if you recognized it as an acronym. Here, too, there would be recollection (of the name of our country) and rules for decoding. That is, to "remember" the ten letters, you would have to envision the phrase ("The United States of America") and read off the first two letters of each word. Because using this semantic code is more complex than simply seeing the entire list (using a visual code), it may take a while to recall (actually, to reconstruct) the list of ten letters. But by using the phrase, you are likely to remember the list of letters permanently.

Now, what if you were not able to remember the list of ten letters? What would have gone wrong? In terms of the three processes of memory, it could be that you had (1) not encoded the list in a useful way, (2) not entered the encoded information into storage, or (3) stored the information but lacked the proper cues for remembering it—such as the phrase "The United States of America" or the rule for decoding the phrase.

By now you may have noticed that I have discussed three kinds of memory and three processes of memory, but I have not yet *defined* memory. No apologies—we weren't ready for a definition yet. Now that we have explored some basic concepts, let us give it a try: **Memory** is the processes by which information is encoded, stored, and retrieved.

Learning Connections
See the Connections *CD-ROM for an animation on mnemonic devices.*

R E F L E C T

How do you remember how to spell the words receive *and* retrieve?

Elaborative Rehearsal
The kind of coding in which new information is related to information that is already known.

Retrieval
The location of stored information and its return to consciousness. The third stage of information processing.

Memory
The processes by which information is encoded, stored, and retrieved.

Learning Connections
See Web site for an interactive version of these review questions.

R E V I E W

(4) _____ is the transforming of information so that we can remember it. (5) One way of storing information is by _____ rehearsal, or by mentally repeating it. (6) Another is by _____ rehearsal, in which we relate new information to things we already know. (7) _____ of information from storage requires knowledge of the proper cues.

Critical Thinking: Why would an author—like me—compare the functioning of memory to the functioning of a computer? Do you find the comparison to be useful or misleading?

STAGES OF MEMORY: MAKING *SENSE* OF THE *SHORT* AND THE *LONG* OF IT

William James (1890) was intrigued by the fact that some memories are unreliable, "going in one ear and out the other," while others could be recalled for a lifetime. He wrote:

> The stream of thought flows on, but most of its elements fall into the bottomless pit of oblivion. Of some, no element survives the instant of their passage. Of others, it is confined to a few moments, hours, or days. Others, again, leave vestiges which are indestructible, and by means of which they may be recalled as long as life endures.

Yes, the world is a constant display of sights and sounds and other sources of sensory stimulation, but only some of these things are remembered. James was correct in observing that we remember various "elements" of thought for different lengths of time, and many we do not remember at all. Psychologists Richard Atkinson and Richard Shiffrin (1968) suggested a model for how some stimuli are lost immediately, others held briefly, and still others for a lifetime. *Question: What is the Atkinson–Shiffrin model of memory?* Atkinson and Shiffrin proposed that there are three stages of memory and suggested that the progress of information through these stages determines whether (and how long) it is retained (see Figure 7.2). These stages are *sensory memory, short-term memory (STM),* and *long-term memory (LTM).*

There is a saying that when you cover a topic completely, you are talking about "the long and short of it." In the case of the stages of memory, we could say that we are trying to "make *sense* of the *short* and the *long* of it."

Sensory Memory: Flashes on the Mental Monitor

William James also wrote about the stream of thought, or consciousness:

> Consciousness . . . does not appear to itself chopped up in bits. A "river" or a "stream" are the metaphors by which it is most naturally described. In talking of it hereafter, let us call it the stream of thought, of consciousness, or of subjective life.

When we look at a visual stimulus, our impressions may seem fluid enough. Actually, however, they consist of a series of eye fixations referred to as **saccadic eye movements.** These movements jump from one point to another about four times each second. Yet the visual sensations seem continuous, or streamlike, because of **sensory memory.** Sensory memory is the type or stage of memory that is first encountered by a stimulus. Although sensory memory holds impressions briefly, it is long enough so that a series of perceptions seem to be connected. *Question: How does sensory memory function?*

To explain the functioning of sensory memory, let us return to our list of letters: THUNSTOFAM. If the list were flashed on a screen for a fraction of a second, the visual impression, or **memory trace,** of the stimulus would also last for only a fraction of a second afterward. Psychologists speak of the memory trace of the list as being held in a visual **sensory register.**

If the letters had been flashed on a screen for, say, 1/10 of a second, your ability to remember them on the basis of sensory memory alone would be limited. Your memory would be based on a single eye fixation, and the trace of the image would vanish before a single second had passed. At the turn of the century, psychologist William McDougall (1904) engaged in research in which he showed people one to twelve

Saccadic Eye Movement
The rapid jumps made by a person's eyes as they fixate on different points.

Sensory Memory
The type or stage of memory first encountered by a stimulus. Sensory memory holds impressions briefly, but long enough so that series of perceptions are psychologically continuous.

Memory Trace
An assumed change in the nervous system that reflects the impression made by a stimulus. Memory traces are said to be "held" in sensory registers.

Sensory Register
A system of memory that holds information briefly, but long enough so that it can be processed further. There may be a sensory register for every sense.

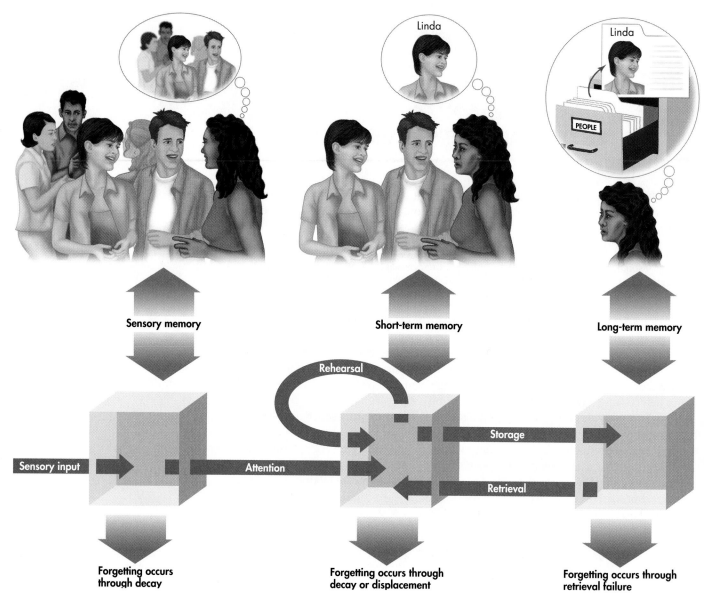

■ **Figure 7.2**
Three Stages of Memory

The Atkinson–Shiffrin model proposes that there are three distinct stages of memory. Sensory information impacts upon the registers of sensory memory, where memory traces are held briefly before decaying. If we attend to the information, much of it is transferred to short-term memory (STM). Information in STM may decay or be displaced if it is not transferred to long-term memory (LTM). We can use rehearsal or elaborative strategies to transfer memories to LTM. If information in LTM is organized poorly, or if we cannot find cues to retrieve it, it may be lost.

letters arranged in rows—just long enough to allow a single eye fixation. Under these conditions, people could typically remember only four or five letters. Thus recollection of THUNSTOFAM, a list of ten letters arranged in a single row, would probably depend on whether one had encoded it so that it could be processed further.

George Sperling (1960) modified McDougall's experimental method and showed that there is a difference between what people can see and what they can report. McDougall had used a *whole-report procedure,* in which people were asked to report every letter they saw in the array. Sperling used a modified *partial-report procedure,* in which people were asked to report the contents of one of three rows of letters. In a typical procedure, Sperling flashed three rows of letters like the following on a screen for 50 milliseconds (1/20 of a second):

A G R E
V L S B
N K B T

Using the whole-report procedure, people could report an average of four letters from the entire display (one out of three). But if immediately after presenting the display Sperling pointed an arrow at a row he wanted viewers to report, they usually reported most of the letters in the row successfully.

If Sperling presented six letters arrayed in two rows, people could usually report either row without error. If people were flashed three rows of four letters each—a total of twelve—they reported correctly an average of three of four letters in the designated row, suggesting that about nine of the twelve letters had been perceived.

Sperling found that the amount of time that elapsed before indicating the row to be reported was crucial. If he delayed pointing to the arrow for a few fractions of a second after presenting the letters, people were much less successful in reporting the letters in the target row. If he allowed a full second to elapse, the arrow did not aid recall at all. From these data, Sperling concluded that the memory trace of visual stimuli *decays* within a second in the visual sensory register (see Figure 7.2). With a single eye fixation, people can *see* most of a display of 12 letters clearly, as shown by their ability to immediately read off most of the letters in a designated row. Yet as the fractions of a single second are elapsing, the memory trace of the letters is fading. By the time a second has elapsed, the trace has vanished.

Iconic Memory

Psychologists believe we possess a sensory register for each one of our senses. The mental representations of visual stimuli are referred to as **icons.** The sensory register that holds icons is labeled **iconic memory.** Iconic memory is one kind of sensory memory. Iconic memories are accurate, photographic memories. So those of us who mentally represent visual stimuli have "photographic memories." However, iconic memories are very brief. What most of us normally think of as a photographic memory—the ability to retain exact mental representations of visual stimuli over long periods of time—is technically referred to as *eidetic imagery.*

Eidetic Imagery

A few individuals retain visual stimuli, or icons, in their sensory memories for remarkably long periods of time. About 5% of children can look at a detailed picture, turn away, and several minutes later recall the particulars of the picture with exceptional clarity—as if they were still seeing it. This extraordinary visual sensory memory is referred to as **eidetic imagery** (Haber, 1980). This ability declines with age, however, all but disappearing by adolescence.

Figure 7.3 provides an example of a test of eidetic imagery. Children are asked to look at the first drawing in the series for 20 to 30 seconds, after which it is removed. The children then continue to gaze at a neutral background. Several minutes later the drawing in the center is placed on the backdrop. When asked what they see, many

Icon
A mental representation of a visual stimulus that is held briefly in sensory memory.

Iconic Memory
The sensory register that briefly holds mental representations of visual stimuli.

Eidetic Imagery
The maintenance of detailed visual memories over several minutes.

R E F L E C T

Do you know anyone with an extraordinary memory? Perhaps a "photographic" memory? What behavior suggests the presence of such a memory? How do you account for it?

■ **Figure 7.3**
A Research Strategy for Assessing Eidetic Imagery

Children look at the first drawing for 20 to 30 seconds, after which it is removed. Next, the children look at a neutral background for several minutes. They are then shown the second drawing. When asked what they see, children with the capacity for eidetic imagery report a face. The face is seen only by children who retain the first image and fuse it with the second, thus perceiving the third image.

Echo

A mental representation of an auditory stimulus (sound) that is held briefly in sensory memory.

Echoic Memory

The sensory register that briefly holds mental representations of auditory stimuli.

report "a face." A face would be seen only if the children had retained a clear image of the first picture and fused it with the second so that they are, in effect, perceiving the third picture in Figure 7.3 (Haber, 1980).

Eidetic imagery appears remarkably clear and detailed. It seems to be essentially a perceptual phenomenon in which encoding or rehearsal is not necessary to continue to "see" a visual stimulus. Although eidetic imagery is rare, iconic memory, as we see in the following section, universally transforms visual perceptions into smoothly unfolding impressions of the world.

Thus people who can see have a photographic memory, which is what is meant technically by a photographic memory. However, only a few people have *eidetic imagery*, which refers to the ability to continue to "see" the memory trace of a visual stimulus in the visual sensory register long after the trace would have decayed in most people.

Iconic Memory and Saccadic Eye Movements

Iconic memory smooths out the bumps in the visual ride. Saccadic eye movements occur about four times every second. Iconic memory, however, holds icons for up to a second. As a consequence, the flow of visual information seems smooth and continuous. Your impression that the words you are reading flow across the page, rather than jumping across in spurts, is a product of your iconic memory. Similarly, motion pictures present 16 to 22 separate frames, or still images, each second. Iconic memory allows you to perceive the imagery in the film as being seamless (G. R. Loftus, 1983).

Echoic Memory

Mental representations of sounds, or auditory stimuli, are called **echoes.** The sensory register that holds echoes is referred to as **echoic memory.**

The memory traces of auditory stimuli (that is, echoes) can last for several seconds, many times longer than the traces of visual stimuli (icons). The difference in the duration of traces is probably based on biological differences between the eye and the ear. This difference is one of the reasons that acoustic codes aid in the retention of information that has been presented visually—or why saying the letters or syllables of THUNSTOFAM makes the list easier to remember.

Yet echoes, like icons, fade with time. If they are to be retained, we must pay attention to them. By selectively attending to certain stimuli, we sort them out from the background noise. For example, in studies on the development of patterns of processing information, young children have been shown photographs of rooms full of toys and then been asked to recall as many of the toys as they can. One such study found that 2-year-old boys are more likely to attend to and remember toys such as cars, puzzles, and trains. Two-year-old girls are more likely to attend to and remember dolls, dishes, and teddy bears (Renninger & Wozniak, 1985). Even by this early age, the things that children attend to frequently fall into stereotypical patterns.

R E F L E C T

Why are girls more likely than boys to remember the dolls and teddy bears they see in a picture?

■ **Echoic Memory**
The mental representations of auditory stimuli are called echoes, and the sensory register that holds echoes is referred to as echoic memory. By encoding visual information as echoes and rehearsing the echoes, we commit them to memory.

Short-Term Memory: Keeping Things "In Mind"

Imagine that you are completing a writing assignment and you keyboard or speak words and phrases into your word-processing program. They appear on your monitor as a sign that your computer has them in *memory.* Your word-processing program allows you to add words, delete words, see if they are spelled correctly, add images, and move whole paragraphs from place to place. So you can manipulate the information in your computer's memory, but it isn't saved. It hasn't been entered into storage. If the program or the computer crashes, the information is gone. The computer's memory is a short-term affair. To maintain a long-term connection with the information, you have to save it. Saving it means giving it a name—hopefully a name that you will remember so that you can later find and retrieve the information—and instructing your computer to save it (keep it in storage until told otherwise).

If you focus on a stimulus in the sensory register, you will tend to retain it in your own **short-term memory**—also referred to as **working memory**—for a minute or so after the trace of the stimulus decays. ***Question: How does short-term memory function?*** As one researcher describes it, "Working memory is the mental glue that links a thought through time from its beginning to its end" (Goldman-Rakic, 1995). When you are given a phone number by the information operator and write it down or immediately dial the number, you are retaining the number in your short-term memory. When you are told the name of someone at a party and then use that name immediately in addressing that person, you are retaining the name in short-term memory. In short-term memory, the image tends to fade significantly after 10 to 12 seconds if it is not repeated or rehearsed. It is possible to focus on maintaining a visual image in the short-term memory, but it is more common to encode visual stimuli as sounds, or auditory stimuli. Then the sounds can be rehearsed, or repeated.

Most of us know that one way of retaining information in short-term memory—and possibly storing it permanently—is to rehearse it. When an information operator tells me a phone number, I usually rehearse it continuously while I am dialing it or running around frantically searching for a pencil and a scrap of paper so that I can "save" it. The more times we rehearse information, the more likely we are to remember it. We have the capacity (if not the will or the time) to rehearse information and thereby keep it in short-term memory indefinitely.

Once information is in our short-term memories, we can work on it. Like the information in the word-processing program, we can manipulate it. But it isn't necessarily saved. If we don't do something to save it (like write down that telephone number on a scrap of paper or in a personal digital assistant), it can be gone forever. We can try to reconstruct it, but it may never be the same. Getting most of the digits in someone's phone number right doesn't get you a date for the weekend—at least not with the person you were thinking of!

Keeping THUNSTOFAM in Short-Term Memory

Let us now return to the task of remembering the first list of letters in the challenges to memory at the beginning of the chapter. If you had encoded the letters as the three-syllable word THUN-STO-FAM, you would probably have recalled them by mentally rehearsing (saying to yourself) the three-syllable "word" and then spelling it out from the sounds. A few minutes later, if someone asked whether the letters had been uppercase (THUNSTOFAM) or lowercase (thunstofam), you might not have been able to answer with confidence. You used an acoustic code to help recall the list, and uppercase and lowercase letters sound alike.

Because it can be pronounced, THUNSTOFAM is not too difficult to retain in short-term memory. But what if the list of letters had been TBXLFNTSDK? This list of letters cannot be pronounced as it is. You would have to find a complex acronym to code these letters, and do so within a fraction of a second—most likely an impossible task. To aid recall, you would probably choose to try to repeat the letters rapidly—to read each one as many times as possible before the memory trace fades. You might visualize each letter as you say it and try to get back to it (that is, to run through the entire list) before it decays.

R E F L E C T

What do you do to try to remember names and telephone numbers? What could you do to improve your memory of them?

Short-Term Memory
The type or stage of memory that can hold information for up to a minute or so after the trace of the stimulus decays. Also called *working memory.*

Working Memory
Same as *short-term memory.*

Serial-Position Effect

The tendency to recall more accurately the first and last items in a series.

Primacy Effect

The tendency to recall the initial items in a series of items.

Recency Effect

The tendency to recall the last items in a series of items.

Chunk

A stimulus or group of stimuli that are perceived as a discrete piece of information.

Let us assume that you encoded the letters as sounds and then rehearsed the sounds. When asked to report the list, you might mistakenly say T-V-X-L-F-N-T-S-T-K. This would be an understandable error because the incorrect *V* and *T* sounds are similar, respectively, to the correct *B* and *D* sounds.

The Serial-Position Effect

If asked to recall the list of letters TBXLFNTSDK, you would also be likely to recall the first and last letters in the series, *T* and *K*, more accurately than the others.   ***Question: Why are we most likely to remember the first and last items in a list?***   The tendency to recall the first and last items in a series is known as the **serial-position effect.** This effect may occur because we pay more attention to the first and last stimuli in a series. They serve as the visual or auditory boundaries for the other stimuli. It may also be that the first items are likely to be rehearsed more frequently (repeated more times) than other items. The last items are likely to have been rehearsed most recently and hence are most likely to be retained in short-term memory.

According to cognitive psychologists, the tendency to recall the initial items in a list is referred to as the **primacy effect.** Social psychologists have also noted a powerful primacy effect in our formation of impressions of other people. In other words, first impressions tend to last. The tendency to recall the last items in a list is referred to as the **recency effect.** If we are asked to recall the last items in a list soon after we have been shown the list, they may still be in short-term memory. As a result, they can be "read off." Earlier items, in contrast, may have to be retrieved from long-term memory.

Chunking

Rapidly rehearsing ten meaningless letters is not an easy task. With TBXLFNTSDK there are ten discrete elements, or **chunks,** of information that must be kept in short-term memory. When we encode THUNSTOFAM as three syllables, there are only three chunks to swallow at once—a memory task that is much easier on the digestion.

George Miller (1956) wryly noted that the average person is comfortable with digesting about seven integers at a time, the number of integers in a telephone number: "My problem is that I have been persecuted by an integer [the number *seven*]. For seven years this number has followed me around, has intruded in my most private data, and has assaulted me from the pages of our most public journals" (1956). ***Question: Is seven a magic number, or did the phone company get lucky?***

It may sound as if Miller was being paranoid or magical, but he was actually talking about research findings. Research shows that most people have little trouble recalling five chunks of information, as in a zip code. Some can remember nine, which is, for all but a few, an upper limit. So seven chunks, plus or minus one or two, is a "magic" number in the sense that the typical person can manage to remember that many chunks of information and not a great deal more.

So how, you ask, do we manage to include area codes in our recollections of telephone numbers, hence making them ten digits long? The truth of the matter is that we usually don't. We tend to recall the area code as a single chunk of information derived from our general knowledge of where a person lives. So we are more likely to remember (or "know") the ten-digit numbers of acquaintances who reside in locales with area codes that we use frequently.

Businesses pay the phone company hefty premiums so that they can attain numbers with two or three zeroes—for example, 592-2000 or 614-3300. These numbers include fewer chunks of information and hence are easier to remember. Customer recollection of business phone numbers increases sales. One financial services company uses the toll-free number CALL-IRA, which reduces the task to two chunks of information that also happen to be meaningfully related (semantically coded) to the nature of the business. Similarly, a clinic that helps people quit smoking arranged for a telephone number that can be reached by dialing the letters NO SMOKE.

Return to the third challenge to memory presented earlier. Were you able to remember the six groups of letters? Would your task have been simpler if you had grouped them differently? How about moving the dashes forward by a letter, so that they read

Harvard University Archives

■ **A Psychologist Hounded by the Number Seven?**

Psychologist George Miller complained, "My problem is that I have been persecuted by an integer [the number *seven*]. For seven years this number has followed me around, has intruded in my most private data, and has assaulted me from the pages of our most public journals." Just what is so special about the number seven?

GM-CBS-IBM-ATT-CIA-FBI? If we do this, we have the same list of letters, but we also have six chunks of information that can be coded semantically (according to what they mean). You may have also been able to generate the list by remembering a rule, such as "big corporations and government agencies."

If we can recall seven or perhaps nine chunks of information, how do children remember the alphabet? The alphabet contains 26 discrete pieces of information. How do children learn to encode the letters of the alphabet, which are visual symbols, as spoken sounds? There is nothing about the shape of an *A* that suggests its sound. Nor does the visual stimulus *B* sound "B-ish." Children learn to associate letters with their spoken names by **rote.** It is mechanical associative learning that takes time and repetition. If you think that learning the alphabet by rote is a simple task, try learning the Russian alphabet.

If you had recognized THUNSTOFAM as an acronym for the first two letters of each word in the phrase "THe UNited STates OF AMerica," you would also have reduced the number of chunks of information that had to be recalled. You could have considered the phrase to be a single chunk of information. The rule that you must use the first two letters of each word of the phrase would be another chunk.

Reconsider the second challenge to memory presented earlier. You were asked to remember nine chunks of visual information. Perhaps you could have used the acoustic codes "L" and "Square" for chunks 3 and 5, but no obvious codes are available for the seven other chunks. Now look at Figure 7.4. If you had recognized that the elements in the challenge could be arranged as the familiar tic-tac-toe grid, remembering the nine elements might have required two chunks of information. The first would have been the mental image of the grid, and the second would have been the rule for decoding: Each element corresponds to the shape of a section of the grid if read like words on a page (from upper left to lower right). The number sequence 1 through 9 would not in itself present a problem, because you learned this series by rote many years ago and have rehearsed it in countless calculations since then.

Interference in Short-Term Memory

I mentioned that I often find myself running around looking for a pencil and a scrap of paper to write down a telephone number that has been given to me. If I keep on rehearsing the number while I'm looking, I'm okay. But I have also often cursed myself for failing to keep a pad and pencil by the telephone, and sometimes this has interfered with my recollection of the number. (The moral of the story? Avoid self-reproach.) It has also happened that I have actually looked up a phone number and been about to dial it when someone has asked me for the time or where I said we were going to dinner. Unless I say, "Hold on a minute!" and manage to jot down the number on something, it's back to the phone book. Attending to distracting information, even briefly, prevents me from rehearsing the number, so it falls through the cracks of my short-term memory.

In an experiment with college students, Lloyd and Margaret Peterson (1959) demonstrated how prevention of rehearsal can wreak havoc with short-term memory. They asked students to remember three-letter combinations such as HGB—normally, three easy chunks of information. They then had the students count backward from an arbitrary number, such as 181, by threes (that is, 181, 178, 175, 172, and so on). The students were told to stop counting and to report the letter sequence after the intervals of time shown in Figure 7.5. The percentage of letter combinations that were recalled correctly fell precipitously within seconds. After 18 seconds of interference, counting had dislodged the letter sequences in almost all of these bright young students' memories.

Psychologists say that the appearance of new information in short-term memory **displaces** the old information. Remember: Only a few bits of information can be retained in short-term memory at the same time. (Unfortunately we cannot upgrade our human memories from, say, 64 megabytes to 128 or 256 megabytes.) Think of short-term memory as a shelf or workbench. Once it is full, some things fall off it when new items are shoved onto it. Here we have another possible explanation for the recency effect: The most recently learned bit of information is least likely to be displaced by additional information.

R E F L E C T

Are you trying to learn anything by rote in the courses you are taking now? Would another strategy also be of help?

Rote
Mechanical associative learning that is based on repetition.

Displace
In memory theory, to cause information to be lost from short-term memory by adding new information.

■ **Figure 7.4**
A Familiar Grid
The nine drawings in the second challenge to memory form this familiar tic-tac-toe grid when the numbers are placed inside them and they are arranged in order. This method for recalling the shapes collapses nine chunks of information into two. One is the tic-tac-toe grid. The second is the rule for decoding the drawings from the grid.

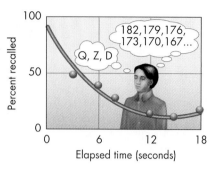

Figure 7.5
The Effect of Interference on Short-Term Memory

In this experiment, college students were asked to remember a series of three letters while they counted backward by threes. After just three seconds, retention was cut by half. Ability to recall the words was almost completely lost by 15 seconds.

Long-Term Memory
The type or stage of memory capable of relatively permanent storage.

Repression
In Freud's psychodynamic theory, the ejection of anxiety-evoking ideas from conscious awareness.

Schema
A way of mentally representing the world, such as a belief or an expectation, that can influence perception of persons, objects, and situations.

Displacement
Information can be lost to short-term memory through displacement. We may have little trouble remembering the names of the first or second person we meet at a gathering. But as introductions continue, new names may displace the old ones and we may forget the names of people we met only a few minutes earlier.

Displacement occurs at cocktail parties, and I'm not referring to jostling by the crowd. The point is this: When you meet Linda or Latrell at the party, you should have little trouble remembering the name. But then you may meet Tamara or Timothy and, still later, Keith or LaToya. By that time you may have a hard time dredging up Jennifer or Jonathan's name—unless, of course, you were very, very attracted to one of them. A passionate response would set a person apart and inspire a good deal of selective attention. According to signal-detection theory, if you were enamored enough, we may predict that you would "detect" the person's name (sensory signals) with a vengeance, and the other names would dissolve into background noise.

Long-Term Memory: Your Memory's "Hard Drive"

Long-term memory is the third stage of information processing. Think of your long-term memory as a vast storehouse of information containing names, dates, places, what Johnny did to you in second grade, and what Susan said about you when you were 12. *Question: How does long-term memory function?*

Some psychologists (Freud was one) used to believe that nearly all of our perceptions and ideas are stored permanently. We might not be able to retrieve all of them, because some memories might be "lost" because of lack of proper cues, or they might be kept unconscious by the forces of **repression.** Adherents to this view often pointed to the work of neurosurgeon Wilder Penfield (1969). When parts of their brains were electrically stimulated, many of Penfield's patients reported the appearance of images that had something of the feel of memories.

Today most psychologists view this notion as exaggerated. Memory researcher Elizabeth Loftus, for example, notes that the "memories" stimulated by Penfield's probes lacked detail and were sometimes incorrect (Loftus & Loftus, 1980; Loftus, 1983). Now let us consider some other questions about long-term memory.

How Accurate Are Long-Term Memories?

Psychologist Elizabeth Loftus notes that memories are distorted by our biases and needs—by the ways in which we conceptualize our worlds. We represent much of our world in the form of **schemas.**

To understand what is meant by the term *schema,* consider the problems of travelers who met up with Procrustes, the legendary highwayman of ancient Greece. Procrustes had a quirk. He was interested not only in travelers' pocketbooks but also in their height. He had a concept—a schema—of how tall people should be, and when people did not fit his schema, they were in trouble. You see, Procrustes also had a bed,

© Norbert Von der Groeben/The Image Works

the famous "Procrustean bed." He made his victims lie down in the bed, and if they were too short for it, he stretched them to make them fit. If they were too long for the bed, he practiced surgery on their legs.

Although the myth of Procrustes may sound absurd, it reflects a quirky truth about each of us. We all carry our cognitive Procrustean beds around with us—our unique ways of perceiving the world—and we try to make things and people fit them.

Let me give you an example. "Retrieve" the fourth sheet of paper you prepared according to the instructions for the challenges to memory. The labels you wrote on the sheet will remind you of the figures. Take a minute or two to draw them now. Then continue reading.

Now that you have made your drawings, turn to Figure 7.6. Are your drawings closer in form to those in group 1 or to those in group 2? I wouldn't be surprised if they were more like those in group 1—if, for example, your first drawing looked more like eyeglasses than a dumbbell. After all, they were labeled like the drawings in group 1. The labels serve as *schemas* for the drawings—ways of organizing your knowledge of them—and these schemas may have influenced your recollections.

Consider another example of the power of schemas in processing information. Loftus and Palmer (1974) showed people a film of a car crash and then asked them to fill out questionnaires that included a question about how fast the cars were going at the time. The language of the question varied in subtle ways, however. Some people were asked to estimate how fast the cars were going when they "hit" each other. Others were asked to estimate the cars' speed when they "smashed into" each other. On average, people who reconstructed the scene on the basis of the cue "hit" estimated a speed of 34 mph. People who watched the same film but reconstructed the scene on the basis of the cue "smashed" estimated a speed of 41 mph! In other words, the use of the word *hit* or *smashed* caused people to organize their knowledge about the crash in different ways. That is, the words served as diverse schemas that fostered the development of very different ways of processing information about the crash.

Subjects in the same study were questioned again a week later: "Did you see any broken glass?" Because there was no broken glass shown in the film, an answer of "yes" would be wrong. Of those who had earlier been encouraged to process information about the accident in terms of one car "hitting" the other, 14% incorrectly answered yes. But 32% of the subjects who had processed information about the crash in terms of one car "smashing into" the other reported, incorrectly, that they had seen broken glass.

An experiment reported by Elizabeth Loftus (1979) shows that people may reconstruct their experiences according to their prejudices. Subjects in the study were shown a picture that contained an African American man who was holding a hat and a European American man who was holding a razor. Later, when they were asked what they

■ **How Fast Were These Cars Going When They Collided?**

Our schemas influence our processing of information. When shown pictures such as these, people who were asked how fast the cars were going when they *smashed* into each other offer higher estimates than people who were told that the cars *hit* each other.

Figures shown	Group 1	Group 2
	Eyeglasses	Dumbbell
	Hourglass	Table
	Seven	Four
	Gun	Broom

■ **Figure 7.6 Memory as Reconstructive**

In their classic experiment, Carmichael, Hogan, and Walter (1932) showed people the figures in the left-hand box and made remarks as suggested in the other boxes. For example, the experimenter might say, "This drawing looks like eyeglasses [or a dumbbell]." When people later reconstructed the drawings, they were influenced by the labels.

had seen, many subjects erroneously recalled the razor as being in the hands of the African American. The subjects recalled information that was consistent with their schemas, but it was wrong.

▶ CONTROVERSY IN PSYCHOLOGY ◀

Can we trust eyewitness testimony?

Jean Piaget, the investigator of children's cognitive development, distinctly remembered an attempt to kidnap him from his baby carriage as he was being wheeled along the Champs Élysées. He recalled the excited throng, the abrasions on the face of the nurse who rescued him, the police officer's white baton, and the flight of the assailant. Although they were graphic, Piaget's memories were false. Years later, the nurse admitted that she had made up the tale.

Can eyewitness testimony be trusted? Is there reason to believe that the statements of eyewitnesses are any more factual than Piaget's? Legal professionals are concerned about the accuracy of our long-term memories as reflected in eyewitness testimony (Wells et al., 2000). Misidentifications of suspects "create a double horror: The wrong person is devastated by this personal tragedy, and the real criminal is still out on the streets" (Loftus, 1993, p. 550). Let us consider what can go wrong—and what can go right—with eyewitness testimony.

One problem with eyewitness testimony is that the words chosen by an experimenter—and those chosen by a lawyer interrogating a witness—have been shown to influence the reconstruction of memories (Wells et al., 2000). For example, as in the experiment described earlier, an attorney for the plaintiff might ask the witness, "How fast was the defendant's car going when it *smashed into* the plaintiff's car?" In such a case, the car might be reported as going faster than if the question had been: "How fast was the defendant's car going when the accident occurred?" (Loftus & Palmer, 1974). Could the attorney for the defendant claim that use of the word *smashed* biased the witness? What about jurors who heard the word *smashed?* Would they be biased toward assuming that the driver had been reckless?

Children tend to be more suggestible witnesses than adults, and preschoolers are more suggestible than older children (Ceci & Bruck, 1993). But when questioned prop-

■ **Eyewitness Testimony?**
How trustworthy is eyewitness testimony? Memories are reconstructive rather than photographic. The wording of questions also influences the content of the memory. Attorneys therefore are sometimes instructed not to phrase questions in such a way that they "lead" the witness.

erly, even young children may be able to provide accurate and useful testimony (Ceci & Bruck, 1993).

There are cases in which the memories of eyewitnesses have been "refreshed" by hypnosis. Sad to say, hypnosis does more than amplify memories; it can also distort them (Loftus, 1994). One problem is that witnesses may accept and embellish suggestions made by the hypnotist. Another is that hypnotized people may report fantasized occurrences as compellingly as if they were real (Loftus, 1994).

There are also problems in the identification of criminals by eyewitnesses. For one thing, witnesses may pay more attention to the suspect's clothing than to more meaningful characteristics such as facial features, height, and weight. In one experiment, viewers of a videotaped crime incorrectly identified a man as the criminal because he wore the eyeglasses and T-shirt that had been worn by the perpetrator on the tape. The man who had actually committed the crime was identified less often (Sanders, 1984).

Other problems with eyewitness testimony include the following:

- Identification is less accurate when suspects belong to ethnic or racial groups that differ from that of the witness (Egeth, 1993).
- Identification of suspects is confused when interrogators make misleading suggestions (Loftus, 1997).
- Witnesses are seen as more credible when they claim to be certain in their testimony, but there is little evidence that claims of certainty are accurate (Wells et al., 2000).

There are thus many problems with eyewitness testimony. Yet even Elizabeth Loftus (1993), who has extensively studied the accuracy of eyewitness testimony, agrees that it is a valuable tool in the courtroom. After all, identifications made by eyewitnesses are frequently correct, and what, Loftus asks, would be the alternative to the use of eyewitnesses? If we were to prevent eyewitnesses from testifying, how many criminals would go free?

How Much Information *Can* Be Stored in Long-Term Memory?

How many gigabytes of storage are there in your most personal computer—your brain? Unlike a computer, the human ability to store information is, for all practical purposes, unlimited (Goldman-Rakic, 1995). Even the largest hard drives fill up quickly when we save Web pages from the Internet, pictures, or movies. Yet how many "movies" of the past have you saved in your own long-term memory? How many thousands of scenes and stories can you rerun at will? And assuming that you have an intact sensory system, the movies in your personal storage bins not only have color and sound, but also aromas, tactile sensations, and much more. *Your long-term memory is a biochemical "hard drive" with no known limits on the gigabytes of information it can store.*

Yes, new information may replace older information in short-term memory, but there is no evidence that long-term memories—those in "storage"—are lost by displacement. Long-term memories may endure for a lifetime. Now and then it may seem that we have forgotten, or "lost," a long-term memory such as the names of our elementary or high-school classmates. Yet it may be that we cannot find the proper cues to help us retrieve them. It is like forgetting a file name when working with a computer. If long-term memories are lost, they may be lost in the same way that a misplaced object or computer file is lost. It is "lost," but we sense that it is still somewhere in the room or on the hard drive. In other words, it is lost but not destroyed or deleted.

Transferring Information from Short-Term to Long-Term Memory: Using the "Save" Function

How can you transfer information from short-term to long-term memory? By and large, the more often chunks of information are rehearsed, the more likely they are to be transferred to long-term memory. Repeating information over and over to prevent it from decaying or being displaced is termed *maintenance rehearsal*. But maintenance rehearsal does not give meaning to information by linking it to past learning. Thus it is not considered the best way to permanently store information (Simpson et al., 1994).

R E F L E C T
Is there any limit to the amount of information you can learn or remember?

A more effective method is to make information more meaningful—to purposefully relate new information to things that are already well known (Woloshyn et al., 1994). For example, to better remember the components of levers, physics students might use seesaws, wheelbarrows, and oars as examples (Scruggs & Mastropieri, 1992). The nine chunks of information in our second challenge to memory were made easier to reconstruct once they were associated with the familiar tic-tac-toe grid in Figure 7.4. Relating new material to well-known material is known as **elaborative rehearsal.** For example, have you seen this word before?

FUNTHOSTAM

Say it aloud. Do you know it? If you had used an acoustic code alone to memorize THUNSTOFAM, the list of letters you first saw on page 252, it might not have been easy to recognize FUNTHOSTAM as an incorrect spelling. Let us assume, however, that by now you have used elaborative rehearsal and encoded THUNSTOFAM semantically (according to its "meaning") as an acronym for "The United States of America." Then you would have been able to scan the spelling of the words in the phrase "The United States of America" to determine that FUNTHOSTAM is an incorrect spelling.

Rote repetition of a meaningless group of syllables, such as thun-sto-fam, relies on maintenance rehearsal for permanent storage. The process might be tedious (continued rehearsal) and unreliable. Elaborative rehearsal—tying THUNSTOFAM to the name of a country—might make storage instantaneous and retrieval foolproof.

Levels of Processing Information

People who use elaborative rehearsal to remember things are *processing information at a deeper level* than people who use maintenance rehearsal. ***Question: What is the levels-of-processing model of memory?*** Fergus Craik and Robert Lockhart (1972) pioneered the levels-of-processing model of memory, which holds that memories tend to endure when information is processed *deeply*—attended to, encoded carefully, pondered, and related to things we already know. Remembering relies on how *deeply* people process information, not on whether memories are transferred from one *stage* of memory to another.

Evidence for the importance of levels of processing information is found in an experiment with three groups of college students, all of whom were asked to study a picture of a living room for one minute (Bransford et al., 1977). The groups' examination of the picture entailed different approaches. Two groups were informed that small *x*'s were imbedded in the picture. The first of these groups was asked to find the *x*'s by scanning the picture horizontally and vertically. The second group was informed that the *x*'s could be found in the edges of the objects in the room and was asked to look for them there. The third group was asked, instead, to think about how it would use the objects pictured in the room. As a result of the divergent sets of instructions, the first two groups (the *x* hunters) processed information about the objects in the picture superficially. But the third group rehearsed the objects elaboratively—that is, members of this group thought about the objects in terms of their meanings and uses. It should not be surprising that the third group remembered many times more objects than the first two groups.

In another experiment, researchers asked subjects to indicate whether they recognized photos of faces they had been shown under one of three conditions: (1) being asked to recall the gender of the person in the photo, (2) being asked to recall the width of the person's nose, or (3) being asked to judge whether the person is honest (Bloom & Mudd, 1991). Subjects asked to form judgments about the persons' honesty recognized more faces. Asking people to judge other people's honesty may stimulate deeper processing of the facial features. That is, subjects may study each face in detail to see if they can relate what they see to their ideas about human nature.

Language arts teachers encourage students to use new vocabulary words in sentences to process them more deeply. Each new usage is an instance of elaborative rehearsal. Usage helps build semantic codes that make it easier to retrieve the meanings of words in the future. When I was in high school, teachers of foreign languages told us that learning classical languages "exercises the mind" so that we would under-

Elaborative Rehearsal
A method for increasing retention of new information by relating it to information that is well known.

stand English better. Not exactly. The mind is not analogous to a muscle that responds to exercise. However, the meanings of many English words are based on foreign ones. A person who recognizes that *retrieve* stems from roots meaning "again" (*re-*) and "find" (*trouver* in French) is less likely to forget that *retrieval* means "finding again" or "bringing back."

Think, too, of all the algebra and geometry problems we were asked to solve in high school. Each problem is an application of a procedure and, perhaps, of certain formulas and theorems. By repeatedly applying the procedures, formulas, and theorems in different contexts, we rehearse them elaboratively. As a consequence, we are more likely to remember them. Knowledge of the ways in which a formula or an equation is used helps us remember the formula. Also, by building one geometry theorem on another, we relate new theorems to ones that we already understand. As a result, we process information about them more deeply and remember them better.

There is also a good deal of biologically oriented research that connects deep processing with activity in certain parts of the brain, notably the prefrontal area of the cerebral cortex (Grady et al., 1999). Fergus Craik and his colleagues (e.g., Grady et al., 1999) are discovering that one reason that older adults show memory loss is that they tend not to process information quite as deeply as younger people do. Deep processing requires sustained attention, and older adults, along with people who have suffered brain injuries and strokes, are apparently not capable of focusing their attention as well as they had previously (Iidaka et al., 2000; Winocur et al., 2000).

Before proceeding to the next section, cover the preceding paragraph with your hand. Which of the following words is spelled correctly: *retrieval* or *retreival*? The spellings sound alike, so an acoustic code for reconstructing the correct spelling would fail. Yet a semantic code, such as the spelling rule "*i* before *e* except after *c*," would allow you to reconstruct the correct spelling: retri*e*val.

Flashbulb Memories: "To Leave a Scar Upon the Cerebral Tissues"

The attention which we lend to an experience is proportional to its vivid or interesting character; and it is a notorious fact that what interests us most vividly at the time is, other things equal, what we remember best. An impression may be so exciting emotionally as almost to leave a scar upon the cerebral tissues.

—William James

Many of us will never forget where we were or what we were doing when we learned of the attacks on the World Trade Center and the Pentagon on September 11, 2001. Some of us will similarly recall where we were and what we were doing when we learned that John F. Kennedy Jr.'s airplane had crashed into the ocean in 1999—or that his father had been assassinated in 1963. Others will recall the day in 1997 when Britain's Princess Diana died in an automobile accident. We may also have a detailed memory of what we were doing when we learned of a relative's death.

Question: Why is it that some events, like the attack of September 11, 2001, can be etched in memory for a lifetime? It appears that we tend to remember events that are surprising, important, and emotionally stirring more clearly. Such events can create "flashbulb memories," which preserve experiences in detail (Conway et al., 1994; Finkenauer et al., 1998). Why is the memory etched when the "flashbulb" goes off? One factor is the distinctness of the memory. It is easier to discriminate stimuli that stand out. Such events are striking in themselves. The feelings caused by them are also special. It is thus relatively easy to pick them out from the storehouse of memories. Major events such as the assassination of a president or the loss of a close relative also tend to have important effects on our lives. We are likely to dwell on them and form networks of associations. That is, we are likely to rehearse them elaboratively. Our rehearsal may include great expectations, or deep fears, for the future.

Biology is intimately connected with psychology. Strong feelings are connected with the secretion of stress hormones, and stress hormones help etch events into our memory—"as almost to leave a scar upon the cerebral tissues," poetically speaking.

REFLECT

Do you have difficulty spelling receive *or* retrieve? *How do you remember how to spell "receive"?*

REFLECT

Do you remember the first time you were in love? Can you remember how the streets and the trees looked transformed? The vibrancy in your step? How generous you felt? How all of life's problems seemed suddenly solved? Are there some things that you feel certain you will never forget? What is special about these memories?

AP/Wide World Photos

■ Flashbulb Memories

Where were you and what were you doing on the morning of September 11, 2001? Many older Americans never forgot where they were and what they were doing when they learned about the attack on Pearl Harbor on December 7, 1941. Major events can illuminate everything about them so that we recall everything that was happening at the time.

Organization in Long-Term Memory

The storehouse of long-term memory is usually well organized. Items are not just piled on the floor or thrown into closets. ***Question: How is knowledge organized in long-term memory?*** We tend to gather information about rats and cats into a certain section of the storehouse, perhaps the animal or mammal section. We put information about oaks, maples, and eucalyptus into the tree section. Such categorization of stimuli is a basic cognitive function. It allows us to make predictions about specific instances and to store information efficiently.

We tend to organize information according to a *hierarchical structure,* as shown in Figure 7.7. A *hierarchy* is an arrangement of items (or chunks of information) into groups or classes according to common or distinct features. As we work our way up the hierarchy shown in Figure 7.7, we find more encompassing, or *superordinate,* classes to which the items below them belong. For example, all mammals are animals, but there are many types of animals other than mammals.[1]

When items are correctly organized in long-term memory, you are more likely to recall—or know—accurate information about them. For instance, do you "remember" whether whales breathe underwater? If you did not know that whales are mammals (or, in Figure 7.7, *subordinate* to mammals), or if you knew nothing about mammals, a correct answer might depend on some remote instance of rote learning. That is, you might be depending on chancy episodic memory rather than on reliable semantic memory. For example, you might recall some details from a TV documentary on whales. If you *did* know that whales are mammals, however, you would also know—or remember—that whales do not breathe underwater. How? You would reconstruct information about whales from knowledge about mammals, the group to which whales are subordinate. Similarly, you would know, or remember, that because they are mammals, whales are warm-blooded, nurse their young, and are a good deal more intelligent than, say, tunas and sharks, which are fish. Had you incorrectly classified whales as fish, you might have searched your memory and constructed the incorrect answer that they do breathe underwater.

[1]A note to biological purists: Figure 7.7 is not intended to represent phyla, classes, orders, and so on accurately. Rather, it shows how an individual's classification scheme might be organized.

■ **Figure 7.7**
The Hierarchical Structure of Long-Term Memory
Where are whales filed in the hierarchical cabinets of your memory? Your classification of whales may influence your answers to these questions: Do whales breathe underwater? Are they warm-blooded? Do they nurse their young?

The Tip-of-the-Tongue Phenomenon

Having something on the tip of your tongue can be a frustrating experience. It is like reeling in a fish but having it drop off the line just before it breaks the surface of the water. Psychologists term this experience the **tip-of-the-tongue (TOT) phenomenon,** or the **feeling-of-knowing experience.** *Question: Why do we sometimes feel that the answer to a question is on the tip of our tongue?*

Research provides insight into the TOT phenomenon. In classic research, Brown and McNeill (1966) defined some rather unusual words for students, such as *sampan,* a small riverboat used in China and Japan. The students were then asked to recall the words they had learned. Some of the students often had the right word "on the tip of their tongue" but reported words with similar meanings such as *junk, barge,* or *house-boat.* Still other students reported words that sounded similar, such as *Saipan, Siam, sarong,* and *sanching.* Why?

To begin with, the words were unfamiliar, so elaborative rehearsal did not take place. The students, that is, did not have an opportunity to relate the words to other things they knew. Brown and McNeill also suggested that our storage systems are indexed according to cues that include both the sounds and the meanings of words—that is, according to both acoustic and semantic codes. By scanning words similar in sound and meaning to the word on the tip of the tongue, we sometimes find a useful cue and retrieve the word for which we are searching.

The feeling-of-knowing experience also seems to reflect incomplete or imperfect learning. In such cases, our answers may be "in the ballpark" if not on the mark. In some feeling-of-knowing experiments, people are often asked trivia questions. When they do not recall an answer, they are then asked to guess how likely it is that they will recognize the right answer if it is among a group of possibilities. People turn out to be very accurate in their estimations about whether or not they will recognize the answer. Similarly, Brown and McNeill found that the students in their TOT experiment proved to be very good at estimating the number of syllables in words that they could not recall. The students often correctly guessed the initial sounds of the words. They sometimes recognized words that rhymed with them.

Sometimes an answer seems to be on the tip of our tongue because our knowledge of the topic is incomplete. We may not know the exact answer, but we know something. (As a matter of fact, if we have good writing skills, we may present our incomplete knowledge so forcefully that we earn a good grade on an essay question on the topic!) At such times, the problem lies not in retrieval but in the original encoding and storage.

Context-Dependent Memory: Been There, Done That?

It's déjà vu all over again.

—Yogi Berra

The context in which we acquire information can also play a role in retrieval. I remember walking down the halls of the apartment building where I had lived as a child. Cooking odors triggered a sudden assault of images of playing under the staircase, of falling against a radiator, of the shrill voice of a former neighbor calling for her child at dinnertime. Have you ever walked the halls of an old school building and been assaulted by memories of faces and names that you had thought would be lost forever? Odors, it turns out, are particularly likely to trigger related memories (Pointer & Bond, 1998).

My experience was an example of a **context-dependent memory.** My memories were particularly clear in the context in which they were formed. *Question: Why may it be useful to study in the room in which we will be tested?* One answer is that being in the proper context—for example, studying in the exam room or under the same conditions—can dramatically enhance recall (Isarida & Isarida, 1999). One fascinating experiment in context-dependent memory included a number of people who were "all wet." Members of a university swimming club were asked to learn lists of words either while they were submerged or while they were literally high and dry

REFLECT

Have you ever been so close to retrieving information that it seemed to be on "the tip of your tongue," yet you could not quite remember it? Were you eventually able to retrieve it? How?

REFLECT

Did you ever have a déjà vu experience? For example, did you ever walk through your old neighborhood and recall people's faces or aromas of cooking that were so real that you actually salivated? How do you explain such experiences?

Tip-of-the-Tongue (TOT) Phenomenon
The feeling that information is stored in memory although it cannot be readily retrieved. Also called the *feeling-of-knowing experience.*

Feeling-of-Knowing Experience
Same as *tip-of-the-tongue phenomenon.*

Context-Dependent Memory
Information that is better retrieved in the context in which it was encoded and stored, or learned.

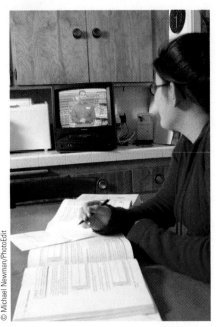

© Michael Newman/PhotoEdit

■ **Should This Student Bring the TV to Class to Take the Test?**

Research on context-dependent memory suggests that we remember information better when we attempt to recall it in the context in which we learned it. If we study with the TV or stereo on, should we also take the test within the "context" of the TV or stereo?

State-Dependent Memory

Information that is better retrieved in the physiological or emotional state in which it was encoded and stored, or learned.

Learning Connections
See Web site for an interactive version of these review questions.

(Godden & Baddeley, 1975). Students who learned the list underwater showed superior recall of the list when immersed. Similarly, those who had rehearsed the list ashore showed better retrieval on terra firma.

According to a study with 20 bilingual Cornell students, the "context" for memory extends to language (Marian & Neisser, 2000). The students emigrated from Russia at an average age of 14 and were an average of about 22 years old at the time of the experiment. They were asked to recall the details of experiences in Russia and the United States. When they were interviewed in Russian, they were better able to retrieve experiences from their lives in Russia. Similarly, when they were interviewed in English, they were better able to recall events that had happened in the United States.

Other studies have found that students do better on tests when they study under the same conditions—either in silence or with the stereo on (Grant et al., 1998). When police are interviewing witnesses to crimes, they ask the witnesses to paint the scene verbally as vividly as possible, or they visit the scene of the crime with the witnesses. People who mentally place themselves in the context in which they encoded and stored information frequently retrieve it more accurately.

One of the more eerie psychological experiences is *déjà vu* (French for "already seen"). Sometimes we meet someone new or find ourselves in a strange place, yet we have the feeling that we know this person or have been there before. The *déjà vu* experience seems to occur when we are in a context similar to one we have been in before—or when we meet someone who has a way of talking or moving similar to that of someone we know or once knew. Familiarity with the context leads us to think, "I've been here before." Some people might even wonder whether they had experienced the situation in a former life, or whether their experience is something supernatural. Although your feelings and ideas are flooding in because of the similarity of the context, the sense that you have been there before, or done this thing before, can be so strong that you just stand back and wonder.

State-Dependent Memory

State-dependent memory is an extension of context-dependent memory. It sometimes happens that we retrieve information better when we are in a physiological or emotional state that is similar to the one in which we encoded and stored the information. Feeling the rush of love may trigger images of other times when we fell in love. The grip of anger may prompt memories of incidents of frustration and rage. The research in this area even extends to states in which we are sober or inebriated!

Gordon Bower (1981) ran experiments in which happy or sad moods were induced by hypnotic suggestion. The subjects then learned lists of words. People who learned a list while in a happy mood showed better recall when a happy state was induced again. But people who had learned the list while in a sad mood showed superior recall when they were saddened again.

Studies of this kind are usually run with normal subjects. However, one study was carried out with people with bipolar disorder (also known as manic-depressive disorder). In this psychological disorder, moods swing from the heights of elation to the depths of depression and back, with no apparent external cause. The researchers found that the participants in the study had better recall of events that occurred when they were "up" or "down" when they were in the same mood (Eich et al., 1997).

Psychologists suggest that in day-to-day life a happy mood influences us to focus on positive events (Eich, 1995; Matt et al., 1992). As a result, we have better recall of these events in the future. A sad mood, unfortunately, leads us to focus on and recall the negative. Happiness may feed on happiness; but, under extreme circumstances, sadness can develop into a vicious cycle and lead to depression.

R E V I E W

(8) The Atkinson–Shiffrin model hypothesizes three stages of memory: sensory memory, _____-term memory, and long-term memory. (9) The mental representations of visual stimuli are referred to as _____. (10) The ability to retain exact mental representations of visual stimuli over long amounts of time is termed _____ imagery. (11) The mental representations of _____ stimuli are called *echoes.*

(12) According to the _____-position effect, we are most likely to recall the first and last items in a series. (13) The Petersons showed that information can be displaced from short-term memory by means of _____. (14) Elizabeth Loftus and other psychologists have shown that we _____ our memories according to our schemas. (15) We need the proper _____ to retrieve information in long-term memory. (16) Detailed memories of surprising, important, and emotional events are termed "_____ memories." (17) Information in long-term memory is organized in a _____ structure. (18) The _____-of-the-tongue phenomenon reflects incomplete learning. (19) _____-dependent memory refers to information that is better retrieved under the circumstances in which it was encoded and stored.

Critical Thinking: Can we know whether our own memories are accurate? Is it possible to function in a world of uncertain memory? (Do you have a choice?)

FORGETTING: WILL YOU REMEMBER HOW WE FORGET?

What do DAL, RIK, BOF, and ZEX have in common? They are all **nonsense syllables.** Nonsense syllables are meaningless sets of two consonants with a vowel sandwiched in between. They were first used by Hermann Ebbinghaus to study memory and forgetting. Because nonsense syllables are intended to be meaningless, remembering them should depend on simple acoustic coding and maintenance rehearsal rather than on elaborative rehearsal, semantic coding, or other ways of making learning meaningful. They are thus well suited for use in the measurement of forgetting. *Question: What types of memory tasks are used in measuring forgetting?*

Memory Tasks Used in Measuring Forgetting

Three basic memory tasks have been used by psychologists to measure forgetting: recognition, recall, and relearning. Nonsense syllables have been used in studying each of them. The study of these memory tasks has led to several conclusions about the nature of forgetting.

Recognition

One aspect of forgetting is failure to recognize something we have experienced. There are many ways of measuring **recognition.** In many studies, psychologists ask subjects to read a list of nonsense syllables. The subjects then read a second list of nonsense syllables and indicate whether they recognize any of the syllables as having appeared on the first list. Forgetting is defined as failure to recognize a syllable that has been read before.

In another kind of recognition study, Harry Bahrick and his colleagues (1975) studied high-school graduates who had been out of school for various lengths of time. They interspersed photos of the graduates' classmates with four times as many photos of strangers. Recent graduates correctly recognized former classmates 90% of the time. Those who had been out of school for 40 years recognized former classmates 75% of the time. A chance level of recognition would have been only 20% (1 photo in 5 was of an actual classmate). Thus even older people showed rather solid long-term recognition ability.

Recognition is the easiest type of memory task. This is why multiple-choice tests are easier than fill-in-the-blank or essay tests. We can recognize correct answers more easily than we can recall them unaided.

Recall

In his own studies of **recall,** another kind of memory task, Ebbinghaus would read lists of nonsense syllables aloud to the beat of a metronome and then see how many he could produce from memory. After reading through a list once, he usually would be able to recall seven syllables—the typical limit for short-term memory.

Psychologists also often use lists of pairs of nonsense syllables, called **paired associates,** to measure recall. A list of paired associates is shown in Figure 7.8. Subjects read

■ **Hermann Ebbinghaus**

While teaching at the University of Berlin, Ebbinghaus constructed some 2,300 nonsense syllables to be used as tools in studying memory. He used himself as his main subject and read through lists of 12 to 16 nonsense syllables repeatedly until he had memorized them. Then he would test himself. On one occasion, he rehearsed 420 lists of 16 nonsense syllables 34 times each. His immense labors led to the commonly used concepts of *savings* and the *forgetting curve.*

R E F L E C T

Are multiple-choice test questions easier for you than fill-in-the-blanks? If so, why?

Nonsense Syllables
Meaningless sets of two consonants, with a vowel sandwiched in between, that are used to study memory.

Recognition
In information processing, the easiest memory task, involving identification of objects or events encountered before.

Recall
Retrieval or reconstruction of learned material.

Paired Associates
Nonsense syllables presented in pairs in experiments that measure recall.

◼ Figure 7.8
Paired Associates

Psychologists often use paired associates to measure recall. Retrieving CEG in response to the cue WOM is made easier by an image of a WOMan smoking a "CEG-arette."

Relearning
A measure of retention. Material is usually relearned more quickly than it is learned initially.

Method of Savings
A measure of retention in which the difference between the number of repetitions originally required to learn a list and the number of repetitions required to relearn the list after a certain amount of time has elapsed is calculated.

through the lists pair by pair. Later they are shown the first member of each pair and asked to recall the second. Recall is more difficult than recognition. In a recognition task, one simply indicates whether an item has been seen before or which of a number of items is paired with a stimulus (as in a multiple-choice test). In a recall task, the person must retrieve a syllable, with another syllable serving as a cue.

Retrieval is made easier if the two syllables can be meaningfully linked—that is, encoded semantically—even if the "meaning" is stretched a bit. Consider the first pair of nonsense syllables in Figure 7.8. The image of a WOMan smoking a CEG-arette may make CEG easier to retrieve when the person is presented with the cue WOM.

It is easier to recall vocabulary words from foreign languages if you can construct a meaningful link between the foreign and English words (Atkinson, 1975). The *peso,* pronounced *pay-so,* is a unit of Mexican money. A link can be formed by finding a part of the foreign word, such as the *pe-* (pronounced *pay*) in *peso,* and constructing a phrase such as "You pay with money." When you read or hear the word *peso* in the future, you recognize the *pe-* and retrieve the link or phrase. From the phrase you then reconstruct the translation, "a unit of money."

Relearning: Is Learning Easier the Second Time Around?

Relearning is a third method of measuring retention. Do you remember having to learn all of the state capitals in grade school? What were the capitals of Wyoming and Delaware? Even when we cannot recall or recognize material that had once been learned, such as Cheyenne for Wyoming and Dover for Delaware, we can relearn it more rapidly the second time. Similarly, as we go through our 30s and 40s we may forget a good deal of our high-school French or geometry. Yet the second time around we could learn what previously took months or years much more rapidly.

To study the efficiency of relearning, Ebbinghaus (1885/1913) devised the **method of savings.** First he recorded the number of repetitions required to learn a list of nonsense syllables or words. Then he recorded the number of repetitions required to relearn the list after a certain amount of time had elapsed. Next he computed the difference in the number of repetitions to determine the savings. If a list had to be repeated 20 times before it was learned, and 20 times again after a year had passed, there were no savings. Relearning, that is, was as tedious as the initial learning. However, if the list could be learned with only 10 repetitions after a year had elapsed, half the number of repetitions required for learning had been saved.

Figure 7.9 shows Ebbinghaus's classic curve of forgetting. As you can see, there was no loss of memory as measured by savings immediately after a list had been learned. However, recollection dropped quite a bit, by half, during the first hour after learning a list. Losses of learning then became more gradual. It took a month (31 days) for retention to be cut in half again. In other words, forgetting occurred most rapidly right after material was learned. We continue to forget material as time elapses, but at a slower pace.

Before leaving this section, I have one question for you: What are the capitals of Wyoming and Delaware?

◼ Figure 7.9
Ebbinghaus's Classic Curve of Forgetting

Recollection of lists of words drops precipitously during the first hour after learning. Losses of learning then becomes more gradual. Retention drops by half within the first hour. However, it takes a month (31 days) for retention to be cut in half again.

Interference Theory

When we do not attend to, encode, and rehearse sensory input, we may forget it through decay of the trace of the image. Material in short-term memory, like material in sensory memory, can be lost through decay. It can also be lost through displacement, as may happen when we try to remember several new names at a party.

Question: Why can learning Spanish make it harder to remember French? The answer may be found in **interference theory.** According to this view, we also forget material in short-term and long-term memory because newly learned material interferes with it. The two basic types of interference are retroactive interference (also called *retroactive inhibition*) and proactive interference (also called *proactive inhibition*).

Retroactive Interference

In **retroactive interference,** new learning interferes with the retrieval of old learning. For example, a medical student may memorize the names of the bones in the leg through rote repetition. Later he or she may find that learning the names of the bones in the arm makes it more difficult to retrieve the names of the leg bones, especially if the names are similar in sound or in relative location on each limb.

Proactive Interference

In **proactive interference,** older learning interferes with the capacity to retrieve more recently learned material. High-school Spanish may pop in when you are trying to retrieve college French or Italian words. All three are Romance languages, with similar roots and spellings. Previously learned Japanese words probably would not interfere with your ability to retrieve more recently learned French or Italian, because the roots and sounds of Japanese differ considerably from those of the Romance languages.

Consider motor skills. You may learn to drive a standard shift on a car with three forward speeds and a clutch that must be let up slowly after shifting. Later you may learn to drive a car with five forward speeds and a clutch that must be released rapidly. For a while, you may make errors on the five-speed car because of proactive interference. (Old learning interferes with new learning.) If you return to the three-speed car after driving the five-speed car has become natural, you may stall it a few times. This is because of retroactive interference (new learning interfering with the old).

Interference Theory
The view that we may forget stored material because other learning interferes with it.

Retroactive Interference
The interference of new learning with the ability to retrieve material learned previously.

Proactive Interference
The interference by old learning with the ability to retrieve material learned recently.

R E F L E C T

Have you experienced retroactive or proactive interference in your own life or academic career?

■ **Interference**
In retroactive interference, new learning interferes with the retrieval of old learning. In proactive interference, older learning interferes with the capacity to retrieve material learned more recently. For example, high-school French vocabulary may "pop in" when you are trying to retrieve words you have learned for a Spanish test in college.

Repression: Ejecting the Unwanted from Consciousness

According to Sigmund Freud, we are motivated to forget painful memories and unacceptable ideas because they produce anxiety, guilt, and shame. *Question: What is the Freudian concept of repression?* Repression, according to Freud, is the automatic ejection of painful memories and unacceptable urges from conscious awareness. It is motivated by the desire to avoid facing painful memories and emotions. Psychoanalysts believe that repression is at the heart of disorders such as **dissociative amnesia** (see Chapter 15). There is a current controversy in psychology as to whether repression (motivated forgetting) exists and, if it does, how it works. One interesting finding is that stress hormones—the kind we secrete when we experience extremes of anxiety, guilt, and shame—*heighten* memory formation (Clayton & Williams, 2000; Ferry et al., 1999). But supporters of the concept of repression do not claim that repressed memories were ill-formed; they say, rather, that we do not focus on them.

There is much research on repression, often in the form of case studies that are found in psychoanalytic journals (e.g., Eagle, 2000). Much has been made of case studies in which veterans have supposedly forgotten traumatic battlefield experiences, developed posttraumatic stress disorder (once called "battlefield neurosis"), and then "felt better" once they recalled and discussed the traumatic events (Karon & Widener, 1998). Critics argue that the evidence for such repression and recovery of memories is weak and that this kind of "memory" can be implanted by the suggestions of interviewers (Lilienfeld & Loftus, 1998; Loftus & Polage, 1999). The issue remains controversial, as highlighted in the following pages.

▶ CONTROVERSY IN PSYCHOLOGY ◀

Do people really recover repressed memories of sexual abuse at an early age, or are these "memories" implanted by interviewers?

There is apparently little doubt that the memory of traumatic events can be repressed. But, as we see in this section, there is also little doubt that many so-called recovered memories, particularly memories of childhood sexual abuse, are sometimes induced by a therapist.[2]

A young woman in psychotherapy recovered the memory that at age 13 she was raped by her teacher, became pregnant, and underwent an abortion. No corroborating evidence for this event existed. In fact, the woman had not reached menarche until 15, so the pregnancy was medically impossible. Still, she filed criminal charges against the teacher, who had to spend his life savings to defend himself against the false accusation. Eventually, the court ruled that recovery of a repressed memory lacked sufficient scientific foundation to be admissible evidence.

There is apparently little question that the memory of traumatic events is sometimes repressed. For example, an otherwise law-abiding man who in a fit of rage committed a heinous crime might report it to police as if someone else had done it and make no attempt to escape or to defend himself when he is accused of the crime. Or a woman who was violently raped may afterward be unable to explain her bruises or shock until perhaps she returns to the crime scene.

Truth or Fiction?

But there is also little question that many so-called recovered memories, particularly those involving allegations of childhood sexual abuse by a parent or other close relative, teacher, or friend, are sometimes fictions induced by the concerted efforts of a therapist who fosters a belief that becomes so deeply held it seems like a real memory. This "false memory syndrome" has resulted in many family tragedies: alienation of children from their parents, loss of jobs, ostracism, and divorces.

"We don't know what percent of these recovered memories are real and what percent are pseudomemories," said psychiatrist Harold Lief, who was one of the first to

Dissociative Amnesia
Amnesia thought to stem from psychological conflict or trauma.

[2]Adapted from Jane E. Brody. (2000, April 25). Memories of things that never were. *The New York Times*, p. F8.

question these induced memories. "But we do know there are hundreds, maybe thousands of cases of pseudomemories and that many families have been destroyed by them. We also know that many therapists who track down these memories and focus on them fail to deal with the patient's real problems." Indeed, many adults who had in treatment recovered a memory of childhood sexual abuse and accused the supposed perpetrator later retracted the claim.

"Making of an Illness"

For example, Gail Macdonald, the author of *Making of an Illness,* had seen a social worker who used hypnosis and guided imagery to convince her that prior sexual abuse by her father was the cause of her current emotional problems. The social worker said she had dissociative identity disorder, a diagnosis he inflicted, she said, on "120 people in my little community."

As a result of the false memory, Ms. Macdonald said she divorced herself from her family, suffered horrible nightmares, wrote compulsively in journals about the abuses her father had supposedly committed and lost so much weight she was described as corpselike until she sought the help of a psychiatrist who said she had developed "post-traumatic stress disorder as a direct result of therapy" and helped her realize that her recovered memory was false.

How can someone tell if a recovered memory is false? Serious questions should be raised when corroborating evidence is lacking, when the so-called memory occurs before a child is able to remember, and when details of the memory are preposterous (like a rape by aliens), said psychiatrist Paul McHugh. McHugh also questioned the reliability of methods typically used to elicit these "memories." Among the most common are hypnosis and guided imagery, during which a therapist may introduce the notion that sexual abuse had occurred and ask the patient to try to remember the circumstances and who the perpetrator might have been. Sometimes patients participate in a recovered memory group where other members pressure the newcomer to recall prior sexual abuse and even suggest how it may have occurred.

Psychologist Elizabeth Loftus cited numerous studies that demonstrated how easy it was to implant a false memory. By asking a series of leading questions and by having a supposed "witness" talk about the made-up experience, it is often possible to convince someone that the event actually happened. In one study, researchers easily convinced half the adult participants that they had been hospitalized in severe pain as children or that they had been lost in a shopping mall at age 5. Several people with these false memories provided detailed embellishments.

This is especially true for young children. In a study conducted by psychologist Stephen J. Ceci, preschool children were asked weekly about whether a fictitious event had ever happened to them. By the tenth week, more than half reported that it had happened and provided cogent details about it.

In one experiment, interviewers told the children: "Think real hard. Did you get your hand caught in a mousetrap and go to the hospital to get it off?" Ceci reported: "So compelling did the children's narrative appear that we suspected that some of the children had come to truly believe they had experienced the fictitious events. Neither parents nor researchers were able to convince 27% of the children that the events never happened."

Based on his research, Ceci concluded, "It is exceedingly, devilishly difficult for professionals to tell fact from fiction when a child has been repeatedly suggestively interviewed over a long period of time. They look and act the way children do when they are trying to be accurate and honest."

Infantile Amnesia: Why Can't Johnny Remember?

Question: Can children remember events from the first couple of years of life?
When he interviewed people about their early experiences, Freud discovered that they could not recall episodes that had happened prior to the age of 3 or so and that recall was cloudy through the age of 5. This phenomenon is referred to as **infantile amnesia.**

Infantile amnesia has little to do with the fact that the episodes occurred in the distant past. Middle-aged and older people have vivid memories from the ages of six and

Infantile Amnesia
Inability to recall events that occurred prior to the age of 2 or 3. Also termed *childhood amnesia.*

REFLECT

Do children really remember little or nothing from the first two years of life? Don't they remember (recognize) their caregivers? Don't they remember language? Don't they remember how to crawl and sit up and walk? To what kinds of memories, then, does the concept of infantile amnesia apply?

ten, yet the events happened many decades ago. But 18-year-olds show steep declines in memory when they try to recall episodes that occurred earlier than the age of six, even though they happened less than 18 years earlier (Wetzler & Sweeney, 1986).

Freud believed that young children have aggressive impulses and perverse lusts toward their parents. He attributed infantile amnesia to repression of these impulses. However, the episodes lost to infantile amnesia are not weighted in the direction of such "primitive" impulses.

Infantile amnesia probably reflects the interaction of physiological and cognitive factors. For example, a structure of the limbic system (the **hippocampus**) that is involved in the storage of memories does not become mature until we are about 2 years old (Squire, 1993, 1996). Also, myelination of brain pathways is incomplete for the first few years, contributing to the inefficiency of information processing and memory formation.

There are also cognitive explanations for infantile amnesia:

- Infants are not particularly interested in remembering the past (Neisser, 1993).
- Infants, in contrast to older children, tend not to weave episodes together into meaningful stories of their own lives. Information about specific episodes thus tends to be lost. Research shows that when parents reminisce about the past with children, infant memories are strengthened (Harley & Reese, 1999; Pillemer, 1998). (Of course, one could question the accuracy of some of these reminiscences.)
- Infants do not make reliable use of language to symbolize or classify events. Their ability to *encode* sensory input—that is, to apply the auditory and semantic codes that facilitate memory formation—is therefore limited. Yet research shows that young infants can recall events throughout the period when infantile amnesia is presumed to occur if they are now and then exposed to nonverbal reminders (Rovee-Collier, 1999).

In any event, we are unlikely to remember episodes from the first two years of life unless we are reminded of them from time to time as we develop. (Really, Allyn, believe me.) Many of the early childhood memories that seem clear today are likely to be reconstructed, and they may hold many inaccuracies. They might also be memories of events that occurred later than the period to which we attribute them. Yet there is no evidence that such early memories are systematically repressed.

Anterograde and Retrograde Amnesia

Question: Why do people frequently have trouble recalling being in accidents?
In so-called **anterograde amnesia,** there are memory lapses for the period following a trauma such as a blow to the head, an electric shock, or an operation. In some cases the trauma seems to interfere with all the processes of memory. The ability to pay attention, the encoding of sensory input, and rehearsal are all impaired. A number of investigators have linked certain kinds of brain damage—such as damage to the hippocampus—to amnesia (Henke et al., 1999; Reed & Squire, 1997; Squire, 1996).

Consider the classic case of a man with the initials H. M. Parts of the brain are sometimes lesioned to help people with epilepsy. In H. M.'s case, a section of the hippocampus was removed (Milner, 1966). Right after the operation, H. M.'s mental functioning appeared normal. As time went on, however, it became clear that he had problems processing new information. For example, two years after the operation, H. M. believed he was 27—his age at the time of the operation. When his family moved to a new address, H. M. could not find his new home or remember the new address. He responded with appropriate grief to the death of his uncle, yet he then began to ask about his uncle and why he did not visit. Each time he was informed of his uncle's passing, he grieved as he had when he first heard of it. All in all, it seems that H. M.'s operation prevented him from transferring information from short-term to long-term memory.

In **retrograde amnesia,** the source of trauma prevents people from remembering events that took place before the accident. A football player who is knocked unconscious or a person in an auto accident may be unable to recall events that occurred for

Hippocampus
A structure in the limbic system that plays an important role in the formation of new memories.

Anterograde Amnesia
Failure to remember events that occur after physical trauma because of the effects of the trauma.

Retrograde Amnesia
Failure to remember events that occur prior to physical trauma because of the effects of the trauma.

several minutes prior to the trauma. The football player may not recall taking the field. The person in the accident may not recall entering the car. It also sometimes happens that the individual cannot remember events that occurred for several years prior to the traumatic incident.

In one well-known case of retrograde amnesia, a man received a head injury in a motorcycle accident (Baddeley, 1982). When he regained consciousness, he had lost memory for all events that had occurred after the age of 11. In fact, he appeared to believe that he was still 11 years old. During the next few months he gradually recovered more knowledge of his past. He moved toward the present year by year, up until the critical motorcycle ride. But he never did recover the events just prior to the accident. The accident had apparently prevented the information that was rapidly unfolding before him from being transferred to long-term memory. In terms of stages of memory, it may be that our perceptions and ideas need to consolidate, or rest undisturbed for a while, if they are to be transferred to long-term memory (Nader et al., 2000).

REVIEW

Learning Connections
See Web site for an interactive version of these review questions.

(20) The German psychologist Hermann _____ originated the use of nonsense syllables in the study of memory and forgetting. (21) According to Ebbinghaus's classic curve of forgetting, recollection drops (gradually or sharply?) during the first hour after learning a list. (22) In _____ interference, new learning interferes with the retrieval of old learning. (23) In _____ interference, older learning interferes with the capacity to retrieve more recently learned material. (24) Infantile amnesia probably reflects immaturity of the brain structure called the _____ and lack of language. (25) In _____ amnesia there are memory lapses for the period following a traumatic event. (26) In _____ amnesia the source of trauma prevents people from remembering events that took place beforehand.

Critical Thinking: Critical thinkers do not accept arguments without sufficient evidence. Does the research evidence adequately support the view that people recover accurate memories of childhood sexual abuse that had been repressed?

THE BIOLOGY OF MEMORY: THE BRAIN AS A LIVING TIME MACHINE

Psychologists assume that mental processes such as the encoding, storage, and retrieval of information—that is, memory—are accompanied by changes in the brain. Early in the century, many psychologists used the concept of the **engram** in their study of memory. Engrams were viewed as electrical circuits in the brain that corresponded to memory traces—neurological processes that paralleled experiences. Yet biological psychologists such as Karl Lashley (1950) spent many fruitless years searching for such circuits or for the structures of the brain in which they might be housed. Much contemporary research on the biology of memory focuses on the roles of neurons, neurotransmitters, hormones, and structures in the brain.

Neural Activity and Memory: "Better Living Through Chemistry"

Question: What neural events are connected with memory? Rats who are reared in richly stimulating environments provide some answers. The animals develop more dendrites and synapses in the cerebral cortex than rats reared in relatively impoverished environments (Neisser, 1997a). It also has been shown that the level of visual stimulation rats receive is associated with the number of synapses they develop in the visual cortex (Turner & Greenough, 1985). In sum, there is reason to believe that the storage of experience requires the number of avenues of communication among brain cells to be increased.

Engram
(1) An assumed electrical circuit in the brain that corresponds to a memory trace. (2) An assumed chemical change in the brain that accompanies learning. (From the Greek *en-*, meaning "in," and *gramma*, meaning "something that is written or recorded.")

Thus, changes occur in the visual cortex as a result of visual experience. Changes are also likely to occur in the auditory cortex as a result of heard experiences. Information received through the other senses is just as likely to lead to corresponding changes in the cortical regions that represent them. Experiences that are perceived by several senses are also stored in numerous areas of the brain. The recollection of experiences, as in the production of visual images, apparently involves neural activity in the appropriate regions of the brain (Kosslyn, 1994).

Research with sea snails such as *Aplysia* and *Hermissenda* has offered insight into the events that take place at existing synapses when learning occurs. *Aplysia,* for example, has only about 20,000 neurons compared with humans' *billions*. As a result, researchers have actually been able to study how experience is reflected at the synapses of specific neurons. The sea snail will reflexively withdraw its gills when it receives electric shock, in the same way that a person will reflexively withdraw a hand from a hot stove or a thorn. In one kind of experiment, researchers have preceded the shock with a squirt of water and noted that after a few repetitions the sea snail becomes conditioned to withdraw its gills when squirted with the water. They have been able to determine that when sea snails are conditioned, they release more of the neurotransmitter serotonin at certain synapses. As a consequence, transmission at these synapses becomes more efficient as trials (learning) progress (Kandel & Hawkins, 1992). This greater efficiency is termed **long-term potentiation (LTP)**. There is a great deal of research on serotonin and LTP. It has also been shown, for example, that rats who are given substances that enhance LTP learn mazes with fewer errors; that is, they are less likely to turn down the wrong alley (Service, 1994).

Serotonin and many other naturally occurring chemical substances, including adrenaline, noradrenaline, acetylcholine, glutamate, antidiuretic hormone, even estrogen have also been shown to play roles in memory. Consider the following examples:

- *Serotonin.* This neurotransmitter increases the efficiency of conditioning in sea snails (Kandel & Hawkins, 1992). It is released when stimuli are paired repeatedly, increasing the efficiency of neural transmission (LPT) at certain synapses. As a result, it appears that neural circuits are sort of carved out to represent or contain the relevant information.

- *Acetylcholine (ACh).* This neurotransmitter is vital in memory formation; low levels of ACh are connected with Alzheimer's disease. Increased levels of ACh promote conditioning in mice (Farr et al., 2000a).

- *Glutamate.* Agents that increase the action of glutamate in the brain promote conditioning in mice (Farr et al., 2000a, 2000b).

- *Adrenaline and noradrenaline (also called epinephrine and norepineprhine).* The hormone adrenaline and the related hormone and neurotransmitter noradrenaline both strengthen memory when they are released into the bloodstream following learning. Stressful events stimulate release of stress hormones from the adrenal glands—adrenaline and steroids—which, in turn, stimulate a structure in the limbic system (the amygdala) to release noradrenaline. These hormones and neurotransmitter, acting together, heighten memory for stressful events (Clayton & Williams, 2000; Ferry et al., 1999; Nader et al., 2000).

- *Vasopressin.* Also known as *antidiuretic hormone,* vasopressin affects fluid retention in the body. But like so many other chemical substances in the body, it has multiple chores, one of which is facilitating memory functioning, particularly working memory (de Wied, 1997; Dietrich & Allen, 1997). Sniffing vasopressin in the form of a nasal spray has complex but generally beneficial effects on memory (Perras et al., 1997).

- *Estrogen and testosterone.* The sex steroids, estrogen and testosterone, facilitate the functioning of working memory in, respectively, females and males (Janowsky et al., 2000). Estrogen replacement helps older, postmenopausal women retain cognitive functioning.

Other research has focused on the potential of the stimulant nicotine to aid in the formation of memories, even to delay the progression of Alzheimer's disease.

R E F L E C T

Can you think of any uses of knowledge about how various neurotransmitters and other substances affect memory formation?

Long-Term Potentiation (LTP)
Enhanced efficiency in synaptic transmission that follows brief, rapid stimulation.

Brain Structures and Memory

Question: What structures in the brain are connected with memory?   Memory does not reside at a single point in the brain or in a single structure of the brain. The ability to recall one's past relies on large-scale neural networks that draw on the functions of various parts of the brain (Nyberg et al., 2000).

Yet various parts of the brain appear to play more or less specific roles in memory. Consider the problems that beset H. M. after his operation. Parts of the brain such as the hippocampus are also involved in the formation of new memories—or the transfer of information from short-term to long-term memory (Rodriguez & Levy, 2001). The hippocampus, a part of the limbic system, does not comprise the "storage bins" for memories themselves, because H. M.'s memories prior to the operation were not destroyed. For example, memory for places learned long ago remains intact after damage to the hippocampus (Teng & Squire, 1999). Rather, it is involved in relaying incoming sensory information to parts of the cortex. Research shows that alcohol interferes with learning and memory by changing cellular activity in the hippocampus and related structures (A. M. White et al., 2000). The hippocampus is vital in storing new information even if we can retrieve old information without it (Reed & Squire, 1997; Squire, 1996).

Where are the storage bins? The brain stores parts of memories in the appropriate areas of the sensory cortex. Sights are stored in the visual cortex, sounds in the auditory cortex, and so on. The limbic system is largely responsible for integrating these pieces of information when we recall an event. However, research with animals and people suggests that an area in the frontal lobe (labeled "Place and Time") stores information about where and when an event occurred (Chafee & Goldman-Rakic, 2000; Goldman-Rakic et al., 2000).

But what of the decision to try to recall something? What of the spark of consciousness that drives us to move backward in time or to strive to remember to perform an action in the future? The prefrontal cortex acts apparently as the executive center in memory. It appears to empower people with consciousness—the ability to mentally represent and become aware of experiences that occur in the past, present, and future. It enables people to mentally travel back in subjective time to reexperience the personal, autobiographical past (Wheeler et al., 1997). It also enables people to focus on the things they intend to do in the future, such as mail a letter on the way to class or brush their teeth before going to bed (Fuster, 2000; McDaniel et al., 1999). People in whom the prefrontal cortex is damaged frequently try to fill in the memory gaps by making up stories about when and where certain events took place.

The hippocampus is much involved in the where and when of things. The hippocampus does not become mature until we are about 2 years old. Immaturity may be connected with infantile amnesia. Adults with hippocampal damage may be able to form new procedural memories, even though they cannot form new episodic ("where and when") memories. For example, they can acquire the skill of reading words backwards even though they cannot recall individual practice sessions (Reed & Squire, 1997; Squire, 1996).

The thalamus is involved in verbal memories. Part of the thalamus of an Air Force cadet known as N. A. was damaged in a freak fencing accident. After the episode, N. A. could no longer form verbal memories. But ability to form visual memories was unimpaired (Squire, 1996).

The encoding, storage, and retrieval of information thus involve biological activity. As we learn, new synapses are developed, and changes occur at existing synapses. Parts of the brain are also involved in the formation of memories. In the next chapter, we see how people manipulate information they have stored to adapt to the environment or create new environments.

REVIEW

(27) Experience enhances the avenues of communication among brain cells by development of dendrites and _____ . (28) Conditioning of sea snails causes more of

Learning Connections
See Web site for an interactive version of these review questions.

the neurotransmitter _____ to be released at certain synapses, making transmission at these synapses more efficient. (29) The hippocampus appears vital to the storage of (new or old?) information. (30) The _____ seems to be involved in the formation of verbal memories.

Critical Thinking: This is a psychology course. Why do we discuss the biology of memory?

Using the Psychology of Memory to Enhance Your Memory

Humans have survived the Ice Age, the Stone Age, the Iron Age, and, a bit more recently, the Industrial Revolution. Now we are trying to cope with the so-called Age of Information, in which there has been an explosion of information. Computers have been developed to process it. Humans, too, process information, and there is more of it to process than ever before. We can always add more memory to our computers, but how can people improve their memory? Fortunately, psychologists have helped devise methods for improving memory. Let us consider some of them.

Drill and Practice: "A, B, C, D . . ."

Repetition (rote maintenance rehearsal) helps transfer information from short-term to long-term memory. Does maintenance rehearsal seem too mechanical for you as a college student? If so, don't forget that this is how you learned the alphabet and how to count! Schoolchildren write spelling words over and over to remember them. Athletes repeat motions so that they will become an implicit memory. When you have memorized formulas, during a test you can use your time to think about when to apply them, rather than using up valuable time trying to recall them.

Some students use flash cards to help them remember facts. For example, they might write "The originator of modern behaviorism is _____" on one side of the card and "John Broadus Watson" on the flip side.

In his book *Super Memory*, Douglas Herrmann (1991) recommends the following methods for remembering a person's name:

1. Say the name out loud.
2. Ask the person a question, using her or his name.
3. Use the person's name as many times as you can during your conversation.
4. Write down the name when the conversation has ended.

Relate New Information to What Is Already Known

Relating new information to what is already known is a form of elaborative rehearsal that helps us to remember it (Willoughby et al., 1994). Herrmann (1991) also suggests that you can better remember the name of a new acquaintance by thinking of a rhyme for it. Now you have done some active thinking about the name, and you also have two tags for the person, not one. If you are trying to retrieve the spelling of the word *retrieve,* do so by retrieving the rule "*i* before *e* except after *c.*" There are exceptions, of course: Remember that "weird" doesn't follow the rule because it's a "weird" word.

We normally expand our knowledge base by relating new items to things already known. Children learn that a cello is like a violin, only bigger. A bass fiddle is also like a violin, but bigger yet. We remember information about whales by relating whales to other mammals. Similarly, we are better able to recall information about porpoises and dolphins if we think of them as small whales (not as bright fish).

The media are filled with stories about people who exhibit psychological disorders of one kind or another. To help remember the disorders discussed in Chapter 15, think of film or TV characters with those disorders. How were the characters' behaviors consistent (or inconsistent) with the descriptions in the text (and those offered by your professor)?

Form Unusual, Exaggerated Associations

Psychologist Charles L. Brewer uses an interesting method to teach psychology students the fundamentals of shaping:

> Dr. Brewer first danced on his desk, then bleated like a sheep and finally got down on "all fours and oinked like a pig," he said. His antics were in response to a session he teaches on "successive approximation"—shaping behavior into a desired response.
>
> To get students to "shape" him, he told them he would try to figure out what they wanted him to do. If he guessed wrong, they'd "boo and hiss," while if he did what they wanted, they'd applaud him—which is why he eventually acted like a pig. "I'll do anything to get them to learn," he said. (DeAngelis, 1994a, p. 40)

It is easier to recall stimuli that stand out from the crowd. We pay more attention to them. Sometimes, therefore, we are better able to remember information when we create unusual, exaggerated associations.

Assume that you are trying to remember the geography of the cerebral cortex, as shown in Figure 2.15 on page 68. Why not think of what you look like in right profile? (Use your left profile if it is better.) Then imagine a new imaging technique in which we can see through your skull and find four brightly colored lobes in the right hemisphere of your cerebral cortex. Not only that, but there are little people (let's call them "homunculi") who are flapping about in the sensory and motor areas (see Figure 2.15 again).

Then you see that the perpetrator of the crime is a very attractive and apologetic stranger! What part of the occipital lobe is flashing the wonderful images?

Use the Method of Loci: Meat Loaf in the Navel

Another way to form unusual associations is the *method of loci* (pronounced LOW-sigh). Select a series of related images such as the parts of your body or the furniture in your home. Then imagine an item from your shopping list, or another list you want to remember, as being attached to each image. Consider this meaty application: Remember your shopping list by imagining meat loaf in your navel and a strip of bacon draped over your nose.

By placing meat loaf or a favorite complete dinner in your navel, rather than a single item such as ground beef, you can combine several items into one chunk of information. At the supermarket, you recall the ingredients for meat loaf and consider whether you need each one.

Use Mediation: Find a Conceptual Bridge

The method of mediation also relies on forming associations: You link two items with a third one that ties them together. What if you are having difficulty remembering that John's wife's name is Tillie? You can mediate between John and Tillie as follows. Reflect that *john* is a slang term for bathroom. Bathrooms often have ceramic *tiles. Tiles,* of course, sounds like *Tillie.* So it goes: John → bathroom tiles → Tillie.

I used a combination of mediation and formation of unusual associations to help me remember foreign vocabulary words in high school. For example, the Spanish word *mujer* (pronounced moo-hair [almost]), means "woman" in English. Women have mo' hair than I do. Woman → mo' hair → mujer. This particular example would no longer work for me because now most men also have more hair than I, but the association was so outlandish that it stuck with me.

Use Mnemonic Devices: "Soak Her Toe"

Broadly speaking, methods for jogging memory can all be termed *mnemonics*, or systems for remembering information. But so-called *mnemonic devices* usually combine chunks of information into a format such as an acronym, jingle, or phrase. (By the way, the word *mnemonic* is derived from Mnemosyne, the Greek goddess of memory. Her name is pronounced Nee-MOS-uh-nee. How can you remember the pronunciation? Why not think of the goddess getting down on her two knees [*nee-nee*] to worship? End of commercial for mnemonic devices.) For example, recalling the phrase "Every Good Boy Does Fine" has helped many people remember the musical keys E, G, B, D, F. In Chapter 3, we saw that the acronym SAME serves as a mnemonic device for distinguishing between afferent and efferent neurons. In Chapter 5, we noted that most psychology students use the acronym Roy G. Biv to remember the colors of the rainbow, even though your "backward" author chose to use the "word" vibgyor.

Acronyms have found applications in many disciplines. Consider geography. The acronym HOMES stands for the Great Lakes: *H*uron, *O*ntario, *M*ichigan, *E*rie, and *S*uperior. In astronomy, the phrase "*M*ercury's *v*ery *e*ager *m*other *j*ust *s*erved *us* nine *p*otatoes" helps students recall the order of the planets Mercury, Venus, Earth, Mars, Jupiter, Saturn, Uranus, Neptune, and Pluto. Table 7.1 lists some of my favorite mnemonic devices.

What about biology? You can remember that Dromedary camels have one hump while Bactrian camels have two by turning the letters *D* and *B* on their sides.

And how can you math students ever be expected to remember the reciprocal of pi (that is, 1 divided by 3.14)? Simple: Just remember the question "Can I remember the reciprocal?" and count the number of letters in each word. The reciprocal of pi, it turns out, is 0.318310. (Remember the last two digits as 10, not as 1 and 0.)

Finally, how can you remember how to spell *mnemonics*? Easy—be willing to grant "a*MN*esty" to those who cannot.

TABLE 7.1 Mnemonic Devices

Mnemonic Device	Encoded Information
HOMES	The names of the Great Lakes: Huron, Ontario, Michigan, Erie, and Superior
No Plan Like Yours to Study History Wisely.	The royal houses of England: Norman, Plantagenet, Lancaster, York, Tudor, Stuart, Hanover, Windsor
X shall stand for playmates Ten. V for Five stalwart men. I for One, D for Five. M for a Thousand soldiers true. And L for Fifty, I'll tell you.	The value of the Roman numerals; "D for Five" means D = 500.
Mary Eats Peanut Butter.	The first four hydrocarbons of the alkane class: methane, ethane, propane, and butane, in ascending order of the number of carbon atoms in their chains
These Ten Valuable Amino Acids Have Long Preserved Life in Man.	Ten vital amino acids: threonine, tryptophan, valine, arginine, histidine, lysine, phenylalanine, leucine, isoleucine, methionine
All Hairy Men Will Buy Razors.	Constituents of soil: air, humus, mineral salts, water, bacteria, rock particles
Soak Her Toe.	Translates into SOHCAHTOA, or: Sine = Opposite/Hypotenuse Cosine = Adjacent/Hypotenuse Tangent = Opposite/Adjacent
Krakatoa Positively Casts Off Fumes; Generally Sulfurous Vapors.	Biological classifications in descending order: kingdom, phylum, class, order, family, genus, species, variety
Never Lower Tillie's Pants; Mother Might Come Home.	The eight bones of the wrist: navicular, lunate, triangular, pisiform, multangular greater, multangular lesser, capitate, hamate
Roy G. Biv	The colors of the spectrum: red, orange, yellow, green, blue, indigo, violet
Lazy French Tarts Sit Naked In Anticipation.	The nerves that pass through the superior orbital fissure of the skull: lachrymal, frontal, trochlear, superior, nasal, inferior, abducent

Recite   Recite   Recite

Learning Connections
See Web site for an interactive version of this chapter summary

1. **What is meant by explicit memory?**

Explicit memories contain specific information—information that can be clearly stated or declared. The information can be autobiographical or general.

2. **What is meant by episodic memory?**

An episodic memory is a memory of a specific event that one has observed or participated in.

3. **What is meant by semantic memory?**

Semantic memory is general knowledge, as in remembering that the United States has 50 states or that Shakespeare wrote *Hamlet*.

4. **What is meant by implicit memory?**

Implicit or procedural memory means knowing how to do things like write with a pencil or ride a bicycle. It is also called *skill memory*.

5. **What is the difference between retrospective memory and prospective memory?**

Retrospective memories concern events in the past that can be explicit or implicit. Prospective memories involve remembering to do things in the future. Prospective memory is affected by factors such as distraction, mood, and age.

6. **What is the role of encoding in memory?**

Encoding information means transforming it so that we can place it in memory. We commonly use visual, auditory, and semantic codes to convert physical and chemical stimulation into psychological formats that can be remembered.

7. **What is the role of storage in memory?**

Storage means the maintenance of information over time. The main methods of storing information are maintenance rehearsal (rote repetition) and elaborative rehearsal (relating it to things we already know).

8. **What is the role of retrieval in memory?**

Retrieval means locating stored information and bringing it back into consciousness. Retrieval requires use of the proper cues (just as to retrieve information stored on a hard drive, we need to know the file name.) Memory is defined as the processes by which information is encoded, stored, and retrieved.

9. **What is the Atkinson–Shiffrin model of memory?**

Atkinson and Shiffrin propose that there are three stages of memory—sensory memory, short-term memory, and long-term memory—and that the progress of information through these stages determines whether and how long it is remembered.

10. **How does sensory memory function?**

Each sense is believed to have a sensory register that briefly holds the *memory traces* of stimuli in sensory memory. The traces then *decay*. Visual sensory memory makes discrete visual sensations—produced by saccadic eye movements—seem continuous. McDougall used the whole-report procedure to demonstrate that visual stimuli are maintained in sensory memory for only a fraction of a second. Sperling used the partial-report procedure to show that we can see more objects than we can report afterward. Icons are mental representations of visual stimuli. Some people, usually children, can maintain icons over long periods of time and are said to have eidetic imagery. Echoes are representations of auditory stimuli (sounds). Echoes can be held in sensory memory for several seconds.

11. **How does short-term memory function?**

Focusing on a stimulus allows us to maintain it in short-term memory—also called *working memory*—for a minute or so after the trace decays. Rehearsal allows us to maintain information indefinitely. Miller showed that we can hold seven chunks of information (plus or minus two) in short-term memory. The appearance of new information in short-term memory *displaces* the old information.

12. **Why are we most likely to remember the first and last items in a list?**

This phenomenon is referred to as the serial-position effect. We tend to remember the initial items in a list because they are rehearsed most often (the primacy effect). We tend to remember the final items in a list because they are least likely to have been displaced by new information (the recency effect).

Recite Recite Recite

13. **Is seven a magic number, or did the phone company get lucky?**

Seven may not be a magic number, but it seems that the typical person can remember about seven chunks of information (juggle that many pieces of information in short-term memory).

14. **How does long-term memory function?**

There is no known limit to the amount of information that can be stored in long-term memory, and memories can be stored for a lifetime. However, long-term memories have not been shown to be perfectly accurate. They are frequently biased because they are reconstructed according to our schemas—that is, our ways of mentally organizing our experiences. The memories of eyewitnesses can also be distorted by leading questions. Information is usually transferred from short-term to long-term memory by one of two paths: maintenance rehearsal (rote repetition) and elaborative rehearsal (relating information to things that are already known).

15. **What is the levels-of-processing model of memory?**

This model views memory in terms of a single dimension—not three stages. It is hypothesized that we encode, store, and retrieve information more efficiently when we have processed it more deeply.

16. **Why is it that some events, like the attack of September 11, 2001, can be etched in memory for a lifetime?**

So-called *flashbulb memories,* as of the terrorist attack of September 11 or the death of a public figure like Princess Diana or JFK, Jr., tend to occur within a web of unusual and emotionally arousing circumstances. We may elaborate them extensively—that is, relate them to many things.

17. **How is knowledge organized in long-term memory?**

We tend to organize information according to a hierarchical structure. That is, we classify or arrange chunks of information into groups or classes according to common features.

18. **Why do we sometimes feel that the answer to a question is on the tip of our tongue?**

Research suggests that the tip-of-the-tongue phenomenon often reflects incomplete learning.

19. **Why may it be useful to study in the room in which we will be tested?**

This is because memories are frequently dependent on the context in which they were formed. That is, context dependence refers to the finding that we often retrieve information more efficiently when we are in the same context we were in when we acquired it. State dependence refers to the finding that we often retrieve information better when we are in the same state of consciousness or mood we were in when we learned it.

20. **What types of memory tasks are used in measuring forgetting?**

Nonsense syllables were developed by Ebbinghaus in the 19th century as a way of measuring the functions of memory. Retention is often tested through three types of memory tasks: recognition, recall, and relearning.

21. **Why can learning Spanish make it harder to remember French?**

This is an example of retroactive interference, in which new learning interferes with old learning. In proactive interference, on the other hand, old learning interferes with new learning. According to interference theory, people can forget because learning can cause cues (such as English words) to be connected with the wrong information (perhaps a Spanish word when a French word is sought).

22. **What is the Freudian concept of repression?**

Repression refers to Freud's concept of motivated forgetting. Freud suggested that we are motivated to forget threatening or unacceptable material. Research on the recovery of repressed memories is quite controversial.

23. **Can children remember events from the first couple of years of life?**

Probably not. This phenomenon is referred to as infantile amnesia. Freud believed that infantile amnesia is due to repression, but modern psychologists believe that infantile amnesia reflects factors such as immaturity of the hippocampus and failure to use acoustic and semantic codes to help remember information.

Recite   Recite   Recite

24. Why do people frequently have trouble recalling being in accidents?

Physical trauma can interfere with memory formation. Two kinds of amnesia are caused by physical trauma. In anterograde amnesia, a traumatic event such as damage to the hippocampus prevents the formation of new memories. In retrograde amnesia, shock or other trauma prevents previously known information from being retrieved.

25. What neural events are connected with memory?

Learning is apparently connected with the proliferation of dendrites and synapses in the brain. Learning and memory are also connected with the release of the neurotransmitters serotonin and acetylcholine and the hormones adrenaline and vasopressin.

26. What structures in the brain are connected with memory?

The hippocampus relays sensory information to the cortex and is therefore vital in formation of new memories. Visual memories appear to be stored in the visual cortex, auditory memories in the auditory cortex, and so on. The thalamus is connected with the formation of visual memories.

Active Learning Resources

Search Online with InfoTrac® College Edition

For additional information on the topics in this chapter, explore InfoTrac College Edition, your online library. Go to **http://www.infotrac.thomsonlearning.com** and use the passcode that came on the card with your book. Try these search terms: episodic memory, implicit memory, metamemory, eidetic imagery, working memory, eyewitness memory, context and memory, repressed memory, and mnemonic devices.

Visit Our Web Site

Go to **http://www.wadsworth.com/psychology**, where you will find online resources directly linked to your book, including interactive exercises related to PQ4R and Power Visuals for mastering and reviewing key concepts. In addition, you will find hints on using InfoTrac College Edition to answer the Critical Thinking questions throughout the text. Start with the **Self Study Assessment** for a customized **Study Plan** generated by taking the **Pre-Test** and **Post-Test.**

Connections CD-ROM

Go to the Wadsworth *Connections* CD-ROM for further study of the concepts in this chapter. The CD-ROM includes videos and animations, quizzes, and additional activities to expand your learning experience, plus interactive self-assessments to help connect the material to your own life.

Psyk.trek™ CD-ROM

The Wadsworth *Psyk.trek* CD-ROM offers tutorials, simulations, videos, multimedia glossary, and quizzing to help you master the material.

PsychNow! CD-ROM

The Wadsworth *PsychNow!* CD-ROM includes interactive exercises, videos, and animations to enhance your learning.

Thinking: The Most Human Aspect of Our Psychology

- IS THE TRIED-AND-TRUE formula always the best way to solve a problem, or is it sometimes better to jump to a conclusion?

- SHOULD YOU KEEP on plugging away at a frustrating problem or stand back from it for a while?

- IF A COUPLE has five sons, is the sixth child likely to be a daughter?

- DO PEOPLE CHANGE their opinions when they are shown to be wrong? (Do you?)

Language: "Of Shoes and Ships and Sealing Wax . . . and Whether Pigs Have Wings"

- BIRDS USE CHIRPS to signal other birds of danger, and bees use waggle dances to communicate the location of food to other bees. Are they using language?

- CAN YOU THINK without using words?

Language Development: The Two-Year Explosion

- LANGUAGE DEVELOPS from mindless crying to sophisticated use of grammar—all within a couple of years.

- YOUNG CHILDREN SAY things like "Daddy goed away" and "Mommy sitted down" because they do understand rules of grammar.

Nature and Nurture in Language Development

- DON'T WASTE YOUR time making threats. House plants won't talk.

Intelligence: The Most Controversial Concept in Psychology?

- ARE MUSICAL TALENT and sensitivity to people's feelings kinds of intelligence?

- DO PEOPLE HAVE to be smart to be creative? Do people have to be creative to be smart?

- TWO CHILDREN CAN answer exactly the same items on an intelligence test correctly, yet one child can be above average and the other one below average in IQ.

- WHY IS IT SO IMPORTANT to distinguish between the concepts of *intelligence* and the *intelligence quotient (IQ)?*

- JUST WHAT DO intelligence tests measure? Why is this question so important?

Nature and Nurture in Intelligence: Where Does Intelligence Come From?

- DO YOU "GET" your intelligence from your parents? If so, how? And how *much?*

Life Connections: Bilingualism and Ebonics—Making Connections or Building Walls?

- IS IT GOOD for children to learn one language in the home and another in the schools of the society in which they live?

When she was 9, my daughter Jordan stumped me with a problem about a bus driver that she had heard in school. Because I firmly believe in exposing students to the kinds of torture I have undergone, see what you can do with her problem:

> You're driving a bus that's leaving from Pennsylvania. To start off with, there were 32 people on the bus. At the next bus stop, 11 people got off and 9 people got on. At the next bus stop, 2 people got off and 2 people got on. At the next bus stop, 12 people got on and 16 people got off. At the next bus stop, 5 people got on and 3 people got off. What color are the bus driver's eyes?

I was not about to be fooled when I was listening to this problem. Although it seemed clear that I should be keeping track of how many people were on the bus, I had an inkling that a trick was involved. Therefore, I told myself to remember that the bus was leaving from Pennsylvania. Being clever, I also kept track of the number of stops rather than the number of people getting on and off the bus. When I was finally hit with the question about the bus driver's eyes, I was at a loss. I protested that Jordan had said nothing about the bus driver's eyes, but she insisted that she had given me enough information to answer the question.

One of the requirements of problem solving is paying attention to relevant information (de Jong & Das-Smaal, 1995). To do that, you need some familiarity with the type of problem you are dealing with. I immediately classified the bus driver problem as a trick question and paid attention to information that apparently was superfluous. But I wasn't good enough.

REFLECT

What strategy did you use to try to solve the bus driver problem? Did it work? Why or why not?

THINKING: THE MOST HUMAN ASPECT OF OUR PSYCHOLOGY

The Greek philosopher Aristotle pointed out that people differ from lower organisms in their capacity for rational thinking. Thinking enables us to build skyscrapers, create computers, and scan the interior of the body without surgery. Some people even manage to keep track of their children and balance their checkbooks.

Question: What is thinking? **Thinking** may be defined as the mental activity involved in understanding, processing, and communicating information. Thinking entails attending to information, representing it mentally, reasoning about it, and making judgments and decisions about it. Thinking is an aspect of cognition and generally refers to conscious, planned attempts to make sense of our world. Other aspects of cognition—for example, dreaming and daydreaming—may be unplanned and seem to proceed more or less on their own.

In this chapter we explore the related topics of thinking, language, and intelligence. We begin with concepts, which provide building blocks for thinking. But before we proceed, I have one question for you: What color were the bus driver's eyes?

Concepts: Building Blocks of Thought

I began the chapter with Jordan's problem. Let me proceed with an oral riddle from my own childhood: "What's black and white and read all over?" Because this riddle was spoken, not written, and involved the colors black and white, you would probably assume that "read" meant "red." Thus, in seeking an answer, you might scan your memory for an object that was red although it also somehow managed to be black and white. The answer to the riddle, "newspaper," was usually met with a groan.

The word *newspaper* is a **concept.** *Red, black,* and *white* are also concepts—color concepts. Concepts are mental categories used to group together objects, relations, events, abstractions, or qualities that have common properties.

Question: How do concepts function as building blocks of thinking? Concepts are crucial to thinking. Concepts can represent objects, events, and activities—and visions of things that never were. Much thinking has to do with categorizing new concepts and manipulating relationships among concepts.

Thinking
Mental activity that is involved in understanding, manipulating, and communicating about information. Thinking entails paying attention to information, mentally representing it, reasoning about it, and making decisions about it.

Concept
A mental category that is used to class together objects, relations, events, abstractions, or qualities that have common properties.

■ Jordan
The author's daughter, Jordan, posed the problem, "A farmer had 17 sheep. All but 9 died. How many sheep were left?" What is the answer?

The Image Maker, Berkeley Heights-Mendham, NJ

We tend to organize concepts in *hierarchies* (Figure 8.1). The newspaper category includes objects such as your school paper and the *Los Angeles Times*. Newspapers, college textbooks, novels, and merchandise catalogs can be combined into higher-order categories such as *printed matter* or *printed devices that store information*. If you add floppy disks and DVDs, you can create a still higher category, *objects that store information*. Now consider a question that requires categorical thinking: How are a newspaper and a DVD alike? Answers to such questions entail supplying the category that includes both objects. In this case, we can say that both objects store information. That is, their functions are similar, even if their technology differs.

Prototypes are examples that best match the essential features of categories. In less technical terms, prototypes are good examples. When new stimuli closely match people's prototypes of concepts, they are readily recognized as examples (Sloman, 1996). Which animal seems more birdlike to you, a robin or an ostrich? Why? Which of the following better fits the prototype of a fish, a sea horse or a shark? Both self-love and maternal love may be forms of love, but more people readily agree that maternal love is a kind of love. Apparently maternal love better fits their prototype of love (Fehr & Russell, 1991).

Many simple prototypes, such as *dog* and *red*, are taught by means of **exemplars.** We point to a dog and say "dog" or "This is a dog" to a child. Dogs represent *positive instances* of the dog concept. *Negative instances*—that is, things that are not dogs—are then shown to the child while we say, "This is *not* a dog." Negative

Prototype
A concept of a category of objects or events that serves as a good example of the category.

Exemplar
A specific example.

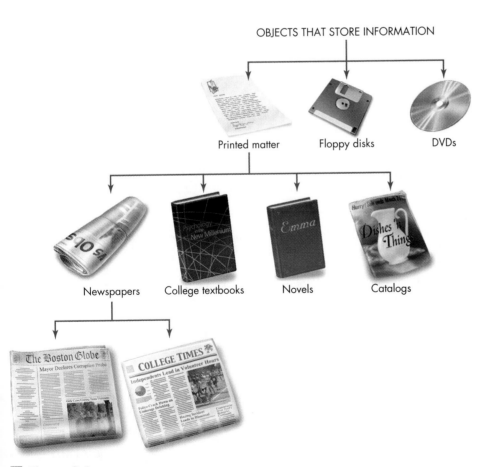

OBJECTS THAT STORE INFORMATION

Printed matter　　　Floppy disks　　　DVDs

Newspapers　　College textbooks　　Novels　　Catalogs

■ Figure 8.1
Organization of Concepts into Hierarchies

People may have a concept "objects that store information." This concept may include concepts such as floppy disk, DVD, and printed matter. Within the concept of printed matter, people may include newspapers, college textbooks (certainly the most important object that stores information!), novels, and catalogs. The concept of newspaper may include one's school newspaper and various commercial newspapers.

REFLECT

When you were a child, some people were probably introduced to you as Aunt Bea or Uncle Harry. Do you remember when you first understood the concept of aunt or uncle? Can you think of ways of teaching these concepts to small children without using verbal explanation?

instances of one concept may be positive instances of another. So in teaching a child we may be more likely to say, "This is not a dog—it's a cat" than simply, "This is not a dog."

Children may at first include horses and other four-legged animals within the dog schema or concept until the differences between dogs and horses are pointed out. (To them, the initial category could be more appropriately labeled "fuzzy-wuzzies.") In language development, such overinclusion of instances in a category (reference to horses as dogs) is labeled *overextension*. Children's prototypes become refined after children are shown positive and negative instances and given explanations. Abstract concepts such as *bachelor* or *square root* tend to be formed through verbal explanations that involve more basic concepts.

Problem Solving

Now I would like to share something personal with you. One of the pleasures I derived from my own introductory psychology course lay in showing friends the textbook and getting them involved in the problems in the section on problem solving. First, of course, I struggled with them myself. Now it's your turn. Get some scrap paper, take a breath, and have a go at them. The answers will be discussed in the following pages, but don't peek. *Try* the problems first.

1. Provide the next two letters in the series for each of the following:
   a. ABABABAB??
   b. ABDEBCEF??
   c. OTTFFSSE??
2. Draw straight lines through all the points in part A of Figure 8.2, using only *four* lines. Do not lift your pencil from the paper or retrace your steps. (See Figure 8.5 for answer.)
3. Move three matches in part B of Figure 8.2 to make four squares of the same size. You must use *all* the matches. (See Figure 8.5 for answer.)
4. You have three jars—A, B, and C—which hold the amounts of water, in ounces, shown in Table 8.1. For each of the seven problems in Table 8.1, use the jars in any way you wish in order to arrive at the indicated amount of water. Fill or empty any jar as often as you wish. How do you obtain the desired amount of water in each problem? (The solutions are discussed on pages 297 and 299.)

Approaches to Problem Solving: Getting from Here to There

Question: How do people go about solving problems? To answer this question, begin by considering the steps you used to try to solve parts a and b of problem 1. Did you first make sure you understood the problem by rereading the instructions? Or did you dive right in as soon as you saw them on the page? Perhaps the solutions to 1a and 1b came easily, but I'm sure you studied 1c very carefully.

After you believed you understood what was required in each problem, you probably tried to discover the structure of the cycles in each series. Series 1a has repeated

A Goat or a Dog?

Yes, yes, you know the answer, but little children may at first include goats, horses, and other four-legged animals within the "dog" concept until they understand the differences among the animals.

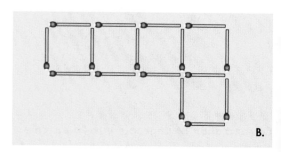

Figure 8.2
Two Problems
Draw straight lines through all the points in Part A, using only four lines. Do not lift your pencil or retrace your steps. Move three matches in Part B to make four squares equal in size. Use all the matches.

TABLE 8.1 Water-Jar Problems: For each problem, how can you use some combination of the three jars given and a tap to obtain precisely the amount of water shown?

	Three Jars Are Present with the Listed Capacity (in Ounces)			
Problem	Jar A	Jar B	Jar C	Goal
1	21	127	3	100
2	14	163	25	99
3	18	43	10	5
4	9	42	6	21
5	20	59	4	31
6	23	49	3	20
7	10	36	7	3

Source: Adapted from *Rigidity of Behavior* (p. 109), by Abraham S. Luchins and Edith H. Luchins (Eugene: University of Oregon Press, 1959).

cycles of two letters: AB, AB, and so on. Series 1b may be seen as having four cycles of two consecutive letters: AB, DE, BC, and so on.

Again, did you solve 1a and 1b in a flash of insight, or did you try to find rules that govern each series? In series 1a, the rule is simply to repeat the cycle. Series 1b is more complicated, and different sets of rules can be used to describe it. One correct set of rules is that odd-numbered cycles (1 and 3, or AB and BC) simply repeat the last letter of the previous cycle (in this case B) and then advance by one letter in the alphabet. The same rule applies to even-numbered cycles (2 and 4, or DE and EF).

If you found rules for problems 1a and 1b, you used them to produce the next letters in the series: AB in series 1a and CD in series 1b. Perhaps you then evaluated the effectiveness of your rules by checking your answers against the solutions in the preceding paragraphs.

Understanding the Problem

Let us begin our discussion of understanding problems by considering a bus driver problem very similar to the one Jordan gave me. This one, however, appeared in the psychological literature:

> Suppose you are a bus driver. On the first stop, you pick up 6 men and 2 women. At the second stop, 2 men leave and 1 woman boards the bus. At the third stop, 1 man leaves and 2 women enter the bus. At the fourth stop, 3 men get on and 3 women get off. At the fifth stop, 2 men get off, 3 men get on, 1 woman gets off and 2 women get on. What is the bus driver's name? (Halpern, 1989, p. 392)

Both versions of the bus driver problem demonstrate that a key to understanding a problem is focusing on the right information. If we assume it is crucial to keep track of the numbers of people getting on and off the bus, we focus on information that turns out to be unessential. In fact, it distracts us from the important information.

When we are faced with a novel problem, how can we know which information is relevant and which is not? Background knowledge helps. If you are given a chemistry problem, it helps if you have taken courses in chemistry. If Jordan gives you a problem, it is helpful to expect the unexpected. (In case you still haven't gotten it, the critical information you need to solve both bus driver problems is provided in the first sentence.)

Successful understanding of a problem generally requires three features:

1. *The parts or elements of our mental representation of the problem relate to one another in a meaningful way.* If we are trying to solve a problem in geometry, our mental triangles should have angles that total 180 degrees, not 360 degrees.
2. *The elements of our mental representation of the problem correspond to the elements of the problem in the outer world.* If we are neutralizing an acid in order to produce water

REFLECT

How did you go about solving (or trying to solve) the problems presented at the beginning of the section? Why?

and a salt, our mental representation of water should be H_2O, not OH. The elements of our mental representations must include the key elements for solving the problem, such as the information in the first sentence of the bus driver problem. We prepare ourselves to solve a problem by familiarizing ourselves with its elements and defining our goals.

3. *We have a storehouse of background knowledge that we can apply to the problem.* We have taken the necessary courses to solve problems in algebra and chemistry. When given a geometry problem involving a triangle, for example, we may think, "Is this problem similar to problems I've solved by using the quadratic equation?"

Algorithms

An **algorithm** is a specific procedure for solving a type of problem. An algorithm invariably leads to the solution—if it is used properly, that is. Mathematical formulas like the Pythagorean theorem are examples of algorithms. They yield correct answers to problems *as long as the right formula is used.* Finding the right formula to solve a problem may require scanning one's memory for all formulas that contain variables that represent one or more of the elements in the problem. The Pythagorean theorem, for example, concerns triangles with right angles. Therefore, it is appropriate to consider using this formula for problems concerning right angles, but not for others.

Consider anagram problems, in which we try to reorganize groups of letters into words. Some anagram problems require us to use every letter from the pool of letters; others allow us to use only some of the letters. How many words can you make from the pool of letters *DWARG*? If you were to use the **systematic random search** algorithm, you would list every possible letter combination, using from one to all five letters. You could use a dictionary or a spell-checking program to see whether each result is, in fact, a word. Such a method might be time-consuming, but it would work.

Heuristics

Question: Is it best to use a tried-and-true formula to solve a problem? Not necessarily. Sometimes people use shortcuts that enable them to jump to conclusions—including the correct conclusion. Such shortcuts are called heuristics, or heuristic devices. **Heuristics** are rules of thumb that help us simplify and solve problems. In contrast to algorithms, heuristics do not guarantee a correct solution to a problem. But when they work, they permit more rapid solutions. A heuristic device for solving the anagram problem would be to look for familiar letter combinations and then check the remaining letters for words that include these combinations. In *DWARG*, for example, we can find the familiar combinations dr and gr. We may then quickly find *draw, drag,* and *grad.* The drawback to this method, however, is that we might miss some words.

One type of heuristic device is the **means–end analysis.** In using this heuristic device, we assess the difference between our current situation and our goals and then do what we can to reduce this discrepancy. Let's say that you are out in your car and have gotten lost. One heuristic device based on analysis of what you need to do to get to where you want to go might be to ask for directions. This approach requires no "sense of direction." An algorithm might be more complicated and require some geographical knowledge. Let us say that you know your destination is west of your current location and on the other side of the railroad tracks. You might therefore drive toward the setting sun (west) and, at the same time, watch for railroad tracks. If the road comes to an end and you must turn left or right, you can scan in both directions for tracks. If you don't see any, turn right or left, but at the next major intersection turn toward the setting sun. Eventually you may get there. If not, you can always ask for directions.

Analogies

An *analogy* is a partial similarity among things that are different in other ways. During the Cold War, some people in the United States believed in the so-called domino theory. Seeing the nations of Southeast Asia as analogous to dominoes, they argued that if one nation were allowed to fall to communism, its neighbor would be likely to follow. In the late 1980s, a sort of reverse domino effect actually occurred as communism

REFLECT

Have you ever gotten lost and asked for directions? Is asking for directions an algorithm or a heuristic device? (And why are so many men reluctant to ask for directions?!)

Algorithm
A systematic procedure for solving a problem that works invariably when it is correctly applied.

Systematic Random Search
An algorithm for solving problems in which each possible solution is tested according to a particular set of rules.

Heuristics
Rules of thumb that help us simplify and solve problems.

Means–End Analysis
A heuristic device in which we try to solve a problem by evaluating the difference between the current situation and the goal.

collapsed in the nations of Eastern Europe. When communism collapsed in one nation, it became more likely to collapse in neighboring nations as well.

The analogy heuristic applies the solution of an earlier problem to the solution of a new one. We use the analogy heuristic whenever we try to solve a new problem by referring to a previous problem (Halpern et al., 1990). Consider the water jar problems in Table 8.1. Problem 2 is analogous to problem 1. Therefore, the approach to solving problem 1 works with problem 2. (Later we consider what happens when the analogy heuristic fails.)

Let us see whether you can use the analogy heuristic to your advantage in the following number series problem: To solve problems 1a, 1b, and 1c on page 294, you had to figure out the rules that govern the order of the letters. Scan the following series of numbers and find the rule that governs their order:

$$8, 5, 4, 9, 1, 7, 6, 3, 2, 0$$

Hint: The problem is somewhat analogous to problem 1c.[1]

Factors That Affect Problem Solving

The way you approach a problem is central to how effective you are at solving it. Other factors also influence your effectiveness at problem solving. ***Question: What factors make it easier or harder to solve problems?*** Three such factors—your level of expertise, whether you fall prey to a mental set, and whether you develop insight into the problem—reside within you. A couple of characteristics of problems also affect your ability to solve them effectively: the extent to which the elements of the problem are fixed in function and the way the problem is defined.

Expertise To appreciate the role of expertise in problem solving, unscramble the following anagrams, taken from Novick and Coté (1992). In each case use all of the letters to form an actual English word:

DNSUO
RCWDO
IASYD

How long did it take you to unscramble each anagram? Would a person whose native language is English—that is, an "expert"—unscramble each anagram more efficiently than a bilingual person who spoke another language in the home? Why or why not?

Experts solve problems more efficiently and rapidly than novices do. Generally speaking, people who are experts at solving a certain kind of problem share the following characteristics:

- They know the particular area well.
- They have a good memory for the elements in the problems.
- They form mental images or representations that facilitate problem solving (Clement, 1991).
- They relate the problem to similar problems.
- They have efficient methods for problem solving (Hershey et al., 1990).

These factors are interrelated. Art historians, for example, acquire a database that permits them to understand the intricacies of paintings. As a result, their memory for paintings—and who painted them—expands vastly.

Novick and Coté (1992) found that the solutions to the anagram problems seemed to "pop out" in under two seconds among experts. The experts apparently used more efficient methods than the novices. Experts seemed to use *parallel processing*. That is, they dealt simultaneously with two or more elements of the problems. In the case of DNSUO, for example, they may have played with the order of the vowels (UO or OU) at the same time that they tested which consonant (D, N, or S) was likely to precede

R E F L E C T
Why do math textbooks have all those problems at the end of each chapter? How is solving them of help to you?

R E F L E C T
Are you an expert at solving math problems? Social problems? Automobile problems? Musical problems? How did you get to be an expert?

[1]The analogous element is that there is a correspondence between these numbers and the first letter in the English word that spells them out.

them, arriving quickly at *sou* and *sound.* Novices were more likely to engage in *serial processing*—that is, to handle one element of the problem at a time.

Mental Sets Jordan hit me with another question: "A farmer had 17 sheep. All but 9 died. How many sheep did he have left?" Being a victim of a mental set, I assumed that this was a subtraction problem and gave the answer 8. She gleefully informed me that she hadn't said "9 died." She had said *"all but* 9 died." Therefore, the correct answer was 9. (Get it?) Put it another way: I had not *understood* the problem. My mental representation of the problem did not correspond to the actual elements of the problem.

Return to problem 1, part c (page 294). To try to solve this problem, did you seek a pattern of letters that involved cycles and the alphabet? If so, it may be because this approach worked in solving parts a and b.

The tendency to respond to a new problem with the same approach that helped solve similar problems is termed a **mental set.** Mental sets usually make our work easier, but they can mislead us when the similarity between problems is illusory, as in part c of problem 1. Here is a clue: Part c is not an alphabet series. Each of the letters in the series *stands for* something. If you can discover what they stand for (that is, if you can discover the rule), you will be able to generate the 9th and 10th letters. (See Figure 8.5 for the answer.)

Insight: Aha! To gain **insight** into the role of insight in problem solving, consider the following problem, posed by Janet Metcalfe (1986):

> A stranger approached a museum curator and offered him an ancient bronze coin. The coin had an authentic appearance and was marked with the date 544 B.C. The curator had happily made acquisitions from suspicious sources before, but this time he promptly called the police and had the stranger arrested. Why? (p. 624)

I'm not going to give you the answer to this problem. Instead, I'll make a guarantee. When you arrive at the solution, it will hit you all at once. You'll think "Aha!" or "Of course!" (or something less polite). It will seem as though the pieces of information in the problem have suddenly been reorganized so that the solution leaps out at you—in a flash.

Bismarck, one of University of Michigan psychologist N. R. F. Maier's rats, provided evidence of insight in laboratory rats (Maier & Schneirla, 1935). Bismarck had been trained to climb a ladder to a tabletop where food was placed. On one occasion Maier used a mesh barrier to prevent the rat from reaching his goal. But, as shown in Figure 8.3, a second ladder was provided and was clearly visible to the animal. At first Bismarck sniffed and scratched and made every effort to find a path through the mesh barrier. Then he spent some time washing his face, an activity that apparently signals frustration in rats. Suddenly he jumped into the air, turned, ran down the familiar lad-

R E F L E C T

Have you ever thought about a problem for a while and then had the solution come to you "in a flash"? Why do you think it happened like that? What was the experience like?

Mental Set
The tendency to respond to a new problem with an approach that was successfully used with similar problems.

Insight
In Gestalt psychology, a sudden perception of relationships among elements of the "perceptual field," permitting the solution of a problem.

■ Figure 8.3
Bismarck Uses a Cognitive Map to Claim His "Just Desserts"

Bismarck has learned to reach dinner by climbing ladder A. But now the food goal (F) is blocked by a wire-mesh barrier B. Bismarck washes his face for a while, but then, in an apparent flash of insight, he runs back down ladder A and up new ladder N to reach the goal.

der and around to the new ladder, ran up the new ladder, and claimed his just desserts. It seems that Bismarck suddenly perceived the relationships between the elements of his problem so that the solution occurred by insight. He seems to have had what Gestalt psychologists have termed an "Aha! experience."

Incubation   Let us return to the problems at the beginning of the section. How did you do with problem 1, part c, and problems 2 and 3? Students tend to fiddle around with them for a while. The solutions, when they come, appear to arrive in a flash. Students set the stage for the flash of insight by studying the elements in the problems carefully, repeating the rules to themselves, and trying to imagine what a solution might look like. If you tried out solutions that did not meet the goals, you may have become frustrated and thought, "The heck with it! I'll come back to it later." Standing back from the problem may allow for the **incubation** of insight. An incubator warms chicken eggs for a while so that they will hatch. Incubation in problem solving refers to standing back from the problem for a while as some mysterious process within us continues to work on it. Later, the answer may occur to us in a flash of insight. When standing back from the problem is helpful, it may be because it distances us from unprofitable but persistent mental sets (Azar, 1995b).

Have another look at the role of incubation in helping us overcome mental sets. Consider the seventh water jar problem in Table 8.1. What if we had tried several solutions involving the three water jars and none had worked? We could distance ourselves from the problem for a day or two. At some point we might recall a 10, a 7, and a 3—three elements of the problem—and suddenly realize that we can arrive at the correct answer by using only two water jars!

Functional Fixedness   **Functional fixedness** may also hinder problem solving. For example, first ask yourself what a pair of pliers is. Is it a tool for grasping, a paperweight, or a weapon? A pair of pliers could function as any of these, but your tendency to think of it as a grasping tool is fostered by your experience with it. You have probably used pliers only for grasping things. Functional fixedness is the tendency to think of an object in terms of its name or its familiar function. It can be similar to a mental set in that it makes it difficult to use familiar objects to solve problems in novel ways.

Now that you know what functional fixedness is, let's see if you can overcome it by solving the Duncker candle problem. You enter a room that has the following objects on a table: a candle, a box of matches, and some thumbtacks (see Figure 8.4). Your task is to use the objects on the table to attach the candle to the wall of the room so that it will burn properly. (See Figure 8.5 for the answer.)

Judgment and Decision Making

Decisions, decisions. Should you go to breakfast before classes begin or catch a few extra winks? Should you get married or remain single? Should you take a job or go on for advanced training when you complete your college program? If you opt for the job, cash will soon be jingling in your pockets. Yet later you may wonder if you have enough education to reach your full potential. By furthering your education, you may have to delay independence and gratification, but you may find a more fulfilling position later on. Ah, decisions, decisions.

Other kinds of decisions are judgments about the nature of the world. We make judgments about which route to school or work will be the least crowded. We make judgments about where it will be safe and convenient to live. We make judgments about what political candidates to vote for and which brand of ice cream to buy.

Question: How do people go about making judgments and decisions?   You might like to think that people are so rational that they carefully weigh all the pros and cons when they make judgments or decisions. Or you might think that they insist on finding and examining all the relevant information. Actually, people make most of their decisions on the basis of limited information. They take shortcuts. They use heuristic devices—rules of thumb—in their judgments and decision making, just as they do in problem solving. For example, they may let a financial adviser select stocks

■ Figure 8.4
The Duncker Candle Problem
Can you use the objects shown on the table to attach the candle to the wall of the room so that it will burn properly?

R E F L E C T
Do you have trouble making decisions? What kinds of decisions? What is the difficulty?

Incubation
In problem solving, a hypothetical process that sometimes occurs when we stand back from a frustrating problem for a while and the solution "suddenly" appears.

Functional Fixedness
The tendency to view an object in terms of its name or familiar usage.

Representativeness Heuristic
A decision-making heuristic in which people make judgments about samples according to the populations they appear to represent.

Availability Heuristic
A decision-making heuristic in which our estimates of frequency or probability of events are based on how easy it is to find examples.

Anchoring and Adjustment Heuristic
A decision-making heuristic in which a presumption or first estimate serves as a cognitive anchor. As we receive additional information, we make adjustments but tend to remain in the proximity of the anchor.

for them rather than research the companies themselves. Or they may see a doctor recommended by a friend rather than examine the doctor's credentials. In this section we consider various factors in judgment and decision making.

Heuristics in Decision Making: If It Works, Must It Be Logical?

Let us begin by asking you to imagine that you flip a coin six times. In the following three possible outcomes, H stands for head and T for tail. Circle the most likely sequence:

H H H H H H

H H H T T T

T H H T H T

Did you select T H H T H T as the most likely sequence of events? Most people do. Why? There are two reasons. First, people recognize that the sequence of six heads in a row is unlikely. (The probability of achieving it is ½ × ½ × ½ × ½ × ½ × ½, or 1/64th.) Three heads and three tails are more likely than six heads (or six tails). Second, people recognize that the sequence of heads and tails ought to appear random. T H H T H T has a random look to it, whereas H H H T T T does not.

People tend to select T H H T H T because of the **representativeness heuristic.** According to this decision-making heuristic, people make judgments about events (samples) according to the populations of events that they appear to represent (Kosonen & Winne, 1995). In this case, the sample of events is six coin tosses. The "population" is an infinite number of random coin tosses. But guess what? *Each* of the sequences is equally likely (or unlikely). If the question had been whether six heads or three heads and three tails had been more likely, the correct answer would have been three and three. If the question had been whether heads and tails would be more likely to be consecutive or in random order, the correct answer would have been random order.

But each of the three sequences shown is a *specific* sequence. What is the probability of attaining the specific sequence T H H T H T? The probability that the first coin toss will result in a tail is ½. The probability that the second will result in a head is ½, and so on. Thus, the probability of attaining the exact sequence T H H T H T is identical to that of achieving any other specific sequence: ½ × ½ × ½ × ½ × ½ × ½ = 1/64th. (Don't just sit there. Try this out on a friend.)

Or consider this question: If a couple has five children, all of whom are boys, is their sixth child more likely to be a boy or a girl? Use of the representativeness heuristic might lead us to imagine that the couple is due for a girl. That is, five boys and one girl is closer to the assumed random distribution that accounts for roughly equal numbers of boys and girls in the world. But people with some knowledge of reproductive biology might predict that another boy is actually more likely because five boys in a row may be too many to be a random biological event. If the couple's conception of a boy or girl were truly random, however, what would be the probability of conceiving another boy? Answer: ½.

Another heuristic device used in decision making is the **availability heuristic.** According to this heuristic, our estimates of frequency or probability are based on how easy it is to find examples of relevant events. Let me ask you whether there are more art majors or sociology majors at your college. Unless you are familiar with the enrollment statistics, you will probably answer on the basis of the numbers of art majors and sociology majors that you know personally.

The **anchoring and adjustment heuristic** suggests that there can be a good deal of inertia in our judgments. In forming opinions or making estimates, we have an initial view, or presumption. This is the anchor. As we receive additional information, we make adjustments, sometimes grudgingly. That is, if you grow up believing that one religion or one political party is the "right" one, that belief serves as a cognitive anchor. When inconsistencies show up in your religion or political party, you may adjust your views of them, but perhaps not very willingly.

Let us illustrate further by means of a math problem. Write each of the following multiplication problems on a separate piece of paper:

R E F L E C T

Do you imagine that you could ever give up or seriously change your political or religious beliefs? Why or why not?

A. $8 \times 7 \times 6 \times 5 \times 4 \times 3 \times 2 \times 1$

B. $1 \times 2 \times 3 \times 4 \times 5 \times 6 \times 7 \times 8$

Show problem A to a few friends. Give them each 5 seconds to estimate the answer. Show problem B to some other friends and give them 5 seconds to estimate the answer.

The answers to the multiplication problems are the same because the order of the quantities being multiplied does not change the outcome. However, when Tversky and Kahneman (1982) showed these problems to high school students, the average estimate given by students who were shown version A was significantly higher than that given by students who were shown version B. Students who saw 8 in the first position offered an average estimate of 2,250. Students who saw 1 in the first position gave an average estimate of 512. That is, the estimate was larger when 8 served as the anchor. By the way, what is the correct answer to the multiplication problems? Can you use the anchoring and adjustment heuristic to explain why both groups of students were so far off?

The Framing Effect: Say That Again?

If you were on a low-fat diet, would you be more likely to choose an ice cream that is 97% fat free or one whose fat content makes up 10% of its calorie content? On one shopping excursion I was impressed with an ice cream package's claims that the product was 97% fat free. Yet when I read the label closely, I noticed that a 4-ounce serving had 160 calories, 27 of which were contributed by fat. Fat, then, accounted for 27/160ths, or about 17%, of the ice cream's calorie content. But fat accounted only for 3% of the ice cream's *weight.* The packagers of the ice cream knew all about the *framing effect.* They understood that labeling the ice cream as "97% fat free" would make it sound more healthful than "Only 17% of calories from fat."

Question: How do people frame information in order to persuade others? The **framing effect** refers to the way in which wording, or the context in which information is presented, can influence decision making. Political groups are as aware as advertisers of the role of the framing effect and choose their words accordingly. For example, proponents of legalized abortion refer to themselves as "pro-choice" and opponents refer to themselves as "pro-life." Thus each group frames itself in a way that is positive ("pro" something) and refers to a value (freedom, life) with which it would be difficult to argue.

Framing Effect
The influence of wording, or the context in which information is presented, on decision making.

■ Figure 8.5
Answers to Problems on Pages 294 and 299

For problem 1C, note that each of the letters is the first letter of the numbers one through eight. Therefore, the two missing letters are NT, for *nine* and *ten.* The solutions to problems 2 and 3 are shown in this illustration (left and center). To solve the Duncker candle problem, use the thumbtack to pin the matchbox to the wall (right). Then set the candle on top of the box. Functional fixedness prevents many people from conceptualizing the matchbox as anything more than a device to hold matches. Commonly given *wrong* answers include trying to affix the bottom of the candle to the wall with melted wax or trying to tack the candle to the wall.

R E F L E C T

Did you ever use the framing effect to try to persuade someone? What did you say?

Parents are also aware of the framing effect. My 3-year-old, Taylor, was invited to a play date at Abigail's house. I asked Taylor, "Would you like to play with Abigail at her house?" The question met with a resounding no. I thought things over and reframed the question: "Would you like to play at Abigail's house and have a real fun time? She has lots of toys and games, and I'll pick you up real soon." This time Taylor's decision was yes.

Overconfidence: Is Your Hindsight 20–20?

Whether our decisions are correct or incorrect, most of us tend to be overconfident about them (Lundeberg et al., 1994). Overconfidence applies to judgments as wide-ranging as whether one will be infected by the virus that causes AIDS (Goldman & Harlow, 1993), predicting the outcome of elections (Hawkins & Hastie, 1990), asserting that one's answers to test items are correct (Lundeberg et al., 1994), and selecting stocks. Many people refuse to alter their judgments even in the face of statistical evidence that shows them to be flawed. (Have you ever known someone to maintain unrealistic confidence in a candidate who was far behind in the polls?)

We also tend to view our situations with 20–20 hindsight. When we are proven wrong, we frequently find a way to show that we "knew it all along." We also become overconfident that we would have known the actual outcome if we had had access to the information that became available after the event (Hawkins & Hastie, 1990). For example, if we had known that a key player would pull a hamstring muscle, we would have predicted a different outcome for the football game. If we had known that it would be blustery on Election Day, we would have predicted a smaller voter turnout and a different outcome.

Question: Why do people tend to be convinced that they are right, even when they are dead wrong? There are several reasons for overconfidence, even when our judgments are wrong. Here are some of them:

- We tend to be unaware of how flimsy our assumptions may be.
- We tend to focus on examples that confirm our judgments and ignore those that do not.
- Because our working memories have limited space, we tend to forget information that runs counter to our judgments.
- We work to bring about the events we believe in, so they sometimes become self-fulfilling prophecies.
- Even when people are told that they tend to be overconfident in their decisions, they usually ignore this information (Gigerenzer et al., 1991).

Before leaving the section on thinking, I have a final problem for you:

> You're driving a bus that's leaving from Pennsylvania. To start off with, there were 32 people on the bus. At the next bus stop, 11 people got off and 9 people got on. At the next bus stop, 2 people got off and 2 people got on. At the next bus stop, 12 people got on and 16 people got off. At the next bus stop, 5 people got on and 3 people got off. How many people are now on the bus?

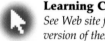

Learning Connections
See Web site for an interactive version of these review questions.

R E V I E W

(1) _____ is defined as mental activity involved in understanding, processing, and communicating information. (2) _____ are mental categories used to class objects, relations, or events with common properties. (3) An _____ is a specific procedure for solving a type of problem. (4) _____ devices are rules of thumb that serve as shortcuts to rapid solutions. (5) We use the _____ heuristic when we solve a new problem by referring to a previous problem. (6) A _____ set is the tendency to respond to a new problem with the same approach that helped solve similar problems. (7) Some problems are solved by rapid "perception of relationships" among the elements of the problem, which is called _____. (8) According to the _____ heuristic, people make judgments about events according to the populations of events that they appear to represent. (9) According to the _____ heuris-

tic, people's estimates of frequency or probability are based on how easy it is to find examples of relevant events. (10) In forming opinions or making estimates, our initial view serves as a _____ anchor. (11) The _____ effect refers to the fact that wording, or the context in which information is presented, can influence decision making.

Critical Thinking: Research suggests that people are reluctant to change their views, even when they are shown to be incorrect. What are the implications of these research findings for professors who desire to encourage their students to become critical thinkers?

LANGUAGE: "OF SHOES AND SHIPS AND SEALING WAX . . . AND WHETHER PIGS HAVE WINGS"

"The time has come," the Walrus said,
   "To talk of many things
Of shoes—and ships—and sealing wax—
   Of cabbages—and kings—
And why the sea is boiling hot—
   And whether pigs have wings."

   —Lewis Carroll, Through the Looking-Glass

Lewis Carroll wasn't quite telling the truth. The sea is not boiling hot—in most places and at most times. Nor do walruses speak. At the risk of alienating walrus fans across the land, let me assert, most boldly, that walruses neither speak nor use other forms of language to communicate.

On the other hand, the time has come indeed to talk of how talking—of how language—permits us to communicate about shoes and ships and . . . you get the idea. When I was in high school, I was taught that humans differ from other creatures that run, swim, or fly because only we can use tools and language. Then I learned that lower animals also use tools. Otters use rocks to open clam shells. Chimpanzees toss rocks as weapons and use sticks to dig out grubs for food.

In recent years our exclusive claim to language has also been questioned because apes have been taught to use symbols to communicate. (*Symbols* such as words stand for or represent other objects, events, or ideas.) Some communicate by making signs with their hands. Others use plastic symbols or press keys on a computer keyboard. Scientists debate how well chimpanzees and gorillas understand and produce language, but there is little doubt that they have learned to use symbols to communicate (Hixon, 1998; Savage-Rumbaugh & Fields, 2000).   *Question: How do we define language?*

Language is the communication of thoughts and feelings by means of symbols that are arranged according to rules of grammar. Language makes it possible for one person to communicate knowledge to another and for one generation to communicate to another. It creates a vehicle for recording experiences. It allows us to put ourselves in the shoes of other people, to learn more than we could ever learn from direct experience. Language also provides many of the basic units of thinking.

In the ongoing struggle for existence, language is one of the human assets that has enabled us to survive and prosper. Other species may be stronger, run faster, smell more keenly, even live longer, but only humans have produced literature, music, mathematics, and science. Language is intricately involved with these achievements.

Do not confuse the complexities of language with the simplicity of the communications systems of many animals. Dogs may communicate their possession of a territory by barking at an intruder, but they are not saying "Excuse me, but you are too

Language
The communication of information by means of symbols arranged according to rules of grammar.

■ An Ape Uses Signs to Communicate

Apes at Emory University's Yerkes Primate Center have been taught to express concepts by pressing keys on a computer-controlled keyboard. Do apes use language in the same way that humans do? Apes have been taught to use sign language, so the issue does not revolve around the fact that apes do not speak. Rather, many psychologists note that apes do not share the apparently inborn human grasp of grammar.

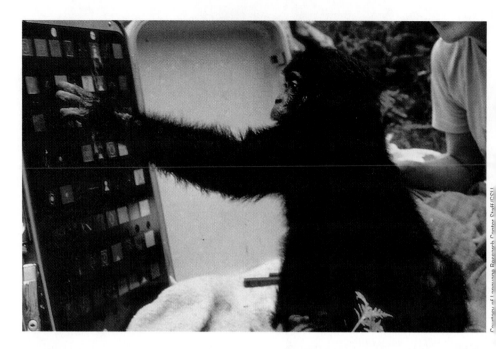

REFLECT

Have you ever known someone to claim that a pet could "speak" or understand English or another language? Did the pet really "speak"? Did the pet "understand" language? What was the nature of the evidence? What is your conclusion?

Semanticity

Meaning. The quality of language in which words are used as symbols for objects, events, or ideas.

Infinite Creativity

The capacity to combine words into original sentences.

Displacement

The quality of language that permits one to communicate information about objects and events in another time and place.

close for comfort." Birds warn other birds of predators. And, through particular types of chirps and shrieks, they communicate that they have taken possession of a certain tree or bush. The "dances" of bees inform other bees of the location of a food source or a predator. Vervet monkeys make sounds that signal the distance and species of predators. But these are all instinctive communication patterns. Swamp sparrows that have been reared in isolation, for example, produce songs that are very similar to those produced by birds that have been reared naturally in the wild. But we humans are ahead of the birds and the bees in communicating, and even the vervet monkeys and walruses. Let us see how.

Question: What are the properties of a "true" language as opposed to an inborn communication system? True language is distinguished from the communication systems of lower animals by properties such as semanticity, infinite creativity, and displacement (Ratner & Gleason, 1993).

Semanticity refers to the fact that the sounds (or signs) of a language have meaning. Words serve as symbols for actions, objects, relational concepts (*over, in, more,* and so on), and other ideas. The communications systems of the birds and the bees lack semanticity. Specific sounds and—in the case of bees—specific waggles do *not* serve as symbols.

Infinite creativity refers to the capacity to create rather than imitate sentences. To produce original sentences, children must have a basic understanding of *syntax,* or the structure of grammar. Two-year-old children string signs (words) together in novel combinations.

Displacement is the capacity to communicate information about events and objects in another time or place. Language makes it possible to transmit knowledge from one person to another and from one generation to another. Therefore, people transmit not only traits from one generation to another, but also information. Information can thus accumulate in the human species, which is another feature of the human capacity to adapt.

Language and Thinking

Let us discuss language in terms of the broader picture: *Question: What are the relationships between language and thinking?* The relationships between language and thinking are complex and not always obvious. For example, can you think *without* using language? (The answer seems to be yes, but of course you would not be able to use thoughts that entail symbols that are arranged according to rules of grammar.) Would you be able to solve problems without using words or sentences? (That depends on the problem.)

Jean Piaget believed that language reflects knowledge of the world but that much knowledge can be acquired without language. For example, it is possible to understand the concepts of roundness or redness even when we do not know or use the words *round* or *red*. **Question: Is it possible for English speakers to share the thoughts experienced by people who speak other languages?**

The Linguistic-Relativity Hypothesis

Different languages have different words for the same concepts, and concepts do not necessarily fully overlap. Can we be certain that English speakers can truly share or understand the ideas of people who speak other languages? This question brings us to the linguistic-relativity hypothesis.

The **linguistic-relativity hypothesis** was proposed by Benjamin Whorf (1956). Whorf believed that language structures the way we perceive the world. That is, the categories and relationships we use to understand the world are derived from our language. Therefore, speakers of various languages conceptualize the world in different ways.

Thus most English speakers' ability to think about snow may be limited compared with that of the Inuit (Eskimos). We have only a few words for snow. The Inuit have many words. They differ according to whether the snow is hard-packed, falling, melting, covered by ice, and so on. When we think about snow, we have fewer words to choose from and have to search for descriptive adjectives. The Inuit, however, can readily find a single word that describes a complex weather condition. It might therefore be easier for them to think about this variety of snow in relation to other aspects of their world. Similarly, the Hanunoo people of the Philippines use 92 words for rice, depending on whether the rice is husked or unhusked and on how it is prepared. And whereas we have one word for camel, Arabs have more than 250.

In English, we have hundreds of words to describe different colors, but people who speak Shona use only three words for colors. People who speak Bassa use only two words for colors; these correspond to light and dark. It may be that there are no universal basic color categories and that our tendency to separate, say, blues from greens as we do is learned within a cultural setting (Wierzbicka, 1999).

The Hopi Indians had two words for flying objects, one for birds and an all-inclusive word for anything else that might be found traveling through the air. Does this mean that the Hopi were limited in their ability to think about bumblebees and airplanes? Are English speakers limited in their ability to think about skiing conditions? Are people who speak Shona and Bassa "color-blind" for practical purposes? Probably not. People who use only a few words to distinguish among colors seem to perceive the same color variations as people with dozens of words. For example, the Dani of New Guinea, like the Bassa, have just two words for colors: one that refers to yellows and reds and one that refers to greens and blues. Yet performance on matching and memory tasks shows that the Dani can discriminate the many colors of the spectrum when they are motivated to do so. English-speaking skiers who are concerned about different skiing conditions have developed a comprehensive vocabulary about snow, including the terms *powder, slush, ice, hard packed,* and *corn snow,* that allows them to communicate and think about snow with the facility of the Inuit. When a need to expand a language's vocabulary arises, the speakers of that language apparently have little difficulty meeting the need.

Modern cognitive scientists generally do not accept the linguistic-relativity hypothesis (Pinker, 1990). For one thing, adults use images and abstract logical propositions, as well as words, as units of thought. Infants, moreover, display considerable intelligence before they have learned to speak. Another criticism is that a language's vocabulary suggests the range of concepts that the speakers of the language have traditionally found important, not their cognitive limits. For example, people who were magically lifted from the 19th century and placed inside an airplane probably would not think they were flying inside a bird or a large insect, even if their language lacked a word for airplane.

Linguistic-Relativity Hypothesis
The view that language structures the way in which we view the world.

LANGUAGE DEVELOPMENT: THE TWO-YEAR EXPLOSION

Question: How does language develop? Languages around the world develop in a specific sequence of steps, beginning with the *prelinguistic* vocalizations of crying, cooing, and babbling. These sounds are not symbols. That is, they do not represent objects or events. Therefore, they are *pre*linguistic, not linguistic.

Prelinguistic Vocalizations

As parents are well aware, newborn children have one inborn, highly effective form of verbal expression: crying—and more crying. During the second month, babies begin *cooing,* which appears to be linked to feelings of pleasure. By the fifth or sixth month, children begin to *babble.* Children babble sounds that occur in many languages, including the throaty German *ch,* the clicks of certain African languages, and rolling *r*'s. Babies' babbling frequently combines consonants and vowels, as in "ba," "ga," and, sometimes, the much-valued "dada." "Dada" at first is purely coincidental (sorry, dads), despite the family's delight over its appearance.

Babbling, like crying and cooing, is inborn. Children from cultures whose languages sound very different all seem to babble the same sounds, including many they could not have heard (Gleason & Ratner, 1993). But children single out the sounds used in the home within a few months. By the age of 9 or 10 months they are repeating them regularly and foreign sounds are dropping out.

Children tend to utter their first word at about 1 year of age, but many parents miss it, often because it is not pronounced clearly or because pronunciation varies from one usage to the next (Nelson et al., 1993). The growth of vocabulary is slow at first. It may take children 3 to 4 months to achieve a 10-word vocabulary after they have spoken their first word. By about 18 months, children are producing a couple of dozen words.

Development of Grammar

The first linguistic utterances of children around the globe are single words that can express complex meanings. These are called **holophrases.** For example, *mama* may be used by the child to signify meanings as varied as "There goes Mama," "Come here, Mama," and "You are my Mama." Similarly, *poo-cat* can signify "There is a pussycat," "That stuffed animal looks just like my pussycat," or "I want you to give me my pussycat right now!" Most children readily teach their parents what they intend by augmenting their holophrases with gestures, intonations, and reinforcers. That is, they act delighted when parents do as requested and howl when they do not.

Toward the end of the second year, children begin to speak two-word sentences. These sentences are termed *telegraphic speech* because they resemble telegrams. Telegrams cut out the "unnecessary" words. "Home Tuesday" might stand for "I expect to be home on Tuesday." Two-word utterances seem to appear at about the same time in the development of all languages (Slobin, 1983). Two-word utterances are brief but grammatically correct. The child says, "Sit chair" to tell a parent to sit in a chair, not "Chair sit." The child says, "My shoe," not "Shoe my," to show possession. "Mommy go" means Mommy is leaving. "Go Mommy" expresses the wish for Mommy to go away. (For this reason, "Go Mommy" is not heard often.)

There are different kinds of two-word utterances. Some, for example, contain nouns or pronouns and verbs ("Daddy sit"). Others contain verbs and objects ("Hit ball"). The sequence of emergence of the various kinds of two-word utterances is also apparently the same in all languages—languages diverse as English, Luo (an African tongue), German, Russian, and Turkish (Slobin, 1983). The invariance of this sequence has implications for theories of language development, as we will see.

Overregularization

An important development for understanding the roles of nature and nurture in language is **overregularization.** Consider the formation of the past tense and of plurals in

Holophrase

A single word used to express complex meanings.

Overregularization

The application of regular grammatical rules for forming inflections (e.g., past tense and plurals) to irregular verbs and nouns.

English. We add *d* or *ed* to make the past tense of regular verbs and *s* or *z* sounds to make regular nouns plural. Thus, *walk* becomes *walked* and *look* becomes *looked*. *Pussy-cat* becomes *pussycats* and *doggy* becomes *doggies*. There are also irregular verbs and nouns. For example, *see* becomes *saw*, *sit* becomes *sat*, and *go* becomes *went*. *Sheep* remains *sheep* (plural), and *child* becomes *children*.

At first children learn a small number of these irregular verbs by imitating their parents. Two-year-olds tend to form them correctly—at first! Then they become aware of the grammatical rules for forming the past tense and plurals. As a result, they tend to make charming errors (Pinker, 1997). A 3- to 5-year-old, for example, may be more likely to say "I seed it" than "I saw it," and more likely to say "Mommy sitted down" than "Mommy sat down." They are likely to talk about the "gooses" and "sheeps" they "seed" on the farm and about all the "childs" they ran into at the playground. This tendency to regularize the irregular is what is meant by overregularization.

Some parents recognize that at one point their children were forming the past tense of irregular verbs correctly and that they later began to make errors. The thing to remember is that overregularization reflects knowledge of grammar, not faulty language development. In another year or two, *mouses* will be boringly transformed into *mice*, and Mommy will no longer have *sitted* down. Parents might as well enjoy overregularization while they can.

Other Developments

By the age of 6, children's vocabularies have expanded to 10,000 words, give or take a few thousand. By 7 to 9, most children realize that words can have more than one meaning, and they are entertained by riddles and jokes that require some sophistication with language ("What's black and white, but read all over?").

Between the elementary school and high school years, language grows more complex and children rapidly add on to their vocabularies. Vocabulary, in fact, can grow for a lifetime, especially in one's fields of specialization and interest.

NATURE AND NURTURE IN LANGUAGE DEVELOPMENT

Since all normal humans talk but no house pets or house plants do, no matter how pampered, heredity must be involved in language. But since a child growing up in Japan speaks Japanese whereas the same child brought up in California would speak English, the environment is also crucial. Thus, there is no question about whether heredity or environment is involved in language, or even whether one or the other is "more important." Instead . . . our best hope [might be] finding out how they interact.

—Steven Pinker (1994a)

Billions of children have acquired the languages spoken by their parents and passed them down, with minor changes, from generation to generation. Language development, like many other areas of development, apparently reflects the interactions between the influences of heredity (nature) and the environment (nurture). **Question: *What are the roles of nature and nurture in language development?***

Learning theorists see language as developing according to laws of learning (Gleason & Ratner, 1993). They usually refer to the concepts of imitation and reinforcement. From a social–cognitive perspective, parents serve as *models*. Children learn language, at least in part, through observation and imitation. It seems likely that many words, especially nouns and verbs (including irregular verbs), are learned by imitation.

At first children accurately repeat the irregular verb forms they observe. This repetition can probably be explained in terms of modeling, but modeling does not explain all the events involved in learning. Children later begin to overregularize irregular verb forms *because of* their knowledge of rules of grammar, not through imitation. Nor does imitative learning explain how children come to utter phrases and sentences that they have *not* observed. Parents, for example, are unlikely to model utterances such as "bye-bye sock" and "allgone Daddy," but children do say them.

Learning theory cannot account for the unchanging sequence of language development and the spurts in children's language acquisition. Even the types of two-word utterances emerge in a consistent pattern in diverse cultures. Although timing differs from one child to another, the types of questions used, passive versus active sentences, and so on, all emerge in the same order.

The nativist theory of language development holds that innate or inborn factors—which make up children's *nature*—cause children to attend to and acquire language in certain ways. From this perspective, children bring neurological "prewiring" to language learning (Baker, 2001; Newport, 1998; Pinker, 1994a, 1999).

According to **psycholinguistic theory,** language acquisition involves the interaction of environmental influences—such as exposure to parental speech and reinforcement—and an inborn tendency to acquire language. Chomsky (1980, 1991) refers to the inborn tendency as a **language acquisition device (LAD).** Evidence for an LAD is found in the universality of human language abilities and in the specific sequence of language development (Baker, 2001).

The LAD prepares the nervous system to learn grammar. On the surface, languages differ a great deal. However, the LAD serves children all over the world because languages share what Chomsky refers to as a "universal grammar"—an underlying set of rules for turning ideas into sentences (Pinker, 1994a). Consider an analogy with computers: According to psycholinguistic theory, the universal grammar that resides in the LAD is the same as a computer's basic operating system (Baker, 2001). The particular language that a child learns to use is the same as a word-processing program.

In the following section we see that some aspects of language development—particularly vocabulary development—are strongly related to intelligence.

Learning Connections
See Web site for an interactive version of these review questions.

REVIEW

(12) Apes (have or have not?) been taught to use symbols to communicate. (13) Language is the communication of thoughts and feelings by means of symbols that are arranged according to rules of _____. (14) According to the _____-relativity hypothesis, language structures (and limits) the way in which we perceive the world. (15) Crying, cooing, and babbling are (prelinguistic or linguistic?) events. (16) _____ are one-word utterances that have the meanings of sentences. (17) Children's use of sentences such as "I standed up" and "Mommy sitted down" are examples of _____. (18) Chomsky refers to the inborn tendency to develop language as a language _____ device (LAD).

Critical Thinking: Let's think about definitions of terms: How do scientists distinguish true language from the communication systems of lower animals? What are the key issues in deciding whether apes can be taught to use language?

Psycholinguistic Theory
The view that language learning involves an interaction between environmental factors and an inborn tendency to acquire language.

Language Acquisition Device (LAD)
In psycholinguistic theory, neural "prewiring" that facilitates the child's learning of grammar.

Intelligence
A complex and controversial concept. According to David Wechsler (1975), the "capacity . . . to understand the world [and] resourcefulness to cope with its challenges."

INTELLIGENCE: THE MOST CONTROVERSIAL CONCEPT IN PSYCHOLOGY?

What form of life is so adaptive that it can survive in desert temperatures of 120° F or Arctic climes of −40° F? What form of life can run, walk, climb, swim, live underwater for months on end, and fly to the moon and back?

I won't keep you in suspense any longer. We are that form of life. Yet our unclad bodies do not allow us to adapt to these extremes of temperature. Brute strength does not allow us to live underwater or travel to the moon. Rather, it is our **intelligence** that permits us to adapt to these conditions and to challenge our physical limitations.

Question: Just what is intelligence? The concept of intelligence is closely related to the concept of thinking. Whereas thinking involves the understanding and manipulating of information, *intelligence* is somewhat more broadly thought of as the underlying ability to understand the world and cope with its challenges. In other words, intelligence is seen as making thinking possible.

Although these concepts overlap, psychologists tend to be concerned with *how* we think, but laypeople and psychologists are often concerned with *how much* intelligence we have. At an early age, we gain impressions of how intelligent or bright we are compared to other people.

Intelligence provides the cognitive basis for academic achievements. It allows us to profit from experiences such as educational experiences. Intelligence allows people to

R E F L E C T

When did you form an impression of how intelligent you are? Has this impression helped you or hurt you? Explain.

A Closer Look

Wired—*The Awesome Future of Artificial Intelligence*

Saying that Deep Blue [an IBM computer] doesn't really think is like saying an airplane doesn't really fly because it doesn't flap its wings.

—Drew McDermott

Science has brought us a number of artificial objects—artificial sweeteners, designer drugs, and artificial limbs, to name a few. But one of the major scientific developments is in the realm of artificial intelligence. Artificial intelligence, or A.I., is the duplication of human intellectual functioning in computers.

The concept of A.I. has a long history both in science fiction and in practice. Think of HAL, the computer in the film *2001.* Not only could HAL coordinate the monitors and controls of a spaceship; it could also engage in such human activities as committing murder, lying with a straight . . . monitor, and striving to save its own . . . memory chips. The robot C3PO in *Star Wars* not only mimicked human intelligence but also displayed remarkably human anxieties and self-doubts. What about the *Terminator* films? The programming in the artificial combination of flesh and metal portrayed by Arnold Schwarzenegger presented him with options that enabled him to size up any situation and efficiently curse, kill, or utter notable Arnoldisms like "I'll be back."

So much for Hollywood. The idea that human intelligence could be copied in computer form originated in the 1950s. It was predicted that machines with A.I. would "one day" be able to understand spoken language, decipher bad handwriting, search their memories for relevant information, reason, solve problems, make decisions, write books, and explain themselves out loud. At the time, these predictions were visionary. No longer. "One day" is today. Within certain limits, today's computers are very, very good at encoding, storing, retrieving, and manipulating information to solve problems and make decisions. And to some degree, they can even learn from experience (Fogel, 2000).

In some ways, A.I. goes beyond human intelligence. "Deep Blue," the IBM computer that defeated Russian grand master Garry Kasparov in chess, examined 200 million possible chess moves *each second* (McDermott, 1997). A.I. can solve problems that would take people years to solve, if they could solve them at all. Given clear direction and the right formulas, computers can carry out complex intellectual functions in a flash. "Who," asks University of Illinois professor Patrick Hayes (1993), "can keep track of 10,000 topics like a computer?"

But Deep Blue was baby steps. Despite its skill at chess, in nearly every other way it was much less than human. Deep Blue did not have the insights, intuitions, and creativity found in people. The sparks of brilliance we find in the best of today's computers turn into dense wood when we ask them to write prose or compose music. (I hope my computer's not reading this.)

We are likely to approach human processing power in most areas within a decade or two (Kurzweil, 2000). At that point we may have moved beyond silicon—the substance of the microchip—to "nanotubes," which are arrays of carbon atoms that would permit one million times the processing power of the human brain to be packed into a cubic inch of circuitry (Kurzweil, 2000). Computing power has been doubling every 12 to 18 months. Therefore, once we reach the human level of information processing, we (or the computers themselves!) will probably quickly push beyond. Moreover, when you learn Spanish or calculus, other people cannot easily "download" the information from you. If they could (as in the science-fiction film *The Matrix*), education as we know it would vanish. Also, one computer that learned something could rapidly share the information with all the other computers on the planet (and elsewhere).

Some futurists speak of the merging of human and computer intelligence. They speak of things like "chipping" the human brain (installing microchips that would boost our knowledge and processing power) or of microscopic robots ("nanobots") that could set up shop at synapses and boost neuronal communication or supplant it with virtual realities that would have all the immediacy of true experience (again, as in the film *The Matrix*?).

It's all stimulating and somewhat scary. We're making computers that think more like people, and we may use computers (or they may use us?) to boost our own intellectual powers. What the worlds of natural and artificial intelligence will look like a century from now is anybody's guess. But for the moment at least, the qualities that make our psychological processes fully human have not been captured by computer science. That thought doesn't bother me a byte.

think—to understand complex ideas, reason, and solve problems—and to learn from experience and adapt effectively to the environment (Neisser et al., 1996). As we see in architecture, in the creation of mechanisms for heating and cooling, and in travel through space and under water, intelligence even permits people to create new environments. Although intelligence, like thinking, cannot be directly seen or touched, psychologists tie the concept to predictors such as school performance and occupational status (Wagner, 1997).

We now discuss theories about the nature of intelligence. We see how intelligence is measured and discuss group differences in intelligence. Finally, we examine the determinants of intelligence: heredity and the environment.

Theories of Intelligence

Many investigators have viewed intelligence as consisting of one or more factors. *Question: What are the various theories of intelligence?* Factor theories argue that intelligence is made up of a number of mental abilities, ranging from one to hundreds.

In 1904, British psychologist Charles Spearman suggested that the behaviors we consider intelligent have a common underlying factor. He labeled this factor *g*, for "general intelligence" or broad reasoning and problem-solving abilities. Spearman supported his view by noting that people rarely score very high in one area (such as knowledge of the meaning of words) and very low in another (such as the ability to compute numbers). People who excel in one area are also likely to excel in others. But he also noted that even the most capable people are relatively superior in some areas—such as music or business or poetry. For this reason, he suggested that specific, or *s*, factors account for specific abilities.

To test his views, Spearman developed **factor analysis.** Factor analysis is a statistical technique that allows researchers to determine which items on tests seem to be measuring the same things. In his research on relationships among scores on tests of verbal, mathematical, and spatial reasoning, Spearman repeatedly found evidence supporting the existence of *s* factors. The evidence for *g* was more limited.

The American psychologist Louis Thurstone (1938) used factor analysis with various tests of specific abilities and also found only limited evidence for the existence of *g*. Thurstone concluded that Spearman had oversimplified the concept of intelligence. Thurstone's data suggested the presence of nine specific factors, which he labeled **primary mental abilities.** They included visual–spatial ability, computational ability, vocabulary, memory, and reasoning.

Over the years, psychologist J. P. Guilford (1988) expanded the numbers of factors found in intellectual functioning to hundreds. The problem with this approach seems to be that the more factors we generate, the more overlap we find among them. For example, several of his "factors" deal with solving math problems and computing numbers.

The Theory of Multiple Intelligences

Howard Gardner (1983/1993) proposes the existence of several kinds of intelligence. *Question: What is meant by multiple intelligences?* Gardner refers to each kind of intelligence in his theory as "an intelligence" because they can be so different from one another (see Figure 8.6). He also believes that each kind of intelligence has its neurological base in a different area of the brain. Two of these "intelligences" are familiar ones: language ability and logical–mathematical ability. However, Gardner also refers to bodily–kinesthetic talents (of the sort shown by dancers, mimes, and athletes), musical talent, spatial-relations skills, and two kinds of personal intelligence: awareness of one's own inner feelings and sensitivity to other people's feelings. Gardner (2001) has recently added "naturalist intelligence," which refers to the type of scientific insight of a Charles Darwin. He is also considering adding "existential intelligence," which refers to dealing with the larger philosophical issues of life. According to Gardner, one can compose symphonies or advance mathematical theory yet be average in, say, language and personal skills. (Are not some academic "geniuses" foolish in their personal lives?)

REFLECT

From your own experiences, what seem to be the relationships between general intelligence (g) and special talents, such as musical or artistic ability? Do you know people who are "good at everything"? Do you know people who are talented in some areas but not in others? In what areas are they talented?

g
Spearman's symbol for general intelligence, which he believed underlay more specific abilities.

s
Spearman's symbol for *specific* factors, or *s factors,* which he believed accounted for individual abilities.

Factor Analysis
A statistical technique that allows researchers to determine the relationships among large number of items such as test items.

Primary Mental Abilities
According to Thurstone, the basic abilities that make up intelligence.

**Figure 8.6
Gardner's Theory of Multiple Intelligences**

According to Gardner, there are several *intelligences,* not one, each based in a different area of the brain. Language ability and logic are familiar aspects of intelligence. But Gardner also refers to bodily talents, musical ability, spatial-relations skills, and two kinds of personal intelligence— sensitivity to one's own feelings (intrapersonal sensitivity) and sensitivity to the feelings of others (interpersonal sensitivity) as *intelligences.* Gardner's critics ask whether such special talents are truly "intelligences" or specific talents.

Critics of Gardner's view agree that people function more intelligently in some aspects of life than in others. They also agree that many people have special talents, such as bodily–kinesthetic talents, even if their overall intelligence is average. But they question whether such special talents are really "intelligences" or . . . special talents (Neisser et al., 1996). Language skills, reasoning ability, and ability to solve math problems seem to be more closely related than musical or gymnastic talent to what most people mean by intelligence. If people have no musical ability, do we really think of them as *unintelligent?*

The Triarchic Theory of Intelligence

Psychologist Robert Sternberg (2000) has constructed a three-pronged, or *triarchic,* theory of intelligence, which is reminiscent of a view proposed by the Greek philosopher Aristotle (Tigner & Tigner, 2000). ***Question: What is Sternberg's triarchic model of intelligence?*** The three types are *analytical, creative,* and *practical* (see Figure 8.7).

Analytical intelligence is similar to Aristotle's "theoretical intelligence" and may be defined as what we generally think of as academic ability. It enables us to solve problems and to acquire new knowledge, and is the type of intelligence best measured by standard intelligence tests. Problem-solving skills include encoding information, combining and comparing pieces of information, and generating a solution. Consider Sternberg's analogy problem:

Washington is to *1* as *Lincoln* is to (a) 5, (b) 10, (c) 15, (d) 50?

To solve the analogy, we must first correctly *encode* the elements—*Washington, 1,* and *Lincoln*—by identifying them and comparing them to other information. We must first encode *Washington* and *Lincoln* as the names of presidents[2] and then try to combine

REFLECT

Do the talents of dancers, gymnasts, artists, and musicians strike you as kinds of intelligences? Why or why not?

[2]There are other possibilities. Both are the names of memorials and cities, for example.

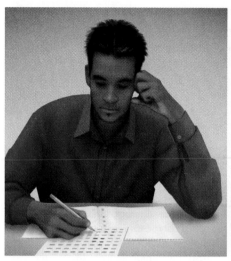

Analytical intelligence
(Academic ability)
Abilities to solve problems,
compare and contrast, judge,
evaluate, and criticize

Creative intelligence
(Creativity and insight)
Abilities to invent, discover,
suppose, or theorize

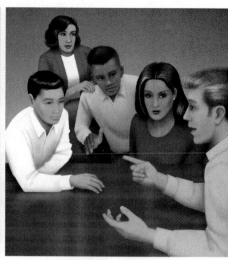

Practical intelligence
("Street smarts")
Abilities to adapt to the demands
of one's environment, apply
knowledge in practical situations

■ **Figure 8.7**
Sternberg's Theory of Intelligence
According to Robert Sternberg, there are three types of intelligence: analytical (academic ability), creative, and practical ("street smarts"). Psychologists discuss the relationships between intelligence and creativity, but within Sternberg's model, creativity is a *type* of intellectual functioning.

Washington and *1* in a meaningful manner. Two possibilities quickly come to mind. Washington was the first president, and his picture is on the $1 bill. We can then generate two possible solutions and try them out. First, was Lincoln the 5th, 10th, 15th, or 50th president? Second, on what bill is Lincoln's picture found? (Do you need to consult a history book or peek into your wallet at this point?)

Creative intelligence is similar to Aristotle's "productive intelligence" and defined by the abilities to cope with novel situations and to profit from experience. The ability to quickly relate novel situations to familiar situations (that is, to perceive similarities and differences) fosters adaptation. Moreover, experience teaches us to solve problems more rapidly. There is only a moderate relationship between academic ability and creativity (Simonton, 2000).

Aristotle and Sternberg both speak of practical intelligence, or "street smarts." Practical intelligence enables people to adapt to the demands of their environment. For example, keeping a job by adapting one's behavior to the employer's requirements is adaptive. But if the employer is making unreasonable demands, reshaping the environment (by changing the employer's attitudes) or selecting an alternate environment (by finding a more suitable job) is also adaptive (Sternberg, 1997b). Street smarts appear to help people get by in the real world, especially with other people, but are not all that predictive of academic success.

▶ CONTROVERSY IN PSYCHOLOGY ◀

Is "emotional intelligence" a form of intelligence? Should it be taught in school?

Psychologists Peter Salovey and John Mayer developed the theory of emotional intelligence, which was popularized by the *New York Times* writer Daniel Goleman (1995). The theory holds that social and emotional skills are a form of intelligence, just as academic skills are. ***Question: Just what is "emotional intelligence"?*** Emotional intelligence bears more than a little resemblance to two of Gardner's "intelligences"—intrapersonal skills and interpersonal skills.

The theory suggests that self-awareness and social awareness are best learned during childhood. Failure to develop emotional intelligence is connected with childhood depression and aggression. Moreover, childhood experiences may even mold the brain's emotional responses to life's challenges. Therefore, it is useful for schools to teach skills related to emotional intelligence as well as academic ability. "I can foresee a day," wrote Goleman (1995), "when education will routinely include [teaching] essential human competencies such as self-awareness, self-control and empathy, and the arts of listening, resolving conflicts and cooperation."

No one argues that self-awareness, self-control, empathy, and cooperation are unimportant. But critics of the theory of emotional intelligence argue that schools may not have the time (or the competence) to teach these skills, and that emotional intelligence may not really be a kind of intelligence at all.

Should emotional intelligence be taught in the schools? Some psychologists believe that "emotional literacy" is as important as literacy (in reading). However, psychologist Robert McCall (1997) echoes the views of other psychologists when he says:

> There are so many hours in a day, and one of the characteristics of American schools is we've saddled them with teaching driver's education, sex education, drug education and other skills, to the point that we don't spend as much time on academics as other countries do. There may be consequences for that.

Is emotional intelligence a form of intelligence? Psychologist Ulric Neisser (1997b) says that "The skills that Goleman describes . . . are certainly important for determining life outcomes, but nothing is to be gained by calling them forms of intelligence."

There are thus many views of intelligence—what intelligence is and how many kinds of intelligence there may be. We do not yet have the final word on the nature of intelligence, but I would like to share with you David Wechsler's definition of intelligence. Wechsler is the originator of the most widely used series of contemporary intelligence tests, and he defined intelligence as the "capacity of an individual to understand the world [and the] resourcefulness to cope with its challenges" (1975, p. 139). To Wechsler, intelligence involves accurate representation of the world and effective problem solving—adapting, profiting from experience, selecting the appropriate strategies, and so on. He leaves room for others to consider the kinds of resourcefulness—academic, practical, emotional, perhaps bodily—that are considered intelligent.

Creativity and Intelligence

Think of artists, musicians, poets, scientists who innovate research methods, and other creative individuals. *Questions: What is creativity? What are the connections between creativity and intelligence?*

Creativity may be defined as the ability to do things that are novel and useful (Sternberg, 2001). Creative people can solve problems to which there are no preexisting solutions, no tried and tested formulas (Simonton, 2000). Creative people share several characteristics (Sternberg & Lubart, 1995, 1996):

- They take chances.
- They refuse to accept limitations and try to do the impossible.
- They appreciate art and music.
- They use the materials around them to make unique things.
- They challenge social norms.
- They take unpopular stands.
- They examine ideas that other people accept at face value.

A professor of mine remarked that there is nothing new under the sun, only new combinations of existing things. Many psychologists agree. They see creativity as the

Creativity
The ability to generate novel and useful solutions to problems.

■ **Pablo Picasso at Work**
We know that the great artist was creative, but what about his academic ability? Academic ability and creativity often go hand in hand, but academic ability is no guarantee of imagination or of specific talents.

 Learning Connections
See the Connections *CD-ROM for an animation on the elevator riddle.*

 Learning Connections
See the Connections *CD-ROM for an animation on the match problem.*

 Learning Connections
See the Connections *CD-ROM for the solution to the elevator riddle.*

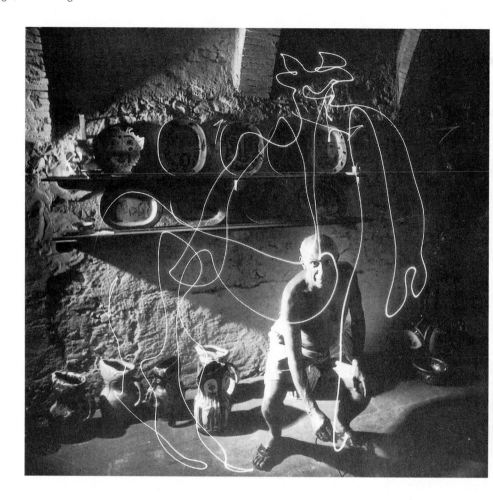

R E F L E C T

Do you know some brilliant people who aren't very creative? Do you know some creative people who are not necessarily brilliant? What is the connection between intelligence and creativity?

Convergent Thinking
A thought process that narrows in on the single best solution to a problem.

Divergent Thinking
A thought process that attempts to generate multiple solutions to problems.

ability to make unusual, sometimes remote, associations to the elements of a problem to generate new combinations. An essential aspect of a creative response is the leap from the elements of the problem to the novel solution. A predictable solution is not creative, even if it is hard to reach.

Creative problem solving demands divergent rather than **convergent thinking.** In convergent thinking, thought is limited to present facts; the problem solver narrows his or her thinking to find the best solution. (You use convergent thinking to arrive at the right answer to a multiple-choice question.) In **divergent thinking,** the problem solver associates freely to the elements of the problem, allowing "leads" to run a nearly limitless course. (You may use divergent thinking when you are trying to generate ideas to answer an essay question on a test.) Problem solving can involve both kinds of thinking. At first divergent thinking helps generate many possible solutions. Convergent thinking is then used to select likely solutions and reject others. The nearby Remote Associates Test may afford you insight into your creativity.

Let's return to the connections between creativity and academic ability. Remember that Aristotle and Sternberg viewed creativity as one aspect of intelligence. To them creativity *is* intelligence, or at least one factor in intelligence. But many, perhaps most, psychologists view creativity as somewhat distinct from the kind of academic ability that is measured by intelligence tests. These psychologists would suggest that many highly creative people do not do all that well on intelligence tests, or in school, and that many brilliant individuals have little interest in art, music, and other creative endeavors. Research findings do suggest that the relationship between intelligence test scores and standard measures of creativity is only moderate (Simonton, 2000; Sternberg & Williams, 1997). Intelligence test questions usually require analytical, convergent thinking to focus in on the one right answer.

Tests of creativity determine how flexible a person's thinking is (Simonton, 2000). Here, for example, is an item from a test used by Getzels and Jackson (1962) to measure associative ability, a factor in creativity: "Write as many meanings as you can for each of the following words: (a) duck; (b) sack; (c) pitch; (d) fair." Those who write several meanings for each word, rather than only one, are rated as potentially more creative.

Another measure of creativity might ask people to produce as many words as possible that begin with T and end with N within a minute. Still another item might give people a minute to classify a list of names in as many ways as possible. How many ways can you classify the following group of names?

MARTHA   PAUL   JEFFRY   SALLY   PABLO   JOAN

The ability to do well on these kinds of items is connected with scores on intelligence tests, but only moderately so.

Speaking of scores on intelligence tests, let's see how psychologists go about measuring intelligence.

The Measurement of Intelligence

Although there are disagreements about the nature of intelligence, laypeople and psychologists are concerned with "how much" intelligence people have, because the question has important implications for their ability to profit from experiences, such as education. Thousands of intelligence tests are administered by psychologists and educators every day. In this section we examine two of the most widely used intelligence tests.

The Stanford–Binet Intelligence Scale

You never would have guessed that Alfred Binet (1857–1911) would invent the method that transformed the testing of intelligence from nonsense into science. It's not that he wasn't, well, intelligent enough. It's that he wasn't quite focused enough.

Binet, the only child of separated parents, was raised by his mother. He grew up introverted, a true loner. He first took a degree in law, then decided that medicine was more interesting. However, he dropped out of medical school when he became bored. He turned to psychology, but because he was independently wealthy he saw no need to earn a degree. In 1883, a former classmate, Joseph Babinski (who would go on to describe the *Babinski reflex*), introduced Binet to Jean Martin Charcot, the director of the Salpêtrière hospital. (This is the hospital where Britain's Princess Diana was taken following her fatal automobile accident in 1997.) Charcot, who would also influence Sigmund Freud, gave Binet a position practicing hypnosis.

■ **Alfred Binet**

Binet toyed with law and medicine, then finally turned to psychology.

Self-Assessment ☑

 Life Connections
See the Connections *CD-ROM for an interactive version of this Self-Assessment and for other Self-Assessments*

Questionnaire: The Remote Associates Test

One aspect of creativity is the ability to associate freely to all aspects of a problem. Creative people take far-flung ideas and piece them together in novel combinations. Following are items from the Remote Associates Test, which measures the ability to find words that are distantly related to stimulus words. For each set of three words, try to think of a fourth word that is related to all three words. For example, the words *rough, resistance,* and *beer* suggest the word *draft,* as in the phrases *rough draft, draft resistance,* and *draft beer.* The answers are given in Appendix B.

1. charming	student	valiant
2. food	catcher	hot
3. hearted	feet	bitter
4. dark	shot	sun
5. Canadian	golf	sandwich
6. tug	gravy	show
7. attorney	self	spending
8. magic	pitch	power
9. arm	coal	peach
10. type	ghost	story

Binet and a colleague conducted some bad experiments in hypnosis. Binet believed he had shown that he could use magnets to shift an action (such as lifting an arm) from one side of the body to the other or to transform an emotion into its opposite. He was criticized for this silliness and later admitted that his "findings" could all be attributed to the power of suggestion. He resigned from the hospital and began writing and producing plays that wallowed in terror, mental illness, and murder.

He later earned a doctorate in natural science and enthusiastically dove into craniometry—skull measurement—as a way of measuring intelligence. But his own data showed him the error of his ways. Only in middle age would he develop a method that he had first used with his own children to assess intelligence for the Ministry of Public Instruction. (For example, he had asked his children to point to parts of their bodies, to explain how things were used, and to show that they understood concepts such as *more* and *less*.) The result was the Binet–Simon scale.

You never would have guessed that it would be Binet.

But it was.

Question: What is the Stanford–Binet Intelligence Scale? Early in the 20th century, the French public school system was looking for a test that could identify children who were unlikely to benefit from regular classroom instruction. If these children were identified, they could be given special attention. The first version of that test, the Binet–Simon scale, came into use in 1905. Since that time it has undergone extensive revision and refinement. The current version is the Stanford–Binet Intelligence Scale (SBIS).

Binet assumed that intelligence increases with age, so older children should get more items right than younger children. Binet therefore included a series of age-graded questions, as in Table 8.2, arranged in order of difficulty.

REFLECT

You have probably taken a number of intelligence tests, most of which were group tests. What were the experiences like? Were you informed as to how well you did on the tests? Do you believe that the test assessed you fairly or arrived at an accurate estimate of your intelligence?

TABLE 8.2 Items Similar to Those on the Stanford–Binet Intelligence Scale

Level (Years)	Item
2	1. Children show knowledge of basic vocabulary words by identifying parts of a doll, such as the mouth, ears, and hair.
	2. Children show counting and spatial skills along with visual–motor coordination by building a tower of four blocks to match a model.
4	1. Children show word fluency and categorical thinking by filling in the missing words when they are asked questions such as: "Father is a man; mother is a _____?" "Hamburgers are hot; ice cream is _____?"
	2. Children show comprehension by answering correctly when they are asked questions such as: "Why do people have automobiles?" "Why do people have medicine?"
9	1. Children can point out verbal absurdities, as in this question: "In an old cemetery, scientists unearthed a skull which they think was that of George Washington when he was only 5 years of age. What is silly about that?"
	2. Children display fluency with words, as shown by answering these questions: "Can you tell me a number that rhymes with snore?" "Can you tell me a color that rhymes with glue?"
Adult	1. Adults show knowledge of the meanings of words and conceptual thinking by correctly explaining the differences between word pairs like "sickness and misery," "house and home," and "integrity and prestige."
	2. Adults show spatial skills by correctly answering questions like: "If a car turned to the right to head north, in what direction was it heading before it turned?"

The Binet–Simon scale yielded a score called a **mental age,** or MA. The MA shows the intellectual level at which a child is functioning. For example, a child with an MA of 6 is functioning intellectually like the average 6-year-old. In taking the test, children earned "months" of credit for each correct answer. Their MA was determined by adding up the years and months of credit they attained.

Louis Terman adapted the Binet–Simon scale for use with children in the United States. The first version of the *Stanford*–Binet Intelligence Scale (SBIS) was published in 1916. (The test is so named because Terman carried out his work at Stanford University.) The SBIS included more items than the original test and was used with children aged 2 to 16. The SBIS also yielded an **intelligence quotient (IQ)** rather than an MA. As a result, American educators developed interest in learning the IQs of their pupils. The SBIS is used today with children from the age of 2 upward and with adults.

The IQ reflects the relationship between a child's mental age and his or her actual or chronological age (CA). Use of this ratio reflects the fact that the same MA score has different implications for children of different ages. That is, an MA of 8 is an above-average score for a 6-year-old but below average for a 10-year-old. In 1912 the German psychologist Wilhelm Stern suggested the IQ as a way to deal with this problem. Stern computed IQ using the formula

$$IQ = \frac{\text{Mental Age (MA)}}{\text{Chronological Age (CA)}} \times 100$$

According to this formula, a child with an MA of 6 and a CA of 6 would have an IQ of 100. Children who can handle intellectual problems as well as older children do have IQs above 100. For instance, an 8-year-old who does as well on the SBIS as the average 10-year-old would attain an IQ of 125. Children who do not answer as many items correctly as other children of the same age attain MAs lower than their CAs. Thus, their IQ scores are below 100.

IQ scores on the SBIS today are derived by comparing their results to those of other people of the same age. People who answer more items correctly than the average for people of the same age attain IQ scores above 100. People who answer fewer items correctly than the average for their age attain scores below 100. Therefore, two children can answer exactly the same items on an intelligence test correctly, yet one can be above average and the other below average in IQ. This is because the ages of the children may differ. The more intelligent child would be the younger of the two.

The Wechsler Scales

David Wechsler developed a series of scales for use with children and adults. *Question: What is different about the Wechsler scales of intelligence?* The Wechsler scales group test questions into a number of separate subtests, such as those shown in Table 8.3. Each subtest measures a different type of intellectual task. For this reason, the test shows how well a person does on one type of task (such as defining words) as compared with another (such as using blocks to construct geometric designs). In this way, the Wechsler scales highlight children's relative strengths and weaknesses, as well as measure overall intellectual functioning.

As you can see in Table 8.3, Wechsler described some of his scales as measuring *verbal* tasks and others as assessing *performance* tasks. In general, verbal subtests require knowledge of verbal concepts, whereas performance subtests require familiarity with spatial-relations concepts. (Figure 8.8 shows items similar to those found on the performance scales of the Wechsler tests.) But it is not that easy to distinguish between the two groupings. For example, associating to the name of the object being pieced together in subtest 11—a sign of word fluency and general knowledge as well as of spatial-relations ability—helps the person construct it more rapidly. In any event, Wechsler's scales permit the computation of verbal and performance IQs. It is not unusual for nontechnically oriented college students to attain higher verbal than performance IQs.

Wechsler also introduced the concept of the deviation IQ. Instead of dividing mental by chronological age to compute an IQ, he based IQ scores on how a person's answers compared with those attained by people in the same age group. The average

Mental Age (MA)
The accumulated months of credit that a person earns on the Stanford–Binet Intelligence Scale.

Intelligence Quotient (IQ)
(1) Originally, a ratio obtained by dividing a child's score (or mental age) on an intelligence test by chronological age. (2) Generally, a score on an intelligence test.

TABLE 8.3 Items Similar to Those on the Wechsler Adult Intelligence Scale

Verbal Subtests	Performance Subtests
1. *Information:* "What is the capital of the United States?" "Who was Shakespeare?"	7. *Digit symbol:* Learning and drawing meaningless figures that are associated with numbers.
2. *Comprehension:* "Why do we have ZIP codes?" "What does 'A stitch in time saves 9' mean?"	8. *Picture completion:* Pointing to the missing part of a picture.
3. *Arithmetic:* "If 3 candy bars cost 25 cents, how much will 18 candy bars cost?"	9. *Block design:* Copying pictures of geometric designs using multicolored blocks.
4. *Similarities:* "How are good and bad alike?" "How are peanut butter and jelly alike?"	10. *Picture arrangement:* Arranging cartoon pictures in sequence so that they tell a meaningful story.
5. *Digit span:* Repeating a series of numbers forwards and backwards.	11. *Object assembly:* Putting pieces of a puzzle together so that they form a meaningful object.
6. *Vocabulary:* "What does *canal* mean?"	

test result at any age level is defined as an IQ score of 100. Wechsler distributed IQ scores so that the middle 50% of them were defined as the "broad average range" of 90 to 110.

As you can see in Figure 8.9, most IQ scores cluster around the average. Only 4% of the population have IQ scores of above 130 or below 70. Table 8.4 indicates the labels that Wechsler assigned to various IQ scores and the approximate percentages of the population who attain IQ scores at those levels.

Group Tests

The SBIS and Wechsler scales are administered to one person at a time. This one-to-one ratio is considered optimal. It allows the examiner to facilitate performance (within the limits of the standardized directions) and to observe the test taker closely. Examiners thus are alerted to factors that impair performance, such as language difficulties, illness, or a noisy or poorly lit room. But large institutions with few trained examiners, such as the public schools and armed forces, require tests that can be administered simultaneously to large groups of people.

Group tests for children, first developed during World War I, were administered to 4 million children by 1921, a couple of years after the war had ended. At first these tests were heralded as remarkable instruments because they helped school administrators place children. However, as the years passed, group tests came under increasing attack, because many administrators relied on them exclusively and did not seek other sources of information about children's abilities and achievements.

At their best, intelligence tests provide just one source of information about individual children. Numbers alone, and especially IQ scores, cannot adequately reflect children's special abilities and talents.

Extremes of Intelligence

The average IQ score in the United States is very close to 100. About 50% of U.S. children obtain IQ scores in the broad average range from 90 to 110. Nearly 95% obtain scores between 70 and 130. But what about the other 5%? Children who obtain IQ scores below 70 are generally labeled as intellectually deficient or mentally retarded. Children who obtain scores of 130 or above are usually labeled as gifted. Both of these labels create certain expectations. Both can place heavy burdens on children and their parents.

© 1988 David E. Dempster/Offshoot

■ **Taking the Wechsler**
The Wechsler intelligence scales consist of verbal and performance subtests such as the one shown in this photograph.

Figure 8.8
Performance Items of an Intelligence Test

These tasks resemble those in the performance subtests of the Wechsler Adult Intelligence Scale.

Mental Retardation

Question: What is mental retardation? According to the American Psychiatric Association (2000), mental retardation refers to substantial limitations in general intellectual functioning that are accompanied by limitations in at least two or more areas of adaptive skills: communication, self-care, maintaining a home life, interpersonal skills, use of community resources, and organization of one's academic life, vocational life, health and safety needs, and leisure activities. Table 8.5 describes levels of mental retardation. Most people who are retarded are mildly retarded. They are capable of adjusting to the demands of educational institutions and, eventually, to society at

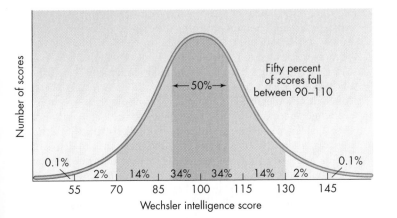

Figure 8.9
Approximate Distribution of IQ Scores

Wechsler defined the deviation IQ so that 50% of scores fall within the broad average range of 90 to 110. This bell-shaped curve is referred to as a *normal curve* by psychologists. It describes the distribution of many traits, including height.

TABLE 8.4 Variations in IQ Scores

Range of Scores	Percentage of Population	Interpretation
130 and above	2	Very superior
120–129	7	Superior
110–119	16	Above average
100–109	25	High average
90–99	25	Low average
80–89	16	Slow learner
70–79	7	Borderline
Below 70	2	Intellectually deficient

large. Mildly retarded children are often taught in regular classrooms, as opposed to being placed in special needs classes. This approach is intended to give them the best possible education and encourage socialization with children at all intellectual levels.

Children with Down syndrome are most likely to fall within the moderately retarded range. Moderately retarded children can learn to speak; to dress, feed, and clean themselves; and eventually to engage in work under supportive conditions, as in sheltered workshops. However, they usually do not learn how to read or compute numbers. Severely and profoundly retarded children may not acquire speech and self-help skills and are likely to remain highly dependent on others throughout their lives.

A Closer Look ◉

Socioeconomic and Ethnic Differences in Intelligence

There is a body of research suggestive of differences in intelligence between socioeconomic and ethnic groups. Lower-class U.S. children obtain IQ scores some 10 to 15 points lower than those obtained by middle- and upper-class children. African American children tend to obtain IQ scores some 15 points lower than those obtained by their European American agemates (Neisser et al., 1996). Latino and Latina American and Native American children also tend to score below the norms for European American children (Neisser et al., 1996).

Several studies of IQ have confused the factors of social class and ethnicity because disproportionate numbers of African Americans, Latino and Latina Americans, and Native Americans are found among the lower socioeconomic classes (Neisser et al., 1996). When we limit our observations to particular ethnic groups, however, we still find an effect for social class. That is, middle-class European Americans outscore lower-class European Americans. Middle-class African Americans, Latino and Latina Americans, and Native Americans also outscore lower-class members of their own ethnic groups.

There may also be cognitive differences between Asians and Caucasians. Asian Americans, for example, frequently outscore European Americans on the math portion of the Scholastic Aptitude Test. Students in China (Taiwan) and Japan also outscore European Americans on standardized achievement tests in math and science (Stevenson et al., 1986). In the United States,

moreover, people of Asian Indian, Korean, Japanese, Filipino, and Chinese descent are more likely to graduate from high school and complete four years of college than European Americans, African Americans, and Latino and Latina Americans (Sue & Okazaki, 1990). Asian Americans are vastly overrepresented in competitive colleges and universities in the United States.

There are differences in mathematics ability between high school students in Germany and Japan. Japanese students, who are Asian, outscore their German counterparts, who are Caucasian (Randel et al., 2000). Most psychologists believe that ethnic differences such as these reflect cultural attitudes toward education rather than inborn racial differences in cognitive ability per se (Neisser et al., 1996). That is, the Asian children may be more motivated to work hard in school. Research shows that Chinese and Japanese students and their mothers tend to attribute academic successes to hard work (Randel et al., 2000). American mothers are more likely to attribute their children's academic successes to "natural" ability (Basic Behavioral Science Task Force, 1996b). Asians are more likely to believe that they can make good scores happen, and they work to do so.

Sue and Okazaki (1990) agree. They note that the achievements of Asian students reflect their values in the home, the school, or the culture at large. They note that Asian Americans have been discriminated against in blue-collar careers. There-

TABLE 8.5 Degrees of Severity of Mental Retardation

Severity of Mental Retardation	IQ Level	Percent of Persons with Mental Retardation	Characteristic Behaviors and Abilities
Mild	50–55 to 70	About 85%	Develop social and communication skills during preschool years. By late teens, often acquire skills up to sixth-grade level. Usually achieve social and vocational skills that permit minimal self-support.
Moderate	35–40 to 50–55	About 10%	Acquire communication skills during early childhood, profit from vocational training, and maintain self-care. Usually do not progress beyond second-grade skills. Can usually perform unskilled or semiskilled work with supervision.
Severe	20–25 to 35–40	3–4%	May learn to talk and engage in elementary self-care. May perform simple work tasks with supervision.
Profound	Below 20–25	1–2%	Impaired sensorimotor development, self-care, and communication skills. May perform simple tasks with close supervision.

Source of information: American Psychiatric Association. (2000). *Diagnostic and statistical manual of mental disorders, 4th ed., text revision (DSM–IV–TR).* Washington, DC: American Psychiatric Association.

Some of the causes of mental retardation, especially profound retardation, are biological. Retardation can stem from chromosomal abnormalities such as Down syndrome, from genetic disorders such as phenylketonuria, or from brain damage. Brain damage may have many origins, including accidents during childhood and problems during pregnancy. Maternal alcohol abuse, malnutrition, or diseases during pregnancy can all lead to retardation in the infant.

fore, they have come to emphasize the importance of education. Looking to other environmental factors, Steinberg and his colleagues (1996) claim that parental encouragement and supervision in combination with peer support for academic achievement partially explain the superior performances of European Americans and Asian Americans as compared with African Americans and Latino and Latina Americans.

■ **Who's Smart?**
Asian children and Asian American children frequently outperform European American children on tests of cognitive skills. Sue and Okazaki suggest that Asian Americans place great value on education because they have been discriminated against in careers that do not require advanced education.

Giftedness

Question: What does it mean to be gifted? Giftedness involves more than excellence in the tasks provided by standard intelligence tests. Most educators include children who have outstanding abilities, are capable of high performance in a specific academic area such as language arts or mathematics, or who show creativity or leadership, distinction in the visual or performing arts, or talent in physical activities such as gymnastics and dancing. This view of giftedness exceeds the realm of intellectual ability alone and is consistent with Gardner's view that there are multiple intelligences, not just one.

Much of our knowledge of the progress of children who are gifted in overall intellectual functioning stems from Louis Terman's classic longitudinal studies of genius (Janos, 1987). In 1921, Terman began to track the progress of some 1,500 California schoolchildren who had attained IQ scores of 135 or above. The average score was 150, which places these children in a very superior group.

As adults, the group was extremely successful, compared with the general population, in terms of level of education (nearly 10% had earned doctoral degrees), socioeconomic status, and creativity (the group had published more than 90 books and many more shorter pieces). Boys were much more likely than girls to climb the corporate ladder or distinguish themselves in science, literature, or the arts. But we must keep in mind that the Terman study began in the 1920s, when it was generally agreed that a woman's place was in the home. As a result, more than two-thirds of the girls became full-time homemakers or office workers (Lips, 1993). Some of the women later expressed regret that they had not fulfilled their potential. But both the women and men in the study were well adjusted, with rates of psychological disorders and suicide below the national average.

The Testing Controversy

► CONTROVERSY IN PSYCHOLOGY ◄

Just what do intelligence tests measure?

As we see in this section, some psychologists and social critics claim that intelligence tests measure many things other than intelligence—including familiarity with the dominant middle-class culture in the United States and motivation to perform well. Is it possible to construct intelligence tests that provide a fair estimate of the intellectual capacity of those who are less familiar with middle-class culture?

It is no secret that during the 1920s intelligence tests were used to prevent many Europeans and others from immigrating to the United States. For example, testing pioneer H. H. Goddard assessed 178 newly arrived immigrants at Ellis Island and claimed that the great majority of Hungarians, Italians, and Russians were "feeble-minded." Apparently it was of little concern to Goddard that these immigrants, by and large, did not understand English—the language in which the tests were administered!

It is now recognized that intelligence tests cannot be considered valid when they are used with people who do not understand the language. But what of cultural differences? ***Question: Do intelligence tests contain cultural biases against ethnic minority groups and immigrants?*** Are the tests valid when used with ethnic minority groups or people who are poorly educated? A survey of psychologists and educational specialists by Mark Snyderman and Stanley Rothman (1987) found that most consider intelligence tests to be **culturally biased** against African Americans and members of the lower classes. Elementary and secondary schools may also place too much emphasis on them in making educational placements.

Intelligence tests measure traits that are required in developed, high-tech societies. The vocabulary and arithmetic subtests on the Wechsler scales, for example, reflect achievements in language skills and computational ability. The broad achievements measured by these tests reflect intelligence, but they also reflect familiarity with the cultural concepts required to answer test questions correctly. In particular, the tests seem to reflect middle-class European American culture.

Cultural Bias
A factor that provides an advantage for test takers from certain cultural backgrounds, such as using test items that are based on middle-class culture in the United States.

 Learning Connections
See Web site for an interactive version of these review questions.

R E V I E W

(19) Spearman suggested that intelligent behaviors have a common underlying factor, which he labeled _____, and specific factors that account for specific abilities. (20) Thurstone suggested that there are nine _____ mental abilities. (21) _____ proposes the existence of multiple intelligences, each of which is based in a different area of the brain. (22) Sternberg constructed a "triarchic" model of

intelligence, including analytical, creative, and _____ intelligence. (23) Creativity involves _____ thinking rather than convergent thinking. (24) The Stanford–Binet Intelligence Scale yields a score called an _____ _____ (IQ). (25) The _____ scales have verbal and performance subtests. (26) Children who obtain IQ scores below _____ are labeled intellectually deficient. (27) Children who obtain scores of _____ or above are labeled gifted. (28) Most psychologists and educational specialists (do or do not?) consider intelligence tests to be biased against African Americans and members of the lower classes.

Critical Thinking: Why is it so important to understand the difference between the concept of intelligence and the term *IQ?*

NATURE AND NURTURE IN INTELLIGENCE: WHERE DOES INTELLIGENCE COME FROM?

Let us now discuss one of the most controversial topics in the field of psychology: the roles of nature (heredity) and nurture (environmental influences) in intellectual functioning. If different ethnic groups tend to score differently on intelligence tests, psychologists—like educators and other people involved in public life—want to know why. We will see that this is one debate that can make use of key empirical findings. Psychologists can point with pride to a rich mine of contemporary research on the roles of nature (genetic influences) and nurture (environmental influences) in the development of intelligence.

Genetic Influences on Intelligence

Question: What are the genetic influences on intelligence? Research on the genetic influences on human intelligence has employed several basic strategies. These include kinship studies, twin studies, and adoptee studies (Neisser et al., 1996). Let us consider each of them to see how genes may affect intellectual functioning.

We can examine the IQ scores of closely and distantly related people who have been reared together or apart. If heredity is involved in human intelligence, closely related people ought to have more similar IQs than distantly related or unrelated people, even when they are reared separately.

Figure 8.10 is a composite of the results of more than 100 studies of IQ and heredity in human beings (Bouchard et al., 1990). The IQ scores of identical (monozygotic, or MZ) twins are more alike than scores for any other pairs, even when the twins have been reared apart. There are moderate correlations between the IQ scores of fraternal (dizygotic, or DZ) twins, between those of siblings, and between those of parents and their children. Correlations between the scores of children and their foster parents and between those of cousins are weak.

The results of large-scale twin studies are consistent with the data in Figure 8.10. For instance, a study of 500 pairs of MZ and DZ twins in Louisville, Kentucky (Wilson, 1983), found that the correlations in intelligence between MZ twins were about the same as that for MZ twins in Figure 8.10. The correlations in intelligence between DZ twin pairs were the same as that between other siblings. Research at the University of Minnesota with sets of twins who were reared together and others who were reunited in adulthood has obtained essentially similar results (Bouchard et al., 1990). In the MacArthur Longitudinal Twin Study, Robert Emde (1993) and his colleagues examined the intellectual abilities of 200 primarily European American, healthy 14-month-old pairs of twins. They found that identical (MZ) twins were more similar than fraternal (DZ) twins in spatial memory, ability to categorize things, and word comprehension. Emde and his colleagues concluded that genes tend to account for about 40% to 50% of differences in children's cognitive skills.

REFLECT

Does your own family seem to be generally similar in overall intellectual functioning? Are there one or more family members who appear to stand out from the others because of intelligence? If so, in what ways? Where do you seem to stand in your family in terms of intellectual functioning?

■ **Figure 8.10**
Findings of Studies of the Relationship Between IQ Scores and Heredity

The data are a composite of studies summarized in *Science*. By and large, correlations are greater between pairs of people who are more closely related. Yet people who are reared together also have more similar IQ scores than people who are reared apart. Such findings suggest that both genetic and environmental factors contribute to IQ scores.

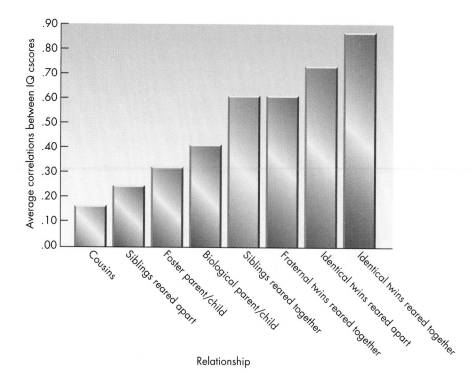

All in all, studies generally suggest that the **heritability** of intelligence is between 40% and 60% (Bouchard et al., 1990; Neisser et al., 1996). In other words, about half of the variations (the technical term is *variance*) in IQ scores can be accounted for by heredity. This is *not* the same as saying that you inherited about half of your intelligence. The implication of such a statement would be that you "got" the other half of your intelligence somewhere else. It means, rather, that about half of the difference between your IQ score and the IQ scores of other people can be explained in terms of genetic factors.

Note, too, that genetic pairs (such as MZ twins) who were reared together show higher correlations in their IQ scores than similar genetic pairs (such as other MZ twins) who were reared apart. This finding holds for DZ twins, siblings, parents and their children, and unrelated people. Being reared together is therefore related with similarities in IQ. *For this reason, the same group of studies used to demonstrate a role for the heritability of IQ scores also suggests that the environment plays a role in determining IQ scores.*

Another strategy for exploring genetic influences on intelligence is to compare the correlations between the IQ scores of adopted children and those of their biological and adoptive parents. When children are separated from their biological parents at an early age, one can argue that strong relationships between their IQs and those of their natural parents reflect genetic influences. Strong relationships between their IQs and those of their adoptive parents might reflect environmental influences.

Several studies with 1- and 2-year-old children in Colorado (Baker et al., 1983), Texas (Horn, 1983), and Minnesota (Scarr & Weinberg, 1983) have found a stronger relationship between the IQ scores of adopted children and those of their biological parents than between the children's scores and those of their adoptive parents. The Scarr and Weinberg report concerns African American children reared by European American adoptive parents. We return to its findings in the section on environmental influences on intelligence.

In sum, genetic factors may account for about half of the variation in intelligence test scores among individuals. Environmental factors also affect scores on intelligence tests.

Heritability
The degree to which the variations in a trait from one person to another can be attributed to, or explained by, genetic factors.

Environmental Influences on Intelligence

Question: What are the environmental influences on intelligence? To answer this question we must consider studies of environmental influences, which also employ a variety of research strategies. These include manipulation of the testing situation, observation of the role of the home environment, and evaluation of the effects of educational programs.

The home environment and styles of parenting also affect IQ scores (Olson et al., 1992; Steinberg et al., 1996; Suzuki & Valencia, 1997). Children of mothers who are emotionally and verbally responsive, furnish appropriate play materials, are involved with their children, encourage independence, and provide varied daily experiences during the early years obtain higher IQ scores later on (Gottfried et al., 1994; Molfese et al., 1997). Organization and safety in the home have also been linked to higher IQs and achievement test scores at later ages (Bradley et al., 1989).

Other studies support the view that children's early environment is linked to IQ scores and academic achievement. For example, Victoria Molfese and her colleagues (1997) found that the home environment was the single most important predictor of scores on IQ tests among children aged 3 to 8.

▶ CONTROVERSY IN PSYCHOLOGY ◀

The Mozart effect—will music provide children with the sweet sounds of success?

Technological innovations are overleaping themselves in the new millennium. Parents are concerned about what they can do to help their children grasp the new technologies. Whatever environmental factors are found to enhance children's intellectual functioning may well be music to parents' ears. But it may also turn out that music will be spatial reasoning to children's ears.

Research suggests that listening to and studying music may enhance at least one aspect of intellectual functioning—spatial reasoning. In 1993, the research team of Frances Rauscher, Gordon Shaw, and Katherine Ky published an intriguing article in *Nature* on the effects of exposure to Mozart's music. They claimed that listening to 10 minutes of Mozart's Piano Sonata K 448 enhanced college students' scores on spatial reasoning tasks. For example, they were better able to perceive the design of a "snowflake," after mentally cutting and folding a piece of paper, and they were better able to rotate and compare objects in space (Hershenson, 2000).

At the 1994 meeting of the American Psychological Association, a research team headed by Rauscher reported the results of a follow-up study with preschoolers in a paper titled "Music and spatial task performance: A causal relationship." They

■ The Sweet Sounds of Success?

Some research suggests that training in music enhances children's intellectual functioning, particularly in visual–spatial areas. Perhaps perceptions of music and spatial relations occupy overlapping neural pathways. However, it should be noted that this field of research is in its infancy and that psychologists disagree as to its implications.

recruited 19 preschool children aged from 3 years to 4 years 9 months and gave them 8 months of music lessons, including singing and use of a keyboard. After the lessons the children's scores on an object assembly task significantly exceeded those of 15 preschoolers who did not receive the musical training.

Cognitive psychologist Lois Hetland (2000) reports that children given keyboard lessons perform better on spatial reasoning tests. She also analyzed research with college students and concluded that they scored higher on spatial-reasoning tests after hearing the music of Mozart, Schubert, and Mendelssohn but not the music of Philip Glass (a contemporary composer of classical-style music) or of Pearl Jam and other rock groups. That is, music with complex structure and rhythm apparently had more beneficial cognitive benefits.

How might listening to music or training in music affect spatial reasoning? It may be that neural pathways involved in processing music overlap those involved in other cognitive functions—such as spatial reasoning (Rauscher, 1998). Musical training thus develops the neural firing patterns used in spatial reasoning, which may eventually help children solve geometry problems, design skyscrapers, navigate ships, perhaps even fit suitcases into the trunk of a car.

The researchers caution that their findings should be considered preliminary. Attempts to replicate the Rauscher studies have met with mixed success (Rauscher & Shaw, 1998). Moreover, it is unclear exactly what aspects of the "treatment" may have influenced students (Nantais & Schellenberg, 1999). Is it the music itself, or could it be related factors like the spatial patterns made by the black and white keys on the keyboard, or even a mood change caused by the music (Hershenson, 2000)? We do not have the answers (Schellenberg, 2000).

But perhaps the findings are enticing enough to encourage school administrators to maintain music programs, which are often among the first to go when school districts tighten the purse strings. Music, after all, may contribute to the sweet sounds of success.

Education

Although intelligence is viewed as permitting people to profit from education, education also apparently contributes to intelligence. For example, government-funded

■ Head Start
Preschoolers who are placed in Head Start programs have shown dramatic improvements in readiness for elementary school and in IQ scores.

efforts to provide preschoolers with enriched early environments have led to measurable intellectual gains. Head Start programs, for example, enhance the IQ scores, achievement test scores, and academic skills of disadvantaged children (Barnett, 1998; Zigler, 1999) by exposing them to materials and activities that middle-class children take for granted. These include letters and words, numbers, books, exercises in drawing, pegs and pegboards, puzzles, toy animals, and dolls. Head Start also helps poor children get medical and dental care, serves nutritious meals, and helps children develop the social skills necessary to succeed in school (Zigler, 1999).

Preschool intervention programs can have long-term positive effects on children. During the elementary and high school years, graduates of preschool programs are less likely to be left back or placed in classes for slow learners. They are more likely to graduate from high school, go on to college, and earn higher incomes.

Schooling at later ages also contributes to intelligence test scores. When children of about the same age start school a year apart because of admissions standards related to their date of birth, children who have been in school longer obtain higher IQ scores (Neisser et al., 1996). Moreover, IQ test scores tend to decrease during the summer vacation (Neisser et al., 1996).

The findings on intelligence, the home environment, and educational experiences show that much indeed can be done enhance intellectual functioning in children.

Adoptee Studies

The Minnesota adoption studies reported by Scarr and Weinberg suggest a genetic influence on intelligence. But the same studies (Scarr & Weinberg, 1976, 1977) also suggest a role for environmental influences. African American children who were adopted during their first year by European American parents with above-average income and education obtained IQ scores some 15 to 25 points higher than those obtained by African American children reared by their natural parents (Scarr & Weinberg, 1976). There are two cautions regarding these findings. One is that the adoptees' average IQ score, about 106, remained below those of their adoptive parents' natural children—117 (Scarr & Weinberg, 1977). The second is that follow-up studies of the adopted children at the age of 17 found that the mean IQ score of the adopted African American children had decreased by 9 points, to 97 (Weinberg et al., 1992). The meaning of the change remains to be unraveled (Neisser, 1997a).

As suggested by Figure 8.11, intellectual functioning would appear to reflect the interaction of genetic, physical, personal, and sociocultural factors (Dickens & Flynn, 2001).

Perhaps we need not be so concerned with whether we can sort out exactly how much of a person's IQ is due to heredity and how much is due to environmental

Life Connections
See the Connections *CD-ROM to take the "Chitling" test.*

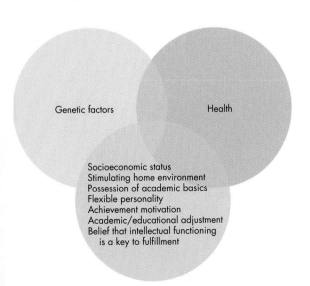

Genetic factors

Health

Socioeconomic status
Stimulating home environment
Possession of academic basics
Flexible personality
Achievement motivation
Academic/educational adjustment
Belief that intellectual functioning
is a key to fulfillment

■ Figure 8.11
The Complex Web of Factors That Appears to Affect Intellectual Functioning

Intellectual functioning appears to be influenced by the interaction of genetic factors, health, personality, and sociocultural factors.

influences. A majority of psychologists and educators believe that IQ reflects the complex interaction of heredity, early childhood experiences, sociocultural factors and expectations, and even the atmosphere in which intelligence tests are conducted. Psychology has traditionally supported the dignity of the individual. It might be more appropriate for us to try to identify children *of all ethnic groups* whose environments place them at risk for failure and do what we can to enrich their environments. As noted by Paul Ehrlich (2000), professor of biology and population studies at Stanford University:

> There is no such thing as a fixed human nature, but rather an interaction between our genotypes—the genetic information we have—and the different environments we live in, with the result that all our natures are unique.

Learning Connections
See Web site for an interactive version of these review questions.

R E V I E W

(29) When children are separated from their biological parents early, strong relationships between their IQs and those of their biological parents probably reflect (genetic or environmental?) influences. (30) Estimates place the _____ of intelligence at 40% to 60%. (31) _____ Start programs enhance IQ scores by exposing poor children to materials and activities that middle-class children take for granted.

Critical Thinking: Why are people so concerned about "how much" of intelligence is inherited?

Bilingualism and Ebonics—Making Connections or Building Walls?

It may be surprising to Americans, most of whom speak only English, that most people throughout the world speak two or more languages. Bilingualism makes it possible to connect with people in other cultures. Lack of ability to speak other peoples' languages can build walls between them. Most countries, in fact, have minority populations whose languages differ from the national tongue. Nearly all Europeans are taught English and the languages of neighboring nations. Consider the Netherlands. Dutch is the native tongue, but all children are also taught French, German, and English and are expected to become fluent in each of them.

For more than 30 million people in the United States, English is a second language (Barringer, 1993). Spanish, French, Chinese, Russian, or Hebrew is spoken in the home and, perhaps, the neighborhood. (See Table 8.6 on page 330.)

Bilingualism and Intellectual Development

A century ago it was widely believed that children reared in bilingual homes were retarded in their intellectual and language development. The theory was that cognitive capacity is limited, so people who store two linguistic systems are crowding their mental abilities. It is true that there is some "mixing" of languages by bilingual children (Patterson, 2000), but they can generally separate the two languages from an early age (Mueller & Hulk, 2001). The U.S. Bureau of the Census reports that more than 75% of Americans who first spoke another language in the home also speak English "well" or "very well" (Barringer, 1993). Moreover, a careful analysis of older studies in bilingualism shows that the bilingual children observed often lived in families with low socioeconomic status and little education. Yet these bilingual children were compared to middle-class monolingual children. In addition, achievement and intelligence tests were conducted in the monolingual child's language, which was the second language of the bilingual child (Reynolds, 1991). Lack of education and inadequate testing methods, rather than bilingualism per se, accounted for the apparent differences in achievement and intelligence.

Today most linguists consider it advantageous for children to be bilingual. For one thing, knowledge of more than one language expands their awareness of different cultures and broadens their perspectives (Cavaliere, 1996). Bilingualism apparently contributes to the complexity of the child's cognitive processes (Bialystock, 1999). For example, bilingual children are more likely to understand that the symbols used in language are arbitrary. Monolingual children are more likely to think—erroneously—that the word *dog* is somehow intertwined with the nature of the beast. Bilingual children may thus have more cognitive flexibility. Second, learning a second language does not crowd children's available "cognitive space." Instead, learning a second language has been shown to increase children's expertise in their first (native) language. Research evidence reveals that learning French enhances knowledge of the structure of English among Canadian children whose native language is English (Lambert et al., 1991).

Ebonics

The term *Ebonics* is derived from the words *ebony* and *phonics*. It was coined by Robert Williams (Burnette, 1997). Ebonics was previously called Black English or Black Dialect (Pinker, 1994a). Williams explains that a group of African American scholars convened "to name our language, which had always been named by White scholars in the past" (Burnette, 1997, p. 12).

According to linguists, Ebonics is rooted in the remnants of the West African dialects used by slaves. It reflects attempts by the slaves, who were denied formal education, to imitate the speech of the dominant European American culture. Some observers believe that Ebonics uses verbs haphazardly, downgrading standard English. As a result, some school systems react to the concept of Ebonics with contempt—which is hurtful to the child who speaks Ebonics. Other observers say that Ebonics has different grammatical rules than standard English, but that the rules are consistent and allow for complex thought (Pinker, 1994a). A few years ago, the Oakland, California, school board

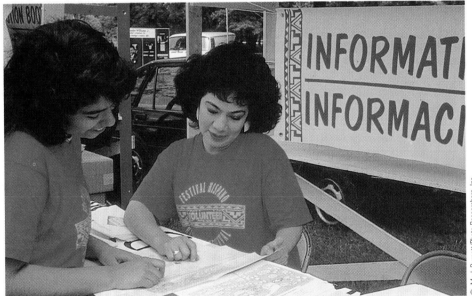

© Mark Burnett/Photo Researchers, Inc.

■ Bilingualism

Throughout the world most people speak two or more languages, and most countries have minority populations whose languages differ from that of the dominant population. It was once thought that children reared in bilingual homes were retarded in their cognitive and language development, but today most linguists consider it advantageous for children to be bilingual. Knowledge of more than one language certainly expands people's awareness of diverse cultures and broadens their perspectives.

TABLE 8.6 Bilingualism in the United States

Language Spoken in the Home	Total Number of Speakers, Age 5 and Above
TOTAL	31,845,000
Spanish	17,339,000
French[1]	1,703,000
German	1,547,000
Italian	1,309,000
Chinese	1,249,000
Tagalog[2]	843,000
Polish	723,000
Korean	626,000
Vietnamese	507,000
Portuguese	430,000
Japanese	428,000
Greek	388,000
Arabic	355,000
Hindi, Urdu	331,000
Russian	242,000
Yiddish	213,000
Thai	206,000
Persian	202,000
French Creole[3]	188,000
Armenian	150,000
Navajo[4]	149,000
Hungarian	148,000
Hebrew	144,000
Dutch	143,000
Mon-Khmer[5]	127,000

[1]Spoken commonly in the home in New Hampshire, Maine, and Louisiana
[2]Main language of the Philippines
[3]Mainly spoken by Haitians
[4]Native American language
[5]Cambodian language

Source: U.S. Bureau of the Census.

recognized Ebonics as the primary language of African American students, just as Spanish had been recognized as the primary language of Latino and Latina American students. "I was honored," said Williams. "And truthfully, I was shocked. It was like the truth that had been covered up in the ground for so long just exploded one day" (Burnette, 1997, p. 12).

"To Be or Not to Be": Use of Verbs in Ebonics

There are differences between Ebonics and standard English in the use of verbs. For example, the Ebonics usage "She-ah touch us" corresponds to the standard English "She will touch us." The Ebonics "He be gone" is the equivalent of the standard English "He has been gone for a long while." "He gone" is the same as "He is not here right now" in standard English.

Consider use of the verb *to be* in Ebonics. In standard English, *be* is part of the infinitive form of the verb and is used to form the future tense, as in "I'll be busy tomorrow." Thus, "I *be* busy" is incorrect. But in Ebonics *be* refers to a continuing state of being. The Ebonics sentence "I be busy" is the same as the standard "I have been busy for a while" and is grammatically correct.

Ebonics leaves out *to be* in cases in which standard English would use a contraction. For example, the standard "She's the one I'm talking about" could be "*She* the one *I* talking about" in Ebonics. Ebonics also often drops *ed* from the past tense and lacks the possessive '*s*.

"Not to Be" or "Not to Be Nothing": Negation in Ebonics

Consider the sentence "I don't want no trouble," which is, of course, commendable. Middle-class European American children would be corrected for using double negation (do*n't* along with *no*) and would be encouraged to say "I don't want *any* trouble." Yet double negation is acceptable in Ebonics (Pinker, 1994a). Nevertheless, many teachers who use standard English have demeaned African American children who speak this way.

Many African Americans are "bilingual." They use standard English in a conference with a teacher or on the job but switch to Ebonics among friends.

Recite Recite Recite

Learning Connections
See Web site for an interactive version of this chapter summary

1. What is thinking?

Thinking is mental activity that is involved in the understanding, processing, and communicating of information. It refers to conscious, planned attempts to make sense of the world.

2. How do concepts function as building blocks of thinking?

Concepts provide mental categories that allow for the grouping together of objects, events, or ideas with common properties. We tend to organize concepts in hierarchies. Prototypes are good examples of particular concepts. Simple prototypes are usually taught by means of exemplars, or positive and negative instances of the concept. Abstract concepts are usually formed through explanations involving more basic concepts.

3. How do people go about solving problems?

People first attempt to understand the problem. Then they use various strategies for attacking the problem, including algorithms, heuristic devices, and analogies. Algorithms are specific procedures for solving problems (such as formulas) that invariably work as long as they are applied correctly.

4. Is it best to use a tried-and-true formula to solve a problem?

Not necessarily. Heuristic devices often help us "jump" to correct conclusions. Heuristics are rules of thumb that help us simplify and solve problems. Heuristics are less reliable than algorithms, but when they are effective, they allow us to solve problems more rapidly. One commonly used heuristic device is means–end analysis, in which we assess the difference between our current situation and our goals and do what we can to reduce the discrepancy. The analogy heuristic applies the solution of an earlier problem to the solution of a new, similar problem.

5. What factors make it easier or harder to solve problems?

Key factors include one's level of expertise, whether one falls prey to a mental set, whether one develops insight into a problem, incubation, and functional fixedness.

6. How do people go about making judgments and decisions?

People sometimes make decisions by carefully weighing the pluses and minuses, but most make decisions on the basis of limited information. Decision makers frequently use rules of thumb or heuristics, which are shortcuts that are correct (or correct enough) most of the time. According to the representativeness heuristic, people make judgments about events according to the populations of events that they appear to represent. According to the availability heuristic, people's estimates of frequency or probability are based on how easy it is to find examples of relevant events. According to the anchoring and adjustment heuristic, we adjust our initial estimates as we receive additional information—but we often do so unwillingly.

7. How do people frame information in order to persuade others?

People frequently phrase or frame arguments in ways to persuade others. For example, people on both sides of the abortion issue present themselves as being in favor of an important value—either pro-life or pro-choice.

8. Why do people tend to be convinced that they are right, even when they are dead wrong?

People tend to retain their convictions, even when proven false, because they are unaware of the flimsiness of their assumptions, focus on events that confirm their judgments, and work to bring about results consistent with their judgments.

9. How do we define language?

Language is the communication of thoughts and feelings by means of symbols that are arranged according to rules of grammar.

10. What are the properties of a "true" language as opposed to an inborn communication system?

True language is distinguished from the communication systems of lower animals by properties such as semanticity, infinite creativity, and displacement. Semanticity means that the symbols of a language have meaning. Infinite creativity is the capacity to combine words into original sentences. Displacement is the ability to communicate information about events and objects from another time or place.

Recite Recite Recite

11. What are the relationships between language and thinking?

Language is not necessary for thinking, but language makes possible cognitive activity that involves use of symbols arranged according to rules of grammar.

12. Is it possible for English speakers to share the thoughts experienced by people who speak other languages?

Perhaps it is. According to the linguistic-relativity hypothesis, the concepts we use to understand the world are derived from our language. Therefore, speakers of various languages would think about the world in different ways. However, modern cognitive scientists suggest that the vocabulary of a language suggests the range of concepts that the users have traditionally found to be useful, not their cognitive limits.

13. How does language develop?

Children make the prelinguistic sounds of crying, cooing, and babbling before true language develops. Single-word utterances occur at about 1 year of age; two-word utterances by the age of 2. Early language is characterized by overextension of familiar words and concepts to unfamiliar objects (calling horses *doggies*), and by overregularization of verbs ("She *sitted* down"). As children develop, their vocabulary grows larger, and their sentence structure grows more complex.

14. What are the roles of nature and nurture in language development?

The two main theories of language development are learning theories and nativist theories. Learning theories focus on the roles of reinforcement and imitation. Nativist theories assume that innate factors cause children to attend to and perceive language in certain ways.

15. Just what is intelligence?

Intelligence underlies (provides the cognitive basis for) thinking and academic achievement. Wechsler defined it as the "capacity . . . to understand the world . . . and . . . resourcefulness to cope with its challenges."

16. What are the various theories of intelligence?

Spearman and Thurstone believed that intelligence is composed of a number of factors. Spearman believed that a common factor, *g*, underlies all intelligent behavior but that people also have specific abilities, or *s* factors. Thurstone suggested that there are several primary mental abilities, including word fluency and numerical ability.

17. What is meant by multiple intelligences?

Gardner believes that people have several intelligences, not one, and that each is based in a different area of the brain. Two such "intelligences" are language ability and logical–mathematical ability, but Gardner also includes bodily–kinesthetic intelligence and others.

18. What is Sternberg's triarchic model of intelligence?

Sternberg's triarchic theory proposes three kinds of intelligence: analytical (academic ability), creative, and practical ("street smarts"). Analytical intelligence is not always the best predictor of success.

19. Just what is "emotional intelligence"?

The theory of emotional intelligence holds that social and emotional skills are a form of intelligence that helps children avert violence and depression. The theory suggests that emotional skills are best learned during childhood.

20. What is creativity? What are the connections between creativity and intelligence?

Creativity is the ability to solve problems without preexisting solutions. Creative people take chances, defy limits, and appreciate art and music. Creative problem solving involves divergent thinking. Many highly creative people do not do all that well on intelligence tests or in school, and many brilliant people have little interest in art, music, and other creative endeavors.

21. What is the Stanford–Binet Intelligence Scale?

This is the test originated by Binet in France and developed by Terman at Stanford University. It includes age-graded questions and yields an IQ score by comparing a mental age score with chronological age.

Recite Recite Recite

22. What is different about the Wechsler scales of intelligence?

The Wechsler scales use deviation IQs, which compare a person's performance with that of age-mates. The Wechsler scales contain verbal and performance subtests that measure information, comprehension, similarities, vocabulary, mathematics, block design, and object assembly.

23. What is mental retardation?

Mental retardation is characterized by an IQ score of no more than 70 to 75 and problems in adaptive skills. Most people who are retarded are mildly retarded.

24. What does it mean to be gifted?

Giftedness combines high scores on IQ along with ability in a specific academic area, creativity, leadership, or special talents.

25. Do intelligence tests contain cultural biases against ethnic minority groups and immigrants?

Intelligence tests were used historically to prevent many people from immigrating to the United States. Many psychologists believe that they are biased against African Americans and people in the lower classes because they require familiarity with concepts that reflect middle-class European American culture.

26. What are the genetic influences on intelligence?

Kinship studies find a stronger relationship between the IQ scores of adopted children and those of their biological parents than between the children's scores and those of their adoptive parents. Studies generally suggest that the heritability of intelligence is between 40% and 60%.

27. What are the environmental influences on intelligence?

Environmental influences on intelligence include the home environment, including styles of parenting; education, including Head Start programs; and, among adults, lifestyle, such as cultural activities. Most psychologists and educators believe that intelligence reflects the interaction of genetics, childhood experiences, and cultural factors.

Active Learning Resources

Search Online with InfoTrac® College Edition

For additional information on the topics in this chapter, explore InfoTrac College Edition, your online library. Go to **http://infotrac.thomsonlearning.com** and use the passcode that came on the card with your book. Try these search terms: cognitive psychology, biases in decision-making, animal communication, language acquisition, Noam Chomsky and language, intelligence tests, multiple intelligences, divergent thinking, and mental retardation.

Visit Our Web Site

Go to **http://www.wadsworth.com/psychology**, where you will find online resources directly linked to your book, including interactive exercises related to PQ4R and Power Visuals for mastering and reviewing key concepts. In addition, you will find hints on using InfoTrac College Edition to answer the Critical Thinking questions throughout the text. Start with the **Self Study Assessment** for a customized **Study Plan** generated by taking the **Pre-Test** and **Post-Test.**

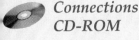

Connections CD-ROM

Go to the Wadsworth *Connections* CD-ROM for further study of the concepts in this chapter. The CD-ROM includes videos and animations, quizzes, and additional activities to expand your learning experience, plus interactive self-assessments to help connect the material to your own life.

Psyk.trek™ CD-ROM

The Wadsworth *Psyk.trek* CD-ROM offers tutorials, simulations, videos, multimedia glossary, and quizzing to help you master the material.

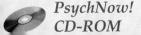

PsychNow! CD-ROM

The Wadsworth *PsychNow!* CD-ROM includes interactive exercises, videos, and animations to enhance your learning.

9 Motivation and Emotion

The Seekers were quite a group. Their brave leader, Marian Keech, dutifully recorded the messages that she believed were sent to her by the Guardians from outer space. One particular message was somewhat disturbing. It specified that the world would come to an end on December 21. A great flood would engulf Lake City, the home of Ms. Keech and many of her faithful followers.

A second message brought good news, however. Ms. Keech received word that the Seekers would be rescued from the flood. You see, Ms. Keech reported that she received messages through "automatic writing." The messengers would communicate through her; she would write down their words, supposedly without awareness. This bit of writing was perfectly clear: The Seekers would be saved by flying saucers at the stroke of midnight on the 21st.

In their classic observational study, Leon Festinger and his colleagues (1956) described how they managed to be present in Ms. Keech's household at the fateful hour by pretending to belong to the group. Their purpose was to observe the behavior of the Seekers during and following (what they assumed would be) the prophecy's failure.

Let us return to the moment of truth. Many Seekers had quit their jobs and gone on spending sprees before the anticipated end. Now they were all gathered together. As midnight approached they fidgeted, awaiting the flying saucers. Midnight came, but no saucers. Anxious glances were exchanged. Silence. Coughs. A few minutes passed tortuously slowly. Watches were checked, more glances exchanged. At 4:00 AM a bitter and frantic Ms. Keech complained that she sensed that members of the group were doubting her. At 4:45 AM, however, she seemed suddenly relieved. A third message was arriving, and Ms. Keech was spelling it out through automatic writing! The Seekers, it turned out, had managed to save the world through their faith. The universal powers had decided to let the world travel on along its sinful way for a while longer. Why? Because of the faith of the Seekers, there was hope!

You guessed it. The faith of most of those present was renewed. They called wire services and newspapers to spread the word. The three psychologists from the University of Minnesota went home, weary but enlightened, and wrote a book entitled *When Prophecy Fails,* which serves as one of the key documents of cognitive-motivational theory.

What about Ms. Keech's husband? He was a tolerant sort. He slept through it all.

R E F L E C T
Are you surprised at the reactions of the Seekers to their leader's failure at prophecy? Why or why not?

THE PSYCHOLOGY OF MOTIVATION: THE *WHYS* OF WHY

Leon Festinger, the lead author of *When Prophecy Fails,* was developing a cognitive theory of motivation called **cognitive-dissonance theory.** The theory suggested that when the prophecy failed, the Seekers would be caught between two key conflicting cognitions: (1) Ms. Keech is a prophet, and (2) Ms. Keech is wrong. Ms. Keech, as it happened, was shown to be wrong. How did the seekers resolve the conflict? One way would have been for the Seekers to lose faith in Ms. Keech—and in their own judgment in following her. But the researchers argued that such a course might be humiliating. (Who likes to admit that he or she has been a fool?) Still, according to cognitive-dissonance theory, the Seekers needed some way to resolve the conflict. Thus they apparently jumped at the "solution" of accepting the "truthfulness" of Ms. Keech's third message—the message that their faith had saved the world. It feels good to save the world now and then. The Seekers went out to spread the word and find additional converts.

The Seekers were *motivated* to resolve the conflict. They *needed* to maintain their self-esteem. They were *driven* to find a way out. They could not ignore the *incentive* provided by accepting Ms. Keech's third message: It erased the conflict and showed that they, the Seekers, retained their special status.

Questions: What is the psychology of motivation? What are motives, needs, drives, and incentives?   The psychology of motivation concerns the whys of behavior. Why do people do this or that? Let us begin our journey with some definitions

Cognitive-Dissonance Theory
The view that we are motivated to make our cognitions or beliefs consistent.

Motives are hypothetical states that activate behavior, propelling one toward goals. Why do we say "hypothetical states"? Because motives are not seen and measured directly. They are inferred from behavior. Motives may take the form of *needs, drives,* and *incentives,* which are also inferred from behavior.

Psychologists speak of physiological and psychological **needs.** We must meet physiological needs to survive. Examples include the needs for oxygen, food, drink, pain avoidance, proper temperature, and elimination of waste products. Some physiological needs, such as hunger and thirst, are states of physical deprivation. When we have not eaten or drunk for a while, we develop needs for food and water. The body also needs oxygen, vitamins, minerals, and so on.

Psychological needs include needs for achievement, power, self-esteem, social approval, and belonging. Psychological needs differ from physiological needs in two ways. First, psychological needs are not necessarily based on states of deprivation. A person with a need for achievement may already have a history of successful achievements. Second, psychological needs may be acquired through experience, or learned. By contrast, physiological needs reside in the physical makeup of the organism. Because people's biological makeups are similar, we share similar physiological needs. But we are influenced by our cultural settings, and our needs may be expressed in various ways. All people need food, but some prefer a vegetarian diet whereas others prefer meat. Because learning enters into psychological needs, they can differ markedly from one person to another.

Needs give rise to **drives.** Depletion of food gives rise to the hunger drive, and depletion of liquids gives rise to the thirst drive. **Physiological drives** are the psychological counterparts of physiological needs. When we have gone without food and water, our body may *need* these substances. However, our *experience* of the drives of hunger and thirst is psychological. Drives arouse us to action. Drives tend to be stronger when we have been deprived longer. We are usually hungrier when we haven't eaten for five hours than for five minutes.

Psychological needs for approval, achievement, and belonging also give rise to drives. We can have a drive to get ahead in the business world just as we can have a drive to eat. The drives for achievement and power consume the daily lives of many people.

An **incentive** is an object, person, or situation that is viewed as capable of satisfying a need or as desirable for its own sake. Money, food, a sexually attractive person, social approval, and attention can all act as incentives that motivate behavior.

In the following section, we explore theories of motivation. We ask: Just what is so motivating about motives?

THEORIES OF MOTIVATION: WHICH WHY IS WHICH?

Although psychologists agree that it is important to understand why humans and lower animals do things, they do not agree about the precise nature of motivation. Let us consider various theoretical perspectives on motivation.

The Evolutionary Perspective: The Fish, the Spiders, and the Bees

The evolutionary perspective notes that many animals are neurally "prewired"—that is, born with preprogrammed tendencies—to respond to certain situations in certain ways. Siamese fighting fish reared in isolation from other fish assume stereotypical threatening stances and attack other males when they are introduced into their tank. Spiders spin webs instinctively. Bees "dance" instinctively to communicate the location of food to other bees.

These behaviors are found in particular species. They are *species-specific.* **Question: What is meant by species-specific behaviors?** Species-specific behaviors are also called **instincts,** or *fixed action patterns* (FAPs). Such behavior patterns are inborn. They are genetically transmitted from generation to generation.

Motive

A hypothetical state within an organism that propels the organism toward a goal. (From the Latin *movere,* meaning "to move.")

Need

A state of deprivation.

Drive

A condition of arousal in an organism that is associated with a need.

Physiological Drives

Unlearned drives with a biological basis, such as hunger, thirst, and avoidance of pain.

Incentive

An object, person, or situation perceived as being capable of satisfying a need.

Instinct

An inherited disposition to activate specific behavior patterns that are designed to reach certain goals.

■ **A Fixed Action Pattern**

In the presence of another male, Siamese fighting fish assume threatening stances in which they extend their fins and gills and circle each other. If neither male retreats, there will be a conflict.

Psychologists have asked whether humans have instincts, and if so, how many. A century ago, psychologists William James (1890) and William McDougall (1908) argued that humans have instincts that foster survival and social behavior. James numbered love, sympathy, and modesty among his social instincts. McDougall compiled 12 "basic" instincts, including hunger, sex, and self-assertion. Other psychologists have made longer lists, and still others deny that people have any instincts. The question remains unresolved.

Drive-Reductionism and Homeostasis: "Steady, Steady . . ."

Sigmund Freud believed that tension motivates us to behave in ways that restore us to a resting state. His views are similar to those of the **drive-reduction theory** of learning, as set forth by psychologist Clark Hull in the 1930s. *Question: What is drive-reduction theory?*

According to Hull, **primary drives** such as hunger, thirst, and pain trigger arousal (tension) and activate behavior. We learn to engage in behaviors that reduce the tension. We also acquire drives through experience. These drives are called **acquired drives.** We may acquire a drive for money because money enables us to obtain food, drink, and homes, which protect us from predators and extremes of temperature. We might acquire drives for social approval and affiliation because other people, and their good will, help us reduce primary drives, especially when we are infants. In all cases, reduction of tension is the goal. Yet some people appear to acquire what could be considered excessive drives for money or affiliation. They gather money long after their material needs have been met, and some people find it difficult to be alone, even briefly.

Primary drives like hunger are triggered when we are in a state of deprivation. Sensations of hunger motivate us to act in ways that will restore the bodily balance. This tendency to maintain a steady state is called **homeostasis.** Homeostasis works much like a thermostat. When the temperature in a room drops below the set point, the heating system is triggered. The heat stays on until the set point is reached. Similarly, most animals eat until they are no longer hungry. (The fact that many people eat "recreationally"—for example, when they are presented with an appealing dessert—suggests that there is more to eating than drive reduction.)

The Search for Stimulation: Is Downtime a Downer?

Physical needs give rise to drives like hunger and thirst. In such cases, we are motivated to *reduce* the tension or stimulation that impinges on us. *Question: Are all motives aimed at the reduction of tension?* No, in the case of *stimulus motives,* organisms seek to *increase* stimulation.

A classic study conducted at McGill University in Montreal during the 1950s suggests the importance of sensory stimulation and activity. Some "lucky" students were paid $20 a day (which, with inflation, would now be well above $100) for doing nothing—literally. Would you like to "work" by doing nothing for $100 a day? Don't answer too quickly. According to the results of classic research on sensory deprivation, you might not like it at all.

In that experiment, student volunteers were placed in quiet cubicles and blindfolded (Bexton et al., 1954). Their arms were bandaged; they could hear nothing but the dull, continuous hum of air conditioning. Many slept for a while, but after a few hours of sensory-deprived wakefulness, most felt bored and irritable. As time went on, many grew more uncomfortable. Many students quit the experiment during the first day despite the financial incentive. Many of those who remained for a few days found it hard to concentrate on simple problems days afterward. For many, the experiment did not provide a relaxing vacation. Instead, it produced boredom and disorientation.

Lower animals and humans appear to be motivated to seek novel stimulation. Even when they have been deprived of food, rats may explore unfamiliar arms of mazes rather than head straight for the spot where they have learned to expect food. Animals that have just copulated and thereby reduced their primary sex drives often show

REFLECT
Do you know people who cannot accumulate enough money? What do you think motivates them?

REFLECT
Why do people go on roller-coasters?

Drive-Reduction Theory
The view that organisms learn to engage in behaviors that have the effect of reducing drives.

Primary Drives
Unlearned, or physiological, drives.

Acquired Drives
Drives acquired through experience, or learned.

Homeostasis
The tendency of the body to maintain a steady state.

renewed interest in sexual behavior when presented with a new sex partner—a novelty. People (and lower animals) tend to take in more calories at buffets and smorgasbords than when they have fewer kinds of food available (Raynor & Epstein, 2001). Children spend hour after hour manipulating the controls of video games for the pleasure of zapping video monsters. Similarly, infants prolong their play with "busy boxes"—boxes filled with objects that honk, squeak, rattle, and buzz when manipulated in certain ways. Finding ways to control the gadgets is fun even though the children are not rewarded with desserts or parental hugs.

Stimulus motives provide an evolutionary advantage. Animals that are active and motivated to learn about and manipulate their environment are more likely to survive. If you know where the nearest tall tree is, you're more likely to be able to escape from a lion. If you've explored where to find food and water, you're more likely to pass your genes to future generations.

Humanistic Theory: "I've Got to Be Me"?

Humanistic psychologists, particularly Abraham Maslow (1908–1970), suggest that human behavior is not just mechanical and aimed toward survival and reduction of tension. *Question: How does humanistic theory differ from other theories of motivation?*

As a humanist, Maslow believed that people are also motivated by the conscious desire for personal growth. Humanists note that people tolerate pain, hunger, and many other sources of tension to obtain personal fulfillment.

Maslow believed that we are separated from so-called lower animals by our capacity for **self-actualization,** or self-initiated striving to become whatever we believe we are capable of being. Maslow considered self-actualization to be as important a need in humans as hunger. The need for self-actualization pushes people to strive to become concert pianists, chief executive officers, or best-selling authors—even when there is money in the family.

Maslow (1970) organized human needs into a hierarchy. *Question: What is Maslow's hierarchy of needs?* Maslow's hierarchy ranges from physiological needs, such as hunger and thirst, through self-actualization (see Figure 9.1). He believed that we naturally strive to travel up through this hierarchy.

Critics of Maslow's theory argue that there is too much individual variation for the hierarchy of motives to apply to everyone. Some people whose physiological, safety, and love needs are met show little interest in achievement and recognition. And some visual and performing artists devote themselves fully to their craft, even if they have to pass up the comforts of a warm home, live in an unsafe part of town, and alienate their friends. Thus many people seek distant, self-actualizing goals, even while their other needs, as outlined by Maslow, have not yet been met.

Cognitive-Dissonance Theory: "I Think, Therefore I Am . . . Consistent"?

The brain within its groove
Runs evenly and true . . .

—Emily Dickinson

"I think, therefore I am," said the French philosopher René Descartes. If he had been a cognitive psychologist, he might have said, "I think, therefore I am *consistent*."

According to cognitive-dissonance theory, people are thinking creatures who seek consistency in their behaviors and their attitudes—their views of the world (Albarracín & Wyer, 2000). *Question: Why are people motivated to eliminate inconsistencies in their worldviews?* The answer seems to be that people must mentally represent the world accurately in order to predict and control events. Consistency in these ideas helps make the world seem like a predictable place. Therefore, if we find ourselves in the uncomfortable spot where two cherished ideas conflict, we are

Harlow Primate Lab/University of Wisconsin

■ **Monkeying Around**
Do organisms have innate drives to obtain sensory stimulation, manipulate objects (like these young rhesus monkeys), and explore the environment? The monkeys appear to monkey around with gadgets just for the fun of it. No external incentives are needed. Children similarly enjoy manipulating gadgets that honk, squeak, rattle, and buzz, even though the resultant honks and squeaks do not satisfy physiological drives such as hunger or thirst.

R E F L E C T
Where would you place yourself in Maslow's hierarchy? Where do you see yourself as being headed? Why?

Self-Actualization
According to Maslow and other humanistic psychologists, self-initiated striving to become what one is capable of being. The motive for reaching one's full potential, for expressing one's unique capabilities.

■ **Figure 9.1**
Maslow's Hierarchy of Needs
Maslow believed we progress toward higher psychological needs once basic survival needs have been met. Where do you fit in this picture?

Power Visual
See Web site for an interactive version of this figure.

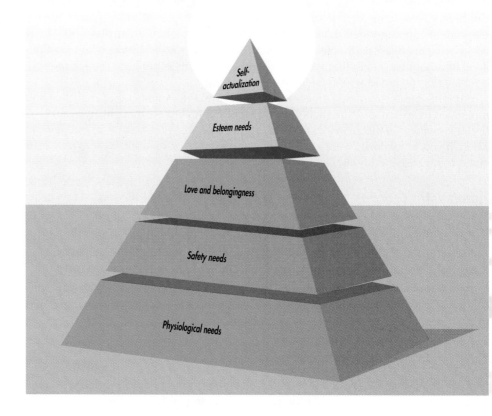

Self-actualization

Esteem needs

Love and belongingness

Safety needs

Physiological needs

REFLECT

Were you ever subjected to difficult hazing upon joining a sorority, fraternity, or other kind of club? Did the experience affect your feelings about being a member of the group? How? Can you connect your experience to the concept of effort justification?

Attitude-Discrepant Behavior
Behavior inconsistent with an attitude that may have the effect of modifying an attitude.

Effort Justification
In cognitive-dissonance theory, the tendency to seek justification (acceptable reasons) for strenuous efforts.

motivated to reduce the discrepancy—just as the Seekers did when the flying saucers did not land on schedule.

In the first and still one of the best-known studies on cognitive dissonance, one group of participants received $1 (worth $5 to $10 today) for telling someone else that a boring task was interesting (Festinger & Carlsmith, 1959). Members of a second group received $20 (worth $100 to $200 today) to describe the chore positively. Both groups were paid to engage in **attitude-discrepant behavior**—that is, behavior that ran counter to what they actually thought. After presenting their fake enthusiasm for the boring task, the participants were asked to rate their own liking for it. Ironically, those who were paid *less* rated the task as actually more interesting than their better-paid colleagues reported. *Question: Why are people who go unrewarded more likely than those who are rewarded to think or say that what they are doing is worthwhile for its own sake?*

According to learning theory (Chapter 6), this result would be confusing. Learning theorists would predict that the more we are reinforced for doing something (given more money, for example), the more we should like it (not find the task quite as boring, that is). But that is not what happened here. The cognitive-dissonance theorists rightly predicted this outcome. Because the ideas (cognitions) of (a) "I was paid very little" and (b) "I told someone that this assignment was interesting" are dissonant, people will tend to engage in **effort justification.** So, according to cognitive-dissonance theorists, the discomfort of cognitive dissonance motivates them to explain their behavior to themselves in such a way that unpleasant undertakings seem worth it. Participants who were paid only $1 may have justified their lie by concluding that they may not have been lying in the first place.

Each theory of motivation may have something to offer. Each might apply to certain aspects of behavior. As the chapter progresses, we will describe research that lends support to each theory. Let us first describe research on the hunger drive. Hunger is based on physiological needs, and drive reduction would appear to explain some—although not all—eating behavior. Then we turn to sexual motivation; in the realm of sex we may enjoy increasing sexual tensions before finding release. Then we switch gears. We consider two powerful motives that push us ahead in life, and sometimes to the front of the line: aggression and achievement. Psychologist Henry Murray (1938) hypothesized that each of these motives reflects a psychological need. He also referred to them as *social motives*, which he believed differ from primary motives such as hunger and sex in that they are learned. However, contemporary researchers believe that heredity may also play a role in these behavior patterns. Evolutionary psychologists believe that "genetic whisperings" influence tendencies toward aggression and achievement and many other aspects of personality and social behavior, even if we can also point to environmental influences (Buss et al., 1998; Plomin, 2002; Rose, 1995).

REVIEW

(1) _____ are hypothetical states that activate behavior and direct organisms toward goals. (2) Physiological needs generally reflect states of physical _____. (3) An _____ is an object, person, or situation that is perceived as being capable of satisfying a need. (4) According to the _____ perspective, animals are born with instinctive tendencies to behave in certain ways. (5) Drives help the body maintain a steady state, a tendency that is called _____. (6) Studies in sensory _____ show that lack of stimulation is aversive and irritating. (7) Humanistic psychologist Maslow argued that people have a hierarchy of needs, the highest of which is the need for _____. (8) _____ psychologists suggest that people strive to predict and control events. (9) According to cognitive-_____ theory, we are motivated to make our cognitions consistent with one another and with our behavior.

Critical Thinking: If we observe a person to be behaving in a certain way, are we justified in assuming that the person is *motivated* to behave in that way?

Learning Connections
See Web site for an interactive version of these review questions.

HUNGER: DO YOU GO BY "TUMMY-TIME"?

I go by tummy-time and I want my dinner.

—Sir Winston Churchill

We need food to survive, but to many of us food means more than survival. Food is a symbol of family togetherness and caring. We associate food with the nurturance of the parent–child relationship, with visits home during holidays. Friends and relatives offer us food when we enter their homes, and saying no may be viewed as a personal rejection. Bacon and eggs, coffee with cream and sugar, meat and mashed potatoes—all seem to be part of sharing American values and abundance. *Questions: What bodily mechanisms regulate the hunger drive? What psychological processes are at work?*

Life Connections
See the Connections *CD-ROM for an animation on hunger and our sensitivity to external cues.*

Biological Influences on Hunger

In considering the bodily mechanisms that regulate hunger, let us begin with the mouth. (After all, we are talking about eating.) Chewing and swallowing provide some sensations of **satiety,** or satisfaction. If they did not, we might eat for a long time after we had taken in enough food. It takes the digestive tract time to metabolize food and provide the brain with signals of satiety by way of the bloodstream.

In classic "sham feeding" experiments with dogs, researchers implanted a tube in the animals' throats so that any food swallowed fell out of the body. Even though no food reached the stomach, the animals stopped feeding after a while (Janowitz &

Satiety
The state of being satisfied; fullness.

■ Hunger

How do *you* feel while waiting for someone to carve the turkey? Hunger is a physiological drive that motivates us to eat. Why do we feel hungry? Why do we feel satiated? Why do many people continue to eat when they have already supplied their bodies with the needed nutrients?

REFLECT

Have you ever eaten because you were anxious or bored or because you passed a bakery window with some enticing pastries? What are the effects on your health?

Ventromedial Nucleus (VMN)
A central area on the underside of the hypothalamus that appears to function as a stop-eating center.

Hyperphagic
Characterized by excessive eating.

Lateral Hypothalamus
An area at the side of the hypothalamus that appears to function as a start-eating center.

Aphagic
Characterized by undereating.

Grossman, 1949). Thus sensations of chewing and swallowing must provide some feelings of satiety. However, the dogs in the study resumed feeding sooner than animals whose food did reach the stomach. Let us proceed to the stomach, too, as we seek further regulatory factors in hunger.

An empty stomach leads to stomach contractions, which we call *hunger pangs.* Classic research suggested that stomach contractions are crucial to hunger. A man (A. L. Washburn) swallowed a balloon that was inflated in his stomach. His stomach contractions squeezed the balloon, so the contractions could be recorded by observers. Washburn also pressed a key when he felt hungry, and the researchers found a correspondence between his stomach contractions and his feelings of hunger (Cannon & Washburn, 1912).

But stomach contractions are not as influential as formerly thought. (We apparently go by more than "tummy-time.") Medical observations and classic research also find that people and animals whose stomachs have been removed still regulate food intake so as to maintain their normal weight (Tsang, 1938). (Food is absorbed through their intestines.) This finding led to the discovery of many other mechanisms that regulate hunger, including the hypothalamus, blood sugar level, and even receptors in the liver. When we are deprived of food, the level of sugar in the blood drops. The drop in blood sugar is communicated to the hypothalamus and apparently indicates that we have been burning energy and need to replenish it by eating.

If you were just reviving from a surgical operation, fighting your way through the fog of the anesthesia, food would probably be the last thing on your mind. But when a researcher uses a probe to destroy the **ventromedial nucleus (VMN)** of a rat's hypothalamus, the rat will grope toward food as soon as its eyes open. Then it eats vast quantities of Purina Rat Chow or whatever.

The VMN seems to be able to function like a "stop-eating center" in the rat's brain. If the VMN is electrically stimulated—that is, "switched on"—the rat stops eating until the current is turned off. When the VMN is destroyed, the rat becomes **hyperphagic** (Figure 9.2). It continues to eat until it has about doubled its normal weight. Then it will level off its eating rate and maintain the higher weight. It is as if the set point of the stop-eating center has been raised to a higher level, like turning up the thermostat in a house from 65°F degrees to 70°F. Hyperphagic rats are also more finicky. They eat more fats or sweet-tasting food, but if their food is salty or bitter they actually eat less. Some people develop tumors near the base of the brain, damaging the VMN and apparently causing them to overeat and grow obese (Miller, 1995).

The **lateral hypothalamus** may function like a "start-eating center." If you electrically stimulate the lateral hypothalamus, the rat starts to eat (Miller, 1995). If you destroy the lateral hypothalamus, the rat may stop eating altogether—that is, become **aphagic.** If you force-feed an aphagic rat for a while, however, it begins to eat on its own and levels off at a relatively low body weight. It is as if you have lowered the rat's set point. It is like turning down the thermostat from, say, 70°F to 40°F.

Psychological Influences on Hunger

Although many areas of the body work in concert to regulate the hunger drive, this is only part of the story. In human beings, the hunger drive is more complex. Psychological as well as physiological factors play an important role. How many times have you been made hungry by the sight or aroma of food? How many times have you eaten not because you were hungry but because you were at a relative's home or hanging around in a cafeteria? Or because you felt anxious or depressed? Or simply because you were bored? The chapter's "Life Connections" feature explores problems connected with eating too much and eating too little.

REVIEW

Learning Connections
See Web site for an interactive version of these review questions.

(10) Biological factors in hunger include stomach contractions, the blood _____ level, and the hypothalamus. (11) The _____ nucleus (VMN) of the hypothalamus functions as a stop-eating center. (12) As time passes after a meal, the _____ sugar level drops and fat is drawn from fat cells to provide nourishment.

Critical Thinking: Is it possible to sort out the relative influences of nature and nurture on eating behavior?

© Dr. Neal Miller/Yale University

■ **Figure 9.2**
A Hyperphagic Rat
This rodent winner of the basketball look-alike contest went on a binge after it received a lesion in the ventromedial nucleus (VMN) of the hypothalamus. It is as if the lesion pushed the "set point" for body weight up several notches; the rat's weight is now about five times normal. But now it eats only enough to maintain its pleasantly plump shape, so you need not be concerned that it will eventually burst. If the lesion had been made in the lateral hypothalamus, the animal might have become the "Twiggy" of the rat world.

SEXUAL MOTIVATION: THE BATTLE BETWEEN CULTURE AND NATURE?

Off the misty coast of Ireland lies the small island of Inis Beag. From the air it is a green jewel, warm and inviting. At ground level, things are somewhat cooler.

For example, the residents of Inis Beag do not believe that women experience orgasm. The woman who chances to find pleasure in sex is considered deviant. Premarital sex is all but unknown. Women engage in sexual relations to conceive children and to appease their husbands' carnal cravings. They need not worry about being called on for frequent performances, however, because the men of Inis Beag believe, erroneously, that sex saps their strength. Sex on Inis Beag is carried out in the dark—both literally and figuratively—and with nightclothes on. The man lies on top in the so-called missionary position. In accordance with local concepts of masculinity, he ejaculates as fast as he can. Then he rolls over and falls asleep.

If Inis Beag does not sound like your cup of tea, you may find the atmosphere of Mangaia more congenial. Mangaia is a Polynesian pearl of an island, lifting lazily from the blue waters of the Pacific. It is on the other side of the world from Inis Beag—in more ways than one.

From an early age, Mangaian children are encouraged to get in touch with their sexuality through masturbation. Mangaian adolescents are expected to engage in sexual intercourse. They may be found on secluded beaches or beneath the swaying fronds of palms, diligently practicing techniques learned from village elders.

REFLECT

In which society would you rather live? Inis Beag or Mangaia? In which society would you rather rear your children? Explain.

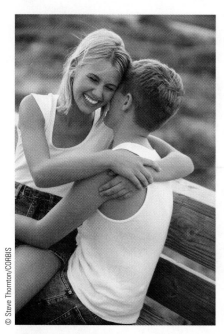

© Steve Thornton/CORBIS

■ How Powerful Is the Sex Drive?

The sex drive is quite powerful among late adolescents and young adults, when sex hormones are at their peak. However, the modes of sexual expression they choose—and whether they express sexual impulses at all—is greatly influenced by cultural factors.

Mangaian women are expected to reach orgasm several times before their partners do. Young men want their partners to reach orgasm, and they compete to see who is more effective at bringing young women to multiple orgasms.

On the island of Inis Beag, a woman who has an orgasm is considered deviant. On Mangaia, multiple orgasms are the norm (Rathus et al., 2002). What turns people on? What makes the sex drive click? What springs people's hearts into their mouths, tightens their throats, and stirs their sex organs? Is it the sight of a lover undressing, a jpg file on a Web site, a sniff of some velvety perfume, a sip of wine? Some people become aroused by remembrances of lovers past. Some are stimulated by fantasies of flings with strangers.

Many factors contribute to the sex drive. People vary greatly in the cues that excite them sexually and in the frequency with which they experience sexual thoughts and feelings. Sex hormones also play their part. In adolescence, when we are flooded with sex hormones, we may seem perpetually aroused or arousable. Yet some people rarely or never entertain sexual thoughts or fantasies. The cultural setting also affects the sex drive. The residents of Inis Beag and Mangaia have similar anatomical features and endocrine systems but vastly different attitudes toward sex. Cultural beliefs influence their sexual behavior and the pleasure they find—or do not find—in sex. Sexual motivation may be natural, but this natural function is strongly influenced by religious and moral beliefs, cultural tradition, folklore, and superstition.

The kinds of sexual behaviors that are considered "normal" depend on the society in which one lives. *Question: What do we know about the sex lives of people in the United States?* What is "normal" in the United States, at least in the statistical sense? There are many difficulties in gathering data, such as the refusal of many individuals to participate in research. As noted in Chapter 1, large-scale magazine surveys of sexual behavior invite readers to fill out and return questionnaires, but only a minority do so, and they are unlikely to represent the entire readership of the magazine. (Nor would the readership of the magazine necessarily represent the nation at large.) People who return surveys differ from those who do not in that they are more willing to disclose intimate information and possibly also more liberal in their sexual behavior (Rathus et al., 2002).

Surveys of Sexual Behavior

The well-known Kinsey reports (Kinsey et al., 1948, 1953) carefully interviewed 5,300 males and 5,940 females in the United States between 1938 and 1949. Interviewers asked about sexual experiences including masturbation, oral sex, and premarital sex. The nation was astounded to be informed that the majority of males masturbated and had engaged in sexual intercourse prior to marriage. Moreover, significant minorities of females reported engaging in these behaviors. But Kinsey had not obtained a random sample of the population either. He chose not to try to do so because he expected a high refusal rate. Thus he recruited participants from organizations and community groups, such as college fraternities and sororities. In general, he secured a high rate of participation. Still, his samples underrepresented people of color, people in rural areas, older people, poor people, and Catholics and Jews. There is thus no way of knowing whether or not Kinsey's results accurately mirrored general American sexual behavior at the time. But the *relationships* Kinsey uncovered, such as the positive link between level of education and premarital sex, may be generalizable.

A more recent and accurate survey—The National Health and Social Life Survey (NHSLS)—interviewed 3,432 people (Laumann et al., 1994) and may offer the most accurate information we have. Of this number, 3,159 were English-speaking adults aged 18 to 59. The other 273 respondents were obtained by purposefully oversampling African American and Hispanic American households in order to obtain more information about these ethnic groups. While the sample probably represents the overall U.S. population aged 18 to 59 quite well, it may include too few Asian Americans, Native Americans, and Jews to offer much information about these groups. The NHSLS team identified sets of households in various locales and obtained an overall participation rate of close to 80%.

The NHSLS considered the sociocultural factors of gender, level of education, religion, and race/ethnicity in many aspects of people's sexual behavior, including their number of sex partners (see Table 9.1). Males in the survey report having higher numbers of sex partners than females do. For example, one male in three (33%) reports having 11 or more sex partners since the age of 18. This compares with fewer than one woman in 10 (9%). One the other hand, most people in the United States appear to limit their numbers of sex partners to a handful or fewer.

Level of education is connected with sexual behavior. Generally speaking, it would appear that education is a liberating influence. People with some college, or who have completed college, are likely to report having more sex partners than those who attended only grade school or high school. But if education has a liberating influence on sexuality, conservative religious experience appears to be a restraining factor. Liberal Protestants (for example, Methodists, Lutherans, Presbyterians, Episcopalians, and United Churches of Christ) and people who say they have no religion report higher numbers of sex partners than Catholics and conservative Protestants (for example, Baptists, Pentecostals, Churches of Christ, and Assemblies of God).

Ethnicity is also connected with sexual behavior. The research findings in Table 9.1 suggest that European Americans and African Americans have the highest numbers of sex partners. Latino and Latina Americans are mostly Catholic. Perhaps Catholicism provides a restraint on sexual behavior. Asian Americans would appear to be the most sexually restrained ethnic group. However, the sample sizes of Asian Americans and Native Americans are relatively small.

Despite our ethnicity, our levels of education, and other factors, our sex drives are connected with sex hormones and our bodies respond in more or less similar ways to sexual stimulation. Let us first consider the roles of sex hormones in sexual behavior. Then we'll look at the ways in which our bodies respond—the sexual response cycle. *Question: What are the effects of sex hormones on sexual motivation?*

TABLE 9.1 Number of Sex Partners Since Age 18 as Found in the NHSLS* Study

Sociocultural Factors	Number of Sex Partners (%)					
	0	1	2–4	5–10	11–20	21+
Gender						
Male	3	20	21	23	16	17
Female	3	32	36	20	6	3
Education						
Less than high school	4	27	36	19	9	6
High school graduate	3	30	29	20	10	7
Some college	2	24	29	23	12	9
College graduate	2	24	26	24	11	13
Advanced degree	4	25	26	23	10	13
Religion						
None	3	16	29	20	16	16
Liberal, moderate Protestant	2	23	31	23	12	8
Conservative Protestant	3	30	30	20	10	7
Catholic	4	27	29	23	8	9
Race/Ethnicity						
European American	3	26	29	22	11	9
African American	2	18	34	24	11	11
Latino and Latina American	3	36	27	17	8	9
Asian American**	6	46	25	14	6	3
Native American**	5	28	35	23	5	5

*National Health and Social Life Survey, conducted by a research team centered at the University of Chicago.
**These sample sizes are quite small.

Source: Laumann et al., 1994.

Hormones and Sexual Motivation: Adding Fuel to the Fire

Yes, sex hormones can be said to fuel the sex drive. Research with men who produce little testosterone—due to age or health problems—shows that their sex drive is increased when they receive testosterone replacement therapy (Sullivan, 2000; Yates, 2000). The most common sexual problem among women is lack of sexual desire or interest, and the sex drive in women is also connected with testosterone levels (Friedrich, 2000). Although men produce 10 to 20 times the testosterone produced by women, women produce androgens ("male" sex hormones) in the adrenal glands. Testosterone injections, patches, or pills can heighten the sex drive in women who do not produce enough of it (Tuiten et al., 2000). Sex hormones are clearly connected with sexual motivation in both women and men.

Sex hormones promote the development of male and female sex organs and regulate the menstrual cycle. They also have activating and organizing effects on sexual behavior. They affect the sex drive and promote sexual response; these are **activating effects.** Female mice, rats, cats, and dogs are receptive to males only during **estrus,** when female sex hormones are plentiful. During estrus, female rats respond to males by hopping, wiggling their ears, and arching their backs with their tails to one side, thus enabling males to penetrate them. But, as noted by Kimble (1988),

> . . . if we were to observe this same pair of animals one day [after estrus], we would see very different behaviors. The male would still be interested (at least at first), but his advances would not be answered with hopping, ear wiggling, and [arching of the back]. The female would be much more likely to "chatter" her teeth at the male (a sure sign of hostility if you are a rat). If the male were to be slow to grasp her meaning, she might turn away from him and kick him in the head, mule fashion. Clearly, it is over between them. (p. 271)

▶ CONTROVERSY IN PSYCHOLOGY ◀

Is the human sex drive affected by pheromones?

For centuries people have searched for a love potion—a magical formula that could make other people fall in love with you or be strongly attracted to you. Some scientists suggest that such potions may already exist in the form of chemical secretions known as **pheromones.** *Question: What are pheromones?* Responses to pheromones would be instinctive. That is, pheromones would release certain fixed action patterns. Do pheromones release instinctive sexual responses in humans? Let us consider the research evidence.

Pheromones are odorless chemicals that are detected through a "sixth sense"—the *vomeronasal organ (VNO).* People possess such an organ, located in the mucous lining of the nose (Rodriguez et al., 2000). During the embryonic period, the VNO acts as a pathway for sex hormones into the brain, aiding in sexual differentiation (Rodriguez et al., 2000). But prior to birth, the VNO in humans shrinks, and there is debate about whether it stops working. If it does continue to work, it might detect pheromones and communicate information about them to the hypothalamus, where certain pheromones might affect sexual response (Cutler, 1999). People might also use pheromones in many ways. Infants might use them to recognize their mothers, and adults might respond to them in seeking a mate. Research clearly shows that lower animals use pheromones to stimulate sexual response, organize food gathering, maintain pecking orders, sound alarms, and mark territories (Cutler, 1999). Pheromones induce mating behavior in insects. Male rodents such as mice are extremely sensitive to several kinds of pheromones (Leinders-Zufall et al., 2000). Male rodents show less sexual arousal when their sense of smell is blocked (Curtis et al., 2001), but the role of pheromones in sexual behavior becomes less vital as one moves upward through the ranks of the animal kingdom.

So what about humans? In a typical study, Winnifred Cutler and her colleagues (1998) had men wear a suspected male pheromone, whereas a control group wore a placebo. The men using the pheromone increased their frequency of sexual intercourse with their female partners but did not increase the frequency of masturbation. The

Activating Effect
The arousal-producing effects of sex hormones that increase the likelihood of sexual behavior.

Estrus
The periodic sexual excitement of many mammals, as governed by levels of sex hormones.

Pheromone
A chemical secretion detected by other members of the same species that stimulates stereotypical behaviors.

researchers conclude that the substance increased the sexual attractiveness of the men to their partners, although they do not claim that it directly stimulated sexual behavior. In fact, it has not been conclusively shown that pheromones—or suspected pheromones—directly affect the behavior of people at all (Wysocki & Preti, 1998).

Even so, some other studies are also of interest. Consider a couple of double-blind studies that exposed men and women to certain steroids (androstadienone produced by males and estratetraenol produced by females) suspected of being pheromones. They found that both steroids enhanced the moods of women but not of men; the substances also apparently reduced feelings of nervousness and tension in women, but again, not in men (Grosser et al., 2000; Jacob & McClintock, 2000). The findings about estratetraenol are not terribly surprising. This substance is related to estrogen, and women tend to function best during the time of the month when estrogen levels are highest (Ross et al., 2000). The fact that the women responded positively to the androstadienone is of somewhat greater interest. It suggests that women may generally feel somewhat better when they are around men (although my wife believes this is nonsense), even if the chemical substances that may be connected with their moods do not have direct sexual effects. Of course, being in a good (or better) mood could indirectly contribute to a woman's interest in sex.

If current studies stand up to the scrutiny of replication and time, we might conclude that certain substances enhance the moods of women and thus make them more receptive to sexual advances. Still, the substances do not "release" sexual fixed action patterns. They do not directly stimulate behavior, as do pheromones with lower animals. If pheromones with such effects on humans exist, they have not yet been isolated. And they may not exist, because the higher we go up the evolutionary ladder, the less important is the role of instinctive behavior.

Sex hormones have not only activating effects, but also directional or **organizing effects** (Crews, 1994). That is, they predispose lower animals toward masculine or feminine mating patterns. Sex hormones are thus likely candidates for influencing the development of sexual orientation (Lalumière et al., 2000). *Question: What is meant by* **sexual orientation**?

Sexual Orientation: Which Way Is Love?

The great majority of people have a *heterosexual* orientation. That is, they are sexually attracted to, and interested in forming romantic relationships with, people of the other sex. However, some people have a **homosexual** orientation. They are attracted to and interested in forming romantic relationships with people of their own sex. Males with a homosexual orientation are referred to as *gay males*. Females with a homosexual orientation are referred to as *lesbians*. However, males and females with a homosexual orientation are sometimes categorized together as "gay people," or "gays." *Bisexual* people are attracted to both females and males.

The concept of **sexual orientation** differs from that of *sexual activity*. Engaging in sexual activity with people of one's own sex does not necessarily mean that one has a homosexual orientation. Sexual activity between males sometimes reflects limited sexual opportunities. Adolescent males may manually stimulate one another while fantasizing about girls. Male Sambian adolescents in New Guinea engage in oral sex with older males because of the cultural belief that they must drink "men's milk" to achieve the fierce manhood of the headhunter (Rathus et al., 2002). Once they marry, however, they engage in sexual activity with females only.

The Origins of Sexual Orientation

Surveys find that about 3% of the males and 2% of the females in the United States identify themselves as being gay (Laumann et al., 1994). Theories of the origins of sexual orientation look both at nature and nurture—the biological makeup of the individual and environmental influences. Several theories bridge the two. *Question: What do we know about the origins of gay male and lesbian sexual orientations?*

R E F L E C T
What are the attitudes of people from your cultural background toward gay males and lesbians? Do you share these attitudes? Why or why not?

Organizing Effect
The directional effect of sex hormones—for example, along stereotypically masculine or feminine lines.

Homosexual
Referring to people who are sexually aroused by, and interested in forming romantic relationships with, people of the same gender. (Derived from the Greek *homos*, meaning "same," not from the Latin *homo*, meaning "man.")

Sexual Orientation
The directionality of one's sexual and romantic interests; that is, whether one is sexually attracted to, and desires to form a romantic relationship with, members of the other sex or of one's own sex.

■ The Two Girlfriends
This drawing by Henri de Toulouse-Lautrec is of lesbian lovers.

© Francis G. Mayer/CORBIS

Let us begin our search for the psychological roots of sexual orientation with psychodynamic theory because of its historic importance. Freudian theory attributes the individual's sexual orientation to identification with male or female figures, particularly one's father or mother. Identification with males or females has to do with the outcome of the Oedipus or Electra complex (Downey & Friedman, 1998). Freud believed that homosexuality represented an abnormal resolution of these complexes. Many psychoanalysts attributed faulty resolution of the Oedipus complex to a "classic pattern" of family life which involves a "close-binding" mother and a "detached-hostile" father. In such a setting, boys are more likely to identify with their mothers that their fathers. Evidence for this view is sketchy, however, relying on a number of case studies. Also, many gay males have good relationships with both parents. Besides, many heterosexuals develop in homes that seem to fit the "classic pattern."

Learning theorists look for the roles of factors such as reinforcement and observational learning. From this perspective, reinforcement of sexual behavior with members of one's own sex—as in reaching orgasm with them when members of the other sex are unavailable—might affect one's sexual orientation. Similarly, childhood sexual abuse by someone of the same gender could lead to fantasies about sex with people of one's own sex and affect sexual orientation. Observation of others engaged in enjoyable male–male or female–female sexual encounters could also affect the development of sexual orientation. But critics point out that most individuals become aware of their sexual orientation before they experience sexual contacts with other people of either sex (Laumann et al., 1994). Moreover, in a society which generally condemns homosexuality, young people are unlikely to believe that male–male or female–female contacts they observe or hear about will have positive effects for them.

There is some evidence for genetic factors in sexual orientation (Bailey et al., 2000; Dawood et al., 2000; Kendler et al., 2000c). One study found that 22% of the brothers of 51 gay men were gay or bisexual, although one would expect to find only 3% of the brothers to also be gay if the relationship were just coincidental (Pillard & Weinrich, 1986). Twin studies also support a role for genes. About 52% of identical (MZ) twin pairs are "concordant" (in agreement) for a gay male sexual orientation, as compared with 22% for fraternal (DZ) twins (Bailey & Pillard, 1991). Monozygotic (MZ) twins fully share their genetic heritage, whereas dizygotic (DZ) twins, like other pairs of siblings, overlap 50%.

In many species, there is little room for thinking about sex and deciding whether an individual will pursue sexual relationships with males or females. Sexual motivation comes under the almost complete governance of sex hormones (Crews, 1994). And much sexual motivation is determined by whether the brains and sex organs of fetuses are bathed in large doses of testosterone in the uterus. In male fetuses, testosterone is normally produced by the developing testes. Yet female fetuses may also be exposed to testosterone. They can be flooded with testosterone naturally if they share the uterus with many male siblings. Researchers can also inject male sex hormones into the uterus. When they do, the sex organs of females become masculinized in appearance, and their brains become organized in the male direction, creating a tendency toward female–female mating efforts and other masculine-typed behavior patterns at maturity (Crews, 1994). Among rodents with such prenatal experience, girls will be boys—although infertile boys.

In other experiments with laboratory animals, boys will be girls. In a typical study, pregnant rats were injected with drugs that block the effects of testosterone. When the drugs were injected during the sexual differentiation of the embryo's brains, male offspring were likely to exhibit feminine mating patterns at maturity (Ellis & Ames, 1987). That is, they made no attempt to mount females and became receptive to the advances of other males.

All right: It has been demonstrated repeatedly that sex hormones predispose lower animals toward stereotypical masculine or feminine mating patterns. Does this research suggest that gay males and lesbians differ from heterosexuals in their levels of sex hormones? Among gay male and lesbian adolescents and adults, the answer is apparently not. Sexual orientation has not been reliably connected with adolescent or adult levels of sex hormones (Friedman & Downey, 1994).

But do sex hormones influence the developing human embryo and fetus in the way that they affect rodents? The evidence is somewhat mixed and this possibility continues to receive intensive study (Dessens et al., 1999; Ellis, 1990). And if prenatal hormone levels affect the sexual orientation of the fetus, what causes the fluctuation in hormone levels? We're not sure. Hormone levels in utero are affected by genetic factors and maternal stress, along with other factors—some suspected, many completely unknown. How does maternal stress fit into the equation? Stressful experiences can trigger the release of stress hormones including *epinephrine* and *cortisol*. Cortisol is a steroid that is chemically similar to testosterone. Cortisol could thus affect the prenatal development of the brain, especially if the mother is under continuous stress. It is possible that the brains of some gay males were feminized in utero and that the brains of some lesbians were masculinized in utero (Collaer & Hines, 1995; Friedman & Downey, 1994).

We have to conclude by confessing that much about the development of sexual orientation remains speculative. There are possible roles for prenatal exposure to certain hormones. Exposure to these hormones, in turn, may be related to genetic factors, use of drugs (prescribed and illicit), even maternal stress. Moreover, the possibility that childhood experiences play a role has not been ruled out. But the interactions among these factors largely remain a mystery. Nor is there any reason to believe that the development of sexual orientation will follow precisely the same pattern for all individuals (Garnets, 2002).

Regardless of one's sexual orientation, and even regardless of one's sex, various things happen to our bodies when we are exposed to sexual stimulation. These events are known as our *sexual response*.

R E F L E C T

Why are people who believe that the origins of sexual orientation are biological generally more accepting of gay male and lesbian sexual orientations?

Sexual Response

Although we may be culturally attuned to focus on gender differences rather than similarities, William Masters and Virginia Johnson (1966) found that the biological responses of males and females to sexual stimulation—that is, their sexual response cycles—are quite similar.   *Question: What is the sexual response cycle?*   Masters and Johnson use the term *sexual response cycle* to describe the changes that occur in the body as men and women become sexually aroused. Masters and Johnson divide the **sexual response cycle** into four phases: *excitement, plateau, orgasm,* and *resolution.*

The sexual response cycle is characterized by vasocongestion and myotonia. **Vasocongestion** is the swelling of the genital tissues with blood. It causes erection of

Sexual Response Cycle
Masters and Johnson's model of sexual response, which consists of four stages or phases.

Vasocongestion
Engorgement of blood vessels with blood, which swells the genitals and breasts during sexual arousal.

the penis and swelling of the area surrounding the vaginal opening. The testes, the nipples, and even the earlobes swell as blood vessels dilate in these areas.

Myotonia is muscle tension. It causes facial grimaces, spasms in the hands and feet, and then the spasms of orgasm.

Excitement Phase

Vasocongestion during the **excitement phase** can cause erection in young men within a few seconds after sexual stimulation begins. The scrotal skin thickens, becoming less baggy. The testes increase in size and become elevated.

In the female, excitement is characterized by vaginal lubrication, which may start 10 to 30 seconds after sexual stimulation begins. Vasocongestion swells the **clitoris** and flattens and spreads the vaginal lips. The inner part of the vagina expands. The breasts enlarge, and blood vessels near the surface become more prominent. The nipples may become erect in both men and women. Heart rate and blood pressure increase.

Plateau Phase

The level of sexual arousal remains somewhat stable during the **plateau phase** of the cycle. Because of vasocongestion, men show some increase in the circumference of the head of the penis, which also takes on a purplish hue. The testes are elevated into position for **ejaculation** and may reach one and a half times their unaroused size.

In women, vasocongestion swells the outer part of the vagina, contracting the vaginal opening in preparation for grasping the penis. The inner part of the vagina expands further. The clitoris withdraws beneath the clitoral hood and shortens.

Breathing becomes rapid, like panting. Heart rate may increase to 100 to 160 beats per minute. Blood pressure continues to rise.

Orgasmic Phase

During the orgasmic phase in the male, muscle contractions propel the ejaculate out of the body. Sensations of pleasure tend to be related to the strength of the contractions and the amount of seminal fluid present. The first three to four contractions are generally most intense and occur at 0.8-second intervals (five contractions every four seconds). Additional contractions occur more slowly.

Orgasm in the female is manifested by 3 to 15 contractions of the pelvic muscles that surround the vaginal barrel. The contractions first occur at 0.8-second intervals. As in the male, they produce release of sexual tension. Weaker and slower contractions follow.

Erection, vaginal lubrication, and orgasm are all reflexes. That is, they occur automatically in response to adequate sexual stimulation. (Of course, the decision to enter a sexual relationship is voluntary, as are the decisions to kiss and pet and so on.)

Blood pressure and heart rate reach a peak, with the heart beating up to 180 times per minute. Respiration may increase to 40 breaths per minute.

Resolution Phase

After orgasm, the body returns to its unaroused state. This is called the **resolution phase.** After ejaculation, blood is released from engorged areas, so that the erection disappears. In women orgasm also triggers the release of blood from engorged areas. Blood pressure, heart rate, and breathing return to normal levels. Both partners may feel relaxed and satisfied.

Unlike women, men enter a **refractory period** during which they cannot experience another orgasm or ejaculate. The refractory period of adolescent males may last only minutes, whereas that of men age 50 and above may last from several minutes to a day. Women do not undergo a refractory period and therefore can become quickly rearoused to the point of repeated (multiple) orgasm if they desire and receive continued sexual stimulation.

We noted that testosterone is connected with the sex drive and sexual response. In the following section we see that this sex hormone is also connected with aggression.

REFLECT

What do you experience when you become sexually aroused? Do your own experiences match the description of Masters and Johnson?

Myotonia
Muscle tension.

Excitement Phase
The first phase of the sexual response cycle, which is characterized by muscle tension, increases in the heart rate, and erection in the male and vaginal lubrication in the female.

Clitoris
The female sex organ that is most sensitive to sexual sensation; a smooth, round knob of tissue that is situated above the urethral opening.

Plateau Phase
The second phase of the sexual response cycle, which is characterized by increases in vasocongestion, muscle tension, heart rate, and blood pressure in preparation for orgasm.

Ejaculation
The process of propelling seminal fluid (semen) from the penis.

Orgasm
The height or climax of sexual excitement, involving involuntary muscle contractions, release of sexual tensions, and, usually, subjective feelings of pleasure.

Resolution Phase
The fourth phase of the sexual response cycle, during which the body gradually returns to its prearoused state.

Refractory Period
In the sexual response cycle, a period of time following orgasm during which an individual is not responsive to sexual stimulation.

REVIEW

Learning Connections
See Web site for an interactive version of these review questions.

(13) The hormone _____ is connected with sex drive in both males and females. (14) Sex hormones have activating and _____ effects on sexual behavior. (15) The sexual response cycle consists of the _____, plateau, orgasm, and resolution phases. (16) A person's sexual _____ involves whether he or she is sexually attracted to, and interested in forming romantic relationships with, people of the same or the other gender. (17) Freudian theory attributes sexual orientation to one's _____ with male or female figures. (18) Twin studies (do or do not?) support a role for genes in sexual orientation. (19) Sex hormones (do or do not?) predispose lower animals toward stereotypical masculine or feminine mating patterns. (20) _____ are odorless chemicals that are detected through the vomeronasal organ. (21) Male (humans or rodents?) have been clearly shown to be responsive to pheromones. (22) Sexual response cycle is generally characterized by _____ and myotonia.

Critical Thinking: If sex is a natural function, do cultures have the right to restrict the expression of sexual impulses? Is sexual response more alike than unalike in men and women?

AGGRESSION: OF AUSTRALOPITHECINES, HUMANS, ROBINS, AND TESTOSTERONE

A murder trial took place in the library of anthropologist Raymond Dart. His guest, Robert Ardrey, held the evidence in his hand—the smashed jawbone of an adolescent. Dart had deduced that the adolescent had been struck in the head with the humerus bone of an antelope—a weapon derived from the animal's leg. The angle of the blow, its intensity—these and other pieces of evidence swept aside any possibility that the death had been by accident.

What was stunning to Ardrey was that the murder had taken place more than 500,000 years ago. The victim was an *australopithecine,* an early hominid who had grown to something over four feet, weighed 90 pounds, and walked upright. Though not a direct ancestor of humans, this primate shared a branch on the evolutionary tree with humans. The murderer would also have been an australopithecine. And here in a flash, to Ardrey, was an explanation of human aggression: murder and warfare were not the products of modern society and the state. Here in the dawn of time, on the hot, dusty African plains, close relatives of humans had stalked antelopes, baboons, and each other with weapons.

There were those who argued that social deprivation and inequality lay at the root of human aggression. If people were to remove poverty, inequality, and social injustice, went the litany, there would be an end to crime, aggression, and war. In his book *African Genesis,* Ardrey (1961) dubbed this view the romantic fallacy. It was founded, in part, by the French philosopher Jean-Jacques Rousseau, who had argued that people were "noble savages" who had been corrupted by twin inventions: private property and the state. Private property created envy—envy experienced by peasants who observed the extravagance of the czars of Russia, by sons of nomads who witnessed the corruption and excesses of the royal families in the Middle East, by jobless youth from ethnic minority groups who saw the wealth amassed by European Americans in the United States. And, said Rousseau, the state provided the social structure that maintained the institution of private property and the riches of the few. Yet Ardrey knew that there were no states on that prehistoric African plain. He asserted that *Australopithecus africanus* was undoubtedly savage but was not noble. Australopithecines bore weapons and used them to brutally take the lives of not only animals, but also other australopithecines.

■ **A Speculative View of the Primate Past, from the Film _2001_**
Researchers have unearthed evidence that the ancestors and relatives of humans used weapons against each other as well as prey. In the film _2001_, a fictitious primate—similar in appearance to _Australopithecus africanus,_ a relative of humans—uses a bone from an antelope as a weapon.

▶ CONTROVERSY IN PSYCHOLOGY ◀

Is aggression "natural"?

The evolutionary view is that aggression is natural. Evolutionary psychologists view much social behavior, including aggressive behavior, as influenced by genetic factors which, for example, give rise to the development of brain structures and to the functioning of the endocrine system, including the determination of levels of testosterone. In his theory of evolution, Charles Darwin noted that many more individuals are produced than can find food and survive into adulthood. Therefore, there is a struggle for survival. Individuals who possess characteristics that give them an advantage in this struggle are more likely to mature and contribute their genes to the next generation. In many species, those characteristics include aggressiveness. Because aggressive individuals are more likely to survive and reproduce, whatever genes are linked to aggressive behavior are more likely to be transmitted to new generations.

Even if aggression is "natural," intelligence is also a key to survival in the case of humans. The capacity to outwit other species may be more important to human survival than aggressiveness. Now that humans have organized themselves into societies in which aggression is either outlawed or confined to athletic contests, it could be that factors such as intelligence and organizational skills are more important than aggressiveness in having one's genes transmitted to future generations.

One kind of property is land. In many species in the animal kingdom, animals act aggressively to establish and defend a piece of land, a piece of turf, a "territory." Privileges are connected with possession of territories, including eating the plants and animals that dwell within the territory and attracting mates to share the territory. Inner-city gangs are also often concerned with protecting their "turf" from invading gangs. Nations, too, protect their borders. "Good fences make good neighbors" wrote the poet Robert Frost. Territory has its privileges—land for farming and industry, homes for rearing one's family. People tend to value their "turf."

Ardrey believed that humans—and their cousins, the australopithecines—had inherited a number of instincts. One is the killer instinct that involves the use of weapons. Another is the instinct to establish and defend a territory, an instinct that Ardrey termed _The Territorial Imperative_ in a book by that name. Ardrey even argued that we created states—nations—to protect ourselves from ourselves. Social controls are our bulwark against instinctive savagery.

When we use critical thinking, we see that Ardrey's reasoning is flawed. Yes, there may have been a murder half a million years earlier. And yes, it may have been committed by a cousin to humankind. We will even report evidence that aggressive behavior and the territorial "imperative" are instinctive in many species. But critical thinking teaches us to search for rival explanations for the behavior we observe—whether we observe it in the present or its record from the distant past, and whether we observe it in humans or other species.

Question: What have psychologists and other scientists learned about the roles of genetics and environmental influences on aggressive behavior?

Biology, Chemistry, and Aggression

Numerous biological structures and chemicals appear to be involved in aggression. In response to certain stimuli, many lower animals show instinctive aggressive reactions. This behavior is automatic, although it can be modified somewhat by learning. For example, the male robin responds aggressively to the red breast of another robin. The hypothalamus appears to be involved in this inborn reaction pattern. Electrical stimulation of part of the hypothalamus triggers stereotypical aggressive behaviors in many lower animals. However, in humans, whose brains are more complex, other brain structures apparently moderate possible aggressive instincts.

Chemistry is also involved in aggression, especially in the form of the male sex hormone testosterone. Testosterone appears to affect the tendencies to dominate and control other people. Men have higher testosterone levels than women do and are also (usually) more aggressive than women, especially with male strangers (Pope et al., 2000). For example, 9- to 11-year-old boys with conduct disorders are likely to have higher testosterone levels than their less aggressive peers (Chance et al., 2000), and members of so-called "rambunctious" fraternities have higher testosterone levels, on average, than members of more "well-behaved" fraternities (Dabbs et al., 1996).

A Closer Look

Cross-Cultural Aspects of Aggression

Anthropological research shows that the stereotype of the aggressive male is not universal. Margaret Mead's (1935) research on the South Pacific island of New Guinea revealed that the sociocultural milieu influences motives such as aggressiveness and nurturance. Among the Mundugumor, a tribe of headhunters and cannibals, both women and men were warlike and aggressive. The women felt that motherhood sidetracked them from more important activities, such as butchering inhabitants of neighboring villages. In contrast, both women and men of the Arapesh tribe were gentle and nurturant of children. Then there were the Tchambuli. In that tribe the women earned a living while the men spent most of their time nurturing the children, primping, and gossiping.

As noted in Chapter 2, there is a 99.9% overlap among people in the genetic code. There is no reason to believe that significant differences in that other 0.1% account for the differences in aggressiveness among the Mundugumor, the Arapesh, and the Tchambuli. Is it not more likely that the people within the various tribes had arrived at a consensus as to proper behavior over the generations, and that they taught their children to behave accordingly?

Library of Congress

■ **What Does Cross-Cultural Research Suggest About Aggressiveness?**
Margaret Mead's anthropological research in New Guinea found wide variety in the incidence of aggressiveness. Among a tribe of headhunters and cannibals, both women and men were warlike. In another tribe, both women and men were gentle and nurturant. A third tribe showed reversal of the masculine and feminine stereotypes: Women earned a living while the men nurtured the children and spent time primping.

Testosterone levels also vary with the occasion: Men's testosterone levels tend to be higher when they are "winning"—whether in athletic competitions such as football or even in chess (Bernhardt et al., 1998).

Psychological Aspects of Aggression

Psychologists have recognized the importance of understanding (and curbing) human aggressiveness for many generations. Let us consider various psychological views of aggression.

▶ CONTROVERSY IN PSYCHOLOGY ◀

The catharsis controversy

Does watching violent sports such as football, boxing, and pro wrestling make viewers more or less likely to engage in violent behavior themselves?

According to psychodynamic theory, the best way to prevent harmful aggression may be to encourage less harmful aggression. In the steam engine analogy, verbal aggression (through wit, sarcasm, or expression of negative feelings) may vent some of the aggressive steam in a person's unconscious mind. So might cheering on a football team or attending a prize fight. Psychoanalysts refer to the venting of aggressive impulses as *catharsis.* Thus, catharsis is viewed as a safety valve. But research findings on the usefulness of catharsis are mixed. Some studies suggest that catharsis leads to pleasant reductions in tension and reduced likelihood of future aggression (e.g., Doob & Wood, 1972). Other studies, however, suggest that "venting" some steam actually encourages more aggression later on (e.g., Bushman et al., 1999). Research evidence has been hard on the psychodynamic perspective, yielding partial support for Freud's views at best.

Psychodynamic Theory and Aggression

Sigmund Freud, the originator of psychodynamic theory, like Ardrey, believed that aggression is natural and instinctive. But Freud viewed aggressive impulses as inevitable reactions to the frustrations of daily life. He was not thinking so much in terms of the evolutionary history of humans. According to Freud, children (and adults) naturally desire to vent aggressive impulses on other people, including parents, because even the most attentive parents cannot gratify all of their demands immediately. Yet children also fear punishment and loss of love, so they repress most aggressive impulses and store them in the unconscious recesses of the mind. Instinctive behavior is thus modified by experience.

The Freudian perspective, in a sense, sees humans as "steam engines." By holding in steam rather than venting it, we set the stage for future explosions. Pent-up aggressive impulses demand an outlet. They may be expressed toward parents in roundabout ways, such as destroying furniture; later in life they may be expressed toward strangers.

Most psychologists believe that Freud's views on aggression remain highly speculative. We will see that there is reason to believe that people *choose* to act aggressively.

Cognitive Psychology and Aggression

Cognitive psychologists assert that it is natural for people to attempt to understand their environments and make decisions. From this perspective, our behavior is influenced by our values, by how we interpret situations, and by choice. From this perspective, people who believe that aggression is necessary and justified—as during wartime—are likely to act aggressively. People who believe that a particular war or act of aggression is unjust, or who oppose aggression regardless of the circumstances, are less likely to behave aggressively (Huesmann & Guerra, 1997).

One cognitive theory suggests that frustration and discomfort trigger unpleasant feelings (Rule et al., 1987). These feelings, in turn, prompt aggression. Aggression is *not* automatic, however. Cognitive factors intervene (Berkowitz, 1994). People *decide*—sometimes making split-second decisions—whether they will strike out or not on the basis of factors such as their previous experiences with aggression and their interpretation of the other person's motives.

But researchers find that many individuals who act aggressively distort other people's motives for their behavior. For example, they assume that other people wish them harm when they actually do not (Dodge et al., 2002; Crick & Dodge, 1994). Cognitive therapists note that we are more likely to respond aggressively to a provocation when we magnify the importance of the "insult" or otherwise stir up feelings of anger (e.g., Lochman & Dodge, 1994). How do you respond when someone bumps into you? If you view it as an intentional insult to your honor, you may respond with aggression. If you view it as an accident, or as a social problem in need of a solution, you are less likely to act aggressively.

REFLECT

Consider people whom you would label "explosive." Do you believe that they actually explode or that they decide where and when to behave violently? Explain.

■ **Catharsis?**
Are these football fans harmlessly venting aggressive impulses, or are they building the likelihood of behaving aggressively themselves? What does Freudian theory say about "catharsis"? Does the research support Freud's theory?

From the cognitive perspective, in sum, it is natural for people to appraise their situations. Whether or not they behave aggressively depends on the outcome of that appraisal.

Learning and Aggression

What do the behavioral and the social–cognitive perspectives have to say about aggression? From the behavioral perspective, learning is acquired through reinforcement. Organisms that are reinforced for aggressive behavior are more likely to behave aggressively in situations similar to those in which reinforcement occurs. Environmental consequences make it more likely that an animal will be rewarded for aggression if it "picks on" a smaller, weaker animal. Strong, agile organisms are likely to be reinforced for aggressive behavior.

Among lower animals, reinforcement is usually physical; for example, food, mating, or escaping a predator. Humans respond to such reinforcements but also to other reinforcers, such as social approval. Research shows that children are less likely to behave aggressively when teachers and fellow students communicate strong disapproval of aggressive behavior (Henry et al., 2000).

The behavioral perspective would describe aggressive behaviors as being instinctive, as in the case of many lower animals, or as acquired by means of reinforcement. From the social–cognitive perspective, aggressive skills are mainly acquired by the observation of other people acting aggressively. Most behaviorists would see aggressive behavior as being mechanical even in humans, either because it is inborn or because the learning of aggressive behaviors is controlled by reinforcements. However, social–cognitive theorists—like other cognitive theorists—believe that consciousness and choice play key roles in aggressive behavior among humans. Social–cognitive theorists believe that we are not likely to act aggressively unless we believe that aggression is appropriate under the circumstances and likely to be reinforced.

Social and Environmental Factors and Aggression

Situational factors can contribute to aggression. For example, aggression sometimes takes place within the context of a mob. When people act as individuals, fear of consequences and awareness of their moral values tend to prevent them from hurting other people. But in a mob, they may experience *deindividuation,* which is a state of reduced self-awareness and focusing on one's values. Factors that lead to deindividuation include anonymity, sharing of responsibility for aggressive behavior (also called *diffusion of responsibility*), a high level of emotional arousal due to noise and crowding, and a focus on the group's norms rather than on one's own concepts of right and wrong (Baron & Byrne, 2003). Under these circumstances crowd members behave more aggressively than they would as individuals.

Environmental factors also contribute to the likelihood of aggressive behavior. Bad-smelling pollutants decrease feelings of attraction and heighten aggression (Baron & Byrne, 2003). Extremes of noise can also trigger violence. If you and your date have had a fight and are then exposed to a tire blowout, look out. Angry people are more likely to behave aggressively when exposed to a sudden noise of 95 dB than one of 55 dB (Donnerstein & Wilson, 1976).

Extreme heat also apparently makes some people hot under the collar (Anderson, 2001). That is, high temperatures are connected with aggression. The frequency of honking at traffic lights in Phoenix increases with the temperature (Kenrick & Mac-Farlane, 1986). In Houston, murders and rapes are most likely to occur when the temperature is in the nineties Fahrenheit (Anderson & DeNeve, 1992). In Raleigh, North Carolina, the incidence of rape and aggravated assault rises with the average monthly temperature (Cohn, 1990; Simpson & Perry, 1990).

Some psychologists (e.g., Anderson & DeNeve, 1992) suggest that the probability of aggressive behavior continues to increase as the temperature soars. Others argue that once temperatures become extremely aversive, people tend to avoid aggressive behavior so that they will not be doubly struck by hot temper and hot temperature (Bell, 1992; Rotton & Cohn, 2000). The evidence does not absolutely eliminate either view, so the issue remains, well, heated.

The overall message seems to be something like this: Yes, some of the foundations of aggression may be embedded in our genes, but that does not mean that aggressive behavior is instinctive in humans. Moreover, human survival on planet Earth no longer requires physical aggressiveness in the way it once may have. Yes, aggression may be affected by testosterone levels and other biological factors, but that does not mean that human aggression is mechanical or automatic. Yes, aggressive behaviors may be learned, but people make decisions about whether or not to act aggressively based on their appraisal of their situations. People's cultural milieus are one source of information people use in making these decisions. When aggression is valued within a culture, or seen as being "normal," people are more likely to choose to act aggressively. Situational factors such as being part of a mob, unpleasant odors, sudden noises, and extremes of temperature also affect the likelihood that a human will behave aggressively.

Learning Connections
See Web site for an interactive version of these review questions.

R E V I E W

(23) Electrical stimulation of part of the brain structure called the _____ triggers stereotypical aggressive behaviors in many lower animals. (24) The male sex hormone _____ affects tendencies to dominate and control other people. (25) Cognitive psychologists assert that our behavior is influenced by our values, by how we _____ situations, and by choice. (26) When individuals are part of an aggressive mob, they may experience _____. (27) Bad odors and extreme heat (increase or decrease?) the likelihood of aggressive behavior.

Critical Thinking: As members of the jury, what can we deduce about humans from the murder trial in Dart's library? Yes, one australopithecine appeared to kill another and to use a weapon to do so. People have also killed other people and used weapons to do so. But is there evidence that aggressive behavior is instinctive in humans, or in australopithecines for that matter? That is, is killing and the use of weapons hard-wired into our nervous systems, or is it learned? Is it automatic and inevitable, or is it premeditated and changeable?

ACHIEVEMENT MOTIVATION: "JUST DO IT"

Many students persist in studying despite being surrounded by distractions. Many people strive relentlessly to get ahead, to "make it," to earn large sums of money, to invent, to accomplish the impossible.   *Question: Why do some people strive to get ahead?*   These people are said to have strong achievement motivation.

Psychologist David McClelland (1958) helped pioneer the assessment of achievement motivation through evaluation of fantasies. One method involves the Thematic Apperception Test (TAT), developed by Henry Murray. The TAT contains cards with pictures and drawings that are subject to various interpretations. Individuals are shown one or more TAT cards and asked to construct stories about the pictured theme: to indicate what led up to it, what the characters are thinking and feeling, and what is likely to happen.

One TAT card is similar to that in Figure 9.3. The meaning of the card is ambiguous—unclear. Is the girl sleeping, thinking about the book, wishing she were out with friends? Consider two stories that could be told about this card:

Story 1: "She's upset that she's got to read the book because she's behind in her assignments and doesn't particularly like to work. She'd much rather be out with her friends, and she may very well sneak out to do just that."

Story 2: "She's thinking, 'Someday I'll be a great scholar. I'll write books like this, and everybody will be proud of me.' She reads all the time."

The second story suggests the presence of more achievement motivation than the first. Classic studies find that people with high achievement motivation earn higher grades than people with comparable learning ability but lower achievement motivation. They are more likely to earn high salaries and be promoted than less motivated people with similar opportunities. They perform better at math problems and at unscrambling anagrams, such as decoding RSTA into STAR, TARS, ARTS, or RATS.

McClelland (1965) used the TAT to sort college students into groups—students with high achievement motivation and students with low achievement motivation. He found that 83% of college graduates with high achievement motivation found jobs in occupations characterized by risk, decision making, and the chance for great success, such as business management, sales, or self-employment. Most (70%) of the graduates who chose nonentrepreneurial positions showed low achievement motivation. People with high achievement motivation seem to prefer challenges and are willing to take moderate risks to achieve their goals.

What Flavor Is Your Achievement Motivation?

Do you want to do well in this course? If you do, why? Carol Dweck (1997) finds that achievement motivation can be driven by different forces. Are you motivated mainly by performance goals? That is, is your grade in the course of most importance? If it is, it may be in part because your motives concern tangible rewards such as getting into graduate school, landing a good job, reaping approval from parents or your instructor, or avoiding criticism. Performance goals are usually met through extrinsic

R E F L E C T

Why do some people seem satisfied to just get by, whereas other people are driven to work and improve despite their achievements?

■ **Figure 9.3**
Tapping Fantasies in Personality Research

This picture is similar to a Thematic Apperception Test card used to measure the need for achievement. What is happening in this picture? What is the person thinking and feeling? What is going to happen? Your answers to these questions reflect your own needs as well as the content of the picture itself.

R E F L E C T

Do you seem to be driven mainly by performance goals or learning goals? Explain.

rewards such as prestige and income. Parents of children who develop performance goals are likely to respond to good grades with tangible rewards such as toys or money and to respond to poor grades with anger and removal of privileges.

Or do learning goals mainly motivate you to do well? That is, is your central motive the enhancing of your knowledge and skills—your ability to understand and master the subject matter? Learning goals usually lead to intrinsic rewards, such as satisfaction with oneself. Students who develop learning goals often have parents with strong achievement motivation, parents who encourage their children to think and act independently from an early age. They help their children develop learning goals by showing warmth and praising them for their efforts to learn, exposing them to novel and stimulating experiences, and encouraging persistence (Dweck, 1997; Ginsburg & Bronstein, 1993; Gottfried et al., 1994). Children of such parents frequently set high standards for themselves, associate their achievements with self-worth, and attribute their achievements to their own efforts rather than to chance or to the intervention of others.

Many of us strive to meet both performance and learning goals in our courses as well as in other areas of life. Grades are important because they are connected with (very) tangible benefits, but learning for its own sake is also of value.

Learning Connections
See Web site for an interactive version of these review questions.

R E V I E W

(28) McClelland used the Thematic _____ Test to measure achievement motivation. (29) Students with _____ goals are mainly motivated by factors such as good grades, rewards from parents, and the prospect of landing a good job. (30) Students with _____ goals are usually more motivated by intrinsic rewards like self-satisfaction.

Critical Thinking: Some people strive harder to get ahead than others. Is it circular reasoning to "explain" the difference in terms of more or less achievement motivation?

Emotion
A state of feeling that has cognitive, physiological, and behavioral components.

Sympathetic Nervous System
The branch of the autonomic nervous system that is most active during processes that spend body energy from stored reserves, such as in a fight-or-flight reaction to a predator or when you are anxious about a big test. When people experience fear, the sympathetic nervous system accelerates the heart rate, raises the blood pressure, tenses muscles, and so on.

Parasympathetic Nervous System
The branch of the autonomic nervous system that is most active during processes that restore reserves of energy to the body, such as relaxing and eating. When people relax, the parasympathetic nervous system decelerates the heart rate, normalizes the blood pressure, relaxes muscles, and so on. The parasympathetic division also stimulates digestion.

EMOTION: ADDING COLOR TO LIFE

Emotions color our lives. We are green with envy, red with anger, blue with sorrow. Poets paint a thoughtful mood as a "brown study." Positive emotions such as love and desire can fill our days with pleasure. Negative emotions such as fear, depression, and anger can fill us with dread and make each day a chore. *Question: Just what is an emotion?*

An emotion can be a response to a situation, in the way that fear is a response to a threat. An emotion can motivate behavior (e.g., anger can motivate us to act aggressively). An emotion can also be a goal in itself. We may behave in ways that will lead us to experience joy or feelings of love.

Emotions are feeling states with physiological, cognitive, and behavioral components (Carlson & Hatfield, 1992). In terms of physiology, strong emotions arouse the autonomic nervous system (LeDoux, 1997) (see Chapter 2). The greater the arousal, the more intense the emotion. It also appears that the type of arousal affects the emotion being experienced. Although the word *emotion* might seem to be about feeling and not about thinking, cognitions—particularly interpretations of the meanings of events—are important aspects of emotions. *Fear,* which usually occurs in response to a threat, involves cognitions that one is in danger as well as arousal of the **sympathetic nervous system** (rapid heartbeat and breathing, sweating, muscle tension). Emotions also involve behavioral tendencies. The emotion of fear is connected with behavioral tendencies to avoid or escape from the situation (see Table 9.2). As a response to a social provocation, *anger* involves cognitions that the provocateur should be paid back, arousal of both the sympathetic and **parasympathetic nervous systems,** and tendencies to attack. *Depression* usually involves cognitions of helplessness and hopelessness,

TABLE 9.2 Components of Emotions

Emotion	Physiological	Cognitive	Behavioral
Fear	Sympathetic arousal	Belief that one is in danger	Avoidance tendencies
Anger	Sympathetic and parasympathetic arousal	Frustration or belief that one is being mistreated	Attack tendencies
Depression	Parasympathetic arousal	Thoughts of helplessness, hopelessness, worthlessness	Inactivity, possible self-destructive tendencies

parasympathetic arousal, and tendencies toward inactivity—or, sometimes, self-destruction. *Joy, grief, jealousy, disgust, embarrassment, liking*—all have cognitive, physiological, and behavioral components.

The Expression of Emotions

Joy and sadness are found in all cultures, but, **Question: How can we tell when other people are happy or sad?** It turns out that the expression of many emotions may be universal (Rinn, 1991). Smiling is apparently a universal sign of friendliness and approval. Baring the teeth, as noted by Charles Darwin (1872) in the 19th century, may be a universal sign of anger. As the originator of the theory of evolution, Darwin believed that the universal recognition of facial expressions would have survival value. For example, in the absence of language, facial expressions could signal the approach of enemies (or friends).

Most investigators (e.g., Buss, 1992; Izard, 1994) concur that certain facial expressions suggest the same emotions in all people. Moreover, people in diverse cultures recognize the emotions manifested by certain facial expressions. In a classic study, Paul Ekman (1980) took photographs of people exhibiting anger, disgust, fear, happiness, sadness, and surprise (see Figure 9.4). He then asked people around the world to indicate what emotions were being depicted. Those queried ranged from European college students to members of the Fore, a tribe that dwells in the New Guinea highlands. All groups, including the Fore, who had almost no contact with Western culture, agreed on the emotions being portrayed. The Fore also displayed familiar facial expressions when

© 1976 Paul Ekman/Human Interaction Laboratory

Figure 9.4
Photographs Used in Research by Paul Ekman

Ekman's research suggests that the facial expressions connected with several important emotions such as happiness, anger, surprise, and fear are universally recognized.

asked how they would respond if they were the characters in stories that called for basic emotional responses. Ekman and his colleagues (1987) obtained similar results in a study of ten cultures. In that study, participants were allowed to identify more than one emotion in facial expressions. The participants generally agreed on which two emotions were being shown and which emotion was more intense.

An interesting study found that women's college yearbook pictures predicted life outcomes as much as 30 years later. LeeAnne Harker and Dacher Keltner (2001) found that women who showed more positive emotions in yearbook photos—as by smiling—were more likely to show social competence, personal well-being, and even happier marriages as the years went by. By the way, their physical attractiveness did not seem to matter; it was the display of positive emotions that told the lifelong tale.

On the other hand, there is no perfect one-to-one relationship between facial expressions and emotions. Facial expressions sometimes occur in the absence of the emotion they are thought to accompany (Camras, 2000). As noted by psychologist Joseph Campos (2000), the voice, posture, and gestures also provide clues as to what people are feeling and about to do.

The Facial-Feedback Hypothesis: Does Smiling Make You Happy?

The face has a special place among visual stimuli. Social animals like humans need to be able to differentiate and recognize members of their group and, in people, the face is the most distinctive key to identity (Parr et al., 2000). Faces are also a key to social communication. Facial expressions reflect emotional states, and our ability to "read" these expressions enables us to interact appropriately with other people.

A Closer Look

"Is Evvvvrybody Happy?" An Excursion into Positive Psychology

Ted Lewis, the Great-Depression-era bandleader, used to begin his act by asking, "Is evvvvrybody happy?" Well, everybody is not happy, but surveys do suggest that the majority of people in developed nations are satisfied with their lives (Cummins & Nistico, 2002). Many people might think that psychologists are only interested in negative emotions such as anxiety, depression, and anger. Not at all. An area of psychology called *positive psychology* deals with positive emotions such as happiness and love.

Question: What factors contribute to happiness? Are some people just "born happy" or do life experiences determine happiness? What factors interfere with happiness?

Some psychologists, such as David Lykken (Lykken & Csikszentmihalyi, 2001), believe that genetic factors play a powerful role in happiness. They note that happiness tends to run in families and that it seems as though we have a more or less stable level of happiness throughout much of our lives (Easterlin, 2002). Positive events such as learning that the person we love also loves us, or recognition for our work, can certainly raise the level of happiness we experience at the moment. Similarly, negative life events, such as the loss of a loved one, financial reverses, or injuries can depress us—and understandably so. Yet we may tend to bounce back to a more or less characteristic level of happiness, as did the actor Christopher Reeve following the accident—being thrown from a horse—that paralyzed him.

Which life experiences contribute to happiness? Despite the saying that "Money can't buy you happiness," surveys in the United States, Russia, China, and Latin America suggest that

people tend to be happier when they live in affluent societies and earn decent incomes (Frey & Stutzer, 2000; Graham & Pettinato, 2001; Schyns, 2001; Tsou & Liu, 2001). It may not be that money makes people happy in itself, but when we have enough money, at least we don't have to worry about money (Cummins, 2000).

U.S. surveys reveal more evidence for a role for social and socioeconomic factors in happiness. For example, European Americans tend to be happier than African Americans, and more-educated people tend to be happier than less-well-educated people (Easterlin, 2001). The persistence of differences according to race and education suggests that socioeconomic circumstances are in fact important contributors to happiness (Easterlin, 2001).

■ **Christopher Reeve**

People who are married (Tsou & Liu, 2001) and who have social support (Lu, 1999) tend to be happier than "loners." There is a difference, of course, between loneliness and solitude, and it could be that people who are extraverted (Cheng & Furn-

It is known that various emotional states give rise to certain patterns of electrical activity in the facial muscles and in the brain (Cacioppo et al., 1988). But can it work the other way around? The **facial-feedback hypothesis** argues that facial expressions can also affect our emotional state, that the causal relationship between emotions and facial expressions can work in the opposite direction. *Questions: Can smiling give rise to feelings of goodwill? Can frowning produce anger?* Perhaps they can.

Psychological research has yielded some interesting findings concerning the facial-feedback hypothesis (Ekman, 1993a). Inducing people to smile, for example, leads them to report more positive feelings (Basic Behavioral Science Task Force, 1996c) and to rate cartoons as more humorous. When induced to frown, they rate cartoons as more aggressive. When they exhibit pain through facial expressions, they rate electric shocks as more painful.

What are the possible links between facial feedback and emotion? One is arousal. Intense contraction of facial muscles such as those used in signifying fear heightens arousal, which, in turn, boosts emotional response. Feedback from the contraction of facial muscles may also induce emotions. Ekman (1993b) has found that engaging in the Duchenne smile, characterized by "crow's feet wrinkles around the eyes and a subtle drop in the eye cover fold so that the skin above the eye moves down slightly toward the eyeball," can induce pleasant feelings.

You may have heard the British expression "Keep a stiff upper lip" as a recommendation for handling stress. It might be that a "stiff" lip suppresses emotional response—as long as the lip is relaxed rather than quivering with fear or tension. But when the lip is stiffened through strong muscle tension, facial feedback may heighten emotional response.

Facial-Feedback Hypothesis
The view that stereotypical facial expressions can contribute to stereotypical emotions.

ham, 2001) and who have the skills to maintain social relationships are generally more capable of finding life satisfaction. Happy people also tend to be open to new experiences; they are more willing to risk becoming involved in new relationships (Rath, 2002).

Research has also suggested that religious people are happier than those who are not, as was found to be the case in a recent study of American and Chinese people (Swinyard et al., 2001). Although having enough money to get by comfortably contributes to life satisfaction, this study found that materialism per se did not contribute to happiness. One's inner life—one's feeling of connectedness to important things outside oneself—was found to be a greater contributor to happiness than material possessions. Chinese college students tend to think about happiness in terms of feelings of contentment, inner harmony, personal achievement, physical wellness, spiritual enrichment, hopefulness about the future, generosity, and self-development (Lu, 2001).

Then there are the attitudinal aspects of happiness (Cheng & Furnham, 2001; Cummins & Nistico, 2002). Numerous studies have shown that people at any income level can make themselves miserable when they compare their incomes to those who bring in more (Schyns, 2001). Happiness also tends to be accompanied by optimism—a cognitive bias toward assuming that things will work out (Diener et al., 2000). But the "bias" is not without some grounds, for happy people often believe in their ability to effect change, and thus they try harder. They are also willing to pat themselves on the back for their successes and are not quick to blame themselves when things go wrong. These attitudes contribute to self-esteem, a factor in happiness.

"Come On! Get Happy!" A Possible or Impossible Dream?

Are there lessons for you in these research findings on happiness? Perhaps. But keep in mind that the studies are correlational; for example, not one of them provided individuals with money to determine whether affluence would affect their mood. Nor did any of them manipulate people's attitudes toward life and measure the outcomes. Still, there might be no harm in placing oneself within the groups of people who are more likely to be happy. Here are some suggestions:

- Take advantage of your education to develop knowledge and skills that can help you be free from want. Even if money does not make you happy in itself, it is good not to have to worry about money.
- Do not let the fact that other people have more impair your ability to appreciate and enjoy what you have.
- Value friendships and other social relationships. Be open to developing new relationships.
- Think about the meaning of your life and whether you can make your life more meaningful to yourself.
- Consider whether you are generally optimistic or pessimistic about your future. If you are pessimistic, examine the reasons for your pessimism and work to overcome them. If you cannot find reasons for your pessimism, challenge yourself to change your outlook.
- Consider whether you blame yourself too much when things go wrong or give yourself too little credit when things go right.

In the section on the facial-feedback hypothesis, we see that you may also find it worthwhile to "put on a happy face."

■ Is Smiling Caused by Feeling Good, or Does Smiling Cause Us to Feel Good?

Smiling is usually a response to feeling good within, but research into the facial feedback hypothesis suggests that the act of smiling can also enhance our moods.

Life Connections
See the Connections *CD-ROM: Can you tell the difference between genuine and false smiles?*

Theories of Emotion: *"How* Do You Feel?"

> David, 32, is not sleeping well. He wakes before dawn and cannot get back to sleep. His appetite is off, his energy level is low, he has started smoking again. He has a couple of drinks at lunch and muses that it's lucky that any more alcohol makes him sick to his stomach—otherwise, he'd probably be drinking too much, too. Then he thinks, "So what difference would it make?" Sometimes he is sexually frustrated; at other times he wonders whether he has any sex drive left. Although he's awake, each day it's getting harder to drag himself out of bed in the morning. This week he missed one day of work and was late twice. His supervisor has suggested in a nonthreatening way that he "do something about it." David knows that her next warning will not be unthreatening. It's been going downhill since Sue walked out. Suicide has even crossed David's mind. He wonder's if he's going crazy.

David is experiencing the emotion of depression, seriously so. Depression is to be expected following a loss, such as the end of a relationship, but David's feelings have lingered. His friends tell him that he should get out and do things, but David is so down that he hasn't the motivation to do much of anything at all. After much prompting by family and friends, David consults a psychologist who, ironically, also pushes him to get out and do things—the things he used to enjoy. The psychologist also shows David that part of his problem is that he sees himself as a failure who cannot make meaningful changes.

*Question: **How do the physiological, situational, and cognitive components of emotions interact to produce feelings and behavior?*** Some psychologists argue that physiological arousal is a more basic component of emotional response than cognition and that the type of arousal we experience strongly influences our cognitive appraisal and our labeling of the emotion (e.g., Izard, 1984). For these psychologists, the body takes precedence over the mind. Do David's bodily reactions—for example, his loss of appetite and energy—take precedence over his cognitions? Other psychologists argue that cognitive appraisal and physiological arousal are so strongly intertwined that cognitive processes may determine the emotional response. Are David's ideas that he is helpless to make meaningful changes more at the heart of his feelings of depression?

The "commonsense theory" of emotions is that something happens (a situation) that is cognitively appraised (interpreted) by the person, and the feeling state (a combination of arousal and thoughts) follows. For example, you meet someone new, appraise that person as delightful, and feelings of attraction follow. Or, as in the case of David, a social relationship comes to an end, you recognize your loss, feel powerless to change it, and feel down in the dumps.

However, both historic and contemporary theories of how the components of emotions interact are at variance with this commonsense view. Let us consider a number of theories and see whether we can arrive at some useful conclusions.

The James–Lange Theory

A century ago, William James suggested that our emotions follow, rather than cause, our behavioral responses to events. At about the same time this view was also proposed by the Danish physiologist Karl G. Lange. It is therefore termed the James–Lange theory of emotion.

According to James and Lange, certain external stimuli instinctively trigger specific patterns of arousal and action, such as fighting or fleeing (see Figure 9.5, part A). We then become angry *because* we are acting aggressively or become afraid *because* we are running away. Emotions are simply the cognitive representations (or by-products) of automatic physiological and behavioral responses.

The James–Lange theory is consistent with the facial-feedback hypothesis. That is, smiling apparently can induce pleasant feelings, even if the effect may not be strong enough to overcome feelings of sadness (Ekman, 1993a). The theory also suggests that we may be able to change our feelings by changing our behavior. Changing one's behavior to change one's feelings is one aspect of behavior therapy. When David's psychologist urges him to get out and do things, she is assuming that by changing his behavior, David can have a positive effect on the way he feels.

Walter Cannon (1927) criticized the James–Lange assertion that each emotion has distinct physiological correlates. He argued that the physiological arousal associated with emotion A is not as distinct from the arousal associated with emotion B as the theory asserts. Note that the James–Lange view downplays the importance of human cognition; it denies the roles of cognitive appraisal, personal values, and personal choice in our behavioral and emotional responses to events.

The Cannon–Bard Theory

Cannon (1927) was not content to criticize the James–Lange theory. Along with Philip Bard (1934), he suggested that an event might *simultaneously* trigger bodily responses (arousal and action) and the experience of an emotion. As shown in Figure 9.5 (part B), when an event is perceived (processed by the brain), the brain stimulates autonomic and muscular activity (arousal and action) *and* cognitive activity (experience of the emotion). Thus, according to the Cannon–Bard theory, emotions *accompany* bodily responses. They are not *produced by* bodily changes, as in the James–Lange theory.

The central criticism of the Cannon–Bard theory focuses on whether bodily responses (arousal and action) and emotions are actually stimulated simultaneously. For example, pain or the perception of danger may trigger arousal before we begin to

Power Visual
See Web site for an interactive version of this figure.

■ **Figure 9.5**
What Theories of Emotion Are There?

Several theories of emotion have been advanced, each of which proposes a different role for the components of emotional response. According to the James–Lange theory (part A), events trigger specific arousal patterns and actions. Emotions result from our appraisal of our bodily responses. According to the Cannon–Bard theory (part B), events are first processed by the brain. Body patterns of arousal, action, and our emotional responses are then triggered simultaneously. According to the theory of cognitive appraisal (part C), events and arousal are appraised by the individual. The emotional response stems from the person's appraisal of the situation and his or her level of arousal.

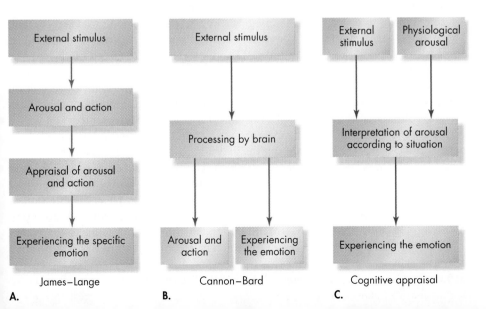

A. James–Lange
B. Cannon–Bard
C. Cognitive appraisal

The Kobal Collection/20ᵗʰ Century Fox

■ Fear, and Behavior, and Cognitive Appraisal, and . . . Fear!

How do we experience the emotion of fear? Do we run from a dangerous stimulus and feel fear as a result? Does a dangerous stimulus trigger fear and running simultaneously? Or do we appraise our situation, decide it is dangerous, and then experience fear and run away?

REFLECT

Were you ever emotionally aroused but uncertain as to exactly what you were feeling? How does such an experience relate to the Schachter–Singer theory of emotional response? And did you eventually decide what you were feeling? How?

feel distress or fear. Also, many of us have had the experience of having a "narrow escape" and becoming aroused and shaky afterward, when we have had time to consider the damage that might have occurred. What is needed is a theory that allows for an ongoing interaction of external events, physiological changes (such as autonomic arousal and muscular activity), and cognitive activities.

The Theory of Cognitive Appraisal

More recent theoretical approaches to emotion have stressed cognitive factors. Among those who argue that thinking comes first are Gordon Bower, Richard Lazarus, Stanley Schachter, and Robert Zajonc.

Stanley Schachter asserts that emotions are associated with similar patterns of bodily arousal that may be weaker or stronger, depending on the level of arousal. The label we give to an emotion depends largely on our cognitive appraisal of the situation. Cognitive appraisal is based on many factors, including our perception of external events and the ways in which other people seem to respond to those events (see Figure 9.5, part C). Given the presence of other people, we engage in social comparison to arrive at an appropriate response.

In a classic experiment, Schachter and Singer (1962) showed that arousal can be labeled quite differently, depending on the situation. The investigators told participants that they wanted to determine the effects of a vitamin on vision. Half of the participants received an injection of adrenaline, a hormone that increases the arousal of the sympathetic branch of the autonomic nervous system. A control group received an injection of an inactive solution. Those who had been given adrenaline then received one of three "cognitive manipulations," as shown in Table 9.3. Group 1 was told nothing about possible emotional effects of the "vitamin." Group 2 was deliberately misinformed; members of this group were led to expect itching, numbness, or other irrelevant symptoms. Group 3 was informed accurately about the increased arousal they would experience. Group 4 was a control group injected with an inactive substance and given no information about its effects.

After receiving injections and cognitive manipulations, the participants were asked to wait in pairs while the experimental apparatus was being set up. The participants did not know that the person with whom they were waiting was a confederate of the experimenter. The confederate's purpose was to exhibit a response that the individual would believe was caused by the injection.

Some of those who took part in the experiment waited with a confederate who acted in a happy-go-lucky manner. He flew paper airplanes about the room and tossed paper balls into a wastebasket. Other participants waited with a confederate who acted angry. He complained about the experiment, tore up a questionnaire, and left the waiting room in a huff. As the confederates worked for their Oscar awards, the real participants were observed through a one-way mirror.

The people in groups 1 and 2 were likely to imitate the behavior of the confederate. Those who were exposed to the happy-go-lucky confederate acted jovial and content. Those who were exposed to the angry confederate imitated that person's complaining, aggressive behavior. But those in groups 3 and 4 were less influenced by the confederate's behavior.

Schachter and Singer concluded that participants in groups 1 and 2 were in an ambiguous situation. Members of these groups felt arousal from the adrenaline injection but couldn't label their arousal as any specific emotion. Social comparison with a confederate led them to attribute their arousal either to happiness or to anger. Members of group 3 expected arousal from the injection, with no particular emotional consequences. These participants did not imitate the confederate's display of happiness or anger because they were not in an ambiguous situation; they knew they felt arousal because of the shot of adrenaline. Members of group 4 had no physiological arousal for which they needed an attribution, except perhaps for some arousal induced by observing the confederate. They also did not imitate the behavior of the confederate.

Now, happiness and anger are quite different emotions. Happiness is a positive emotion, whereas anger, for most of us, is a negative emotion. Yet Schachter and Singer suggest that any physiological differences between these two emotions are so

A Closer Look 👁

Just What Do Lie Detectors Detect?

The connection between autonomic arousal and emotions has led to the development of many kinds of lie detectors. Such instruments detect something, but do they detect specific emotional responses that signify lies? Let us take a closer look at the problem of lying.

Lying—for better or worse—is a part of life. A *New York Times* poll found that 60% of American adults believe that it is sometimes necessary to lie, especially to protect people's feelings (Smiley, 2000). Political leaders lie to get elected. Some students lie about why they have not completed assignments (Saxe, 1991). ('Fess up!) The great majority of people lie to their lovers—most often about other relationships (Rowatt et al., 1999; Saxe, 1991). (Is it really true that you never kissed anyone before?) People also lie about their qualifications to obtain jobs, and, of course, some people lie in denying guilt for crimes. Although we are unlikely to subject political leaders, students, and lovers to lie detector tests, such tests are frequently used in hiring and in police investigations.

Facial expressions often offer clues to deceit, but some people can lie with a straight face—or a smile. As Shakespeare pointed out in *Hamlet*, "One may smile, and smile, and be a villain." The use of devices to detect lies has a long, if not laudable, history:

> The Bedouins of Arabia . . . until quite recently required conflicting witnesses to lick a hot iron; the one whose tongue was burned was thought to be lying. The Chinese, it is said, had a similar method for detecting lying: Suspects were forced to chew rice powder and spit it out; if the powder was dry, the suspect was guilty. A variation of this test was used during the Inquisition. The suspect had to swallow a "trial slice" of bread and cheese; if it stuck to the suspect's palate or throat he or she was not telling the truth. (Kleinmuntz & Szucko, 1984, pp. 766–767)

These methods may sound primitive, even bizarre, but they are broadly consistent with modern psychological knowledge. Anxiety about being caught in a lie is linked to arousal of the sympathetic division of the autonomic nervous system. One sign of sympathetic arousal is lack of saliva, or dryness in the mouth. The emotions of fear and guilt are also linked to sympathetic arousal and, hence, to dryness in the mouth.

Questions: How do lie detectors work? How reliable are they? Modern lie detectors, or polygraphs, monitor indicators of sympathetic arousal while a witness or suspect is being examined. These indicators include heart rate, blood pressure, respiration rate, and electrodermal response (sweating) (Figure 9.6). Questions have been raised about the validity of assessing truth or fiction in this way, however (Saxe & Ben-Shakhar, 1999).

The American Polygraph Association claims that use of the polygraph is 85% to 95% accurate. Critics find polygraph testing to be less accurate and claim that it is sensitive to more than lies (Saxe & Ben-Shakhar, 1999). Factors such as tense muscles, drugs, and previous experience with polygraph tests can significantly reduce their accuracy rate. In one experiment, people were able to reduce the accuracy of polygraph-based judgments to about 50% by biting their tongue (to produce pain) or by pressing their toes against the floor (to tense muscles) while being interviewed (Honts et al., 1985). Thus you might be able to fool a lie detector by wiggling your toes.

Iacono and Lykken (1997) conducted a mail survey of members of the Society for Psychophysiological Research and the General Psychology division of the American Psychological Association. Response rates were high—91% and 74%, respectively. Most respondents replied that polygraph lie detection was not theoretically sound, that claims for its validity were overstated, that people can easily learn to beat the test, and that polygraph results should not be admitted as evidence in courts of law.

It appears that no identifiable pattern of bodily responses pinpoints lying (Iacono & Lykken, 1997; Saxe & Ben-Shakhar, 1999). Because of validity problems, results of polygraph examinations are no longer admitted as evidence in many courts.

■ Figure 9.6
What Do "Lie Detectors" Detect?

The polygraph monitors heart rate, blood pressure, respiration rate, and sweat in the palms of the hands. Is the polygraph sensitive to lying only? Is it foolproof? Because of the controversy surrounding these questions, many courts no longer admit polygraph evidence.

© Mark Burnett/Stock Boston

TABLE 9.3 Injected Substances and Cognitive Manipulations in the Schachter–Singer Study

Group	Substance	Cognitive Manipulation
1	Adrenaline	No information given about effects
2	Adrenaline	Misinformation given: itching, numbness, etc.
3	Adrenaline	Accurate information given: physiological arousal
4	Inactive	None

Source: Schachter & Singer (1962).

slight that different views of the situation can lead one person to label arousal as happiness and another person to label it as anger. The Schachter–Singer view could not be further removed from the James–Lange theory, which holds that each emotion is associated with specific and readily recognized body sensations.

The truth, it happens, may lie somewhere in between.

In science, it must be possible to replicate experiments and attain identical or similar results; otherwise, a theory cannot be considered valid. The Schachter and Singer study has been replicated, but with *different* results (Ekman, 1993a). For instance, a number of studies found that participants were less likely to imitate the behavior of the confederate and were likely to perceive unexplained arousal in negative terms, attributing it to nervousness, anger, even jealousy (Zimbardo et al., 1993).

Evaluation

What can we make of all this? Research by Paul Ekman and his colleagues (1993a) suggests that the patterns of arousal connected with various emotions are more specific than suggested by Schachter and Singer—although less so than suggested by James and Lange. Research with brain imaging suggests that different emotions, such as happiness and sadness, involve different structures within the brain (Goleman, 1995). Moreover, lack of control over our emotions and lack of understanding of what is happening to us are disturbing experiences (Zimbardo et al., 1993). Thus our cognitive appraisals of situations apparently do affect our emotional responses, even if not quite in the way envisioned by Schachter.

Learning Connections
See Web site for an interactive version of these review questions.

R E V I E W

(31) An emotion is a _____ state. (32) The emotion of anxiety mainly involves arousal of the _____ division of the autonomic nervous system (ANS). (33) The expression of emotions such as anger, fear, happiness, and surprise appears to be (culture-specific or universal?). (34) Genetic factors (do or do not?) appear to be involved in happiness. (35) Comapring one's income to that of people who make more money contributes to feelings of (happiness or unhappiness?). (36) According to the James–Lange theory, emotions have specific patterns of arousal and _____. (37) According to the theory of _____ appraisal, the emotion a person will experience reflects his or her appraisal of the situation. (38) Lie detectors assess heart rate, blood _____, respiration rate, and electrodermal response (sweating).

Critical Thinking: Should lie detectors be used in screening candidates for mortgages or jobs?

Obesity and Eating Disorders: This Meal Is Too Big; This Meal Is Too Little—Can You Ever Get It Just Right?

Millions upon millions of Americans are eating too much and putting on more weight than is healthful for them. Hundreds of thousands of people—mainly adolescent girls and young women, but boys and men as well—are eating less than is healthful for them. Some eat too much and then purposefully throw it up. Eating has become a traumatic experience for many Americans, a continuous test of willpower—or won't-power. Dieting has become the "normal"—at least in the statistical sense of the word—way of eating for women in the United States today.

In this section we focus on obesity and on the eating disorders of anorexia nervosa and bulimia nervosa, and what to do about them. The section may apply directly to you in one way or another. If not, it is almost certain to apply to people you know and care about.

Obesity—A Serious and Pervasive Problem

There is no sincerer love than the love of food.

—George Bernard Shaw

The two biggest sellers in any bookstore are the cookbooks and the diet books. The cookbooks tell you how to prepare the food and the diet books tell you how not to eat any of it.

—Andy Rooney

Consider some facts about obesity:

- More than six out of ten adult Americans are overweight, according to the National Body Mass Index (BMI)[1] guidelines, and three in ten are obese (Flegal et al., 2002).
- Problems with unhealthy weight gain are on the upswing in the United States; for example, 64% to 65% of Americans were overweight in 1999–2000, as compared with 60% in 1988–1994 (Flegal et al., 2002).
- More than 80% of African American women aged 40 or above are overweight, and more than half are obese, possibly because they have lower metabolic rates than European American women (Flegal et al., 2002).
- Americans eat more than a total of 800 billion calories of food each day (200 billion calories more than they need to maintain their weights). The extra calories could feed the nation of Germany—80 million people.
- About 300,000 Americans die each year because of health problems related to excess weight (Pinel et al., 2000).
- Weight control is elusive for most people, who regain most of the weight they have lost, even when they have dieted "successfully" (Cooper & Fairburn, 2001).

[1] You can calculate your Body Mass Index as follows. Write down your weight in pounds. Multiply it by 703. Divide the product by your height in inches squared. For example, if you weigh 160 lbs and are 5'8" tall, your BMI is $(160 \times 703)/68^2$, or 24.33. A BMI of 25 or higher is defined as overweight. A BMI of 30 or higher is defined as obese.

American culture idealizes slender heroes and heroines. For those who "more than measure up" to TV and film idols, food may have replaced sex as the central source of guilt. Obese people encounter more than their fair share of illnesses, including heart disease, stroke, diabetes, gall bladder disease, gout, respiratory problems, even certain kinds of cancer (Kenchaiah et al., 2002; Pinel et al., 2000). Research has contributed to our understanding of obesity and what can be done about it.

Origins of Obesity

We are in real trouble. Having a culture bombarded with rushed lifestyles, fast foods, and physical inactivity has caught up with us.

—Carmen Nevarez, vice president of the Berkeley, California, Public Health Institute (Californians losing fight, 2000)

Numerous biological and psychological factors are involved in obesity. On the biological side, we can point to the influences of heredity, adipose tissue (body fat), and metabolism (the rate at which the individual converts calories to energy).

Obesity runs in families. It was once assumed that obese parents encouraged their children to be overweight by serving fattening foods and setting poor examples. However, a study of Scandinavian adoptees by Stunkard and his colleagues (1990) found that children bear a closer resemblance in weight to their biological parents than to their adoptive parents. Today it is widely accepted that heredity plays a role in obesity (Wadden et al., 2002).

The efforts of obese people to maintain a slender profile may also be sabotaged by microscopic units of life within their own bodies: fat cells. No, fat cells are not overweight cells. They are adipose tissue, or cells that store fat. Hunger might be related to the amount of fat stored in these cells. As time passes after a meal, the blood sugar level drops. Fat is then drawn from these cells to provide further nourishment. At some point, referred to as the *set point*, fat deficiency in these cells is communicated to the hypothalamus in the brain, triggering the hunger drive.

People with more adipose tissue than others feel food-deprived earlier, even though they may be equal in weight. This might occur because more signals are being sent to the brain. Obese and *formerly* obese people tend to have more adipose tissue than people of normal weight. Thus many people who have lost weight complain that they are always hungry when they try to maintain normal weight levels.

Fatty tissue also metabolizes (burns) food more slowly than muscle does. For this reason, a person with a high fat-to-muscle ratio metabolizes food more slowly than a person of the same weight with a lower fat-to-muscle ratio. That is, two people who are identical in weight metabolize food at different rates, depending on the distribution of muscle and fat in their bodies. Obese people therefore are doubly handicapped in their efforts to lose weight—not only by their extra weight but by the fact that much of their body is composed of adipose tissue.

In a sense, the normal distribution of fat cells could be considered "sexist." The average man is 40% muscle and 15% fat. The average woman is 23% muscle and 25% fat. If a man and a woman with typical distributions of muscle and fat are of equal weight, therefore, the woman—who has more fat cells—has to eat less to maintain that weight.

Ironically, the very act of dieting can make it progressively more difficult to lose additional weight. This is because people on diets and those who have lost substantial amounts of weight burn fewer calories. That is, their metabolic rates slow down (Wadden et al., 2002). The slowdown appears to be a built-in mechanism that helps preserve life in times of famine. However, it also makes it more difficult for dieters to continue to lose weight. The pounds seem to come off more and more reluctantly.

Psychological factors, such as observational learning, stress, and emotional states, also "bombard" us and play a role in obesity (Greeno & Wing, 1994). Children in the United States are exposed to an average of 10,000 food commercials a year. More than nine out of ten of these commercials are for fast foods (like McDonald's fries), sugared cereals, candy, and soft drinks (Wadden et al., 2002). Situations also play a role. Family celebrations, watching TV, arguments, and tension at work can all lead to overeating or going off a diet (Drapkin et al., 1995). Efforts to diet may be also impeded by negative emotions such as depression and anxiety, which can lead to binge eating (Cools et al., 1992; Stice et al., 2000a).

The Skinny on Weight Control

All right, all right. Many factors—biological, psychological, and sociocultural—contribute to obesity. People can do many things, but first be advised that psychologists warn that not everyone should be trying to slim down. Women in the United States today are under social pressure to conform to an unnaturally slender female ideal. As a result, they tend to set unrealistic weight loss goals (Sherwood & Neumark-Sztainer, 2001). Moreover, many attempts to lose weight are ineffective. For many obese people, however, especially those who are severely obese, shedding excess pounds lowers the risks of health problems such as diabetes and heart disease.

Research on motivation and on methods of therapy has enhanced our knowledge of healthful ways to lose weight. Sound

■ A Sampler of Dietary Methods

At any given time nearly half of the adult American population is on a diet. Dieting has become the "normal" pattern of eating for women. Dozens of diets vie for attention on bookstore shelves. How can we know which ones contain truth and which ones contain fiction?

© Dion Ogust/The Image Works

weight-control programs do not involve fad diets such as fasting, eliminating carbohydrates, or eating excessive amounts of one particular food (Goldschmidt & Reuters, 2000; Kolata, 2000). Nor have effective and safe drugs to treat obesity yet emerged (Yanovski & Yanovski, 2002). Today's most effective weight-control programs involve improving nutritional knowledge, decreasing calorie intake, exercising, and changing eating habits (see Table 9.4).

Most people in the United States eat too much fat and not enough fruits and vegetables (Stampfer et al., 2000). Eating foods low in saturated fats and cholesterol not only is good for the heart but also can contribute to weight loss. Because dietary fat is converted into bodily fat more efficiently than carbohydrates are, a low-fat diet also leads to weight loss. Nutritional knowledge leads to suggestions for taking in fewer calories, which results in lower weight. Taking in fewer calories does not just mean eating smaller portions. It means switching to some lower-calorie foods—relying more on fresh, unsweetened fruits and vegetables (eating apples rather than apple pie), fish and poultry, and skim milk and cheese. It means cutting down on—or eliminating—butter, margarine, oils, and sugar.

The same foods that help control weight also tend to be high in vitamins and fiber and low in fats. Such foods therefore may also reduce the risk of heart disease, cancer, and other illnesses.

Dieting plus exercise is more effective than dieting alone for shedding pounds and keeping them off. When we restrict our intake of calories, our metabolic rate compensates by slowing down (Wadden et al., 2002). Exercise burns calories and builds muscle tissue, which metabolizes more calories than fatty tissue does (Dubbert, 2002).

Cognitive and behavioral methods have also provided many strategies for losing weight. Among them are the following:

- Establish calorie-intake goals and keep track of whether you are meeting them. Get a book that shows how many calories are found in foods. Keep a diary of your calorie intake.
- Substitute low-calorie, low-fat foods for high-calorie, high-fat

TABLE 9.4 Dietary Recommendations of the American Heart Association

- Limit your total fat intake to 30% or less of your total calorie intake.
- Limit your intake of saturated fats to less than 10% of your total calorie intake.
- Keep your cholesterol intake under 300 mg per day.
- Eat five or more servings of vegetables and fruits each day.
- Eat six or more servings of grains, breads, cereals, and legumes each day, including whole grains.
- Eat at least two servings of fish per week.
- Limit intake of sodium (salt) to less than 6 g per day.
- Limit intake of alcohol to two drinks per day for men and one drink per day per women.
- Take in enough calcium.

Source: Krauss, et al. (2000).

foods. Fill your stomach with celery rather than cheesecake and enchiladas. Eat preplanned low-calorie snacks instead of binge-eating peanuts or ice cream.

- Take a five-minute break between helpings. Ask yourself "Am I still hungry?" If not, stop eating.
- Avoid temptations that have sidetracked you in the past. Shop at the mall with the Alfalfa Sprout Café, not the Cheesecake Factory. Plan your meal before entering a restaurant. (Avoid ogling that tempting full-color menu.) Attend to your own plate, not to the sumptuous dish at the next table. (Your salad probably looks greener to them, anyhow.) Shop from a list. Walk briskly through the supermarket, preferably after dinner when you're no longer hungry. Don't be sidetracked by pretty packages (fattening things may come in them). Don't linger in the kitchen. Study, watch TV, or write letters elsewhere. Don't bring fattening foods into the house. Prepare only enough food to keep within your calorie goals.
- Exercise to burn more calories and increase your metabolic rate. Reach for your mate, not your plate (to coin a phrase). Take a brisk walk instead of eating an unplanned snack. Build exercise routines by adding a few minutes each week.
- Reward yourself for meeting calorie goals (but not with food). Imagine how great you'll look in that new swimsuit next summer. Do not go to the latest movie unless you have met your weekly calorie goal. When you meet your weekly calorie goal, put cash in the bank toward a vacation or a new camera.
- Use imagery to help yourself lose weight. Tempted by a fattening dish? Imagine that it's rotten, that you would be nauseated by it and have a sick taste in your mouth for the rest of the day.
- Mentally walk through solutions to problem situations. Consider what you will do when cake is handed out at the office party. Rehearse your next visit to relatives who tell you how painfully thin you look and try to stuff you with food (Drapkin et al., 1995). Imagine how you will politely (but firmly) refuse seconds and thirds, despite their objections.
- Above all, if you slip from your plan for a day, don't blow things out of proportion. Dieters are often tempted to binge, especially when they rigidly see themselves either as perfect successes or as complete failures or when they experience powerful emotions—either positive or negative (Cools et al., 1992). Consider the weekly or monthly trend, not just a single day. Credit yourself for the long-term trend. If you do binge, resume dieting the next day.

Losing weight—and keeping it off—is not easy, but it can be done. Making a commitment to losing weight and establishing a workable plan for doing so are two of the keys.

Anorexia Nervosa and Bulimia Nervosa

Most of us either deprive ourselves or consume vast quantities of food now and then. This is normal. The eating disorders listed in the *DSM* are characterized by persistent, gross disturbances in eating patterns. The major eating disorders are anorexia nervosa and bulimia nervosa.

Anorexia Nervosa

The Duchess of Windsor once said, "You can never be too rich or too thin." Most people make no objection to having a fat bank account, but the fact is that one can most certainly be too skinny, as in the case of anorexia nervosa. Anorexia nervosa is a life-threatening eating disorder characterized by extreme fear of being too heavy, dramatic weight loss, a distorted body image, and resistance to eating enough to reach or maintain a healthful weight, as we see in the case of Rachel:

I wanted to be a runner. Runners were thin and I attributed this to dieting, not training. So I began restricting my diet: No butter, red meat, pork, dessert, candy, or snacking. If I ate any of the forbidden items I obsessed about it and felt guilty for days.

As a high school freshman, I wanted to run with the fastest girls so I trained hard, really hard and ate less. Lunch was lettuce sandwiches, carrots, and an apple. By my senior year, I was number three on the team and lunch was a bagel and an orange.

I maintained a rigid schedule—running cross country and track, having a seat on student council, volunteering, and maintaining a 3.9 GPA throughout high school—while starving myself (1,000 calories per day), trying to attain the impossible perfection I thought couldn't be far away if I only slimmed down a little bit more.

Several teammates were concerned, but I shrugged them off saying family members were tall and slender; I was a health nut, I didn't like fatty foods; I was a vegetarian; I didn't like sweets; I wasn't hungry; I wasn't starving.

A psychiatrist didn't help at all. I went in, sat on the couch and told her what she wanted to hear: I would eat more, run less, stop restricting myself, and quit obsessing about being thin. I was very good at knowing exactly what to tell others.

I dropped 10 pounds my freshman year—from 125 to 115 lbs. I was 5' 8" tall and wore a size five. I hated my body so I starved myself and ran like a mad woman.

In quiet moments, I was sad and worried about what might be going on inside me.

I was already taking birth control to regain my menstrual cycle; my weight was 15% below what was recommended for my height; I was always cold; I had chest pains and an irregular heartbeat; my hair was limp and broke off; my skin was colorless.

It wasn't until I came to the University of Iowa and joined the varsity women's cross country team that I began to see what I was doing to myself. A teammate had an eating problem. Every time I saw her, I felt sick to my stomach. She had sunken cheeks, eyes so big they swallowed her face. She was an excellent student and a college-level varsity athlete. Many people wondered at her determination, but I understood. She used the same excuses I did.

For one sick instant, I wondered if I would be happier if I were that thin. That is when I started to realize I was slowly killing myself.

At the urging of my coach, I saw the team nutritionist who recommended a psychiatrist who felt no pity for me and made me take a brutally honest look at who I was and why I was starving myself. She didn't accept any of my excuses. She helped me realize that there are other things to think about besides food and body image. About this time I decided to quit the cross country team. The pressure I felt to be thin and competition at the college level were too much when I needed to focus on getting well.

After two months of therapy, my weight had dropped again. I'm not sure how far because I refused to step on a scale, but my size five pants were falling off. My psychiatrist required weekly weigh-ins.

I wasn't putting into practice any of the things my nutritionist and counselor suggested. They told me that if I wanted to have children someday I needed to eat. They warned me of osteoporosis at age 30. Then my psychiatrist scared me to death. She told me I needed to start eating more or I would be checked into the hospital and hooked up to an IV. That would put me on the same level as my Iowa teammate. I had looked at her with such horror and never realized that I was in the same position.

My psychiatrist asked how my family would feel if they had to visit me in the hospital because I refused to eat. It was enough to make me think hard the next time I went through the food service lines.

Of course, I didn't get better the next day. But it was a step in the right direction. It's taken me three years to get where I am now. At 5′ 8 ¾″ (I even grew as I got healthier) and 145 lbs, I look and feel healthier, have better eating and exercise habits, and I don't obsess about food as much as I used to. On rare occasions, I think about controlling my food intake. My eating disorder will haunt me for the rest of my life. If I'm not careful, it could creep back.

Rachel, like other people with anorexia nervosa, weighed less than 85% of her desirable body weight, and "desirable" body weights are already too slender for many individuals. By and large, anorexia nervosa afflicts women during adolescence and young adulthood (Winzelberg et al., 2000; Zagar & Rubenstein, 2002). The typical person with anorexia is a young European American female of higher socioeconomic status (McLaren, 2002). Affluent females have greater access to fitness centers and health clubs and are more likely to read the magazines which idealize slender bodies and shop in the boutiques that cater to females with svelte figures. All in all, they are regularly confronted with unrealistically high standards of slimness that make them extremely unhappy with their own physiques (McLaren, 2002). The incidences of anorexia nervosa and bulimia nervosa have increased markedly in recent years. Women with these disorders greatly outnumber the men who have them by more than six to one, but we lack precise data on their prevalence because so many people deny their disorder (Goode, 2000; Striegel-Moore & Cachelin, 2001).

Females with anorexia nervosa can drop 25% or more of their weight within a year. Severe weight loss triggers abnormalities in the endocrine system (that is, with hormones) that prevent ovulation (Treasure & Serpell, 2001). General health deteriorates. Nearly every system in the body is affected. There are problems with the respiratory system (Key et al., 2001) and with the cardiovascular system (Eidem et al., 2001). Females with anorexia are also at risk for premature development of osteoporosis, a condition characterized by loss of bone density that usually afflicts people in late adulthood (Geiser et al., 2001; Treasure & Serpell, 2001). Given all these problems, it is not surprising that the mortality rate for females with anorexia nervosa is approximately 5%.

In one common pattern, the girl sees that she has gained some weight after reaching puberty, and she resolves that she must lose it. But even after the weight is gone, she maintains her pattern of dieting and, in many cases, exercises at a fever pitch. This pattern continues as she plunges below her "desirable" weight—according to standardized weight charts—and even after those who care about her tell her that she is becoming all skin and bones. Denial is a huge part of anorexia nervosa. Girls with the disorder tragically tend to deny that they are losing too much weight.

They are in denial about any health problems, pointing to their feverish exercise routines as evidence of their strength. Distortion of the body image is a major feature of the disorder (Winzelberg et al., 2000). In one study, researchers recruited women who weighed an average of 31% below their desirable weight according to Metropolitan Life Insurance Company charts (Penner et al., 1991). They found that the women overestimated the size of their bodies by exactly 31%! Friends, coworkers, and families see females with anorexia nervosa as skin and bones. Meanwhile, the women fix their gaze into the mirror and believe that they are looking at a body shape that is too heavy.

Ironically, individuals with anorexia do not literally distance themselves from food. They may become as preoccupied with food as they are with their own body shape. They may develop a fascination with cookbooks, shop for their families, and prepare gourmet feasts—for other people, that is.

Bulimia Nervosa

Bulimia nervosa is sort of a companion disorder to anorexia nervosa, as we see in the case of Nicole:

> Nicole awakens in her cold dark room and already wishes it was time to go back to bed. She dreads the thought of going through this day, which will be like so many others in her recent past. She asks herself the question every morning, "Will I be able to make it through the day without being totally obsessed by thoughts of food, or will I blow it again and spend the day [binge eating]"? She tells herself that today she will begin a new life, today she will start to live like a normal human being. However, she is not at all convinced that the choice is hers. (Boskind-White & White, 1983, p. 29)

So, does Nicole begin a new life today? No. Despite her pledge to herself, Nicole begins the day with eggs and toast—butter included. Then she downs cookies; bagels smothered with cream cheese, butter, and jelly; doughnuts; candy bars; bowlfuls of cereal and milk—all in less than an hour. When her body cries "No more!" she turns to the next step: purging. Purging also is a routine. In the bathroom, she ties back her hair. She runs the shower to mask noise, drinks some water, and then makes herself throw it all up. Afterward she makes another pledge to herself: "Starting tomorrow, I'm going to change." Will she change? In truth, she doubts it.

Bulimia nervosa, Nicole's eating disorder, entails recurrent cycles of binge eating and purging. Binge eating often follows on the heels of food restriction—as in dieting (Lowe et al., 1996). There are various methods of purging. Nicole vomited. Other avenues include strict dieting or fasting, laxatives, and demanding, prolonged exercise regimes. Individuals with eating disorders, like Rachel and Nicole, tend to be perfectionistic about their bodies. They will not settle for less than their idealized body shape and weight (Halmi et al., 2000; Santonastaso et al., 2001). Bulimia, like anorexia, triggers hormonal imbalances: One study found that nearly half of the females with bulimia nervosa have irregular menstrual cycles (Gendall et al., 2000).

Bulimia nervosa, like anorexia nervosa, tends to afflict women during adolescence and young adulthood (Lewinsohn et al., 2000b; Winzelberg et al., 2000). Eating disorders are upsetting and dangerous in themselves, of course, but they are also often connected with deep depression (Stice et al., 2000b). However, it seems that depression is more likely to co-occur with eating disorders than to be caused by them (Wade et al., 2000).

On a Binge

Bulimia nervosa is characterized by recurrent cycles of binge eating and purging, as by means of vomiting. Why are women more likely than men to have eating disorders?

Origins of the Eating Disorders

Health professionals have done a great deal of research into the origins of eating disorders. Yet they will be the first to admit that many questions about these disorders remain unanswered (Striegel-Moore & Cachelin, 2001).

According to some psychoanalysts, anorexia nervosa may symbolize a young woman's efforts to cope with sexual fears, especially the possibility of becoming pregnant. Keep in mind that anorexia is connected with *amenorrhea* (lack of menstruation). Some psychoanalysts interpret the behavior pattern as a female's attempt to regress to her lifestyle prior to puberty. Anorexia nervosa prevents some adolescents from separating from their families and assuming adult responsibilities. Their breasts and hips flatten once more due to the loss of fatty tissue. In the adolescent's fantasies, perhaps, she remains a sexually undifferentiated child.

Many parents are obsessed with getting their children—especially their infants—to eat. Thus some psychoanalysts suggest that children now and then refuse to eat as a way of engaging in warfare with their parents. ("You have to eat something!" "I'm not hungry!") It often seems that warfare does occur in the families of adolescents with eating disorders. Parents in such families are often unhappy with the family's functioning. They frequently have issues with eating and dieting themselves. They also "act out" against their daughters—letting them know that they consider them unattractive, and, prior to the development of the eating disorder, letting them know that they think they should lose weight (Baker et al., 2000; Cooper et al., 2001; Fairburn et al., 1998). The family environment, in other words, is negative, negative, negative.

A particularly disturbing risk factor for eating disorders in adolescent females is a history of child abuse, particularly sexual abuse (Fairburn et al., 1998). One study found a history of childhood sexual abuse in about half of women with bulimia nervosa, as opposed to a rate of about 7% among women without the disorder (Deep et al., 1999). Another study compared 45 pairs of sisters, one of whom was diagnosed with anorexia nervosa (Karwautz et al., 2001). Those with anorexia were significantly more likely to be exposed to high parental expectations and to sexual abuse.

Also consider the sociocultural features of eating disorders. Slimness is idealized in the United States, but when you check out *Cosmopolitan, Glamour,* or the *Victoria's Secret* catalog, you are looking at models who, on average, are 9% taller and 16% thinner than the typical female—and who still manage to have ample bustlines. Miss America, the annually renewed American role model, has also been slenderizing herself across the years. The pageant began in 1922. Over the past 80 years, the winner has added only 2% in height but has lost 12 lbs in weight. In the early days of the 1920s, Miss America's weight relative to her height yielded a Body Mass Index (BMI) of 20 to 25, which is considered normal by the World Health Organization (WHO). WHO labels people as malnourished when their BMIs are lower than 18.5. However, recent Miss Americas come in at a BMI near 17 (Rubinstein & Caballero, 2000). So Miss America adds to the woes of "normal" young women, and even to those of young women who hover near the WHO "malnourished" borderline. As the cultural ideal slenderizes, women with desirable body weights according to the health charts feel overweight, and overweight women feel gargantuan (Winzelberg et al., 2000). As a group, men are more likely than women to believe that their body shape is desirable (Rozin & Fallon, 1988).

Many individuals with eating disorders, like Rachel, are involved in activities that demand weight limits, such as dancing, acting, and modeling. Male wrestlers also feel the pressure to stay within an "acceptable" weight range (Goode, 2000). Men, like women, experience pressure to create an ideal body, one with power in the upper torso and a trim abdomen (Goode, 2000).

Eating disorders tend to run in families, which raises the possibility of the involvement of genetic factors (DeAngelis, 2002; Strober et al., 2000). Genetic factors might not directly cause eating disorders but are likely to involve obsessionistic and perfectionistic personality traits, which are at least partly heritable (Bellodi et al., 2001; Halmi et al., 2000; Kaye et al., 2000; Speranza et al., 2001). In a society in which so much attention is focused on the ideal of the slender body, these personality traits encourage dieting (Wade et al., 2000). Anorexia also often co-occurs with depression (Lewinsohn et al., 2000b; Wade et al., 2000). We can note that perfectionistic people are likely to be disappointed in themselves, giving rise to feelings of depression. But it may also be that both disorders share genetic factors. Genetically inspired perfectionism, cultural emphasis on slimness, self-absorption, and family conflict may create a perfect recipe for development of eating disorders (Baker et al., 2000).

Treatment and Prevention of Eating Disorders

Treatment of the eating disorders—particularly anorexia nervosa—is a great challenge (Stein et al., 2001). The disorders are connected with serious health problems, and the low weight of individuals with anorexia is often life-threatening. Many children and adolescents are admitted to the hospital for treatment against their will (Watson et al., 2000). Denial is a feature of anorexia nervosa, and many do not recognize—or do not admit—that they have a problem. When the individual with anorexia does not—or cannot—eat adequately through the mouth, measures such as nasogastric (tube) feeding may be used. Nasogastric feeding is unpleasant, but some children and adolescents understand and appreciate its value (Niederman et al., 2001).

What are the outcomes of hospitalization? They vary, and they are not always good. A British study attempted to contact 84 women who had been hospitalized 21 years earlier for anorexia (Zipfel et al., 2000; Figure 9.7). The researchers found that about half of the women had achieved complete recovery; nearly 16% had died from causes related to anorexia, such as weakness or imbalances in body chemistry; about 10% were still anorexic; and the remaining 23% could not be contacted or had outcomes that were unclear. These outcomes seem rather severe, but they resulted only from women who had been hospitalized for anorexia. Women with less serious cases may not require hospitalization.

Medication, especially antidepressants, is frequently used in the treatment of eating disorders. Eating disorders are frequently accompanied by depression, and it may be that the common culprit in the eating and mood disorders is a lower-than-normal level of the neurotransmitter serotonin. Antidepressants such as Prozac and Zoloft enhance the activity of serotonin in the brain, often increasing food intake in anorexic individuals and decreasing binge eating in bulimic people. In one study, 10 of 11 anorexic patients showed significant weight gain after 14 weeks of treatment with an antidepressant, and they maintained the gain at a

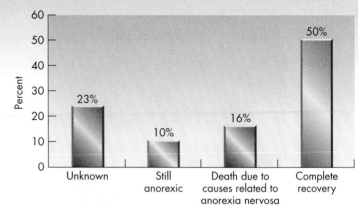

■ **Figure 9.7**
Results of a British Study of Outcomes for Women Diagnosed with Anorexia Nervosa, 21 Years After First Hospitalization (in Percents)

Although the outcomes shown here are pessimistic, note that they apply only to women who were hospitalized for anorexia nervosa. In many cases, the psychological disorder is treated on an outpatient basis. Women who are hospitalized with the disorder impress their physicians as being in relatively greater danger.

64-week follow-up (Santonastaso et al., 2001). They were also evaluated as being significantly less depressed and perfectionistic (obsessive) than they had been.

Because family problems are commonly connected with eating disorders, family therapy is often used to treat these disorders (Diamond & Siqueland, 2001; Lock & Le Grange, 2001). Family therapy has positive outcomes in many cases but is not an appropriate setting for dealing with childhood sexual abuse.

Cognitive–behavioral therapy has been used to help anorexic and bulimic individuals challenge their perfectionism and their attitudes toward their bodies. It has also been used to systematically reinforce appropriate eating behavior. But let us remember that all of this is connected with cultural attitudes that idealize excessive thinness. "Prevention" will have to address cultural values as well as potential problems in individuals.

Recite Recite Recite

Learning Connections
See Web site for an interactive version of this chapter summary

1. **What is the psychology of motivation? What are motives, needs, drives, and incentives?**

The psychology of motivation is concerned with why people behave in certain ways. Motives are hypothetical states within an organism that propel the organism toward goals. Physiological needs include those for oxygen and food. Psychological needs include those for achievement and self-esteem. Needs give rise to drives; for example, depletion of food gives rise to the hunger drive. An incentive is a desirable object, person, or situation.

2. **What is meant by species-specific behaviors?**

According to the evolutionary perspective, organisms are born with preprogrammed tendencies—called instincts, species-specific behaviors, or fixed action patterns (FAPs)—to behave in certain ways in certain situations. FAPs occur in the presence of stimuli called releasers. Male members of many species are sexually aroused by pheromones secreted by females. Psychologists debate whether humans have instincts, and if so, what they are.

3. **What is drive-reduction theory?**

According to drive-reduction theory, we are motivated to engage in behavior that reduces drives. Primary drives such as hunger and pain are based on the biological makeup of the organism. Acquired drives such as the drive for money are learned. We learn to do what reduces drives. The body has a tendency called homeostasis to maintain a steady state; food deprivation thus leads to the hunger drive and eating, which reduces hunger.

4. **Are all motives aimed at the reduction of tension?**

Apparently not. Stimulus motives aim to increase rather than decrease the amount of stimulation acting on the organism. Sensory-deprivation studies suggest that inactivity and lack of stimulation are aversive in humans. People and many lower animals have needs for stimulation, activity, exploration, and manipulation. Many psychologists believe that exploration is reinforcing in itself.

5. **How does humanistic theory differ from other theories of motivation?**

Instincts and drives are mainly defensive, aimed at survival and reproduction. Humanistic psychologists argue that people are self-aware and that behavior can be growth-oriented; people are motivated to strive for self-actualization.

6. **What is Maslow's hierarchy of needs?**

Maslow hypothesized that people have a hierarchy of needs. Once lower-level needs such as physiological and safety needs are met, people strive to meet needs for love, esteem, and self-actualization.

7. **Why are people motivated to eliminate inconsistencies in their worldviews?**

According to cognitive theory, people are motivated to understand and predict events. People must represent the world accurately in order to attain these goals. Therefore, their cognitions need to be consistent with one another.

8. **Why are people who go unrewarded more likely than those who are rewarded to think or say that what they are doing is worthwhile for its own sake?**

Cognitive-dissonance theory hypothesizes that people dislike situations in which their attitudes and behavior are inconsistent. Such situations apparently induce cognitive dissonance, which people can reduce by changing their attitudes. For example, people engage in effort justification; that is, they tend to justify boring or fruitless behavior to themselves by concluding that their efforts are worthwhile, even when they go unrewarded.

9. **What bodily mechanisms regulate the hunger drive? What psychological processes are at work?**

Hunger is regulated by several internal factors, including stomach contractions, blood sugar level, receptors in the mouth and liver, and the hypothalamus. The ventromedial nucleus the hypothalamus functions as a stop-eating center. Damage to the area leads to hyperphagia in rats (gross overweight). The lateral hypothalamus may function as a start-eating center. External stimuli such as the aroma of food can also trigger hunger. Chewing and swallowing provide some satiety.

Recite Recite Recite

10. **What do we know about the sex lives of people in the United States?**

Sex may be a natural function, but it is influenced by religious beliefs and tradition. Males are generally more likely than females to masturbate, engage in premarital sex, and have a large number of sex partners. Education appears to have a liberating influence on sexual behavior, whereas conservative religious belief appears to have a constraining effect.

11. **What are the effects of sex hormones on sexual motivation?**

Sex hormones have activating and organizing effects on behavior. "Male" sex hormones appear to fuel the sex drive, even in women, who produce much less of them. Many female animals are receptive to males only during estrus, when female sex hormones are plentiful.

12. **What are pheromones?**

Pheromones are chemical secretions that are detected through a vomeronasal organ. Pheromones trigger sexual and other behaviors in many mammals, but their role in human sexuality is controversial.

13. **What is meant by sexual orientation?**

Sexual orientation is the directionality of erotic interests. People with a homosexual orientation are attracted to and interested in forming romantic relationships with people of their own sex. In the United States, about 3% of males and 2% of females consider themselves gay or lesbian.

14. **What do we know about the origins of gay male and lesbian sexual orientations?**

According to Freudian theory, sexual orientation is determined by identification with male or female figures, and identification reflects the outcome of the Oedipus or Electra complex. Learning theorists explain sexual orientation in terms of reinforcement and observational learning. Biological psychologists find evidence for genetic factors in sexual orientation, as found in comparisons of MZ and DZ twins. In many species, sexual motivation is almost completely regulated by sex hormones.

15. **What is the sexual response cycle?**

Vasocongestion and myotonia take people through a four-phase sexual response cycle: excitement, plateau, orgasm, and resolution.

16. **What have psychologists and other scientists learned about the roles of genetics and environmental influences on aggressive behavior?**

Many lower animals show instinctive aggressive reactions. Electrical stimulation of part of the hypothalamus triggers stereotypical aggressive behaviors in many animals. Testosterone appears to affect the tendencies to dominate and control other people and is also involved in aggression. Freud believed that accumulating frustrations could trigger explosions, but that catharsis would help prevent them. Cognitive psychologists assert that our behavior is influenced by our values, by our interpretation of our situations, and by choice. From the social–cognitive perspective, aggressive skills are mainly acquired by observation. Situational factors that contribute to aggression include membership in a mob and aversive environmental stimuli.

17. **Why do some people strive to get ahead?**

One reason may be that they have more achievement motivation than others. McClelland studied achievement motivation by means of responses to TAT cards. People with high achievement motivation earn higher grades and more money than people of comparable ability but less achievement motivation. Academic achievement may be motivated by performance or learning goals. Performance goals are tangible rewards, such as getting into graduate school. Learning goals involve the enhancement of knowledge or skills.

18. **What is an emotion?**

An emotion is a state of feeling with physiological, cognitive, and behavioral components. Emotions motivate behavior and also serve as goals. Fear, for example, is connected with arousal of the sympathetic division of the autonomic nervous system, cognitions that one is in danger, and behavioral tendencies to escape.

19. How can we tell when other people are happy or sad?	Facial expressions are one factor in the expression of emotion. According to Ekman, the expression of several basic emotions is recognized in cultures around the world. Darwin believed that universal recognition of facial expressions has survival value.
20. What factors contribute to happiness?	Happiness may have a genetic component, but environmental and attitudinal factors also make their contributions. Affluence helps, and so do social relationships, a sense of meaning, optimism, and self-esteem.
21. Can smiling give rise to feelings of goodwill? Can frowning produce anger?	Facial expressions might influence one's experience of emotion. The contraction of facial muscles might be influential.
22. How do the physiological, situational, and cognitive components of emotions interact to produce feelings and behavior?	According to the James–Lange theory, emotions are associated with specific patterns of arousal and action that are triggered by certain external events. The emotion follows the behavioral response. The Cannon–Bard theory proposes that processing of events by the brain gives rise simultaneously to feelings and bodily responses; that is, feelings accompany bodily responses. According to Schachter and Singer's theory of cognitive appraisal, emotions are associated with similar patterns of arousal. The emotion a person experiences reflects a person's appraisal of the situation. Research evidence suggests that patterns of arousal are more specific than suggested by the theory of cognitive appraisal, but that cognitive appraisal plays a role in determining our responses to events.
23. How do lie detectors work? How reliable are they?	Lie detectors—also called polygraphs—monitor indicators of sympathetic arousal: heart rate, blood pressure, respiration rate, and sweating while a person is being questioned. These responses are presumed to indicate the presence of emotions—anxiety and/or guilt—that might be caused by lying. Critics find polygraph testing to be unreliable.

Active Learning Resources

Search Online with InfoTrac® College Edition

For additional information on the topics in this chapter, explore InfoTrac College Edition, your online library. Go to **http://www.infotrac.thomsonlearning.com** and use the passcode that came on the card with your book. Try these search terms: cognitive dissonance, incentives, self-actualization, sexual motivation, pheromones, sexual orientation, testosterone and aggression, lie detectors, and eating disorders.

Visit Our Web Site

Go to **http://www.wadsworth.com/psychology**, where you will find online resources directly linked to your book, including interactive exercises related to PQ4R and Power Visuals for mastering and reviewing key concepts. In addition, you will find hints on using InfoTrac College Edition to answer the Critical Thinking questions throughout the text. Start with the **Self Study Assessment** for a customized **Study Plan** generated by taking the **Pre-Test** and **Post-Test.**

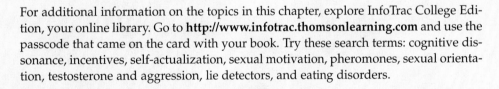

Connections CD-ROM

Go to the Wadsworth *Connections* CD-ROM for further study of the concepts in this chapter. The CD-ROM includes videos and animations, quizzes, and additional activities to expand your learning experience, plus interactive self-assessments to help connect the material to your own life.

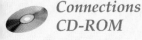

Psyk.trek™ CD-ROM

The Wadsworth *Psyk.trek* CD-ROM offers tutorials, simulations, videos, multimedia glossary, and quizzing to help you master the material.

PsychNow! CD-ROM

The Wadsworth *PsychNow!* CD-ROM includes interactive exercises, videos, and animations to enhance your learning.

Health Psychology

- **HEALTH PSYCHOLOGISTS** study the links between psychological factors and the prevention and treatment of health problems.

Stress: Presses, Pushes, and Pulls

- **STRESS CRUSHES**, smashes, and stretches—So now what?

Sources of Stress: Don't Hassle Me? (Right)

- **WHY ARE DAILY** hassles . . . hassles?

- **GOING ON VACATION** is a source of stress. Should you stay at home?

- **PEOPLE WITH** a strong need for social approval may be setting themselves up for feelings of anxiety and depression.

- **ARE YOU** Type A?

Psychological Moderators of Stress

- **IS IT TRUE THAT** "A merry heart doeth good like a medicine"?

- **IF YOU CAN STOP** the roller coaster, you're less likely to want to get off.

- **STRESSED OUT?** Get a friend.

Stress and the Body: The War Within

- **WHEN STRESS COMES** along, your body sounds a biological alarm.

- **AT ANY GIVEN MOMENT,** countless microscopic warriors within our bodies are carrying out search-and-destroy missions against foreign agents.

Psychology and Health: Headaches, Heart Disease, Cancer, and Sexually Transmitted Infections

- **CAN BLOWING THINGS** out of proportion give you a headache?

- **CAN HANDING ASSIGNMENTS** in early be bad for your health?

- **SOME OF US HAVE** inherited predispositions to develop cancer. Should we resign ourselves to our fate?

- **WHO IS AT RISK** of being infected with HIV? (Are you sure?)

Life Connections: Preventing and Coping with Health Problems—Stress, Headaches, Heart Disease, Cancer, and Sexually Transmitted Infections

- **HOW DO YOU CHANGE** those nagging irrational thoughts? By changing them.

- **WANT TO RELAX** a little? We can show you how.

- **KETCHUP IS** a health food. (Really.)

- **IF YOU ARE AWARE** of the threat of AIDS, will you change your behavior to protect your partner and yourself?

irens. Ambulances. Stretchers. The emergency room at Dallas's public Parkland Memorial Hospital is a busy place. Sirens wail endlessly as ambulances pull up to the doors and discharge people who need prompt attention. Because of the volume of patients, beds line the halls, and people who do not require immediate care cram the waiting room. Many hours may pass before they are seen by a doctor. It is not unusual for people who are not considered in danger to wait 10 to 12 hours.

All this may sound rather foreboding, but good things are happening at Parkland as well. One of them is the attention physicians are devoting to patients' psychological needs as well as to their physical needs. For example, influenced both by his own clinical experience and by Native American wisdom about the healing process, Dr. Ron Anderson teaches his medical students that caring about patients is not an outdated ideal. Rather, it is a powerful weapon against disease.

TV journalist Bill Moyers describes Anderson on his medical rounds with students:

> I listen as he stops at the bedside of an elderly woman suffering from chronic asthma. He asks the usual questions: "How did you sleep last night?" "Is the breathing getting any easier?" His next questions surprise the medical students: "Is your son still looking for work?" "Is he still drinking?" "Tell us what happened right before the asthma attack." He explains to his puzzled students. "We know that anxiety aggravates many illnesses, especially chronic conditions like asthma. So we have to find out what may be causing her episodes of stress and help her find some way of coping with it. Otherwise she will land in here again, and next time we might not be able to save her. We cannot just prescribe medication and walk away. That is medical neglect. We have to take the time to get to know her, how she lives, her values, what her social supports are. If we don't know that her son is her sole support and that he's out of work, we will be much less effective in dealing with her asthma." (Moyers, 1993, p. 2)

HEALTH PSYCHOLOGY

Note some key concepts from the slice of hospital life reported by Moyers: "Anxiety aggravates many illnesses." "We have to find out what may be causing . . . stress and . . . find some way of coping with it." "We cannot just prescribe medication and walk away." "We have to take the time to get to know [patients], how [they] live, [their] values, what [their] social supports are."

Anderson and Moyers have provided us with an introduction to the field of health psychology. *Question: What is health psychology?* **Health psychology** studies the relationships between psychological factors and the prevention and treatment of physical health problems. The case of the woman with asthma is a useful springboard for discussion because health psychologists study the ways in which

- psychological factors such as stress, behavior patterns, and attitudes can lead to or aggravate illness.
- people can cope with stress.
- stress and **pathogens** (disease-causing organisms such as bacteria and viruses) interact to influence the immune system.
- people decide whether or not to seek health care.
- psychological forms of intervention such as health education (for example, concerning nutrition, smoking, and exercise) and behavior modification can contribute to physical health.

In this chapter we consider a number of issues in health psychology: sources of stress, factors that moderate the impact of stress, and the body's response to stress.

Health Psychology
The field of psychology that studies the relationships between psychological factors (e.g., attitudes, beliefs, situational influences, and behavior patterns) and the prevention and treatment of physical illness.

Pathogen
A microscopic organism (e.g., bacterium or virus) that can cause disease.

STRESS: PRESSES, PUSHES, AND PULLS

Question: What is stress?   In physics, stress is defined as a pressure or force exerted on a body. Tons of rock pressing on the earth, one car smashing into another, a rubber band stretching—all are types of physical stress. Psychological forces, or stresses, also press, push, or pull. We may feel "crushed" by the weight of a big decision, "smashed" by adversity, or "stretched" to the point of snapping.

In psychology, **stress** is the demand made on an organism to adapt, cope, or adjust. Some stress is healthful and necessary to keep us alert and occupied. Stress researcher Hans Selye (1980) referred to such healthful stress as **eustress.** But intense or prolonged stress can overtax our adjustive capacity, affect our moods, impair our ability to experience pleasure, and harm the body (Harkness & Luther, 2001; Kiecolt-Glaser et al., 2002a, 2002b).

SOURCES OF STRESS: DON'T HASSLE ME? (RIGHT)

There are many sources of stress. In this section we consider daily hassles, life changes, conflict, irrational beliefs, and Type A behavior.

Daily Hassles—The Stress of Everyday Life

Which straw will break the camel's back? The last straw, according to the saying. Similarly, stresses can pile up until we can no longer cope with them. Some of these stresses are **daily hassles.**   *Question: What are daily hassles?*   Daily hassles are regularly occurring conditions and experiences that can threaten or harm our well-being. Others are life changes. Lazarus and his colleagues (1985) analyzed a scale that measures daily hassles and their opposites—termed **uplifts**—and found that hassles could be grouped as follows:

- *Household hassles:* preparing meals, shopping, and home maintenance.
- *Health hassles:* Physical illness, concern about medical treatment, and side effects of medication.
- *Time-pressure hassles:* Having too many things to do, too many responsibilities, and not enough time.
- *Inner concern hassles:* Being lonely and fearful of confrontation.

Stress
The demand that is made on an organism to adapt.

Eustress
(YOU-stress). Stress that is healthful.

Daily Hassles
Notable daily conditions and experiences that are threatening or harmful to a person's well-being.

Uplifts
Notable pleasant daily conditions and experiences.

■ **A Daily Hassle**
Daily hassles are notable daily conditions and experiences that are threatening or harmful to a person's well-being. What are some of the daily hassles in your life?

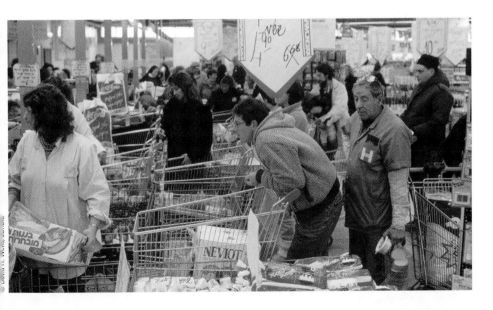

- *Environmental hassles:* Crime, neighborhood deterioration, and traffic noise.
- *Financial responsibility hassles:* Concern about owing money such as mortgage payments and loan installments.
- *Work hassles:* Job dissatisfaction, not liking one's duties at work, and problems with coworkers.
- *Future security hassles:* Concerns about job security, taxes, property investments, stock market swings, and retirement.

These hassles are linked to psychological variables such as nervousness, worrying, inability to get started, feelings of sadness, and feelings of loneliness.

Life Changes—Variety May Be the Very Spice of Life, But Does Too Much Spice Leave an Ill Taste?

You might think that marrying Mr. or Ms. Right, finding a good job, and moving to a better neighborhood all in the same year would propel you into a state of bliss. It might. But too much of a good thing may also make you ill. **Question: How is it that too much of a good thing can make you ill?** It is because all of these events are life changes. As pleasant as they may be, they require adjustment. Coming one after another, life changes, even positive ones, can lead to headaches, high blood pressure, and other health problems.

Life changes differ from daily hassles in two key ways:

1. Many life changes are positive and desirable. Hassles, by definition, are negative.
2. Hassles occur regularly. Life changes occur at irregular intervals.

Peggy Blake and her colleagues (1984) constructed a scale to measure the impact of life changes among college students. Surveys with students revealed that death of a spouse or parent was considered the most stressful life change (94 and 88 life-change units, respectively; see Table 10.1). Academic failure (77 units) and graduation from college (68 units) were also considered highly stressful, even though graduation from college is a positive event—considering the alternative. Positive life changes such as an outstanding personal achievement (49 units) and going on vacation (30 units) also made the list. Although vacations can be good for your health (Gump & Matthews, 2000), they remain a life change that requires adjustment.

■ Life Changes
Life changes differ from daily hassles in that they tend to be more episodic. Also, life changes can be positive as well as negative. What is the relationship between life changes and illness? Is the relationship causal?

TABLE 10.1 Life-Change Units Connected with Various Events

Event	Life-Change Units
1. Death of a spouse, lover, or child	94
2. Death of a parent or sibling	88
3. Beginning formal higher education	84
4. Jail sentence	82
5. Divorce or marital separation	82
6. Unwanted pregnancy of self, spouse, or lover	80
7. Abortion of unwanted pregnancy of self, spouse, or lover	80
8. Academic failure	77
9. Marrying or living with lover against parents' wishes	75
10. Change in love relationship or important friendship	74
11. Change in marital status of parents	73
12. Hospitalization of a parent or sibling	70
13. Graduation from college	68
14. Major personal injury or illness	68
15. Wanted pregnancy of self, spouse, or lover	67
16. Preparing for an important exam or writing a major paper	65
17. Major financial difficulties	65
18. Change in academic status	64
19. Change in relationship with members of your immediate family	62
20. Hospitalization of yourself or a close relative	61
21. Change in course of study, major field, vocational goals, or work status	60
22. Change in own financial status	59
23. Beginning or ceasing service in the armed forces	57
24. Change in living arrangements, conditions, or environment	55
25. Change in frequency or nature of sexual experiences	55
26. Change in degree of interest in college or attitudes toward education	55
27. Academic success	54
28. Change to a new college or university	54
29. Change in number or type of arguments with roommate	52
30. Change in responsibility at work	50
31. Change in amount or nature of social activities	50
32. Change in routine at college or work	49
33. Change in amount of leisure time	49
34. Outstanding personal achievement	49
35. Improvement of own health	47
36. Change in study habits	46
37. Change in religious affiliation	44
38. Change in address or residence	43
39. Change in weight or eating habits	39
40. Vacation or travel	30

Source: Adapted from *Self-Assessment and Behavior Change Manual* (pp. 43–47), by Peggy Blake, Robert Fry, and Michael Pesjack, 1984, New York: Random House. Reprinted by permission of Random House, Inc.

Hassles, Life Changes, and Health Problems

Hassles and life changes—especially negative life changes—affect us psychologically. They can cause us to worry and affect our moods (Harkness & Luther, 2001). Stressors such as hassles and life changes also predict health problems such as heart disease and cancer, even athletic injuries (Smith et al., 1990). Holmes and Rahe (1967) found that people who "earned" 300 or more life-change units within a year, according to their scale, were at greater risk for health problems. Eight of ten developed health problems, compared with only one of three people whose totals of life-change units for the year were below 150.

Moreover, people who remain married to the same person live longer than people who experience marital breakups and remarry (Tucker et al., 1996). Apparently the life changes of divorce and remarriage—or the instability associated with them—can be harmful to health.

REFLECT

Can you think of positive life changes in your own life that have caused you stress?

■ Figure 10.1
What Are the Relationships Among Daily Hassles, Life Changes, and Physical Illness?

There are positive correlations between daily hassles and life events, on the one hand, and illness on the other. It may seem logical that hassles and life changes cause illness, but research into the issue is correlational and not experimental. The results are therefore subject to rival interpretations. One is that people who are predisposed toward medical or psychological problems encounter or generate more hassles and amass more life-change units.

▶ CONTROVERSY IN PSYCHOLOGY ◀

Just how are daily hassles and life changes connected with health problems?

The links between daily hassles, life changes, and health problems are supported by research. But what leads to what? Although it may appear obvious that hassles and life changes should *cause* health problems, what is obvious can be incomplete, even wrong. In this case, researchers are not convinced that the causal connections are all that clear. Let us consider a number of limitations in the research on the connections between daily, hassles, life changes, and health problems:

- *Correlational evidence.* The links that have been uncovered between hassles, life changes, and illness are correlational rather than experimental. It may seem logical that the hassles and life changes caused the disorders, but these variables were not manipulated experimentally. Other explanations of the data are possible (Figure 10.1). One possible explanation is that people who are predisposed toward medical or psychological problems encounter more hassles and amass more life-change units (Harkness & Luther, 2001). For example, undiagnosed medical disorders may contribute to sexual problems, arguments with spouses or in-laws, changes in living conditions and personal habits, and changes in sleeping habits.

- *Positive versus negative life changes.* Other aspects of the research on the relationship between life changes and illness have also been challenged. For instance, positive life changes may be less disturbing than hassles and negative life changes, even though the number of life-change units assigned to them is high (Lefcourt et al., 1981).

- *Personality differences.* People with different personalities respond to stress in different ways. People who are easygoing or psychologically hardy are less likely to become ill under the impact of stress.

Optimism also helps people cope with stress. A study of 586 people whose siblings had heart problems found that those who were optimistic were half as likely as those who were pessimistic to develop a heart "event"—sudden death, a heart attack, or chest pain that required surgery—over a 7½-year period (Nagourney, 2001). Another study followed 39 healthy women for three months (Cohen et al., 1999). Repeated measures were taken of stressors they encountered, life events, and several biological measures of immune system functioning. Overall, serious stressors depressed the women's moods, but optimism appeared to buffer the effects of stress to some degree. An optimistic outlook helps people marshal social support and find other ways of coping with stress (Brissette et al., 2002).

- *Cognitive appraisal.* The stress of an event reflects the meaning of the event to the individual (Folkman & Moskowitz, 2000a; Kiecolt-Glaser et al., 2002a). Pregnancy, for example, can be a positive or negative life change, depending on whether one wants and is prepared to have a child. We appraise the hassles, traumatic experiences, and life changes that we encounter. In responding to them, we take into account their perceived danger, our values and goals, our beliefs in our coping ability, our social support, and so on. The same event will be less taxing to someone with greater coping ability and support than to someone who lacks these advantages.

Despite these methodological flaws, hassles and life changes require adjustment. It seems wise to be aware of hassles and life changes and how they may affect us. Now let us consider a particular source of stress that affects people from ethnic minority groups.

Conflict—Darned If You Do, Darned If You Don't

Should you eat dessert or try to stick to your diet? Should you live on campus, which is more convenient, or should you rent an apartment, where you may have more independence? Choices like these can place us in **conflict**. *Question: What is conflict?* In psychology, conflict is the feeling of being pulled in two or more directions by opposing motives. Conflict is frustrating and stressful. Psychologists often classify

Conflict
Being torn in different directions by opposing motives. Feelings produced by being in conflict.

conflicts into four types: approach–approach, avoidance–avoidance, approach–avoidance, and multiple approach–avoidance.

Approach–approach conflict (Figure 10.2, part A) is the least stressful type. Here, each of two goals is desirable, and both are within reach. You may not be able to decide between pizza or tacos, Tom or Dick, or a trip to Nassau or Hawaii. Such conflicts are usually resolved by making a decision. People who experience this type of conflict may vacillate until they make a decision.

Avoidance–avoidance conflict (Figure 10.2, part B) is more stressful because you are motivated to avoid each of two negative goals. However, avoiding one of them requires approaching the other. You may be fearful of visiting the dentist but also afraid that your teeth will decay if you do not make an appointment and go. You may not want to contribute to the Association for the Advancement of Lost Causes, but you fear that your friends will consider you cheap or uncommitted if you do not. Each goal in an avoidance–avoidance conflict is negative. When an avoidance–avoidance conflict is highly stressful and no resolution is in sight, some people withdraw from the conflict by focusing on other matters or doing nothing. Highly conflicted people have been known to refuse to get up in the morning and start the day.

When the same goal produces both approach and avoidance motives, we have an **approach–avoidance conflict** (Figure 10.2, part C). People and things have their pluses and minuses, their good points and their bad points. Cream cheese pie may be delicious, but oh, the calories! Goals that produce mixed motives may seem more attractive from a distance but undesirable from up close. Many couples repeatedly break up and then reunite. When they are apart and lonely, they may recall each other fondly and swear that they could make the relationship work if they got together again. But after they spend time together again, they may find themselves thinking, "How could I ever have believed that this so-and-so would change?"

The most complex form of conflict is the **multiple approach–avoidance conflict,** in which each of several alternative courses of action has pluses and minuses. An

REFLECT

Have you ever felt "damned if you do and damned if you don't"? Regretted that you couldn't do two things, or be in two places, at the same time? How did you resolve the conflict? (Or didn't you?)

Approach–Approach Conflict
A type of conflict in which the goals that produce opposing motives are positive and within reach.

Avoidance–Avoidance Conflict
A type of conflict in which the goals are negative, but avoidance of one requires approaching the other.

Approach–Avoidance Conflict
A type of conflict in which the same goal produces approach and avoidance motives.

Multiple Approach–Avoidance Conflict
A type of conflict in which each of a number of goals produces approach and avoidance motives.

■ **Figure 10.2
Models for Conflict**

Part A shows an approach–approach conflict, in which a person (P) has motives (M) to reach two goals (G) that are desirable, but approach of one requires exclusion of the other. Part B shows an avoidance–avoidance conflict in which both goals are negative, but avoiding one requires approaching the other. Part C shows an approach–avoidance conflict, in which the same goal has desirable and undesirable properties. Part D shows a double approach–avoidance conflict, which is the simplest kind of *multiple* approach–avoidance conflict. In a multiple approach–avoidance conflict, two or more goals have mixed properties.

A. Approach–
approach
conflict

B. Avoidance–
avoidance
conflict

C. Approach–
avoidance
conflict

D. Double
approach–
avoidance
conflict

example with two goals is shown in Figure 10.2, part D. This sort of conflict might arise on the eve of an examination, when you are faced with the choice of studying or, say, going to a film. Each alternative has both positive and negative aspects: "Studying's a bore, but I won't have to worry about flunking. I'd love to see the movie, but I'd just be worrying about how I'll do tomorrow."

All forms of conflict entail motives that aim in opposite directions. When one motive is much stronger than the other—such as when you feel starved and are only slightly concerned about your weight—it will probably not be too stressful to act in accordance with the powerful motive—in this case, to eat. When each conflicting motive is powerful, however, you may experience stress and confusion about the proper course of action. At such times you need to make a decision. Yet decision making can also be stressful, especially when there is no clear correct choice.

Irrational Beliefs: Ten Doorways to Distress

Psychologist Albert Ellis notes that our beliefs about events, as well as the events themselves, can be stressors (Ellis, 2002; Ellis & Dryden, 1996). Consider a case in which a person is fired from a job and is anxious and depressed about it. It may seem logical that losing the job is responsible for the misery, but Ellis points out how the individual's beliefs about the loss compound his or her misery.

Question: How do irrational beliefs create or compound stress? Let us examine this situation according to Ellis's A→B→C approach: Losing the job is an *activating event* (A). The eventual outcome, or *consequence* (C), is misery. Between the activating event (A) and the consequence (C), however, lie *beliefs* (B), such as these: "This job was the most important thing in my life," "What a no-good failure I am," "My family will starve," "I'll never find a job as good," "There's nothing I can do about it." Beliefs such as these compound misery, foster helplessness, and divert us from planning and deciding what to do next. The belief that "There's nothing I can do about it" fosters helplessness. The belief that "I am a no-good failure" internalizes the blame and may be an exaggeration. The belief that "My family will starve" may also be an exaggeration.

Let's diagram the situation like this:

$$\text{Activating events} \rightarrow \text{Beliefs} \rightarrow \text{Consequences}$$
$$\text{or } A \rightarrow B \rightarrow C$$

Anxieties about the future and depression over a loss are normal and to be expected. However, the beliefs of the person who lost the job tend to **catastrophize** the extent of the loss and contribute to anxiety and depression—and thus raise the blood pressure. By heightening the individual's emotional reaction to the loss and fostering feelings of helplessness, these beliefs also impair coping ability. They lower the person's self-efficacy expectations.

Ellis proposes that many of us carry with us the irrational beliefs shown in Table 10.2. They are our personal doorways to distress. In fact, they can give rise to problems in themselves. When problems assault us from other sources, these beliefs can magnify their effect.

R E F L E C T
How many of Albert Ellis's irrational beliefs do you harbor? (Are you sure?) How do they affect your life?

Ellis finds it understandable that we would want the approval of others but irrational to believe that we cannot survive without it. It would be nice to be competent in everything we do, but it's unreasonable to *expect* it. Sure, it would be nice to be able to serve and volley like a tennis pro, but most of us haven't the time or natural ability to perfect the game. Demanding perfection prevents us from going out on the court on weekends and batting the ball back and forth just for fun (Ellis, 2002). Belief number 5 is a prescription for perpetual emotional upheaval. Beliefs numbers 7 and 9 lead to feelings of helplessness and demoralization. Sure, Ellis might say, childhood experiences can explain the origins of irrational beliefs, but it is our own cognitive appraisal—here and now—that causes us to be miserable.

Research findings confirm the connections between irrational beliefs (e.g., excessive dependence on social approval and perfectionism) and feelings of anxiety and depression (Chang & Sanna, 2001; Rice & Dellwo, 2001; Wiebe & McCabe, 2002).

Catastrophize
To interpret negative events as being disastrous; to "blow out of proportion."

TABLE 10.2 Irrational Beliefs—Cognitive Doorways to Distress

Irrational belief 1: You must have sincere love and approval almost all the time from the people who are important to you.

Irrational belief 2: You must prove yourself to be thoroughly competent, adequate, and achieving at something important.

Irrational belief 3: Things must go the way you want them to go. Life is awful when you don't get your first choice in everything.

Irrational belief 4: Other people must treat everyone fairly and justly. When people act unfairly or unethically, they are rotten.

Irrational belief 5: When there is danger or fear in your world, you must be preoccupied with and upset by it.

Irrational belief 6: People and things should turn out better than they do. It's awful and horrible when you don't find quick solutions to life's hassles.

Irrational belief 7: Your emotional misery stems from external pressures that you have little or no ability to control. Unless these external pressures change, you must remain miserable.

Irrational belief 8: It is easier to evade life's responsibilities and problems than to face them and undertake more rewarding forms of self-discipline.

Irrational belief 9: Your past influenced you immensely and must therefore continue to determine your feelings and behavior today.

Irrational belief 10: You can achieve happiness by inertia and inaction, or by just enjoying yourself from day to day.

The Type A Behavior Pattern—Burning Out from Within?

Some people create stress for themselves through the **Type A behavior** pattern. *Question: What is Type A behavior?* Type A people are highly driven, competitive, impatient, and aggressive—so much so that they are prone to getting into auto accidents (Karlberg et al., 1998; Magnavita et al., 1997). They feel rushed and under pressure all the time and keep one eye firmly glued to the clock. They are not only prompt for appointments but often early. They eat, walk, and talk rapidly and become restless when others work slowly. They attempt to dominate group discussions. Type A people find it difficult to give up control or share power. They are often reluctant to delegate authority in the workplace, and because of this they increase their own workloads.

Type A people find it difficult just to go out on the tennis court and bat the ball back and forth. They watch their form, perfect their strokes, and demand continual self-improvement. They hold to the irrational belief that they must be perfectly competent and achieving in everything they undertake.

Type B people, in contrast, relax more readily and focus more on the quality of life. They are less ambitious and less impatient, and they pace themselves. Type A people earn higher grades and more money than Type B's who are equal in intelligence.

Learning Connections
See Web site for an interactive version of these review questions.

REVIEW

(1) Daily _____ are regularly occurring conditions and experiences that threaten or harm our well-being. (2) Life changes, even pleasant ones, are stressful because they require _____. (3) The links among hassles, life changes, and physical health problems are (experimental or correlational?). (4) The feeling of being pulled in two or more directions by opposing motives is called _____.

Type A Behavior
Behavior characterized by a sense of time urgency, competitiveness, and hostility.

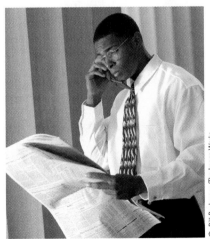

© Bill Bachmann/The Image Works

■ **Type A Behavior**

The Type A behavior pattern is characterized by a sense of time urgency, competitiveness, and hostility.

(5) Albert _____ notes that our beliefs about events, as well as the events themselves, can be stressors. (6) Type A behavior is characterized by a sense of time _____, competitiveness, and aggressiveness.

Critical Thinking: Life changes are stressful. Should people therefore avoid life changes?

Self-Efficacy Expectations
Our beliefs that we can bring about desired changes through our own efforts.

Psychological Hardiness
A cluster of traits that buffer stress and are characterized by commitment, challenge, and control.

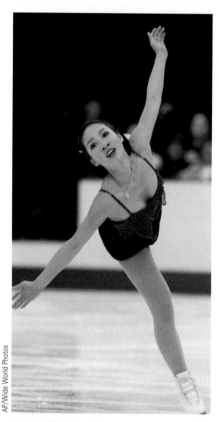

AP/Wide World Photos

■ **Self-Efficacy Expectations and Performance**

Outstanding athletes tend to have high self-efficacy expectations. That is, they believe in themselves. Self-efficacy expectations are one of the psychological factors that moderate the effects of stress on us.

PSYCHOLOGICAL MODERATORS OF STRESS

There is no one-to-one relationship between stress and physical or psychological health problems. Physical factors account for some of the variability in our responses: Some people inherit predispositions toward specific disorders. Psychological factors also play a role, however (Holahan & Moos, 1990). They can influence, or *moderate,* the effects of stress. In this section we discuss several psychological moderators of stress: self-efficacy expectations, psychological hardiness, a sense of humor, predictability, and social support.

Self-Efficacy Expectations: "The Little Engine That Could"

Our **self-efficacy expectations** affect our ability to withstand stress (Basic Behavioral Science Task Force, 1996a; Maciejewski et al., 2000). *Question: How do our self-efficacy expectations affect our ability to withstand stress?* Classic research shows that when we are faced with fear-inducing objects, high self-efficacy expectations are accompanied by relatively *lower* levels of adrenaline and noradrenaline in the bloodstream (Bandura et al., 1985). Adrenaline is secreted when we are under stress. It arouses the body in several ways, such as accelerating the heart rate and releasing glucose from the liver. As a result, we may have "butterflies in the stomach" and feel nervous. Excessive arousal can impair our ability to manage stress by boosting our motivation beyond optimal levels and by distracting us from the tasks at hand. People with higher self-efficacy expectations thus have biological as well as psychological reasons for remaining calmer.

People who are self-confident are less prone to be disturbed by adverse events (Kaslow et al., 2002; Lang & Heckhausen, 2001). People with higher self-efficacy expectations are more likely to lose weight or quit smoking and less likely to relapse afterward (Anderson et al., 2000, 2001; Shiffman et al., 2000). They are better able to function in spite of pain (Lackner et al., 1996). A study of Native Americans found that alcohol abuse was correlated with self-efficacy expectations (M. J. Taylor, 2000). That is, individuals with feelings of powerlessness were more likely to abuse alcohol, perhaps as a way of lessening the stresses in their lives.

People are more likely to comply with medical advice when they believe that it will work (Schwartzer & Renner, 2000). Women, for example, are more likely to engage in breast self-examination when they believe that they will really be able to detect abnormal growths (Miller et al., 1996). People are more likely to try to quit smoking when they believe that they can do so successfully (Mischel & Shoda, 1995).

Psychological Hardiness—Tough Enough?

Psychological hardiness also helps people resist stress (Richardson, 2002). Our understanding of this phenomenon is derived largely from the pioneering work of Suzanne Kobasa and her colleagues (1994). They studied business executives who seemed able to resist illness despite stress. In one phase of the research, executives completed a battery of psychological tests. Kobasa (1990) found that the psychologically hardy executives had three key characteristics. *Question: What characteristics are connected with psychological hardiness?* The characteristics include commitment, challenge, and control.

. Kobasa found that psychologically hardy executives were high in *commitment.* They tended to involve themselves in, rather than feel alienated from, whatever they were doing or encountering.

.. They were also high in *challenge.* They believed that change, rather than stability, is normal in life. They appraised change as an interesting incentive to personal growth, not as a threat to security.

. They were high in perceived *control* over their lives. A sense of control is one of the keys to psychological hardiness (Folkman & Moskowitz, 2000b; Tennen & Affleck, 2000). Hardy participants felt and behaved as though they were influential, rather than helpless, in facing the various rewards and punishments of life. Psychologically hardy people tend to have what Julian B. Rotter (1990) terms an internal **locus of control.**

Hardy people are more resistant to stress because they *choose* to face it (Kobasa, 1990). They also interpret stress as making life more interesting. For example, they see a conference with a supervisor as an opportunity to persuade the supervisor rather than as a risk to their position.

Sense of Humor: "A Merry Heart Doeth Good Like a Medicine"

The idea that humor lightens the burdens of life and helps people cope with stress has been with us for millennia (Lefcourt & Martin, 1986). Consider the biblical maxim "A merry heart doeth good like a medicine" (Proverbs 17:22).

Question: Is there any evidence that "A merry heart doeth good like a medicine"? Yes, both anecdotes and controlled research support this ancient maxim. In *Anatomy of an Illness,* Norman Cousins (1979) reported his bout with a painful illness that was similar to arthritis. He found that ten minutes of belly laughter of the sort he experienced while watching Marx Brothers movies relieved much of his pain. Laughter allowed him to sleep. It may also have reduced the inflammation he suffered. This is consistent with some findings that positive affect—for example, feelings of happiness—may have beneficial effects on the immune system (Salovey et al., 2000).

Research has also shown that humor can moderate the effects of stress. In one study, students completed a checklist of negative life events and a measure of mood disturbance (Martin & Lefcourt, 1983). The measure of mood disturbance also yielded a stress score. The students also rated their sense of humor. Behavioral assessments were made of their ability to produce humor under stress. Overall, there was a significant relationship between negative life events and stress scores: High accumulations of negative life events predicted higher levels of stress. However, students who had a greater sense of humor and produced humor in difficult situations were less affected by negative life events than other students. In other studies, Lefcourt (1997) found that watching humorous videotapes raised the level of immunoglobin A (a measure of the functioning of the immune system) in students' saliva.

How does humor help people cope with stress? We are uncertain, but there has been speculation. One possibility, which might apply to the case of Norman Cousins, is that laughter stimulates the output of endorphins, which might enhance the functioning of the immune system. Another is more psychological: that the benefits of humor may be explained in terms of the sudden cognitive shifts they entail and the emotional changes that accompany them.

Predictability and Control: "If I Can Stop the Roller Coaster, I Don't Want to Get Off"

The ability to predict a stressor apparently moderates its impact. *Question: How do predictability and control help us cope with stress?* Predictability allows us to brace ourselves for the inevitable and, in many cases, plan ways of coping with it. Control—even the illusion of being in control—allows us to feel that we are not at the mercy of the fates (Folkman & Moskowitz, 2000b; Tennen & Affleck, 2000). There is also a relationship between the desire to assume control over one's situation and the

REFLECT

Are you committed to your undertakings—including college? Do you seek or avoid challenges? Are you in control of your life? What do your answers suggest about your psychological hardiness?

REFLECT

Do you have a sense of humor? Has it ever helped you get through hard times?

Locus of Control
The place (locus) to which an individual attributes control over the receiving of reinforcers—either inside or outside the self.

"Internals"
People who perceive the ability to attain reinforcements as being largely within themselves.

"Externals"
People who perceive the ability to attain reinforcements as being largely outside themselves.

REFLECT

When you are stressed out, do you seek out the company of others or do you tend to withdraw into yourself? Does research support the effectiveness of your social behavior under stress? Explain.

Learning Connections
See Web site for an interactive version of these review questions.

usefulness of information about impending stressors. Predictability is of greater benefit to **"internals"**—that is, to people who wish to exercise control over their situations—than to **"externals."** People who want information about medical procedures and what they will experience cope better with pain when they undergo those procedures (Ludwick-Rosenthal & Neufeld, 1993).

Social Support: On Being in It Together

People are social beings, and social support also seems to act as a buffer against the effects of stress (Cohen et al., 2001a; Folkman & Moskowitz, 2000a).

Sources of social support include the following:

- *Emotional concern:* Listening to people's problems and expressing feelings of sympathy, caring, understanding, and reassurance.
- *Instrumental aid:* The material supports and services that facilitate adaptive behavior. For example, after a disaster the government may arrange for low-interest loans so that survivors can rebuild. Relief organizations may provide foodstuffs, medicines, and temporary living quarters.
- *Information:* Guidance and advice that enhance people's ability to cope.
- *Appraisal:* Feedback from others about how one is doing. This kind of support involves helping people interpret, or "make sense of," what has happened to them.
- *Socializing:* Simple conversation, recreation, even going shopping with another person. Socializing has beneficial effects, even when it is not oriented specifically toward solving problems.

Question: Is there evidence that social support helps people cope with stress? Yes, research does support the value of social support. Introverts, people who lack social skills, and people who live by themselves seem more prone to developing infectious diseases such as colds under stress (Cohen & Williamson, 1991). Social support helps people cope with the stresses of cancer and other health problems (Azar, 1996b; Wilcox et al., 1994). Social support helps Mexican Americans and other immigrants to cope with the stresses of acculturation (Hovey, 2000). Social support helped children cope with the stresses of Hurricane Andrew (Vernberg et al., 1996) and Chinese villagers cope with an earthquake (X. Wang et al., 2000). It has been found to help women cope with the aftermath of rape (Valentiner et al., 1996). Stress is also less likely to lead to high blood pressure or alcohol abuse in people who have social support (Linden et al., 1993).

How does stress contribute to the development of physical health problems? Let us gain insight into this question by examining the effects of stress on the body.

REVIEW

(7) People with (higher or lower?) self-efficacy expectations tend to cope better with stress. (8) Psychologically hardy executives are high in _____, challenge, and control. (9) Being able to predict and control the onset of a stressor (increases or decreases?) its impact on us.

Critical Thinking: Social support helps most people cope with stress. What does this research finding suggest about human nature?

STRESS AND THE BODY: THE WAR WITHIN

Stress is more than a psychological event. It is more than "knowing" it is there; it is more than "feeling" pushed and pulled. Stress also has very definite effects on the body. Stress researcher Hans Selye outlined a number of them in his concept of the *general adaptation syndrome (GAS).*

The General Adaptation Syndrome

How can stress make us ill? Hans Selye suggested that under stress the body is like a clock with an alarm system that does not shut off until its energy has been depleted.

Selye (1976) argued that the body's response to different stressors shows certain similarities whether the stressor is a bacterial invasion, perceived danger, or a major life change. For this reason, he labeled this response the **general adaptation syndrome (GAS).** *Question: What is the general adaptation syndrome?* The GAS is a cluster of bodily changes that occur in three stages: an alarm reaction, a resistance stage, and an exhaustion stage.

The Alarm Reaction

The **alarm reaction** is triggered by perception of a stressor. This reaction mobilizes or arouses the body, biologically speaking. Early in the 20th century, physiologist Walter B. Cannon (1932) argued that this mobilization was the basis for an instinctive **fight-or-flight reaction.** But contemporary psychologists question whether the fight-or-flight reaction is instinctive in humans (Updegraff et al., 2002). In any event, the alarm reaction involves bodily changes that are initiated by the brain and regulated by the endocrine system and the sympathetic division of the autonomic nervous system (ANS). Let us consider the roles of these systems.

Stress has a domino effect on the endocrine system (Figure 10.3). The hypothalamus secretes corticotrophin-releasing hormone (CRH). CRH causes the pituitary gland to secrete adrenocorticotrophic hormone (ACTH). ACTH then causes the adrenal cortex to secrete cortisol and other corticosteroids (steroidal hormones

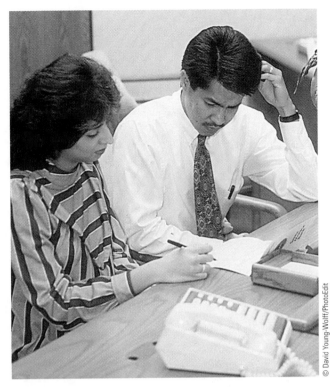

© David Young-Wolff/PhotoEdit

■ Are Their Alarm Systems Going Off as They Take Out a Loan?
The alarm reaction of the general adaptation syndrome can be triggered by daily hassles and life changes—such as taking out a large loan—as well as by physical threats. When the stressor persists, diseases of adaptation may develop.

■ Figure 10.3
Stress and the Endocrine System

Stress has a domino effect on the endocrine system, leading to the release of corticosteroids and a mixture of adrenaline and noradrenaline. Corticosteroids combat allergic reactions (such as difficulty in breathing) and cause inflammation. Adrenaline and noradrenaline arouse the body to cope by accelerating the heart rate and providing energy for the fight-or-flight reaction.

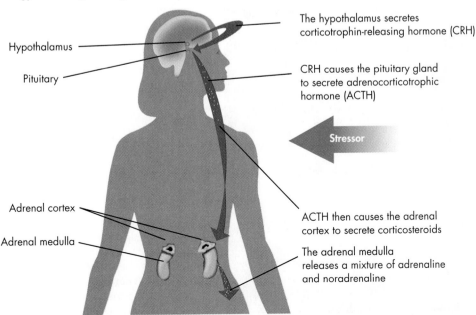

Hypothalamus

Pituitary

The hypothalamus secretes corticotrophin-releasing hormone (CRH)

CRH causes the pituitary gland to secrete adrenocorticotrophic hormone (ACTH)

Stressor

Adrenal cortex

Adrenal medulla

ACTH then causes the adrenal cortex to secrete corticosteroids

The adrenal medulla releases a mixture of adrenaline and noradrenaline

General Adaptation Syndrome (GAS)
Selye's term for a hypothesized three-stage response to stress.

Alarm Reaction
The first stage of the GAS, which is triggered by the impact of a stressor and characterized by sympathetic activity.

Fight-or-Flight Reaction
An innate adaptive response to the perception of danger.

REFLECT

What do you experience happening in your body when you are under stress? How do those sensations fit the description of the general adaptation syndrome?

produced by the adrenal cortex). Corticosteroids help protect the body by combating allergic reactions (such as difficulty breathing) and producing inflammation. (However, corticosteroids can be harmful to the cardiovascular system, which is one reason that chronic stress can impair one's health and why athletes who use steroids to build the muscle mass can experience cardiovascular problems.) Inflammation increases circulation to parts of the body that are injured. It ferries in hordes of white blood cells to fend off invading pathogens.

Two other hormones that play a major role in the alarm reaction are secreted by the adrenal medulla. The sympathetic division of the ANS activates the adrenal medulla, causing it to release a mixture of adrenaline and noradrenaline. This mixture arouses the body by accelerating the heart rate and causing the liver to release glucose (sugar). This provides the energy that fuels the fight-or-flight reaction, which activates the body so that it is prepared to fight or flee from a predator.

The fight-or-flight reaction stems from a period in human prehistory when many stressors were life-threatening. It was triggered by the sight of a predator at the

A Closer Look 👁

"Fight or Flight" or "Tend and Befriend"? Gender Differences in Response to Stress

Nearly a century ago, Harvard University physiologist Walter Cannon labeled the body's response to stress the "fight-or-flight" reaction. He believed that the body was prewired to become mobilized or aroused in preparation for combat when faced with a predator or a competitor; or, if the predator was

threatening enough, that "discretion"—that is, a "strategic retreat"—would sometimes be the "better part of valor." Although the biology of his day did not allow Cannon to be as precise as we, we now know that the fight-or-flight reaction includes bodily changes that involve the brain (perceptions, neurotransmitters), the endocrine system (hormones), and the sympathetic division of the autonomic nervous system (rapid heart rate, rapid breathing, muscle tension). The sum of these bodily changes pumps us up to fight like demons or, when advisable, to beat a hasty retreat.

■ "Fight-or-Flight" or "Tend-and-Befriend"?

Walter Cannon labeled the body's response to stress the "fight-or-flight" reaction. He thought that evolution prewired the body to become mobilized in preparation for combat or rapid retreat when faced with a threat. It has been assumed that this reaction applies to both men and women, but research by Shelley Taylor and her colleagues suggests that women may be "prewired" to take care of others ("tend") or affiliate with others ("befriend") when they encounter threats.

Or does it?

According to a review of the literature by UCLA psychologist Shelley E. Taylor and her colleagues (2000b), at least half of us are more likely to tend to the kids or "interface" with family and friends than to fight or flee. Which half of us would that be? The female half.

Why Are All Those Rats Males?

Taylor explains that the study was prompted by an offhand remark of a student who had noticed that nearly all of the rats in studies of the effects of stress on animals were male. Taylor did an overview of the research on stress with humans and noted that prior to 1995, when federal agencies began requiring more equal representation of women if they were to fund research, edge of a thicket or by a sudden rustling in the undergrowth. Today it may be aroused when you are caught in stop-and-go traffic or learn that your mortgage payments are going to increase. Once the threat is removed, the body returns to a lower state of arousal. Many of the bodily changes that occur in the alarm reaction are outlined in Table 10.3 on page 392.

We noted that many contemporary theorists do not believe that the fight-or-flight reaction is not universal. In "A Closer Look" (below) Shelley Taylor and her colleagues report evidence that many women experience a tend-and-befriend response to threats, rather than a fight-or-flight response. Margaret Kemeny and her colleagues (e.g., Updegraff et al., 2002) also observe that some people attempt to respond productively to stress by pulling back from the situation in order to better appraise it and conserve their resources while they are doing so. This response pattern to stress is described by two theories that are currently under development: "cognitive adaptation theory" and "conservation of resources theory."

---

only 17% of the subjects were female. Quite a gender gap—and one that had allowed researchers to ignore the question as to whether females responded to stress in the same way as males.

Taylor and her colleagues then dug more deeply into the literature and found that "Men and women do have some reliably different responses to stress," notes S. E. Taylor (2000). "I think we've really been missing the boat on one of the most important responses."

This response to stress can be called the "tend-and-befriend" response. It involves nurturing and seeking the support of others rather than fighting or fleeing. The studies that were reviewed showed that when females faced a predator, a disaster, or even an especially bad day at the office, they often responded by caring for their children and seeking contact and support from others, particularly other women. After a bad day at the office, men are more likely to withdraw from the family or start arguments.

An Evolutionary Perspective

This response may be prewired in female humans and in females of other mammalian species. Evolutionary psychologists might suggest that the tend-and-befriend response might have become sealed in our genes because it promotes the survival of females who are tending to their offspring. (Females who choose to fight may often die or at least be separated from their offspring—no evolutionary brass ring here.)

Gender differences in behavior are frequently connected with gender differences in hormones and other biological factors. This one is no different. Taylor and her colleagues point to the effects of the pituitary hormone oxytocin. Oxytocin stimulates labor and causes the breasts to eject milk when women nurse. It is also connected with nurturing behaviors such as affiliating with and cuddling one's young in many mammals (Taylor et al., 2000b). The literature also shows that when oxytocin is released during stress, it tends to have a calming effect on both rats and humans. It makes them less afraid and more social.

But wait a minute! Men also release oxytocin when they are under stress. So why the gender difference? The answer may lie in the presence of other hormones, the sex hormones estrogen and testosterone. Female have more estrogen than males do, and estrogen appears to enhance the effects of oxytocin. Males, on the other hand, have more testosterone than females, and testosterone may mitigate the effects of oxytocin by prompting feelings of self-confidence (which may be exaggerated) and fostering aggression (Sullivan, 2000).

It is thus possible that males are more aggressive than females under stress because of the genetic balance of hormones in their bodies, while females are more affiliative and nurturant. It makes evolutionary sense, at least. In order to perpetuate the human species and even make it tougher as the generations progress, it only takes a few tough men (does this sound like a commercial for the Marines?) to impregnate a large number of women.

But men, even tough ones, may not outlive women. "Men are more likely than women to respond to stressful experiences by developing certain stress-related disorders, including hypertension, aggressive behavior, or abuse of alcohol or hard drugs," Taylor added in a UCLA press release (May 18, 2000). "Because the tend-and-befriend regulatory system may, in some ways, protect women against stress, this biobehavioral pattern may provide insights into why women live an average of seven and a half years longer than men."

Another View

Not all psychologists agree with an evolutionary or biological explanation. Psychologist Alice H. Eagly (2000) allows that gender differences in response to stress may be rooted in hormones but suggests an alternative: The differences may reflect learning and cultural conditioning. "I think we have a certain amount of evidence that women are in some sense more affiliative, but what that's due to becomes the question. Is it biologically hardwired? Or is it because women have more family responsibility and preparation for that in their development? That is the big question for psychologists."

A very big question, indeed.

TABLE 10.3 Components of the Alarm Reaction*

Corticosteroids are secreted	Muscles tense
Adrenaline is secreted	Blood shifts from internal organs to the skeletal musculature
Noradrenaline is secreted	Digestion is inhibited
Respiration rate increases	Sugar is released from the liver
Heart rate increases	Blood coagulability increases
Blood pressure increases	

*The alarm reaction is triggered by various types of stressors. It is defined by the release of corticosteroids and adrenaline and by activity of the sympathetic branch of the autonomic nervous system. It prepares the body to fight or flee from a source of danger.

The Resistance Stage

According to Selye's theory, if the alarm reaction mobilizes the body and the stressor is not removed, we enter the adaptation or **resistance stage** of the GAS. Levels of endocrine and sympathetic activity are lower than in the alarm reaction but still higher than normal. In this stage the body attempts to restore lost energy and repair bodily damage.

The Exhaustion Stage

If the stressor is still not dealt with adequately, we may enter the **exhaustion stage** of the GAS. Individual capacities for resisting stress vary, but anyone will eventually become exhausted when stress continues indefinitely. The muscles become fatigued. The body is depleted of the resources required for combating stress. With exhaustion, the parasympathetic division of the ANS may predominate. As a result, our heartbeat and respiration rate slow down and many aspects of sympathetic activity are reversed. It might sound as if we would profit from the respite, but remember that we are still under stress—possibly an external threat. Continued stress in the exhaustion stage may lead to what Selye terms "diseases of adaptation." These are connected with constriction of blood vessels and alteration of the heart rhythm, and can range from allergies to hives and coronary heart disease (CHD)—and, ultimately, death.

Discussion of the effects of stress on the immune system paves the way for understanding the links between psychological factors and physical illness.

Effects of Stress on the Immune System

Research shows that stress suppresses the **immune system,** as measured by the presence of various substances in the blood that make up the immune system (Cohen et al., 2001b). Psychological factors such as feelings of control and social support moderate these effects (Cohen et al., 2001a).

The Immune System

Given the complexity of the human body and the fast pace of scientific change, we often feel that we are dependent on trained professionals to cope with illness. Yet we actually do most of this coping by ourselves, by means of the immune system. *Question: How does the immune system work?*

The immune system has several functions that combat disease (Delves & Roitt, 2000). One of these is the production of white blood cells, which engulf and kill pathogens such as bacteria, fungi, and viruses, and worn-out and cancerous body cells. The technical term for white blood cells is **leukocytes.** Leukocytes carry on microscopic warfare. They engage in search-and-destroy missions in which they "recognize" and eradicate foreign agents and unhealthy cells.

Leukocytes recognize foreign substances by their shapes. The foreign substances are termed **antigens** because the body reacts to them by generating specialized pro-

Resistance Stage

The second stage of the GAS, characterized by prolonged sympathetic activity in an effort to restore lost energy and repair damage. Also called the *adaptation stage.*

Exhaustion Stage

The third stage of the GAS, characterized by weakened resistance and possible deterioration.

Immune System

The system of the body that recognizes and destroys foreign agents (antigens) that invade the body.

Leukocytes

White blood cells. (Derived from the Greek words *leukos,* meaning "white," and *kytos,* literally meaning "a hollow" but used to refer to cells.)

Antigen

A substance that stimulates the body to mount an immune system response to it. (The contraction for *anti*body *gen*erator.)

■ Microscopic Warfare

The immune system helps us to combat disease. It produces white blood cells (leukocytes), such as that shown here, which routinely engulf and kill pathogens like bacteria and viruses.

teins, or **antibodies.** Antibodies attach themselves to the foreign substances, deactivating them and marking them for destruction. The immune system "remembers" how to battle antigens by maintaining their antibodies in the bloodstream, often for years.[1]

Inflammation is another function of the immune system. When injury occurs, blood vessels in the area first contract (to stem bleeding) and then dilate. Dilation increases the flow of blood, cells, and natural chemicals to the damaged area, causing the redness, swelling, and warmth that characterize inflammation (Duenwald, 2002). The increased blood supply also floods the region with white blood cells to combat invading microscopic life forms such as bacteria, which otherwise might use the local damage as a port of entry into the body.

Stress and the Immune System

Psychologists, biologists, and medical researchers have combined their efforts in a field of study that addresses the relationships among psychological factors, the nervous system, the endocrine system, the immune system, and disease. This field is called **psychoneuroimmunology.** One of its major concerns is the effect of stress on the immune system (Kiecolt-Glaser et al., 2002a). *Question: How does stress affect the functioning of the immune system?*

One of the reasons that stress eventually exhausts us is that it stimulates the production of steroids. Steroids suppress the functioning of the immune system. Suppression has negligible effects when steroids are secreted occasionally. But persistent secretion of steroids decreases inflammation and interferes with the formation of antibodies. As a consequence, we become more vulnerable to various illnesses, including the common cold (Cohen et al., 1993). By weakening the immune system, stress may also be connected with a more rapid progression of HIV infection to AIDS (Leserman et al., 2000).

In one study, dental students showed lower immune system functioning, as measured by lower levels of antibodies in their saliva, during stressful periods of the school year than immediately following vacations (Jemmott et al., 1983). In contrast, social support buffers the effects of stress and enhances the functioning of the immune

Antibodies

Substances formed by white blood cells that recognize and destroy antigens.

Inflammation

Increased blood flow to an injured area of the body, resulting in redness, warmth, and an increased supply of white blood cells.

Psychoneuroimmunology

(sigh-coe-new-row-im-you-NOLL-oh-gee). The field that studies the relationships between psychological factors (e.g., attitudes and overt behavior patterns) and the functioning of the immune system.

[1]Vaccination is the introduction of a weakened form of an antigen (usually a bacteria or a virus) into the body to stimulate the production of antibodies. Antibodies can confer immunity for many years, in some cases for a lifetime. Smallpox has been eradicated by means of vaccination.

system (Cohen et al., 2001a). In the Jemmott study, students who had many friends showed less suppression of immune system functioning than students with few friends.

Other studies with students have shown that the stress of exams depresses the immune system's response to the Epstein-Barr virus, which causes fatigue and other problems (Glaser et al., 1993). Here too, students who were lonely showed greater suppression of the immune system than students who had more social support. All in all, however, there is only modest evidence that psychological interventions enhance the functioning of the immune system. A review of the research found that hypnosis (intended to help people relax), stress management methods, and conditioning methods were of some use, but less than reliable (Miller & Cohen, 2001).

Learning Connections
See Web site for an interactive version of these review questions.

R E V I E W

(10) The general adaptation syndrome has three stages: _____, resistance, and exhaustion. (11) Cannon dubbed the alarm reaction the _____-or-_____ reaction. (12) Women may show a tend-and-_____ response to stress rather than fight-or-flight. (13) Under stress, pituitary ACTH causes the adrenal cortex to release _____ that help the body respond to stress by fighting inflammation and allergic reactions. (14) Two hormones that play a role in the alarm reaction are secreted by the adrenal medulla: _____ and noradrenaline. (15) The immune system produces (red or white?) blood cells, called leukocytes, that routinely engulf and kill pathogens. (16) _____ are pathogens that are recognized and destroyed by leukocytes. (17) Some leukocytes produce _____, or specialized proteins that bind to their antigens and mark them for destruction.

Critical Thinking: Prolonged stress is connected with health problems. Must you avoid stress to remain healthy, or can you do something to become psychologically hardy?

PSYCHOLOGY AND HEALTH: HEADACHES, CARDIOVASCULAR DISORDERS, CANCER, AND SEXUALLY TRANSMITTED INFECTIONS

Why do people become ill? Why do some people develop cancer? Why do others have heart attacks? Why do still others seem to be immune to these illnesses? Why do some of us seem to come down with everything that is going around, while others ride out the roughest winters with nary a sniffle? *Question: What is the multifactorial approach to health?* The multifactorial approach recognizes that there is no single, simple answer to these questions. The likelihood of contracting an illness—be it a case of the flu or cancer—can reflect the interaction of many factors, including genetic factors (Hoover, 2000).

Biological factors such as pathogens, inoculations, injuries, age, gender, and a family history of disease may strike us as the most obvious causes of illness. Genetics, in particular, tempts some people to assume there is little they can do about their health. It is true that there are some severe health problems that are unavoidable for people with certain genes. "There is this kind of fatalistic approach to genes that the general public seems to have now—that if your mom, dad, sister or brother had something that you're doomed to have it too," writes Dr. Robert N. Hoover (2000) of the National Cancer Institute. But in many cases, especially with cardiovascular problems and cancer, genes only create *predispositions* toward the health problem.

► CONTROVERSY IN PSYCHOLOGY ◄

Can you maintain your health if your genes are "against" you?

As we see in this section, genes create predispositions, but we may be able to prevent their expression.

As Jane Brody (1995b) notes, predispositions "need a conducive environment in which to express themselves. A bad family medical history should not be considered a portent of doom. Rather, it should be welcomed as an opportunity to keep those nasty genes from expressing themselves." For example, genetic factors are involved in breast cancer. However, rates of breast cancer among women who have recently immigrated to the United States from rural Asia are similar to those in their countries of origin and nearly 80% lower than the rates among third-generation Asian American women, whose rates are similar to those of European American women (Hoover, 2000). Thus factors related to one's lifestyle are also intimately connected with the risk of breast cancer—and most other kinds of cancer.

As shown in Figure 10.4, psychological (behavior and personality) factors, sociocultural factors, environmental factors, and stressors all play roles in health and illness. Many health problems are affected by psychological factors, such as attitudes,

Figure 10.4
Factors in Health and Illness

Various factors figure into a person's state of health or illness. Which of the factors in this figure are you capable of controlling? Which are beyond your control?

Biological Factors
Family history of illness
Exposure to infectious organisms (e.g., bacteria and viruses)
Functioning of the immune system
Inoculations
Medication history
Congenital disabilities, birth complications
Physiological conditions (e.g., hypertension, serum cholesterol level)
Reactivity of the cardiovascular system to stress (e.g., "hot reactor")
Pain and discomfort
Age
Gender
Ethnicity (e.g., genetic vulnerability to Tay-Sachs disease or sickle-cell anemia)

Environmental Factors
Vehicular safety
Architectural features (e.g., crowding, injury-resistant design, nontoxic construction materials, aesthetic design, air quality, noise insulation)
Aesthetics of residential, workplace, and communal architecture and landscape architecture
Water quality
Solid waste treatment and sanitation
Pollution
Radiation
Global warming
Ozone depletion
Natural disasters (earthquakes, blizzards, floods, hurricanes, drought, extremes of temperature, tornadoes)

Behavior
Diet (intake of calories, fats, fiber, vitamins, etc.)
Consumption of alcohol
Cigarette smoking
Level of physical activity
Sleep patterns
Safety practices (e.g., using seat belts; careful driving; practice of sexual abstinence, monogamy, or "safer sex"; adequate prenatal care)
Having (or not having) regular medical and dental checkups
Compliance with medical and dental advice
Interpersonal/social skills

Sociocultural Factors
Socioeconomic status
Family circumstances (social class, family size, family conflict, family disorganization)
Access to health care (e.g., adequacy of available health care, availability of health insurance, availability of transportation to health care facilities)
Prejudice and discrimination
Health-related cultural and religious beliefs and practices
Health promotion in the workplace or community
Health-related legislation

Personality
Seeking (or avoiding) information about health risks and stressors
Self-efficacy expectations
Psychological hardiness
Psychological conflict (approach-approach, avoidance-avoidance, approach-avoidance)
Optimism or pessimism
Attributional style (how one explains one's failures and health problems to oneself)
Health locus of control (belief that one is or is not in charge of one's own health)
Introversion/extraversion
Coronary-prone (Type A) personality
Tendencies to express or hold in feelings of anger and frustration
Depression/anxiety
Hostility/suspiciousness

Stressors
Daily hassles (e.g., preparing meals, illness, time pressure, loneliness, crime, financial insecurity, problems with coworkers, day care)
Major life changes such as divorce, death of a spouse, taking out a mortgage, losing a job
Frustration
Pain and discomfort
Availability and use of social support vs. peer rejection or isolation
Climate in the workplace (e.g., job overload, sexual harassment)

TABLE 10.4 Annual Preventable Deaths in the United States*

- Elimination of tobacco use could prevent 400,000 deaths each year from cancer, heart and lung diseases, and stroke.

- Improved diet and exercise could prevent 300,000 deaths from conditions like heart disease, stroke, diabetes, and cancer.

- Control of underage and excess drinking of alcohol could prevent 100,000 deaths from motor vehicle accidents, falls, drownings, and other alcohol-related injuries.

- Immunizations for infectious diseases could prevent up to 100,000 deaths.

- Safer sex or sexual abstinence could prevent 20,000 deaths from sexually transmitted infections (STIs).

*Other measures for preventing needless deaths include improved worker training and safety to prevent accidents in the workplace, wider screening for breast and cervical cancer, and control of high blood pressure and elevated blood cholesterol levels.

emotions, and behavior (Kiecolt-Glaser et al., 2002b; Salovey et al., 2000). Table 10.4 reveals that nearly 1 million deaths each year in the United States are preventable (National Center for Health Statistics, 1996). Stopping smoking, eating right, exercising, and controlling alcohol use would prevent nearly 80% of these. Psychological states such as anxiety and depression can impair the functioning of the immune system, rendering us more vulnerable to physical disorders ranging from viral infections to cancer (McGuire et al., 2002; Salovey et al., 2000).

Let us now discuss a number of health problems, including headaches, heart disease, cancer, and sexually transmitted infections (STIs). In each case we find an interplay of biological, psychological, and environmental factors—including the social and technological environments. Although these are medical problems, we also explore ways in which psychologists have contributed to their prevention and treatment.

Headaches: When Stress Presses and Pounds

Headaches are among the most common stress-related physical ailments. Nearly 20% of people in the United States suffer severe headaches. *Question: How has psychology contributed to the understanding and treatment of headaches?* To answer this question, let us consider the common muscle-tension headache and the more severe migraine headache.

Muscle Tension Headache

The single most frequent kind of headache is the muscle tension headache. During the first two stages of the GAS we are likely to contract muscles in the shoulders, neck, forehead, and scalp. Persistent stress can lead to constant contraction of these muscles, causing muscle tension headaches. Psychological factors, such as the tendency to catastrophize negative events—that is, blow them out of proportion—can bring on a tension headache (Ukestad & Wittrock, 1996). Tension headaches usually come on gradually. They are most often characterized by dull, steady pain on both sides of the head and feelings of tightness or pressure.

Migraine Headache

The **migraine headache** usually has a sudden onset and is identified by severe throbbing pain on one side of the head. Migraines affect one American in ten (Mulvihill, 2000). They may last for hours, or days. Sensory and motor disturbances often precede the pain; a warning "aura" may include vision problems and perception of unusual odors. The migraines themselves are often accompanied by sensitivity to light, loss of appetite, nausea, vomiting, sensory and motor disturbances such as loss of balance, and changes in mood. Imaging techniques suggest that

R E F L E C T

Do you suffer from headaches? What kind? What can you do about them?

Migraine Headaches
Throbbing headaches that are connected with changes in the supply of blood to the head.

when something triggers a migraine, neurons at the back of the brain fire in waves that ripple across the top of the head and then down to the brain stem, the site of many pain centers.

Triggers for migraines include barometric pressure; pollen; certain drugs; monosodium glutamate (MSG), a chemical which is often used to enhance flavor; chocolate; aged cheese; beer, champagne, and red wine; and the hormonal changes connected with menstruation (Goadsby et al., 2002; Mulvihill, 2000).

The behaviors connected with migraine headaches serve as a mini-textbook in health psychology (Holroyd, 2002). For example, the Type A behavior pattern apparently contributes to migraines. In one study, 53% of people who had migraine headaches showed the Type A behavior pattern, compared with 23% of people who had muscle tension headaches (Rappaport et al., 1988). Another study compared 26 women who had regular migraines with women who had none. The migraine sufferers were more sensitive to pain, more self-critical, more likely to catastrophize stress and pain, and less likely to seek social support when under stress (Hassinger et al., 1999).

Regardless of the source of the headache, we can unwittingly propel ourselves into a vicious cycle. Headache pain is a stressor that can lead us to increase, rather than relax, muscle tension in the neck, shoulders, scalp, and face.

Coronary Heart Disease: Taking Stress to Heart

Coronary heart disease (CHD) is the leading cause of death in the United States, most often from heart attacks (American Heart Association, 2000a). *Question: How has psychology contributed to the understanding and treatment of coronary heart disease?* Let us begin by considering the risk factors for CHD. We will see that people's choices and behavior have a great deal to do with their risk of incurring CHD.

- *Family history:* People with a family history of CHD are more likely to develop the disease themselves (American Heart Association, 2000a).
- *Physiological conditions:* Obesity, high **serum cholesterol** levels, and **hypertension** are risk factors for CHD (American Heart Association, 2000a; Stamler et al., 2000; Xin et al., 2001). Even "high normal" blood pressure increases the risk for CHD (Ramachandran et al., 2001).

About one American in five has hypertension, or abnormally high blood pressure (Blumenthal et al., 2002). When high blood pressure has no identifiable cause, it is referred to as *essential hypertension.* This condition has a genetic component (Levy et al., 2000; Williams et al., 2000). However, blood pressure is also connected with emotions like depression and anxiety (Kazuomi Kario et al., 2001). It also rises when we inhibit the expression of strong feelings or are angry or on guard against threats (Jorgensen et al., 1996). When we are under stress, we may believe that we can feel our blood pressure "pounding through the roof," but this notion is usually false. Most people cannot recognize hypertension. Therefore it is important to check the blood pressure regularly.

- *Patterns of consumption:* Patterns include heavy drinking, smoking, overeating, and eating high-fat foods (Stampfer et al., 2000; Xin et al., 2001). On the other hand, a little alcohol seems to be good for the heart (Blanco-Colio et al., 2000).
- *Type A behavior:* Most studies suggest that there is at least a modest relationship between Type A behavior and CHD (Smith & Ruiz, 2002). It also seems that alleviating Type A behavior patterns may reduce the risk of *recurrent* heart attacks (Friedman & Ulmer, 1984).
- *Hostility and holding in feelings of anger:* Hostility seems to be the component of the Type A behavior pattern that is most harmful to physical health (Birks & Roger, 2000; Smith & Ruiz, 2002). One study that controlled for the influences of other risk factors, like high blood pressure and cholesterol levels, smoking, and obesity, found that people who are highly prone to anger are about three times as likely as other people to have heart attacks (Williams et al., 2000). The stress hormones connected

REFLECT
Does CHD run in your family? If so, what can you do about it?

Serum Cholesterol
Cholesterol in the blood.

Hypertension
High blood pressure.

with anger can constrict blood vessels to the heart, leading to a heart attack. Chronically hostile and angry people also have higher cholesterol levels (Richards et al., 2000). Highly hostile young adults—as young as 18 to 30—are already at greater risk for calcification (hardening) of the arteries, which increases the risk of heart attacks (Iribarren et al., 2000).

- *Job strain:* Overtime work, assembly-line labor, and exposure to conflicting demands can all contribute to CHD. High-strain work, which makes heavy demands on workers but gives them little personal control, puts workers at the highest risk (Krantz et al., 1988; Smith & Ruiz, 2002). As shown in Figure 10.5, the work of waiters and waitresses may best fit this description.
- *Chronic fatigue and chronic emotional strain.*
- *Sudden stressors:* For example, after the 1994 Los Angeles earthquake there was an increased incidence of death from heart attacks in people with heart disease (Leor et al., 1996).
- *A physically inactive lifestyle* (Stampfer et al., 2000).

African Americans are more likely than European Americans to have heart attacks and to die from them (Freeman & Payne, 2000). Figure 10.6 compares the death rates from heart disease of African American women and women from other ethnic backgrounds in the United States (Smith, 2000). Early diagnosis and treatment might help decrease the racial gap. However, African Americans with heart disease are less likely than European Americans to obtain complex procedures such as bypass surgery and simple measures such as aspirin, even when they would benefit equally from them (Freeman & Payne, 2000; Rathore et al., 2000). Moreover, when European Americans and African Americans show up in the emergency room with heart attacks and other severe cardiac problems, physicians are more likely to misdiagnose the conditions among the African Americans (J. H. Pope et al., 2000).

■ Figure 10.5
The Job-Strain Model

This model highlights the psychological demands made by various occupations and the amount of personal (decision) control they allow. Occupations characterized by high demand and low decision control place workers at greatest risk for heart disease.

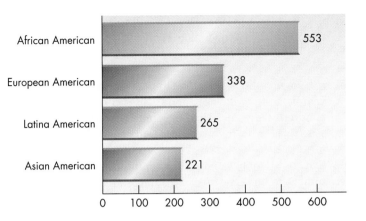

■ **Figure 10.6**
Deaths from Heart Disease per 100,000 Women Aged 35 and Above

African American women have experienced a higher annual death rate from heart attacks (553 per 100,000) than women from any other ethnic group in the United States.

Cancer: Swerving Off Course

Cancer is the number-one killer of women in the United States and the number-two killer of men (Andersen, 1996). Cancer is characterized by the development of abnormal, or mutant, cells that may take root anywhere in the body: in the blood, bones, digestive tract, lungs, and sex organs. If their spread is not controlled early, the cancerous cells may *metastasize*—that is, establish colonies elsewhere in the body. It appears that our bodies develop cancerous cells frequently. However, these are normally destroyed by the immune system. People whose immune system is damaged by physical or psychological factors may be more likely to develop tumors (Azar, 1996b).

Question: How has psychology contributed to our understanding and treatment of cancer?   Health psychologists have conducted research into the origins and treatment of cancer.

Risk Factors

As with many other disorders, people can inherit a disposition toward cancer (Lichtenstein et al., 2000). Carcinogenic genes may remove the brakes from cell division, allowing cells to multiply wildly. Or they may allow mutations to accumulate unchecked. However, many behavior patterns markedly heighten the risk for cancer (Hoover, 2000). These include smoking, drinking alcohol (especially in women), eating animal fats, and sunbathing (which may cause skin cancer due to exposure to ultraviolet light). Agents in cigarette smoke, such as benzopyrene, may damage a gene that would otherwise block the development of many tumors, including lung cancer ("Damaged gene," 1996). Prolonged psychological conditions such as depression or stress also apparently heighten the risk of some kinds of cancer by depressing the functioning of the immune system (McGuire et al., 2002; Salovey et al., 2000).

African Americans are also more likely than European Americans to contract most forms of cancer (Freeman & Payne, 2000). Possibly because of genetic factors, the incidence of lung cancer is significantly higher among African Americans than European Americans (Blakeslee, 1994). Once they contract cancer, African Americans are more likely than European Americans to die from it (Freeman & Payne, 2000). The results for African Americans are connected with their lower socioeconomic status and relative lack of access to health care (Whitfield et al., 2002).

Also consider cultural differences in health. Death rates from cancer are higher in such nations as the Netherlands, Denmark, England, Canada, and—yes—the United States, where average rates of daily fat intake are high (Cohen, 1987). Death rates from cancer are lower in such nations Thailand, the Philippines, and Japan, where fat intake is lower. Thailand, the Philippines, and Japan are Asian nations, but do not assume that the difference is racial! The diets of Japanese Americans are similar in fat content to those of other Americans—and so are their rates of death from cancer. According to the British Heart Foundation (Reaney, 2000), it turns out that there are also significant differences among Europeans. French, Spanish, and Portuguese people enjoy the lowest death rates from coronary heart disease (CHD) and also eat diets that are relatively low in fat and

REFLECT
Are you prone to developing any type of cancer? What are you doing to prevent or treat cancer?

high in fruits and vegetables. People in Ireland, Finland, and Britain suffer the most deaths from CHD and also eat high-fat diets and relatively fewer fruits and vegetables.

Stress and Cancer

Researchers have uncovered possible links between stress and cancer (Azar, 1996b; Salovey et al., 2000). For example, a study by Jacob and Charles (1980) revealed that a significant percentage of children with cancer had encountered severe life changes within a year of the diagnosis. These often involved the death of a loved one or loss of a close relationship.

Experimental research that could not be conducted with humans has been carried out using rats and other animals. In one type of study, animals are injected with cancerous cells or with viruses that cause cancer and then exposed to various conditions. In this way researchers can determine which conditions influence the likelihood that the animals' immune systems will be able to fend off the disease. Such experiments suggest that once cancer has developed, stress can influence its course. In one study, for example, rats were implanted with small numbers of cancer cells so that their own immune systems would have a chance to combat them (Visintainer et al., 1982). Some of the rats were then exposed to inescapable shocks. Others were exposed to escapable shocks or to no shock. The rats that were exposed to the most stressful condition—the inescapable shock—were half as likely as the other rats to reject the cancer and twice as likely to die from it. Therefore, it may be that in some cases, stress can influence the course of cancer, although not the eventual outcome.

A Closer Look 👁

Psychological Factors in the Treatment of Cancer

People with cancer not only must cope with the biological aspects of their illnesses; they may also face a host of psychological problems. These include feelings of anxiety and depression about treatment methods and the eventual outcome, changes in body image after the removal of a breast or testicle, feelings of vulnerability, and family problems (Azar, 1996b). For example, some families criticize members with cancer for feeling sorry for themselves or not fighting the disease hard enough (Andersen et al., 1994; Rosenthal, 1993). Psychological stress due to cancer can weaken the immune system, setting the stage for other health problems, such as respiratory tract infections (Andersen, 2002).

There are also psychological treatments for the nausea that often accompanies chemotherapy. People undergoing chemotherapy who also obtain relaxation training and guided imagery techniques experience significantly less nausea and vomiting than patients who do not use these methods (Azar, 1996c). Distraction helps (Cohen, 2002). Studies with children find that playing video games reduces the discomfort of chemotherapy (Kolko & Rickard-Figueroa, 1985; Redd et al., 1987). Children focus on battling computer-generated enemies rather than the side effects of drugs.

Of course, cancer is a medical disorder. However, health psychologists have improved the methods used to treat people with cancer. For example, a crisis like cancer can lead people to feel that life has spun out of control (Merluzzi & Martinez Sanchez, 1997). Control is a factor in psychological hardiness. A sense of loss of control can heighten stress and impair the immune system. Health psychology therefore stresses the value of encouraging people with cancer to remain in charge of their lives (Jacox

et al., 1994). Even measures such as training physicians to listen more attentively, convey warmth, and provide feedback (as opposed to saying nothing) can help (Andersen, 2002).

Cancer requires medical treatment, and in many cases there are few treatment options. However, people with cancer can still choose how they will deal with the disease. Patients' moods are connected with the functioning of the immune system, and we know that prolonged stress, depression, and feelings of tension depress the immune system (McGuire et al., 2002). However, we should point out that the literature is mixed as to whether patients' attitudes and moods can actually affect the course of cancer (Kiecolt-Glaser et al., 2002b). Still, there are some encouraging notes. For example, one ten-year follow-up of women with breast cancer found a significantly higher survival rate for women who responded to their diagnosis with anger and a "fighting spirit" rather than with stoic acceptance (Pettingale et al., 1985). A five-year follow-up of nearly 600 women with early-stage breast cancer found that the survival rate was significantly higher for women who showed a fighting spirit as compared with women who reported feeling helpless and hopeless—that is, depressed (Faller et al., 1999; Watson et al., 1999).

Psychologists are teaching coping skills to people with cancer in order to relieve psychological distress as well as pain. One study of 235 women with metastatic breast cancer found that group therapy aimed at providing support and helping the women express their feelings enhanced the women's moods and decreased the amount of pain they experienced (Goodwin et al., 2001). Unfortunately, the therapy did not affect their survival rate. But psychological methods such as relaxation train-

HIV/AIDS and Other Sexually Transmitted Infections (STIs)

Sexual relationships can be sources of pleasure and personal fulfillment. They also carry some risks and responsibilities. One of the risks is that of contracting **AIDS** or other sexually transmitted infections (STIs). ***Question: What kinds of sexually transmitted infections are there?*** What are their effects? Although media attention usually focuses on AIDS and **HIV** (the virus that causes AIDS), other STIs are more widespread. Nearly 4 million new chlamydia infections occur each year, with the incidence among college students especially high (CDC, 2001). Chlamydia is a major cause of pelvic inflammatory disease, which often leads to infertility.

Most college students are informed about HIV transmission and AIDS, yet many are unaware that chlamydia can go undetected for years. A survey of first-year college students found a great deal of ignorance about human papilloma virus (HPV) and genital warts (Baer et al., 2000). The findings were ironic: Although nearly all (96% of the males and 95% of the females) had heard of genital warts, only 4% of the males and 12% of the females knew that HPV caused them. Moreover, the students were generally ignorant of the modes of transmission of HPV. Ignorance in this case is danger rather than bliss because HPV infection is linked to cervical cancer (Josefsson et al., 2000). Yet as many as 1 million new cases of HPV infection occur each year in the United States—more than syphilis, genital herpes, and AIDS combined.

Women experience the effects of most STIs disproportionately (Glynn et al., 2001). They are more likely to develop infertility if an STI spreads through the reproductive

AIDS
Acronym for *acquired immunodeficiency syndrome*.

HIV
Acronym for *human immunodeficiency virus*.

■ **How Have Health Psychologists Helped This Youngster Cope with Cancer?** Cancer is a medical disorder, but psychologists have contributed to the treatment of people with cancer. For example, psychologists help people with cancer remain in charge of their lives, combat feelings of hopelessness, manage stress, and cope with the side effects of chemotherapy.

ing, meditation, biofeedback training, and exercise can all help patients cope with their disorders (Andersen, 2002).

Yet another psychological application is helping people undergoing chemotherapy keep up their strength by eating. The problem is that chemotherapy often causes nausea. Nausea then becomes associated with foods eaten during the day, causing taste aversions (Azar, 1996c). So people with cancer, who may already be losing weight because of their illness, may find that taste aversions aggravate the problems caused by lack of appetite. To combat these conditions, Bernstein (1996) recommends eating unusual ("scapegoat") foods prior to chemotherapy. If taste aversions develop, they are associated with the unusual food and not the patient's normal diet.

system. STIs are believed to account for 15 to 30% of cases of infertility among U.S. women.

One of the reasons for discussing STIs in a psychology textbook involves psychological risk factors, which are cognitive and behavioral:

- *Cognitive:* People tend to deny or underestimate their risk of infection. For example, AIDS has been characterized as mainly transmitted by anal intercourse (a practice that is fairly common among gay males) and the sharing of contaminated needles. Therefore, many heterosexual Americans who do not use these drugs dismiss the threat of AIDS. Yet male–female sexual intercourse accounts for the majority of cases around the world (United Nations Special Session on AIDS, 2001).

TABLE 10.5 Causes, Transmission, Symptoms, Diagnosis, and Treatment of Sexually Transmitted infections (STIs)

STI and Cause	Methods of Transmission	Symptoms	Diagnosis	Treatment
Acquired immune deficiency syndrome (AIDS): Human immunodeficiency virus (HIV)	Sexual intercourse; injection of contaminated blood; from mother to child during childbirth or breast-feeding.	AIDS kills white blood cells and weakens the immune system, leaving the body vulnerable to "opportunistic" lethal diseases.	Blood, saliva, and urine tests can detect HIV antibodies in the bloodstream. Other tests detect the virus itself.	A "cocktail" of antiviral drugs including protease inhibitors usually reduces the amount of HIV in the bloodstream. Long-term outcomes of treatment remain unclear.
Bacterial vaginosis: *Gardnerella vaginalis* bacterium and others	Sexual contact	In women, a vaginal discharge, genital irritation, and mild pain during urination. In men, inflammation of the penis, urethritis, and cystitis. May be asymptomatic.	Culture and examination of bacterium	Oral treatment with metronidazole (Flagyl)
Candidiasis (moniliasis, thrush, "yeast infection"): *Candida albicans*—a yeastlike fungus	Sexual contact (or sharing a washcloth with an infected person)	In women, vulval itching, discharge, soreness or swelling of genital tissues. In men, itching and burning on urination, or inflammation of the penis.	Diagnosis usually made on basis of symptoms	Vaginal suppositories, creams, or tablets containing miconazole, clotrimazole, or teraconazole
Chlamydia and nongonococcal urethritis (NGU): *Chlamydia trachomatis* bacterium in women, and several in men	Vaginal, oral, or anal sexual activity	In women, frequent and painful urination, lower abdominal pain and inflammation, and vaginal discharge. In men, burning or painful urination, slight discharge. May be asymptomatic.	The Abbott Testpack analyzes a cervical smear in women	Antibiotics
Genital herpes: Herpes simplex virus–type 2 (HSV–2)	Vaginal, oral, or anal sexual activity; most contagious during outbreaks	Painful, reddish bumps around the genitals. Bumps become blisters or sores that fill with pus and break, shedding viral particles. Burning urination, fever, aches and pains, swollen glands, and vaginal discharge possible.	Clinical inspection of sores; culture and examination of fluid drawn from sore	Antiviral drugs may provide relief and prompt healing but are not cures

- *Behavioral:* Despite their knowledge of the effects of infection by HIV and other disease organisms, many people do not change their behavior in an effort to prevent infection (Dailard, 2001; Santelli et al., 2000).

More information about STIs is found in Table 10.5. For the latest on HIV/AIDS, you can call the National AIDS Hotline at 1-800-342-AIDS. If you want to receive information in Spanish, call 1-800-344-SIDA. Or go to the Web site of the Centers for Disease Control and Prevention: www.cdc.gov. Once you're there, click on "Health Topics A–Z," and then on "AIDS/HIV." Information on preventing and coping with STIs is presented in this chapter's "Life Connections" section.

TABLE 10.5 Causes, Transmission, Symptoms, Diagnosis, and Treatment of Sexually Transmitted infections (STIs)—continued

STI and Cause	Methods of Transmission	Symptoms	Diagnosis	Treatment
Genital warts (venereal warts): Human papilloma virus (HPV)	Sexual and other forms of contact, as with infected towels or clothing	Painless warts, often resembling cauliflowers, on the genitals or anus or in the rectum.	Clinical inspection; regular Pap tests	Removal by freezing, podophyllin, burning, and surgery
Gonorrhea ("clap," "drip"): Gonococcus bacterium (*Neisseria gonorrhoeae*)	Vaginal, oral, or anal sexual activity	In men, thick discharge, burning urination. In women, may be symptom-free or there may be increased discharge, burning urination, irregular menstrual bleeding.	Clinical inspection, culture of sample discharge	Antibiotics
Pubic lice ("crabs"): *Phthirus pubis* (an insect, not a crab)	Sexual contact or contact with an infested towel, sheet, or toilet seat	Intense itching in pubic area and other hairy regions to which lice can attach	Clinical examination	Prescriptions or over-the-counter drugs containing pyrethrins or piperonal butoxide (e.g., NIX, A200, RID, Triple X)
Syphilis: *Treponema pallidum*	Vaginal, oral, or anal sexual activity	Hard, round, painless chancre (sore) appears at site of infection within 2 to 4 weeks. May progress through additional stages if left untreated. Potentially lethal.	Clinical examination or examination of fluid from a chancre. Blood test (the VDRL).	Antibiotics
Trichomoniasis ("trich"): *Trichomonas vaginalis*— a protozoan (one-celled animal)	Almost always transmitted sexually	In women, a discharge, itching, or burning in vulva. Mild urethritis in men. May be asymptomatic in both women and men.	Microscopic examination of vaginal secretions or of culture of the sample	Metronidazole (Flagyl)

Learning Connections
See Web site for an interactive version of these review questions.

REVIEW

(18) Psychological states such as anxiety and depression impair the functioning of the _____ system, rendering us more vulnerable to health problems. (19) The most common kind of headache is the _____-_____ headache. (20) The _____ headache has a sudden onset and is identified by throbbing pain on one side of the head. (21) Risk factors for coronary heart disease include family history, obesity, hypertension, high levels of serum _____, heavy drinking, smoking, hostility, Type A behavior, and job strain. (22) African Americans have (more or less?) access to health care than European Americans do. (23) African Americans are (more or less?) likely than European Americans to have heart attacks and contract most forms of cancer. (24) Genetic factors (play or do not play?) a role in cancer. (25) HIV is the virus that causes _____ immunodeficiency syndrome. (26) HPV causes _____ warts and is linked to cervical cancer. (27) HIV weakens the immune system, leaving the body vulnerable to _____ diseases. (28) HIV is transmitted by infected _____, semen, vaginal and cervical secretions, and breast milk.

Critical Thinking: Agree or disagree with the following statement and support your answer: "Bad genes" doom people to health problems.

Preventing and Coping with Health Problems—Stress, Headaches, Heart Disease, Cancer, and Sexually Transmitted Infections

Health psychologists have engaged in a wealth of research concerning the ways in which mental processes and behavior can help people prevent and cope with health problems. In this "Life Connections" section, we highlight ways of preventing and coping with stress, headaches, heart disease, cancer, and sexually transmitted infections. Because stress depresses the functioning of the immune system, it may be that alleviating stress has beneficial effects on the immune system, thus making us less vulnerable to some health problems. Still, do not assume that stress-management is the cure-all. This area of research is in its infancy (Miller & Cohen, 2001). But at the very least, stress reduction reduces feelings of stress! Moreover, the strategies for preventing and coping with heart disease, cancer, and sexually transmitted infections involve significant improvements in your lifestyle. By following them, there is an excellent chance that you will live longer. It is almost a certainty that you will live *better*.

Coping with Stress

What do these things have in common: (1) telling yourself that you can live with another person's disappointment, (2) taking a deep breath and telling yourself to relax, (3) taking the scenic route to work, and (4) jogging for half an hour? These are all methods suggested by psychologists to help people cope with the stresses of modern life.

Stress takes many forms and can harm our psychological well-being and physical health. Here we highlight ways of coping with stress.

Controlling Irrational Thoughts—How to Change Your Mind for the Better

People often feel pressure from their own thoughts. Consider the following experiences:

1. You have difficulty with the first item on a test and become convinced that you will flunk.

2. You want to express your genuine feelings but think that if you do so you might make another person angry or upset.
3. You haven't been able to get to sleep for 15 minutes and assume that you will lie awake all night and feel "wrecked" in the morning.
4. You're not sure what decision to make, so you try to put the problem out of your mind by going out, playing cards, or watching TV.
5. You decide not to play tennis because your form isn't perfect and you're in less than perfect condition.

If you have had these or similar experiences, it may be because you harbor some of the irrational beliefs identified by Albert Ellis (see Table 10.2). These beliefs may make you overly concerned about the approval of others (item 2 in the preceding list) or perfectionistic (item 5). They may lead you to think that you can solve problems by pretending that they do not exist (item 4) or that a minor setback will invariably lead to greater problems (items 1 and 3).

How do we change the irrational thoughts that create and compound stress? The answer is deceptively simple: We just change them. However, this may require work. Moreover, before we can change our thoughts we must become aware of them.

Cognitive–behavioral psychologists (e.g., Marks & Dar, 2000) outline a multistep procedure for controlling the irrational or catastrophizing thoughts that often accompany feelings of anxiety, conflict, or tension:

1. Develop awareness of the thoughts that seem to be making you miserable by careful self-examination. Study the examples at the beginning of this section or in Table 10.6 to see if they apply to you. (Also consider Ellis's list of irrational beliefs in Table 10.2 and ask yourself whether any of them governs your behavior.) Also: When you encounter anxiety or frustration, pay close attention to your thoughts.

TABLE 10.6 Controlling Irrational Beliefs and Thoughts*

Irrational (Upsetting) Thoughts	Rational (Calming) Thoughts
"Oh my God, I'm going to completely lose control!"	"This is painful and upsetting, but I don't have to go to pieces over it."
"This will never end."	"This will end even if it's hard to see the end right now."
"It'll be awful if Mom gives me that look again."	"It's more pleasant when Mom's happy with me, but I can live with it if she isn't."
"How can I go out there? I'll look like a fool."	"So you're not perfect. That doesn't mean that you're going to look stupid. And so what if someone thinks you look stupid? You can live with that, too. Just stop worrying and have some fun."
"My heart's going to leap out of my chest! How much can I stand?"	"Easy—hearts don't leap out of chests. Stop and think! Distract yourself. Breathe slowly, in and out."
"What can I do? There's nothing I can do!"	"Easy—stop and think. Just because you can't think of a solution right now doesn't mean there's nothing you can do. Take it a minute at a time. Breathe easy."

*Do irrational beliefs or catastrophizing thoughts compound your feelings of anxiety and tension? Cognitive psychologists suggest that you can cope with stress by becoming aware of your irrational, upsetting thoughts and replacing them with rational, calming thoughts.

2. Evaluate the accuracy of the thoughts. Are they guiding you toward a solution, or are they compounding your problems? Do they reflect reality or do they blow things out of proportion? Do they misplace the blame for failure or shortcomings? and so on.
3. Prepare thoughts that are incompatible with the irrational or catastrophizing thoughts and practice saying them firmly to yourself. (If nobody is nearby, why not say them firmly aloud?)
4. Reward yourself with a mental pat on the back for making effective changes in your beliefs and thought patterns.

Lowering Arousal: Turning Down the Inner Alarm

Stress tends to trigger intense activity in the sympathetic branch of the autonomic nervous system—in other words, arousal. Arousal is a sign that something may be wrong. It is a message telling us to survey the situation and take appropriate action. But once we are aware that a stressor is acting upon us and have developed a plan to cope with it, it is no longer helpful to have blood pounding fiercely through our arteries.

Psychologists and other scientists have developed many methods for teaching people to reduce arousal. These include meditation, biofeedback, and progressive relaxation. In progressive relaxation, people purposefully tense a particular muscle group before relaxing it. This sequence allows them to develop awareness of their muscle tensions and also to differentiate between feelings of tension and relaxation.

The following instructions will help you to try meditation as a means for lowering the arousal connected with stress:

1. Begin by meditating once or twice a day for 10 to 20 minutes.
2. In meditation, what you *don't* do is more important than what you *do* do. Adopt a passive, "what happens, happens" attitude.
3. Create a quiet, nondisruptive environment. For example, don't face a light directly.
4. Do not eat for an hour beforehand; avoid caffeine for at least two hours.
5. Assume a comfortable position. Change it as needed. It's okay to scratch or yawn.
6. As a device to aid concentrating, you may focus on your breathing or seat yourself before a calming object such as a plant or burning incense. Benson suggests "perceiving" (rather than mentally saying) the word *one* on every out-breath. This means thinking the word, but "less actively" than usual (good luck). Others suggest thinking or perceiving the word *in* as you are inhaling and *out*, or *ah-h-h*, as you are exhaling.
7. If you are using a mantra (like the syllable "om," pronounced *oammm*), you can prepare for meditation and say the mantra out loud several times. Enjoy it. Then say it more and more softly. Close your eyes and only think the mantra. Allow yourself to perceive, rather than actively think, the mantra. Again, adopt a passive attitude. Continue to perceive the mantra. It may grow louder or softer, disappear for a while, and then return.
8. If disruptive thoughts enter your mind as you are meditating, you can allow them to "pass through." Don't get wrapped up in trying to squelch them, or you may raise your level of arousal.
9. Allow yourself to drift. (You won't go too far.) What happens, happens.

10. Above all, take what you get. You cannot force the relaxing effects of meditation. You can only set the stage for it and allow it to happen.

Exercising: Run for Your Life?

I like long walks, especially when they are taken by people who annoy me.

—Fred Allen

Exercise, particularly aerobic exercise, enhances the functioning of the immune system, contributes to our psychological well-being, and helps us cope with stress (Jonsdottir et al., 2000; Tkachuk & Martin, 1999). *Aerobic exercise* refers to exercise that requires a sustained increase in consumption of oxygen. Aerobic exercise promotes cardiovascular fitness. Aerobic exercises include, but are not limited to, running and jogging, running in place, walking (at more than a leisurely pace), aerobic dancing, jumping rope, swimming, bicycle riding, basketball, racquetball, and cross-country skiing.

Anaerobic exercises, in contrast, involve short bursts of muscle activity. Examples of anaerobic exercises are weight training, calisthenics (which usually allow rest periods between exercises), and sports such as baseball, in which there are infrequent bursts of strenuous activity. Anaerobic exercises can strengthen muscles and improve flexibility.

Exercise helps people cope by enhancing their physical fitness, or "condition." Fitness includes muscle strength; muscle endurance; suppleness or flexibility; cardiorespiratory, or aerobic, fitness; and a higher ratio of muscle to fat (usually due to both building muscle and reducing fat). Fitness also enhances our natural immunity and boosts our levels of endorphins (Jonsdottir et al., 2000). Cardiovascular fitness, or "condition," means that the body can use more oxygen during vigorous activity and pump more blood with each heartbeat. Because conditioned athletes' hearts pump more blood with each beat, they usually have a slower pulse rate—that is, fewer heartbeats per minute. However, during aerobic exercise they may double or triple their resting heart rate for minutes at a time.

Sustained physical activity does more than promote fitness. It reduces hypertension (Blumenthal et al., 2002; Taylor-Tolbert et al., 2000) and the risk of heart attacks (Stampfer et al., 2000) and strokes (Hu et al., 2000). In one research program, Ralph Paffenbarger and his colleagues (1993; Lee et al., 2000; Sesso et al., 2000) have been tracking several thousand Harvard University alumni by means of university records and questionnaires. They have correlated the incidence of heart attacks in this group with their levels of physical activity. As shown in Figure 10.7, the incidence of heart attacks declines as physical activity rises to a level at which about 2,000 calories are used per week—the equivalent of jogging about 20 miles a week. Inactive alumni have the highest risk of heart attacks. Alumni who burn at least 2,000 calories a week through exercise live two years longer, on the average, than their less active counterparts.

Of course, there is an important limitation to Paffenbarger's research: It is correlational, not experimental. It is possible that people who are in better health *choose* to engage in higher levels of physical activity. If such is the case, then their lower incidence of heart attacks and their lower mortality rates would be attributable to their initial superior health, not to their physical activity.

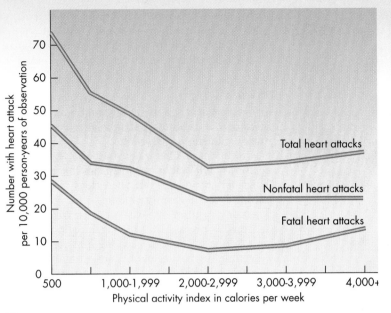

Number with heart attack per 10,000 person-years of observation

Total heart attacks

Nonfatal heart attacks

Fatal heart attacks

500 | 1,000-1,999 | 2,000-2,999 | 3,000-3,999 | 4,000+
Physical activity index in calories per week

■ Figure 10.7
Heart Attacks and Physical Activity
Paffenbarger and his colleagues have correlated the incidence of heart attacks with level of physical activity among 17,000 Harvard alumni. The incidence of heart attacks declines as the activity level rises to burning about 2,000 calories a week by means of physical activity. Above 2,000 calories a week, however, the incidence of heart attacks begins to climb again, although gradually, not steeply.

Aerobic exercise raises blood levels of high-density lipoproteins (HDL, or "good cholesterol") (Stampfer et al., 2000). HDL lowers the amount of low-density lipoproteins (LDL, or "bad cholesterol") in the blood. This is another way in which exercise may reduce the risk of heart attacks.

How about you? Are you thinking of climbing onto the exercise bandwagon? If so, consider these suggestions:

1. Unless you have engaged in sustained and vigorous exercise recently, seek the advice of a medical expert. If you smoke, have a family history of heart disease, are overweight, or are over 40, get a stress test.
2. Consider joining a beginner's aerobics class. Group leaders are not usually experts in physiology, but at least they "know the steps." You'll also be among other beginners and derive the benefits of social support.
3. Get the proper equipment to facilitate performance and avert injury.
4. Read up on the activity you are considering. Books, magazines, and newspaper articles will give you ideas as to how to get started and how fast to progress.
5. Try to select activities that you can sustain for a lifetime. Don't worry about building yourself up rapidly. Enjoy yourself. Your strength and endurance will progress on their own. If you do not enjoy what you're doing, you're not likely to stick to it.
6. If you feel severe pain, don't try to exercise "through" it. Soreness is to be expected for beginners (and for old-timers now and then). In that sense, soreness, at least when it is intermittent, is normal. But sharp pain is abnormal and a sign that something is wrong.
7. Have fun!

Preventing and Coping with Headaches

Because many headaches are related to stress, one way to fight headaches is to lessen the stress in your life. All the methods mentioned here—challenging irrational beliefs, lowering the physical alarm, and exercising—may be of help. We described the method of meditation for lowering arousal. Progressive relaxation focuses on decreasing muscle tension and has been shown to be highly effective in relieving muscle tension headaches (Blanchard et al., 1990; Holden et al., 1999). Biofeedback training has also helped many people with migraine headaches (Powers et al., 2001; Scharff et al., 2002).

Aspirin, acetaminophen, ibuprofen, and many prescription drugs are also used to fight headache pain. Some inhibit the production of the prostaglandins that help initiate transmission of pain messages to the brain. Newer prescription drugs can help prevent many migraines (Bateman, 2000); ask your doctor. People who are sensitive to MSG or red wine can request meals without MSG and switch to white wine.

Reducing the Risk of CHD Through Behavior Modification

Once CHD has been diagnosed, a number of medical treatments, including surgery and medication, are available. However, people who have not had CHD (as well as those who have) can profit from behavior modification techniques designed to reduce the risk factors. These methods include:

- *Stopping smoking* (see Chapter 5).
- *Controlling weight* (See Chapter 9).
- *Reducing hypertension:* There is medication for reducing hypertension, but behavioral changes such as the following help and are sometimes enough: meditation (Alexander et al., 1996; Schneider et al., 1995), aerobic exercise (Danforth et al., 1990), taking in more fruits and vegetables, fish, and folic acid (a B vitamin) but less saturated fat (Stampfer et al., 2000) and less salt (Sacks et al., 2001).
- *Lowering low-density lipoprotein (harmful) serum cholesterol:* Major methods involve exercise, medication, and cutting down on foods that are high in cholesterol and saturated fats (Stampfer et al., 2000). Lowering LDL is helpful at any time of life, even during older adulthood. However, even young adults should think about their LDL levels, because elevated LDL in young adulthood can establish a pattern that places one at risk for cardiovascular disease later in life (Stamler et al., 2000).
- *Modifying Type A behavior.*
- *Managing feelings of anger.*
- *Exercising:* Sustained physical activity protects people from CHD as well as cope with stress (Stampfer et al., 2000).

Preventing and Coping with Cancer

Cancer is a frightening disease; and, in many cases, there may be little that can be done about its eventual outcome. However, we are not helpless in the face of cancer. We can take measures like the following:

- Limit exposure to behavioral risk factors for cancer (Chlebowski, 2000).

■ **They're in Love—Will They Be Careful?**
What are the risk factors in contracting sexually transmitted infections? What can people do to protect their partners and themselves?

- Modify diet by reducing intake of fats and increasing intake of fruits and vegetables (Kant et al., 2000; Mangelsdorf, 2002). Tomatoes (especially cooked tomatoes, such as we find in tomato sauce and ketchup—yes, ketchup!), broccoli, cauliflower, and cabbage appear to be especially helpful (Angier, 1994a). (Yes, Grandma was right about veggies.)
- Exercise regularly. (Yes, exercise not only helps us cope with stress. It also lowers the risk of developing CHD and cancer. Just do it.)
- Have regular medical checkups so that cancer will be detected early. Cancer is most treatable in the early stages.
- Regulate exposure to stress (Folkman & Moskowitz, 2000a).
- If we are struck by cancer, we can fight it energetically.

Preventing HIV/AIDS and Other STIs

Prevention is the primary weapon against STIs. People need to learn about the transmission, symptoms, and consequences of STIs. They need to learn about "safer sex" techniques, including abstinence, and, if they are sexually active, the use of condoms. Educating people to use condoms is associated with lower levels of infection (Ford et al., 2000; Fylkesnes et al., 2001).

But there remains what social psychologists call the A–B problem; that is, people do not always behave (B) in accord with their attitudes (A). Thus knowledge may not be enough to change behavior (Parsons et al., 2000). For example, many female adolescents lack power in their relationships. Males are likely to pressure females into unwanted sexual relations or to pressure them into unprotected sexual relations (Friedman et al., 2001; Garcia-Moreno & Watts, 2000). In many cases, that is, prevention involves the empowerment of adolescent females (United Nations Special Session on AIDS, 2001).

What can *you* do to prevent the transmission of HIV and other STI-causing organisms? A number of things.

1. *The first aspect of prevention is psychological: Don't ignore the threat of STIs.* Don't simply assume that your partner is uninfected or believe it would hurt the relationship to ask about STIs.
2. *Remain abstinent.* One way to curb the sexual transmission of HIV and other organisms that cause STIs is sexual abstinence. But what does "abstinence" mean? Does it mean avoiding sexual intercourse (yes) or any form of sexual activity with another person (not necessarily)? Kissing, hugging, and petting to orgasm (without coming into contact with semen or vaginal secretions) are generally considered safe in terms of HIV transmission. However, kissing can transmit oral herpes (as shown by cold sores) and some bacterial STIs.
3. *Engage in a monogamous relationship with someone who is not infected.* Sexual activity within a monogamous relationship with an uninfected person is safe.

   Readers who do not abstain from sexual relationships or limit themselves to a monogamous relationship can do some things to make sex safer—if not perfectly safe:
4. *Be selective.* Engage in sexual activity only with people you know well. Consider whether they are likely to have engaged in the kinds of behaviors that transmit HIV or other STIs.
5. *Inspect your partner's genitals.* People who have STIs often have a variety of symptoms. Examining your partner's genitals for blisters, discharges, chancres, rashes, warts, lice, and unpleasant odors during foreplay may reveal signs of such diseases.
6. *Wash your own genitals before and after contact.* Washing beforehand helps protect your partner. Washing promptly afterward with soap and water helps remove germs.
7. *Use condoms.* Latex condoms (but not condoms made from animal membrane) protect the woman from having HIV-infected semen enter the vagina and the man from contact with HIV-infected vaginal (or other) body fluids. Condoms also prevent transmission of bacterial STIs.
8. *If you fear that you have been exposed to HIV or another infectious organism, talk to your doctor about it.* Early treatment is usually more effective than later treatment. There is a difference between exposure to HIV and infection by HIV; early treatment may prevent infection.
9. *When in doubt, stop.* If you are not sure that sex is safe, stop and think things over or seek expert advice.

We conclude this section with good news for readers of this book: *Better-educated* people—that means *you*—are more likely to modify health-impairing behavior and reap the benefits of change (Pappas et al., 1993).

Recite Recite Recite

Learning Connections
See Web site for an interactive version of this chapter summary

1. **What is health psychology?**

Health psychology studies the relationships between psychological factors and the prevention and treatment of physical health problems.

2. **What is stress?**

Stress is the demand made on an organism to adjust. Whereas some stress—called eustress—is desirable to keep us alert and occupied, too much stress can tax our adjustive capacities and contribute to physical health problems.

3. **What are daily hassles?**

Daily hassles are regularly occurring experiences that threaten or harm our well-being. There are several kinds of hassles, including household, health, time pressure, inner concern, environmental, financial responsibility, work, and future security hassles.

4. **How is it that too much of a good thing can make you ill?**

Too many positive life changes can affect one's health because life changes require adjustment, whether they are positive or negative. In contrast to daily hassles, life changes occur irregularly. Research shows that hassles and life changes are connected with health problems such as heart disease and cancer. However, the demonstrated connection between life changes and health is correlational; thus causality remains clouded.

5. **What is conflict?**

Conflict is the stressful feeling of being pulled in two or more directions by opposing motives. There are four kinds of conflict: approach–approach, avoidance–avoidance, approach–avoidance (in the case of a single goal), and multiple approach–avoidance, when each alternative has its pluses and minuses.

6. **How do irrational beliefs create or compound stress?**

Albert Ellis shows that negative activating events (A) can be made more aversive (C) when irrational beliefs (B) compound their effects. People often catastrophize negative events. Two common irrational beliefs are excessive needs for social approval and perfectionism. Both set the stage for disappointment and increased stress.

7. **What is Type A behavior?**

Type A behavior is connected with a sense of time urgency and characterized by competitiveness, impatience, and aggressiveness. Type B people relax more readily.

8. **How do our self-efficacy expectations affect our ability to withstand stress?**

Self-efficacy expectations encourage us to persist in difficult tasks and to endure discomfort. Self-efficacy expectations are also connected with lower levels of adrenaline and noradrenaline, thus having a braking effect on bodily arousal.

9. **What characteristics are connected with psychological hardiness?**

Kobasa found that psychological hardiness among business executives is characterized by commitment, challenge, and control.

10. **Is there any evidence that "A merry heart doeth good like a medicine"?**

Yes. Research evidence shows that students who produce humor under adversity experience less stress. Moreover, watching humorous videos apparently enhances the functioning of the immune system.

11. **How do predictability and control help us cope with stress?**

Predictability allows us to brace ourselves, and control permits us to plan ways of coping with it.

12. **Is there evidence that social support helps people cope with stress?**

Social support has been shown to help people resist infectious diseases such as colds. It also helps people cope with the stress of cancer and other health problems. Kinds of social support include expression of emotional concern, instrumental aid, information, appraisal, and simple socializing.

Recite Recite Recite

13. What is the general adaptation syndrome?

The GAS is a cluster of bodily changes triggered by stressors. The GAS consists of three stages: alarm, resistance, and exhaustion. Corticosteroids help resist stress by fighting inflammation and allergic reactions. Adrenaline arouses the body by activating the sympathetic nervous system, which is highly active during the alarm and resistance stages of the GAS. Sympathetic activity is characterized by rapid heartbeat and respiration rate, release of stores of sugar, muscle tension, and other responses that deplete the body's supply of energy. The parasympathetic division of the ANS predominates during the exhaustion stage of the GAS and is connected with depression and inactivity. Prolonged stress is dangerous.

14. How does the immune system work?

Leukocytes (white blood cells) engulf and kill pathogens, worn-out body cells, and cancerous cells. The immune system also "remembers" how to battle antigens by maintaining their antibodies in the bloodstream. The immune system also facilitates inflammation, which increases the number of white blood cells that are transported to a damaged area.

15. How does stress affect the functioning of the immune system?

Stress depresses the functioning of the immune system by stimulating the release of corticosteroids. Steroids counter inflammation and interfere with the formation of antibodies.

16. What is the multifactorial approach to health?

This view recognizes that many factors, including biological, psychological, sociocultural, and environmental factors, affect our health. Nearly 1 million preventable deaths occur each year in the United States. Measures such as quitting smoking, eating properly, exercising, and controlling alcohol intake would prevent nearly 80% of them.

17. How has psychology contributed to our understanding and treatment of headaches?

Psychologists participate in research concerning the origins of headaches, including stress and tension. Psychologists help people alleviate headaches by reducing tension. They have also developed biofeedback training methods for helping people cope with migraines.

18. How has psychology contributed to our understanding and treatment of coronary heart disease?

Psychologists have participated in research that shows that the risk factors for coronary heart disease include family history; physiological conditions such as hypertension and high levels of serum cholesterol; behavior patterns such as heavy drinking, smoking, eating fatty foods, and Type A behavior; work overload; chronic tension and fatigue; and physical inactivity. They help people achieve healthier cardiovascular systems by stopping smoking, controlling weight, reducing hypertension, lowering LDL levels, changing Type A behavior, reducing hostility, and exercising.

19. How has psychology contributed to our understanding and treatment of cancer?

Psychologists have participated in research that shows that the risk factors for cancer include family history, smoking, drinking alcohol, eating animal fats, sunbathing, and stress. The following measures can be helpful in preventing and treating cancer: controlling exposure to behavioral risk factors for cancer, having regular medical check-ups, regulating exposure to stress, and vigorously fighting cancer if it develops.

20. What kinds of sexually transmitted infections are there? What are their effects?

Viral infections include HIV/AIDS, genital herpes, and HPV (cause of genital warts). HIV/AIDS is lethal but controlled to some degree by a cocktail of antiviral drugs. Herpes responds to some degree to antiviral drugs, and genital warts—linked with cervical cancer—can be removed. Bacterial infections such as chlamydia, gonorrhea, and syphilis are connected with discomfort and infertility; untreated syphilis is potentially lethal. Bacterial infections are treated with antibiotics.

Active Learning Resources

Search Online with InfoTrac® College Edition

For additional information on the topics in this chapter, explore InfoTrac College Edition, your online library. Go to **http://www.infotrac.thomsonlearning.com** and use the passcode that came on the card with your book. Try these search terms: college stress, stress and health, and coping and life-skills.

Visit Our Web Site

Go to **http://www.wadsworth.com/psychology**, where you will find online resources directly linked to your book, including interactive exercises related to PQ4R and Power Visuals for mastering and reviewing key concepts. In addition, you will find hints on using InfoTrac College Edition to answer the Critical Thinking questions throughout the text. Start with the **Self Study Assessment** for a customized **Study Plan** generated by taking the **Pre-Test** and **Post-Test.**

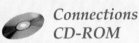

Connections CD-ROM

Go to the Wadsworth *Connections* CD-ROM for further study of the concepts in this chapter. The CD-ROM includes videos, animations, quizzes, and additional activities to expand your learning experience, plus interactive self-assessments to help connect the material to your own life.

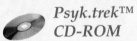

Psyk.trek™ CD-ROM

The Wadsworth *Psyk.trek* CD-ROM offers tutorials, simulations, videos, multimedia glossary, and quizzing to help you master the material.

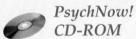

PsychNow! CD-ROM

The Wadsworth *PsychNow!* CD-ROM includes interactive exercises, videos, and animations to enhance your learning.

PowerPreview®

■ **Introduction to Personality: "Why Are They Sad and Glad and Bad?"**

   ■ YOU'VE GOT PERSONALITY. So what does that mean?

■ **The Psychodynamic Perspective: Excavating the Iceberg**

   ■ ACCORDING TO FREUD, the human mind is like a vast submerged iceberg. Only its tip rises above the surface into conscious awareness.

   ■ FREUD BELIEVED that biting one's fingernails or smoking cigarettes as an adult was a sign of childhood conflict.

■ **The Trait Perspective: The Five-Dimensional Universe**

   ■ THE ANCIENT GREEK physician Hippocrates devised a way of looking at personality that—with a little "tweaking"—remains in use today.

   ■ WHY WERE BLOODLETTING and vomiting once recommended as ways of coping with depression?

   ■ YOU MAY HAVE HEARD of the Big Ten athletic conference. Your personality may be made up of the Big Five.

■ **Learning-Theory Perspectives: All the Things You Do**

   ■ JOHN WATSON BELIEVED he could select any infant at random and train him or her to become a doctor, lawyer, or merchant-chief—even a "beggar-man" or thief.

   ■ DOES SOCIETY CONDITION us to want what is good for society?

■ SOCIAL–COGNITIVE THEORISTS admit that the environment influences you, but they also believe that you influence the environment—in fact, that you can create environments.

■ **The Humanistic–Existential Perspective: How Becoming?**

   ■ ABRAHAM MASLOW believed that you keep on wanting to go higher . . . and higher and higher.

   ■ CARL ROGERS believed that if people around you are supportive, you will strive to become everything you are capable of being.

■ **The Sociocultural Perspective: Personality in Context**

   ■ HOW HAVE YOU BEEN influenced by your cultural background?

■ **Measurement of Personality**

   ■ CAN PSYCHOLOGISTS determine whether a person has told the truth on a personality test?

   ■ THERE IS A TEST of personality made up of inkblots, and test-takers are asked to say what the blots look like to them.

■ *Life Connections: Gender-Typing—On Becoming a Woman or a Man*

   ■ WHAT DOES IT MEAN to be "masculine"? To be "feminine"?

   ■ ARE MALES AND females more alike, or more different, in their personalities?

   ■ ARE GENDER DIFFERENCES hardwired by evolutionary forces?

I was reading Dr. Seuss's *One Fish, Two Fish, Red Fish, Blue Fish* to my daughter Taylor when she was 2 years old. The sneaky author had set up a trap for fathers. A part of the book reads "Some [fish] are sad. And some are glad. And some are very very bad. Why are they sad and glad and bad? I do not know. Go ask your dad."

Thanks, Dr. Seuss.

For many months I had just recited this section and then moved on. One day, however, Taylor's cognitive development had apparently flowered, and she would not let me get away with glossing over this. Why, indeed, she wanted to know, were some fish sad whereas others were glad and bad? I paused and then, being a typical American dad, I gave the answer I'm sure has been given by thousands of other fathers:

"Uh, some fish are sad and others are glad or bad because of, uh, the interaction of nature and nurture—I mean, you know, heredity and environmental factors."

At which Taylor laughed and replied, "Not!"

INTRODUCTION TO PERSONALITY: "WHY ARE THEY SAD AND GLAD AND BAD?"

I'm still not certain whether Taylor thought my words came out silly or that my psychological theorizing was simplistic or off base. When applied to people—that is, why are people sad or glad or bad—this is the kind of question that is of interest to psychologists who study personality.

Question: Just what **is** *personality?* People do not necessarily agree on what the word **personality** means. Many equate personality with liveliness, as in "She's got a lot of personality." Others characterize a person's personality as consisting of one's most striking traits, as in a "shy personality" or a "happy-go-lucky personality." Psychologists define personality as the reasonably stable patterns of emotions, motives, and behavior that distinguish one person from another.

Psychologists also seek to explain how personality develops—that is, why some (people) are sad or glad or bad—and to predict how people with certain personality traits respond to life's demands. In this chapter we explore five perspectives on personality: the psychodynamic, trait, learning, humanistic–existential, and sociocultural perspectives. Then we discuss personality tests—the methods used to measure whether people are sad, glad, bad, and lots of other things.

REFLECT

Think of a friend who is single. If you were trying to fix him or her up on a date and you were asked what kind of "personality" he or she had, what would you answer? As you read through the chapter, ask yourself whether your description would change.

THE PSYCHODYNAMIC PERSPECTIVE: EXCAVATING THE ICEBERG

There are several **psychodynamic theories** of personality, each of which owes its origin to the thinking of Sigmund Freud. These theories have a number of features in common. Each teaches that personality is characterized by conflict—by a dynamic struggle. At first the conflict is external: Drives like sex, aggression, and the need for superiority come into conflict with laws, social rules, and moral codes. But at some point laws and social rules are brought inward, or *internalized*. After that the conflict is between opposing *inner* forces. At any given moment our behavior, thoughts, and emotions represent the outcome of these inner contests. *Question: What is Freud's theory of psychosexual development?*

Sigmund Freud's Theory of Psychosexual Development

Sigmund Freud (1856–1939) was a mass of contradictions. He has been lauded as the greatest thinker of the 20th century, the most profound of psychologists. He has been criticized as overrated, even a "false and faithless prophet." He preached liberal views on sexuality but was himself a model of sexual restraint. He invented a popular form of psychotherapy but experienced lifelong psychologically related problems such as

Personality
The distinct patterns of behavior, thoughts, and feelings that characterize a person's adaptation to life.

Psychodynamic Theory
Sigmund Freud's perspective, which emphasizes the importance of unconscious motives and conflicts as forces that determine behavior. *Dynamic* refers to the concept of (psychological) forces being in motion.

migraine headaches, bowel problems, fainting under stress, hatred of the telephone, and an addiction to cigars. He smoked 20 cigars a day and could not or would not break the habit even after he developed cancer of the jaw.

Freud saw himself as an outsider. He was born to Jewish parents in a small town in the Austro-Hungarian empire, at a time when Jews were prevented from holding high offices or practicing most professions. His father, a poor merchant, had become a "free-thinker." Freud, although he considered himself Jewish, proclaimed himself to be an atheist. He spent nearly all of his adult life in Vienna, fleeing to England to escape the Nazi threat only a year before his death.

Although he was rejected by his fellow students because of his religion, he excelled in medical school at the University of Vienna. His interests lay in neurology and then in psychotherapy. He first practiced hypnotherapy, then developed psychoanalysis, the method that has had such a profound influence in psychology and the arts. He borrowed ideas from others, but his own contributions have made him the person that most people think of when asked to name a psychologist.

Early in his practice, Freud was astounded to find that some people apparently experience loss of feeling in a hand or paralysis of the legs in the absence of any medical disorder. These odd symptoms often disappear once the person has recalled and discussed stressful events and feelings of guilt or anxiety that seem to be related to the symptoms. For a long time, these events and feelings have lain hidden beneath the surface of awareness. Even so, they have the capacity to influence behavior.

From this sort of clinical evidence, Freud concluded that the human mind is like an iceberg. Only the tip of an iceberg rises above the surface of the water; the great mass of it is hidden in the depths (see Figure 11.1). Freud came to believe that people, similarly, are aware of only a small portion of the ideas and impulses that dwell within their minds. He argued that a much greater portion of the mind—our deepest images, thoughts, fears, and urges—remains beneath the surface of conscious awareness, where little light illumines them.

Freud labeled the region that pokes through into the light of awareness the **conscious** part of the mind. He called the regions below the surface the *preconscious*

■ **Sigmund Freud**
Freud is one of the key figures in the history of psychology—the first person who comes to mind when most people are asked to name a psychologist. Today many see his teachings as unscientific and even question whether they should be included in a scientific psychology textbook.

Conscious
Self-aware.

■ **Figure 11.1**
The Human Iceberg According to Freud
According to psychodynamic theory, only the tip of human personality rises above the surface of the mind into conscious awareness. Material in the preconscious can become conscious if we direct our attention to it. Unconscious material tends to remain shrouded in mystery.

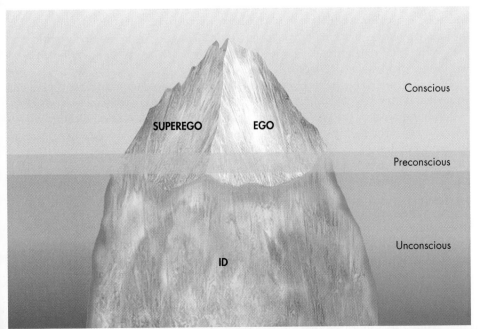

and the *unconscious*. The **preconscious** mind contains elements of experience that are out of awareness but can be made conscious simply by focusing on them. The **unconscious** mind is shrouded in mystery. It contains biological instincts such as sex and aggression. Some unconscious urges cannot be experienced consciously because mental images and words could not portray them in all their color and fury. Other unconscious urges may be kept below the surface through repression.

Repression is the automatic ejection of anxiety-evoking ideas from awareness. Research evidence suggests that many people repress bad childhood experiences (Myers & Brewin, 1994). Perhaps "something shocking happens, and the mind pushes it into some inaccessible corner of the unconscious" (Loftus, 1993). Repression may also protect us from perceiving morally unacceptable impulses.

In the unconscious mind, primitive drives seek expression, while internalized values try to keep them in check. The conflict can arouse emotional outbursts and psychological problems.

To explore the unconscious mind, Freud engaged in a form of mental detective work called **psychoanalysis.** For this reason, his theory of personality is also referred to as *psychoanalytic theory.* In psychoanalysis, people are prodded to talk about anything that pops into their mind while they remain comfortable and relaxed. They may gain self-insight by pursuing some of the thoughts that pop into awareness. But they are also motivated to evade threatening subjects. The same repression that ejects unacceptable thoughts from awareness prompts **resistance,** or the desire to avoid thinking about or discussing those thoughts. Repression and resistance can make psychoanalysis a tedious process that lasts for years, or even decades.

The Structure of Personality

Freud spoke of mental or **psychic structures** to describe the clashing forces of personality. Psychic structures cannot be seen or measured directly, but their presence is suggested by behavior, expressed thoughts, and emotions. Freud believed that there are three psychic structures: the id, the ego, and the superego.

The **id** is present at birth. It represents physiological drives and is entirely unconscious. Freud described the id as "a chaos, a cauldron of seething excitations" (1927/1964, p. 73). The conscious mind might find it inconsistent to love and hate the same person, but Freud believed that conflicting emotions could dwell side by side in the id. In the id, one can feel hatred for one's mother for failing to gratify immediately all of one's needs, while also feeling love for her.

The id follows what Freud termed the **pleasure principle.** It demands instant gratification of instincts without consideration of law, social custom, or the needs of others.

The **ego** begins to develop during the first year of life, largely because a child's demands for gratification cannot all be met immediately. The ego stands for reason and good sense, for rational ways of coping with frustration. It curbs the appetites of the id and makes plans that fit social conventions. Thus, a person can find gratification yet avoid social disapproval. The id informs you that you are hungry, but the ego decides to microwave enchiladas.

The ego is guided by the **reality principle.** It takes into account what is practical along with what is urged by the id. The ego also provides the person's conscious sense of self.

Although most of the ego is conscious, some of its business is carried out unconsciously. For instance, the ego also acts as a censor that screens the impulses of the id. When the ego senses that improper impulses are rising into awareness, it may use psychological defenses to prevent them from surfacing. Repression is one such psychological defense, or **defense mechanism.** Several defense mechanisms are described in Table 11.1.

The **superego** develops throughout early childhood, usually incorporating the moral standards and values of parents and important members of the community through **identification.** The superego functions according to the **moral principle.** The superego holds forth shining examples of an ideal self and also acts like the conscience, an internal moral guardian. Throughout life, the superego monitors the intentions of the ego and hands out judgments of right and wrong. It floods the ego with feelings of guilt and shame when the verdict is negative.

REFLECT

Freud chose the term id *because* id *is the Latin word meaning "it." Would it make a difference if we referred to "the id" simply as "it"? Explain.*

Preconscious
Capable of being brought into awareness by the focusing of attention.

Unconscious
In psychodynamic theory, not available to awareness by simple focusing of attention.

Repression
A defense mechanism that protects the person from anxiety by ejecting anxiety-evoking ideas and impulses from awareness.

Psychoanalysis
In this usage, Freud's method of exploring human personality.

Resistance
A blocking of thoughts whose awareness could cause anxiety.

Psychic Structure
In psychodynamic theory, a hypothesized mental structure that helps explain different aspects of behavior.

Id
The psychic structure, present at birth, that represents physiological drives and is fully unconscious.

Pleasure Principle
The governing principle of the id—the seeking of immediate gratification of instinctive needs.

Ego
The second psychic structure to develop, characterized by self-awareness, planning, and delay of gratification.

TABLE 11.1 Defense Mechanisms

Defense Mechanism	Definition	Examples
Repression	Ejection of anxiety-evoking ideas from awareness	• A student forgets that a difficult term paper is due. • A person in therapy forgets an appointment when anxiety-evoking material is to be discussed.
Regression	The return, under stress, to a form of behavior characteristic of an earlier stage of development	• An adolescent cries when forbidden to use the family car. • An adult becomes highly dependent on his parents after the breakup of his marriage.
Rationalization	The use of self-deceiving justifications for unacceptable behavior	• A student blames her cheating on her teacher's leaving the room during a test. • A man explains his cheating on his income tax by saying "Everyone does it."
Displacement	The transfer of ideas and impulses from threatening or unsuitable objects to less threatening objects	• A worker picks a fight with her spouse after being sharply criticized by her supervisor.
Projection	The thrusting of one's own unacceptable impulses onto others so that others are assumed to have those impulses	• A hostile person perceives the world as a dangerous place. • A sexually frustrated person interprets innocent gestures as sexual advances.
Reaction formation	Engaging in behavior that opposes one's genuine impulses in order to keep those impulses repressed	• A person who is angry with a relative behaves in a "sickly sweet" manner toward that relative. • A sadistic individual becomes a physician.
Denial	The refusal to face the true nature of a threat	• Belief that one will not contract cancer or heart disease even though one smokes heavily. • "It can't happen to me."
Sublimation	The channeling of primitive impulses into positive, constructive efforts	• A person paints nudes for the sake of "beauty" and "art." • A hostile person becomes a tennis star.

The ego hasn't an easy time of it. It stands between the id and the superego, striving to satisfy the demands of the id and the moral sense of the superego. From the Freudian perspective, a healthy personality has found ways to gratify most of the id's demands without seriously offending the superego. Most of the id's remaining demands are contained or repressed. If the ego is not a good problem solver, or if the superego is too stern, the ego will have a hard time of it.

Stages of Psychosexual Development

Freud stirred controversy by arguing that sexual impulses are a central factor in personality development, even among children. Freud believed that sexual feelings are closely linked to children's basic ways of relating to the world, such as sucking on their mother's breasts and moving their bowels.

Reality Principle
Consideration of what is practical and possible in gratifying needs; the governing principle of the ego.

Defense Mechanism
In psychodynamic theory, an unconscious function of the ego that protects it from anxiety-evoking material by preventing accurate recognition of this material.

Superego
The third psychic structure, which functions as a moral guardian and sets forth high standards for behavior.

Identification
In psychodynamic theory, the unconscious assumption of the behavior of another person.

Moral Principle
The governing principle of the superego, which sets moral standards and enforces adherence to them.

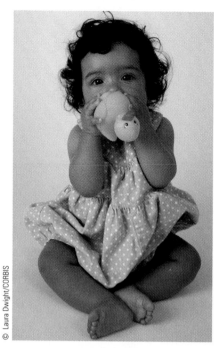

© Laura Dwight/CORBIS

■ The Oral Stage?

According to Sigmund Freud, during the first year the child is in the oral stage of development. If it fits, into the mouth it goes. What, according to Freud, are the effects of insufficient or excessive gratification during the oral stage? Is there evidence to support his views?

Eros

In psychodynamic theory, the basic instinct to preserve and perpetuate life.

Libido

(1) In psychodynamic theory, the energy of eros; the sexual instinct. (2) Generally, sexual interest or drive.

Erogenous Zone

An area of the body that is sensitive to sexual sensations.

Psychosexual Development

In psychodynamic theory, the process by which libidinal energy is expressed through different erogenous zones during different stages of development.

Oral Stage

The first stage of psychosexual development, during which gratification is hypothesized to be attained primarily through oral activities.

Fixation

In psychodynamic theory, arrested development. Attachment to objects of an earlier stage.

Freud believed that a major instinct, which he termed **eros,** is aimed at preserving and perpetuating life. Eros is fueled by psychological, or psychic, energy, which Freud labeled **libido.** Libidinal energy involves sexual impulses, so Freud considered it to be *psychosexual.* As the child develops, libidinal energy is expressed through sexual feelings in different parts of the body, or **erogenous zones.** To Freud, human development involves the transfer of libidinal energy from one erogenous zone to another. He hypothesized five periods of **psychosexual development:** oral, anal, phallic, latency, and genital.

During the first year of life a child experiences much of its world through the mouth. If an object fits, into the mouth it goes. This is the **oral stage.** Freud argued that oral activities such as sucking and biting give the child sexual gratification as well as nourishment.

Freud believed that children encounter conflict during each stage of psychosexual development. During the oral stage, conflict centers on the nature and extent of oral gratification. Early weaning (cessation of breast feeding) could lead to frustration. Excessive gratification, on the other hand, could lead an infant to expect that it will routinely be given anything it wants. Insufficient or excessive gratification in any stage could lead to **fixation** in that stage and to the development of traits that are characteristic of that stage. Oral traits include dependency, gullibility, and excessive optimism or pessimism (depending on the child's experiences with gratification).

REFLECT

If you were fixated in a stage of psychosocial development, which stage would it be? Explain.

REFLECT

At what age do you believe children should be toilet-trained? Why?

Freud theorized that adults with an *oral fixation* could experience exaggerated desires for "oral activities," such as smoking, overeating, alcohol abuse, and nail biting. Like the infant whose very survival depends on the mercy of an adult, adults with oral fixations may be disposed toward clinging, dependent relationships.

During the **anal stage** sexual gratification is attained through contraction and relaxation of the muscles that control elimination of waste products from the body. Elimination, which was controlled reflexively during most of the first year of life, comes under voluntary muscular control, even if such control is not reliable at first. The anal stage is said to begin in the second year of life.

During the anal stage children learn to delay the gratification that comes from eliminating as soon as they feel the urge. The general issue of self-control may become a source of conflict between parent and child. *Anal fixations* may stem from this conflict and lead to two sets of traits in adulthood. So-called *anal-retentive* traits involve excessive use of self-control. They include perfectionism, a strong need for order, and exaggerated neatness and cleanliness. *Anal-expulsive* traits, on the other hand, "let it all hang out." They include carelessness, messiness, even sadism.

Children enter the **phallic stage** during the third year of life. During this stage the major erogenous zone is the phallic region (the penis in boys, and the **clitoris** in girls). Parent–child conflict is likely to develop over masturbation, to which parents may respond with threats or punishment. During the phallic stage children may develop strong sexual attachments to the parent of the other gender and begin to view the parent of the same gender as a rival for the other parent's affections. Thus boys may want to marry Mommy, and girls may want to marry Daddy.

Children have difficulty dealing with feelings of lust and jealousy. Home life would be tense indeed if they were aware of them. These feelings, therefore, remain unconscious, but their influence is felt through fantasies about marriage with the parent of the other gender and hostility toward the parent of the same gender. In boys, this conflict is labeled the **Oedipus complex,** after the legendary Greek king who unwittingly killed his father and married his mother. Similar feelings in girls give rise to the **Electra complex.** According to Greek legend, Electra was the daughter of King Agamemnon. She longed for him after his death and sought revenge against his slayers—her mother and her mother's lover.

The Oedipus and Electra complexes are resolved by about the ages of 5 or 6. Children then repress their hostilities toward the parent of the same gender and begin to identify with her or him. Identification leads them to play the social and gender roles of that parent and to internalize his or her values. Sexual feelings toward the parent of the other gender are repressed for a number of years. When the feelings emerge again during adolescence, they are **displaced,** or transferred, to socially appropriate members of the other gender.

Freud believed that by the age of 5 or 6, children have been in conflict with their parents over sexual feelings for several years. The pressures of the Oedipus and Electra complexes cause them to repress all sexual urges. In so doing, they enter a period of **latency** during which their sexual feelings remain unconscious. During the latency phase it is not uncommon for children to prefer playmates of their own gender.

Freud believed that we enter the final stage of psychosexual development, the **genital stage,** at puberty. Adolescent males again experience sexual urges toward their mother and adolescent females experience such urges toward their father. However, the **incest taboo** causes them to repress these impulses and displace them onto other adults or adolescents of the other gender. Boys might seek girls "just like the girl that married dear old Dad." Girls might be attracted to boys who resemble their fathers.

People in the genital stage prefer, by definition, to find sexual gratification through intercourse with a member of the other gender. In Freud's view, oral or anal stimulation, masturbation, and sexual activity with people of the same gender all represent *pregenital* fixations and immature forms of sexual conduct. They are not consistent with the life instinct, eros.

Other Psychodynamic Theorists

Several personality theorists are among Freud's intellectual heirs. Their theories, like his, include dynamic movement of psychological forces, conflict, and defense mechanisms. In other respects, their theories differ considerably. *Questions: Who are some other psychodynamic theorists? What are their views on personality?*

■ Carl Jung

Many of Carl Jung's concepts—such as those of the collective unconscious and of archetypes—remain highly popular among the general population. However, Jung's concepts, like Freud's, have been labeled as unscientific by most psychologists.

Carl Jung

Carl Jung (1875–1961) was a Swiss psychiatrist who had been a member of Freud's inner circle. He fell into disfavor with Freud when he developed his own psychodynamic theory—**analytical psychology.** In contrast to Freud (for whom, he said, "the brain is viewed as an appendage of the genital organs"), Jung downplayed the importance of the sexual instinct. He saw it as just one of several important instincts.

Jung, like Freud, was intrigued by unconscious processes. He believed that we not only have a *personal* unconscious that contains repressed memories and impulses but also an inherited **collective unconscious.** The collective unconscious contains primitive images, or **archetypes,** that reflect the history of our species. Examples of archetypes are the all-powerful God, the young hero, the fertile and nurturing mother, the wise old man, the hostile brother—even fairy godmothers, wicked witches, and themes of rebirth or resurrection. Archetypes themselves remain unconscious, but Jung declared that they influence our thoughts and emotions and cause us to respond to cultural themes in stories and films.

Anal Stage
The second stage of psychosexual development, when gratification is attained through anal activities.

Phallic Stage
The third stage of psychosexual development, characterized by a shift of libido to the phallic region. (From the Greek *phallos,* referring to an image of the penis. However, Freud used the term *phallic* to refer both to boys and girls.)

Clitoris
An external female sex organ that is highly sensitive to sexual stimulation.

Oedipus Complex
A conflict of the phallic stage in which the boy wishes to possess his mother sexually and perceives his father as a rival in love.

Electra Complex
A conflict of the phallic stage in which the girl longs for her father and resents her mother.

Displaced
Transferred.

Latency
A phase of psychosexual development characterized by repression of sexual impulses.

Genital Stage
The mature stage of psychosexual development, characterized by preferred expression of libido through intercourse with an adult of the other gender.

Incest Taboo
The cultural prohibition against marrying or having sexual relations with a close blood relative.

Analytical Psychology
Jung's psychodynamic theory, which emphasizes the collective unconscious and archetypes.

Collective Unconscious
Jung's hypothesized store of vague racial memories.

Archetypes
Basic, primitive images or concepts hypothesized by Jung to reside in the collective unconscious.

Inferiority Complex

Feelings of inferiority hypothesized by Adler to serve as a central motivating force.

Drive for Superiority

Adler's term for the desire to compensate for feelings of inferiority.

Creative Self

According to Adler, the self-aware aspect of personality that strives to achieve its full potential.

Individual Psychology

Adler's psychodynamic theory, which emphasizes feelings of inferiority and the creative self.

■ **Karen Horney**

Horney, like many of Freud's intellectual descendants, took issue with Freud on many issues. For one thing, Horney did not believe that little girls had penis envy or felt inferior to boys in any other way. She also believed that children's social relationships are more important in their development than unconscious sexual and aggressive impulses.

Alfred Adler

Alfred Adler (1870–1937), another follower of Freud, also felt that Freud had placed too much emphasis on sexual impulses. Adler believed that people are basically motivated by an **inferiority complex.** In some people, feelings of inferiority may be based on physical problems and the need to compensate for them. Adler believed, however, that all of us encounter some feelings of inferiority because of our small size as children, and that these feelings give rise to a **drive for superiority.** For instance, the English poet Lord Byron, who had a crippled leg, became a champion swimmer. As a child Adler was crippled by rickets and suffered from pneumonia, and it may be that his theory developed in part from his own childhood striving to overcome repeated bouts of illness.

Adler believed that self-awareness plays a major role in the formation of personality. He spoke of a **creative self,** a self-aware aspect of personality that strives to overcome obstacles and develop the individual's potential. Because each person's potential is unique, Adler's views have been termed **individual psychology.**

Karen Horney

She was drummed out of the New York Psychoanalytic Institute because she took issue with the way in which psychoanalytic theory portrayed women. Early in the century, psychoanalytic theory taught that a woman's place was in the home. Women who sought to compete with men in the business world were assumed to be suffering from unconscious penis envy. Psychoanalytic theory taught that little girls feel inferior to boys when they learn that boys have a penis and they do not. Karen Horney (1885–1952) argued that little girls do *not* feel inferior to boys, and that these views were founded on Western cultural prejudice, not scientific evidence.

Horney was born in Germany and emigrated to the United States before the outbreak of World War II. Trained in psychoanalysis, she agreed with Freud that childhood experiences are important factors in the development of adult personality. Like other neoanalysts, however, she asserted that unconscious sexual and aggressive impulses are less important than social relationships in children's development. She also believed that genuine and consistent love can alleviate the effects of even the most traumatic childhood.

Erik Erikson

Erik Erikson's natural father deserted his mother just before his birth, and the boy was raised by his mother and his stepfather, a physician named Theodor Homburger. They did not want the boy to feel different, so he was not told about his father until many years later. Though both his mother and his stepfather were Jewish, Erikson resembled his father, a Dane with blond hair and blue eyes. In his stepfather's synagogue, he was considered a Gentile. To his classmates, he was a Jew. He began to feel different from other children and alienated from his family. He fantasized that he was the offspring of special parents who had abandoned him. The question "Who am I?" permeated his adolescent quest for identity. As he matured, Erikson faced another identity issue: "What am I to do in life?" His stepfather encouraged him to attend medical school, but Erikson sought his own path. As a youth he studied art and traveled through Europe, leading the Bohemian life of an artist. This was a period of soul-searching that Erikson came to label an *identity crisis.* As a result of his own search for identity, he became oriented toward his life's work—psychotherapy. He left his wanderings and plunged into psychoanalytic training under the supervision of Sigmund Freud's daughter, Anna Freud.

Despite Erikson's grueling search for identity, he appears to have denied his own children information about their family. He and his wife institutionalized their fourth child, Neil, who was born with Down syndrome. But his biographer (Friedman, 1999) writes that the Eriksons told their older children that Neil had died after birth. Perhaps Erikson's upbeat view of life did not prepare him to handle such harsh reality, so he pushed it away (Edmundson, 1999).

Like many other modern psychoanalysts, Erik Erikson (1902–1994) believed that Freud had placed undue emphasis on sexual instincts. He asserted that social relationships are more crucial determinants of personality than sexual urges. To Erikson, the nature of the mother–infant relationship is more important than the details of the feeding process or the sexual feelings that might be stirred by contact with the mother. Erikson also argued that to a large extent we are the conscious architects of our own personalities. His view grants more powers to the ego than Freud did. In Erikson's theory, it is possible for us to make real choices. In Freud's theory, we may think that we are making choices when we are actually merely rationalizing the compromises forced upon us by internal conflicts.

Erikson, like Freud, is known for devising a comprehensive theory of personality development. But whereas Freud proposed stages of psycho*sexual* development, Erikson proposed stages of psycho*social* development. Rather than label stages for various erogenous zones, Erikson labeled them for the traits that might be developed during them (see Table 3.4). Each stage is named according to its possible outcomes. For example, the first stage of **psychosocial development** is labeled the stage of trust versus mistrust because of its two possible outcomes: (1) A warm, loving relationship with the mother (and others) during infancy might lead to a sense of basic trust in people and the world. (2) On the other hand, a cold, ungratifying relationship might generate a pervasive sense of mistrust. Erikson believed that most people would wind up with some blend of trust and mistrust—hopefully more trust than mistrust. A basic sense of mistrust could interfere with the formation of relationships unless it was recognized and challenged.

For Erikson, the goal of adolescence is the attainment of **ego identity,** not genital sexuality. The focus is on who we see ourselves as being and what we stand for, not on sexual interests.

Evaluation of the Psychodynamic Perspective

Psychodynamic theories have tremendous appeal. They involve many concepts and explain many varieties of human behavior and traits. *Question: What are the strengths and weaknesses of the psychodynamic perspective?*

Although today concepts such as "the id" and "libido" strike many psychologists as unscientific, Freud fought for the idea that human personality and behavior are subject to scientific analysis. He developed his theories at a time when many people still viewed psychological problems as signs of possession by the devil or evil spirits, as they had during the Middle Ages. Freud argued that psychological disorders stem from problems within the individual—not evil spirits. His thinking contributed to the development of compassion for people with psychological disorders and methods for helping them.

Psychodynamic theory has also focused attention on the far-reaching effects of childhood events. Freud and other psychodynamic theorists are to be credited for suggesting that personality and behavior *develop* and that it is important for parents to be aware of the emotional needs of their children.

Freud has helped us recognize that sexual and aggressive urges are commonplace and that there is a difference between acknowledging these urges and acting on them. As W. Bertram Wolfe put it, "Freud found sex an outcast in the outhouse, and left it in the living room an honored guest."

Freud also noted that people have defensive ways of looking at the world. His defense mechanisms have become part of everyday speech. Whether or not we attribute these cognitive distortions to unconscious ego functioning, our thinking may be distorted by our efforts to avert anxiety and guilt. Because defense mechanisms are unconscious, they have been difficult to assess and were rejected by academic psychologists in the 1950s and 1960s. However, the cognitive revolution of more recent years has again made them the subject of scientific investigation, and cognitive, developmental, and personality psychologists have found some evidence for their existence (Cramer, 2000; Somerfield & McCrae, 2000). The debate is unresolved.

A number of critics note that "psychic structures" such as the id, ego, and superego are too vague to measure scientifically (Hergenhahn, 2001). Nor can they be used to predict behavior with precision. They are little more than useful fictions—poetic ways

■ **Erik Erikson**
Erikson's preoccupation with the issue of self identity seems to reflect the conflicts he experienced about his own identity in his youth. He was reared as a Jew by his stepfather, but he had the Gentile appearance of his natural father. Like other modern-day analysts, Erikson believed that Freud had placed too much emphasis on sex and unconscious conflict. Erikson believed that social relationships were the key to healthful development.

Psychosocial Development
Erikson's theory of personality and development, which emphasizes social relationships and eight stages of growth.

Ego Identity
A firm sense of who one is and what one stands for.

to express inner conflict. Freud's critics thus have the right to use other descriptive terms.

Nor have the stages of psychosexual development escaped criticism. Children begin to masturbate as early as the first year, not in the phallic stage. As parents know from discovering their children play "doctor," the latency stage is not as sexually latent as Freud believed. Much of Freud's thinking about the Oedipus and Electra complexes remains little more than speculation. The evidence for some of Erikson's developmental views seems somewhat sturdier. For example, people who fail to develop ego identity in adolescence seem to encounter problems developing intimate relationships later on.

Freud's method of gathering evidence from clinical sessions is also suspect (Hergenhahn, 2001). In subtle ways, therapists may influence clients to produce memories and feelings they expect to find. Therapists may also fail to separate what they are told from their own interpretations. Also, Freud and many other psychodynamic theorists restricted their evidence gathering to case studies with individuals who sought help for psychological problems. Their clients were also mostly European and European American and from the middle and upper classes. People who seek therapy are likely to have more problems than the general population.

REFLECT

If Freud's theory is riddled with scientific shortcomings, why do you think it remains popular among the general population?

Learning Connections
See Web site for an interactive version of these review questions.

REVIEW

(1) Psychodynamic theories of personality teach that personality is characterized by _____ between primitive drives and laws, social rules, and moral codes. (2) According to Freud, the unconscious psychic structure called the _____ is present at birth and operates according to the pleasure principle. (3) The _____ is the sense of self and operates according to the reality principle. (4) The ego uses _____ mechanisms such as repression to protect itself from anxiety. (5) The _____ is the moral sense and develops by internalizing the standards of parents and others. (6) The stages of psychosexual development include the oral, _____, phallic, latency, and genital stages. (7) _____ in a stage may lead to the development of traits associated with the stage. (8) In the Oedipus and Electra complexes, children long to possess the parent of the (same or other?) gender and resent the parent of the same gender. (9) Jung believed that in addition to a personal unconscious mind, people also have a _____ unconscious. (10) Adler believed that people are motivated by an _____ complex. (11) Karen _____, like Freud, saw parent–child relationships as paramount in importance. (12) Erikson extended Freud's five developmental stages to (how many?).

Critical Thinking: Is your behavior controlled by conscious choice or by forces deep within? How would you be able to determine the answer?

THE TRAIT PERSPECTIVE: THE FIVE-DIMENSIONAL UNIVERSE

In most of us by the age of thirty, the character has set like plaster, and will never soften again.

—William James

The notion of **traits** is very familiar. If I asked you to describe yourself, you would probably do so in terms of traits such as bright, sophisticated, and witty. (That is you, is it not?) We also describe other people in terms of traits. **Question: What are traits?** Traits are reasonably stable elements of personality that are inferred from behavior. If you describe a friend as "shy," it may be because you have observed social anxiety or withdrawal in that person's encounters with others. Traits are assumed to account for consistent behavior in diverse situations. You probably expect your "shy" friend to be retiring in most social confrontations—"all across the board," as the saying goes.

Trait
A relatively stable aspect of personality that is inferred from behavior and assumed to give rise to consistent behavior.

The concept of traits is also found in other approaches to personality. Freud linked the development of certain traits to children's experiences in each stage of psychosexual development.

From Hippocrates to the Present

Question: What is the history of the trait perspective?   The trait perspective dates back to the Greek physician Hippocrates (ca. 460–377 BCE) and could be even older (Maher & Maher, 1994). It has generally been assumed that traits are embedded in people's bodies, but *how*? Hippocrates believed that traits are embedded in bodily fluids, which give rise to certain types of personalities. In his view, an individual's personality depends on the balance of four basic fluids, or "humors," in the body. Yellow bile is associated with a choleric (quick-tempered) disposition; blood with a sanguine (warm, cheerful) one; phlegm with a phlegmatic (sluggish, calm, cool) disposition; and black bile with a melancholic (gloomy, pensive) temperament. Disease was believed to reflect an imbalance among the humors. Methods such as bloodletting and vomiting were recommended to restore the balance (Maher & Maher, 1994). Although Hippocrates' theory was pure speculation, the terms *choleric, sanguine,* and so on are still used in descriptions of personality.

More enduring trait theories assume that traits are heritable and are embedded in the nervous system. They rely on the mathematical technique of factor analysis in attempting to determine which traits are basic.

Sir Francis Galton was among the first scientists to suggest that many of the world's languages use single words to describe fundamental differences in personality. More than 60 years ago, Gordon Allport and a colleague (Allport & Oddbert, 1936) catalogued some 18,000 human traits from a search through word lists like dictionaries. Some were physical traits such as *short, black,* and *brunette.* Others were behavioral traits such as *shy* and *emotional.* Still others were moral traits such as *honest.* This exhaustive list has served as the basis for personality research by many other psychologists.   *Question: How have contemporary researchers used factor analysis to reduce the universe of traits to smaller lists of traits that show common features?*

Hans Eysenck's Trait Theory: A Two-Dimensional View

Psychologist Hans J. Eysenck (1916–1997) was born in Berlin but moved to England in 1934 to escape the Nazi threat. Ironically, he was not allowed to enter the British military to fight the Nazis during World War II because he was still a German citizen (Farley, 2000).

Eysenck developed the first English training program for clinical psychologists and focused much of his research on the relationships between two personality traits: **introversion–extraversion** and emotional stability–instability (Eysenck & Eysenck, 1985). (Emotional *in*stability is also known as **neuroticism.**) Carl Jung was first to distinguish between introverts and extraverts. Eysenck added the dimension of emotional stability–instability to introversion–extraversion. He catalogued various personality traits according to where they are situated along these dimensions or factors (see Figure 11.2). For instance, an anxious person would be high in both introversion and neuroticism—that is, preoccupied with his or her own thoughts and emotionally unstable.

Eysenck noted that his scheme is reminiscent of that suggested by Hippocrates. According to Eysenck's dimensions, the choleric type would be extraverted and unstable; the sanguine type, extraverted and stable; the phlegmatic type, introverted and stable; and the melancholic type, introverted and unstable.

The Five-Factor Model

More recent research suggests that there may be five basic personality factors, not two. These include the two found by Eysenck—extraversion and neuroticism—along with conscientiousness, agreeableness, and openness to experience (see Table 11.2). Many personality theorists, especially Robert McCrae and Paul T. Costa, Jr., have played a role in the development of the five-factor model. Cross-cultural research has found

Introversion
A trait characterized by intense imagination and the tendency to inhibit impulses.

Extraversion
A trait characterized by tendencies to be socially outgoing and to express feelings and impulses freely.

Neuroticism
Eysenck's term for emotional instability.

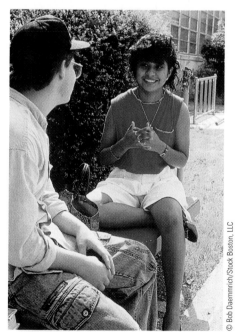

© Bob Daemmrich/Stock Boston, LLC

■ **An Extraverted Individual**

Hans Eysenck based much of his research on the relationships between two personality traits: introversion–extraversion and emotional stability–instability. Extraversion is characterized by tendencies to be socially outgoing and to freely express feelings and impulses. Some people are mostly extraverted, others mostly introverted, and some are balanced—both outgoing (extraverted) and reflective (introverted).

■ **Figure 11.2**
Eysenck's Personality Dimensions and Hippocrates' Personality Types

Various personality traits shown in the outer ring fall within the two major dimensions of personality suggested by Hans Eysenck. The inner circle shows how Hippocrates' four major personality types—choleric, sanguine, phlegmatic, and melancholic—fit within Eysenck's dimensions.

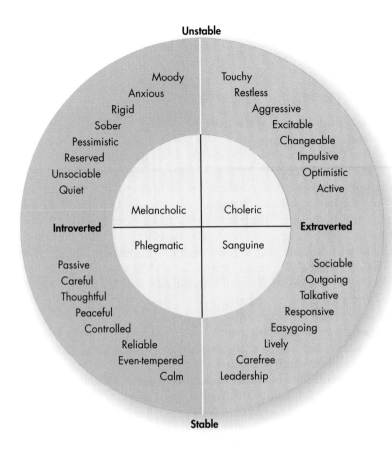

REFLECT

Are you conscientious? Are you open to experience? Is there such as thing as being too conscientious? As being too open to experience? Explain.

that these five factors appear to define the personality structure of American, German, Portuguese, Hebrew, Chinese, Korean, Japanese, and Philippine people (Katigbak et al., 2002; McCrae & Costa, 1997). A study of more than 5,000 German, British, Spanish, Czech, and Turkish people suggests that the factors are related to people's basic temperaments, which are considered to be largely inborn (McCrae et al., 2000). The researchers interpret the results to suggest that our personalities tend to mature rather than be shaped by environmental conditions, although the expression of personality traits is certainly affected by culture. (A person who is "basically" open to new experience is likely to behave less openly in a restrictive society than in an open society.)

The five-factor model—also known as the "Big Five" model—is hot right now. There are hundreds of studies correlating scores on the five factors, according to a psychological test constructed by Costa and McCrae (the *NEO Five-Factor Inventory*), with various behavior patterns, psychological disorders, and kinds of "personalities." Consider driving. Significant negative correlations have been found between the numbers

TABLE 11.2 The Five-Factor Model

Factor	Name	Traits
I	Extraversion	Contrasts talkativeness, assertiveness, and activity with silence, passivity, and reserve
II	Agreeableness	Contrasts kindness, trust, and warmth with hostility, selfishness, and distrust
III	Conscientiousness	Contrasts organization, thoroughness, and reliability with carelessness, negligence, and unreliability
IV	Neuroticism	Contrasts traits such as nervousness, moodiness, and sensitivity to negative stimuli with coping ability
V	Openness to experience	Contrasts imagination, curiosity, and creativity with shallowness and lack of perceptiveness

of tickets people get and accidents people get into, on the one hand, and the factor of agreeableness on the other (Cellar et al., 2000). As we have long suspected, it's safer to share the freeway with agreeable people. People who are not judgmental—who will put up with your every whim, like puppy dogs—tend to score low on conscientiousness (they don't examine you too closely) and high on agreeableness (you can be yourself; that's cool) (Bernardin et al., 2000).

A firm handshake is positively correlated with extraversion and negatively correlated with neuroticism (Chaplin et al., 2000). It is also connected with openness to experience—in women. Message? If you want to make a positive first impression, "Shake, baby, shake!" (Those are song lyrics, not sexism.)

The five-factor model is being used in the realm of politics. For example, studies in the United States (Butler, 2000) and Belgium and Poland (van Hiel et al., 2000) show that people who are right-wing authoritarians ("Do it the way it's always been done! Why? Because I say so!") score low on openness to experience ("Turn off that TV! Get off the Net now!" "There's no dancing in Beaumont!").

Researchers are also studying the way in which the five factors are connected with the ways in which people interact with their friends, lovers, and families (e.g., Wan et al., 2000; Wintre & Sugar, 2000). In the realm of psychological disorders, researchers are also studying links between the factors and disorders such as anxiety disorders, hypochondriasis (Cox et al., 2000), depression and suicide attempts (Duberstein et al., 2000), schizophrenia (Gurrera et al., 2000), and personality disorders (Widiger & Costa, 1994). The five-factor model is apparently helping us describe these disorders. It remains to be seen how well the model will enable us to explain, predict, and control them (that is, prevent them or come to the aid of people who develop them).

Evaluation of the Trait Perspective

Trait theories, like psychodynamic theories, have their pluses and minuses. ***Question: What are the strengths and weaknesses of trait theory?*** Trait theorists have focused much attention on the development of personality tests. They have also given rise to theories about the fit between personality and certain kinds of jobs (Holland, 1996). The qualities that suit a person for various kinds of work can be expressed in terms of abilities, personality traits, and interests. By using interviews and tests to learn about an individual's abilities and traits, testing and counseling centers can make valuable suggestions about that person's chances of success and fulfillment in various kinds of jobs.

One limitation of trait theory is that it has tended to be more descriptive than explanatory. It has historically focused on describing traits rather than on tracing their origins or finding out how they may be modified. Moreover, the "explanations" provided by trait theory are sometimes criticized as being **circular.** That is, they restate what is observed and do not explain it. Saying that John failed to ask Marsha on a date *because* of shyness is an example of a circular explanation: We have merely restated John's (shy) behavior as a trait (shyness). If asked to account for the shyness, it can be of little help to be told whether or not it is a "basic" trait, and suggesting that shyness is largely inborn does not quite explain *how* it is inborn or what we can do about it.

Circular
Descriptive of an explanation that restates its own concepts instead of offering additional information.

R E V I E W

(13) _____ are personality elements that endure and account for behavioral consistency. (14) Eysenck used factor analysis to derive two basic traits: introversion–extraversion and emotional _____. (15) Five-factor theory suggests that there are five basic personality factors: introversion–extraversion, emotional stability, _____, agreeableness, and openness to experience.

Learning Connections
See Web site for an interactive version of these review questions.

Critical Thinking: The trait theories of Hippocrates and Eysenck are similar. Is one more scientific than the other?

LEARNING-THEORY PERSPECTIVES: ALL THE THINGS YOU DO

Learning theory not only contributes to our understanding of the acquisition of behavior. It also contributes to our understanding of personality. *Question: What does learning theory have to contribute to our understanding of personality?* In this section we focus on the contributions of two learning-theory approaches to personality: behaviorism and social–cognitive theory.

Behaviorism

You have freedom when you're easy in your harness.

—Robert Frost

In 1924, at Johns Hopkins University, John B. Watson raised the battle cry of the behaviorist movement:

> Give me a dozen healthy infants, well-formed, and my own specified world to bring them up in and I'll guarantee to take any one at random and train him to become any type of specialist I might suggest—doctor, lawyer, merchant-chief and, yes, even beggar-man and thief, regardless of his talents, penchants, tendencies, abilities, vocations, and the race of his ancestors. (p. 82)

Question: What is Watson's contribution to personality theory? Watson's view is extreme and inconsistent with the thrust of evidence concerning the heritability of various personality traits. But his proclamation underscores the behaviorist view that personality is plastic—that situational variables or environmental influences, not internal, individual variables, are the key shapers of human preferences and behaviors. In contrast to the psychoanalysts and structuralists of his day, Watson argued that unseen, undetectable mental structures must be rejected in favor of that which can be seen and measured.

In the 1930s Watson's battle cry was taken up by B. F. Skinner, who agreed that psychologists should avoid trying to see into the "black box" of the organism and instead emphasized the effects that reinforcements have on behavior.

The views of Watson and Skinner largely ignored the notions of personal freedom, choice, and self-direction. Most of us assume that our wants originate within us. But Skinner suggested that environmental influences such as parental approval and social custom shape us into *wanting* certain things and *not wanting* others.

Question: How did Skinner develop Watson's views? In his novel *Walden Two*, Skinner (1948) described a Utopian society in which people are happy and content because they are allowed to do as they please. However, from early childhood, they have been trained or conditioned to be cooperative. Because of their reinforcement histories, they *want* to behave in decent, kind, and unselfish ways. They see themselves as free because society makes no effort to force them to behave in particular ways.

Some object to behaviorist notions because they play down the importance of consciousness and choice. Others argue that humans are not blindly ruled by pleasure and pain. In some circumstances people have rebelled against the so-called necessity of survival by choosing pain and hardship over pleasure, or death over life. Many people have sacrificed their own lives to save those of others.

The behaviorist defense might be that the apparent choice of pain or death is forced on altruistic individuals just as conformity to social custom is forced on others. The altruist is also shaped by external influences, even if those influences differ from those that affect many other people.

Social–Cognitive Theory

Social–cognitive theory[1] is a contemporary view of learning developed by Albert Bandura (1986, 1999) and other psychologists (e.g., Mischel & Shoda, 1995). It focuses on the importance of learning by observation and on the cognitive processes that underlie individual differences. *Question: How does social–cognitive theory differ from the behaviorist view?* Social–cognitive theorists differ from behaviorists in that they see people as influencing their environment just as their environment influences them. Bandura terms this mutual pattern of influence **reciprocal determinism.** Social–cognitive theorists agree with behaviorists and other empirical psychologists that discussions of human nature should be tied to observable experiences and behaviors. They assert, however, that variables within people—which they call **person variables**—must also be considered if we are to understand them.

One goal of psychological theories is the prediction of behavior. We cannot predict behavior from situational variables alone. Whether a person will behave in a certain way also depends on the person's **expectancies** about the outcomes of that behavior and the perceived or **subjective values** of those outcomes.

To social–cognitive theorists, people are not simply at the mercy of the environment. Instead, they are self-aware and purposefully engage in learning. They seek to learn about their environment and to alter it in order to make reinforcers available.

Observational Learning

Observational learning (also termed **modeling** or *cognitive learning*) refers to acquiring knowledge by observing others. For operant conditioning to occur, (1) an organism must engage in a response, and (2) that response must be reinforced. But observational learning occurs even when the learner does not perform the observed behavior. Therefore, direct reinforcement is not required either. Observing others extends to reading about them or seeing what they do and what happens to them in books, TV, radio, and film.

[1]The name of this theory is in flux. It was formerly referred to as social-learning theory. Today it is also sometimes referred to as *cognitive social theory* (Miller et al., 1996).

Social–Cognitive Theory
A cognitively oriented learning theory in which observational learning and person variables such as values and expectancies play major roles in individual differences.

Reciprocal Determinism
Bandura's term for the social–cognitive view that people influence their environment just as their environment influences them.

Person Variables
Factors within the person, such as expectancies and competencies, that influence behavior.

Expectancies
Personal predictions about the outcomes of potential behaviors.

Subjective Value
The desirability of an object or event.

Model
In social–cognitive theory, an organism that exhibits behaviors that others will imitate or acquire through observational learning.

Our expectations stem from our observations of what happens to ourselves and other people. For example, teachers are more likely to call on males and more accepting of "calling out" in class by males than by females (Sadker & Sadker, 1994). As a result, many males expect to be rewarded for calling out. Females, however, may learn that they will be reprimanded for behaving in what some might term an "unladylike" manner.

Social–cognitive theorists believe that behavior reflects person variables and situational variables. Person variables include competencies, encoding strategies, expectancies, emotions, and self-regulatory systems and plans (Cervone & Mischel, 2002; Mischel & Shoda, 1995; see Figure 11.3).

Competencies: What Can You Do?

Competencies include knowledge of rules that guide conduct, concepts about ourselves and other people, and skills. Our ability to use information to make plans depends on our competencies. Knowledge of the physical world and of cultural codes of conduct are important competencies. So are academic skills such as reading and writing, athletic skills such as swimming and tossing a football, social skills such as knowing how to ask someone out on a date, and many others. Individual differences in competencies reflect genetic variation, learning opportunities, and other environmental factors. People do not perform well at given tasks unless they have the competencies needed to do so.

Encoding Strategies: How Do You See It?

Different people **encode** (symbolize or represent) the same stimuli in different ways. Their encoding strategies are an important factor in their behavior. One person might encode a tennis game as a chance to bat the ball back and forth and have some fun. Another person might encode the game as a demand to perfect his or her serve. One person might encode a date that doesn't work out as a sign of her or his social incompetence. Another person might encode the date as reflecting the fact that people are not always "made for each other."

Some people make themselves miserable by encoding events in self-defeating ways. A linebacker may encode an average day on the field as a failure because he didn't make any sacks. Cognitive therapists foster adjustment by challenging people to view life in more optimistic ways.

REFLECT

What competencies do you have? How did they develop?

Competencies
Knowledge and skills.

Encode
Interpret; transform.

■ **Figure 11.3**
Person Variables and Situational Variables in Social–Cognitive Theory

According to social–cognitive theory, person variables and situational variables interact to influence behavior.

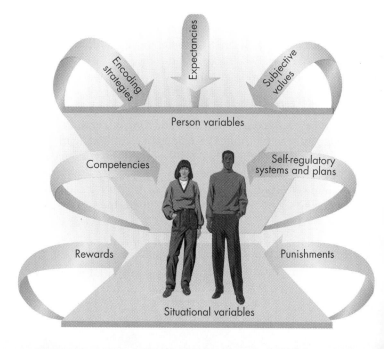

Expectancies: What Will Happen?

There are various kinds of expectancies. Some are predictions about what will follow various stimuli or signs. For example, some people predict other people's behavior on the basis of signs such as "tight lips" or "shifty eyes" (Ross & Nisbett, 1991). Other expectancies involve what will happen if we engage in certain behaviors. **Self-efficacy expectations** are beliefs that we can accomplish certain things, such as speaking before a group, doing a backflip into a swimming pool, or solving math problems (Bandura, 1997).

Competencies influence expectancies. Expectancies, in turn, influence motivation to perform. People with positive self-efficacy expectations have higher self-esteem (Sanna & Meier, 2000) and are more likely to try difficult tasks than people who do not believe that they can master those tasks (Heimpel et al., 2002). Lack of belief in self-efficacy is often associated with depression and hopelessness (Bandura et al., 1999). One way that psychotherapy helps people is by changing their self-efficacy expectations from "I can't" to "I can" (Bandura, 1999). As a result, people are motivated to try new things.

Emotions: How Does It Feel?

Because of our different learning histories, similar situations can arouse different feelings in us—anxiety, depression, fear, hopelessness, and anger. What frightens one person may entice another. What bores one person may excite another. From the social–cognitive perspective, in contrast to the behaviorist perspective, we are not controlled by stimuli. Instead, stimuli arouse feelings in us, and feelings influence our behavior. Hearing Chopin may make one person weep and another person switch to a rock 'n' roll station.

Self-Regulatory Systems and Plans: How Can You Achieve It?

We tend to regulate our own behavior, even in the absence of observers and external constraints. We set our own goals and standards. We make plans to achieve them. We congratulate or criticize ourselves, depending on whether or not we achieve them (Bandura, 1999).

Self-regulation helps us influence our environments. We can select the situations to which we expose ourselves and the arenas in which we will compete. Depending on our expectancies, we may choose to enter the academic or athletic worlds. We may choose marriage or the single life. And when we cannot readily select our environment, we can to some degree select our responses within an environment—even an aversive one. For example, if we are undergoing an uncomfortable medical procedure, we may try to reduce the stress by focusing on something else—an inner fantasy or an environmental feature such as the cracks in the tiles on the ceiling. This is one of the techniques used in prepared or "natural" childbirth.

Evaluation of the Learning Perspective

Learning theorists have made monumental contributions to the scientific understanding of behavior, but they have left some psychologists dissatisfied. *Question: What are the strengths and weaknesses of learning theories as they apply to personality?*

Psychodynamic theorists and trait theorists propose the existence of psychological structures that cannot be seen and measured directly. Learning theorists—particularly behaviorists—have dramatized the importance of referring to publicly observable variables, or behaviors, if psychology is to be accepted as a science.

Similarly, psychodynamic theorists and trait theorists focus on internal variables such as unconscious conflict and traits to explain and predict behavior. Learning theorists emphasize the importance of environmental conditions, or situational variables, as determinants of behavior. They have also elaborated on the conditions that foster learning—even automatic kinds of learning. They have shown that we can learn to do things because of reinforcements and that many behavior patterns are acquired by observing others.

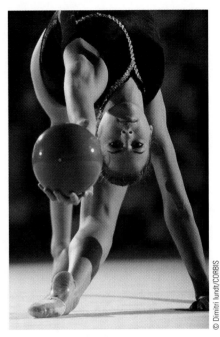

© Dimitri Iundt/CORBIS

■ **How Do Competencies Contribute to Performance?**
What factors contribute to this girl's performance? Individual differences in competencies stem from variations in genetic endowment, nutrition, and learning opportunities.

R E F L E C T

Do you expect that you will succeed? Do you believe in your abilities? How do your attitudes toward yourself affect your self-esteem and your behavior?

Self-Efficacy Expectations
Beliefs to the effect that one can handle a task.

On the other hand, behaviorism is limited in its ability to explain personality. Behaviorism does not describe, explain, or even suggest the richness of inner human experience. We experience thoughts and feelings and browse through our complex inner maps of the world, but behaviorism does not deal with these. To be fair, the so-called limitations of behaviorism are self-imposed. Personality theorists have traditionally dealt with thoughts, feelings, and behavior, whereas behaviorism, which insists on studying only that which is observable and measurable, deals with behavior alone.

Critics of social–cognitive theory cannot accuse its supporters of denying the importance of cognitive activity and feelings. But they often contend that social–cognitive theory has not come up with satisfying statements about the development of traits or accounted for self-awareness. Also, social–cognitive theory—like its intellectual forebear, behaviorism—may not pay enough attention to genetic variation in explaining individual differences in behavior. Learning theories have done very little to account for the development of traits or personality types.

Learning Connections
See Web site for an interactive version of these review questions.

REVIEW

(16) The behaviorists John B. Watson and B. F. _____ argued that environmental contingencies shape people into wanting to do the things that are required of them. (17) _____–cognitive theory argues that people can shape the environment and learn by intention. (18) Social–cognitive theorists believe that we must consider situational and _____ variables to predict behavior. (19) _____ variables include competencies, which refer to knowledge and skills; encoding strategies; expectancies; emotions; and self-regulatory systems and plans.

Critical Thinking: Given cultural and social conditioning, is true freedom possible? To behaviorists, even our telling ourselves that we have free will is determined by the environment. Is free will merely an illusion? Explain.

THE HUMANISTIC–EXISTENTIAL PERSPECTIVE: HOW BECOMING?

You are unique, and if that is not fulfilled, then something has been lost.

—Martha Graham

REFLECT
Do you know anyone who seems to be alienated? How is the person alienated? What do you think led to feelings of alienation?

Humanism
The view that people are capable of free choice, self-fulfillment, and ethical behavior.

Existentialism
The view that people are completely free and responsible for their own behavior.

Humanists and existentialists dwell on the meaning of life. Self-awareness is the hub of the humanistic–existential search for meaning. *Questions: What is humanism? What is existentialism?*

The term **humanism** has a long history and many meanings. It became a third force in American psychology in the 1950s and 1960s, partly in response to the predominant psychodynamic and behavioral models. Humanism puts people and self-awareness at the center of consideration and argues that they are capable of free choice, self-fulfillment, and ethical behavior. Humanism also represented a reaction to the "rat race" spawned by industrialization and automation. Humanists felt that work on assembly lines produced "alienation" from inner sources of meaning. The humanistic views of Abraham Maslow and Carl Rogers emerged from these concerns.

Existentialism in part reflects the horrors of mass destruction of human life through war and genocide, frequent events in the 20th century. The European existentialist philosophers Jean-Paul Sartre and Martin Heidegger saw human life as trivial in the grand scheme of things. But psychiatrists like Viktor Frankl, Ludwig Binswanger, and Medard Boss argued that seeing human existence as meaningless could give rise to withdrawal and apathy—even suicide. Psychological salvation therefore requires giving personal meaning to things and making personal choices. Yes, there is pain in life, and yes, sooner or later life ends, but people can see the world for what it is and make genuine choices.

Freud argued that defense mechanisms prevent us from seeing the world as it is. Therefore, the concept of free choice is meaningless. Behaviorists view freedom as an illusion determined by social forces. Social–cognitive theorists also speak of external or situational forces that influence us. To existentialists, we are really and painfully free to do what we choose with our lives. Moreover, the meaning of our lives is the meaning that we give to our lives.

Abraham Maslow and the Challenge of Self-Actualization

Humanists see Freud as preoccupied with the "basement" of the human condition. Freud wrote that people are basically motivated to gratify biological drives and that their perceptions are distorted by their psychological needs. ***Question: How do humanistic psychologists differ from psychodynamic theorists?*** The humanistic psychologist Abraham Maslow argued that people also have a conscious need for **self-actualization**—to become all that they can be—and that people can see the world as it is. Because people are unique, they must follow unique paths to self-actualization. People are not at the mercy of unconscious, primitive impulses. Rather, one of the main threats to individual personality development is control by other people. We must each be free to get in touch with and actualize our selves. But self-actualization requires taking risks. Many people prefer to adhere to the tried and . . . what may be

Self-Actualization

In humanistic theory, the innate tendency to strive to realize one's potential.

Self-Assessment ☑

Questionnaire: Do You Strive to Be All That You Can Be?

Are you a self-actualizer? Do you strive to be all that you can be? Psychologist Abraham Maslow attributed the following eight characteristics to the self-actualizing individual. How many of them describe you? Why not check them and undertake some self-evaluation?

Yes   No

1. *Do you fully experience life in the present—the here and now?* (Self-actualizers do not focus excessively on the lost past or wish their lives away as they stride toward distant goals.)

2. *Do you make growth choices rather than fear choices?* (Self-actualizers take reasonable risks to develop their unique potentials. They do not bask in the dull life of the status quo. They do not "settle.")

3. *Do you seek to acquire self-knowledge?* (Self-actualizers look inward. They search for values, talents, and meaningfulness. It might be enlightening to take an interest inventory—a test frequently used to help make career decisions—at your college testing and counseling center.)

4. *Do you strive toward honesty in interpersonal relationships?* (Self-actualizers strip away the social facades and games that stand in the way of self-disclosure and the formation of intimate relationships.)

5. *Do you behave self-assertively and express your own ideas and feelings, even at the risk of occasional social disapproval?* (Self-actualizers do not bottle up their feelings for the sake of avoiding social disapproval.)

Yes   No

6. *Do you strive toward new goals? Do you strive to be the best that you can be in a chosen life role?* (Self-actualizers do not live by the memory of past accomplishments. Nor do they present second-rate efforts.)

7. *Do you seek meaningful and rewarding life activities?* Do you experience moments of actualization that humanistic psychologists call *peak experiences*? (Peak experiences are brief moments of rapture filled with personal meaning. Examples might include completing a work of art, falling in love, redesigning a machine tool, suddenly solving a complex problem in math or physics, or having a baby. Note that we differ as individuals; one person's peak experience might bore another person silly.)

8. *Do you remain open to new experiences?* (Self-acualizers do not hold themselves back for fear that novel experiences might shake their views of the world, or of right and wrong. Self-actualizers are willing to revise their expectations, values, and opinions.)

■ Unique

According to humanistic psychologists like Carl Rogers, each of us views the world from a unique frame of reference. What matters to one person may mean little to another.

R E F L E C T

How is your own frame of reference unique? Think of some things that are unique about you. (Yes—you can!)

Were you shown unconditional or conditional positive regard as a child? What were the effects on you?

Frame of Reference

One's unique patterning of perceptions and attitudes according to which one evaluates events.

Unconditional Positive Regard

A persistent expression of esteem for the value of a person, but not necessarily an unqualified acceptance of all of the person's behaviors.

Conditional Positive Regard

Judgment of another person's value on the basis of the acceptability of that person's behaviors.

Conditions of Worth

Standards by which the value of a person is judged.

untrue for them. But people who adhere to the "tried and true" may find their lives degenerating into monotony and predictability.

Let us learn more about the nature of the self by examining Carl Rogers's self theory. Rogers offers insights into the ways in which the self develops—or fails to develop—in the real social world.

Carl Rogers's Self Theory

The humanistic psychologist Carl Rogers (1902–1987) wrote that people shape themselves—their selves—through free choice and action. ***Questions: Just what is your self? What is self theory?***

Rogers defined the *self* as the center of experience. Your self is your ongoing sense of who and what you are, your sense of how and why you react to the environment and how you choose to act on the environment. Your choices are made on the basis of your values, and your values are also part of your self. Rogers's self theory focuses on the nature of the self and the conditions that allow the self to develop freely. Two of his major concerns are the self-concept and self-esteem.

The Self-Concept and Frames of Reference

Our self-concepts consist of our impressions of ourselves and our evaluations of our adequacy. It may be helpful to think of us as rating ourselves according to various scales or dimensions such as good–bad, intelligent–unintelligent, strong–weak, and tall–short.

Rogers believed that we all have unique ways of looking at ourselves and the world—that is, unique **frames of reference.** It may be that we each use a different set of dimensions in defining ourselves and that we judge ourselves according to different sets of values. To one person, achievement–failure may be the most important dimension. To another person, the most important dimension may be decency–indecency. A third person may not even think in terms of decency.

Self-Esteem and Positive Regard

Rogers assumed that we all develop a need for self-regard, or self-esteem, as we develop and become aware of ourselves. At first, self-esteem reflects the esteem in which others hold us. Parents help children develop self-esteem when they show them **unconditional positive regard**—that is, when they accept them as having intrinsic merit regardless of their behavior at the moment. But when parents show children **conditional positive regard**—that is, when they accept them only when they behave in a desired manner—children may develop **conditions of worth.** That is, they may come to think that they have merit only if they behave as their parents wish them to behave.

Because each individual is thought to have a unique potential, children who develop conditions of worth must be somewhat disappointed in themselves. We cannot fully live up to the wishes of others and remain true to ourselves. This does not mean that the expression of the self inevitably leads to conflict. Rogers was optimistic about human nature. He believed that we hurt others or act in antisocial ways only when we are frustrated in our efforts to develop our potential. But when parents and others are loving and tolerant of our differentness, we, too, are loving—even if some of our preferences, abilities, and values differ from those of our parents.

However, children in some families learn that it is bad to have ideas of their own, especially about sexual, political, or religious matters. When they perceive their caregivers' disapproval, they may come to see themselves as rebels and label their feelings as selfish, wrong, or evil. If they wish to retain a consistent self-concept and self-esteem, they may have to deny many of their feelings or disown aspects of themselves. In this way the self-concept becomes distorted. According to Rogers, anxiety often stems from recognition that people have feelings and desires that are inconsistent with their distorted self-concept. Because anxiety is unpleasant, people may deny the existence of their genuine feelings and desires.

According to Rogers, the path to self-actualization requires getting in touch with our genuine feelings, accepting them, and acting on them. This is the goal of Rogers's method of psychotherapy, *client-centered therapy.*

Rogers also believed that we have mental images of what we are capable of becoming. These are termed **self-ideals.** We are motivated to reduce the discrepancy between our self-concepts and our self-ideals.

Evaluation of the Humanistic–Existential Perspective

Question: What are the strengths and weaknesses of humanistic–existential theory?   Humanistic–existential theories have tremendous appeal for college students because of their focus on the importance of personal experience. We tend to treasure our conscious experiences (our "selves") and those of the people we care about. For lower organisms, to be alive is to move, to process food, to exchange oxygen and carbon dioxide, and to reproduce. But for human beings, an essential aspect of life is conscious experience—the sense of oneself as progressing through space and time.

Psychodynamic theories see individuals largely as victims of their childhood. Learning theories, to some degree, see people as "victims of circumstances"—or at least as victims of situational variables. But humanistic–existential theorists see humans as free to make choices. Psychodynamic theorists and learning theorists wonder whether our sense of freedom is merely an illusion. Humanistic–existential theorists, in contrast, begin by assuming personal freedom.

Ironically, the primary strength of the humanistic–existential approaches—their focus on conscious experience—is also their main weakness. Conscious experience is private and subjective. Therefore, the validity of formulating theories in terms of consciousness has been questioned. On the other hand, some psychologists (e.g., Bevan & Kessel, 1994) believe that the science of psychology can afford to loosen its methods somewhat if this will help it address the richness of human experience.

Self-actualization, like trait theory, yields circular explanations for behavior. When we see someone engaging in what seems to be positive striving, we gain little insight by attributing this behavior to a self-actualizing force. We have done nothing to account for the origins of the force. And when we observe someone who is not engaging in growth-oriented striving, it seems arbitrary to "explain" this outcome by suggesting that the self-actualizing tendency has been blocked or frustrated.

Humanistic–existential theories, like learning theories, have little to say about the development of traits and personality types. They assume that we are all unique, but they do not predict the sorts of traits, abilities, and interests we will develop.

REVIEW

(20) The humanistic view argues that people (are or are not?) capable of free choice and self-fulfillment. (21) _____ assert that our lives have the meaning we give to them. (22) Maslow argued that people have growth-oriented needs for self-_____. (23) Rogers's theory begins with the assumption of the existence of the _____. (24) We see the world through unique frames of _____.

Critical Thinking: If humanistic–existential theory is less scientific than some other views of personality, how do we explain its enduring popularity?

Self-Ideal
A mental image of what we believe we ought to be.

Learning Connections
See Web site for an interactive version of these review questions.

THE SOCIOCULTURAL PERSPECTIVE: PERSONALITY IN CONTEXT

Thirteen-year-old Hannah brought her lunch tray to the table in the cafeteria. Her mother, Julie, eyed with horror the french fries, the plate of mashed potatoes in gravy, the bag of potato chips, and the large paper cup brimming with soda. "You can't eat that!" she said. "It's garbage!"

"Oh come on, Mom! Chill, okay?" Hannah rejoined before taking her tray to sit with some friends rather than with us.

I used to spend Saturdays with my children at the Manhattan School of Music. Not only do they study voice and piano. They—and I—have widened our cultural perspective by relating to families and students from all parts of the world.

Julie and Hannah are Korean Americans. Flustered, Julie shook her head and said, "I've now been in the United States longer than I was in Korea, and I still can't get used to the way children act here." Dimitri, a Russian American parent, chimed in. "I never would have spoken to my parents the way Michael speaks to me. I would have been . . . whipped or beaten."

"I try to tell Hannah she is part of the family," Julie continued. "She should think of other people. When she talks that way, it's embarrassing."

"Over here children are not part of the family," said Ken, an African American parent. "They are either part of their own crowd or they are 'individuals.'"

"Being an individual does not mean you have to talk back to your mother," Julie said. "What do you think, Spencer? You're the psychologist."

I think I made some unhelpful comments about the ketchup on the french fries having antioxidants and some slightly helpful comments about what is typical of teenagers in the United States. But I'm not sure, because I was thinking deeply about Hannah at the time. Not about her lunch, but about the formation of her personality and the influences on her behavior.

Question: Why is the sociocultural perspective important to the understanding of personality? As I thought about Hannah, I realized that in our multicultural society, personality cannot be understood without reference to the **sociocultural perspective.** According to a *New York Times* poll, 91% of people in the United States agree that "being an American is a big part" of who they are (Powers, 2000). Seventy-nine percent say that their religion has played a big role or some role in making them who they are, and 54% say that their race has played a big role or some role (Powers, 2000). Different cultural groups within the United States have different attitudes, beliefs, norms, self-definitions, and values (Basic Behavioral Science Task Force, 1996c; Phinney, 2000).

Back to Hannah. Perhaps there were some unconscious psychodynamic influences operating on her. Her traits included exceptional academic ability and musical talent, which were at least partly determined by her heredity. Clearly, she was consciously striving to become a great violinist. But one could not fully understand her personality without also considering the sociocultural influences acting on her.

Here was a youngster who was strongly influenced by her peers—she was completely at home with blue jeans and french fries. She was also a daughter in an Asian American immigrant group that views education as the key to success in our culture (Gibson & Ogbu, 1991; Ogbu, 1993). Belonging to this ethnic group had certainly contributed to her ambition. But being a Korean American had not prevented her from becoming an outspoken American teenager. (Would she have been outspoken if she had been reared in Korea? I wondered. Of course, this question cannot be answered with certainty.) Her outspoken behavior had struck her mother as brazen and inappropriate. Julie was deeply offended by behavior that I consider acceptable in my own children. She reeled off the things that were "wrong" with Hannah from her Korean American perspective. I listed some things that were very right with Hannah and encouraged Julie to worry less.

Let us consider how sociocultural factors can affect one's sense of self.

Individualism Versus Collectivism

Sociocultural Perspective
The view that focuses on the roles of ethnicity, gender, culture, and socioeconomic status in personality formation, behavior, and mental processes.

Individualist
A person who defines herself or himself in terms of personal traits and gives priority to her or his own goals.

One could say that Julie's complaint was that Hannah saw herself as an individual and an artist to a greater extent than as a family member and a Korean girl. *Questions: What does it mean to be individualistic? What is meant by individualism and collectivism?* Cross-cultural research reveals that people in the United States and many northern European nations tend to be individualistic. **Individualists** tend to define themselves in terms of their personal identities and to give priority to their personal goals (Triandis, 2001). When asked to complete the statement "I am . . . ," they are likely to respond in terms of their personality traits ("I am outgoing," "I am artistic") or their occupations ("I am a nurse," "I am a systems analyst") (Triandis & Suh, 2002). In contrast, many people from cultures in Africa, Asia, and Central and South America tend to be collectivistic (Basic Behavioral Science Task Force, 1996c). **Collectivists** tend to define themselves in terms of the groups to which they belong and to give priority to the group's goals (Triandis, 2001). They feel complete in terms of their relationships with others (Markus & Kitayama, 1991; see Figure 11.4). They are more likely than individualists to conform to group norms and judgments (Triandis & Suh, 2002). When asked to complete the statement "I am . . . ," they are more likely to respond in terms of their families, gender, or nation ("I am a father," "I am a Buddhist," "I am a Japanese") (Triandis, 2001).

The seeds of individualism and collectivism are found in the culture in which a person grows up. The capitalist system fosters individualism to some degree. It assumes that individuals are entitled to amass personal fortunes and that the process of doing so creates jobs and wealth for large numbers of people. The individualist perspective is found in the self-reliant heroes and antiheroes of Western literature and mass media—from Homer's Odysseus to Clint Eastwood's gritty cowboys and Walt Disney's Pocahontas. The traditional writings of the East have exalted people who resisted personal temptations in order to do their duty and promote the welfare of the group.

Another issue from the sociocultural perspective is acculturation. Just how much acculturation is good for you? *Question: How does acculturation affect the psychological well-being of immigrants and their families?*

▶ CONTROVERSY IN PSYCHOLOGY ◀

Just how much acculturation is enough?

Should Hindu women who emigrate to the United States surrender the sari in favor of California casuals? Should Russian immigrants try to teach their children English at home? Should African American children be acquainted with the music and art of African peoples or those of Europe? Such activities are examples of **acculturation,** in which immigrants become acclimated to the customs and behavior patterns of their new host culture.

How do various patterns of acculturation affect the individual? The answer to the question probably depends on the variables one chooses to measure. Consider that catch-all of psychological well-being: self-esteem. Self-esteem has been shown to be connected with patterns of acculturation among immigrants (Phinney et al., 1997). Those patterns take various forms. Some immigrants are completely assimilated by the dominant culture. They lose the language and customs of their country of origin and become like the dominant culture in the new host country. Others maintain almost complete separation. They retain the language and customs of their country of origin and never acclimate to those of the new country. Still others become bicultural (Ryder et al., 2000). For example, they remain fluent in the language of their country of origin but also become conversant in the language of their new country. They also blend the

REFLECT
Do you see yourself as individualistic or collectivistic? Explain.

Collectivist
A person who defines her- or himself in terms of relationships to other people and groups and gives priority to group goals.

Acculturation
The process of adaptation in which immigrants and native groups identify with a new, dominant culture by learning about that culture and making behavioral and attitudinal changes.

■ Figure 11.4
The Self in Relation to Others from the Individualist and Collectivist Perspectives

To an individualist, the self is separate from other people (Part A). To a collectivist, the self is complete only in terms of relationships to other people (Part B). (Based on Markus & Kitayama, 1991).

A. Independent View of Self

B. Interdependent View of Self

■ Personality and Acculturation

This Latina American is highly accultur-ated to life in the United States. Some immigrants are completely assimilated by the dominant culture and abandon the language and customs of their country of origin. Others retain the lan-guage and customs of their country of origin and never become comfortable with those of their new country. Still others become bicultural. They become fluent in both languages and blend the customs and values of both cultures.

Learning Connections
See Web site for an interactive version of these review questions.

Behavior-Rating Scale

A systematic means for recording the frequency with which target behaviors occur.

customs and values of both cultures. They can switch "mental gears"—that is, they apply the values of one culture under some circumstances and apply the values of the other culture under others (Hong et al., 2000). Perhaps they relate to other people in one way at work or in school, and in another way at home or in the neighborhood.

Research evidence suggests that people who identify with the bicultural pattern have the highest self-esteem (Phinney et al., 1997; Phinney & Devich-Navarro, 1997). For example, Mexican Americans who are more proficient in English are less likely to be anxious and depressed than less-proficient Mexican Americans (Salgado de Snyder et al., 1990). The ability to adapt to the ways of the new society, combined with a sup-portive cultural tradition and a sense of ethnic identity, apparently helps people adjust.

Evaluation of the Sociocultural Perspective

The sociocultural perspective provides valuable insights into the roles of ethnicity, gender, culture, and socioeconomic status in personality formation. When we ignore sociocultural factors, we deal only with the core of the human being—the potentials that allow the person to adapt to external forces. Sociocultural factors are external forces that are internalized. They run through us deeply, touching many aspects of our cognitions, motives, emotions, and behavior. Without reference to sociocultural fac-tors, we may be able to understand generalities about behavior and cognitive processes. However, we will not be able to understand how individuals think, behave, and feel about themselves within a given cultural setting. The sociocultural perspec-tive enhances our sensitivity to cultural differences and expectations and allows us to appreciate the richness of human behavior and mental processes.

The "In Review" chart on pages 438–439 summarizes various theories of personality.

REVIEW

(25) The _____ perspective considers the influences of ethnicity, gender, and socioeconomic status on personality. (26) _____ define themselves in terms of their personal identities and give priority to their personal goals. (27) _____ define themselves in terms of the groups to which they belong and give priority to group goals. (28) Immigrants who identify with the bicultural pattern of assimilation have the (highest or lowest?) self-esteem.

Critical Thinking: Can one "believe in" more than one theory of personality? For example, could one accept the sociocultural perspective *along with* another perspective?

MEASUREMENT OF PERSONALITY

Methods of personality assessment take a sample of behavior to predict future behav-ior. Standardized interviews are often used. Some psychologists use computers to con-duct routine interviews. **Behavior-rating scales** assess behavior in settings such as classrooms or mental hospitals. With behavior-rating scales, trained observers usually check off each occurrence of a specific behavior within a certain time frame—say, 15 minutes. Behavior-rating scales are growing in popularity, especially for use with chil-dren (Kamphaus et al., 2000). However, standardized objective and projective tests are used more frequently, and we focus on them in this section.

Question: How are personality measures used? Measures of personality are used to make important decisions, such as whether a person is suited for a certain type of work, a particular class in school, or a drug to reduce agitation. As part of their admissions process, graduate schools often ask professors to rate prospective students on scales that assess traits such as intelligence, emotional stability, and cooperation.

Students may take tests to measure their **aptitudes** and interests to gain insight into whether they are suited for certain occupations. It is assumed that students who share the aptitudes and interests of people who function well in certain positions are also likely to function well in those positions.

Let us consider the two most widely used types of personality tests: objective tests and projective tests.

Objective Tests

Question: What are objective personality tests?   **Objective tests** present respondents with a **standardized** group of test items in the form of a questionnaire. Respondents are limited to a specific range of answers. One test might ask respondents to indicate whether items are true or false for them. Another might ask respondents to select the preferred activity from groups of three.

Some tests have a **forced-choice format,** in which respondents are asked to indicate which of two statements is more true for them or which of several activities they prefer. The respondents are not usually given the option of answering "none of the above." Forced-choice formats are frequently used in interest inventories, which help predict whether the person would function well in a certain occupation. The following item is similar to those found in occupational interest inventories:

> I would rather
> a. be a forest ranger.
> b. work in a busy office.
> c. play a musical instrument.

The Minnesota Multiphasic Personality Inventory (MMPI) contains hundreds of items presented in a true–false format. The MMPI is designed to be used by clinical and counseling psychologists to help diagnose psychological disorders. Accurate measurement of an individual's problems should point to appropriate treatment. The MMPI is the most widely used psychological test in clinical work (Watkins et al., 1995). It is also the most widely used instrument for personality measurement in psychological research.

Psychologists can score tests by hand, send them to computerized scoring services, or have them scored by on-site computers. Computers generate reports by interpreting the test record according to certain rules or by comparing it with records in memory.

The MMPI is usually scored for the four **validity scales** and ten **clinical scales** described in Table 11.3 on page 440. The validity scales suggest whether answers actually represent the person's thoughts, emotions, and behaviors. However, they cannot guarantee that deception will be disclosed.

The validity scales in Table 11.3 assess different **response sets,** or biases, in answering the questions. People with high L scores, for example, may be attempting to present themselves as excessively moral and well-behaved individuals. People with high F scores may be trying to seem bizarre or are answering haphazardly. Many personality measures have some kind of validity scale. The clinical scales of the MMPI assess the problems shown in Table 11.3, as well as stereotypical masculine or feminine interests and introversion.

The MMPI scales were constructed *empirically*—that is, on the basis of actual clinical data rather than on the basis of psychological theory. A test-item bank of several hundred items was derived from questions that are often asked in clinical interviews. Here are some examples of the kinds of items that were used:

- My father was a good man.   T F
- I am very seldom troubled by headaches.   T F
- My hands and feet are usually warm enough.   T F
- I have never done anything dangerous for the thrill of it.   T F
- I work under a great deal of tension.   T F

The items were administered to people with previously identified symptoms, such as depressive or schizophrenic symptoms. Items that successfully set these people apart were included on scales named for these conditions. Confidence in the MMPI has developed because of its extensive use.

Aptitude
A natural ability or talent.

Objective Tests
Tests whose items must be answered in a specified, limited manner; tests whose items have concrete answers that are considered correct.

Standardized Test
A test that is given to a large number of respondents so that data concerning the typical responses can be accumulated and analyzed.

Forced-Choice Format
A method of presenting test questions that requires a respondent to select one of a number of possible answers.

Validity Scales
Groups of test items that indicate whether a person's responses accurately reflect that individual's traits.

Clinical Scales
Groups of test items that measure the presence of various abnormal behavior patterns.

Response Set
A tendency to answer test items according to a bias—for instance, to make oneself seem perfect or bizarre.

© Bob Daemmrich/The Image Works

■ **Is This Test Taker Telling the Truth?**

How can psychologists determine whether or not people answer test items honestly? What are the validity scales of the MMPI?

IN REVIEW

	Psychodynamic Perspective	**Trait Perspective**

PERSPECTIVE

Psychodynamic Perspective

Preconscious and unconscious elements drive personality.

Trait Perspective

Personality is determined by a limited number of fundamental inherent traits. Hippocrates divides these traits into four types (inner circle), while Eysenck groups them into two major dimensions—extraversion/introversion) and neuroticism (unstable/stable).

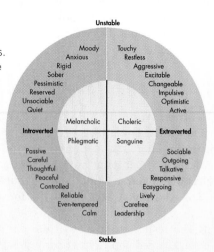

The current five-factor theory includes the two factors found by Eysenck, along with conscientiousness, agreeableness, and openness to experience.

THE BIG FIVE

Extraversion
Neuroticism
Conscientiousness
Agreeableness
Openness to Experience

KEY THEORISTS

Sigmund Freud (1856–1939)
Carl Jung (1875–1961)
Alfred Adler (1870–1937)
Karen Horney (1885–1952)
Erik Erikson (1902–1994)
Margaret Mahler (1897–1985)

Hippocrates (460–377 BCE)
Hans Eysenck (1916–1997)
Paul T. Costa, Jr.
Robert McCrae

FOCUS OF RESEARCH

Unconscious conflict, in which drives such as sex, aggression, and the need for superiority come into conflict with laws, social rules, and moral codes. Based on interpretations of responses of clients in psychoanalysis.

Use of mathematical techniques to catalogue and organize basic human personality traits. Connected with the tradition of psychological measurement, as early championed by Sir Francis Galton. Based on use of personality inventories.

VIEW OF PERSONALITY

Freud hypothesized three structures of personality (id, ego, superego) and five states of psychosexual development (oral, anal, phallic, latency, genital).

Whereas Freud focused on unconscious motives, neo-analysts pay more attention to subconscious motives and ideas and are often called ego analysts.

Hippocrates hypothesized the existence of four basic traits (melancholic, choleric, phlegmatic, sanguine), organized into two dimensions of personality (unstable/stable; introverted/extraverted). This was updated by Eysenck. Contemporary researchers find five (the five-factor model).

arning–Theory Perspective

uational and personal
riables mold personality.

Humanistic–Existential Perspective

Maslow believed we progress toward
higher psychological needs once
basic survival needs have been met.

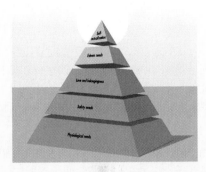

Sociocultural Perspective

To a collectivist, the self is complete only in
terms of relationships to other people.

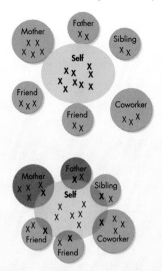

---

nn Watson (1878–1958)
F. Skinner (1904–1990)
bert Bandura

Abraham Maslow (1908–1970)
Carl Rogers (1902–1987)

Jean Phinney
Harry Triandis
Lillian Comas-Diaz
Stanley Sue

---

ictors that determine behavior. Based
experiments using mainly animals
ch as rats and pigeons but also
mans. Focus on situational influences
ther than individual differences,
hough allowance is made for different
ehaviors based on different
einforcement histories."

The process of how individuals
develop their own unique potential
even within a hostile environment.
Based mainly on clinical observations.

The roles of ethnicity, gender, culture,
and socioeconomic status in
personality formation and behavior.
Based on research and the
development of ethnic identity, effects
of prejudice and discrimination, and
studies of individualist versus collectivist
societies.

---

ehaviorists see personality as plastic and
etermined by external, situational
riables. Social–cognitive theorists also
ok for variables within the person, such
s competencies, encoding strategies,
xpectancies, emotions, and self-
gulatory systems, that affect behavior.

People have inborn drives to become
what they are capable of being.
Unconditional positive regard leads to
self-esteem, facilitating development of
unique talents, abilities, and ways of
viewing the world.

Development differs in individualistic
and collectivist societies. Discrimination,
poverty, and acculturation affect self-
concept and self-esteem.

TABLE 11.3 Minnesota Multiphasic Personality Inventory (MMPI) Scales

	Scale	Abbreviation	Possible Interpretations
Validity Scales	Question	?	Corresponds to number of items left unanswered
	Lie	L	Lies or is highly conventional
	Frequency	F	Exaggerates complaints or answers items haphazardly; may have bizarre ideas
	Correction	K	Denies problems
Clinical Scales	Hypochondriasis	Hs	Has bodily concerns and complaints
	Depression	D	Is depressed; has feelings of guilt and helplessness
	Hysteria	Hy	Reacts to stress by developing physical symptoms; lacks insight
	Psychopathic deviate	Pd	Is immoral, in conflict with the law; has stormy relationships
	Masculinity/ femininity	Mf	High scores suggest interests and behavior considered stereotypical of the other gender
	Paranoia	Pa	Is suspicious and resentful, highly cynical about human nature
	Psychasthenia	Pt	Is anxious, worried, high-strung
	Schizophrenia	Sc	Is confused, disorganized, disoriented; has bizarre ideas
	Hypomania	Ma	Is energetic, restless, active, easily bored
	Social introversion	Si	Is introverted, timid, shy; lacks self-confidence

Now that we have defined objective tests and surveyed the MMPI, we may ask— *Questions: How do projective tests differ from objective tests? What are some of the more widely used projective tests?*

Projective Tests

In **projective tests** there are no clear, specified answers. People are shown ambiguous stimuli such as inkblots or ambiguous drawings and asked to say what they look like or to tell stories about them. There is no one correct response. It is assumed that people *project* their own personalities into their responses. The meanings they attribute to these stimuli are assumed to reflect their personalities as well as the drawings or blots themselves.

The Rorschach Inkblot Test

You may have heard that there is a personality test that asks people what a drawing or inkblot looks like and that people commonly answer "a bat." There are a number of such tests, the best known of which is the Rorschach inkblot test, named after its originator, Hermann Rorschach.

People are given the inkblots, one by one, and are asked what they look like or what they could be. A response that reflects the shape of the blot is considered a sign of ade-

Projective Test

A psychological test that presents ambiguous stimuli onto which the test-taker projects his or her own personality in making a response.

quate **reality testing.** A response that richly integrates several features of the blot is considered a sign of high intellectual functioning. Supporters of the Rorschach believe that it provides insight into a person's intelligence, interests, cultural background, personality traits, psychological disorders, and many other variables. Critics argue that there is little empirical evidence to support the test's validity (Goode, 2001; Hunsley & Bailey, 1999).

Although there is no single "correct" response to the Rorschach inkblot shown in Figure 11.5, some responses are not in keeping with the features of the blots. Figure 11.5 could be a bat or a flying insect, the pointed face of an animal, the face of a jack-o'-lantern, or many other things. But responses like "an ice cream cone," "diseased lungs," or "a metal leaf in flames" are not suggested by the features of the blot and may indicate personality problems.

The Thematic Apperception Test

The Thematic Apperception Test (TAT) was developed in the 1930s by Henry Murray and Christiana Morgan. It consists of drawings, like the one shown in Figure 9.3 (see p. 357), that are open to a variety of interpretations. Individuals are given the cards one at a time and asked to make up stories about them.

The TAT is widely used in research on motivation and in clinical practice (Watkins et al., 1995). The notion is that we are likely to project own needs into our responses to ambiguous situations, even if we are unaware of them or reluctant to talk about them. The TAT is also widely used to assess attitudes toward other people, especially parents, lovers, and spouses.

In this chapter, we laid the foundations for the understanding of personality. In Chapter 12 we consider connections between personality and psychological disorders.

R E V I E W

(29) Personality tests sample _____ to predict future behavior. (30) _____ tests present standardized sets of test items in the form of questionnaires. (31) Projective tests present _____ stimuli and permit the respondent a broad range of answers. (32) The MMPI is an objective test that uses a _____–false format to assess psychological disorders. (33) The foremost projective technique is the _____ inkblot test.

Critical Thinking: Do the measurement methods discussed in this section seem to be associated with any particular theory or theories of personalty? Explain.

Figure 11.5
A Rorschach Inkblot
The Rorschach is the most widely used projective personality test.

Reality Testing
The capacity to perceive one's environment and oneself according to accurate sensory impressions.

Learning Connections
See Web site for an interactive version of these review questions.

LIFE CONNECTIONS

Gender-Typing—On Becoming a Woman or a Man

The French have an expression "Vive la différence," which means "Long live the difference" (between men and women). The anatomical differences between women and men are obvious and are connected with the biological aspects of reproduction. To reproduce, women and men have to be biologically different. Biologists therefore have a relatively easy time of it describing and interpreting the physical gender differences they study.

Throughout history and in many cultures, it has also been assumed that women and men must be different in personality in order to fulfill different roles in the family and society (Bem, 1993). But the task of psychologists who would explore these differences is more complex and is wrapped up with cultural and political issues. Gender differences in personality are not as obvious as biological gender differences. In fact, in many ways women and men are more similar psychologically than different. On the other hand, stereotypes of what it means to be masculine and feminine are widespread (see Table 11.4). For example, in their survey of 30 countries, John Williams and Deborah Best (1994) found that the traits *active, adventurous, aggressive, arrogant,* and *autocratic* are more likely to be ascribed to men. Women are more likely to be seen as *fearful, affectionate, appreciative,* and *emotional.*

Gender differences is an area that directly connects with students. Students are female or male, and there are key questions about what it means to be female or to be male. Are there differences in personality between females and males? If so, what are they? How large are they? Where do they come from? And, if they get in one's way, can they be surmounted?

Gender Differences in Personality

It was once a dominant myth in European/Western cultures that males were more intelligent than females because of their greater knowledge of world affairs and their skill in science and industry. However, that apparent greater male knowledge and skill did not reflect differences in cognitive ability. Rather, it reflected the systematic exclusion of females from world affairs, science, and industry. For example, assessments of intelligence do not show overall gender differences in cognitive abilities (Halpern & LaMay, 2000). However, reviews of the research suggest that girls are somewhat superior to boys in verbal abilities, such as verbal fluency, ability to generate words that are similar in meaning to other words, spelling, knowledge of foreign languages, and pronunciation (Halpern, 1997). Males seem to be somewhat superior in the ability to manipulate visual images in working memory.

Girls seem to acquire language somewhat faster than boys do. Also, in the United States far more boys than girls have reading problems, ranging from reading below grade level to severe disabilities (Halpern, 1997; Neisser et al., 1996).

Males seem to excel in visual–spatial abilities of the sort used in math, science, and reading maps (Grön et al., 2000; Halpern & LaMay, 2000). One study compared the navigation strategies of 90 male and 104 female university students (Dabbs et al., 1998). In giving directions, men more often referred to miles and directional coordinates (north, south, east, and west). Women were more likely to refer to landmarks and turning right or left. Psychological tests of spatial ability assess skills such as mentally rotating figures in space (see Figure 11.6) and finding figures embedded within larger designs (see Figure 11.7).

Studies in the United States and elsewhere find that males generally obtain higher scores on math tests than females (Beller & Gafni, 2000; Gallagher et al., 2000; Halpern & LaMay, 2000). Females tend to excel in computational ability in elementary school, however. Males tend to excel in mathematical problem solving in high school and college. Boys largely outperform girls on the math section of the Scholastic Assessment Test.

TABLE 11.4 Gender Role Stereotypes Around the World: Psychologists John Williams and Deborah Best (1994) found that people in 30 nations around the world tended to agree on the nature of masculine and feminine gender-role stereotypes. Men are largely seen as more adventurous and hardheaded than women. Women are generally seen as more emotional and dependent.

Stereotypes of Males		Stereotypes of Females	
Active	Opinionated	Affectionate	Nervous
Adventurous	Pleasure-	Appreciative	Patient
Aggressive	seeking	Cautious	Pleasant
Arrogant	Precise	Changeable	Prudish
Autocratic	Quick	Charming	Self-pitying
Capable	Rational	Complaining	Sensitive
Coarse	Realistic	Complicated	Sentimental
Conceited	Reckless	Confused	Sexy
Confident	Resourceful	Dependent	Shy
Courageous	Rigid	Dreamy	Softhearted
Cruel	Robust	Emotional	Sophisticated
Determined	Sharp-witted	Excitable	Submissive
Disorderly	Show-off	Fault-finding	Suggestible
Enterprising	Steady	Fearful	Superstitious
Hardheaded	Stern	Fickle	Talkative
Individualistic	Stingy	Foolish	Timid
Inventive	Stolid	Forgiving	Touchy
Loud	Tough	Frivolous	Unambitious
Obnoxious	Unscrupulous	Fussy	Understanding
		Gentle	Unstable
		Imaginative	Warm
		Kind	Weak
		Mild	Worrying
		Modest	

Source of data: Williams & Best, 1994, p. 193, Table 1.

■ Figure 11.6
Rotating Figures in Space

Males as a group outperform females on spatial relations tasks, such as rotating figures in space and picturing the results. However, females do as well as males when they receive training in the task.

However, these statistics do not confirm absolute gender differences. Psychologists note that:

- In most cases, the differences are small (Hyde & Plant, 1995). Differences in verbal, math, and visual–spatial abilities also appear to be narrowing as more females pursue course work in fields that had been typically reserved for males.
- Gender differences are *group* differences. There is greater variation in these skills between individuals *within* the groups than between males and females (Maccoby, 1990). That is, there may be a greater difference in, say, verbal skills between two women than between a woman and a man. Millions of females outdistance the "average" male in math and spatial abilities. Men have produced their verbally adept Shakespeares. Women have produced their scientific Marie Curies.
- Some differences reflect cultural influences (Fredericks & Eccles, 2002). In our culture spatial and math abilities are stereotyped as masculine. But when women are trained in spatial skills for just a few hours—for example, rotating geometric figures or studying floor plans—they perform at least as well men on tests of these skills (Baenninger & Elenteny, 1997; Lawton & Morrin, 1999).

There are other differences in personality between males and females. In analyses that average the results of multiple studies in gender differences, Alan Feingold (1994, 1998) has found that women are perceived as exceeding men in sociability, happiness, anxiety, trust, and nurturance. Men are perceived as exceeding women in social dominance and tough-mindedness.

According to a survey of 565 university students, men's friendships with other men tend to be shallower and less supportive than women's friendships with other women (Bank & Hansford, 2000). Despite the Western stereotype of women as very talkative, research in communication styles suggests that in many situations men spend more time talking than women do. Men are more likely to introduce new topics and to interrupt (Hall, 1984). An analysis of 205 studies involving 23,702 participants found that women are generally more willing to discuss feelings and personal experiences (Dindia & Allen, 1992).

There are key gender differences in areas of social behavior such as sex and aggression. Women are more likely to want to combine sex with a romantic relationship (Fisher, 2000). A survey of more than 1,000 undergraduates by David Schmitt and his colleagues (2001) found that men reported being more interested than women in casual sex and in multiple sex partners.

■ Figure 11.7
Items from an Embedded-Figures Test

Although there are exceptions (see the discussion below on whether men are really more aggressive than women), in most cultures, it is the males who march off to war and battle for glory

► CONTROVERSY IN PSYCHOLOGY ◄

Are men really more aggressive than women?

Despite the stereotype of male aggressiveness, the research reveals that women are actually somewhat more likely to hit, kick, or use a weapon against their spouses, cohabitants, or dating partners (Archer, 2000; Felson, 2002). Even so, the women are more likely to be injured.

How do we interpret the data? For one thing, the findings were limited to intimate partners. Men remain more likely to act violently toward strangers and other people of the same gender (Frieze, 2000). You usually need not be concerned about running into a woman on a deserted street. The difference in injury rate is also instructive: Men on average are stronger than women, choose more harmful weapons, and may be more likely to intend injury. So even if women engage in aggressive acts more often with their intimate partners, men remain more dangerous. It should also be noted that feminists are concerned by the reporting of research findings that focus on the frequency of violent acts, because the incidence of injury is more important (O'Leary, 2000; S. W. White et al., 2000).

But critical thinkers do not ignore research findings because they stir controversy. They suggest that women, like men, can turn to violence when they are frustrated. To be human is . . . to be human.

(and sneaker commercials). Males generally behave more aggressively than females (Archer, 1996; Felson, 2002).

In her classic review of the experimental research on gender differences in aggression, Ann Frodi and her colleagues (1977) found that females behave as aggressively as males when they have the means to do so and believe that aggression is justified. The Frodi group also found that:

1. Females are more likely to feel anxious or guilty about aggression. Such feelings inhibit aggressive behavior.
2. Females are more likely to empathize with the victim—to put themselves in the victim's place. Empathy encourages helping behavior, not aggression.
3. Gender differences in aggression tend to decrease when the victim is anonymous. Anonymity may prevent females from empathizing with their victims.

Gender Differences in Mate Selection

Your Daddy's rich

And your Ma is good lookin',

So hush, little baby,

Don't you cry.

From "Summertime" (from the opera Porgy & Bess)

How important to you is your partner's physical appearance? Cross-cultural reviews of the research on strategies for mate selection find that women tend to place greater emphasis than men on traits such as professional status, consideration, dependability, kindness, and fondness for children. Men tend to place relatively greater emphasis on physical allure, cooking ability (can't they turn on the microwave oven themselves?), even thrift (Buss, 1994; Feingold, 1992a). A study of about 300 male and 350 female university students in China also found that females place relatively more emphasis on earning potential in selecting a mate, and males place more emphasis on physical attractiveness (Chuang, 2002).

Susan Sprecher and her colleagues (1994) surveyed more than 13,000 Americans, attempting to represent the ethnic diversity we find in the United States. They asked how willing their subjects would be to marry someone who was older, younger, of a different religion, unlikely to hold a steady job, not good looking, and so on. Each item was answered by checking off a 7-point scale in which 1 meant "not at all" and 7 meant "very willing." Women were more willing than men to marry someone who was not good-looking (see Figure 11.8). But they were less willing to marry someone who was unlikely to hold a steady job.

Thus, although there are no absolute psychological gender differences, there are some intriguing patterns. They include minor differences in cognitive functioning and differences in personality and social behavior. The process by which these differences develop is termed *gender-typing*. In this section we explore several possible sources of gender-typing: evolutionary, genetic, and psychological.

Evolutionary and Genetic Aspects of Gender-Typing

According to evolutionary psychologists like David Buss (2000), gender differences were fashioned by natural selection in response to problems in adaptation that were repeatedly encountered by humans over thousands

How willing would you be to marry someone who . . .

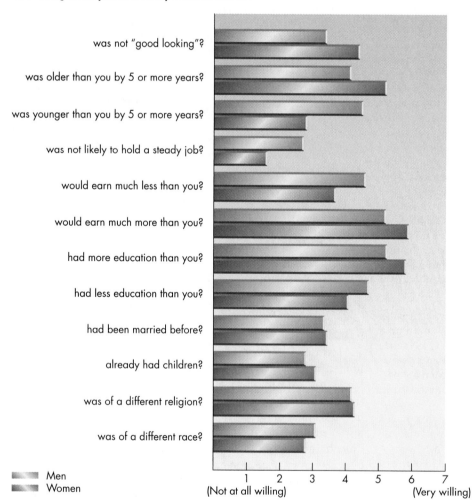

was not "good looking"?

was older than you by 5 or more years?

was younger than you by 5 or more years?

was not likely to hold a steady job?

would earn much less than you?

would earn much more than you?

had more education than you?

had less education than you?

had been married before?

already had children?

was of a different religion?

was of a different race?

Men
Women

1   2   3   4   5   6   7
(Not at all willing)   (Very willing)

■ **Figure 11.8**
Gender Differences in Mate Preferences
Susan Sprecher and her colleagues found that men are more willing than women to marry someone who is several years younger and less well educated. Women, on the other hand, are more willing than men to marry someone who is not good looking and who earns more money than they do.

of generations. The evolutionary process is expressed through structural differences between males and females, as are found in the brain, and through differences in body chemistry, as are found in the endocrine system.

Organization of the Brain

Researchers have found gender differences in the functioning and organization of the brain. Males and females have the same structures in the brain, but they seem to use them somewhat differently. For example, Matthias Riepe and his colleagues (Grön et al., 2000) found that men use the hippocampus in both hemispheres when they are trying to navigate through mazes, whereas women use only the hippocampus in the right hemisphere along with the right prefrontal cortex (Figure 11.9). It has also been found that most women tend to rely on landmarks to navigate ("Turn right at the drugstore, then left at the grocery"), whereas men use geometry, as in deriving information from a map ("The museum should be two blocks to the north") (Ritter, 2000). Riepe (2000) speculates that the women's activity in the cortex might be due to processing landmark cues, whereas the hippocampal activity in men might reflect the more geometric approach. Riepe (2000) has found the same gender difference in brain functioning in rats that are navigating mazes.

Then too, some psychological activities, such as language, seem to be controlled largely by the left side of the brain. Other psychological activities, such as aesthetic and emotional responses, seem to be controlled largely by the right side. Research with brain-imaging techniques suggests that the brain hemispheres may be more specialized in males than in females (Shaywitz et al., 1995). For example, men with damage to the left hemisphere are more likely to experience difficulties in verbal functioning than women with similar damage. Men with damage to the right hemisphere are more likely to have problems with spatial relations than women with similar injuries. Women appear to be able to use both sides of their brains for these functions and hence have a greater chance of recovery.

Gender differences in brain organization might explain, in part, why women tend to excel in verbal skills that require some spatial organization, such as reading, spelling, and crisp articulation of speech. Men, however, tend to excel at more specialized spatial-relations tasks such as interpreting road maps and visualizing objects in space.

Sex Hormones

Sex hormones and other chemical substances are responsible for the prenatal differentiation of sex organs (Davis et al., 2000). These substances may also "masculinize" or "feminize" the brain by creating predispositions consistent with some gender-role tendencies (Collaer & Hines, 1995; Crews, 1994). Evidence for the possible role of hormonal influences has been obtained from studies with lower animals (Collaer & Hines, 1995; Crews, 1994). For example, male rats are generally superior to females in maze-learning ability, a task that requires spatial skills. Female rats that are exposed to androgens in the uterus (e.g., because they have several male siblings in the uterus with them) or soon after birth learn maze routes as rapidly as males, however. They also roam larger distances and mark larger territories than most females do (Vandenbergh, 1993).

Men are generally more aggressive than women, and aggressiveness appears to be at least in part connected with testosterone (Pope et al., 2000; A. Sullivan, 2000). However, cognitive psychologists argue that boys (and girls) can choose whether or not to act aggressively, regardless hormone levels in the blood.

Are There Evolutionary Factors in Mate Selection?

Why do males tend to place relatively more emphasis than females on physical appearance in mate selection? Why do females tend to place relatively more emphasis on personal factors such as financial status and reliability?

Evolutionary psychologists believe that evolutionary forces favor the survival of women who desire status in their mates and men who emphasize physical allure because these preferences provide reproductive advantages. Some physical features such as cleanliness, good complexion, clear eyes, strong teeth and healthy hair, firm muscle tone, and a steady gait are found to be universally appealing to both genders (Buss, 1999). Perhaps such traits have value as markers of better reproductive potential in prospective mates. According to the "parental investment model," a woman's appeal is more strongly connected with her age and health, both of which are markers of reproductive capacity. The value of men as reproducers, however, is more intertwined with factors that contribute to a stable environment for child rearing—such as social standing and reliability (Feingold, 1992a). For such reasons, evolutionary psychologists speculate that these qualities may have grown relatively more alluring to women over the millennia (e.g., Buss, 1994).

This theory is largely speculative, however, and not fully consistent with all the evidence. Women, like men, are attracted to physically appealing partners, and women tend to marry men similar to them in physical attractiveness and socioeconomic standing. Aging men are more likely than younger men to die from natural causes. The wealth they accrue may not always be transmitted to their spouses and children, either. Many women may be more able to find reproductive success by mating with a

REFLECT

So why are women more willing than men to ask for directions?

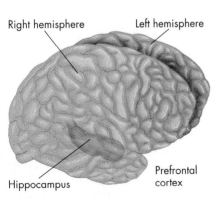

■ Figure 11.9
How Do People Navigate?

Brain-scanning research suggests that when women are navigating their way through mazes, they use only the hippocampus in the right hemisphere along with the right prefrontal cortex. Men apparently use the hippocampus in both hemispheres. What should we take away from such findings? It is apparently the case that different strategies for solving problems may be connected with activity in different parts of the brain. Moreover, the pattern of usage of parts of the brain may be at least in part genetically determined.

fit, younger male than with an older, higher-status male. Even evolutionary psychologists allow that despite any innate predispositions, many men desire older women.

Psychodynamic Theory and Gender-Typing

The two most prominent psychological perspectives on gender-typing today are social–cognitive theory and gender-schema theory. Both portray human nature as inquisitive. Both suggest that people—even in early childhood—attempt to understand their environments and to behave in ways that are consistent with their understanding. However, we begin with psychodynamic theory because of its historic interest.

Sigmund Freud explained the acquisition of gender roles in terms of identification. He believed that gender-related behaviors remain flexible until the age of 5 or 6. Freud argued that it was natural for boys to want to possess their mothers and view their fathers as rivals in love. It was natural for girls to wish they had a penis. In Freud's speculative theme, appropriate gender-typing requires that boys identify with their fathers and give up the wish to possess their mothers. Girls have to surrender the wish to have a penis and identify with their mothers.

But research evidence reveals that boys and girls are inclined to develop gender-typed preferences for toys and activities earlier than predicted by psychodynamic theory. Even within the first year, boys tend to be more explorative and active than girls (Rathus, 2003). A Canadian study of 77 infants found that infants showed preferences for gender-stereotyped toys by the age of 18 months (Serbin et al., 2001). That is, girls gazed longer at photos of dolls, and boys gazed longer at photos of transportation toys. Freud connected gender-typing with the resolution of highly emotional inner conflicts. We will see that more recent theories of gender-typing allow for the earlier ages of gender-typing by noting that all that is necessary is for children to understand whether they are boys or girls and what boys and girls "do."

Learning Theories and Gender-Typing

Behaviorists explain gender-typing in terms of the selective reinforcement of behavior patterns deemed appropriate for boys and girls within a given culture. But there is no evidence that boys and girls "try out" all possible behavior patterns, nor that they are so accurately reinforced.

Social–cognitive theory does not agree that reinforcement mechanically induces stereotypical gender-related behaviors. They assert, instead, that experience helps the individual create concepts of gender-appropriate behavior (Bussey & Bandura, 1999). Reinforcement helps—but by providing information as to what other people deem to be appropriate behavior.

According to social–cognitive theory, children learn much of what is considered masculine or feminine by observational learning. Whom do young children observe most frequently? Usually, their parents. Research evidence shows that children's views of what is masculine and feminine are related to those of their parents (Tenenbaum & Leaper, 2002). This finding is consistent with social–cognitive theory and, as we will see, also with gender-schema theory.

The importance of observational learning is also supported by the findings of experiments such as a classic experiment conducted by David Perry and Kay Bussey (1979). In this study, children learned how behaviors are gender-typed by observing the *relative frequencies* with which men and women performed them. The adult role models expressed arbitrary preferences for one item from each of 16 pairs of items—pairs such as oranges versus apples and toy cows versus toy horses—while 8- and 9-year-old boys and girls watched them. The children were then asked to show their own preferences. Boys selected an average of 14 of 16 items that agreed with the "preferences" of the men. Girls selected an average of only 3 of 16 items that agreed with the choices of the men. In other words, boys and girls learned gender-typed preferences even though those preferences were completely arbitrary.

Social–cognitive theorists also see a role for "identification." However, social–cognitive theorists view identification not as a

■ **Acquiring Gender Roles**

How do people develop gender roles? What contributions are made by biological and psychological factors? Social–cognitive theory focuses on imitation of the behavior of adults of the same gender and reinforcement by parents and peers.

© Myrleen Ferguson/PhotoEdit

© Andy Sacks

Figure 11.10
Mean Shock Settings Selected by Women in Retaliation Against Male Opponents

Women in the Richardson study chose higher shock levels for their opponents when they were alone or when another person (a "supportive other") urged them on. Could it be that women are as aggressive as men when they have the means to be aggressive, are provoked, and believe that the social environment will support their aggressive behavior?

sort of one-shot swallowing of the personality of another human being, but rather as a continuous learning process in which children are influenced by reinforcements to imitate adults of the same gender—particularly the parent of the same gender. In identification, as opposed to imitation, children do not simply imitate a certain behavior pattern. They strive to become as much like the model as they can.

Socialization also plays a role within social–cognitive theory. Parents and other adults—even other children—inform children about how they are expected to behave. They reinforce or reward children for behavior they consider appropriate for their gender. They punish (or fail to reinforce) children for behavior they consider inappropriate. Girls, for example, are given dolls while they are still sleeping in their cribs. They are encouraged to use the dolls to rehearse caretaking behaviors in preparation for traditional feminine adult roles.

Classic experiments point up the importance of social learning in female aggressiveness. In one study, for example, American college women competed with men to see who could respond to a stimulus more quickly (Richardson et al., 1979). There were four blocks of trials, with six trials in each block. The subjects could not see their opponents. The loser of each trial received an electric shock whose intensity was set by the opponent. Women competed under one of three experimental conditions: public, private, or with a supportive other. In the public condition, another woman observed the subject silently. In the private condition, there was no observer. In the supportive-other condition, another woman urged the subject to retaliate strongly when her opponent selected high shock levels. As shown in Figure 11.10, women in the private and supportive-other conditions selected increasingly higher levels of shock in retaliation. Presumably, the women assumed that an observer, though silent, would frown on aggressive behavior. This assumption is likely to reflect the women's own early socialization experiences. Women who were not observed or who were urged on by another person apparently felt free to violate the gender norm of nonaggressiveness when their situations called for aggressive responses.

Social–cognitive theory outlines ways in which experience leads to concepts of gender and how people try to regulate their own behavior to conform to what they believe is appropriate. Gender-schema theory suggests that it is human nature to assume gender-appropriate behavior by blending one's self-concept with cultural expectations.

Gender-Schema Theory and Gender-Typing

You have probably heard the expression, "looking at the world through rose-colored glasses." According to Sandra Bem (1993), the originator of *gender-schema theory*, people look at the social world through "the lenses of gender." Bem argues that cultures tend to polarize females and males by organizing social life around mutually exclusive gender roles. Children come to accept the polarizing scripts without realizing it. Unless parents or unusual events encourage them to challenge the validity of gender polarization, children attempt to construct identities that are consistent with the "proper" script. Most children reject behavior—in others and in themselves—that deviates from it. Children's self-esteem soon becomes wrapped up in the ways in which they measure up to the gender schema. For example, most boys learn early to hold a high opinion of themselves if they excel in sports.

Once children understand the labels *boy* and *girl*, they have a basis for blending their self-concepts with the gender schema of their culture. The desire to do so is natural. No external pressure is required. Children who have developed a sense of being male or being female, which usually occurs by the age of 3, actively seek information about their gender schema. As in social–cognitive theory, children seek to learn through observation what is considered appropriate for them.

A review of the research literature suggests that polarized female–male scripts serve as cognitive anchors within Western culture (Bowes & Goodnow, 1996). Researchers in one study showed 5- and 6-year-old boys and girls pictures of actors engaged in "gender-consistent" or "gender-inconsistent" activities. The gender-consistent pictures showed boys playing with trains or sawing wood. Girls were shown cooking and cleaning. Gender-inconsistent pictures showed actors of the other gender engaged in these gender-typed activities. Each child was shown a randomized set of pictures that included only one picture of each activity. One week later, the children were asked who had engaged in the activity, a male or a female. Both boys and girls gave wrong answers more often when the picture they had seen showed gender-*inconsistent* activity. In other words, they distorted what they had seen to conform to the gender schema.

In sum, the organization of the brain and sex hormones appear to contribute to gender-typed behavior and play roles in verbal ability, math skills, and aggression. Gender-typed behavior patterns are unlikely to result simply from the resolution of deep-seated conflict as the Freudians would assert, or from just mechanical reinforcement of selected behaviors. Social–cognitive theory assumes that children actively seek information about the environment and outlines ways in which children obtain information about which behaviors are considered masculine or feminine. Gender-schema theory focuses on how children blend their self-identities with the gender schema of their culture.

Today, most researchers would agree that both genetic and environmental factors affect most areas of behavior and mental processes—including the complex processes in gender-typing. But there is also the element of choice. Yes, you may be "stronger" in some traits than others because of evolutionary and genetic factors. Yes, you may have been influenced by cultural and social expectations. But traits tend to be dimensions, like the volume control on your stereo. It is not often that the volume is set as low or as high as it can go. When you want to pursue a course of study, a profession, a hobby, a social relationship, go for it—regardless of whether it is stereotyped as masculine or feminine, regardless of whether you are a man or a woman. Motivation matters as well as the strength of stereotyped traits.

Recite Recite Recite

Learning Connections
See Web site for an interactive version of this chapter summary

1. What *is* personality?

Personality is defined as the reasonably stable patterns of behavior, including thoughts and emotions, that distinguish one person from another.

2. What is Freud's theory of psychosexual development?

Freud's theory is termed psycho*dynamic* because it assumes that we are driven largely by unconscious motives and by the movement of unconscious forces within our minds. People experience conflict as basic instincts of hunger, sex, and aggression come up against social pressures to follow laws, rules, and moral codes. At first this conflict is external, but as we develop, it is internalized. The unconscious id represents psychological drives and seeks instant gratification. The ego, or the sense of self or "I," develops through experience and takes into account what is practical and possible in gratifying the impulses of the id. Defense mechanisms such as repression protect the ego from anxiety by repressing unacceptable ideas or distorting reality. The superego is the conscience and develops largely through the Oedipus complex and identification with others. People undergo psychosexual development as psychosexual energy, or libido, is transferred from one erogenous zone to another during childhood. There are five stages of development: oral, anal, phallic, latency, and genital. Fixation in a stage leads to development of traits associated with the stage.

3. Who are some other psychodynamic theorists? What are their views on personality?

Carl Jung's theory, analytical psychology, features a collective unconscious and numerous archetypes, both of which reflect the history of our species. Alfred Adler's theory, individual psychology, features the inferiority complex and the compensating drive for superiority. Karen Horney's theory focuses on parent–child relationships and the possible development of feelings of anxiety and hostility. Erik Erikson's theory of psychosocial development highlights the importance of early social relationships rather than the gratification of childhood sexual impulses. Erikson extended Freud's five developmental stages to eight, including stages that occur in adulthood.

4. What are the strengths and weaknesses of the psychodynamic perspective?

Freud fought for the idea that personality is subject to scientific analysis at a time when many people still viewed psychological problems as signs of possession. He also focused attention on the importance of sexuality, the effects of child rearing, and the fact that people distort perceptions according to their needs. On the other hand, there is no evidence for the existence of psychic structures, and his theory is fraught with inaccuracies about child development.

5. What are traits?

Traits are personality elements that are inferred from behavior and that account for behavioral consistency. Trait theory adopts a descriptive approach to personality.

6. What is the history of the trait perspective?

Hippocrates, the ancient Greek physician, believed that personality reflects the balance of liquids ("humors") in the body. Galton in the 19th century and Allport in the 20th century surveyed traits by studying words that referred to them in dictionaries.

7. How have contemporary researchers used factor analysis to reduce the universe of traits to smaller lists of traits that show common features?

Hans Eysenck used factor analysis to arrive at two broad, independent personality dimensions: introversion–extraversion and emotional stability–instability (neuroticism). More recent mathematical analyses point to the existence of five key factors (five-factor theory): extraversion, agreeableness, conscientiousness, emotional stability, and openness to experience.

8. What are the strengths and weaknesses of trait theory?

Trait theorists have helped develop personality tests and used them to predict adjustment in various lines of work. Critics argue that trait theory is descriptive, not explanatory.

9. What does learning theory have to contribute to our understanding of personality?

Behaviorists believe that we should focus on observable behavior rather than hypothesized unconscious forces and that we should emphasize the situational determinants of behavior.

Recite Recite Recite

10. What is Watson's contribution to personality theory?

John B. Watson, the "father" of modern behaviorism, rejected notions of mind and personality altogether. He also argued that he could train any child to develop into a professional or a criminal by controlling the child's environment.

11. How did Skinner develop Watson's views?

B. F. Skinner, like Watson, opposed the idea of personal freedom. In *Walden Two*, Skinner argued that environmental contingencies can shape people into wanting to do the things that are required of them.

12. How does social–cognitive theory differ from the behaviorist view?

Social–cognitive theory has a cognitive orientation and focuses on learning by observation. To predict behavior, social–cognitive theorists consider situational variables (rewards and punishments) and person variables (competencies, encoding strategies, expectancies, emotions, and self-regulatory systems and plans).

13. What are the strengths and weaknesses of learning theories as they apply to personality?

Learning theorists have highlighted the importance of referring to publicly observable behaviors in theorizing. However, behaviorism does not describe, explain, or suggest the richness of inner human experience. Critics of social–cognitive theory note that it does not address self-awareness or adequately account for the development of traits. It may also not pay enough attention to genetic variation in explaining individual differences in behavior.

14. What is humanism? What is existentialism?

Humanism argues that we are capable of free choice, self-fulfillment, and ethical behavior. Existentialists argue that our lives have meaning when we give them meaning.

15. How do humanistic psychologists differ from psychodynamic theorists?

Whereas Freud wrote that people are motivated to gratify unconscious drives, humanistic psychologists believe that people have a conscious need for self-actualization.

16. What is your *self*? What is self theory?

According to Rogers, the self is an organized and consistent way in which a person perceives his or her "I" in relation to others. Self theory begins by assuming the existence of the self and each person's unique frame of reference. The self attempts to actualize (develop its unique potential) and best does so when the person receives unconditional positive regard. Conditions of worth may lead to a distorted self-concept, to disowning of parts of the self, and to anxiety.

17. What are the strengths and weaknesses of humanistic–existential theory?

Humanistic–existential theory is appealing because of its focus on self-awareness and freedom of choice, but critics argue that concepts such as conscious experience and self-actualization are unscientific.

18. Why is the sociocultural perspective important to the understanding of personality?

One cannot fully understand the personality of an individual without understanding the cultural beliefs and socioeconomic conditions that have affected that individual. The sociocultural perspective encourages us to consider the roles of ethnicity, gender, culture, and socioeconomic status in personality formation, behavior, and mental processes.

19. What does it mean to be individualistic? What is meant by individualism and collectivism?

Individualists define themselves in terms of their personal identities and to give priority to their personal goals. Collectivists define themselves in terms of the groups to which they belong and to give priority to the group's goals. Many Western societies are individualistic and foster individualism in personality. Many Eastern societies are collectivist and foster collectivism in personality.

20. How does acculturation affect the psychological well-being of immigrants and their families?

Immigrants who retain the customs and values of their country of origin, but who also learn those of their new host country and blend the two, tend to have higher self-esteem than immigrants who either become completely assimilated or who maintain complete separation from the new dominant culture.

Recite Recite Recite

21. How are personality measures used?

Personality measures are used in many ways, including assessing psychological disorders, predicting the likelihood of adjustment in various lines of work, measuring aptitudes, and determining academic placement.

22. What are objective personality tests?

Objective tests present test-takers with a standardized set of test items to which they must respond in specific, limited ways (as in multiple-choice or true–false tests). A forced-choice format asks respondents to indicate which of two or more statements is true for them or which of several activities they prefer. The Minnesota Multiphasic Personality Inventory (MMPI) is widely used in the assessment of psychological disorders.

23. How do projective tests differ from objective tests? What are some of the more widely used projective tests?

Projective tests do not have specific correct answers. They present ambiguous stimuli and allow the test-taker to give a range of responses that reflect individual differences. Examples include the Rorschach inkblot test and the Thematic Apperception Test.

Active Learning Resources

Search Online with InfoTrac® College Edition

For additional information on the topics in this chapter, explore InfoTrac College Edition, your online library. Go to **http://www.infotrac.thomsonlearning.com** and use the passcode that came on the card with your book. Try these search terms: Sigmund Freud, repression, libido, Carl Jung, Erik Erikson, five-factor model, self-efficacy, individualism and collectivism, and personality tests.

Visit Our Web Site

Go to **http://www.wadsworth.com/psychology** where you will find online resources directly linked to your book, including interactive exercises related to PQ4R and Power Visuals for mastering and reviewing key concepts. In addition, you will find hints on using InfoTrac College Edition to answer the Critical Thinking questions throughout the text. Start with the **Self Study Assessment** for a customized **Study Plan** generated by taking the **Pre-Test** and **Post-Test.**

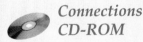

Connections CD-ROM

Go to the Wadsworth *Connections* CD-ROM for further study of the concepts in this chapter. The CD-ROM includes videos and animations, quizzes, and additional activities to expand your learning experience, plus interactive self-assessments to help connect the material to your own life.

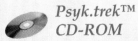

Psyk.trek™ CD-ROM

The Wadsworth *Psyk.trek* CD-ROM offers tutorials, simulations, videos, multimedia glossary, and quizzing to help you master the material.

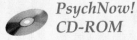

PsychNow! CD-ROM

The Wadsworth *PsychNow!* CD-ROM includes interactive exercises, videos, and animations to enhance your learning.

What Are Psychological Disorders?

- WHERE DOES run-of-the-mill anxiety or depression end and a psychological disorder begin?

Perspectives on Psychological Disorders: "The Devil Made Me Do It"?

- IN THE MIDDLE AGES, innocent people were drowned to prove that they were not possessed by the devil.

Anxiety Disorders

- HOW DO YOU KNOW when you are feeling anxious?

- SOME PEOPLE WILL not leave the house for fear of falling apart in public.

Dissociative Disorders

- SOME PEOPLE HAVE more than one identity, and each one may have different allergies and eyeglass prescriptions.

Somatoform Disorders

- SOME PEOPLE BELIEVE they have every disease that's "going around," and then some.

- OTHER PEOPLE HAVE lost the function of their limbs, although nothing was physically wrong with them.

Mood Disorders

- FEELING "UP" is not always a good thing.

- WOMEN ARE MORE likely than men to be depressed. (With good reason, many would say.)

Schizophrenia

- A MAN SHOT the president of the United States in front of millions of television witnesses, yet was found not guilty by a court of law.

- PEOPLE WITH schizophrenia may see and hear things that are not there.

Personality Disorders

- SOME PEOPLE CAN injure or kill others with no feelings of guilt at all.

Life Connections: Understanding and Preventing Suicide

- WHO COMMITS SUICIDE? Younger people, older people? Men, women?

- ARE PEOPLE WHO threaten suicide only seeking attention?

- WHAT CAN YOU DO if somebody tells you he or she is going to commit suicide?

uring one long fall semester, the Ohio State campus lived in terror. Four college women were abducted, forced to cash checks or obtain money from automatic teller machines, and then raped. A mysterious phone call led to the arrest of a 23-year-old drifter—let's call him "William"—who had been dismissed from the Navy.

William was not the boy next door.

Psychologists and psychiatrists who interviewed William concluded that 10 personalities—8 male and 2 female—resided within him (Scott, 1994). His personality had been "fractured" by an abusive childhood. His several personalities displayed distinct facial expressions, speech patterns, and memories. They even performed differently on psychological tests.

Arthur, the most rational personality, spoke with a British accent. Danny and Christopher were quiet adolescents. Christine was a 3-year-old girl. Tommy, a 16-year-old, had enlisted in the Navy. Allen was 18 and smoked. Adelena, a 19-year-old lesbian personality, had committed the rapes. Who had made the mysterious phone call? Probably David, 9, an anxious child.

The defense claimed that William's behavior was caused by a psychological disorder termed **dissociative identity disorder** (also referred to as **multiple personality disorder**). Several distinct identities or personalities dwelled within him. Some of them were aware of the others. Some believed that they were unique. Billy, the core identity, had learned to sleep as a child in order to avoid his father's abuse. A psychiatrist asserted that Billy had also been "asleep," or in a "psychological coma," during the abductions. Billy should therefore be found not guilty by reason of **insanity**.

William was found not guilty. He was committed to a psychiatric institution and released six years later.

In 1982, John Hinckley was also found not guilty of the assassination attempt on President Reagan's life. Expert witnesses testified that he should be diagnosed with **schizophrenia.** Hinckley, too, was committed to a psychiatric institution.

Dissociative identity disorder and schizophrenia are psychological disorders. *Question: What, exactly, are psychological disorders?*

WHAT ARE PSYCHOLOGICAL DISORDERS?

Dissociative Identity Disorder
A disorder in which a person appears to have two or more distinct identities or personalities that may alternately emerge.

Multiple Personality Disorder
The previous term for *dissociative identity disorder.*

Insanity
A legal term descriptive of a person judged to be incapable of recognizing right from wrong or of conforming his or her behavior to the law.

Schizophrenia
A psychotic disorder characterized by loss of control of thought processes and inappropriate emotional responses.

Psychological Disorders
Patterns of behavior or mental processes that are connected with emotional distress or significant impairment in functioning.

Psychology is the study of behavior and mental processes. **Psychological disorders** are behaviors or mental processes—like those of "William" and John Hinckley—that are connected with various kinds of distress or disability. However, they are not predictable responses to specific events.

For example, some psychological disorders are characterized by anxiety, but many people are anxious now and then without being considered disordered. It is appropriate to be anxious before an important date or on the eve of a midterm exam. When, then, are feelings like anxiety deemed to be abnormal or signs of a psychological disorder? For one thing, anxiety may suggest a disorder when it is not appropriate to the situation. It is inappropriate to be anxious when entering an elevator or looking out of a fourth-story window. The magnitude of the problem may also suggest disorder. Some anxiety is usual before a job interview. However, feeling that your heart is pounding so intensely that it might leap out of your chest—and then avoiding the interview—are not usual.

Behavior or mental processes are suggestive of psychological disorders when they meet some combination of the following criteria:

1. *They are unusual.* Although people with psychological disorders are a minority, uncommon behavior or mental processes are not abnormal in themselves. Only one person holds the record for running or swimming the fastest mile. That person is different from you and me but is not abnormal. Only a few people qualify as geniuses in mathematics, but mathematical genius is not a sign of a psychological disorder.

Rarity or statistical deviance may not be sufficient for behavior or mental processes to be labeled abnormal, but it helps. Most people do not see or hear things that are not there. "Seeing things" and "hearing things," as Hinckley did, are abnormal. We must also consider the situation. Although many of us feel "panicked" when we realize that a term paper or report is due the next day, most of us do not have panic attacks "out of the blue." Unpredictable panic attacks thus are suggestive of psychological disorder.

2. *They suggest faulty perception or interpretation of reality.* Our society considers it normal to be inspired by religious beliefs but abnormal to believe that God is literally speaking to you. "Hearing voices" and "seeing things" are considered **hallucinations.** Similarly, **ideas of persecution,** such as believing that the Mafia or the FBI are "out to get you," are considered signs of disorder. (Unless, of course, they *are* out to get you.) Hinckley's view, that he would be impressing a popular actress with his behavior, was delusional.

3. *They suggest severe personal distress.* Anxiety, exaggerated fears, and other psychological states cause personal distress, and severe personal distress may be considered abnormal. William and Hinckley were in distress—although, of course, they victimized other people. Anxiety, of course, may be an appropriate response to a situation, as when a big test or a big date is coming up.

4. *They are self-defeating.* Behavior or mental processes that cause misery rather than happiness and fulfillment may suggest psychological disorder. Chronic drinking that impairs work and family life and cigarette smoking that impairs health may therefore be deemed abnormal.

5. *They are dangerous.* Behaviors or mental processes that are hazardous to the self or others may be considered suggestive of psychological disorders. People who threaten or attempt suicide may be considered abnormal, as may people who threaten or attack others, like William and Hinckley. Yet criminal behavior or aggressive behavior in sports need not imply a psychological disorder.

6. *The individual's behavior is socially unacceptable.* We must consider the cultural context of a behavior pattern in judging whether or not it is normal (Lopez & Guarnaccia, 2000). In the United States, it is deemed normal for males to be aggressive in sports and in combat. In other situations warmth and tenderness are valued. Many people in the United States admire women who are self-assertive, yet Latino and Latina

REFLECT

Have you ever felt anxious? Did your anxiety strike you as being normal under the circumstances? Why or why not?

Hallucination

A perception in the absence of sensory stimulation that is confused with reality.

Ideas of Persecution

Erroneous beliefs that one is being victimized or persecuted.

■ **Hallucinations**

Hallucinations are a feature of schizophrenia. They are perceptions that occur in the absence of external stimulation, as in "hearing voices" or "seeing things." Hallucinations cannot be distinguished from real perceptions. Are the cats in this Sandy Skoglund photograph real or hallucinatory?

American, Asian American, and "traditional" European American groups may see outspoken women as disrespectful.

Classifying Psychological Disorders

Toss some people, apes, seaweed, fish, and sponges into a room—preferably a well ventilated one. Stir slightly. What do you have? It depends on how you classify this hodgepodge.

Classify them as plants versus animals and you lump the people, chimpanzees, fish, and, yes, sponges together. Classify them as stuff that carries on its business on land or underwater, and we throw in our lot with the chimps and none of the others. How about those that swim and those that don't? Then the chimps, the fish, and some of us are grouped together.

Classification is at the heart of science. Without classifying psychological disorders, investigators would not be able to communicate with each other and scientific progress would come to a standstill. The most widely used classification scheme for psychological disorders[1] is the *Diagnostic and Statistical Manual (DSM)* of the American Psychiatric Association (2000). **Question: How are psychological disorders grouped or classified?**

The *DSM-IV-TR* groups disorders on the basis of observable behaviors or symptoms. However, early editions of the *DSM,* which was first published in 1952, grouped many disorders on the basis of assumptions about their causes. Because Freud's psychodynamic theory was widely accepted at the time, one major diagnostic category contained so-called neuroses.[2] According to Freud, all neuroses—no matter how differently people with various neuroses might behave—were caused by unconscious neurotic conflict. Each neurosis was thought to reflect a way of coping with the unconscious fear that primitive impulses might break loose. As a result, sleepwalking was included as a neurosis (psychoanalysts assumed that sleepwalking reduced unconscious fear by permitting partial expression of impulses). Now that the focus is on observable behaviors, sleepwalking is classified as a sleep disorder, not a neurosis. The psychological disorders discussed in the chapter are listed in Table 12.1.

Some professionals, such as psychiatrist Thomas Szasz, believe that the categories described in the *DSM* are really "problems in living" rather than "disorders." At least, they are not disorders in the sense that high blood pressure, cancer, and the flu are disorders. Szasz argues that labeling people with problems in living as being "sick" degrades them and encourages them to evade their personal and social responsibilities. Because sick people are encouraged to obey doctors' orders, Szasz (1999, 2000) also contends that labeling people as "sick" accords too much power to health professionals. Instead, he believes, troubled people need to be encouraged to take greater responsibility for solving their own problems.

PERSPECTIVES ON PSYCHOLOGICAL DISORDERS: "THE DEVIL MADE ME DO IT"?

REFLECT

Have you ever heard anyone say, "Something got into me" or, "The devil made me do it"? What were the circumstances? Was the person trying to evade responsibility for wrongdoing?

Dissociative identity disorder and schizophrenia are two psychological disorders. **Question: How do people explain psychological disorders?** If William and Hinckley had lived in Salem, Massachusetts, in 1692, just 200 years after Columbus set foot in the New World, they might have been hanged as witches. At that time, most people assumed that psychological disorders were caused by possession by the Devil. A score of people were executed in Salem that year for allegedly practicing the arts of Satan.

Throughout human history people have attributed unusual behavior and psychological disorders to demons. The ancient Greeks believed that the gods punished humans by causing confusion and madness. An exception was the physician Hippocrates, who

[1]The American Psychiatric Association refers to psychological disorders as *mental disorders.*
[2]The neuroses included what are today referred to as anxiety disorders, dissociative disorders, somatoform disorders, mild depression, and some other disorders, such as sleepwalking.

TABLE 12.1 Psychological Disorders

Class	Major Subtypes	Comments
Anxiety disorders	Phobic, panic, generalized anxiety, obsessive–compulsive, and stress disorders	Generally characterized by worrying, fear of the worst happening, fear of losing control, nervousness, and inability to relax
Dissociative disorders	Dissociative amnesia, dissociative fugue, and dissociative identity disorder (multiple personality)	Generally characterized by separation of mental processes such as thoughts, emotions, identity, memory, or consciousness
Somatoform disorders	Conversion disorder and hypochondriasis	Generally characterized by complaints of physical problems such as paralysis or pain, or the persistent belief that one has a serious disease in the absence of medical findings
Mood disorders	Major depression and bipolar disorder	Generally characterized by disturbance in expressed emotions
Schizophrenia	Paranoid, disorganized, and catatonic schizophrenia	Generally characterized by disturbances in language and thought (e.g., delusions, loose associations), attention and perception (e.g., hallucinations), motor activity, and mood, and by withdrawal and absorption in daydreams or fantasy
Personality disorders	Paranoid, schizotypal, schizoid, antisocial, and avoidant personality disorders	Generally characterized by inflexible and maladaptive patterns of behavior that impair personal or social functioning and are a source of distress to oneself or others

made the radical suggestion that psychological disorders are caused by an abnormality of the brain. The notion that biology could affect thoughts, feelings, and behavior was to lie dormant for about 2,000 years.

During the Middle Ages in Europe, as well as during the early period of European colonization of Massachusetts, it was generally believed that psychological disorders were signs of possession by the devil. Possession could stem from retribution, in which God caused the devil to possess a person's soul as punishment for committing certain kinds of sins. Agitation and confusion were ascribed to such retribution. Possession was also believed to result from deals with the devil, in which people traded their souls for earthly gains. Such individuals were called witches. Witches were held responsible for unfortunate events ranging from a neighbor's infertility to a poor harvest. In Europe, as many as 500,000 accused witches were killed during the next two centuries (Hergenhahn, 2001). The goings on at Salem were trivial by comparison.

A document authorized by Pope Innocent VIII, *The Hammer of Witches*, proposed ingenious "diagnostic" tests to identify those who were possessed. The water-float test was based on the principle that pure metals sink to the bottom during smelting. Impurities float to the surface. Suspects were thus placed in deep water. Those who sank to the bottom and drowned were judged to be pure. Those who managed to keep their heads above water were assumed to be "impure" and in league with the devil. Then they were in real trouble. This ordeal is the origin of the phrase "Damned if you do, and damned if you don't."

Few people in the United States today would argue that unusual or unacceptable behavior is caused by demons. Still, we continue to use "demonic" language. How many times have you heard the expressions "Something got into me" or "The devil made me do it"?

Throughout history, most people have explained disorders like those of William and Hinckley from a demonological perspective. Today, however, psychologists and other health professionals tend to explain psychological disorders from various psychological perspectives: the evolutionary and biological perspectives, the cognitive perspective, the humanistic–existential perspective, the psychodynamic perspective, and the learning perspective.

■ **Exorcism**

This medieval woodcut represents the practice of exorcism, in which a demon is expelled from a person who has been "possessed."

© PIERRE PERRIN/CORBIS SYGMA

■ **A Person with a Phobia for Spiders**

Phobias are excessive, irrational fears that can interfere with the person's functioning. A phobia for needles can prevent a person from seeking needed medical assistance.

We will see how these various perspectives explain each of the disorders covered in the chapter. In many cases we will see that there is an *interaction* between perspectives, such as the biological perspective and the cognitive perspective. We will also frequently find an interaction between the biological *nature* of the individual and his or her life experiences, or *nurture*. The origins of psychological disorders are often complex. We cannot pretend that they are simple, but we can present them clearly.

Let us now consider the kinds of psychological disorders. Some of them, like anxiety disorders, are common. Others, like dissociative identity disorder, are rare.

Learning Connections
See Web site for an interactive version of these review questions.

REVIEW

(1) Behavior is labeled abnormal when it is unusual, is socially unacceptable, involves faulty _____ of reality (as with hallucinations), is dangerous, self-defeating, or distressing. (2) The *DSM* was written by the American _____ Association. (3) Thomas _____ argues that labeling people with problems in living as "sick" degrades them and encourages them to evade responsibility. (4) Since the Middle Ages, Europeans have largely explained psychological disorders in terms of _____ by the devil. (5) The document called *The* _____ *of Witches* proposed tests to identify people who were "possessed."

Critical Thinking: When does a psychological problem become a "psychological disorder"? Is the border clearly defined?

REFLECT

Do you know anyone with a phobia? What kind of phobia? Does the phobia seriously interfere with his or her life? How so?

Specific Phobia
Persistent fear of a specific object or situation.

Claustrophobia
Fear of tight, small places.

Acrophobia
Fear of high places.

ANXIETY DISORDERS

Anxiety has psychological and physical features. Psychological features include worrying, fear of the worst things happening, fear of losing control, nervousness, and inability to relax. Physical features reflect arousal of the sympathetic branch of the autonomic nervous system. They include trembling, sweating, a pounding or racing heart, elevated blood pressure (a flushed face), and faintness. Anxiety is an appropriate response to a real threat. It can be abnormal, however, when it is excessive or when it comes out of nowhere—that is, when events do not seem to warrant it. *Question: What kinds of anxiety disorders are there?* There are different kinds of anxiety disorders, but all of them are characterized by excessive or unwarranted anxiety.

Types of Anxiety Disorders

The anxiety disorders include phobias, panic disorder, generalized anxiety, obsessive–compulsive disorder, and stress disorders.

Phobias

There are several types of phobias, including specific phobias, social phobia, and agoraphobia. Some of them, such as social phobia, can be highly detrimental to one's quality of life (Stein & Kean, 2000). **Specific phobias** are excessive, irrational fears of specific objects or situations, such as snakes or heights. One specific phobia is fear of elevators. Some people will not enter elevators despite the hardships they incur as a result (such as walking up six flights of steps). Yes, the cable *could* break. The ventilation *could* fail. One *could* be stuck in midair waiting for repairs. These problems are uncommon, however, and it does not make sense for most people to walk up and down several flights of stairs to elude them. Similarly, some people with a specific phobia for hypodermic needles will not have injections, even to treat profound illness. Injections can be painful, but most people with a phobia for needles would gladly suffer an even more painful pinch if it would help them fight illness. Other specific phobias include **claustrophobia** (fear of tight or enclosed places), **acrophobia** (fear of heights), and fear of mice, snakes, and other creepy-crawlies. Fears of animals and imaginary creatures are common among children.

Social phobias are persistent fears of scrutiny by others or of doing something that will be humiliating or embarrassing. Fear of public speaking is a common social phobia.

Agoraphobia is also widespread among adults. Agoraphobia is derived from the Greek words meaning "fear of the marketplace," or fear of being out in open, busy areas. Persons with agoraphobia fear being in places from which it might be difficult to escape or in which help might not be available if they get upset. In practice, people who receive this diagnosis often refuse to venture out of their homes, especially by themselves. They find it difficult to hold a job or to maintain an ordinary social life.

Panic Disorder

My heart would start pounding so hard I was sure I was having a heart attack. I used to go to the emergency room. Sometimes I felt dizzy, like I was going to pass out. I was sure I was about to die.

—Kim Weiner

Panic disorder is an abrupt attack of acute anxiety that is not triggered by a specific object or situation. People with panic disorder have strong physical symptoms such as shortness of breath, heavy sweating, tremors, and pounding of the heart. Like Kim Weiner (1992), they are particularly aware of cardiac sensations (Wilhelm et al., 2001). It is not unusual for them to think they are having a heart attack. Saliva levels of cortisol (a stress hormone) are elevated during attacks (Bandelow et al., 2000). Many fear suffocation. People with the disorder may also experience choking sensations, nausea, numbness or tingling, flushes or chills, and fear of going crazy or losing control. Panic attacks may last minutes or hours. Afterwards, the person usually feels drained.

Many people panic now and then. The diagnosis of panic disorder is reserved for those who undergo a series of attacks or live in fear of attacks.

Panic attacks seem to come from nowhere. Thus, some people who have had them stay home for fear of having an attack in public. They are diagnosed as having panic disorder with agoraphobia.

Generalized Anxiety Disorder

The central feature of **generalized anxiety disorder** is persistent anxiety. As with panic disorder, the anxiety cannot be attributed to a phobic object, situation, or activity. Rather, it seems to be free floating. The core of the disorder appears to be pervasive worrying about numerous stressors (Aikins & Craske, 2001). Features of the disorder include motor tension (shakiness, inability to relax, furrowed brow, fidgeting); autonomic overarousal (sweating, dry mouth, racing heart, light-headedness, frequent urinating, diarrhea); and excessive vigilance, as shown by irritability, insomnia, and a tendency to be easily distracted.

Obsessive–Compulsive Disorder

Obsessions are recurrent, anxiety-provoking thoughts or images that seem irrational and beyond control. They are so compelling and recurrent that they disrupt daily life. They may include doubts about whether one has locked the doors and shut the windows or images such as one mother's repeated fantasy that her children had been run over on the way home from school. One woman became obsessed with the idea that she had contaminated her hands with toilet cleaner and that the chemicals were spreading to everything she touched. A 16-year-old boy found "numbers in his head" when he was about to study or take a test.

Compulsions are thoughts or behaviors that tend to reduce the anxiety connected with obsessions. They are seemingly irresistible urges to engage in specific acts, often repeatedly, such as elaborate washing after using the bathroom. The impulse is recurrent and forceful, interfering with daily life. The woman who felt contaminated by toilet cleaner spent three to four hours at the sink each day and complained, "My hands look like lobster claws."

REFLECT

Do you know people who repeatedly check that the doors are locked or the gas jets are turned off before they leave home? Or people who refuse to step on the cracks in the sidewalk? Does their behavior seem to fit the definition of obsessive–compulsive disorder?

Social Phobia
An irrational, excessive fear of public scrutiny.

Agoraphobia
Fear of open, crowded places.

Panic Disorder
The recurrent experiencing of attacks of extreme anxiety in the absence of external stimuli that usually elicit anxiety.

Generalized Anxiety Disorder
Feelings of dread and foreboding and sympathetic arousal of at least six months' duration.

Obsession
A recurring thought or image that seems beyond control.

Compulsion
An apparently irresistible urge to repeat an act or engage in ritualistic behavior such as hand washing.

Stress Disorders

Darla, who lives in Oregon, dreamed that she was trapped in a World Trade Center tower when it was hit by an airplane on September 11, 2001. Kelly, a Californian, dreamed of a beautiful bald eagle that was suddenly transformed into a snarling bird that with glowing red eyes ("Sleepers Suffer WTC Nightmares," 2001).

The all-too-real nightmare of the events of September 11 have caused many people to have bad dreams. Such dreams are part of the experience of posttraumatic stress disorder.

Posttraumatic stress disorder (PTSD) is characterized by a rapid heart rate and feelings of anxiety and helplessness that are caused by a traumatic experience. Such experiences may include a natural or humanmade disaster, a threat or assault, or witnessing a death. PTSD may occur months or years after the event. It frequently occurs among firefighters, combat veterans, and people whose homes and communities have been swept away by natural disasters or who have been victims of violence (Vasterling et al., 2002; Waelde et al., 2001; Weinstein et al., 2001). A study of former political prisoners found that PTSD was connected with feelings of mental defeat during the traumatic experience, feelings of alienation from other people, and perceived permanent change in personality or life aspirations (Ehlers et al., 2000).

The traumatic event is revisited in the form of intrusive memories, recurrent dreams, and flashbacks—the sudden feeling that the event is recurring (Rutkowski, 2001; Yehuda, 2002). People with PTSD typically try to avoid thoughts and activities connected to the traumatic event. They may also find it more difficult to enjoy life (Beckham et al., 2000) and have sleep problems (Lavie, 2001), irritable outbursts, difficulty concentrating, extreme vigilance, and an intensified "startle" response (Shayley et al., 2000). The terrorist attacks of September 11, 2001, took their toll on sleep. According to a poll taken by the National Sleep Foundation (2001) two months after the attacks, nearly half of Americans had difficulty falling asleep, as compared with about one-quarter of Americans before the attacks (Figure 12.1). Women respondents were more likely than men to report sleep problems—for example, difficulty falling asleep (50% vs. 37%).

Posttraumatic Stress Disorder (PTSD)
A disorder that follows a distressing event outside the range of normal human experience and that is characterized by features such as intense fear, avoidance of stimuli associated with the event, and reliving of the event.

■ **A Traumatic Experience**
Traumatic experiences like the terrorist attack on of the World Trade Center can lead to posttraumatic stress disorder (PTSD). PTSD is characterized by intrusive memories of the experience, recurrent dreams about it, and the sudden feeling that it is, in fact, recurring (as in "flashbacks").

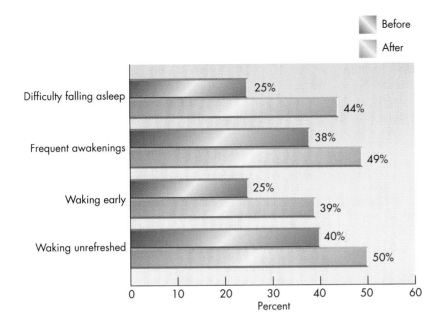

Before
After

- Difficulty falling asleep — 25% / 44%
- Frequent awakenings — 38% / 49%
- Waking early — 25% / 39%
- Waking unrefreshed — 40% / 50%

Percent (0, 10, 20, 30, 40, 50, 60)

Figure 12.1
Sleep Problems Among Americans Before and After September 11, 2001
Insomnia is one of the symptoms of stress disorders. A poll by the National Sleep Foundation found that Americans had a greater frequency of sleep problems after the terrorist attacks of September 11.

Acute stress disorder, like PTSD, is characterized by feelings of anxiety and help-lessness that are caused by a traumatic event. However, PTSD can occur six months or more after the traumatic event and tends to persist. Acute stress disorder occurs within a month of the event and lasts from two days to four weeks. Women who have been raped, for example, experience acute distress that tends to peak in severity about three weeks after the assault (Davidson & Foa, 1991; Rothbaum et al., 1992).

Theoretical Views

There are thus several kinds of anxiety disorders. *Question: What is known about the origins of anxiety disorders?*

Psychological Views

According to the psychodynamic perspective, phobias symbolize conflicts originating in childhood. Psychodynamic theory explains generalized anxiety as persistent diffi-culty in repressing primitive impulses. Obsessions are explained as leakage of uncon-scious impulses, and compulsions are seen as acts that allow people to keep such impulses partly repressed. For example, fixation in the anal stage is theorized to be connected with development of traits such as excessive neatness of the sort that could explain some cases of obsessive–compulsive disorder.

Some learning theorists—particularly behaviorists—consider phobias to be condi-tioned fears that were acquired in early childhood. Therefore, their origins are beyond memory. Avoidance of feared stimuli is reinforced by the reduction of anxiety.

Other learning theorists—social–cognitive theorists—note that observational learn-ing plays a role in the acquisition of fears (Basic Behavioral Science Task Force, 1996b). If parents squirm, grimace, and shudder at the sight of mice, blood, or dirt on the kitchen floor, children might assume that these stimuli are awful and imitate their par-ents' behavior.

Cognitive theorists suggest that anxiety is maintained by thinking that one is in a terrible situation and helpless to change it. People with anxiety disorders may be cog-nitively biased toward paying a good deal of attention to threats (Fox et al., 2001; Sookman et al., 2001). Psychoanalysts and learning theorists agree that compulsive behavior reduces anxiety.

Cognitive theorists note that people's appraisals of the magnitude of threats help determine whether they are traumatic and can lead to PTSD (Folkman & Moskowitz, 2000a). People with panic attacks tend to misinterpret bodily cues and to view them as

REFLECT
Have you ever heard anyone described as being "anal"? How does the description relate to the psychodynamic explanation of obsessive–compulsive disorder?

Acute Stress Disorder
A disorder, like PTSD, that is charac-terized by feelings of anxiety and helplessness and caused by a trau-matic event. Acute stress disorder occurs within a month of the event and lasts from two days to four weeks.

threats. Obsessions and compulsions may serve to divert attention from more frightening issues, such as "What am I going to do with my life?" When anxieties are acquired at a young age, we may later interpret them as enduring traits and label ourselves as "people who fear _____" (you fill it in). We then live up to the labels. We also entertain thoughts that heighten and perpetuate anxiety, such as "I've got to get out of here," or "My heart is going to leap out of my chest." Such ideas intensify physical signs of anxiety, disrupt planning, make stimuli seem worse than they really are, motivate avoidance, and decrease self-efficacy expectations. The belief that we will not be able to handle a threat heightens anxiety. The belief that we are in control reduces anxiety (Bandura et al., 1985).

Biological Views

Biological factors play a role in anxiety disorders. Genetic factors are implicated in most psychological disorders, including anxiety disorders (Kendler et al., 2001; Nestadt et al., 2000; Schmidt et al., 2000). For one thing, anxiety disorders tend to run in families. Twin studies find a higher **concordance** rate for anxiety disorders among identical twins than among fraternal twins (Kendler et al., 2001). Studies of adoptees who are anxious similarly show that the biological parent places the child at risk for anxiety and related traits.

Anxiety may reflect natural selection. Susan Mineka (Oehman & Mineka, 2001) suggests that humans (and nonhuman primates) are genetically predisposed to fear stimuli that may have posed a threat to their ancestors. Evolutionary forces would have favored the survival of individuals who were predisposed toward acquiring fears of large animals, spiders, snakes, heights, entrapment, sharp objects, and strangers.

Perhaps a predisposition toward anxiety—in the form of a highly reactive autonomic nervous system—can be inherited. What might make a nervous system "highly reactive"? In the case of panic disorder, faulty regulation of levels of serotonin and norepinephrine may be involved. In other anxiety disorders, receptor sites in the brain may not be sensitive enough to **gamma-aminobutyric acid (GABA),** a neurotransmitter that may help calm anxiety reactions (Stroele et al., 2002). The **benzodiazepines,** a class of drugs that reduce anxiety, may work by increasing the sensitivity of receptor sites to GABA.

In many cases anxiety disorders may reflect the interaction of biological and psychological factors. In panic disorder, biological imbalances may initially trigger attacks. However, subsequent fear of attacks—and of the bodily cues that signal their onset—may heighten discomfort and give one the idea there is nothing one can do about them (Craske & Zucker, 2001). Feelings of helplessness increase fear. People with panic disorder therefore can be helped by psychological methods that provide ways of reducing physical discomfort—including regular breathing—and show them that there are, after all, things they can do to cope with attacks (Craske & Zucker, 2001).

Learning Connections
See the Connections *CD-ROM for an animation on the interaction of GABA and barbiturates.*

Concordance
Agreement.

Gamma-Aminobutyric Acid (GABA)
An inhibitory neurotransmitter that is implicated in anxiety reactions.

Benzodiazepines
A class of drugs that reduce anxiety; minor tranquilizers.

Learning Connections
See Web site for an interactive version of these review questions.

R E V I E W

(6) A _____ is an irrational fear. (7) _____ disorder is characterized by sudden attacks in which people typically fear that they may be losing control or going crazy. (8) In obsessive–_____ disorder people are troubled by intrusive thoughts or impulses to repeat some activity. (9) _____ is caused by a traumatic experience and characterized by reliving it the form of intrusive memories, recurrent dreams, and flashbacks. (10) Psychodynamic theory explains generalized anxiety as persistent difficulty in maintaining _____ of primitive impulses. (11) _____ see phobias as conditioned fears. (12) Anxiety disorders (do or do not?) tend to run in families.

Critical Thinking: Critical thinkers attend to the definitions of terms. For example, is anxiety abnormal? What is the difference between run-of-the-mill anxiety and an *anxiety disorder?*

DISSOCIATIVE DISORDERS

William's disorder, described at the beginning of the chapter, was a dissociative disorder. In the **dissociative disorders** there is a separation of mental processes such as thoughts, emotions, identity, memory, or consciousness—the processes that make the person feel whole.   *Question: What kinds of dissociative disorders are there?*

Types of Dissociative Disorders

The *DSM* lists several dissociative disorders. Among them are dissociative amnesia, dissociative fugue, and dissociative identity disorder (also termed multiple personality).

Dissociative Amnesia

In **dissociative amnesia** the person is suddenly unable to recall important personal information (that is, explicit episodic memories). The loss of memory cannot be attributed to organic problems such as a blow to the head or alcoholic intoxication. It is thus a psychological dissociative disorder and not an organic one. In the most common example, the person cannot recall events for a number of hours after a stressful incident, as in warfare or in the case of an uninjured survivor of an accident. In generalized amnesia, people forget their entire lives. Amnesia may last for hours or years.

Dissociative Fugue

In **dissociative fugue,** the person abruptly leaves his or her home or place of work and travels to another place, having lost all memory of his or her past life. While at the new location, the person either does not think about the past or reports a past filled with invented memories. The new personality is often more outgoing and less inhibited than the "real" identity. Following recovery, the events that occurred during the fugue are not recalled.

Dissociative Identity Disorder

Dissociative identity disorder (formerly termed *multiple personality disorder*) is the name given to William's disorder. In dissociative identity disorder, two or more identities or personalities, each with distinct traits and memories, "occupy" the same person. Each identity may or may not be aware of the others.

The identities of people with dissociative identity disorder can be very different from one another. They might even have different eyeglass prescriptions (Braun, 1988). Braun reports cases in which assorted identities showed different allergic responses. In one person, an identity named Timmy was not sensitive to orange juice. But when other identities gained control over him and drank orange juice, he would break out with hives. Hives would also erupt if another identity emerged while the juice was being digested. If Timmy reappeared when the allergic reaction was present, the itching of the hives would cease, and the blisters would start to subside. In other cases reported by Braun, different identities within a person might show various responses to the same medicine. Or one identity might exhibit color blindness while others have normal color vision.

A few celebrated cases of this disorder have been portrayed in the popular media. One of them became the subject of the film *The Three Faces of Eve.* A timid housewife named Eve White harbored two other identities. One was Eve Black, a sexually aggressive, antisocial personality. The third was Jane, an emerging identity who was able to accept the existence of her primitive impulses yet engage in socially appropriate behavior. Finally the three faces merged into one—Jane. Ironically, later on, Jane (Chris Sizemore in real life) reportedly split into 22 identities. Another well-publicized case is that of Sybil, a woman with 16 identities who was portrayed by Sally Field in the film *Sybil.*

> ▶ CONTROVERSY IN PSYCHOLOGY ◀
>
> ### Do dissociative disorders really exist?
>
> There is a good deal of skepticism about whether dissociative disorders exist (Thomas, 2001). For example, there were about 50 known cases of dissociative identity disorder before the public learned about "Sybil." By the 1990s, however, this number had mushroomed to more than 20,000 ("Tapes raise new doubts," 1998). Moreover, psychologists who have listened carefully to tapes of Sybil's therapy have raised the possibility that some of her psychiatrists may have "coached" her into reporting the symptoms. Sybil herself is reported to have vacillated as to whether or not her story was true ("Tapes raise new doubts," 1998). It is possible that many or even most people who are diagnosed with dissociative amnesia or dissociative identity disorder are faking. The technical term for faking in order to obtain some benefit—such as being excused from responsibility for a crime or for family obligations—is *malingering.*

Dissociative Disorders
Disorders in which there are sudden, temporary changes in consciousness or self-identity.

Dissociative Amnesia
A dissociative disorder marked by loss of memory or self-identity; skills and general knowledge are usually retained. Previously termed *psychogenic amnesia.*

Dissociative Fugue
A dissociative disorder in which one experiences amnesia and then flees to a new location. Previously termed *psychogenic fugue.*

■ Dissociative Identity Disorder

In the film *The Three Faces of Eve*, Joanne Woodward played three personalities in the same woman: the shy, inhibited Eve White (lying on couch); the flirtatious, promiscuous Eve Black (in dark dress); and a third personality (Jane) who could accept her sexual and aggressive impulses and still maintain her sense of identity.

REFLECT

Have you seen a film or a TV show in which a character was supposed to have dissociative identity disorder (perhaps it was called "multiple personality")? What kind of behavior did the character display? Does the behavior seem consistent with the description of the disorder in the text? In the film or TV show, what were the supposed origins of the disorder?

 Learning Connections
See Web site for an interactive version of these review questions.

Theoretical Views

The dissociative disorders are some of the odder psychological disorders. *Question: What is known about the origins of dissociative disorders?*

Psychologists of different theoretical persuasions have offered hypotheses about the origins of dissociative identity disorder and other dissociative disorders. According to psychodynamic theory, for example, people with dissociative disorders use massive repression to prevent them from recognizing improper impulses or remembering ugly events (Vaillant, 1994). In dissociative amnesia and fugue, the person forgets a profoundly disturbing event or impulse. In dissociative identity disorder, the person expresses unacceptable impulses through alternate identities.

According to learning theorists, people with dissociative disorders have learned *not to think* about bad memories or disturbing impulses in order to avoid feelings of anxiety, guilt, and shame. Both psychodynamic and learning theories suggest that dissociative disorders help people keep disturbing memories or ideas out of mind. Of what could such memories be? Research suggests that many—perhaps most—cases involve memories of sexual or physical abuse during childhood, usually by a relative or caretaker (Coons, 1994; Martinez-Taboas & Bernal, 2000; Weaver & Clum, 1995). Yet some studies find no connection between dissociative disorders in adulthood and abuse in childhood (Elzinga et al., 2002).

Perhaps all of us are capable of dividing our awareness so that we become unaware, at least temporarily, of events that we usually focus more attention on. The dissociative disorders raise fascinating questions about the nature of human self-identity and memory. Perhaps it is no surprise that attention can be divided. Perhaps the surprising thing is that human consciousness normally integrates an often chaotic set of experiences into a meaningful whole.

REVIEW

(13) Dissociative _____ is characterized by motivated forgetting. (14) In dissociative _____ disorder, the person behaves as if distinct personalities occupy the body. (15) According to learning theory, people learn not to _____ about disturbing acts or impulses in dissociative disorders. (16) Many people with dissociative disorders have a history of physical or sexual _____.

Critical Thinking: What is malingering? Can you think of a way to determine whether someone who claims to have a dissociative disorder is malingering?

SOMATOFORM DISORDERS

Somatoform Disorders
Disorders in which people complain of physical (somatic) problems even though no physical abnormality can be found.

People with **somatoform disorders** complain of physical problems such as paralysis, pain, or a persistent belief that they have a serious disease. Yet no evidence of a physical abnormality can be found. *Question: What kinds of somatoform disorders are there?* In this section we discuss two somatoform disorders: conversion disorder and hypochondriasis.

Types of Somatoform Disorders

Conversion disorder is characterized by a major change in, or loss of, physical functioning, although there are no medical findings to explain the loss of functioning. The behaviors are not intentionally produced. That is, the person is not faking. Conversion disorder is so named because it appears to "convert" a source of stress into a physical difficulty.

If you lost the ability to see at night, or if your legs became paralyzed, you would understandably show concern. But some people with conversion disorder show indifference to their symptoms, a remarkable feature referred to as **la belle indifférence.**

During World War II, some bomber pilots developed night blindness. They could not carry out their nighttime missions, although no damage to the optic nerves was found. In rare cases, women with large families have been reported to become paralyzed in the legs, again with no medical findings. More recently, a Cambodian woman who had witnessed atrocities became blind as a result.

Another more common type of somatoform disorder is **hypochondriasis** (also called *hypochondria*). People with this disorder insist that they are suffering from a serious physical illness, even though no medical evidence of illness can be found. They become preoccupied with minor physical sensations and continue to believe that they are ill despite the reassurance of physicians that they are healthy. They may run from doctor to doctor, seeking the one who will find the causes of the sensations. Fear of illness may disrupt their work or home life.   *Question: What is known about the origins of somatoform disorders?*

Theoretical Views

There is evidence that people with conversion disorder are susceptible to being hypnotized. In fact, some investigators consider conversion disorder to be a form of self-hypnosis (Roelofs et al., 2002). The idea here would seem to be that individuals with conversion disorder bring themselves to focus intently on an imaginary physical problem, to the point where they exclude conflicting information.

There is research evidence that people who develop hypochondriasis are particularly sensitive to bodily sensations and tend to ruminate about them (Lecci & Cohen, 2002). However, the history of the name of the somatoform disorders affords us insight into an interesting former sexist explanation of them. Consistent with psychodynamic theory, early versions of the *DSM* labeled somatoform disorders as "hysterical neuroses."

Conversion Disorder
A disorder in which anxiety or unconscious conflicts are "converted" into physical symptoms that often have the effect of helping the person cope with anxiety or conflict.

La Belle Indifférence
A French term descriptive of the lack of concern sometimes shown by people with conversion disorders.

Hypochondriasis
Persistent belief that one has a medical disorder despite lack of medical findings.

▶ CONTROVERSY IN PSYCHOLOGY ◀

Are somatoform disorders the special province of women?

"Hysterical" derives from the word *hystera*, the Greek word for uterus or womb. Like many other Greeks, Hippocrates believed that hysteria was a sort of female trouble that was caused by a wandering uterus. It was erroneously thought that the uterus could roam through the body—that it was not anchored in place! As the uterus meandered, it could cause pains and odd sensations almost anywhere. The Greeks also believed that pregnancy anchored the uterus and ended hysterical complaints. What do you think Greek physicians prescribed to end monthly aches and pains? Good guess.

Even in the earlier years of the 20th century, it was suggested that strange sensations and medically unfounded complaints were largely the province of women. Moreover, viewing the problem as a neurosis suggested that it stemmed from unconscious childhood conflicts. The psychodynamic view of conversion disorders is that the symptoms protect the individual from feelings of guilt or shame, or from another source of stress. Conversion disorders, like dissociative disorders, often seem to serve a purpose. For example, the "blindness" of the World War II pilots may have enabled them to avoid feelings of fear of being literally shot down or of guilt for killing civilians. The night blindness of the pilots shows that conversion disorders are not the special province of women—whether they were once labeled hysterical or not.

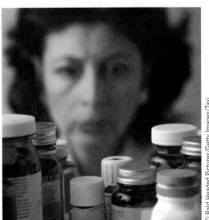

© Bald Headed Pictures/Getty Images/Taxi

■ **Hypochondriasis**
People with hypochondriasis are irrationally concerned that they have contracted illnesses. Such people appear to be unusually sensitive to physical sensations. Do they also focus on their physical symptoms as an alternative to dealing with the social and other problems in their lives?

Learning Connections
See Web site for an interactive version of these review questions.

REVIEW

(17) In _____ disorders, people complain of physical problems or persist in believing they have a serious disease, even though no medical problem can be found. (18) In a _____ disorder, there is a major change in or loss of physical functioning with no organic basis.

Critical Thinking: Why have somatoform disorders been considered "hysterical"? What are the social problems in labeling them as hysterical?

MOOD DISORDERS

Mood disorders are characterized by disturbance in expressed emotions. The disruption generally involves sadness or elation. Most instances of sadness are normal, or "run-of-the-mill." If you have failed an important test, if you have lost money in a business venture, or if your closest friend becomes ill, it is understandable and fitting for you to be sad about it. It would be odd, in fact, if you were *not* affected by adversity.

Types of Mood Disorders

Question: What kinds of mood disorders are there? In this section we discuss two mood disorders: major depression and bipolar disorder.

Major Depression

Depression is the common cold of psychological problems, affecting upwards of 10% of adults at any time (Alloy et al., 1990). People with run-of-the-mill depression may feel sad, blue, or "down in the dumps." They may complain of lack of energy, loss of self-esteem, difficulty concentrating, loss of interest in activities and other people (Nezlek et al., 2000), pessimism, crying, and thoughts of suicide.

These feelings are more intense in people with **major depression.** People with this disorder may also show poor appetite, serious weight loss, and agitation or **psychomotor retardation.** They may be unable to concentrate and make decisions. They may say that they "don't care" anymore and in some cases attempt suicide. They may also display faulty perception of reality—so-called psychotic behaviors. These include delusions of unworthiness, guilt for imagined wrongdoings, even the notion that one is rotting from disease. There may also be delusions, as of the devil administering deserved punishment, or hallucinations, as of strange bodily sensations.

Bipolar Disorder

People with **bipolar disorder,** formerly known as *manic–depressive disorder,* have mood swings from ecstatic elation to deep depression. The cycles seem to be unrelated to external events. In the elated, or **manic** phase, the person may show excessive excitement or silliness, carrying jokes too far. The manic person may be argumentative. He or she may show poor judgment, destroying property, making huge contributions to charity, or giving away expensive possessions. People often find manic individuals abrasive and avoid them. They are often oversexed and too restless to sit still or sleep restfully. They often speak rapidly (showing "pressured speech") and jump from topic to topic (showing **rapid flight of ideas**). It can be hard to get a word in edgewise.

Depression is the other side of the coin. People with bipolar depression often sleep more than usual and are lethargic. People with major (or unipolar) depression are more likely to have insomnia and agitation. Those with bipolar depression also exhibit social withdrawal and irritability. Some people with bipolar disorder attempt suicide when the mood shifts from the elated phase toward depression (Jamison, 2000). They will do almost anything to escape the depths of depression that lie ahead.

REFLECT

Do you think that you would find it easy or difficult to admit to having feelings of depression? Explain.

Major Depression
A severe depressive disorder in which the person may show loss of appetite, psychomotor behaviors, and impaired reality testing.

Psychomotor Retardation
Slowness in motor activity and (apparently) in thought.

Bipolar Disorder
A disorder in which the mood alternates between two extreme poles (elation and depression). Also referred to as *manic–depression.*

Manic
Elated, showing excessive excitement.

Rapid Flight of Ideas
Rapid speech and topic changes, characteristic of manic behavior.

Theoretical Views

Question: What is known about the origins of mood disorders? Although the mood disorders are connected with processes within the individual, let us begin by noting that many kinds of situations are also connected with depression. For example, depression may be a reaction to losses and stress (Cowen, 2002; Mazure et al., 2000). Sources of chronic strain such as marital discord, physical discomfort, incompetence, and failure or pressure at work all contribute to feelings of depression (Nolen-Hoeksema et al., 1999). We tend to be more depressed by things we bring on ourselves, such as academic problems, financial problems, unwanted pregnancy, conflict with the law, arguments, and fights (Greenberger et al., 2000; Simons et al., 1995). However, some people recover from depression less readily than others. People who remain

R E F L E C T
How would you distinguish between "normal" depression or "normal" enthusiasm and a mood disorder?

A Closer Look

The Case of Women and Depression

Women are about two times more likely to be diagnosed with depression than men (Depression Research, 2000; Greenberger et al., 2000). This gender difference begins to emerge during adolescence, at about the age of 13 (Hankin & Abramson, 2001).

Many people assume that biological gender differences largely explain why women are more likely to become depressed. Low levels of estrogen are widely seen as the culprit. Estrogen levels plummet prior to menstruation, and how often do we hear degrading remarks such as "It must be that time of the month" when a woman expresses feelings of anger or irritation? But part of the gender difference may be due to the fact that men are less likely than women to admit to depression or seek treatment for depression. "I'm the John Wayne generation," admitted one man, a physician. "'It's only a flesh wound'; that's how you deal with it. I thought depression was a weakness—

■ **Women and Depression**

Women are much more likely than men to be diagnosed with depression. Does the gender difference reflect biases among the mental-health professionals who make the diagnoses, women's (frequent) status as second-class citizens, the fact that women are often expected to take care of the family as well as earn a living, hormonal and other biological differences between women and men, other factors—or all of the above or some of the above?

there was something disgraceful about it. A real man would just get over it" (cited in Wartik, 2000).

Still, in any given year, about 12% of women and 7% of men in the United States are estimated to be diagnosable with depression (Depression Research, 2000). It was once assumed that depression was most likely to accompany menopause in women, because women could no longer carry out their "natural" function of childbearing. However, women are more likely to encounter severe depression during the childbearing years (Depression Research, 2000).

Yes, hormonal changes during adolescence, the menstrual cycle, and childbirth may contribute to depression in women (Cyranowski et al., 2000; McGrath et al., 1990). The bodies and brains of males, on the other hand, are stoked by testosterone during adolescence. High testosterone levels are connected with feelings of self-confidence, high activity levels, and aggressiveness, a cluster of traits and behaviors that are more connected with elation (even if sometimes misplaced) than with depression (Pope et al., 2000; Sullivan, 2000).

However, some theorists suggest that women may also have a "cognitive vulnerability" to depression as well, connected, for example, with greater tendencies than men to ruminate about stresses and other negative events (Hankin & Abramson, 2001).

A panel convened by the American Psychological Association attributed most of the gender difference to the greater stresses placed on women, which tend to be greatest when they are trying to meet the multiple demands of childbearing, child rearing, and financial support of the family (McGrath et al., 1990). Women are more likely to experience physical and sexual abuse, poverty, single parenthood, and sexism. Single mothers, in particular, have lower socioeconomic status than men, and depression and other psychological disorders are more common among poor people (Hobfoll et al., 1995). Women are also more likely than men to help other people who are under stress. Supporting other people heaps additional caregiving burdens on themselves. A part of "therapy" for depressed women, then, is to modify the overwhelming demands that are placed on women today (Comas-Diaz, 1994). The pain may lie in the individual, but the cause often lies in society.

Learning Connections
See the Connections *CD-ROM for a video on depression and bipolar disorder.*

REFLECT

When you fall short of your goals, do you tend to be merciless in your self-criticism or to blame other people or "circumstances"? Do your views of your shortcomings tend to worsen or to ease your feelings of depression?

Learned Helplessness
A model for the acquisition of depressive behavior, based on findings that organisms in aversive situations learn to show inactivity when their operants go unreinforced.

Attributional Style
The tendency to attribute one's behavior to internal or external factors, stable or unstable factors, and so on.

Neuroticism
A personality trait characterized largely by persistent anxiety.

depressed have lower self-esteem (Andrews, 1998; Sherrington et al., 2001), are less likely to be able to solve social problems (Reinecke et al., 2001), and have less social support.

What are the origins of depression?

Psychological Views

Psychoanalysts suggest various explanations for depression. In one, people who are at risk for depression are overly concerned about hurting other people's feelings or losing their approval. As a result, they hold in feelings of anger rather than expressing them. Anger is turned inward and experienced as misery and self-hatred. From the psychodynamic perspective, bipolar disorder may be seen as alternating states in which the personality is first dominated by the superego and then by the ego. In the depressive phase of the disorder, the superego dominates, producing exaggerated ideas of wrongdoing and associated feelings of guilt and worthlessness. After a while the ego asserts supremacy, producing the elation and self-confidence often seen in the manic phase. Later, in response to the excessive display of ego, feelings of guilt return and plunge the person into depression once again.

Many learning theorists suggest that depressed people behave as though they cannot obtain reinforcement. For example, they appear to be inactive and apathetic. Many people with depressive disorders have an external locus of control. That is, they do not believe they can control events so as to achieve reinforcements (Tong, 2001; Weinmann et al., 2001).

Research conducted by learning theorists has also found links between depression and **learned helplessness.** In classic research, psychologist Martin Seligman taught dogs that they were helpless to escape an electric shock. The dogs were prevented from leaving a cage in which they received repeated shocks. Later, a barrier to a safe compartment was removed, offering the animals a way out. When they were shocked again, however, the dogs made no effort to escape. They had apparently learned that they were helpless. Seligman's dogs were also, in a sense, reinforced for doing nothing. That is, the shock *eventually* stopped when the dogs were showing helpless behavior—inactivity and withdrawal. "Reinforcement" might have increased the likelihood of repeating the "successful behavior"—that is, doing nothing—in a similar situation. This helpless behavior resembles that of people who are depressed.

Other cognitive factors also contribute to depression. For example, perfectionists set themselves up for depression by making irrational demands on themselves. They are likely to fall short of their (unrealistic) expectations and to feel depressed as a result (Flett & Hewitt, 2002; Hewitt et al., 1996).

Cognitive psychologists also note that people who ruminate about feelings of depression are more likely to prolong them (Nolen-Hoeksema, 2000; Spasojevic & Alloy, 2001). Women are more likely than men to ruminate about feelings of depression (Nolen-Hoeksema, 2001). Men seem more likely to try to fight off negative feelings by distracting themselves. Men are also more likely to distract themselves by turning to alcohol (Nolen-Hoeksema, 2001). They thus expose themselves and their families to further problems.

Still other cognitions involve the ways in which people explain their failures and shortcomings to themselves. Seligman (1996) suggests that when things go wrong we may think of the causes of failure as either *internal* or *external, stable* or *unstable, global* or *specific*. These various **attributional styles** can be illustrated using the example of having a date that does not work out. An internal attribution involves self-blame, as in "I really loused it up." An external attribution places the blame elsewhere (as in "Some couples just don't take to each other," or "She was the wrong sign for me"). A stable attribution ("It's my personality") suggests a problem that cannot be changed. An unstable attribution ("It was because I had a head cold") suggests a temporary condition. A global attribution of failure ("I have no idea what to do when I'm with other people") suggests that the problem is quite large. A specific attribution ("I have problems making small talk at the beginning of a relationship") chops the problem down to a manageable size. Research has shown that people who are depressed are more likely to attribute the causes of their failures to internal, stable, and global factors—factors that they are relatively powerless to change (Lewinsohn et al., 2000b; Ziegler & Hawley, 2001).

Let's add one remarkable note about attributional styles and the mind–body connection. Shelley Taylor and her colleagues (2000a) found that self-blame for negative events is connected with poorer functioning of the immune system. Too much self-blame, in other words, is not only depressing; it can also make us physically ill.

Biological Factors

Researchers are also searching for biological factors in mood disorders. Depression, for example, is often associated with the trait of **neuroticism,** which is heritable (Mulder, 2002). Anxiety is also connected with neuroticism, and mood and anxiety disorders are frequently found in the same person (Mulder, 2002).

Genetic factors appear to be involved in major depression and bipolar disorder (Jamison, 2000; Lewinsohn et al., 2000b; Nurnberger et al., 2001; Sullivan et al., 2000). Support for a role for genetic factors in bipolar disorder is found in twin and adoption studies (Craddock & Jones, 2001).

Research into depression focuses on underutilization of the neurotransmitter serotonin in the brain (Yatham et al., 2000). It has been shown, for example, that learned helplessness is connected with lower serotonin levels in the brains of rats (Wu et al., 1999). Moreover, people with severe depression often respond to drugs that heighten the action of serotonin.

Relationships between mood disorders and biological factors are complex and under intense study. Even if people are biologically predisposed toward depression, self-efficacy expectations and attitudes—particularly attitudes about whether one can change things for the better—may also play a role.

■ **Why Did He Miss That Tackle?**

This football player is compounding his feelings of depression by attributing his shortcomings on the field to factors that he cannot change. For example, he tells himself that he missed the tackle out of stupidity and lack of athletic ability. He ignores the facts that his coaching was poor and his teammates failed to support him.

R E V I E W

(19) Mood disorders are characterized by disturbance in expressed _____. (20) _____ depression can reach psychotic proportions, with grossly impaired reality testing. (21) In bipolar disorder there are mood swings between _____ and depression. (22) Manic people may have grand, delusional schemes and show rapid _____ of ideas. (23) Seligman and his colleagues have explored links between depression and learned _____. (24) Depressed people are more likely than other people to make (internal or external?), stable, and global attributions for failures. (25) Mood disorders (do or do not?) tend to run in families. (26) Deficiency in the neurotransmitter _____ may create a predisposition toward depression.

Critical Thinking: When is depression to be considered a psychological disorder? How does bipolar disorder differ from responses to the "ups and downs" of life?

Learning Connections
See Web site for an interactive version of these review questions.

SCHIZOPHRENIA

Jennifer was 19. Her husband David brought her into the emergency room because she had cut her wrists. When she was interviewed, her attention wandered. She seemed distracted by things in the air, or something she might be hearing. It was as if she had an invisible earphone.

She explained that she had cut her wrists because the "hellsmen" had told her to. Then she seemed frightened. Later she said that the hellsmen had warned her not to reveal their existence. She had been afraid that they would punish her for talking about them.

David and Jennifer had been married for about one year. At first they had been together in a small apartment in town. But Jennifer did not want to be near other people and had convinced him to rent a bungalow in the country. There she would make fantastic drawings of goblins and monsters during the days. Now and then she would become agitated and act as if invisible things were giving her instructions.

"I'm bad," Jennifer would mutter. "I'm bad." She would begin to jumble her words. David would then try to convince her to go to the hospital, but she would refuse. Then the wrist-cutting would begin. David thought he had made the cottage safe by removing knives and blades. But Jennifer would always find something.

Then Jennifer would be brought to the hospital, have stitches put in, be kept under observation for a while, and medicated. She would explain that she cut herself because the hellsmen had told her that she was bad and must die. After a few days she would deny hearing the hellsmen, and she would insist on leaving the hospital.

David would take her home. The pattern continued.

When the emergency room staff examined Jennifer's wrists and heard that she believed she had been following the orders of "hellsmen," they suspected that she could be diagnosed with schizophrenia. ***Question: What is schizophrenia?*** Schizophrenia is a severe psychological disorder that touches every aspect of a person's life. It is characterized by disturbances in thought and language, perception and attention, motor activity, and mood, and withdrawal and absorption in daydreams or fantasy.

Schizophrenia has been referred to as the worst disorder affecting human beings. It afflicts nearly 1% of the population worldwide. Its onset occurs relatively early in life, and its adverse effects tend to endure.

People with schizophrenia have problems in memory, attention, and communication. Their thinking and communication ability become unraveled (Kerns & Kerenbaum, 2002). Unless we are allowing our thoughts to wander, our thinking is normally tightly knit. We start at a certain point, and associated thoughts tend to be logically connected. But people with schizophrenia often think illogically. Their speech may be jumbled. They may combine parts of words into new words or make meaningless rhymes. They may jump from topic to topic, conveying little useful information. They usually do not recognize that their thoughts and behavior are abnormal.

Many people with schizophrenia have **delusions**—for example, delusions of grandeur, persecution, or reference. In the case of delusions of grandeur, a person may believe that he is a famous historical figure such as Jesus, or a person on a special mission. He may have grand, illogical plans for saving the world. Delusions tend to be unshakable even in the face of evidence that they are not true. People with delusions of persecution may believe that they are sought by the Mafia, CIA, FBI, or some other group. A woman with delusions of reference said that news stories contained coded information about her. A man with such delusions complained that neighbors had "bugged" his walls with "radios." Other people with schizophrenia have had delusions that they have committed unpardonable sins, that they were rotting away from disease, or that they or the world did not exist.

The perceptions of people with schizophrenia often include hallucinations—imagery in the absence of external stimulation that the person cannot distinguish from reality. In Shakespeare's *Macbeth*, for example, after killing King Duncan, Macbeth apparently experiences a hallucination:

> *Is this a dagger which I see before me,*
>
> *The handle toward my hand? Come, let me clutch thee:*
>
> *I have thee not, and yet I see thee still.*
>
> *Art thou not, fatal vision, sensible*
>
> *To feeling as to sight? or art thou but*
>
> *A dagger of the mind, a false creation,*
>
> *Proceeding from the heat-oppressed brain?*

Jennifer apparently hallucinated the voices of "hellsmen." Other people who experience hallucinations may see colors or even obscene words spelled out in midair. Auditory hallucinations are the most common type.

In individuals with schizophrenia, motor activity may become wild or become so slow that the person is said to be in a **stupor.** There may be strange gestures and facial expressions. The person's emotional responses may be flat or blunted, or inappropriate—as in giggling upon hearing bad news. People with schizophrenia tend to withdraw from social contacts, and become wrapped up in their own thoughts and fantasies. ***Question: What kinds of schizophrenia are there?***

 Learning Connections
See the Connections *CD-ROM for a video on the symptoms of schizophrenia.*

 Learning Connections
See the Connections *CD-ROM for a video on the causes of schizophrenia.*

REFLECT

Have you ever heard the expression "split personality"? Does the expression seem to apply more to dissociative identity disorder or schizophrenia? Explain.

Delusions
False, persistent beliefs that are unsubstantiated by sensory or objective evidence.

Stupor
A condition in which the senses and thought are dulled.

Types of Schizophrenia

There are three major types of schizophrenia: paranoid, disorganized, and catatonic.

Paranoid Type

People with **paranoid schizophrenia** have systematized delusions and, frequently, related auditory hallucinations. They usually have delusions of grandeur and persecution, but they may also have delusions of jealousy, in which they believe that a spouse or lover has been unfaithful. They may show agitation, confusion, and fear, and may experience vivid hallucinations that are consistent with their delusions. People with paranoid schizophrenia often construct complex or systematized delusions involving themes of wrongdoing or persecution. John Nash, the character in the true story *A Beautiful Mind,* believed that the government was recruiting him to decipher coded messages by our Cold War enemies.

Disorganized Type

People with **disorganized schizophrenia** show incoherence, loosening of associations, disorganized behavior, disorganized delusions, fragmentary delusions or hallucinations, and flat or highly inappropriate emotional responses. Extreme social impairment is common. People with this type of schizophrenia may also exhibit silliness and giddiness of mood, giggling, and nonsensical speech. They may neglect their appearance and personal hygiene and lose control of their bladder and bowels.

Catatonic Type

People with **catatonic schizophrenia** show striking impairment in motor activity. It is characterized by a slowing of activity into a stupor that may suddenly change into an agitated phase. Catatonic individuals may maintain unusual, even difficult postures for hours, even as their limbs grow swollen or stiff. A striking feature of this condition is **waxy flexibility,** in which the person maintains positions into which he or she has been manipulated by others. Catatonic individuals may also show **mutism,** but afterward they usually report that they heard what others were saying at the time.

Schizophrenia is thus characterized by extremely unusual behavior. ***Question: What is known about the origins of schizophrenia?***

Theoretical Views

Psychologists have investigated various factors that may contribute to schizophrenia. They include psychological and biological factors.

Psychological Views

According to the psychodynamic perspective, schizophrenia occurs because the ego is overwhelmed by sexual or aggressive impulses from the id. The impulses threaten the ego and cause intense inner conflict. Under this threat, the person regresses to an early phase of the oral stage in which the infant has not yet learned that it and the world are separate. Fantasies become confused with reality, giving rise to hallucinations and delusions. Yet critics point out that schizophrenic behavior is not the same as infantile behavior.

Most learning theorists explain schizophrenia in terms of conditioning and observational learning. From this perspective, people engage in schizophrenic behavior when it is more likely to be reinforced than normal behavior. This may occur when a person is reared in a socially unrewarding or punitive situation. Inner fantasies then become more reinforcing than social realities.

Patients in a psychiatric hospital may learn what is "expected" by observing others. Hospital staff may reinforce schizophrenic behavior by paying more attention to patients who behave bizarrely. This view is consistent with folklore that the child who disrupts the class attracts more attention from the teacher than the "good" child.

Although quality of parenting is connected with the development of schizophrenia (Buckley et al., 2000), critics note that many people who are reared in socially punitive

Paranoid Schizophrenia
A type of schizophrenia characterized primarily by delusions—commonly of persecution—and by vivid hallucinations.

Disorganized Schizophrenia
A type of schizophrenia characterized by disorganized delusions and vivid hallucinations.

Catatonic Schizophrenia
A type of schizophrenia characterized by striking motor impairment.

Waxy Flexibility
A feature of catatonic schizophrenia in which people can be molded into postures that they maintain for quite some time.

Mutism
Refusal to talk.

■ **Schizophrenia in *A Beautiful Mind***

In the film *A Beautiful Mind*, Russell Crowe played the role of the mathematician John Forbes Nash, Jr. Nash struggled with schizophrenia for more than three decades and was eventually awarded a Nobel Prize for work he had done as a graduate student decades earlier. People with paranoid schizophrenia may have hallucinations and systematized delusions, often involving the idea that they are being persecuted or are on a special mission. Although they cannot be argued out of their delusions, their cognitive functioning is relatively intact compared to that of disorganized and catatonic schizophrenics. In the film, Nash's hallucinations are presented as being just as real to him as the actual external world. For example, he believed he had a roommate in graduate school who never really existed.

© Grunnitus/Photo Researchers, Inc.

■ **Catatonic Schizophrenia**

People with catatonic schizophrenia show striking motor impairment and may hold unusual positions for hours.

R E F L E C T

There is evidence for a genetic role in schizophrenia. What would you tell the son or daughter of a person with schizophrenia about the likelihood of his or her developing schizophrenia? Explain.

settings are apparently immune to the extinction of socially appropriate behavior. Other people develop schizophrenic behavior without having had opportunities to observe other people with schizophrenia.

Many investigators have considered whether and how social and cultural factors such as poverty, discrimination, and overcrowding contribute to schizophrenia—especially among people who are genetically vulnerable to the disorder. Classic research in New Haven, Connecticut, showed that the rate of schizophrenia was twice as high in the lowest socioeconomic class as in the next-higher class on the socioeconomic ladder (Hollingshead & Redlich, 1958). It appears that poor-quality housing contributes to psychological disorder (Evans et al., 2000). Some sociocultural theorists therefore suggest that treatment of schizophrenia requires alleviation of poverty and other social ills, rather than changing people whose behavior is deviant.

Critics of this view suggest that low socioeconomic status may be a result, rather than a cause, of schizophrenia. People with schizophrenia may drift toward low social status because they lack the social skills and cognitive abilities to function at higher social class levels. Thus, they may wind up in poor neighborhoods in disproportionately high numbers.

Evidence for the hypothesis that people with schizophrenia drift downward to lower socioeconomic status is mixed. Many people with schizophrenia do drift downward occupationally in comparison with their fathers' occupations. Many others, however, were reared in families in which the father came from the lowest socioeconomic class. Because the stresses of poverty may play a role in the development of schizophrenia, many researchers are interested in the possible interactions between psychosocial stressors and biological factors (Buckley et al., 2000; Sawa & Snyder, 2002).

Biological Views

Schizophrenia appears to be a brain disorder (Egan et al., 2001). Many studies have been done to determine how the brains of schizophrenic people differ from those of others. Some studies have focused on structures in the brain, such as the size of ventricles (hollow spaces), others on activity levels in the brain, still others on brain chemistry (e.g., neurotransmitters).

One avenue of brain research connects the major deficits we find in schizophrenia—problems in attention, working memory, abstract thinking, and language—with dysfunction in the prefrontal cortex of the brain. Imaging of the brain has shown that people with schizophrenia have smaller brains than other people and, in particular, a smaller prefrontal region of the cortex (Flashman et al., 2000; Selemon, 2000; Staal et al., 2000). On the other hand, people with schizophrenia tend to have larger ventricles in the brain than other people (Wright et al., 2000). PET scans reveal that people with schizophrenia also tend to have a lower level of activity in the frontal region of the brain (Kim et al., 2000; Meyer-Lindenberg et al., 2001; Lahti et al., 2001). Still other research connects the lower activity levels with a loss in synapses (the structures that permit communication between neurons) in the region (Glantz & Lewis, 2000; McGlashan & Hoffman, 2000; Selemon, 2000).

What might account for differences in brain structure and functioning? Research evidence suggests that there are a number of biological risk factors for schizophrenia, such as heredity, complications during pregnancy and birth, and birth during winter (Buckley et al., 2000; Sawa & Snyder, 2002). Schizophrenia, like many other psychological disorders, runs in families (Conklin & Iacono, 2002; Egan et al., 2001). People with schizophrenia constitute about 1% of the population. Yet children with one parent who has been diagnosed with schizophrenia have about a 10% chance of being diagnosed with schizophrenia themselves. Children with two such parents have about a 35% to 40% chance of being so diagnosed (Gottesman, 1991; Straube & Oades, 1992). Twin studies also find about a 45% concordance rate for the diagnosis among pairs of identical (MZ) twins, whose genetic codes are the same, compared with a 17% rate among pairs of fraternal (DZ) twins (Plomin & Crabbe, 2000). Moreover, adoptee studies find that the biological parent typically places the child at greater risk for schizophrenia than the adoptive parent—even though the child has been reared by the adoptive parent (Gottesman, 1991). Sharing genes with relatives who have schizophrenia apparently places a person at risk of developing the disorder. Many studies have been carried out to try to isolate the gene or genes involved in schizophrenia. Some studies find locations for multiple genes on several chromosomes.

But heredity is not the only factor that creates a vulnerability to schizophrenia. If it were, we would expect a 100% concordance rate between identical twins, as opposed to the 40% to 50% rate we find. It also turns out that many people with schizophrenia have undergone complications during pregnancy and birth (Rosso et al., 2000). For example, the mothers of many people with schizophrenia had the flu during the sixth or seventh month of pregnancy (Brown & Susser, 2002). Poor maternal nutrition has also been implicated (Hulshoff et al., 2000; Pol et al., 2000). Complications during childbirth, especially prolonged labor, seem to be connected with the larger ventricles we find among people with schizophrenia (McNeil et al., 2000). People with schizophrenia are also somewhat more likely to have been born during winter than would be predicted by chance (Pol et al., 2000; Suvisaari et al., 2002). Alcohol abuse may also lead to differences in brain structures among people with schizophrenia (Sullivan et al., 2000). Taken together, these biological risk factors suggest that schizophrenia involves atypical development of the central nervous system. Problems in the nervous system may involve brain chemistry as well as brain structures, and research along these lines has led to the dopamine theory of schizophrenia.

The Dopamine Theory of Schizophrenia

Numerous chemical substances have been suspected of playing a role in schizophrenia, and much research has focused on the neurotransmitter dopamine. According to the dopamine theory of schizophrenia, people with schizophrenia overutilize dopamine (use more of it than other people do) although they may not produce more of it (Gijsman et al., 2002; Tsai & Coyle, 2002). Why? Research suggests that they have increased concentrations of dopamine at the synapses in the brain and also larger numbers of dopamine receptors (Butcher, 2000). It's a sort of "double hit" of neural transmission that may be connected with the confusion that characterizes schizophrenia.

Because many psychological and biological factors have been implicated in schizophrenia, most investigators today favor a *multifactorial* model. According to this model, genetic factors create a predisposition toward schizophrenia (see Figure 12.2). Genetic vulnerability to the disorder interacts with other factors, such as complications of pregnancy and birth, stress, and quality of parenting, to give rise to the disorder (Buckley et al., 2000; Sawa & Snyder, 2002).

Because the perceptions and judgment of people with schizophrenia are impaired, the diagnosis is sometimes associated with the insanity plea in the criminal courts. The nearby "A Closer Look" feature offers insight into the insanity plea.

Learning Connections
See Web site for an interactive version of these review questions.

REVIEW

(27) Schizophrenic disorders are characterized by disturbances in _____ and language (as in the loosening of associations and in delusions); in perception and attention (as in hallucinations); in motor activity; in mood; and by withdrawal and autism. (28) Paranoid schizophrenia is characterized by paranoid _____. (29) _____ schizophrenia is characterized by impaired motor activity and waxy flexibility. (30) Schizophrenia (does or does not?) tend to run in families. (31) The prefrontal region of the brain of people with schizophrenia has (more or fewer?) synapses than those of other people. (32) People with schizophrenia utilize more of the neurotransmitter _____ than other people do.

Critical Thinking: Agree or disagree with the following statement and support your answer: Schizophrenia is a disease of the brain.

■ **Figure 12.2**
A Multifactorial Model of Schizophrenia

According to the multifactorial model of schizophrenia, people with a genetic vulnerability to the disorder experience increased risk for schizophrenia when they encounter problems such as viral infections, birth complications, stress, and poor parenting. People without the genetic vulnerability would not develop schizophrenia despite such problems.

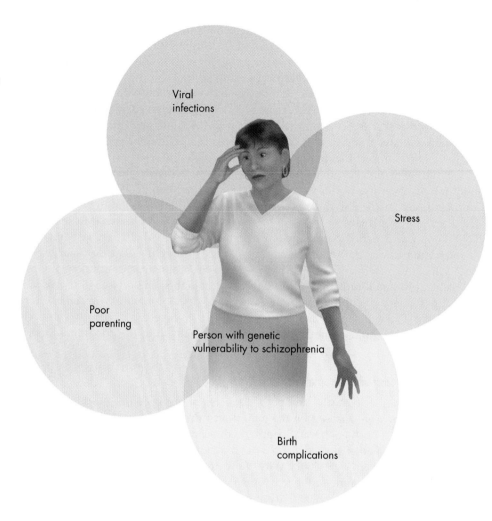

Viral infections

Stress

Poor parenting

Person with genetic vulnerability to schizophrenia

Birth complications

A Closer Look

The Insanity Plea

Forensic psychologists apply psychological knowledge in the evaluation of people who commit crimes. They testify about defendants' competence to stand trial or participate in their own defense, as well as about whether defendants should be found not guilty by reason of insanity. For example, John Hinckley was found not guilty of a 1981 assassination attempt on President Ronald Reagan by reason of insanity. Hinckley was diagnosed with schizophrenia and committed to a psychiatric institution rather than given a prison term. He remains there to this day.

In pleading insanity, lawyers use the M'Naghten rule, named after Daniel M'Naghten, who tried to assassinate the British prime minister, Sir Robert Peel, in 1843. M'Naghten had delusions that Peel was persecuting him, and he killed Peel's secretary in the attempt. The court found M'Naghten not guilty by reason of insanity, referring to what has become the M'Naghten rule. It states that the accused did not understand what she or he was doing at the time of the act, did not realize it was wrong, or was succumbing to an irresistible impulse. Today the insanity plea tends to be used in much the same way—when the person accused of the crime could not under-

stand that the criminal act was illegal or wrong, or when he or she could not control his or her behavior (Follingstad & McCormick, 2002).

Many people would like to ban the insanity plea (DeAngelis, 1994b). Such banning "is an attempt to deal with a perception that the world is getting more violent," notes psychologist/lawyer Donald Bersoff (1994, p. 28). "That's combined with the perception that people are literally getting away with murder because of the insanity defense."

Practically speaking, there may not be all that much cause for concern, however. Although the public estimates that the insanity defense is used in about 37% of felony cases, it is actually raised in only 1% (Silver, 1994). Moreover, the insanity plea may be no bargain for people who use it. People found to be not guilty by reason of insanity are institutionalized for indefinite terms—supposedly until they are no longer insane. If it can be difficult to prove that someone is insane, it can also be difficult to prove that he or she is no longer insane. Hinckley remains institutionalized more than two decades after he attempted to kill President Reagan. If he had been convicted of attempted murder, he might already have completed a specific sentence.

PERSONALITY DISORDERS

Personality disorders, like personality traits, are characterized by enduring patterns of behavior. Personality disorders, however, are inflexible and maladaptive. They impair personal or social functioning and are a source of distress to the individual or to other people. *Question: What kinds of personality disorders are there?*

Types of Personality Disorders

There are a number of personality disorders. They include the paranoid, schizotypal, schizoid, antisocial, and avoidant personality disorders. The defining trait of the **paranoid personality disorder** is a tendency to interpret other people's behavior as threatening or demeaning. People with the disorder do not show the grossly disorganized thinking of paranoid schizophrenia. However, they are mistrustful of others, and their relationships suffer for it. They may be suspicious of coworkers and supervisors, but they can generally hold a job.

Schizotypal personality disorder is characterized by peculiarities of thought, perception, or behavior, such as excessive fantasy and suspiciousness, feelings of being unreal, or odd usage of words. The bizarre behaviors that characterize schizophrenia are absent, so this disorder is schizo*typal,* not schizophrenic.

The **schizoid personality** is defined by indifference to relationships and flat emotional response. People with this disorder are "loners." They do not develop warm, tender feelings for others. They have few friends and rarely get married. Some people with schizoid personality disorder do very well on the job provided that continuous social interaction is not required. They do not have hallucinations or delusions.

People with **antisocial personality disorder** persistently violate the rights of others and are often in conflict with the law (see the "In Review" chart on pages 476–477). They often show a superficial charm and are at least average in intelligence. Striking features are their lack of guilt or anxiety about their misdeeds and their failure to learn from punishment or to form meaningful bonds with other people (Levenston et al., 2000; Romero et al., 2001). Though they are often heavily punished by their parents and rejected by peers, they continue in their impulsive, careless styles of life. Women are more likely than men to have anxiety and

REFLECT

Sick people may be excused from school or work. If some criminals are "sick" in the sense of being diagnosed with antisocial personality disorder, does the disorder relieve them of responsibility for criminal behavior? Explain.

Personality Disorders
Enduring patterns of maladaptive behavior that are sources of distress to the individual or others.

Paranoid Personality Disorder
A disorder characterized by persistent suspiciousness but not involving the disorganization of paranoid schizophrenia.

Schizotypal Personality Disorder
A disorder characterized by oddities of thought and behavior but not involving bizarre psychotic behaviors.

Schizoid Personality Disorder
A disorder characterized by social withdrawal.

Antisocial Personality Disorder
The diagnosis given a person who is in frequent conflict with society, yet who is undeterred by punishment and experiences little or no guilt and anxiety.

■ **A Person with an Antisocial Personality**
Some people with antisocial personalities fit the stereotype of the amoral, violent career criminal. Is it possible that mass murderer Henry Lee Lucas, shown here in prison along with photographs of his victims, was simply born with the wrong kind of genes?

IN REVIEW

	Anxiety Disorders	**Dissociative Disorders**	**Somatoform Disorders**

CLASS

Anxiety Disorders

Generally characterized by worrying, fear of the worst happening, fear of losing control, nervousness, and inability to relax.

Possible contributing factors for anxiety disorders

Dissociative Disorders

Generally characterized by separation of mental processes such as thoughts, emotions, identity, memory, or consciousness.

Dissociative amnesia is marked by loss of memory or self-identity.

Somatoform Disorders

Generally characterized by complaints of physical problems such as paralysis and pain, or the persistent belief that one has a serious disease in the absence of medical findings.

MAJOR SUBTYPES

Anxiety Disorders

Phobia: an irrational, excessive fear of an object or situation
Panic: recurrent extreme anxiety attacks in the absence of external stimuli that usually elicit anxiety
Generalized Anxiety: enduring general feelings of dread and foreboding
Obsessive–Compulsive Disorder: characterized by recurring thoughts or images that seem beyond control and irresistible urges to repeat an act or engage in ritualistic behavior
Stress Disorder: Following a distressing event outside the range of normal human experience; characterized by intense fear, avoidance of stimuli associated with the event, and reliving of the event. Acute stress disorders occur immediately after the event; posttraumatic stress disorder (PTSD) occurs after some time has elapsed.

Dissociative Disorders

Dissociative Amnesia: a disorder marked by loss of memory or self-identity, while skills and general knowledge are usually retained
Dissociative Fugue: amnesia connected with fleeing to a new location
Dissociative Identity (multiple personality): a disorder in which a person appears to have two or more distinct identities or personalities that may alternately emerge

Somatoform Disorders

Conversion Disorder: the "conversion" of anxiety or unconscious conflicts into physical symptoms
Hypochondriasis: the persistent belief that one is physically ill despite absence of medical findings

POSSIBLE CAUSES

Anxiety Disorders

Biopsychologists note a genetic vulnerability to anxiety disorders that may involve a highly reactive autonomic nervous system due to insensitivity to GABA, a neurotransmitter that can quell anxiety.
Cognitive theorists suggest that individuals with anxiety disorders tend to focus on and overestimate the magnitude of threats.
Learning theorists suggest that anxieties are learned through conditioning or observation.
Psycholanalysts attribute anxiety disorders to failure to adequately repress childhood conflicts.

Dissociative Disorders

Learning theorists suggest that people may learn *not to think* about such impulses and events because of feelings of guilt.
Psychodynamic theorists attribute dissociative disorders to massive repression that prevents individuals from recognizing improper impulses or remembering ugly events.

Somatoform Disorders

Some theorists view conversion disorder as a form of self-hypnosis in which people focus only on physical sensations. Research suggests that hypochondriacs are particularly sensitive to physical sensations.

ood Disorders

enerally characterized by
sturbance in expressed emotions.

ajor Depression: severe
epression in which the person may
ow loss of appetite and impaired
ality testing
polar Disorder: alternation of the
ood between two extremes, elation
nd depression

opsychologists note that there may be
genetic vulnerability toward mood
sorders and that depression is
aracterized by underuse of the
eurotransmitter serotonin.
ognitive theorists suggest that
epressed people engage in excessive
elf-blame, expect the worst, and tend to
minate about their problems.
earning theorists suggest that depressed
eople cannot obtain adequate
einforcement or give up on trying to
otain reinforcement.

Schizophrenia

Generally characterized by
disturbances in language and thought
(i.e., delusions, loose associations),
attention and perception (i.e.,
hallucinations), motor activity, and
mood, and by withdrawal and
absorption in daydreams or fantasies.

A multifactorial model of schizophrenia.

Paranoid Schizophrenia: a form of
schizophrenia characterized by
delusions, as of persecution, and
hallucinations
Disorganized Schizophrenia: a
form of schizophrenia characterized
by disorganized delusions and
hallucinations
Catatonic Schizophrenia: a form of
schizophrenia characterized by motor
impairment, such as a stupor and
waxy flexibility

Although **psychoanalysts** and **learning
theorists** have suggested possible
psychological origins for schizophrenia,
most theorists today argue in favor of a
genetic vulnerability and other
biological and situational factors. There
is also evidence that people with
schizophrenia tend to overuse the
neurotransmitter dopamine.

Personality Disorders

Generally characterized by inflexible
and maladaptive patterns of behavior
that impair personal or social
functioning and are a source of distress
to oneself or others.

© Trinette Reed/CORBIS

Paranoid: characterized by
persistent suspiciousness
Schizotypal: characterized by
oddities of thought and behavior,
but not bizarre behavior
Schizoid: characterized by social
withdrawal
Antisocial: characterized by
frequent conflict with society, lack of
deterrance by punishment, and lack
of guilt or anxiety
Avoidant: characterized by
unwillingness to enter relationships
because of fears of rejection and
criticism

Biopsychologists see personality
disorders as exaggerated personality
traits with a key genetic component.
Also, people with antisocial personality
disorder may have less arousable
nervous systems, making them less
susceptible to feelings of guilt or
deterrence by punishment.
Cognitive theorists find that antisocial
people interpret social interactions to
support their misdeeds, such as
assuming that others are "out to get"
them.
Learning theorists speak of childhood
experiences, such as inconsistent
discipline, possibly leading to antisocial
personality disorder.
Psychoanalysts tend to explain
personality disorders in terms of
Oedipal conflict.

Avoidant Personality Disorder
A personality disorder in which the person is generally unwilling to enter relationships without assurance of acceptance because of fears of rejection and criticism.

depressive disorders. Men are more likely than women to have antisocial personality disorder (K. G. Anderson et al., 2001).

People with **avoidant personality disorder** are generally unwilling to enter a relationship without some assurance of acceptance because they fear rejection and criticism. As a result, they may have few close relationships outside their immediate families. Unlike people with schizoid personality disorder, however, they have some interest in, and feelings of warmth toward, other people. ***Question: What is known about the origins of personality disorders?***

Theoretical Views

Many of the theoretical explanations of personality disorders are derived from the psychodynamic model. Traditional Freudian theory focuses on Oedipal problems as the source of many psychological disorders, including personality disorders. Faulty resolution of the Oedipus complex might lead to antisocial personality disorder, because the moral conscience, or superego, is believed to depend on proper resolution of the Oedipus complex. Research evidence supports the theory that lack of guilt, a frequent characteristic of people with antisocial personality disorder, is more likely to develop among children who are rejected and punished by their parents rather than given warmth and affection (Denham et al., 2000; Hastings et al. 2000).

Learning theorists suggest that childhood experiences can contribute to maladaptive ways of relating to others in adulthood—that is, can lead to personality disorders. Cognitive psychologists find that antisocial adolescents encode social information in ways that bolster their misdeeds. For example, they tend to interpret other people's behavior as threatening, even when it is not (Crick & Dodge, 1994; Lochman, 1992). Cognitive therapists have encouraged some antisocial adolescents to view social provocations as problems to be solved rather than as threats to their "manhood," with some favorable initial results (Lochman, 1992).

Genetic factors are apparently involved in some personality disorders (Eaves et al. 2000; Rutter & Silberg, 2002). Personality traits are to some degree heritable (Plomin, 2000), and many personality disorders seem to be extreme variations of normal personality traits. An analysis of 51 twin and adoption studies estimated that genetic factors were the greatest influences on antisocial behavior (Rhee & Waldman, 2002). Referring to the five-factor model of personality, people with schizoid personalities tend to be highly introverted (Widiger & Costa, 1994). People with avoidant personalities tend to be both introverted and emotionally unstable (neurotic) (Widiger & Costa, 1994).

Perhaps the genetics of antisocial personality disorder involve the prefrontal cortex of the brain, a part of the brain connected with emotional responses. There is some evidence that people with antisocial personality disorder, as a group, have less gray matter (associative neurons) in the prefrontal cortex of the brain than other people (Damasio, 2000; Raine et al., 2000). The lesser amount of gray matter could lessen the level of arousal of the nervous system. As a result, it would be more difficult to condition fear responses (Blair & James, 2001). People with the disorder would then be unlikely to show guilt for their misdeeds and would seem to be unafraid of punishment. But a biological factor such as a lower-than-normal level of arousal might not in itself cause the development of an antisocial personality (Rutter & Silberg, 2002). Perhaps a person must also be reared under conditions that do not foster the self-concept of a law-abiding citizen.

Although the causes of psychological disorders remain in dispute, various methods of therapy have been devised to deal with them. Those methods are the focus of Chapter 13.

Learning Connections
*See Web site for an interactive
version of these review questions.*

REVIEW

(33) _____ disorders are inflexible, maladaptive behavior patterns that impair personal or social functioning and are a source of distress to the individual or to others. (34) The defining trait of the _____ personality is suspiciousness. (35) Social _____ is the major characteristic of the schizoid personality. (36) Persons with _____ personality disorder violate the rights of others, show little or no guilt for their misdeeds, and are undeterred by punishment. (37) Research suggests that people with antisocial personalities have (higher or lower?)-than-normal levels of arousal than most people. (38) Their levels of arousal may be connected with lower-than-normal levels of (white or gray?) matter in the prefrontal cortex.

Critical Thinking: What is the difference between people with "bad personalities" and people with personality disorders?

Understanding and Preventing Suicide

In January 2002, 15-year-old Charles Bishop flew his small airplane into the side of a bank building in Tampa, Florida. It was no accident. He left a suicide note expressing sympathy for what terrorists had done four months earlier, flying passenger jets into the towers of the World Trade Center in New York and the Pentagon, outside Washington, DC. His teachers and friends expressed shock and dismay.

Terrorist examples and politics aside, his teachers and friends were trying to understand how Charles could have intentionally flown into the side of an—in this case—extremely unforgiving skyscraper. After all, he, like so many people, had "so much to live for." Didn't he? Apparently Charles didn't think so. Neither do the other thousands of other Americans who take their own lives each year.

About 30,000 people each year take their lives in the United States (CDC, 2000c). Suicide is the third or fourth leading cause of death among older teenagers (National Center for Health Statistics, 2002). What prompts people to take their own lives? Who is most at risk of attempting or committing suicide?

Risk Factors in Suicide

Most suicides are linked to feelings of depression and hopelessness (Leslie et al., 2002; Sampaio et al., 2001). Jill Rathus—who has presented your author with grandchildren and research articles—and her colleagues (Miller et al., 2000; Velting et al., 2000) have found that suicidal adolescents experience four areas of psychological problems: (1) confusion about the self, (2) impulsiveness, (3) emotional instability, and (4) interpersonal problems. Some suicidal teenagers, like suicidal adults, are highly achieving, rigid perfectionists who have set impossibly high expectations for themselves (Miller et al., 2000; Wu et al., 2001). Many people throw themselves into feelings of depression and hopelessness by comparing themselves negatively with others, even when the comparisons are inappropriate (Barber, 2001).

("Yes, you didn't get the promotion, but you got a raise of ten thousand dollars, and that's nothing to sneeze at.")

Suicide attempts are more common following stressful life events, especially "exit events." Exit events entail loss of social support, as in the death of a parent or friend, divorce, or a family member's leaving home, and result in what Shneidman (2001) refers to as psychological pain, or "psychache." Other contributors to suicidal behavior among adolescents include concerns over sexuality, pressures to achieve in school, problems at home, and substance abuse (Miller et al., 2000; Wu et al., 2001). It is not always a stressful event itself that precipitates suicide but the individual's anxiety or fear of being "found out" about something, such as failing a course or getting arrested (Marttunen, 1998). Problem-solving ability—or lack of it—is connected with suicide. People who consider suicide are apparently less capable of solving problems, especially their social problems, than others (Miller et al., 2000; Townsend et al., 2001). People contemplating suicide are thus less likely to find productive ways of changing the stressful situation. They have borne the "psychache"; now they want a magical solution to problems that require work, or else a quick way out (Shneidman, 2001).

There is a tendency for suicide to run in families (Bongar, 2002; Joiner, 2002). Many suicide attempters have family members with serious psychological problems, and about 25% have family members who have taken their lives (Segal & Roy, 2001; Sorensen & Rutter, 1991). The causal connections are unclear, however. Do people who attempt suicide inherit disorders that can lead to suicide? Does the family environment subject family members to feelings of hopelessness? Does the suicide of a family member give a person the idea of committing suicide or create the impression that he or she is somehow fated to commit suicide? Perhaps these possibilities and others—such as poor problem-solving ability—form a complex web of contributing factors.

Let us consider some myths about suicide.

A Closer Look ◉

Ethnicity, Gender, and Suicide

Suicide is connected not only with feelings of depression and stressful events, but also with age, educational status, ethnicity, and gender. Consider some facts about suicide:

- Suicide is the third leading cause of death among young people aged 15 to 24 (National Center for Health Statistics, 2002). More teenagers and young adults die from suicide than from cancer, heart disease, AIDS, birth defects, stroke, pneumonia and influenza, and chronic lung disease combined (National Center for Health Statistics, 2002).
- Suicide is more common among college students than among people of the same age who do not attend college. Each year about 10,000 college students attempt suicide.

- Although teenage suicides loom large in the media spotlight, older people are actually more likely to commit suicide (National Center for Health Statistics, 2002). The suicide rate among older people who are unmarried or divorced is double that of older people who are married (CDC, 2000c).

Rates of suicide and suicide attempts also vary among different ethnic groups and according to gender. For example, one in every four Native Americans (17%) has attempted suicide—a rate higher than that of other Americans. About one in eight Latino and Latina Americans has attempted suicide and three in ten have considered it (National Center for Health Statistics, 2002). European Americans are next, with 8% attempting and

Myths About Suicide

You may have heard that individuals who threaten suicide are only seeking attention. Those who are serious "just do it." Actually, it is not true that people who threaten suicide are only seeking attention. Most people who commit suicide give warnings about their intentions (Jackson & Nuttall, 2001; Waters, 2000).

Some believe that those who fail at suicide attempts are only seeking attention. But many people who commit suicide have made prior attempts (Jackson & Nuttall, 2001; Waters, 2000). Contrary to widespread belief, discussing suicide with a person who is depressed does not prompt the person to attempt suicide (CDC, 1995). Extracting a promise not to commit suicide before calling or visiting a helping professional seems to prevent some suicides.

Some believe that only "insane" people (meaning people who are out of touch with reality) would take their own lives. However, suicidal thinking is not necessarily a sign of psychosis, neurosis, or personality disorder. Instead, people may consider suicide when they think they have run out of options (Nock & Kazdin, 2002; Townsend et al., 2001).

Warning Signs of Suicide

The great majority of people who commit suicide send out a variety of signals about their impending act (Bongar, 2002; Hendin et al., 2001). Sad to say, these signals often are overlooked, sometimes because other people do not recognize them, sometimes because other people do not have adequate access to health care (MacDonald, 1999; Wu et al., 2001). Sometime people do not receive help until they actually attempt suicide, and sometimes not even then (Gili-Planas et al., 2001; Wu et al., 2001). Here are some clues that a person may be at risk of committing suicide (Hendin et al., 2001):

- Changes in eating and sleeping patterns.
- Difficulty concentrating on schoolwork.
- A sharp decline in school performance and attendance.
- Loss of interest in previously enjoyed activities.
- Giving away prized possessions.
- Complaints about physical problems when no medical basis for the problems can be found.
- Withdrawal from social relationships.
- Personality or mood changes.
- Talking or writing about death or dying.
- Abuse of drugs or alcohol.
- An attempted suicide.
- Availability of a handgun.
- A precipitating event such as an argument, a broken romantic relationship, academic difficulties, problems on the job, loss of a friend, or trouble with the law.
- In the case of adolescents, knowing or hearing about another teenager who has committed suicide (which can lead to so-called "cluster" suicides).
- Threatening to commit suicide.

What Can You Do?

Imagine that you are having a heart-to-heart talk with Jamie, one of your best friends. Things haven't been going well. Jamie's grandmother died a month ago, and they were very close. Jamie's course work has been suffering, and things have also been going downhill with the person Jamie has been seeing. But you are not prepared when Jamie looks you in the eye and says, "I've been thinking about this for days, and I've decided that the only way out is to kill myself."

If someone tells you that he or she is considering suicide, you may become frightened and flustered or feel that an enormous burden has been placed on you. You are right: It has. In such a case your objective should be to encourage the person to consult a health care provider, or to consult one yourself, as soon as possible. But if the person refuses to talk to anyone else, and you feel that you can't break free for a consultation, there are a number of

28% contemplating suicide. African Americans are least likely to attempt suicide (6.5%) or to think about it (20%). The actual suicide rates for African Americans are only about two-thirds of those for European Americans, despite the fact that African Americans are more likely to live in poverty and suffer from discrimination (National Center for Health Statistics, 2002). How can we explain this "disconnect" between hope for the future and suicide rates? One possibility is that some suicidal African American males may engage in risk-taking behaviors that lead to early death by homicide or accident. Another possibility is that cultural factors such as the support offered by extended families and the important role of religion may have a protective effect. Yet another possibility is that when African Americans are feeling low, they tend to blame social circumstances, including discrimination. Many European Americans, on the other hand, may feel that there is no one to blame but themselves.

About three times as many females as males attempt suicide, but about five times as many males succeed (National Center for Health Statistics, 2002). In part, males are more likely to "succeed" because of the methods they choose. The methods preferred by males are more deadly and more rapid: Males are more likely to shoot or hang themselves; females more often use drugs, such as overdoses of tranquilizers or sleeping pills, or poisons. Females often do not take enough of these chemicals. It also takes a while for them to work, giving people the opportunity to find them and intervene.

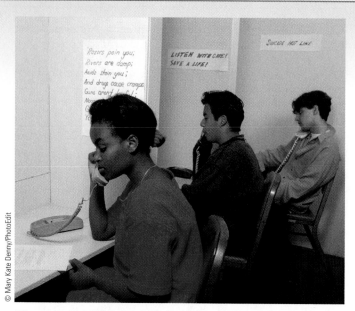

■ A Suicide-Prevention Hot Line

At suicide-prevention centers, staff members stand by hot lines around the clock. If you know someone who is threatening to commit suicide, consult a professional as soon as possible.

things you can do (Hendin et al., 2001; Omer & Elitzur, 2001; Shneidman, 2001):

1. Keep talking. Encourage the person to talk to you or to some other trusted person (Los Angeles Unified School District, 2000). Draw the person out with questions like "What's happening?" "Where do you hurt?" "What do you want to happen?" Questions like these may encourage the person to express frustrated needs and provide some relief. They also give you time to think.
2. Be a good listener. Be supportive with people who express suicidal thoughts or feel depressed, hopeless, or worthless. They may believe their condition is hopeless and will never improve, but let them know that you are there for them and willing to help them get help. Show that you understand how upset the person is. Do *not* say, "Don't be silly."
3. Suggest that something other than suicide might solve the problem, even if it is not evident at the time. Many suicidal people see only two solutions—either death or a magical

resolution of their problems. Therapists try to "remove the mental blinders" from suicidal people.

4. Emphasize as concretely as possible how the person's suicide would be devastating to you and to other people who care.
5. Ask how the person intends to commit suicide. People with concrete plans and a weapon are at greater risk. Ask if you might hold on to the weapon for a while. Sometimes the answer is yes.
6. Suggest that the person go *with you* to obtain professional help *now*. The emergency room of a general hospital, the campus counseling center or infirmary, or the campus or local police station will do. Some campuses have hot lines you can call. Some cities have suicide prevention centers with hot lines that people can use anonymously.
7. Extract a promise that the person will not commit suicide before seeing you again. Arrange a specific time and place to meet. Get professional help as soon as you are apart.
8. Do *not* tell people threatening suicide that they're silly or crazy. Do *not* insist on contact with specific people, such as parents or a spouse. Conflict with these people may have led to the suicidal thinking in the first place.

Resources

You can also check out the following resources:

- *The national suicide hot line:* 1-800-SUICIDE (1-800-784-2433).
- *American Association of Suicidology:* Their Web site, www.suicidology.org, provides information on ways to prevent suicide. You will also find a list of crisis centers.
- *American Foundation for Suicide Prevention:* Their Web site, www.afsp.org, offers information about suicide and links to other suicide and mental health sites.
- *American Psychological Association (APA):* The APA Web site, www.apa.org, provides information about risk factors, warning signs, and prevention.
- *National Institute of Mental Health (NIMH):* The Web site, www.nimh.nih.gov, contains information on depression and other psychological disorders.
- *Suicide Awareness–Voices of Education (SAVE):* SAVE's Web site, www.save.org, offers educational and practical information on suicide and depression. It highlights ways in which family members and friends can help suicidal people.
- *Suicide Information & Education Centre (SIEC):* SIEC's Web site, www.siec.ca, offers a specialized library on suicide.

Recite Recite Recite

Learning Connections
See Web site for an interactive version of this chapter summary

1. What are psychological disorders?	Psychological disorders are characterized by unusual behavior, socially unacceptable behavior, faulty perception of reality, personal distress, dangerous behavior, or self-defeating behavior.
2. How are psychological disorders grouped or classified?	The most widely used classification scheme is found in the *Diagnostic and Statistical Manual (DSM)* of the American Psychiatric Association. The current edition of the *DSM*—the *DSM-IV-TR*—groups disorders on the basis of observable symptoms and no longer uses the category of neuroses.
3. How do people explain psychological disorders?	People throughout history have mainly attributed psychological disorders to spiritual intervention, such as possession by the devil. Today psychologists apply their theoretical perspectives to the explanation of these disorders.
4. What kinds of anxiety disorders are there?	Anxiety disorders are characterized by motor tension, feelings of dread, and over-arousal of the sympathetic branch of the autonomic nervous system. These disorders include irrational, excessive fears, or phobias; panic disorder, characterized by sudden attacks in which people typically fear that they may be losing control or going crazy; generalized or pervasive anxiety; obsessive–compulsive disorder, in which people are troubled by intrusive thoughts or impulses to repeat some activity; and stress disorders, in which a stressful event is followed by persistent fears and intrusive thoughts about the event. Posttraumatic stress disorder can occur six months or more after the event, whereas acute stress disorder occurs within a month.
5. What is known about the origins of anxiety disorders?	The psychodynamic perspective tends to view anxiety disorders as representing difficulty in repressing primitive impulses. Many learning theorists view phobias as conditioned fears. Cognitive theorists focus on ways in which people interpret threats. Some people may also be genetically predisposed to acquire certain kinds of fears. Anxiety disorders tend to run in families. Some psychologists suggest that biochemical factors—which could be inherited—may create a predisposition toward anxiety disorders. One such factor is faulty regulation of neurotransmitters.
6. What kinds of dissociative disorders are there?	Dissociative disorders are characterized by sudden, temporary changes in consciousness or self-identity. They include dissociative amnesia; dissociative fugue, which involves forgetting plus fleeing and adopting a new identity; and dissociative identity disorder (multiple personality), in which a person behaves as if more than one personality occupies his or her body.
7. What is known about the origins of dissociative disorders?	Many psychologists suggest that dissociative disorders help people keep disturbing memories or ideas out of mind. These memories may involve episodes of childhood sexual or physical abuse.
8. What kinds of somatoform disorders are there?	People with somatoform disorders exhibit or complain of physical problems, although no medical evidence of such problems can be found. The somatoform disorders include conversion disorder and hypochondriasis. In conversion disorder, stress is converted into a physical symptom, and the individual may show la belle indifférence (indifference to the symptom).
9. What is known about the origins of somatoform disorders?	These disorders were once called "hysterical neuroses" and were expected to be found more often among women. However, they are also found among men and may reflect the relative benefits of focusing on physical symptoms rather than fears and conflicts.

Recite Recite Recite

10. What kinds of mood disorders are there?

Mood disorders involve disturbances in expressed emotions. Major depression is characterized by persistent feelings of sadness, loss of interest, feelings of worthlessness or guilt, inability to concentrate, and physical symptoms that may include disturbances in regulation of eating and sleeping. Feelings of unworthiness and guilt may be so excessive that they are considered delusional. Bipolar disorder is characterized by dramatic swings in mood between elation and depression; manic episodes include pressured speech and rapid flight of ideas.

11. What is known about the origins of mood disorders?

Research emphasizes possible roles for learned helplessness, attributional styles, and underutilization of serotonin in depression. People who are depressed are more likely than other people to make internal, stable, and global attributions for failures. Genetic factors involving regulation of neurotransmitters may also be involved in mood disorders. For example, bipolar disorder has been linked to inappropriate levels of the neurotransmitter glutamate. Moreover, people with severe depression often respond to drugs that heighten the action of serotonin.

12. What is schizophrenia?

Schizophrenia is a most severe psychological disorder that is characterized by disturbances in thought and language, such as loosening of associations and delusions; in perception and attention, as found in hallucinations; in motor activity, as shown by a stupor or by excited behavior; in mood, as in flat or inappropriate emotional responses; and in social interaction, as in social withdrawal and absorption in daydreams or fantasy.

13. What kinds of schizophrenia are there?

The major types of schizophrenia are paranoid, disorganized, and catatonic. Paranoid schizophrenia is characterized largely by systematized delusions; disorganized schizophrenia by incoherence; and catatonic schizophrenia by motor impairment.

14. What is known about the origins of schizophrenia?

Schizophrenia is connected with smaller brains, especially fewer synapses in the prefrontal region, and larger ventricles in the brain. According to the multifactorial model, genetic vulnerability to schizophrenia may interact with other factors, such as stress, complications during pregnancy and childbirth, and quality of parenting, to cause the disorder to develop. According to the dopamine theory of schizophrenia, people with schizophrenia *use* more dopamine than other people do, perhaps because they have more dopamine in the brain along with more dopamine receptors than other people.

15. What kinds of personality disorders are there?

Personality disorders are inflexible, maladaptive behavior patterns that impair personal or social functioning and cause distress for the individual or others. The defining trait of paranoid personality disorder is suspiciousness. People with schizotypal personality disorders show oddities of thought, perception, and behavior. Social withdrawal is the major characteristic of schizoid personality disorder. People with antisocial personality disorders persistently violate the rights of others and are in conflict with the law. They show little or no guilt or shame over their misdeeds and are largely undeterred by punishment. People with avoidant personality disorder tend to avoid entering relationships for fear of rejection and criticism.

16. What is known about the origins of personality disorders?

Psychodynamic theory connected many personality disorders with hypothesized Oedipal problems. Genetic factors may be involved in some personality disorders. Antisocial personality disorder may develop from some combination of genetic vulnerability (less gray matter in the prefrontal cortex of the brain, which may provide lower-than-normal levels of arousal), inconsistent discipline, and cynical processing of social information.

Active Learning Resources

*Search Online
with InfoTrac®
College Edition*

For additional information on the topics in this chapter, explore InfoTrac College Edition, your online library. Go to **http://www.infotrac.thomsonlearning.com** and use the passcode that came on the card with your book. Try these search terms: panic disorder, posttraumatic stress disorder, compulsive behavior, dissociative identity disorder, conversion disorder, hypochondriasis, major depression, learned helplessness, and antisocial personality disorder.

Visit Our Web Site

Go to **http://www.wadsworth.com/psychology**, where you will find online resources directly linked to your book, including interactive exercises related to PQ4R and Power Visuals for mastering and reviewing key concepts. In addition, you will find hints on using InfoTrac College Edition to answer the Critical Thinking questions throughout the text. Start with the **Self Study Assessment** for a customized **Study Plan** generated by taking the **Pre-Test** and **Post-Test.**

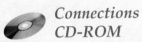

*Connections
CD-ROM*

Go to the Wadsworth *Connections* CD-ROM for further study of the concepts in this chapter. The CD-ROM includes videos, animations, quizzes, and additional activities to expand your learning experience, plus interactive self-assessments to help connect the material to your own life.

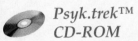

Psyk.trek™
CD-ROM

The Wadsworth *Psyk.trek* CD-ROM offers tutorials, simulations, videos, multimedia glossary, and quizzing to help you master the material.

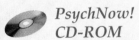

*PsychNow!
CD-ROM*

The Wadsworth *PsychNow!* CD-ROM includes interactive exercises, videos, and animations to enhance your learning.

J asmine is a 19-year-old college sophomore. She has been crying almost without letup for several days. She feels that her life is falling apart. Her college dreams are in a shambles. She has brought shame upon her family. Thoughts of suicide have crossed her mind. She can barely drag herself out of bed in the morning. She is avoiding her friends. She can pinpoint some sources of stress in her life: a couple of poor grades, an argument with a boyfriend, friction with roommates. Still, her misery seemed to descend on her out of nowhere.

Jasmine is depressed—so depressed that her family and friends have finally prevailed on her to seek professional help. Had she broken her leg, her treatment by a qualified professional would have followed a fairly standard course. Yet treatment of psychological problems and disorders like depression may be approached from very different perspectives. Depending on the therapist Jasmine sees, she may be doing the following:

- Lying on a couch talking about anything that pops into her awareness and exploring the possible meaning of a recurrent dream.
- Sitting face to face with a warm, gentle therapist who accepts Jasmine as she is and expresses faith in Jasmine's ability to make the right decisions for herself.
- Listening to a frank, straightforward therapist assert that Jasmine is depressing herself with her self-defeating attitudes and perfectionistic beliefs.
- Taking antidepressant medication.
- Participating in some combination of these approaches.

These methods, although different, all represent methods of therapy. In this chapter we explore various methods of psychotherapy and biological therapy. *Question: What is psychotherapy?*

WHAT IS THERAPY? THE SEARCH FOR A "SWEET OBLIVIOUS ANTIDOTE"[1]

There are many kinds of psychotherapy, but they all have certain common characteristics. **Psychotherapy** is a systematic interaction between a therapist and a client that applies psychological principles to affect the client's thoughts, feelings, or behavior in order to help the client overcome psychological disorders, adjust to problems in living, or develop as an individual.

Quite a mouthful? True. But note the essentials:

1. *Systematic interaction:* Psychotherapy is a systematic interaction between a client and a therapist. The therapist's theoretical point of view interacts with the client's to determine how the therapist and client relate to each other.
2. *Psychological principles:* Psychotherapy is based on psychological theory and research in areas such as personality, learning, motivation, and emotion.
3. *Thoughts, feelings, and behavior:* Psychotherapy influences clients' thoughts, feelings, and behavior. It can be aimed at any or all of these aspects of human psychology.
4. *Psychological disorders, adjustment problems, and personal growth:* Psychotherapy is often used with people who have psychological disorders. Other people seek help in adjusting to problems such as shyness, weight problems, or loss of a spouse. Still other clients want to learn more about themselves and to reach their full potential as individuals, parents, or creative artists.

The History of Therapies

Psychotherapy

A systematic interaction between a therapist and a client that brings psychological principles to bear on influencing the client's thoughts, feelings, or behavior to help that client overcome abnormal behavior or adjust to problems in living.

Historically speaking, "treatments" of psychological disorders often reflected demonological thinking. *Question: How, then, have people with psychological problems and disorders been treated throughout the ages?* Because of this belief, treatment tended to involve cruel practices such as exorcism and death by hanging or burning. Some people who could not meet the demands of everyday life were tossed

[1]The phrase is from Shakespeare's *Macbeth.*

into prisons. Others begged in the streets, stole food, or became prostitutes. A few found their way to monasteries or other retreats that offered a kind word and some support. Generally speaking, they died early.

Asylums

Asylums originated in European monasteries. They were the first institutions meant primarily for people with psychological disorders. But their function was warehousing, not treatment. Their inmate populations mushroomed until the stresses created by noise, overcrowding, and disease aggravated the problems they were meant to ease. Inmates were frequently chained and beaten.

The word *bedlam* derives from St. Mary's of *Bethlehem,* the London asylum that opened its gates in 1547. Here unfortunate people with psychological disorders were chained, whipped, and allowed to lie in their own waste. And here the ladies and gentlemen of the British upper class might stroll on a lazy afternoon to be amused by the inmates' antics. The price of admission was one penny.

Humanitarian reform movements began in the 18th century. In Paris, the physician Philippe Pinel unchained the patients at La Bicêtre. Rather than run amok, most patients profited from kindness and freedom. Many eventually reentered society. Later movements to reform institutions were led by the Quaker William Tuke in England and by Dorothea Dix in America.

Mental Hospitals

In the United States mental hospitals gradually replaced asylums. In the mid-1950s more than a million people resided in state, county, Veterans Administration, or private facilities. The mental hospital's function is treatment, not warehousing. Still, because of high patient populations and understaffing, many patients received little attention. Even today, with somewhat improved conditions, one psychiatrist may be responsible for the welfare of several hundred residents on a weekend when other staff members are absent.

The Community Mental Health Movement

Since the 1960s, efforts have been made to maintain people with serious psychological disorders in their communities. Community mental health centers attempt to maintain new patients as outpatients and to serve patients who have been released from mental hospitals. Today most people with chronic psychological disorders live in the community, not the hospital.

Asylum
(uh-SIGH-lum) An institution for the care of the mentally ill.

■ **The Unchaining of the Patients at La Bicêtre**
Philippe Pinel sparked the humanitarian reform movement by unchaining the patients at this asylum in Paris.

Critics note that many people who had resided in hospitals for decades were suddenly discharged to "home" communities that seemed foreign and forbidding to them. Many do not receive adequate follow-up care. Many join the ranks of the homeless (Francis, 2000; Lam & Rosenheck, 2000).

Learning Connections
See Web site for an interactive version of these review questions.

R E V I E W

(1) Psychotherapy is a systematic interaction between a therapist and a client that applies _____ principles to influence clients' thoughts, feelings, or behavior. (2) Historic treatments of psychological disorders were based on the demonological model and included the _____ of evil spirits.

Critical Thinking: Trace the evolution of thinking about psychological disorders in Western culture. How do current views reflect a more scientific view?

PSYCHODYNAMIC THERAPIES: DIGGING DEEP WITHIN

Psychodynamic therapies are based on the thinking of Sigmund Freud, the founder of psychodynamic theory. They assume that psychological problems reflect early childhood experiences and internal conflicts. According to Freud, these conflicts involve the shifting of psychic, or libidinal, energy among the three psychic structures—the id, ego, and superego. These shifts of psychic energy determine our behavior. When primitive urges threaten to break through from the id or when the superego floods us with excessive guilt, defenses are established and distress is created. Freud's psychodynamic therapy method—psychoanalysis—aims to modify the flow of energy among these structures, largely to bulwark the ego against the torrents of energy loosed by the id and the superego. With impulses and feelings of guilt and shame placed under greater control, clients are freer to develop adaptive behavior. *Question: How, then, do psychoanalysts conduct a traditional Freudian psychoanalysis?*

Traditional Psychoanalysis: "Where Id Was, There Shall Ego Be"

> *Canst thou not minister to a mind diseas'd,*
> *Pluck out from the memory a rooted sorrow,*
> *Raze out the written troubles of the brain,*
> *And with some sweet oblivious antidote*
> *Cleanse the stuff'd bosom of that perilous stuff*
> *Which weighs upon the heart?*

Shakespeare, Macbeth

In this passage, Macbeth asks a physician to help Lady Macbeth after she has gone mad. In the play, her madness is caused partly by events—namely, her role in murders designed to seat her husband on the throne of Scotland. There are also hints of mysterious, deeply rooted problems, such as conflicts about infertility.

If Lady Macbeth's physician had been a traditional psychoanalyst, he might have asked her to lie on a couch in a slightly darkened room. He would have sat behind her and encouraged her to talk about anything that came to mind, no matter how trivial, no matter how personal. To avoid interfering with her self-exploration, he might have said little or nothing for session after session. That would have been par for the course. A traditional **psychoanalysis** can extend for months, even years.

Psychoanalysis is the clinical method devised by Freud for plucking "from the memory a rooted sorrow," for razing "out the written troubles of the brain." It aims to provide *insight* into the conflicts that are presumed to lie at the roots of a person's

Psychoanalysis
Freud's method of psychotherapy.

problems. Insight means many things, including knowledge of the experiences that lead to conflicts and maladaptive behavior, recognition of unconscious feelings and conflicts, and conscious evaluation of one's thoughts, feelings, and behavior.

Psychoanalysis also aims to help the client express feelings and urges that have been repressed. By so doing, Freud believed that the client spilled forth the psychic energy that had been repressed by conflicts and guilt. He called this spilling forth **catharsis.** Catharsis would provide relief by alleviating some of the forces assaulting the ego.

Freud was also fond of saying, "Where id was, there shall ego be." In part, he meant that psychoanalysis could shed light on the inner workings of the mind. He also sought to replace impulsive and defensive behavior with coping behavior. In this way, for example, a man with a phobia for knives might discover that he had been repressing the urge to harm someone who had taken advantage of him. He might also find ways to confront the person verbally.

Free Association

Early in his career as a therapist, Freud found that hypnosis allowed his clients to focus on repressed conflicts and talk about them. The relaxed "trance state" provided by hypnosis seemed to allow clients to "break through" to topics of which they would otherwise be unaware. Freud also found, however, that many clients denied the accuracy of this material once they were out of the trance. Other clients found them to be premature and painful. Freud therefore turned to **free association,** a more gradual method of breaking through the walls of defense that block a client's insight into unconscious processes.

In free association, the client is made comfortable—for example, lying on a couch—and asked to talk about any topic that comes to mind. No thought is to be censored—that is the basic rule. Psychoanalysts ask their clients to wander "freely" from topic to topic, but they do not believe that the process occurring *within* the client is fully free. Repressed impulses clamor for release.

The ego persists in trying to repress unacceptable impulses and threatening conflicts. As a result, clients might show **resistance** to recalling and discussing threatening ideas. A client about to entertain such thoughts might claim, "My mind is blank." The client might accuse the analyst of being demanding or inconsiderate. He or she might "forget" the next appointment when threatening material is about to surface.

The therapist observes the dynamic struggle between the compulsion to utter certain thoughts and the client's resistance to uttering them. Through discreet remarks,

REFLECT
Does it make you feel good to talk with someone about your problems? Are there some "deep secrets" you are unwilling to talk about or share with others? How do you think a psychoanalyst would respond if you brought them up? Why?

Catharsis
(cuh-THAR-sis) In psychoanalysis, the expression of repressed feelings and impulses to allow the release of the psychic energy associated with them.

Free Association
In psychoanalysis, the uncensored uttering of all thoughts that come to mind.

Resistance
The tendency to block the free expression of impulses and primitive ideas—a reflection of the defense mechanism of repression.

■ A View of Freud's Consulting Room
Freud would sit in a chair by the head of the couch while a client free-associated. The basic rule of free association is that no thought is censored. Freud did not believe that free association was really "free"; he assumed that significant feelings would rise to the surface and demand expression.

Interpretation
An explanation of a client's utterance according to psychoanalytic theory.

Transference
Responding to one person (such as a spouse or the psychoanalyst) in a way that is similar to the way one responded to another person (such as a parent) in childhood.

the analyst subtly tips the balance in favor of utterance. A gradual process of self-discovery and self-insight ensues. Now and then the analyst offers an **interpretation** of an utterance, showing how it suggests resistance or deep-seated feelings and conflicts.

Transference

Freud believed that clients not only responded to him as an individual but also in ways that reflected their attitudes and feelings toward other people in their lives. He labeled this process **transference.** For example, a young woman client might respond to him as a father figure and displace her feelings toward her father onto Freud, perhaps seeking affection and wisdom. A young man could also see Freud as a father figure, but rather than wanting affection from Freud, he might view Freud as a rival, responding to Freud in terms of his own unresolved Oedipal complex.

Analyzing and working through transference has been considered a key aspect of psychoanalysis. Freud believed that clients reenact their childhood conflicts with their parents when they are in therapy. Clients might thus transfer the feelings of anger, love, or jealousy they felt toward their own parents onto the analyst. Childhood conflicts often involve unresolved feelings of love, anger, or rejection. A client may interpret a suggestion by the therapist as a criticism and see it as a devastating blow, transferring feelings of self-hatred that he had repressed because his parents had rejected him in childhood. Transference can also distort clients' relationships with other people here and now, such as relationships with spouses or employers. The following therapeutic dialogue illustrates the way in which an analyst may interpret a client's inability to communicate his needs to his wife as a function of transference. The purpose is to provide his client, a Mr. Arianes, with insight into how his relationship with his wife has been colored by his childhood relationship with his mother:

Arianes:	I think you've got it there, Doc. We weren't communicating. I wouldn't tell [my wife] what was wrong or what I wanted from her. Maybe I expected her to understand me without saying anything.
Therapist:	Like the expectations a child has of its mother.
Arianes:	Not my mother!
Therapist:	Oh?
Arianes:	No, I always thought she had too many troubles of her own to pay attention to mine. I remember once I got hurt on my bike and came to her all bloodied up. When she saw me she got mad and yelled at me for making more trouble for her when she already had her hands full with my father.
Therapist:	Do you remember how you felt then?
Arianes:	I can't remember, but I know that after that I never brought my troubles to her again.
Therapist:	How old were you?
Arianes:	Nine, I know that because I got that bike for my ninth birthday. It was a little too big for me still, that's why I got hurt on it.
Therapist:	Perhaps you carried this attitude into your marriage.
Arianes:	What attitude?
Therapist:	The feeling that your wife, like your mother, would be unsympathetic to your difficulties. That there was no point in telling her about your experiences because she was too preoccupied or too busy to care.
Arianes:	But she's so different from my mother. I come first with her.
Therapist:	On one level you know that. On another, deeper level there may well be the fear that people—or maybe only women, or maybe only women you're close to—are all the same, and you can't take a chance at being rejected again in your need.
Arianes:	Maybe you're right, Doc, but all that was so long ago, and I should be over that by now.
Therapist:	That's not the way the mind works. If a shock, or a disappointment is strong enough it can permanently freeze our picture of ourselves and our expectations of the world. The rest of us grows up—that is, we let ourselves learn about life from experience and from what we see, hear, or read of the experiences of others, but that one area where we really got hurt stays unchanged. So what I mean when I say you might be carrying that attitude into your relationship with your wife is that when it comes to your hopes of being understood and catered to when you feel hurt or abused by life, you still feel very

much like that nine-year-old boy who was rebuffed in his need and gave up hope that anyone would or could respond to him. (Basch, 1980, pp. 29–30)

Dream Analysis

Freud often asked clients to jot down their dreams upon waking so that they could discuss them in therapy. Freud considered dreams the "royal road to the unconscious." He believed that the content of dreams is determined by unconscious processes as well as by the events of the day. Unconscious impulses tend to be expressed in dreams as a form of **wish fulfillment.**

But unacceptable sexual and aggressive impulses are likely to be displaced onto objects and situations that reflect the client's era and culture. These objects become symbols of unconscious wishes. For example, long, narrow dream objects might be **phallic symbols,** but whether the symbol takes the form of a spear, rifle, stick shift, or spacecraft partially reflects the dreamer's cultural background.

In Freud's theory, the perceived content of a dream is called its visible, or **manifest content.** Its presumed hidden or symbolic content is its **latent content.** If a man dreams he is flying, flying is the manifest content of the dream. Freud usually interpreted flying as symbolic of erection, so concerns about sexual potency might make up the latent content of the dream.

Modern Psychodynamic Approaches

Some psychoanalysts adhere faithfully to Freud's techniques. They engage in protracted therapy that continues to rely heavily on free association, interpretation of dreams, and other traditional methods. In recent years, however, more modern forms of psychodynamic therapy have been devised. *Question: How do modern psychodynamic approaches differ from traditional psychoanalysis?* Modern psychodynamic therapy is briefer and less intense and makes treatment available to clients who do not have the time or money for long-term therapy. Many modern psychodynamic therapists do not believe that prolonged therapy is needed or justifiable in terms of the ratio of cost to benefits.

Some modern psychodynamic therapies continue to focus on revealing unconscious material and breaking through psychological defenses. Nevertheless, they differ from traditional psychoanalysis in several ways (Prochaska & Norcross, 2003). One is that the client and therapist usually sit face to face (the client does not lie on a couch). The therapist is usually directive. That is, modern therapists often suggest helpful behavior instead of focusing on insight alone. Finally, there is usually more focus on the ego as the "executive" of personality and less emphasis on the id. For this reason, many modern psychodynamic therapists are considered **ego analysts.**

Many of Freud's followers, the "second generation" of psychoanalysts—from Jung and Adler to Horney and Erikson—believed that Freud had placed too much emphasis on sexual and aggressive impulses and underestimated the role of the ego. For example, Freud aimed to establish conditions under which clients could spill forth psychic energy and eventually shore up the ego. Erikson, in contrast, spoke to clients directly about their values and concerns, encouraging them to develop desired traits and behavior patterns. Even Freud's daughter, the psychoanalyst Anna Freud (1895–1982), was more concerned with the ego than with unconscious forces and conflicts.

Wish Fulfillment
A primitive method used by the id to attempt to gratify basic instincts.

Phallic Symbol
A sign that represents the penis.

Manifest Content
In psychodynamic theory, the reported content of dreams.

Latent Content
In psychodynamic theory, the symbolized or underlying content of dreams.

Ego Analyst
A psychodynamically oriented therapist who focuses on the conscious coping behavior of the ego instead of the hypothesized unconscious functioning of the id.

 Learning Connections
See Web site for an interactive version of these review questions.

R E V I E W

(3) Freud's method of psychoanalysis attempts to shed light on _____ conflicts that are presumed to lie at the roots of clients' problems. (4) Freud believed that psychoanalysis would promote _____, that is, the spilling forth of repressed psychic energy. (5) The chief psychoanalytic method is _____ association. (6) Freud considered _____ to be the "royal road to the unconscious."

Critical Thinking: Are "modern" psychoanalytic approaches psychodynamic? Do "Freudians" have a "right" to use different techniques?

HUMANISTIC THERAPIES: STRENGTHENING THE SELF

Psychodynamic therapies focus on internal conflicts and unconscious processes. Humanistic therapies focus on the quality of the client's subjective, conscious experience (Cain & Seeman, 2002). Traditional psychoanalysis focuses on early childhood experiences. Humanistic therapies usually focus on what clients are experiencing "here and now."

These differences, however, are mainly a matter of emphasis. The past has a way of influencing current thoughts, feelings, and behavior. Carl Rogers, the originator of client-centered therapy, believed that childhood experiences gave rise to the conditions of worth that troubled his clients here and now. He and Fritz Perls, the originator of Gestalt therapy, recognized that early incorporation of other people's values often leads clients to "disown" parts of their own personalities.

Client-Centered Therapy: Removing Roadblocks to Self-Actualization

Carl Rogers spent his early years in a wealthy Chicago suburb, where he attended school with Ernest Hemingway and Frank Lloyd Wright's children. His family, with its six children, was religious and close-knit. His father viewed such activities as smoking, drinking, playing cards, and going to the movies as questionable. It was all right to be tolerant of them, but relationships with those who engaged in them were discouraged. When Carl Rogers was 12, his family moved to a farm farther from the city to protect the children from such unwholesome influences.

Rogers (1902–1987) took refuge in books and developed an interest in science. His first college major was agriculture. During a student visit to Peking in 1922, he was exposed for the first time to people from different ethnic backgrounds. He wrote his parents to proclaim his independence from their conservative views. Shortly thereafter he developed an ulcer and had to be hospitalized.

Rogers then attended New York's Union Theological Seminary with the goal of becoming a minister. At the same time he took courses in psychology and education across the street at Columbia University. After a couple of years he came to believe that psychology might be a better way of helping people, so he transferred to Columbia. Perhaps in response to his parents' efforts to "protect" him from other ways of thinking, Rogers developed a form of therapy—**client-centered therapy**—that is intended to help people get in touch with their genuine feelings and pursue their own interests, regardless of other people's wishes.

Question: What is Carl Rogers's method of client-centered therapy? Rogers believed that we are free to make choices and control our destinies, despite the burdens of the past. He also believed that we have natural tendencies toward health, growth, and fulfillment. Psychological problems arise from roadblocks placed in the path of self-actualization—that is, what Rogers believed was an inborn tendency to strive to realize one's potential. If, when we are young, other people approve of us only when we are doing what they want us to do, we may learn to disown the parts of ourselves to which they object. We may learn to be seen but not heard—not even by ourselves. As a result, we may experience stress and discomfort and the feeling that we—or the world—are not real.

Client-centered therapy aims to provide insight into the parts of us that we have disowned so that we can feel whole. It creates a warm, therapeutic atmosphere that encourages self-exploration and self-expression. The therapist's acceptance of the client is thought to foster self-acceptance and self-esteem. Self-acceptance frees the client to make choices that develop his or her unique potential.

Client-centered therapy is nondirective. The client takes the lead, stating and exploring problems. An effective client-centered therapist has several qualities:

- *Unconditional positive regard:* Respect for clients as human beings with unique values and goals.

Client-Centered Therapy
Carl Rogers's method of psychotherapy, which emphasizes the creation of a warm, therapeutic atmosphere that frees clients to engage in self-exploration and self-expression.

Unconditional Positive Regard
Acceptance of the value of another person, although not necessarily acceptance of everything the person does.

© Bettman/CORBIS

■ **Carl Rogers**
Rogers's form of psychotherapy—*client-centered therapy*—is another example of how one's life experiences can shape one's views of human nature and methods of psychotherapy. Rogers's father attempted to restrict the young Rogers to a puritanically narrow lifestyle. Rogers's form of therapy attempts to enable clients to develop their own unique ideas and feelings and to act on them.

- *Empathic understanding:* Recognition of the client's experiences and feelings. Therapists view the world through the client's **frame of reference** by setting aside their own values and listening closely.
- *Genuineness:* Openness and honesty in responding to the client. Client-centered therapists must be able to tolerate differentness because they believe that every client is different in important ways.

The following excerpt from a therapy session shows how Carl Rogers uses empathic understanding and paraphrases a client's (Jill's) feelings. His goal is to help her recognize feelings that she has partially disowned:

Jill: I'm having a lot of problems dealing with my daughter. She's 20 years old; she's in college; I'm having a lot of trouble letting her go. . . . And I have a lot of guilt feelings about her; I have a real need to hang on to her.

C.R.: A need to hang on so you can kind of make up for the things you feel guilty about. Is that part of it?

Jill: There's a lot of that. . . . Also, she's been a real friend to me, and filled my life. . . . And it's very hard. . . . a lot of empty places now that she's not with me.

C.R.: The old vacuum, sort of, when she's not there.

Jill: Yes. Yes. I also would like to be the kind of mother that could be strong and say, you know, "Go and have a good life," and this is really hard for me, to do that.

C.R.: It's very hard to give up something that's been so precious in your life, but also something that I guess has caused you pain when you mentioned guilt.

Jill: Yeah. And I'm aware that I have some anger toward her that I don't always get what I want. I have needs that are not met. And, uh, I don't feel I have a right to those needs. You know. . . . she's a daughter; she's not my mother. Though sometimes I feel as if I'd like her to mother me . . . it's very difficult for me to ask for that and have a right to it.

C.R.: So, it may be unreasonable, but still, when she doesn't meet your needs, it makes you mad.

Jill: Yeah I get very angry, very angry with her.

C.R.: (Pauses) You're also feeling a little tension at this point, I guess.

Jill: Yeah. Yeah. A lot of conflict. . . . (C.R.: M-hm.) A lot of pain.

C.R A lot of pain. Can you say anything more about what that's about? (Farber et al., 1996, pp. 74-75).

Client-centered therapy is practiced widely in college and university counseling centers, not just to help students experiencing, say, anxieties or depression but also to help them make decisions. Many college students have not yet made career choices or wonder whether they should become involved with particular people or in sexual activity. Client-centered therapists do not tell clients what to do. Instead, they help clients arrive at their own decisions.

Empathic Understanding
(em-PATH-ick) Ability to perceive a client's feelings from the client's frame of reference. A quality of the good client-centered therapist.

Frame of Reference
One's unique patterning of perceptions and attitudes, according to which one evaluates events.

Genuineness
Recognition and open expression of the therapist's own feelings.

■ **Client-Centered Therapy**
By showing the qualities of unconditional positive regard, empathic understanding, genuineness, and congruence, client-centered therapists create an atmosphere in which clients can explore their feelings.

■ **Fritz Perls**

Known to friends, clients, and peers alike as "Fritz," Perls put clients through structured experiences in the effort to help them understand how their feelings might be in conflict with one another. He believed that people had to accept the responsibility of making the importance choices in their lives.

R E F L E C T

Have you heard the expression "getting it together"? How might it relate to Gestalt therapy?

Gestalt Therapy

Fritz Perls's form of psychotherapy, which attempts to integrate conflicting parts of the personality through directive methods designed to help clients perceive their whole selves.

Gestalt Therapy: Getting It Together

Gestalt therapy was originated by Fritz Perls (1893–1970). *Question: What is Fritz Perls's method of Gestalt therapy?* Like client-centered therapy, Gestalt therapy assumes that people disown parts of themselves that might meet with social disapproval or rejection. People also don social masks, pretending to be things that they are not. Therapy aims to help individuals integrate conflicting parts of their personality. Perls used the term *Gestalt* to signify his interest in giving the conflicting parts of the personality an integrated form or shape. He aimed to have his clients become aware of inner conflict, accept the reality of conflict rather than deny it or keep it repressed, and make productive choices despite misgivings and fears. People in conflict frequently find it difficult to make choices, and Perls sought to encourage—*compel* might be a better word—them to do so.

Although Perls's ideas about conflicting personality elements owe much to psychodynamic theory, his form of therapy, unlike psychoanalysis, focuses on the here and now. In Gestalt therapy, clients perform exercises to heighten their awareness of their current feelings and behavior, rather than exploring the past. Perls also believed, along with Rogers, that people are free to make choices and to direct their personal growth. But the charismatic and forceful Perls was unlike the gentle and accepting Rogers in temperament (Prochaska & Norcross, 2003). Thus, unlike client-centered therapy, Gestalt therapy is highly directive. The therapist leads the client through planned experiences.

There are a number of Gestalt exercises and games, including the following:

- *The dialogue:* In this game, the client undertakes verbal confrontations between opposing wishes and ideas to heighten awareness of internal conflict. An example of these clashing personality elements is "top dog" and "underdog." One's top dog might conservatively suggest, "Don't take chances. Stick with what you have or you might lose it all." One's frustrated underdog might then rise up and assert, "You never try anything. How will you ever get out of this rut if you don't take on new challenges?" Heightened awareness of the elements of conflict can clear the path toward resolution, perhaps through a compromise of some kind.
- *I take responsibility:* Clients end statements about themselves by adding, "and I take responsibility for it."
- *Playing the projection:* Clients role-play people with whom they are in conflict, expressing, for example, the ideas of their parents.

Body language also provides insight into conflicting feelings. Clients might be instructed to attend to the ways in which they furrow their eyebrows and tense their facial muscles when they express certain ideas. In this way, they often find that their body language asserts feelings they have been denying in their spoken statements.

The following excerpt from a therapy session with a client named Max shows how Perls would make clients take responsibility for what they experience. One of his techniques is to show how clients are treating something they are doing (a "verb") like something that is just out there and beyond their control (a "noun"):

Max: I feel the tenseness in my stomach and in my hands.
Perls: *The* tenseness. Here we've got a noun. Now *the* tenseness is a noun. Now change the noun, the thing, into a verb.
Max: I am tense. My hands are tense.
Perls: Your hands are tense. They have nothing to do with you.
Max: I am tense.
Perls: You are tense. How are you tense? What are you doing?
Max: I am tensing myself.
Perls: That's it. (Perls, 1971, p. 115).

Once Max understands that he is tensing himself and takes responsibility for it, he can choose to stop tensing himself. The tenseness is no longer something out there that is victimizing him; it is something he is doing to himself.

Psychodynamic theory views dreams as the "royal road to the unconscious." Perls saw the content of dreams as representing disowned parts of the personality. Perls would often ask clients to role-play elements of their dreams in order to get in touch with these parts of their personality.

REVIEW

Learning Connections
See Web site for an interactive version of these review questions.

(7) _____ therapies focus on clients' subjective, conscious experience. (8) Client-centered therapy is a (directive or nondirective?) method that provides clients with an accepting atmosphere that enables them to overcome roadblocks to self-actualization. (9) The client-centered therapist shows (conditional or unconditional?) positive regard, empathic understanding, and genuineness. (10) Gestalt therapy provides (directive or nondirective?) methods that are designed to help clients accept responsibility and integrate conflicting parts of the personality.

Critical Thinking: Why are the therapies of Rogers and Perls placed in the same category? What do they have in common? How do they differ?

BEHAVIOR THERAPY: ADJUSTMENT IS WHAT YOU DO

Psychodynamic and humanistic forms of therapy tend to focus on what people think and feel. Behavior therapists tend to focus on what people *do*.   ***Question: What is behavior therapy?*** **Behavior therapy**—also called *behavior modification*—applies principles of learning to directly promote desired behavioral changes (Wolpe & Plaud, 1997). Behavior therapists rely heavily on principles of conditioning and observational learning. They help clients discontinue self-defeating behavior patterns such as overeating, smoking, and phobic avoidance of harmless stimuli. They also help clients acquire adaptive behavior patterns such as the social skills required to start social relationships or say no to insistent salespeople.

Behavior therapists may help clients gain "insight" into maladaptive behavior in the sense of fostering awareness of the circumstances in which it occurs. They do not foster insight in the psychoanalytic sense of unearthing the childhood origins of problems and the symbolic meanings of maladaptive behavior. Behavior therapists, like other therapists, may also build warm, therapeutic relationships with clients, but they see the efficacy of behavior therapy as deriving from specific, learning-based procedures (Wolpe, 1990). They insist that their methods be established by experimentation and that the outcomes be assessed in terms of measurable behavior. In this section we consider some frequently used behavior-therapy techniques.

Fear-Reduction Methods

Many people seek therapy because of fears and phobias that interfere with their functioning. This is one of the areas in which behavior therapy has made great inroads. ***Question: What are some behavior-therapy methods for reducing fears?***   These include flooding (see Chapter 6), systematic desensitization, and modeling.

Systematic Desensitization

Adam has a phobia for receiving injections. His behavior therapist treats him as he reclines in a comfortable padded chair. In a state of deep muscle relaxation, Adam observes slides projected on a screen. A slide of a nurse holding a needle has just been shown three times, 30 seconds at a time. Each time Adam has shown no anxiety. So now a slightly more discomforting slide is shown: one of the nurse aiming the needle toward someone's bare arm. After 15 seconds, our armchair adventurer notices twinges of discomfort and raises a finger as a signal (speaking might disturb his relaxation). The projector operator turns off the light, and Adam spends 2 minutes imagining his "safe scene"—lying on a beach beneath the tropical sun. Then the slide is shown again. This time Adam views it for 30 seconds before feeling anxiety.

Behavior Therapy
Systematic application of the principles of learning to the direct modification of a client's problem behaviors.

■ **Overcoming Fear of Flying**
One way behavior therapists help clients overcome phobias is by having them gradually approach the feared object or situation while they remain relaxed.

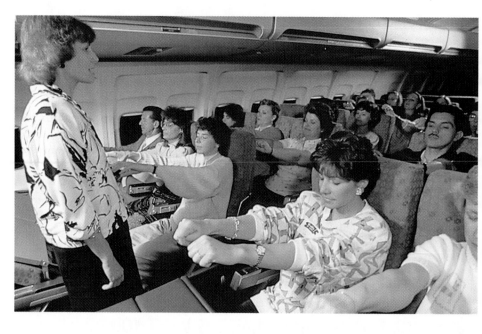

Life Connections
See the Connections *CD-ROM for an animation on the behavioral treatment of phobias.*

Adam is undergoing **systematic desensitization,** a method for reducing phobic responses originated by psychiatrist Joseph Wolpe (1915–1997). Systematic desensitization is a gradual process in which the client learns to handle increasingly disturbing stimuli while anxiety to each one is being counterconditioned. About 10 to 20 stimuli are arranged in a sequence, or **hierarchy,** according to their capacity to elicit anxiety. In imagination or by being shown photos, the client travels gradually up through this hierarchy, approaching the target behavior. In Adam's case, the target behavior was the ability to receive an injection without undue anxiety.

Wolpe (1990) developed systematic desensitization on the assumption that anxiety responses, like other behaviors, are learned or conditioned. He reasoned that they can be unlearned by means of counterconditioning or extinction. In counterconditioning, a response that is incompatible with anxiety is made to appear under conditions that usually elicit anxiety. Muscle relaxation is incompatible with anxiety. For this reason, Adam's therapist is teaching him to relax in the presence of (usually) anxiety-evoking slides of needles.

Remaining in the presence of phobic imagery, rather than running away from it, is also likely to enhance self-efficacy expectations (Galassi, 1988). Self-efficacy expectations are negatively correlated with levels of adrenaline in the bloodstream (Bandura et al., 1985). Raising clients' self-efficacy expectations thus may help lower their adrenaline levels and reduce their feelings of nervousness.

And What If a (Virtual) Spider Sat Down Beside Her? Use of Virtual Reality in Desensitization

Some psychologists are now conducting desensitization to phobic stimuli by means of virtual reality. In the case of using virtual reality, clients don goggles and headphones such that they perceive themselves to be in the fearful setting, although they are "safe" in the office or laboratory of the therapist. Barbara Rothbaum and her colleagues (2001, 2002) have used the method to treat clients with problems such as posttraumatic stress due to combat and fear of flying. David Ready, one of Rothbaum's colleagues, notes that "You're not watching something, you're in something. All you see is what's in the goggles and all you hear is what's on the headphones" (cited in Robbins, 2000).

Virtual reality was also used to help desensitize Joanne Cartwright, who had a debilitating phobia for spiders. "I washed my truck every night before I went to work in case there were webs," says Cartwright (cited in Robbins, 2000). "I put all my clothes in plastic bags and taped duct tape around my doors so spiders couldn't get in. I thought I was going to have a mental breakdown. I wasn't living." Twelve sessions of desensitization by means of virtual reality apparently changed her life. "I'm amazed," notes Cartwright, "because I am doing all this stuff I could never do—camping, hunting and hiking."

Systematic Desensitization
Wolpe's method for reducing fears by associating a hierarchy of images of fear-evoking stimuli with deep muscle relaxation.

Hierarchy
An arrangement of stimuli according to the amount of fear they evoke.

Modeling

Modeling relies on observational learning. In this method clients observe, and then imitate, people who approach and cope with the objects or situations that the clients fear. Bandura and his colleagues (1969) found that modeling worked as well as systematic desensitization—and more rapidly—in reducing fear of snakes. Like systematic desensitization, modeling is likely to increase self-efficacy expectations in coping with feared stimuli.

Aversive Conditioning

Many people also seek behavior therapy because they want to break bad habits, such as smoking, excessive drinking, nail biting, and the like. One behavior-therapy approach to helping people do so is **aversive conditioning.** *Question: How do behavior therapists use aversive conditioning to help people break bad habits?* Aversive conditioning is a controversial procedure in which painful or aversive stimuli are paired with unwanted impulses, such as desire for a cigarette or desire to engage in antisocial behavior, in order to make the impulse less appealing. For example, to help people control alcohol intake, tastes of different alcoholic beverages can be paired with drug-induced nausea and vomiting or with electric shock.

Aversive conditioning has been used with problems as diverse as cigarette smoking, sexual abuse (Rice et al., 1991), and retarded children's self-injurious behavior. **Rapid smoking** is an aversive-conditioning method designed to help smokers quit. In this method, the would-be quitter inhales every six seconds. In another method the hose of a hair dryer is hooked up to a chamber containing several lit cigarettes. Smoke is blown into the quitter's face as he or she also smokes a cigarette. A third method uses branching pipes so that the smoker draws in smoke from several cigarettes at the same time. In these methods, overexposure makes once-desirable cigarette smoke aversive. The quitter becomes motivated to avoid, rather than seek, cigarettes. However, the effectiveness of aversive conditioning for helping people quit smoking is uncertain (Lancaster et al., 2000), and interest in aversive conditioning for quitting smoking has waned because of side effects such as raising blood pressure and the availability of nicotine-replacement techniques.

In one study of aversive conditioning in the treatment of alcoholism, 63% of the 685 people treated remained abstinent for one year afterward, and about a third remained abstinent for at least three years (Wiens & Menustik, 1983). It may seem ironic that punitive aversive stimulation is sometimes used to stop children from punishing

R E F L E C T

Do you think that aversive conditioning is an ethical form of therapy? Explain.

Modeling
A behavior-therapy technique in which a client observes and imitates a person who approaches and copes with feared objects or situations.

Aversive Conditioning
A behavior-therapy technique in which undesired responses are inhibited by pairing repugnant or offensive stimuli with them.

Rapid Smoking
An aversive conditioning method for quitting smoking in which the smoker inhales every six seconds, thus rendering once-desirable cigarette smoke aversive.

■ Aversive Conditioning

In aversive conditioning, unwanted behaviors take on a noxious quality as a result of being repeatedly paired with aversive stimuli. Overexposure is making cigarette smoke aversive to this smoker.

Token Economy

A controlled environment in which people are reinforced for desired behaviors with tokens (such as poker chips) that may be exchanged for privileges.

Successive Approximations

In operant conditioning, a series of behaviors that gradually become more similar to a target behavior.

Self-Monitoring

Keeping a record of one's own behavior to identify problems and record successes.

Behavior Rehearsal

Practice.

Feedback

In assertiveness training, information about the effectiveness of a response.

themselves, but people sometimes hurt themselves in order to obtain sympathy and attention. If self-injury leads to more pain than anticipated and no sympathy, it might be discontinued.

Operant Conditioning Procedures

We usually prefer to relate to people who smile at us rather than ignore us and to take courses in which we do well rather than fail. We tend to repeat behavior that is reinforced. Behavior that is not reinforced tends to become extinguished. Behavior therapists have used these principles of operant conditioning with psychotic patients as well as with clients with milder problems. *Question: How do behavior therapists apply principles of operant conditioning in behavior modification?*

The staff at one mental hospital was at a loss about how to encourage withdrawn schizophrenic patients to eat regularly. Ayllon and Haughton (1962) observed that staff members were making the problem worse by coaxing patients into the dining room and even feeding them. Staff attention apparently reinforced the patients' lack of cooperation. Some rules were changed. Patients who did not arrive at the dining hall within 30 minutes after serving were locked out. Staff could not interact with patients at mealtime. With uncooperative behavior no longer reinforced, patients quickly changed their eating habits. Then patients were required to pay one penny to enter the dining hall. Pennies were earned by interacting with other patients and showing other socially appropriate behaviors. These target behaviors also became more frequent.

Health professionals are concerned as to whether people who are, or have been, dependent on alcohol can exercise control over their drinking. One study showed that rewards for remaining abstinent from alcohol can exert a powerful effect (Petry et al., 2000). In the study, one group of alcohol-dependent veterans was given a standard treatment while another group received the treatment *plus* the chance to win prizes for remaining alcohol-free, as measured by a Breathalyzer test. By the end of the eight-week treatment period, 84% of the veterans who could win prizes remained in the program, as compared with 22% of the standard treatment group. The prizes had an average value of $200, far less than what alcohol-related absenteeism from work and other responsibilities can cost.

The Token Economy

Many psychiatric wards and hospitals now use **token economies** in which patients must use tokens such as poker chips to purchase TV viewing time, extra visits to the canteen, or a private room (Comaty et al., 2001). The tokens are reinforcements for productive activities such as making beds, brushing teeth, and socializing. Token economies have not eliminated all symptoms of schizophrenia but have enhanced patient activity and cooperation. Tokens have also been used to modify the behavior of children with conduct disorders. In one program, for example, children received tokens for helpful behaviors such as volunteering and lost tokens for behaviors such as arguing and failing to pay attention (Schneider & Byrne, 1987).

Successive Approximations

The operant conditioning method of **successive approximations** is often used to help clients build good habits. Let us use a (not uncommon!) example: You want to study three hours each evening but can concentrate for only half an hour. Rather than attempting to increase your study time all at once, you could do so gradually by adding, say, five minutes each evening. After every hour or so of studying, you could reinforce yourself with five minutes of people-watching in a busy section of the library.

Social Skills Training

In social skills training, behavior therapists decrease social anxiety and build social skills through operant-conditioning procedures that employ **self-monitoring**, coaching, modeling, role-playing, **behavior rehearsal,** and **feedback.** Social skills training has been used to help formerly hospitalized mental patients maintain jobs and apartments in the community. For example, a worker can rehearse politely asking a supervisor for assistance or asking a landlord to fix the plumbing in an apartment.

Social skills training is effective in groups. Group members can role-play important people—such as parents, spouses, or potential dates—in the lives of other members.

Biofeedback Training

Through **biofeedback training (BFT),** therapists help clients become more aware of, and gain control over, various bodily functions. Therapists attach clients to devices that measure bodily functions such as heart rate. "Bleeps" or other electronic signals are used to indicate (and thereby reinforce) changes in the desired direction—for example, a slower heart rate. (Knowledge of results is a powerful reinforcer.) One device, the electromyograph (EMG), monitors muscle tension. It has been used to augment control over muscle tension in the forehead and elsewhere, thereby alleviating anxiety, stress, and headaches.

BFT also helps clients voluntarily regulate functions once thought to be beyond conscious control, such as heart rate and blood pressure. Hypertensive clients use a blood pressure cuff and electronic signals to gain control over their blood pressure. The electroencephalograph (EEG) monitors brain waves and can be used to teach people how to produce alpha waves, which are associated with relaxation. Some people have overcome insomnia by learning to produce the kinds of brain waves associated with sleep.

Self-Control Methods

Do mysterious forces sometimes seem to be at work in your life? Forces that delight in wreaking havoc on New Year's resolutions and other efforts to put an end to your bad habits? Just when you go on a diet, that juicy pizza stares at you from the TV set. Just when you resolve to balance your budget, that sweater goes on sale.   *Question: How can you—yes, you—use behavior therapy to deal with temptation and enhance your self-control?*

Functional Analysis of Behavior

Behavior therapists usually begin with a **functional analysis** of the problem behavior. In this way, they help determine the stimuli that trigger the behavior and the reinforcers that maintain it. Then clients are taught how to manipulate the antecedents and consequences of their behavior and how to increase the frequency of desired responses and decrease the frequency of undesired responses. You can use a diary to jot down each instance of a problem behavior. Note the time of day, location, your activity at the time (including your thoughts and feelings), and reactions (yours and others'). Functional analysis serves a number of purposes. It makes you more aware of the environmental context of your behavior and can increase your motivation to change.

Brian used functional analysis to master his nail biting. Table 13.1 shows a few items from his notebook. He discovered that boredom and humdrum activities

Biofeedback Training (BFT)
The systematic feeding back to an organism of information about a bodily function so that the organism can gain control of that function.

Functional Analysis
A systematic study of behavior in which one identifies the stimuli that trigger problem behavior and the reinforcers that maintain it.

REFLECT
Do you have any habits you would like to change? Can you use any of the methods of self-control discussed here to help you do so?

TABLE 13.1 Excerpts from Brian's Diary of Nail Biting for April 14

Incident	Time	Location	Activity (Thoughts, Feelings)	Reactions
1	7:45 AM	Freeway	Driving to work, bored, not thinking	Finger bleeds, pain
2	10:30 AM	Office	Writing report	Self-disgust
3	2:25 PM	Conference	Listening to dull financial report	Embarrassment
4	6:40 PM	Living room	Watching evening news	Self-disgust

Note: A functional analysis of problem behavior like nail biting increases awareness of the environmental context in which it occurs, spurs motivation to change, and, in highly motivated people, might lead to significant behavioral change.

seemed to serve as triggers for nail biting. He began to watch out for feelings of boredom as signs to practice self-control. He also made some changes in his life so that he would feel bored less often.

There are numerous self-control strategies aimed at the stimuli that trigger behavior, the behaviors themselves, and reinforcers. Table 5.8 describes some of them.

Learning Connections
See Web site for an interactive version of these review questions.

R E V I E W

(11) Behavior therapy applies principles of _____ to bring about desired behavioral changes. (12) Behavior-therapy methods for reducing fears include flooding; systematic _____, in which a client is gradually exposed to more fear-arousing stimuli; and modeling. (13) _____ conditioning associates undesired behavior with painful stimuli to decrease the frequency of the behavior. (14) _____ conditioning methods reinforce desired responses and extinguish undesired responses. (15) In self-control methods, clients first engage in a _____ analysis of problem behavior. (16) Clients are then taught how to change the behavior by manipulating its antecedents and _____.

Critical Thinking: How do behavior therapists attempt to ensure that their methods are scientific?

COGNITIVE THERAPIES: ADJUSTMENT IS WHAT YOU THINK (AND DO)

There is nothing either good or bad, but thinking makes it so.

—Shakespeare, *Hamlet*

In this line from *Hamlet,* Shakespeare did not mean to suggest that injuries and misfortunes are painless or easy to manage. Rather, he meant that our appraisals of unfortunate events can heighten our discomfort and impair our coping ability. In so doing, Shakespeare was providing a kind of motto for cognitive therapists. **Question: What is cognitive therapy?**

Cognitive therapy focuses on changing the beliefs, attitudes, and automatic types of thinking that create and compound their clients' problems (Beck, 1993; Ellis & Dryden, 1996). Cognitive therapists, like psychodynamic and humanistic therapists, aim to foster self-insight, but they aim to heighten insight into *current cognitions* as well as those of the past. Cognitive therapists also aim to directly change maladaptive cognitions in order to reduce negative feelings, provide insight, and help the client solve problems.

You may have noticed that many behavior therapists incorporate cognitive procedures in their methods. For example, techniques such as systematic desensitization, covert sensitization, and covert reinforcement ask clients to focus on visual imagery. Behavioral methods for treating bulimia nervosa focus on clients' irrational attitudes toward their weight and body shape as well as foster healthful eating habits. Let us look at the approaches and methods of some major cognitive therapists.

Cognitive Therapy: Correcting Cognitive Errors

Aaron Beck used cognitive and behavioral techniques on himself before he became a psychiatrist. One of the reasons Aaron Beck went into medicine was to confront his own fear of blood. He had had a series of operations as a child, and from then on the sight of blood had made him feel faint. During his first year of medical school, he forced himself to watch operations. In his second year, he became a surgical assistant. Soon the sight of blood became normal to him. Later he essentially argued himself out of an irrational fear of tunnels. He convinced himself that the tunnels did not cause the fear because the symptoms of faintness and shallow breathing would appear before he entered them.

Cognitive Therapy
A form of therapy that focuses on how clients' cognitions (expectations, attitudes, beliefs, etc.) lead to distress and may be modified to relieve distress and promote adaptive behavior.

As a psychiatrist, Beck first practiced psychoanalysis. However, he could not find scientific evidence for psychoanalytic beliefs. Psychoanalytic theory explained depression as anger turned inward, so that it is transformed into a need to suffer. Beck's own clinical experiences led him to believe that it is more likely that depressed people experience cognitive distortions such as the *cognitive triad.* That is, they expect the worst of themselves ("I'm no good"), the world at large ("This is an awful place"), and their future ("Nothing good will ever happen"). Beck's approach to therapy is active. Beck encourages clients to challenge beliefs that are not supported by evidence.

Beck also challenges his own points of view. "I am a big self-doubter," Beck (2000) admits. "I always doubt what I do, which is one of the reasons I do so much research and encourage research." Beck teaches health professionals his form of therapy—and scientific skepticism—at the University of Pennsylvania.

Cognitive therapy is the name of a general approach to therapy as well as Aaron Beck's specific methods. Beck (1991, 1993) focuses on clients' cognitive distortions. *Question: What is Aaron Beck's method of cognitive therapy?* Beck encourages clients to become their own personal scientists and challenge beliefs that are not supported by evidence.

Beck questions people in a way that encourages them to see the irrationality of their ways of thinking. For example, depressed people tend to minimize their accomplishments and to assume that the worst will happen. Both distortions heighten feelings of depression. Cognitive distortions can be fleeting and automatic, difficult to detect (Persons et al., 2001). Beck's therapy methods help clients become aware of distortions and challenge them.

Beck notes how cognitive errors contribute to clients' miseries:

- Clients may *selectively perceive* the world as a harmful place and ignore evidence to the contrary.
- Clients may *overgeneralize* on the basis of a few examples. For example, they may perceive themselves as worthless because they were laid off at work or as unattractive because they were refused a date.
- Clients may *magnify,* or blow out of proportion, the importance of negative events. They may catastrophize failing a test by assuming they will flunk out of college, or catastrophize losing a job by believing that they will never find another one and that serious harm will befall their family as a result.
- Clients may engage in *absolutist thinking,* or looking at the world in black and white rather than in shades of gray. In doing so, a rejection on a date takes on the meaning of a lifetime of loneliness; an uncomfortable illness takes on life-threatening proportions.

■ Cognitive Therapists Aaron Beck and Albert Ellis

Psychiatrist Aaron Beck's (left) method of therapy grew out of his early life experiences, in which he argued himself out of fear of tunnels and overcame his fear of blood by exposing himself repeatedly to assisting in surgical operations. Psychologist Albert Ellis (right) was originally trained in psychoanalysis but became frustrated with the slow rate of progress made by clients. He also found himself uncomfortable with the psychoanalyst's laid-back approach and took to engaging in sometimes heated discussions with his clients about their irrational and self-defeating ways of viewing themselves and other people.

The concept of pinpointing and modifying errors may become clearer from the following excerpt from a case in which a 53-year-old engineer obtained cognitive therapy for severe depression. The engineer had left his job and become inactive. As reported by Beck and his colleagues, the first goal of treatment was to foster physical activity—even things like raking leaves and preparing dinner—because activity is incompatible with depression. Then:

> [The engineer's] cognitive distortions were identified by comparing his assessment of each activity with that of his wife. Alternative ways of interpreting his experiences were then considered.
>
> In comparing his wife's résumé of his past experiences, he became aware that he had (1) undervalued his past by failing to mention many previous accomplishments, (2) regarded himself as far more responsible for his "failures" than she did, and (3) concluded that he was worthless since he had not succeeded in attaining certain goals in the past. When the two accounts were contrasted, he could discern many of his cognitive distortions. In subsequent sessions, his wife continued to serve as an "objectifier."
>
> In midtherapy, [he] compiled a list of new attitudes that he had acquired since initiating therapy. These included:
>
> 1. "I am starting at a lower level of functioning at my job, but it will improve if I persist."
> 2. "I know that once I get going in the morning, everything will run all right for the rest of the day."
> 3. "I can't achieve everything at once."
> 4. "I have my periods of ups and downs, but in the long run I feel better."
> 5. "My expectations from my job and life should be scaled down to a realistic level."
> 6. "Giving in to avoidance [e.g., staying away from work and social interactions] never helps and only leads to further avoidance."
>
> He was instructed to reread this list daily for several weeks even though he already knew the content. (Rush et al., 1975)

The engineer gradually became less depressed and returned to work and an active social life. Along the way, he learned to combat inappropriate self-blame for problems, perfectionistic expectations, magnification of failures, and overgeneralization from failures.

Becoming aware of cognitive errors and modifying catastrophizing thoughts helps us cope with stress. Internal, stable, and global attributions of failure lead to depression and feelings of helplessness. Cognitive therapists also alert clients to cognitive errors such as these so that the clients can change their attitudes and pave the way for more effective overt behavior.

Rational Emotive Behavior Therapy: Overcoming "Musts" and "Shoulds"

REFLECT

Do you believe that you must have the love and approval of people who are important to you? Do you believe that you must prove yourself to be thoroughly competent, adequate, and achieving? Do such beliefs make you miserable? What can you do about them?

In **rational emotive behavior therapy (REBT),** Albert Ellis (2002) points out that our beliefs *about* events, not only the events themselves, shape our responses to them. Moreover, many of us harbor a number of irrational beliefs that can give rise to problems or magnify their impact. Two of the most important ones are the belief that we must have the love and approval of people who are important to us and the belief that we must prove ourselves to be thoroughly competent, adequate, and achieving. *Question: What is Albert Ellis's method of rational emotive behavior therapy (REBT)?*

Albert Ellis, like Aaron Beck, began as a psychoanalyst. But he became disturbed by the passive role of the analyst and by the slow rate of obtaining results—if they were obtained at all. Still, Ellis finds a role for Freud's views: "One of the main things [Freud] did was point out the importance of unconscious thinking. Freud pointed out that when people are motivated to do things, that they unconsciously think, and even feel, certain things. We use that concept," Ellis (2000) admits, "although Freud, as usual, ran it into the ground."

Ellis's REBT methods are active and directive. He does not sit back like the traditional psychoanalyst and occasionally offer an interpretation. Instead, he urges clients to seek out their irrational beliefs, which can be unconscious, though not as deeply buried as Freud believed. Nevertheless, they can be hard to pinpoint without some direction. Ellis shows clients how those beliefs lead to misery and challenges clients to

Rational Emotive Behavior Therapy (REBT)
Albert Ellis's form of therapy that encourages clients to challenge and correct irrational expectations and maladaptive behaviors.

change them. When Ellis sees clients behaving according to irrational beliefs, he may refute the beliefs by asking "Where is it written that you must . . . ?" or "What evidence do you have that . . . ?" According to Ellis, we need less misery and less blaming in our lives, and more action.

Ellis straddles behavioral and cognitive therapies. He originally dubbed his method of therapy *rational–emotive therapy,* because his focus was on the cognitive—irrational beliefs and how to change them. However, Ellis has also always promoted behavioral changes to cement cognitive changes. In keeping with his broad philosophy, he recently changed the name of rational–emotive therapy to rational emotive *behavior* therapy.

Many theorists consider cognitive therapy to be a collection of techniques that are part of the overall approach known as behavior therapy, which is discussed in the following section. Some members of this group use the term "cognitive *behavioral* therapy." Others argue that the term *behavior therapy* is broad enough to include cognitive techniques. Many cognitive therapists and behavior therapists differ in focus, however. Behavior therapists deal with client cognitions in order to change *overt* behavior. Cognitive therapists also see the value of tying treatment outcomes to observable behavior, but they believe that cognitive change is a key goal in itself.

See the "In Review" chart on pages 506–507.

R E V I E W

Learning Connections
See Web site for an interactive version of these review questions.

(17) _____ therapists focus on the beliefs, attitudes, and automatic thoughts that create and compound their clients' problems. (18) Beck notes four types of cognitive errors that contribute to clients' miseries: selective abstraction of the world as a harmful place; overgeneralization; magnification of the importance of negative events, and _____ thinking, or looking at the world in black and white rather than shades of gray. (19) Ellis's REBT confronts clients with the ways in which _____ beliefs contribute to problems such as anxiety and depression.

Critical Thinking: Many therapists call themselves cognitive behavior therapists. Does it seem possible to combine behavior therapy and cognitive therapy?

GROUP THERAPIES

When a psychotherapist has several clients with similar problems—anxiety, depression, adjustment to divorce, lack of social skills—it often makes sense to treat them in a group rather than in individual sessions. The methods and characteristics of the group reflect the needs of the members and the theoretical orientation of the leader. In group psychoanalysis, clients might interpret one another's dreams. In a client-centered group, they might provide an accepting atmosphere for self-exploration. Members of behavior therapy groups might be jointly desensitized to anxiety-evoking stimuli or might practice social skills together.   *Question: What are the advantages and disadvantages of group therapy?*

Group therapy has the following advantages:

- It is economical (Davison, 2000; Haaga, 2000). It allows the therapist to work with several clients at once.
- Compared with one-to-one therapy, group therapy provides more information and life experience for clients to draw upon.
- Appropriate behavior receives group support. Clients usually appreciate an outpouring of peer approval.
- When we run into troubles, it is easy to imagine that we are different from other people or inferior to them. Affiliating with people with similar problems is reassuring.
- Group members who show improvement provide hope for other members.
- Many individuals seek therapy because of problems in relating to other people. People who seek therapy for other reasons also may be socially inhibited. Members of groups

IN REVIEW

	Biological Therapies	**Cognitive Therapies**

TYPE OF THERAPY

Assume that disorders reflect the interaction of genetic vulnerability with other factors such as imbalances of neurotransmitters or hormones, or situational stressors; for example, depression may reflect interaction of genetic vulnerability with low levels of serotonin and with a personal failure.

Assume disorders reflect cognitive errors such as excessive self-blame, pessimism, and selective focus on negative events.

Many drugs have been used to combat psychological disorders.

The therapist seeks to guide the client to correct cognitive errors and recognize irrational beliefs.

GOALS

To decrease anxiety, alleviate depression, lessen mood swings in bipolar disorder, eliminate or lessen symptoms of schizophrenia

To make clients aware of the beliefs, attitudes, and automatic types of thinking that create and compound their problems; to help them correct these kinds of thinking to reduce negative feelings and solve problems.

METHODS

Antianxiety drugs (also known as *anxiolytic* drugs or "minor tranquilizers"), antidepressant drugs, lithium and other drugs for treatment of bipolar disorder, antipsychotic drugs ("major tranquilizers"), electroconvulsive shock therapy (ECT) for treatment of depression that is unresponsive to drug therapy, psychosurgery

Aaron Beck's cognitive therapy helps people recognize and correct cognitive errors such as selective perception, overgeneralization, magnification of negative events, and absolutist thinking. Rational emotive behavior therapists show clients how irrational beliefs catastrophize events and make them miserable.

ABOUT ...

Most psychologists prefer psychotherapy to biological therapies as being more helpful in developing strategies for solving problems. There is controversy as to whether cognitive therapy is as effective as biological therapy for depression. Most psychologists agree that biological therapies may be appropriate when disorders are severe and unresponsive to psychotherapy.

Many theorists consider cognitive therapy to be part of behavior therapy, and some call it cognitive–*behavioral* therapy.

Principle proponents: Aaron Beck introduced his approach, "cognitive therapy," in the 1960s. Albert Ellis first developed what he called "rational-emotive therapy" (RET) in the late 1950s and 1960s. More recently, he changed the name to "rational emotive behavior therapy" (REBT).

Electroconvulsive therapy is used mainly in cases of major depression where other therapies have failed.

...vior Therapies

...he disorders reflect learning of ...aptive responses (such as ...aptive fear responses, or ...as) or failure to acquire adaptive ...nses (such as social skills).

...ay behavior therapists help clients ...me phobias is to have them gradually ...ch the feared object or sitation while ...main relaxed.

...e principles of learning to help ...s engage in adaptive behavior ...discontinue maladaptive ...vior.

...vior therapy is directive and uses ...eduction methods (including ...matic desensitization) to overcome ...ias such as fear of flying, aversive ...itioning (to help clients discontinue ...habits), operant conditioning ...edures (e.g., social skills training), ...elf-control methods (beginning with ...onal analysis of behavior).

...vior therapists have developed ...nent for problems (e.g., smoking, ...ias, sexual dysfunctions) for which ...previously were no effective ...nent methods.

...iple proponents: Joseph Wolpe ...5–1997) introduced systematic ...nsitization in the late 1950s. Albert ...ura integrated behavioral and ...itive factors in forming his therapeutic ...ods, such as modeling.

Humanistic Therapies

Assume that disorders reflect feelings of alienation from one's genuine beliefs and feelings.

Client-centered therapists provide a warm atmosphere in which clients feel free to explore their genuine feelings.

To help clients get in touch with parts of themselves that they have "disowned" and actualize their unique desires and abilities

Client-centered therapy is nondirective. It provides an atmosphere of "unconditional positive regard" from the therapist in which clients can engage in self-exploration without fear. Gestalt therapy uses highly directive methods to help clients integrate conflicting parts of the personality into a healthy "Gestalt," or whole.

Client-centered therapy is practiced widely in college and university counseling centers to help students make academic and personal decisions.

Principle proponents: Carl Rogers (1902–1970) developed client-centered therapy in the mid-20th century. Fritz Perls (1893–1970) originated Gestalt therapy, which reached its greatest prominence in the 1960s.

Psychodynamic Therapies

Assume disorders stem from unresolved unconscious conflict.

Freud's consulting room.

To strengthen the ego; to provide self-insight into unconscious conflict

Traditional psychoanalysis is lengthy and nondirective and involves methods such as free association and dream analysis.

Most effective with verbal, "upscale" clients. Modern ego-analytic approaches are briefer and more directive than traditional psychoanalysis.

Principle proponent: Sigmund Freud (1856–1939) formulated his psychodynamic theory of personality a century ago. His method of therapy, psychoanalysis, achieved greatest prominence in the 1940s and 1950s.

■ Group Therapy

Group therapy has a number of advantages over individual therapy for many clients. It's economical, provides a fund of experience for clients to draw upon, elicits group support, and provides an opportunity to relate to other people. On the other hand, some clients do need individual attention.

have the opportunity to practice social skills in a relatively nonthreatening atmosphe In a group consisting of men and women of different ages, group members can ro play one another's employers, employees, spouses, parents, children, and frien Members can role-play asking one another out on dates, saying no (or yes), and so

But group therapy is not for everyone. Some clients fare better with individ treatment. Many prefer not to disclose their problems to a group. They may be ove shy or want individual attention. It is the responsibility of the therapist to insist th group disclosures be kept confidential, to establish a supportive atmosphere, and ensure that group members obtain the attention they need.

Many types of therapy can be conducted either individually or in group Encounter groups and family therapy are conducted only in groups.

Encounter Groups

Encounter groups are not appropriate for treating serious psychological problen Rather, they are intended to promote personal growth by heightening awareness one's own needs and feelings and those of others. This goal is sought through inter confrontations, or encounters, between strangers. *Questions: What are encount groups? What are their effects?*

Like ships in the night, group members come together out of the darkness, tou one another briefly, then sink back into the shadows of one another's lives. But son thing is gained from the passing.

Encounter groups stress interactions between group members in the here and no Discussion of the past may be outlawed. Interpretation is out. However, expression genuine feelings toward others is encouraged. When group members think a perso social mask is phony, they may descend en masse to rip it off.

Encounter groups can be damaging when they urge overly rapid disclosure of in mate matters or when several members attack one member. Responsible leaders do r tolerate these abuses and try to keep the group moving in a growth-enhancing directic

R E F L E C T

Do you share the power in your relationships? How does your power sharing—or lack of it!—affect your relationships?

Encounter Group
A type of group that aims to foster self-awareness by focusing on how group members relate to each other in a setting that encourages open expression of feelings.

Couple Therapy

Couple therapy helps couples enhance their relationship by improving their comm nication skills and helping them manage conflict (Markman et al., 1993). There a often power imbalances in relationships, and couple therapy helps individuals fi "full membership" in the couple. Correcting power imbalances increases happine and can decrease the incidence of domestic violence. Ironically, in situations of dome tic violence, the partner with *less* power in the relationship is usually the violent one. Violence sometimes appears to be a way of compensating for inability to share power in other aspects of the relationship (Rathus & Sanderson, 1999).

Today the main approach to couple therapy today is cognitive–behavioral (Rathus & Sanderson, 1999). It teaches couples communications skills (such as how to listen and how to express feelings), ways of handling feelings like depression and anger, and ways of solving problems.

Family Therapy

Question: What is family therapy?   **Family therapy** is a form of group therapy in which one or more families constitute the group. Family therapy may be undertaken from various theoretical viewpoints. One is the "systems approach," in which family interaction is studied and modified to enhance the growth of individual family members and of the family unit as a whole (Prochaska & Norcross, 2003).

Family members with low self-esteem often cannot tolerate different attitudes and behaviors in other family members. Faulty communication within the family also creates problems. In addition, it is not uncommon for the family to present an "identified patient"—that is, the family member who has *the* problem and is *causing* all the trouble. Yet family therapists usually assume that the identified patient is a scapegoat for other problems within and among family members. It is a sort of myth: Change the bad apple—or identified patient—and the barrel—or family—will be functional once more.

The family therapist—often a specialist in this field—attempts to teach the family to communicate more effectively and encourage growth and autonomy in each family member.

R E V I E W

(20) Group therapy is (more or less?) economical than individual therapy. (21) _____ groups promote personal growth by heightening awareness of people's needs and feelings through intense confrontations. (22) In the _____ approach to family therapy, family interaction is modified to enhance the growth of family members and the family unit as a whole.

Critical Thinking: Critical thinkers avoid overgeneralization. Is it accurate to say that individual therapy is preferable to group therapy, or is the statement an overgeneralization?

Learning Connections
See Web site for an interactive version of these review questions.

DOES PSYCHOTHERAPY WORK?

In 1952, the British psychologist Hans Eysenck published a review of psychotherapy research—"The Effects of Psychotherapy"—that sent shock waves through the psychotherapy community. On the basis of his review of the research, Eysenck concluded that the rate of improvement among people in psychotherapy was no greater than the rate of "spontaneous remission"—that is, the rate of improvement that would be shown by people with psychological disorders who received no treatment at all. Eysenck was not addressing people with schizophrenia, who typically profit from biological forms of therapy, but he argued that whether or not people with problems such as anxiety and depression received therapy, two of three reported substantial improvement within two years.

That was half a century ago. Since that time, sophisticated research studies—many of them employing a statistical averaging method called **meta-analysis**—have strongly suggested that psychotherapy is, in fact, effective. (Luborsky et al., 2002; Shadish et al., 2002).

Family Therapy
A form of therapy in which the family unit is treated as the client.

Meta-Analysis
A method for combining and averaging the results of individual research studies.

Before we report on the research dealing with the effectiveness of therapy, let us review some of the problems of this kind of research (Shadish, 2002). ***Question: What kinds of problems do researchers encounter when they conduct research on psychotherapy?***

Problems in Conducting Research on Psychotherapy

It is not an easy matter to evaluate the effectiveness of psychotherapy. Many problems bedevil the effort.

Problems in Running Experiments on Psychotherapy

The ideal method for evaluating a treatment—such as a method of therapy—is the experiment (Chambless & Hollon, 1998; Shadish, 2002). However, experiments on therapy methods are difficult to arrange and control. The outcomes can be difficult to define and measure.

Consider psychoanalysis. In well-run experiments, people are assigned at random to experimental and control groups. A true experiment on psychoanalysis would require randomly assigning people seeking therapy to psychoanalysis and to a control group or other kinds of therapy for comparison. But a person may have to remain in traditional psychoanalysis for years to attain beneficial results. Could we create control treatments that last as long? Moreover, some people seek psychoanalysis per se, not psychotherapy in general. Would it be ethical to assign them at random to other treatments or to a no-treatment control group? Clearly not.

In an ideal experiment, subjects and researchers are "blind" with regard to the treatment the subjects receive. Blind research designs allow researchers to control for subjects' expectations. In an ideal experiment on therapy, individuals would be blind regarding the type of therapy they are obtaining—or whether they are obtaining a placebo. However, it is difficult to mask the type of therapy clients are obtaining (Seligman, 1995). Even if we could conceal it from clients, could we hide it from therapists?

Problems in Measuring Outcomes of Therapy

Consider the problems we run into when measuring outcomes of therapy (Shadish, 2002). Behavior therapists define their goals in behavioral terms—such as a formerly phobic individual being able to obtain an injection or look out of a 20th-story window. Therefore, behavior therapists do not encounter many problems in this area. But what about the client-centered therapist who fosters insight and self-actualization? We cannot directly measure these qualities. The psychoanalytic process is educational as well as therapeutic, and some argue that different standards must be applied in evaluating what the client gains from treatment (Strupp, 2001).

Are Clinical Judgments Valid?

Because of problems like these, many clinicians believe that important clinical questions cannot be answered through research (Silberschatz, 1998). For them, clinical judgment is the basis for evaluating the effectiveness of therapy. Unfortunately, therapists have a stake in believing that their clients profit from treatment. They are not unbiased judges, even when they try to be.

Does Therapy Help Because of the Method or Because of "Nonspecific Factors"?

Even when psychotherapy helps, we're often not sure why (Marks, 2002). Sorting out the benefits of therapy per se from other aspects of the therapy situation is a staggering task. These other aspects are termed *nonspecific factors.* They refer to features that are found in most therapies, such as the client's relationship with the therapist. Most therapists, regardless of theoretical outlook, show warmth and empathy, encourage exploration, and instill hope (Perlman, 2001; Scaturo, 2001). Many of the benefits of therapy could stem from interactions such as these. In such cases, the method itself might have little more value than a "sugar pill" in combating physical ailments.

What Is the Experimental Treatment in Psychotherapy Outcome Studies?

We may also ask, what exactly is the experimental "treatment" being evaluated? Various therapists may say that they are practicing psychoanalysis, but they differ both as individuals and in their training. It is therefore difficult to specify just what is happening in the therapeutic session.

Analyses of the Effectiveness of Therapy

Despite these evaluation problems, research on the effectiveness of therapy has been encouraging (Luborsky et al., 2002; Shadish et al., 2000). Some of this research has relied on meta-analysis. Meta-analysis combines and averages the results of individual studies. Generally speaking, the studies included in the analysis address similar issues in a similar way. Moreover, the analysts judge them to have been conducted in a valid manner. *Question: What, then, do we know about the effectiveness of psychotherapy?*

In their classic early use of meta-analysis, Mary Lee Smith and Gene Glass (1977) analyzed the results of dozens of outcome studies of various types of therapies. They concluded that people who obtained psychodynamic therapy showed greater well-being, on the average, than 70% to 75% of those who did not obtain treatment. Similarly, nearly 75% of the clients who obtained client-centered therapy were better off than people who did not obtain treatment. Psychodynamic and client-centered therapies appear to be most effective with well-educated, verbal, strongly motivated clients who report problems with anxiety, depression (of light to moderate proportions), and interpersonal relationships. Neither form of therapy appears to be effective with people with severe disorders such as major depression, bipolar disorder, and schizophrenia. Smith and Glass (1977) found that people who obtained Gestalt therapy showed greater well-being than about 60% of those who did not obtain treatment. The effectiveness of psychoanalysis and client-centered therapy thus was reasonably comparable. Gestalt therapy fell behind.

Smith and Glass (1977) did not include cognitive therapies in their meta-analysis because at the time of their study many cognitive approaches were relatively new. Because behavior therapists also incorporate many cognitive techniques, it can be difficult to sort out which aspects—cognitive or otherwise—of behavioral treatments are most effective. However, many meta-analyses of cognitive–behavioral therapy have been conducted since the early work of Smith and Glass. Their results are encouraging.

A more recent meta-analysis of 90 studies by William R. Shadish and his colleagues (2000) concurred that psychotherapy is generally effective. Generally speaking, the more therapy the better; that is, people who have more psychotherapy tend to fare better than people who have less of it. Therapy also appears to be more effective when the outcome measures reflect the treatment (e.g., when the effects of treatment aimed at fear-reduction are measured in terms of people's ability to approach fear-inducing objects and situations).

Studies of cognitive therapy have shown that modifying irrational beliefs of the type described by Albert Ellis helps people with problems such as anxiety and depression (Engels et al., 1993; Haaga & Davison, 1993). Modifying self-defeating beliefs of the sort outlined by Aaron Beck also frequently alleviates anxiety and depression (Butler & Beck, 2001). Cognitive therapy may be helpful with people with severe depression, who had been thought responsive only to biological therapies (Hollon & Shelton, 2001; Simons et al., 1995). Cognitive therapy has also helped people with personality disorders (Beck & Freeman, 1990).

Behavioral and cognitive therapies have provided strategies for treating anxiety disorders, social skills deficits, and problems in self-control (DeRubeis & Crits-Christoph, 1998). These two kinds of therapies—which are often integrated as *cognitive–behavioral therapy*—have also provided empirically supported methods for helping couples and families in distress (Baucom et al., 1998), and for modifying behaviors related to health problems such as headaches (Blanchard, 1992), smoking, chronic pain, and bulimia nervosa (Agras et al., 2000; Compas et al., 1998). Cognitive–

behavioral therapists have also innovated treatments for sexual dysfunctions for which there previously were no effective treatments. Cognitive therapy has helped many people with schizophrenia (who are also using drug therapy) modify their delusional beliefs (Chadwick & Lowe, 1990). Behavior therapy has helped to coordinate the care of institutionalized patients, including people with schizophrenia and mental retardation (Spreat & Behar, 1994). However, there is little evidence that psychological

A Closer Look

Diversity: Ethnicity, Gender, and Psychotherapy

The United States, they are a-changing. The numbers of African Americans, Asian Americans, and Latino and Latina Americans are growing rapidly (U.S. Bureau of the Census, 2003), yet most of the "prescriptions" for psychotherapy discussed in this chapter were originated by, and intended for use with, European Americans (Hall, 1997)—and especially for males.

People from ethnic minority groups are less likely than European Americans to seek therapy (Penn et al., 1995). Reasons for their lower participation rate include:

- Unawareness that therapy would help.
- Lack of information about the availability of professional services, or inability to pay for them (DeAngelis, 1995).
- Distrust of professionals, particularly European American professionals and (for women) male professionals (Basic Behavioral Science Task Force, 1996c).
- Language barriers (American Psychological Association, 1993).

REFLECT

Consider your part of the country and your sociocultural background. Do people in your area and from your background frequently go for "therapy"? Is psychotherapy considered a normal option for people having problems in your area, or is it stigmatized?

- A reluctance to open up about personal matters to strangers—especially strangers who are not members of one's own ethnic group (LaFramboise, 1994).
- Cultural inclinations toward other approaches to problem solving, such as religious approaches and psychic healers (LaFramboise, 1994).

- Negative experiences with professionals and authority figures.

Women have also sometimes found therapy to be insensitive to their needs. Let us consider ways in which psychotherapy can be of more use to people from ethnic minority groups and to women.

Psychotherapy and Ethnic Minority Groups

Clinicians need to be sensitive to the cultural heritage, language, and values of the people they see in therapy (American Psychological Association, 1993; Comas-Diaz, 1994). That is, they need to develop *multicultural competence* (Sue et al., 1999).

Let us consider some of the issues involved in conducting psychotherapy with African Americans, Asian Americans, Latino and Latina Americans, and Native Americans.

In addition to addressing the psychological problems of African American clients, therapists often need to help them cope with the effects of prejudice and discrimination. Beverly Greene (1993) notes that some African Americans develop low self-esteem because they internalize negative stereotypes.

African Americans often are reluctant to seek psychological help because of cultural assumptions that people should manage their own problems and because of mistrust of the therapy process. They tend to assume that people are supposed to solve their own problems. Signs of emotional weakness such as tension, anxiety and depression are stigmatized (Boyd-Franklin, 1995; Greene, 1993).

Many African Americans are also suspicious of their therapists—especially when the therapist is a European American. They may withhold personal information because of the society's history of racial discrimination (Boyd-Franklin, 1995; Greene, 1993).

Asian Americans tend to stigmatize people with psychological disorders. As a result, they may deny problems and refuse to seek help for them (Sue, 1991). Asian Americans, especially recent immigrants, also may not understand or believe in Western approaches to psychotherapy. For example, Western psychotherapy typically encourages people to express their feelings openly. This mode of behavior may conflict with the Asian tradition of restraint in public. Many Asians prefer to receive concrete advice rather than Western-style encouragement to develop their own solutions (Isomura et al., 1987).

Because of a cultural tendency to turn away from painful thoughts, many Asians experience and express psychological complaints as physical symptoms (Zane & Sue, 1991). Rather than thinking of themselves as being anxious, they may focus on physical features of anxiety such as a pounding heart and heavy sweating. Rather than thinking of themselves as depressed, they may focus on fatigue and low energy levels.

Therapists need to be aware of potential conflicts between the traditional Latino and Latina American value of interdependency in the family and the typical European American belief in independence and self-reliance (De la Cancela & Guzman, 1991). Measures like the following may help bridge the gaps between psychotherapists and Latino and Latina American clients:

- Interacting with clients in the language requested by them or, if this is not possible, referring them to professionals who can do so.

therapy alone is effective in treating the quirks of thought exhibited in people with severe psychotic disorders (Wolpe, 1990).

Thus, it is not enough to ask which type of therapy is most effective. We must ask which type is most effective for a particular problem and a particular patient. What are its advantages? Its limitations? Clients may successfully use systematic desensitization to overcome stage fright, as measured by ability to speak to a group of people. If

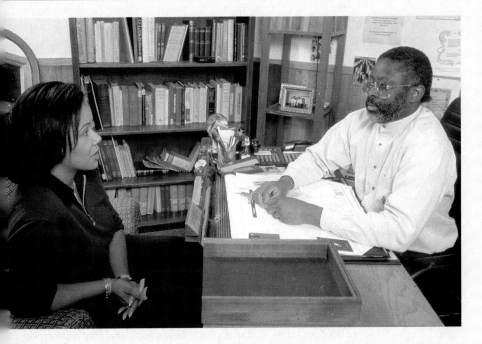

■ Is Psychotherapy for Everyone?

Why are members of some ethnic groups more willing to seek therapy than members of other ethnic groups? Do members of all ethnic groups have the same kinds of needs in therapy? Must therapists be from the same ethnic group as their clients? Can therapists from the dominant culture be sensitive to the life issues of people from ethnic minority groups?

Using methods that are consistent with the client's values and levels of acculturation, as suggested by fluency in English and level of education.

Developing therapy methods that incorporate clients' cultural values. Malgady and his colleagues (1990), for example, use *cuento therapy* with Puerto Ricans. *Cuento therapy* uses Latino and Latina folktalkes (*cuentos*) with characters who serve as models for adaptive behaviors.

Many psychological disorders experienced by Native Americans involve the disruption of their traditional culture caused by European colonization (LaFramboise, 1994). Native Americans have also been denied full access to key institutions in Western culture (LaFramboise, 1994). Loss of cultural identity and social disorganization have set the stage for problems such as alcoholism, substance abuse, and depression. Theresa LaFramboise (1994) argues that if psychologists are to help Native Americans cope with psychological disorders, they must do so in a way that is sensitive to their culture, customs, and values. Efforts to prevent psychological disorders should focus on strengthening Native American cultural identity, pride, and cohesion.

Some therapists use ceremonies that reflect clients' cultural or religious traditions. Purification and cleansing rights are therapeutics for many Native Americans (Lefley, 1990). Such rites are commonly sought by Native Americans who believe

that their problems are caused by failure to placate malevolent spirits or perform required rituals (Lefley, 1990).

Feminist Psychotherapy

Feminist psychotherapy is not a particular method of therapy. It is an approach to therapy rooted in feminist political theory and philosophy. Feminism challenges the validity of gender-role stereotypes and the tradition of male dominance (Greene, 1993).

Feminist therapy developed as a response to male dominance of health professions and institutions. It suggested that the mental health establishment often worked to maintain inequality between men and women by trying to help women "adjust" to traditional gender roles when they wished to challenge these roles in their own lives. Feminist therapists note that many women experience depression and other psychological problems as a result of being treated as second-class citizens, and they argue that society rather than the individual woman must change if these psychological problems are to be alleviated.

Psychotherapy is most effective when therapists attend to and respect people's sociocultural as well as individual differences. Although it is the individual who experiences psychological anguish, the fault often lies in the cultural setting and not the individual.

clients also want to know *why* they have stage fright, however, behavior therapy alone will not provide the answer.

As we see in the "Closer Look" on pages 512–513, we must also consider the sociocultural features of clients in determining how to make therapy most effective. Failure to do so leaves many people who would profit from therapy on the wayside. And in some cases, inappropriate methods of therapy may do more harm than good.

Learning Connections
See Web site for an interactive version of these review questions.

R E V I E W

(23) Smith and Glass used the method of _____-analysis to analyze the results o dozens of outcome studies of various types of therapies. (24) Current research show: that psychotherapy (is or is not?) effective in the treatment of psychological disorders (25) _____ therapy appears to be helpful for people with severe depression who had been thought to respond only to biological therapies. (26) African Americans ma be reluctant to seek therapy because of cultural assumptions that people (should o should not?) manage their own problems and because they mistrust European Ameri can professionals. (27) There may be conflict between the traditional Latino and Latina American value of _____ in the family and the typical European American belief in independence. (28) _____ psychotherapists challenge the validity o stereotypical gender-role stereotypes and the traditional of male dominance.

Critical Thinking: Justin swears he feels much better because of psychoanalysis Deborah swears by her experience with Gestalt therapy. Are these anecdotal endorse ments acceptable as scientific evidence? Why or why not?

BIOLOGICAL THERAPIES

The kinds of therapy we have discussed are psychological in nature—forms of *ps chotherapy*. Psychotherapies apply *psychological* principles to treatment, principle based on psychological knowledge of matters such as learning and motivation. Peopl with psychological disorders are also often treated with biological therapies. Biolog cal therapies apply what is known of people's *biological* structures and processes to th amelioration of psychological disorders. For example, they may work by alterin events in the nervous system, as by changing the action of neurotransmitters. In th section, we discuss three biological, or medical, approaches to treating people wit psychological disorders: drug therapy, electroconvulsive therapy, and psychosurger *Question: What kinds of drug therapy are available for psychological disorders*

Drug Therapy: In Search of the Magic Pill?

In the 1950s Fats Domino popularized the song "My Blue Heaven." Fats was singin about the sky and happiness. Today "blue heavens" is one of the street names for th 10-milligram dose of the antianxiety drug Valium. Clinicians prescribe Valium an other drugs for people with various psychological disorders.

Antianxiety Drugs

Most antianxiety drugs (also called *minor tranquilizers*) belong to the chemical cla: known as *benzodiazepines*. Valium (diazepam) is a benzodiazepine. Other benzod azepines include chlordiazepoxide (for example, Librium), oxazepam (Serax), ar alprazolam (Xanax). Antianxiety drugs are usually prescribed for outpatients wh complain of generalized anxiety or panic attacks, although many people also use the as sleeping pills. Valium and other antianxiety drugs depress the activity of the centr nervous system (CNS). The CNS, in turn, decreases sympathetic activity, reducing th heart rate, respiration rate, and feelings of nervousness and tension.

■ **An Arsenal of Chemical Therapies**

Many drugs have been developed to combat psychological disorders. They include antianxiety drugs, antipsychotic drugs, antidepressants, and lithium.

© P. Peterson/Custom Medical Stock

Many people come to tolerate antianxiety drugs very quickly. When tolerance occurs, dosages must be increased for the drug to remain effective.

Sedation (feelings of being tired or drowsy) is the most common side effect of antianxiety drugs. Problems associated with withdrawal from these drugs include **rebound anxiety.** That is, some people who have been using these drugs regularly report that their anxiety becomes worse than before once they discontinue them. Antianxiety drugs can induce physical dependence, as evidenced by withdrawal symptoms such as tremors, sweating, insomnia, and rapid heartbeat.

Antipsychotic Drugs

People with schizophrenia are often given antipsychotic drugs (also called *major tranquilizers*). In most cases these drugs reduce agitation, delusions, and hallucinations. Many antipsychotic drugs, including phenothiazines (for example, Thorazine) and clozapine (Clozaril) are thought to act by blocking dopamine receptors in the brain (Buckley et al., 2000; Sawa & Snyder, 2002). Research along these lines supports the theory that schizophrenia is connected with overactivity of the neurotransmitter dopamine.

Antidepressants

People with major depression often take so-called **antidepressant** drugs. These drugs are also helpful for some people with eating disorders, panic disorder, obsessive–compulsive disorder, and social phobia (Bacaltchuk et al., 2000; Barlow et al., 2000; McElroy et al., 2000). Problems in the regulation of noradrenaline and serotonin may be involved in eating and panic disorders as well as in depression. Antidepressants are believed to work by increasing levels of one or both of these neurotransmitters, which can affect both depression and the appetite (C. L. White et al., 2000). However, cognitive–behavior therapy addresses irrational attitudes concerning weight and body shape, fosters normal eating habits, and helps people resist the urges to binge and purge. This form of therapy therefore apparently is more effective with people with bulimia than antidepressants (Wilson et al., 2002). But when cognitive behavioral therapy does not help people with bulimia nervosa, drug therapy may (Walsh et al., 2000).

There are various kinds of antidepressant drugs. Each increases the concentration of noradrenaline or serotonin in the brain. **Monoamine oxidase (MAO) inhibitors** such as Nardil and Parnate block the activity of an enzyme that breaks down noradrenaline and serotonin. **Tricyclic antidepressants** such as Tofranil and Elavil prevent the reuptake of noradrenaline and serotonin by the axon terminals of the transmitting neurons. Selective **serotonin-reuptake inhibitors** such as Prozac and Zoloft also block the reuptake of serotonin by presynaptic neurons. As a result, serotonin remains in the synaptic cleft longer, influencing receiving neurons. Serotonin-reuptake inhibitors appear to be more effective than tricyclics (Bech et al., 2000).

Antidepressant drugs must usually build up to a therapeutic level over several weeks. Because overdoses can be lethal, some people stay in a hospital during the buildup to prevent suicide attempts. There are also side effects, such as nausea, agitation, and weight gain. The first two are usually temporary.

Lithium

The ancient Greeks and Romans were among the first to use the metal lithium as a psychoactive drug. They prescribed mineral water—which contains lithium—for people with bipolar disorder. They had no inkling as to why this treatment sometimes helped. A salt of the metal lithium (lithium carbonate), in tablet form, flattens out cycles of manic behavior and depression in most people. Lithium can also be used to strengthen the effects of antidepressant medication (Bauer et al., 2000). It is not known exactly how lithium works, although it affects the functioning of neurotransmitters, including glutamate (Hokin et al., 1998).

People with bipolar disorder may have to use lithium indefinitely, as a person with diabetes must use insulin to control the illness. Lithium also has been shown to have side effects such as hand tremors, memory impairment, and excessive thirst and urination (Price & Heninger, 1994). Memory impairment is reported as the main reason why people discontinue lithium.

Rebound Anxiety
Strong anxiety that can attend the suspension of usage of a tranquilizer.

Antidepressant
(ant-eye-dee-PRESS-ant) Acting to relieve depression.

Monoamine Oxidase (MAO) Inhibitors
(MON-oh-ah-mean OX-see-dase) Antidepressant drugs that work by blocking the action of an enzyme that breaks down noradrenaline and serotonin.

Tricyclic Antidepressants
(try-SIGH-click) Antidepressant drugs that work by preventing the reuptake of noradrenaline and serotonin by transmitting neurons.

Serotonin-Reuptake Inhibitors
Antidepressant drugs that work by blocking the reuptake of serotonin by presynaptic neurons.

Electroconvulsive Therapy

Question: What is electroconvulsive therapy (ECT)? **Electroconvulsive therapy (ECT)** is a biological form of therapy for psychological disorders that was introduced by the Italian psychiatrist Ugo Cerletti in 1939. Cerletti had noted that some slaughterhouses used electric shock to render animals unconscious. The shocks also produced convulsions. Along with other European researchers of the period, Cerletti erroneously believed that convulsions were incompatible with schizophrenia and other major psychological disorders.

ECT was originally used for a variety of psychological disorders. Because of the advent of antipsychotic drugs, however, it is now used mainly for people with major depression who do not respond to antidepressants (Thase & Kupfer, 1996).

People typically obtain one ECT treatment three times a week for up to 10 sessions. Electrodes are attached to the temples, and an electrical current strong enough to produce a convulsion is induced. The shock causes unconsciousness, so the patient does not recall it. Nevertheless, patients are given a **sedative** so that they are asleep during the treatment.

Electroconvulsive Therapy (ECT)
Treatment of disorders like major depression by passing an electric current (that causes a convulsion) through the head.

Sedative
A drug that relieves nervousness or agitation, or puts one to sleep.

▶ CONTROVERSY IN PSYCHOLOGY ◀

Should health professionals use electroconvulsive therapy?

ECT is controversial for many reasons, such as the fact that many professionals are distressed by the thought of passing an electric shock through a patient's head and producing convulsions. But there are side effects, including memory problems in the form of retrograde amnesia (Lisanby et al., 2000; Weiner, 2000). (Some researchers argue that stronger shock to one side of the head may be as effective yet have fewer side effects as compared with weaker shock to both sides of the head [Sackeim et al., 2000].) However, research suggests that for most people, cognitive impairment tends to be temporary. One study followed up 10 adolescents who had received ECT an average of 3½ years earlier. Six of the 10 had complained of memory impairment immediately after treatment, but only one complained of continued problems at the follow-up. Nevertheless, psychological tests did not reveal any differences in cognitive functioning between severely depressed adolescents who had received ECT and others who had not (Cohen et al., 2000).

■ **Electroconvulsive Therapy**
In ECT, electrodes are placed on each side of the patient's head and a current is passed between them, inducing a seizure. ECT is used mainly in cases of major depression when antidepressant drugs and psychotherapy are not sufficient.

© Najlah Feanny/Stock Boston, LLC

Psychosurgery

Psychosurgery is more controversial than ECT. *Questions: What is psychosurgery?* How is it used to treat psychological disorders? The best-known modern technique, **prefrontal lobotomy,** has been used with people with severe disorders. In this method, a picklike instrument severs the nerve pathways that link the prefrontal lobes of the brain to the thalamus. This method was pioneered by the Portuguese neurologist Antonio Egas Moniz and was brought to the United States in the 1930s. The theoretical rationale for the operation was vague and misguided, and Moniz's reports of success were exaggerated. Nevertheless, by 1950 prefrontal lobotomies had been performed on more than a thousand people in an effort to reduce violence and agitation. Anecdotal evidence of the method's unreliable outcomes is found in an ironic footnote to history: One of Dr. Moniz's "failures" shot the doctor, leaving a bullet lodged in his spine and paralyzing his legs.

Prefrontal lobotomy also has a host of side effects, including hyperactivity and distractibility, impaired learning ability, overeating, apathy and withdrawal, epileptic-type seizures, reduced creativity, and, now and then, death. Because of these side effects, and because of the advent of antipsychotic drugs, this method has been largely discontinued in the United States.

Does Biological Therapy Work?

There are thus a number of biological approaches to the therapy of psychological disorders. *Question: What do we know about the effectiveness of biological therapies?*

There is little question that drug therapy has helped many people with severe psychological disorders. For example, antipsychotic drugs largely account for the reduced need for the use of restraint and supervision (padded cells, straitjackets, hospitalization, and so on) with people diagnosed with schizophrenia. Antipsychotic drugs have allowed hundreds of thousands of former mental hospital residents to lead largely normal lives in the community, hold jobs, and maintain family lives. Most of the problems related to these drugs concern their side effects.

But many comparisons of psychotherapy (in the form of cognitive therapy) and drug therapy for depression suggest that cognitive therapy is as effective as, or more effective than, antidepressants (Antonuccio, 1995; Muñoz et al., 1994). For one thing, cognitive therapy provides coping skills that reduce the risk of recurrence of depression once treatment ends (Hollon & Shelton, 2001). Then again, at least one study suggests that a combination of cognitive therapy and antidepressant medication is superior to either treatment alone with chronically depressed people (Keller et al., 2000). The chapter's "Life Connections" section discusses cognitive–behavioral methods for tackling depression.

A similar story holds for cognitive–behavior therapy and "antidepressant" medication in the treatment of panic disorder. A carefully controlled study found that cognitive–behavior therapy and the antidepressant imipramine are both helpful in treating panic disorder, but a combination of the psychological and biological treatments appears to be somewhat more helpful in the long run (Barlow et al., 2000).

Many psychologists and psychiatrists are comfortable with the short-term use of antianxiety drugs in helping clients manage periods of unusual anxiety or tension. However, many people use antianxiety drugs routinely to dull the arousal stemming from anxiety-producing lifestyles or interpersonal problems. Rather than make the often painful decisions required to confront their problems and change their lives, they prefer to take a pill.

One study found that both tranquilizers and cognitive–behavior therapy (stress management training plus imagined exposure to the fearful stimuli) helped phobic people get through a dental session. However, 70% of those who received cognitive–behavior therapy continued to go for dental treatment, as compared with only 20% of those who took the tranquilizer (Thom et al., 2000). The cognitive–behavior therapy apparently taught the individuals in the study coping skills, whereas the tranquilizers afforded only temporary relief.

REFLECT

Are you disturbed by the thought of ECT or psychosurgery? Explain.

Psychosurgery
Surgery intended to promote psychological changes or to relieve disordered behavior.

Prefrontal Lobotomy
The severing or destruction of a section of the frontal lobe of the brain.

Despite the controversies surrounding ECT, it helps many people who do not respond to antidepressant drugs (Thase & Kupfer, 1996).

In sum, drug therapy and perhaps ECT seem to be effective for some disorders that do not respond to psychotherapy alone. Yet common sense and research evidence suggest that psychotherapy is preferable for problems such as anxiety, mild depression, and interpersonal conflict. No chemical can show a person how to change an idea or solve an interpersonal problem.

Learning Connections
See Web site for an interactive version of these review questions.

R E V I E W

(29) (Minor or Major?) tranquilizers are usually prescribed for people who complain of anxiety or tension. (30) _____ tranquilizers are used to reduce agitation, delusions, and hallucinations. (31) Major tranquilizers that belong to the chemical class of phenothiazines are thought to work by blocking the action of the neurotransmitter _____. (32) Antidepressants heighten the action of the neurotransmitter _____. (33) ECT is mainly used to treat severe cases of _____. (34) The best-known psychosurgery technique is the _____ lobotomy.

Critical Thinking: Are there times when it is appropriate to prescribe medical treatment for a psychological disorder? How would you make that decision?

Alleviating Depression—Getting Out of the Dumps

Be not afraid of life. Believe that life is worth living and your belief will help create the fact.

—William James

We began the chapter with the case of a depressed college sophomore, Jasmine. We noted that various kinds of therapists might treat her depression in different ways.

Depression is characterized by inactivity, feelings of sadness, and cognitive distortions. When we suspect that our feelings may fit the picture of a major depressive episode or bipolar disorder, it may be helpful to talk things over with our instructor or visit the college counseling or health center. Some of us may also want to try to get at the deep-seated roots of our feelings of depression, and doing so in some cases might require long-term talk therapy. On the other hand, cognitive–behavioral therapists have pointed out that there are many things we can do on our own to cope with milder feelings of depression. These methods attempt to directly reverse the characteristics of depression. They include:

- Engaging in pleasant events.
- Thinking rationally.
- Exercising.
- Asserting ourselves.

Engaging in Pleasant Events

There is a relationship between our moods and what we do. Losses, failures, and tension can trigger feelings of depression. Pleasant events can generate feelings of happiness and joy. You may be able to use pleasant events to lift your mood purposefully by taking the following steps:

1. Check off items in Table 13.2 that appeal to you.
2. Engage in at least three pleasant events each day.
3. Record your activities in a diary. Add other activities and events that strike you as pleasant, even if they are unplanned.
4. Toward the end of each day, rate your response to each activity, using a scale like this one:

    +3 Wonderful
    +2 Very nice
    +1 Somewhat nice
     0 No particular response
    −1 Somewhat disappointing
    −2 Rather disappointing
    −3 The pits

5. After a week or so, check the items in the diary that received positive ratings.
6. Repeat successful activities and experiment with new ones.

Rational Thinking

Public opinion is a weak tyrant compared with our own private opinion. What a man thinks of himself, that it is which determines . . . his fate.

—Henry David Thoreau, *Walden*

Depressed people tend to blame themselves for failures and problems, even when they are not at fault. They *internalize* blame and see their problems as *stable* and *global*—as all but impossible to change. Depressed people also make cognitive errors such as *catastrophizing* their problems and *minimizing* their accomplishments.

Column 1 in Table 13.3 illustrates a number of irrational, depressing thoughts. How many of them have you had? Column 2 indicates the type of cognitive error being made (such as internalizing or catastrophizing), and column 3 shows examples of rational alternatives.

You can pinpoint irrational, depressing thoughts by identifying the kinds of thoughts you have when you feel low. Look for the fleeting thoughts that can trigger mood changes. It helps to jot them down. Then challenge their accuracy. Do you characterize difficult situations as impossible and hopeless? Do you expect too much from yourself and minimize your achievements? Do you internalize more than your fair share of blame?

You can use Table 13.3 to classify your cognitive errors and construct rational alternatives. Write these next to each irrational thought. Review them from time to time. When you are alone, you can read the irrational thought aloud. Then follow it by saying to yourself firmly, "No, that's irrational!" Then read the rational alternative aloud twice, *emphatically*.

After you have thought or read aloud the rational alternative, think, "That makes more sense! That's a more accurate view of things! I feel better now that I have things in perspective."

Exercising

Exercise not only fosters physical health. It can enhance psychological well-being and help us cope with depression. Depression is characterized by inactivity and feelings of helplessness. Exercise is, in a sense, the opposite of inactivity. Exercise might also

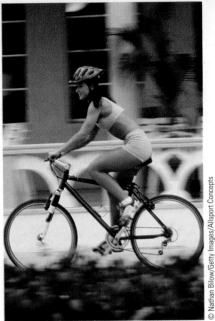

© Nathan Bilow/Getty Images/Allsport Concepts

■ Tackling Depression or Just Having Fun?

Many cognitive–behavioral therapists tackle depression directly, by focusing on what depressed people do (or don't do) and think. Depressed people are often inactive, withdrawn from the activities that typically delighted them. Therefore, cognitive–behavioral therapists may prescribe such activities as part of the treatment for depression.

TABLE 13.2 A Catalog of Pleasant Events

1. Being in the country
2. Wearing expensive or formal clothes
3. Making contributions to religious, charitable, or political groups
4. Talking about sports
5. Meeting someone new
6. Going to a rock concert
7. Playing baseball, softball, football, or basketball
8. Planning trips or vacations
9. Buying things for yourself
10. Being at the beach
11. Doing art work (painting, sculpture, drawing, moviemaking, etc.)
12. Rock climbing or mountaineering
13. Reading the scriptures
14. Playing golf
15. Rearranging or redecorating your room or house
16. Going naked
17. Going to a sports event
18. Going to the races
19. Reading stories, novels, poems, plays, magazines, newspapers
20. Going to a bar, tavern, club
21. Going to lectures or talks
22. Creating or arranging songs or music
23. Boating
24. Restoring antiques, refinishing furniture
25. Watching television or listening to the radio
26. Camping
27. Working in politics
28. Working on machines (cars, bikes, radios, television sets)
29. Playing cards or board games
30. Doing puzzles or math games
31. Having lunch with friends or associates
32. Playing tennis
33. Driving long distances
34. Woodworking, carpentry
35. Writing stories, novels, poems, plays, articles
36. Being with animals

37. Riding in an airplane
38. Exploring (hiking away from known routes, spelunking, etc.)
39. Singing
40. Going to a party
41. Going to church functions
42. Playing a musical instrument
43. Snow skiing, ice skating
44. Wearing informal clothes, "dressing down"
45. Acting
46. Being in the city, downtown
47. Taking a long, hot bath
48. Playing pool or billiards
49. Bowling
50. Watching wild animals
51. Gardening, landscaping
52. Wearing new clothes
53. Dancing
54. Sitting or lying in the sun
55. Riding a motorcycle
56. Just sitting and thinking
57. Going to a fair, carnival, circus, zoo, amusement park
58. Talking about philosophy or religion
59. Gambling
60. Listening to sounds of nature
61. Dating, courting
62. Having friends come to visit
63. Going out to visit friends
64. Giving gifts
65. Getting massages or backrubs
66. Photography
67. Collecting stamps, coins, rocks, etc.
68. Seeing beautiful scenery
69. Eating good meals
70. Improving your health (having teeth fixed, changing diet, having a checkup, etc.)
71. Wrestling or boxing
72. Fishing
73. Going to a health club, sauna
74. Horseback riding
75. Protesting social, political, or environmental conditions
76. Going to the movies
77. Cooking meals

78. Washing your hair
79. Going to a restaurant
80. Using cologne, perfume
81. Getting up early in the morning
82. Writing a diary
83. Giving massages or backrubs
84. Meditating or doing yoga
85. Doing heavy outdoor work
86. Snowmobiling, dune buggying
87. Being in a body-awareness, encounter, or "rap" group
88. Swimming
89. Running, jogging
90. Walking barefoot
91. Playing frisbee or catch
92. Doing housework or laundry, cleaning things
93. Listening to music
94. Knitting, crocheting
95. Making love
96. Petting, necking
97. Going to a barber or beautician
98. Being with someone you love
99. Going to the library
100. Shopping
101. Preparing a new or special dish
102. Watching people
103. Bicycling
104. Writing letters, cards, or notes
105. Talking about politics or public affairs
106. Watching attractive women or men
107. Caring for houseplants
108. Having coffee, tea, or Coke, etc., with friends
109. Beachcombing
110. Going to auctions, garage sales, etc.
111. Water skiing, surfing, diving
112. Traveling
113. Attending the opera, ballet, or a play
114. Looking at the stars or the moon
115. Surfing the Net
116. Playing video games

Source: Adapted from D. J. MacPhillamy & P. M. Lewinsohn, *Pleasant Events Schedule, Form III-S*, University of Oregon, Mimeograph, 1971.

help alleviate feelings of helplessness. In one experiment, 156 adult volunteers who were depressed were randomly assigned to four months of either aerobic exercise, antidepressant medication, or a combination of the two (Babyak et al., 2000). Following treatment, all three groups showed comparable relief from depression. But at a further six-month follow-up, subjects from the exercise groups who had continued to exercise showed the greatest improvement. Other experiments also find that exercise alleviates feelings of depression (Jorm et al., 2002; Tkachuk & Martin, 1999). Exercise has also been shown to decrease anxiety and hostility and to boost self-esteem (Hansen et al., 2001; Norvell & Belles, 1993).

TABLE 13.3 Irrational, Depressing Thoughts and Rational Alternatives

Irrational Thought	Type of Thought	Rational Alternative
"There's nothing I can do."	Catastrophizing (the size of the problem), minimizing (one's coping ability), stabilizing	"I can't think of anything to do right now, but if I work at it, I may."
"I'm no good."	Internalizing, globalizing, stabilizing	"I did something I regret, but that doesn't make me evil or worthless as a person."
"This is absolutely awful."	Catastrophizing	"This is pretty bad, but it's not the end of the world."
"I just don't have the brains for college."	Stabilizing, globalizing	"I guess I really need to go back over the basics in that course."
"I just can't believe I did something so disgusting!"	Catastrophizing	"That was a bad experience. Well, I won't be likely to try that again soon."
"I can't imagine ever feeling right."	Stabilizing, catastrophizing	"This is painful, but if I try to work it through step by step, I'll probably eventually see my way out of it."
"It's all my fault."	Internalizing	"I'm not blameless, but I wasn't the only one involved. It may have been my idea, but he went into it with his eyes open."
"I can't do anything right."	Globalizing, stabilizing, catastrophizing, minimizing	"I sure screwed this up, but I've done a lot of things well, and I'll do other things well."
"I hurt everybody who gets close to me."	Internalizing, globalizing, stabilizing	"I'm not totally blameless, but I'm not responsible for the whole world. Others make their own decisions, and they have to live with the results, too."
"If people knew the real me, they would have it in for me."	Globalizing, minimizing (the positive in yourself)	"I'm not perfect, but nobody's perfect. I have positive as well as negative features, and I am entitled to self-interests."

Many of us create or compound feelings of depression because of cognitive errors such as those in this table. Have you had any of these irrational, depressing thoughts? Are you willing to challenge them?

Asserting Ourselves: Stand Up!

We humans are social creatures, and social interactions are important to us. Nonassertive behavior patterns are linked to feelings of depression. Learning to express our feelings and relate to others has been shown to alleviate feelings of depression (Hersen et al., 1984). Assertive behavior permits more effective interactions with family members, friends, coworkers, and strangers. In this way we remove sources of frustration and expand our social support. Expressions of positive feelings—saying you love someone or simply saying "Good morning" cheerfully—help reduce feelings of hostility and pave the way toward further social involvement.

Assertive behavior involves the expression of one's genuine feelings, standing up for one's legitimate rights, and refusing unreasonable requests. It means resisting undue social influences, disobeying *arbitrary* authority figures, and resisting conformity to *arbitrary* group standards. But many feelings such as love and admiration are positive, so assertive behavior also

means expressing positive feelings ("That was great!" "You're wonderful!").

Assertive people also influence others to join them in worthwhile social and political activities. They may become involved in political campaigns, consumer groups, conservationist organizations, and other groups to advance their causes.

Alternatives to assertive behavior include submissive, or *unassertive*, behavior and *aggressive* behavior. When we are submissive, our self-esteem plummets. Unexpressed feelings sometimes smolder as resentments and then catch fire as socially inappropriate outbursts. Aggressive behavior includes physical and verbal attacks, threats, and insults. Sometimes we get our way through aggression, but we also earn the condemnation of others. And, unless we are unfeeling, we condemn ourselves for bullying others. You may wish to take the nearby questionnaire to gain insight into how assertive you are as part of the process of deciding whether to become more assertive.

Perhaps you can't become completely assertive overnight, but you can decide *now* that you have been unassertive long enough and plan to change. There may be times when you want to quit and revert to your unassertive ways. Expressing your genuine beliefs may lead to some immediate social disapproval. Others may have a stake in your remaining a doormat, and the people we wind up confronting are sometimes those who are closest to us: parents, spouses, supervisors, and friends.

Perhaps the strategies presented here will work for you. I they don't, why not talk things over with your professor or visi the college health or counseling center?

Self-Assessment

Life Connections
See the Connections *CD-ROM for an interactive version of this Self-Assessment and for other Self-Assessments*

Do You Speak Your Mind or Do You Wimp Out? The Assertiveness Schedule

What about you? Do you enrich the pockets of every telemarketer, or do you say no? Do you stick up for your rights, or do you allow others to walk all over you? Do you say what you feel or what you think other people want you to say? Do you initiate relationships with attractive people, or do you shy away from them?

One way to gain insight into how assertive you are is to take the following Assertiveness Schedule. Once you have finished, turn to the appendix to find out how to calculate your score. A table in the appendix will also allow you to compare your assertiveness to that of a sample of 1,400 students drawn from 35 college campuses across the United States.

If you believe that you are not assertive enough, why not take the quick course in self-assertion offered here? You need not spend your life imitating a doormat.

Directions: Indicate how well each item describes you by using this code:

```
 3 = very much like me
 2 = rather like me
 1 = slightly like me
-1 = slightly unlike me
-2 = rather unlike me
-3 = very much unlike me
```

_____ 1. Most people seem to be more aggressive and assertive than I am.*

_____ 2. I have hesitated to make or accept dates because of "shyness."*

_____ 3. When the food served at a restaurant is not done to my satisfaction, I complain about it to the waiter or waitress.

_____ 4. I am careful to avoid hurting other people's feelings, even when I feel that I have been injured.*

_____ 5. If a salesperson has gone to considerable trouble to show me merchandise that is not quite suitable, I have a difficult time saying "No."*

_____ 6. When I am asked to do something, I insist upon knowing why.

_____ 7. There are times when I look for a good, vigorous argument.

_____ 8. I strive to get ahead as well as most people in my position.

_____ 9. To be honest, people often take advantage of me.*

_____ 10. I enjoy starting conversations with new acquaintances and strangers.

_____ 11. I often don't know what to say to people who are sexually attractive to me.*

_____ 12. I will hesitate to make phone calls to business establishments and institutions.*

_____ 13. I would rather apply for a job or for admission to a college by writing letters than by going through with personal interviews.*

_____ 14. I find it embarrassing to return merchandise.*

_____ 15. If a close and respected relative were annoying me, I would smother my feelings rather than express my annoyance.*

_____ 16. I have avoided asking questions for fear of sounding stupid.*

_____ 17. During an argument I am sometimes afraid that I will get so upset that I will shake all over.*

_____ 18. If a famed and respected lecturer makes a comment which I think is incorrect, I will have the audience hear my point of view as well.

_____ 19. I avoid arguing over prices with clerks and salespeople.*

_____ 20. When I have done something important or worthwhile, I manage to let others know about it.

_____ 21. I am open and frank about my feelings.

_____ 22. If someone has been spreading false and bad stories about me, I see him or her as soon as possible and "have a talk" about it.

_____ 23. I often have a hard time saying "No."*

_____ 24. I tend to bottle up my emotions rather than make a scene.*

_____ 25. I complain about poor service in a restaurant and elsewhere.

_____ 26. When I am given a compliment, I sometimes just don't know what to say.*

_____ 27. If a couple near me in a theater or at a lecture were conversing rather loudly, I would ask them to be quiet or to take their conversation elsewhere.

_____ 28. Anyone attempting to push ahead of me in a line is in for a good battle.

_____ 29. I am quick to express an opinion.

_____ 30. There are times when I just can't say anything.*

Reprinted from Rathus, 1973, pp. 398–406.

Recite Recite Recite

1. **What is psychotherapy?**

Psychotherapy is a systematic interaction between a therapist and a client that uses psychological principles to help the client overcome psychological disorders or adjust to problems in living.

2. **How have people with psychological problems and disorders been treated throughout the ages?**

Mostly badly. It has been generally assumed that psychological disorders represented possession due to witchcraft or divine retribution, and cruel methods such as exorcism were used to try to rid the person of evil spirits. Asylums were the first institutions for people with psychological disorders, and eventually mental hospitals and the community mental health movement came into being.

3. **How do psychoanalysts conduct a traditional Freudian psychoanalysis?**

The goals of psychoanalysis are to provide self-insight, encourage the spilling forth (catharsis) of psychic energy, and replace defensive behavior with coping behavior. The main method is free association, but dream analysis and interpretations are used as well. For example, a psychoanalyst may help clients gain insight into the ways in which they are transferring feelings toward their parents onto a spouse or even onto the analyst.

4. **How do modern psychodynamic approaches differ from traditional psychoanalysis?**

Modern approaches are briefer and more directive, and the therapist and client usually sit face to face.

5. **What is Carl Rogers's method of client-centered therapy?**

Client-centered therapy uses nondirective methods to help clients overcome obstacles to self-actualization. The therapist shows unconditional positive regard, empathic understanding, and genuineness.

6. **What is Fritz Perls's method of Gestalt therapy?**

Perls's highly directive method aims to help people integrate conflicting parts of their personality. He aimed to make clients aware of conflict, accept its reality, and make choices despite fear.

7. **What is behavior therapy?**

Behavior therapy relies on psychological learning principles (for example, conditioning and observational learning) to help clients develop adaptive behavior patterns and discontinue maladaptive ones.

8. **What are some behavior-therapy methods for reducing fears?**

These include flooding, systematic desensitization, and modeling. Flooding exposes a person to fear-evoking stimuli without aversive consequences until fear is extinguished. Systematic desensitization counterconditions fears by gradually exposing clients to a hierarchy of fear-evoking stimuli while they remain relaxed. Modeling encourages clients to imitate another person (the model) in approaching fear-evoking stimuli.

9. **How do behavior therapists use aversive conditioning to help people break bad habits?**

This is a behavior-therapy method for discouraging undesirable behaviors by repeatedly pairing clients' self-defeating goals (for example, alcohol, cigarette smoke, deviant sex objects) with aversive stimuli so that the goals become aversive rather than tempting.

10. **How do behavior therapists apply principles of operant conditioning in behavior modification?**

These are behavior-therapy methods that foster adaptive behavior through principles of reinforcement. Examples include token economies, successive approximation, social skills training, and biofeedback training.

11. **How can you use behavior therapy to deal with temptation and enhance your self-control?**

Behavior-therapy methods for adopting desirable behavior patterns and breaking bad habits begin with a functional analysis to determine the antecedents and consequences of the problem behavior, along with the details of the behavior itself. They then focus on modifying the antecedents (stimuli that act as triggers) and consequences (reinforcers) of behavior and on modifying the behavior itself.

Recite Recite Recite

12. What is cognitive therapy?	Cognitive therapies aim to give clients insight into irrational beliefs and cognitive distortions and replace these cognitive errors with rational beliefs and accurate perceptions.
13. What is Aaron Beck's method of cognitive therapy?	Aaron Beck notes that clients develop emotional problems such as depression because of cognitive errors that lead them to minimize accomplishments and catastrophize failures. He found that depressed people experience cognitive distortions such as the cognitive triad; that is, they expect the worst of themselves, the world at large, and the future. Beck teaches clients how to scientifically dispute cognitive errors.
14. What is Albert Ellis's method of rational emotive behavior therapy (REBT)?	Albert Ellis originated rational emotive behavior therapy, which holds that people's beliefs *about* events, not only the events themselves, shape people's responses to them. Ellis points out how irrational beliefs, such as the belief that we must have social approval, can worsen problems. Ellis literally argues clients out of irrational beliefs.
15. What are the advantages and disadvantages of group therapy?	Group therapy is more economical than individual therapy. Moreover, group members benefit from the social support and experiences of other members. However, some clients cannot disclose their problems in the group setting or risk group disapproval. They need individual attention.
16. What are encounter groups? What are their effects?	Encounter groups attempt to foster personal growth by heightening awareness of people's needs and feelings through intense confrontations between strangers. Encounter groups can be harmful when they urge too rapid disclosure of personal matters or when several members attack an individual.
17. What is family therapy?	In family therapy, one or more families make up the group. Family therapy undertaken from the "systems approach" modifies family interactions to enhance the growth of individuals in the family and the family as a whole.
18. What kinds of problems do researchers encounter when they conduct research on psychotherapy?	It is difficult and perhaps impossible to randomly assign clients to therapy methods such as traditional psychoanalysis. Moreover, clients cannot be kept blind as to the treatment they are receiving. Further, it can be difficult to sort out the effects of nonspecific therapeutic factors such as instillation of hope from the effects of specific methods of therapy.
19. What do we know about the effectiveness of psychotherapy?	Statistical analyses such as meta-analysis show that people who obtain most forms of psychotherapy fare better than people who do not. Psychodynamic and client-centered approaches are particularly helpful with highly verbal and motivated individuals. Cognitive and behavior therapies are probably most effective. Cognitive therapy appears to be as effective as drug therapy in the treatment of depression.
20. What kinds of drug therapy are available for psychological disorders?	Antipsychotic drugs help many people with schizophrenia by blocking the action of dopamine receptors. Antidepressants often help people with severe depression, apparently by raising levels of serotonin available to the brain. Lithium often helps people with bipolar disorder, apparently by regulating levels of glutamate. The use of antianxiety drugs for daily tensions and anxieties is not recommended because people who use them rapidly build tolerance for the drugs. Also, these drugs do not solve personal or social problems, and people attribute their resultant calmness to the drug and not to self-efficacy.
21. What is electroconvulsive therapy (ECT)?	In ECT an electrical current is passed through the temples, inducing a seizure and frequently relieving severe depression. ECT is controversial because of side effects such as loss of memory and because nobody knows why it works.

Recite Recite Recite

22. What is psychosurgery? How is it used to treat psychological disorders?

Psychosurgery is a controversial method for alleviating agitation by severing nerve pathways in the brain. The best-known psychosurgery technique, prefrontal lobotomy, has been largely discontinued because of side effects.

24. What do we know about the effectiveness of biological therapies?

There is controversy as to whether psychotherapy or drug therapy should be used with people with anxiety disorders or depression. Drugs do not teach people how to solve problems and build relationships. Having said that, antidepressants are apparently advisable when psychotherapy does not help people with depression; furthermore, ECT appears to be helpful in some cases in which neither psychotherapy nor drug therapy (antidepressants) is of help. Psychosurgery is all but discontinued because of questions about whether it is effective and because of side effects. Most health professionals agree that antipsychotic drugs are of benefit to large numbers of people with schizophrenia.

Active Learning Resources

Search Online with InfoTrac® College Edition

For additional information on the topics in this chapter, explore InfoTrac College Edition, your online library. Go to **http://www.infotrac.thomsonlearning.com** and use the passcode that came on the card with your book. Try these search terms: Sigmund Freud, catharsis, dream content, virtual reality and therapy, biofeedback, functional analysis, rational–emotive therapy, electroconvulsive therapy, and antidepressants.

Visit Our Web Site

Go to **http://www.wadsworth.com/psychology**, where you will find online resources directly linked to your book, including interactive exercises related to PQ4R and Power Visuals for mastering and reviewing key concepts. In addition, you will find hints on using InfoTrac College Edition to answer the Critical Thinking questions throughout the text. Start with the **Self Study Assessment** for a customized **Study Plan** generated by taking the **Pre-Test** and **Post-Test**.

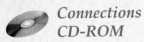

Connections CD-ROM

Go to the Wadsworth *Connections* CD-ROM for further study of the concepts in this chapter. The CD-ROM includes videos, animations, quizzes, and additional activities to expand your learning experience, plus interactive self-assessments to help connect the material to your own life.

Psyk.trek™ CD-ROM

The Wadsworth *Psyk.trek* CD-ROM offers tutorials, simulations, videos, multimedia glossary, and quizzing to help you master the material.

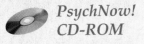

PsychNow! CD-ROM

The Wadsworth *PsychNow!* CD-ROM includes interactive exercises, videos, and animations to enhance your learning.

14 *Social Psychology*

© Mary Kate Denny/PhotoEdit

Social Psychology: Individuals Among Others

- **HOW IS YOUR BEHAVIOR** affected by other people?

Attitudes—"The Good, the Bad, and the Ugly"

- **PEOPLE ACT** in accordance with their consciences—sometimes.

- **DOES AIRING A TV** commercial repeatedly increase or decrease sales?

- **WHEN OLDER PEOPLE** are reminded that they are, well, older, they tend to live up to the stereotype by walking more slowly.

Social Perception: Looking Out, Looking Within

- **SHOULD YOU** "just be yourself," or should you get dressed up and watch your language in a job interview?

- **WE TAKE OTHERS** to task for their misdeeds but tend to see ourselves as victims of circumstances when our conduct falls short of our ideal.

- **SHOULD WE PUT** the arm on people when we . . . "put the arm on" people?

Interpersonal Attraction: On Liking and Loving

- **IS BEAUTY** "in the eye of the beholder"?

- **DO "OPPOSITES ATTRACT"** or do "birds of a feather flock together"?

- **IS IT A GOOD IDEA** to "put on a happy face" when you're meeting someone for the first time?

- **AFTER READING THIS** section, you will be one of the enlightened who can explain what romantic love is!

Social Influence: Are You an Individual or One of the Crowd?

- **MOST PEOPLE TEND** to obey authority figures. (Are you one of them?)

- **IS SEEING BELIEVING?** What if the group disagrees with what you see?

Group Behavior

- **DO YOU RUN FASTER** or slower when you are in a group of runners?

- **IS A CAMEL A HORSE** made by a committee?

- **NEARLY 40 PEOPLE** stood by and did nothing while a woman was being stabbed to death.

Life Connections: Understanding and Combating Prejudice

- **PEOPLE HAVE CONDEMNED** billions of other people without ever meeting them or learning their names.

- **HOW DO PREJUDICES DEVELOP?** What can we do about them?

andy and Stretch: a new technique for controlling weight gains? No, these are the names of a couple who have just met at a camera club. Candy and Stretch stand above the crowd—literally. Candy, an attractive woman in her early 30s, is almost 6 feet tall. Stretch is more plain looking, but wholesome, in his late 30s, and 6 feet 5 inches tall.

Stretch has been in the group for some time. Candy is a new member. Let's listen in on them as they make conversation during a coffee break.[1] Note some differences between what they say and what they are thinking:

THEY SAY	THEY THINK
Stretch: Well, you're certainly a welcome addition to our group.	(Can't I ever say something clever?)
Candy: Thank you. It certainly is friendly and interesting.	(He's cute.)
Stretch: My friends call me Stretch. It's left over from my basketball days. Silly, but I'm used to it.	(It's safer than saying my name is David Stein.)
Candy: My name is Candy.	(At least my nickname is. He doesn't have to hear Hortense O'Brien.)
Stretch: What kind of camera is that?	(Why couldn't a girl named Candy be Jewish? It's only a nickname, isn't it?)
Candy: Just this old German one of my uncle's. I borrowed it from the office.	(He could be Irish. And that camera looks expensive.)
Stretch: May I? (He takes her camera, brushing her hand and then tingling with the touch.) Fine lens. You work for your uncle?	(Now I've done it. Brought up work.)
Candy: Ever since college. It's more than being just a secretary. I get into sales, too.	(So okay, what if I only went for a year. If he asks what I sell, I'll tell him anything except underwear.)
Stretch: Sales? That's funny. I'm in sales, too, but mainly as an executive. I run our department. I started using cameras on trips. Last time I was in the Bahamas. I took—	(Is there a nice way to say used cars? I'd better change the subject.) (Great legs! And the way her hips move . . .)
Candy: Oh! Do you go to the Bahamas, too? I love those islands.	(So I went just once, and it was for the brassiere manufacturers' convention. At least we're off the subject of jobs.)
Stretch: I did a little underwater work there last summer. Fantastic colors. So rich in life.	(She's probably been around. Well, at least we're off the subject of jobs.) (And lonelier than hell.)
Candy: I wish I'd had time when I was there. I love the water.	(Look at that build. He must swim like a fish. I should learn.) (Well, I do. At the beach, anyway, where I can wade in and not go too deep.)

So begins a relationship. Candy and Stretch have a drink and talk, sharing their likes and dislikes. Amazingly, they seem to agree on everything—from cars to clothing to politics. The attraction is very strong, and neither is willing to risk turning the other off by disagreeing. They scrupulously avoid one topic: religion. Their religious differences become apparent when they exchange last names. But that doesn't mean they have to talk about it.

[1]From *Pairing*, by G. R. Bach and R. M. Deutsch, 1970, New York: Peter H. Wyden.

They also put off introductions to their parents. The O'Briens and the Steins are narrow-minded about religion. If the truth be known, so are Candy and Stretch.

What happens in this tangled web of deception? After some deliberation, and not without misgivings, they decide to get married. Do they live happily ever after? We can't say. "Ever after" isn't here yet. We do not have all the answers, but we have some questions. Candy and Stretch pretended to share each other's attitudes. What are *attitudes*? Why didn't Candy and Stretch introduce each other to their parents? Candy and Stretch were attracted to one another. What is *attraction*? Who is attracted to whom? Did they fear that their parents would want them to *conform* to their own standards? Would their parents try to *persuade* them to limit dating to people of their own religions? Would they *obey*?

SOCIAL PSYCHOLOGY: INDIVIDUALS AMONG OTHERS

Attitudes, conformity, persuasion, obedience—these are some of the topics we find in **social psychology.** Candy and Stretch went to dinner at a restaurant where they served fine wine and soft music swelled in the background. The ways the environment influenced their behavior and mental processes are also part of social psychology. *Question: What is social psychology?* Social psychology studies the nature and causes of behavior and mental processes in social situations. The social psychological topics we discuss in this chapter include attitudes, social perception, interpersonal attraction, social influence, and group behavior.

ATTITUDES—"THE GOOD, THE BAD, AND THE UGLY"

How do you feel about abortion, Japanese cars, and the Republican party? The only connection I draw among these items is that people have *attitudes* toward them. They each give rise to cognitive evaluations (such as approval or disapproval), feelings (liking, disliking, or something stronger), and behavioral tendencies (such as approach or avoidance). Although I asked you how you "feel," attitudes are not just feelings or emotions. Many psychologists view thinking—or judgment—as primary. Feelings and behavior follow (Eagly & Chaiken, 1993). *Question: What are attitudes?*

Attitudes are behavioral and cognitive tendencies that are expressed by evaluating particular people, places, or things with favor or disfavor (Petty et al., 1997). Attitudes are learned, and they affect behavior (Petty et al., 1997). They can foster love or hate. They can give rise to helping behavior or to mass destruction. They can lead to social conflict or to the resolution of conflicts. Attitudes can change, but not easily. Most people do not change their religion or political affiliation without serious reflection or coercion.

The A–B Problem: Do We Do as We Think?

Our definition of attitude implies that our behavior is consistent with our cognitions—that is, with our beliefs and feelings. *Question: Do people do as they think?* (For example, do people really vote their consciences?) When we are free to do as we wish, our behavior is often consistent with our cognitions. But, as indicated by the term **A–B problem,** there are exceptions. In fact, the links between attitudes (A) and behaviors (B) tend to be weak to moderate (Eagly & Chaiken, 1993). For example, research reveals that attitudes toward health-related behaviors such as use of alcohol, smoking, and drunken driving are not consistent predictors of these behaviors (Stacy et al., 1994).

It also appears that we tend to live up to our **stereotypes**—even our stereotypes of ourselves. For example, when older people are reminded that they are "elderly," they tend to walk more slowly (Wheeler & Petty, 2001).

R E F L E C T

Is what you say and do always consistent with your beliefs? Can you think of examples when your behavior was inconsistent with your attitudes? Why was it inconsistent?

Social Psychology
The field of psychology that studies the nature and causes of people's thoughts and behavior in social situations.

Attitude
An enduring mental representation of a person, place, or thing that evokes an emotional response and related behavior.

A–B Problem
The issue of how well we can predict behavior on the basis of attitudes.

Stereotype
A fixed, conventional idea about a group.

■ Do People Always Vote Their "Conscience"?

The so called A–B problem refers to the research finding that people do not always act in accord with their attitudes.

Joseph Sohm; ChromoSohm Inc./CORBIS

A number of factors influence the likelihood that we can predict behavior from attitudes:

- *Specificity:* We can better predict specific behavior from specific attitudes than from global attitudes. For example, we can better predict church attendance by knowing people's attitudes toward church attendance than by knowing whether they are Christian.
- *Strength of attitudes:* Strong attitudes are more likely to determine behavior than weak attitudes (Petty et al., 1997). A person who believes that the nation's destiny depends on Republicans taking control of Congress is more likely to vote than a person who leans toward the Republican party but does not believe that the outcome of elections makes much difference.
- *Vested interest:* People are more likely to act on their attitudes when they have a vested interest in the outcome (Lehman & Crano, 2002). People are more likely to vote for (or against) unionization of their workplace, for example, when they believe that their job security depends on the outcome.
- *Accessibility:* People are more likely to behave in accord with their attitudes when they are accessible—that is, when they are brought to mind (Kallgren et al., 2000; Petty et al., 1997). This is why politicians attempt to "get out the vote" by means of media blitzes just prior to an election. It does them little good to have supporters who forget them on election day. Attitudes with a strong emotional impact are more accessible, which is one reason that politicians strive to get their supporters "worked up" over the issues.

Candy and Stretch avoided discussing matters on which they differed. One motive might have been to avoid heightening the *accessibility* of their clashing attitudes. By keeping them under the table, they might be less likely to act on them and go their separate ways.

REFLECT

What are your political attitudes? Liberal? Conservative? Middle of the road? How did you develop these attitudes? (Are you sure?)

Origins of Attitudes

You were not born a Republican or a Democrat. You were not born a Catholic or a Jew—although your parents may have practiced one of these religions when you came along. ***Question: Where do attitudes come from?*** Political, religious, and other attitudes are learned or derived from cognitive processes. In this section we describe some of the processes that result in acquiring attitudes.

Conditioning

Conditioning may play a role in acquiring attitudes. Experiments have shown that attitudes toward national groups can be influenced by associating them with positive words (such as *gift* or *happy*) or negative words (such as *ugly* or *failure*) (De Houwer et al., 2001). Parents often reward children for saying and doing things that agree with their own attitudes. Patriotism is encouraged by showing approval to children when they sing the national anthem or wave the flag.

Attitudes formed through direct experience may be stronger and easier to recall, but we also acquire attitudes by observing others. The approval or disapproval of peers leads adolescents to prefer short or long hair, baggy jeans, or preppie sweaters. The media inform us that body odor and bad breath are dreaded diseases—and, perhaps, that people who use harsh toilet paper are somehow un-American.

Cognitive Appraisal

Despite what we have said, the acquisition of attitudes is not so mechanical. People are also motivated to have a valid understanding of reality, so that they can make predictions and exercise some control over their environment (Wood, 2000). So people also evaluate information and form or change attitudes, including stereotypes, on the basis of new information (Petty et al., 1997, 1999). For example, we may believe that a car is more reliable than we had thought if a survey by *Consumer Reports* finds that it has an excellent repair record. Even so, initial attitudes act as cognitive anchors (Wegener et al., 2001; Wood, 2000). We often judge new ideas in terms of how much they deviate from our existing attitudes. Accepting larger deviations requires more information processing—in other words, more intellectual work (Petty et al., 1997, 1999). For this reason, perhaps, great deviations—such as changes from liberal to conservative attitudes, or vice versa—are apt to be resisted.

Changing Attitudes Through Persuasion

Let advertisers spend the same amount of money improving their product that they do on advertising and they wouldn't have to advertise it.

—Will Rogers

Rogers's social comment sounds on the mark, but he was probably wrong. It does little good to have a wonderful product if its existence remains a secret. ***Question: Can you really change people?—their attitudes and behavior, that is?***

The **elaboration likelihood model** describes the ways in which people respond to persuasive messages (Crano, 2000). Consider two routes to persuading others to change attitudes. The first, or central, route inspires thoughtful consideration of arguments and evidence. The second, or peripheral, route associates objects with positive or negative cues. When politicians avow that "This bill is supported by Jesse Jackson (or Jesse Helms)," they are seeking predictable, knee-jerk reactions, not careful consideration of a bill's merits. Other cues are rewards (such as a smile or a hug), punishments (such as parental disapproval), and such factors as the trustworthiness and attractiveness of the communicator.

Advertisements, which are a form of persuasive communication, also rely on central and peripheral routes. Some ads focus on the quality of the product (central route). Others attempt to associate the product with appealing images (peripheral route). Ads for Total cereal, which highlight its nutritional benefits, provide information about the quality of the product. So, too, did the "Pepsi Challenge" taste-test ads, which claimed that Pepsi tastes better than Coca-Cola. Marlboro cigarette ads that focus on the masculine, rugged image of the "Marlboro man"[2] offer no information about the product itself. Nor do ads that show football players heading for Disney World or choosing a brand of beer.

[2]The rugged actor in the original TV commercials died of lung cancer. Apparently cigarettes were more rugged than he was.

REFLECT

Are you entertained by radio or TV commercials? Which ones? Why? Did these commercials ever convince you to buy a product? Which one? Was the commercial accurate?

Elaboration Likelihood Model
The view that persuasive messages are evaluated (elaborated) on the basis of central and peripheral cues.

In this section we look at one central factor in persuasion—the nature of the message—and three peripheral factors: the messenger, the context of the message, and the audience. We also examine the foot-in-the-door technique.

The Persuasive Message: Say What? Say How? Say How Often?

How do we respond when TV commercials are repeated until we have memorized every dimple on the actors' faces? Research suggests that familiarity breeds content, not contempt (Macrae et al., 2002; Zajonc, 2001).

You might not be crazy about *zabulon*s and *afworbu*s at first, but Robert Zajonc (1968) found that people began to react favorably toward these foreign words on the basis of repeated exposure. In fact, repeated exposure to people and things as diverse as the following enhances their appeal (Baron & Byrne, 2003):

- Political candidates (who are seen in repeated TV commercials).
- Photographs of African Americans.
- Photographs of college students.
- Abstract art.
- Classical music.

The more complex the stimuli, the more likely it is that frequent exposure will have favorable effects (Smith & Dorfman, 1975). The 100th playing of a Bach fugue may be less tiresome than the 100th performance of a pop tune.

When trying to persuade someone, is it helpful or self-defeating to alert them to the arguments by the opposition? In two-sided arguments, the communicator recounts the arguments of the opposition in order to refute them. In research concerning a mock trial, college undergraduates were presented with two-sided arguments—those of the prosecution and those of the defendant (McKenzie et al., 2002). When one argument was weak, the college "jurors" expressed more confidence in their decision than when they did not hear the other side at all. Theologians and politicians sometimes forewarn their followers about the arguments of the opposition and then refute each one. Forewarning creates a kind of psychological immunity to them (Jacks & Devine, 2000).

It would be nice to think that people are too sophisticated to be persuaded by a **fear appeal**. However, many women who are warned of the dire risk they run if they fail to be screened for breast cancer are more likely to obtain mammograms than women who are informed of the *benefits* of mammography (Ruiter et al., 2001). Interestingly, although suntanning has been shown to increase the likelihood of skin cancer, warnings against suntanning were shown to be more effective when students were warned of risks to their *appearance* (premature aging, wrinkling, and scarring of the skin) than when the warning dealt with the risk to their health (Jones & Leary, 1994). That is, students informed of tanning's cosmetic effects were more likely to say they would protect themselves from the sun than were students informed about the risk of cancer. Fear appeals are most effective when the audience believes that the risks are serious—as in causing wrinkles!—and that the audience members can change their behavior to avert the risks—as in preventing cancer or wrinkling (Schneider et al., 2001).

Audiences also tend to believe arguments that appear to run counter to the vested interests of the communicator (Lehman & Crano, 2002). If the president of Chrysler or General Motors said that Toyotas and Hondas were superior, you can bet that we would prick up our ears.

The Persuasive Communicator: Whom Do You Trust?

Would you buy a used car from a person who had been convicted of larceny? Would you leaf through fashion magazines featuring homely models? Probably not. Research shows that persuasive communicators are characterized by expertise, trustworthiness, attractiveness, or similarity to their audiences (Petty et al., 1997). Because of the adoration of their fans, sports superstars such as Tiger Woods are highly valued as endorsers.

TV news anchors enjoy high prestige. One study (Mullen et al., 1987) found that before the 1984 presidential election, Peter Jennings of ABC News had shown significantly more favorable facial expressions when reporting on Ronald Reagan than when reporting on Walter Mondale. Tom Brokaw of NBC and Dan Rather of CBS had

R E F L E C T

Do you shut off the TV or switch channels when certain politicians or talk show hosts come on? Why? What are the advantages and potential dangers of such selective avoidance?

Fear Appeal

A type of persuasive communication that influences behavior on the basis of arousing fear instead of rational analysis of the issues.

© Duomo/CORBIS

not shown favoritism. The researchers also found that viewers of ABC News voted for Reagan in greater proportions than viewers of NBC or CBS News. It is tempting to conclude that Jennings subtly persuaded viewers to vote for Reagan—and maybe this did happen in a number of cases. But viewers do not simply absorb, spongelike, whatever the media feed them. People find it painful when they are confronted with information that discredits their own stereotypes and prejudices (Foerster et al., 2000). Therefore, they often show **selective avoidance** and **selective exposure** (Perse, 1998). That is, they switch channels when the news coverage runs counter to their own attitudes. They also seek communicators whose outlook coincides with their own. Thus, it may simply be that Reaganites favored Jennings over Brokaw and Rather.

The Context of the Message: "Get 'Em in a Good Mood"

You are too shrewd to let someone persuade you by buttering you up, but perhaps someone you know would be influenced by a sip of wine, a bite of cheese, and a sincere compliment. Aspects of the immediate environment, such as music, increase the likelihood of persuasion. When we are in a good mood, we apparently are less likely to evaluate the situation carefully (Park & Banaji, 2000; Petty et al., 1997).

It is also counterproductive to call your dates fools when they differ with you—even though their ideas are bound to be foolish if they do not agree with yours. Agreement and praise are more effective ways to encourage others to embrace your views. Appear sincere, or else your compliments will look manipulative. (It seems unfair to let out this information.)

The Persuaded Audience

Why do some people have sales resistance? Why do others enrich the lives of every door-to-door salesperson? It may be that people with high self-esteem and low social anxiety are more likely to resist social pressure (Ellickson et al., 2001).

A classic study by Schwartz and Gottman (1976) reveals the cognitive nature of the social anxiety that can make it difficult for some people to refuse requests. The researchers found that people who comply with unreasonable requests are more apt to report thoughts like the following:

- "I was worried about what the other person would think of me if I refused."
- "It is better to help others than to be self-centered."
- "The other person might be hurt or insulted if I refused."

Selective Avoidance
Diverting one's attention from information that is inconsistent with one's attitudes.

Selective Exposure
Deliberately seeking and attending to information that is consistent with one's attitudes.

People who refuse unreasonable requests reported thoughts like these:

- "It doesn't matter what the other person thinks of me."
- "I am perfectly free to say no."
- "This request is unreasonable."

Learning Connections
See Web site for an interactive version of these review questions.

REVIEW

(1) _____ psychology is the study of the nature and causes of our behavior and mental processes in social situations. (2) An _____ is a behavioral and cognitive tendency that is expressed by evaluating people or things with favor or disfavor. (3) When we are free to do as we wish, our behavior (is or is not?) usually consistent with our attitudes. (4) Attitudes are acquired through conditioning, observational learning, and _____ appraisal. (5) Early attitudes serve as _____ anchors. (6) According to the _____ likelihood model, there are central and peripheral routes to persuasion. (7) According to the _____-in-the-door effect, people are more likely to agree to large requests after they have agreed to smaller ones.

Critical Thinking: How would you use the information in this section to understand and resist persuasive arguments?

SOCIAL PERCEPTION: LOOKING OUT, LOOKING WITHIN

An important area of social psychology concerns the ways in which we perceive other people—for example, the importance of the first impressions they make on us. Next we explore some factors that contribute to **social perception:** the primacy and recency effects, attribution theory, and body language.

Primacy and Recency Effects: The Importance of First Impressions

Why do you wear a suit to a job interview? Why do defense attorneys make sure that their clients dress neatly and get their hair cut before they are seen by the jury? *Questions: Do first impressions really matter? What are the primacy and recency effects?* Apparently first impressions do matter—a great deal.

Social Perception
A subfield of social psychology that studies the ways in which we form and modify impressions of others.

Foot-in-the-Door Technique
A method for inducing compliance in which a small request is followed by a larger request.

A Closer Look

The Foot-in-the-Door Technique

You might suppose that contributing money to door-to-door solicitors for charity will get you off the hook. Perhaps they'll take the cash and leave you alone for a while. Actually, the opposite is true. The next time they mount a campaign, they may call on you to go door to door on their behalf! Organizations compile lists of people they can rely on. Because they have gotten their "foot in the door," this is known as the **foot-in-the-door technique.**

Consider a classic experiment by Freedman and Fraser (1966). Groups of women received phone calls from a consumer group requesting that they let a six-person crew come to their home to catalog their household products. The job could take hours. Only 22% of one group acceded to this irksome request.

But 53% of another group of women assented to a visit from this wrecking crew. Why was the second group more compliant? They had been phoned a few days earlier and had agreed to answer a few questions about the soap products they used. Thus they had been primed for the second request: The caller had gotten a foot in the door.

Research suggests that people who accede to small requests become more amenable to larger ones for a variety of reasons, including conformity and self-perception as the kind of people who help in this way (Burger, 1999). Regardless of how the foot-in-the-door technique works, if you want to say no, it may be easier to do so (and stick to your guns) the first time a request is made. Later may be too late.

Whether we are talking about the business or social worlds, or even the relationship between a therapist and a client, first impressions are important (Bidell et al., 2002; Laungani, 2002). First impressions are an example of the primacy effect. Let's have a look at the primacy and recency effects.

When I was a teenager, a young man was accepted or rejected by his date's parents the first time they were introduced. If he was considerate and made small talk, her parents might allow the couple to stay out past curfew—perhaps even to watch submarine races at the beach during the early morning hours. If he was boorish or uncommunicative, he was seen as a cad forever after. Her parents would object to him, no matter how hard he worked to gain their favor.

My experiences demonstrated to me that first impressions often make or break us. This phenomenon is known as the **primacy effect.** Why are first impressions so important? The answer may be because we infer traits from behavior. If we act considerately at first, we are labeled considerate. The *trait* of consideration is used to explain and predict our future behavior. If, after being labeled considerate, one keeps a date out past curfew, this lapse is likely to be seen as an exception to a rule—excused by circumstances or external causes. If one is first seen as inconsiderate, however, several months of considerate behavior may be perceived as a cynical effort to "make up for it."

Subjects in a classic experiment on the primacy effect read different stories about "Jim" (Luchins, 1957). The stories consisted of one or two paragraphs. The one-paragraph stories portrayed Jim as either friendly or unfriendly. These paragraphs were also used in the two-paragraph stories, but in this case the paragraphs were read in the reverse order. Of those reading only the "friendly" paragraph, 95% rated Jim as friendly. Of those who read just the "unfriendly" paragraph, 3% rated him as friendly. Seventy-eight percent of those who read two-paragraph stories in the "friendly–unfriendly" order labeled Jim as friendly. When they read the paragraphs in the reverse order, only 18% rated Jim as friendly.

How can we encourage people to pay more attention to impressions occurring after the first encounter? Abraham Luchins accomplished this by allowing time to elapse between the presentations of the two paragraphs. In this way, fading memories allowed more recent information to take precedence. This is known as the **recency effect.** Luchins found a second way to counter first impressions: He simply asked subjects to avoid making snap judgments and to weigh all the evidence.

There is some interesting research on the role of the handshake in making a first impression. In our culture, a firm handshake is a key to making a good first impression, by women as well as men. Researchers find that a firm handshake is perceived as an indication of being outgoing and open to new experience. A weak handshake was perceived as indicative of shyness and social anxiety (Chaplin et al., 2000). Thus women in the business world are well-advised to shake hands of new acquaintances firmly.

■ **First Impressions**

Why is it so important to make a good first impression? What are some ways of doing so?

R E F L E C T

Did you ever try to "make a good first impression"? Why? What did you do? Did it work? Explain.

Attribution Theory: You're Free, but I'm Caught in the Middle?

When she was 3 years old, one of my daughters believed that a friend's son was a boy because he *wanted* to be a boy. Since she was 3 years old at the time, this error in my daughter's **attribution** of the boy's gender is understandable. Adults tend to make somewhat similar attribution errors, however. Although they do not believe that people's preferences have much to do with their gender, they do tend to exaggerate the role of choice in their behavior. ***Questions: What is attribution theory? Why do we assume that other people intend the mischief that they do?***

An attribution is an assumption about why people do things. When you assume that one child is mistreating another child because she is "mean," you are making an attribution. The process by which we make inferences about the motives and traits of others through observation of their behavior is the **attribution process.** This section focuses on *attribution theory,* or the processes by which people draw conclusions about the factors that influence one another's behavior. Attribution theory is important because attributions lead us to perceive others either as purposeful actors or as victims of circumstances.

Primacy Effect
The tendency to evaluate others in terms of first impressions.

Recency Effect
The tendency to evaluate others in terms of the most recent impression.

Attribution
A belief concerning why people behave in a certain way.

Attribution Process
The process by which people draw inferences about the motives and traits of others.

Dispositional and Situational Attributions

Social psychologists describe two types of attributions. **Dispositional attributions** ascribe a person's behavior to internal factors such as personality traits and free will. **Situational attributions** attribute a person's actions to external factors such as social influence or socialization. If you assume that one child is mistreating the other because her parents have given her certain attitudes toward the other child, you are making a situational attribution.

The Fundamental Attribution Error

In cultures that view the self as independent, such as ours, people tend to attribute other people's behavior primarily to internal factors such as personality, attitudes, and free will (Gilovich & Eibach, 2001; Reeder, 2001). This bias in the attribution process is known as the **fundamental attribution error.** In such individualistic societies, people tend to focus on the behavior of others rather than on the circumstances surrounding their behavior. For example, if a teenager gets into trouble with the law, individualistic societies are more likely to blame the teenager than the social environment in which the teenager lives. When involved in difficult negotiations, there is a tendency to attribute the toughness to the personalities of the negotiators on the other side rather than the nature of the process of negotiation (Morris et al., 1999).

One reason for the fundamental attribution error is that we tend to infer traits from behavior. But in cultures that stress interdependence, such as Asian cultures, people are more likely to attribute other people's behavior to their social roles and obligations (Basic Behavioral Science Task Force, 1996c). For example, Japanese people might be more likely to attribute a businessperson's extreme competitiveness to the "culture of business" rather than to his or her personality.

The Actor–Observer Effect

When we see people (including ourselves) doing things that we do not like, we tend to see the others as willful actors but to see ourselves as victims of circumstances (Baron & Byrne, 2003). The tendency to attribute other people's behavior to dispositional factors and our own behavior to situational influences is called the **actor–observer effect.**

Consider an example. Parents and children often argue about the children's choice of friends or dates. When they do, the parents tend to infer traits from behavior and to see the children as stubborn and resistant. The children also infer traits from behavior.

REFLECT

Did you ever try to excuse your behavior by making a situational attribution? Do you make the fundamental attribution error of attributing too much of other people's behavior to choice? Give examples.

Dispositional Attribution
An assumption that a person's behavior is determined by internal causes such as personal attitudes or goals.

Situational Attribution
An assumption that a person's behavior is determined by external circumstances such as the social pressure found in a situation.

Fundamental Attribution Error
The assumption that others act predominantly on the basis of their dispositions, even when there is evidence suggesting the importance of their situations.

Actor–Observer Effect
The tendency to attribute our own behavior to situational factors but to attribute the behavior of others to dispositional factors.

■ The Actor–Observer Effect
Who is at fault here? People tend to make dispositional attributions for other people's behavior, but they tend to see their own behavior as motivated by situational factors. Thus people are aware of the external forces acting on themselves when they behave, but tend to attribute other people's behavior to choice and will.

Thus they may see their parents as bossy and controlling. Parents and children alike attribute the others' behavior to internal causes. That is, both make dispositional attributions about other people's behavior.

How do the parents and children perceive themselves? The parents probably see themselves as being forced into combat by their children's foolishness. If they become insistent, it is in response to the children's stubbornness. The children probably see themselves as responding to peer pressures and, perhaps, to sexual urges that may have come from within but seem like a source of outside pressure. The parents and the children both tend to see their own behavior as motivated by external forces. That is, they make situational attributions for their own behavior.

The actor–observer effect extends to our perceptions of both the in-group (an extension of ourselves) and the out-group. Consider conflicts between nations, for example. Both sides may engage in brutal acts of violence. Each side usually considers the other to be calculating, inflexible, and—not infrequently—sinister. Each side also typically views its own people as victims of circumstances and its own violent actions as justified or dictated by the situation. After all, we may look at the other side as being in the wrong, but can we expect them to agree with us?[3]

The Self-Serving Bias

There is also a **self-serving bias** in the attribution process. We are likely to ascribe our successes to internal, dispositional factors but our failures to external, situational influences (Duval & Silvia, 2002; Pronin et al., 2002). When we have done well on a test or impressed a date, we are likely to credit our intelligence and charm. But when we fail, we are likely to blame bad luck, an unfair test, or our date's bad mood.

We can extend the self-serving bias to sports. A study with 27 college wrestlers found that they tended to attribute their wins to stable and internal conditions such as their abilities, but their losses to unstable and external conditions such as an error by a referee (De Michele et al., 1998). Sports fans fall into the same trap. They tend to attribute their team's victories to internal conditions and their losses to external conditions (Wann & Shrader, 2000).

There are exceptions to the self-serving bias. In accord with the bias, when we work in groups, we tend to take the credit for the group's success but to pin the blame for group failure on someone else. But the outcome is different when we are friends with other group members: Then we tend to share the credit for success or the blame for failure (Campbell et al., 2000). Another exception is found in the fact that depressed people are more likely than other people to ascribe their failures to internal factors, even when external forces are mostly to blame.

Another interesting attribution bias is a gender difference in attributions for friendly behavior. Men are more likely than women to interpret a woman's smile or friendliness toward a man as flirting (Abbey, 1987; Buss, 2000). Perhaps traditional differences in gender roles still lead men to expect that a "decent" woman will be passive.

Factors Contributing to the Attribution Process

Our attribution of behavior to internal or external causes can apparently be influenced by three factors: *consensus, consistency,* and *distinctiveness* (Kelley & Michela, 1980). When few people act in a certain way—that is, when **consensus** is low—we are likely to attribute behavior to dispositional (internal) factors. Consistency refers to the degree to which the same person acts in the same way on other occasions. Highly consistent behavior can often be attributed to dispositional factors. Distinctiveness is the extent to which the person responds differently in different situations. If the person acts similarly in different situations, distinctiveness is low. We therefore are likely to attribute his or her behavior to dispositional factors.

Let us apply the criteria of consensus, consistency, and distinctiveness to the behavior of a customer in a restaurant. She takes one bite of her blueberry cheesecake and

REFLECT

Do you ever do anything that is wrong? (Be honest!) How do you explain your misdeeds to yourself? Are other people harsher in their judgment of you than you yourself are? If so, why?

Self-Serving Bias
The tendency to view one's successes as stemming from internal factors and one's failures as stemming from external factors.

Consensus
General agreement.

[3]I am not suggesting that all nations are equally blameless (or blameworthy) for their brutality toward other nations. I am pointing out that there is a tendency for the people of a nation to perceive themselves as being driven to undesirable behavior. Yet they are also likely to perceive other nations' negative behavior as willful.

calls the waiter. She tells him that her food is inedible and demands that it be replaced. Now, has she complained as a result of internal causes (for example, because she is hard to please) or external causes (that is, because the food really is bad)? Under the following circumstances, we are likely to attribute her behavior to internal, dispositional causes: (1) No one else at the table is complaining, so consensus is low. (2) She has returned her food on other occasions, so consistency is high. (3) She complains in other restaurants also, so distinctiveness is low (see Table 14.1).

Under the following circumstances, however, we are likely to attribute the customer's behavior to external, situational causes: (1) Everyone else at the table is also complaining, so consensus is high. (2) She does not usually return food, so consistency is low. (3) She usually does not complain at restaurants, so distinctiveness is high. Given these conditions, we are likely to believe that the blueberry cheesecake really is awful and that the customer is justified in her response.

Body Language: The Body Speaks

Body language is important in social perception. *Question: What is body language?* Body language is nonverbal language; it refers to the meanings we infer from the ways in which people carry themselves and the gestures they make (Flack et al., 1999; McClave, 2000). At an early age we learn that the way people carry themselves provides cues to how they feel and are likely to behave. You may have noticed that when people are "uptight" they may also be rigid and straight-backed. People who are relaxed are more likely to "hang loose." Factors such as eye contact, posture, and the distance between two people provide cues to the individuals' moods and their feelings toward their companions. When people face us and lean toward us, we may assume that they like us or are interested in what we are saying. If we overhear a conversation between a couple and observe that the woman is leaning toward the man but the man is sitting back and toying with his hair, we are likely to infer that he is not interested in what she is saying.

Touching: Put the Arm on People (Literally)

Touching also communicates. Women are more likely than men to touch other people when they are interacting with them (Stier & Hall, 1984). In one "touching" experiment, Kleinke (1977) showed that appeals for help can be more effective when the distressed person makes physical contact with people who are asked for aid. A woman obtained more coins for phone calls when she touched the arm of the person she was asking for money. In another experiment, waitresses obtained higher tips when they touched patrons on the hand or the shoulder while making change (Crusco & Wetzel, 1984).

In these experiments, the touching was noncontroversial. It was usually gentle, brief, and done in familiar settings. However, when touching suggests greater intimacy than is desired, it can be seen as negative. A study in a nursing home found that responses to being touched depended on factors such as the status of the staff member, the type of touch, and the part of the body that was touched (Hollinger & Buschmann, 1993). Touching was considered positive when it was appropriate to the situation and did not appear to be condescending. It was seen as negative when it was controlling, unnecessary, or overly intimate.

REFLECT

Look around. Can you tell whether other people are enjoying being with one another, or whether they are finding the experience annoying? How can you tell?

TABLE 14.1 Factors Leading to Internal or External Attributions of Behavior

	Internal Attribution	External Attribution
Consensus	Low: Few people behave this way.	High: Most people behave this way.
Consistency	High: The person behaves this way frequently.	Low: The person does not behave this way frequently.
Distinctiveness	Low: The person behaves this way in many situations.	High: The person behaves this way in few situations.

Body language can also be used to establish and maintain territorial control, as anyone knows who has had to step aside because a football player was walking down the hall. Werner and her colleagues (1981) found that players in a game arcade used touching as a way of signaling others to keep their distance. Solo players engaged in more touching than did groups, perhaps because they were surrounded by strangers.

Gazing and Staring: The Eyes Have It

We usually feel that we can learn much from eye contact. When other people "look us squarely in the eye," we may assume that they are being assertive or open with us. Avoidance of eye contact may suggest deception or depression. Gazing is interpreted as a sign of liking or friendliness (Kleinke, 1986). In one penetrating study, men and women were asked to gaze into each other's eyes for two minutes (Kellerman et al., 1989). After doing so, they reported having passionate feelings toward one another. (Watch out!)

Of course, a gaze is not the same thing as a persistent hard stare. A hard stare is interpreted as a provocation or a sign of anger. Adolescent males sometimes engage in staring contests as an assertion of dominance. The male who looks away first loses the contest. In a classic series of field experiments, Phoebe Ellsworth and her colleagues (1972) subjected drivers stopped at red lights to hard stares by riders of motor scooters (see Figure 14.1). When the light changed, people who were stared at crossed the intersection more rapidly than people who were not. People who are stared at exhibit higher levels of physiological arousal than people who are not (Strom & Buck, 1979).

■ **Gazing Versus Staring**

Gazing into an attractive person's eyes can give rise to feelings of passion, but people interpret a hard stare as an aversive challenge.

R E V I E W

(8) The psychology of social _____ involves the ways in which we perceive other people and ourselves. (9) The tendency to perceive others in terms of first impressions is an example of the _____ effect. (10) Our inference of the motives and traits of others through observation of their behavior is called the _____ process. (11) People who feel (positively or negatively?) toward one another tend to position themselves close together. (12) Gazing into another's eyes can be a sign of love, but a hard _____ is an aversive challenge.

Critical Thinking: Why is it that we tend to hold others accountable for their misdeeds but excuse ourselves for the bad things we do? How can you use this information to enhance your social relationships?

Learning Connections
See Web site for an interactive version of these review questions.

■ **Figure 14.1**
Diagram of an Experiment in Hard Staring and Avoidance

In the Greenbaum and Rosenfeld (1978) study, the confederate of the experimenter stared at some drivers and not at others. Recipients of the stares drove across the intersection more rapidly once the light turned green. Why?

Traffic signal

Flow of traffic

Flow of traffic

Confederate C

Observers (these persons record drivers' behavior)

Auto

One-way street

INTERPERSONAL ATTRACTION: ON LIKING AND LOVING

Sexual interactions usually take place within relationships. Feelings of **attraction** can lead to liking and perhaps to love, and to a more lasting relationship. *Question: What factors contribute to attraction in our culture?* Among the factors contributing to attraction are physical appearance, similarity, and reciprocity.

Physical Appearance: How Important Is Looking Good?

Physical appearance is a key factor in attraction and in the consideration of partners for dates and marriage (Langlois et al., 2000; Sangrador & Yela, 2000). What determines physical allure? Are our standards subjective—that is, "in the eye of the beholder"? Or is there general agreement on what is appealing?

Many aspects of beauty appear to be cross-cultural (Langlois et al., 2000; Little & Perrett, 2002). For example, a study of people in England and Japan found that both British and Japanese men consider women with large eyes, high cheekbones, and narrow jaws to be most attractive (Perret, 1994). In his research, Perret created computer composites of the faces of 60 women and, as shown in part A of Figure 14.2, of the 15 women who were rated the most attractive. He then used computer enhancement to exaggerate the differences between the composite of the 60 and the composite of the 15 most attractive women. He arrived at the image shown in part B of Figure 14.2. Part B, which shows higher cheekbones and a narrower jaw than part A, was rated as the most attractive image. Similar results were found for the image of a Japanese woman. Works of art suggest that the ancient Greeks and Egyptians favored similar facial features.

In our society, tallness is an asset for men (Hensley, 1994; Pierce, 1996). Although women may be less demanding than men concerning a variety of physical features, height—that is, tallness—is more important to women in the selection of dates and mates than it is to men.

Although preferences for facial features may transcend time and culture, preferences for body weight and shape may be more culturally determined. For example,

Attraction
In social psychology, an attitude of liking or disliking (negative attraction).

■ **Figure 14.2**
What Features Contribute to Facial Attractiveness?

In both England and Japan, features such as large eyes, high cheekbones, and narrow jaws contribute to perceptions of the attractiveness of women. Part A shows a composite of the faces of 15 women rated as the most attractive of a group of 60. Part B is a composite in which the features of these 15 women are exaggerated—that is, developed further in the direction that separates them from the average of the entire 60.

A.

B.

© Science Photo Library/Photo Researchers, Inc.

"Looking Good"
Models like these are among those who set the standards for beauty in contemporary American culture. How important is physical attractiveness in interpersonal attraction and social and vocational success?

plumpness has been valued in many cultures. Grandmothers who worry that their granddaughters are starving themselves often come from cultures in which stoutness is acceptable or desirable. In contemporary Western society, there is pressure on both males and females to be slender (Goode, 2000; Wade et al., 2000). Women generally favor men with a V-taper—broad shoulders and a narrow waist.

Gender Differences

Although both genders perceive overweight people as unappealing, there are fascinating gender differences in perceptions of desirable body shapes. College men tend to consider their current physique similar to the ideal male build and to the one that women find most appealing (Fallon & Rozin, 1985). College women, in contrast, generally see themselves as markedly heavier than the figure that is most appealing to men and heavier still than the ideal (see Figure 14.3). Both mothers and fathers of college students see themselves as heavier than their ideal weight (Rozin & Fallon, 1988). Both genders err in their estimates of the other gender's preferences, however. Men of both generations actually prefer women to be heavier than the women presume. Both college women and their mothers prefer men who are slimmer than the men presume.

"Pretty Is as Pretty Does?"

Both men and women are perceived as more attractive when they are smiling (Reis et al., 1990). When you're smiling, observers expect to have positive social interactions with you (Harker & Keltner, 2001). There is thus ample reason to, as the song goes, "put on a happy face" when you are meeting people or looking for a date.

Other aspects of behavior also affect interpersonal attraction. Women who are shown videotapes of prospective dates or asked to describe ideal partners tend to prefer men who are outgoing, self-assertive, and self-confident (Burger & Cosby, 1999). However, college men respond negatively to women who show self-assertion and social dominance (Sadalla et al., 1987). Despite the liberating trends of recent years, the cultural stereotype of the ideal woman still includes modesty. I am *not* suggesting that self-assertive women should take a back seat in order to make themselves more appealing to traditional men. Assertive women might find nothing but conflict in their interactions with such men in any case.

R E F L E C T
Does it matter if your date or your mate is taller or shorter than you are? Explain.

■ **Figure 14.3**
Can You Ever Be Too Thin?

Research suggests that most college women believe that they are heavier than is ideally attractive. However, men actually prefer women to be a bit heavier than women assume the men would like them to be. And what of the college men? They tend to believe that their physiques are just about where they should be; college women, however, would prefer them to be somewhat slimmer.

REFLECT

Could you maintain a relationship with a partner whose attitudes toward religion, politics, education, and child-rearing differed significantly from your own? Would you want to?

Matching Hypothesis

The view that people tend to choose persons similar to themselves in attractiveness and attitudes in the formation of interpersonal relationships.

The Matching Hypothesis: Do "Opposites Attract" or Do "Birds of a Feather Flock Together"?

Although we may rate highly attractive people as most desirable, most of us are not left to blend in with the wallpaper. According to the **matching hypothesis,** we tend to date people who are similar to ourselves in physical attractiveness rather than the local Will Smith or Sandra Bullock look-alike. One motive for asking out "matches" seems to be fear of rejection by more attractive people (Bernstein et al., 1983).

The quest for similarity extends beyond physical attractiveness. Our marital and sex partners tend to be similar to us in race/ethnicity, age, level of education, and religion. Consider some findings of the National Health and Social Life Survey (Michael et al., 1994, pp. 45–47):

- Nearly 94% of single European American men have European American women as their sex partners; 2% are partnered with Latina Americans, 2% with Asian American women, and less than 1% with African American women.
- About 82% of African American men have African American women as their sex partners; nearly 8% are partnered with European American women and almost 5% with Latina Americans.
- About 83% of the women and men in the study chose partners within five years of their own age and of the same or a similar religion.
- Of nearly 2,000 women in the study, not one with a graduate college degree had a partner who had not finished high school.

■ The Matching Hypothesis

Do opposites attract, or do we tend to pair off with people who look and think the way we do? As suggested by these photographs, similarity often runs at least skin-deep.

Why do most people have partners from the same background as their own? One reason is that marriages are made in the neighborhood and not in heaven (Michael et al., 1994). We tend to live among people who are similar to us in background, and we therefore come into contact with them more often than with people from other backgrounds. Another reason is that we are drawn to people whose attitudes are similar to ours (Michinov & Michinov, 2001; Singh & Ho, 2000; Watson et al., 2000). People from similar backgrounds are more likely to have similar attitudes.

Reciprocity: If You Like Me, You Must Have Excellent Judgment

Has anyone told you how good-looking, brilliant, and mature you are? That your taste is refined? That all in all, you are really something special? If so, have you been impressed by his or her fine judgment?

Reciprocity is a powerful determinant of attraction (Bruce & Sanders, 2001; Sprecher, 1998). We tend to return feelings of admiration. We tend to be more open, warm, and helpful when we are interacting with strangers who seem to like us (Curtis & Miller, 1986).

Feelings of attraction are influenced by factors such as physical appearance and similarity. Let us explore what we mean when we say that feelings of attraction have blossomed into love.   *Questions: Just what is love? What is romantic love?*

Love: Doing What Comes . . . Culturally?

Love—the ideal for which we make great sacrifice. Love—the sentiment that launched a thousand ships in Homer's epic poem *The Iliad*. Through the millennia, poets have sought to capture love in words. Dante, the Italian poet, wrote of "the love that moves the sun and the other stars." The Scottish poet Robert Burns wrote that his love was like "a red, red rose." Love is beautiful and elusive. Passion and romantic love are also lusty, surging with sexual desire.

The Love Triangle

No, this love triangle does not refer to two men wooing the same woman. It refers to Robert Sternberg's **triangular model of love.** Sternberg (1988) believes that love can include combinations of three components: intimacy, passion, and commitment (see Figure 14.4).

Intimacy refers to a couple's closeness, to their mutual concern and sharing of feelings and resources. **Passion** means romance and sexual feelings. Commitment means deciding to enhance and maintain the relationship. Passion is most crucial in short-term relationships. Intimacy and commitment are more important in enduring relationships. The ideal form of love combines all three: **consummate love.** Consummate love is made up of romantic love plus commitment.

REFLECT

How do you know when you are in love? Can you express the feelings in words? Can you think of a way that psychologists can measure them?

Reciprocity
In interpersonal attraction, the tendency to return feelings and attitudes that are expressed about us.

Triangular Model of Love
Sternberg's view that love involves combinations of three components: intimacy, passion, and decision/commitment.

Intimacy
Close acquaintance and familiarity; a characteristic of a relationship in which partners share their inmost feelings.

Passion
Strong romantic and sexual feelings.

Consummate Love
The ideal form of love within Sternberg's model, which combines passion, intimacy, and commitment.

■ **Figure 14.4**
The Triangular Model of Love
According to this model, love has three components: intimacy, passion, and commitment. The ideal of consummate love consists of romantic love plus commitment.

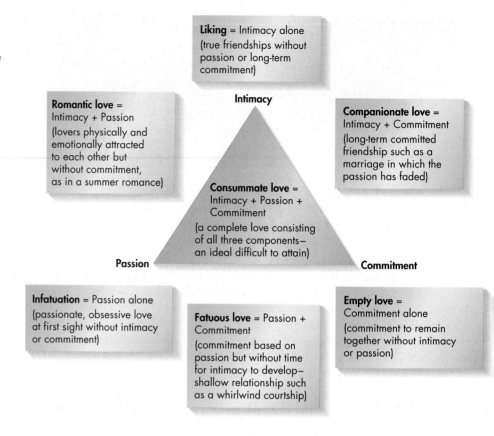

Liking = Intimacy alone (true friendships without passion or long-term commitment)

Romantic love = Intimacy + Passion (lovers physically and emotionally attracted to each other but without commitment, as in a summer romance)

Companionate love = Intimacy + Commitment (long-term committed friendship such as a marriage in which the passion has faded)

Intimacy

Consummate love = Intimacy + Passion + Commitment (a complete love consisting of all three components— an ideal difficult to attain)

Passion

Commitment

Infatuation = Passion alone (passionate, obsessive love at first sight without intimacy or commitment)

Fatuous love = Passion + Commitment (commitment based on passion but without time for intimacy to develop— shallow relationship such as a whirlwind courtship)

Empty love = Commitment alone (commitment to remain together without intimacy or passion)

REFLECT

Have you ever had the experience of being so in love that you were convinced the person was wonderful, or perfect, while others were pointing out flaws? Have you later wondered why you were so smitten? How do you explain it all?

Romantic Love
An intense, positive emotion that involves sexual attraction, feelings of caring, and the belief that one is in love.

Affective Shift Hypothesis
The view that men and women tend to experience different shifts in the emotions following initiation of sexual activity, such that women feel more love and commitment, and many men experience less love and commitment.

Romantic love is characterized by passion and intimacy. Passion involves fascination (preoccupation with the loved one); sexual craving; and the desire for exclusiveness (a special relationship with the loved one). Intimacy involves caring—championing the interests of the loved one, even if it entails sacrificing one's own. People are cognitively biased toward evaluating their dating partners positively (Loving & Agnew, 2001). In plain English, we idealize the people we love. People tend to pay attention to information that confirms their romantic interests. Romantic lovers often magnify each other's positive features and overlook their flaws.

To experience romantic love, in contrast to attachment or sexual arousal, one must be exposed to a culture that idealizes the concept. In Western culture, romantic love blossoms in fairy tales about Sleeping Beauty, Cinderella, Snow White, and all their princes charming. It matures with romantic novels, television tales and films, and the personal accounts of friends and relatives about dates and romances.

The Affective Shift Hypothesis

Men are generally more reluctant than women to make commitments in their romantic relationships (Buss, 1995). The **affective shift hypothesis,** developed by evolutionary psychologist David Buss and his colleagues (Haselton & Buss, 2001), offers one possible explanation of men's lesser willingness to commit themselves to relationships. In a study of nearly 200 subjects, the psychologists found that women tend to experience greater feelings of love and commitment—a positive affective shift—after first-time sex than men do. But not all men are alike. (Really.) As a group, men are more likely than women to be interested in short-term relationships and multiple sex partners. And it seems accurate to say that men with high numbers of sex partners tend to experience a negative affective shift following first-time sex. The negative shift in feelings motivates them to end the relationship and curbs tendencies toward making a commitment. However, men with fewer sex partners and more of an interest in developing long-term relationships also tend to experience the positive affective shift after first-time sex.

Evolutionary psychologists also suggest that men may be naturally more promiscuous than women because they are the genetic heirs of ancestors whose reproductive success was connected with the number of women they could impregnate (Buss, 1994, 1999; Schmitt et al., 2001). But women can produce relatively few children in their lifetimes. Thus, the theory suggests, women need to be more selective with respect to their mating partners. Is it possible that the man's "roving eye" and the woman's selectivity are embedded in their genes? (This possibility is *not* intended to provide male readers with the excuse: "But how can I make a commitment? Running around is in my genes.")

Learning Connections
See Web site for an interactive version of these review questions.

R E V I E W

(13) Physical attractiveness (is or is not?) a key factor in the selection of dates and mates. (14) According to the _____ hypothesis, we tend to date people who are similar to ourselves. (15) According to the _____ model of love, love can include combinations of intimacy, passion, and commitment.

Critical Thinking: How might the features found attractive by males and females provide humans with an evolutionary advantage? Can you think of alternative explanations as to why people tend to find these features attractive?

© Helen King/CORBIS

■ Uh, Oh—What Will Happen if They Make Love?

According to the "affective shift hypothesis," most women experience stronger feelings of love and commitment toward their partners after they make love for the first time. The picture is mixed for men. Men with few dating partners may, like most women, experience greater love and commitment. But the feelings of men with many dating partners often turn negative. That is, they want out.

SOCIAL INFLUENCE: ARE YOU AN INDIVIDUAL OR ONE OF THE CROWD?

Most people would be reluctant to wear blue jeans to a funeral, walk naked on city streets, or, for that matter, wear clothes at a nudist colony. This is because other people and groups can exert enormous pressure on us to behave according to their norms. **Social influence** is the area of social psychology that studies the ways in which people alter the thoughts, feelings, and behavior of others (Crano, 2000). We already learned how attitudes can be changed through persuasion. In this section we describe a couple of classic experiments that demonstrate how people influence others to engage in destructive obedience or conform to social norms.

Obedience to Authority: Does Might Make Right?

Throughout history soldiers have followed orders—even when it comes to slaughtering innocent civilians. The Turkish slaughter of Armenians, the Nazi slaughter of Jews, the mutual slaughter of Hutus and Tutsis in Rwanda—these are all examples of the tragedies that can arise from simply following orders. We may say we are horrified by such crimes and we cannot imagine why people engage in them. But how many of us would refuse to follow orders issued by authority figures? *Questions: Why will so many people commit crimes against humanity if they are ordered to do so? (Why don't they refuse?)*

The Milgram Studies: Shocking Stuff at Yale

Yale University psychologist Stanley Milgram also wondered how many people would resist immoral requests made by authority figures. To find out, he undertook a series of classic experiments at the university that have become known as the Milgram studies on obedience.

In an early phase of his work, Milgram (1963) placed ads in New Haven (Connecticut) newspapers for people who would be willing to participate in studies on learning and memory. He enlisted 40 people ranging in age from 20 to 50—teachers, engineers, laborers, salespeople, people who had not completed elementary school, people with graduate degrees.

R E F L E C T
Do you believe that it is good to be obedient? That children should be trained to be obedient? Explain.

Social Influence
The area of social psychology that studies the ways in which people influence the thoughts, feelings, and behavior of others.

Let's suppose that you have answered the ad. You show up at the university in exchange for a reasonable fee ($4.50, which in the early 1960s might easily fill your gas tank) and to satisfy your own curiosity. You may be impressed. After all, Yale is a venerable institution that dominates the city. You are no less impressed by the elegant labs, where you meet a distinguished behavioral scientist dressed in a white coat and another person who has responded to the ad. The scientist explains that the purpose of the experiment is to study the *effects of punishment on learning*. The experiment requires a "teacher" and a "learner." By chance, you are appointed the teacher and the other recruit the learner.

You, the scientist, and the learner enter a laboratory room containing a threatening chair with dangling straps. The scientist straps the learner in. The learner expresses some concern, but this is, after all, for the sake of science. And this is Yale University, isn't it? What could happen to a person at Yale?

You follow the scientist to an adjacent room, from which you are to do your "teaching." This teaching promises to have an impact. You are to punish the learner's errors by pressing levers marked from 15 to 450 volts on a fearsome-looking console (see Figure 14.5). Labels describe 28 of the 30 levers as running the gamut from "Slight Shock" to "Danger: Severe Shock." The last two levers are simply labeled "XXX." Just in case you have no idea what electric shock feels like, the scientist gives you a sample 45-volt shock. It stings. You pity the person who might receive more.

Your learner is expected to learn pairs of words, which are to be read from a list. After hearing the list once, the learner is to produce the word that pairs with the stimulus word from a list of four alternatives. This is done by pressing a switch that lights one of four panels in your room. If it is the correct panel, you proceed to the next stimulus word. If not, you are to deliver an electric shock. With each error, you are to increase the voltage of the shock (Figure 14.5).

You probably have some misgivings. Electrodes have been strapped to the learner's wrists, and the scientist has applied electrode paste "to avoid blisters and burns." You have also been told that the shocks will cause "no permanent tissue damage," although they might be extremely painful. Still, the learner is going along. And after all, this is Yale.

The learner answers some items correctly and then makes some errors. With mild concern you press the levers up through 45 volts. You've tolerated that much yourself. Then a few more mistakes are made. You press the 60-volt lever, then 75. The learner makes another mistake. You pause and look at the scientist, who is reassuring: "Although the shocks may be painful, there is no permanent tissue damage, so please go on." The learner makes more errors, and soon you are up to a shock of 300 volts. But now the learner is pounding on the other side of the wall! Your chest tightens and you begin to perspire. "Damn science and the $4.50!" you think. You hesitate and the scientist says, "The experiment requires that you continue." After the delivery of the next stimulus word, the learner chooses no answer at all. What are you to do? "Wait for 5 to

■ **Figure 14.5**
The Experimental Setup in the Milgram Studies on Obedience

When the "learner" made an error, the experimenter prodded the "teacher" to deliver a painful electric shock.

Overbearing experimenter

"Learner" who to be receivin

"Teacher" with "aggression" machine

10 seconds," the scientist instructs, "and then treat no answer as a wrong answer." But after the next shock the pounding on the wall resumes! Now your heart is racing, and you are convinced you are causing extreme pain and discomfort. Is it possible that no lasting damage is being done? Is the experiment that important, after all? What to do? You hesitate again, and the scientist says, "It is absolutely essential that you continue." His voice is very convincing. "You have no other choice," he says, "you *must* go on." You can barely think straight, and for some unaccountable reason you feel laughter rising in your throat. Your finger shakes above the lever. *What are you to do?*

Milgram had foreseen that some "teachers" in his experiment would hesitate. He had therefore conceived standardized statements that his assistants would use when subjects balked—for example: "Although the shocks may be painful, there is no permanent tissue damage, so please go on." "The experiment requires that you continue." "It is absolutely essential that you continue." "You have no other choice; you *must* go on."

To repeat: If you are a "teacher" in the Milgram study, what do you do? Milgram (1963, 1974) found out what most people in his sample would do. The sample was a cross-section of the male population of New Haven. Of the 40 men in this phase of his research, only 5 refused to go beyond the 300-volt level, the level at which the learner first pounded the wall. Nine other "teachers" defied the scientist within the 300-volt range. But 65% of the subjects complied with the scientist throughout the series, believing they were delivering 450-volt, XXX-rated shocks.

Were these subjects unfeeling? Not at all. Milgram was impressed by their signs of stress. They trembled, they stuttered, they bit their lips. They groaned, they sweated, they dug their fingernails into their flesh. Some had fits of laughter, although laughter was inappropriate. One salesperson's laughter was so convulsive that he could not continue with the experiment.

Milgram's initial research on obedience was limited to a sample of New Haven men. Could he generalize his findings to other men or to women? Would college students, who are considered to be independent thinkers, show more defiance? A replication of Milgram's study with a sample of Yale men yielded similar results. What about women, who are supposedly less aggressive than men? In subsequent research, women, too, administered shocks to the learners. All this took place in a nation that values independence and free will.

In various phases of Milgram's research, nearly half or the majority of the subjects complied throughout the series, believing that they were delivering 450-volt, XXX-rated shocks. These findings held for men from the New Haven community, for male students at Yale, and for women.

On Deception and Truth at Yale

I have said that the "teachers" in the Milgram studies *believed* that they were shocking other people when they pressed the levers on the console. They weren't. The only real shock in this experiment was the 45-volt sample given to the teachers. Its purpose was to make the procedure believable.

The learners in the experiment were actually confederates of the experimenter. They had not answered the newspaper ads but were in on the truth from the start. The "teachers" were the only real subjects. They were led to believe they had been chosen at random for the teacher role, but the choosing was rigged so that newspaper recruits would always become teachers.

Milgram debriefed his subjects after the experiment was complete. He explained the purpose and methods of his research in detail. He emphasized the fact that they had not actually harmed anyone. But of course the subjects did believe that they were hurting other people as the experiment was being carried out. As you can imagine, the ethics of the Milgram studies has been debated by psychologists for four decades.

Why Did People in the Milgram Studies Obey the Experimenters?

In any event, many people obey the commands of others even when they are required to perform immoral tasks. But *why*? Why did Germans "just follow orders" during the Holocaust? Why did "teachers" obey the experimenter in Milgram's study? We do not have all the answers, but we can offer a number of hypotheses:

REFLECT

How do you think you would have behaved if you had been a "teacher" in the Milgram studies? Are you sure?

Are you surprised that women in the Milgram study obeyed orders and shocked "learners" just as men did? Why or why not?

- *Socialization:* Despite the expressed American ideal of independence, we are socialized from early childhood to obey authority figures such as parents and teachers. Obedience to immoral demands may be the ugly sibling of socially desirable respect for authority figures (Blass, 1999).
- *Lack of social comparison:* In Milgram's experimental settings, experimenters displayed command of the situation. Teachers (subjects), however, were on the experimenter's ground and very much on their own so they did not have the opportunity to compare their ideas and feelings with those of other people in the same situation. They therefore were less likely to have a clear impression of what to do.
- *Perception of legitimate authority:* One phase of Milgram's research took place within the hallowed halls of Yale University. Subjects might have been overpowered by the reputation and authority of the setting. An experimenter at Yale might have appeared to be a highly legitimate authority figure—as might a government official or a high-ranking officer in the military (Blass & Schmitt, 2001). Yet further research showed that the university setting contributed to compliance but was not fully responsible for it. The percentage of individuals who complied with the experimenter's demands dropped from 65% to 48% when Milgram (1974) replicated the study in a dingy storefront in a nearby town. At first glance, this finding might seem encouraging. But the main point of the Milgram studies is that most people are willing to engage in morally reprehensible acts at the behest of a legitimate-looking authority figure. Hitler and his henchmen were authority figures in Nazi Germany. "Science" and Yale University legitimized the authority of the experimenters in the Milgram studies.
- *The foot-in-the-door technique:* The foot-in-the-door technique might also have contributed to the obedience of the teachers. Once they had begun to deliver shocks to learners, they might have found it progressively more difficult to extricate themselves from the situation. Soldiers, similarly, are first taught to obey orders unquestioningly in unimportant matters such as dress and drill. By the time they are ordered to risk their lives, they have been saluting smartly and following commands without question for a long time.
- *Inaccessibility of values:* People are more likely to act in accordance with their attitudes when their attitudes are readily available, or accessible. Most people believe that it is wrong to harm innocent people. But strong emotions interfere with clear thinking. As the teachers in the Milgram experiments became more aroused, their attitudes might thus have become less "accessible." As a result, it might have become progressively more difficult for them to behave according to these attitudes.
- *Buffers:* Several buffers decreased the effect of the learners' pain on the teachers. For example, the "learners" (actually confederates of the experimenter) were in another room. When they were in the same room with the teachers, the teachers' compliance rate dropped from 65% to 40%. Moreover, when the teacher held the learner's hand on the shock plate, the compliance rate dropped to 30%. In modern warfare, opposing military forces may be separated by great distances. They may be little more than a blip on a radar screen. It is one thing to press a button to launch a missile or aim a piece of artillery at a distant troop carrier or a faraway mountain ridge. It is another to hold a weapon to a victim's throat.

Conformity: Do Many Make Right?

We are said to **conform** when we change our behavior in order to adhere to social norms. **Social norms** are widely accepted expectations concerning social behavior. Explicit social norms are often made into rules and laws such as those that require us to whisper in libraries and to slow down when driving past a school. There are also unspoken or implicit social norms, such as those that cause us to face the front in an elevator or to be "fashionably late" for social gatherings.

The tendency to conform to social norms is often good. Many norms have evolved because they promote comfort and survival. Group pressure can also promote maladaptive behavior, as when people engage in risky behavior because "everyone is doing it." ***Question: Why do so many people tend to follow the crowd?***

REFLECT

There are many possible explanations for obedience. Milgram's research has alerted us to a real danger—the tendency of many, if not most, people to obey the orders of an authority figure even when they run counter to moral values. It has happened before. It is happening now. What will you do to stop it?

Conform

To changes one's attitudes or overt behavior to adhere to social norms.

Social Norms

Explicit and implicit rules that reflect social expectations and influence the ways people behave in social situations.

Conformity

In the military, individuals are taught to conform until the group functions in machinelike fashion. What pressures to conform do you experience? Do you surrender to them? Why or why not?

To answer this question, let us look at a classic experiment on conformity conducted by Solomon Asch in the early 1950s. We then examine factors that promote conformity.

Seven Line Judges Can't Be Wrong: The Asch Study

Can you believe what you see with your own eyes? Seeing is believing, isn't it? Not if you were a subject in Asch's (1952) study.

You entered a laboratory room with seven other subjects, supposedly taking part in an experiment on visual discrimination. At the front of the room stood a man holding cards with lines drawn on them.

The eight of you were seated in a series. You were given the seventh seat, a minor fact at the time. The man explained the task. There was a single line on the card on the left. Three lines were drawn on the card at the right (Figure 14.6). One line was the same length as the line on the other card. You and the other subjects were to call out, one at a time, which of the three lines—1, 2, or 3—was the same length as the one on the card on the left. Simple.

The subjects to your right spoke out in order: "3," "3," "3," "3," "3," "3." Now it was your turn. Line 3 was clearly the same length as the line on the first card, so you said "3." The fellow after you then chimed in: "3." That's all there was to it. Then two other cards were set up at the front of the room. This time line 2 was clearly the same length as the line on the first card. The answers were "2," "2," "2," "2," "2," "2." Again it was your turn. You said "2," and perhaps your mind began to wander. Your stomach was gurgling a bit. The fellow after you said "2."

Another pair of cards was held up. Line 3 was clearly the correct answer. The six people on your right spoke in turn: "1," "1 . . ." Wait a second! ". . . 1," "1." You forgot about dinner and studied the lines briefly. No, line 1 was too short by a good half inch.

A. Standard line   **B.** Comparison lines

Figure 14.6
Cards Used in the Asch Study on Conformity

Which line on card B—1, 2, or 3—is the same length as the line on card A? Line 2, right? But would you say "2" if you were a member of a group and six people answering ahead of you all said "3"? Are you sure?

But the next two subjects said "1" and suddenly it was your turn. Your hands had become sweaty, and there was a lump in your throat. You wanted to say "3," but was it right? There was really no time, and you had already paused noticeably. You said "1," and so did the last fellow.

Now your attention was riveted on the task. Much of the time you agreed with the other seven judges, but sometimes you did not. And for some reason beyond your understanding, they were in perfect agreement even when they were wrong—assuming you could trust your eyes. The experiment was becoming an uncomfortable experience, and you began to doubt your judgment.

The discomfort in the Asch study was caused by the pressure to conform. Actually, the other seven recruits were confederates of the experimenter. They prearranged a number of incorrect responses. The sole purpose of the study was to see whether you would conform to the erroneous group judgments.

How many people in Asch's study caved in? How many went along with the crowd rather than give what they thought to be the right answer? Seventy-five percent. *Three out of four agreed with the majority's wrong answer at least once.*

Factors That Influence Conformity

Several factors increase the tendency to conform. They include the following:

- Belonging to a collectivist rather than an individualistic society (Phalet & Schoenpflug, 2001).
- The desire to be liked by other members of the group (but valuing being right over being liked *decreases* the tendency to conform).
- Low self-esteem.
- Social shyness (Santee & Maslach, 1982).
- Lack of familiarity with the task.

Other factors in conformity include group size and social support. The likelihood of conformity, even to incorrect group judgments, increases rapidly as group size grows to five members, then rises more slowly as the group grows to about eight members. At about that point the maximum chance of conformity is reached. Yet finding just one other person who supports your minority opinion apparently is enough to encourage you to stick to your guns (Morris et al., 1977).

Learning Connections
See Web site for an interactive version of these review questions.

R E V I E W

(16) Most people (do or do not?) comply with the demands of authority figures, even when the demands are immoral. (17) The following factors contribute to obedience: socialization, lack of _____ comparison, perception of experimenters as legitimate authority figures, and inaccessibility of values. (18) In Asch's studies of conformity, _____% of the subjects agreed with an incorrect majority judgment at least once.

Critical Thinking: How will the information in this section affect your own tendency to obey authority figures? How will it affect your tendency to conform to group norms?

GROUP BEHAVIOR

To be human is to belong to groups. Groups have much to offer us. They help us satisfy our needs for affection, attention, and belonging. They empower us to do things we could not manage by ourselves. But groups can also pressure us into doing things we might not do if we were acting alone, such as taking great risks or attacking other people.

This section considers ways in which people behave differently as group members than they would as individuals. We begin with social facilitation.

Social Facilitation: Monkey See, Monkey Do Faster?

One effect of groups on individual behavior is **social facilitation,** or the effects on performance that result from the presence of others.   *Question: Do we run faster when we are in a group?*   Apparently so. Runners and bicycle riders tend to move faster when they are members of a group. This effect is not limited to people. Dogs and cats eat more rapidly around others. Even roaches—yes, roaches—run more rapidly when other roaches are present (Zajonc, 1980).

Research suggests that the presence of other people increases our levels of arousal, or motivation (Platania & Moran, 2001; Thomas et al., 2002). At high levels of arousal, our performance of simple tasks is facilitated. Our performance of complex responses may be impaired, however. For this reason, a well-rehearsed speech may be delivered more masterfully before a larger audience. An offhand speech or a question-and-answer session may be hampered by a large audience.

Social facilitation may be influenced by **evaluation apprehension** as well as arousal (Platania & Moran, 2001; Thomas et al., 2002). Our performance before a group is affected not only by the presence of others but also by concern that they are evaluating us. When giving a speech, we may "lose our thread" if we are distracted by the audience and focus too much on its apparent reaction. If we believe that we have begun to flounder, evaluation apprehension may skyrocket. As a result, our performance may falter even more.

The presence of others can also impair performance—not when we are acting *before* a group but when we are anonymous members *of* a group (Guerin, 1999). Workers, for example, may "goof off" or engage in *social loafing* on humdrum jobs when they believe they will not be found out and held accountable. Under these conditions there is no evaluation apprehension. There may also be **diffusion of responsibility** in groups. Each person may feel less obligation to help because others are present, especially if the others are perceived as being capable of doing the job (Hart et al., 2001). Group members may also reduce their efforts if an apparently capable member makes no contribution but "rides free" on the efforts of others.

How would you perform in a tug-of-war? Would the presence of other people pulling motivate you to pull harder? (If so, we might attribute the result to "social facilitation," unless you personally enjoy tugging [Smith et al., 2001].) Or would the

REFLECT

Families, classes, religious groups, political parties, nations, circles of friends, bowling teams, sailing clubs, conversation groups, therapy groups— how many groups do you belong to? How does belonging to groups influence your behavior?

REFLECT

When you are given a group assignment, do you work harder or less hard than you would alone? Why?

Social Facilitation
The process by which a person's performance is increased when other members of a group engage in similar behavior.

Evaluation Apprehension
Concern that others are evaluating our behavior.

Diffusion of Responsibility
The spreading or sharing of responsibility for a decision or behavior within a group.

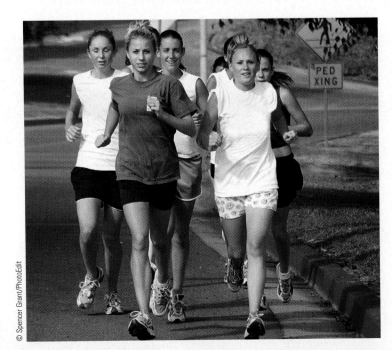

■ **Social Facilitation**
Runners tend to move faster when they are members of a group. Does the presence of other people raise our levels of arousal or produce "evaluation apprehension"?

© Spencer Grant/PhotoEdit

fact that no one can tell how hard you are pulling encourage you to "loaf"? (If so, should we attribute the result to "diffusion of responsibility"?)

Group Decision Making: Is a Camel a Horse Made by a Committee?

Organizations use groups such as committees or juries to make decisions in the belief that group decisions are more accurate than individual decisions (Gigone & Hastie, 1997). *Question: How do groups make decisions?* Social psychologists have discovered a number of "rules," or **social decision schemes,** that govern much of group decision making (Stasser, 1999). Here are some examples:

- *The majority-wins scheme:* In this commonly used scheme, the group arrives at the decision that was initially supported by the majority. This scheme appears to guide decision making most often when there is no single objectively correct decision. An example would be a decision about which car models to build when their popularity has not been tested in the court of public opinion.
- *The truth-wins scheme:* In this scheme, as more information is provided and opinions are discussed, the group comes to recognize that one approach is objectively correct. For example, a group deciding whether to use SAT scores in admitting students to college would profit from information about whether the scores do predict college success.
- *The two-thirds majority scheme:* Juries tend to convict defendants when two-thirds of the jury initially favors conviction.
- *The first-shift rule:* In this scheme, the group tends to adopt the decision that reflects the first shift in opinion expressed by any group member. If a car-manufacturing group is divided on whether to produce a convertible, it may opt to do so after one member of the group who initially was opposed to the idea changes her mind. Similarly, if a jury is deadlocked, the members may eventually follow the lead of the first juror to switch his position.

Polarization and the "Risky Shift"

We might think that a group decision would be more conservative than an individual decision. After all, shouldn't there be an effort to compromise, to "split the difference"? We might also expect that a few mature individuals would be able to balance the opinions of daredevils. *Questions: Are group decisions more risky or more conservative than those of the individual members of the group? Why?*

R E F L E C T

Have you been part of a group decision-making process? How did the group arrive at its decisions? Do you believe that the group decision reflected the judgments of the individuals in the group? Explain.

Social Decision Schemes
Rules for predicting the final outcome of group decision making on the basis of the members' initial positions.

■ **How Will This Jury Make Their Decision?**
Will the majority prevail? Will someone point to a significant piece of evidence that sways the day? Will the group follow the lead of the first person to change his or her mind? What other possibilities are there?

© Royalty-Free/CORBIS

Groups do not always appear to work as we might expect, however. Consider the **polarization** effect. As an individual, you might recommend that your company risk an investment of $500,000 to develop or market a new product. Other company executives, polled individually, might risk similar amounts. If you were gathered together to make a group decision, however, you would probably recommend either an amount well above this figure or nothing at all (Kamalanabhan et al., 2000; Mordock, 1997). This group effect is called *polarization,* or the taking of an extreme position. If you had to gamble on which way the decision would go, however, you would do better to place your money on movement toward the higher sum—that is, to bet on a **risky shift.** Why?

One possibility is that one member of the group may reveal information that the others were not aware of. This information may clearly point in one direction or the other. With doubts removed, the group becomes polarized. It moves decisively in the appropriate direction. It is also possible that social facilitation occurs in the group setting and that the resulting greater motivation prompts more extreme decisions.

Why, however, do groups tend to take *greater* risks than those their members would take as individuals? One answer is diffusion of responsibility (Kamalanabhan et al., 2000; Mordock, 1997). If the venture flops, the blame will not be placed on you alone. Remember the self-serving bias: You can always say (and think) that the failure was the result of a group decision. You thus protect your self-esteem (Larrick, 1993). If the venture pays off, however, you can attribute the outcome to your cool analysis and boast of your influence on the group. Note that all this behavior fits right in with what is known about the self-serving bias.

Groupthink

Groupthink, a concept originated by Irving Janis (1982), is a problem that sometimes arises in group decision making. *Question: What is groupthink?* In **groupthink,** group members tend to be more influenced by group cohesiveness and a dynamic leader than by the realities of the situation (Eaton, 2001; Postmes et al., 2001). Group problem solving may degenerate into groupthink when a group senses an external threat (Rempel & Fisher, 1998). Groupthink is usually fueled by a dynamic group leader. The threat heightens the cohesiveness of the group and is a source of stress. Under stress, group members tend not to consider all their options carefully. Flawed decisions are frequently made as a result.

Groupthink has been connected with fiascos such as the Bay of Pigs invasion of Cuba, the Watergate scandal, the Iran–Contra affair, and NASA's decision to launch the *Challenger* space shuttle despite engineers' warnings about the dangers created by unusually cold weather (Raven, 1998; Turner & Pratkanis, 1998). Janis (1982) and other researchers (Turner & Pratkanis, 1998) note several characteristics of groupthink that contribute to flawed group decisions:

- *Feelings of invulnerability:* Each decision-making group might have believed that it was beyond the reach of critics or the law—in some cases, because the groups consisted of powerful people who were close to the president of the United States.
- *The group's belief in its rightness:* These groups apparently believed in the rightness of what they were doing. In some cases, they were carrying out the president's wishes. In the case of the *Challenger* launch, NASA had a track record of successful launches.
- *Discrediting of information contrary to the group's decision:* The government group involved in the Iran–Contra affair knowingly broke the law. Its members apparently discredited the law by (1) deciding that it was inconsistent with the best interests of the United States and (2) enlisting private citizens to do the dirty work so that the government was not directly involved.
- *Pressures on group members to conform:* Group cohesiveness and a dynamic leader pressure group members to conform.
- *Stereotyping of members of the out-group:* Members of the group that broke the law in the Iran–Contra affair reportedly stereotyped people who would oppose them as "communist sympathizers" and "knee-jerk liberals."

Polarization
In social psychology, taking an extreme position or attitude on an issue.

Risky Shift
The tendency to make riskier decisions as a member of a group than as an individual acting independently.

Groupthink
A process in which group members are influenced by cohesiveness and a dynamic leader to ignore external realities as they make decisions.

Groupthink can be averted if group leaders encourage members to remain skeptical about options and to feel free to ask probing questions and disagree with one another.

Mob Behavior and Deindividuation: The "Beast with Many Heads"

The Frenchman Gustave Le Bon (1895/1960) branded mobs and crowds as irrational, resembling a "beast with many heads." Mob actions such as race riots and lynchings sometimes seem to operate on a psychology of their own. **Questions: Do mobs bring out the beast in us? How is it that mild-mannered people commit mayhem when they are part of a mob?** In seeking an answer, let us examine a lynching.

The Lynching of Arthur Stevens

In their classic volume *Social Learning and Imitation,* Neal Miller and John Dollard (1941) vividly described a lynching that occurred in the South in the 1930s. Arthur Stevens, an African American, was accused of murdering his lover, a European American woman, when she wanted to break up with him. Stevens was arrested, and he confessed to the crime. Fearing violence, the sheriff moved Stevens to a town 200 miles away during the night. But his location was discovered. On the next day a mob of a hundred people stormed the jail and returned Stevens to the scene of the crime.

Outrage spread from one member of the mob to another like a plague bacillus. Laborers, professionals, women, adolescents, and law-enforcement officers alike were infected. Stevens was tortured and murdered. His corpse was dragged through the streets. The mob then went on a rampage, chasing and assaulting other African Americans. The riot ended only when troops were sent in to restore law and order.

Deindividuation

When people act as individuals, fear of consequences and self-evaluation tend to prevent them from engaging in antisocial behavior. But in a mob, they may experience **deindividuation,** a state of reduced self-awareness and lowered concern for social evaluation. Many factors lead to deindividuation. These include anonymity, diffusion of responsibility, arousal due to noise and crowding, and a focus on emerging group norms rather than on one's own values (Baron & Byrne, 2003). Under these circumstances, crowd members behave more aggressively than they would as individuals.

Police know that mob actions are best averted early by dispersing small groups that could gather into a crowd. On an individual level, perhaps we can resist deindividua-

Deindividuation
The process by which group members may discontinue self-evaluation and adopt group norms and attitudes.

■ **An Angry Mob Is Contained by Police**
The French social thinker Gustave Le Bon branded mobs as irrational, like a "beast with many heads." Police are taught that it's useful to confront groups as early as possible, to prevent them from becoming so highly emotionally aroused that they forget their values as individuals and focus on the emerging group norms.

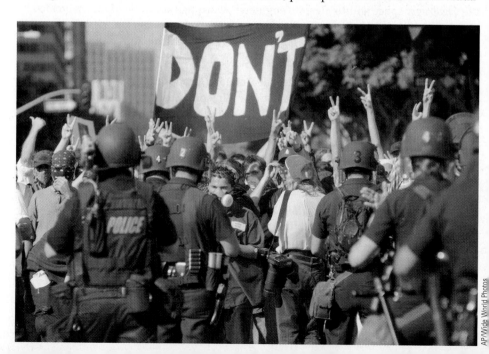

tion by instructing ourselves to stop and think whenever we begin to feel highly aroused in a group. If we dissociate ourselves from such groups when they are forming, we are more likely to remain critical and avoid behavior that we might later regret.

Altruism and the Bystander Effect: Some Watch While Others Die

Altruism—selfless concern for the welfare of others—is connected with some heroic and some very strange behavior throughout the animal kingdom. Humans have been known to sacrifice themselves to ensure the survival of their children or of comrades in battle. Primates sometimes suicidally attack the leopard to give others the opportunity to escape.

These behaviors are heroic. But consider the red spider's strange ways (Begley & Check, 2000). After depositing its sperm into a female red spider, the male of the species flips into her mouth and becomes her dinner! Clearly, the red spider is not bothered by the spark of consciousness, and it certainly is blind to the light of reason. But evolutionary psychologists might argue that the self-sacrificing behavior of the male red spider is actually selfish from an evolutionary point of view. How, you might wonder, can individuals sacrifice themselves and at the same time be acting in their own self-interests? To answer the question, you should also know that female red spiders are promiscuous; they will mate with multiple suitors. However, eating a "lover" slows them down, increasing the probability that his sperm will fertilize her eggs, and that his genes will survive and be transmitted to the next generation. We could thus say that the male red spider is altruistic in that he puts the welfare of future generations ahead of his own. Fatherhood ain't easy.

Red spiders, of course, do not think—at least, not in any humanly understandable sense of the concept of thinking. But people do. So how, one might ask, could the murder of 28-year-old Kitty Genovese have happened? It took place in New York City more than a generation ago. Murder was not unheard of in the Big Apple, but Kitty had screamed for help as her killer stalked her for more than half an hour and stabbed her in three separate attacks (Rosenthal, 1994). Thirty-eight neighbors heard the commotion. Twice the assault was interrupted by their voices and bedroom lights. Each time the attacker returned. Yet nobody came to the victim's aid. No one even called the police. Why? Some witnesses said matter-of-factly that they did not want to get involved. One said that he was tired. Still others said "I don't know." As a nation, are we a callous bunch who would rather watch than help when others are in trouble?

Question: Why do people sometimes sacrifice themselves for others and, at other times, ignore people who are in trouble?   Why did 38 bystanders allow Kitty Genovese to die? When do we decide to come to the aid of someone who is in trouble?

The Helper: Who Helps?

It turns out that many factors are involved in helping behavior. The following are among them:

- Observers are more likely to help when they are in a good mood (Baron & Byrne, 2003). Perhaps good moods impart a sense of personal power—the feeling that we can handle the situation (Cunningham et al., 1990).
- People who are empathic are more likely to help people in need (Darley, 1993). Empathic people feel the distress of others, feel concern for them, and can imagine what it must be like to be in need. Women are more likely than men to be empathic, and thus more likely to help people in need (Trobst et al., 1994).
- Bystanders may not help unless they believe that an emergency exists (Baron & Byrne, 2003). Perhaps some people who heard Kitty Genovese's calls for help were not certain as to what was happening. (But remember that others admitted they did not want to get involved.)
- Observers must assume the responsibility to act (Baron & Byrne, 2003). It may seem logical that a group of people would be more likely to have come to the aid of Kitty Genovese than a lone person. After all, a group could more effectively have overpowered her attacker. Yet research by Darley and Latané (1968) suggests that a lone person may have been more likely to try to help her.

Altruism
Unselfish concern for the welfare of others.

In their classic experiment, male subjects were performing meaningless tasks in cubicles when they heard a (convincing) recording of a person apparently having an epileptic seizure. When the men thought that four other persons were immediately available, only 31% tried to help the victim. When they thought that no one else was available, however, 85% of them tried to help. As in other areas of group behavior, it seems that *diffusion of responsibility* inhibits helping behavior in groups or crowds. When we are in a group, we are often willing to let George (or Georgette) do it. When George isn't around, we are more willing to help others ourselves. (Perhaps some who heard Kitty Genovese thought, "Why should I get involved? Other people can hear her too.")

- Observers must know what to do (Baron & Byrne, 2003). We hear of cases in which people impulsively jump into the water to save a drowning child and then drown themselves. Most of the time, however, people do not try to help unless they know what to do. For example, nurses are more likely than people without medical training to try to help accident victims (Cramer et al., 1988). Observers who are not sure that they can take charge of the situation may stay on the sidelines for fear of making a social blunder and being ridiculed. Or they may fear getting hurt themselves. (Perhaps some who heard Kitty Genovese thought, "If I try to intervene, I may get killed or make an idiot of myself.")

- Observers are more likely to help people they know (Rutkowski et al., 1983). Aren't we also more likely to give to charity when asked directly by a coworker or supervisor in the socially exposed situation of the office as compared with a letter received in the privacy of our own homes?

   Evolutionary psychologists suggest that altruism is a natural aspect of human nature—even if not in the same way as in the case of the red spider! Self-sacrifice sometimes helps close relatives or others who are similar to us to survive. Self-sacrifice is "selfish" from a genetic or evolutionary point of view (Bruene & Ribbert, 2002). It helps us perpetuate a genetic code similar to our own. This view suggests that we are more likely to be altruistic with our relatives rather than strangers, however. The Kitty Genoveses of the world may remain out of luck unless they are surrounded by kinfolk or friends.

- Observers are more likely to help people who are similar to themselves. Being able to identify with the person in need appears to promote helping behavior (Cialdini et al., 1997). Poorly dressed people are more likely to succeed in requests for a dime with poorly dressed strangers. Well-dressed people are more likely to get money from well-dressed strangers (Hensley, 1981).

The Victim: Who Is Helped?

Although women are more likely than men to help people in need, it is traditional for men to help women, particularly in the South—at least a generation ago. Women were more likely than men to receive help, especially from men, when they dropped coins in Atlanta (a southern city) than in Seattle or Columbus (northern cities) (Latané & Dabbs, 1975). Why? The researchers suggest that traditional gender roles persist more strongly in the South.

Women are also more likely than men to be helped when their cars have broken down on the highway or they are hitchhiking. Is this gallantry or are there sexual overtones to some of this "altruism"? There may be, because attractive and unaccompanied women are most likely to be helped by men (Benson et al., 1976).

REFLECT

Research concerning altruism and the bystander effect highlight the fact that we are members of a vast, interdependent social fabric. The next time you see a stranger in need, what will you do? Are you sure?

Learning Connections
See Web site for an interactive version of these review questions.

REVIEW

(19) Social _____ refers to the enhancement of performance that results from the presence of others. (20) However, performance may decline when we are _____ members of a group. (21) Social-_____ schemes seem to govern group decision making: the majority-wins scheme, the truth-wins scheme, the two-thirds majority scheme, and the first-shift rule. (22) Groups are (more or less?) likely than individuals

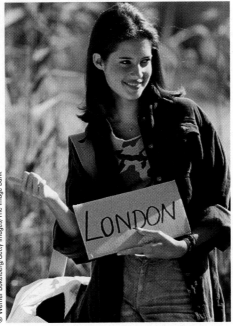

© Werner Bokelberg/Getty Images/The Image Bank

■ So, Which One Would You Give a Ride?

Social psychologists note that we are more willing to help people who are similar to ourselves. On the other hand, women are more likely to be helped than men. Is it because women appear to pose less of a threat or to be more in need? Is it chivalry? Or is something else at work?

to take extreme positions. (23) That is, people in a group are likely to experience a _____ shift. (24) Members of a group may experience _____, which is a state of reduced self-awareness and lowered concern for social evaluation. (25) Group-think is usually (realistic or unrealistic?). (26) Helping behavior is also known as _____.

Critical Thinking: What factors affect the decision to help other people? Does it seem likely that genetic "whisperings" play a role in altruism? Explain.

Understanding and Combating Prejudice

People have condemned billions of other people. Without ever meeting them. Without ever learning their names. In this section, we discuss some of the reasons for this. We will be dealing with a particularly troubling kind of attitude: prejudice. What is prejudice? Why are people prejudiced?

Prejudice is an attitude toward a group that leads people to evaluate members of that group negatively—even though they have never met them. On a cognitive level, prejudice is linked to expectations that members of the target group will behave poorly, say, in the workplace, or engage in criminal behavior. On an emotional level, prejudice is associated with negative feelings such as fear, dislike, or hatred. In behavioral terms, it is connected with avoidance, aggression, and discrimination. Prejudice is the most troubling kind of attitude. It is connected with the genocide of millions upon millions of people.

Discrimination

One form of negative behavior that results from prejudice is discrimination. Many groups in the United States have experienced discrimination—women, gay males and lesbians, older people, and ethnic groups such as African Americans, Asian Americans, Latino and Latina Americans, Irish Americans, Jewish Americans, and Native Americans. Discrimination takes many forms, including denial of access to jobs, housing, and the voting booth.

Stereotypes

Are Jewish Americans shrewd and ambitious? Are African Americans superstitious and musical? Are Californians "airheads"? Such ideas are *stereotypes*—prejudices about certain groups that lead people to view members of those groups in a biased fashion.

Some stereotypes are positive rather than negative, such as the cultural stereotypes about physically attractive people. By and large, we assume that "good things come in pretty packages." Attractive children and adults are judged and treated more posi-

tively than their unattractive peers (Langlois et al., 2000). We expect attractive people to be poised, sociable, popular, intelligent, mentally healthy, fulfilled, persuasive, and successful in their jobs and marriages (Eagly et al., 1991; Feingold, 1992b). Research shows that attractiveness is positively correlated with popularity, social skills, and sexual experience (Feingold, 1992b; Langlois et al., 2000).

Attractive people are even more likely to be judged innocent of crimes in mock jury experiments and observational studies (Mazzella & Feingold, 1994). When they are found guilty, they are given less severe sentences. Perhaps we assume that attractive people have less need to resort to deviant behavior to achieve their goals. Even when they have erred, perhaps they will be more likely to change their evil ways.

Sources of Prejudice

The sources of prejudice are many and varied:

REFLECT

How do you treat people of different religions or races? Do you treat them as individuals or are your expectations based on stereotypes? Explain.

- *Dissimilarity:* We are apt to like people who share our attitudes. In forming impressions of others, we are influenced by attitudinal similarity and dissimilarity (Duckitt, 1992). People of different religions and races often have different backgrounds, however, giving rise to dissimilar attitudes. Even when people of different races share important values, they may assume that they do not.
- *Social conflict:* There is often social and economic conflict between people of different races and religions. For example, for many decades Southern European Americans and African Americans have competed for jobs, giving rise to negative attitudes and even lynchings (Green et al., 1998).

■ **Stereotyping**
How well is this child doing? Research shows that our expectations concerning a child's performance on a test are linked to our awareness of that child's socioeconomic background.

© Jeff Greenberg/Index Stock Imagery

- *Social learning:* Children acquire some attitudes from other people, especially their parents. Children tend to imitate their parents, and parents reinforce their children for doing so (Duckitt, 1992). In this way prejudices can be transmitted from generation to generation.

The mass media also perpetuate stereotypes. TV commercials tend to portray European Americans, especially men, as being more prominent and wielding more authority than African Americans (Coltraine & Messineo, 2000). European Americans, especially women, are portrayed as being more likely to obtain romantic and domestic fulfillment. In general, European American men tend to be portrayed as powerful, European American women as sex objects, African American men as aggressive, and African American women as unimportant.

- *Information processing:* One cognitive view is that prejudices act as cognitive filters through which we perceive the social world. The brain tends to automatically place people into categories such as "familiar" and "foreign," and "good" and "bad." Such categorization may then bias people's feelings and reactions toward others (Azar, 2002). It is also easier to attend to, and remember, instances of behavior that are consistent with our biases than it is to reconstruct our mental categories (Kashima, 2000; Sherman & Frost, 2000). If you believe that Jewish Americans are stingy, it is easier to recall a Jewish American's negotiation of a price than a Jewish American's charitable donation. If you believe that Californians are airheads, it may be easier to recall TV images of surfing than of scientific conferences at Caltech and Berkeley. On the other hand, people are often likely to evaluate messages from stigmatized groups such as gay males or African Americans extra carefully, in an effort to make sure that they are judging on the basis of the message and not the deliverer of the message (Petty et al., 1999).

- *Social categorization:* A second cognitive perspective focuses on the tendency to divide our social world into "us" and "them." People usually view those who belong to their own groups—the "in-group"—more favorably than those who do not—the "out-group" (Duckitt, 1992). Moreover, there is a tendency to assume that members of the out-group are more similar in their attitudes and behavior than members of our own groups (Mussweiler & Bodenhausen, 2002). Our isolation from the out-group makes it easier to maintain our stereotypes.

Combating Prejudice

Prejudice has been with us throughout history, and it is unlikely that a miracle cure is at hand. Yet we need not stand idly by when we witness prejudice. We can create millions of mini-miracles—changes in those of us who wish to end prejudice. Here are some things we can do to combat prejudice:

- *Encourage intergroup contact and cooperation.* Prejudice encourages us to avoid other groups, which is unfortunate because intergroup contact is one way of breaking down prejudices (Baron & Byrne, 2003). Intergroup contact reveals that members of religious and racial groups have varying values, abilities, interests, and personalities. That is, contact heightens awareness of individual variation, and this knowledge can

■ Intergroup Contact

Intergroup contact can reduce feelings of prejudice when people work together toward common goals.

lead us to abandon stereotypical thinking (Hewstone & Hamberger, 2000; Sherman & Frost, 2000). Intergroup contact is especially effective when people are striving to meet common goals. Playing on the same team, working together on a joint educational project or the yearbook are examples.

A classic experiment by Muzafer Sherif and his colleagues (1961/1988) showed how feelings of prejudice can be created and reduced. They randomly divided 11-year-old male campers at Oklahoma's Robbers Cave State Park into two groups, who labeled themselves the Eagles and the Rattlers. After being kept apart for a week, the Eagles and Rattlers met in competitive games. A bitter rivalry quickly erupted, in which the Eagles burned the Rattlers' flag and the Rattlers retaliated by trashing the Eagles' cabin. Eating and watching movies together were not enough to overcome the feelings of hostility felt by the groups. The Eagles and the Rattlers became friends only after they had worked together to achieve common goals, such as repairing the camp's water supply and fixing a truck that was carrying food to the camp (both of which had been sabotaged by the experimenters).

- *Present examples of admired individuals within groups that are often stigmatized.* Nilanjana Dasgupta and Anthony G. Greenwald (2001) found that they could modify negative attitudes toward African Americans by presenting photographs of admired African American individuals. Similarly, they could combat automatic preference for European Americans by presenting pictures of Europeans who were disliked. The effects of bringing admired individuals to mind will presumably work with verbal reminders as well.

- *Attack discriminatory behavior.* It is sometimes easier to change people's behavior than to alter their feelings. Yet cognitive dissonance theory suggests that when we change people's behavior, their feelings may follow along. It is illegal to deny access to an education and jobs on the basis of gender, religion, race, or disability. Seek legal remedies if you have been discriminated against. Have you been denied access to living accommodations or a job because of prejudice? Talk about it to your academic advisor, the college equal opportunity office, or the dean of students. Unfortunately, many members of ethnic minority groups are reluctant to discuss instances of discrimination with members of majority groups, such as European American males (Stangor et al., 2002).

- *Hold discussion forums.* Many campuses conduct workshops and discussion groups on gender, race, and diversity. Talk to your dean of students about holding such workshops.
- *Examine your own beliefs.* Prejudice isn't "out there." Prejudice dwells within us. It is easy to focus on the prejudices of others, but what about our own? Have you examined your own attitudes and rejected stereotyping and prejudice?

Even if we do not personally harbor feelings of racial or religious enmity, are we doing anything to counter such feelings in others? Do we confront people who make prejudiced remarks? Do we belong to organizations that deny access to members of other racial and religious groups? Do we strike up conversations with people from other groups or avoid them? College is meant to be a broadening experience, and we deny ourselves much of the education we could be receiving when we limit our encounters to people who share our own backgrounds.

Recite Recite Recite

Learning Connections
See Web site for an interactive version of this chapter summary

---

1. **What is social psychology?**

Social psychology is the field of psychology that studies the factors that influence people's thoughts, feelings, and behaviors in social situations.

2. **What are attitudes?**

Attitudes are behavioral and cognitive tendencies expressed by evaluating particular people, places, or things with favor or disfavor.

3. **Do people do as they think? (For example, do people really vote their consciences?)**

When we are free to act as we wish, our behavior is often consistent with our beliefs and feelings. But as indicated by the term *A–B problem,* the links between attitudes (A) and behaviors (B) are often weak to moderate. The following strengthen the A–B connection: specificity of attitudes, strength of attitudes, whether people have a vested interest in the outcome of their behavior, and the accessibility of the attitudes.

4. **Where do attitudes come from?**

Attitudes are acquired (not inborn). They can be learned somewhat mechanically by means of conditioning or learning by observation. However, people also appraise and evaluate situations and often form their own judgments.

5. **Can you really change people?— their attitudes and behavior, that is?**

People attempt to change other people's attitudes and behavior by means of persuasion. According to the elaboration likelihood model, persuasion occurs through both central and peripheral routes. Change occurs through the central route by means of consideration of arguments and evidence. Peripheral routes involve associating the objects of attitudes with positive or negative cues, such as attractive or unattractive communicators. Repeated messages generally "sell" better than messages delivered only once. People tend to show greater response to fear appeals than to purely factual presentations. This is especially so when the appeals offer concrete advice for avoiding negative outcomes. Persuasive communicators tend to show expertise, trustworthiness, attractiveness, or similarity to the audience. In the foot-in-the-door technique, people are asked to comply with larger requests after they have complied with smaller ones.

6. **Do first impressions really matter? What are the primacy and recency effects?**

First impressions can last (the primacy effect) because we tend to label or describe people in terms of the behavior we see initially. The recency effect appears to be based on the fact that—other things being equal—recently learned information is easier to remember.

7. **What is attribution theory? Why do we assume that other people intend the mischief that they do?**

The tendency to infer the motives and traits of others through observation of their behavior is referred to as the attribution process. In dispositional attributions, we attribute people's behavior to internal factors such as their personality traits and decisions. In situational attributions, we attribute people's behavior to their circumstances or external forces. According to the actor–observer effect, we tend to attribute the behavior of others to internal, dispositional factors. However, we tend to attribute our own behavior to external, situational factors. The so-called fundamental attribution error is the tendency to attribute too much of other people's behavior to dispositional factors. The self-serving bias refers to the finding that we tend to attribute our successes to internal, stable factors and our failures to external, unstable factors. The attribution of behavior to internal or external causes is influenced by three factors: consensus, consistency, and distinctiveness. For example, when few people act in a certain way—that is, when the consensus is low—we are likely to attribute behavior to internal factors.

8. **What is body language?**

Body language refers to the tendency to infer people's thoughts and feelings from their postures and gestures. For example, people who feel positively toward one another position themselves closer together and are more likely to touch. Touching results in a negative reaction when it suggests more intimacy than is desired. Gazing into another's eyes can be a sign of love, but a hard stare is an aversive challenge. Women are more likely than men to touch people with whom they are interacting.

Recite Recite Recite

9. What factors contribute to attraction in our culture?

Men seem to find large eyes and narrows jaws to be attractive in women. In our culture, slenderness is considered attractive in both men and women, and tallness is valued in men. Women tend to see themselves as being heavier than the cultural ideal. We are more attracted to good-looking people. Similarity in attitudes and sociocultural factors (ethnicity, education, and so on), and reciprocity in feelings of admiration, also enhance attraction. According to the matching hypothesis, we tend to seek dates and mates at our own level of attractiveness, largely because of fear of rejection.

10. Just what is love? What is romantic love?

Sternberg's theory suggests that love has three components: intimacy, passion, and commitment. Different kinds of love combine these components in different ways. Romantic love is characterized by the combination of passion and intimacy. Consummate love has all three factors.

11. Why will so many people commit crimes against humanity if they are ordered to do so? (Why don't they refuse?)

The majority of subjects in the Milgram studies complied with the demands of authority figures, even when the demands required that they hurt innocent people by means of electric shock. Factors contributing to obedience include socialization, lack of social comparison, perception of legitimate authority figures, the foot-in-the-door technique, inaccessibility of values, and buffers between the perpetrator and the victim.

12. Why do so many people tend to follow the crowd?

Asch's research in which subjects judged the lengths of lines suggests that the majority of people will follow the crowd, even when the crowd is wrong. Personal factors such as desire to be liked by group members, low self-esteem, high self-consciousness, and shyness contribute to conformity. Belonging to a collectivist society and group size also contribute to conformity.

13. Do we run faster when we are in a group?

The concept of social facilitation refers to the effects on performance that result from the presence of other people. The presence of others may facilitate performance for reasons such as increased arousal and evaluation apprehension. However, when we are anonymous group members, we may experience diffusion of responsibility and task performance may fall off. This phenomenon is termed *social loafing*.

14. How do groups make decisions?

Social psychologists have identified several decision-making schemes, including the majority-wins scheme, the truth-wins scheme, the two-thirds majority scheme, and the first-shift rule.

15. Are group decisions more risky or more conservative than those of the individual members of the group? Why?

Group decisions tend to be more polarized and riskier than individual decisions, largely because groups diffuse responsibility. Group decisions may be highly productive when group members are knowledgeable, there is an explicit procedure for arriving at decisions, and there is a process of give and take.

16. What is groupthink?

Groupthink is an unrealistic kind of decision making that is fueled by the perception of external threats to the group or to those whom the group wishes to protect. It is facilitated by a dynamic group leader, feelings of invulnerability, the group's belief in its rightness, the discrediting of information that contradicts the group's decision, conformity, and the stereotyping of members of the out-group.

17. Do mobs bring out the beast in us? How is it that mild-mannered people commit mayhem when they are part of a mob?

Highly emotional crowds may induce attitude-discrepant behavior through the process of *deindividuation*, which is a state of reduced self-awareness and lowered concern for social evaluation. The high emotions are connected with arousal that makes it more difficult to access one's own values.

Recite Recite Recite

18. Why do people sometimes sacrifice themselves for others and, at other times, ignore people who are in trouble?

A number of factors contribute to altruism (the tendency to help others). Among them are empathy, being in a good mood, feelings of responsibility, knowledge of how to help, and acquaintance with—and similarity to—the person in need of help. According to the bystander effect, we are unlikely to aid people in distress when we are members of crowds. Crowds tend to diffuse responsibility.

Active Learning Resources

 Search Online with InfoTrac® College Edition

For additional information on the topics in this chapter, explore InfoTrac College Edition, your online library. Go to **http://infotrac.thomsonlearning.com** and use the passcode that came on the card with your book. Try these search terms: stereotypes, mere exposure, fear appeal, attribution theory, self-serving bias, Milgram and authority, social loafing, groupthink, and prejudice and discrimination.

 Visit Our Web Site

Go to **http://www.wadsworth.com/psychology**, where you will find online resources directly linked to your book, including interactive exercises related to PQ4R and Power Visuals for mastering and reviewing key concepts. In addition, you will find hints on using InfoTrac College Edition to answer the Critical Thinking questions throughout the text. Start with the **Self Study Assessment** for a customized **Study Plan** generated by taking the **Pre-Test** and **Post-Test.**

 Connections CD-ROM

Go to the Wadsworth *Connections* CD-ROM for further study of the concepts in this chapter. The CD-ROM includes videos, animations, quizzes, and additional activities to expand your learning experience, plus interactive self-assessments to help connect the material to your own life.

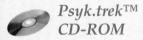 *Psyk.trek™ CD-ROM*

The Wadsworth *Psyk.trek* CD-ROM offers tutorials, simulations, videos, multimedia glossary, and quizzing to help you master the material.

 PsychNow! CD-ROM

The Wadsworth *PsychNow!* CD-ROM includes interactive exercises, videos, and animations to enhance your learning.

A Statistics

Statistics

- STATISTICS IS the science of obtaining and organizing numerical data.

- IF YOUR POPULATION is "people on planet Earth," how do you get a representative sample of them?

Descriptive Statistics

- BASKETBALL PLAYERS could be said to be abnormal. How so?

- BEING A "10" is not always a good thing.

- DON'T ASSUME you can walk across a river with an average depth of 4 feet.

- ADDING PEOPLE'S incomes and then dividing them by the number of people can be an awful way of showing the average income.

- HOW VARIABLE are the heights of women and men?

The Normal Curve

- A NORMAL CURVE is shaped like a bell.

- PSYCHOLOGISTS MAY express your IQ score in terms of how deviant you are.

- AN IQ SCORE of 130 is more impressive than an SAT score of 500.

The Correlation Coefficient

- DO INTROVERTED people go on more or fewer dates than extraverted people?

- CAN CORRELATIONAL research show that smoking cigarettes causes cancer?

Inferential Statistics

- INFERENTIAL STATISTICS tell us how confident we can be that we can apply measurements of a sample to the population that the sample represents.

- WE CANNOT CONCLUDE that men are taller than women unless we know the average heights of men and women and how much the heights within each group vary.

STATISTICS

Imagine that some visitors from outer space arrive outside Madison Square Garden in New York City. Their goal this dark and numbing winter evening is to learn all they can about planet Earth. They are drawn inside the Garden by lights, shouts, and warmth. The spotlighting inside rivets their attention to a wood-floored arena where the New York Big Apples are hosting the California Quakes in a briskly contested basketball game.

Our visitors use their sophisticated instruments to take some measurements of the players. Some interesting statistics are sent back to their planet of origin: It appears that (1) 100% of Earthlings are male, and (2) the height of Earthlings ranges from 6 feet 1 inch to 7 feet 2 inches.

These measurements are called **statistics.**   *Question: What is statistics?*   Statistics is the name given the science concerned with obtaining and organizing numerical information or measurements. Our imagined visitors have sent home statistics about the gender and size of human beings that are at once accurate and misleading. Although they accurately measured the basketball players (we have translated their units of measurement into feet and inches for readers' convenience), their small **sample** of Earth's **population** was, shall we say, distorted.

Question: What are samples and populations?   A population is a complete group of people, other animals, or measures from which a sample is drawn. For example, all people on Earth could be defined as the population of interest. So could all women, or all women in the United States. A sample is a group of measures drawn from a population. Fortunately for us Earthlings, about half of the world's population is female. And the **range** of heights observed by the aliens, of 6 feet 1 inch to 7 feet 2 inches, is both restricted and too high—much too high. People vary in height by more than 1 foot and 1 inch. And our **average** height is not between 6 feet 1 inch and 7 feet 2 inches; rather, it is a number of inches below.

Psychologists, like our imagined visitors, are vitally concerned with measuring human as well as animal characteristics and traits—not just physical characteristics like height, but also psychological traits like intelligence, sociability, aggressiveness, neatness, anxiety, and depression. By observing the central tendencies (averages) and variations in measurement from person to person, psychologists can say that one person is average or above average in intelligence or that someone else is less anxious than, say, 60% of the population.

But psychologists, unlike our aliens, are careful in their attempts to select a sample that accurately represents the entire population. Professional basketball players do not represent the entire human species. They are taller, stronger, and more agile than the rest of us. They also make appreciably more commercials for sneakers. (Fans consider these abnormalities to be assets, not deficits.)

In this appendix we survey some of the statistical methods used by psychologists to draw conclusions about the measurements they take in research activities. First we discuss *descriptive statistics* and learn what types of statements we can make about height and other human traits. Then we discuss the *normal curve* and learn why basketball players are abnormal—at least in terms of height. We explain *correlation coefficients* and provide you with some less-than-shocking news: As a group, students who study obtain higher grades than students who do not study. Finally, we have a look at *inferential statistics,* and we see why we can be bold enough to say that the difference in height between basketball players and other people is not a chance fluctuation or fluke. Basketball players are in fact *statistically significantly* taller than the general population.

REFLECT

Why would the observations of the basketball players give the aliens a distorted impression of the traits of Earthlings?

Statistics
Numerical facts assembled in such a manner that they provide useful information about measures or scores. (From the Latin *status,* meaning "standing" or "position.")

Sample
Part of a population.

Population
A complete group from which a sample is selected.

Range
A measure of variability defined as the high score in a distribution minus the low score.

Average
The central tendency of a group of measures, expressed either as the mean, median, or mode of a distribution.

REVIEW

(1) The science that obtains and organizes numerical information or measurements is called _____. (2) The _____ of heights of the basketball players discussed in this section was restricted and too high to represent the general population. (3) By observing the _____ tendencies (averages) and variations in measurement from person to person, psychologists can say that an individual is average or above average in some trait or behavior.

Critical Thinking: What is the relationship between a population and a sample?

Learning Connections
See Web site for an interactive version of these review questions.

DESCRIPTIVE STATISTICS

Being told that someone is a "10" may sound great at first. However, it is not very descriptive unless you know something about how the scores on the scale are distributed and how frequently one finds a 10. Fortunately—for 10s, if not for the rest of us—one usually means that the person is a 10 on a scale of from 1 to 10, and that 10 is the highest possible score on the scale. If this is not sufficient, one will also be told that 10s are few and far between—rather unusual statistical events. But note that the scale could also vary from 0 to 100, in which case a score of 10 would place one nearer to the bottom of the scale and make a score of 50 the center point of the scale. With such a scale, being a 10 would be much less impressive.

The idea of the scale from 1 to 10 may not be very scientific, but it does suggest something about **descriptive statistics**. *Question: What is descriptive statistics? (Why isn't it always good to be a "10"?)* Descriptive statistics is the branch of statistics that provides information about distributions of scores. We can use descriptive statistics to clarify our understanding of a distribution of scores such as heights, test grades, IQs, or even increases or decreases in measures of aggressive behavior following the drinking of alcohol. For example, descriptive statistics can help us determine measures of central tendency (averages), and to determine how much fluctuation or variability there is in the scores. Being a 10 loses much of its charm if the average score is an 11. Being a 10 is more remarkable in a distribution whose scores range from 1 to 10 than it is in a distribution whose scores range from 9 to 11.

Let us now consider some of the concerns of descriptive statistics: the frequency distribution, measures of central tendency (types of averages), and measures of variability.

The Frequency Distribution

Question: What is a frequency distribution? A **frequency distribution** takes scores or items of raw data, puts them into order as from the lowest to the highest, and indicates how often a score appears. A frequency distribution groups data according to class intervals, although the class may be a single unit (one), as in Table A.2. Table A.1 shows the rosters for a recent basketball game between the California Quakes and the New York Big Apples. The players are listed according to the numbers on their uniforms. Table A.2 shows a frequency distribution of the heights of the players, with the two teams combined. The class interval in Table A.2 is 1 inch.

It would also be possible to use other class intervals, such as 3 inches, as shown in Table A.3. In determining the size of a class interval, the researcher tries to collapse the

REFLECT

Would it take a 3.00, 4.00, or 5.00 grade point average for you to be a perfect student? Would yet another number be required? Explain?

Descriptive Statistics
The branch of statistics that is concerned with providing descriptive information about a distribution of scores.

Frequency Distribution
An ordered set of data that indicates the frequency (how often) with which scores appear.

TABLE A.1 Rosters of Quakes Versus Big Apples at New York: A glance at the rosters for a recent basketball game in which the New York Big Apples "entertained" the California Quakes shows that the heights of the team members, combined, ranged from 6 feet 1 inch to 7 feet 2 inches. Do the heights of the team members represent those of the general male population? What do you think?

California Quakes		New York Big Apples	
2 Callahan	6'7"	3 Roosevelt	6'1"
5 Daly	6'11'	12 Chaffee	6'5"
6 Chico	6'2"	13 Baldwin	6'9"
12 Capistrano	6'3"	25 Delmar	6'6"
21 Brentwood	6'5"	27 Merrick	6'8"
25 Van Nuys	6'3"	28 Hewlett	6'6"
31 Clemente	6'9"	33 Hollis	6'9"
32 Whittier	6'8"	42 Bedford	6'5"
41 Fernando	7'2"	43 Coram	6'2"
43 Watts	6'9"	45 Hampton	6'10"
53 Huntington	6'6"	53 Ardsley	6'10"

data into a small enough number of classes to ensure that they will be meaningful at a glance. But the researcher also tries to keep a large enough number of categories (classes) to ensure that important differences are not obscured.

Table A.3 obscures the fact that no players are 6 feet 4 inches tall. If the researcher believes that this information is extremely important, a class interval of 1 inch may be maintained.

TABLE A.2 Frequency Distribution of Basketball Players (Quakes and Big Apples Combined), with a One-Inch Class Interval

Class Interval	Number of Players in Class
6'1"–6'1.9"	1
6'2"–6'2.9"	2
6'3"–6'3.9"	2
6'4"–6'4.9"	0
6'5"–6'5.9"	3
6'6"–6'6.9"	3
6'7"–6'7.9"	1
6'8"–6'8.9"	2
6'9"–6'9.9"	4
6'10"–6'10.9"	2
6'11"–6'11.9"	1
7'0"–7'0.9"	0
7'1"–7'1.9"	0
7'2"–7'2.9"	1

TABLE A.3 Frequency Distribution of Heights of Basketball Players, Using a Three-Inch Class Interval

Class Interval	Number of Players in Class
6′1″–6′3.9″	5
6′4″–6′6.9″	6
6′7″–6′9.9″	7
6′10″–7′0.9″	3
7′1″–7′3.9″	1

Figure A.1 shows two methods of graphing the information in Table A.3: the **frequency histogram** and the **frequency polygon.** Students sometimes have difficulty interpreting graphs, but the purpose of graphs is to reveal key information about frequency distributions at a glance. Note that in both kinds of graph, the frequency histogram and the frequency polygon, the class intervals are usually drawn along the horizontal line. The horizontal line is also known as the X-axis. The numbers of cases (scores, persons, or events) in each class interval are shown along the vertical line, which is also known as the Y-axis. In the histogram, the number of scores in each class interval is represented by a bar—a rectangular solid—so that the graph looks like a series of steps. In the polygon, the number of scores in each class interval is plotted as a point. The points are connected to form a many-sided geometric figure (polygon). Note that empty class intervals were added at each end of the frequency polygon so that the sides of the figure could be brought down to the X-axis to close the geometric figure.

Measures of Central Tendency

Never try to walk across a river just because it has an average depth of four feet.

—Martin Friedman

As you see in the quip by Martin Friedman, a measure of central tendency can sometimes be misleading. ***Question: What are measures of central tendency?*** Measures of central tendency are "averages" that show the center or balancing points of a frequency distribution. There are three commonly used types of measures of central tendency: the *mean, median,* and *mode*. Each attempts to describe something about the scores in a frequency distribution through the use of a typical or representative number.

Frequency Histogram
A graphic representation of a frequency distribution that uses rectangular solids (bars) to represent the frequency with which scores appear.

Frequency Polygon
A graphic representation of a frequency distribution that connects the points that show the frequencies with which scores appear, thereby creating a multisided geometric figure.

■ **Figure A.1**
Two Graphical Representations of the Data in Table A.3
The graph on the left is called a frequency histogram, or bar graph. The graph on the right is called a frequency polygon.

Learning Connections
See the Connections *CD-ROM to step through a tutorial on measures of central tendency.*

R E F L E C T

Can you think of examples in your own experience in which the median or the mode would be a more accurate indicator of a central tendency than the mean? (Hint: Possibilities include class grades, IQ scores, and special abilities, as in music, art, and athletics.)

Mean

A type of average that is calculated by adding all the scores and then dividing by the number of scores.

Median

The central score in a frequency distribution; the score beneath which 50% of the cases fall.

Mode

The most frequently occurring number or score in a distribution.

Bimodal

Having two modes.

The **mean** is what most people think of as "the average." We obtain the mean of a distribution by adding up the scores and then dividing the sum by the number of scores. In the case of the basketball players, it would be advisable to first convert the heights into a single unit, such as inches (6'1" becomes 73", and so on). If we add all the heights in inches and then divide by the number of players (22), we obtain a mean height of 78.73". If we convert that number back into units of feet and inches, we obtain 6'6.73".

The **median** is the score of the middle case in a distribution. It is the score beneath which 50% of the cases fall. In a distribution with an even number of cases, such as the distribution of the heights of the 22 basketball players shown in Table A.2, we obtain the median by finding the mean of the two middle cases. When we list the 22 cases in ascending order (moving from lowest to highest), the 11th case is 6'6" and the 12th case is 6'7". Therefore, the median of the distribution is (6'6" + 6'7")/2, or 6'6½".

When we analyze the heights of the basketball players, we find that the mean and median are similar. Either one serves as a useful indicator of the central tendency of the data. But suppose we are trying to find the average savings of 30 families living on a suburban block. Let us assume that 29 of the 30 families have savings between $8,000 and $12,000, adding up to $294,000. But the 30th family has savings of $1,400,000! The mean savings for a family on this block would thus be $56,467. The mean can be greatly distorted by one or two extreme scores. An IQ score of 145 would similarly distort the mean of the IQ scores of a class of 20 students, among whom the other 19 IQ scores ranged from 93 to 112. Then, too, if a few basketball players signed up for one of your classes, the mean of the students' heights would be distorted in an upward direction. Therefore, adding people's incomes and then dividing them by the number of people can be an awful way of showing the average income. A few extremely high incomes, or IQ scores, or heights can distort the average of a group in an upward direction.

When there are a few extreme scores in a distribution, the median is a better indicator of central tendency. The median savings on our hypothetical block would lie between $8,000 and $12,000. Thus it would be more representative of the central tendency of savings. Studies of the incomes of families in the United States usually report median rather than mean incomes just to avoid the distortion of findings that would occur if the incomes of a handful of billionaires were treated in the same way as more common incomes. On the other hand, one could argue that choosing the median as the average obscures or hides the extreme scores, which are just as "real" as the other scores. Perhaps it is best to use the median and a footnote—a rather big footnote.

The **mode** is simply the most frequently occurring score or measure in a distribution. The mode of the data in Table A.1 is 6'9" because this height occurs most often among the players on the two teams. The median class interval for the data shown in Table A.3 is 6'6½" to 6'9½". With this particular distribution, the mode is somewhat higher than the mean or median.

In some cases the mode is a more appropriate description of the central tendency of a distribution than the mean or the median. Figure A.2 shows a **bimodal** distribution—that is, a distribution with two modes. This is a hypothetical distribution of test scores obtained by a class. The mode at the left indicates the most common class interval (45–49) for students who did not study, and the mode to the right shows the most common class interval (65–69) for students who did study. (Don't be alarmed. I'm sure that the professor, who is extremely fair, will be delighted to curve the grades so that the interval of 75–79 is an A+ and the interval of 65–69 is at least a B.) The mean and median test scores would probably lie within the 55–59 class interval, yet use of that interval as the measure of central tendency could obscure rather than reveal the important aspects of this distribution of test scores. It might suggest that the test was too hard, not that a number of students chose not to study. Similarly, one of the distribution's modes might be a bit larger than the other, so one could follow the exact rule for finding the mode and report just one of them. But this approach would also hide the meaning of this particular distribution of scores. All in all, it is clearly best to visualize this distribution of scores as bimodal. Even when the modes are not exactly equal, it is often most accurate to report distributions as bimodal, or when there are three or more modes, as multimodal. One chooses one's measure or measures of central tendency to describe the essential features of a frequency distribution, not to hide them.

Measures of Variability

Our hypothetical class obtained test scores ranging from class intervals of 35–39 to 75–79. That is, the scores *varied* from the lower class interval to the higher class interval. Now, if all the students had obtained scores from 55–59 to 65–69, the scores would not have varied as much; that is, they would have clustered closer to one another and would have had lower variability.

Question: What are measures of variability? The measures of the variability of a distribution inform us about the spread of scores—that is, about the typical distances of scores from the average score. Two commonly used measures of variability are the *range* of scores and the *standard deviation* of scores.

The range of scores in a distribution is defined as the difference between the highest score and the lowest score. The range is obtained by subtracting the lowest score from the highest score. The range of heights in Table A.2 is obtained by subtracting 6′1″ from 7′2″, or 1′1″. It is useful to know the range of temperatures when we move to an area with a different climate so that we may anticipate the weather and dress for it appropriately. A teacher must have some understanding of the range of abilities or skills in a class in order to teach effectively. An understanding of the range of human heights can be used to design doorways, beds, and headroom in automobiles. Even so, the typical doorway is 6′8″ high; and, as we saw with the California Quakes and New York Big Apples, some people will have to duck to get through.

The range is an imperfect measure of variability because of the manner in which it is influenced by extreme scores. The range of savings of the 30 families on our suburban block is $1,400,000 minus $8,000, or $1,392,000. This is a large number, and it is certainly true. However, it tells us little about the *typical* variation of savings accounts, which lie within a more restricted range of $8,000 to $12,000.

The **standard deviation** is a statistic that does a better job of showing how the scores in a distribution are distributed (spread) about the mean. It is usually better than the range because it considers every score in the distribution, not just the extreme (highest and lowest) scores. Consider Figure A.3. Each distribution in the figure has the same number of scores, the same mean, and the same range of scores. However, the scores in the distribution on the right side cluster more closely about the mean. Therefore, the standard deviation of the distribution on the right is smaller. That is, the typical score deviates less from the mean score.

The standard deviation is usually abbreviated as S.D. It is calculated by the formula

$$\text{S.D.} = \sqrt{\frac{\text{Sum of } d^2}{N}}$$

where *d* equals the deviation of each score from the mean of the distribution and *N* equals the number of scores in the distribution.

Figure A.2
A Bimodal Distribution

This hypothetical distribution represents students' scores on a test. The mode at the left represents the central tendency of the test scores of students who did not study. The mode at the right represents the mode of the test scores of students who did study. (I'm allowed to be moralistic about studying; I wrote the book.)

R E F L E C T

What is the range of test grades in your class? What is the standard deviation? Which measure gives a more accurate impression of the variability of grades? Explain.

Standard Deviation

A measure of the variability of a distribution, obtained by the formula

$$\text{S.D.} = \sqrt{\frac{\text{Sum of } d^2}{N}}$$

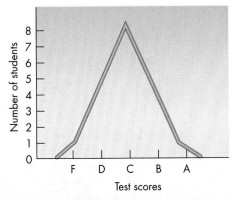

Figure A.3
Hypothetical Distributions of Student Test Scores

Each distribution has the same number of scores, the same mean, even the same range, but the standard deviation (a measure of variability) is greater for the distribution on the left because the scores tend to be farther from the mean.

Let us find the mean and standard deviation of the IQ scores listed in column 1 of Table A.4. To obtain the mean we add all the scores, attain 1,500, and then divide by the number of scores (15) to obtain a mean of 100. We obtain the deviation score (*d*) for each IQ score by subtracting the score from 100. The *d* for an IQ score of 85 equals 100 minus 85, or 15, and so on. Then we square each *d* and add the squares. The S.D. equals the square root of the sum of squares (1,426) divided by the number of scores (15), or 9.75.

As an additional exercise, we can show that the S.D. of the test scores on the left (in Figure A.3) is greater than that for the scores on the right. First we assign the grades a number according to a 4.0 system. Let A = 4, B = 3, C = 2, D = 1, and F = 0. The S.D. for each distribution is computed in Table A.5. The larger S.D. for the distribution on the left indicates that the scores in that distribution are more variable, or tend to be farther from the mean.

Learning Connections
See Web site for an interactive version of these review questions.

R E V I E W

(4) _____ statistics provides information about distributions of scores. (5) Descriptive statistics helps us determine measures of central tendency and how much fluctuation or _____ there is in a distribution. (6) A _____ distribution takes items of data, puts them into order, and indicates how often a score appears. (7) A frequency distribution groups data according to _____ intervals. (8) In the frequency histogram and polygon, the class intervals are usually drawn

TABLE A.4 Hypothetical Scores Obtained from an IQ Testing

IQ Score	d (Deviation Score)	d² (Deviation Score Squared)
85	15	225
87	13	169
89	11	121
90	10	100
93	7	49
97	3	9
97	3	9
100	0	0
101	−1	1
104	−4	16
105	−5	25
110	−10	100
112	−12	144
113	−13	169
117	−17	289

Sum of IQ scores = 1,500   Sum of d² scores = 1,426

$$\text{Mean} = \frac{\text{Sum of scores}}{\text{Number of scores}} = \frac{1,500}{15} = 100$$

$$\text{Standard Deviation (S.D.)} = \sqrt{\frac{\text{Sum of } d^2}{N}} = \sqrt{\frac{1,426}{15}} = \sqrt{95.07} = 9.75$$

TABLE A.5 Computation of Standard Deviations for Test-Score Distributions in Figure A.3

	Distribution at Left			Distribution to the Right	
Grade	d	d^2	Grade	d	d^2
A (4)	2	4	A (4)	2	4
A (4)	2	4	B (3)	1	1
A (4)	2	4	B (3)	1	1
B (3)	1	1	B (3)	1	1
B (3)	1	1	B (3)	1	1
B (3)	1	1	C (2)	0	0
B (3)	1	1	C (2)	0	0
C (2)	0	0	C (2)	0	0
C (2)	0	0	C (2)	0	0
C (2)	0	0	C (2)	0	0
C (2)	0	0	C (2)	0	0
D (1)	−1	1	C (2)	0	0
D (1)	−1	1	C (2)	0	0
D (1)	−1	1	D (1)	−1	1
D (1)	−1	1	D (1)	−1	1
F (0)	−2	4	D (1)	−1	1
F (0)	−2	4	D (1)	−1	1
F (0)	−2	4	F (0)	−2	4

Sum of grades = 36
Mean grade = 36/18 = 2
Sum of d^2 = 32
S.D. = $\sqrt{32/18}$ = 1.33

Sum of grades = 36
Mean grade = 36/18 = 2
Sum of d^2 = 16
S.D. = $\sqrt{16/18}$ = 0.94

along the X-axis, or (horizontal or vertical?) line. (9) The numbers of cases in each class interval are shown along the Y-axis, or (horizontal or vertical?) line. (10) We obtain the _____ of a distribution by adding the scores and then dividing the sum by the number of scores. (11) The _____ is the score beneath which 50% percent of the cases fall. (12) The _____ is the most frequently occurring measure in a distribution. (13) The range of scores is obtained by subtracting the _____ score from the highest score. (14) The standard deviation is calculated by the formula:

$$\text{S.D.} = \sqrt{\frac{\text{Sum of }\_\_^2}{N}}$$

Critical Thinking: Provide examples of distributions in which the median and mode are better measures of central tendency than the mean. Why is being a "10" more remarkable in a distribution whose scores range from 1 to 10 than in a distribution whose scores range from 9 to 11?

THE NORMAL CURVE

Many human traits and characteristics, including height and intelligence, seem to be distributed in a pattern known as a normal distribution. ***Question: What is a normal distribution?*** In a **normal distribution,** the mean, median, and mode all fall at the same data point or score. Scores cluster most heavily about the mean, fall off rapidly in either direction at first (as shown in Figure A.4), and then taper off more gradually.

The curve in Figure A.4 is bell-shaped. This type of distribution is also called a **normal curve** or bell-shaped curve. This curve is the hypothesized distribution of variables in which different scores are determined by chance variation. Height is thought to be largely determined by chance combinations of genetic material. A distribution of the heights of a random sample of the population approximates normal distributions for men and women, with the mean of the distribution for men a few inches higher than the mean for women.

Test developers traditionally assumed that intelligence was also randomly or normally distributed among the population. For that reason, they constructed intelligence tests so that scores would be distributed as close to "normal" as possible. In actuality, IQ scores are also influenced by environmental factors and chromosomal abnormalities, so that the resultant curves are not perfectly normal. The means of most IQ tests are defined as scores of 100 points. The Wechsler scales are constructed to have standard deviations of 15 points, as shown in Figure A.4. A standard deviation of 15 points causes 50% of the Wechsler scores to fall between 90 and 110, which is called the "broad average" range. About 68% of scores (two out of three) fall between 85 and 115 (within a standard deviation of the mean), and more than 95% fall between 70 and 130—that is, within two standard deviations of the mean. Psychologists, therefore, may express your IQ score in terms of how deviant you are. The more extreme high (and low) IQ scores deviate more from the mean score.

The Scholastic Assessment Tests (SATs) were constructed so that the mean scores would be 500 points and the S.D. would be 100 points. Thus a score of 600 would equal or exceed that of some 84% to 85% of the test takers. Because of the complex interaction of variables that determine SAT scores, their distribution is not exactly normal either. Moreover, the actual mean scores and standard deviations tend to vary from year to year and, in the case of the SAT IIs, from test to test. The normal curve is an idealized curve.

An IQ score of 130 may therefore be more impressive than an SAT score of 500. The IQ score of 130 is two standard deviations above the mean and exceeds that of more than 97% of the population. An SAT score of 500 is the mean SAT score and thus equals or surpasses that of about 50% of the population.

REFLECT

Do you tend to place yourself on the normal curve according to traits like nurturance, conscientiousness, and openness to new experience? Explain. Do you feel that people should be informed of their IQ scores? Explain.

Do you feel that your SAT scores (or SAT II scores, or ACT scores) represent you accurately as a person? Explain.

Normal Distribution

A symmetrical distribution that is assumed to reflect chance fluctuations; approximately 68% of cases lie within a standard deviation of the mean.

Normal Curve

Graphic presentation of a normal distribution, which shows a characteristic bell shape.

■ **Figure A.4**
A Bell-Shaped or Normal Curve

In a normal curve, approximately two out of three cases (68%) lie within a standard deviation (S.D.) from the mean. The mean, median, and mode all lie at the same score. IQ tests and the Scholastic Assessment Tests (SATs) are constructed so that their distributions approximate the normal curve.

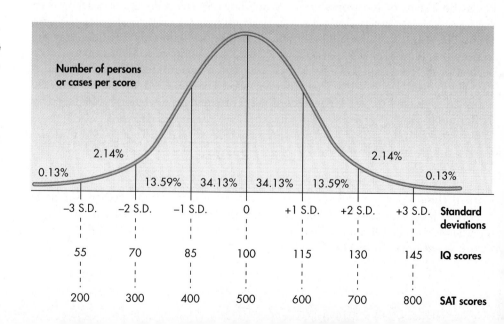

Learning Connections
See Web site for an interactive version of these review questions.

REVIEW

(15) In a _____ distribution, the mean, median, and mode all fall at the same score. (16) A normal distribution yields a graph which has the shape of a _____. (17) The means of most IQ tests are defined as scores of _____ points. (18) The Wechsler scales have standard deviations of _____ points.

Critical Thinking: Why can we say that a Wechsler IQ score of 150 is "higher" than an SAT score of 400?

THE CORRELATION COEFFICIENT

What is the relationship between intelligence and educational achievement? Between cigarette smoking and lung cancer among humans? Between the personality trait of introversion and numbers of dates among college students? We cannot run experiments to determine whether the relationships between these variables are causal, because we cannot manipulate the independent variable. That is, we cannot assign high or low intelligence at random. Nor can we (ethically) assign some people to smoke cigarettes and others not to smoke. People must be allowed to make their own decisions, so it is possible that the same factors that lead some people to smoke—or to continue to smoke after they have experimented with cigarettes—also lead to lung cancer. (Even if we were to assign a group of people to a nonsmoking condition, could we monitor them continuously to make sure that they weren't sneaking puffs?) Nor can we designate who will be introverted and who will be extraverted. True, we could encourage people to act as if they are introverted or extraverted, but behavior is not the same thing as a personality trait. We cannot run true experiments to answer any of these questions, but the **correlation coefficient** can be used to reveal whether there is a relationship between intelligence and achievement, a relationship between smoking and cancer, or a relationship between personality and dating. Correlational research shows that smoking and cancer are related but does not reveal cause and effect. However, experimental research with animals does strongly suggest that smoking will cause cancer in humans.

Question: What is the correlation coefficient? The correlation coefficient is a statistic that describes the relationship between two variables. A correlation coefficient can vary from +1.00 to −1.00. A correlation coefficient of +1.00 is called a perfect positive correlation, and it describes the relationship between temperatures as measured by the Fahrenheit and Centigrade scales. A correlation coefficient of −1.00 is a perfect negative correlation, and a correlation of 0 (zero) reveals no relationship between variables.

As suggested by Figures A.5 and A.6, most correlation coefficients in psychological research are less than perfect. The left-hand graph in Figure A.5 reveals a positive relationship between time spent studying and grade point averages. Because there is a positive correlation between the variables but the relationship is not perfect, the correlation coefficient will lie between 0.00 and +1.00. Perhaps it is about +0.6 or +0.7. However, we cannot absolutely predict what a person's GPA will be if we know the hours per week that he or she spends studying (nor can we predict exactly how much time the person spends studying on the basis of his or her GPA). Nevertheless, it would seem advisable to place oneself among those who spend a good deal of time studying if one wishes to achieve a good GPA.

The right-hand drawing in Figure A.5 reveals a negative relationship between number of delinquent acts committed per year and GPA. The causal connection is less than perfectly clear. Does delinquency interfere with studying and academic achievement? Does poor achievement weaken a student's commitment to trying to get ahead through work? Do feelings of distance from "the system" contribute both to delinquent behavior and a low GPA? The answers are not to be found in Figure A.5, but

REFLECT
How would you explain the correlation between studying and grades?

Correlation Coefficient
A number between −1.00 and +1.00 that indicates the direction (negative or positive) and extent (from none to perfect) of the relationship between two variables.

■ Figure A.5
Positive and Negative Correlations

When there is a positive correlation between variables, as there is between intelligence and achievement, one increases as the other increases. By and large, the more time students spend studying, the better their grades are likely to be, as suggested in the diagram to the left. (Each dot represents the amount of time a student spends studying each week and his or her grade point average.) But there is a negative correlation between grades and juvenile delinquency. As the number of delinquent acts per year increases, one's grade point average tends to decline. Correlational research may suggest but does not demonstrate cause and effect.

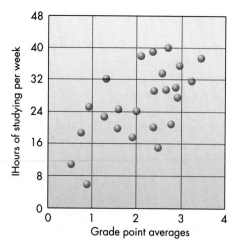

Positive correlation, as found between intelligence and academic achievment

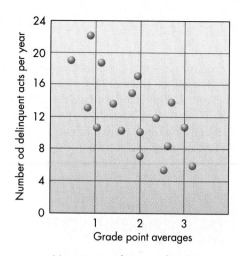

Negative correlation, as found between delinquency and academic achievment

Learning Connections
See Web site for an interactive version of these review questions.

the negative correlation between delinquent behavior and GPA does suggest that it is worthwhile to study the issues involved and—for a student—to distance himself or herself from delinquent behavior if he or she wishes to achieve in the academic world.

R E V I E W

(19) The correlation _____ is a statistic that describes the relationship between two variables. (20) Correlational research (does or does not?) reveal cause and effect. (21) Correlation coefficients vary from +1.00 to _____.

Critical Thinking: Why is the correlation between grades at your college and the price of eggs in the local supermarket likely to be close to zero?

■ Figure A.6
Correlational Relationships, Cause and Effect

Correlational relationships may suggest but do not demonstrate cause and effect. In part A, there is a correlation between variables X and Y. Does this mean that either variable X causes variable Y or that variable Y causes variable X? Not necessarily. Other factors could affect both variables X and Y. Consider the examples of academic grades (variable X) and time spent studying (variable Y) in part B. There is a positive correlation between the two. Does this mean that studying contributes to good grades? Perhaps. Does it mean that good grades encourage studying? Again, perhaps. But there could also be other variables—such as cultural belief in the value of education, enjoyment of learning, even parental pressure to do well—that contribute both to time spent studying and good grades.

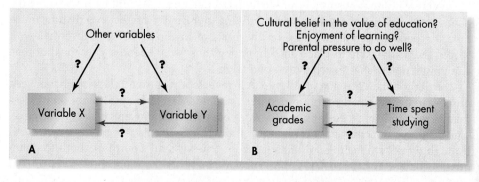

INFERENTIAL STATISTICS

Head Start programs have apparently raised children's intellectual functioning as reflected in their grades and IQ scores. In one such study, children enrolled in a Head Start program obtained a mean IQ score of 99, whereas children similar in background who were not enrolled in Head Start obtained a mean IQ score of 93 (Palmer, 1976). Is this difference of six points in IQ *significant,* or does it represent a chance fluctuation in scores? In a study reported in Chapter 1, college students were provoked by people in league with the researchers. Some of the students believed they had drunk alcohol (in a cocktail with tonic water); others believed they had drunk tonic water only. The students were then given the opportunity to shock the individuals who had provoked them. Students who believed they had drunk alcohol chose higher levels of shock than students who believed they had drunk tonic water only. Did the mean difference in shock level chosen by the two groups of students represent actual differences between the groups, or might it have been a chance fluctuation? The individuals in the Head Start study were a sample of young children. The individuals in the alcohol study were a sample of college students. Inferential statistics helps us determine whether we can conclude that the differences between such samples reflect real differences that are found in the populations that they represent.

Descriptive statistics enables us to provide descriptive information about samples of scores. *Question: What are inferential statistics?* **Inferential statistics** assist us in determining whether we can generalize differences among samples to the populations that they represent.

Figure A.7 shows the distribution of heights of 1,000 men and 1,000 women who were selected at random from the general U.S. population. The mean height for men is greater than the mean height for women. Can we conclude, or **infer,** that this difference in height is not just a chance fluctuation but represents an actual difference between the general populations of men and women? Or must we avoid such an inference and summarize our results by stating only that the mean height of the sample of men in the study was greater than the mean height of the sample of women in the study?

If we could not draw inferences about populations from studies of samples, our research findings would be limited indeed. We could only speak about the specific individuals studied. There would be no point to learning about any study in which you did not participate because it would not apply to you! Fortunately, that is not the case. Inferential statistics permits us to extend findings with samples to the populations from which they were drawn.

Inferential Statistics
The branch of statistics that is concerned with confidence with which conclusions drawn about samples can be extended to the populations from which the samples were drawn.

Infer
To go from the particular to the general; to draw a conclusion.

Statistically Significant Differences

We asked whether the differences in height between our samples of men and women were simply a chance fluctuation or whether they represented actual differences between the heights of men and women. Researchers tend not to talk about "real differences" or "actual differences" between groups, however. Instead, they speak of statistically significant differences. Similarly, researchers asked whether differences in IQ scores between children in Head Start programs and other children from similar backgrounds were chance fluctuations or statistically significant differences. *Question: What are "statistically significant" differences?* Statistically significant differences are differences that are unlikely to be due to chance fluctuation. Psychologists usually do not accept a difference as being statistically significant unless the probability (p) that it is due to chance fluctuation is less than 1 in 20 (i.e., $p < .05$). They are more comfortable labeling a difference as statistically significant when the probability (p) that it is due to chance fluctuation is less than 1 in 100 (i.e., $p < .01$).

Psychologists use formulas involving the means (e.g., mean IQ scores of 93 versus 99) and the standard deviations of sample groups to determine whether differences in means are statistically significant. As you can see in Figure A.8, the farther apart group means are, the more likely it is that they are statistically significant. In other words, if the men are on the average 5 inches taller than the women, it is more likely

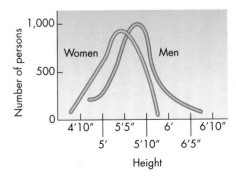

■ **Figure A.7**
Distribution of Heights for Random Samples of Men and Women
Note that the mean height of the men is greater than that of the women. Is the group mean difference in height statistically significant? Researchers use a tool called inferential statistics to determine the answer.

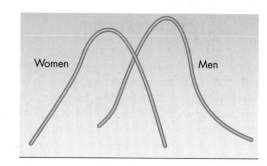

■ **Figure A.8**
Decreasing and Increasing the Mean Group Difference in Heights
Everything else being equal, the greater the difference in group means, the greater the probability that the difference is statistically significant. The distribution on the right shows a greater difference in group means; therefore, there is a greater probability that the difference is statistically significant.

that the difference is statistically significant than if the men are only one-quarter of an inch taller on average. Principle 1: Everything else being equal, the greater the difference between means, the greater the probability that the difference is statistically significant. This makes common sense. After all, if you were told that your neighbor's car had gotten one-tenth of a mile more per gallon of gas than your car in the past year, you would probably attribute the difference to chance fluctuation. But if the difference were greater, say 14 miles per gallon, you would probably assume that the difference reflected an actual difference in driving habits or the efficiency of the automobile.

As you can see in Figure A.9, the smaller the standard deviations (a measure of variability) of the groups, the more likely it is that the difference between means is statistically significant. Consider the extreme example in which there is *no* variability within each group. That is, imagine that every woman in the randomly selected sample of 1,000 women is exactly 5'5" tall. Similarly, imagine that every man in the randomly selected sample of 1,000 men is exactly 5'10" tall. In such a case the heights of the men and women would not overlap at all, and it would appear that the differences were statistically significant. Consider the other extreme—one with unnaturally large variability. Imagine that the heights of the women vary from 2' to 14' and that the heights of the men vary from 2'1" to 14'3". In such a case we might be more likely to assume that the difference in group means of 5" was a chance fluctuation. Principle 2: Every-

■ **Figure A.9**
Decreasing and Increasing the Variability of the Distributions of Scores
Everything else being equal, the smaller the variability in group scores, the greater the probability that the difference in groups means is statistically significant. The distribution on the right shows a greater difference in the variability of the groups; therefore, there is a *lower* probability that the difference in group means is statistically significant.

thing else being equal, the smaller the variability of the distributions of scores, the greater the probability that the difference in group means is statistically significant.

Therefore, we cannot conclude that men are taller than women unless we know the average heights of men and women and how much the heights within each group vary. We must know both the central tendencies (means) and variability of the two distributions of heights in order to infer that the mean heights are statistically significantly different.

We have been "eyeballing" the data and making assumptions. We have been relying on what one professor of mine called the "Wow!" effect. As noted, psychologists and other researchers actually use mathematical techniques that take group means and standard deviations into account to determine whether group differences are statistically significant. It is often the case that eyeballing real data does not yield clear results or even good guesses.

Samples and Populations

Inferential statistics are mathematical tools that psychologists apply to samples of scores to determine whether they can generalize or extend their findings to populations of scores. They must therefore be quite certain that the samples involved actually represent the populations from which they were drawn. Sampling techniques are crucial. Random sampling is the best method, and sampling is random only if every member of the target population has an equal chance of being selected.

It matters little how sophisticated our statistical methods are if the samples studied do not represent the target populations. We could use a variety of sophisticated statistical techniques to analyze the heights of the New York Big Apples and the California Quakes, but none of these methods would tell us much about the height of the general population. Or about the height of women. (Or about the height of people who can't pass the ball, shoot, or play defense.)

R E V I E W

(22) _____ statistics enables us to provide descriptive information about samples of scores. (23) _____ statistics helps us decide whether we can generalize differences among samples to their populations. (24) Psychologists usually do not accept a difference as being statistically significant unless the probability that it is due to chance fluctuation is less than one in _____. (25) Psychologists use formulas involving the means and _____ deviations of sample groups to determine whether differences in means are statistically significant.

Critical Thinking: What does it mean to say that the difference in heights between men and women is *statistically significant?* (Does it mean that all men are taller than all women?)

Learning Connections
See Web site for an interactive version of these review questions.

Recite   Recite   Recite

Learning Connections
See Web site for an interactive version of this chapter summary

1. **What is statistics?**

   Statistics is the science that assembles data in such a way that they provide useful information about measures or scores. Such measures or scores include people's height, weight, and scores on psychological tests such as IQ tests.

2. **What are samples and populations?**

   A sample is part of a population. A population is a complete group from which a sample is drawn. The example with basketball players shows that a sample must represent its population if it is to provide accurate information about the population.

3. **What is descriptive statistics? (Why isn't it always good to be a "10"?)**

   Descriptive statistics is the branch of statistics that provides information about the central tendencies and variabilities of distributions of scores.

4. **What is a frequency distribution?**

   A frequency distribution organizes a set of data, usually from low scores to high scores, and indicates how frequently a score appears. Class intervals may be used on large sets of data to provide a quick impression of how the data tend to cluster. The histogram and frequency polygon are two ways of graphing data to help people visualize the way in which the data are distributed.

5. **What are measures of central tendency?**

   Measures of central tendency are "averages" that show the center or balancing points of a frequency distribution. The mean—which is what most people consider the average—is obtained by adding the scores in a distribution and dividing by the number of scores. The median is the score of the middle or central case in a distribution. The mode is the most common score in a distribution. Distributions can be bimodal (having two modes) or multimodal.

6. **What are measures of variability?**

   Measures of variability provide information about the spread of scores in a distribution. The range is defined as the difference between the highest and lowest scores. The standard deviation is a statistic that shows how scores cluster around the mean. Distributions with higher standard deviations are more spread out.

7. **What is a normal distribution?**

   The normal or bell-shaped curve is hypothesized to occur when the scores in a distribution occur by chance. The normal curve has one mode, and approximately two of three scores (68%) are found within one standard deviation of the mean. Fewer than 5% of cases are found beyond two standard deviations from the mean.

8. **What is the correlation coefficient?**

   The correlation coefficient is a statistic that describes how variables such as IQ and grade point averages are related. It varies from +1.00 to −1.00. When correlations between two variables are positive, it means that one (such as school grades) tends to rise as the other (such as IQ) rises.

9. **What are inferential statistics?**

   Inferential statistics is the branch of statistics that indicates whether researchers can extend their findings with samples to the populations from which they were drawn.

10. **What are "statistically significant" differences?**

    Statistically significant differences are believed to represent real differences between groups and not chance fluctuation.

Active Learning Resources

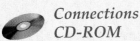

**Search Online
with InfoTrac®
College Edition**

For additional information on the topics in this chapter, explore InfoTrac College Edition, your online library. Go to **http://www.infotrac.thomsonlearning.com** and use the passcode that came on the card with your book. Try these search terms: statistics in psychology, correlation and causation, and achievement tests.

Visit Our Web Site

Go to **http://www.wadsworth.com/psychology**, where you will find online resources directly linked to your book, including interactive exercises related to PQ4R and Power Visuals for mastering and reviewing key concepts. In addition, you will find hints on using InfoTrac College Edition to answer the Critical Thinking questions throughout the text. Start with the **Self Study Assessment** for a customized **Study Plan** generated by taking the **Pre-Test** and **Post-Test.**

**Connections
CD-ROM**

Go to the Wadsworth *Connections* CD-ROM for further study of the concepts in this chapter. The CD-ROM includes videos, animations, quizzes, and additional activities to expand your learning experience, plus interactive self-assessments to help connect the material to your own life.

**Psyk.trek™
CD-ROM**

The Wadsworth *Psyk.trek* CD-ROM offers tutorials, simulations, videos, multimedia glossary, and quizzing to help you master the material.

**PsychNow!
CD-ROM**

The Wadsworth *PsychNow!* CD-ROM includes interactive exercises, videos, and animations to enhance your learning.

B Answer Keys to Self-Assessments

SCORING KEY FOR "SLEEP QUIZ: ARE YOU GETTING YOUR Z'S?" (CHAPTER 5, p. 209)

Psychologist James Maas, the author of *Power Sleep* (HarperCollins, 1998), writes that an answer of "true" to two or more of the statements in the questionnaire may be a sign of a sleep problem.

SCORING KEY FOR "REMOTE ASSOCIATES TEST" (CHAPTER 8, p. 315)

1. Prince	5. Club	9. Pit
2. Dog	6. Boat	10. Writer
3. Cold	7. Defense	
4. Glasses	8. Black	

SCORING KEY FOR "DO YOU STRIVE TO BE ALL THAT YOU CAN BE?" (CHAPTER 11, p. 431)

"Yes" answers indicate a tendency toward self-actualization. There are no norms for this self-assessment, but your number of "yes" answers will help you undertake some meaningful self-evaluation.

SCORING KEY FOR "DO YOU SPEAK YOUR MIND OR DO YOU WIMP OUT? THE ASSERTIVENESS SCHEDULE" (CHAPTER 13, p. 522)

Tabulate your score as follows: For those items followed by an asterisk (*), change the signs (plus to minus; minus to plus). For example, if the response to an asterisked item was 2, place a minus sign (−) before the 2. If the response to an asterisked item was −3, change the minus sign to a plus sign (+) by adding a vertical stroke. Then add up the scores of the 30 items.

Scores on the assertiveness schedule can vary from +90 to −90. Table B.1 will show you how your score compares to those of 764 college women and 637 men from 35 campuses across the United States. For example, if you are a woman and your score was 26, it exceeded that of 80% of the women in the sample. A score of 15 for a male exceeds that of 55–60% of the men in the sample.

TABLE B.1 Percentiles for Scores on the RAS

Women's Scores	Percentile	Men's Scores
55	99	65
48	97	54
45	95	48
37	90	40
31	85	33
26	80	30
23	75	26
19	70	24
17	65	19
14	60	17
11	55	15
8	50	11
6	45	8
2	40	6
−1	35	3
−4	30	1
−8	25	−3
−13	20	−7
−17	15	−11
−24	10	−15
−34	5	−24
−39	3	−30
−48	1	−41

Source: Nevid, J. S., & Rathus, S. A. (1978). Multivariate and normative data pertaining to the RAS with the college population. *Behavior Therapy, 9, 675.*

C Anwers to Reviews

CHAPTER 1 THE SCIENCE OF PSYCHOLOGY

(1) Behavior; (2) Predict; (3) Theories; (4) Pure; (5) Applied; (6) Solving problems, changing behavior, etc.; (7) Counseling; (8) School; (9) Educational; (10) Developmental; (11) Social; (12) Experimental; (13) Industrial; (14) Aristotle; (15) Socrates; (16) Wundt; (17) Functionalism; (18) Watson; (19) Gestalt; (20) Freud; (21) Biologically; (22) Evolutionary; (23) Cognitive; (24) Existential; (25) Social; (26) Sociocultural; (27) Hypothesis; (28) Population; (29) Random; (30) Stratified; (31) Case; (32) Survey; (33) Naturalistic; (34) Correlational; (35) Cause; (36) Experiment; (37) Independent; (38) Control; (39) Blind; (40) Ethical; (41) Informed; (42) Debriefed; (43) Animals

CHAPTER 2 BIOLOGY AND BEHAVIOR

(1) Selection; (2) Existence; (3) Random; (4) Adapted, fitted, etc.; (5) Evolutionary; (6) Instincts, fixed action patterns; (7) Behavioral; (8) Molecular; (9) Genes; (10) Down; (11) Monozygotic, identical; (12) Maze; (13) Neurotransmitters; (14) Dendrites; (15) Myelin; (16) Efferent; (17) Firing; (18) Synapse; (19) Hippocampus; (20) Schizophrenia; (21) Serotonin; (22) Peripheral; (23) Autonomic; (24) Electroencephalograph; (25) Resonance; (26) Cerebellum; (27) Hypothalamus; (28) Callosum; (29) Occipital; (30) Frontal; (31) Left; (32) More; (33) Epilepsy; (34) Hypothalamus; (35) Prolactin; (36) Thyroxin; (37) Cortex; (38) Medulla

CHAPTER 3 VOYAGE THROUGH THE LIFESPAN

(1) Ovulation; (2) Zygote; (3) Uterus; (4) Embryonic; (5) Five; (6) Assimilation; (7) Sensorimotor; (8) Concrete; (9) Three; (10) Psychosocial; (11) Initial-preattachment; (12) Contact; (13) Instinct, fixed action pattern; (14) Authoritative; (15) Secondary; (16) Testosterone; (17) Formal; (18) Imaginary; (19) Universal; (20) Stress; (21) Diffusion; (22) Young; (23) Programmed senescence; (24) Wear; (25) Crystallized; (26) Fluid; (27) Is not; (28) Generativity; (29) Do not; (30) Integrity

CHAPTER 4 SENSATION AND PERCEPTION

(1) Sensation; (2) Perception; (3) Absolute; (4) Difference; (5) Signal; (6) Electromagnetic; (7) Wavelength; (8) Cornea; (9) Iris; (10) Lens; (11) Cones; (12) Optic; (13) Color; (14) Whole; (15) Figure; (16) Top-down; (17) Retina; (18) Stroboscopic; (19) Compress; (20) 20,000; (21) Pitch; (22) Decibels; (23) "Anvil"; (24) Basilar; (25) Corti; (26) Auditory; (27) Olfactory; (28) Bitter; (29) Taste; (30) Two-point; (31) Roots; (32) Position; (33) Muscles; (34) Upright; (35) Semicircular canals; (36) Extrasensory perception; (37) Zener; (38) File

CHAPTER 5 CONSCIOUSNESS

(1) Behavior; (2) Awareness; (3) Freud; (4) Brain; (5) Paradoxical; (6) Five; (7) REM; (8) Activation; (9) Deep (Stage 3 or 4); (10) Magnetism; (11) Hypermnesia; (12) Response; (13) Mantra; (14) Blood; (15) Heart; (16) Autonomic, automatic, involuntary; (17) Dependence; (18) Abstinence, withdrawal; (19) More; (20) Pain; (21) Anxiety, pain, high blood pressure, epilepsy, insomnia; (22) Attention; (23) Cocaine; (24) Nicotine; (25) Hallucinogenic; (26) Marijuana; (27) Hallucinations

CHAPTER 6 LEARNING

(1) Behavior; (2) Represent; (3) Stimulus; (4) Unconditioned; (5) Conditioned; (6) Only one; (7) Extinguish; (8) Spontaneous; (9) Generalization; (10) Discrimination; (11) Higher; (12) Effect; (13) Rewards; (14) Reinforcement; (15) Positive; (16) Negative; (17) Primary; (18) Secondary; (19) Extinction; (20) Punishments; (21) Discriminative; (22) Fixed-interval; (23) Variable-ratio; (24) Successive; (25) Contingency; (26) Cognitive; (27) Latent

CHAPTER 7 MEMORY: REMEMBRANCE OF THINGS PAST—AND FUTURE

(1) Explicit; (2) Episodic; (3) Semantic; (4) Encoding; (5) Maintenance; (6) Elaborative; (7) Retrieval; (8) Short; (9) Icons; (10) Eidetic; (11) Auditory; (12) Serial; (13) Interference; (14) Distort, bias, etc.; (15) Cues; (16) Flashbulb; (17) Hierarchical; (18) Tip; (19) Context; (20) Ebbinghaus; (21) Sharply; (22) Retroactive; (23) Proactive; (24) Hippocampus; (25) Anterograde; (26) Retrograde; (27) Synapses; (28) Serotonin; (29) New; (30) Thalamus

CHAPTER 8 THINKING, LANGUAGE, AND INTELLIGENCE

(1) Thinking; (2) Concepts; (3) Algorithm; (4) Heuristic; (5) Analogy; (6) Mental; (7) Insight; (8) Representativeness; (9) Availability; (10) Cognitive; (11) Framing; (12) Have; (13) Grammar; (14) Linguistic; (15) Prelinguistic; (16) Holophrases; (17) Overregularization; (18) Acquisition; (19) g; (20) Primary; (21) Gardner; (22) Practical; (23) Divergent; (24) Intelligence quotient; (25) Wechsler; (26) 70; (27) 130; (28) Do; (29) Genetic; (30) Heritability; (31) Head

CHAPTER 9 MOTIVATION AND EMOTION

(1) Motives; (2) Deprivation; (3) Incentive; (4) Evolutionary; (5) Homeostasis; (6) Deprivation; (7) Self-actualization; (8) Cognitive; (9) Dissonance; (10) Sugar; (11) Ventromedial; (12) Blood; (13) Testosterone; (14) Organizing; (15) Excitement; (16) Orientation; (17) Identification; (18) Do; (19) Do; (20) Pheromones; (21) Rodents; (22) Vasocongestion; (23) Hypothalamus; (24) Testosterone; (25) Evaluate, interpret, appraise, perceive, etc.; (26) Deindividuation; (27) Increase; (28) Apperception; (29) Performance; (30) Learning; (31) Feeling; (32) Sympathetic; (33) Universal; (34) Do; (35) Unhappiness; (36) Action; (37) Cognitive; (38) Pressure

CHAPTER 10 STRESS, HEALTH, AND ADJUSTMENT

(1) Hassles; (2) Adjustment; (3) Correlational; (4) Conflict; (5) Ellis; (6) Urgency; (7) Higher; (8) Commitment; (9) Decreases; (10) Alarm; (11) Fight-or-flight; (12) Befriend; (13) Cortisol, corticosteroids; (14) Adrenaline; (15) White; (16) Antigens; (17) Antibodies; (18) Immune; (19) Muscle-tension; (20) Migraine; (21) Cholesterol; (22) Less; (23) More; (24) Play; (25) Acquired; (26) Genital; (27) Opportunistic; (28) Blood

CHAPTER 11 PERSONALITY: THEORY AND MEASUREMENT

(1) Conflict; (2) Id; (3) Ego; (4) Defense; (5) Superego; (6) Anal; (7) Fixation; (8) Other; (9) Collective; (10) Inferiority; (11) Horney; (12) Eight; (13) Traits; (14) Stability–instability; (15) Conscientiousness; (16) Skinner; (17) Social; (18) Person, personal; (19) Person; (20) Are; (21) Existentialists; (22) Actualization; (23) Self; (24) Reference; (25) Sociocultural; (26) Individualists; (27) Collectivists; (28) Highest; (29) Behavior; (30) Objective; (31) Ambiguous; (32) True; (33) Rorschach

CHAPTER 12 PSYCHOLOGICAL DISORDERS

(1) Perception; (2) Psychiatric; (3) Szasz; (4) Possession; (5) *Hammer;* (6) Phobia; (7) Panic; (8) Compulsive; (9) Posttraumatic stress disorder, acute stress disorder; (10) Repression; (11) Behaviorists, learning theorists; (12) Do; (13) Amnesia; (14) Identity; (15) Think; (16) Abuse; (17) Somatoform; (18) Conversion; (19) Emotions; (20) Major; (21) Elation; (22) Flight; (23) Helplessness; (24) Internal; (25) Do; (26) Serotonin; (27) Thought; (28) Delusions; (29) Catatonic; (30) Does; (31) Fewer; (32) Dopamine; (33) Personality; (34) Paranoid; (35) Indifference, withdrawal; (36) Antisocial; (37) Lower; (38) Gray

CHAPTER 13 METHODS OF THERAPY

(1) Psychological; (2) Exorcism; (3) Unconscious; (4) Catharsis; (5) Free; (6) Dreams; (7) Humanistic; (8) Nondirective; (9) Unconditional; (10) Directive; (11) Learning; (12) Desensitization; (13) Aversive; (14) Operant; (15) Functional; (16) Consequences; (17) Cognitive; (18) Absolutist; (19) Irrational; (20) More; (21) Encounter; (22) Systems; (23) Meta; (24) Is; (25) Cognitive; (26) Should; (27) Interdependency; (28) Feminist; (29) Minor; (30) Major; (31) Dopamine; (32) Serotonin; (33) Depression; (34) Prefrontal

CHAPTER 14 SOCIAL PSYCHOLOGY

(1) Social; (2) Attitude; (3) Is; (4) Cognitive; (5) Cognitive; (6) Elaboration; (7) Foot; (8) Perception; (9) Primacy; (10) Attribution; (11) Positively; (12) Stare; (13) Is; (14) Matching; (15) Triangular; (16) Do; (17) Social; (18) 75; (19) Facilitation; (20) Anonymous; (21) Decision; (22) More; (23) Risky; (24) Deindividuation; (25) Unrealistic; (26) Altruism

APPENDIX A STATISTICS

(1) Statistics; (2) Distribution; (3) Central; (4) Descriptive; (5) Variability; (6) Frequency; (7) Class; (8) Horizontal; (9) Vertical; (10) Mean; (11) Median; (12) Mode; (13) Lowest; (14) d; (15) Normal; (16) Bell; (17) 100; (18) 15; (19) Coefficient; (20) Does not; (21) -1.00; (22) Descriptive; (23) Inferential; (24) 20; (25) Standard

References

Abbey, A. (1987). Misperceptions of friendly behavior as sexual interest. *Psychology of Women Quarterly, 11,* 173–194.

Abbey, A., et al. (2001). Alcohol and sexual assault. *Alcohol Research & Health, 25*(1), 43–51.

Abeles, N. (1997). Memory problems in later life. *APA Monitor, 28*(6), 2.

Aber, J. L., & Allen, J. P. (1987). Effects of maltreatment of young children on young children's socioemotional development. *Developmental Psychology, 23,* 406–414.

Abraham, H. D., & Duffy, F. H. (2001). EEG coherence in post-LSD visual hallucinations. *Psychiatry Research: Neuroimaging, 107*(3), 151–163.

Ader, D. N., & Johnson, S. B. (1994). Sample description, reporting, and analysis of sex in psychological research. *American Psychologist, 49,* 216–218.

Adler, T. (1990). Distraction, relaxation can help "shut off" pain. *APA Monitor, 21*(9), 11.

Agras, W. S., Walsh, T., Fairburn, C. G., Wilson, G. T., & Kraemer, H. C. (2000). A multicenter comparison of cognitive–behavioral therapy and interpersonal psychotherapy for bulimia nervosa. *Archives of General Psychiatry, 57*(5), 459–466.

Aikins, D. E., & Craske, M. G. (2001). Cognitive theories of generalized anxiety disorder. *Psychiatric Clinics of North America, 24*(1), 57–74.

Ainsworth, M. D. S., Blehar, M. C., Waters, E., & Wall, S. (1978). *Patterns of attachment: A psychological study of the strange situation.* Hillsdale, NJ: Erlbaum.

Ainsworth, M. D. S., & Bowlby, J. (1991). An ethological approach to personality development. *American Psychologist, 46,* 333–341.

Alarcon, A., Capafons, A., Bayot, A., & Cardena, E. (1999). Preference between two methods of active-alert hypnosis: Not all techniques are created equal. *American Journal of Clinical Hypnosis, 41*(3), 269–276.

Albarracín, D., & Wyer, Jr., R. S. (2000).The cognitive impact of past behavior: Influences on beliefs, attitudes, and future behavioral decisions. *Journal of Personality and Social Psychology, 79*(1), 5–22.

Alexander, C. N., et al. (1996). Trial of stress reduction for hypertension in older African Americans: II. Sex and risk Subgroup analysis. *Hypertension, 28,* 228–237.

Allen, L. (1993, August). Integrating a sociocultural perspective into the psychology curriculum. G. Stanley Hall lecture presented to the American Psychological Association, Toronto, Canada.

Alloy, L. B., Abramson, L. Y., & Dykman, B. M. (1990). Depressive realism and nondepressive optimistic illusions. In R. E. Ingram (Ed.), *Contemporary psychological approaches to depression.* New York: Plenum.

Allport, G. W., & Oddbert, H. S. (1936). Trait names: A psycholexical study. *Psychological Monographs, 47,* 1–36.

American Heart Association online (2000). *2000 Heart and stroke statistical update.* http://www.americanheart.org.

American Lung Association (2000). Smoking fact sheet, http://www.lungusa.org

American Psychiatric Association (2000). *Diagnostic and statistical manual of mental disorders* (4th ed., text revision). *DSM-IV-TR.* Washington, DC: Author.

American Psychological Association (1992a). Ethical principles of psychologists and code of conduct. *American Psychologist, 47,* 1597–1611.

American Psychological Association (1992b). *Guidelines for ethical conduct in the care and use of animals.* Washington, DC: Author.

American Psychological Association. (1993). Guidelines for providers of psychological services to ethnic, linguistic, and culturally diverse populations. *American Psychologist, 48,* 45–48.

American Psychological Association Research Office (2000). First-year (full-time) students in doctoral-level departments of psychology by race/ethnicity: 1999–2000. *Graduate Study in Psychology 2000.* Washington, D.C.: American Psychological Association.

Andersen, B. L. (1996). Psychological and behavioral studies in cancer prevention and control. *Health Psychology, 15,* 411–412.

Andersen, B. L. (2002). Biobehavioral outcomes following psychological interventions for cancer patients. *Journal of Consulting and Clinical Psychology, 70*(3), 590–610.

Andersen, B. L., Kiecolt-Glaser, J. K., & Glaser, R. (1994). A biobehavioral model of cancer stress and disease course. *American Psychologist, 49,* 389–404.

Anderson, C. A. (2001). Heat and violence. *Current Directions in Psychological Science, 10*(1), 33–38.

Anderson, C. A., & DeNeve, K. M. (1992). Temperature, aggression, and the negative affect escape model. *Psychological Bulletin, 111,* 347–351.

Anderson, C. A., & Dill, K. E. (2000). Video games and aggressive thoughts, feelings, and behavior in the laboratory and in life. *Journal of Personality and Social Psychology, 78*(4), 772–790.

Anderson, E. S., Winett, R. A., & Wojcik, J. R. (2000). Social-cognitive determinants of nutrition behavior among supermarket food shoppers: A structural equation analysis. *Health Psychology, 19*(5), 479–486.

Anderson, E. S., Winett, R. A., Wojcik, J. R., Winett, S. G., & Bowden, T. (2001). A computerized social cognitive intervention for nutrition behavior: Direct and mediated effects on fat, fiber, fruits and vegetables, self-efficacy and outcome expectations among food shoppers. *Annals of Behavioral Medicine, 23*(2), 88–100.

Anderson, K. G., Sankis, L. M., & Widiger, T. A. (2001). Pathology versus statistical infrequency: Potential sources of gender bias in personality disorder criteria. *Journal of Nervous & Mental Disease, 189*(10), 661–668.

Andrews, B. (1998). Self-esteem. *Psychologist, 11*(7), 339–342.

Andrews, J. A., Tildesley, E., Hops, H., & Li, F. (2002). The influence of peers on young adult substance use. *Health Psychology, 21*(4), 349–357.

Angier, N. (1994a). Benefits of broccoli confirmed as chemical blocks tumors. *The New York Times,* p. C11.

Antonuccio, D. (1995). Psychotherapy for depression: No stronger medicine. *American Psychologist, 50,* 452–454.

Archer, J. (1996). Sex differences in social behavior. *American Psychologist, 51,* 909–917.

Archer, J. (2000). Sex differences in aggression between heterosexual partners: A meta-analytic review. *Psychological Bulletin, 126*(5), 651–680.

Ardrey, R. (1961). *African genesis: A personal investigation into the animal origins and nature of man.* London: Collins.

Arendt, J. (2000). Melatonin, circadian rhythms, and sleep. *The New England Journal of Medicine online, 343*(159), 1114–1116.

Arkin, R. M., & Hermann, A. D. (2000). Constructing desirable identities—Self-presentation in psychotherapy and daily life: Comment on Kelly (2000). *Psychological Bulletin, 126*(4), 501–504.

Armeli, S., Carney. M. A., Tennen, H., Affleck, G., & O'Neil, T. (2000). Stress and alcohol use: A daily process examination of the stressor-vulnerability model. *Journal of Personality and Social Psychology, 78*(5), 979–994.

Arnett, J. J. (1999). Adolescent storm and stress, reconsidered. *American Psychologist, 54*(5), 317–326.

Arthritis Foundation. (2000, April 6). Pain in America: Highlights from a Gallup survey. http://www.arthritis.org/answers/sop_factsheet.asp

Asch, S. E. (1952). *Social psychology.* Englewood Cliffs, NJ: Prentice-Hall.

Ashton, C. H. (2001). Pharmacology and effects of cannabis: a brief review. *The British Journal of Psychiatry, 178*, 101–*f*106.

Atkinson, R. C. (1975). Mnemotechnics in second-language learning. *American Psychologist, 30*, 821–828.

Atkinson, R. C., & Shiffrin, R. M. (1968). Human memory: A proposed system and its control processes. In K. Spence (Ed.), *The psychology of learning and motivation* Vol. 2. New York: Academic Press.

Ayllon, T., & Haughton, E. (1962). Control of the behavior of schizophrenic patients by food. *Journal of the Experimental Analysis of Behavior, 5*, 343–352.

Azar, B. (1995b). Breaking through barriers to creativity. *APA Monitor, 26*(8), 1, 20.

Azar, B. (1996b). Scientists examine cancer patients' fears. *APA Monitor, 27*(8), 32.

Azar, B. (1996c). Training is enhanced by virtual reality. *APA Monitor, 26*(3), 24.

Azar, B. (1997a). Poor recall mars research and treatment. *APA Monitor, 28*(1), 1, 29.

Azar, B. (2002). At the frontier of science. *Monitor on Psychology online, 33*(1).

Babyak, M., et al. (2000). Exercise treatment for major depression: Maintenance of therapeutic benefit at 10 months. *Psychosomatic Medicine, 62*(5), 633–638.

Bacaltchuk, J., Hay, P., & Mari, J. J. (2000). Antidepressants versus placebo for the treatment of bulimia nervosa: A systematic review. *Australian & New Zealand Journal of Psychiatry, 34*(2), 310–317.

Baddeley, A. (1982). *Your memory: A user's guide.* New York: Macmillan.

Baenninger, M. A., & Elenteny, K. (1997). Cited in Azar, B. (1997). Environment can mitigate differences in spatial ability. *APA Monitor, 28*(6), 28.

Baer, H., Allen, S., & Braun, L. (2000). Knowledge of human papillomavirus infection among young adult men and women: Implications for health education and research. *Journal of Community Health: The Publication for Health Promotion & Disease Prevention, 25*(1), 67–78.

Bahrick, H. P., Bahrick, P. O., & Wittlinger, R. P. (1975). Fifty years of memory for names and faces. *Journal of Experimental Psychology: General, 104*, 54–75.

Bailey, J. M., Dunne, M. P., & Martin, N. G. (2000). Genetic and environmental influences on sexual orientation and its correlates in an Australian twin sample. *Journal of Personality and Social Psychology, 78*(3), 524–536.

Bailey, J. M., & Pillard, R. C. (1991). A genetic study of male sexual orientation. *Archives of General Psychiatry, 48*, 1089–1096.

Baker, C. W., Whisman, M. A., & Brownell, K. D. (2000). Studying intergenerational transmission of eating attitudes and behaviors: Methodological and conceptual questions. *Health Psychology, 19*(4), 376–381.

Baker, F., et al. (2000). Health risks associated with cigar smoking. *Journal of the American Medical Association, 284*(6), 735–740.

Baker, L. A., DeFries, J. C., & Fulker, D. W. (1983). Longitudinal stability of cognitive ability in the Colorado adoption project. *Child Development, 54*, 290–297.

Baker, M. C. (2001). *The atoms of language: The mind's hidden rules of grammar.* New York: Basic Books.

Baltes, P. B. (1997). On the incomplete architecture of human ontogeny: Selection, optimization, and compensation as foundation of developmental theory. *American Psychologist, 52*, 366–80.

Baltes, P. B., & Staudinger, U. M. (2000). Wisdom: A metaheuristic (pragmatic) to orchestrate mind and virtue toward excellence. *American Psychologist, 55*, 122–136.

Bandelow, B., et al. (2000). Salivary cortisol in panic attacks. *American Journal of Psychiatry, 157*, 454–456.

Bandura, A. (1997). *Self efficacy: The exercise of control.* New York: Freeman.

Bandura, A. (1999). Social cognitive theory: An agentic perspective. *Asian Journal of Social Psychology, 2*(1), 21–41.

Bandura, A., Blanchard, E. B., & Ritter, B. (1969). The relative efficacy of desensitization and modeling approaches for inducing behavioral, affective, and cognitive changes. *Journal of Personality and Social Psychology, 13*, 173–199.

Bandura, A., & McDonald, F. J. (1963). Influence of social reinforcement and the behavior of models in shaping children's moral judgments. *Journal of Abnormal and Social Psychology, 67*, 274–281.

Bandura, A., Pastorelli, C., Barbaranelli, C., & Caprara, G. V. (1999). Self-efficacy pathways to childhood depression. *Journal of Personality & Social Psychology, 76*(2), 258–269.

Bandura, A., Ross, S. A., & Ross, D. (1963). Imitation of film-mediated aggressive models. *Journal of Abnormal and Social Psychology, 66*, 3–11.

Bandura, A., Taylor, C. B., Williams, S. L., Medford, I. N., & Barchas, J. D. (1985). Catecholamine secretion as a function of perceived coping self-efficacy. *Journal of Consulting and Clinical Psychology, 53*, 406–414.

Bank, B. J., & Hansford, S. L. (2000). Gender and friendship: Why are men's best same-sex friendships less intimate and supportive? *Personal Relationships, 7*(1), 63–78.

Banks, M. S., & Shannon, E. (1993). Spatial and chromatic visual efficiency in human neonates. In C. E. Granrud (Ed.), *Visual perception and cognition in infancy.* Hillsdale, NJ: Erlbaum.

Barber, J. G. (2001). Relative misery and youth suicide. *Australian & New Zealand Journal of Psychiatry, 35*(1), 49–57.

Barber, T. X. (2000). A deeper understanding of hypnosis: Its secrets, its nature, its essence. *American Journal of Clinical Hypnosis, 42*(3–4), 208–272.

Bard, P. (1934). The neurohumoral basis of emotional reactions. In C. A. Murchison (Ed.), *Handbook of general experimental psychology.* Worcester, MA: Clark University Press.

Barlow, D. H., Gorman, J. M., Shear, M. K., Woods, S. W. (2000). Cognitive–behavioral therapy, imipramine, or their combination for panic disorder: A randomized controlled trial. *Journal of the American Medical Association, 283*, 2529–2536.

Barnett, W. S. (1998). Long-term cognitive and academic effects of early childhood education of children in poverty. *Preventive Medicine: An International Journal Devoted to Practice & Theory, 27*(2), 204–207.

Baron, R. A., & Byrne, D. (2003). *Social psychology, 10th ed.* Boston: Allyn & Bacon.

Barringer, F. (1993, April 28). For 32 million Americans, English is a second language. *The New York Times*, p. A18.

Bartoshuk, L. M. (2000). Psychophysical advances aid the study of genetic variation in taste. *Appetite, 34*(1), 105.

Basch, M. F. (1980). *Doing psychotherapy.* New York: Basic Books.

Basic Behavioral Science Task Force of the National Advisory Mental Health Council. (1996a). Basic behavioral science research for mental health: Vulnerability and resilience. *American Psychologist, 51*, 22–28.

Basic Behavioral Science Task Force of the National Advisory Mental Health Council. (1996b). Basic behavioral science research for mental health: Perception, attention, learning, and memory. *American Psychologist, 51*, 133–142.

Basic Behavioral Science Task Force of the National Advisory Mental Health Council. (1996c). Basic behavioral science research for mental health: Sociocultural and environmental practices. *American Psychologist, 51*, 722–731.

Bassetti, C., Vella, S., Donati, F., Wielepp, P., & Weder, B. (2000). SPECT during sleepwalking. *Lancet, 356*, 484–485.

Bateman, D. N. (2000). Triptans and migraine. *The Lancet, 355*, 860–861.

Baucom, D. H., Shoham, V., Mueser, K. T., Daiuto, A. D., & Stickle, T. R. (1998). Empirically supported couple and family interventions for marital distress and adult mental health problems. *Journal of Consulting and Clinical Psychology, 66*, 53–88.

Bauer, M., et al. (2000). Double-blind, placebo-controlled trial of the use of lithium to augment antidepressant medication in continuation treatment of unipolar major depression. *American Journal of Psychiatry, 157*, 1429–1435.

Baumrind, D. (1973). The development of instrumental competence through socialization. In A. D. Pick (Ed.), *Minnesota Symposia on Child Development, Vol. 7*. Minneapolis: University of Minnesota Press.

Baumrind, D. (1991a). The influence of parenting style on adolescent competence and substance abuse. *Journal of Early Adolescence, 11*, 56–95.

Baumrind, D., Larzelere, R. E., & Cowan, P. A. (2002). Ordinary physical punishment: Is it harmful? Comment on Gershoff (2002). *Psychological Bulletin, 128*(4), 580–589.

Baydar, N., & Brooks-Gunn, J. (1991). Effects of maternal employment and child-care arrangements on preschoolers' cognitive and behavioral outcomes: Evidence from the Children of the National Longitudinal Survey of Youth. *Developmental Psychology, 27*, 932–945.

Bech., P. et al. (2000). Meta-analysis of randomised controlled trials of fluoxetine *v.* placebo and tricyclic antidepressants in the short-term treatment of major depression. *British Journal of Psychiatry, 176*, 421–428.

Beck, A. T. (1991). Cognitive therapy: A 30-year retrospective. *American Psychologist, 46*, 368–375.

Beck, A. T. (1993). Cognitive therapy: Past, present, and future. *Journal of Consulting and Clinical Psychology, 61*, 194–198.

Beck, A. T. (2000). Cited in Chamberlin, J. (2000). An historic meeting of the minds. *Monitor on Psychology, 31*(9), 27.

Beck, A. T., & Freeman, A. (1990). *Cognitive therapy of personality disorders*. New York: Guilford.

Beckham, J. C., et al. (2000). Ambulatory cardiovascular activity in Vietnam combat veterans with and without posttraumatic stress disorder. *Journal of Consulting and Clinical Psychology, 68*, 269–276.

Begley, S., & Check, E. (2000, August 5). Sex and the single fly. *Newsweek magazine*, pp. 44–45.

Beitchman, J. H., et al. (2001). Comorbidity of psychiatric and substance use disorders in late adolescence: A cluster analytic approach. *American Journal of Drug & Alcohol Abuse, 27*(3), 421–440.

Bekoff, M. (2002). *Minding animals: Awareness, emotions, and heart*. New York: Oxford University Press.

Bell, P. A. (1992). In defense of the negative affect escape model of heat and aggression. *Psychological Bulletin, 111*, 342–346.

Beller, M., & Gafni, N. (2000). Can item format (multiple choice vs. open-ended) account for gender differences in mathematics achievement? *Sex Roles, 42*(1–2), 1–21.

Bellodi, L., et al. (2001). Morbidity risk for obsessive-compulsive spectrum disorders in first-degree relatives of patients with eating disorders. *American Journal of Psychiatry, 158*, 563–569.

Belsky, J. (1990a). Developmental risks associated with infant day care: Attachment insecurity, noncompliance and aggression? In S. Cherazi (Ed.), *Psychosocial issues in day care*. New York: American Psychiatric Press.

Belsky, J. (1990b). The "effects" of infant day care reconsidered. In N. Fox & G. G. Fein (Eds.), *Infant day care: The current debate*. Norwood, NJ: Ablex.

Belsky, J. (1993). Etiology of child maltreatment. *Psychological Bulletin, 114*, 413–434.

Belsky, J., Weinraub, M., Owen, M., & Kelly, J. (2001, April). Quantity of child care and problem behavior. In J. Belsky (Chair), *Early childcare and children's development prior to school entry*. Symposium conducted at the 2001 Biennial Meetings of the Society for Research in Child Development, Minneapolis, MN.

Bem, D. J., & Honorton, C. (1994). Does Psi exist? Replicable evidence for an anomalous process of information transfer. *Psychological Bulletin, 115*, 4–18.

Bem, D. J., Palmer, J., & Broughton, R. S. (2001). Updating the ganzfeld database: A victim of its own success? *Journal of Parapsychology, 65*(3), 207–218.

Bem, S. L. (1993). *The lenses of gender*. New Haven: Yale University Press.

Benda, B. B., & Corwyn, R. F. (2002).The effect of abuse in childhood and in adolescence on violence among adolescents. *Youth & Society, 33*(3), 339–365.

Benson, H. (1975). *The relaxation response*. New York: Morrow.

Benson, P. L., Karabenick, S. A., & Lerner, R. M. (1976). Pretty pleases: The effects of physical attractiveness, race, and sex on receiving help. *Journal of Experimental Social Psychology, 12*, 409–415.

Berkowitz, L. (1994). Is something missing? Some observations prompted by the cognitive–neoassociationist view of anger and emotional aggression. In L. R. Huesmann (Ed.), *Aggressive behavior: Current perspectives*. New York: Plenum.

Bernardin, H. J., Cooke, D. K., & Villanova, P. (2000). Conscientiousness and agreeableness as predictors of rating leniency. *Journal of Applied Psychology, 85*(2) 232–236.

Bernhardt, P. C., Dabbs, J. M., Jr., Fielden, J. A., & Lutter, C. D. (1998). Testosterone changes during vicarious experiences of winning and losing among fans at sporting events. *Physiology & Behavior, 65*(1) 59–62.

Bernstein, I. (1996). Cited in Azar, B. (1996). Research could help patients cope with chemotherapy. *APA Monitor, 27*(8), 33.

Bernstein, W. M., Stephenson, B. O., Snyder, M. L., & Wicklund, R. A. (1983). Causal ambiguity and heterosexual affiliation. *Journal of Experimental Social Psychology, 19*, 78–92.

Berquier, A., & Ashton, R. (1992). Characteristics of the frequent nightmare sufferer. *Journal of Abnormal Psychology, 101*, 246–250.

Bersoff, D. (1994). Cited in DeAngelis, T. (1994). Experts see little impact from insanity plea ruling. *APA Monitor, 25*(6), 28.

Bevan, W., & Kessel, F. (1994). Plain truths and home cooking. *American Psychologist, 49*, 505–509.

Bexton, W. H., Heron, W., & Scott, T. H. (1954). Effects of decreased variation in the sensory environment. *Canadian Journal of Psychology, 8*, 70–76.

Bialystock, E. (1999). Cognitive complexity and attentional control in the bilingual mind. *Child Development, 70*(3), 636–644.

Bidell, M. P., Turner, J. A., & Casas, J. M. (2002). First impressions count: Ethnic/racial and lesbian/gay/bisexual content of professional psychology application materials. *Professional Psychology: Research & Practice, 33*(1), 97–103.

Birks, Y., & Roger, D. (2000). Identifying components of type-A behaviour: "Toxic" and "non-toxic" achieving. *Personality & Individual Differences, 28*(6), 1093–1105.

Bjorklund, D. F. (2000). *Children's thinking* (3rd ed). Pacific Grove, CA: Brooks/Cole.

Blair, R., & James, R. (2001). Neurocognitive models of aggression, the antisocial personality disorders, and psychopathy. *Journal of Neurology, Neurosurgery & Psychiatry, 71*(6), 727–731.

Blake, S. M., Amaro, H., Schwartz, P. M., & Flinchbaugh, L. J. (2001). A review of substance abuse prevention interventions for young adolescent girls. *Journal of Early Adolescence, 21*(3), 294–324.

Blanchard, E. B. (1992). Psychological treatment of benign headache disorders. *Journal of Consulting and Clinical Psychology, 60*, 537–551.

Blanchard, E. B., et al. (1990). Placebo-controlled evaluation of abbreviated progressive muscle relaxation and of relaxation combined with cognitive therapy in the treatment of tension headache. *Journal of Consulting and Clinical Psychology, 58*, 210–215.

Blanco, C., Ibanez, A., Saiz-Ruiz, J., Blanco-Jerez, C., & Nunes, E. V. (2000). Epidemiology, pathophysiology, and treatment of pahtological gambling. *CNS Drugs, 13*(6), 397–407

Blanco-Colio, L. M., et al. (2000). Red wine intake prevents nuclear factor-B activation in peripheral blood mononuclear cells of healthy volunteers during postprandial lipemia. *Circulation, 102*, 1020–1026.

Blass, T. (1999). The Milgram Paradigm after 35 years: Some things we now know about obedience to authority. *Journal of Applied Social Psychology, 29*(5), 955–978.

Blass, T., & Schmitt, C. (2001). The nature of perceived authority in the Milgram paradigm: Two replications. *Current Psychology: Developmental, Learning, Personality, Social, 20*(2), 115–121.

Block, R. I., et al. (2000). Effects of frequent marijuana use on brain tissue volume and composition. *Neuroreport: For Rapid Communication of Neuroscience Research, 11*(3), 491–496.

Bloom, L., & Mudd, S. A. (1991). Depth of processing approach to face recognition. *Journal of Experimental Psychology: Learning, Memory, and Cognition, 17,* 556–565.

Blum, D. (1997). *Sex on the brain: The biological differences between men and women.* New York: Viking.

Blumenthal, J. A., Sherwood, A., Gullette, E. C. D., Georgiades, A., & Tweedy, D. (2002). Biobehavioral approaches to the treatment of essential hypertension. *Journal of Consulting and Clinical Psychology, 70*(3), 569–589.

Bogen, J. E. (1969). The other side of the brain II: An appositional mind. *Bulletin of the Los Angeles Neurological Society, 34,* 135–162.

Bogen, J. E. (1998). My developing understanding of Roger Wolcott Sperry's philosophy. *Neuropsychologia, 36*(10), 1089–1096.

Bogen, J. E. (2000). Split-brain basics: Relevance for the concept of one's other mind. *Journal of the American Academy of Psychoanalysis, 28*(2), 341–369.

Bohlin, G., Hagekull, B., & Rydell, A. (2000). Attachment and social functioning: A longitudinal study from infancy to middle childhood. *Social Development, 9*(1), 24–39.

Bongar, B. (2002). *The suicidal patient: Clinical and legal standards of care (2nd ed.).* Washington, DC: American Psychological Association.

Bonin, M. F., McCreary, D. R., & Sadava, S. W. (2000). Problem drinking behavior in two community-based samples of adults: Influence of gender, coping, loneliness, and depression. *Psychology of Addictive Behaviors, 14*(2), 151–161.

Boskind-White, M., & White, W. C. (1983). *Bulimarexia: The binge/purge cycle.* New York: W. W. Norton.

Bouchard, T. J., Jr., & Loehlin, J. C. (2001). Genes, evolution, and personality. *Behavior Genetics, 31*(3), 243–273.

Bouchard, T. J., Jr., Lykken, D. T., McGue, M., Segal, N. L., & Tellegen, A. (1990). Sources of human psychological differences: The Minnesota study of twins reared apart. *Science, 250,* 223–228.

Bower, G. H. (1981). Mood and memory. *American Psychologist, 36,* 129–148.

Bowers, K. S., & Woody, E. Z. (1996). Hypnotic amnesia and the paradox of intentional forgetting. *Journal of Abnormal Psychology, 105,* 381–390.

Bowes, J. M., & Goodnow, J. J. (1996). Work for home, school, or labor force. *Psychological Bulletin, 119,* 300–321.

Bowlby, J. (1988). *A secure base.* New York: Basic Books.

Boyatzis, R. E. (1974). The effect of alcohol consumption on the aggressive behavior of men. *Quarterly Journal for the Study of Alcohol, 35,* 959–972.

Boyd-Franklin, N. (1995). A multisystems model for treatment interventions with inner-city African American families. Master lecture delivered to the meeting of the American Psychological Association, New York, August 12.

Bradley, R. H., et al. (1989). Home environment and cognitive development in the first 3 years of life. *Developmental Psychology, 25,* 217–235.

Brand, J. (2000). Cited in McFarling, U. L. (2000, August 27). Sniffing out genes' role in our senses of taste and smell. *The Los Angeles Times online.*

Bransford, J. D., Nitsch, K. E., & Franks, J. J. (1977). Schooling and the facilitation of knowing. In R. C. Anderson, R. J. Spiro, & W. E. Montague (Eds.), *Schooling and the acquisition of knowledge.* Hillsdale, NJ: Erlbaum.

Braun, B. G. (1988). *Treatment of multiple personality disorder.* Washington, DC: American Psychiatric Press.

Brewin, C. R., Andrews, B., & Gotlib, I. H. (1993). Psychopathology and early experience. *Psychological Bulletin, 113,* 82–98.

Brissette, I., Scheier, M. F., & Carver, C. S. (2002). The role of optimism in social network development, coping, and psychological adjustment during a life transition. *Journal of Personality & Social Psychology, 82*(1), 102–111.

Broberg, A. G., Wessels, H., Lamb, M. E., & Hwang, C. P. (1997). Effects of day care on the development of cognitive abilities in 8-year-olds: A longitudinal study. *Developmental Psychology, 33*(1), 62–69.

Broder, S. (2000, July 29). Fighting media violence! www.FamilyEducation.com.

Brody, J. E. (1995b). Cited in DeAngelis, T. (1995), Eat well, keep fit, and let go of stress. *APA Monitor, 26*(10), 20.

Brody, J. E. (1996, August 28). PMS need not be the worry it was just decades ago. *The New York Times,* p. C9.

Brody, J. E. (2000, April 25). Memories of things that never were. *The New York Times,* p. F8.

Brook, J. S., Zheng, L., Whiteman, M., & Brook, D. W. (2001). Aggression in toddlers: Associations with parenting and marital relations. *Journal of Genetic Psychology, 162*(2), 228–241.

Brown, A. S., & Susser, E. S. (2002). In utero infection and adult schizophrenia. *Mental Retardation & Developmental Disabilities Research Reviews, 8*(1), 51–57.

Brown, M. W. (1995, June 6). Scientists deplore flight from reason. *The New York Times,* pp C1, C7.

Brown, R., & McNeill, D. (1966). The tip-of-the-tongue phenomenon. *Journal of Verbal Learning and Verbal Behavior, 5,* 325–337.

Bruce, N. W., & Sanders, K. A. (2001). Incidence and duration of romantic attraction in students progressing from secondary to tertiary education. *Journal of Biosocial Science, 33*(2), 173–184.

Bruene, M., & Ribbert, H. (2002). Grundsaetzliches zur Konzeption einer evolutionaeren Psychiatrie. *Schweizer Archiv für Neurologie und Psychiatrie, 153*(1), 4–11.

Buchanan, C. M., Eccles, J. S., & Becker, J. B. (1992). Are adolescents the victims of raging hormones? Evidence for activational effects of hormones on moods and behavior at adolescence. *Psychological Bulletin, 111,* 62–107.

Buckley, P. F., Buchanan, R. W., Tamminga, C. A., & Schulz, S. C. (2000). Schizophrenia research. *Schizophrenia Bulletin, 26*(2), 411–419.

Burger, J. M. (1999). The foot-in-the-door compliance procedure: A multiple-process analysis and review. *Personality & Social Psychology Review, 3*(4), 303–325.

Burger, J. M., & Cosby, M. (1999). Do women prefer dominant men? The case of the missing control condition. *Journal of Research in Personality, 33*(3), 358–368.

Burgess, R. L., & Drais, A. A. (2001). Explaining child maltreatment: From behavior analysis to behavioral biology. *Revista Mexicana de Analisis de la Conducta, 27*(2), 201–224.

Burnette, E. (1997). "Father of Ebonics" continues his crusade. *APA Monitor, 28*(4), 12.

Bushman, B. J. (1998). Priming effects of media violence on the accessibility of aggressive constructs in memory. *Personality & Social Psychology Bulletin, 24*(5), 537–545.

Bushman, B. J., Baumeister, R. F., & Stack, A. D. (1999). Catharsis, aggression, and persuasive influence: Self-fulfilling or self-defeating prophecies? *Journal of Personality & Social Psychology, 76*(3), 367–376.

Buss, D. M. (1992). Is there a universal human nature? *Contemporary Psychology, 37,* 1262–1263.

Buss, D. M. (1994). *The evolution of desire.* New York: Basic Books.

Buss, D. M. (1995). Psychological sex differences. *American Psychologist, 50,* 164–168.

Buss, D. M. (1999). Adaptive individual differences revisited. *Journal of Personality, 67*(2), 259–264.

Buss, D. M. (2000). The evolution of happiness. *American Psychologist, 55,* 15–23.

Buss, D. M., Haselton, M. G., Shackelford, T. K., Bleske, A. L., & Wakefield, J. C. (1998). Adaptations, exaptations, and spandrels. *American Psychologist, 53,* 533–548.

Bussey, K., & Bandura, A. (1999). Social cognitive theory of gender development and differentiation. *Psychological Review, 106*(4), 676–713.

Butcher, J. (2000). Dopamine hypothesis gains further support. *The Lancet, 356,* 139–146.

Butler, A. C., & Beck, J. S. (2001). Cognitive therapy outcomes. A review of meta-analyses. *Tidsskrift for Norsk Psykologforening, 38*(8), 698–706.

Butler, J. C. (2000). Personality and emotional correlates of right-wing authoritarianism. *Social Behavior & Personality, 28*(1), 1–14.

Butler, R. (1998). Cited in CD-ROM that accompanies Nevid, J. S., Rathus, S. A., & Rubenstein, H. (1998). *Health in the new millennium.* New York: Worth Publishers.

Cacioppo, J. T., Martzke, J. S, Petty, R. E., & Tassinary, L. G. (1988). Specific forms of facial EMG response index emotions during an interview. *Journal of Personality and Social Psychology, 54,* 552–604.

Cain, D. J., & Seeman, J. (2002). *Humanistic psychotherapies: Handbook of research and practice.* Washington, DC: American Psychological Association.

Californians losing fight against flab. (2000, June 14). Reuters News Agency online.

Campbell, W. K., Sedikides, C., Reeder, G. D., & Elliott, A. J. (2000). Among friends? An examination of friendship and the self-serving bias. *British Journal of Social Psychology, 39*(2), 229–239.

Campos, J. J. (2000). Cited in Azar, B. (2000). What's in a face? *Monitor on Psychology, 31*(1), 44–45.

Campos, J. J., Hiatt, S., Ramsey, D., Henderson, C., & Svejda, M. (1978). The emergence of fear on the visual cliff. In M. Lewis & L. Rosenblum (Eds.), *The origins of affect.* New York: Plenum.

Camras, L. (2000). Cited in Azar, B. (2000). What's in a face? *Monitor on Psychology, 31*(1), 44–45.

Canalis, R. F., & Lambert, P. R. (2000). *The ear: Comprehensive otology.* Philadelphia: Lippincott Williams & Wilkins.

Cann, R. E. (2002). Human evolution: Tangled genetic routes. *Nature, 416,* 6876.

Cannon, W. B. (1927). The James–Lange theory of emotions: A critical examination and an alternative theory. *American Journal of Psychology, 39,* 106–124.

Cannon, W. B. (1932). *The wisdom of the body.* New York: Norton.

Cannon, W. B., & Washburn, A. (1912). An explanation of hunger. *American Journal of Physiology, 29,* 441–454.

Cantor, J. (1997). Cited in Seppa, N. (1997). Children's TV remains steeped in violence. *APA Monitor, 28*(6), 36.

Carey, G., & DiLalla, D. L. (1994). Personality and psychopathology: Genetic perspectives. *Journal of Abnormal Psychology, 103,* 32–43.

Carlson, J. G., & Hatfield, E. (1992). *Psychology of emotion.* Fort Worth: Harcourt Brace Jovanovich.

Carlsson, K., et al. (2000). Tickling expectations: Neural processing in anticipation of a sensory stimulus. *Journal of Cognitive Neuroscience, 12,* 691–703.

Carmichael, L. L., Hogan, H. P., & Walter, A. A. (1932). An experimental study of the effect of language on the reproduction of visually perceived form. *Journal of Experimental Psychology, 15,* 73–86.

Carpenter, W. T., Kirkpatrick, B., & Buchanan, R. W. (1999). Schizophrenia: Syndromes and diseases. *Journal of Psychiatric Research, 33*(6), 473–475.

Carroll, M. E., & Overmier, J. B. (2001). *Animal research and human health.* Washington, DC: American Psychological Association.

Carstensen, L. (1997, August 17). The evolution of social goals across the life span. Paper presented to the American Psychological Association, Chicago.

Case, R. (1992). *The mind's staircase.* Hillsdale, NJ: Erlbaum.

Castillo-Richmond, A., et al. (2000). Effects of stress reduction on carotid atherosclerosis in hypertensive African Americans. *Stroke, 31,* 568.

Caughy, M. O., DiPietro, J. A., & Strobino, D. M. (1994). Day-care participation as a protective factor in the cognitive development of low-income children. *Child Development, 65*(2), 457–471.

Cavaliere, F. (1996). Bilingual schools face big political challenges. *APA Monitor, 27*(2), 36.

Cavanaugh, J. C., & Green, E. E. (1990). I believe, therefore I can: Self-efficacy beliefs in memory aging. In E. A. Lovelace (Ed.), *Aging and cognition: Mental processes, self-awareness, and interventions.* North-Holland, Elsevier.

Cavelaars, A. E. J. M., et al. (2000). Educational differences in smoking: International comparison. *British Medical Journal, 320,* 1102–1107.

CDC (See Centers for Disease Control and Prevention.)

Ceci, S. J., & Bruck, M. (1993). Suggestibility of the child witness. *Psychological Bulletin, 113,* 403–439.

Cellar, D. F., Nelson, Z. C., & Yorke, C. M. (2000). The five-factor model and driving behavior: Personality and involvement in vehicular accidents. *Psychological Reports, 86*(2) 454–456.

Centers for Disease Control and Prevention (1995). *Suicide surveillance: 1980–1990.* Washington, DC: USDHHS.

Centers for Disease Control and Prevention. (2000b, June 9). Youth risk behavior surveillance: United States, 1999. *Morbidity and Mortality Weekly Report, 49*(SS05); 1–96.

Centers for Disease Control and Prevention. (2000c). Suicide in the United States. Page updated January 28, 2000. (http://www.cdc.gov/ncipc/factsheets/suifacts.htm)

Centers for Disease Control and Prevention. (2000d). National and state-specific pregnancy rates among adolescents: United States, 1995–1997. *Morbidity and Mortality Weekly Report, 49*(270.

Centers for Disease Control and Prevention. (2001, December 3). Sexually transmitted disease surveillance 2000. Atlanta, GA: Division of STD Prevention, National Center for HIV, STD and TB Prevention.

Cervilla, J. A., et al. (2000). Long-term predictors of cognitive outcome in a cohort of older people with hypertension. *British Journal of Psychiatry, 177,* 66–71.

Cervone, D., & Mischel, W. (2002). Personality science. In Cervone, D., & Mischel, W. (Eds.), *Advances in personality science* (pp. 1–26). New York: Guilford Press.

Chadwick, P. D. J., & Lowe, C. F. (1990). Measurement and modification of delusional beliefs. *Journal of Consulting and Clinical Psychology, 58,* 225–232.

Chafee, M. V., & Goldman-Rakic, P. S. (2000). Inactivation of parietal and prefrontal cortex reveals interdependence of neural activity during memory-guided saccades. *Journal of Neurophysiology, 83*(3), 1550–1566.

Chambless, D. L., & Hollon, S. D. (1998). Defining empirically supported therapies. *Journal of Consulting and Clinical Psychology, 66,* 7–18.

Chance, S. E., Brown, R. T., Dabbs, J. M., Jr., & Casey, R. (2000). Testosterone, intelligence and behavior disorders in young boys. *Personality & Individual Differences, 28*(3) 437–445.

Chang, E. C., & Sanna, L. J. (2001). Negative attributional style as a moderator of the link between perfectionism and depressive symptoms: Preliminary evidence for an integrative model. *Journal of Counseling Psychology, 48*(4), 490–495.

Chaplin, W. F., Phillips, J. B., Brown, J. D., Clanton, N. R., & Stein, J. L. (2000). Handshaking, gender, personality, and first impressions. *Journal of Personality and Social Psychology, 79*(1), 110–117.

Chassin, L., Presson, C. C., Pitts, S. C., & Sherman, S. J. (2000). The natural history of cigarette smoking from adolescence to adulthood in a Midwestern community sample: Multiple trajectories and their psychological correlates. *Health Psychology, 19,* 223–231.

Chassin, L., Presson, C. C., Rose, J. S., & Sherman, S. J. (2001). From adolescence to adulthood: Age-related changes in beliefs about cigarette smoking in a Midwestern community sample. *Health Psychology, 20*(5), 377–386.

Chavez, M. L., & Spitzer, M. F. (2002). Herbals and other dietary supplements for premenstrual syndrome and menopause. *Psychiatric Annals, 32*(1), 61–71.

Cheng, H., & Furnham, A. (2001). Attributional style and personality as predictors of happiness and mental health. *Journal of Happiness Studies, 2*(3), 307–327.

Cherry, K. E., & LeCompte, D. C. (1999). Age and individual differences influence prospective memory. *Psychology & Aging, 14*(1) 60–76.

Chlebowski, R. T. (2000). Primary care: Reducing the risk of breast cancer. *The New England Journal of Medicine online, 343*(3).

Chomsky, N. (1980). Rules and representations. *Behavioral and Brain Sciences, 3,* 1–16.

Chomsky, N. (1991). Linguistics and cognitive science. In A. Kasher (Ed.), *The Chomskyan turn.* Cambridge, MA: Blackwell.

Chuang, Y. (2002). Sex differences in mate selection preference and sexual strategy: Tests for evolutionary hypotheses. *Chinese Journal of Psychology, 44*(1), 75–93.

Cialdini, R. B. (2000). Cited in McKinley, J. C., Jr. (2000, August 11). It isn't just a game: Clues to avid rooting. *The New York Times online.*

Cialdini, R. B., et al. (1997). Reinterpreting the empathy-altruism relationship: When one into one equals oneness. *Journal of Personality & Social Psychology, 73*(3), 481–494.

Cigars increase lung cancer risk fivefold: Study. (2000, February 15). Reuters News Agency online.

Clancy, S. A., Schacter, D. L., McNally, R. J., & Pitman, R. K. (2000). False recognition in women reporting recovered memories of sexual abuse. *Psychological Science, 11*(1), 26–31.

Clarke-Stewart, K. A. (1989). Infant day care: Maligned or malignant? *American Psychologist, 44*, 266–273.

Clarke-Stewart, K. A. (1991). A home is not a school: The effects of child care on children's development. *Journal of Social Issues, 47*, 105–123.

Clay, R. A. (2000). Staying in control. *Monitor on Psychology, 31*(1), 32–34.

Clayton, E. C., & Williams, C. L. (2000). Adrenergic activation of the nucleus tractus solitarius potentiates amygdala norepinephrine release and enhances retention performance in emotionally arousing and spatial memory tasks. *Behavioural Brain Research, 112*(1–2), 151–158.

Clement, J. (1991). Nonformal reasoning in experts and in science students. In J. Voss, D. Perkins, & J. Siegel (Eds.), *Informal reasoning and education.* Hillsdale, NJ: Erlbaum.

Cohen, D., et al. (2000). Absence of cognitive impairment at long-term follow-up in adolescents treated with ECT for severe mood disorder. *American Journal of Psychiatry, 157*, 460–462.

Cohen, F., et al., (1999). Differential immune system changes with acute and persistent stress for optimists vs pessimists. *Brain, Behavior & Immunity, 13*(2), 155–174.

Cohen, L. A. (1987, November). Diet and cancer. *Scientific American,* pp. 42–48, 53–54.

Cohen, L. L. (2002). Reducing infant immunization distress through distraction. *Health Psychology, 21*(2), 207–211.

Cohen, S., Tyrrell, D. A. J., & Smith, A. P. (1993). Negative life events, perceived stress, negative affect, and susceptibility to the common cold. *Journal of Personality and Social Psychology, 64*, 131–140.

Cohen, S., & Williamson, G. M. (1991). Stress and infectious disease in humans. *Psychological Bulletin, 109*, 5–24.

Cohen, S., Gottlieb, B. H., & Underwood, L. G. (2001a). Social relationships and health: Challenges for measurement and intervention. *Advances in Mind-Body Medicine, 17*(2), 129–141.

Cohen, S., Miller, G. E., & Rabin, B. S. (2001b). Psychological stress and antibody response to immunization: A critical review of the human literature. *Psychosomatic Medicine, 63*(1), 7–18.

Cohn, E. G. (1990). Weather and violent crime. *Environment and Behavior, 22*, 280–294.

Cohn, L. D., Macfarlane, S., Yanez, C., & Imai, W. K. (1995). Risk-perception: Differences between adolescents and adults. *Health Psychology, 14*, 217–222.

Collaer, M. L., & Hines, M. (1995). Human behavioral sex differences: A role for gonadal hormones during early development? *Psychological Bulletin, 118*, 55–107.

Collier, G. (1994). *Social origins of mental ability.* New York: Wiley.

Coltraine, S., & Messineo, M. (2000). The perpetuation of subtle prejudice: Race and gender imagery in 1990s television advertising. *Sex Roles, 42*(5–6), 363–389.

Comas-Diaz, L. (1994, February). Race and gender in psychotherapy with women of color. *Winter roundtable on cross-cultural counseling and psychotherapy: Race and gender.* New York: Teachers College, Columbia University.

Compas, B. E., Haaga, D. A. F., Keefe, F. J., Leitenberg, H., & Williams, D. A. (1998). Sampling of empirically supported psychological treatments from health psychology: Smoking, chronic pain, cancer, and bulimia nervosa. *Journal of Consulting and Clinical Psychology, 66*, 89–112.

Concar, D. (2002, April 20). Ecstasy on the brain. NewScientist.com.

Condon, J. T. (2001). Premenstrual syndrome in primary care: An update. *Primary Care Psychiatry, 7*(3), 85–90.

Conklin, H. M., & Iacono, W. G. (2002). Schizophrenia: A neuro-developmental perspective. *Current Directions in Psychological Science, 11*(1), 33–37.

Constantinidis, C., Franowicz, M. N., & Goldman-Rakic, P. S. (2001). Coding specificity in cortical microcircuits: A multiple-electrode analysis of primate prefontal cortex. *Journal of Neuroscience, 21*(10), 3646–3655.

Conway, M. A., et al. (1994). The formation of flashbulb memories. *Memory & Cognition, 22*(3), 326–343.

Cools, J., Schotte, D. E., & McNally, R. J. (1992). Emotional arousal and overeating in restrained eaters. *Journal of Abnormal Psychology, 101*, 348–351.

Coons, P. M. (1994). Confirmation of childhood abuse in child and adolescent cases of multiple personality disorder and dissociative disorder not otherwise specified. *Journal of Nervous and Mental Disease, 182*, 461–464.

Cooper, Z., & Fairburn, C. G. (2001). A new cognitive behavioural approach to the treatment of obesity. *Behaviour Research & Therapy, 39*(5), 499–511.

Corballis, M. C. (1998). Sperry and the Age of Aquarius: Science, values and the split brain. *Neuropsychologia, 36*(10), 1083–1087.

Cotman, C. W. (2000, July). Amyloid toxicity. Paper presented to the World Alzheimer Congress 2000, Washington, DC.

Courtenay, W. H. (2000) Engendering health: A social constructionist examination of men's health beliefs and behaviors. *Psychology of Men & Masculinity, 1*(1), 4–15.

Cousins, N. (1979). *Anatomy of an illness as perceived by the patient.* New York: W. W. Norton.

Cowen, P. J. (2002). Cortisol, serotonin and depression: All stressed out? *British Journal of Psychiatry, 180*(2), 99–100.

Cox, B. J., Borger, S. C., Asmundson, G. J. G., & Taylor, S. (2000). Hypochondriasis: Dimensions of hypochondriasis and the five-factor model of personality. *Personality & Individual Differences, 29*(1), 99–108.

Craddock, N., & Jones, I. (2001). Molecular genetics of bipolar disorder. *British Journal of Psychiatry, 178*(Suppl41), s128–s133.

Craik, F. I. M., & Lockhart, R. S. (1972). Levels of processing. *Journal of Verbal Learning and Verbal Behavior, 11*, 671–684.

Cramer, P. (2000). Defense mechanisms in psychology today. *American Psychologist, 55*(6), 637–646.

Cramer, R. E., McMaster, M. R., Bartell, P. A., & Dragna, M. (1988). Subject competence and minimization of the bystander effect. *Journal of Applied Social Psychology, 18*, 1133–1148.

Crano, W. D. (2000) Milestones in the psychological analysis of social influence. *Group Dynamics, 4*(1), 68–80.

Craske, M. G., & Zucker, B. G. (2001). Consideration of the APA practice guideline for the treatment of patients with panic disorder: Strengths and limitations for behavior therapy. *Behavior Therapy, 32*(2), 259–281.

Crews, D. (1994). Animal sexuality. *Scientific American, 270*(1), 108–114.

Crick, F., & Koch, C. (1997). The problem of consciousness. *Scientific American mysteries of the mind, Special Issue Vol. 7, No. 1,* 18–26.

Crick, N. R., & Dodge, K. A. (1994). A review and reformulation of social information-processing mechanisms in children's social adjustment. *Psychological Bulletin, 115*, 74–101.

Crowe, R. A. (1990). Astrology and the scientific method. *Psychological Reports, 67*, 163–191.

Crusco, A. H., & Wetzel, C. G. (1984). The Midas touch: The effects of interpersonal touch on restaurant tipping. *Personality and Social Psychology Bulletin, 10*, 512–517.

Cummins, R. A. (2000). Personal income and subjective well-being: A review. *Journal of Happiness Studies, 1*(2), 133–158.

Cummins, R. A., & Nistico, H. (2002). Maintaining life satisfaction: The role of positive cognitive bias. *Journal of Happiness Studies, 3*(1), 37–69.

Cumsille, P. E., Sayer, A. G., & Graham, J. W. (2000). Perceived exposure to peer and adult drinking as predictors of growth in positive alcohol expectancies during adolescence. *Journal of Consulting and Clinical Psychology, 68*(3), 531–536.

Cunningham, M. R., Shaffer, D. R., Barbee, A. P., Wolff, P. L., & Kelley, D. J. (1990). Separate processes in the relation of elation and depression to helping. *Journal of Experimental Social Psychology, 26*, 13–33.

Curtis, J. T., Liu, Y., & Wang, Z. (2001). Lesions of the vomeronasal organ disrupt mating-induced pair bonding in female prairie voles (Microtus ochrogaster). *Brain Research, 901*(1-2), 167–174.

Curtis, R. C., & Miller, K. (1986). Believing another likes or dislikes you: Behavior making the beliefs come true. *Journal of Personality and Social Psychology, 51*, 284–290.

Cutler, W. B. (1999). Human sex-attractant hormones: Discovery, research, development, and application in sex therapy. *Psychiatric Annals, 29*(1), 54–59.

Cutler, W. B., Friedmann, E., & McCoy, N. L. (1998). Pheromonal influences on sociosexual behavior in men. *Archives of Sexual Behavior, 27*(1), 1–13.

Cyranowski, J. M., Frank, E., Young, E., & Shear, M. M. (2000). Adolescent onset of the gender difference in lifetime rates of major depression: A theoretical model. *Archives of General Psychiatry, 57*(1), 21–27.

Dabbs, J. M., Jr., Chang, E-L., Strong, R. A., & Milun, R. (1998). Spatial ability, navigation strategy, and geographic knowledge among men and women. *Evolution & Human Behavior, 19*(2), 89–98.

Dabbs, J. M., Jr., Hargrove, M. F., & Heusel, C. (1996). Testosterone differences among college fraternities: Well-behaved vs. rambunctious. *Personality & Individual Differences, 20*(2), 157–161.

Dailard, C. (2001, February). Sex education: Politicians, parents, teachers and teens. *The Guttmacher Report on Public Policy.* New York: The Alan Guttmacher Institute.

Damaged gene is linked to lung cancer. (1996, April 6.) *The New York Times,* p. A24.

Damasio, A. R. (2000). A neural basis for sociopathy. *Archives of General Psychiatry online, 57*(2).

Danforth, J. S., et al. (1990). Exercise as a treatment for hypertension in low-socioeconomic-status black children. *Journal of Consulting and Clinical Psychology, 58*, 237–239.

Darley, J. M. (1993). Research on morality. *Psychological Science, 4*, 353–357.

Darley, J. M., & Latané, B. (1968). Bystander intervention in emergencies: Diffusion of responsibility. *Journal of Personality and Social Psychology, 8*, 377–383.

Darwin, C. A. (1872). *The expression of the emotions in man and animals.* London: J. Murray.

Dasgupta, N., & Greenwald, A. G. (2001). On the malleability of automatic attitudes: Combating automatic prejudice with images of admired and disliked individuals. *Journal of Personality and Social Psychology, 81*(5), 800–814.

Davidson, J. R., & Foa, E. G. (1991). Diagnostic issues in posttraumatic stress disorder. *Journal of Abnormal Psychology, 100*, 346–355.

Davidson, N. E. (1995). Hormone-replacement therapy—Breast versus heart versus bone. *New England Journal of Medicine, 332*, 1638–1639.

Davis, A. M., Grattan, D. R., & McCarthy, M. M. (2000). Decreasing GAD neonatally attenuates steroid-induced sexual differentiation of the rat brain. *Behavioral Neuroscience, 114*(5) 923–933.

Davis, S. (2000). Testosterone and sexual desire in women. *Journal of Sex Education & Therapy, 25*(1), 25–32.

Davison, G. C. (2000). Stepped care: Doing more with less? *Journal of Consulting and Clinical Psychology, 68*(4), 580–585.

Dawood, K., Pillard, R. C., Horvath, C., Revelle, W., & Bailey, J. M. (2000). Familial aspects of male homosexuality. *Archives of Sexual Behavior, 29*(2), 155–163.

Day, S. J., & Altman, D. G. (2000). Statistics notes: Blinding in clinical trials and other studies *British Medical Journal, 321*, 504.

DeAngelis, T. (1994a). Educators reveal keys to success in classroom. *APA Monitor, 25*(1), 39–40.

DeAngelis, T. (1994b). Experts see little impact from insanity plea ruling. *APA Monitor, 25*(6), 28.

DeAngelis, T. (1995). Mental health care is elusive for Hispanics. *APA Monitor, 26*(7), 49.

DeAngelis, T. (2002). A genetic link to anorexia. *APA Monitor, 33*(3), 34–36.

DeCasper, A. J., & Prescott, P. A. (1984). Human newborns' perception of male voices. *Developmental Psychobiology, 17*, 481–491.

Deep, A. L., et al. (1999). Sexual abuse in eating disorder subtypes and control women: The role of comorbid substance dependence in bulimia nervosa. *International Journal of Eating Disorders, 25*(1), 1–10.

DeGrandpre, R. J. (2000). A science of meaning: Can behaviorism bring meaning to psychological science? *American Psychologist, 55*(7), 721–739.

De Houwer, J., Thomas, S., & Baeyens, F. (2001). Associative learning of likes and dislikes: A review of 25 years of research on human evaluative conditioning. *Psychological Bulletin, 127*(6), 853–869.

de Jong, P. F., & Das-Smaal, E. A. (1995). Attention and intelligence. *Journal of Educational Psychology, 87*, 80–92.

De La Cancela, V., & Guzman, L. P. (1991). Latino mental health service needs. In H. F. Myers and others (Eds.), *Ethnic minority perspectives on clinical training and services in psychology* (pp. 59–64). Washington, DC: American Psychological Association.

Delgado, J. M. R. (1969). *Physical control of the mind.* New York: Harper & Row.

Delves, P. J., & Roitt, I. M. (2000). Advances in immunology: The immune system. *The New England Journal of Medicine online, 343*(1).

De Michele, P. E., Gansneder, B., & Solomon, G. B. (1998). Success and failure attributions of wrestlers: Further evidence of the self-serving bias. *Journal of Sport Behavior, 21*(3), 242–255.

Denham, S. A., et al. (2000). Prediction of externalizing behavior problems from early to middle childhood: The role of parental socialization and emotion expression. *Development & Psychopathology, 12*(1), 23–45.

Denmark, F. L. (1998). Women and psychology: An international perspective. *American Psychologist, 53*(4), 465–473.

Dennis, H. (2000). Cited in Stewart, J. Y., & Armet, E. (2000, April 3). Aging in America: Retirees reinvent the concept. *Los Angeles Times online.*

Dennis, W., & Dennis, M. G. (1940). The effect of cradling practices upon the onset of walking in Hopi children. *Journal of Genetic Psychology, 56*, 77–86.

den Tonkelaar, I. & Oddens, B. J. (2000). Determinants of long-term hormone replacement therapy and reasons for early discontinuation. *Obstetrics & Gynecology, 95*(4), 507–512.

Depression Research at the National Institute of Mental Health. (2000). NIH Publication No. 00-4501. http://www.nimh.nih.gov/publicat/depresfact.cfm.

DeRubeis, R. J., & Crits-Christoph, P. (1998). Empirically supported individual and group psychological treatments for adult mental disorders. *Journal of Consulting and Clinical Psychology, 66*, 37–52.

Dessens, A. B., et al. (1999). Prenatal exposure to anticonvulsants and psychosexual development. *Archives of Sexual Behavior, 28*(1) 31–44.

de Toledo-Morrell, L. (2000, July). Hippocampal and entorhinal atrophy in aging and Alzheimer's disease: Relation to function. Paper presented to the World Alzheimer Congress 2000, Washington, DC.

DeValois, R. L., & Jacobs, G. H. (1984). Neural mechanisms of color vision. In I. Darian-Smith (Ed.), *Handbook of physiology* (Vol. 3). Bethesda, MD: American Physiological Society.

de Wied, D. (1997). Neuropeptides in learning and memory processes. *Behavioural Brain Research. 83*(1–2), 83–90.

de Wit, H., Crean, J., & Richards, J. B. (2000). Effects of *d*-amphetamine and ethanol on a measure of behavioral inhibition in humans. *Behavioral Neuroscience, 114*(4), 830–837.

Diamond, G., & Siqueland, L. (2001). Current status of family intervention science. *Child & Adolescent Psychiatric Clinics of North America, 10*(3), 641–661.

Dickens, W. T., & Flynn, J. R. (2001). Heritability estimates versus large environmental effects: The IQ paradox resolved. *Psychological Review, 108*(2), 346–369.

Dickson, N., Paul, C., Herbison, P., & Silva, P. (1998). First sexual intercourse: age, coercion, and later regrets reported by a birth cohort. *British Medical Journal, 316*, 29–33.

Diener, E., Napa Scollon, C. K., Oishi, S., Dzokoto, V., & Suh, E. M. (2000). Positivity and the construction of life satisfaction judgments: Global happiness is not the sum of its parts. *Journal of Happiness Studies, 1*(2), 159–176.

Dierker, L. C., et al. (2001). Association between psychiatric disorders and the progression of tobacco use behaviors. *Journal of the American Academy of Child & Adolescent Psychiatry, 40*(10), 1159–1167.

Dietrich, A., & Allen, J. D. (1997). Vasopressin and memory: I. The vasopressin analogue AVP-sub(4-9) enhances working memory as well as reference memory in the radial arm maze. *Behavioural Brain Research, 87*(2), 195–200.

DiLalla, D. L., Carey, G., Gottesman, I. I., & Bouchard, T. J., Jr. (1996). Heritability of MMPI personality indicators of psychopathology in twins reared apart. *Journal of Abnormal Psychology, 105,* 491–499.

Dill, C. A., Gilden, E. R., Hill, P. C., & Hanselka, L. L. (1982). Federal human subjects regulations. *Personality and Social Psychology Bulletin, 8,* 417–425.

Dindia, K., & Allen, M. (1992). Sex differences in self-disclosure. *Psychological Bulletin, 112,* 106–124.

Dodge, K. A., Laird, R., Lochman, J. E., Zelli, A., & Conduct Problems Prevention Research Group US (2002). Multidimensional latent-construct analysis of children's social information processing patterns: Correlations with aggressive behavior problems. *Psychological Assessment, 14*(1), 60–73.

Dogil, G., et al. (2002). The speaking brain: A tutorial introduction to fMRI experiments in the production of speech, prosody and syntax. *Journal of Neurolinguistics, 15*(1), 59–90.

Dollard, J., Doob, L. W., Miller, N. E., Mowrer, O. H., & Sears, R. R. (1939). *Frustration and aggression.* New Haven, CT: Yale University Press.

Domhoff, G. W. (2001). A new neurocognitive theory of dreams. *Dreaming: Journal of the Association for the Study of Dreams, 11*(1), 13–33.

Donnerstein, E. I., & Wilson, D. W. (1976). Effects of noise and perceived control on ongoing and subsequent aggressive behavior. *Journal of Personality and Social Psychology, 34,* 774–781.

Doob, A. N., & Wood, L. (1972). Catharsis and aggression. *Journal of Personality and Social Psychology, 22,* 236–245.

Downey, J. I., & Friedman, R. C. (1998). Female homosexuality: Classical psychoanalytic theory reconsidered. *Journal of the American Psychoanalytic Association, 46*(2), 471–506.

Drapkin, R. G., Wing, R. R., & Shiffman, S. (1995). Responses to hypothetical high risk situations. *Health Psychology, 14,* 427–434.

Dubbert, P. M. (2002). Physical activity and exercise: Recent advances and current challenges. *Journal of Consulting and Clinical Psychology, 70*(3), 526–536.

Duberstein, P. R., et al. (2000). Personality traits and suicidal behavior and ideation in depressed inpatients 50 years of age and older. *Journals of Gerontology: Series B: Psychological Sciences & Social Sciences, 55B*(1), P18–P26.

Duckitt, J. (1992). Psychology and prejudice. *American Psychologist, 47,* 1182–1193.

Duenwald, M. (2002, January 22). Body's defender goes on the attack. *The New York Times,* pp. F1, F9.

Duka, T., Tasker, R., & McGowan, J. F. (2000). The effects of 3-week estrogen hormone replacement on cognition in elderly healthy females. *Psychopharmacology, 149*(2), 129–139.

Duncan, J., et al. (2000). A neural basis for general intelligence. *Science, 289*(5478), 457–460.

Durbin, D. L., Darling, N., Steinberg, L., & Brown, B. B. (1993). Parenting style and peer group membership among European-American adolescents. *Journal of Research on Adolescence, 3*(1), 87–100.

Duval, T. S., & Silvia, P. J. (2002). Self-awareness, probability of improvement, and the self-serving bias. *Journal of Personality & Social Psychology, 82*(1), 49–61.

Dweck, C. (1997). Paper presented to the meeting of the Society for Research in Child Development. Cited in Murray, B. (1997). Verbal praise may be the best motivator of all. *APA Monitor, 28*(6), 26.

d'Ydewalle, G., Luwel, K., & Brunfaut, E.. (1999). The importance of on-going concurrent activities as a function of age in time- and event-based prospective memory. *European Journal of Cognitive Psychology, 11*(2), 219–237.

Eagle, M. (2000). Repression, part I of II. *Psychoanalytic Review, 87*(1), 1–38.

Eagly, A. H. (2000). Cited in Goode, E. (2000, May 19). Response to stress found that's particularly female. *The New York Times,* p. A20.

Eagly, A. H., Ashmore, R. D., Makhijani, M. G., & Longo, L. C. (1991). What is beautiful is good, but . . . *Psychological Bulletin, 110,* 109–128.

Eagly, A. H., & Chaiken, S. (1993). *The psychology of attitudes.* Fort Worth: Harcourt Brace Jovanovich.

Easterlin, R. A. (2001). Life cycle welfare: Trends and differences. *Journal of Happiness Studies, 2*(1), 1–2.

Easterline, R. A. (2002). Is reported happiness five years ago comparable to present happiness? A cautionary note. *Journal of Happiness Studies, 3*(2), 193–198.

Eaton, J. (2001). Management communication: The threat of groupthink. *Corporate Communications, 6*(4), 183–192.

Eaves, L., et al. (2000). Genetic and environmental causes of covariation in interview assessments of disruptive behavior in child and adolescent twins. *Behavior Genetics, 30*(4), 321–334.

Eberly, M. B., & Montemayor, R. (1999). Adolescent affection and helpfulness toward parents: A 2-year follow-up. *Journal of Early Adolescence, 19*(2), 226–248.

Ebbinghaus, H. (1913). *Memory: A contribution to experimental psychology.* (H. A. Roger & C. E. Bussenius, Trans.). New York: Columbia University Press. (Original work published 1885).

Edinger, J. D., Wohlgemuth, W. K., Radtke, R. A., Marsh, G. R., & Quillian, R. E. (2001). Cognitive behavioral therapy for treatment of chronic primary insomnia: A randomized controlled trial. *Journal of the American Medical Association, 285*(14), 1856–1864.

Edmundson, M. (1999, August 22). Psychoanalysis, American style. *The New York Times online.*

Egan, M.. F., et al. (2001). Relative risk of neurological signs in siblings of patients with schizophrenia. *American Journal of Psychiatry, 158,* 1827–1834.

Egeth, H. E. (1993). What do we *not* know about eyewitness identification? *American Psychologist, 48,* 577–580.

Ehlers, A., Maercker, A., & Boos, A. (2000). Posttraumatic stress disorder following political imprisonment: The role of mental defeat, alienation, and perceived permanent change. *Journal of Abnormal Psychology, 109*(1), 45–55.

Ehrlich, P. R. (2000). Cited in Angier, N. (2000, October 10). A conversation with Dr. Paul R. Ehrlich: On human nature, genetics and the evolution of culture. *The New York Times online.*

Eich, E. (1995). Searching for mood dependent memory. *Psychological Science, 6,* 67–75.

Eich, E., Macaulay, D., & Lam, R. W. (1997). Mania, depression, and mood dependent memory. *Cognition & Emotion, 11*(5-6), 607–618.

Eidem, B. W., et al. (2001). Early detection of cardiac dysfunction: Use of the myocardial performance index in patients with anorexia nervosa. *Journal of Adolescent Health, 29*(4), 267–270.

Einstein, G. O., McDaniel, M. A., Smith, R., & Shaw, P. (1998). Habitual prospective memory and aging: Remembering instructions and forgetting actions. *Psychological Science, 9*(4), 284–288.

Ekman, P. (1980). *The face of man.* New York: Garland.

Ekman, P. (1993a). Facial expression and emotion. *American Psychologist, 48,* 384–392.

Ekman, P. (1993b). Cited in D. Goleman (1993, October 26). One smile (only one) can lift a mood. *The New York Times,* p. C11.

Ekman, P., et al. (1987). Universals and cultural differences in the judgments of facial expressions of emotion. *Journal of Personality and Social Psychology, 53,* 712–717.

Elkind, D. (1967). Egocentrism in adolescence. *Child Development, 38,* 1025–1034.

Elkind, D. (1985). Egocentrism redux. *Developmental Review, 5,* 218–226.

Elkind, D., & Bowen, R. (1979). Imaginary audience behavior in children and adolescents. *Developmental Psychology, 15*(1), 38–44.

Ellenbroek, B. A., Sluyter, F., & Cools, A. R. (2000). The role of genetic and early environmental factors in determining apomorphine susceptibility. *Psychopharmacology, 148*(2), 124–131.

Ellickson, P. L., Hays, R. D., & Bell, R. M. (1992). Stepping through the drug use sequence. *Journal of Abnormal Psychology, 101,* 441–451.

Ellickson, P. L., Tucker, J. S., Klein, D. J., & McGuigan, K. A. (2001). Prospective risk factors for alcohol misuse in late adolescence. *Journal of Studies on Alcohol, 62*(6), 773–782.

Ellis, A. (2000). Cited in Chamberlin, J. (2000). An historic meeting of the minds. *Monitor on Psychology, 31*(9), 27.

Ellis, A. (2002). The role of irrational beliefs in perfectionism. In G. L. Flett & P. L. Hewitt (eds.), *Perfectionism: Theory, research, and treatment.* Washington, DC: American Psychological Association.

Ellis, A., & Dryden, W. (1996). *The practice of rational emotive behavior therapy.* New York: Springer.

Ellis, L. (1990). Prenatal stress may effect sex-typical behaviors of a child. *Brown University Child Behavior and Development Letter, 6*(1), pp. 1–3.

Ellis, L., & Ames, M. A. (1987). Neurohormonal functioning and sexual orientation. *Psychological Bulletin, 101,* 233–258.

Ellsworth, P. C., Carlsmith, J. M., & Henson, A. (1972). The stare as a stimulus to flight in human subjects. *Journal of Personality and Social Psychology, 21,* 302–311.

Elzinga, B. M., Bermond, B., & van Dyck, R. (2002). The relationship between dissociative proneness and alexithymia. *Psychotherapy & Psychosomatics, 71*(2), 104–111.

Emde, R. (1993). Cited in Adler, T. (1993). Shy, bold temperament? It's mostly in the genes. *APA Monitor, 24*(1), 7, 8.

Engel, J. (1996). Surgery for seizures. *New England Journal of Medicine, 334,* 647–652.

Engels, G. I., Garnefski, N., & Diekstra, R. F. W. (1993). Efficacy of rational–emotive therapy. *Journal of Consulting and Clinical Psychology, 61,* 1083–1090.

Erel, O., Oberman, Y., & Yirmiya, N. (2000). Maternal versus nonmaternal care and seven domains of children's development. *Psychological Bulletin, 126*(5), 727–747.

Erikson, E. H. (1963). *Childhood and society.* New York: W. W. Norton.

Eron, L. D. (1982). Parent–child interaction, television violence, and aggression of children. *American Psychologist, 37,* 197–211.

Eron, L. D. (1993). Cited in DeAngelis, T. (1993). It's baaack: TV violence, concern for kid viewers. *APA Monitor, 24*(8), 16.

Ertem, I. O., Leventhal, J. M., & Dobbs, S. (2000). Intergenerational continuity of child physical abuse: How good is the evidence? *Lancet, 356,* 814–819.

Evans, G. W., Lepore, S. J., & Allen, K. M. (2000). Cross-cultural differences in tolerance for crowding: Fact or fiction? *Journal of Personality & Social Psychology, 79*(2), 204–210.

Evans, S. W., et al. (2001). Dose-response effects of methylphenidate on ecologically valid measures of academic performance and classroom behavior in adolescents with ADHD. *Experimental & Clinical Psychopharmacology, 9*(2), 163–175.

Eysenck, H. J., & Eysenck, M. W. (1985). *Personality and individual differences.* New York: Plenum.

Fairburn, C. G., et al. (1998). Risk factors for binge eating disorder: A community-based, case-control study. *Archives of General Psychiatry, 55*(5), 425–432.

Faller, H., Buelzebruck, H., Drings, P., & Lang, H. (1999). Coping, distress, and survival among patients with lung cancer. *Archives of General Psychiatry, 56*(8) 756–762.

Fallon, A. E., & Rozin, P. (1985). Sex differences in perceptions of desirable body shape. *Journal of Abnormal Psychology, 94,* 102–105.

Fantz, R. L. (1961). The origin of form perception. *Scientific American, 204*(5), 66–72.

Farber, B. A., Brink, D. C., & Raskin, P. M. (1996). *The psychotherapy of Carl Rogers: Cases and commentary* (pp. 74–75). New York: The Guilford Press.

Farley, F. (2000). Hans J. Eysenck (1916–1997). *American Psychologist, 55*(6), 674–675.

Farr, S. A., Flood, J. F., & Morley, J. E. (2000a). The effect of cholinergic, GABAergic, serotonergic, and glutamatergic receptor modulation on posttrial memory processing in the hippocampus. *Neurobiology of Learning & Memory, 73*(2), 150–167.

Farr, S. A., Uezu, K., Creonte, T. A., Flood, J. F., & Morley, J. E. (2000b). Modulation of memory processing in the cingulate cortex of mice. *Pharmacology, Biochemistry & Behavior, 65*(3), 363–368.

Fehr, B., & Russell, J. A. (1991). The concept of love viewed from a prototype perspective. *Journal of Personality and Social Psychology, 60,* 425–438.

Feingold, A. (1992a). Gender differences in mate selection preferences. *Psychological Bulletin, 112,* 125–139.

Feingold, A. (1992b). Good-looking people are not what we think. *Psychological Bulletin, 111,* 304–341.

Feingold, A. (1994). Gender differences in personality: A meta-analysis. *Psychological Bulletin, 116,* 429–456.

Feingold, A. (1998). Gender stereotyping for sociability, dominance, character, and mental health: A meta-analysis of findings from the bogus stranger paradigm. *Genetic, Social, & General Psychology Monographs, 124*(3), 253–270.

Felson, R. B. (2002). *Violence and gender reexamined.* Washington, DC: American Psychological Association.

Feola, T. W., de Wit, H., & Richards, J. B. (2000). Effects of *d*-amphetamine and alcohol on a measure of behavioral inhibition in rats. *Behavioral Neuroscience, 114*(4), 838–848.

Ferry, B., Roozendaal, B., & McGaugh, J. L. (1999). Role of norepinephrine in mediating stress hormone regulation of long-term memory storage: A critical involvement of the amygdala. *Biological Psychiatry, 46*(9), 1140–1152.

Festinger, L., & Carlsmith, J. M. (1959). Cognitive consequences of forced compliance. *Journal of Abnormal and Social Psychology, 58,* 203–210.

Festinger, L., Riecken, H. W., Jr., & Schachter, S. (1956). *When prophecy fails.* Minneapolis: University of Minnesota Press.

Field, T. M. (1991). Young children's adaptations to repeated separations from their mothers. *Child Development, 62,* 539–547.

Fiellin, D. A., et al. (2001). Methadone maintenance in primary care: A randomized controlled trial. *Journal of the American Medical Association, 286*(14), 1724–1731.

Finkenauer, C., et al. (1998). Flashbulb memories and the underlying mechanisms of their formation: Toward an emotional-integrative model. *Memory & Cognition, 26*(3), 516–531.

Finn, P. R., Sharkansky, E. J., Brandt, K. M., & Turcotte, N. (2000). The effects of familial risk, personality, and expectancies on alcohol use and abuse. *Journal of Abnormal Psychology, 109*(1), 122–133.

Fisher, H. E. (2000). Brains do it: Lust, attraction and attachment. *Cerebrum, 2,* 23–42.

Flack, W. F., Jr., Laird, J. D., & Cavallaro, L. A. (1999). Separate and combined effects of facial expressions and bodily postures on emotional feelings. *European Journal of Social Psychology, 29*(2–3), 203–217.

Flashman, L. A., McAllister, T. W., Andreasen, N. C., & Saykin, A. J. (2000). Smaller brain size associated with unawareness of illness in patients with schizophrenia. *American Journal of Psychiatry, 157,* 1167–1169.

Flavell, J. H. (2000). Development of children's knowledge about the mental world. *International Journal of Behavioral Development, 24*(1), 15–23.

Flavell, J. H., Miller, P. H., & Miller, S. A. (2002). *Cognitive development* (4th ed.). Upper Saddle River, NJ: Prentice Hall.

Flegal, K. M., Carroll, M. D., Ogden, C. L., & Johnson, C. L. (2002). Prevalence and trends in obesity among U.S. adults, 1999–2000. *Journal of the American Medical Association, 288*(14), 1723–1727.

Flemons, W. W. (2002). Obstructive sleep apnea. *New England Journal of Medicine online, 347*(7), 498–504.

Flett, G. L., & Hewitt, P. L. (2002). *Perfectionism.* Washington, DC: American Psychological Association.

Flor, H., & Birbaumer, N. (1993). Comparison of the efficacy of electromyographic biofeedback, cognitive-behavioral therapy, and conservative medical intervention in the treatment of chronic musculoskeletal pain. *Journal of Consulting and Clinical Psychology, 61,* 653–658.

Foerster, J., Higgins, E. T., & Strack, F. (2000). When stereotype disconfirmation is a personal threat: How prejudice and prevention focus moderate incongruency effects. *Social Cognition, 18*(2), 178–197.

Fogel, D. B. (2000, July). Paper presented at the 2000 Congress on Evolutionary Computation, San Diego.

Folkman, S., & Moskowitz, T. (2000a). Positive affect and the other side of coping. *American Psychologist, 55*(6), 647–654.

Folkman, S., & Moskowitz, J. T. (2000b). The context matters. *Personality & Social Psychology Bulletin, 26*(2), 150–151.

Follingstad, D., & McCormick, M. (2002). *Law and mental health professionals.* Washington, DC: American Psychological Association.

Ford, K., Wirawan, D. N., Reed, B. D., Muliawan, P., & Sutarga, M. (2000). AIDS and STD knowledge, condom use, and HIV/STD infection among female sex workers in Bali, Indonesia. *AIDS Care, 12*(5), 523–534.

Fox, E., Russo, R., Bowles, R., & Dutton, K. (2001). Do threatening stimuli draw or hold visual attention in subclinical anxiety? *Journal of Experimental Psychology: General, 130*(4), 681–700.

Francis, L. E. (2000). Conflicting bureaucracies, conflicted work: Dilemmas in case management for homeless people with mental illness. *Journal of Sociology & Social Welfare, 27*(2) 97–112.

Frangione, B. (2000, July). Amyloid and dementia: To be or not to be. Paper presented to the World Alzheimer Congress 2000, Washington, DC.

Frankel, K. A., & Bates, J. E. (1990). Mother–toddler problem solving. *Child Development, 61,* 810–819.

Fraser, A. M., Brockert, J. E., & Ward, R. H. (1995). Association of young maternal age with adverse reproductive outcomes. *New England Journal of Medicine, 332,* 1113–1117.

Fredricks, J. A., & Eccles, J. S. (2002). Children's competence and value beliefs from childhood through adolescence: Growth trajectories in two male-sex-typed domains. *Developmental Psychology, 38*(4), 519–533.

Freedman, J. L., & Fraser, S. C. (1966). Compliance without pressure: The foot-in-the-door technique. *Journal of Personality and Social Psychology, 4,* 195–202.

Freeman, E. W., et al. (2001). Evaluation of a unique oral contraceptive in the treatment of premenstrual dysphoric disorder. *Journal of Women's Health & Gender-Based Medicine, 10*(6), 561–569.

Freeman, H. P., & Payne, R. (2000). Racial injustice in health care. *The New England Journal of Medicine, 342,* 1045–1047.

Freeman, M. S., Spence, M. J., & Oliphant, C. M. (1993, June). *Newborns prefer their mothers' low-pass filtered voices over other female filtered voices.* Paper presented at the annual convention of the American Psychological Society, Chicago.

Freud, S. (1927). A religious experience. In *Standard edition of the complete psychological works of Sigmund Freud, Vol. 21.* London: Hogarth Press, 1964.

Frey, B. S., & Stutzer, A. (2000). Happiness prospers in democracy. *Journal of Happiness Studies, 1*(3), 79–102.

Friedman, L. J. (1999). *Identity's architect: A biography of Erik H. Erikson.* New York: Scribner.

Friedman, M., & Ulmer, D. (1984). *Treating Type A behavior and your heart.* New York: Fawcett Crest.

Friedman, R. C., & Downey, J. I. (1994). Homosexuality. *New England Journal of Medicine, 331,* 923–930.

Friedman, S. R., et al. (2001). Correlates of anal sex with men among young adult women in an inner city minority neighborhood. *AIDS, 15*(15), 2057–2060.

Friedrich, M. J. (2000). Can male hormones really help women? *Journal of the American Medical Association online, 283*(20).

Frieze, I. H. (2000). Violence in close relationships: Development of a research area. *Psychological Bulletin, 126*(5), 681–684.

Frisch, R. (1997). Cited in Angier, N. (1997). Chemical tied to fat control could help trigger puberty. *The New York Times,* pp. C1, C3.

Fritsch, G., & Hitzig, E. (1870). On the electrical excitability of the cerebrum. In G. von Bonin (Ed.), *Some papers on the cerebral cortex.* Springfield, IL: Charles C Thomas. (1960).

Frodi, A. M., Macauley, J., & Thome, P. R. (1977). Are women always less aggressive than men? A review of the experimental literature. *Psychological Bulletin, 84,* 634–660.

Funk, J. B., Buchman, D., Myers, M., & Jenks, J. (2000, August 7). Asking the right question in research on violent electronic games. Paper presented to the annual meeting of the American Psychological Association, Washington, D.C.

Fuster, J. M. (2000). The prefrontal cortex of the primate: A synopsis. *Psychobiology, 28*(2), 125–131.

Fylkesnes, K., et al. (2001). Declining HIV prevalence and risk behaviours in Zambia: Evidence from surveillance and population-based surveys. *AIDS, 15*(7), 907–916.

Galambos, N. L., & Turner, P. K. (1999). Parent and adolescent temperaments and the quality of parent–adolescent relations. *Merrill-Palmer Quarterly, 45*(3), 493–511.

Galassi, J. P. (1988). Four cognitive-behavioral approaches. *The Counseling Psychologist, 16*(1), 102–105.

Gallagher, A. M., et al. (2000). Gender differences in advanced mathematical problem solving. *Journal of Experimental Child Psychology, 75*(3), 165–190.

Gallup, G. H., & Newport, F. (1991). Belief in paranormal phenomena among adult Americans. *Skeptical Inquirer, 15*(4), 137–146.

Garcia, J. (1993). Misrepresentation of my criticism of Skinner. *American Psychologist, 48,* 1158.

Garcia, J., Brett, L. P., & Rusiniak, K. W. (1989). Limits of Darwinian conditioning. In S. B. Klein & R. R. Mowrer (Eds.), *Contemporary learning theories: Instrumental conditioning theory and the impact of biological constraints on learning.* Hillsdale, NJ: Erlbaum.

Garcia, J., & Koelling, R. A. (1966). Relation of cue to consequences in avoidance learning. *Psychonomic Science 4,* 123–124.

Garcia-Moreno, C., & Watts, C. (2000). Violence against women: Its importance for HIV/AIDS. *AIDS, 14*(Suppl 3), S253–S265.

Gardner, H. (1983/1993). *Frames of mind.* New York: Basic Books.

Gardner, H. (2001, April 5). Multiple intelligence. *The New York Times,* p. A20.

Garfinkel, R. (1995). Cited in Margoshes, P. (1995). For many, old age is the prime of life. *APA Monitor, 26*(5), 36–37.

Garnets, L. D. (2002). Sexual orientations in perspective. *Cultural Diversity and Ethnic Minority Psychology, 8*(2), 115–129.

Gazzaniga, M. S. (1995). Consciousness and the cerebral hemispheres. In M. S. Gazzaniga (Ed.), *The cognitive neurosciences.* Cambridge, MA: MIT Press.

Geers, A., Spehar, B., & Sedey, A. (2002). Use of speech by children from total communication programs who wear cochlear implants. *American Journal of Speech-Language Pathology, 11*(1), 50–58.

Geiser, F., et al. (2001). Magnetic resonance spectroscopic and relaxometric determination of bone marrow changes in anorexia nervosa. *Psychosomatic Medicine, 63*(4), 631–647.

Gendall, K. A., Bulik, C. M., Joyce, P. R., McIntosh, V. V., & Carter, F. A. (2000). Menstrual cycle irregularity in bulimia nervosa: Associated factors and changes with treatment. *Journal of Psychosomatic Research, 49*(6), 409–415.

Gentry, M. V., et al. (2000). Nicotine patches improve mood and response speed in a lexical decision task. *Addictive Behaviors, 25*(4), 549–557.

Gershoff, E. T. (2002). Corporal punishment by parents and associated child behaviors and experiences: A meta-analytic and theoretical review. *Psychological Bulletin, 128*(4), 539–579.

Geschwind, D. H. (2000) Cited in Rosenbaum, D. E. (2000, May 16). On left-handedness, its causes and costs. *The New York Times,* pp. F1, F6.

Geschwind, N., & Galaburda, A. M. (1987). *Cerebral lateralization: Biological mechanisms, associations, and pathology.* Cambridge, MA: Harvard University Press.

Gesell, A. (1929). Maturation and infant behavior patterns. *Psychological Review, 36,* 307–319.

Getzels, J. W., & Jackson, P. W. (1962). *Creativity and intelligence.* New York: Wiley.

Gibson, M., & Ogbu, J. (Eds.). (1991). *Minority status and schooling.* New York: Garland.

Gigerenzer, G., Hoffrage, U., & Kleinbölting, H. (1991). Probabilistic mental models. *Psychological Review, 98,* 506–528.

Gigone, D., & Hastie, R. (1997). Proper analysis of the accuracy of group judgments. *Psychological Bulletin, 121,* 149–167.

Gijsman, H. J., et al. (2002). A dose-finding study on the effects of branch chain amino acids on surrogate markers of brain dopamine function. *Psychopharmacology, 160*(2), 192–197.

Gili-Planas, M., Roca-Bennasar, M., Ferrer-Perez, V., & Bernardo-Arroyo, M. (2001). Suicidal ideation, psychiatric disorder, and medical illness in a community epidemiological study. *Suicide & Life-Threatening Behavior, 31*(2), 207–213.

Gilligan, C. (1982). *In a different voice.* Cambridge, MA: Harvard University Press.

Gilligan, C., Ward, J. V., & Taylor, J. M. (1989). *Mapping the moral domain: A contribution of women's thinking to psychological theory and education.* Cambridge, MA: Harvard University Press.

Gilovich, T., & Eibach, R. (2001). The fundamental attribution error where it really counts. *Psychological Inquiry, 12*(1), 23–26.

Ginsburg, G., & Bronstein, P. (1993). Family factors related to children's intrinsic/extrinsic motivational orientation and academic performance. *Child Development, 64,* 1461–1474.

Glantz, L. A., & Lewis, D. A. (2000). Decreased dendritic spine density on prefrontal cortical pyramidal neurons in schizophrenia. *Archives of General Psychiatry, 57*(1), 65–73.

Glaser, R., et al. (1993). Stress and the memory T-cell response to the Epstein–Barr virus. *Health Psychology, 12,* 435–442.

Gleason, J. B., & Ratner, N. B. (1993). Language development in children. In J. B. Gleason & N. B. Ratner (Eds.), *Psycholinguistics.* Fort Worth: Harcourt Brace Jovanovich.

Glenn, S. S., Ellis, J., & Greenspoon, J. (1992). On the revolutionary nature of the operant as a unit of behavioral selection. *American Psychologist, 47,* 1326–1329.

Glynn, J. R., et al. (2001). Why do young women have a much higher prevalence of HIV than young men? A study of Kisumu, Kenya and Ndola Zambia. *AIDS, 15*(Suppl4), S51–S60.

Goadsby, P. J., Lipton, R. B., & Ferrari, M. D. (2002). Drug therapy: Migraine: Current understanding and treatment. *New England Journal of Medicine, 346,* 257–270.

Godden, D. R., & Baddeley, A. D. (1975). Context-dependent memory in two natural environments: On land and underwater. *British Journal of Psychology, 66,* 325–331.

Goldman, J. A., & Harlow, L. L. (1993). Self-perception variables that mediate AIDS-preventive behavior in college students. *Health Psychology, 12,* 489–498.

Goldman-Rakic, P. S. (1995). Cited in Goleman, D. (1995, May 2). Biologists find site of working memory. *The New York Times,* pp. C1, C9.

Goldman-Rakic, P. S., Muly, E. C., III, & Williams, G. V. (2000). D-sub-1 receptors in prefrontal cells and circuits. *Brain Research Reviews, 31*(2-3), 295–301.

Goldschmidt, D., & Reuters. (2000). Portions, foods in a diet won't determine weight loss, study says. Web posted on www.CNN.com on October 20, 2000.

Goleman, D. J. (1995). *Emotional intelligence.* New York: Bantam Books.

Goodall, J. (2000). *My life with the chimpanzees.* Minstrel Books.

Goodall, J., & Peterson, D. (2000). *Africa in my blood: An autobiography in letters.* Boston: Houghton Mifflin.

Goode, E. (2000, June 25). Thinner: The male battle with anorexia. *The New York Times,* p. MH8.

Goode, E. (2001, February 20). What's in an inkblot? Some say, not much. *The New York Times,* pp. F1, F4.

Goodwin, P. J., et al. (2001). The effect of group psychosocial support on survival in metastatic breast cancer. *New England Journal of Medicine, 345*(24), 1719–1726.

Gorman, J. M. (2001). A call to action: Overcoming anxiety through active coping. *American Journal of Psychiatry, 158*(12), 1953–1955.

Gottesman, I. I. (1991). *Schizophrenia genesis.* New York: Freeman.

Gottfried, A. E., Fleming, J. S., & Gottfried, A. W. (1994). Role of parental motivational practices in children's academic intrinsic motivation and achievement. *Journal of Educational Psychology, 86,* 104–113.

Gould, S. J. (2002). *The structure of evolutionary theory.* Cambridge, MA: The Belknap Press/Harvard University Press.

Grady, C. L., McIntosh, A. R., Rajah, M. N., Beig, S., & Craik, F. I. M. (1999). The effects of age on the neural correlates of episodic encoding. *Cerebral Cortex, 9*(8), 805–814.

Grady, D., et al. (2002). Cardiovascular disease outcomes during 6.8 years of hormone therapy. Heart and Estrogen/progestin Replacement Study follow-up (HERS II). *Journal of the American Medical Association, 288*(1), 49–57.

Graf, P. (1990). Life-span changes in implicit and explicit memory. *Bulletin of the Psychonomic Society, 28,* 353–358.

Graham, C., & Pettinato, S. (2001). Happiness, markets, and democracy: Latin America in comparative perspective. *Journal of Happiness Studies, 2*(3), 237–268.

Granot, D., & Mayseless, O. (2001). Attachment security and adjustment to school in middle childhood. *International Journal of Behavioral Development, 25*(6), 530–541.

Grant, H. M., et al. (1998). Context-dependent memory for meaningful material: Information for students. *Applied Cognitive Psychology, 12*(6), 617–623.

Green, D. P., Glaser, J., & Rich, A. (1998). From lynching to gay bashing: The elusive connection between economic condition and hate crime. *Journal of Personality and Social Psychology, 75,* 82–92.

Green, J. P., & Lynn, S. J. (2000). Hypnosis and suggestion-based approaches to smoking cessation: An examination of the evidence. *International Journal of Clinical & Experimental Hypnosis, 48*(2), 195–224.

Greenbaum, P., & Rosenfeld, H. M. (1978). Patterns of avoidance in response to interpersonal staring and proximity: Effects of bystanders on drivers at a traffic intersection. *Journal of Personality & Social Psychology, 36*(6), 575–587.

Greenberger, E., Chen, C., Tally, S. R., & Dong, Q. (2000). Family, peer, and individual correlates of depressive symptomology among U.S. and Chinese adolescents. *Journal of Consulting and Clinical Psychology, 68,* 209–219.

Greene, B. (1993). African American women. In L. Comas-Diaz & B. A. Greene (Eds.), *Women of color and mental health.* New York: Guilford.

Greeno, C. G., & Wing, R. R. (1994). Stress-induced eating. *Psychological Bulletin, 115,* 444–464.

Griffin, C. (2001). Imagining new narratives of youth: Youth research, the "new Europe" and global youth culture. *Childhood: A Global Journal of Child Research, 8*(2), 147–166.

Grinspoon, L. (2000). Medical cannabis: The patient's and the doctor's dilemmas. *Addiction Research, 8*(1), 1–4.

Grön, G., Wunderlich, A. P., Spitzer, M., Tomczak, R., & Riepe, M. W. (2000). Brain activation during human navigation: Gender-different neural networks as substrate of performance. *Nature Neuroscience, 3*(4), 404–408.

Grosser, B. I., Monti-Bloch, L., Jennings-White, C., & Berliner, D. L. (2000). Behavioral and electrophysiological effects of androstadienone, a human pheromone. *Psychoneuroendocrinology, 25*(3), 289–300.

Guerin, B. (1999). Social behaviors as determined by different arrangements of social consequences: Social loafing, social facilitation, deindividuation, and a modified social loafing. *Psychological Record, 49*(4), 565–578.

Guilford, J. P. (1988). Some changes in the structure-of-intellect model. *Educational and Psychological Measurement, 48,* 1–4.

Gump, B. B., & Matthews, K. A. (2000). Are vacations good for your health? The 9-year mortality experience after the Multiple Risk Factor Intervention Trial. *Psychosomatic Medicine, 62*(5), 608–612.

Gupta, V. B., Nwosa, N. M., Nadel, T. A., & Inamdar, S. (2001). Externalizing behaviors and television viewing in children of low-income minority parents. *Clinical Pediatrics, 40*(6), 337–341.

Guralnik, O., Schmeidler, J., & Simeon, D. (2000). Feeling unreal: Cognitive processes in depersonalization. *American Journal of Psychiatry, 157,* 103–109.

Gurrera, R. J., Nestor, P. G., & O'Donnell, B. F. (2000). Personality traits in schizophrenia: Comparison with a community sample. *Journal of Nervous & Mental Disease, 188*(1), 31–35.

Haaf, R. A., Smith, P. H., & Smitley, S. (1983). Infant response to facelike patterns under fixed trial and infant-control procedures. *Child Development, 54,* 172–177.

Haaga, D. A. F. (2000). Introduction to the special section on Stepped Care Models in Psychotherapy. *Journal of Consulting and Clinical Psychology, 68*(4), 547–548.

Haaga, D. A. F., & Davison, G. C. (1993). An appraisal of rational-emotive therapy. *Journal of Consulting and Clinical Psychology, 61,* 215–220.

Haan, M. N. (2000, July). Cognitive decline is not normal in aging. Paper presented to the World Alzheimer Congress 2000, Washington, DC.

Haber, R. N. (1980). Eidetic images are not just imaginary. *Psychology Today, 14*(11), 72–82.

Hakim, A. A., et al. (1998). Effects of walking on mortality among nonsmoking retired men. *New England Journal of Medicine, 338,* 94–99.

Hall, C. S. (1984). A "ubiquitous sex difference in dreams" revisited. *Journal of Personality and Social Psychology, 46,* 1109–1117.

Hall, G. C. N. (1997). Cultural malpractice: The growing obsolescence of psychology with the changing U.S. population. *American Psychologist, 52,* 642–651.

Halmi, K. A., et al. (2000). Perfectionism in anorexia nervosa: Variation by clinical subtype, obsessionality, and pathological eating behavior. *American Journal of Psychiatry, 157,* 1799–1805.

Halpern, D. F. (1989). *Thought and knowledge.* (2nd ed.). Hillsdale, NJ: Erlbaum.

Halpern, D. F. (1997). Sex differences in intelligence: Implications for education. *American Psychologist, 52,* 1091–1102.

Halpern, D. F., Hansen, C., & Riefer, D. (1990). Analogies as an aid to understanding and memory. *Journal of Educational Psychology, 82,* 298–305.

Halpern, D. F., & LaMay, M. L. (2000). The smarter sex: A critical review of sex differences in intelligence. *Educational Psychology Review, 12*(2), 229–246.

Hamilton, M. (2001). Who believes in astrology? Effect of favorableness of astrologically derived personality descriptions on acceptance of astrology. *Personality & Individual Differences, 31*(6), 895–902.

Hankin, B. L., & Abramson, L. Y. (2001). Development of gender differences in depression: An elaborated cognitive vulnerability-transactional stress theory. *Psychological Bulletin, 127*(6), 773–796.

Hansell, N. K., et al. (2001). Genetic influence on ERP slow wave measures of working memory. *Behavior Genetics, 31*(6), 603–614.

Hansen, C. J., Stevens, L. C., & Coast, J. R. (2001). Exercise duration and mood state: How much is enough to feel better? *Health Psychology, 20*(4), 267–275.

Harker, L., & Keltner, D. (2001). Expressions of positive emotion in women's college yearbook pictures and their relationship to personality and life outcomes across adulthood. *Journal of Personality and Social Psychology, 80*(1), 112–124.

Harkness, K. L., & Luther, J. (2001). Clinical risk factors for the generation of life events in major depression. *Journal of Abnormal Psychology, 110*(4), 564–572.

Harley, K., & Reese, E. (1999). Origins of autobiographical memory. *Developmental Psychology, 35*(5), 1338–1348.

Harlow, H. F. (1959). Love in infant monkeys. *Scientific American, 200,* 68–86.

Harlow, H. F., & Zimmermann, R. R. (1959). Affectional responses in the infant monkey. *Science, 130,* 421–432.

Hart, A. J., et al. (2000). Differential response in the human amygdala to racial outgroup vs. ingroup face stimuli. *NeuroReport, 11*(11), 2351–2355.

Hart, J. W., Bridgett, D. J., & Karau, S. J. (2001). Coworker ability and effort as determinants of individual effort on a collective task. *Group Dynamics, 5*(3), 181–190.

Haselton, M. G., & Buss, D. M. (2001). The affective shift hypothesis: The functions of emotional changes following sexual intercourse. *Personal Relationships, 8*(4), 357–369.

Hashimoto, N. (1991). Memory development in early childhood. *Journal of Genetic Psychology, 152,* 101–117.

Hassinger, H. J., Semenchuk, E. M., & O'Brien, W. H. (1999). Appraisal and coping responses to pain and stress in migraine headache sufferers. *Journal of Behavioral Medicine, 22*(4), 327–340.

Hastings, P. D., Zahn-Waxler, C., Robinson, J., Usher, B., & Bridges, D. (2000). The development of concern for others in children with behavior problems. *Developmental Psychology, 36*(5), 531–546.

Hawkins, S. A., & Hastie, R. (1990). Hindsight: Biased judgments of past events after the outcomes are known. *Psychological Bulletin, 107,* 311–327.

Hayes, P. (1993). Cited in Chartrand, S. (1993, July 18). A split in thinking among keepers of artificial intelligence. *The New York Times,* p. E6.

Health, United States (2002). http:/www.cdc.gov/nchs. (National Center for Health Statistics.)

Heim, C., et al. (2000). Pituitary-adrenal and autonomic responses to stress in women after sexual and physical abuse in childhood. *Journal of the American Medical Association, 284,* 592–597.

Heimpel, S. A., Wood, J. V., Marshall, M. A., & Brown, J. D. (2002). Do people with low self-esteem really want to feel better? Self-esteem differences in motivation to repair negative moods. *Journal of Personality & Social Psychology, 82*(1), 128–147.

Heller, D. A., de Faire, U., Pedersen, N. L., Dahlén, G., & McClearn, G. E. (1993). Genetic and environmental influences on serum lipid levels in twins. *New England Journal of Medicine, 328,* 1150–1156.

Helson, R., Stewart, A. J., & Ostrove, J. (1995). Identity in three cohorts of midlife women. *Journal of Personality and Social Psychology, 69,* 544–557.

Henderson, V. W., et al. (2000). Estrogen for Alzheimer's disease in women: Randomized, double-blind, placebo-controlled trial. *Neurology, 54,* 295–301.

Hendin, H., Maltsberger, J. T., Lipschitz, A., Pollinger H., & Kyle, J. (2001). Recognizing and responding to a suicide crisis. *Suicide & Life-Threatening Behavior, 31*(2), 115–128.

Henke, K., et al. (1999). Memory lost and regained following bilateral hippocampal damage. *Journal of Cognitive Neuroscience, 11*(6), 682–697.

Henry, D., et al. (2000). Normative influences on aggression in urban elementary school classrooms. *American Journal of Community Psychology, 28*(1) 59–81.

Hensley, W. E. (1981). The effects of attire, location, and sex on aiding behavior. *Journal of Nonverbal Behavior, 6,* 3–11.

Hepper, P. G., Shahidullah, S., & White, R. (1990, October 4). Origins of fetal handedness. *Nature, 347,* 431.

Hergenhahn, B. R. (2001). *An introduction to the history of psychology,* 4th ed. Pacific Grove, CA: Brooks/Cole.

Herman-Giddens, M. E., et al. (1999). Underascertainment of child abuse mortality in the United States. *Journal of the American Medical Association, 282,* 463–467.

Herrington, D. M., et al. (2000). Effects of estrogen replacement on the progression of coronary-artery atherosclerosis. *The New England Journal of Medicine online, 343*(8).

Herrmann, D. J. (1991). *Super memory.* Emmaus, PA: Rodale.

Hersen, M., Bellack, A. S., Himmelhoch, J. M., & Thase, M. E. (1984). Effect of social skill training, amitriptyline, and psychotherapy in unipolar depressed women. *Behavior Therapy, 15,* 21–40.

Hershenson, R. (2000, August 6). Debating the Mozart theory. *The New York Times magazine online.*

Hershey, D. A., Walsh, D. A., Read, S. J., & Chulef, A. S. (1990). Relationships between metamemory, memory predictions, and memory task performance in adults. *Psychology and Aging, 5,* 215–227.

Hetland, L. (2000). Cited in Hershenson, R. (2000, August 6). Debating the Mozart theory. *The New York Times magazine online.*

Hewitt, P. L., Flett, G. L., & Ediger, E. (1996). Perfectionism and depression. *Journal of Abnormal Psychology, 105,* 276–280.

Hewstone, M., & Hamberger, J. (2000). Perceived variability and stereotype change. *Journal of Experimental Social Psychology, 36*(2), 103–124.

Hilgard, E. R. (1994). Neodissociation theory. In S. J. Lynn & J. W. Rhue. *Dissociation: Clinical, theoretical and research perspectives.* New York: Guilford Press.

Hingson, R., et al. (2002). A call to action: Changing the culture of drinking at U.S. colleges. Washington, DC: National Institutes of Health: National Institute of Alcohol Abuse and Alcoholism.

Hixon, M. D. (1998). Ape language research: A review and behavioral perspective. *Analysis of Verbal Behavior, 15,* 17–39.

Hobfoll, S. E., Ritter, C., Lavin, J., Hulsizer, M. R., & Cameron, R. P. (1995). Depression prevalence and incidence among inner-city pregnant and postpartum women. *Journal of Consulting and Clinical Psychology, 63,* 445–453.

Hobson, J. A. (1999). Arrest of firing of aminergic neurones during REM sleep: Implications for dream theory. *Brain Research Bulletin, 50*(5–6), 333–334.

Hobson, J. A. (2003). *Dreaming: An introduction to the science of sleep.* New York: Oxford University Press.

Hodis, J. Cited in Kolata, G. (2002, December 22). Chasing youth, many gamble on hormones. *The New York Times* online.

Hokin, L., et al. (1998). *Proceedings of the National Academy of Sciences, 95*(14), 8363–8368. Cited in Azar, B. (1998). Lithium's mood-stabilizing effect is explained. *APA Monitor, 29*(9), 8.

Holahan, C. J., & Moos, R. H. (1990). Life stressors, resistance factors, and psychological health. *Journal of Personality and Social Psychology, 58,* 909–917.

Holden, C. (1980). Identical twins reared apart. *Science, 207*(4437), 1323–1328.

Holden, E. W., Deichmann, M. M., & Levy, J. D. (1999). Empirically supported treatments in pediatric psychology: Recurrent pediatric headache. *Journal of Pediatric Psychology, 24*(2), 91–109.

Holland, J. J. (2000, July 25). Groups link media to child violence. The Associated Press online.

Holland, J. L. (1996). Exploring careers with a typology. *American Psychologist, 51,* 397–406.

Hollinger, L. M., & Buschmann, M. B. (1993). Factors influencing the perception of touch by elderly nursing home residents and their health caregivers. *International Journal of Nursing Studies, 30,* 445–461.

Hollingshead, A. B., & Redlich, F. C. (1958). *Social class and mental illness.* New York: Wiley.

Hollon, S. D., & Shelton, R. C. (2001). Treatment guidelines for major depressive disorder. *Behavior Therapy, 32*(2), 235–258.

Holmes, T. H., & Rahe, R. H. (1967). The social readjustment rating scale. *Journal of Psychosomatic Research, 11,* 213–218.

Holroyd, K. A. (2002). Assessment and psychological management of recurrent headache disorders. *Journal of Consulting & Clinical Psychology, 70*(3), 656–677.

Holt, J. (2002, April 14). Supernatural selection. *The New York Times online.*

Hong, Y., Morris, M. W., Chiu, C., & Benet-Martinez, V. (2000). A dynamic constructivist approach to culture and cognition. *American Psychologist, 55*(7), 709–720.

Honorton, C. (1985). Meta-analysis of psi Ganzfeld research. *Journal of Parapsychology, 49,* 51–91.

Honorton, C., et al. (1990). Psi communication in the Ganzfeld. *Journal of Parapsychology, 54,* 99–139.

Honts, C. R., Hodes, R. L., & Raskin, D. C. (1985). Effects of physical countermeasures on the physiological detection of deception. *Journal of Applied Psychology, 70*(1), 177–187.

Hoover, R. N. (2000). Cancer: Nature, nurture, or both. *New England Journal of Medicine online, 343*(2).

Hopper, J. L., & Seeman, E. (1994). The bone density of female twins discordant for tobacco use. *New England Journal of Medicine, 330,* 387–392.

Horn, J. M. (1983). The Texas adoption project. *Child Development, 54,* 268–275.

Hovey, J. D. (2000). Acculturative stress, depression, and suicidal ideation in Mexican immigrants. *Cultural Diversity and Ethnic Minority Psychology, 6*(2), 134–151.

Hu, F. B., et al. (2000). Physical activity and risk of stroke in women. *Journal of the American Medical Association, 283,* 2961–2967.

Hubel, D. H., & Wiesel, T. N. (1979). Brain mechanisms of vision. *Scientific American, 241,* 150–162.

Huesmann, L. R., Eron, L. D., Klein, R., Brice, P., & Fischer, P. (1983). Mitigating the imitation of aggressive behaviors by changing children's attitudes about media violence. *Journal of Personality and Social Psychology, 44,* 899–910.

Huesmann, L. R., & Guerra, N. G. (1997). Children's normative beliefs about aggression and aggressive behavior. *Journal of Personality & Social Psychology, 72*(2), 408–419.

Huesmann, L. R., & Miller, L. S. (1994). Long-term effects of repeated exposure to media violence in childhood. In L. R. Huesmann (Ed.), *Aggressive behavior.* New York: Plenum.

Hulshoff, P., et al. (2000). Prenatal exposure to famine and brain morphology in schizophrenia. *American Journal of Psychiatry, 157*(7), 1170–1172.

Hunsley, J., & Bailey, J. M. (1999). The clinical utility of the Rorschach: Unfulfilled promises and an uncertain future. *Psychological Assessment, 11*(3), 266–277.

Hyde, J. S., & Plant, E. A. (1995). Magnitude of psychological gender differences. *American Psychologist, 50,* 159–161.

Iacono, W. G., & Lykken, D. T. (1997). The validity of the lie detector: Two surveys of scientific opinion. *Journal of Applied Psychology, 82*(3), 426–433.

Iidaka, T., Anderson, N. D., Kapur, S., Cabeza, R., & Craik, F. I. M. (2000). The effect of divided attention on encoding and retrieval in episodic memory revealed by positron emission tomography. *Journal of Cognitive Neuroscience, 12*(2), 267–280.

Insel, T. R. (2000). Toward a neurobiology of attachment. *Review of General Psychology, 4*(2), 176–185.

International Human Genome Sequencing Consortium. (2001). Initial sequencing and analysis of the human genome. *Nature, 409,* 860–921.

Iribarren, C., et al. (2000). Association of hostility with coronary artery calcification in young adults: The CARDIA study. *Journal of the American Medical Association, 283,* 2546–2551.

Isabella, R. A. (1998). Origins of attachment: The role of context, duration, frequency of observation, and infant age in measuring maternal behavior. *Journal of Social & Personal Relationships, 15*(4), 538–554.

Isarida, T., & Isarida, T. (1999). Effects of contextual changes between class and intermission on episodic memory. *Japanese Journal of Psychology, 69*(6), 478–485.

Isomura, T., Fine, S., & Lin, T. (1987). Two Japanese families. *Canadian Journal of Psychiatry, 32,* 282–286.

Izard, C. E. (1984). Emotion-cognition relationships and human development. In C. E. Izard, J. Kagan, & R. B. Zajonc (Eds.), *Emotions, cognition, and behavior.* New York: Cambridge University Press.

Izard, C. E. (1994). Basic emotions, relations among emotions, and emotion-cognition relations. *Psychological Bulletin, 115,* 561–565.

Jacks, J. Z., & Devine, P. G. (2000). Attitude importance, forewarning of message content, and resistance to persuasion. *Basic & Applied Social Psychology, 22*(1) 19–29.

Jackson, H., & Nuttall, R. L. (2001). Risk for preadolescent suicidal behavior: An ecological model. *Child & Adolescent Social Work Journal, 18*(3), 189–203.

Jacob, S., & McClintock, M. K. (2000). Psychological state and mood effects of steroidal chemosignals in women and men. *Hormones and Behavior, 37*(1), 57–78.

Jacob, S., McClintock, M. K., Zelano, B., & Ober, C. (2002, January 22). Paternally inherited HLA alleles are associated with women's choice of male odor. *Nature Genetics online.*

Jacob, T. J., & Charles, E. (1980). Life events and the occurrence of cancer in children. *Psychosomatic Medicine, 42,* 11–24.

Jacox, A., Carr, D. B., & Payne, R. (1994). New clinical-practice guidelines for the management of pain in patients with cancer. *New England Journal of Medicine, 330,* 651–655.

Jaffee, S., & Hyde, J. S. (2000). Gender differences in moral orientation. *Psychological Bulletin, 126*(5), 703–726.

James, W. (1890). *The principles of psychology.* New York: Henry Holt.

Jamison, K. R. (1997). Manic-depressive illness and creativity. *Scientific American mysteries of the mind, Special Issue Vol. 7,* No. 1, 44–49.

Jamison, K. R. (2000). Suicide and bipolar disorder. *Journal of Clinical Psychiatry, 61*(Suppl 9), 47–51.

Janerich, D. T., et al. (1990). Lung cancer and exposure to tobacco smoke in the household. *New England Journal of Medicine, 323,* 632–636.

Janis, I. L. (1982). *Groupthink* (2nd ed.). Boston: Houghton Mifflin.

Janos, P. M. (1987). A fifty-year follow-up of Terman's youngest college students and IQ-matched agemates. *Gifted Child Quarterly, 31,* 55–58.

Janowitz, H. D., & Grossman, M. I. (1949). Effects of variations in nutritive density on intake of food in dogs and cats. *American Journal of Physiology, 158,* 184–193.

Janowsky, J. S., Chavez, B., & Orwoll, E. (2000). Sex steroids modify working memory. *Journal of Cognitive Neuroscience, 12,* 407–414.

Janus, C., et al. (2000). A peptide immunization reduces behavioural impairment and plaques in a model of Alzheimer's disease. *Nature, 408*(6815), 979–981.

Jeffery, R. W., Hennrikus, D. J., Lando, H. A., Murray, D. M., & Liu, J. W. (2000). Reconciling conflicting findings regarding postcessation weight concerns and success in smoking cessation. *Health Psychology, 19,* 242–246.

Jemmott, J. B., et al. (1983). Academic stress, power motivation, and decrease in secretion rate of salivary secretory immunoglobin A. *Lancet, 1,* 1400–1402.

Jensen, M. P., Turner, J. A., & Romano, J. M. (1994). Correlates of improvement in multidisciplinary treatment of chronic pain. *Journal of Consulting and Clinical Psychology, 62,* 172–179.

Johns, A. (2001). Psychiatric effects of cannabis. *The British Journal of Psychiatry, 178,* 116–122.

Johnston, L. D., O'Malley, P. M., & Bachman, J. G. (2001). *Monitoring the Future national survey results on drug use, 1975–2000. Volume I: Secondary school students* (NIH Publication No. 01-4924). Bethesda, MD: National Institute on Drug Abuse.

Joiner, T. E., Jr. (2002). The trajectory of suicidal behavior over time. *Suicide & Life-Threatening Behavior, 32*(1), 33–41.

Jones, J. L., & Leary, M. R. (1994). Effects of appearance-based admonitions against sun exposure on tanning intentions in young adults. *Health Psychology, 13,* 86–90.

Jones, M. C. (1924). Elimination of children's fears. *Journal of Experimental Psychology, 7,* 381–390.

Jonsdottir, I. H., Hellstrand, K., Thoren, P., & Hoffman, P. (2000). Enhancement of natural immunity seen after voluntary exercise in rats. Role of central opioid receptors. *Life Sciences, 66*(13), 1231–1239.

Joranson, D. E., Ryan, K. M., Gilson, A. M., & Dahl, J. L. (2000). Trends in medical use and abuse of opioid analgesics. *Journal of the American Medical Association, 283,* 1710–1714.

Jorgensen, R. S., Johnson, B. T., Kolodziej, M. E., & Schreer, G. E. (1996). Elevated blood pressure and personality. *Psychological Bulletin, 120,* 293–320.

Jorm, A. F., et al. (2002). Sexual orientation and mental health: Results from a community survey of young and middle-aged adults. *British Journal of Psychiatry, 180,* 423–427.

Josefsson, A. M., et al. (2000). Viral load of human papilloma virus 16 as a determinant for development of cervical carcinoma in situ: A nested case-control study. *The Lancet, 355,* 2189–2193.

Kail, R. (2000). Speed of information processing: Developmental change and links to intelligence. *Journal of School Psychology, 38*(1), 51–61.

Kallgren, C. A., Reno, R. R., & Cialdini, R. B. (2000). A focus theory of normative conduct: When norms do and do not affect behavior. *Personality & Social Psychology Bulletin, 26*(8), 1002–1012.

Kamalanabhan, T. J., Sunder, D. L., & Vasanthi, M. (2000). An evaluation of the Choice Dilemma Questionnaire as a measure of risk-taking propensity. *Social Behavior & Personality, 28*(2), 149–156.

Kamphaus, R. W., Petoskey, M. D., & Rowe, E. W. (2000). Current trends in psychological testing of children. *Professional Psychology: Research and Practice, 31*(2), 155–164.

Kandel, E. R., & Hawkins, R. D. (1992). The biological basis of learning and individuality. *Scientific American, 267*(3), 78–86.

Kant, A. K., et al. (2000). A prospective study of diet quality and mortality in women. *Journal of the American Medical Association, 283,* 2109–2115.

Karl, A., Birbaumer, N., Lutzenberger, W., Cohen, L. G., & Flor, H. (2001). Reorganization of motor and somatosensory cortex in upper extremity amputees with phantom limb pain. *Journal of Neuroscience, 21*(10), 3609–3618.

Karlberg, L., et al. (1998). Is there a connection between car accidents, near accidents, and Type A drivers? *Behavioral Medicine, 24*(3), 99–106.

Karon, B. P., & Widener, A. (1998). Repressed memories: The real story. *Professional Psychology: Research & Practice, 29*(5), 482–487.

Karwautz, A., et al. (2001). Individual-specific risk factors for anorexia nervosa: A pilot study using a discordant sister-pair design. *Psychological Medicine, 31*(2), 317–329.

Kashima, Y. (2000). Maintaining cultural stereotypes in the serial reproduction of narratives. *Personality & Social Psychology Bulletin, 26*(5), 594–604.

Kaslow, N. J., et al. (2002). Risk and protective factors for suicidal behavior in abused African American women. *Journal of Consulting & Clinical Psychology, 70*(2), 311–319.

Katigbak, M. S., Church, A. T., Guanzon-Lapena, M. A., Carlota, A. J., & del Pilar, G. H. (2002). Are indigenous personality dimensions culture specific? Philippine inventories and the five-factor model. *Journal of Personality & Social Psychology, 82*(1), 89–101.

Katzman, R. (2000, July). Epidemiology of Alzheimer's disease. Paper presented to the World Alzheimer Congress 2000, Washington, DC.

Kaufman, J., & Zigler, E. (1989). The intergenerational transmission of child abuse. In D. Cicchetti & V. Carlson (Eds.), *Child maltreatment* (pp. 129–150). Cambridge, U.K.: Cambridge University Press.

Kawas, C. (2000, July). Estrogen and the prevention of Alzheimer's disease. Paper presented at the World Alzheimer Congress 2000, Washington, DC.

Kaye, W. H., Klump, K. L., Frank, G. K. W., & Strober, M. (2000). Anorexia and bulimia nervosa. *Annual Review of Medicine, 51,* 299–313.

Kazuomi Kario, J. E., et al. (2001). Gender differences in associations of diurnal blood pressure variation, awake physical activity, and sleep quality with negative affect: The Work Site Blood Pressure Study. *Hypertension, 38,* 997–1002.

Keller, M. B., et al. (2000). A Comparison of nefazodone, the cognitive behavioral–analysis system of psychotherapy, and their combination for the treatment of chronic depression. *The New England Journal of Medicine, 342*(20), 1462–1470.

Kellerman, J., Lewis, J., & Laird, J. D. (1989). Looking and loving: The effects of mutual gaze on feelings of romantic love. *Journal of Research in Personality, 23,* 145–161.

Kelley, H. H., & Michela, J. L. (1980). Attribution theory and research. *Annual Review of Psychology, 31,* 457–501.

Kellman, P. J., & von Hofsetn, C. (1992). The world of the moving infant. In C. Rovee-Collier & L. P. Lipsitt (Eds.), *Advances in Infancy Research* (Vol. 7). Norwood, NJ: Ablex.

Kelly, A. (2000). Helping construct desirable identities: A self-presentational view of psychotherapy. *Psychological Bulletin, 126*(4), 475–494.

Kenchaiah, S., et al. (2002). Obesity and the risk of heart failure. *New England Journal of Medicine online, 347*(5), 305–313.

Kendler, K. S., et al. (2000a). Illicit psychoactive substance use, heavy use, abuse, and dependence in a US population-based sample of male twins. *Archives of General Psychiatry, 57,* 261–269.

Kendler, K. S., Myers, J. M., Neale, M. C. (2000b). A multidimensional twin study of mental health in women. *American Journal of Psychiatry, 157,* 506–513.

Kendler, K. S., Thornton, L. M., Gilman, S. E., & Kessler, R. C. (2000c). Sexual orientation in a U.S. national sample of twin and nontwin sibling pairs. *American Journal of Psychiatry, 157,* 1843–1846.

Kendler, K. S., Thornton, L. M., & Pedersen, N. L. (2000d). Tobacco consumption in Swedish twins reared apart and reared together. *Archives of General Psychiatry, 57,* 886–892.

Kendler, K. S., Myers, J., Prescott, C. A., & Neale, M. C. (2001). The genetic epidemiology of irrational fears and phobias in men. *Archives of General Psychiatry, 58*(3), 257–265.

Kennedy, C. H. (2002). Effects of REM sleep deprivation on a multiple schedule of appetitive reinforcement. *Behavioural Brain Research, 128*(2), 205–214.

Kenrick, D. T., & MacFarlane, S. W. (1986). Ambient temperature and horn honking. *Environment and Behavior, 18,* 179–191.

Keppel, B. (2002). Kenneth B. Clark in the patterns of American culture. *American Psychologist, 57*(1), 29–37.

Kerns, J. G., & Berenbaum, H. (2002). Cognitive impairments associated with formal thought disorder in people with schizophrenia. *Journal of Abnormal Psychology, 111*(2), 211–224.

Key, A., Lacey, J. H., & Nussey, S. (2001). Do starvation diets lead to irreversible lung changes? *European Eating Disorders Review, 9*(5), 348–353.

Kiecolt-Glaser, J. K., Marucha, P. T., Atkinson, C., & Glaser, R. (2001). Hypnosis as a modulator of cellular immune dysregulation during acute stress. *Journal of Consulting & Clinical Psychology, 69*(4), 674–682.

Kiecolt-Glaser, J. K., McGuire, L., Robles, T. F., & Glaser, R. (2002a). Psychoneuroimmunology and psychosomatic medicine: Back to the future. *Psychosomatic Medicine, 64*(1), 15–28.

Kiecolt-Glaser, J. K., McGuire, L., Robles, T. F., & Glaser, R. (2002b). Emotions, morbidity, and mortality: New perspectives from psychoneuroimmunology. *Annual Review of Psychology, 53*(1), 83–107.

Kilshaw, D., & Annett, M. (1983). Right- and left-hand skill: Effects of age, sex, and hand preferences showing superior in left-handers. *British Journal of Psychology, 74*, 253–268.

Kim, J., et al. (2000). Regional neural dysfunctions in chronic schizophrenia studied with positron emission tomography. *American Journal of Psychiatry, 157*, 542–548.

Kim, K., & Rohner, R. P. (2002). Parental warmth, control, and involvement in schooling: Predicting academic achievement among Korean American adolescents. *Journal of Cross-Cultural Psychology, 33*(2), 127–140.

Kimble, D. P. (1988). *Biological psychology.* New York: Holt, Rinehart and Winston.

King, R. (2000). Cited in Frazier, L. (2000, July 16). The new face of HIV is young, black. *The Washington Post*, p. C01.

Kinnunen, T., Zamansky, H. S., & Block, M. L. (1994). Is the hypnotized subject lying? *Journal of Abnormal Psychology, 103*, 184–191.

Kinsey, A. C., Pomeroy, W. B., & Martin, C. E. (1948). *Sexual behavior in the human male.* Philadelphia: W. B. Saunders.

Kinsey, A. C., Pomeroy, W. B., Martin, C. E., & Gebhard, P. H. (1953). *Sexual behavior in the human female.* Philadelphia: W. B. Saunders.

Kirsch, I. (2000). The response set theory of hypnosis. *American Journal of Clinical Hypnosis, 42*(3-4), 274–292.

Kirsch, I., Montgomery, G., & Sapirstein, G. (1995). Hypnosis as an adjunct to cognitive-behavioral psychotherapy. *Journal of Consulting and Clinical Psychology, 63*, 214–220.

Kite, M. E., et al. (2001). Women psychologists in academe: Mixed progress, unwarranted complacency. *American Psychologist, 56*(12), 1080–1098.

Kleinke, C. L. (1977). Compliance to requests made by gazing and touching experimenters in field settings. *Journal of Experimental Social Psychology, 13*, 218–223.

Kleinke, C. L. (1986). Gaze and eye contact. *Psychological Review, 100*, 78–100.

Kleinmuntz, B., & Szucko, J. J. (1984). Lie detection in ancient and modern times. *American Psychologist, 39*, 766–776.

Klüver, H., & Bucy, P. C. (1939). Preliminary analysis of functions of the temporal lobe in monkeys. *Archives of Neurology and Psychiatry, 42*, 979–1000.

Kobasa, S. C. O. (1990). Stress-resistant personality. In R. E. Ornstein & C. Swencionis (Eds.), *The healing brain* (pp. 219–230). New York: The Guilford Press.

Kobasa, S. C. O., Maddi, S. R., Puccetti, M. C., & Zola, M. A. (1994). Effectiveness of hardiness, exercise, and social support as resources against illness. In A. Steptoe & J. Wardle (Eds.), *Psychosocial processes and health* (pp. 247–260). Cambridge, England: Cambridge University Press.

Kohlberg, L. (1969). *Stages in the development of moral thought and action.* New York: Holt, Rinehart and Winston.

Kohlberg, L. (1981). *The philosophy of moral development.* San Francisco: Harper & Row.

Kolata, G. (2000, January 18). True secret of fad diets: It's calories. *The New York Times*, p. F7.

Kolata, G. (2002, December 22). Chasing youth, many gamble on hormones. *The New York Times* online.

Kolko, D. J., & Rickard-Figueroa, J. L. (1985). Effects of video games on the adverse corollaries of chemotherapy in pediatric oncology patients. *Journal of Consulting and Clinical Psychology, 53*, 223–228.

Kollins, S. H., & Rush, C. R. (2002). Sensitization to the cardiovascular but not subject-rated effects of oral cocaine in humans. *Biological Psychiatry, 51*(2), 143–150.

Kooijman, C. M., et al. (2000). Phantom pain and phantom sensations in upper limb amputees: An epidemiological study. *Pain, 87*(1), 33–41.

Kosonen, P., & Winne, P. H. (1995). Effects of teaching statistical laws on reasoning about everyday problems. *Journal of Educational Psychology, 87*, 33–46.

Kosslyn, S. M. (1994). *Image and brain.* Cambridge, MA: The MIT Press, a Bradford Book.

Krantz, D. S., Contrada, R. J., Hill, D. R., & Friedler, E. (1988). Environmental stress and biobehavioral antecedents of coronary heart disease. *Journal of Consulting and Clinical Psychology, 56*, 333–341.

Krauss, R. M., et al. (2000). AHA dietary guidelines: Revision 2000: A statement for healthcare professionals from the Nutrition Committee of the American Heart Association. *Circulation, 102*, 2284–2299.

Krcmar, M., & Cooke, M. C. (2001). Children's moral reasoning and their perceptions of television violence. *Journal of Communication, 51*(2), 300–316.

Kuczmarski, R. J., et al. (2000, December 4). CDC Growth charts: United States. Advance data from vital and health statistics; no. 314. Hyattsville, MD: National Center for Health Statistics.

Kurzweil, R. (2000, June 19). Will my PC be smarter than I am? *Time Magazine*, pp. 82–83.

Kyle, T. M., & Williams, S. (2000, May). Results of the 1998–1999 APA survey of graduate departments of psychology. APA Research Office. Washington, D.C.: American Psychological Association.

Lackner, J. M., Carosella, A. M., & Feuerstein, M. (1996). Pain expectancies, pain, and functional self-efficacy expectancies as determinants of disability in patients with chronic low back disorders. *Journal of Consulting and Clinical Psychology, 64*, 212–220.

LaFramboise, T. (1994). Cited in DeAngelis, T. (1994). History, culture affect treatment for Indians. *APA Monitor, 27*(10), 36.

Lahti, A. C., et al. (2001). Abnormal patterns of regional cerebral blood flow in schizophrenia with primary negative symptoms during an effortful auditory recognition task. *American Journal of Psychiatry, 158*, 1797–1808.

Lal, S. (2002). Giving children security: Mamie Phipps Clark and the radicalization of child psychology. *American Psychologist, 57*(1), 20–28.

Lalumière, M. L., Blanchard, R., & Zucker, K. J. (2000). Sexual orientation and handedness in men and women: A meta-analysis. *Psychological Bulletin, 126*(4), 575–592.

Lam, J. A., & Rosenheck, R. A. (2000). Correlates of improvement in quality of life among homeless persons with serious mental illness. *Psychiatric Services, 51*(1), 116–118.

Lamb, M. E., & Baumrind, D. (1978). Socialization and personality development in the preschool years. In M. E. Lamb (Ed.), *Social and personality development.* New York: Holt, Rinehart and Winston.

Lamb, M. E., Sternberg, K. J., & Prodromidis, M. (1992). Nonmaternal care and the security of infant–mother attachment. *Infant Behavior and Development, 15*, 71–83.

Lambert, W. E., Genesee, F., Holobow, N., & Chartrand, L. (1991). *Bilingual education for majority English-speaking children.* Montreal: McGill University.

Lancaster, T., Stead, L., Silagy, C., & Sowden, A. (2000). Regular review: Effectiveness of interventions to help people stop smoking: Findings from the Cochrane Library. *British Medical Journal, 321*, 355–358.

Lang, A. R., Goeckner, D. J., Adesso, V. J., & Marlatt, G. A. (1975). Effects of alcohol on aggression in male social drinkers. *Journal of Abnormal Psychology, 84*, 508–518.

Lang, E. V., et al. (2000). Adjunctive non-pharmacological analgesia for invasive medical procedures: A randomised trial. *The Lancet, 355*, 1486–1490.

Lang, F. R., & Heckhausen, J. (2001). Perceived control over development and subjective well-being: Differential benefits across adulthood. *Journal of Personality & Social Psychology, 81*(3), 509–523.

Langer, E. J., Rodin, J., Beck, P., Weinan, C., & Spitzer, L. (1979). Environmental determinants of memory improvement in late adulthood. *Journal of Personality and Social Psychology, 37*, 2003–2013.

Langlois, J. H., et al. (2000). Maxims or myths of beauty? A meta-analytic and theoretical review. *Psychological Bulletin, 126*(3), 390–423.

Larkin, M. (2000). Can lost hearing be restored? *The Lancet, 356*, 741–748.

Larrick, R. P. (1993). Motivational factors in decision theories. *Psychological Bulletin, 113*, 440–450.

Larson, R., & Richards, M. H. (1991). Daily companionship in late childhood and early adolescence. *Child Development, 62*, 284–300.

Lashley, K. S. (1950). In search of the engram. In *Symposium of the Society for Experimental Biology* (Vol. 4). New York: Cambridge University Press.

Latané, B., & Dabbs, J. M. (1975). Sex, group size, and helping in three cities. *Sociometry, 38*, 180–194.

Latimer, W. W., Winters, K. C., Stinchfield, R., & Traver, R. E. (2000). Demographic, individual, and interpersonal predictors of adolescent alcohol and marijuana use following treatment. *Psychology of Addictive Behaviors, 14*(2), 162–173.

Laumann, E. O., Gagnon, J. H., Michael, R. T., & Michaels, S. (1994). *The social organization of sexuality.* Chicago: University of Chicago Press.

Laungani, P. (2002). The counselling interview: First impressions. *Counselling Psychology Quarterly, 15*(1), 107–113.

Lavie, P. (2001). Current concepts: Sleep disturbances in the wake of traumatic events. *New England Journal of Medicine, 345*, 1825–1832.

Lawton, C. A., & Morrin, K. A. (1999). Gender differences in pointing accuracy in computer-simulated 3D mazes. *Sex Roles, 40*(1–2), 73–92.

Lazarus, R. S., DeLongis, A., Folkman, S., & Gruen, R. (1985). Stress and adaptational outcomes. *American Psychologist, 40*, 770–779.

Le Bon, G. (1960). *The crowd.* New York: Viking. (Original work published 1895)

Lecci, L., & Cohen, D. J. (2002). Perceptual consequences of an illness-concern induction and its relation to hypochondriacal tendencies. *Health Psychology, 21*(2), 147–156.

LeDoux, J. E. (1997). Emotion, memory, and the brain. *Scientific American mysteries of the mind, Special Issue Vol. 7*, No. 1, 68–75.

LeDoux, J. E. (1998). Fear and the brain: Where have we been, and where are we going? *Biological Psychiatry, 44*(12), 1229–1238.

Lee, I-M., Sesso, H. D., & Paffenbarger, R. S., Jr. (2000). Physical activity and coronary heart disease risk in men: Does the duration of exercise episodes predict risk? *Circulation, 102*, 981–986.

Lefcourt, H. M. (1997). Cited in Clay, R. A. (1997). Researchers harness the power of humor. *APA Monitor, 28*(9), 1, 18.

Lefcourt, H. M., & Martin, R. A. (1986). *Humor and life stress.* New York: Springer-Verlag.

Lefcourt, H. M., Miller, R. S., Ware, E. E., & Sherk, D. (1981). Locus of control as a modifier of the relationship between stressors and moods. *Journal of Personality and Social Psychology, 41*, 357–369.

Lefley, H. P. (1990). Culture and chronic mental illness. *Hospital and Community Psychiatry, 41*, 277–286.

Lehman, B. J., & Crano, W. D. (2002). The pervasive effects of vested interest on attitude-criterion consistency in political judgment. *Journal of Experimental Social Psychology, 38*(2), 101–112.

Leibowitz, H. W. (1996). The symbiosis between basic and applied research. *American Psychologist, 51*, 366–370.

Leinders-Zufall, T., et al. (2000). Ultrasensitive pheromone detection by mammalian vomeronasal neurons. *Nature, 405*, 792–796.

Leinwand, D. (2000, August 24). 20% say they used drugs with their mom or dad, Among reasons: Boomer culture and misguided attempts to bond. *USA TODAY online.*

Le Marec, N., Beaulieu, I., & Godbout, R. (2001). Four hours of paradoxical sleep deprivation impairs alternation performance in a water maze in the rat. *Brain & Cognition, 46*(1–2), 195–197.

Lensvelt-Mulders, G., & Hettema, J. (2001). Genetic analysis of autonomic reactivity to psychologically stressful situations. *Biological Psychology, 58*(1), 25–40.

Leor, J., Poole, K., & Kloner, R. A. (1996). Sudden cardiac death triggered by an earthquake. *New England Journal of Medicine, 334*, 413–419.

Lerner, A. G., et al. (2000). LSD-induced hallucinogen persisting perception disorder treatment with clonidine: An open pilot study. *International Clinical Psychopharmacology, 15*(1), 35–37.

Leserman, J., et al. (2000). Impact of stressful life events, depression, social support, coping, and cortisol on progression to AIDS. *American Journal of Psychiatry, 157*, 1221–1228.

Leslie, M. B., Stein, J. A., & Rotheram-Borus, M. J. (2002). Sex-specific predictors of suicidality among runaway youth. *Journal of Community Psychology, 31*(1), 27–40.

Levenston, G. K., Patrick, C. J., Bradley, M. M., & Lang, P. J. (2000). The psychopath as observer: Emotion and attention in picture processing. *Journal of Abnormal Psychology, 109*(3), 373–385.

Levinson, D. J. (1996). *The seasons of a woman's life.* New York: Knopf.

Levinson, D. J., Darrow, C. N., Klein, E. B., Levinson, M. H., & McKee, B. (1978). *The seasons of a man's life.* New York: Knopf.

Levy, D., et al. (2000). Evidence for a gene influencing blood pressure on chromosome 17 : Genome scan linkage results for longitudinal blood pressure phenotypes in subjects from the Framingham Heart Study. *Hypertension, 36*, 477–483.

Lewin, T. (1995, December 7). Parents poll shows higher incidence of child abuse. *The New York Times*, p. B16.

Lewinsohn, P. M., Brown, R. A., Seeley, J. R., & Ramsey, S. E. (2000a). Psychological correlates of cigarette smoking abstinence, experimentation, persistence, and frequency during adolescence. *Nicotine & Tobacco Research, 2*(2), 121–131.

Lewinsohn, P. M., Rohde, P., Seeley, J. R., Klein, D. N., & Gotlib, I. H. (2000b). Natural course of adolescent major depressive disorder in a community sample: Predictors of recurrence in young adults. *American Journal of Psychiatry, 157*, 1584–1591.

Lewis-Fernández, R., & Kleinman, A. (1994). Culture, personality, and psychopathology. *Journal of Abnormal Psychology, 103*, 67–71.

Leyton, M., et al. (2000). Acute tyrosine depletion and alcohol ingestion in healthy women. *Alcoholism: Clinical & Experimental Research, 24*(4) 459–464.

Li, G., Baker, S. P., Smialek, J. E., & Soderstrom, C. A. (2001). Use of alcohol as a risk factor for bicycling injury. *Journal of the American Medical Association, 284*, 893–896.

Lichtenstein, P., et al. (2000). Environmental and heritable factors in the causation of cancer: Analyses of cohorts of twins from Sweden, Denmark, and Finland. *New England Journal of Medicine, 343*(2), 78–85.

Lidow, M. S., et al. (2001). Antipsychotic treatment induces alterations in dendrite- and spine-associated proteins in dopamine-rich areas of the primate cerebral cortex. *Biological Psychiatry, 49*(1), 1–12.

Lieber, C. S. (1990). Cited in Barroom biology: How alcohol goes to a woman's head (January 14). *The New York Times*, p. E24.

Lilienfeld, S. O., & Loftus, E. F. (1998). Repressed memories and World War II: Some cautionary notes. *Professional Psychology: Research & Practice, 29*(5), 471–475.

Lillqvist, O., & Lindeman, M. (1998). Belief in astrology as a strategy for self-verification and coping with negative life-events. *European Psychologist, 3*(3), 202–208.

Lin, J., & Thompson, D. S. (2001). Treating premenstrual dysphoric disorder using serotonin agents. *Journal of Women's Health & Gender-Based Medicine, 10*(8), 745–750.

Lincoln, G. A. (2001). The irritable male syndrome. *Reproduction, Fertility and Development, 13*(7&8), 567–576.

Lindeman, M. (1998). Motivation, cognition and pseudoscience. *Scandinavian Journal of Psychology, 39*(4), 257–265.

Linden, W., Chambers, L., Maurice, J., & Lenz, J. W. (1993). Sex differences in social support, self-deception, hostility, and ambulatory cardiovascular activity. *Health Psychology, 12*, 376–380.

Lips, H. (1993). *Sex and gender* (2nd ed.). Mountain View, CA: Mayfield.

Lisanby, S. H., et al. (2000). The effects of electroconvulsive therapy on memory of autobiographical and public events. *Archives of General Psychiatry, 57*(6), 581–590.

Little, A. C., & Perrett, D. I. (2002). Putting beauty back in the eye of the beholder. *Psychologist, 15*(1), 28–32.

Littner, M., et al. (2001). Practice parameters for the treatment of narcolepsy: An update for 2000. *Sleep: Journal of Sleep & Sleep Disorders Research, 24*(4), 451–466.

Lochman, J. E. (1992). Cognitive–behavioral intervention with aggressive boys. *Journal of Consulting and Clinical Psychology, 60*, 426–432.

Lochman, J. E., & Dodge, K. A. (1994). Social-cognitive processes of severely violent, moderately aggressive, and nonaggressive boys. *Journal of Consulting and Clinical Psychology, 62,* 366–374.

Lock, J., & Le Grange, D. (2001). Can family based treatment of anorexia nervosa be manualized? *Journal of Psychotherapy Practice & Research, 10*(4). 253–261.

Loftus, E. F. (1979). The malleability of human memory. *American Scientist, 67*(3), 312–320.

Loftus, E. F. (1983). Silence is not golden. *American Psychologist, 38,* 564–572.

Loftus, E. F. (1993). Psychologists in the eyewitness world. *American Psychologist, 48,* 550–552.

Loftus, E. F. (1994). Conference on memory, Harvard Medical School. Cited in D. Goleman (1994, May 31). Miscoding is seen as the root of false memories. *The New York Times,* pp. C1, C8.

Loftus, E. F. (1997). Cited in Loftus consulting in Oklahoma City bombing trial. *APA Monitor, 28*(4), 8–9.

Loftus, E. F., & Loftus, G. R. (1980). On the permanence of stored information in the brain. *American Psychologist, 35,* 409–420.

Loftus, E. F., & Palmer, J. C. (1974). Reconstruction of automobile destruction. *Journal of Verbal Learning and Verbal Behavior, 13,* 585–589.

Loftus, G. R. (1983). The continuing persistence of the icon. *Behavioral and Brain Sciences, 6,* 28.

Loftus, E. F., & Polage, D. C. (1999). Repressed memories: When are they real? How are they false? *Psychiatric Clinics of North America, 22*(1), 61–70.

Longer, healthier, better. (1997, March 9). *The New York Times Magazine,* pp. 44–45.

Los Angeles Unified School District. (2000). Youth Suicide Prevention Information. http://www.sanpedro.com/spyc/suicide.htm.

López, P., Martín, J., & Cuadrado, M. (2002). Pheromone-mediated intrasexual aggression in male lizards, *Podarcis hispanicus. Aggressive Behavior, 28,* 154–163.

Lopez, S. R., & Guarnaccia, P. J. J. (2000). Cultural psychopathology: Uncovering the social world of mental illness. *Annual Review of Psychology, 51,* 571–598.

Lorenz, K. Z. (1981). *The foundations of ethology.* New York: Springer-Verlag.

Loving, T. J., & Agnew, C. R. (2001). Socially desirable responding in close relationships: A dual-component approach and measure. *Journal of Social & Personal Relationships, 18*(4), 551–573.

Lowe, M. R., et al. (1996). Restraint, dieting, and the continuum model of bulimia nervosa. *Journal of Abnormal Psychology, 105,* 508–517.

Lu, L. (1999). Personal or environmental causes of happiness: A longitudinal analysis. *Journal of Social Psychology, 139*(1), 79–90.

Lu, L. (2001). Understanding happiness: A look into the Chinese folk psychology. *Journal of Happiness Studies, 2*(4), 407–432.

Luborsky, L., et al. (2002). The dodo bird verdict is alive and well—mostly. *Clinical Psychology: Science & Practice, 9*(1), 2–12.

Luchins, A. S. (1957). Primacy-recency in impression formation. In C. I. Hovland (Ed.), *The order of presentation in persuasion.* New Haven, CT: Yale University Press.

Luchins, A. S., & Luchins, E. H. (1959). *Rigidity of behavior.* Eugene: University of Oregon Press.

Ludwick-Rosenthal, R., & Neufeld, R. W. J. (1993). Preparation for undergoing an invasive medical procedure. *Journal of Consulting and Clinical Psychology, 61,* 156–164.

Lundeberg, M. A., Fox, P. W., & Puncochar, J. (1994). Highly confident but wrong. *Journal of Educational Psychology, 86,* 114–121.

Lykken, D., & Csikszentmihalyi, M. (2001). Happiness—Stuck with what you've got? *Psychologist, 14*(9), 470–472.

Lykken, D., & Tellegen, A. (1996). Happiness is a stochastic phenomenon. *Psychological Science, 7*(3), 186–189.

Lykken, D. T., McGue, M., Tellegen, A., & Bouchard, T. J., Jr. (1992). Emergenesis: Genetic traits that may not run in families. *American Psychologist, 47,* 1565–1577.

Maas, J. B. (1998). *Power sleep: Revolutionary strategies that prepare your mind and body for peak performance.* New York: Villard.

Maccoby, E. E. (1990). Gender and relationships. *American Psychologist, 45,* 513–520.

MacDonald, K. (1992). Warmth as a developmental construct. *Child Development, 63,* 753–773.

MacDonald, M. G. (1999). Suicide-intervention trainees' perceptions of awareness for warning signs of suicide. *Psychological Reports, 85*(3, Pt 2 [Spec Issue]), 1195–1198.

MacDonald, T. K., MacDonald, G., Zanna, M. P., & Fong, G. T. (2000). Alcohol, sexual arousal, and intentions to use condoms in young men: Applying alcohol myopia theory to risky sexual behavior. *Health Psychology, 19,* 290–298.

Macfarlane, J. A. (1975). Olfaction in the development of social preferences in the human neonate. In M. A. Hofer (Ed.), *Parent-infant interaction.* Amsterdam: Elsevier.

Maciejewski, P. K., Prigerson, H. G., & Mazure, C. M. (2000). Self-efficacy as a mediator between stressful life events and depressive symptoms: Differences based on history of prior depression. *British Journal of Psychiatry, 176,* 373–378.

MacKenzie, T. D., Bartecchi, C. E., & Schrier, R. W. (1994). The human costs of tobacco use. *New England Journal of Medicine, 330,* 975–980.

Macrae, C. N., Mitchell, J. P., & Pendry, L. F. (2002). What's in a forename? Cue familiarity and stereotypical thinking. *Journal of Experimental Social Psychology, 38*(2), 186–193.

Magnavita, N., et al. (1997). Type A behaviour pattern and traffic accidents. *British Journal of Medical Psychology, 70*(1), 103–107.

Maher, B. A., & Maher, W. B. (1994). Personality and psychopathology. *Journal of Abnormal Psychology, 103,* 72–77.

Maier, N. R. F., & Schneirla, T. C. (1935). *Principles of animal psychology.* New York: McGraw-Hill.

Male PMT behind men behaving badly. (2002, March 6). http://iafrica.com/highlife/hislife/features/903658.htm

Malgady, R. G., Rogler, L. H., & Constantino, G. (1990). Hero/heroine modeling for Puerto Rican adolescents. *Journal of Consulting and Clinical Psychology, 58,* 469–474.

Mangelsdorf, D. (2002). Cited in Study shows how vitamin D prevents colon cancer. (2002, May 16). Reuters.

Maquet, P. (2001). The role of sleep in learning and memory. *Science, 294*(5544), 1048–1052.

Marchbanks, P. A., et al. (2002). Oral contraceptives and the risk of breast cancer. *New England Journal of Medicine, 346*(26), 2025–2032.

Marian, V., & Neisser, U. (2000). Language-dependent recall of autobiographical memories. *Journal of Experimental Psychology: General, 129*(3), 361–368.

Markman, H. J., Renick, M. J., Floyd, F. J., Stanley, S. M., & Clements, M. (1993). Preventing marital distress through communication and conflict management training. *Journal of Consulting and Clinical Psychology, 61,* 70–77.

Marks, I. M. (2002). The maturing of therapy: Some brief psychotherapies help anxiety/depressive disorders but mechanisms of action are unclear. *British Journal of Psychiatry, 180*(3), 200–204.

Marks, I. M., & Dar, R. (2000). Fear reduction by psychotherapies: Recent findings, future directions. *The British Journal of Psychiatry, 176,* 507–511.

Markus, H., & Kitayama, S. (1991). Culture and the self. *Psychological Review, 98*(2), 224–253.

Martin, R. A., & Lefcourt, H. M. (1983). Sense of humor as a moderator of the relation between stressors and moods. *Journal of Personality and Social Psychology, 45,* 1313–1324.

Martin, S. (2002). Easing migraine pain. *Monitor on Psychology, 33*(4), 71.

Martinez-Taboas, A., & Bernal, G. (2000). Dissociation, psychopathology, and abusive experiences in a nonclinical Latino university student group. *Cultural Diversity & Ethnic Minority Psychology, 6*(1), 32–41.

Marttunen, M. J., et al. (1998). Completed suicide among adolescents with no diagnosable psychiatric disorder. *Adolescence, 33*(131), 669–681.

Maslow, A. H. (1970). *Motivation and personality* (2nd ed.). New York: Harper & Row.

Masters, W. H., & Johnson, V. E. (1966). *Human sexual response.* Boston: Little, Brown.

Matlin, M. W., & Foley, H. J. (1995). *Sensation and perception* (4th ed.). Boston: Allyn & Bacon.

Matt, G. E., Vasquez, C., & Campbell, W. K. (1992). Mood-congruent recall of affectively toned stimuli: A meta-analytic review. *Clinical Psychology Review, 12,* 227–255.

Mazure, C. M., et al. (2000). Adverse life events and cognitive–personality characteristics in the prediction of major depression and antidepressant response. *American Journal of Psychiatry, 157,* 896–903.

Mazzella, R., & Feingold, A. (1994). The effects of physical attractiveness, race, socioeconomic status, and gender of defendants and victims on judgments of mock jurors. *Journal of Applied Social Psychology, 24*(15), 1315–1344.

McCall, R. (1997). Cited in Sleek, S. (1997). Can "emotional intelligence" be taught in today's schools? *APA Monitor, 28*(6), 25.

McCarley, R. W. (1992). Cited in Blakeslee, S. (1992, January 7). Scientists unraveling chemistry of dreams. *The New York Times,* pp. C1, C10.

McClave, E. Z. (2000). Linguistic functions of head movements in the context of speech. *Journal of Pragmatics, 32*(7), 855–878.

McClelland, D. C. (1958). Methods of measuring human motivation. In J. W. Atkinson (Ed.), *Motives in fantasy, action, and society.* Princeton, NJ: Van Nostrand.

McClelland, D. C. (1965). Achievement and entrepreneurship. *Journal of Personality and Social Psychology, 1,* 389–392.

McCourt, K., et al. (1999). Authoritarianism revisited: Genetic and environmental influences examined in twins reared apart and together. *Personality & Individual Differences, 27*(5), 985–1014.

McCrae, R. R., & Costa, P. T., Jr. (1997). Personality trait structure as a human universal. *American Psychologist, 52,* 509–516.

McCrae, R. R., et al. (2000). Nature over nurture: Temperament, personality, and life span development. *Journal of Personality & Social Psychology, 78*(1), 173–186.

McDaniel, M. A., Glisky, E. L., Guynn, M. J., & Routhieaux, B. C. (1999). Prospective memory: A neuropsychological study. *Neuropsychology, 13*(1), 103–110.

McDermott, D. (1997, May 14). Yes, computers *can* think. *The New York Times,* p. A21.

McDonald-Miszczak, L., Gould, O. N., & Tychynski, D. (1999). Metamemory predictors of prospective and retrospective memory performance. *Journal of General Psychology, 126*(1) 37–52.

McDougall, W. (1904). The sensations excited by a single momentary stimulation of the eye. *British Journal of Psychology, 1,* 78–113.

McDougall, W. (1908). *An introduction to social psychology.* London: Methuen.

McElroy, S. L., et al. (2000). Placebo-controlled trial of sertraline in the treatment of binge eating disorder. *American Journal of Psychiatry, 157,* 1004–1006.

McGlashan, T. H., & Hoffman, R. E. (2000). Schizophrenia as a disorder of developmentally reduced synaptic connectivity. *Archives of General Psychiatry, 57,* 637–648.

McGovern, T. V. (1989). Task force eyes the making of a major. *APA Monitor, 20*(7), 50.

McGrath, E., Keita, G. P., Strickland, B. R., & Russo, N. F. (1990). *Women and depression.* Washington DC: American Psychological Association.

McGue, M., Pickens, R. W., & Svikis, D. S. (1992). Sex and age effects on the inheritance of alcohol problems: A twin study. *Journal of Abnormal Psychology, 101,* 3–17.

McGuire, L., Kiecolt-Glaser, J. K., & Glaser, R. (2002). Depressive symptoms and lymphocyte proliferation in older adults. *Journal of Abnormal Psychology, 111*(1), 192–197.

McKenzie, C. R. M., Lee, S. M., & Chen, K. K. (2002). When negative evidence increases confidence: Changes in belief after hearing two sides of a dispute. *Journal of Behavioral Decision Making, 15*(1), 1–18.

McLaren, L. (2002). Cited in Wealthy women most troubled by poor body image. (2002, February 11). Reuters online.

McNeil, T. F., Cantor-Graae, E., & Weinberger, D. R. (2000). Relationship of obstetric complications and differences in size of brain structures in monozygotic twin pairs discordant for schizophrenia. *American Journal of Psychiatry, 157,* 203–212.

Mead, M. (1935). *Sex and temperament in three primitive societies.* New York: Dell.

Meltzoff, A. N. (1997). Cited in Azar, B. (1997). New theory on development could usurp Piagetian beliefs. *APA Monitor, 28*(6), 9.

Meltzoff, A. N., & Gopnik, A. (1997). *Words, thoughts, and theories.* Cambridge, MA: MIT Press.

Melzack, R. (1999, August). From the gate to the neuromatrix. *Pain* Suppl. 6, S121–S126.

Merluzzi, T. V., & Martinez Sanchez, M. (1997). Assessment of self efficacy and coping with cancer. *Health Psychology, 16,* 163–170.

Metcalfe, J. (1986). Premonitions of insight predict impending error. *Journal of Experimental Psychology: Learning, Memory, and Cognition, 12,* 623–634.

Meyer-Lindenberg, A., et al. (2001). Evidence for abnormal cortical functional connectivity during working memory in schizophrenia. *American Journal of Psychiatry, 158,* 1809–1817.

Michael, R. T., Gagnon, J. H., Laumann, E. O., & Kolata, G. (1994). *Sex in America: A definitive survey.* Boston: Little, Brown.

Michinov, E., & Michinov, N. (2001). The similarity hypothesis: A test of the moderating role of social comparison orientation. *European Journal of Social Psychology, 31*(5), 549–555.

Middleman, M. A. (2000, May). Paper presented to the 40th Annual Conference on Cardiovascular Disease Epidemiology and Prevention of the American Heart Association, San Diego.

Milar, K. S. (2000). The first generation of women psychologists and the psychology of women. *American Psychologist, 55*(6), 616–619.

Milgram, S. (1963). Behavioral study of obedience. *Journal of Abnormal and Social Psychology, 67,* 371–378.

Milgram, S. (1974). *Obedience to authority.* New York: Harper & Row.

Miller, A. L., Wyman, S. E., Huppert, J. D., Glassman, S. L., & Rathus, J. H. (2000). Analysis of behavioral skills utilized by suicidal adolescents receiving dialectical behavior therapy. *Cognitive & Behavioral Practice, 7*(2), 183–187.

Miller, G. A. (1956). The magical number seven, plus or minus two: Some limits on our capacity for processing information. *Psychological Review, 63,* 81–97.

Miller, G. E., & Cohen, S. (2001). Psychological interventions and the immune system: A meta-analytic review and critique. *Health Psychology, 20*(1), 47–63.

Miller, J. L. (1992). Trouble in mind. *Scientific American, 267*(3), 180.

Miller, M. E., & Bowers, K. S. (1993). Hypnotic analgesia. *Journal of Abnormal Psychology, 102,* 29–38.

Miller, M. F., Barabasz, A. F., & Barabasz, M. (1991). Effects of active alert and relaxation hypnotic inductions on cold pressor pain. *Journal of Abnormal Psychology, 100,* 223–226.

Miller, N. B., Cowan, P. A., Cowan, C. P., Hetherington, E. M., & Clingempeel, W. G. (1993). Externalizing in preschoolers and early adolescents. *Developmental Psychology, 29,* 3–18.

Miller, N. E. (1969). Learning of visceral and glandular responses. *Science, 163,* 434–445.

Miller, N. E. (1995). Clinical-experimental interactions in the development of neuroscience. *American Psychologist, 50,* 901–911.

Miller, N. E., & Dollard, J. (1941). *Social learning and imitation.* New Haven, CT: Yale University Press.

Miller, S. M., Shoda, Y., & Hurley, K. (1996). Applying cognitive–social theory to health-protective behavior: Breast self-examination in cancer screening. *Psychological Bulletin, 199,* 70–94.

Milner, B. R. (1966). Amnesia following operation on temporal lobes. In C. W. M. Whitty & O. L. Zangwill (Eds.), *Amnesia.* London: Butterworth.

Milstead, M., Lapsley, D., & Hale, C. (1993, March). *A new look at imaginary audience and personal fable.* Paper presented at the meeting of the Society for Research in Child Development, New Orleans, LA.

Milton, J., & Wiseman, R. (1999). Does psi exist? Lack of replication of an anomalous process of information transfer. *Psychological Bulletin, 125*(4), 387–391.

Mimeault, V., & Morin, C. M. (1999). Self-help treatment for insomnia: Bibliotherapy with and without professional guidance. *Journal of Consulting & Clinical Psychology, 67*(4), 511–519.

Mindell, J. A. (1993). Sleep disorders in children. *Health Psychology, 12*, 151–162.

Minton, H. L. (2000). Psychology and gender at the turn of the century. *American Psychologist, 55*(6), 613–615.

Mischel, W., & Shoda, Y. (1995). A cognitive-affective system theory of personality. *Psychological Review, 102*, 246–268.

Moeller, F. G., et al. (2001). Psychiatric aspects of impulsivity. *American Journal of Psychiatry, 158*(11), 1783–1793.

Molfese, V. J., DiLalla, L. F., & Bunce, D. (1997). Prediction of the intelligence test scores of 3- to 8-year-old children by home environment, socioeconomic status, and biomedical risks. *Merrill-Palmer Quarterly, 43*(2) 219–234.

Moliterno, D. J., et al. (1994). Coronary-artery vasoconstriction induced by cocaine, cigarette smoking, or both. *New England Journal of Medicine, 330*, 454–459.

Montgomery, G. H., DuHamel, K. N., & Redd, W. H. (2000). A meta-analysis of hypnotically induced analgesia: How effective is hypnosis? *International Journal of Clinical & Experimental Hypnosis, 48*(2), 138–153.

Mordock, B. (1997). Skepticism, data, risky shift, polarization, and attitude change: Their role in implementing innovations. *Psychologist-Manager Journal, 1*(1), 41–46.

Morgan, D., et al. (2000). A peptide vaccination prevents memory loss in an animal model of Alzheimer's disease. *Nature, 408*(6815), 982–984.

Morin, C. M., Colecchi, C., Stone, J., Sood, R., & Brink, D. (1999). Behavioral and pharmacological therapies for late-life insomnia: A randomized controlled trial. *Journal of the American Medical Association, 281*(11), 991–999.

Morley, J. E., & van den Berg, L, Eds. (2000). *Endocrinology of aging.* Totowa, N.J., Humana Press.

Morris, M. W., Larrick, R. P., & Su, S. K. (1999). Misperceiving negotiation counterparts: When situationally determined bargaining behaviors are attributed to personality traits. *Journal of Personality & Social Psychology, 77*(1), 52–67.

Morris, W. N., Miller, R. S., & Spangenberg, S. (1977). The effects of dissenter position and task difficulty on conformity and response conflict. *Journal of Personality, 45*, 251–256.

Morrison, E. S., et al. (1980). *Growing up sexual.* New York: Van Nostrand Reinhold Co.

Moruzzi, G., & Magoun, H. W. (1949). Brain stem reticular formation and activation of the EEG. *Electroencephalography & Clinical Neurophysiology, 1*, 455–473.

Moss, D. P. (2002). Cited in Clay, R. A. (2002). A renaissance for humanistic psychology. *Monitor on Psychology, 33*(8), 42–43.

Moss, E., & St-Laurent, D. (2001). Attachment at school age and academic performance. *Developmental Psychology, 37*(6), 863–874.

Moyers, B. (1993). *Healing and the mind.* New York: Doubleday.

Mueller, N., & Hulk, A. (2001). Crosslinguistic influence in bilingual language acquisition: Italian and French as recipient languages. *Bilingualism: Language & Cognition, 4*(1), 1–21.

Muir, G. D. (2000). Early ontogeny of locomotor behaviour: A comparison between altricial and precocial animals. *Brain Research Bulletin, 53*(5), 719–726.

Mukamal, K. J., Maclure, M., Muller, J. E., Sherwood, J. B., & Mittleman, M. A. (2001). Prior alcohol consumption and mortality following acute myocardial infarction. *Journal of the American Medical Association, 285*(15), 1965–1970.

Mulder, R. T. (2002). Personality pathology and treatment outcome in major depression: A review. *American Journal of Psychiatry, 159*(3), 359–371.

Mullen, B., et al. (1987). Newscasters' facial expressions and voting behavior of viewers. *Journal of Personality and Social Psychology, 51*(2), 291–295.

Mulnard, R. A., et al. (2000). Estrogen replacement therapy for treatment of mild to moderate Alzheimer disease. *Journal of the American Medical Association, 283*, 1007–1015.

Mulvihill, K. (2000, March 14). Many miss out on migraine remedies. *The New York Times online.*

Muñoz, R. F., Hollon, S. D., McGrath, E., Rehm, L. P., & VandenBos, G. R. (1994). On the AHCPR *Depression in Primary Care* guidelines: Further considerations for practitioners. *American Psychologist, 49,* 42–61.

Munro, G. D., & Munro, J. E. (2000). Using daily horoscopes to demonstrate expectancy confirmation. *Teaching of Psychology, 27*(2), 114–116.

Murray, H. A. (1938). *Explorations in personality.* New York: Oxford University Press.

Murtagh, D. R. R., & Greenwood, K. M. (1995). Identifying effective psychological treatments for insomnia: A meta-analysis. *Journal of Consulting and Clinical Psychology, 63*, 79–89.

Mussweiler, T., & Bodenhausen, G. V. (2002). I know you are, but what am I? Self-evaluative consequences of judging in-group and out-group members. *Journal of Personality & Social Psychology, 82*(1), 19–32.

Myers, L. B., & Brewin, C. R. (1994). Recall of early experience and the repressive coping style. *Journal of Abnormal Psychology, 103*, 288–292.

Nader, K., Schafe, G. E., & Le Doux, J. E. (2000). Fear memories require protein synthesis in the amygdala for reconsolidation after retrieval. *Nature, 406*, 722–726.

Nahas, G., Sutin, K., & Bennett, W. M. (2000). Review of "Marihuana and Medicine." *The New England Journal of Medicine online, 343*(7).

Nagourney, E. (2001, November 27). Mind and body: In heart disease, head can be an ally. *The New York Times*, p. F9.

Nagourney, E. (2002, April 2). Neal E. Miller is dead at 92; studied brain and behavior. *The New York Times*, p. A21.

Nagtegaal, J. E., et al. (2000). Effects of melatonin on the quality of life in patients with delayed sleep phase syndrome. *Journal of Psychosomatic Research, 48*(1), 45–50.

Nantais, K. M., & Schellenberg, E. G. (1999). The Mozart effect: An artifact of preference. *Psychological Science, 10*(4), 370–373.

National Center for Health Statistics (1996, March.). News Releases and Fact Sheets. *Monitoring Health Care in America: Quarterly Fact Sheet.*

National Center for Health Statistics. (2002, April 21). Abstracted from Suicide statistics by age, race, and sex. *Monthly Vital Statistics Report, 48*(11). Atlanta: Centers for Disease Control and Prevention. http://www.cdc.gov/nchs/fastats/suicide.htm.

National Institute of Child Health & Human Development (2001, July 6). America's children: Key national indicators of well-being. http://156.40.88.3/publications/pubs/report2001.pdf

National Science Foundation (2002). Cited in Associated Press. (2002, April 30). Study: Science literacy poor in U.S. Associated Press.

National Sleep Foundation (2000a). Helping yourself to a good night's sleep. http://www.sleepfoundation.org/publications/goodnights.html.

National Sleep Foundation (2000b). 2000 Omnibus Sleep in America Poll. http://www.sleepfoundation.org/publications/2000poll.html#3.

National Sleep Foundation (2001, November 19). Events of 9-11 took their toll on Americans' sleep, particularly for women, according to new National Sleep Foundation poll. http://www.sleepfoundation.org/whatsnew/crisis_poll.html.

Neisser, U. (1993). Cited in Goleman, D. J. (1993, April 6). Studying the secrets of childhood memory. *The New York Times*, pp. C1, C11.

Neisser, U. (1997a). Never a dull moment. *American Psychologist, 52*, 79–81.

Neisser, U. (1997b). Cited in Sleek, S. (1997). Can "emotional intelligence" be taught in today's schools? *APA Monitor, 28*(6), 25.

Neisser, U., et al. (1996). Intelligence: Knowns and unknowns. *American Psychologist, 51*, 77–101.

Nelson, K., Hampson, J., & Shaw, L. K. (1993). Nouns in early lexicons: Evidence, explanations, and implications. *Journal of Child Language, 20*, 228.

Nestadt, G., et al. (2000). A family study of obsessive-compulsive disorder. *Archives of General Psychiatry, 57*(4), 358–363.

Newcomb, P. A., & Storer, B. E. (1995). Postmenopausal hormone use and risk of large-bowel cancer. *Journal of the National Cancer Institute, 87*(14), 1067–1071.

Newport, E. L. (1998). Cited in Azar, B. (1998). Acquiring sign language may be more innate than learned. *APA Monitor, 29*(4), 12.

Nezlek, J. B., Hampton, C. P., & Shean, G. D. (2000). Clinical depression and day-to-day social interaction in a community sample. *Journal of Abnormal Psychology, 109*(1), 11–19.

Niaura, R., & Abrams, D. B. (2002). Smoking cessation: Progress, priorities, and prospectus. *Journal of Consulting and Clinical Psychology, 70*(3), 494–509.

Niederman, M., Farley, A., Richardson, J., & Lask, B. (2001). Nasogastric feeding in children and adolescents with eating disorders: Toward good practice. *International Journal of Eating Disorders, 29*(4), 441–448.

Nieto, J. J., Cogswell, D., Jesinger, D., & Hardiman, P. (2000). Lipid effects of hormone replacement therapy with sequential transdermal 17-beta-estradiol and oral dydrogesterone. *Obstetrics & Gynecology, 95*, 111–114.

NIMH. See National Institute of Mental Health.

Nock, M. K., & Kazdin, A. E. (2002). Examination of affective, cognitive, and behavioral factors and suicide-related outcomes in children and young adolescents. *Journal of Community Psychology, 31*(1), 48–58.

Nolen-Hoeksema, S. (2000). The role of rumination in depressive disorders and mixed anxiety/depressive symptoms. *Journal of Abnormal Psychology, 109*(3), 504–511.

Nolen-Hoeksema, S. (2001). Gender differences in depression. *Current Directions in Psychological Science, 10*(5), 173–176.

Norton, A. (2000, July 21). A drink a day keeps brain in tip-top shape. Reuters News Agency online.

Norvell, N., & Belles, D. (1993). Psychological and physical benefits of circuit weight training in law enforcement personnel. *Journal of Consulting and Clinical Psychology, 61*, 520–527.

Novick, L. R., & Coté, N. (1992). The nature of expertise in anagram solution. *In Proceedings of the Fourteenth Annual Conference of the Cognitive Science Society*. Hillsdale, NJ: Erlbaum.

Nurnberger, J. I., Jr., et al. (2001). Evidence for a locus on chromosome 1 that influences vulnerability to alcoholism and affective disorder. *American Journal of Psychiatry, 158*, 718–724.

Nyberg, L., et al. (2000). Large scale neurocognitive networks underlying episodic memory. *Journal of Cognitive Neuroscience, 12*(1), 163–173.

O'Brien, C. P. (1996). Recent developments in the pharmacotherapy of substance abuse. *Journal of Consulting and Clinical Psychology, 64*, 677–686.

Oehman, A., & Mineka, S. (2001). Fears, phobias, and preparedness: Toward an evolved module of fear and fear learning. *Psychological Review, 108*(3), 483–522.

Ogbu, J. U. (1993). Differences in cultural frame of reference. *International Journal of Behavioral Development, 16*, 483–506.

Ohayon, M. M., Guilleminault, C., & Priest, R. G. (1999). Night terrors, sleepwalking, and confusional arousals in the general population: Their frequency and relationship to other sleep and mental disorders. *Journal of Clinical Psychiatry, 60*(4), 268–276.

Oktedalen, O., Solberg, E. E., Haugen, A. H., & Opstad, P. K. (2001). The influence of physical and mental training on plasma beta-endorphin level and pain perception after intensive physical exercise. *Stress & Health: Journal of the International Society for the Investigation of Stress, 17*(2), 121–127.

Olanow, W. M. (2000, July). Clinical and pathological perspective on Parkinsonism. Paper presented to the World Alzheimer Congress 2000, Washington, DC.

Olds, J. (1969). The central nervous system and the reinforcement of behavior. *American Psychologist, 24*, 114–132.

Olds, J., & Milner, P. (1954). Positive reinforcement produced by electrical stimulation of the septal area and other regions of the rat brain. *Journal of Comparative and Physiological Psychology, 47*, 419–427.

O'Leary, K. D. (2000). Are women really more aggressive than men in intimate relationships? *Psychological Bulletin, 126*(5), 685–689.

Olson, S. L., Bates, J. E., & Kaskie, B. (1992). Caregiver–infant interaction antecedents of children's school-age cognitive ability. *Merrill-Palmer Quarterly, 38*, 309–330.

Olthof, A., & Roberts, W. A. (2000). Summation of symbols by pigeons (*Columba livia*): The importance of number and mass of reward items. *Journal of Comparative Psychology, 114*(2), 158–166.

Omer, H., & Elitzur, A. C. (2001). What would you say to the person on the roof? A suicide prevention text. *Suicide & Life-Threatening Behavior, 31*(2), 129–139.

Ouimette, P. C., Finney, J. W., & Moos, R. H. (1997). Twelve-step and cognitive–behavioral treatment for substance abuse. *Journal of Consulting and Clinical Psychology, 65*, 230–240.

Paffenbarger, R. S., Jr., and others (1993). The association of changes in physical-activity level and other lifestyle characteristics with mortality among men. *New England Journal of Medicine, 328*, 538–545.

Pappas, G., Queen, S., Hadden, W., & Fisher, G. (1993). The increasing disparity of mortality between socioeconomic groups in the United States, 1960 and 1986. *New England Journal of Medicine, 329*, 103–109.

Park, J., & Banaji, M. R. (2000). Mood and heuristics: The influence of happy and sad states on sensitivity and bias in stereotyping. *Journal of Personality & Social Psychology, 78*(6), 1005–1023.

Parker, A. (2000). A review of the ganzfeld work at Gothenburg University. *Journal of the Society for Psychical Research, 64*(858), 1–15.

Parker, J. G., & Herrera, C. (1996). Interpersonal processes in friendship: A comparison of abused and nonabused children's experience. *Developmental Psychology, 32*, 1025–1038.

Parker, K. J., Kinney, L. F., Phillips, K. M., & Lee, T. M. (2001). Paternal behavior is associated with central neurohormone receptor binding patterns in meadow voles (*Microtus pennsylvanicus*). *Behavioral Neuroscience, 115*(6), 1341–1348.

Parr, L. A., Winslow, J. T., Hopkins, W. D., & de Waal, F. B. M. (2000). Recognizing facial cues: Individual discrimination by chimpanzees (*Pan troglodytes*) and Rhesus monkeys (*Macaca mulatta*). *Journal of Comparative Psychology, 114*(1), 47–60.

Parsons, J. T., Halkitis, P. N., Bimbi, D., & Borkowski, T. (2000). Perceptions of the benefits and costs associated with condom use and unprotected sex among late adolescent college students. *Journal of Adolescence, 23*(4), 377–391.

Patterson, D. R., & Ptacek, J. T. (1997). Baseline pain as a moderator of hypnotic analgesia for burn injury treatment. *Journal of Consulting and Clinical Psychology, 65*, 60–67.

Patterson, J. L. (2000). Observed and reported expressive vocabulary and word combinations in bilingual toddlers. *Journal of Speech, Language, & Hearing Research, 43*(1), 121–128.

Pavlov, I. (1927). *Conditioned reflexes*. London: Oxford University Press.

Pear, R. (2000, March 20). White House seeks to curb pills used to calm young. *The New York Times online*.

Penfield, W. (1969). Consciousness, memory, and man's conditioned reflexes. In K. H. Pribram (Ed.), *On the biology of learning*. New York: Harcourt Brace Jovanovich.

Penn, N. E., Kar, S., Kramer, J., Skinner, J., & Zambrana, R. E. (1995). Panel VI. Ethnic minorities, health care systems, and behavior. *Health Psychology, 14*, 641–648.

Penner, L. A., Thompson, J. K., & Coovert, D. L. (1991). Size overestimation among anorexics: Much ado about very little? *Journal of Abnormal Psychology, 100*, 90–93.

Pennock, R. T. (2002). *Intelligent design: Creationism and its critics. Philosophical, theological, and scientific perspectives.* Cambridge, MA: A Bradford Book/The MIT Press.

Penton-Voak, I. S., & Perrett, D. I. (2000). Female preference for male faces changes cyclically: Further evidence. *Evolution & Human Behavior, 21*(1), 39–48.

Perlman, L. M. (2001). Nonspecific, unintended, and serendipitous effects of psychotherapy. *Professional Psychology: Research & Practice, 32*(3), 283–288.

Perls, F. S. (1971). *Gestalt therapy verbatim*. New York: Bantam.

Perras, B., et al. (1997). Verbal memory after three months of intranasal vasopressin in healthy old humans. *Psychoneuroendocrinology, 22*(6), 387–396.

Perrett, D. I. (1994). *Nature*. Cited in Brody, J. E. (1994, March 21). Notions of beauty transcend culture, new study suggests. *The New York Times*, p. A14.

Perry, D. G., & Bussey, K. (1979). The social learning theory of sex differences. *Journal of Personality and Social Psychology, 37*, 1699–1712.

Perse, E. M. (1998). Implications of cognitive and affective involvement for channel changing. *Journal of Communication, 48*(3), 49–68.

Persons, J. B., Davidson, J., & Tompkins, M. A. (2001). *Essential components of cognitive–behavior therapy for depression.* Washington, D.C.: American Psychological Association.

Peterson, L. R., & Peterson, M. J. (1959). Short-term retention of individual verbal items. *Journal of Experimental Psychology, 58,* 193–198.

Petrov, E. S., Varlinskaya, E. I., & Spear, N. E. (2001). Self-administration of ethanol and saccharin in newborn rats: Effects on suckling plasticity. *Behavioral Neuroscience, 115*(6), 1318–1331.

Petry, N. M., Martin, B., Cooney, J. L., & Kranzler, H. R. (2000). Give them prizes and they will come: Contingency management for treatment of alcohol dependence. *Journal of Consulting and Clinical Psychology, 68,* 250–257.

Pettingale, K. W., et al. (1985). Mental attitudes to cancer. *Lancet, 1,* 750.

Petty, R. E., Fleming, M. A., & White, P. H. (1999). Stigmatized sources and persuasion: Prejudice as a determinant of argument scrutiny. *Journal of Personality & Social Psychology, 76*(1), 19–34.

Petty, R. E., Wegener, D. T., & Fabrigar, L. R. (1997). Attitudes and attitude change. *Annual Review of Psychology, 48,* 609–647.

Phalet, K., & Schoenpflug, U. (2001). Intergenerational transmission of collectivism and achievement values in two acculturation contexts: The case of Turkish families in Germany and Turkish and Moroccan families in the Netherlands. *Journal of Cross-Cultural Psychology, 32*(2), 186–201.

Phelps, E. A., O'Connor, K. J., Cunningham, W. A., Funayama, E. S., & Banaji, M. R. (2000). Performance on indirect measures of race evaluation predicts amygdala activation. *Journal of Cognitive Neuroscience, 12*(5).

Phinney, J. S. (1996). When we talk about American ethnic groups, what do we mean? *American Psychologist, 51,* 918–927.

Phinney, J. S. (2000). Identity formation across cultures: The interaction of personal, societal, and historical change. *Human Development, 43*(1), 27–31.

Phinney, J. S., Cantu, C. L., & Kurtz, D. A. (1997). Ethnic and American identity as predictors of self-esteem among African American, Latino, and white adolescents. *Journal of Youth & Adolescence, 26*(2), 165–185.

Phinney, J. S., & Devich-Navarro, M. (1997). Variations in bicultural identification among African American and Mexican American adolescents. *Journal of Research on Adolescence, 7*(1), 3–32.

Piaget, J. (1963). *The origins of intelligence in children.* New York: W. W. Norton.

Piaget, J. (1997, Ed.) *The moral judgment of the child.* Trans. by Marjorie Gabain. New York: Free Press.

Pihl, R. O., Peterson, J. B., & Finn, P. (1990). Inherited predisposition to alcoholism. *Journal of Abnormal Psychology, 99,* 291–01.

Pillard, R. C., & Weinrich, J. D. (1986). Evidence of familial nature of male homosexuality. *Archives of Sexual Behavior, 43,* 808–812.

Pillemer, D. B. (1998). What is remembered about early childhood events? *Clinical Psychology Review, 18*(8), 895–913.

Pinel, J. P. J., Assanand, S., & Lehman, D. R. (2000). Hunger, eating, and ill health. *American Psychologist, 55*(10), 1105–1116.

Pinker, S. (1990). Language acquisition. In D. N. Osherson, & H. Lasnik (Eds.), *An invitation to cognitive science: Language* (Vol. 1). Cambridge, MA: The MIT Press, a Bradford Book.

Pinker, S. (1994). *The language instinct.* New York: William Morrow.

Pinker, S. (1997). Words and rules in the human brain. *Nature, 387*(6633), 547–548.

Pinker, S. (1999). Out of the minds of babes. *Science, 283*(5398), 40–41.

Pinquart, M., & Sörensen, S. (2000). Influences of socioeconomic status, social network, and competence on subjective well-being in later life: A meta-analysis. *Psychology and Aging, 15*(2), 187–224.

Pinnell, C. M., & Covino, N. A. (2000). Empirical findings on the use of hypnosis in medicine: A critical review. *International Journal of Clinical & Experimental Hypnosis, 48*(2), 170–194.

Platania, J., & Moran, G. P. (2001). Social facilitation as a function of mere presence of others. *Journal of Social Psychology, 141*(2), 190–197.

Plomin, R. (2000). Behavioural genetics in the 21st century. *International Journal of Behavioral Development, 24*(1), 30–34.

Plomin, R. (2001). Genetics and behaviour. *Psychologist, 14*(3), 134–139.

Plomin, R., & Crabbe, J. (2000). DNA. *Psychological Bulletin, 126*(6), 806–828.

Plomin, R., DeFries, J. C., McClearn, G. E., & Rutter, M. (1997). *Behavioral genetics.* New York: Freeman.

Plous, S. (1996). Attitudes toward the use of animals in psychological research and education. *American Psychologist, 51,* 1167–1180.

Poe, G. R., Nitz, D. A., McNaughton, B. L., & Barnes, C. A. (2000). Experience-dependent phase-reversal of hippocampal neuron firing during REM sleep. *Brain Research, 855*(1), 176–180.

Pointer, S. C., & Bond, N. W. (1998). Context-dependent memory: Colour versus odor. *Chemical Senses, 23*(3), 359–362.

Pol, H. E. H., et al. (2000). Prenatal exposure to famine and brain morphology in schizophrenia. *American Journal of Psychiatry, 157,* 1170–1172.

Pollock, B., Prior, H., & Güntürkün, O. (2000). Development of object permanence in food-storing magpies (*Pica pica*). *Journal of Comparative Psychology, 114*(2), 148–157.

Pope, H. G., Kouri, E. M., & Hudson, J. I. (2000). Effects of supraphysiologic doses of testosterone on mood and aggression in normal men: A randomized controlled trial. *Archives of General Psychiatry, 57,* 133–140.

Pope, J. H., et al. (2000). Missed diagnoses of acute cardiac ischemia in the emergency department. *The New England Journal of Medicine, 342,* 1163–1170.

Porter, R. H., Makin, J. W., Davis, L. B., & Christensen, K. M. (1992). Breast-fed infants respond to olfactory cues from their own mother and unfamiliar lactating females. *Infant Behavior and Development, 15,* 85–93.

Posada, G., et al. (2002). Maternal caregiving and infant security in two cultures. *Developmental Psychology, 38*(1), 67–78.

Postmes, T., Spears, R., & Cihangir, S. (2001). Quality of decision making and group norms. *Journal of Personality & Social Psychology, 80*(6), 918–930.

Powers, R. (2000, May 7). American dreaming. *The New York Times Magazine,* pp. 66–67.

Powers, S. W., et al. (2001). A pilot study of one-session biofeedback training in pediatric headache. *Neurology, 56*(1), 133.

Preti, A., De Biasi, F., & Miotto, P. (2001). Musical creativity and suicide. *Psychological Reports, 89*(3), 719–727.

Preti, A., & Miotto, P. (1999). Suicide among eminent artists. *Psychological Reports, 84*(1), 291–301.

Price, L. H., & Heninger, G. R. (1994). Lithium in the treatment of mood disorders. *New England Journal of Medicine, 331,* 591–598.

Prochaska, J. O., & Norcross, J. C. (2003). *Systems of psychotherapy* (5th ed.). Belmont, CA: Wadsworth.

Pronin, E., Lin, D. Y., & Ross, L. (2002). The bias blind spot: Perceptions of bias in self versus others. *Personality & Social Psychology Bulletin, 28*(3), 369–381.

Pryce, C. R., Bettschen, D., Bahr, N. I., & Feldon, J. (2001). Comparison of the effects of infant handling, isolation, and nonhandling on acoustic startle, prepulse inhibition, locomotion, and HPA activity in the adult rat. *Behavioral Neuroscience, 115*(1), 71–83.

Pugh, K. R., et al., (2000). The angular gyrus in developmental dyslexia: Task-specific differences in functional connectivity within posterior cortex. *Psychological Science, 11*(1). 51–56.

Pulley, B. (1998, June 16). Those seductive snake eyes: Tales of growing up gambling. *The New York Times,* A1, A28.

Raichle, M. E. (1994). Visualizing the mind. *Scientific American, 270*(4), 58–64.

Raine, A., et al. (2000). Reduced prefrontal gray matter volume and reduced autonomic activity in antisocial personality disorder. *Archives of General Psychiatry, 57*(2), 119–127.

Rakowski, W. (1995). Cited in Margoshes, P. (1995). For many, old age is the prime of life. *APA Monitor, 26*(5), 36–37.

Ramachandran S. V., et al. (2001). Impact of high-normal blood pressure on the risk of cardiovascular disease. *New England Journal of Medicine, 345*(18),1291–1297.

Randel, B., Stevenson, H. W., & Witruk, E. (2000). Attitudes, beliefs, and mathematics achievement of German and Japanese high school students. *International Journal of Behavioral Development, 24*(2), 190–198.

Rappaport, N. B., McAnulty, D. P., & Brantley, P. J. (1988). Exploration of the Type A behavior pattern in chronic headache sufferers. *Journal of Consulting and Clinical Psychology, 56,* 621–623.

Rath, N. (2002). The power to feel fear and the one to feel happiness are the same. *Journal of Happiness Studies, 3*(1), 1–21.

Rathore, S. S., et al. (2000). Race, sex, poverty, and the medical treatment of acute myocardial infarction in the elderly. *Circulation, 102,* 642–648.

Rathus, J. H., & Sanderson, W. C. (1999). *Marital distress: Cognitive behavioral interventions for couples.* Northvale, NJ: Jason Aronson.

Rathus, S. A. (1973). A 30-item schedule for assessing assertive behavior. *Behavior Therapy, 4,* 398–406.

Rathus, S. A. (2003). *Voyages: Childhood and adolescence.* Belmont, CA: Wadsworth Publishing Company.

Rathus, S. A., Nevid, J. S., & Fichner-Rathus, L. (2002). *Human sexuality in a world of diversity* (5th ed.). Boston: Allyn & Bacon.

Ratner, N. B., & Gleason, J. B. (1993). An introduction to psycholinguistics. In J. B. Gleason & N. B. Ratner (Eds.), *Psycholinguistics.* Fort Worth: Harcourt Brace Jovanovich.

Rauscher, F. H. (1998). Response to Katie Overy's paper, Can music really improve the mind? *Psychology of Music, 26*(2), 197–199.

Rauscher, F. H., & Shaw, G. L. (1998). Key components of the Mozart effect. *Perceptual & Motor Skills, 86*(3), 835–841.

Raven, B. H. (1998). Groupthink, Bay of Pigs, and Watergate reconsidered. *Organizational Behavior & Human Decision Processes, 73*(2–3), 352–361.

Raynor, H. A., & Epstein, L. H. (2001). Dietary variety, energy regulation, and obesity. *Psychological Bulletin, 127*(3), 325–341.

Ready, T. (2000, June 7). Meditation apparently good for the heart as well as the mind. Healtheon/WebMD.

Reaney, P. (1998, March 16.) Acupuncture can work but is not totally safe. Reuters News Agency online.

Reaney, P. (2000, February 14). In matters of the heart, France tops EU neighbors. Reuters News Agency online.

Redd, W. H., et al. (1987). Cognitive/attentional distraction in the control of conditioned nausea in pediatric cancer patients receiving chemotherapy. *Journal of Consulting and Clinical Psychology, 55,* 391–395.

Reed, J. M., & Squire, L. R. (1997). Impaired recognition memory in patients with lesions limited to the hippocampal formation. *Behavioral Neuroscience, 111*(4) 667–675.

Reeder, G. D. (2001). On perceiving multiple causes and inferring multiple internal attributes. *Psychological Inquiry, 12*(1), 34–36.

Reid, P. T. (1994). The real problem in the study of culture. *American Psychologist, 49,* 524–525.

Reinecke, M. A., DuBois, D. L., & Schultz, T. M. (2001). Social problem solving, mood, and suicidality among inpatient adolescents. *Cognitive Therapy & Research, 25*(6), 743–756.

Reis, H. T., et al. (1990). What is smiling is beautiful and good. *European Journal of Social Psychology, 20,* 259–267.

Reiser, M. (2001). The dream in contemporary psychiatry. *American Journal of Psychiatry, 158*(3), 351–359.

Rempel, M. W., & Fisher, R. J. (1998). Perceived threat, cohesion, and group problem solving in intergroup conflict. *International Journal of Conflict Management, 8*(3), 216–234.

Renninger, K. A., & Wozniak, R. H. (1985). Effect of interest on attentional shift, recognition, and recall in young children. *Developmental Psychology, 21,* 624–632.

Rescorla, R. A. (1988). Pavlovian conditioning: It's not what you think it is. *American Psychologist, 43,* 151–160.

Rescorla, R. A. (1999). Partial reinforcement reduces the associative change produced by nonreinforcement. *Journal of Experimental Psychology: Animal Behavior Processes, 25*(4), 403–414.

Rest, J. R. (1983). Morality. In P. H. Mussen, J. Flavell, & E. Markman (Eds.), *Handbook of child psychology: Vol. 3. Cognitive development.* New York: Wiley.

Reynolds, A. G. (1991). The cognitive consequences of bilingualism. In A. G. Reynolds (Ed.), *Bilingualism, multiculturalism, and second language learning.* Hillsdale, NJ: Erlbaum.

Rezvani, A. H., & Levin, E. D. (2001). Cognitive effects of nicotine. *Biological Psychiatry, 49*(3), 258–267.

Rhee, S. H., & Waldman, I. D. (2002). Genetic and environmental influences on antisocial behavior: A meta-analysis of twin and adoption studies. *Psychological Bulletin, 128*(3), 490–529.

Rice, K. G., & Dellwo, J. P. (2001). Within-semester stability and adjustment correlates of the Multidimensional Perfectionism Scale. *Measurement & Evaluation in Counseling & Development, 34*(3), 146–156.

Rice, M. E., Quinsey, V. L., & Harris, G. T. (1991). Sexual recidivism among child molesters released from a maximum security psychiatric institution. *Journal of Consulting and Clinical Psychology, 59,* 381–386.

Richards, J. C., Hof, A., & Alvarenga, M. (2000). Serum lipids and their relationships with hostility and angry affect and behaviors in men. *Health Psychology, 19*(4) 393–398.

Richardson, D. C., Bernstein, S., & Taylor, S. P. (1979). The effect of situational contingencies on female retaliative behavior. *Journal of Personality and Social Psychology, 37,* 2044–2048.

Richardson, G. E. (2002). The metatheory of resilience and resiliency. *Journal of Clinical Psychology, 58*(3), 307–321.

Rickard, T. C., et al., (2000). The calculating brain: An fMRI study. *Neuropsychologia, 38*(3), 325–335.

Riepe, M. (2000). Cited in Ritter, M. (2000, March 21). Brains differ in navigation skills. The Associated Press online.

Rigotti, N. A., Lee, J. E., & Wechsler, H.. (2000). US college students' use of tobacco products: Results of a national survey. *Journal of the American Medical Association, 284*(6), 699–705.

Rinn, W. E. (1991). Neuropsychology of facial expression. In R. S. Feldman & B. Rime (Eds.), *Fundamentals of nonverbal behavior.* Cambridge, England: Cambridge University Press.

Ritter, M. (2000, March 21). Brains differ in navigation skills. The Associated Press online.

Ritvo, E. R., Freeman, B. J., Mason-Brothers, A., Mo, A., & Ritvo, A. M. (1985). Concordance for the syndrome of autism in 40 pairs of afflicted twins. *American Journal of Psychiatry, 142,* 74–77.

Robbins, J. (2000, July 4). Virtual reality finds a real place as a medical aid. *The New York Times online.*

Robins, R. W., Gosling, S. D., & Craik, K. H. (1999). An empirical analysis of trends in psychology. *American Psychologist, 54*(2), 117–128.

Robson, P. (2001). Therapeutic aspects of cannabis and cannabinoids. *The British Journal of Psychiatry, 178,* 107–115.

Rodriguez, I., Greer, C. A., Mok, M. Y., & Mombaerts, P. (2000). A putative pheromone receptor gene expressed in human olfactory mucosa. *Nature Genetics, 26*(1), 18–19.

Rodriguez, P., & Levy, W. B. (2001). A model of hippocampal activity in trace conditioning: Where's the trace? *Behavioral Neuroscience, 115*(6), 1224–1238.

Roediger, H. L., Weldon, M. S., Stadler, M.. L., & Riegler, G. L. (1992). Direct comparison of two implicit memory tests: Word fragment and word stem completion. *Journal of Experimental Psychology: Learning, Memory, & Cognition, 18*(6), 1251–1269.

Roelofs, K., et al. (2002). Hypnotic susceptibility in patients with conversion disorder. *Journal of Abnormal Psychology, 111*(2), 390–395.

Rogers, C. R. (1951). *Client-centered therapy.* Boston: Houghton Mifflin.

Romero, E., Luengo, M. A., & Sobral, J. (2001). Personality and antisocial behaviour: Study of temperamental dimensions. *Personality & Individual Differences, 31*(3), 329–348.

Roncesvalles, M. N. C., Woollacott, M. H., & Jensen, J. L. (2001). Development of lower extremity kinetics for balance control in infants and young children. *Journal of Motor Behavior, 33*(2), 180–192.

Rose, J. S., Chassin, L., Presson, C. C., & Sherman, S. J. (1996). Prospective predictors of quit attempts and smoking cessation in young adults. *Health Psychology, 15,* 261–268.

Rose, R. J. (1995). Genes and human behavior. *Annual Review of Psychology, 46,* 625–654.

Rosenbaum, D. E. (2000, May 16). On left-handedness, its causes and costs. *The New York Times,* pp. F1, F6.

Rosenstein, D., & Oster, H. (1988). Differential facial responses to four basic tastes. *Child Development, 59,* 1555–1568.

Rosenthal, A. M. (1994, March 15). The way she died. *The New York Times,* p. A23.

Rosenthal, E. (1993, July 20). Listening to the emotional needs of cancer patients. *The New York Times,* pp. C1, C7.

Ross, J. L., Roeltgen, D., Feuillan, P., Kushner, H., & Cutler, W. B. (2000). Use of estrogen in young girls with Turner syndrome: Effects on memory. *Neurology, 54*(1), 164–170.

Ross, L., & Nisbett, R. E. (1991). *The person and the situation.* New York: McGraw-Hill.

Ross, M. J., & Berger, R. S. (1996). Effects of stress inoculation training on athletes' postsurgical pain and rehabilitation after orthopedic injury. *Journal of Consulting and Clinical Psychology, 64,* 406–410.

Rosso, I. M., et al. (2000). Obstetric risk factors for early-onset schizophrenia in a Finnish birth cohort. *American Journal of Psychiatry, 157,* 801–807.

Roth, D. B., & Gellert, M. (2000). Cancer: New guardians of the genome. *Nature, 404,* 823–824.

Rothbart, M. K., & Ahadi, S. A. (1994). Temperament and the development of personality. *Journal of Abnormal Psychology, 103,* 55–66.

Rothbaum, B. O., Foa, E. B., Riggs, D. S., Murdock, T., & Walsh, W. (1992). A prospective examination of post-traumatic stress disorder in rape victims. *Journal of Traumatic Stress, 5,* 455–475.

Rothbaum, B. O., Hodges, L. F., Ready, D., Graap, K., & Alarcon, R. D. (2001). Virtual reality exposure therapy for Vietnam veterans with posttraumatic stress disorder. *Journal of Clinical Psychiatry, 62*(8), 617–622.

Rothbaum, B. O., Hodges, L., Anderson, P. L., Price, L., & Smith, S. (2002). Twelve-month follow-up of virtual reality and standard exposure therapies for the fear of flying. *Journal of Consulting & Clinical Psychology, 70*(2), 428–432.

Rotter, J. B. (1990). Internal versus external control of reinforcement. *American Psychologist, 45,* 489–493.

Rotton, J., & Cohn, E. G. (2000). Violence is a curvilinear function of temperature in Dallas: A replication. *Journal of Personality and Social Psychology, 78*(6), 1074–1081.

Rovee-Collier, C. (1999). The development of infant memory. *Current Directions in Psychological Science, 8*(3), 80–85.

Rowatt, W. C., Cunningham, M. R., & Druen, P. B. (1999). Lying to get a date: The effect of facial physical attractiveness on the willingness to deceive prospective dating partners. *Journal of Social & Personal Relationships, 16*(2) 209–223.

Rozin, P., & Fallon, A. (1988). Body image, attitudes to weight, and misperceptions of figure preferences of the opposite sex. *Journal of Abnormal Psychology, 97,* 342–345.

Rubinstein, S., & Caballero, B. (2000). Is Miss America an undernourished role model? *Journal of the American Medical Association online, 283*(12).

Rude, S. S., Hertel, P. T., Jarrold, W., Covich, J., & Hedlund, S. (1999). Depression-related impairments in prospective memory. *Cognition & Emotion, 13*(3), 267–276.

Ruiter, R. A. C., Abraham, C., & Kok, G. (2001). Scary warnings and rational precautions: A review of the psychology of fear appeals. *Psychology & Health, 16*(6), 613–630.

Rule, B. G., Taylor, B. R., & Dobbs, A. R. (1987). Priming effects of heat on aggressive thoughts. *Social Cognition, 5,* 131–143.

Rush, A. J., Khatami, M., & Beck, A. T. (1975). Cognitive and behavior therapy in chronic depression. *Behavior Therapy, 6,* 398–404.

Rutkowski, G. K., Gruder, C. L., & Romer, D. (1983). Group cohesiveness, social norms, and bystander intervention. *Journal of Personality and Social Psychology, 44,* 545–552.

Rutkowski, K. (2001). Anxiety, depression and nightmares in PTSD. *Archives of Psychiatry & Psychotherapy, 3*(2), 41–50.

Rutter, M. (1997). Nature–nurture integration. *American Psychology, 52,* 390–398.

Rutter, M., & Silberg, J. (2002). Gene–environment interplay in relation to emotional and behavioral disturbance. *Annual Review of Psychology, 53*(1), 463–490.

Ryder, A. G., Alden, L. E., & Paulhus, D. L. (2000). Is acculturation unidimensional or bidimensional? A head-to-head comparison in the prediction of personality, self-identity, and adjustment. *Journal of Personality and Social Psychology, 79*(1), 49–65.

Sackeim, H. A., et al. (2000). A prospective, randomized, double-blind comparison of bilateral and right unilateral electroconvulsive therapy at different stimulus intensities. *Archives of General Psychiatry, 57*(5), 425–434.

Sacks, F. M., et al. (2001). Effects on blood pressure of reduced dietary sodium and the Dietary Approaches to Stop Hypertension (DASH) Diet. *The New England Journal of Medicine, 344*(1), 3–10.

Sadalla, E. K., Kenrick, D. T., & Vershure, B. (1987). Dominance and heterosexual attraction. *Journal of Personality and Social Psychology, 52,* 730–738.

Sadker, M., & Sadker, D. (1994). *How America's schools cheat girls.* New York: Scribners.

Sagrestano, L. M., McCormick, S. H., Paikoff, R. L., & Holmbeck, G. N. (1999). Pubertal development and parent–child conflict in low-income, urban, African American adolescents. *Journal of Research on Adolescence, 9*(1), 85–107.

Salgado de Snyder, V. N., Cervantes, R. C., & Padilla, A. M. (1990). Gender and ethnic differences in psychosocial stress and generalized distress among Hispanics. *Sex Roles, 22,* 441–453.

Salovey, P., Rothman, A. J., Detweiler, J. B., & Steward, W. T. (2000). Emotional states and physical health. *American Psychologist, 55,* 110–121.

Sampaio, D., et al. (2001). Representacoes sociais do suicidio em estudantes do ensino secundario. *Analise Psicologica, 18*(2), 139–155.

Sanders, G. S. (1984). Effects of context cues on eyewitness identification responses. *Journal of Applied Social Psychology, 14,* 386–397.

Sandman, C., & Crinella, F. (1995) Cited in Margoshes, P. (1995). For many, old age is the prime of life. *APA Monitor, 26*(5), 36–37.

Sangrador, J. L., & Yela, C. (2000). What is beautiful is loved: Physical attractiveness in love relationships in a representative sample. *Social Behavior & Personality, 28*(3), 207–218.

Sanna, L. J., & Meier, S. (2000). Looking for clouds in a silver lining: Self-esteem, mental simulations, and temporal confidence changes. *Journal of Research in Personality, 34*(2), 236–251.

Sano, M. (2000, July). Estrogen in Alzheimer's disease: Treatment or prevention. Paper presented to the World Alzheimer Congress 2000, Washington, DC.

Santelli, J. S., Lowry, R., Brener, N. D., & Robin, L. (2000). The association of sexual behaviors with socioeconomic status, family structure, and race/ethnicity among U.S. adolescents. *American Journal of Public Health, 90*(10), 1582–1588.

Santonastaso, P., Friederici, S., & Favaro, A. (2001). Sertraline in the treatment of restricting anorexia nervosa: An open controlled trial. *Journal of Child & Adolescent Psychopharmacology, 11*(2), 143–150.

Sarbin, T. R., & Coe, W. C. (1972). *Hypnosis.* New York: Holt, Rinehart and Winston.

Savage, C. R., et al. (2001). Prefrontal regions supporting spontaneous and directed application of verbal learning strategies. Evidence from PET. *Brain, 124*(1), 219–231.

Savage-Rumbaugh, E. S., & Fields, W. M. (2000). Linguistic, cultural and cognitive capacities of bonobos (Pan paniscus). *Culture & Psychology, 6*(2), 131–153.

Sawa, A., & Snyder, S. H. (2002, April 26). Schizophrenia: Diverse approaches to a complex disease. *Science,* pp. 692–695.

Saxe, L. (1991). Lying. *American Psychologist, 46,* 409–415.

Saxe, L., & Ben-Shakhar, G. (1999). Admissibility of polygraph tests: The application of scientific standards post-Daubert. *Psychology, Public Policy, & Law, 5*(1), 203–223.

Saywitz, K. J., Mannarino, A. P., Berliner, L., & Cohen, J. A. (2000). Treatment for sexually abused children and adolescents. *American Psychologist, 55*(9), 1040–1049.

Scarr, S., & Kidd, K. K. (1983). Developmental behavior genetics. In M. Haith & J. J. Campos (Eds.), *Handbook of child psychology.* New York: Wiley.

Scarr, S., & Weinberg, R. A. (1976). IQ test performance of black children adopted by white families. *American Psychologist, 31,* 726–739.

Scarr, S., & Weinberg, R. A. (1977). Intellectual similarities within families of both adopted and biological children. *Intelligence, 1,* 170–191.

Scarr, S., & Weinberg, R. A. (1983). The Minnesota adoption studies: Genetic differences and malleability. *Child Development, 54,* 260–267.

Scaturo, D. J. (2001). The evolution of psychotherapy and the concept of manualization: An integrative perspective. *Professional Psychology: Research & Practice, 32*(5), 522–530.

Schachter, S., & Singer, J. E. (1962). Cognitive, social, and physiological determinants of emotional state. *Psychological Review, 69,* 379–399.

Schacter, D. L. (1992). Understanding implicit memory: A cognitive neuroscience approach. *American Psychologist, 47*(4), 559–569.

Schacter, D. L. (1999). The seven sins of memory: Insights from psychology and cognitive neuroscience. *American Psychologist, 54*(3), 182–203.

Schacter, D. L., Badgaiyan, R. D., & Alpert, N. M. (1999). Visual word stem completion priming within and across modalities: A PET study. *Neuroreport: For Rapid Communication of Neuroscience Research, 10*(10), 2061–2065.

Schacter, D. L., & Badgaiyan, R. D. (2001). Neuroimaging of priming: New perspectives on implicit and explicit memory. *Current Directions in Psychological Science, 10*(1), 1–4.

Schaie, K. W. (1994). The course of adult intellectual development. *American Psychologist, 49,* 304–313.

Scharff, L., Marcus, D. A., & Masek, B. J. (2002). A controlled study of minimal-contact thermal biofeedback treatment in children with migraine. *Journal of Pediatric Psychology, 27*(2), 109–119.

Schellenberg, E. G. (2000). Cited in Hershenson, R. (2000, August 6). Debating the Mozart theory. *The New York Times magazine online.*

Schenk, D. (2000, July). A possible vaccine for Alzheimer's disease. Paper presented to the World Alzheimer Congress 2000, Washington, DC.

Schmidt, N. B., et al. (2000). Evaluating gene–psychological risk factor effects in the pathogenesis of anxiety: A new model approach. *Journal of Abnormal Psychology, 109*(2), 308–320.

Schmitt, D. P., Shackelford, T. K., Duntley, J., Tooke, W. & Buss, D. M. (2001). The desire for sexual variety as a key to understanding basic human mating strategies. *Personal Relationships, 8*(4), 425–455.

Schneider, B. H., & Byrne, B. M. (1987). Individualizing social skills training for behavior-disordered children. *Journal of Consulting and Clinical Psychology, 55,* 444–445.

Schneider, K. J., Bugental, J. F. T., & Pierson, J. F. (Eds.). (2001). *The handbook of humanistic psychology: Leading edges in theory, research, and practice.* Thousand Oaks, CA: Sage Publications.

Schneider, R. H., et al. (1995). A randomized controlled trial of stress reduction for hypertension in older African Americans. *Hypertension, 26,* 820.

Schuckit, M. A. (1996). Recent developments in the pharmacotherapy of alcohol dependence. *Journal of Consulting and Clinical Psychology, 64,* 669–676.

Schuckit, M. A., et al. (2001) A genome-wide search for genes that relate to a low level of response to alcohol. *Alcoholism: Clinical & Experimental Research, 25*(3), 323–329.

Schulz, R., & Heckhausen, J. (1996). A life span model of successful aging. *American Psychologist, 51,* 702–714.

Schupf, N. (2000, July). Epidemiology of dementia in Down syndrome. Paper presented to the World Alzheimer Congress 2000, Washington, DC.

Schwartz, R. M., & Gottman, J. M. (1976). Toward a task analysis of assertive behavior. *Journal of Consulting and Clinical Psychology, 44,* 910–920.

Schwartzer, R., & Renner, B. (2000). Social-cognitive predictors of health behavior: Action self-efficacy and coping self-efficacy. *Health Psychology, 19*(5), 487–495.

Schyns, P. (2001). Income and satisfaction in Russia. *Journal of Happiness Studies, 2*(2), 173–204.

Scott, J. (1994, May 9). Multiple personality cases perplex legal system. *The New York Times,* pp. A1, B10, B11.

Scruggs, T. E., & Mastropieri, M. A. (1992). Remembering the forgotten art of memory. *American Educator, 16*(4), 31–37.

Segal, N. L., & Roy, A. (2001). Suicidal attempts and ideation in twins whose co-twins' deaths were non-suicides: Replication and elaboration. *Personality & Individual Differences, 31*(3), 445–452.

Selemon, L. D. (2000). A measured milestone in schizophrenia research. *Archives of General Psychiatry, 57*(1), 74–75.

Seligman, M. E. P. (1995). The effectiveness of psychotherapy: The *Consumer Reports* study. *American Psychologist, 50,* 965–974.

Seligman, M. E. P. (1996, August). Predicting and preventing depression. Master lecture presented to the meeting of the American Psychological Association, Toronto.

Selye, H. (1976). *The stress of life* (Rev. ed.). New York: McGraw-Hill.

Selye, H. (1980). The stress concept today. In I. L. Kutash et al. (Eds.), *Handbook on stress and anxiety.* San Francisco: Jossey-Bass.

Serbin, L. A., Poulin-Dubois, D., Colburne, K. A., Sen, M. G., & Eichstedt, J. A. (2001). Gender stereotyping in infancy: Visual preferences for and knowledge of gender-stereotyped toys in the second year. *International Journal of Behavioral Development, 25*(1), 7–15.

Service, R. F. (1994). Will a new type of drug make memory-making easier? *Science, 266,* 218–219.

Sesso, H. D., Paffenbarger, R. S., Jr., & Lee, I-M. (2000). Physical activity and coronary heart disease in men: The Harvard Alumni Health Study. *Circulation, 102,* 975–980.

Shadish, W. R. (2002). Revisiting field experiments: Field notes for the future. *Psychological Methods, 7*(1), 3–18.

Shadish, W. R., Matt, G. E., Navarro, A. M., & Phillips, G. (2000). The effects of psychological therapies under clinically representative conditions: A meta-analysis. *Psychological Bulletin, 126*(4), 512–529.

Shayley, A. Y., et al. (2000). Auditory startle response in trauma survivors with posttraumatic stress disorder: A prospective study. *American Journal of Psychiatry, 157,* 255–261.

Shaywitz, B. A., et al. (1995). Sex differences in the functional organization of the brain for language. *Nature, 373,* 607–609.

Shaywitz, B. A., & Shaywitz, S., E. (2000). Estrogen and Alzheimer disease: Plausible theory, negative clinical trial. *Journal of the American Medical Association, 283*(8), 1055–1056.

Sherif, M., Harvey, O. J., White, B. J., Hood, W. R., & Sherif, C. W. (1961/1988). *The Robbers Cave experiment: Intergroup conflict and cooperation.* Middletown, CT: Wesleyan University Press.

Sherman, J. W., & Frost, L. A. (2000). On the encoding of stereotype-relevant information under cognitive load. *Personality & Social Psychology Bulletin, 26*(1), 26–34.

Sherrington, J. M., Hawton, K. E., Fagg, J., Andrews, B., & Smith, D. (2001). Outcome of women admitted to hospital for depressive illness: Factors in the prognosis of severe depression. *Psychological Medicine, 31*(1), 115–125.

Sherwood, N. E., & Neumark-Sztainer, D. (2001). Internalization of the sociocultural ideal: Weight-related attitudes and dieting behaviors among young adolescent girls. *American Journal of Health Promotion, 15*(4), 228–231.

Shiffman, S., et al. (1997). A day at a time: Predicting smoking lapse from daily urge. *Journal of Abnormal Psychology, 106,* 104–116.

Shiffman, S., et al. (2000). Dynamic effects of self-efficacy on smoking lapse and relapse. *Health Psychology, 19*(4), 315–323.

Shlipak, M. G., et al. (2000). Estrogen and progestin, lipoprotein(a), and the risk of recurrent coronary heart disease events after menopause. *Journal of the American Medical Association, 283,* 1845–1852.

Shneidman, E. S. (1998). Perspectives on suicidology: Further reflections on suicide and psychache. *Suicide & Life-Threatening Behavior, 28*(3), 245–250.

Shneidman, E. S. (2001). *Comprehending suicide.* Washington, DC: American Psychological Association.

Silberschatz, G. (1998). In Persons, J. B., & Silberschatz, G. (1998). Are results of randomized controlled trials useful to psychotherapists? *Journal of Consulting and Clinical Psychology, 66,* 126–135.

Silver, E. (1994). Cited in DeAngelis, T. (1994). Experts see little impact from insanity plea ruling. *APA Monitor, 25*(6), 28.

Simons, A. D., Gordon, J. S., Monroe, S. M., & Thase, M. E. (1995). Toward an integration of psychologic, social, and biologic factors in depression. *Journal of Consulting and Clinical Psychology, 63,* 369–377.

Simonsen, G., Blazina, C., & Watkins, C. E., Jr. (2000). Gender role conflict and psychological well-being among gay men. *Journal of Counseling Psychology, 47*(1), 85–89.

Simonton, D. K. (2000). Creativity: Cognitive, personal, developmental, and social aspects. *American Psychologist, 55*, 151–158.

Simpson, M., & Perry, J. D. (1990). Crime and climate. *Environment and Behavior, 22*, 295–300.

Simpson, M. L., Olejnik, S., Tam, A. Y., & Supattathum, S. (1994). Elaborative verbal rehearsals and college students' cognitive performance. *Journal of Educational Psychology, 86*, 267–278.

Singh, R., & Ho, S. Y. (2000). Attitudes and attraction: A new test of the attraction, repulsion and similarity–dissimilarity asymmetry hypotheses. *British Journal of Social Psychology, 39*(2), 197–211.

Singletary, K. W., & Gapstur, S. M. (2001). Alcohol and breast cancer: Review of epidemiologic and experimental evidence and potential mechanisms. *Journal of the American Medical Association, 286*(17), 2143–2151.

Skinner, B. F. (1938). *The behavior of organisms: An experimental analysis.* New York: Appleton.

Skinner, B. F. (1948). *Walden two.* New York: Macmillan.

Skinner, B. F. (1983). Intellectual self-management in old age. *American Psychologist, 38*, 239–244.

Sleek, S. (1996). Side effects undermine drug compliance. *APA Monitor, 26*(3), 32.

Sleepers suffer WTC nightmares. (2001, November 22). The Associated Press.

Slobin, D. I. (1983). Crosslinguistic evidence for basic child grammar. Paper presented to the biennial meeting of the Society for Research in Child Development, Detroit.

Sloman, S. A. (1996). The empirical case for two systems of reasoning. *Psychological Bulletin, 119*, 3–22.

Smetana, J., & Gaines, C. (1999). Adolescent–parent conflict in middle-class African American families. *Child Development, 70*(6), 1447–1463.

Smiley, J. (2000, May 7). The good life. *The New York Times Magazine,* pp. 58–59.

Smith, B. N., Kerr, N. A., Markus, M. J., & Stasson, M. F. (2001). Individual differences in social loafing: Need for cognition as a motivator in collective performance. *Group Dynamics, 5*(2), 150–158.

Smith, D. E., & Seymour, R. B. (1994). LSD: History and toxicity. *Psychiatric Annals, 24*(3), 145–147.

Smith, G. F., & Dorfman, D. (1975). The effect of stimulus uncertainty on the relationship between frequency of exposure and liking. *Journal of Personality and Social Psychology, 31*, 150–155.

Smith, M. L., & Glass, G. V. (1977). Meta-analysis of psychotherapy outcome studies. *American Psychologist, 32*, 752–760.

Smith, R. E., Smoll, F. L., & Ptacek, J. T. (1990). Conjunctive moderator variables in vulnerability and resiliency research. *Journal of Personality and Social Psychology, 58*, 360–370.

Smith, T. W., & Ruiz, J. M. (2002). Course of coronary heart disease: Current status and implications for research and practice. *Journal of Consulting and Clinical Psychology, 70*(3), 548–568.

Smith, V. (2000, February 16). Female heart, geography link shown. The Associated Press.

Snyderman, M., & Rothman, S. (1987). Survey of expert opinion on intelligence and aptitude testing. *American Psychologist, 42*, 137–144.

Solowij, N., et al., for the Marijuana Treatment Project Research Group. (2002). Cognitive functioning of long-term heavy cannabis users seeking treatment. *Journal of the American Medical Association, 287*(9), 1123–1131.

Solomon, E. P., Berg, L. R., & Martin, D. W. (2002). *Biology* (6th ed.). Pacific Grove, CA: Brooks/Cole.

Somerfield, M. R., & McCrae, R. R. (2000). Stress and coping research: Methodological challenges, theoretical advances, and clinical applications. *American Psychologist, 55*(6), 620–625.

Sommerfeld, J. (2000, April 18). Lifting the curse: Should monthly periods be optional? MSNBC online.

Sookman, D., Pinard, G., & Beck, A. T. (2001). Vulnerability schemas in obsessive-compulsive disorder. *Journal of Cognitive Psychotherapy, 15*(2), 109–130.

Sorenson, S. B., & Rutter, C. M. (1991). Transgenerational patterns of suicide attempt. *Journal of Consulting and Clinical Psychology, 59*, 861–866.

Spasojevic, J., & Alloy, L. B. (2001). Rumination as a common mechanism relating depressive risk factors to depression. *Emotion, 1*(1), 25–37.

Sperling, G. (1960). The information available in brief visual presentations. *Psychological Monographs, 74*, 1–29.

Speranza, M., et al. (2001). Obsessive compulsive disorders in eating disorders. *Eating Behaviors, 2*(3), 193–207.

Sperry, R. W. (1998). A powerful paradigm made stronger. *Neuropsychologia, 36*(10), 1063–1068.

Spreat, S., & Behar, D. (1994). Trends in the residential (inpatient) treatment of individuals with a dual diagnosis. *Journal of Consulting and Clinical Psychology, 61*, 43–48.

Sprecher, S. (1998). Insiders' perspectives on reasons for attraction to a close other. *Social Psychology Quarterly, 61*(4), 287–300.

Sprecher, S., Sullivan, Q., & Hatfield, E. (1994). Mate selection preferences. *Journal of Personality and Social Psychology, 66*(6), 1074–1080.

Squire, L. R. (1993). Memory and the hippocampus. *Psychological Review, 99*, 195–231.

Squire, L. R. (1996, August). Memory systems of the brain. Master lecture presented to the meeting of the American Psychological Association, Toronto.

Staal, W. G., et al. (2000). Structural brain abnormalities in patients with schizophrenia and their healthy siblings. *American Journal of Psychiatry, 157*, 416–421.

Stacy, A. W., Bentler, P. M., & Flay, B. R. (1994). Attitudes and health behavior in diverse populations: Drunk driving, alcohol use, binge eating, marijuana use, and cigarette use. *Health Psychology, 13*(1), 73–85.

Stacy, A. W., & Newcomb, M. D. (1999). Adolescent drug use and adult drug problems in women: Direct, interactive, and mediational effects. *Experimental & Clinical Psychopharmacology, 7*(2), 160–173.

Stamler, J., et al. (2000). Relationship of baseline serum cholesterol levels in 3 large cohorts of younger men to long-term coronary, cardiovascular, and all-cause mortality and to longevity. *Journal of the American Medical Association, 284*, 311–318.

Stampfer, M. J., Hu, F. B., Manson, J. E., Rimm, E. B., & Willett, W. C. (2000). Primary prevention of coronary heart disease in women through diet and lifestyle. *New England Journal of Medicine, 343*(1), 16–22.

Stangor, C., Swim, J. K., Van Allen, K. L., & Sechrist, G. B. (2002). Reporting discrimination in public and private contexts. *Journal of Personality & Social Psychology, 82*(1), 69–74.

Stasser, G. (1999). A primer of social decision scheme theory: Models of group influence, competitive model-testing, and prospective modeling. *Organizational Behavior & Human Decision Processes, 80*(1), 3–20.

Steele, C. M., & Josephs, R. A. (1990). Alcohol myopia. *American Psychologist, 45*, 921–933.

Stein, M. B., & Kean, Y. M. (2000). Disability and quality of life in social phobia: Epidemiologic findings. *American Journal of Psychiatry, 157*, 1606–1613.

Stein, R. I., et al. (2001). Treatment of eating disorders in women. *Counseling Psychologist, 29*(5), 695–732.

Steinberg, L. (1996). *Beyond the classroom.* New York: Simon & Schuster.

Steinberg, L. (2001). We know some things: Parent–adolescent relationships in retrospect and prospect. *Journal of Research on Adolescence, 11*(1), 1–19.

Steinberg, L., Brown, B. B., & Dornbusch, S. M. (1996). Ethnicity and adolescent achievement. *American Educator, 20*(2), 28–35.

Steiner, M., & Pearlstein, T. (2000). Premenstrual dysphoria and the serotonin system pathophysiology and treatment. *Journal of Clinical Psychiatry, 61*(Suppl 12), 17–21.

Sternberg, R. J. (1988). Triangulating love. In R. J. Sternberg & M. J. Barnes (Eds.), *The psychology of love.* New Haven, CT: Yale University Press.

Sternberg, R. J. (1997). The concept of intelligence and its role in lifelong learning and success. *American Psychologist, 52*, 1030–1037.

Sternberg, R. J. (2000). In search of the zipperump-a-zoo. *Psychologist, 13*(5), 250–255.

Sternberg, R. J. (2001). What is the common thread of creativity? *American Psychologist, 56*(4), 360–362.

Sternberg, R. J., & Lubart, T. I. (1995). *Defying the crowd: Cultivating creativity in a culture of conformity.* New York: Free Press.

Sternberg, R. J., & Lubart, T. I. (1996). Investing in creativity. *American Psychologist, 51,* 677–688.

Sternberg, R. J., Wagner, R. K., Williams, W. M., & Horvath, J. A. (1995). Testing common sense. *American Psychologist, 50,* 912–927.

Sternberg, R. J., & Williams, W. M. (1997). Does the Graduate Record Examination predict meaningful success in the graduate training of psychologists? *American Psychologist, 52,* 630–641.

Stevenson, H. W., Lee, S. Y., & Stigler, J. W. (1986). Mathematics achievement of Chinese, Japanese, and American children. *Science, 231,* 693–699.

Stewart, A. J., & Ostrove, J. M. (1998). Women's personality in middle age: Gender, history, and midcourse corrections. *American Psychologist, 53*(11), 1185–1194.

Stewart, J. Y., & Armet, E. (2000, April 3). Aging in America: Retirees reinvent the concept. *Los Angeles Times online.*

Stice, E., Akutagawa, D., Gaggar, A., & Agras, W. S. (2000a). Negative affect moderates the relation between dieting and binge eating. *International Journal of Eating Disorders, 27*(2), 218–229.

Stice, E., & Bearman, S. K. (2001). Body-image and eating disturbances prospectively predict increases in depressive symptoms in adolescent girls: A growth curve analysis. *Developmental Psychology, 37*(5), 597–607.

Stice, E., Hayward, C., Cameron, R. P., Killen, J. D., & Taylor, C. B. (2000b). Body-image and eating disturbances predict onset of depression among female adolescents: A longitudinal study. *Journal of Abnormal Psychology, 109*(3), 438–444.

Stickgold, R., Whidbee, D., Schirmer, B., Patel, V., & Hobson, J. A. (2000). Visual discrimination task improvement: A multi-step process occurring during sleep. *Journal of Cognitive Neuroscience, 12*(2), 246–254.

Stier, D. S., & Hall, J. A. (1984). Gender differences in touch. *Journal of Personality and Social Psychology, 47,* 440–459.

Straneva, P. A., et al. (2002). Menstrual cycle, beta-endorphins, and pain sensitivity in premenstrual dysphoric disorder. *Health Psychology, 21*(4), 358–367.

Straube, E. R., & Oades, R. D. (1992). *Schizophrenia.* San Diego: Academic Press.

Straus, M. (1995). Cited in Collins, C. (1995, May 11). Spanking is becoming the new don't. *The New York Times,* p. C8.

Striegel-Moore, R. H., & Cachelin, F. M. (2001). Etiology of eating disorders in women. *Counseling Psychologist, 29*(5), 635–661.

Strober, M., Freeman, R., Lampert, C., Diamond, J., & Kaye, W. (2000). Controlled family study of anorexia nervosa and bulimia nervosa: Evidence of shared liability and transmission of partial syndromes. *American Journal of Psychiatry, 157,* 393–401.

Stroele, A., et al. (2002). GABA-sub(A) receptor-modulating neuroactive steroid composition in patients with panic disorder before and during paroxetine treatment. *American Journal of Psychiatry, 159*(1), 145–147.

Strom, J. C., & Buck, R. W. (1979). Staring and participants' sex. *Personality and Social Psychology Bulletin, 5,* 114–117.

Stroud, M. W., Thorn, B. E., Jensen, M. P., & Boothby, J. L. (2000). The relation between pain beliefs, negative thoughts, and psychosocial functioning in chronic pain patients. *Pain, 84*(2-3), 347–352.

Strupp, H. H. (2001). Implications of the empirically supported treatment movement for psychoanalysis. *Psychoanalytic Dialogues, 11*(4), 605–619.

Stunkard, A. J., Harris, J. R., Pedersen, N. L., & McLearn, G. E. (1990). A separated twin study of the body mass index. *New England Journal of Medicine, 322,* 1483–1487.

Sue, D. W., Bingham, R. P., Porché-Burke, L, & Vasquez, M. (1999). The diversification of psychology: A multicultural revolution. *American Psychologist, 54,* 1061–1069.

Sue, S. (1991). In J. D. Goodchilds (Ed.), *Psychological perspectives on human diversity in America.* Washington, DC: American Psychological Association.

Sue, S., & Okazaki, S. (1990). Asian-American educational achievements. *American Psychologist, 45,* 913–920.

Sullivan, A. (2000, April 2). The He hormone. *The New York Times Magazine,* pp. 46–51ff.

Sullivan, E. V., et al. (2000). Contribution of alcohol abuse to cerebellar volume deficits in men with schizophrenia. *Archives of General Psychiatry, 57,* 894–902.

Sullivan, J. M. (2000) Cellular and molecular mechanisms underlying learning and memory impairments produced by cannabinoids. *Learning & Memory, 7*(3), 132–139.

Suvisaari, J. M., Haukka, J. K., & Loennqvist, J. K. (2002). Seasonal fluctuation in schizophrenia: Dr. Suvisaari and colleagues reply. *American Journal of Psychiatry, 159*(3), 500.

Suzuki, L. A., & Valencia, R. R. (1997). Race-ethnicity and measured intelligence: Educational implications. *American Psychologist, 52,* 1103–1114.

Swinyard, W. R., Kau, A., & Phua, H. (2001). Happiness, materialism, and religious experience in the U.S. and Singapore. *Journal of Happiness Studies, 2*(1), 13–32.

Szasz, T. (1999). Medical incapacity, legal incompetence and psychiatry. *Psychiatric Bulletin, 23*(9), 517–519.

Szasz, T. (2000). Second commentary on Aristotle's function argument. *Philosophy, Psychiatry, & Psychology, 7*(1), 3–16.

Tailoring treatments for alcoholics is not the answer. (1997). *APA Monitor, 28*(2), 6–7.

Tan, R. S. (2001). *The andropause mystery: Unraveling truths about the male menopause.* Houston: Amred Publishing.

Tan, R. S. (Accessed March 23, 2002). Managing the andropause in aging men. *Clinical Geriatrics.* http://www.mmhc.com/cg/articles/CG9907/Tan.html

Tapes raise new doubts about Sybil's personalities. (1998, August 19). *The New York Times* online.

Tattersall, I. (2002). Cited in Gugliotta, G. (2002, July 10). Skull of oldest human ancestor found in Africa. *The Washington Post online.*

Taylor, M. J. (2000). The influence of self-efficacy on alcohol use among American Indians. *Cultural Diversity and Ethnic Minority Psychology, 6*(2), 152–167.

Taylor, S. E. (2000). Cited in Goode, E. (2000, May 19). Response to stress found that's particularly female. *The New York Times,* p. A20.

Taylor, S. E., Kemeny, M. E., Reed, G. M., Bower, J. E., & Gruenewald, T. L. (2000a). Psychological resources, positive illusions, and health. *American Psychologist, 55*(1), 99–109.

Taylor, S. E., et al. (2000b). Biobehavioral responses to stress in females: Tend-and-befriend, not fight-or-flight. *Psychological Review, 107*(3), 411–429.

Taylor-Tolbert, N. S., et al. (2000). Exercise reduces blood pressure in heavy older hypertensive men. *American Journal of Hypertension, 13,* 44–51.

Teachout, T. (2000, April 2). For more artists, a fine old age. *The New York Times online.*

Teller, D. Y. (1998). Spatial and temporal aspects of infant color vision. *Vision Research, 38*(21), 3275–3282.

Tenenbaum, H. R., & Leaper, C. (2002). Are parents' gender schemas related to their children's gender-related cognitions? A meta-analysis. *Developmental Psychology, 38*(4), 615–630.

Teng, E., & Squire, L. R. (1999). Memory for places learned long ago is intact after hippocampal damage. *Nature, 400*(6745), 675–677.

Tennen, H., & Affleck, G. (2000). The perception of personal control: Sufficiently important to warrant careful scrutiny. *Personality & Social Psychology Bulletin, 26*(2), 152–156.

Thase, M. E., & Kupfer, D. J. (1996). Recent developments in the pharmacotherapy of mood disorders. *Journal of Consulting and Clinical Psychology, 64,* 646–659.

Thom, A., Sartory, G., & Jöhren, P. (2000). Comparison between one-session psychological treatment and benzodiazepine in dental phobia. *Journal of Consulting and Clinical Psychology, 68*(3), 378–387.

Thomas, A. (2001). Factitious and malingered dissociative identity disorder: Clinical features observed in 18 cases. *Journal of Trauma & Dissociation, 2*(4), 59–77.

Thomas, S. L., Skitka, L. J., Christen, S., & Jurgena, M. (2002). Social facilitation and impression formation. *Basic & Applied Social Psychology, 24*(1), 67–70.

Thurstone, L. L. (1938). Primary mental abilities. *Psychometric Monographs, 1.*

Tigner, R. B., & Tigner, S. S. (2000). Triarchic theories of intelligence: Aristotle and Sternberg. *History of Psychology, 3*(2), 168–176.

Tkachuk, G. A., & Martin, G. L. (1999). Exercise therapy for patients with psychiatric disorders: Research and clinical implications. *Professional Psychology: Research and Practice, 30*(3), 275–282.

Tolman, E. C., & Honzik, C. H. (1930). Introduction and removal of reward, and maze performance in rats. *University of California Publications in Psychology, 4,* 257–275.

Tong, H. (2001). Loneliness, depression, anxiety, and the locus of control. *Chinese Journal of Clinical Psychology, 9*(3), 196–197.

Tooley, G. A., Armstrong, S. M., Norman, T. R., & Sali, A. (2000). Acute increases in night-time plasma melatonin levels following a period of meditation. *Biological Psychology, 53*(1) 69–78.

Townsend, E., et al. (2001). The efficacy of problem-solving treatments after deliberate self-harm: Meta-analysis of randomized controlled trials with respect to depression, hopelessness and improvement in problems. *Psychological Medicine, 31*(6), 979–988.

Treasure, J., & Serpell, L. (2001). Osteoporosis in young people: Research and treatment in eating disorders. *Psychiatric Clinics of North America, 24*(2), 359–370.

Triandis, H. C. (2001). Individualism–collectivism and personality. *Journal of Personality, 69*(6), 907–924.

Triandis, H. C., & Suh, E. M. (2002). Cultural influences on personality. *Annual Review of Psychology, 53*(1), 133–160.

Trobst, K. K., Collins, R. L., & Embree, J. M. (1994). The role of emotion in social support provision. *Journal of Social and Personal Relationships, 11,* 45–62.

Tryon, R. C. (1940). Genetic differences in maze learning in rats. *Yearbook of the National Society for Studies in Education, 39,* 111–119.

Tsai, G., & Coyle, J. T. (2002). Glutamatergic mechanisms in schizophrenia. *Annual Review of Pharmacology & Toxicology, 42,* 165–179.

Tsang, Y. C. (1938). Hunger motivation in gastrectomized rats. *Journal of Comparative Psychology, 26,* 1–17.

Tsou, M., & Liu, J. (2001). Happiness and domain satisfaction in Taiwan. *Journal of Happiness Studies, 2*(3), 269–288.

Tucker, J. S., Friedman, H. S., Wingard, D. L., & Schwartz, J. E. (1996). Marital history at midlife as a predictor of longevity. *Health Psychology, 15,* 94–101.

Tuiten, A., et al. (2000). Time course of effects of testosterone administration on sexual arousal in women. *Archives of General Psychiatry, 57,* 149–153.

Tulving, E. (1985). How many memory systems are there? *American Psychologist, 40,* 385–398.

Tulving, E., & Markowitsch, H. J. (1998). Episodic and declarative memory: Role of the hippocampus. *Hippocampus, 8*(3), 198–204.

Turk, D. C., & Okifuji, A. (2002). Psychological factors in chronic pain: Evolution and revolution. *Journal of Consulting and Clinical Psychology, 70*(3), 678–690.

Turner, A. M., & Greenough, W. T. (1985). Differential rearing effects on rat visual cortex synapses: I. Synaptic and neuronal density and synapses per neuron. *Brain Research, 329,* 195–203.

Turner, M. E., & Pratkanis, A. R. (1998). A social identity maintenance model of groupthink. *Organizational Behavior & Human Decision Processes, 73*(2–3), 210–235.

Tversky, A., & Kahneman, D. (1982). Judgment under uncertainty. In D. Kahneman, P. Slovic, & A. Tversky (Eds.), *Judgment under uncertainty: Heuristics and biases.* New York: Cambridge University Press.

Ukestad, L. K., & Wittrock, D. A. (1996). Pain perception and coping in female tension headache sufferers and headache-free controls. *Health Psychology, 15,* 65–68.

Unger, J. B., Rohrbach, L. A., Howard-Pitney, B., Ritt-Olson, A., & Mouttapa, M. (2001a). Peer influences and susceptibility to smoking among Californian adolescents. *Substance Use & Misuse, 36*(5), 551–571.

Unger, J. B., et al. (2001b) Stressful life events among adolescents in Wuhan, China: Associations with smoking, alcohol use, and depressive symptoms. *International Journal of Behavioral Medicine, 8*(1), 1–18.

United Nations Special Session on AIDS. (2001, June 25–27). Preventing HIV/AIDS among young people. New York: United Nations.

USBC (U.S. Bureau of the Census). (2002). *Statistical abstract of the United States* (122nd ed.). Washington, DC: U.S. Government Printing Office.

USBC (U.S. Bureau of the Census). (2003). *Statistical abstract of the United States* (123rd ed.). Washington, DC: U.S. Government Printing Office.

Updegraff, J. A., Taylor, S. E., Kemeny, M. E., & Wyatt, G. E. (2002). Positive and negative effects of HIV infection in women with low socioeconomic resources. *Personality & Social Psychology Bulletin, 28*(3) 382–394.

Vaillant, G. E. (1994). Ego mechanisms of defense and personality psychopathology. *Journal of Abnormal Psychology, 103,* 44–50.

Valentiner, D. P., Foa, E. B., Riggs, D. S., & Gershuny, B. S. (1996). Coping strategies and posttraumatic stress disorder in female victims of sexual and nonsexual assault. *Journal of Abnormal Psychology, 105,* 455–458.

Vandenbergh, J. G. (1993). Cited in Angier, N. (1993, August 24). Female gerbil born with males is found to be begetter of sons. *The New York Times,* p. C4.

van Hiel, A., Kossowska, M., & Mervielde, I. (2000). The relationship between openness to experience and political ideology. *Personality & Individual Differences, 28*(4) 741–751.

Van Raalte, J. L., & Brewer, B. W. (2002). *Exploring sport and exercise psychology (2nd ed.).* Washington, DC: American Psychological Association.

Varas-Lorenzo, C., García-Rodríguez, L. A., Perez-Gutthann, S., Duque-Oliart, A. (2000). Hormone replacement therapy and incidence of acute myocardial infarction: A population-based nested case-control study. *Circulation online, 101.*

Vasterling, J. J., et al. (2002). Attention, learning, and memory performances and intellectual resources in Vietnam veterans: PTSD and no disorder comparisons. *Neuropsychology, 16*(1), 5–14.

Velting, D. M., Rathus, J. H., & Miller, A. L. (2000). MACI personality scale profiles of depressed adolescent suicide attempters: A pilot study. *Journal of Clinical Psychology, 56*(10), 1381–1385.

Vermeer, H. J., Boekaerts, M., & Seegers, G. (2000). Motivational and gender differences: Sixth-grade students' mathematical problem-solving behavior. *Journal of Educational Psychology, 92*(2), 308–315.

Vernberg, E. M., La Greca, A. M., Silverman, W. K., & Prinstein, M. J. (1996). Prediction of posttraumatic stress symptoms in children after Hurricane Andrew. *Journal of Abnormal Psychology, 105,* 237–248.

Vgontzas, A. N., & Kales, A. (1999). Sleep and its disorders. *Annual Review of Medicine, 50,* 387–400.

Vik, P. W., Carrello, P., Tate, S. R., & Field, C. (2000). Progression of consequences among heavy-drinking college students. *Psychology of Addictive Behaviors, 14*(2), 91–101.

Villa, K. K., & Abeles, N. (2000). Broad spectrum intervention and the remediation of prospective memory declines in the able elderly. *Aging & Mental Health, 4*(1), 21–29.

Villani, S. (2001). Impact of media on children and adolescents: A 10-year review of the research. *Journal of the American Academy of Child & Adolescent Psychiatry, 40*(4), 392–401.

Visintainer, M. A., Volpicelli, J. R., & Seligman, M. E. P. (1982). Tumor rejection in rats after inescapable or escapable shock. *Science, 216*(23), 437–439.

Volkow, N. D., et al. (2001a). Association of dopamine transporter reduction with psychomotor impairment in methamphetamine abusers. *American Journal of Psychiatry, 158,* 377–382.

Volkow, N. D., et al. (2001b). Higher cortical and lower subcortical metabolism in detoxified methamphetamine abusers. *American Journal of Psychiatry, 158,* 383–389.

Volz, J. (2000). Successful aging: The second 50. *Monitor on Psychology, 30*(1), 24–28.

Von Békésy, G. (1957, August). The ear. *Scientific American, 66–78.*

Voneida, T. J. (1998). Sperry's concept of mind as an emergent property of brain function and its implications for the future of humankind. *Neuropsychologia, 36*(10), 1077–1082.

Wadden, T. A., Brownell, K. D., & Foster, G. D. (2002). Obesity: Responding to the global epidemic. *Journal of Consulting and Clinical Psychology, 70*(3), 510–525.

Wade, N. (1998, January 6). Was Freud wrong? Are dreams the brain's start-up test? *The New York Times online.*

Wade, T. D., Bulik, C. M., Neale, M., & Kendler, K. S. (2000). Anorexia nervosa and major depression: Shared genetic and environmental risk factors. *American Journal of Psychiatry, 157*(3), 469–471.

Waelde, L. C., Koopman, C., Rierdan, J., & Spiegel, D. (2001). Symptoms of acute stress disorder and posttraumatic stress disorder following exposure to disastrous flooding. *Journal of Trauma & Dissociation, 2*(2), 37–52.

Wagner, R. K. (1997). Intelligence, training, and employment. *American Psychologist, 52,* 1059–1069.

Waldron, H. B., Slesnick, N., Brody, J. L., & Peterson, T. R. (2001). Treatment outcomes for adolescent substance abuse at 4- and 7-month assessments. *Journal of Consulting & Clinical Psychology, 69*(5), 802–813.

Walk, R. D., & Gibson, E. J. (1961). A comparative and analytical study of visual depth perception. *Psychological Monographs, 75*(15, Whole No. 519), 44.

Walsh, B. T., et al. (2000). Fluoxetine for bulimia nervosa following poor response to psychotherapy. *American Journal of Psychiatry, 157,* 1332–1334.

Wan, W. W. N., Luk, C., & Lai, J. C. L. (2000). Personality correlates of loving styles among Chinese students in Hong Kong. *Personality & Individual Differences, 29*(1), 169–175.

Wang, H., et al. (2000). Nicotine as a potent blocker of the cardiac A-type K$^+$ channels: Effects on cloned Kv4.3 channels and native transient outward current. *Circulation, 102,* 1165–1171.

Wang, X., et al. (2000). Longitudinal study of earthquake-related PTSD in a randomly selected community sample in North China. *American Journal of Psychiatry, 157,* 1260–1266.

Wann, D. L., & Schrader, M. P. (2000). Controllability and stability in the self-serving attributions of sport spectators. *Journal of Social Psychology, 140*(2), 160–168.

Warman, D. M., & Cohen, R. (2000). Stability of aggressive behaviors and children's peer relationships. *Aggressive Behavior, 26*(4), 277–290.

Wartik, N. (2000, June 25). Depression comes out of hiding. *The New York Times,* pp. MH1, MH4.

Waters, M. (2000). Psychologists spotlight growing concern of higher suicide rates among adolescents. *Monitor on Psychology, 31*(6), 41.

Watkins, C. E., Jr., Campbell, V. L., Nieberding, R., & Hallmark, R. (1995). Contemporary practice of psychological assessment by clinical psychologists. *Professional Psychology: Research and Practice, 26,* 54–60.

Watson, D., Hubbard, B., & Wiese, D. (2000). Self-other agreement in personality and affectivity: The role of acquaintanceship, trait visibility, and assumed similarity. *Journal of Personality & Social Psychology, 78*(3), 546–558.

Watson, J. B. (1913). Psychology as the behaviorist views it. *Psychological Review, 20,* 158–177.

Watson, M., Haviland, J. S., Greer, S., Davidson, J., & Bliss, J. M. (1999). Influence of psychological response on survival in breast cancer: A population-based cohort study. *The Lancet, 354*(9187), 1331–1336.

Weaver, T. L., & Clum, G. A. (1995). Psychological distress associated with interpersonal violence: A meta-analysis. *Clinical Psychology Review, 15,* 115–140.

Webb, W. (1993). Cited in Adler, T. (1993). Sleep loss impairs attention—and more. *APA Monitor, 24*(9), 22–23.

Wechsler, D. (1975). Intelligence defined and undefined. *American Psychologist, 30,* 135–139.

Weekes, J. R., Lynn, S. J., Green, J. P., & Brentar, J. T. (1992). Pseudomemory in hypnotized and task-motivated subjects. *Journal of Abnormal Psychology, 101,* 356–360.

Wegener, D. T., Petty, R. E., Detweiler-Bedell, B. T., & Jarvis, W. B. G. (2001). Implications of attitude change theories for numerical anchoring: Anchor plausibility and the limits of anchor effectiveness. *Journal of Experimental Social Psychology, 37*(1), 62–69.

Weinberg, R. A., Scarr, S., & Waldman, I. D. (1992). The Minnesota Transracial Adoption Study: A follow-up of IQ test performance at adolescence. *Intelligence, 16,* 117–135.

Weiner, B. (1991). Metaphors in motivation and attribution. *American Psychologist, 46,* 921–930.

Weiner, K. (1992). Cited in Goleman, D. J. (1992, January 8). Heart seizure or panic attack? *The New York Times,* p. C12.

Weiner, R. D. (2000). Retrograde amnesia with electroconvulsive therapy. *Archives of General Psychiatry online, 57*(6).

Weinmann, M., Bader, J., Endrass, J., & Hell, D. (2001). Sind Kompetenz- und Kontrollueberzeugungen depressionsabhaengig? Eine Verlaufsuntersuchung. *Zeitschrift fuer Klinische Psychologie und Psychotherapie, 30*(3), 153–158.

Weinstein, C. S., Fucetola, R., & Mollica, R. (2001). Neuropsychological issues in the assessment of refugees and victims of mass violence. *Neuropsychology Review, 11*(3), 131–141.

Wells, G. L., et al. (2000). From the lab to the police station: A successful application of eyewitness research. *American Psychologist, 55*(6), 581–598.

Wenger, N. K., et al. (2002, June). International position paper on women's health and menopause. Washington, DC: National Heart, Lung and Blood Institute.

Werner, C. M., Brown, B. B., & Damron, G. (1981). Territorial marking in a game arcade. *Journal of Personality and Social Psychology, 41,* 1094–1104.

West, R., & Craik, F. I. M. (1999). Age-related decline in prospective memory: The roles of cue accessibility and cue sensitivity. *Psychology & Aging, 14*(2), 264–272.

Wetzler, S. E., & Sweeney, J. A. (1986). Childhood amnesia. In D. C. Rubin (Ed.), *Autobiographical memory.* New York: Cambridge University Press.

Wheeler, J. (2000) Cited in Larkin, M. (2000). Toxic noise attacked. *Lancet, 356,* 605–606.

Wheeler, M. A., Stuss, D. T., & Tulving, E. (1997). Toward a theory of episodic memory: The frontal lobes and autonoetic consciousness. *Psychological Bulletin, 121,* 331–354.

Wheeler, S. C., & Petty, R. E. (2001). The effects of stereotype activation on behavior: A review of possible mechanisms. *Psychological Bulletin, 127*(6), 797–826.

White, A. M., Matthews, D. B., & Best, P. J. (2000). Ethanol, memory, and hippocampal function: A review of recent findings. *Hippocampus, 10*(1), 88–93.

White, C. L., Kashima, K., Bray, G. A., & York, D. A. (2000). Effect of a serotonin 1-A agonist on food intake of Osborne-Mendel and S5B/PI rats. *Physiology & Behavior, 68*(5), 715–722.

White, J. W., Smith, P. H., Koss, M. P., & Figueredo, A. J. (2000). Intimate partner aggression: What have we learned? *Psychological Bulletin, 126*(5), 690–696.

Whorf, B. (1956). *Language, thought, and reality.* New York: Wiley.

Widiger, T. A., & Costa, P. T., Jr. (1994). Personality and personality disorders. *Journal of Abnormal Psychology, 103,* 78–91.

Wiebe, R. E., & McCabe, S. B. (2002). Relationship perfectionism, dysphoria, and hostile interpersonal behaviors. *Journal of Social & Clinical Psychology, 21*(1), 67–91.

Wiens, A. N., & Menustik, C. E. (1983). Treatment outcome and patient characteristics in an aversion therapy program for alcoholism. *American Psychologist, 38,* 1089–1096.

Wierzbicka, A. (1999). "Universals of colour" from a linguistic point of view. *Behavioral & Brain Sciences, 22*(4), 724–725.

Wilcox, V. L., Kasl, S. V., & Berkman, L. F. (1994). Social support and physical disability in older people after hospitalization. *Health Psychology, 13,* 170–179.

Wilgoren, J. (2000, March 15). Effort to curb binge drinking in college falls short. *The New York Times,* p. A16.

Wilhelm, F. H., Gevirtz, R., & Roth, W. T. (2001). Respiratory dysregulation in anxiety, functional cardiac, and pain disorders: Assessment, phenomenology, and treatment. *Behavior Modification, 25*(4), 513–545.

Williams, J. E., & Best, D. L. (1994). Cross-cultural views of women and men. In W. J. Lonner & R. Malpass (Eds.), *Psychology and culture*. Boston: Allyn & Bacon.

Williams, J. E., et al. (2000). Anger proneness predicts coronary heart disease risk: Prospective analysis from the Atherosclerosis Risk In Communities (ARIC) study. *Circulation, 101*(17), 2034–2039.

Willoughby, T., Wood, E., & Khan, M. (1994). Isolating variables that impact on or detract from the effectiveness of elaboration strategies. *Journal of Educational Research, 86*, 279–289.

Wills, T. A., Sandy, J. M., & Yaeger, A. M. (2002). Moderators of the relation between substance use level and problems: Test of a self-regulation model in middle adolescence. *Journal of Abnormal Psychology, 111*(1), 3–21.

Wilson, B. (1997). Cited in Seppa, N. (1997). Children's TV remains steeped in violence. *APA Monitor, 28*(6), 36.

Wilson, G. T., Fairburn, C. C., Agras, W. S., Walsh, B. T., & Kraemer, H. (2002). Cognitive–behavioral therapy for bulimia nervosa: Time course and mechanisms of change. *Journal of Consulting & Clinical Psychology, 70*(2), 267–274.

Wilson, R. S. (1983). The Louisville twin study: Developmental synchronies in behavior. *Child Development, 54*, 298–316.

Wilson, W., et al. (2000). Brain morphological changes and early marijuana use: A magnetic resonance and positron emission tomography study. *Journal of Addictive Diseases, 19*(1), 1–22.

Winocur, G., et al. (2000). Cognitive rehabilitation in clinical neuropsychology. *Brain & Cognition, 42*(1), 120–123.

Winter, W. E. (2001). The use of a skill-based activity in therapeutic induction. *American Journal of Clinical Hypnosis, 44*(2), 119–126.

Wintre, M. G., & Sugar, L. A. (2000). Relationships with parents, personality, and the university transition. *Journal of College Student Development, 41*(2), 202–214.

Winzelberg, A. J., et al. (2000). Effectiveness of an Internet-based program for reducing risk factors for eating disorders. *Journal of Consulting and Clinical Psychology, 68*, 346–350.

Witt, K., Nuhsman, A., & Deuschl, G. (2002). Dissociation of habit-learning in Parkinson's and cerebellar disease. *Journal of Cognitive Neuroscience, 14*(3), 493–499.

Wolkow, C. A., Kimura, K. D., Lee, M-S., & Ruvkun, G. (2000). Regulation of *C. elegans* lifespan by insulinlike signaling in the nervous system. *Science, 290*(5489), 147–150.

Woloshyn, V. E., Paivio, A., & Pressley, M. (1994). Use of elaborative interrogation to help students acquire information consistent with prior knowledge and information inconsistent with prior knowledge. *Journal of Educational Psychology, 86*, 79–89.

Wolpe, J. (1990). *The practice of behavior therapy* (4th ed.). New York: Pergamon.

Wolpe, J., & Plaud, J. J. (1997). Pavlov's contributions to behavior therapy: The obvious and the not so obvious. *American Psychologist, 52*, 966–972.

Wood, J. M., & Bootzin, R. R. (1990). The prevalence of nightmares and their independence from anxiety. *Journal of Abnormal Psychology, 99*, 64–68.

Wood, W. (2000). Attitude change: Persuasion and social influence. *Annual Review of Psychology, 51*, 539–570.

Woody, E., & Szechtman, H. (2000). Hypnotic hallucinations: Towards a biology of epistemology. *Contemporary Hypnosis, 17*(1), 4–14.

Wright, I. C., et al. (2000). Meta-analysis of regional brain volumes in schizophrenia. *American Journal of Psychiatry 157*, 16–25.

Writing Group for the Women's Health Initiative Investigators. (2002). Risks and benefits of estrogen plus progestin in healthy postmenopausal women: Principal results from the Women's Health Initiative Randomized Controlled Trial. *Journal of the American Medical Association, 288*(3), 321–333.

Wu, J., et al. (1999). Serotonin and learned helplessness: A regional study of 5-HT-sub(1A), 5-HT-sub(2A) receptors and the serotonin transport site in rat brain. *Journal of Psychiatric Research, 33*(1), 17–22.

Wu, P., et al. (2001). Factors associated with use of mental health services for depression by children and adolescents. *Psychiatric Services, 52*(2), 189–195.

Wysocki, C. J., & Preti, G. (1998). Pheromonal influences. *Archives of Sexual Behavior, 27*(6), 627–629.

Xin, X., et al. (2001). Effects of alcohol reduction on blood pressure: A meta-analysis of randomized controlled trials. *Hypertension, 38*, 1112–1117.

Yaffe, K., et al. (2000). Cognitive decline in women in relation to non-protein-bound oestradiol concentrations. *Lancet, 356*, 708–712.

Yanovski S. Z., & Yanovski J. A. (2002). Drug therapy: Obesity. *New England Journal of Medicine, 346*, 591–602.

Yates, W. R. (2000). Testosterone in psychiatry: Risks and benefits. *Archives of General Psychiatry, 58*, 12.

Yatham, L. N., et al. (2000). Brain serotonin$_2$ receptors in major depression: A positron emission tomography study. *Archives of General Psychiatry, 57*, 850–858.

Ybarra, G. J., Passman, R. H., & Eisenberg, C. S. L. (2000). The presence of security blankets or mothers (or both) affects distress during pediatric examinations. *Journal of Consulting and Clinical Psychology, 68*, 322–330.

Yehuda, R. (2002). Post-traumatic stress disorder. *New England Journal of Medicine, 346*(2), 108–114.

Yokota, F., & Thompson, K. M. (2000). Violence in G-rated animated films. *Journal of the American Medical Association, 283*, 2716–2720.

Zagar, K., & Rubenstein, A. (2002). *The inside story on teen girls*. Washington, DC: American Psychological Association.

Zajonc, R. B. (1968). Attitudinal effects of mere exposure. *Journal of Personality and Social Psychology, Monograph Supplement 2*(9), 1–27.

Zajonc, R. B. (1980). Compresence. In P. Paulus (Ed.), *The psychology of group influence*. Hillsdale, NJ: Erlbaum.

Zajonc, R. B. (2001). Mere exposure: A gateway to the subliminal. *Current Directions in Psychological Science, 10*(6), 224–228.

Zane, N., & Sue, S. (1991). Culturally responsive mental health services for Asian Americans. In H. F. Myers et al. (Eds.), *Ethnic minority perspectives on clinical training and services in psychology* (pp. 49–58). Washington, DC: American Psychological Association.

Zelazo, N. A., Zelazo, P. R., Cohen, K. M., & Zelazo, P. D. (1993). Specificity of practice effects on elementary neuromotor patterns. *Developmental Psychology, 29*, 686–691.

Zelazo, P. R. (1998). McGraw and the development of unaided walking. *Developmental Review, 18*(4), 449–471.

Ziegler, D. J., & Hawley, J. L. (2001). Relation of irrational thinking and the Pessimistic Explanatory Style. *Psychological Reports, 88*(2), 483–488.

Zigler, E. (1999). Head Start is not child care. *American Psychologist, 54*(2), 142.

Zimbardo, P. G., LaBerge, S., & Butler, L. D. (1993). Psychophysiological consequences of unexplained arousal. *Journal of Abnormal Psychology, 102*, 466–473.

Zipfel, S., et al. (2000). Long-term prognosis in anorexia nervosa: Lessons from a 21-year follow-up study. *The Lancet, 355*(9205), 721–722.

Zuger, A. (1997, August 19). Removing half of brain improves young epileptics' lives. *The New York Times*, p. C4.

Glossary

A–B Problem The issue of how well we can predict behavior on the basis of attitudes.

Absolute Threshold The minimal amount of energy that can produce a sensation.

Abstinence Syndrome A characteristic cluster of symptoms that results from sudden decrease in an addictive drug's level of usage.

Accommodation According to Piaget, the modification of schemes so that information inconsistent with existing schemes can be integrated or understood.

Acculturation The process of adaptation in which immigrants and native groups identify with a new, dominant culture by learning about that culture and making behavioral and attitudinal changes.

Acetylcholine (ACh) A neurotransmitter that controls muscle contractions.

Acoustic Code Mental representation of information as a sequence of sounds.

Acquired Drives Drives acquired through experience, or learned.

Acrophobia Fear of high places.

Action Potential The electrical impulse that provides the basis for the conduction of a neural impulse along an axon of a neuron.

Activating Effect The arousal-producing effects of sex hormones that increase the likelihood of sexual behavior.

Activation-Synthesis Model The view that dreams reflect activation of cognitive activity by the reticular activating system and synthesis of this activity into a pattern by the cerebral cortex.

Actor–Observer Effect The tendency to attribute our own behavior to situational factors but to attribute the behavior of others to dispositional factors.

Acupuncture The ancient Chinese practice of piercing parts of the body with needles to deaden pain and treat illness.

Acute Stress Disorder A disorder, like PTSD, that is characterized by feelings of anxiety and helplessness and caused by a traumatic event. Acute stress disorder occurs within a month of the event and lasts from two days to four weeks.

Adolescence The period of life bounded by puberty and the assumption of adult responsibilities.

Affective Shift Hypothesis The view that men and women tend to experience different shifts in the emotions following initiation of sexual activity, such that women feel more love and commitment, and many men experience less love and commitment.

Afferent Neurons Neurons that transmit messages from sensory receptors to the spinal cord and brain. Also called *sensory neurons*.

Afterimage The lingering visual impression made by a stimulus that has been removed.

Age-30 Transition Levinson's term for the ages from 28 to 33, which are characterized by reassessment of the goals and values of the 20s.

Agoraphobia Fear of open, crowded places.

AIDS Acronym for acquired immunodeficiency syndrome.

Alarm Reaction The first stage of the GAS, which is triggered by the impact of a stressor and characterized by sympathetic activity.

Algorithm A systematic procedure for solving a problem that works invariably when it is correctly applied.

Alpha Waves Rapid low-amplitude brain waves that have been linked to feelings of relaxation.

Altruism Unselfish concern for the welfare of others.

Alzheimer's Disease (AHLTS-high-mers). A progressive form of mental deterioration characterized by loss of memory, language, problem solving, and other cognitive functions.

Amniotic Sac A sac within the uterus that contains the embryo or fetus.

Amphetamines Stimulants derived from alpha-methyl-beta-phenyl-ethyl-amine, a colorless liquid consisting of carbon, hydrogen, and nitrogen.

Amygdala A part of the limbic system that apparently facilitates stereotypical aggressive responses.

Anal Stage The second stage of psychosexual development, when gratification is attained through anal activities.

Analytical Psychology Jung's psychodynamic theory, which emphasizes the collective unconscious and archetypes.

Anchoring and Adjustment Heuristic A decision-making heuristic in which a presumption or first estimate serves as a cognitive anchor. As we receive additional information, we make adjustments but tend to remain in the proximity of the anchor.

Androgens Male sex hormones.

Animism The belief that inanimate objects move because of will or spirit.

Anterograde Amnesia Failure to remember events that occur after physical trauma because of the effects of the trauma.

Antibodies Substances formed by white blood cells that recognize and destroy antigens.

Antidepressant (ant-eye-dee-PRESS-ant) Acting to relieve depression.

Antidiuretic Hormone A pituitary hormone that conserves body fluids by increasing reabsorption of urine and is connected with paternal behavior in some mammals. Also called *vasopressin*.

Antigen A substance that stimulates the body to mount an immune system response to it. (The contraction for antibody generator.)

Antisocial Personality Disorder The diagnosis given a person who is in frequent conflict with society, yet who is undeterred by punishment and experiences little or no guilt and anxiety.

Aphagic Characterized by undereating.

Aphasia A disruption in the ability to understand or produce language.

Apnea Temporary absence or cessation of breathing. (From Greek and Latin roots meaning "without" and "breathing.")

Applied Research Research conducted in an effort to find solutions to particular problems.

Approach–Approach Conflict A type of conflict in which the goals that produce opposing motives are positive and within reach.

Approach–Avoidance Conflict A type of conflict in which the same goal produces approach and avoidance motives.

Aptitude A natural ability or talent.

Archetypes Basic, primitive images or concepts hypothesized by Jung to reside in the collective unconscious.

Artificialism The belief that natural objects have been created by human beings.

Assimilation According to Piaget, the inclusion of a new event into an existing scheme.

Asylum (uh-SIGH-lum) An institution for the care of the mentally ill.

Attachment The enduring affectional tie that binds one person to another.

Attachment-in-the-Making Phase The second phase in forming bonds of attachment, characterized by preference for familiar figures.

Attention-Deficit/Hyperactivity Disorder A disorder that begins in childhood and is characterized by a persistent pattern of lack of attention, with or without hyperactivity and impulsive behavior.

Attitude An enduring mental representation of a person, place, or thing that evokes an emotional response and related behavior.

Attitude-Discrepant Behavior Behavior inconsistent with an attitude that may have the effect of modifying an attitude.

Attraction In social psychology, an attitude of liking or disliking (negative attraction).

Attribution A belief concerning why people behave in a certain way.

Attribution Process The process by which people draw inferences about the motives and traits of others.

Attributional Style The tendency to attribute one's behavior to internal or external factors, stable or unstable factors, and so on.

Auditory Nerve The axon bundle that transmits neural impulses from the organ of Corti to the brain.

Authoritarian Parents Parents who are rigid in their rules and who demand obedience for the sake of obedience.

Authoritative Parents Parents who are strict and warm. Authoritative parents demand mature behavior but use reason rather than force in discipline.

Autokinetic Effect The tendency to perceive a stationary point of light in a dark room as moving.

Autonomic Nervous System (ANS) The division of the peripheral nervous system that regulates glands and activities such as heartbeat, respiration, digestion, and dilation of the pupils.

Autonomy Self-direction.

Availability Heuristic A decision-making heuristic in which our estimates of frequency or probability of events are based on how easy it is to find examples.

Average The central tendency of a group of measures, expressed either as the mean, median, or mode of a distribution.

Aversive Conditioning A behavior-therapy technique in which undesired responses are inhibited by pairing repugnant or offensive stimuli with them.

Avoidance–Avoidance Conflict A type of conflict in which the goals are negative, but avoidance of one requires approaching the other.

Avoidant Personality Disorder A personality disorder in which the person is generally unwilling to enter relationships without assurance of acceptance because of fears of rejection and criticism.

Axon A long, thin part of a neuron that transmits impulses to other neurons from branching structures called *terminal buttons*.

Barbiturate An addictive depressant used to relieve anxiety or induce sleep.

Basilar Membrane A membrane that lies coiled within the cochlea.

Behavior Rehearsal Practice.

Behavior Therapy Systematic application of the principles of learning to the direct modification of a client's problem behaviors.

Behavioral Genetics The area of biology and psychology that focuses on the transmission of traits that give rise to behavior. Behavioral genetics also addresses individual differences in behavior.

Behaviorism The school of psychology that defines psychology as the study of observable behavior and studies relationships between stimuli and responses.

Behavior-Rating Scale A systematic means for recording the frequency with which target behaviors occur.

Benzodiazepines A class of drugs that reduce anxiety; minor tranquilizers.

Bimodal Having two modes.

Biofeedback Training (BFT) The systematic feeding back to an organism of information about a bodily function so that the organism can gain control of that function.

Biofeedback Training (BFT) The systematic feeding back to an organism of information about a bodily function so that the organism can gain control of that function.

Bipolar Cells Neurons that conduct neural impulses from rods and cones to ganglion cells.

Bipolar Disorder A disorder in which the mood alternates between two extreme poles (elation and depression). Also referred to as manic–depression.

Blind In experimental terminology, unaware of whether or not one has received a treatment.

Blind Spot The area of the retina where axons from ganglion cells meet to form the optic nerve.

Bottom-Up Processing The organization of the parts of a pattern to recognize, or form an image of, the pattern they compose.

Brightness Constancy The tendency to perceive an object as being just as bright even though lighting conditions change its intensity.

Broca's Aphasia A language disorder characterized by slow, laborious speech.

Case Study A carefully drawn biography that may be obtained through interviews, questionnaires, and psychological tests.

Catastrophize To interpret negative events as being disastrous; to "blow out of proportion."

Catatonic Schizophrenia A type of schizophrenia characterized by striking motor impairment.

Catharsis (cuh-THAR-sis) In psychoanalysis, the expression of repressed feelings and impulses to allow the release of the psychic energy associated with them.

Center According to Piaget, to focus one's attention.

Central Nervous System The brain and spinal cord.

Cerebellum A part of the hindbrain involved in muscle coordination and balance.

Cerebral Cortex The wrinkled surface area (gray matter) of the cerebrum.

Cerebrum The large mass of the forebrain, which consists of two hemispheres.

Chromosome A microscopic rod-shaped body in the cell nucleus that carries genes that transmit hereditary traits from generation to generation. Humans normally have 46 chromosomes.

Chunk A stimulus or group of stimuli that are perceived as a discrete piece of information.

Circadian Rhythm Referring to cycles that are connected with the 24-hour period of the earth's rotation.

Circular Descriptive of an explanation that restates its own concepts instead of offering additional information.

Cirrhosis of the Liver A disease caused by protein deficiency in which connective fibers replace active liver cells, impeding circulation of the blood. Alcohol does not contain protein; therefore, persons who drink excessively may be prone to this disease.

Classical Conditioning A simple form of learning in which an organism comes to associate or anticipate events. A neutral stimulus comes to evoke the response usually evoked by another stimulus by being paired repeatedly with the other stimulus. (Cognitive theorists view classic

Claustrophobia Fear of tight, small places.

Clear-Cut-Attachment Phase The third phase in forming bonds of attachment, characterized by intensified dependence on the primary caregiver.

Client-Centered Therapy Carl Rogers's method of psychotherapy, which emphasizes the creation of a warm, therapeutic atmosphere that frees clients to engage in self-exploration and self-expression.

Clinical Scales Groups of test items that measure the presence of various abnormal behavior patterns.

Clitoris The external female sex organ that is most sensitive to sexual sensation; a smooth, round knob of tissue that is situated above the urethral opening.

Closure The tendency to perceive a broken figure as being complete or whole.

Cochlea The inner ear; the bony tube that contains the basilar membrane and the organ of Corti.

Cognitive Having to do with mental processes such as sensation and perception, memory, intelligence, language, thought, and problem solving.

Cognitive-Dissonance Theory The view that we are motivated to make our cognitions or beliefs consistent.

Cognitive Therapy A form of therapy that focuses on how clients' cognitions (expectations, attitudes, beliefs, etc.) lead to distress and may be modified to relieve distress and promote adaptive behavior.

Collective Unconscious Jung's hypothesized store of vague racial memories.

Collectivist A person who defines her- or himself in terms of relationships to other people and groups and gives priority to group goals.

Color Constancy The tendency to perceive an object as being the same color even though lighting conditions change its appearance.

Common Fate The tendency to perceive elements that move together as belonging together.

Competencies Knowledge and skills.

Compulsion An apparently irresistible urge to repeat an act or engage in ritualistic behavior such as hand washing.

Concept A mental category that is used to class together objects, relations, events, abstractions, or qualities that have common properties.

Concordance Agreement.

Concrete-Operational Stage Piaget's third stage, characterized by logical thought concerning tangible objects, conservation, and subjective morality.

Conditional Positive Regard Judgment of another person's value on the basis of the acceptability of that person's behaviors.

Conditioned Reinforcer Another term for a secondary reinforcer.

Conditioned Response (CR) In classical conditioning, a learned response to a conditioned stimulus.

Conditioned Stimulus (CS) A previously neutral stimulus that elicits a conditioned response because it has been paired repeatedly with a stimulus that already elicited that response.

Conditions of Worth Standards by which the value of a person is judged.

Conductive Deafness The forms of deafness in which there is loss of conduction of sound through the middle ear.

Cones Cone-shaped photoreceptors that transmit sensations of color.

Confident Power Feelings of self-confidence, self-efficacy.

Conflict Being torn in different directions by opposing motives. Feelings produced by being in conflict.

Conform To changes one's attitudes or overt behavior to adhere to social norms.

Conscious Self-aware.

Consensus General agreement.

Conservation According to Piaget, recognition that basic properties of substances such as weight and mass remain the same when superficial features change.

Consummate Love The ideal form of love within Sternberg's model, which combines passion, intimacy, and commitment.

Contact Comfort A hypothesized primary drive to seek physical comfort through contact with another.

Context-Dependent Memory Information that is better retrieved in the context in which it was encoded and stored, or learned.

Continuity The tendency to perceive a series of points or lines as having unity.

Continuous Reinforcement A schedule of reinforcement in which every correct response is reinforced.

Control Groups In experiments, groups whose members do not obtain the treatment, while other conditions are held constant.

Conventional Level According to Kohlberg, a period during which moral judgments largely reflect social conventions. A "law and order" approach to morality.

Convergent Thinking A thought process that narrows in on the single best solution to a problem.

Conversion Disorder A disorder in which anxiety or unconscious conflicts are "converted" into physical symptoms that often have the effect of helping the person cope with anxiety or conflict.

Cornea Transparent tissue forming the outer surface of the eyeball.

Corpus Callosum A thick fiber bundle that connects the hemispheres of the cortex.

Correlation Coefficient A number between 11.00 and 21.00 that expresses the strength and direction (positive or negative) of the relationship between two variables.

Correlational Method A mathematical method of determining whether one variable increases or decreases as another variable increases or decreases. For example, there is a correlation between intelligence test scores and grades in school.

Corticosteroids Steroids produced by the adrenal cortex that regulate carbohydrate metabolism and increase resistance to stress by fighting inflammation and allergic reactions. Also called *cortical steroids*.

Creative Self According to Adler, the self-aware aspect of personality that strives to achieve its full potential.

Creativity The ability to generate novel and useful solutions to problems.

Critical Period A period of time when an instinctive response can be elicited by a particular stimulus.

Crystallized Intelligence One's lifetime of intellectual achievement, as shown largely through vocabulary and knowledge of world affairs.

Cultural Bias A factor that provides an advantage for test takers from certain cultural backgrounds, such as using test items that are based on middle-class culture in the United States.

Daily Hassles Notable daily conditions and experiences that are threatening or harmful to a person's well-being.

Dark Adaptation The process of adjusting to conditions of lower lighting by increasing the sensitivity of rods and cones.

Debrief To provide information about a completed procedure.

Decentration Simultaneous focusing on more than one dimension of a problem, so that flexible, reversible thought becomes possible.

Defense Mechanism In psychodynamic theory, an unconscious function of the ego that protects it from anxiety-evoking material by preventing accurate recognition of this material.

Deindividuation The process by which group members may discontinue self-evaluation and adopt group norms and attitudes.

Delirium Tremens A condition characterized by sweating, restlessness, disorientation, and hallucinations. The DTs occur in some chronic alcohol users when there is a sudden decrease in usage.

Delta Waves Strong, slow brain waves usually emitted during stage 4 sleep.

Delusions False, persistent beliefs that are unsubstantiated by sensory or objective evidence.

Dendrites Rootlike structures, attached to the cell body of a neuron, that receive impulses from other neurons.

Deoxyribonucleic Acid (DNA) A substance that forms the basic material of chromosomes, takes the form of a double helix, and contains the genetic code.

Dependent Variable A measure of an assumed effect of an independent variable.

Depolarize To reduce the resting potential of a cell membrane from about 270 millivolts toward zero.

Depressant A drug that lowers the rate of activity of the nervous system.

Descriptive Statistics The branch of statistics that is concerned with providing descriptive information about a distribution of scores.

Desensitization The type of sensory adaptation in which we become less sensitive to constant stimuli. Also called *negative adaptation*.

Dichromat A person who is sensitive to black–white and either red–green or blue–yellow and hence partially color-blind.

Difference Threshold The minimal difference in intensity required between two sources of energy so that they will be perceived as being different.

Diffusion of Responsibility The spreading or sharing of responsibility for a decision or behavior within a group.

Direct Inner Awareness Knowledge of one's own thoughts, feelings, and memories without use of sensory organs.

Discrimination In conditioning, the tendency for an organism to distinguish between a conditioned stimulus and similar stimuli that do not forecast an unconditioned stimulus.

Discriminative Stimulus In operant conditioning, a stimulus that indicates that reinforcement is available.

Disorganized Schizophrenia A type of schizophrenia characterized by disorganized delusions and vivid hallucinations.

Displace In memory theory, to cause information to be lost from short-term memory by adding new information.

Displaced Transferred.

Displacement The quality of language that permits one to communicate information about objects and events in another time and place.

Dispositional Attribution An assumption that a person's behav-

ior is determined by internal causes such as personal attitudes or goals.

Dissociative Amnesia A dissociative disorder marked by loss of memory or self-identity; skills and general knowledge are usually retained. Thought to stem from psychological conflict or trauma. Previously termed psychogenic amnesia.

Dissociative Disorders Disorders in which there are sudden, temporary changes in consciousness or self-identity.

Dissociative Fugue A dissociative disorder in which one experiences amnesia and then flees to a new location. Previously termed psychogenic fugue.

Dissociative Identity Disorder A disorder in which a person appears to have two or more distinct identities or personalities that may alternately emerge.

Divergent Thinking A thought process that attempts to generate multiple solutions to problems.

Dizygotic (DZ) Twins Twins that develop from two fertilized ova and who are thus as closely related as brothers and sisters in general. Also called *fraternal twins*.

Dopamine A neurotransmitter that is involved in Parkinson's disease and that appears to play a role in schizophrenia.

Double-Blind Study A study in which neither the subjects nor the observers know who has received the treatment.

Down Syndrome A condition caused by an extra chromosome on the 21st pair and characterized by cognitive impairment, a broad face, and slanting eyes.

Dream In this usage, Levinson's term for the overriding drive of youth to become someone important, to leave one's mark on history.

Drive A condition of arousal in an organism that is associated with a need.

Drive for Superiority Adler's term for the desire to compensate for feelings of inferiority.

Drive-Reduction Theory The view that organisms learn to engage in behaviors that have the effect of reducing drives.

Eardrum A thin membrane that vibrates in response to sound waves, transmitting the waves to the middle and inner ears.

Echo A mental representation of an auditory stimulus (sound) that is held briefly in sensory memory.

Echoic Memory The sensory register that briefly holds mental representations of auditory stimuli.

"Ecstasy" A synthetic drug that possesses the properties of stimulant and hallucinogenic drugs. Also referred to as MDMA (the acronym for 3, 4-Methylenedioxymethamphetamine).

Efferent Neurons Neurons that transmit messages from the brain or spinal cord to muscles and glands. Also called *motor neurons*.

Effort Justification In cognitive-dissonance theory, the tendency to seek justification (acceptable reasons) for strenuous efforts.

Ego The second psychic structure to develop, characterized by self-awareness, planning, and delay of gratification.

Ego Analyst A psychodynamically oriented therapist who focuses on the conscious coping behavior of the ego instead of the hypothesized unconscious functioning of the id.

Ego Identity Erikson's term for a firm sense of who one is and what one stands for.

Ego Integrity Versus Despair Erikson's term for the crisis of late adulthood, characterized by the task of maintaining one's sense of identity despite physical deterioration.

Egocentrism According to Piaget, the assumption that others view the world as one does oneself.

Eidetic Imagery The maintenance of detailed visual memories over several minutes.

Ejaculation The process of propelling seminal fluid (semen) from the penis.

Elaboration Likelihood Model The view that persuasive messages are evaluated (elaborated) on the basis of central and peripheral cues.

Elaborative Rehearsal A method for increasing retention of new information by relating it to information that is well known.

Electra Complex A conflict of the phallic stage in which the girl longs for her father and resents her mother.

Electroconvulsive Therapy (ECT) Treatment of disorders like major depression by passing an electric current (that causes a convulsion) through the head.

Electromyograph (EMG) An instrument that measures muscle tension.

Embryonic Stage The baby from the third through the eighth weeks following conception, during which time the major organ systems undergo rapid differentiation.

Emotion A state of feeling that has cognitive, physiological, and behavioral components.

Empathic Understanding (em-PATH-ick) Ability to perceive a client's feelings from the client's frame of reference. A quality of the good client-centered therapist.

Empty-Nest Syndrome A sense of depression and loss of purpose felt by some parents when the youngest child leaves home.

Encode Interpret; transform.

Encoding Modifying information so that it can be placed in memory. The first stage of information processing.

Encounter Group A type of group that aims to foster self-awareness by focusing on how group members relate to each other in a setting that encourages open expression of feelings.

Endocrine System The body's system of ductless glands that secrete hormones and release them directly into the bloodstream.

Endorphins Neurotransmitters that are composed of amino acids and that are functionally similar to morphine.

Engram (1) An assumed electrical circuit in the brain that corresponds to a memory trace. (2) An assumed chemical change in the brain that accompanies learning. (From the Greek en-, meaning "in," and gramma, meaning "something that is written or recorded.")

Epilepsy Temporary disturbances of brain functions that involve sudden neural discharges.

Epinephrine A hormone produced by the adrenal medulla that stimulates sympathetic ANS activity. Also called *adrenaline*.

Episodic Memory Memories of events experienced by a person or that take place in the person's presence.

Erogenous Zone An area of the body that is sensitive to sexual sensations.

Eros In psychodynamic theory, the basic instinct to preserve and perpetuate life.

Estrogen A generic term for several female sex hormones that promote growth of female sex characteristics and regulate the menstrual cycle.

Estrus The periodic sexual excitement of many mammals, as governed by levels of sex hormones.

Ethical Moral; referring to one's system of deriving standards for determining what is moral.

Ethics Review Committee A group found in an institutional setting that helps researchers consider the potential harm of their methods and reviews proposed studies according to ethical guidelines.

Ethnic Group A group characterized by common features such as cultural heritage, history, race, and language.

Ethologist A scientist who studies the characteristic behavior patterns of species of animals.

Eustress (YOU-stress). Stress that is healthful.

Evaluation Apprehension Concern that others are evaluating our behavior.

Evolutionary Psychology The branch of psychology that studies the ways in which adaptation and natural selection are connected with mental processes and behavior.

Excitement Phase The first phase of the sexual response cycle, which is characterized by muscle tension, increases in the heart rate, and erection in the male and vaginal lubrication in the female.

Exemplar A specific example.

Exhaustion Stage The third stage of the GAS, characterized by weakened resistance and possible deterioration.

Existentialism The view that people are completely free and responsible for their own behavior.

Expectancies Personal predictions about the outcomes of potential behaviors.

Experiment A scientific method that seeks to confirm cause-and-effect relationships by introducing independent variables and observing their effects on dependent variables.

Experimental Groups In experiments, groups whose members obtain the treatment.

Explicit Memory Memory that clearly and distinctly expresses (explicates) specific information.

"Externals" People who perceive the ability to attain reinforcements as being largely outside themselves.

Extinction An experimental procedure in which stimuli lose their ability to evoke learned responses because the events that had followed the stimuli no longer occur. (The learned responses are said to be extinguished.)

Extraversion A trait characterized by tendencies to be socially outgoing and to express feelings and impulses freely.

Facial-Feedback Hypothesis The view that stereotypical facial expressions can contribute to stereotypical emotions.

Factor Analysis A statistical technique that allows researchers to determine the relationships among large number of items such as test items.

Family Therapy A form of therapy in which the family unit is treated as the client.

Fear Appeal A type of persuasive communication that influences behavior on the basis of arousing fear instead of rational analysis of the issues.

Feature Detectors Neurons in the sensory cortex that fire in response to specific features of sensory information such as lines or edges of objects.

Feedback In assertiveness training, information about the effectiveness of a response.

Feeling-of-Knowing Experience Same as tip-of-the-tongue phenomenon.

Fetal Stage The baby from the third month following conception through childbirth, during which time there is maturation of organ systems and dramatic gains in length and weight.

Fight-or-Flight Reaction An innate adaptive response to the perception of danger.

Fixation In psychodynamic theory, arrested development. Attachment to objects of an earlier stage.

Fixation Time The amount of time spent looking at a visual stimulus.

Fixed-Interval Schedule A schedule in which a fixed amount of time must elapse between the previous and subsequent times that reinforcement is available.

Fixed-Ratio Schedule A schedule in which reinforcement is provided after a fixed number of correct responses.

Flashbacks Distorted perceptions or hallucinations that occur days or weeks after LSD usage but mimic the LSD experience.

Fluid Intelligence Mental flexibility as shown in learning rapidly to solve new kinds of problems.

Foot-in-the-Door Technique A method for inducing compliance in which a small request is followed by a larger request.

Forced-Choice Format A method of presenting test questions that

requires a respondent to select one of a number of possible answers.

Formal-Operational Stage Piaget's fourth stage, characterized by abstract logical thought; deduction from principles.

Fovea An area near the center of the retina that is dense with cones and where vision is consequently most acute.

Frame of Reference One's unique patterning of perceptions and attitudes according to which one evaluates events.

Framing Effect The influence of wording, or the context in which information is presented, on decision making.

Free Association In psychoanalysis, the uncensored uttering of all thoughts that come to mind.

Frequency Distribution An ordered set of data that indicates the frequency (how often) with which scores appear.

Frequency Histogram A graphic representation of a frequency distribution that uses rectangular solids (bars) to represent the frequency with which scores appear.

Frequency Polygon A graphic representation of a frequency distribution that connects the points which show the frequencies with which scores appear, thereby creating a multisided geometric figure.

Frequency Theory The theory that the pitch of a sound is reflected in the frequency of the neural impulses that are generated in response to the sound.

Frontal Lobe The lobe of the cerebral cortex that lies to the front of the central fissure.

Functional Analysis A systematic study of behavior in which one identifies the stimuli that trigger problem behavior and the reinforcers that maintain it.

Functional Fixedness The tendency to view an object in terms of its name or familiar usage.

Functionalism The school of psychology that emphasizes the uses or functions of the mind rather than the elements of experience.

Fundamental Attribution Error The assumption that others act predominantly on the basis of their dispositions, even when there is evidence suggesting the importance of their situations.

g Spearman's symbol for general intelligence, which he believed underlay more specific abilities.

Gamma-aminobutyric Acid (GABA) An inhibitory neurotransmitter that apparently helps calm anxiety.

Ganglion Cells Neurons whose axons form the optic nerve.

Gender The culturally defined concepts of *masculinity* and *femininity*.

Gene A basic unit of heredity, which is found at a specific point on a chromosome.

General Adaptation Syndrome (GAS) Selye's term for a hypothesized three-stage response to stress.

Generalization In conditioning, the tendency for a conditioned response to be evoked by stimuli that are

similar to the stimulus to which the response was conditioned.

Generalize To extend from the particular to the general; to apply observations based on a sample to a population.

Generalized Anxiety Disorder Feelings of dread and foreboding and sympathetic arousal of at least six months' duration.

Generativity Versus Stagnation Erikson's term for the crisis of middle adulthood, characterized by the task of being productive and contributing to younger generations.

Genes The basic building blocks of heredity.

Genetics The area of biology that focuses on heredity.

Genital Stage The mature stage of psychosexual development, characterized by preferred expression of libido through intercourse with an adult of the other gender.

Genuineness Recognition and open expression of the therapist's own feelings.

Germinal Stage The first stage of prenatal development, during which the dividing mass of cells has not become implanted in the uterine wall.

Gestalt Psychology The school of psychology that emphasizes the tendency to organize perceptions into wholes and to integrate separate stimuli into meaningful patterns.

Gestalt Therapy Fritz Perls's form of psychotherapy, which attempts to integrate conflicting parts of the personality through directive methods designed to help clients perceive their whole selves.

Gland An organ that secretes one or more chemical substances such as hormones, saliva, or milk.

Glial Cells Cells that nourish and insulate neurons, direct their growth, and remove waste products from the nervous system.

Gray Matter In the spinal cord, the grayish neurons and neural segments that are involved in spinal reflexes.

Groupthink A process in which group members are influenced by cohesiveness and a dynamic leader to ignore external realities as they make decisions.

Growth Hormone A pituitary hormone that regulates growth.

Hallucination A perception in the absence of sensory stimulation that is confused with reality.

Hallucinogenic Giving rise to hallucinations.

Hashish A drug derived from the resin of Cannabis sativa. Often called "hash."

Health Psychology The field of psychology that studies the relationships between psychological factors (e.g., attitudes, beliefs, situational influences, and behavior patterns) and the prevention and treatment of physical illness.

Heredity The transmission of traits from parent to offspring by means of genes.

Heritability The degree to which the variations in a trait from one

person to another can be attributed to, or explained by, genetic factors.

Heuristics Rules of thumb that help us simplify and solve problems.

Hierarchy An arrangement of stimuli according to the amount of fear they evoke.

Higher-Order Conditioning (1) According to behaviorists, a classical conditioning procedure in which a previously neutral stimulus comes to elicit the response brought forth by a *conditioned* stimulus by being paired repeatedly with that conditioned stimulus. (2) According to cognitive psychologists, the learning of relationships among events, none of which evoke an unlearned response.

Hippocampus A structure in the limbic system that plays an important role in the formation of new memories.

HIV Acronym for human immunodeficiency virus.

Holophrase A single word used to express complex meanings.

Homeostasis The tendency of the body to maintain a steady state.

Homosexual Referring to people who are sexually aroused by, and interested in forming romantic relationships with, people of the same gender. (Derived from the Greek homos, meaning "same," not from the Latin homo, meaning "man.")

Hormone A substance secreted by an endocrine gland that regulates various body functions.

Hue The color of light, as determined by its wavelength.

Humanism The view that people are capable of free choice, self-fulfillment, and ethical behavior.

Hyperphagic Characterized by excessive eating.

Hypertension High blood pressure.

Hypnagogic State The drowsy interval between waking and sleeping, characterized by brief, hallucinatory, dreamlike experiences.

Hypnosis A condition in which people appear to be highly suggestible and behave as though they are in a trance.

Hypochondriasis Persistent belief that one has a medical disorder despite lack of medical findings.

Hypothalamus A bundle of nuclei below the thalamus involved in body temperature, motivation, and emotion.

Hypothesis In psychology, a specific statement about behavior or mental processes that is tested through research.

Icon A mental representation of a visual stimulus that is held briefly in sensory memory.

Iconic Memory The sensory register that briefly holds mental representations of visual stimuli.

Id The psychic structure, present at birth, that represents physiological drives and is fully unconscious.

Ideas of Persecution Erroneous beliefs that one is being victimized or persecuted.

Identification In psychodynamic theory, the unconscious assumption of the behavior of another person.

Identity Certainty A strong and clear sense of who one is and what one stands for.

Illusions Sensations that give rise to misperceptions.

Imaginary Audience An aspect of adolescent egocentrism; the belief that other people are as concerned with our thoughts and behaviors as we are.

Immune System The system of the body that recognizes and destroys foreign agents (antigens) that invade the body.

Implicit Memory Memory that is suggested (implied) but not plainly expressed, as illustrated in the things that people do but do not state clearly.

Imprinting A process occurring during a critical period in the development of an organism, in which that organism responds to a stimulus in a manner that will afterward be difficult to modify.

Incentive An object, person, or situation perceived as being capable of satisfying a need.

Incest Taboo The cultural prohibition against marrying or having sexual relations with a close blood relative.

Incubation In problem solving, a hypothetical process that sometimes occurs when we stand back from a frustrating problem for a while and the solution "suddenly" appears.

Independent Variable A condition in a scientific study that is manipulated so that its effects may be observed.

Indiscriminate Attachment Showing attachment behaviors toward any person.

Individual Psychology Adler's psychodynamic theory, which emphasizes feelings of inferiority and the creative self.

Individualist A person who defines herself or himself in terms of personal traits and gives priority to her or his own goals.

Infantile Amnesia Inability to recall events that occurred prior to the age of 2 or 3. Also termed childhood amnesia.

Infer To go from the particular to the general; to draw a conclusion.

Inferential Statistics The branch of statistics that is concerned with confidence with which conclusions drawn about samples can be extended to the populations from which the samples were drawn.

Inferiority Complex Feelings of inferiority hypothesized by Adler to serve as a central motivating force.

Infinite Creativity The capacity to combine words into original sentences.

Inflammation Increased blood flow to an injured area of the body, resulting in redness, warmth, and an increased supply of white blood cells.

Informed Consent A subject's agreement to participate in research after receiving information about the purposes of the study and the nature of the treatments.

Initial-Preattachment Phase The first phase in forming bonds of attachment, characterized by indiscriminate attachment.

Insanity A legal term descriptive of a person judged to be incapable of recognizing right from wrong or of conforming his or her behavior to the law.

Insight In Gestalt psychology, the sudden reorganization of perceptions, allowing the sudden solution of a problem.

Instinct An inherited disposition to activate specific behavior patterns that are designed to reach certain goals.

Instrumental Competence Ability to manipulate one's environment to achieve one's goals.

Intelligence A complex and controversial concept. According to David Wechsler (1975), the "capacity . . . to understand the world [and] resourcefulness to cope with its challenges."

Intelligence Quotient (IQ) (1) Originally, a ratio obtained by dividing a child's score (or mental age) on an intelligence test by chronological age. (2) Generally, a score on an intelligence test.

Interference Theory The view that we may forget stored material because other learning interferes with it.

"Internals" People who perceive the ability to attain reinforcements as being largely within themselves.

Interneuron A neuron that transmits a neural impulse from a sensory neuron to a motor neuron.

Interpretation An explanation of a client's utterance according to psychoanalytic theory.

Intimacy Close acquaintance and familiarity; a characteristic of a relationship in which partners share their inmost feelings.

Intimacy Versus Isolation Erikson's life crisis of young adulthood, which is characterized by the task of developing abiding intimate relationships.

Introspection Deliberate looking into one's own cognitive processes to examine one's thoughts and feelings.

Introversion A trait characterized by intense imagination and the tendency to inhibit impulses.

Iris A muscular membrane whose dilation regulates the amount of light that enters the eye.

Just Noticeable Difference (jnd) The minimal amount by which a source of energy must be increased or decreased so that a difference in intensity will be perceived.

Kinesthesis The sense that informs us about the positions and motion of parts of our bodies.

La Belle Indifférence A French term descriptive of the lack of concern sometimes shown by people with conversion disorders.

Language The communication of information by means of symbols arranged according to rules of grammar.

Language Acquisition Device (LAD) In psycholinguistic theory, neural "prewiring" that facilitates the child's learning of grammar.

Latency A phase of psychosexual development characterized by repression of sexual impulses.

Latent Hidden or concealed.

Latent Content In psychodynamic theory, the symbolized or underlying content of dreams.

Lateral Hypothalamus An area at the side of the hypothalamus that appears to function as a start-eating center.

Law of Effect Thorndike's principle that responses are "stamped in" by rewards and "stamped out" by punishments.

Learned Helplessness A model for the acquisition of depressive behavior, based on findings that organisms in aversive situations learn to show inactivity when their operants go unreinforced.

Learning (1) According to behaviorists, a relatively permanent change in behavior that results from experience. (2) According to cognitive theorists, the process by which organisms make relatively permanent changes in the way they represent the environment because of experience. These changes influence the organism's behavior but do not fully determine it.

Lens A transparent body behind the iris that focuses an image on the retina.

Lesion (LEE-shun). An injury that results in impaired behavior or loss of a function.

Leukocytes White blood cells. (Derived from the Greek words leukos, meaning "white," and kytos, literally meaning "a hollow" but used to refer to cells.)

Libido (1) In psychodynamic theory, the energy of eros; the sexual instinct. (2) Generally, sexual interest or drive.

Limbic System A group of structures involved in memory, motivation, and emotion that forms a fringe along the inner edge of the cerebrum.

Linguistic-Relativity Hypothesis The view that language structures the way in which we view the world.

Locus of Control The place (locus) to which an individual attributes control over the receiving of reinforcers—either inside or outside the self.

Long-Term Memory The type or stage of memory capable of relatively permanent storage.

Long-Term Potentiation (LTP) Enhanced efficiency in synaptic transmission that follows brief, rapid stimulation.

LSD Lysergic acid diethylamide. A hallucinogenic drug.

Maintenance Rehearsal Mental repetition of information in order to keep it in memory.

Major Depression A severe depressive disorder in which the person may show loss of appetite, psychomotor behaviors, and impaired reality testing.

Manic Elated, showing excessive excitement.

Manifest Content In psychodynamic theory, the reported content of dreams.

Marijuana The dried vegetable matter of the Cannabis sativa plant.

Matching Hypothesis The view that people tend to choose persons similar to themselves in attractiveness and attitudes in the formation of interpersonal relationships.

Maturation The process of development as guided by the unfolding of the genetic code.

Mean A type of average that is calculated by adding all the scores and then dividing by the number of scores.

Means–End Analysis A heuristic device in which we try to solve a problem by evaluating the difference between the current situation and the goal.

Median The central score in a frequency distribution; the score beneath which 50% of the cases fall.

Medulla An oblong area of the hindbrain involved in regulation of heartbeat and respiration.

Melatonin A pineal hormone that helps regulate the sleep–wake cycle and may affect the onset of puberty.

Memory The processes by which information is encoded, stored, and retrieved.

Memory Trace An assumed change in the nervous system that reflects the impression made by a stimulus. Memory traces are said to be "held" in sensory registers.

Menarche The beginning of menstruation.

Menopause The cessation of menstruation.

Mental Age (MA) The accumulated months of credit that a person earns on the Stanford–Binet Intelligence Scale.

Mental Set The tendency to respond to a new problem with an approach that was successfully used with similar problems.

Mescaline A hallucinogenic drug derived from the mescal (peyote) cactus.

Meta-Analysis A method for combining and averaging the results of individual research studies.

Metamemory Self-awareness of the ways in which memory functions, allowing the person to encode, store, and retrieve information effectively.

Methaqualone An addictive depressant. Often called "ludes."

Method of Savings A measure of retention in which the difference between the number of repetitions originally required to learn a list and the number of repetitions required to relearn the list after a certain amount of time has elapsed is calculated.

Midlife Crisis A crisis experienced by many people during the midlife transition when they realize that life may be more than halfway over and reassess their achievements in terms of their dreams.

Midlife Transition Levinson's term for the ages from 40 to 45, which are characterized by a shift in psychological perspective from viewing ourselves in terms of years lived to viewing ourselves in terms of the years we have left.

Migraine Headaches Throbbing headaches that are connected with changes in the supply of blood to the head.

Mode The most frequently occurring number or score in a distribution.

Model An organism that engages in a response that is then imitated by another organism.

Modeling A behavior-therapy technique in which a client observes and imitates a person who approaches and copes with feared objects or situations.

Molecular Genetics The area of genetics that focuses on the identification of specific genes that are connected with the development of traits, behavior, and mental processes.

Monoamine Oxidase (MAO) Inhibitors (MON-oh-ah-mean OX-see-dase) Antidepressant drugs that work by blocking the action of an enzyme that breaks down noradrenaline and serotonin.

Monochromat A person who is sensitive to black and white only and hence color-blind.

Monocular Cues Stimuli suggestive of depth that can be perceived with only one eye.

Monozygotic (MZ) Twins Twins that develop from a single fertilized ovum that divides in two early in prenatal development. MZ twins thus share the same genetic code. Also called *identical twins*.

Moral Principle The governing principle of the superego, which sets moral standards and enforces adherence to them.

Motive A hypothetical state within an organism that propels the organism toward a goal. (From the Latin movere, meaning "to move.")

Motor Cortex The section of cortex that lies in the frontal lobe, just across the central fissure from the sensory cortex. Neural impulses in the motor cortex are linked to muscular responses throughout the body.

Multiple Approach–Avoidance Conflict A type of conflict in which each of a number of goals produces approach and avoidance motives.

Multiple Personality Disorder The previous term for dissociative identity disorder.

Mutation A sudden variation in an inheritable characteristic, as distinguished from a variation that results from generations of gradual selection.

Mutism Refusal to talk.

Myelin A fatty substance that encases and insulates axons, facilitating transmission of neural impulses.

Myotonia Muscle tension.

Narcolepsy A "sleep attack" in which a person falls asleep suddenly and irresistibly.

Narcotics Drugs used to relieve pain and induce sleep. The term is usually reserved for opiates.

Natural Selection A core concept of the theory of evolution that holds that adaptive genetic variations among members of a species enable individuals with those variations to survive and reproduce. As a result, such variations tend to be preserved, whereas nonadaptive variations tend to drop out.

Naturalistic Observation A scientific method in which organisms are observed in their natural environments.

Nature The inborn, innate character of an organism.

Need A state of deprivation.

Negative Correlation A relationship between two variables in which one variable increases as the other decreases.

Negative Reinforcer A reinforcer that when removed increases the frequency of an operant.

Neodissociation Theory A theory of hypnotic events as the splitting of consciousness.

Neonate A newly born child.

Nerve A bundle of axons from many neurons.

Neural Impulse The electrochemical discharge of a nerve cell, or neuron.

Neuron A nerve cell.

Neuroticism Eysenck's term for emotional instability.

Neurotransmitters Chemical substances involved in the transmission of neural impulses from one neuron to another.

Nonconscious Descriptive of bodily processes such as the growing of hair, of which we cannot become conscious. We may "recognize" that our hair is growing but cannot directly experience the biological process.

Non-Rapid-Eye-Movement (NREM) Sleep Stages of sleep 1 through 4.

Nonsense Syllables Meaningless sets of two consonants, with a vowel sandwiched in between, that are used to study memory.

Norepinephrine A neurotransmitter whose action is similar to that of the hormone epinephrine and that may play a role in depression.

Normal Curve Graphic presentation of a normal distribution, which shows a characteristic bell shape.

Normal Distribution A symmetrical distribution that is assumed to reflect chance fluctuations; approximately 68% of cases lie within a standard deviation of the mean.

Nurture The sum total of the environmental factors that affect an organism from conception onward. (In another usage, *nurture* refers to the act of nourishing and otherwise promoting the development of youngsters.)

Object Permanence Recognition that objects removed from sight still exist, as demonstrated in young children by continued pursuit.

Objective Responsibility According to Piaget, the assignment of blame according to the amount of damage done rather than the motives of the actor.

Objective Tests Tests whose items must be answered in a specified, limited manner; tests whose items have concrete answers that are considered correct.

Observational Learning The acquisition of knowledge and skills through the observation of others (who are called models) rather than by means of direct experience.

Obsession A recurring thought or image that seems beyond control.

Occipital Lobe The lobe that lies behind and below the parietal lobe and behind the temporal lobe.

Oedipus Complex A conflict of the phallic stage in which the boy wishes to possess his mother sexually and perceives his father as a rival in love.

Olfactory Having to do with the sense of smell.

Olfactory Nerve The nerve that transmits information concerning odors from olfactory receptors to the brain.

Operant Behavior Voluntary responses that are reinforced.

Operant Conditioning A simple form of learning in which an organism learns to engage in behavior because it is reinforced.

Operant The same as an operant behavior.

Opiates A group of narcotics derived from the opium poppy that provide a euphoric rush and depress the nervous system.

Opioids Chemicals that act on opiate receptors but are not derived from the opium poppy.

Opponent-Process Theory The theory that color vision is made possible by three types of cones, some of which respond to red or green light, some to blue or yellow, and some only to the intensity of light.

Optic Nerve The nerve that transmits sensory information from the eye to the brain.

Oral Stage The first stage of psychosexual development, during which gratification is hypothesized to be attained primarily through oral activities.

Organ of Corti The receptor for hearing that lies on the basilar membrane in the cochlea.

Organizing Effect The directional effect of sex hormones—for example, along stereotypically masculine or feminine lines.

Orgasm The height or climax of sexual excitement, involving involuntary muscle contractions, release of sexual tensions, and, usually, subjective feelings of pleasure.

Overregularization The application of regular grammatical rules for forming inflections (e.g., past tense and plurals) to irregular verbs and nouns.

Oxytocin A pituitary hormone that stimulates labor and lactation.

Paired Associates Nonsense syllables presented in pairs in experiments that measure recall.

Panic Disorder The recurrent experiencing of attacks of extreme anxiety in the absence of external stimuli that usually elicit anxiety.

Paranoid Personality Disorder A disorder characterized by persistent suspiciousness but not involving the disorganization of paranoid schizophrenia.

Paranoid Schizophrenia A type of schizophrenia characterized primarily by delusions—commonly of persecution—and by vivid hallucinations.

Parasympathetic Nervous System The branch of the autonomic nervous system that is most active during processes that restore reserves of energy to the body, such as relaxing and eating. When people relax, the parasympathetic nervous system decelerates the heart rate, normalizes the blood pressure, relaxes muscles, and so on. The parasympathetic division also stimulates digestion.

Parietal Lobe The lobe that lies just behind the central fissure.

Partial Reinforcement One of several reinforcement schedules in which not every correct response is reinforced.

Passion Strong romantic and sexual feelings.

Passive Smoking Inhaling of smoke from the tobacco products and exhalations of other people; also called secondhand smoking.

Pathogen A microscopic organism (e.g., bacterium or virus) that can cause disease.

Perception The process by which sensations are organized into an inner representation of the world.

Perceptual Organization The tendency to integrate perceptual elements into meaningful patterns.

Period of the Ovum Another term for the *germinal stage.*

Peripheral Nervous System The part of the nervous system consisting of the somatic nervous system and the autonomic nervous system.

Permissive Parents Parents who impose few, if any, rules and who do not supervise their children closely.

Person Variables Factors within the person, such as expectancies and competencies, that influence behavior.

Personal Fable Another aspect of adolescent egocentrism; the belief that our feelings and ideas are special and unique and that we are invulnerable.

Personality The distinct patterns of behavior, thoughts, and feelings that characterize a person's adaptation to life.

Personality Disorders Enduring patterns of maladaptive behavior that are sources of distress to the individual or others.

Perspective A monocular cue for depth based on the convergence (coming together) of parallel lines as they recede into the distance.

Phallic Stage The third stage of psychosexual development, characterized by a shift of libido to the phallic region. (From the Greek phallos, referring to an image of the penis. However, Freud used the term phallic to refer both to boys and girls.)

Phallic Symbol A sign that represents the penis.

Phencyclidine (PCP) Another hallucinogenic drug whose name is an acronym for its chemical structure.

Pheromone A chemical secretion detected by other members of the same species that stimulates stereotypical behaviors.

Phi Phenomenon The perception of movement as a result of sequential presentation of visual stimuli.

Photoreceptors Cells that respond to light.

Physiological Drives Unlearned drives with a biological basis, such as hunger, thirst, and avoidance of pain.

Pitch The highness or lowness of a sound, as determined by the frequency of the sound waves.

Pituitary Gland The gland that secretes growth hormone, prolactin, antidiuretic hormone, and other hormones.

Place Theory The theory that the pitch of a sound is determined by the section of the basilar membrane that vibrates in response to the sound.

Placebo A bogus treatment that has the appearance of being genuine.

Placenta A membrane that permits the exchange of nutrients and waste products between the mother and her developing child but does not allow the maternal and fetal bloodstreams to mix.

Plateau Phase The second phase of the sexual response cycle, which is characterized by increases in vasocongestion, muscle tension, heart rate, and blood pressure in preparation for orgasm.

Pleasure Principle The governing principle of the id—the seeking of immediate gratification of instinctive needs.

Polarization In social psychology, taking an extreme position or attitude on an issue.

Polarize To ready a neuron for firing by creating an internal negative charge in relation to the body fluid outside the cell membrane.

Pons A structure of the hindbrain involved in respiration, attention, and sleep and dreaming.

Population A complete group of organisms or events.

Positive Correlation A relationship between variables in which one variable increases as the other also increases.

Positive Reinforcer A reinforcer that when presented increases the frequency of an operant.

Postconventional Level According to Kohlberg, a period during which moral judgments are derived from moral principles and people look to themselves to set moral standards.

Posttraumatic Stress Disorder (PTSD) A disorder that follows a distressing event outside the range of normal human experience and that is characterized by features such as intense fear, avoidance of stimuli associated with the event, and reliving of the event.

Preconscious Capable of being brought into awareness by the focusing of attention.

Preconventional Level According to Kohlberg, a period during which moral judgments are based largely on expectation of rewards or punishments.

Prefrontal Lobotomy The severing or destruction of a section of the frontal lobe of the brain.

Preoperational Stage The second of Piaget's stages, characterized by illogical use of words and symbols, spotty logic, and egocentrism.

Primacy Effect The tendency to evaluate others in terms of first impressions; also, the tendency to recall the initial items in a series of items.

Primary Drives Unlearned, or physiological, drives.

Primary Mental Abilities According to Thurstone, the basic abilities that make up intelligence.

Primary Reinforcer An unlearned reinforcer.

Proactive Interference The interference of old learning with the ability to retrieve material learned recently.

Progesterone A female sex hormone that promotes growth of the sex organs and helps maintain pregnancy.

Programmed Senescence The view that aging is determined by a biological clock that ticks at a rate governed by genes.

Projective Test A psychological test that presents ambiguous stimuli onto which the test-taker projects his or her own personality in making a response.

Prolactin A pituitary hormone that regulates production of milk and, in lower animals, maternal behavior.

Prospective Memory Memory to perform an act in the future, as at a certain time or when a certain event occurs.

Prototype A concept of a category of objects or events that serves as a good example of the category.

Proximity Nearness. The perceptual tendency to group together objects that are near one another.

Psychedelic Causing hallucinations, delusions, or heightened perceptions.

Psychic Structure In psychodynamic theory, a hypothesized mental structure that helps explain different aspects of behavior.

Psychoactive Substances Drugs that have psychological effects such as stimulation or distortion of perceptions.

Psychoanalysis Freud's method of psychotherapy; emphasizes the importance of unconscious motives and conflicts as determinants of human behavior.

Psychodynamic Referring to Freud's theory, which proposes that the motion of underlying forces of personality determines our thoughts, feelings, and behavior.

Psychodynamic Theory Sigmund Freud's perspective, which emphasizes the importance of unconscious motives and conflicts as forces that determine behavior. Dynamic refers to the concept of (psychological) forces being in motion.

Psycholinguistic Theory The view that language learning involves an interaction between environmental factors and an inborn tendency to acquire language.

Psychological Disorders Patterns of behavior or mental processes that are connected with emotional distress or significant impairment in functioning.

Psychological Hardiness A cluster of traits that buffer stress and are characterized by commitment, challenge, and control.

Psychology The science that studies behavior and mental processes.

Psychomotor Retardation Slowness in motor activity and (apparently) in thought.

Psychoneuroimmunology (sigh-coe-new-row-im-you-NOLL-oh-gee). The field that studies the relationships between psychological factors (e.g., attitudes and overt behavior patterns) and the functioning of the immune system.

Psychophysicist A person who studies the relationships between physical stimuli (such as light or sound) and their perception.

Psychosexual Development In psychodynamic theory, the process by which libidinal energy is expressed through different erogenous zones during different stages of development.

Psychosocial Development Erikson's theory of personality and development, which emphasizes social relationships and eight stages of growth.

Psychosurgery Surgery intended to promote psychological changes or to relieve disordered behavior.

Psychotherapy A systematic interaction between a therapist and a client that brings psychological principles to bear on influencing the client's thoughts, feelings, or behavior to help that client overcome abnormal behavior or adjust to problems in living.

Puberty The period of physical development during which sexual reproduction first becomes possible.

Punishment An unpleasant stimulus that suppresses the behavior it follows.

Pupil The apparently black opening in the center of the iris, through which light enters the eye.

Pure Research Research conducted without concern for immediate applications.

Random Sample A sample drawn so that each member of a population has an equal chance of being selected to participate.

Range A measure of variability defined as the high score in a distribution minus the low score.

Rapid Flight of Ideas Rapid speech and topic changes, characteristic of manic behavior.

Rapid Smoking An aversive conditioning method for quitting smoking in which the smoker inhales every six seconds, thus rendering once-desirable cigarette smoke aversive.

Rapid-Eye-Movement (REM) Sleep A stage of sleep characterized by rapid eye movements, which have been linked to dreaming.

Rational Emotive Behavior Therapy (REBT) Albert Ellis's form of therapy that encourages clients to challenge and correct irrational expectations and maladaptive behaviors.

Reaction Time The amount of time required to respond to a stimulus.

Reality Principle Consideration of what is practical and possible in gratifying needs; the governing principle of the ego.

Reality Testing The capacity to perceive one's environment and oneself according to accurate sensory impressions.

Rebound Anxiety Strong anxiety that can attend the suspension of usage of a tranquilizer.

Recall Retrieval or reconstruction of learned material.

Recency Effect The tendency to evaluate others in terms of the most recent impressions; also, the tendency to recall the last items in a series of items.

Receptor Site A location on a dendrite of a receiving neuron tailored to receive a neurotransmitter.

Reciprocal Determinism Bandura's term for the social–cognitive view that people influence their environment just as their environment influences them.

Reciprocity In interpersonal attraction, the tendency to return feelings and attitudes that are expressed about us.

Recognition In information processing, the easiest memory task, involving identification of objects or events encountered before.

Reflex A simple unlearned response to a stimulus.

Refractory Period In the sexual response cycle, a period of time following orgasm during which an individual is not responsive to sexual stimulation.

Reinforce To follow a response with a stimulus that increases the frequency of the response.

Reinforcement A stimulus that follows a response and increases the frequency of the response.

Relearning A measure of retention. Material is usually relearned more quickly than it is learned initially.

Replicate Repeat, reproduce, copy.

Representativeness Heuristic A decision-making heuristic in which people make judgments about samples according to the populations they appear to represent.

Repression In Freud's psychodynamic theory, the ejection of anxiety-evoking ideas from conscious awareness.

Resistance A blocking of thoughts whose awareness could cause anxiety.

Resistance Stage The second stage of the GAS, characterized by prolonged sympathetic activity in an effort to restore lost energy and repair damage. Also called the adaptation stage.

Resolution Phase The fourth phase of the sexual response cycle, during which the body gradually returns to its prearoused state.

Response Set A tendency to answer test items according to a bias—for instance, to make oneself seem perfect or bizarre.

Response Set Theory The view that response expectancies play a key role in the production of the experiences suggested by the hypnotist.

Resting Potential The electrical potential across the neural membrane when it is not responding to other neurons.

Reticular Activating System (RAS) A part of the brain involved in attention, sleep, and arousal.

Retina The area of the inner surface of the eye that contains rods and cones.

Retrieval The location of stored information and its return to consciousness. The third stage of information processing.

Retroactive Interference The interference of new learning with the ability to retrieve material learned previously.

Retrograde Amnesia Failure to remember events that occur prior to physical trauma because of the effects of the trauma.

Retrospective Memory Memory for past events, activities, and learning experiences, as shown by explicit (episodic and semantic) and implicit memories.

Reversibility According to Piaget, recognition that processes can be undone, that things can be made as they were.

Risky Shift The tendency to make riskier decisions as a member of a group than as an individual acting independently.

Rods Rod-shaped photoreceptors that are sensitive only to the intensity of light.

Role Diffusion Erikson's term for lack of clarity in one's life roles (due to failure to develop ego identity).

Role Theory A theory that explains hypnotic events in terms of the person's ability to act as though he or she were hypnotized. Role theory differs from faking in that subjects cooperate and focus on hypnotic suggestions instead of pretending to be hypnotized.

Romantic Love An intense, positive emotion that involves sexual attraction, feelings of caring, and the belief that one is in love.

Rooting The turning of an infant's head toward a touch, such as by the mother's nipple.

Rote Mechanical associative learning that is based on repetition.

s Spearman's symbol for specific factors, or s factors, which he believed accounted for individual abilities.

Saccadic Eye Movement The rapid jumps made by a person's eyes as they fixate on different points.

Sample Part of a population.

Satiety The state of being satisfied; fullness.

Schema A way of mentally representing the world, such as a belief or an expectation, that can influence perception of persons, objects, and situations.

Scheme According to Piaget, a hypothetical mental structure that permits the classification and organization of new information.

Schizoid Personality Disorder A disorder characterized by social withdrawal.

Schizophrenia A psychotic disorder characterized by loss of control of thought processes and inappropriate emotional responses.

Schizotypal Personality Disorder A disorder characterized by oddities of thought and behavior but not involving bizarre psychotic behaviors.

Secondary Reinforcer A stimulus that gains reinforcement value through association with established reinforcers.

Secondary Sex Characteristics Characteristics that distinguish the sexes, such as distribution of body hair and depth of voice, but that are not directly involved in reproduction.

Sedative A drug that relieves nervousness or agitation, or puts one to sleep.

Selection Factor A source of bias that may occur in research findings when subjects are allowed to choose for themselves a certain treatment in a scientific study.

Selective Avoidance Diverting one's attention from information that is inconsistent with one's attitudes.

Selective Exposure Deliberately seeking and attending to information that is consistent with one's attitudes.

Self-Actualization According to Maslow and other humanistic psychologists, self-initiated striving to become what one is capable of being. The motive for reaching one's full potential, for expressing one's unique capabilities.

Self-Efficacy Expectations Our beliefs that we can bring about desired changes through our own efforts.

Self-Ideal A mental image of what we believe we ought to be.

Self-Monitoring Keeping a record of one's own behavior to identify problems and record successes.

Self-Serving Bias The tendency to view one's successes as stemming from internal factors and one's failures as stemming from external factors.

Semantic Code Mental representation of information according to its meaning.

Semantic Memory General knowledge, as opposed to episodic memory.

Semanticity Meaning. The quality of language in which words are used as symbols for objects, events, or ideas.

Semicircular Canals Structures of the inner ear that monitor body movement and position.

Sensation The stimulation of sensory receptors and the transmission of sensory information to the central nervous system.

Sensitization The type of sensory adaptation in which we become more sensitive to stimuli that are low in magnitude. Also called *positive adaptation*.

Sensorimotor Stage The first of Piaget's stages of cognitive development, characterized by coordination of sensory information and motor activity, early exploration of the environment, and lack of language.

Sensorineural Deafness The forms of deafness that result from damage to hair cells or the auditory nerve.

Sensory Adaptation The processes by which organisms become more sensitive to stimuli that are low in magnitude and less sensitive to stimuli that are constant or ongoing in magnitude.

Sensory Memory The type or stage of memory first encountered by a stimulus. Sensory memory holds impressions briefly, but long enough so that series of perceptions are psychologically continuous.

Sensory Register A system of memory that holds information briefly, but long enough so that it can be processed further. There may be a sensory register for every sense.

Serial-Position Effect The tendency to recall more accurately the first and last items in a series.

Serotonin A neurotransmitter, deficiencies of which have been linked to affective disorders, anxiety, and insomnia.

Serotonin-Reuptake Inhibitors Antidepressant drugs that work by blocking the reuptake of serotonin by presynaptic neurons.

Serum Cholesterol Cholesterol in the blood.

Sex Chromosomes The 23rd pair of chromosomes, whose genetic material determines the sex of the individual.

Sexual Orientation The directionality of one's sexual and romantic interests; that is, whether one is sexually attracted to, and desires to form a romantic relationship with, members of the other sex or of one's own sex.

Sexual Response Cycle Masters and Johnson's model of sexual response, which consists of four stages or phases.

Shape Constancy The tendency to perceive an object as being the same shape although the retinal image varies in shape as it rotates.

Shaping A procedure for teaching complex behaviors that at first reinforces approximations of the target behavior.

Short-Term Memory The type or stage of memory that can hold information for up to a minute or so after the trace of the stimulus decays. Also called working memory.

Signal-Detection Theory The view that the perception of sensory stimuli involves the interaction of physical, biological, and psychological factors.

Similarity The perceptual tendency to group together objects that are similar in appearance.

Situational Attribution An assumption that a person's behavior is determined by external circumstances such as the social pressure found in a situation.

Size Constancy The tendency to perceive an object as being the same size even as the size of its retinal image changes according to the object's distance.

Sleep Terrors Frightening dreamlike experiences that occur during the deepest stage of NREM sleep. Nightmares, in contrast, occur during REM sleep.

Social Decision Schemes Rules for predicting the final outcome of group decision making on the basis of the members' initial positions.

Social Facilitation The process by which a person's performance is increased when other members of a group engage in similar behavior.

Social Influence The area of social psychology that studies the ways in which people influence the thoughts, feelings, and behavior of others.

Social Norms Explicit and implicit rules that reflect social expectations and influence the ways people behave in social situations.

Social Perception A subfield of social psychology that studies the ways in which we form and modify impressions of others.

Social Phobia An irrational, excessive fear of public scrutiny.

Social Psychology The field of psychology that studies the nature and causes of people's thoughts and behavior in social situations.

Social–Cognitive Theory A school of psychology in the behaviorist tradition that includes cognitive factors in the explanation and prediction of behavior. Formerly termed *social-learning theory.*

Sociocultural Perspective The view that focuses on the roles of ethnicity, gender, culture, and socioeconomic status in personality formation, behavior, and mental processes.

Somatic Nervous System The division of the peripheral nervous system that connects the central nervous system with sensory receptors, skeletal muscles, and the surface of the body.

Somatoform Disorders Disorders in which people complain of physical (somatic) problems even though no physical abnormality can be found.

Somatosensory Cortex The section of cortex in which sensory stimulation is projected. It lies just behind the central fissure in the parietal lobe.

Species A category of biological classification consisting of related organisms who are capable of interbreeding. *Homo sapiens*—humans—make up one species.

Specific Phobia Persistent fear of a specific object or situation.

Spinal Cord A column of nerves within the spine that transmits messages from sensory receptors to the brain and from the brain to muscles and glands throughout the body.

Spinal Reflex A simple, unlearned response to a stimulus that may involve only two neurons.

Spontaneous Recovery The recurrence of an extinguished response as a function of the passage of time.

Standard Deviation A measure of the variability of a distribution, obtained by the formula

$$S.D. = \sqrt{\frac{\text{Sum of } d^2}{N}}$$

Standardized Test A test that is given to a large number of respondents so that data concerning the typical responses can be accumulated and analyzed.

State-Dependent Memory Information that is better retrieved in the physiological or emotional state in which it was encoded and stored, or learned.

Statistics Numerical facts assembled in such a manner that they provide useful information about measures or scores. (From the Latin *status*, meaning "standing" or "position.")

Stereotype A fixed, conventional idea about a group.

Stimulant A drug that increases activity of the nervous system.

Stimulus An environmental condition that elicits a response.

Storage The maintenance of information over time. The second stage of information processing.

Stratified Sample A sample drawn so that identified subgroups in the population are represented proportionately in the sample. How can stratified sampling be carried out to ensure that a sample represents the ethnic diversity we find in the population at large?

Stress The demand that is made on an organism to adapt.

Stroboscopic Motion A visual illusion in which the perception of motion is generated by a series of stationary images that are presented in rapid succession.

Structuralism The school of psychology that argues that the mind consists of three basic elements—sensations, feelings, and images—that combine to form experience.

Stupor A condition in which the senses and thought are dulled.

Subjective Moral Judgment According to Piaget, moral judgments that are based on the motives of the perpetrator.

Subjective Value The desirability of an object or event.

Substance Abuse Persistent use of a substance even though it is causing or compounding problems in meeting the demands of life.

Successive Approximations Behaviors that are progressively closer to a target behavior.

Superego The third psychic structure, which functions as a moral guardian and sets forth high standards for behavior.

Suppression The deliberate, or conscious, placing of certain ideas, impulses, or images out of awareness.

Survey A method of scientific investigation in which a large sample of people answer questions about their attitudes or behavior.

Sympathetic The branch of the ANS that is most active during emotional responses, such as fear and anxiety, that spend the body's reserves of energy.

Sympathetic Nervous System The branch of the autonomic nervous system that is most active during processes that spend body energy from stored reserves, such as in a fight-or-flight reaction to a predator or when you are anxious about a big test. When people experience fear, the sym

Synapse A junction between the axon terminals of one neuron and the dendrites or cell body of another neuron.

Systematic Desensitization Wolpe's method for reducing fears by associating a hierarchy of images of fear-evoking stimuli with deep muscle relaxation.

Systematic Random Search An algorithm for solving problems in which each possible solution is tested according to a particular set of rules.

Taste Buds The sensory organs for taste. They contain taste cells and are located on the tongue.

Taste Cells Receptor cells that are sensitive to taste.

Temporal Lobe The lobe that lies below the lateral fissure, near the temples of the head.

Testosterone A male sex hormone produced by the testes that promotes growth of male sexual characteristics and sperm.

Thalamus An area near the center of the brain involved in the relay of sensory information to the cortex and in the functions of sleep and attention.

Theory A formulation of relationships underlying observed events.

Theta Waves Slow brain waves produced during the hypnagogic state.

Thinking Mental activity that is involved in understanding, manipulating, and communicating about information. Thinking entails paying attention to information, mentally representing it, reasoning about it, and making decisions about it.

Thyroxin The thyroid hormone that increases metabolic rate.

Time Out Removal of an organism from a situation in which reinforcement is available when unwanted behavior is shown.

Tip-of-the-Tongue (TOT) Phenomenon The feeling that information is stored in memory although it cannot be readily retrieved. Also called the feeling-of-knowing experience.

Token Economy A controlled environment in which people are reinforced for desired behaviors with tokens (such as poker chips) that may be exchanged for privileges.

Tolerance Habituation to a drug, with the result that increasingly higher doses of the drug are needed to achieve similar effects.

Top-Down Processing The use of contextual information or knowledge of a pattern in order to organize parts of the pattern.

Trait A relatively stable aspect of personality that is inferred from behavior and assumed to give rise to consistent behavior.

Transcendental Meditation (TM) The simplified form of meditation brought to the United States by the Maharishi Mahesh Yogi and used as a method for coping with stress.

Transduction The process by which we transform physical energy (in the cases of light, sound, and touch) or chemicals (in the cases of odors and tastes) into neural impulses.

Transference Responding to one person (such as a spouse or the psychoanalyst) in a way that is similar to the way one responded to another person (such as a parent) in childhood.

Treatment In experiments, a condition received by subjects so that its effects may be observed.

Triangular Model of Love Sternberg's view that love involves combinations of three components: intimacy, passion, and decision/commitment.

Trichromat A person with normal color vision.

Trichromatic Theory The theory that color vision is made possible by three types of cones, some of which respond to red light, some to green, and some to blue. (From the Greek roots *treis*, meaning "three," and *chroma*, meaning "color.")

Tricyclic Antidepressants (try-SIGH-click) Antidepressant drugs that work by preventing the reuptake of noradrenaline and serotonin by transmitting neurons.

Trust Versus Mistrust Erikson's first stage of psychosexual development, during which children do—or do not—come to trust that primary caregivers and the environment will meet their needs.

Two-Point Threshold The least distance by which two rods touching the skin must be separated before the person will report that there are two rods, not one, on 50% of occasions.

Type A Behavior Behavior characterized by a sense of time urgency, competitiveness, and hostility.

Umbilical Cord A tube between the mother and her developing child through which nutrients and waste products are conducted.

Unconditional Positive Regard Acceptance of the value of another person, although not necessarily acceptance of everything the person does.

Unconditioned Response (UR) An unlearned response to an unconditioned stimulus.

Unconditioned Stimulus (US) A stimulus that elicits a response from an organism prior to conditioning.

Unconscious In psychodynamic theory, descriptive of ideas and feelings that are not available to awareness.

Uninvolved Parents Parents who generally leave their children to themselves.

Uplifts Notable pleasant daily conditions and experiences.

Validity Scales Groups of test items that indicate whether a person's responses accurately reflect that individual's traits.

Variable-Interval Schedule A schedule in which a variable amount of time must elapse between the previous and subsequent times that reinforcement is available.

Variable-Ratio Schedule A schedule in which reinforcement is provided after a variable number of correct responses.

Vasocongestion Engorgement of blood vessels with blood, which swells the genitals and breasts during sexual arousal.

Ventromedial Nucleus (VMN) A central area on the underside of the hypothalamus that appears to function as a stop-eating center.

Vestibular Sense The sense of equilibrium that informs us about our bodies' positions relative to gravity.

Visible Light The part of the electromagnetic spectrum that stimulates the eye and produces visual sensations.

Visual Acuity Sharpness of vision.

Visual Code Mental representation of information as a picture.

Volunteer Bias A source of bias or error in research reflecting the prospect that people who offer to participate in research studies differ systematically from people who do not.

Waxy Flexibility A feature of catatonic schizophrenia in which people can be molded into postures that they maintain for quite some time.

Wear-and-Tear Theory The view that factors such as pollution, disease, and ultraviolet light contribute to wear and tear on the body, so that the body loses the ability to repair itself.

Weber's Constant The fraction of the intensity by which a source of physical energy must be increased or decreased so that a difference in intensity will be perceived.

Wernicke's Aphasia A language disorder characterized by difficulty comprehending the meaning of spoken language.

Wernicke-Korsakoff Syndrome A cluster of symptoms associated with chronic alcohol abuse and characterized by confusion, memory impairment, and filling in gaps in memory with false information (confabulation).

White Matter In the spinal cord, axon bundles that carry messages from and to the brain.

Wisdom Expert knowledge concerning the meaning of life, concern for people's welfare, and a push toward excellence.

Wish Fulfillment A primitive method used by the id to attempt to gratify basic instincts.

Working Memory Same as short-term memory.

Zygote A fertilized ovum (egg cell).

Author Index

Credits

Chapter One Outline

I. **Psychology as a science/Defining Psychology**
   1. Psychology is defined as the scientific study of behavior and mental processes.
   2. Theories: formulations of apparent relationships among observed events. Allows for prediction.
   3. Controversy in Psychology 1: Controlling behavior and mental processes in people? Helping people not controlling them.

II. **What Psychologists do/Fifteen Fields of Psychology**
   A. What Psychologists Do:
      1. Pure research: no immediate application, research for its own sake.
      2. Applied research: designed to find solutions to specific personal or social problems.
      3. Practice psychology: applying psychological knowledge to help individuals change their behavior.
      4. Teaching: share psychological knowledge in classrooms, seminars, and workshops.
   B. Fifteen Fields of Psychology
      1. Clinical psychologist: help people with psychological disorders adjust to the demands of life. Largest subgroup of psychologists.
      2. Psychiatrists: medical doctors who specialize in the treatment of psychological disorders.
      3. Counseling psychologists: similar to clinical psychologist but clients typically have adjustment problems and not serious psychological disorders. More than half of all doctoral students are in programs of clinical or counseling.
      4. School psychologists: employed by school systems to assist students with problems that interfere with learning. One focus is that of placement of students in special classes.
      5. Educational psychologists: like school psychologists, attempt to facilitate learning but focus on course planning, instructional methods. They focus on motivation, intelligence, testing, and student and teacher behavior.
      6. Developmental psychologists: study the changes, physical, cognitive, social and personality, that occur throughout the life span.
      7. Personality psychologists: focus on identifying and measuring human traits, determining influences on human thought processes, feelings, and behavior and explaining psychological disorders.
      8. Social psychologists: primarily concerned with individual's thoughts, feelings, and behavior in social situations.
      9. Experimental psychologists: conduct experiments and specialize in basic processes such as the nervous system, sensation and perception, learning and memory, thought, motivation, and emotion.
      10. Industrial psychologists focus on the relationship between people and work.
      11. Organizational psychologists focus on the relationship between people and organizations such as business.

12. Human factors psychologists provide suggestions and create technical systems such as dashboards, computer keyboards, etc. to be more user friendly.
13. Consumer psychologists: study the behavior of shoppers in an effort to predict and influence their behavior.
14. Health psychologists: examine the ways in which behavior and mental processes are related to health.
15. Sport psychologists: help people improve their performance in various sports.

III. Where Psychology Comes From: A History
  A. Philosophical Contributions
    1. Aristotle: (384-322 BCE)
      a. Wrote a book titled "About the Psyche" covering topics such as personality, sensation, perception, thought, intelligence, needs, motives, feelings, emotions and memory. All of these topics are covered in this text.
      b. A proponent of empiricism: science could rationally treat only information gathered through the senses.
      c. He outlined the laws of associationism or how experience leads to expectations and how thoughts lead to behaviors
    2. Democritus (around 400 BCE)
      a. Suggested that we could think of behavior in terms of a body and mind (interaction of biological and mental processes).
    3. Plato (ca.427-347 BCE)
      a. Recorded Socrates' advice to "Know Thyself" which is a motto of psychology. Also advanced Socrates suggestion of relying on rational thought and introspection - careful examination of one's own thoughts and emotions to achieve self knowledge.
  B. 19th Century Contributions
    1. Gustav Theodore Fechner (1801-1887)
      a. Published his landmark book titled "Elements of Psychophysics" in 1860, which showed how physical events (light and sounds) are related to psychological sensations and perceptions. Some consider this to be the beginning of psychology.
    2. Wilhelm Wundt (1832-1920)
      a. Gets the credit for being the founder of psychology when in 1879 he established the first psychological laboratory in Leipzig, Germany.
  C. Structuralism: The Elements of Experience
    1. Structuralism: attempts to break conscious experience down into objective sensations such as sight, or taste, and the subjective feelings such as emotional responses. They believed that the mind functions by combining objective and subjective elements of experience.
      a. Wundt was considered to be a Structuralist.
  D. Functionalism: Making Psychology a Habit
    1. William James (1842-1919)
      a. Often considered the first true American Psychologist. Made a career teaching at Harvard University. He described his views in textbook he

wrote titled "The Principles of Psychology" a two volume book published in 1890.

    b. James was the founder of functionalism or the idea that in the study of individuals the focus should be on behavior as well as the mind and consciousness. Functionalist look at how experience helps us function more adaptively in our environments.

E. Behaviorism: Practicing Psychology in Public
1. John Broadus Watson (1878-1958)
    a. Considered to be the founder of American Behaviorism. Functionalism was the dominant view in psychology. Watson believed that if psychology wanted to be a science then it must limit itself to observable, measurable events- behavior- and nothing else.
2. B.F. Skinner (1904-1990)
    a. Believed that organisms learn to behave in certain ways because they have been reinforced for their actions. Behavior that has a positive outcome will tend to be repeated.

F. Gestalt Psychology: Making Psychology Whole
1. Wertheimer (1880-1943), Koffka (1886-1941), and Kohler (1887-1967); the three founders of Gestalt psychology.
2. Gestalt translates to "pattern" or "organized whole".
3. Demonstrated that learning is a accomplished by **insight**, not by mechanical repetition.

G. Psychoanalysis: Digging beneath the surface.
1. Founded by Sigmund Freud. Often called psychodynamic.
2. Focus on the unconscious - a seething cauldron of conflicting impulses, urges and wishes.

IV. How Today's Psychologists View Behavior and Mental Processes.

A. The Evolutionary and Biological Perspectives
1. Focus on the evolution of behavior and mental processes.
2. Genes can be transmitted from generation to generation.
3. Biological perspective seek the links between the electrical and chemical activity of the brain. Use of PET and CAT scans.

B. The Cognitive Perspective: Keeping Psychology "In Mind".
1. Venture into the realm of mental processes to understand human nature.
2. Cognitive psychologists study those things we refer to as the mind.

C. The Humanistic-Existential Perspective.
1. Humanism stresses the human capacity for self-fulfillment.
2. Existentialism views people as free to choose and be responsible for choosing ethical conduct.
3. Humanistic-Existential psychologists stress the importance of subjective experience.
4. Abraham Maslow and Carl Rogers; two prominent psychologists in this area.

D. The Psychodynamic Perspective.
1. Freud's influence continues to be felt though contemporary psychodynamic theorists would likely call themselves neoanalysts.

2. Famous neoanalysts include Karen Horney (1885-1952) and Erik Erikson (1902-1994). Also the former APA president Dorothy Cantor.
E. Perspectives on Learning.
   1. Learning through repetition and reinforcement.
   2. Social-cognitive theorists (formerly termed social learning theorists) suggest that people can modify or even create their environments.
   3. Intentional learning by observing others.
F. The Sociocultural Perspective.
   1. Addresses the many ways in which people differ from one another.
   2. Influences of ethnicity, gender, culture, and socioeconomic status on behavior and mental processes are studied.
      a. Ethnicity
         i. Ethnic groups are united by their cultural heritage, race, language, and common history.
         ii. Study cultural heritages and ethnic differences in vulnerability to problems.
      b. Gender
         i. Refers to the culturally defined concepts of masculinity and femininity.
         ii. Involves a complex web of cultural expectations and social roles.

V. **How Psychologists Study Behavior and Mental Processes.**
   A. A Famous Researcher
      1. Sir Francis Galton (1822-1911).
         a. Founded eugenics which proposed that only bright people should mate.
         b. Invented the correlational method.
         c. Empirical science.
   B. The Scientific Method: Putting Ideas to the Test.
      1. Scientific method is an organized way of using experience and testing ideas in order to expand and refine knowledge.
      2. Hypothesis: is a specific statement about behavior or mental processes that is tested through research.
      3. Test the hypothesis through controlled methods such as the experiment.
      4. Replication: repeating a study to see if the findings hold up over time with different subjects.
   C. Samples and Populations: Hitting the Target Population.
      1. Samples must be drawn so that they accurately represent the population. This allows for generalization or extending results from samples to populations.
      2. Individuals who are studied are referred to as a sample. A sample is a segment of the population. The population is the group targeted for study.
         a. Problems in generalizing from psychological research: many factors must be considered in interpreting the accuracy of results of scientific research.
         b. Random and Stratified Sampling.
            i. Random sample: each member of the population has an equal chance of being selected to participate.

  ii. Stratified sample: selection is made so that identified subgroups in the population are represented proportionately in the sample.

 c. Volunteer bias: people who volunteer as participants differ systematically from people who do not.

D. Methods of Observation: The Better to See You.

 1. The Case Study.

  a. Information collected about individuals and small groups.

  b. Typically unscientific accounts of people's behavior referred to as anecdotes.

  c. Provide compelling portraits but may have factual inaccuracies.

 2. The Survey.

  a. Used to study individuals who cannot be observed in the natural setting or studied scientifically.

  b. Employs questionnaires and interviews. Also uses the examination of public records.

  c. Famous Kinsey survey results: *Sexual Behavior in the Human Male* and *Sexual Behavior in the Human Female*.

 3. Naturalistic Observation.

  a. Observe people in their natural habitats.

  b. Unobtrusive measures are used to avoid interfering with the behaviors that are being observed.

E. Correlation: On How Things Go Together-Or Not.

 1. Investigates whether one observed behavior or trait is related to (correlated) with another.

 2. Mathematically expressed as a correlation coefficient; a number the varies between +1.00 and -1.00.

 3. Positive correlation: the higher scores on one variable tend to correspondw ith higher scores on the second variable. Low with low. (e.g. Intelligence test scores and academic performance).

 4. Negative correlation: Higher scores on one variable tend to correspond with lower scores on the second. (e.g. Amount of experience stress and functioning of the immune system).

 5. Correlational studies may suggest but do not prove cause and effect.

F. The Experimental Method: Trying Things Out.

 1. The preferred method for answering questions about cause and effect.

  a. Independent and Dependent Variables.

   i. Independent variable: manipulated by the experimenters so that the effects of various levels may be determined.

   ii. Dependent variable: the measured outcome or result.

  b. Experimental and Control Groups

   i. Experimental groups obtain the treatment.

   ii. Control groups do not receive the treatment.

  c. Blind and Double Blind Experiments.

   i. Placebo or "sugar pill".

   ii. Blind: control for the expectations of effects by creating conditions where the subjects are unaware of the treatment.

          iii.   Double blind: neither the subjects nor the experimenters know who has obtained the treatment.

VI. Ethical Issues in Psychological Research and Practice.
    A. Basic standards.
       1. Intended to promote individual dignity, human welfare and scientific integrity.
       2. Do not undertake research methods that are harmful.
    B. Research with Humans.
       1.   Ethics review committees are found in colleges, hospitals, etc. to help researchers consider the potential harm of their methods. Review research according to ethical guidelines.

Chapter Two Outline

I. **Evolution.**
   A. Charles Darwin: The Man.
      1. The HMS Beagle voyage.
      2. Cousin of Sir Francis Galton.
      3. Influenced by Thomas Malthus's "Essay of the Principle of Population".
      4. Presented "On the Origin of the Species by Natural Selection" in 1859.
         a. Book sold out in the first day.

II. **Evolution and Evolutionary Psychology: "Survivor" Is More Than Just a Game.**
   A. Theory of Evolution.
      1. Published "The Descent of Man" in 1871.
      2. Natural Selection: Survival of the fittest.
      3. Biology serves as the material base for our behaviors, emotions and cognitions.
   B. "Doing What Comes Naturally".
      1. Mutations: differences in individual traits and/or adaptations for survival?
      2. Evolutionary Psychology: Applying adaptation and natural selection to mental processes and behavior.
      3. Instincts: stereotyped pattern of behavior that is triggered in specific situations
         a. Examples of instincts: The Egg Zone; Stickl eback Fish; Song of the Sparrow.

III. **Heredity: The Nature of Nature.**
   A. Heredity: one's biological structures and processes transmitted from generation to generation.
   B. Genetics and Behavioral Genetics.
      1. Behavioral Genetics: Bridges the sciences of psychology and biology. Concerned with the genetic transmission of traits that give rise to patterns of behaviors.
      2. Molecular Genetics: attempts to identify specific genes that are connected with behavior and mental processes.
         a. Examples of this include: sociability, shyness, aggressiveness, thrill seeking, anxiety, depression, schizophrenia, bipolar disorder, alcoholism, and criminal behavior.
   C. Genes and Chromosomes: The Building Blocks of Heredity".
      1. Genes: basic building blocks of heredity. 30,000 - 40,000 genes within every cell of a person's body.
      2. Chromosomes: strings of genes. Each cell contains 46 arranged in 23 pairs.

3. DNA: Chromosomes are large complex molecules of deoxyribonucleic acid (DNA).
4. Human Genome Project: has learned that the sequencing of your DNA consists of about 3 billion DNA sequences.
    a. Genetic Code: The DNA sequences that "define" each person.
        i. Sperm and Egg: 23 chromosomes from the father's sperm and 23 chromosomes from the mother's egg. When the egg is fertilized by the sperm they form 23 pairs.
        ii. Sex Chromosomes: The 23rd pair of chromosomes which determine a person's sex, male or female. X female; Y male.
        iii. Determined by father.
5. Down Syndrome.
    a. Down Syndrome: an extra chromosome on the 21st pair. Usually contributed by mother.
    b. Characteristics: downward sloping fold of skin at the inner corner of the eyes, a round face, a protruding tongue, broad flat nose, mental retardation, and physical problems that can result in death by middle age.
D. Kinship Studies: Is the Behavior of Relatives Related?
1. Parents and Children: 50% of their genes in common. Aunts and Uncles have a 25% overlap with nieces and nephews. 12.5% overlap with cousins.
2. Kinship Studies: Studies which attempt to compare the presence of traits and behavior patterns in people who are biologically related or unrelated to help determine the role of genetic factors.
3. Twin Studies: Looking Into the Genetic Mirror.
    a. Monozygotic Twins (MZ): Identical twins from the same fertilized egg.
    b. Dizygotic Twins (DZ): Fraternal twins, two separate fertilized eggs.
    c. Twin studies compare the presence of traits in MZ twins, DZ twins and others to help determine the role of genetic factors.
        i. If MZ twins show greater similarity on a trait than DZ twins a genetic basis for the trait has been suggested.
        ii. The case of the Jims.... MZ twins raised apart, both named Jim, both were married and divorced, both trained to be policemen, first sons named James Allen, drove same kind of car, vacationed at the same beach, enjoyed carpentry as a hobby.
4. Adoption Studies.
    a. Adoption studies: look for similarities between children and th eir natural and adoptive parents.
        i. When children reared by adoptive parents are more similar to their natural parents in a particular trait, strong evidence exists for a genetic role.
E. Selective Breeding: The Nurture of Nature.

1. Selective breeding: selective breeding to enhance desired physical and behavioral traits.
   a. Examples: cattle, chicken, dogs.
   b. Tryon rat studies: Bred rats to become "maze dull" and "maze bright".
      i. By the seventh generation maze bright rats are making only one error per trial, maze dull are making 9-10 errors per trial.

IV. **The Nervous System: On Being Wired.**
   A. Phineas Gage story: The brain's influence on personality; the nervous system serves as the base for behaviors, emotions, and cognitions.
   B. Neurons: Into the Fabulous Forest.
      1. Neurons: the nerve cells of the body; the metaphoric tree.
         a. Cell Body: contains the nucleus which generates energy
         b. Dendrites: receive incoming messages from adjourning cells (roots).
         c. Axon: carry messages away from the cell body (trunk).
         d. Terminals (terminal buttons): bulb shaped structure at the end of the axon.
         e. Myelin: fatty substance around axons that facilitate conduction.
         f. Glial cells: remove d ead neurons and waste products from the nervous system.
         g. Afferent neurons: sensory input.
         h. Efferent neurons: motor output.
            i. SAME: Sensory = Afferent, and Motor = Efferent.
   C. The Neural Impulse: Let Us "Sing the Body Electric".
      1. Neural Impulse: message traveling along the neuron; between 2 and 225 miles an hour.
      2. An Electrochemical Voyage.
         a. Neuron resting potential: -70 millivolts (negative charge).
         b. Depolarized: action of the cell while it becomes positively charged.
         c. Action potential: positively charged neuron returning to the resting state of being negatively charged. The "message" is sent.
      3. Firing: How Messages Voyage from Neuron to Neuron.
         a. Neuron Firing: neurons attempt to transmit messages to other neurons, muscles or glands.
         b. Threshold: Each neuron has a threshold; the cell will not fire until the threshold is reached.
         c. All or None Principle: When the threshold is reached the neuron fires an impulse of the same strength.
         d. Refractory Period: a period of time when the neuron will not fire; period of recovery during which positive sodium is not allowed to pass through the neural membrane.
   D. The Synapse: On Being Well Connected.
      1. Synapse: junction (fluid filled gap) between neurons.

E. Neurotransmitters: The Chemical Keys to Communication.
1. Synaptic Vesicles: sacs in the axon terminals which contain neurotransmitters.
2. Neurotransmitters: the chemical keys to communication; spilled into the synaptic cleft (synapse) and influence the receiving neuron
3. Receptor Site: specifically tailored site on the receiving neuron where the chemical key (neurotransmitter) fits.
4. Reuptake: reabsorption of neurotransmitters by the sending neuron.
5. Excitatory: neurotransmitter influence on the receiving cell causing it to fire.
6. Inhibitory: neurotransmitter influence on the receiving cell preventing it from firing.
7. Some Key Chemical Keys.
   a. Acetylcholine (ACh): controls muscle contractions; can be both excitatory and inhibitory.
      i. Example of Curare and Botulism both leading to paralysis
      ii. Hippocampus: ACh is also found in the hippocampus and facilitates memory; decreases with Alzheimer's disease leading to memory problems.
   b. Dopamine: affects voluntary movements, learning, memory and arousal.
      i. Deficiencies are linked to Parkinson's Disease in which people progressively lose control over their muscles; Muhammad Ali and Michael J. Fox.
      ii. Schizophrenia: people with schizophrenia may have more receptor sites for dopamine leading to confusion and false perceptions.
   c. Norepinephrine: produced largely in the brain stem; acts as a neurotransmitter and as a hormone; involved in general arousal, learning and memory, and eating; linked to mood disorders.
      i. Example of cocaine which creates an excess of norepinephrine leading to persistent arousal.
   d. Serotonin: involved in emotional arousal and sleep. Deficiencies have been linked to eating disorders, alcoholism, depression, aggression, and insomnia.
      i. Example: LSD which inhibits this inhibitory neurotransmitter leading to increased brain activity including hallucinations
   e. Gamma-aminobutyric acid (GABA): inhibitory neurotransmitter that may help calm anxiety reactions. Tranquilizers and alcohol may quell anxiety by binding with GABA receptors.
   f. Endorphins: inhibitory neurotransmitter; endogenous morphine. Natural painkiller.
      i. Experienced by runners as the runner's high.
   g. Billions and billions of vesicles pouring neurotransmitters into synaptic clefts at any given time; several hundred times every second.

F. The Parts of the Nervous System.
  1. Nerve: a bundle of axons.
  2. Central Nervous System: brain and spinal cord.
  3. Peripheral Nervous System: afferent and efferent neurons which transmit messages from the brain or spinal cord to muscles and glands.
  4. The Peripheral Nervous System: The Body's Peripheral Devices.
     a. Somatic Nervous System: afferent and efferent neurons that transmit sights, sounds, smells, temperature, body positions, etc.
        i. Purposeful body movements.
     b. Autonomic Nervous System: "Automatic" r egulates the glands and internal organ muscles; heartbeat, respiration, digestion, dilation of the pupils, etc.
        i. Sympathetic Division: active during processes that involve spending body energy; fight or flight.
        ii. Parasympathetic Division: active during processes that replenish reserves of energy.
  5. The Central Nervous System: The Body's Central Processing Unit.
     a. Spinal Cord: column of nerves transmits messages from sensory receptors to the brain and from the brain to muscles and glands throughout the body
        i. Spinal Reflexes: unlearned response to a stimulus that may involve only two neurons: afferent and efferent.
        ii. Interneuron: a third neuron that transmits the neural impulse from the sensory neuron through the spinal cord to the motor neuron.
        iii. Gray Matter: non-myelinated neurons; found in brain and spinal cord.
        iv. White Matter: myelinated neurons; found in brain and spinal cord.

V. The Brain: The Star of the Human Nervous System.
  A. Gender differences: Men brains are 15% larger than women's brains; Women's brains run hotter (metabolize more glucose).
  B. Seeing the Brain Through the Eyes of the Psychologist.
    1. Paul Broca: hobby of craniometry or measurement of the skull.
       a. Patient named Leborgne who could understand language but could utter only meaningless sounds. After his death Broca performed an autopsy and found a part of his brain had deteriorated.
       b. Broca tied this into speech, now called Broca's area.
    2. &n bsp; Accidents.
       a. Accidents provide unplanned, uncontrolled opportunities of studying the brain (see Phineas Gage).
    3. Experimenting with the Brain.
       a. Lesioning: damaging part of the brain.
    4. The Electroencephalograph (EEG).
       a. EEG detects minute amounts of electrical activity in the brain.
    5. Brain Imaging Techniques.

a. CAT (computerized axial tomograph): a scan which passes a narrow X-ray beam through the head and measures brain structures, generating a three dimensional image of the brain.
   i. Reveals deformities in shape and structure that are connected with blood clots, tumors, and other health problems.
b. PET (positron emission tomography): computer generated image of the activity of parts of the brain by tracing the amount of glucose used. A harmless amount of radioactive compound (tracer) is mixed with glucose and injected into the blood stream.
   i. Used to see which parts of the brain are most active when we are engaged in various activities (listening to music, working out math problems, etc.)
c. MRI (magnetic reasoning imaging): the person lies in a powerful magnetic field and is exposed to radio waves that cause parts of the brain to emit signals; relies on subtle shifts in blood flow.
   i. MRI has shown people with schizophrenia have smaller prefrontal regions but larger ventricles.
C. A Voyage Through the Brain.
   1. Hindbrain: where the spinal cord meets the brain. Contains three structures, the medulla, pons, and cerebellum.
      a. Medulla: regulates vital functions such as heart rate, blood pressure, and respiration.
      b. Pons: transmits information about body movements and is involved in functions related to attention, sleep/alertness and respiration.
      c. Cerebellum: involved in maintaining balance and controlling motor behavior.
   2. Reticular Activating System (RAS): vital in the functions of attention, sleep and arousal.
   3. Forebrain: forward most part of the brain containing the thalamus, hypothalamus, limbic system and the cerebrum.
      a. Thalamus: relay station for sensory stimulation.
      b. Hypothalamus: vital for the regulation of body temperature, concentration of fluids, storage of nutrients, and various aspects of motivation and emotion.
         i. Also involved in hunger, thirst and sexual behavior. (Pleasure center of the brain see the rat experiment).
      c. Limbic System: made up of several structures including the amygdala, hippocampus, and parts of the hypothalamus.
         i. Involved in memory, emotion and in the drives of hunger, sex and aggression.
         ii. Amygdala: connected with aggression, fear response, and vigilance.
      d. Cerebrum: responsible for thinking and language.
   4. Corpus Callosum: a bundle of some 200 million nerve fibers connecting the two hemispheres.

VI. The Cerebral Cortex.
   A. Cerebral Cortex: outer layer of the cerebrum; about 1/8 of an inch thick.
      1. Involved in almost every bodily activity, including most sensations, and most responses.
      2. Frontal Lobe: in front of the central fissure, contains the motor cortex, which causes our body to move.
      3. Parietal Lobe: behind central fissure, contains the somatosensory cortex which receives messages from skin senses all over the body.
      4. Temporal Lobe: lies below the lateral fissure, contains the auditory area (hearing).
      5. Occipital Lobe: lies behind the temporal lobe and is involved with vision.
   B. Thinking, Language, and the Cortex.
      1. Association Areas: areas of the cerebral cortex that are not primarily involved in sensation or motor activity.
         a. Make possible the breadth and depth of human learning, thought, memory and language.
      2. Language Functions.
         a. Aphasia: disruption in the ability to understand or produce language.
         b. Wernicke's Area: in the temporal lobe responds mainly to auditory information.
         c. Broca's area: processes information and sends it to the motor cortex.
         d. Wernicke's aphasia: impaired ability to comprehend speech and to think of the proper words to express.
         e. Broca's aphasia: Damage to this area results; people can understand language but will speak slowly in simple sentences.
   C. Left Brain, Right Brain.
      1. Left brain: primarily logical and intellectual.
      2. Right brain: primarily intuitive, creative, and emotional.
         a. At best this is exaggerated. The hemispheres do not act independently as they are connected by the corpus callosum.
   D. Handedness: Is It Gauche or Sinister to Be Left Handed?
      1. Lefties: 8-10% of people are left handed; more common in males.
         a. Has been connected with language problems, dyslexia, stuttering, migraine headaches, allergies, schizophrenia.
         b. On the other side being left handed is associated with artists, musicians, and mathematicians.
      2. Handedness runs in families.
   E. Split Brain Experiments: How Many Brains Do You Have?
      1. Split brain: some people with epilepsy have split brain operations in which much of their corpus callosum is severed.
         a. Characteristics of split brain: each hemisphere has a mind of it's own.

i.   One patient described a situation he encountered, as one hemisphere liking reading and other not. If he shifted the book from his right hand to his left, his left hand would put the book down.

VII.   The Endocrine System: Chemicals in the Blood.
  A. Glands: secrete hormones. Two types:
    1. With ducts (saliva, sweat, tears).
    2. Without ducts (released into the blood stream).
  B. Pituitary Gland: implicated in growth, sometimes referred to as the Master Gland as it influ ences other glands in the endocrine system.
  C. Examples of hormones:
    1. Growth Hormone: regulates growth of muscles, bones and glands.
    2. Prolactin: regulates maternal behavior in lower animals such as rats, also produces milk in women.
    3. Antidiuretic Hormone (ADH): inhibits production of urine when fluid levels in the body are low.
    4. Oxytocin: stimulates labor in pregnant women.
    5. Melatonin: secreted by the Pineal gland and helps regulate the sleep-wake cycle.
    6. Thyroxin: secreted by the thyroid and affects the body's metabolism.
      a. Hypothyroidism is too little thyroxin and results in being overweight.
      b. Hyperthyroidism is too much thyroxin and is characterized by excitability, insomnia, and weight loss.
      c. Cretinism is a conditioned caused by a deficiency in thyroxin in children which leads to stunted growth and mental retardation.
    7. Adrenal glands: release hormones to increase resistance to stress.
      a. Promote muscle development and the release of sugar in the liver making more energy available.
      b. Epinephrine: is also known as adrenaline; produced by the adrenal glands.
    8. Testosterone: produced by the testes and in small amounts by the ovaries.
      a. Considered to be the male sex hormone as it aids in the development of male sex organs.
      b. During puberty the release of testosterone promotes the development of primary and secondary sex characteristics.
        i. Primary sex characteristics: those characteristics involved in reproduction: increased penis size, sperm producing ability of the testes.
        ii. Secondary sex characteristics: Not directly related to reproduction: presence of a beard, deeper voice.
    9. Estrogen and Progesterone: produced by the ovaries and in small amounts by the testes.

a. Fosters female reproductive capacity and secondary sex characteristics. The levels of estrogen and progesterone vary and regulate the woman's menstrual cycle.

VIII. Life Connections: Raging Hormones. Premenstrual Syndrome (PMS).

A. Premenstrual Syndrome (PMS): three out of four women report having some psychological and physical problems such as depression, anxiety, and headaches during the four to six days that precede menstruation.

1. However only one in ten has symptoms severe enough to impair academic, occupational, or social functioning.

B. PMS may be a complex interaction between ovarian hormones and neurotransmitters. Once seen as something a woman must tolerate, today there are many treatment options (diet, exercise, hormone treatments).

C. How to Handle Menstrual Discomfort.

1. Don't blame yourself.
2. Keep track of your menstrual symptoms to help you and your doctor identify patterns.
3. Develop strategies for dealing with days on which you experience the most distress.
4. Ask yourself whether you harbor self-defeating attitudes that might be compounding distress.
5. See a doctor about y our symptoms.
6. Develop nutritious eating habits.
7. If you feel bloated, eat smaller meals.
8. Vigorous exercise.
9. Check with your doctor about herbal, vitamin and mineral supplements.
10. Ibuprofen and other medications available over the counter may be helpful for cramping.
11. Menstruation is triggered by a sharp drop off in sex hormones. Some gynecologists prescribe estrogen replacement though this is not hazard free.
12. Remind yourself that menstrual problems are time limited.

D. Menopause: When the Decline in Sex Hormones Becomes Permanent.

1. Menopause: when the drop off in female sex hormones becomes permanent.
   a. Characterized by the cessation of menstruation. Climacteric caused by the falling off in the secretion of estrogen and progesterone. Loss of reproductive ability.
      i. Other characteristics: hot flashes, perspiration, loss of sleep, feelings of anxiety and depression.
      ii. The majority of women get through the menopause transition with little or no problems.
      iii. Some women do experience physical and emotional problems.

2. Hormone Replacement Therapy (HRT).
    a. HRT: consists of synthetic estrogen and progesterone used to offset the effects of declining of naturally occurring hormones.
        i. Positives: May help reduce hot flashes, lower the risk of osteoporosis, colon cancer, and age related cognitive declines. Possibly raises the levels of "good" cholesterol and lowers the levels of "bad" cholesterol.
        ii. Negatives: Increases in some kinds of cancers including breast and endometrial cancer. No cardiac benefits, possible increased risk of stroke and heart attacks.
E. Andropause (Viropause or Manopause).
    1. Andropause: suggests a fall off of levels of the male sex hormone androgens.
        a. The decline is typically more gradual in men than in women.
        b. Characteristics include loss of fertility, problems in achieving and maintaining an erection, loss of bone mass loss of muscle, loss of height, body fat percent nearly doubles and loss of some hearing and vision.
        c. To help alleviate the symptoms try:
            i. Exercise.
            ii. Diet rich in calcium and vitamin D.
            iii. Hormone replacement therapy.
    2. Irritable Male Syndrome.
        a. Characteristics: the drop off of testosterone may lead to anxiety, depression, or irritability in men.
    3. Hormone Replacement Therapy (HRT) in Men.
        a. Each year 1 million prescriptions are written for testosterone.
            i. Positives: May boost strength, energy, and the sex drive.
            ii. Negatives: connected with risk of prostrate cancer and cardiovascular disease.

Chapter Three Outline

I. Prenatal Development: The Beginning of Our Life Story

1. Neonate: newborn
2. Zygote: the union of sperm and egg.
3. Germinal stage: the period from conception to implantation. Also known as the "period of the ovum".
4. Embryonic stage: the prenatal period of development from implantation until about the eighth week of development.
5. XY or XX: the genetic code that begins to assert itself about the seventh week of development.
6. Androgens: male sex hormones produced by the testes.
7. Amniotic sac: The embryo is suspended within this protective sac.
8. Umbilical cord: connects the embryo to the placenta.
9. Fetal stage: the period of development beginning in the third month until birth.
10. Newborns weigh on average 7 ½ pounds for boys and 7 pounds for girls.

II. Childhood: Physical, Cognitive, and Social Developments

A. Physical Development: Babies usually double their birth weight in about 5 months and triple it by their first birthday.

1. Reflexes: are simple unlearned, stereotypical responses elicited by specific stimuli. Essential to survival; do not involve higher brain functions.
   a. Rooting: Infants turning their head toward stimuli that prod or stroke the cheek, chin, or corner of the mouth.
   b. Withdrawal: Infants withdraw from painful stimuli.
   c. Moro: startle reflex.
   d. Babinski: Infants fan their toes when the soles of their feet are stimulated.

B. Perceptual Development: On Not Going Off the Deep End
1. Fixation time: the amount of time spent looking at one stimulus instead of another. 2-month old infants prefer stimuli that resemble a human face.
2. Visual Cliff experiments: 6-8 month old infants develop depth perception and avoid crawling off the "cliff".
3. 3-day old infants prefer to hear their mother's voice to those of other women.
4. Shortly after birth infants can discriminate tastes and distinguish tastes .

C. CONTROVERSY IN PSYCHOLOGY: Is Development Continuous of Discontinuous?
1. Psychologists disagree more strongly on whether aspects of development occur in stages.
2. Piaget and Freud both believed discontinuous.

D. Cognitive Development
   1. The ways in which children mentally represent and think about the world.

E. Jean Piaget's Cognitive-Developmental Theory
   1. Piaget hypothesized that children's cognitive proce sses develop in an orderly sequence of stages.
   2. Assimilation and Accomodation
      a. Assimilation: responding to new stimuli through a reflex or existing habit.
      b. Scheme: a pattern of action or a mental structure involved in acquiring or organizing knowledge.
      c. Accomodation: the creation of new ways of responding to objects or looking at the world.
   3. The Sensorimotor Stage
      a. The newborn is capable of assimilation.
      b. By about 8-12 months of age the infant realizes that objects that are removed from sight still exist. This is called object permanence.
   4. The Preoperational Stage
      a. Characterized by the use of words and symbols to represent objects and relationships among them.
      b. Egocentrism: One dimensional thinking.
      c. Animism: attribute life and consciousness to physical objects like the sun and moon.
      d. Artificialism: believe that the environmental events like rain and thunder are human inventions.
      e. Conservation: Basic properties of substances remain the same (conserve) when you change superficial properties such as shape. Children in the preoperational stage are developing this ability.
   5. The Concrete-Operational Stage
      a. Children ages 7-12; show the beginnings of the capacity for adult logic.
      b. Children typically do bet ter with tangible (concrete) rather than abstract ideas.
      c. Children become subjective in their moral judgments, less egocentric.
      d. Reversibility: the recognition that many processes can be reversed or undone, returning to their previous condition.

F. Lawrence Kohlberg's Theory of Moral Development
      a. Kohlberg proposed that one must pay attention more to one's own conscience than to law and authority figures in determining what is right and wrong.
      b. Research methods including presenting subjects with moral dilemmas. Interested in how the subject arrived at their decision, not by the decision alone.
      c. Proposed that moral reasoning follows a specific sequence.
   2. The Preconventional Level
      a. Applies to most children through the age of 9.
      b. Stage 1 is oriented toward obedience and punishment

       c.   Stage 2 Good behavior allows people to satisfy their needs and those of others.

   3. The Conventional Level

       a.   Moral reasoning is judged by conformity to conventional standards of right and wrong.

       b.   Stage 3: moral behavior is that which meets the expectations of others.

       c.   Stage 4: moral judgments are based on rules that maintain the social order.

   4. The Postconventional Level

       a.   Moral reasoning is more complex and focuses on dilemmas in which individual needs are pitted against the need to maintain social order and on personal conscience.

G. Social and Emotional Development

   1. Social relationships are crucial; as children, are very survival depends on them.

H. Erik Erikson's Stages of Psychosocial Development

   1. First stage: Trust versus Mistrust.

       a.   Based on interactions with primary caregivers.

       b.   Come to expect that our environment will (or will not) meet our needs.

   2. Early childhood and preschool years our relationships encourage us to develop autonomy or feelings of shame and guilt (stage 2)

   3. During the school years friends and teachers encourage us to become industrious or to develop feelings of inferiority.

I. Attachment: Ties that Bind

   1. Attachment is an emotional tie that is formed between one person and another specific individual. Behaviors include:

       a.   Attempts to maintain contact or nearness

       b.   Show anxiety when separated.

   2. The Strange Situation and Patterns of Attachment research

       a.   Secure attachment: infants mildly protest their mother's departure, seek interaction upon return and are readily comforted.

            i.   Children with secure attachment are happier, more sociable, more cooperative, have longer attention spans, less impulsive, liked better by peers and teachers, have fewer behavior problems.

       b.   Avoidant attachment: infants are least distressed by their mother's departure. Play by themselves and ignore their mothers when they return.

       c.   Ambivalent/resistant attachment: infants are the most emotional showing severe signs of distress when their mothers leave and show ambivalence upon reunion by alternately clinging to and pushing their mother away.

   3. Stages of Attachment

       a.   Three Stages of Attachment

            i.   Initial-Preattachment Phase: birth to 3 months characterized by indiscriminant attachment (they prefer being held or being with someone but show no preferences for particular people. Specific attachment begins to form about 4 months of age).

  ii. Attachment-in-the-Making Phase: 3 to 4 months of age, is characterized by preference for familiar figures.

  iii. Clear-Cut-Attachment Phase: 6 to 7 months of age, is characterized by intensified dependence on the primary caregiver.

 b. Fear of Strangers (stranger anxiety): 8-10 months of age, children may cry and cling to their parents when strangers try to befriend them.

4. Theoretical Views of Attachment

 a. Behaviorists believe that attachment is learned through experience.

 b. Harry Harlow suggests that skin contact may be more important than learning experiences.

  i. Rhesus monkey research with the wire mesh and terrycloth mothers demonstrated that monkeys in danger prefer the terrycloth mother.

  ii. Concluded that there may be an inborn need for contact comfort.

 c. Konrad Lorenz (etiologist) noted that attachment is an instinct.

  i. Cr itical period: a period during which the animal is sensitive to stimuli. If is moves it must be mother.

  ii. The formation of attachment in this manner is called imprinting.

5. Parenting Styles

 a. Instrumental Competence: the ability to manipulate the environment to achieve goals.

 b. Parental behavior researched by Baumrind focused n four aspects of parental behavior: 1) strictness, 2) demands for a child to achieve intellectual, emotional and social maturity, 3) communication ability, and 4) warmth and involvement. Based on research in this area four parenting styles have been proposed:

  i. Authoritative: strict but are willing to reason with their children. Most competent children come from this type.

  ii. Authoritarian: strict and rely on force; poor communication, cold and rejecting.

  iii. Permissive: easygoing, warm and supportive, but poor at communicating.

  iv. Uninvolved: leave children on their own. Make few demands, show little warmth or encouragement.

6. Child Abuse

 a. Nearly 3 million children in U.S. neglected or abused by parents or caregivers.

 b. Contributors to child abuse include:

  i. Stress

  ii. History of child abuse

  iii. Acceptance of violence as a coping mechanism

  iv. Failure to attach to children

  v. &n bsp; Substance abuse

  vi. Rigid attitudes toward child rearing

  vii. Unemployment, and low socioeconomic status

 c. Children who are abused are likely to develop personal and social problems, and psychological disorders.

d. There is not an identifiable syndrome for children who have been sexually abused, though they are more likely to develop physical and psychological health problems.

e. Why does abuse run in families?
   i. Parents serve as role models
   ii. Children adopt their parent's strict philosophies
   iii. Abuse creates feelings of hostility that are expressed against others

III. Adolescence: Physical, Cognitive, and Social Developments

A. Definition
   1. Except for infancy, more changes occur during adolescence than during any other time of life.
   2. Neither children nor adults; a period of transition.

B. Physical Development
   1. Growth spurts last for 2-3 years. Grow 8-12 inches.
   2. Puberty: a period during which the body becomes sexually mature.
      a. Secondary sex characteristics: body hair, deepening of the voice in males, rounding of the breasts and hips in females.
      b. Beginning of menarche (menstruation) in women, usually occurs between the ages of 11 and 14.
      c. Ovulation may begin as much as two years after menarche.

C. Cognitive Development
   1. Adolescents are able to deal with the abstract and hypothetical.
   2. Piaget's stage of Formal Operations
      a. The final stage of Piaget's theory beginning about the age of 11 or 12.
      b. Abstract thought
   3. Adolescent Egocentrism
      a. Press for acceptance of their logic without recognizing exceptions; egocentric thought
      b. Imaginary Audience: the belief that other people are as concerned with our thoughts and behavior as we are.
      c. Personal Fable: the belief that our feelings and ideas are special. We are unique and invulnerable. Behaviors such as showing off and taking risks are seen.
   4. Evaluation of Piaget's Theory
      a. Was Piaget's timing accurate?
      b. Does cognitive development occur in stages?
      c. Are developmental sequences always the same?
   5. The Postconventional Level of Moral Reasoning
      a. Highest level is based on person's own moral standards.
         i. Stage 5: legalistic o rientation; law is good for society.
         ii. Stage 6: moral reasoning demands adherence to supposed universal universal ethics.
         iii. Conscience is the highest moral authority.
      b. Evaluation of Kohlberg's Theory
         i. Moral reasoning does not follow a developmental sequence.

  ii. Formal operations is a prerequisite for postconventional reasoning.

  iii. Children do not seem to skip stages as they progress.

6. CONTROVERSY IN PSYCHOLOGY: Are there gender differences in moral development?

 a. Using the Heinz dilemma boys show higher levels of moral development than girls.

 b. Carol Gilligan proposes that this is due to different socialization patterns for boys and girls not differences in morality.

 c. Girls are socialized to focus on the needs of others and forgo simplistic judgments of right and wrong. Boys make judgments based on logic.

D. Social and Emotional Development

1. G. Stanley Hall described adolescence as a time of Sturm and Drang - Storm and Stress.

 a. Need to take into account individual differences and cultural variations.

2. 72% of all deaths among people aged 10-24 years result from:

 a. motor vehicle crashes

 b. homicide

 c. &nb sp; suicide

 d. other unintentional injuries

3. Research evidence suggests that hormonal changes affect activity levels but sociocultural influences have a relatively greater impact.

4. Striving for Independence: Adolescents strive for independence which often leads to:

 a. Fighting with parents

 b. Withdrawal from family life; though most adolescents continue to feel love, respect and loyalty toward their parents.

 c. Adolescents who feel close to their parents show:

  i. Greater self reliance

  ii. Independence

  iii. Fare better in school

  iv. Have fewer adjustment problems

5. Ego Identity Versus Role Diffusion: Who Am I?

 a. The fifth stage of Erikson's theory.

 b. Ego Identity: a firm sense of who one is and what one stands for. If this isn't accomplished then role diffusion is experienced.

E. Adolescent Sexuality-When? What?....Should I?

1. Statistics.

 a. According to the CDC (2000) about half of U.S. high school students have engaged in sexual intercourse.

 b. Fewer than half of those use contraception reliably.

 c. Nearly 800,000 teenage girls get pregnant each year.

 d. Nearly 3 million teenage boys and girls contract a sexually transmitted infection (STI) each year.

2. Problems:

 a. Adolescents often misunderstand reproduction and contraception.

 b. Top reason for engaging in sexual relations is peer pressure.

c. Pregnancies are more likely to be characterized by medical complications, prolonged labor, premature births.

d. Teenage mothers are less likely to graduate from high school, have a lower standard of living, and have a greater need for public assistance.

e. The final decade of the 20th century saw a decline in teenage pregnancy due to increased use of contraception and educational campaigns.

IV. Adulthood: Physical, Cognitive, and Social Developments.

A. Physical development.

1. People are living longer than ever before.

2. Young adulthood characteristics:

a. Height of sensory sharpness, strength, reaction time, and cardiovascular fitness.

b. Sexually, most people are easily aroused and able to perform.

3. Middle adulthood characteristics:

a. Diminished strength, coordination, and stamina but it is minor.

b. Can still maintain excellent cardiorespiratory condition.

c. Menopause: final phase of the climacteric.

i. Decline in female sex hormone secretion.

ii. Ovulation comes to an end.

iii. Loss of bone density.

iv. Hot flashes, loss of sleep, some anxiety and depression.

4. Late adulthood characteristics:

a. Increased numbers of people in this age range.

b. Increased brittleness in the bones.

c. See and hear less acutely.

d. Reaction time diminishes.

e. Immune system functions less efficiently.

5. Theories of Aging:

a. Programmed Senescence: aging is determined by a biological clock that is governed by our genes.

i. Evidence to support this is the longevity runs in families.

b. Wear and Tear Theory: environmental factors such as pollution, disease and ultra violet light contribute to the wear and tear on the body. The body is a machine that is going to wear out.

c. Hakim (1998) researched the value of exercise and found walking at least two miles a day helps.

B. Cognitive Development.

1. &nb sp; Characteristics include: creativity, memory functioning and intelligence all of which are at their height in adulthood.

a. Memory function does decline with age. People tend to retain their verbal skills and general knowledge into advanced age.

2. Crystallized versus Fluid Intelligence.

a. Crystallized intelligence represents a lifetime of attainment including vocabulary and accumulated facts.

i. Typically increases over the decades.

        b. Fluid intelligence represents mental flexibility. This is the ability to process information rapidly; learning and solving new problems.

3. The Seattle Longitudinal Study (Schaie, 1994).
    a. Studied the cognitive development of adults for four decades and found factors that contribute to intellectual functioning:
        i. General health.
        ii. Socioeconomic status (SES).
        iii. Stimulating activities.
        iv. Marriage to a spouse with a high level of intellectual functioning.
        v. Openness to new experience.

4. Alzheimer's Disease.
    a. Alzheimer's disease is a progressive form of mental deterioration that affects about 10% of people over the age of 65. It is a disease, not a normal part of aging.
    b. Characterized by:
        i. Deterioration in memory, language, and pr oblem solving.
        ii. Becoming helpless.
        iii. Inability to communicate or walk.
        iv. More isolated memory losses.
        v. Serious impairment of vocational and social functioning.
    c. Seems to be a result of reduced levels of acetylcholine (ACh) and the build up of sticky plaque on the brain.

C. Social and Emotional Development.
1. Characteristics include social and emotional development being the most fluid in adulthood.
2. Psychologically adults are healthier as they advance from adolescence.
3. Adults are more productive and have better interpersonal relationships.
4. Young Adulthood: adults establish themselves as independent members of society.
    a. Fueled by ambition; wanting to advance their careers.
    b. Dream: the drive to become someone, to leave their mark on history; a tentative blueprint for their life.
    c. Erikson proposed that young adults enter a stage of intimacy versus isolation. This is marked by the establishment of intimate relationships.
    d. Levinson labeled this time period as the "age-30 transition. Young adults ask themselves, "Where am I going?" and "Why am I doing this?".
5. Middle Adulthood: key changes in social and emotional development take place.
    a. Erikson labeled this time of life as the generativity versus stagnation.
        i. Generativity is doing things that we believe are worthwhile. This enhances self-esteem and helps shape a new generation.
        ii. Stagnation is "treading water" and has powerful destructive effects on self esteem.
    b. Levinson called this time period "midlife transition". There is a shift in psychological perspective as people begin to think of how many years they have left.

        c.   Women may undergo a midlife transition a number of years earlier than men do.
            i.   Winding down the biological clock; the ability to conceive and bear children.
        d.   Levinson proposed that this period may trigger for some, a midlife crisis. Feelings include a sense of entrapment and loss of purpose; some encounter severe depression.
        e.   Many Americans find these years full of opportunities for new direction, they feel confident, secure, productive, and powerful.
    6.   CONTORVERSY IN PSYCHOLOGY: Do Women experience an "Empty Nest Syndrome"?
        a.   Empty nest syndrome characterized by profound sense of loss when the youngest child leaves.
        b.   Many mothers report increased marital satisfaction and greater mellowness, self confidence and stability.
        c.   Stewart (1998) developed a scale to assess four personality variables:
            i.   Identity certainty: feeling of having a strong and clear identity.
            ii.   Confident power: feeling of self efficacy.
            iii. Generativity: similar to Erikson's.
            iv. Awareness of aging.
               v.   They found that middle age frees many women from gender-related, traditional, roles.
    7.   Late Adulthood.
        a.   Erikson proposed a stage of ego integrity versus despair.
            i.   Ego integrity derives from wisdom; expert knowledge, balance, and excellence.
    8.   Successful Aging.
        a.   Most people in their 70s report being generally satisfied with their lives.
        b.   Three factors are connected with subjective well-being (Pinquart & Sorensen, 2000):
            i.   Socioeconomic status.
            ii.   Social network.
            iii. Competence.
        c.   Volz (2000) proposes three components for successful aging:
            i.   Reshaping one's life to concentrate on what one finds to be important and meaningful.
            ii.   A positive outlook.
            iii. Self challenge.

V. On Death and Dying.

    A. A book written by Kubler-Ross where five stages of dying are proposed:
        1.   Denial.
        2.   Anger.
        3.   Bargaining.
        4.   Depression.
        5.   Final acceptance.

VI. Life Connections: Day Care- Blessing, Headache, or both?
  A. A great majority of mothers are now in the workforce.
  B. How does day care affect the bonds of attachment?
   1. Children in daycare are somewhat more likely to show insecure attachment, though infants are likely to be securely attached.
  C. How does day care influence social and cognitive development?
   1. Day care experienced children are more peer oriented, play at higher developmental levels, are more likely to share toys, are more independent, self-confident, outgoing, helpful and affectionate. These results are contingent on high quality day care.
   2. Other research has shown the opposite; less cooperation and more aggressiveness. The debate (and research continues).
  D. The Child Care H-Bomb of 2001.
   1. Research findings from the National Institute of Child Health and Human Development showed that children in day care were more likely to exhibit:
     a. Behavioral problems in kindergarten.
     b. Be defiant, aggressive, and disobedient.
   2. Results were correlational thus the reasons for behavioral problems were not clear. Also most of the children's behavior fell within the normal range.
   3. Statistics show that:
     a. 17% of kindergartners who had been in child care acted more aggressively. That is the norm for the general population of children.
     b. The nature of the family-child interactions had a greater impact than child care hours.
     c. Cruelty is never acceptable but some aggressiveness may be children adapting responses to limited resources.
     d. Most of the problems that were observed were not that serious.
   4. Finding Child Care You Can Live With.
     a. Does the day care have a license?
     b. How many children are cared for by the day care center?
     c. How were the caregivers hired?
     d. Is the environment child proofed and secure?
     e. When are meals served?
     f. Is it possible to meet the caregivers?
     g. With what children will your child interact and play?
     h. Does the center seem to have an enriching environment?
     i. Are there facilities and objects like swings, tricycles, etc.?
     j. Does the center's schedule coincide with your needs?
     k. Is the center location convenient for you?
     l. Are parents permitted to visit unannounced?
     m. Do you like the overall environment?

VII.   A Closer Look: Motor Development-Laboratory for the nature-nuture controversy.

1. Maturation: unfolding of traits and behaviors at determined by the genetic code. Gesell argued that all areas of development are self-regulated by the unfolding of natural plans and processes.
2. Maturation and experience both play indispensable roles in motor development.

VIII.   A Closer Look: How Child Abuse May Set the Stage for Psychological Disorders in Adulthood.
1. Women who reported a history of child abuse were significantly more likely to show higher blood levels of ACTH in response to stressors.
2. The combination of early abuse and current depression apparently make the body most sensitive to stress.

IX.   A Closer Look: Aging, Gender, and Ethnicity: Different Patterns of Aging.
1. Women in our society tend to outlive men by about six years.
2. European Americans outlive Latino, African American and Native Americans.
3. Heart disease typically develops later in women. Men are more likely to die because of accidents, cirrhosis of the liver, strokes, suicide, homicide, AIDS and cancer.
4. There is a seven year difference in life expectancy between people in the highest income brackets and those in the lowest.

Chapter Four Outline

I. **Sensation and Perception: Your Ticket of Admission to the World Outside.**
  A. Sensation: is the stimulation of sensory receptors and the transmission of sensory information to the central nervous system.
  B. Perception: is an active process in which sensations are organized and interpreted to form an inner representation of the world.
  C. Five Senses:
    1. Vision.
    2. Hearing.
    3. Smell.
    4. Taste.
    5. Touch.
  D. Concepts that apply to sensation include: absolute threshold, difference threshold, signal-detection theory, and sensory adaptation.
  E. Fechner founded a discipline known as psychophysics which focuses on ways in which we translate physical events such as light and sounds into psychological experiences.
    1. Absolute threshold: refers to the weakest amount of a stimulus that a person can distinguish from no stimulus at all 50% of the time. Examples include:
      a. Vision: a candle flame viewed from about 30 miles on a clear, dark night.
      b. Hearing: a watch ticking from about 20 feet away in a quiet room.
      c. Taste: 1 teaspoon of sugar dissolved in 2 gallons of water.
      d. Smell:& nbsp; about one drop of perfume diffused throughout a small house (1 part in 500 million).
      e. Touch: the pressure of the wing of a fly falling on a cheek from a distance of about 0.4 inch.
  F. Difference Threshold: Is It the Same or Is It Different?
    1. Difference Threshold: is the minimum difference in magnitude of two stimuli required to tell them apart 50% of the time. Similar to the just noticeable difference (jnd).
    2. Weber found that for:
      a. Light the fraction is $1/60^{th}$.
      b. Weight the fraction is $1/53^{rd}$.
      c. Constant pitch the fraction is 1/333.
  G. Signal-Detection Theory: Is Being Bright Enough?
    1. Signal-detection theory considers the human aspects of sensation, and perception and also assumes that the relationship between a physical stimulus and a sensory response is not just mechanical. Other factors include:
      a. Training (learning).
      b. Motivation (desire to perceive).

c. Psychological states such as fatigue or alertness.
H. Feature Detectors in the Brain: Firing on Cue.
1. Feature detectors are brain cells that respond to different aspects of features of a scene (e.g. angles, vertical, horizontal).
I. Sensory Adaptation: Where Did It Go?
1. Sensory adaptation refers to the sensory process of adjustment.

a. Becoming more sensitive to stimulation is referred to as sensitization or positive adaptation.

b. Becoming less sensitive to stimulation is referred to as desensitization or negative adaptation.

II. Vision: Letting the Sun Shine In.
A. More than half of our brain's cerebral cortex is devoted to visual functions.
B. Light: How Dazzling?
1. All forms of electromagnetic energy moves in waves.
a. Visible light at about 400 billionths of a meter in length (violet) to 700 billionths of a meter (red).
b. Radio waves extend for miles.
c. Cosmic rays: wavelengths are only a few trillionths of an inch long.
2. Sir Isaac Newton discovered the prism that could break light into different colors. Colors of the spectrum include:
a. Red, orange, yellow, green, blue, indigo, violet.
b. (Roy G. Biv)
c. The wavelength of visible light determines the color or hue.
C. The Eye: The Better to See You With.
1. Light first passes through the transparent cornea.
2. The amount of light that is allowed to enter is controlled by the muscle called the iris (the colored part of the eye).
3. The actual opening in the i ris is called the pupil.
4. The lens adjusts or accommodates to the image by changing its thickness. The thickness permits a clear image of the object to be projected onto the retina.
5. The retina consists of cells called photoreceptors that are sensitive to light (photosensitive). There are two types of photoreceptors: rods and cones.
a. The retina contains several layers of cells; the rods and cones, bipolar cells, and ganglion cells. All of these are neurons.
i. The rods and cones respond to light with chemical changes that create neural impulses that are picked up by the bipolar cells. These then activate the ganglion cells.
ii. The axons of the million or so ganglion cells in our retina ultimately converge to form the optic nerve.

       iii.   The optic nerve conducts sensory input to the brain where it is
             relayed to the visual area of the occipital lobe.
   6.   Rods and Cones.
       a.   About 125 million rods and 6.4 million cones are distributed
            across the retina.
           i.   Cones are most densely packed in a small spot at the center of
                 the retina called the fovea.
           ii.   Visual acuity (sharpness and detail) is greatest at this spot.
           iii. Rods are most dense just outside the fovea toward the
                 periphery of the retina.
       b.   Rods allow us to see in black and white.
       c.   Cones provide color vision.
       d.   In contrast to visual acuity is the blind spot which is the part of the
            optic nerve which leaves the eye.
       e. &n bsp; Nearsighted: People who have to be unusually close to a
            distant object to discriminate its details.
       f.   Farsighted: People who see distant objects clearly but have
            difficulty focusing on nearby objects.
       g.   When a person is in their late 30s to mid 40s the lenses start to
            grow brittle, making it more difficult to accommodate to, or focus
            on, objects. This condition is called presbyopia.
   7.   Light Adaptation.
       a.   Dark adaptation: the process of adjusting to lower lighting
            conditions.
       b.   Adaptation to brighter lighting takes place much more rapidly.
D. Color Vision: Creating an Inner World of Color.
   1.   The wavelength of light determines its color or hue.
   2.   The value of color is its degree of lightness or darkness.
   3.   Saturation refers to how intense a color appears.
   4.   Warm and Cold Colors.
       a.   Colors on the green-blue side of the color wheel are considered to
            be cool in temperature.
       b.   Colors on the yellow-red side are considered to be warm.
   5.   Complementary Colors.
       a.   The colors across from one another on the color wheel are
            complementary. These include:
           i.   Red-green.
           ii.   Blue-yellow.
           iii. If the complementary colors are mixed they dissolve into
                 gray.
           iv.   (remember we are mixing lights not pigments).
   6.   Afterimages.
       a.   Persistent sensations of color are followed by perception of the
            complimentary color when the first color is removed.
E.   Theories of Color Vision.

1. Our ability to perceive color depends on the eye's transmission of different messages to the brain when lights with different wavelengths stimulate the cones in the retina.

F. CONTROVERSY IN PSYCHOLOGY: What Happens In The Eye And In The Brain When Light With Different Wavelengths Stimulate The Retina?
   1. Trichromatic Theory.
      a. Young found that he could create any color from the visible spectrum by simply varying the intensities of three lights: red, green, and blue-violet.
      b. Hemholtz suggested that the retina in the eye must have three different types of color photoreceptors or cones.
      c. The trichromatic theory is known as the Young-Helmholtz theory.
   2. Opponent-Process theory.
      a. Hering proposed that there are three types of color receptors but they don't respond just to red, green and blue-violet.
      b. They are pairs including red-green; blue-yellow; and a type that perceives differences in brightness.
      c. These pairs of receptors are what make afterimages possible.
   3. Research suggests that each theory of color vision is partially correct.
      a. The cones may be as Helmholtz claimed.
      b. The transmission of the signals to the brain are as Hering proposed.

G. Color Blindness: What Kind of "Chromat" Are You?
   1. If you can discriminate among the colors of the visible spectrum, you have normal color vision and are labeled a trichromat.
   2. People who are totally color blind are called monochromats.
   3. Partial color blindness is a sex-linked trait that affects mostly males. Partially color-blind people are called dichromats as they can discriminate only among two colors-red and green or blue and yellow-and the colors derived from mixing these colors.

III. **Visual Perception: How Perceptive?**
   A. Visual perception is the process by which we organize or make sense of the sensory impressions caused by the light that strikes our eyes.
      1. Visual perception involves our knowledge, expectations, and motivations.
      2. Visual perception is an active process through which we interpret the world around us.
      3. Gestalt psychologists refer to closure as being the integration of disconnected pieces of information into a meaningful whole or the tendency to perceive a complete or whole figure even when there are gaps in the sensory input.
   B. Perceptual Organization: Getting It Together.
      1. Gestalt psychologists are interested in the way we integrate bits and pieces of sensory stimulation into meaningful wholes.

a. Wertheimer discovered many rules that we use to do this called the laws of perceptual organization.
2. Figure-Ground Perception.
   a. When figure-ground relationships are ambiguous, or capable of being interpreted in various ways, our perceptions tend to be unstable, shifting back and forth.
   b. Examples include the Rubin vase and the Necker Cube.
3. Other Gestalt Rules for Organization include proximity, similarity, continuity, and common fate.
   a. Proximity: nearness.
   b. Similarity: we perceive similar objects as belonging together.
   c. Continuity: we perceive a series of points or a broken line as having unity.
   d. Common Fate: elements seen as moving together are perceived as belonging together.
4. Top-Down Versus Bottom-Up Processing.
   a. Top-Down processing: use the larger pattern to guide subordinate tasks.
   b. Bottom-Up processing: begin with bits and pieces of information and become aware of the pattern formed only after you've worked on it awhile.
C. Life On the Move-Perception of Motion.
   1. The visual perception of movement is based on change of position relative to other objects.
   2. Psychologists have studied several types of apparent movement (illusions of movement). These include: autokinetic effect, stroboscopic motion, and the phi phenomenon.
      a. The Autokinetic Effect is the tendency to perceive a stationary point of light as moving in a dark room.
      b. Stoboscopic Motion is what makes motion pictures possible.
         i. The illusion of movement is provided by the presentation of a rapid progression of images of stationary objects.
      c. The Phi Phenomenon occurs as the on-off process of lights is perceived as movement.
         i. We tend to perceive a series of points as having unity, so each series of lights is perceived as a moving line.
D. Depth Perception: How Far Is Far?
   1. Monocular and binocular cues both help us perceive the depth of objects.
      a. Monocular Cues: are cues that can be perceived by one eye. They include: perspective, relative size, clearness, interposition, shadows, and texture gradients.
      b. Perspective: distances between far off objects appear to be smaller than equivalent distances between nearby objects.
      c. Relative size: the fact that distant objects look smaller than nearby objects of the same size.

d. Clearness of an object: We sense more details of nearby objects.
e. Interposition: Nearby objects can block our view of more distant objects. Interposition is placing of one object in front of another.
f. Shadows: opaque objects block light and produce shadows giving us a relationship to the source of light.
g. Texture Gradient: close objects are perceived as having rougher textures.
h. Motion Parallax: the tendency of objects to seem to move backward or forward as a function of their distance.
2. Binocular Cues: include retinal disparity and convergence.
a. Reti nal disparity: the difference between projected images (e.g. different angles).
i. Closer objects have greater retinal disparity.
b. Convergence: causes feelings of tension in the eye muscles and provides another binocular cue for depth.
E. Perceptual Constancies: Keeping the World a Stable Place.
1. Size constancy allows us to perceive objects to be the same size even when viewed from different distances.
a. Experiences teach us about perspective.
2. Color constancy is the tendency to perceive objects as retaining their color even though lighting conditions may alter their appearance.
3. Brightness constancy is similar to color constancy.
4. Shape constancy is the tendency to perceive objects as maintaining their shape, even if we look at them from different angles so that the shape of their image on the retina changes dramatically.

IV. Hearing: Making Sense of Sound.
A. Sound or auditory stimulation, travels through the air like waves.
1. The changes in air pressure are vibrations that approach your ears in waves.
a. The human ear is sensitive to sound waves with frequencies from 20 to 20,000 cycles per second.
B. Pitch and Loudness-All Sorts of Vibes.
1. Pitch and loudness are two psychological dimensions of sound.
a. The pitch of a sound is determined by its frequency, or the number of cycles per second as expressed in the unit hertz (Hz).
i. The greater the number of cycles per second the higher the pitch of the sound.
b. The loudness of a sound roughly corresponds to the height or amplitude of sound waves and is expressed in decibels (dB).
i. 25 dB is equivalent in loudness to a whisper at 5 feet.
ii. 30 dB is equivalent in loudness to what your librarian would like at your college library.
iii. 85-90 dB a person may experience hearing damage with prolonged exposure.
C. The Ear: The Better to Hear You With.

1. The ear has three parts: the outer ear, middle ear, and the inner ear.
2. The outer ear is shaped to funnel sound waves to the eardrum.
    a. The eardrum is a thin membrane that vibrates in response to sound waves and thereby transmits them to the middle and inner ears.
3. The middle ear contains the eardrum and three small bones: the hammer, the anvil, and the stirrup. The middle ear functions as an amplifier.
    a. The stirrup is attached to another vibrating membrane the oval window. The oval window transmits vibrations into the inner ear to a bony tube called the cochlea.
    b. The cochlea is a snail shaped structure that contains longitudinal membranes that divide in into three fluid filled chambers. One of the membranes that lies within the cochlea is the basilar membrane.
    c. Attached to the basilar membrane is the organ of Corti sometimes referred to as the command post of hearing. Here there are 16,000 receptor cells called hair cells.
    d. Hair cells dance in response to the vibrations of the basilar membrane. Their up and down m ovements generate neural impulses which are transmitted to the brain via the auditory nerve.
    e. Auditory input is then projected onto the hearing areas of the temporal lobes of the cerebral cortex.
D. Locating Sounds-Up, Down, and Around.
    1. A sound that is louder in the right ear is perceived as coming from the right.
    2. Both loudness and the sequence in which the sounds reach the ears provide directional cues.
E. Perception of Loudness and Pitch.
    1. The loudness and pitch of sounds appear to be related to the number of receptor neurons on the organ of Corti that fire and how often they fire.
    2. Psychologists generally agree that sounds are perceived as louder when more of these sensory neurons fire.
F. CONTROVERSY IN PSYCHOLOGY: How Do We Explain Pitch Perception? What Happens When the Basilar Membrane Runs Out of Places to Vibrate? What Happens When It Cannot Vibrate Fast Enough?
    1. Place theory: holds that the pitch of a sound is sensed according to the place along the basilar membrane that vibrates in response to it.
    2. Frequency theory: notes that for us to perceive lower pitches, we need the stimulation of neural impulses that match the frequency of the sound waves.
    3. The volley principle states that in response to sound waves groups of neurons take turns firing.
G. Deafness.
    1. More than 1 in 10 Americans has a hearing impairment, and 1 in 100 cannot hear at all.

2. Two major types of deafness are conductive and sensorineural deafness.
   a. Conductive deafness: stems from damage to the structures of the middle ear.
      i. This is the hearing impairment often found among older people.
   b. Sensorineural deafness usually stems from damage to the structures of the inner ear, most often the loss of hair cells, which normally do not regenerate.
      i. Acoustic trauma: prolonged exposure to very loud noises.
      ii. The ringing sensation that often follows exposure to loud noises probably means that hair cells have been damaged.

V. The Chemical Senses: Smell and Taste.
   A. Smell and taste are chemical senses.
   B. Smell: Sampling Molecules in the Air.
      1. If you did not have a sense of smell an onion and an apple would taste the same to you.
      2. Humans can detect the odor of 1 one-millionth of a milligram of vanilla in a liter of air.
      3. An odor is a sample of the substance being sensed.
         a. Odors are detected by sites on receptor neurons in the olfactory membrane high in each nostril.
         b. Their firing transmits information about odors to the brain via the olfactory nerve.
      4. The sense of smell adapts rapidly to odors such that we lose awareness of them.
   C. Taste: Yes, You've Got Taste.
      1. Dogs can perceive the taste quality of sweetness as can pigs, but cats cannot.
      2. There are four primary taste qualities: sweet, sour, salty, and bitter.
      3. The flavor of food depends on its odor, texture, and temperature as well as on its taste.
      4. Taste is sensed through taste cells, receptor neurons located on taste buds.
         a. Humans have approximately 10,000 taste buds most of which are located on the edge and back of your tongue.
            i. Catfish can detect food through murky water and across long distances because their bodies are studded with nearly 150,000 taste buds.
         b. Sensitivities to different tastes apparently have a strong genetic component.
         c. Taste cells reproduce rapidly enough to completely renew themselves about once a week.
         d. Because the flavor of food represents both its taste and its odor, older people experience loss in the flavor on their food, not taste.

VI. The Skin Senses (Yes, It Does).
   A. The skin senses include touch, pressure, warmth, cold, and pain.
   B. Touch and Pressure: How Touching
      1. Active touching involves reception of information concerning not only touch per se but also pressure, temperature, and feedback from the muscles involved in movements of our hands.
      2. Psychphysicists use methods such as the two-point threshold to assess sensitivity to pressure.
         a. Sensory nerve endings are more densely packed in the fingertips and face than in other locations.
         b. The sense of pressure, like the sense of touch undergoes rapid adaptation. < /p>
   C. Temperature: Sometimes Everything Is Relative.
      1. The receptors for temperature are neurons located just beneath the skin.
         a. Sensations of temperatures are relative.

VII. Kinesthesis and the Vestibular Sense.
   A. Kinesthesis: How Moving?
      1. Kinesthesis is the sense that informs you about the position and motion of parts of the body.
         a. Sensory information is fed back to the brain from sensory organs in the joints, tendons, and muscles.
   B. The Vestibular Sense: How Upright?
      1. Your vestibular sense tells you whether you are upright.
         a. Sensory organs located in the semicircular canals and elsewhere in the ears monitor your body's motion and position in relation to gravity.
            i. They tell you if you are falling and if your body is changing speed.

VIII. Extrasensory Perception: Is There Perception Without Sensation?
   A. Hard research does not support the existence of ESP.
      1. Nonetheless 60% of Americans believe that some people have psychic powers or ESP.
   B. Precognition, Psychokinesis, Telepathy, and Clairvoyance.
      1. Precognition: able to perceive future events in advance.
      2. Psychokinesis: mentally manipulating or moving objects.
      3. Telepathy: direct transmission of thoughts or ideas from one person to another.
      4. Clairvoyance: the perception of objects that do not stimulate the sensory organs.
      5. Psi communication refers to the perception of objects or events through means other than sensory organs.

6. Rhine studied ESP for several decades with the conclusion that some people might have some degree of ESP.
    a. Ganzfeld Procedure: one person acts as the "sender" and the other as the "receiver". Receivers correctly identified the visual stimulus 38% of the time, a percentage unlikely to be due to chance.
    b. File drawer problem: ESP researchers are less likely to report research results that show failure.
7. People who have demonstrated ESP with one researcher have failed to do so with another researcher. Not one person has emerged who can reliably show psi communication from one occasion to another and from one researcher to another.

IX. LIFE CONNECTIONS: Pain, Pain, Go Away-Don't Come Again Another Day.

A. A Gallup survey of 2,002 adults in the U.S. showed that 89% experience pain at least once a month.
B. Pain means that something is wrong in the body.
    1. Pain is adaptive.
    2. There are no nerve endings for pain in the brain.
    3. Postaglandins (substance P) facilitate transmission of the pain message to the brain and heighten circulation to the injured area.
        a.& nbsp; Inflammation serves the biological function of attracting infection-fighting blood cells to the affected area to protect it against invading germs.
        b. The pain message is relayed from the spinal cord to the thalamus and then projected to the cerebral cortex.
    4. Other aspects influence pain:
        a. Visual and other sensory inputs tell us what is happening and influence the cognitive interpretation of the situation.
C. Phantom Limb Pain.
    1. About 2 out of 3 combat veterans with amputated limbs report feeling pain in missing or phantom limbs.
        a. Seems to involve activation of nerves in the stump of the missing limb.
D. Gate Theory.
    1. Melzack originated the gate theory of pain.
        a. The nervous system can process only a limited amount of stimulation at a time.
        b. In a sense, there is competition for the attention of neurons.
E. Acupuncture.
    1. Research has shown that acupuncture stimulates nerves that reach the hypothalamus and may also result in the release of endorphins.
F. Modern Psychological Methods for Coping with Pain.
    1. The primary treatment has been chemical; pain-killing drugs.

2. Accurate Information: giving people accurate information and thorough information about their condition often helps them manage pain.
3. Knowledge of medical procedures reduces stress by helping people maintain control over their situation.
4. Distraction and Fantasy: The Nintendo Approach to Coping With Pain?
    a. Diverting attention from pain helps many people cope with it.
5. Hypnosis has been used to reduce chronic pain, as an anesthetic in dentistry, childbirth, even in some forms of surgery.
    a. Hypnosis can also aid in the use of distraction and fantasy.
6. Relaxation Training and Biofeedback.
    a. Tensing muscles is uncomfortable in itself, arouses the sympathetic nervous system, and focuses our attention on the pain.
    b. Some psychological methods of relaxation focus on relaxing muscle groups, breathing exercises, and using relaxing imagery.
    c. Biofeedback is also used to help people relax targeted muscle groups.
        i. Relaxation training with biofeedback seems to be at least as effective as most medications for migraine headaches.
        ii. Also effect for helping chronic pain in the lower back and jaw.
7. Coping with Irrational Beliefs.
    a. Some patients may be unwilling to allow themselves to be distracted from pain and discomfort. Cognitive methods aimed at changing irrational beliefs hold some promise.
8. Other methods.
    a. One is a sense of commitment. It might be helpful to recall that we chose to participate rather than see ourselves as helpless victims. This gives a sense of control of the situation.
    b. Supportive social networks help as well.

X. FEATURES: A CLOSER LOOK: Visual Illusions: Is Seeing Believing?
A. The Hering-Helmholtz and Muller-Lyer illusions are named after the people who devised them.
B. These illusions work because of our life experience.
    1. Lifelong use of perceptual cues.
    2. Experience with perspectives.
C. The Ponzo illusions seems to work because of size constancy.

XI. FEATURES: A CLOSER LOOK: Advances in Science? The Case of the Aromatic T-shirts.
A. Men wore shirts for two days without deodorant, eating spicy foods, pets, and sex.

B. Women were then asked to smell the shirts. By and large the shirts selected as favorites had been worn by men who were similar in genetic makeup to the women's father.

Chapter Five Outline

I. **Just What is Consciousness?**
   A. How can we attempt to understand consciousness?
      1. Psychological Construct: a concept that is devised to help us understand our observations of behavior.
      2. CONTROVERSY IN PSYCHOLOGY: Is consciousness a proper area for psychological study?
      3. William James wrote an article proposing that consciousness was not an area of study for psychologists. John Watson the father of behaviorism agreed.
      4. Today, many psychologists believe that we cannot capture the richness of the human experience without referring to consciousness.
   B. Consciousness as Sensory Awareness.
      1. Consciousness: sensory awareness of the environment.
   C. Consciousness as the Selective Aspect of Attention.
      1. Selective Attention: focusing on a particular stimulus.
         a. Adapting to our environment involves learning which stimuli must be attended to and which ones can be safely ignored.
         b. Various stimuli capture our attention, including:
            i. Sudden changes.
            ii. Novel stimuli.
            iii. Intense stimuli.
            iv. Repetitive stimuli.
   D. Consciousness as Direct Inner Awareness.
      1. Direct inner awareness involved being aware of thoughts, images, emotions and memories.
      2. Sigmund Freud proposed three levels of consciousness:
         a. Consciousness: awareness of our environment.
         b. Preconscious: material that is not currently in awareness but is readily available.
         c. Unconscious: material unavailable to awareness under most circumstances.
            i. Freud believed that we use repression to eject feelings, guilt, and shame from conscious awareness. This is automatic and unconsciously done.
            ii. Suppression is when we consciously eject unwanted events from awareness.
      3. Nonconscious: processes that we cannot experience through our sensory awareness (e.g. firing neurons, growing hair).
   E. Consciousness as Personal Unity: The Sense of Self.
      1. We differentiate ourselves from that which is not us. In this usage, consciousness is "self".
   F. Consciousness as the Waking State.
      1. Consciousness also applies to our waking state compared to sleep.
      2. Also, distorted perceptions of reality called "altered states of consciousness".
         a. Hypnosis, meditation, biofeedback and the effects of psychoactive drugs.

II. Sleep and Dreams.

A. Facts about sleep.
1. One-third of our adult lives are spent in sleep.
2. Experts recommend 8 hours of sleep a night.
   a. A typical adult in the U.S. gets a little less than 7 hours a night.
3. Circadian rhythm: a cycle that is connected with the 24 hour period of the earth's rotation.
   a. Without cues from the environment, the cycle increases to 25 hours, and we sleep about 10 of those hours.

B. The Stages of Sleep.
1. Instruments used in the study of sleep include:
   a. Electroencephalograph (EEG) which measures electrical activity of the brain.
2. Brain waves:
   a. Frequencies: number of waves per second.
   b. Amplitude: height of wave; an index of strength.
      i. High in frequency associated with being awake.
3. Five Stages of Sleep:
   a. When we begin to relax our brain emits alpha waves; low amplitude, 8 to 13 cycles per second.
   b. Stage 1: Brain waves slow down from alpha waves and enter a pattern of 6 to 8 cycles per second called theta waves.
      i. Hypnagogic state: we may experience brief dreamlike images that resemble photographs.
      ii. &n bsp; Stage 1 lasts about 30-40 minutes.
   c. Stage 2: Brain waves slow to 4 to 7 cycles per second. There are also sleep spindles.
      i. Sleep spindles: brief bursts of rapid brain activity; 12 to 16 cycles per second.
   d. Stage 3 and 4: Brain waves slow to 1 to 3 cycles per second called delta waves in stage 3 and slow even more in stage 4 to 0.5 to 2 cycles per second.
      i. Difficult to awake a person in stage 4 sleep and lasts about ½ hour.
   e. Then we begin a journey back upward through the stages until we enter REM (rapid eye movement) sleep. Often called paradoxical sleep because:
      i. EEG patterns look like an awake person's waves.
      ii. Difficult to awaken a person in REM.
      iii. If you do wake a person up, 80% of the time they report having been dreaming.
   f. Each night we tend to undergo five trips through the stages of sleep.

C. Functions of Sleep.
1. We do not have all of the answers as to why we sleep.
2. There seems to be some impairment in concentration ability and performance. Also, attention, learning and memory deteriorate when deprived of sleep for several nights.

3. The amount of sleep we need may be partially determined genetically.
4. Sleep seems to help us recover from stress.
5. Sleep, Learning and Memory
   a.&n bsp;   REM and deep sleep are both connected with the consolidation of learning and memory.
   b. Being REM deprived interferes with memory.
      i.   If REM deprived the person will experience REM rebound where they spend more time in REM sleep during subsequent sleep periods.

D. Dreams: What Is The Stuff of Dreams?
   1. Dreams involve imagery in the absence of external stimulation.
   2. Most likely to experience vivid imagery in dreams during REM sleep.
   3. Theories of the Content of Dreams.
      a. Most dreams involve memories of the activities and problems of the day.
      b. Freud theorized that dreams reflect unconscious wishes and urges.
      c. Activation-synthesis model: ACh and the pons stimulate responses that lead to dreaming.
      d. PET scans show that the frontal lobes of the brain, where we make sense of experience, are pretty much shut down during sleep.
      e. Memories are replayed and consolidated during sleep.
   4. Nightmares: generally products of REM sleep are "bad" dreams.
      a. Traumatic events can spawn nightmares.
      b. Frequent nightmares are related to anxieties, depression and other psychological discomfort.

E. Sleep Disorders.
   1. Insomnia: National Sleep Foundation reports that as many as 58% of American adults are affected by insomnia in a given year.< /p>
      a. Women 61% compared to men 53%.
      b. You cannot force yourself to fall asleep, on set the stage for sleep.
   2. Narcolepsy: Sudden and irresistibly falling asleep.
      a. Affects 100,000 people in a given year.
      b. Typically lasts 15 minutes.
      c. Can be accompanied by sleep paralysis, a sudden collapse of muscle groups.
      d. Thought to be a disorder of REM sleep.
      e. Stimulants and antidepressant drugs have helped.
   3. Apnea: a dangerous sleep disorder in which air passages are obstructed. People stop breathing periodically, upwards of 10 times an hour.
      a. 10 million Americans have apnea, associated obesity and chronic loud snoring.
      b. Related to high blood pressure, heart attacks, and strokes.
      c. Causes may include anatomical deformities that clog air passages and problems in the breathing centers of the brain.
   4. Deep Sleep Disorders: Sleep Terrors, Bed Wetting, and Sleep Walking.
      a. Typically occur in stage 3 or 4 sleep, more common among children and may reflect an immaturity of the nervous system.

III. Altering Consciousness Through Hypnosis: On Being Entranced.
- a.   Sleep Terrors: similar to nightmares but are more severe.
    - i.   Mild tranquilizers help.
- b.   Bed Wetting: stem from immaturity of the nervous system.
    - i.   Behavior therapy methods help. Children often outgrow this.
- c.   Sleep Walking: 15% of children walk in their sleep.
    - i.   Typically don't remember their excursions, though they may respond to questions.
    - ii.   Mild tranquilizers and maturity typically put an end to sleepwalking.

- B.   Definition and History:
    1.   An altered state of consciousness where people appear to be highly suggestible.
    2.   Began with Franz Mesmer (mesmerize) in the 18th century.
        - a.   Mesmer proposed that the universe is connected by forms of magnestism.
    3.   Today hypnosis is popular in nightclubs but it is also used as an anesthetic in dentistry, childbirth and surgery.
        - a.   Psychologists use it to help people reduce anxiety or overcome fears.
        - b.   Also used to help people deal with pain, stress, enhance the functioning of the immune system, losing weight, and prompting memories of witnesses.
    4.   Hypnosis is not sleep though it has been called a hypnotic trance.
    5.   Characteristics of people who are readily hypnotizable are:
        - a.   Suggestibility, prone to fantasy, they compartmentalize unwanted memories, and cooperation with the hypnotist.
        - b.   It is extremely unlikely that someone could be hypnotized against their will.
- C.   CONTROVERSY IN PSYCHOLOGY: How do Psychologist Explain Hypnosis?
    1.   Role Theory: People allow themselves to enact this role under the hypnotist's direction. Behaviors seem while hypnotized can be easily replicated when people are asked to behave as though you are hypnotized.
    2.   Response Set Theory: Response expectancies play a role in the production of personal experiences.
    3.   Neodissociation Theory: People can selectively focus their attention on one thing and dissociate from the things going on around them.
        - a.   This is how hypnotized people avoid the perception of pain.

IV. Altering Consciousness Through Meditation: Letting the World Fade Away.
- A.   Definition:
    1.   Meditation refers to the various ways of focusing one's consciousness to alter one's relationship to the world.
    2.   Can also refer to a process in which people seem to suspend thinking and allow the world to fade away.
    3.   Transcendental meditation (TM) is a simplified form of Far Eastern meditation.
        - a.   Characterized by repeating and concentrating on mantras – words or sounds that aid the person in achieving an altered state of consciousness.

      i.   May have spiritual goals, goals of reducing anxiety and normalizing blood pressure.

      ii.   TM was shown to reduce heart rate and respiration rates as well as blood pressure.

      iii. Meditators produce more frequent alpha waves and can help people sleep.

V. Altering Consciousness Through Biofeedback: Getting in Touch With the Untouchable.

  A. Definition and Usage:

     1. Biofeedback training (BFT) is a system that provides information about a bodily function.

     2. Used to help people combat stress, tension, and anxiety.

  B. Electromyograph (EMG) are often used to monitor muscle tension.

VI. Altering Consciousness Through Drugs.

  A. Definitions:

     1. Psychoactive drugs: drugs that can distort perceptions and change mood.

  B. Substance Abuse and Dependence: Crossing the line.

     1. Substance Abuse: repeated use of a substance despite the fact that it is causing or compounding social, occupational, psychological, physical problems.

     2. Dependence: more severe than abuse is often characterized by tolerance, withdrawal symptoms or both.

        a. Tolerance: The body's habituation to a substance so that higher doses are required to achieve similar effects.

        b. Withdrawal or abstinence syndrome is the effects that are seen when the level of usage suddenly drops off. Symptoms may include anxiety, tremors, restlessness, weakness, rapid pulse, and high blood pressure.

          i.   Psychological dependence signs include anxiety.

          ii.   Delirium Tremens (DTs) experienced by chronic alcoholics when they suddenly lower their intake of alcohol. Symptoms include: heavy sweating, restlessness, general disorientation and terrifying hallucinations.

  C. Causal Factors in Substance Abuse and Dependence.

     1. Some common answers as to why people experiment with drugs include: curiosity, conformity to peer pressure, parental use, rebelliousness, escape from boredom or pressure, and seeking of excitement or pleasure.

        a. CDC survey indicated that drug and cigarette use as increased over the past decade with teenagers.

     2. Psychological views:

        a. Expectations about the effects of a drug are powerful predictors of its use.

        b. Many people use drugs to self-medicate for anxiety and depression.

     3. Biological views:

        a. Genetic predispositions.

  D. Depressants.

1. Generally act by slowing the activity of the central nervous system.
2. Alcohol is considered to be a depressant.
    a. Provides relief from anxiety, depression or loneliness, and lowers inhibitions
    b. 10-20 million Americans are alcoholics. Alcohol is the most abused drug.
    c. Binge drinking (males having 5 or more drinks in a row; 4 for females) is connected with aggressive behavior, poor grades, sexual promiscuity, and serious accidents.
        i. 44% of college students binge at least twice a month.
    d. Low doses of alcohol may feel stimulating but large doses have a clear sedative effect.
        i. Impairs cognitive functioning, slurs speech, and reduces motor coordination.
        ii. Induces feelings of elation and euphoria that may wash away doubts.
    e. Regular drinking leads to physiological dependence.
E. CONTROVERSY IN PSYCHOLOGY: Is a Drink a Day Good For You?
    a. Light drinking can be beneficial as it increases levels of HDL (good cholesterol) and thus decreases the risk of cardiovascular disease.
        i. Other benefits include: less cognitive decline with age, and decreased risk of Alzheimer's disease.
    b. The positive effects disappear with heavy drinking.
        i. Alcohol is fattening.
        ii. Can interfere with the body's absorption of vitamins.
        iii. Can lead to disorders including cirrhosis of the liver and Wernicke-Korsakoff syndrome which is linked to a vitamin B deficiency.
        iv. Heavy drinking has been linked to cancer and cardiovascular disease.
        v. Drinking by pregnant women may harm the embryo.
    c. Alcoholics Anonymous (AA) is the most widely used program to treat alcoholism. Other programs include cognitive-behavioral therapy and motivational-enhancement therapy. All seem to be equally effective unless there are co-morbid psychological problems in which C-B tended to work better.
    d. Disulfiram (Antabuse) a drug which makes people ill if combined with alcohol is used as a treatment.
F. Depressants continued…
1. Opiates: a narcotic derived from the opium poppy.
    a. Opioids are similar in structure but are synthetically derived.
    b. Include: morphine, heroin, codeine, and Demerol. Major application is relief from pain.
        i. Heroin: can cause strong euphoric rushes. Can cause drowsiness and stupor, alter perceptions of time and impair judgement.
        ii. Methadone: synthetic opiod, used to treat heroin dependence.
    c. Withdrawal can be distressing and include flu like symptoms, tremors, cramps, chills, alternating with sweating, rapid pulse, high blood pressure, insomnia, vomiting and diarrhea.
2. Barbiturates and Methaqualone.

a. Barbiturates are depressants which provide relief of anxiety and tension, relief from pain, treatment of epilepsy, high blood pressure and insomnia.
   i. Rapidly lead to both physiological and psychological dependence.
   ii. Both barbiturates and methaqualone produce relaxing and mild euphoric states. High doses result in drowsiness, motor impairment, slurred speech, irritability and poor judgement.
b. Withdrawal can be severe and can include convulsions and death.

G. Stimulants increase activity in the central nervous system.
   1. Amphetamines help people remain alert through the night. Sometimes referred to as "speed", "uppers" or "bennies".
      a. Often abused because of the euphoric rush they provide.
      b. Ritalin (methylphenidate) is a stimulant used to treat attention-deficit disorder.
         i. Has been shown to increase attention span, decrease aggressive and disruptive behavior and can lead to academic gains.
         ii. The hyperactivity may be connected with immaturity of the cerebral cortex.
      c. High doses of amphetamines may cause restlessness, insomnia, loss of appetite, hallucinations, and paranoid delusions, and irritability.
   2. Cocaine: (side note: Coka-Cola stopped putting cocaine in its formula in 1906; Freud used it to help him fight his own depression. He published an article about cocaine titled, "Song of Praise").
      a. Cocaine is a stimulant that produces euphoria, reduces hunger, deadens pain, and bolsters self-confidence.
         i. Stimulates sudden rises in blood pressure; overdoses can lead to restlessness, insomnia, tremors, headaches, convulsions, nausea, hallucinations, and delusions.
         ii. Causes both physical and psychological dependence.
   3. Nicotine stimulates discharge of the hormone adrenaline.
      a. Appears to enhance memory and attention, improve performance on simple repetitive tasks and enhance mood. It also seems to help people relax and reduce stress.
         i. Nicotine depresses appetite and raises the metabolic rate.
      b. Nicotine is addictive and is what causes the physiological dependence people have with tobacco products.
         i. Withdrawal symptoms include nervousness, drowsiness, loss of energy, headaches, irregular bowel movements, lightheadedness, insomnia, dizziness, cramps, palpitations, tremors, and sweating.
      c. Nearly 430,000 Americans die from smoking related illnesses each year (American Lung Association, 2000).
      d. Every cigarette smoked steals about 7 minutes of a person's life.
         i. Hydrocarbons (tars) are what lead to lung cancer.
      e. Pregnant women who smoke have a higher risk of miscarriage, preterm births, low birth weight babies, and still born babies.
      f. Cigar smokers are five times as likely to develop lung cancer and increase the risk of cancers of the mouth, throat, and esophagus.

      g.   Passive smoking is also of concern. This has been connected to respiratory illnesses, asthma, and other health problems.

H. Hallucinogenics.

    1. Hallucinogenics produce hallucinations. They also produce relaxation, euphoria, or in some cases, panic.

    2. Marijuana is produced from the Cannabis sativa plant. It helps some people relax and can elevate mood. It sometimes produces mild hallucinations.

        a. Impairs perceptual-motor coordination, short term memory, and slows learning. Also seen are disturbances in anxiety, confusion, and psychotic reactions.

        b. Strong intoxication can produce nausea and vomiting. People can become psychologically dependent and experience tolerance and withdrawal symptoms.

I. CONTROVERSY IN PSYCHOLOGY: Is marijuana harmful? Should it be available as a medicine?

    1. Marijuana has been used to treat health problems such as glaucoma, and the nausea experienced by cancer patients undergoing chemotherapy. It is reasonable safe, inexpensive and versatile.

J. SOMETHING GOES IN HERE. Strategies for Gaining Control and Maintaining Control

    1. Detoxification is a procedure which can take a week and is best carried out under medical supervision.

    2. Cognitive behavioral approaches to sub stance abuse focus on modifying abusive and dependent ideas and behavior patterns.

    3. By making a public commitment to quit you shore up your own resolve.

        a. Getting there without drugs: don't just say no, do something else.

        b. If you are (from textbook):

            i. Feeling tense try relaxation, exercise or music.

            ii. Feeling bored find a new activity or interest.

            iii. Feeling angry, write down your feelings.

            iv. Feeling worthless seek assistance from loved ones.

            v. Wanting to probe the inner depths of your consciousness try meditation.

            vi. Pressured into using drugs learn how to say "no" politely but firmly.

            vii. Seeking to heighten your sensations, try extreme sports.

            viii. Feeling stressed out? Sit down and figure out the pressures acting upon you and prioritize your actions.

            ix. Wanting to discover new insights take classes or workshops.

            x. Searching for deeper meaning then become more involved in spiritual activities.

        c. Do things that don't involve drugs!

K. CLOSER LOOK: Alcoholism, Gender and Ethnicity.

    1. Men are more likely than women to become alcoholics.

    2. Native Americans and Irish Americans have the highest rate of alcoholism in the U.S.

Chapter Six Outline

I. **Learning: Experience, Change, Adaptation, and...**
   A. Definition:
      1. Learning is a relatively permanent change in behavior that arises from practice or experience.
      2. According to cognitive psychologists, learning may be a mental change that may not be associated with changes in behavior.
         a. Learning is demonstrated by changes in behavior, but learning itself is a mental process.

II. **Classical Conditioning: Learning What Comes After What.**
   A. Definition:
      1. Classical conditioning is a simple form of associative learning that enables organisms to anticipate events.
   B. Ivan Pavlov Rings a Bell.
      1. Reflexes: simple automatic responses to stimuli.
      2. Stimulus: an environmental condition that evokes a response from an organism.
      3. Pavlov discovered that reflexes can also be learned through association.
      4. These learned reflexes are referred to as conditioned responses (CR).
   C. CONTROVERSY IN PSYCHOLOGY: Why did Pavlov's dogs learn to salivate in response to the bell?
      1. Organisms form associations between stimuli because the stimuli are contiguous – that is they occur at about the same time.
      2. Cognitive psychologists view classical conditioning as the learning of relationships among events.
         a. The focus is on the information gained by the organism which is not how the behaviorists see it (Stimulus leads to response).
   D. Stimuli and Responses in Classical Conditioning.
      1. Unconditioned stimulus (US) is unlearned: Pavlov's meat powder elicits salivation, an unconditioned response (UR).
      2. When the dogs learned to salivate to the sound of a bell (previously neutral) the bell became the conditioned stimulus (CS) and the salivation in response to the bell is a conditioned response (CR).
   E. Taste Aversion: Are All Stimuli Created Equal?
      1. Taste aversions are examples of classical conditioning.
         a. Taste aversions are adaptive to the organism as they motivate them to avoid potentially harmful food.
         b. Different than classical conditioning because:
            i. Only one association may be required.
            ii. The US and CS do not have to be contiguous.
      2. The Evolution of Taste Aversion.
         a. The evolutionary perspective suggests that animals and humans would be biologically predisposed to develop aversions that are adaptive in their environmental settings.

III. Factors in Classical Conditioning.

A. Extinction and Spontaneous Recovery are both aspects of conditioning that help us adapt by updating our expectations about the changing environment.
  1. Extinction: the process by which a CS lose the ability to elicit CRs because the CS is no longer paired with the US.
     a. Acquisition trials: initial pairings of a US and CS associated with conditioning.
     b. Extinction trials: initial trials without the UC and CS pairings.
  2. Spontaneous Recovery: recovery of a CR after extinction. A function of the passage of time.
     a. Spontaneous recovery, like extinction, is adaptive.
B. Generalization and Discrimination.
  1. Generalization is the tendency for a conditioned response to be evoked by stimuli similar to the stimulus to which the response was conditioned.
  2. Discrimination: organisms must learn that:
     a. Many stimuli perceived as being similar are functionally different.
     b. The organism must respond adaptively to each.
C. Higher Order Conditioning
  1. In Higher Order Conditioning a previously neutral stimulus comes to serve as a learned or CS after being paired repeatedly with a stimulus that has already become learned.
D. Example of classical conditioning: Little Albert.

IV. Operant Conditioning: Learning What Does What to What.

A. Edward L. Thorndike
  1. The Law of Effect: a response is strengthened in a particular situation by a reward (stamped in). Punishments stamp out stimulus-response connections.
B. Burrhus Frederic Skinner (1904-1990).
  1. Historical contributions: Skinner Box, programmed learning, and Walden II.
C. Concepts of Reinforcement
  1. Organisms learn to do something because of the effects or consequences of that behavior.
  2. Operant conditioning is a simple form of learning in which an organism learns to engage in certain behavior because of the effects of that behavior.
D. Methods of Operant Conditioning
  1. Skinner's book titled "The Behavior of Organisms" (1938).
  2. Skinner devised an operant chamber (Skinner Box); a cage for animals used to study operant conditioning. The chambers had a lever that the animals could press to obtain reinforcements and a turning drum or cumulative recorder to measure behavior (lever presses).
  3. The First Correct Response: it matters little how the first response that is reinforced is made. It could be random or guided.
     a. People can be verbally guided into the desired response.
E. Types of Reinforcers
  1. Any stimulus which increases the probability that responses preceding it will be repeated serves as a reinforcer.

2. Positive Reinforcers: increase the probability that the behavior will occur when they are applied.
3. Negative Reinforcers: increase the probability of a behavior when the reinforcer is removed.
4. With sufficient reinforcement operants become habits.
5. Immediate Versus Delayed Reinforcers.
   a. Immediate reinforcers are more effective than delayed reinforcers.
6. Primary and Secondary Reinforcers.
   a. Primary reinforcers are effective because of an organism's biological makeup (e.g. food and water).
   b. Secondary reinforcers acquire their value through being associated with established reinforcers. Sometimes called conditioned reinforcers.

V. Factors in Operant Conditioning.
A. Extinction and Spontaneous Recovery in Operant Conditioning.
1. Extinction occurs as a result of repeated performance of operant behavior without reinforcement.
2. Spontaneous recovery occurs in operant conditioning. The reward returns and the behavior increases.
B. Reinforcers Versus Rewards and Punishments.
1. Reinforcers are known by their effects.
2. Rewards and punishments are known by how they feel.
   a. Some psychologists refer to reward and positive reinforcement as being synonymous.
   b. Punishments are aversive events that suppress or decrease the frequency of behavior they follow.
      i. Punishment often fails to achieve the goals of parents, teachers, and others.
   c. Results of using punishment:
      i. Children are less likely to develop internal moral standards.
      ii. Physical punishment is connected with poorer parent-child relationships.
      iii. Physically punished children are more likely to be aggressive toward other children.
      iv. Physically punished children are more likely to abuse their spouses or their own children.
   d. Why not use physical punishment:
      i. It hurts.
      ii. Punished individuals may withdraw from the situation (families, school, etc.)
      iii. Children learn the responses that are punished.
   e. Psychologists recommend rewarding good behavior or ignoring misbehavior by using time out.
      i. We must pay attention to children when they are behaving well.
      ii. We must be certain that children are capable of performing desired behavior.

C. Discriminative Stimuli: Do You Step On the Accelerator When the Light is Green or Red.
   1. Discriminative stimuli act as cues by providing information about when an operant will be reinforced.
D. Schedules of Reinforcement: How Often? Under What Conditions?
   1. Some responses are maintained by means of continuous reinforcement; reinforcement after every response. New behaviors are acquired more rapidly through continuous reinforcement.
   2. Partial reinforcement can also maintain behavior. Behavior is more resistant to extinction when partial reinforcement is used.
   3. Interval Schedules.
      a. Fixed Interval: a fixed amount of time must elapse between the previous and subsequent times when reinforcement occurs.
      b. Variable Interval: a variable amount of time occurs between reinforcements.
   4. Ratio schedules.
      a. Fixed ratio: reinforcement is provided after a fixed number of correct responses have been made.
      b. Variable ratio: Reinforcement is provided after a variable number of correct responses.
      c. Both ratio schedules maintain high rates of responding.
   5. Shaping reinforces progressive steps toward the behavioral goal.
      a. Reinforce successive approximations of the goal.

VI. **Cognitive Factors in Learning: Is It Natural to Mentally Represent the Environment?**
   A. Terms:
      1. Cognitive psychologists use concepts such as mental structures, schemas, templates, and information processing.
   B. Latent Learning: Forming Cognitive Maps.
      1. Tolman showed that rats learn about their environment in the absence of reinforcement.
         a. Learning might remain hidden or latent until they were motivated to behave.
   C. Observational Learning: Monkey See, Monkey May Choose to Do?
      1. Albert Bandura proposed that we can acquire operants by observing the behavior of others.
         a. ; A person who engages in a response to be imitated is a model.
         b. Observers are said to be vicariously reinforced.

VII. **LIFE CONNECTIONS: Violence in the media and aggression.**
   A. Statistics.
      1. If a child watches 2 to 4 hours of TV a day, they will have seen 8,000 murders and 100,000 acts of violence by the time they finish elementary school.

B. Bandura, Ross and Ross (1963) conducted a study using a BoBo doll. They found that children who had observed the aggressive model showed significantly more aggressive behavior toward the doll themselves.
   1. Observing the model also disinhibited previously learned aggressive responses.
C. Violence is often shown to have only temporary or minimal effects.
D. Few TV programs show harmful long-term effects.
E. Ways in which depictions of violence make contributions:
   1. Observational learning.
   2. Disinhibition.
   3. Increased emotional arousal.
   4. Priming of aggressive thoughts and memories.
   5. Habituation.
   6. Assumption that violence is acceptable.
   7. Decreases the likelihood that one will take action on behalf of a victim.
   8. May lead to real-life violence.
F. There is no simple one-to-one connection between media violence and violence in real life.
G. Family constellations may also contribute:
   1. Parental substance abuse.
   2. Paternal physical punishments.
   3. Single motherhood.
   4. Parental rejection.
H. Teaching Children Not to Imitate Media Violence.
   1. Children who watch violent shows act less aggressively when they are informed that:
      a. The violent behavior they observe in the media does not represent the behavior of most people.
      b. The apparently aggressive behaviors they watch are not real.
      c. Most people resolve conflicts by nonviolent means.
      d. The real-life consequences of violence are harmful to the victim.

VIII. **A CLOSER LOOK: Applications of Classical Conditioning: Are Cookies Psychological Health Food?**
A. Counterconditioning: a pleasant stimulus is repeatedly paired with a fear-evoking object, thereby counteracting the fear response.
B. Flooding and Systematic Desensitization.
   1. Flooding: the client is exposed to the fear-evoking stimulus until the fear response is extinguished.
      a. Flooding is usually effective but unpleasant.
   2. Systematic desensitization: the client is gradually exposed to fear-evoking stimuli under circumstances in which they remain relaxed.
C. The Bell and Pad Treatment for Bed Wetting.
   1. Children are taught to wake up in response to bladder tension.

IX. A CLOSER LOOK: Applications of Operant Conditioning: Bleeps, Behavior Mod, and Programmed Learning.

   A. Biofeedback Training: Gaining Bleep Control.

     1. BFT has enabled people to learn to control autonomic responses in order to attain reinforcement.

       a. An important innovation in the treatment of health-related problems.

       b. Reinforcement is given in the form of information.

     2. Behavior Modification in the Classroom.

       a. Teachers are taught to pay attention to children when they are behaving appropriately. Works well with younger children.

       b. Older children: peer approval is often more powerful than teacher approval.

   B. Programmed Learning: Step by Step.

     1. This method assumes that any complex task involving conceptual learning as well as motor skills can be broken down into a number of small steps. The steps can be combined in sequence to form the correct behavioral chain.

     2.

X. A CLOSER LOOK: Contingency Theory.

   A. Contingen cy theory: suggests that learning occurs only when the conditioned stimulus provides information about the unconditioned stimulus.

   B. Rescorla concluded that the co-appearance of two events cannot in itself explain classical conditioning. Instead, learning occurs only when the conditioned stimulus provides information about the unconditioned stimulus. Learning theory occurs because a conditioned stimulus indicates that the unconditioned stimulus is likely to follow.

Chapter Seven Outline

I. **Kinds of Memory: Looking Back, Looking Forward.**

   A. Psychologists debate whether there are different systems of memory or just different examples of the same system.

   B. Explicit Versus Implicit Memories.

      1. Explicit memory: referred to as declarative memory is memory for specific information.

      2. Implicit memory: referred to as nondeclarative memory is memory of how to perform a task, how to do something.

      3. Episodic Memory: a form of explicit memory, memories of the things that happen to us or take place in our presence. Also referred to as autobiographical memory. "I remember….."

      4. Semantic Memory: On Not Getting Personal. Memories of general knowledge. Semantics concerns meanings. "I know…"

      5. Implicit Memory: When Remembering Is Doing.

         a. Characteristics:

            i. Implicit memories are suggested (implied) not declared.

            ii. Implicit memories are illustrated by the things that people do but not by the things they state.

            iii. Implicit memories involve skills, both cognitive and physical: they reveal habits and involve effects of conditioning.

            iv. Implicit memories can persist even when we have not used them for many years.

            v. Implicit memories can become relatively automatic referred to as priming.

   C: Retrospective Memory Versus Prospective Memory.

      1. Retrospective memory is the recalling of information that has been previously learned. This includes:

         a. Episodic

         b. Semantic

         c. Implicit

      2. Prospective memory involves remembering to do things in the future.

         a. Prospective memory tends to fail when we are:

            i. Preoccupied

            ii. Distracted

            iii. Feeling stress of time pressure.

         b. Various types of prospective memory tasks include:

            i. Habitual tasks

            ii. Event based tasks

            iii. Time based tasks

3. There is an age related decline in both retrospective and prospective memory.
4. Moods and attitudes have an effect on prospective memory.
   a. Negative emotional states impair prospective memory.

II. Processes of Memory: Processing Information in Our Most Personal Computers.
A. Psychologists and computer scientists speak of processing information.
   1. When we perceive information we must convert it into a form that can be remembered.
   2. Memory is the processes by which information is encoded, stored, and retrieved.
B. Encoding: The Memory's "Transformer".
   1. Information about the outside world reaches our senses in the form of physical and chemical stimuli.
   2. When we encode information we transform it into psychological formats that can be represented mentally.
      a. Visual code: remembering things as a picture.
      b. Acoustic code: remembering things as a sequence of sounds.
      c. Semantic code: remembering things in terms of their meaning.
C. Storage: The Memory's "Save" Function.
   1. Storage: maintaining information over time.
      a. Maintenance rehearsal: mentally repeating information.
      b. Metamemory: our awareness of the functioning of our memory.
      c. Elaborative rehearsal: elaborating or extending the semantic meaning of the what you are trying to remember.
D. Retrieval: The Memory's "Find" Function.
   1. Retrieval of stored information requires locating it and returning it to consciousness.

III. Stages of Memory: Making Sense of the Short and the Long of It.
A. Atkinson-Shiffrin model of memory:
   1. There are three stages of memory and information progresses through these stages determining how whether and how long the information will be retained.
      a. Sensory memory
      b. Short-term memory
      c. Long-term memory
B. Sensory Memory: The Flashes on the Mental Monitor.
   1. Sensory Memory is the type of memory that is first encountered by a stimulus.
      a. Vision example:
         i. Saccadic eye movements: series of eye fixations; movements which jump from one point to another about four times each second.
         ii. Memory trace: visual impression left by the stimulus.

           iii.   Held in visual sensory register.

           iv.   Research has used the whole report procedure and the partial report procedure in memory tasks.

     b.   Memory trace for visual stimuli decay within a second.

  2.   Iconic Memory

     a.   Visual stimuli are referred to as icons. The sensory register that holds icons is labeled iconic memory.

     b.   Iconic memories are accurate, photographic memories but briefly stored.

           i.   Photographic memory is technically referred to as eidetic imagery.

           ii.   Eidetic imagery: photographic memory; having the ability to store visual stimuli for remarkably long periods of time.

  3.   Iconic Memory and Saccadic Eye Movements.

     a.   Saccadic eye movements occur about four times every second.

     b.   Iconic memory holds icons for up to a second.

     c.   The combination is what allows us to perceive imagery in film as being seamless.

  4.   Echoic Memory.

     a.   Mental representations of sounds, or auditory stimuli, are called echoes.

     b.   The sensory register that holds echoes is called echoic memory.

           i.   Echoic memory can last for several seconds.

           ii.   By selectively attending to certain stimuli we sort them out from background noise.

C. Short-Term Memory: Keeping Things "In Mind".

  1.   If one focuses on a stimulus in the sensory register, they will tend to retain it in short-term memory (also referred to as working memory).

  2.   In short term memory the image tends to significantly fade after 10-12 seconds if it is not rehearsed.

  3.   To retain the information then rehearsal is needed.

  4.   The Serial-Position Effect.

     a.   The tendency to recall the first and last items in a series is known as the serial-position effect.

     b.   Primacy effect: tendency to recall the initial items in a list.

     c.   Recency effect: tendency to recall the last items in a list.

  5.   Chunking: discrete elements of information.

     a.   Seven chunks, plus or minus one or two, is a "magic" number of the amount of information a typical person can remember.

     b.   Rote learning: mechanical associative learning that takes time and repetition.

  6.   Interference in Short-Term Memory.

     a.   Prevention of rehearsal can inhibit short term memory.

     b.   Appearance of new information can displace the old information.

D. Long-Term Memory: Your Memory's "Hard Drive".

  1.   Long-term memory is the third stage of information processing.

     a.   The vast storehouse of information.

     b.   Information can be kept in the unconscious; long-term memory by the forces of repression.

  2. How Accurate Are Long-Term Memories?

     a.   Loftus notes that memories are distorted by our biases and needs.

     b.   We represent our world in the form of schemas.

     c.   Loftus and Palmer and the experiment of the car crash. Words served as diverse schemas that fostered the developed the very different ways of processing information.

E.   CONTROVERSY IN PSYCHOLOGY: Can We Trust Eyewitness Testimony?

  1. & nbsp; The words chosen by an experimenter and those chosen by a lawyer interrogating a witness have been shown to influence the reconstruction of memories.

  2. Children tend to be more suggestible witnesses than adults.

     a.   When questioned properly, young children can provide accurate and useful testimony.

  3. Hypnosis does more than amplify memories; it can also distort them

     a.   Witnesses may accept and embellish suggestions made by the hypnotist.

  4. Witnesses may pay more attention to the suspect's clothing than to more meaningful characteristics such as facial features, height and weight.

  5. Other problems with eye-witness testimony are:

     a.   Identification is less accurate when suspects belong to ethnic groups that differ from that of the witness.

     b.   Identification of suspects is confused when interrogators make misleading suggestions.

     c.   Witnesses are seen as more credible when they claim to be certain in their testimony but there is little evidence that claims of certainty are accurate.

F.   How Much Information Can Be Stored in Long-Term Memory?

     a.   For all practical purposes, long-term memory is unlimited.

     b.   The information can endure for a lifetime.

     c.   Information can become lost but not destroyed or deleted.

  2. Transferring Information from Short-Term to Long-Term Memory: Using the "Save" Function.

     a.   The more often chunks of information are rehearsed, the more likely they are to be transferred to lo ng-term memory.

     b.   Repeating information over and over to prevent it from decaying is termed maintenance rehearsal.

     c.   A more effective method is to make information more meaningful; relating information to well-known material is termed elaborative rehearsal.

  3. Levels of Processing Information.

a. Elaborative rehearsal to remember things are processing information at a deeper level than people who use maintenance rehearsal.

b. Information is remembered if processed deeply-attended to, encoded carefully, pondered, and related to things we already know. Remembering relies on how deeply we processes information.

c. Research has shown that deep processing is related to activity in the prefrontal area of the cerebral cortex.

4. Flashbulb Memories: "To Leave a Scar Upon the Cerebral Tissues"

   a. People tend to remember events that are surprising, important, and emotionally stirring. These memories are termed flashbulb memories.

      i. One factor is the distinctness of the memory.

      ii. The feelings caused by them are special.

      iii. We are likely to dwell on them and form networks of associations.

5. Organizations in Long-Term Memory.

   a. People tend to organize information according to a hierarchical structure.

      i. A hierarchy is an arrangement of items into groups or classes according to common or distinct features.

6. The Tip-of-the-Tongue-Phenomenon.

   a. The tip-of-the-tongue-phenomenon is the feeling of knowing experience. Why?

      i. Words were unfamiliar so elaborative rehearsal did not take place.

      ii. Seems to reflect incomplete learning.

      iii. Our knowledge of the topic may be incomplete, we don't know the specific answer but we know something.

7. Context-Dependent Memory: Been There, Done That?

   a. The context in which we acquire information can also play a role in retrieval.

   b. Context-dependent memories are clear in the context in which they were formed.

      i. Being in the proper context can dramatically enhance recall.

   c. Context for memory extends to language.

   d. Déjà vu: the feeling that we know this person or have been there before.

      i. Seems to occur when we are in a context similar to the one we have been in before.

8. State-Dependent Memory.

   a. State-dependent memory is an extension of context-dependent memory.

i.   We retrieve information better when we are in the physiological or emotional state that is similar to the one in which we encoded and stored the information.
   ii. There is evidence of support for this with love, anger, frustration, rage, sober or inebriated, happy, sad, and bipolar.

IV. Forgetting: Will You Remember How We Forget?
   A. Ebbinghaus and the research with nonsense syllables.
      1. Remembering should depend on simple acoustic coding and maintenance rehearsal rather than on elaborative rehearsal.
      2. This research is well suited for the measurement of forgetting.
   B. Memory Tasks Used in Measuring Forgetting.
      1. Three basic memory tasks have been used to measure forgetting:
         a. Recognition
         b. Recall
         c. Learning
      2. Recognition.
         a. Failure to recognize something we have experienced.
         b. The easiest type of memory task.
      3. Recall.
         a. Remembering information from memory without cues.
         b. Research conducted in this area used paired associates.
         c. Recall is more difficult than recognition.
      4. Relearning: Is Learning Easier the Second Time Around?
         a. We can relearn information more rapidly the second time.
         b. Ebbinghaus devised the method of savings.
            i.   Record the number of repetitions needed to learn.
            ii. Record the number of repetitions to relearn the list.
            iii. Compute the difference; called savings.
   C. Interference Theory.
      1. We may forget information in short-term and long-term memory because newly learned material interferes with it.
         a. Two types:
            i.   Retroactive
            ii. Proactive
      2. Retroactive interference: new learning interferes with the retrieval of old learning.
      3. Proactive interference: older learning interferes with the capacity to retrieve more recently learned material.
   D. Repression: Ejecting the Unwanted from Consciousness.
      1. Freud suggested that we are motivated to forget painful memories because they produce anxiety, guilt, and shame. (Repression)
         a. This is the heart of disorders such as dissociative amnesia.
         b. Stress hormones released when we experience extremes of anxiety actually heighten memory.

        c.   Repressed memories may not be ill-formed we just don't focus on them.

E. CONTROVERSY IN PSYCHOLOGY: Do People Really Recover Repressed Memories of Sexual Abuse at an Early Age, Or Are These "Memories" Implanted by Interviewers?

    1. Many recovered memories are sometime induced by therapists.

    2. Techniques used to recover memories: hypnosis and guided imagery.

F. Infantile Amnesia: Why Can't Johnny Remember?

    1. Infantile amnesia is difficulty in remembering episodes that happened prior to age 3 or so.

        a. Has little to do with the fact that the episodes occurred in the distant past.

    2. Reflects the interaction of physiological and cognitive factors.

        a. The hippocampus does not become mature until we are about 2 years of age.

        b. Cognitive factors include:

            i.   Infants are not particularly interested in remembering their past.

           ii. Infants don't weave episodes together into meaningful stories.

           iii. Infants don't make reliable use of language to symbolize their events.

        c. We are unlikely to remember episodes unless we are reminded of them from time to time as we develop.

        d. There is no evidence to suggest that early memories are systematically repressed.

G. Anterograde and Retrograde Amnesia.

    1. Anterograde amnesia is memory lapses for the period following a trauma.

        a. This memory loss has been linked to damage to the hippocampus.

        b. The case of H.M.

    2. Retrograde amnesia is memory lapses for the period before the accident.

V. The Biology of Memory: The Brain as a Living Time Machine.

A. Engrams are viewed as electrical circuits in the brain the correspond to memory traces.

B. Neural Activity and Memory: "Better Living Through Chemistry".

    1. There is reason to believe that the storage of experience requires the number of avenues of communication among brain cells to be increased.

    2. Research conducted with sea snails shows that they can be conditioned, they release more of the neurotransmitter serotonin at certain synapses.

a. As a result the transmission at the synapses becomes more efficient as trials progress. This greater efficiency is termed long-term potentiation (LTP).

3. Acetylcholine (ACh) is vital in memory formation. Low levels of ACh are connected with Alzheimer's disease.

4. Glutamate in the brain promotes conditioning.

5. Adrenaline and noradrenaline both strengthen memory when they are released into the bloodstream following learning.

6. Vasopressin facilitates memory functioning particularly working memory.

7. Estrogen and testosterone facilitate the functioning of working memory.

C. Brain Structures and Memory.

1. Hippocampus is involved in the formation of new memories.

2. Parts of memories are stored in appropriate areas of the sensory cortex.

a. Sight in the visual cortex; sounds in the auditory cortex, etc.

3. The limbic system is largely responsible for integrating these pieces of information when we recall an event.

4. The prefrontal cortex acts apparently as the executive center in memory.

5. Thalamus is involved in verbal memories.

VI. LIFE CONNECTIONS: Using the Psychology of Memory to Enhance Your Memory.

A. Psychologists have developed methods for improving memory.

B. Drill and Practice: "A, B, C, D, …"

C. Recommendations from Herrmann (1991) to remember a person's name:

1. Say the name out loud.

2. Ask the person a question, using her or his name.

3. Use the person's name as many times as you can during your conversation.

4. Write down the name when the conversation has ended.

D. Relate New Information to What Is Already Known.

1. Elaborative rehearsal.

E. Form Unusual, Exaggerated Associations.

1. It is easier to recall stimuli that stand out.

2. Create unusual associations.

F. Use the Method of Loci: Meatloaf in the Navel.

1. Method of Loci: select a series of related images and then attaché information t hat you want to remember to those images. (e.g. parts of the body).

G. Use Mediation: Find a Conceptual Bridge.

1. The method of mediation also relies on forming associations.

a. Lind two items with a third one that ties them together.

H. Use Mnemonic Devices: "Soak Her Toe"

1. Mnemonics are systems for remembering information typically using chunks of information combined into an acronym.

Chapter Eight Outline

I. **Thinking: The Most Human Aspect of Our Psychology.**
    A. Thinking may be defined as:
        1. The mental activity involved in understanding, processing, and communicating information.
        2. Thinking entails attending to information, representing it mentally, reasoning about it, and making judgments and decisions about it.
        3. Conscious, planned attempts to make sense of our world.
    B. Concepts: Building Blocks of Thinking.
        1. Concepts are mental categories used to group together:
            a. Objects
            b. Relations
            c. Events
            d. Abstractions
            e. Qualities that have common properties.
        2. Thinking has to do with categorizing new concepts and manipulating relationships among concepts.
        3. We tend to organize concepts in hierarchies.
        4. Prototypes: are examples that best match the essential features of categories. Prototypes are good examples.
            a. Simple prototypes are taught by exemplars. These include:
                i. Positive instances.
                ii. Negative instances.
        5. Overextension is overinclusion of instances in a category.
    C. Problem Solving.
        1. Approaches to Problem Solving: Getting From Here to There.
            a. Flash of insight.
            b. Finding rules.
        2. Understanding the Problem.
            a. Focus on the right information.
            b. Background knowledge helps.
            c. Successful understanding of a problem requires three features:
                i. The parts or elements of our mental representation of the problem relate to one another in a meaningful way.
                ii. The elements of our mental representations of the problem correspond to the elements of the problem in the outer world.
                iii. We have a storehouse of background knowledge that we can apply to the problem.
        3. Algorithms: is a specific procedure for solving a type of problem.
            a. Algorithms invariable lead to the solution.
            b. Systematic random search algorithm: every possible combination is examined.
        4. Heuristics: are rules of thumb that help us simplify and solve problems.

a. Heuristics do not guarantee a correct solution to a problem.
    i. Heuristics permit more rapid solutions.
b. Means-end analysis: assess the difference between our current situation and our goals and then do what we can to reduce this discrepancy.
5. An analogy is a partial similarity among things that are different in other ways.
    a. The analogy heuristic applies the solution of an earlier problem to the solution of a new one.
6. Factors That Affect Problem Solving.
    a. Three such factors:
        i. Level of expertise.
        ii. Whether you fall prey to a mental set.
        iii. Whether you develop insight into the problem.
    b. Experts solve problems more efficiently and rapidly than novices do. Expert characteristics include:
        i. They know the particular area well.
        ii. They have a good memory for the elements in the problem.
        iii. They form mental images or representations that facilitate problem solving.
        iv. They relate the problem to similar problems.
        v. They have efficient methods for problem solving.
    c. Mental Sets: is the tendency to respond to a new problem with the same approach that helped solve similar problems.
        i. Usually this makes the work easier but they can mislead us.
    d. Insight: Aha!: It seems as if pieces of information in the problem have suddenly been reorganized so that the solution leaps out at you.
    e. Incubation: standing back from the problem may allow for insight.
        i. Some mysterious process within us continues to work on it.
    f. Functional Fixedness: hinder problem solving by:
        i. Tending to think of an object in terms of its name or its familiar function.
D. Judgment and Decision Making.
    1. People make most of their decisions on the basis of limited information. They take shortcuts.
    2. Heuristics in Decision Making: If It Works, Must It Be Logical?
        a. Representative Heuristic: people make judgments about events according to the populations of events that they appear to represent.
        b. Availability heuristic: our estimates of frequency or probability are based on how easy it is to find examples of relevant events.
        c. Anchoring and Adjustment heuristics: suggest that there can be a good deal of inertia in our judgments.

          i.   We have an initial view or presumption that is an anchor.

    3.   The Framing Effect: Say That Again?

        a.   The framing effect refers to the way in which wording, or the context in which information is presented, can influence decision making.

    4.   Overconfidence: Is Your Hindsight 20-20?

        a.   Overconfidence applies to judgments.

            i.   Many people refuse to alter their judgments even in the face of statistical evidence that shows them to be flawed.

           ii.   20-20 hindsight: "we knew it all along".

        b.   There are several reasons for overconfidence:

            i.   We tend to be unaware of how flimsy our assumptions may be.

           ii.   We tend to focus on examples that confirm our judgments and ignore those that do not.

          iii.   Because our working memories have limited space, we tend to forget information that runs counter to our judgments.

          iv.   We work to bring about the events we believe n, so they sometimes become self-fulfilling prophecies.

            v.   Even when people are told that they tend to be overconfident in their decisions, they usually ignore this information.

II. Language: "Of Shoes and Ships and Sealing Wax,… and Whether Pigs Have Wings".

    A.   Language is the communication of thoughts and feelings by means of symbols that are arranged to rules of grammar.

        1.   In recent years our exclusive claim to language has also been questioned.

        2.   Language is one of the human assets that has enabled us to survive and prosper.

        3.   True language is distinguished from the communication systems of lower animals by properties such as semanticity, infinite creativity, and displacement.

           a.   p; Semanticity: refers to the fact that the sounds of a language have meaning.

           b.   Infinite creativity: refers to the capacity to create rather than imitate sentences.

           c.   Displacement is the capacity to communicate information about events and objects in another time or place.

    B.   Language Development: The Two-Year Explosion.

        1.   Prelinguistic vocalizations include crying, cooing, and babbling.

           a.   These are inborn.

        2.   Children tend to utter their first word at about 1 year of age.

           a.   At about 18 months, children are producing a couple dozen words.

        3.   Development of Grammar.

           a.   Holophrases: single words that can express complex meanings.

          i.   Holophrases are often augmented with gestures, intonations, and reinforcers.

    b.   Toward the end of the second year children begin to speak two-word sentences termed telegraphic speech.

          i.   Telegraphic speech is similar to telegrams where the unnecessary words are cut out.

4.   Overregularization.

    a.   Grammatical rules for forming the past tense and plurals.

    b.   The tendency to regularize the irregular is what is meant by overregularization.

    c.   Overregularization reflects knowledge of grammar not faulty language development.

    d. By the age of 6, children's vocabularies have expanded to 10,000 words. By 7 to 9, most children realize that words can have more than one meaning.

C. Genetic and Environmental Factors In Language Development.

1.   Language development reflects the interactions between the influences of heredity (nature) and the environment (nurture).

2.   Learning theorists see language developing according to imitation and reinforcement. Parents serve as models.

    a.   Learning theory cannot account for the unchanging sequence of language development and the spurts in children's language acquisition.

3.   Nativist theory of language hold that language development is innate or inborn.

    a.   Nature – cause children to attend to and acquire language in certain ways.

4.   Psycholinguistic theory: language acquisition involves the interaction of environmental influences such as exposure to parental speech and reinforcement and an inborn tendency to acquire language.

5.   Language acquisition device (LAD) prepares the nervous system to learn grammar.

    a.   Universal grammar: an underlying set of rules for turning ideas into sentences.

D. Language and Thinking.

1.   Can a person think without using language?

2.   Jean Piaget believed that language reflects knowledge of the world but that much knowledge can be acquired without language.

E. The Linguistic-Relativity Hypothesis.

1.   The linguistic-relativity hypothesis: language structures the way we percei ve the world.

    a.   Speakers of various languages conceptualize the world in different ways. (e.g. we have one word for camel; Arabs have more than 250).

2.   Infants display considerable intelligence before they have learned to speak.

III. Intelligence: The Most Controversial Concept on Psychology.

A. Definitions of intelligence include:
1. Intelligence permits us to adapt to conditions and to challenge our physical limitations.
2. Intelligence is broadly thought of as the underlying ability to understand the world and cope with its challenges.
   a. Making things possible.
   b. Profit from experience.
3. Intelligence allows people to:
   a. Think.
   b. Understand complex ideas.
   c. Reason.
   d. Solve problems.
   e. Learn from experience.
   f. Adapt to the environment.

B. Theories of Intelligence.
1. Factor theories argue that intelligence is made up of a number of mental abilities ranging from one to hundreds.
2. Charles Spearman suggested that intelligence has an underlying factor called "g" for general intelligence. "g" is broad reasoning and problem solving skills.
   a. Some people are relatively superior in some areas. This would be an "s" factor for specific abilities.
   b. Spearman used factor analysis, a statistical technique, to test his views.
3. Louis Thurstone used factor analysis and suggested eight specific factors which he labeled primary mental abilities.
   a. Visual and spatial abilities.
   b. Perceptual speed.
   c. Numerical ability.
   d. Verbal meaning.
   e. Memory.
   f. Word Fluency.
   g. Deductive reasoning.
   h. Inductive reasoning.
4. J.P. Guilford expanded the number of factors to hundreds.
5. The Theory of Multiple Intelligences.
   a. Howard Gardner proposed that intelligence is comprised of different kinds of intelligences.
   b. He proposed that each intelligence has its neurological base in a different area of the brain.
   c. Critics of Gardner's view wonder if special talents really are intelligences or special talents.
6. The Triarchic Theory of Intelligence.

     a.   Robert Sternberg proposed an intelligence with three types: analytical, creative, and practical.
         i.   Analytical intelligence is what we generally thing of as academic ability.
         ii.   Creative intelligence is ability to cope with novel situations and to profit from experience.
         iii. Practical intelligence is "street smarts" that enable people to adapt to the demands of their environment.

C. CONTROVERSY IN PSYCHOLOGY: Is "Emotional Intelligence" a form of intelligence? Should it be taught in schools?
  1. Social and emotional skills are a form of intelligence.
     a.   These are similar to Gardner's proposed intrapersonal and interpersonal skills.
  2. Should these be taught in schools? There are only so many hours in a day.
  3. Critics state that these areas are important for determining life outcomes but there is nothing to gain by calling them intelligences.

D. Creativity and Intelligence.
  1. Creativity may be defined as the ability to do things that are novel and useful. Creative people share characteristics that include:
     a.   They take chances.
     b.   They refuse to accept limitations.
     c.   They appreciate art and music.
     d.   They use materials around them to make unique things.
     e.   They challenge social norms.
     f.   They take unpopular stands.
     g.   They examine ideas that other people accept at face value.
  2. Two types of thinking:
     a.   Convergent thinking: thought is limited to present facts.
     b.   Divergent thinking: the problem solver associates freely to the elements of the problem.
     c.   Problem solving can involve both kinds of thinking.
  3. Research indicates that relationships between intelligence test scores and standard measures of creativity is only moderate.

E. The Measurement of Intelligence.
  1. The Stanford-Binet Intelligence Scale.
     a.   French public school system wanted to identify children who were unlikely to benefit from regular classroom instruction.
     b.   In 1905 the Binet-Simon scale was created.
     c.   The Binet-Simon scale yielded a score called a mental age (MA). The MA indicates the intellectual level at which the child is functioning.
     d.   Louis Terman, working at Stanford University, adapted the test for use with children in the U.S. The test came to be known as the Stanford-Binet Intelligence Scale (SBIS).
         i.   The test was used with children aged 2 to 16.

ii. The SBIS yielded an intelligence quotient (IQ) rather than a mental age. IQ reflects the relationship between a child's mental age and their actual chronological age.

iii. IQ = mental age (MA) / chronological age (CA) X 100.

e. Today IQ scores are derived by comparing results to those of other people of the same age.

2. The Wechsler Scales.

a. David Wechsler developed a series of scales where each subtest measures a different intellectual task.

b. These scales can be grouped into:

i. Verbal tasks: require knowledge of verbal concepts.

ii. Performance tasks: require familiarity with spatial-relations concepts.

c. Wechseler introduced the concept of the deviation IQ. He based IQ on how a person's answers compared with those attained by people in the same age group. The average level is defined as an IQ score of 100.

i. IQ scores were distributed so that the middle 50% of them were defined as the broad average range of 90 to 110.

3. Group Tests.

a. Group tests were first developed during World War I for use with large numbers of people in schools and the armed forces.

b. Numbers alone cannot adequately reflect children's abilities and talents.

F. Extremes of Intelligences.

1. IQ scores below 70 are generally labeled as intellectually deficient.

2. IQ scores of 130 or above are usually labeled as gifted.

3. Mental Retardation.

a. According to the American Association on Mental Retardation, mental retardation refers to substantial limitations in present functioning characterized by significantly sub-average intellectual functioning existing concurrently with related limitations in two or more of the following applicable adaptive skill areas:

i. Communication.

ii. Self care.

iii. Home living.

iv. Social skills.

v. Community use.

vi. Self direction.

vii. Health and safety.

viii. Functional academics.

ix. Leisure and work.

b. Most children who are retarded are mildly retarded. They are likely to be taught in regular classrooms and are capable of adjusting to the demands of society at large.

       i.   Children with Down syndrome are most likely to fall within the moderately retarded range. They can learn to speak; to dress, feed and clean themselves.

      ii.   Severely and profoundly retarded children may not acquire speech and self-help skills and are likely to remain highly dependent on others throughout their lives.

   c.   Causes of mental retardation include:

       i.   Chromosomal abnormalities such as Down syndrome.

      ii.   Genetic disorders such as phenylketonuria.

     iii.   Brain damage.

4.   Giftedness.

   a.   Children who have outstanding abilities, are capable of high performance in a specific academic area such as language arts or mathematics, or who show creativity or leadership, or have talent in physical activities.

   b.   Terman's study of geniuses:

       i.   Studied children with IQ scores above 135; average score was 150.

      ii.   As a group they were extremely successful in terms of level of education, socioeconomic status, and creativity.

     iii.   They were well adjusted with rates of psychological disorders and suicide below the national average.

G. The Testing Controversy.

   1.   A survey of psychologists in 1987 found that most consider intelligence tests to be culturally biased against African Americans and member so the lower classes.

   2.   Intelligence tests measure traits that are required in developed, high-tech societies.

   3.   The tests seem to reflect middle-class European American culture.

H. Determinants of Intelligence: Where Does Intelligence Come From?

   1.   One controversial topic in psychology is the role that nature and nurture play in intellectual functioning.

   2.   Genetic Influences on Intelligence.

     a.   Research includes kinship studies, twin studies and adoptee studies.

     b.   IQ scores of identical twins are more alike than scores for any other pairs.

     c.   All in all, studies generally suggest that the heritability of intelligence is between 40% and 60%.&n bsp;

   3.   Environmental Influences on Intelligence.

     a.   Research methods include: manipulation of the testing situation, observation of the role of the home environment, and the evaluation of the effects of educational programs.

     b.   The Home Environment and Style of Parenting.

       i.   Children of mothers who are emotionally and verbally responsive, furnish appropriate play materials, are involved

with their children, encourage independence, and provide varied daily experiences during the early years obtain higher IQ scores later on.
  ii. Organization and safety in the home have also been linked to higher IQs and achievement test scores at later ages.
I. CONTROVERSY IN PSYCHOLOGY: The Mozart Effect.
  1. Listening to and studying music may enhance spatial reasoning.
   a. Claims that listening to 10 minutes of Mozart's Piano Sonata K 448 enhanced college students' scores on spatial reasoning tasks.
   b. Musical training develops the neural firing patterns used in spatial reasoning.
J. Education.
  1. Education contributes to intelligence.
   a. Head Start programs enhance IQ scores, achievement scores and academic skills of disadvantaged children.
   b. Children who have been in school longer obtain higher IQ scores.
    i. IQ scores tend to decrease during summer vacations.
K. Adoptee Studies.
  1. Adoptee studies suggest a genetic influence on intelligence. But they also suggest a role for environmental influence.
  2. Intellectual functioning would appear to reflect the interaction of genetic physical, personal and sociocultural.
L. Ethnicity and Intelligence: A Concluding Note.
  1. Forty-five percent of a sample of 1,020 psychologists and educational specialists believe that differences in IQ between African Americans and European Americans are a product of both genetic and environmental variation.
  2. Parents are most effective when they believe that their efforts will improve their children's functioning.

IV. LIFE CONNECTION: Bilingualism and Bilingual Education – Making Connections or Building Walls?
A. Most people throughout the world speak two or more languages.
  1. For more than 30 million people in the U.S. English is a second language.
B. Bilingualism and Intellectual Development.
  1. Most linguists consider it advantageous for children to be bilingual.
   a. Expands children's awareness of different cultures.
   b. Broadens their perspectives.
   c. Shown to increase children's expertise in their first language.
C. Bilingual Education.
  1. Total Immersion: sink-or-swim method.
  2. Bilingual education legislation requires that non-English speaking children be given the chance to study in their own language to smooth the transition to life i n the U.S.

a. Transitional programs shoot children into regular English speaking classrooms as quickly as possible.
b. Maintenance method programs require rapid mastery of English.
c. Two-way immersion encourages native-born American Cildren to achieve fluency in a foreign language at the same time immigrant children are learning English.

V. FEATURES: Diversity: Ebonics.

A. Williams, a psychologist, developed a test that was culturally sensitive to African American children called the Black Intelligence Test of Cultural Homogeneity (BITCH).
B. Ebonics derives from the word ebony and phonics.
   1. Was previously called Black English or Black Dialect.
   2. The Oakland, California School Board recognized Ebonics as the primary language of African American students.
      a. There are differences between Ebonics and standard English in the use of verbs.
      b. In this case many African Americans are in effect bilingual.

VI. DIVERSITY: Socioeconomic and Ethnic Differences in Intelligence.

A. Lower-class U.S. children obtain IQ scores 10 to 15 points lower than those obtained by middle and upper class children.
B. African American children tend to obtain IQ scores 15 points lower than those obtained by European American age-mates.
   1. Most psychologists believe that ethnic differences such as these reflect cultural attitudes toward education rather than inborn racial differences.
   2. &nbs p; Steinberg claims that parental encouragement, supervision, and peer support for academic achievement partially explain the superior performance of European Americans and Asian Americans.

Chapter Nine Outline

I. **The Psychology of Motivation: The Whys of Why.**
  A. The psychology of motivation concerns the whys of behavior.
    1. Motives are hypothetical states that activate behavior towards goals.
       a. Motives may take the form of:
          i. Needs
          ii. Drives
          iii. Incentives
       b. Needs come in two types: physiological and psychological.
          i. Physiological are needs necessary for survival (e.g. oxygen, food, etc.)
          ii. Psychological include needs for achievement, power, self-esteem, etc.)
       c. Physiological and psychological needs differ in two ways:
          i. Psychological needs are not necessarily based on deprivation.
          ii. Psychological needs may be acquired through experience.
       d. Needs give rise to drives which arouse us to action.
       e. Incentives: are objects, persons, or situations viewed as capable of satisfying a need or as desirable for its own sake.

II. **Theories of Motivation: Which Why is Which?**
  A. Psychologists do not agree about the precise nature of motivation.
  B. The Evolutionary Perspective: The Fish, the Spiders, and the Bees.
    1. Animals are naturally prewired to respond to certain stimuli in certain ways.
    2. Species-specific behaviors are called instincts or fixed action patterns.
       a. Instincts are genetically transmitted from generation to generation.
       b. William James and William McDougal argued that humans have instincts.
          i. Love, sympathy, modesty, hunger, sex, self assertion.
  C. Drive Reductionism and Homeostasis: "Steady, Steady..."
    1. Primary drives trigger arousal (tension) and activate behavior. We engage in behaviors that reduce the tension.
    2. Acquired drives are acquired through experience.
    3. Homeostasis is a steady state. People are motivated to maintain a steady state.
  D. The Search for Stimulation: Is Downtime a Downer?
    1. Stimulus motives: the organism is motivated to increase stimulation not reduce a drive.
       a. Lower animals and humans appear to be motivated to seek novel stimulation.
       b. Stimulus motivation provides an evolutionary advantage. Animals that are active and motivated to learn about their environment are more likely to survive.

E. Humanistic Theory: "I've Got to Be Me"?
   1. Abraham Maslow believed that people are motivated by the conscious desire for personal growth.
      a. Self-actualization: self initiated striving to become whatever we believe we are capable of being.
      b. Maslow's hierarchy of needs ranges from physiological needs such as hunger and thirst through self actualization.
      c. Critics argue that there is too much individual variation for the hierarchy of motives to apply to everyone.
F. Cognitive Dissonance Theory: "I Think, Therefore I Am....Consistent"?
   1. People seek consistency in their behaviors and attitudes. Consistency helps make the world seem predictable.
   2. Attitude-discrepant behavior is behavior that runs counter to what people actually thought.
   3. Effort justification or justifying efforts (behavior) in an attempt for consistency.

III. Hunger: Do You Go by "Tummy-Time"?
   A. Importance of food.
      1. Necessary for survival.
      2. Symbol of family togetherness and caring.
      3. We associate food with the nurturance of the parent-child relationship.
   B. Biological Influences on Hunger.
      1. Satiety or satisfaction.
      2. Hunger pangs are stomach contractions.
      3. Ventromedial nucleus of the hypothalamus. The stop eating center of the brain. Research with rats has shown that:

         a. When destroyed the rat continues to eat (becomes hyperphagic).

         b. When stimulated the rat stops eating.
      4. Lateral hypothalamus is the start eating center of the brain.
         a. When destroyed the rat may stop eating altogether (aphagic).
         b. When stimulated the rat starts to eat.
   C. Psychological Influences of Hunger.
      1. Other factors that influence hunger include the aroma of food, because a person feels anxious or depressed, or bored.

IV. Sexual Motivation: The Battle Between Culture and Nature?
   A. Sexual motivation may be natural but is strongly influenced by religious, moral beliefs, cultural tradition, folklore and superstition.
      1. What is considered "normal" depends on the society in which one lives.
   B. Surveys of Sexual Behavior.
      1. Kinsey reports: interviews with 5,300 males and 5,940 females in the U.S. between 1938 and 1949.

      a.   There is no way of knowing whether or not Kinsey's results accurately mirrored general American sexual behavior at the time.

      b.   Did find a positive link between level of education and premarital sex.

  2. The National Health and Social Life Survey: interviewed 3,432 people and considered subject's gender, level of education, religion and ethnicity.

      a.   Males report having a higher number of sex partners.

      b.   Most people in the U.S. limit the number of sexual partners to a few.

      c.   Level of education is connected with sexual behavior. Education is more liberating.

      d.   European and African Americans have the highest number of sex partners.

  3. Hormones and Sexual Motivation: Adding Fuel to the Fire.

      a.   Testosterone replacement therapy increases sex drive.

      b.   Sex drive in women is also connected with testosterone levels.

      c.   Sex hormones have activating effects: they affect the sex drive and promote sexual response.

      d.   Sex hormones also have organizing effects that is they motivate lower animals toward masculine or feminine mating patterns.

C. CONTROVERSY IN PSYCHOLOGY: Is the human sex drive affected by pheromones?

  1. Pheromones are odorless chemicals that are detected through a "sixth sense" the vomeronasal organ (VNO).

      a.   There is a debate about whether or not the VNO works.

      b.   It has not been conclusively shown that pheromones directly affect the behavior of people.

      c.   Steroids suspected of being pheromones enhanced the moods of women and reduced feelings of nervousness and tension but not in men.

         i.   This steroid is related to estrogen.

      d.   The substances do not release sexual fixed action patterns (instincts).

D. Sexual Orientation: Which Way Is Love?

  1. Heterosexual orientation: sexual attraction to people of the other sex.

  2. Homosexual orientation: attracted to and interested in forming romantic relationships with people of their own sex.

      a.   Males are referred to as gay males.

      b.   Females are referred to as lesbians.

      c.   Bisexual people are attracted to both females and males.

  3. Sexual orientation differs from sexual activity.

  4. The Origins of Sexual Orientation.

      a.   3% of males and 2% of females in the U.S. identify themselves as being gay.

b. Freudian theory attributes sexual orientation to identification with male or female figures.
c. Learning theorists look for roles of factors such as reinforcement and observational learning.
d. Some evidence for genetic factors.
    i. 22% of the brothers of gay men were gay or bisexual.
    ii. 52% of identical twins were both gay.
e. Sexual orientation has not been reliably linked with adolescent or adult levels of sex hormones.
f. Much about the development of sexual orientation remains speculative.

E. Sexual Response.
1. Sexual response cycle. The changes that occur in the body of men and women when they become sexually aroused.
    a. Vasocongestion is swelling of the genital tissues with blood.
    b. Myotonia is muscle tension; causes facial grimaces, spasms in the hands and feet and the spasm of orgasm.
    c. Excitement Phase:
        i. Vasocongestion causes erection in men and swells the clitoris and flattens and spreads the vaginal lips.
        ii. Nipples become erect in men and women.
        iii. Heart rate and blood pressure increase.
    d. Plateau Phase:
        i. Testes are elevated into position for ejaculation.
        ii. Vasocongestion swells the outer part of the vagina opening in preparation for grasping the penis. The clitoris withdraws beneath the clitoral hood and shortens.
        iii. Breathing becomes rapid, heart rate increases to 100-160 beats per minute. Blood pressure continues to rise.
    e. Orgasmic Phase:
        i. Muscle contractions propel the ejaculate out of the body.
        ii. Orgasm in females is manifested by 3 to 15 contractions of the pelvic muscles that surround the vaginal barrel.
        iii. Release of sexual tension in males and females.
        iv. Blood pressure and heart rate reach a peak; 180 times per minute.
    f. Resolution Phase:
        i. The body returns to its unaroused state.
        ii. Feelings of relaxation and satisfaction.
        iii. Men enter a refractory period during which they cannot experience another orgasm or ejaculate.
        iv. Women do not undergo a refractory period.

V. Aggression: Of Australopithecines, Humans, Robins, and Testosterone.
A. Australopithecines are early humanoids. More than 500,000 years ago.
1. Not a direct ancestor of humans.

2. Evidence that they did have murder.
B. Explanations for Aggression:
1. Social deprivation and inequality.
2. Act aggressively to establish and defend land (territory).
   a. Killer instinct to establish and defend territory.
C. CONTROVERSY IN PSYCHOLOGY: Is Aggression Natural?
1. The evolutionary view is that aggression is natural.
2. Even if it is natural, intelligence is also a key to survival. The capacity to outwit other species may be more important.
D. Biology, Chemistry, and Aggression.
1. Instinctive aggressive reactions in lower animals may be automatic.
2. Chemistry:
   a. Testosterone appears to affect the tendencies to dominate and control other people.
E. Psychological Aspects of Aggression.
1. Psychodynamic Theory and Aggression.
   a. Freud believed that aggression is natural and instinctive.
      i. Reactions to the frustrations of daily life.
      ii. Steam engine analogy; by holding in steam rather than venting it we set the stage for future explosions.
F. CONTROVERSY IN PSYCHOLOGY: The Catharsis Controversy.
1. Venting of aggressive impulses is termed catharsis. This is a safety valve.
   a. Possibly leading to pleasant reductions in tension, though some research indicates that it may encourage more aggression later.

2. Cognitive Psychology and Aggression.
   a. Behavior is influenced by our values, by how we interpret situations, and by choice.
   b. Aggression is not automatic: people decide.
3. Learning and Aggression.
   a. Learning is acquired through reinforcement thus reinforced aggression is more likely to be repeated.
   b. Aggressive skills are mainly acquired by the observation of other people.
G. Situational Factors and Aggression.
1. Situational factors can contribute to aggression.
   a. In mobs people may experience deindividuation which is a state of reduced self awareness.
      i. This includes anonymity, sharing of responsibility (diffusion of responsibility), high level of emotional arousal, and a focus on the group's norms.
   b. Environmental factors leading to aggressive behavior include:
      i. Bad smelling pollutants.
      ii. Extreme noise.
      iii. Extreme heat.

VI. Achievement Motivation: "Just Do It".

A. Assessment of Motivation.
1. Henry Murray developed the Thematic Apperception Test (TAT).
   a. TAT contains cards with pictures and drawings that are subject to various interpretations.
   b. Subjects are to construct stories about the picture.
B. What Flavor is Your Achievement Motivation?
1. People with high motivation:
   a. Earn higher grades.
   b. Likely to earn higher salaries and be promoted.
   c. Better at math.
2. Different Forces that drive motivation:
   a. &nbs p; Tangible rewards.
   b. Performance goals are usually met through extrinsic rewards.
   c. Learning goals usually lead to intrinsic rewards.

VII. Emotion: Adding Color to Life.

A. Emotions are feeling states with physiological, cognitive, and behavioral components.
1. Arousal of the autonomic nervous system.
   a. Sympathetic nervous system: rapid heartbeat, breathing, sweating, muscle tension.
2. Behavioral tendencies occur with emotions. For example fear leads to avoidance or escape and anger may lead to "pay back" behaviors.
3. Parasympathetic nervous system arousal can also occur. Joy, grief, jealousy, disgust, etc. all have cognitive, physiological, and behavioral components.
B. The Expression of Emotions.
1. Expression of many emotions may be universal. Certain facial expressions suggest the same emotions in all people.
   a. Smiling is a universal sign of friendliness and approval.
C. The Facial-Feedback Hypothesis: Does Smiling Make You Happy?
1. The Facial-Feedback Hypothesis argues that facial expressions can also affect our emotional state.
   a. Inducing people to smile leads them to report more positive feelings.
   b. When induced to frown subjects rate cartoons as more aggressive.
D. Theories of Emotions: "How Do You Feel?"
1. Various perspectives.
   a. Some psychologists believe that the body takes precedence over the mind.
   b. Cognitive processes may determine the emotional response.
   c. Some psychologists state a combination of arousal and thoughts.
2. James-Lange Theory.

a.   Our emotions follow rather than cause our behavioral response to events.

b.   We become angry because we are acting aggressively.

c.   We may be able to change our feelings by changing our behavior.

3.   Cannon-Bard Theory.

a.   An event might simultaneously trigger bodily responses and the experience of emotion.

b.   Emotions accompany bodily responses.

4.   Theory of Cognitive Appraisal (Schachter and Singer)

a.   The label we give to an emotion depends on our cognitive appraisal of the situation.

b.   Happiness and anger are different emotions. Schachter and Singer suggest that the physiological difference between the two is small so the different views of the situation, the label that people put on the event, is what is important.

5.   Evaluation.

a.   All three theories have aspects of correctness but none fully explain emotions.

VIII.   LIFE CONNECTIONS: Obesity and Eating Disorders: This Meal Is Too Big; This Meal Is Too Little – Can You Ever Get It Just Right?

A.   Obesity-A Serious and Pervasive Problem.

1.   Facts about obesity:

a.   More than six out of ten American adults are overweight.

b.   Problems associated with unhealthy weight are on the upswing.

c.   More than 80% of African American women age 40 or above are overweight.

d.   Americans eat more than a total of 800 billion calories each day (200 billion calories more than they need to maintain their weights). The extra calories could feed the nation of Germany.

e.   About 300,000 Americans die each year because of health problems related to excess weight.

f.   Weight control for most people is elusive.

B.   Origins of Obesity.

1.   Biological side points to the influence of heredity.

a.   Obesity runs in families.

b.   Set point: the point at which the hunger drive kicks in because of fat deficiency in cells.

c.   Fatty tissue also metabolizes food more slowly than muscle does.

d.   Dieting slows down the metabolic rate thus making it more difficult to lose weight.

C.   The Skinny on Weight Control.

1.   Shedding excess pounds lowers the risk of health problems such as diabetes and h eart disease.

2.   The most effective weight control programs involve:

a. Improving nutritional knowledge.
b. Decreasing caloric intake.
c. Exercising.
d. Changing eating habits.
e. Eating more fresh fruits and vegetables.
f. Cutting down on butter, margarine, oils, and sugar.
g. Strategies include:
    i. Establishing calorie intake goals.
    ii. Substitute low calorie foods.
    iii. Take a 5-minute break between helpings.
    iv. Avoid temptations.
    v. Exercise
    vi. Reward yourself but not with food.
    vii. Use imagery.
    viii. Mentally walk through various scenarios.
    ix. Above all if you slip don't blow it out of proportion.

D. Anorexia Nervosa and Bulimia Nervosa.
  1. Anorexia Nervosa.
    a. Anorexia Nervosa is a life threatening eating disorder characterized by:
        i. Extreme fear of being too heavy.
        ii. Dramatic weight loss.
        iii. Distorted body image.
        iv. Resistance to eating enough to maintain a healthy weight.
    b. Afflicts:
        i. Women during adolescence and young adulthood.
        ii. European American females of higher socioeconomic status.
        iii. Increase in numbers in recent years.
        iv. 6 to 1 gender ratio.
    c. Risks:
        i. Mortality rate is approximately 5%.
        ii. Osteoporosis.
  2. Bulimia Nervosa.
    a. Bulimia Nervosa is characterized by recurrent cycles of binging and purging.
        i. Purging can include vomiting, strict dieting, fasting, laxatives, and prolonged exercise.

E. Origins of Eating Disorders.
  1. Psychoanalysts: coping with sexual fear, regressing to life prior to puberty.
    a. The family environment is negative.
        i.< span style="font:7.0pt "Times New Roman""> Typically a history of child abuse.
    b. Exposure to high parental expectations.
  2. Sociocultural features.
    a. Slimness is idealized.

i.   BMI lower than 18.5 is malnourished. Recent Miss Americas come in at a BMI near 17.

    b.   Tend to run in families.

        i.   Genetic factors might not directly cause eating disorders but are likely to involve obsessionistic and perfectionistic personality traits.

F.   Treatment and Prevention of Eating Disorders.

    1.   Characteristics:

        a.   Eating disorders can lead to serious health problems and can be life threatening.

        b.   Denial is a key feature.

    2.   Treatments.

        a.   Antidepressants.

        b.   Family Therapy.

        c.   Cognitive-behavioral Therapy.

IX. A CLOSER LOOK: Cross Cultural Aspects of Aggression

A.   Cultural Characteristics.

    1.   Stereotype of aggressive male is not universal.

        a.   ; Likely that people arrive at consensus as to what proper behavior is and teach their children accordingly.

X. A CLOSER LOOK: "Is Evvvvrybody Happy?" An Excursion Into Positive Psychology.

A.   Positive Psychology deals with positive emotions such as happiness and love.

B.   Statistics of those who are happy.

    1.   Majority of people in developed nations are satisfied with their lives.

    2.   Happiness tends to run in families.

    3.   People tend to be happier when they live in affluent societies and earn decent incomes.

    4.   Money does not make people happy but when we have enough money at least we don't have to worry about money.

    5.   More educated people tend to be happier.

    6.   People who are married are happier.

    7.   People who have a social support are happier.

    8.   Happy people are more open to new experiences and are more willing to risk.

    9.   Religious people are happier.

    10. Happiness tends to be accompanied by optimism.

C.   "Come On! Get Happy!" A Possible or Impossible Dream?

    1.   Suggestions to be happy include:

        a.   Take advantage of your education to develop skills so that you can be free from want.

        b.   Do not le t the fact that other people have more impair your ability to appreciate what you have.

      c.   Value friendships and other social relationships.

      d.   Think about the meaning of your life and make your life more meaningful.

      e.   Consider whether you blame yourself too much when things go wrong.

      f.   Consider if you are generally optimistic or pessimistic about your future.

XI. A CLOSER LOOK: Just What Do Lie Detectors Detect?

  A.   Lying.

     1.   Survey by the New York Times found that 60% of American adults believe that it is sometimes necessary to lie, especially to protect people's feelings.

     2.   Body Reactions to Lying:

       a.   Facial expressions often offer clues to deceit.

       b.   Sympathetic arousal symptoms include dry mouth (lack of saliva).

     3.   Lie detector tests (Polygraphs) monitor sympathetic arousal.

       a.   Indicators include:

         i.   Heart rate.

         ii.   Blood pressure.

         iii.   Respiration rate.

         iv.   Electrodermal response (sweating).

       b.   American Polygraph Association claims that polygraphs are 85-95% accurate.

         i.   Factors that influence accuracy are tense muscles, drugs, previous experience with the test.

       c.   Research on psychologists opinion of accuracy indicate that most think it is not theoretically sound and should not be used in a court of law.

Chapter Ten Outline

I. **Health Psychology.**
   A. Health Psychology studies the relationship between psychological factors and the prevention and treatment of physical health problems.
      1. Psychological factors such as stress, behavior patterns and attitudes can lead to or aggravate illness.
      2. People can cope with stress.
      3. Stress and pathogens interact to influence the immune system.
      4. People decide whether or not to seek health care.
      5. Psychological forms of intervention can contribute to physical health.

II. **Stress: Presses, Pushes, and Pulls.**
   A. Stress is the demand made on an organism to adapt, cope, or adjust.
      1. Some stress is healthful (eustress).
      2. Intense of prolonged stress can harm the body.

III. **Sources of Stress: Don't Hassle Me? (Right)**
   A. Daily Hassles-The Stress of Everyday Life.
      1. Daily hassles are regularly occurring conditions and experiences that can threaten or harm our well-being.
      2. Daily hassles and uplifts can be grouped as follows:
         a. Household hassles.
         b. Health hassles.
         c. Time-pressure hassles.
         d. Inner concern hassles.
         e. Environmental hassles.
         f. Financial responsibility hassles.
         g. Work hassles.
         h. Future security hassles.
      3. These hassles are linked to psychological variables such as nervousness, worrying, inability to get started, feelings of sadness, and feelings of loneliness.
   B. Life Changes-Variety May Be the Very Spice of Life, But Does Too Much Spice Leave an Ill Taste?
      1. Life changes require adjustment. Even positive ones can lead to headaches, high blood pressure, and other health problems.
      2. Life changes differ from daily hassles in two key ways:
         a. Many life changes are positive and desirable. Hassles are negative.
         b. Hassles occur regularly. Life changes occur at irregular intervals.
            i. Example of life change: death of a spouse is considered the most stressful life change.
      3. Hassles, Life Changes, and Health Problems.

a. Hassles and life changes can predict health problems such as heart disease, cancer and athletic injuries.

b. Holmes and Rahe (1967) researched this area a nd developed a scale to measure a person's life change units.

C. CONTOVERSY IN PSYCHOLOGY: Just How Are Daily Hassles and Life Changes Connected With Health Problems?

1. It may appear obvious that hassles and life changes should cause health problems. But some researchers are not convinced that the causal connections are there.

   a. Correlational evidence.

   b. Positive versus negative life changes.

   c. Personality differences.

   d. Cognitive appraisal.

2. Optimism also helps people cope with the effects of stress.

D. Conflict-Darned If You Do, Darned If You Don't.

1. Conflict is the feeling of being pulled in two or more directions by opposing motives.

2. Conflict is frustrating and stressful.

3. There are four types of conflicts:

   a. Approach-approach

   b. Avoidance-avoidance

   c. Approach-avoidance

   d. Multiple approach-avoidance

4. Approach-approach conflict.

   a. The least stressful type.

   b. Each of two goals is desirable and both are within reach.

5. Avoidance-avoidance conflict.

   a. More stressful.

   b. A person is motivated to avoid each of two negative goals. Avoiding one of them requires approaching the other.

6. Approach-avoidance conflict.

   a. The same goal produces both approach and avoidance motives.

      i. Pluses and minuses, good points and bad points.

7. Multiple approach-avoidance conflict.

   a. Each of several alternative courses of action has pluses and minuses.

      i. Decision making can also be stressful especially when there is no clear correct choice.

E. Irrational Beliefs: Ten Doorways to Distress.

1. Ellis notes that our beliefs about events as well as the events themselves can be stressors.

2. Ellis's A-B-C approach.

   a. A is the activating event.

   b. C is the consequence.

   c. B is the belief.

    i. If the belief of someone who loses a job is to catastrophize the extent of the loss, then anxiety and depression is more likely.
   d. Ellis proposes that many of us carry with us irrational beliefs; doorways to distress.
  F. The Type A Behavior Pattern-Burning Out From Within.
   1. Type A people are:
    a. Highly driven
    b. Competitive
    c. Impatient
    d. Aggressive
    e. Feel rushed and under pressure
    f. Find it difficult to give up control or power
    g. They hold to the irrational belief that they must be perfectly competent and achieving in everything they undertake.
   2. Type B people in contrast are:
    a. Relaxed
    b. More focused on the quality of life
    c. Less ambitious and less impatient

IV. Psychological Moderators of Stress.
  A. Psychological factors can influence or moderate the effects of stress.
  B. Self-efficacy Expectations: "The Little Engine That Could".
   1. Self-efficacy expectations affect our ability to withstand stress.
    a. High self-efficacy expectations are accompanied by relatively lower levels of adrenaline and noradrenaline in the bloodstream.
   2. People who are self-confident are less prone to be disturbed by adverse events.
  C. Psychological Hardiness-Tough Enough?
   1. Psychological hardiness also helps people resist stress.
   2. Characteristics include:
    a. High in commitment.
    b. High in challenge.
    c. High in perceived control.
     i. Hardy people are high in internal locus of control.
    d. Hardy people are more resistant to stress because they choose to fact it.
  D. Sense of Humor: "A Merry Heart Doeth Good Like a Medicine".
   1. Feelings of happiness may have beneficial effects on the immune system.
   2. Humor can moderate the effects of stress.
    a. Laughter stimulates the output of endorphins.
   3. There is a significant relationship between negative life events and stress scores.
  E. Predictability and Control: "If I Can Stop the Roller Coaster, I Don't Want to Get Off".
   1. The ability to predict a stressor apparently moderates its impact.

a. Control and even the illusion of control can moderate impact.
b. Internals: people who wish to exercise control over their situations.
c. Externals: people who do not wish to exercise control over their situations.

F. Social Support: On Being In It Together.
1. Social support also seems to act as a buffer against the effects of stress.
2. Sources of social support include:
   a. Emotional concern.
   b. Instrumental aid.
   c. Information.
   d. Appraisal.
   e. Socializing.

V. Stress and the Body: The War Within.

A. The General Adaptation Syndrome.
1. The general adaptation syndrome was proposed by Selye.
2. The syndrome is a cluster of bodily changes that occur in three stages:
   a. Alarm
   b. Resistance
   c. Exhaustion
3. The Alarm Reaction.
   a. The alarm reaction is triggered by perception of a stressor.
      i. The reaction mobilizes or arouses the body.
      ii. This mobilization is the basis for the instinctive fight-or-flight reaction.
   b. The alarm reaction involves bodily changes that are initiated by the brain and regulated by the endocrine system and the sympathetica division of the ANS.
4. The Resistance Stage.
   a. If the stressor isn't removed we enter the adaptation or resistance stage.
      i. The body attempts to restore lost energy and repair bodily damage.
5. The Exhaustion Stage.
   a. If the stressor isn't dealt with we may enter the exhaustion stage.
   b. We become exhausted if the stressor continues indefinitely.
   c. The body is depleted of the resources required for combating stress.
   d. Symptoms may include:
      i. Allergies.
      ii. Hives.
      iii. Coronary heart disease.
      iv. Death.

B. Effects of Stress on the Immune System.

1. Stress suppresses the immune system.
2. Feelings of control and social support moderate these effects.
3. The Immune System.
   a. The immune system has several functions that combat disease.
      i. Production of white blood cells (leukocytes). They recognize and eradicate foreign agents and unhealthy cells.
      ii. Foreign substances are called antigens. The body generates specialized proteins or antibodies to fight antigens.
   b. Inflammation: is another function of the immune system. This is increased blood supply which floods the region with white blood cells.
4. Stress and the Immune System.
   a. Psychoneuroimmunology is the study of the relationship among psychological factors, the nervous system, the endocrine system, the immune system, and disease.
   b. One of the reasons stress exhausts us is that it stimulates the production of steroids. Steroids suppress the functioning of the immune system.
      i. Persistent secretion of steroids decreases inflammation and interferes with the formation of antibodies. We become more vulnerable to various illnesses.

VI. Psychology and Health: Headaches, Cardiovascular Disorders, Cancer, and Sexually Transmitted Infections.

A. Biological factors such as pathogens, inoculations, injuries, age, gender, and a family history of disease may be the most obvious cause of disease. Genetics plays a role.
   1. Genes only create the predisposition toward the health problem.
   2. Many health problems are affected by psychological factors, such as attitudes, emotions, and behavior.
   3. Stopping smoking, eating right, exercising and controlling alcohol use would prevent a number of types of deaths.
B. Headaches: When Stress Presses and Pounds.
   1. Headaches are the most common stress-related physical ailments.
   2. Muscle Tension Headaches.
      a. We contract muscles in the shoulders, neck, forehead, and scalp when we get stressed.
      b. Most often characterized by dull, steady pain on both sides of the head and feelings of tightness or pressure.
   3. Migraine Headaches.
      a. Characterized by:
         i. A sudden onset.
         ii. Severe throbbing pain on one side of the head.
         iii. May last for hours or days.
         iv. Visual problems.
         v. Perceptual of unusual odors.

                vi.   Sensitivity to light.
                vii. Loss of balance.
                viii. Vomiting.
                ix.   Loss of appetite.
                x.   Changes in mood.

        b. Triggers include:
           i.   Barometric pressure.
           ii.   Pollen.
           iii. Certain drugs.
           iv. Chocolate.
           v.   Aged cheese.
           vi.   Beer, champagne and red wine.
           vii. Hormonal changes.

C. Coronary Heart Disease: Taking Stress to Heart.
    1. Coronary Heart Disease (CHD) is the leading cause of death in the United States.
    2. Risks include:
        a. Family history.
        b. Physiological conditions.
        c. Patterns of consumption.
        d. Type A behavior.
        e. Hostility and holding in feelings of anger.
        f. Job strain.
        g. Chronic fatigue and chronic emotional strain.
        h. Sudden stressors.
        i. A physically inactive lifestyle.

D. Cancer: Swerving Off Course.
    1. Cancer is the number one killer of women in the United States and the number two killer of men.
    2. Cancer is characterized by the development of abnormal, or mutant cells that may take root anywhere in the body.
        a. If not controlled early, the cancerous cells may metastasize- establish colonies elsewhere in the body.
    3. Risk Factors.
        a. People can inherit a disposition toward cancer.
        b. Behaviors also contributing are:
           i.   Smoking.
           ii.   Drinking alcohol.
           iii. Eating animal fats.
           iv. Sunbathing.
           v.   Prolonged psychological conditions such as depression.
    4. Stress and Cancer.
        a. Researchers have uncovered possible links between stress and cancer.
        b. Once cancer has developed stress can influence its course.

E. AIDS and Other Sexually Transmitted Infections (STIs).

1. There are nearly 4 million new chlamydia infections each year.
   a. Chlamydia leads to infertility.
2. STIs are believed to account for 15-30% of cases of intertility among U.S. women.
3. Psychological risk factors are:
   a. Cognitive: people tend to deny or underestimate their risk of infection.
   b. Behavioral: many people do not change their behavior in an effort to prevent infection.

VII. **LIFE CONNECTIONS: Preventing and Coping with Health Problems-Stress, Headaches, Heart Disease, Cancer, and Sexually Transmitted Infections.**
A. Alleviating stress may have beneficial effects on the immune system.
   1. Don't assume that stress-management is the cure-all.
B. Coping with Stress.
   1. Methods suggested by psychologists to help people cope with stress include:
      a. Telling yourself that you can live with another person's disappointment.
      b. Taking a deep breath and telling yourself to relax.
      c. Taking the scenic route to work.
      d. Jogging for half an hour.
   2. Controlling Irrational Thoughts-How to Change Your Mind for the Better.
      a. People often feel pressure from their own thoughts (harboring irrational thoughts).
      b. A multi-step procedure for controlling irrational thoughts include:
         i. Develop awareness of the thoughts by careful self-examination.
         ii. Evaluate the accuracy of the thoughts.
         iii. Prepare thoughts that are incompatible with the irrational.
         iv. Reward yourself with a mental pat on the back.
   3. Lowering Arousal: Turning Down the Inner Alarm.
      a. Stress tends to trigger intense activity in the sympathetic branch of the ANS.
      b. Arousal is a sign that something may be wrong.
      c. Tools that help include:
         i. Meditation.
         ii. Biofeedback.
         iii. Progressive relaxation.
      d. 10 steps of meditation.
         i. Begin by meditating once or twice a day for 10-20 minutes.
         ii. In meditation what you don't do is more important than what you do do.
         iii. Create a quiet, nondisruptive environment.
         iv. Do not eat for an hour beforehand.

       v.   Assume a comfortable position.

      vi. As a device to aid in concentrating, focus on your breathing.

     vii. If you are using a mantra prepare by saying the mantra out loud several times.

   viii. If disruptive thoughts enter your mind don't allow them to pass through.

      ix. Allow yourself to drift.

       x. Above all, take what you can get.

4. Exercising: Run For Your Life?
   a. Exercising, particularly aerobic exercise, enhances the functioning of the immune system, contributes to our psychological well-being, and helps us cope with stress.
   b. Aerobic exercise refers to exercise that requires a sustained increase in consumption of oxygen.
   c. Anaerobic exercise involves short bursts of muscle activity.
      i. Anaerobic exercise can strengthen muscles and improve flexibility.
   d. Sustained physical activity reduces hypertension, the risk of heart attacks and strokes.
5. If you are considering beginning an exercise program:
   a. Unless you have engaged in exercise recently seek the advice of a medical expert.
   b. Consider joining a beginner's aerobics class.
   c. Get the proper equipment.
   d. Read up on the activity you are considering.
   e. Try to select activities that you can sustain for a lifetime.
   f. If you feel severe pain, don't exercise through it.
   g. Have fun.

C. Preventing and Coping with Headaches.
   1. Suggestions for preventing headaches.
      a. Challenging irrational beliefs.
      b. Exercising.
      c. Meditation.
      d. Progressive relaxation.
      e. Biofeedback training.

D. Reducing the Risk of CHD Through Behavior Modification.
   1. Behavior modification techniques are designed to aid with:
      a. Stopping smoking.
      b. Controlling weight.
      c. Reducing hypertension.
      d. Lowering cholesterol.
      e. Modifying Type A behavior.
      f. Managing feelings of anger.
      g. Exercising.

E. Preventing and Coping with Cancer.
   1. Suggestions include:

        a. Limit exposure to behavioral risk factors.
        b. Modify diet.
        c. Exercise regularly.
        d. Have regular medical checkups.
        e. Regulate exposure to stress.
        f. If struck with cancer, fight it energetically.
    F. Preventing HIV/AIDS and other STIs.
        1. Prevention is the primary weapon against STIs.
            a. Learn about safer sex.
            b. Don't ignore the threat.
            c. Remain abstinent.
            d. Engage in monogamous relationships with someone who is not infected.
            e. Be selective.
            f. Inspect your partners genitals.
            g. Wash your genitals before and after contact.
            h. Use condoms.
            i. If you fear you have been exposed, talk to your doctor.
            j. When in doubt, stop.
            k.

VIII. A CLOSER LOOK: "Fight or Flight" or "Tend and Befriend"? Gender Differences in Response to Stress.

    A. Cannon labeled the body's response to stress as the "fight or flight" reaction.
    B. Half of us are more likely to tend to kids (interface with family and friends) than to fight or flee….the female half.
        1. Females tend to "tend and befriend" which involves nurturing and seeking the support of others.
        2. Males are more likely to withdraw from the family or start arguments.
        C. Evolutionary Perspective.
        1. Tend and Befriend promotes the survival of females who are tending to their offspring.
        2. Oxytocin is released during stress and tends to have a calming effect.
        3. This biobehavioral pattern may provide insights into why women live an average of seven and a half years longer than men.
    D. Another View.
        1. Differences may reflect learning and culture instead of being genetically based.

IX. A CLOSER LOOK: Psychological Factors in the Treatment of Cancer.

    A. Feelings of anxiety and depression are often found in individuals suffering with cancer.
    B. Psychological stress due to cancer can weaken the immune system, setting the stage for other health problems.
    C. Additional treatments/suggestions include:

1. Relaxation training.
2. Guided imagery.
3. Control is a factor in hardiness.
4. Patient's moods are connected with the functioning of the immune system.
5. Having a fighting spirit

Chapter Eleven Outline

I. **Introduction to Personality: "Why Are They Sad and Glad, and Bad?"**
    A. Psychologists define personality as the reasonably stable patterns of emotions, motives, and behavior that distinguish one person from another.

II. **The Psychodynamic Perspective: Excavating the Iceberg.**
    A. Sigmund Freud characterized personality as conflict, a dynamic struggle.
        1. Drives like sex, aggression and the need for superiority conflict with laws, social rules and moral codes. At some time the laws are internalized.
        2. The conflict is between opposing inner forces.
    B. Sigmund Freud's Theory of Psychosexual Development.
        1. Freud's interests were in neurology.
        2. Worked with people who, for example, had paralysis of the legs in absence of any medical disorder.
            a. The symptoms often would disappear once the person recalled and discussed stressful events and feelings of guilt or anxiety that seem to be related to the symptoms.
        3. The human mind is like an iceberg.
            a. The region that pokes through into the light of awareness is called the conscious.
            b. Preconscious mind contains elements of experience that are out of awareness but can be made conscious simply by focusing on them.
            c. Unconscious mind is shrouded in mystery. Contains biological instincts of:
                i.   Sex
                ii. Aggression.
        4. Repression is the automatic ejection of anxiety-evoking ideas from awareness.
        5. To explore the unconscious mind, Freud engaged in a form of mental detective work called psychoanalysis.
            a. Talk about anything that pops into their mind.
            b. Resistance: the desire to avoid thinking about or discussing thoughts.
        6. The Structure of Personality.
            a. Psychic structures or mental structures that are the clashing forces of personality. Freud proposed that there are three psychic structures:
                i.   Id
                ii. Ego
                iii. Superego
            b. The id is present at birth and represents physiological drives and is entirely unconscious.
                i.   Freud described it as chaos, a cauldron of seething excitations.

        ii.   The id follows the pleasure principle: demands instant gratification.
- c. The ego stands for reason and good sense, for rational ways of coping with frustration.
    - i. Curbs the appetites of the id and makes plans that fit social conventions.
    - ii. The ego is guided by the reality principle. The ego may use psychological defenses to prevent improper impulses from arising. Repression is one such psychological defe nse.
- d. The superego develops throughout childhood, usually incorporating the moral standards and values of parents through identification.
    - i. The superego functions according to the moral principle.
    - ii. The superego holds out the ideal self and acts as your conscience.
    - iii. The superego floods the ego with feelings of guilt and shame if necessary.

7. Stages of Psychosexual Development.
    - a. Eros: is aimed at preserving and perpetuating life.
    - b. Libido: psychic energy involving sexual impulses.
        - i. Focused on sexual feelings in different parts of the body or erogenous zones.
    - c. Five periods of psychosexual development:
        - i. Oral
        - ii. Anal
        - iii. Phallic
        - iv. Latency
        - v. Genital
    - d. Oral stage: during the first year of life. If it fits into the mouth then it goes in the mouth (e.g. sucking and biting).
        - i. Conflict centers on the nature and extent of oral gratification. Insufficient or excessive gratification in any stage could lead to fixation in that stage.
        - ii. Adults with oral fixations could experience exaggerated desires for ora l activities such as smoking, overeating, alcohol abuse, nail biting.
    - e. Anal stage: gratification is attained through contraction and relaxation of the muscles that control elimination of waste products from the body.
        - i. The general issue of self-control.
        - ii. Anal fixations may stem from conflict and lead to anal retentive (excessive self control) or anal expulsive (careless, messiness, and even sadism).
    - f. Phallic stage: during the third year of life. The major erogenous zone is the phallic region.

    i. Oedipus complex: boys want to marry Mommy; hostility towards Dad.

    ii. Electra complex: girls want to marry Daddy; hostility towards Mom.

    iii. Resolution comes when children begin to identify with their same sex parent.

  g. Latency stage: sexual feelings remain unconscious.

  h. Genital stage: final stage, find sexual gratification through intercourse with a member of the other gender.

C. Other Psychodynamic Theorists.

 1. Carl Jung, a Swiss psychiatrist developed his own psychodynamic theory called analytical psychology.

  a. Jung downplayed the importance of the sexual instinct.

  b. Collective unconscious: contains primitive images called archetypes that reflect the history of our species.

    i. Archetypes influence our thoughts and emotions and cause us to respond to cultural themes in stories and films.

 2. Alfred Adler (1870-1937).

  a. Inferiority complex: people are motivated by this complex.

    i. Feelings of inferiority may lead to a drive for superiority.

  b. Creative self: a self aware aspect of personality that strives to overcome obstacles and develop the individual's potential.

  c. Adler's view has been termed individual psychology.

 3. Karen Horney.

  a. Horney argued that little girls do not feel inferior to boys and the view that girls are inferior is founded on Western cultural prejudice, not scientific evidence.

  b. Unconscious sexual and aggressive impulses are less important than social relationships in children's development. Genuineness and consistent love can alleviate the effects of even the most traumatic childhood.

 4. Erik Erikson.

  a. Social relationships are more crucial than sexual urges.

  b. We are the conscious architects of our own personalities.

  c. Proposed stages of psychosocial development.

    i. First stage is trust versus mistrust. Mistrust could interfere with the formation of relationships.

    ii. Goal of adolescence is the attainment of ego identity.

D. Evaluation of the Psychodynamic Perspective.

 1. Psychodynamic theory focused attention on the far-reaching effects of childhood events.

 2. Important for parents to be aware of emotional needs of children.

 3. Defense mechanisms have become part of everyday speech.

 4. Psychic structures may be too vague to measure scientifically.

 5. Oedipus and Electra complexes remain little more than speculation.

III. The Trait Perspective: The Five-Dimensional Universe.
  A. Traits are reasonably stable elements of personality that are inferred from behavior.
  B. From Hippocrates to the Present.
    1. Hippocrates believed that traits are embedded in bodily fluids. There are four basic fluids (humors):
       a. Yellow bile is associated with a choleric (quick tempered) disposition.
       b. Blood is associated with a sanguine (warm, cheerful) disposition.
       c. Phlegm is associated with the phlegmatic (sluggish, calm, cool) disposition.
       d. Black bile is associated with a melancholic (gloomy, pensive) temperament.
    2. Gordon Allport catalogued approximately 18,000 human traits from dictionaries. The list has been used in research by many psychologists.
  C. Hans Eysenck's Trait Theory: A Two-Dimensional View.
    1. Eysenck focused his research on two personality traits:
       a. Introversion-extraversion
       b. Emotional stability-instability (neuroti cism).
          i. An anxious person would be high in both introversion and neuroticism.
          ii. The choleric type would be extraverted and unstable.
          iii. The sanguine would be extroverted and stable.
          iv. The phlegmatic would be introverted and stable.
          v. The melancholic would be introverted and unstable.
  D. The Five-Factor Model (The Big Five).
    1. Recent research has focused on five basic personality factors:
       a. Extraversion
       b. Conscientiousness
       c. Agreeableness
       d. Openness
       e. Neuroticism
    2. The factors are related to basic temperaments and are largely inborn.
       a. Personalities tend to mature rather than be shaped by environmental conditions.
       b. Personalities are affected by culture.
    3. McCrae and Costa created the NEO Five Factor Inventory which has been used in numerous research projects.
  E. Evaluation of the Trait Perspective.
    1. Trait theorists have focused much attention on the development of personality tests.
    2. Trait theory has tended to be more descriptive than explanatory. Sometimes criticized as being circular.

IV. Learning-Theory Perspectives: All the Things You Do.

A. Behaviorism views that personality is plastic-that situational variables and environmental influences are the key shapers of human preference and behaviors.

  1. Skinner suggested that environmental influences such as parental approval and social custom shape us into wanting certain things and not wanting others.

  2. Some object to behaviorist notions because they play down the importance of consciousness and choice.

B. Social-Cognitive Theory is a contemporary view of learning developed by Bandura. Focuses on the importance of learning by observation.

  1. Social-cognitive theorists see people as influencing their environment just as their environment influences them.

    a. Bandura termed this reciprocal determinism.

  2. Person variables are variables within people that must be considered if we are to understand them.

  3. Expectancies: whether a person will behave in a certain way also depends on what the person expects about the outcomes of that behavior and the subjective values of those outcomes.

  4. Observational Learning (modeling).

    a. Acquiring knowledge by observing others.

    b. Our expectations stem from our observations of what happens to ourselves and other people.

    c. Person variable include competencies, encoding strategies, expectancies, emotions, and self-regulatory systems and plans.

  5. Competencies: What Can You Do?

    a. Competencies include knowledge of rules that guide conduct, concepts about ourselves and other people, and skills.

    b. Individual differences in competencies reflect genetic variation, learning opportunities, and other environmental factors.

  6. Encoding Strategies: How Do You See It?

    a. Some people make themselves miserable by encoding events in self-defeating ways.

      i. Cognitive therapists foster adjustment by challenging people to view life in more optimistic ways.

  7. Expectancies: What Will Happen?

    a. Self Efficacay are beliefs that we can accomplish certain things. Expectancies involve what will happen if we engage in certain behaviors.

      i. Competencies influence expectancies. Expectancies in turn influence motivation to perform.

      ii. People with positive self-efficacy expectations have higher self-esteem.

      iii. Lack of belief in self-efficacy is often associated with depression and hopelessness.

  8. Emotions: How Does It Feel?

      a.   Because of different learning histories, similar situations can arouse different feelings in us.

      b.   Stimuli arouse feelings in us, and feelings influence our behavior

   9.   Self-Regulatory Systems and Plans: How Can You Achieve It?

      a.   Self-regulation helps us influence our environments. We can select the situations to which we expose ourselves .

      b.   We can to some degree select our responses within an environment.

C.   Evaluation of the Learning Perspective.

   1.   Emphasized the importance of publicly observable variables or behaviors, if psychology is to be a science.

   2.   Learning theorists emphasized the importance of environmental conditions as determinants of behavior.

   3.   Behaviorism is limited in its ability to explain personality. Behaviorism does not describe, explain or even suggest the richness of inner human experience.

   4.   Behaviorism may not pay enough attention to genetic variation.

V.   The Humanistic-Existential Perspective: How Becoming?

A.   Humanists and existentialists dwell on the meaning of life. Self awareness is the hub of this search for meaning.

B.   The third force in American Psychology, Humanism puts people and self-awareness at the center of consideration. People are capable of:

   1.   Free choice.

   2.   Self fulfillment.

   3.   Ethical behavior.

C.   Existentialism: giving personal meaning to things and making personal choices.

D.   Abraham Maslow and the Challenge of Self-Actualization.

   1.   Maslow argued that people also have a conscious need for self-actualization-to become all that they can be.

E.   Carl Roger's Self Theory.

   1.   Rogers wrote that people shape themselves through free choice and action.

   2.   Rogers defined the self as the center of experience.

   3.   Choices are made on the basis of your values.

   4.   The Self-Concept and Frames of Reference.

      a.   Self-concepts consist of our impressions of ourselves and our evaluations of our adequacy

      b.   Frames of Reference: unique ways of looking at ourselves and the world.

   5.   Self-esteem and Positive Regard.

      a.   Unconditional positive regard: accept people as having intrinsic merit regardless of their behavior at the moment.

          i.   If parents show conditional positive regard, then children may develop conditions of worth-come to think that they have merit only if they behave as their parents wish them to behave.

          ii.   Some children deny many of their feelings or disown aspects of themselves. The self concept becomes distorted which results in anxiety.

      b. Rogers suggested that the path to self-actualization requires getting in touch with our genuine feelings, accepting them, and acting upon them.

      c. Roger's believed that we have mental images of what we are capable of becoming. These are termed self-ideals. We are motivated to reduce the discrepancy between our self-concepts and our self-ideals.

F.   Evaluation of the Humanistic-Existential Perspective.
1. Humanistic-Existential perspective helped emphasize the importance of personal experience.
2. Humanistic-existential perspecti ve see humans as free to make choices, assuming personal freedom.
3. Conscious experience is private and subjective. Therefore the validity of formulating theories in terms of the consciousness has been questioned.
4. Self-actualization yields circular explanations for behavior.
5. Humanistic-existential perspective has little to say about the development of traits and personality types.

VI. The Sociocultural Perspective: Personality in Context.

A. Some psychologists believe that personality cannot be understood without reference to the sociocultural perspective.
1. Aspects of culture, religion, race should be considered.

B. Individualism Versus Collectivism.
1. Individualsits: tend to define themselves in terms of their personal identities and to give priority to their personal goals.
    a. People in the United States and many northern European nations tend to be individualistic.
    b. Capitalist systems tend to foster individualism to a degree.
2. Collectivists: tend to define themselves in terms of the groups to which they belong and to give priority to the group's goals.
    a. Many people from Africa, Asia and Central and South America tend to be collectivists.

C. Evaluation of the Sociocultural Pespective.
1. The sociocultural perspective provides valuable insights into the roles of ethnicity, gender, culture, and socioeconomic status in personality formation.
2. Sociocultural factors are external forces that are internalized.
3. The sociocultural perspective enhances our sensitivity to cultural differences.

a. Enhances the appreciation of the richness of human behavior and mental processes.
D. CONTROVERSY IN PSYCHOLOGY: Just How Much Acculturation Is Enough?
   1. Acculturation: activities in which immigrants become acclimated to the customs and behavior patterns of their new host culture.
   2. Self-esteem has been shown to be connected with patterns of acculturation among immigrants.
   3. People who identify with the bicultural pattern have the highest self-esteem.

VII. **Measurement of Personality**
A. Personality Assessment: take a sample of behavior to predict future behavior.
   1. Behavior-rating scales: trained observers check off each occurrence of a specific behavior within a certain time frame.
   2. Aptitude assessment aids in gaining insight into whether individuals are suited for certain occupations.
B. Objective Tests.
   1. Objective tests present respondents with a standardized group of test items in the form of a questionnaire.
      a. Responses are limited to a specific range of answers.
      b. Forced-choice format: respondents are asked to indicate which of two statements is more true for them.
   2. Minnesota Multiphasic Personality Inventory (MMPI) contains hundreds of items in a true-false format.
a. Used to diagnose psychological disorders.
      b. Most widely used test in clinical work.
      c. Most widely used personality measurement in psychological research.
      d. MMPI contains:
         i. 4 validity scales
         ii. 10 clinical scales
      e. Response set: biases in answering questions.
      f. MMPI scales were empirically constructed; based on actual clinical data rather than on psychological theory.
      g. Confidence in the MMPI has developed because of its extensive use.
C. Projective Tests.
   1. People are shown ambiguous stimuli such as inkblots or ambiguous drawings and asked to say what they look like.
      a. People project their own personalities into their responses.
   2. The Rorschach Inkblot Test.
      a. Individuals are shown inkblots and asked what they look like.
         i. A response that reflects the shape of the blot is considered a sign of adequate reality testing.

        ii.   A response that integrates several features of the blot is considered a sign of high intellectual functioning.

    b.   Critics argue that there is little evidence to support the test's validity.

    3.   The Thematic Apperception Test.

    a.   Developed by Murray and Morgan; the test consists of drawings and subjects are asked to make up stories about them.

        i.   Widely used in research on motivation.

VIII.   LIFE CONNECTIONS: Gender Typing-On Becoming A Woman or a Man.

A.   Gender differences in personality are not as obvious as biological gender differences.

    1.   What is masculine versus feminine?

    a.   Characteristics of men: active, adventurous, aggressive, arrogant, and autocratic.

    b.   Characteristics of women: fearful, affectionate, appreciative, and emotional.

B.   Gender Differences in Personality.

    1.   Assessment of intelligence does not show overall gender differences in cognitive abilities.

    2.   Males seem to be somewhat superior in the ability to manipulate visual images in working member. Males seem to excel in visual-spatial abilities used in math, science, and reading maps. Males exceed women in social dominance and tough-mindedness.

    3.   Females tend to acquire language faster. Women exceed men in sociability, happiness, anxiety, trust and nurturance.

    4.   Overall summary:

    a.   In most cases the differences between males and females are small.

    b.   Gender differences are group differences.

    c.   Some differences reflect cultural influences.

    d.   Frodi (1977) found that:

        i.   Females do act as aggressively as males when they have the means to do so.

        ii.   Females are more likely to feel anxious or guilty about aggression.

        iii.   Females are more likely to empathize with the victim.

        iv. Gender differences in aggression tend to decrease when the victim is anonymous.

    e.   Gender Differences in Mate Selection.

        i.   Women tend to place greater emphasis than men on traits such as professional status, consideration, dependability, kindness, and fondness for children.

        ii.   Men tend to place relatively greater emphasis on physical allure, cooking ability and thrift.

C.   Evolutionary and Genetic Aspects of Gender–Typing.

1. Buss (2000) suggests that gender differences were fashioned by natural selection.
2. Organization of the Brain.
   a. Gender differences in the functioning and organization of the brain do exist.
      i. Men use the hippocampus in both hemispheres when they are trying to navigate whereas women use only the hippocampus in the right hemisphere.
      ii. Men with damage to the left hemisphere are more likely to experience difficulties in verbal functioning than women with similar damage.
      iii. Men with damage to the right hemisphere are more likely to have problems with spatial relations than women with similar injuries.
3. Sex Hormones: substances that may masculinize or feminize the brain. These include: androgens and testosterone.
   a. However, psychologists argue that boys and girls can choose whether or not to act aggressively regardless of hormone levels.
4. Are There Evolutionary Factors in Mate Selection?
   a. Differences may suggest preferences that provide reproductive advantages. These may include:
      i. Cleanliness, good complexion, clear eyes, strong teeth, healthy hair, firm muscle tone, and a steady gait, have universal appeal to both genders.
      ii. Women tend to marry men similar to them in physical attractiveness an socioeconomic standing.
D. Psychodynamic Theory and Gender-Typing.
   1. Freud explained the acquisition of gender roles in terms of identification.
   2. Research has shown that boys and girls are inclined to develop gender-typed preferences for toys and activities earlier than predicted by psychodynamic theory.
E. Learning Theories and Gender-Typing.
   1. Experience helps the individual create concepts of gender-appropriate behavior.
   2. Children can learn what is masculine and feminine by observational learning.
   3. Children are reinforced to imitate adults of the same gender.
F. Gender-Schema Theory and Gender-Typing.
   1. Gender-schema theory proposes that people look at the world through the lenses of gender.
      a. Cultures tend to polarize females and males by organizing social life around mutually exclusive gender roles.

Research suggests that polarized female-male scripts serve as cognitive anchors within Western culture.

Chapter Twelve Outline

I. **Historic Views of Psychological Disorders: "The Devil Made Me Do It"?**
   A. In the past people believed that psychological disorders were caused by possession by the Devil.
      1. People attributed unusual behavior and psychological disorders to demons.
      2. The Hammer of Witches: A document authorized by Pope Innocent VIII proposed to diagnose those who were possessed.

II. **What Are Psychological Disorders?**
   A. Psychological disorders are behaviors or mental processes that are connected with various kinds of distress or disability.
   B. Disorders are characterized on the following criteria:
      1. They are unusual.
      2. They suggest faulty perception or interpretation of reality.
         a. Hearing voices, seeing things, hallucinations, ideas of persecution.
      3. They suggest severe personal distress.
      4. They are self-defeating.
      5. They are dangerous.
      6. The individual's behavior is socially unacceptable.

III. **Classifying Psychological Disorders.**
   A. The most widely used classification scheme for psychological disorders is the Diagnostic and Statistical Manual (DSM) of the American Psychiatric Association.
      1. The current edition of the DSM is the DSM-IV-TR.
      2. People may receive Axis I or Axis II diagnoses or a combination of the two.
      3. Axis III is general medical conditions.
      4. Axis IV is psychosocial and environmental problems.
      5. Axis V is an assessment of global functioning.
      6. The DSM-IV-TR groups disorders on the basis of observable behaviors or symptoms.
      7. Thomas Szasz believes that disorders are really just problems in living rather than disorders.
         a. Labeling people degrades them, encourages them to evade their personal and social responsibilities.
         b. Labeling people as sick accords too much power to health professionals.
         c. Troubled people need to be encouraged to take greater responsibility for solving their own problems.
   B. CONTROVERSY IN PSYCHOLOGY: Is a Gay Male or Lesbian Sexual Orientation A Psychological Disorder?

1. Until 1973 a gay male or lesbian sexual orientation was considered to be a psychological disorder.
   a. A category for people who are distressed about their sexual orientation remains in place.
2. Gay males and lesbians are more likely than heterosexuals to experience feelings of anxiety and depression and they are more prone to suicide.
3. Bailey proposed interpretations of the issues surrounding homosexuality:
   a. Societal oppression causes the higher incidence of depression and suicidality.
   b. Homosexuality reflects a departure from typical development.
   c. Sexual orientation reflects prenatal sex hormones.
   d. Homosexual people could reflect differences in lifestyle.

IV. Anxiety Disorders.
A. Anxiety has psychological and physical features.
   1. Psychological features include:
      a. Worrying.
      b. Fear of the worst things happening.
      c. Fear of losing control.
      d. Nervousness.
      e. Inability to relax.
   2. Physical features include:
      a. Arousal of the sympathetic branch of the autonomic nervous system:
         i. Trembling.
         ii. Sweating.
         iii. Pounding heart.
         iv. Elevated blood pressure.
         v. Faintness.
   3. Anxiety is an appropriate response to a real threat.
B. Types of Anxiety Disorders.
   1. Phobias.
      a. Specific phobias are excessive, irrational fears of specific objects or situations, such as snakes or heights.
      b. Social phobias are persistent fears of scrutiny by others or of doing something that will be humiliating or embarrassing.
         i. Agoraphobia: fear of being out in open, busy areas.
   2. Panic Disorder is an abrupt attack of acute anxiety that is not triggered by a specific object or situation.
      a. Symptoms include:
         i. Shortness of breath.
         ii. Heavy sweating.
         iii. Tremors.
         iv. Pounding of heart.

       v.   Many fear suffocation.

      vi.   Choking sensations.

     vii.   Nausea.

    viii.   Numbness.

      ix.   Fear of going crazy or losing control.

  b.   Symptoms may last minutes or hours.

3. Generalized Anxiety Disorder is persistent anxiety that cannot be attributed to a phobic object, situation or a ctivity. It seems to be free-floating.

  a.   Symptoms include:

      i.   Autonomic nervous system overarousal.

     ii.   Feelings of dread and foreboding.

    iii.   Excessive vigilance.

4. Obsessive-Compulsive Disorder.

  a.   Obsessions are recurrent, anxiety provoking thoughts or images that seem irrational and disrupt daily life.

  b.   Compulsions are thought or behaviors that tend to reduce the anxiety connected with obsessions.

5. Stress Disorders.

  a.   Posttraumatic stress disorder (PTSD) is characterized by a rapid heart rate and feelings of anxiety and helplessness that are caused by a traumatic experience.

      i.   Traumatic experiences include natural or man-made disasters, threats, or assault, or witnessing a death.

     ii.   The traumatic event is revisited in the form of intrusive memories, recurrent dreams, and flashbacks.

  b.   Acute stress disorder is characterized by feelings of anxiety and helplessness that are caused by a traumatic event.

      i.   Acute stress disorder occurs within a month of the event and lasts from 2 days to 4 weeks.

C. Theoretical Views.

  1. Psychological views.

    a.   Psychodynamic:

       i. &n bsp; Phobias symbolize conflicts originating in childhood.

      ii.   Generalized anxiety as persistent difficulty in repressing primitive impulses.

     iii.   Obsessions are explained as leakage of unconscious impulses.

    b.   Learning theorists:

       i.   Phobias are conditioned fears that were acquired in childhood. Observational learning also plays a role.

    c.   Cognitive theorists:

       i.   Anxiety is maintained by thinking that one is in a terrible situation and helpless to change it.

  2. Biological Views.

    a.   Anxiety tends to run in families.

           i.   Twin studies shoe a higher concordance rate for anxiety disorders among identical twins than among fraternal twins.
      b.   Mineka (1991) suggest that humans are genetically predisposed to fear stimuli that may have posed a threat to their ancestors.
      c.   The brain may not be sensitive enough to GABA, a neurotransmitter that may help calm anxiety reactions.

V. Dissociative Disorders.

A. Dissociative disorders are characterized by a separation of mental processes such as thoughts, emotions, identity, memory, or consciousness.

B. Types of Dissociative Disorders include: dissociative amnesia, dissociative fugue, dissociative identity disorder, and depersonalization.

1. Dissociative amnesia is characterized by the person suddenly being unable to recall important personal information.

2. Dissociative Fugue is characterized by the person abruptly leaving their home or place of work and traveling to another place, having lost all memory of their past. The new personality is often more outgoing than the less inhibited one.

3. Dissociative identity disorder (formerly termed multiple personality disorder) is characterized by two or more identities or personalities, each with distinct traits and memories, occupying the same person. Each identity may or may not be aware of the others.

4. Depersonalization Disorder is characterized by persistent feelings that one is detached from one's own body, as if one is observing one's thought processes from the outside.

C. Theoretical Views.

1. Psychodynamic theory explains this as massive repression.

2. Learning theorists suggest that people have learned not to think about bad memories or disturbing impulses in order to avoid feelings of anxiety, guilt or shame.

VI. Somatoform Disorders.

A. Somatoform disorders are characterized by physical problems in people, such as paralysis, pain, or a persistent belief that they have a serious disease. Yet no evidence of a physical abnormality can be found.

B. Types of somatoform disorders include:

1. Conversion disorder which is characterized by a major change in, or loss of, physical functioning although there are no medical findings to explain the loss of functioning.
      a.   The person is not faking as they seem to be converting a source of stress into a physical difficulty.
      b.   Some people with this disorder show indifference to their symptoms.

2. Hypochondriasis is characterized by people insisting that they are suffering with a serious physical illness even though no medical evidence of illness c an be found.

a. They become preoccupied with minor physical sensations and continue to believe that they are ill despite the reassurance of physicians that they are healthy.
C. Theoretical Views.
1. There is research evidence that people who develop hypochondriasis are particularly sensitive to bodily sensations and tend to ruminate about them.
D. CONTROVERSY IN PSYCHOLOGY: Are somatoform disorders the special province of women?
1. Hippocrates believed that hysteria was caused by a wandering uterus.
2. Psychodynamic view suggests that conversion disorders protect the individual from feelings of guilt, shame or from another source of stress.
3. Conversion disorders are not the special province of women.

VII. **Mood Disorders.**
A. Mood disorders are characterized by disturbance in expressed emotions generally involving sadness or elation.
B. Types of Mood Disorders.
1. Major depression is the common cold of psychological problems. Characteristics include:
a. Lack of energy.
b. Loss of self-esteem.
c. Difficulty concentrating.
d. Loss of interest in activities and other people.
e. Pessimism, crying, and thoughts of suicide.
f. Poor appetite and serious weight loss.
g. Psychomotor retardation.
h. Faulty perception including delusions of unworthiness, guilt for imagined wrong doings and possible hallucinations of strange bodily sensations.
2. Bipolar Disorder is formerly known as manic-depressive disorder and is characterized by:
a. Mood swings from ecstatic elation to deep depression.
i. In the manic phase the person may show excessive excitement, silliness, show poor judgment, destroying property and giving away expensive possessions. They are too restless to sit still or sleep restfully.
ii. Depression often includes sleeping more than usual and being lethargic. Individuals also tend to withdraw and experience irritability.
C. CONTROVERSY IN PSYCHOLOGY: Is there a thin line between genius and madness?
1. Researchers have found links between creative genius and the psychological disorders of depression and bipolar disorder.

2. Jamison found that artists are 18 times more likely to commit suicide than the general population.
D. Theoretical Views.
   1. Depression may be a reaction to losses and stress.
      a. We tend to be depressed by things we bring on ourselves.
   2. Psychological Views:
      a. Psychoanalysts suggest that anger is turned inward.
         i. Bipolar disorder may be seen as the personality being dominated by the superego and then b y the ego.
      b. Learning theorists suggest that depressed people behave as though they cannot obtain reinforcement.
         i. They have an external locus of control.
         ii. Researchers have found links between depression and learned helplessness.
      c. Cognitive factors contributing to depression include making irrational demands on themselves.
         i. Depressed people tend to ruminate about feelings of depression.
         ii. Attribution styles include: internal vs. external; stable vs. unstable; and global vs. specific. People who are depressed tend to think of their situation as internal, stable, and global. They are powerless to change.
   3. Biological Factors.
      a. Depression is heritable.
      b. Genetic factors appear to be involved.
         i. Bipolar disorder may be connected with genetic material found on Chromosome 18.
      c. Depression research focuses on the underutilization of the neurotransmitter serotonin in the brain.

VIII. Schizophrenia.

A. Schizophrenia is a severe psychological disorder that touches every aspect of a person's life. It is characterized by:
   1. Disturbances in thought and language.
   2. Disturbances in perception and attention.
   3. Disturbances in motor activity and mood.
   4. Withdrawal and absorption in daydreams or fantasy.
   5. Jumbled speech.
   6. Delusions.
   7. Hallucinations.
   8. Stupors: slow motor activity.
   9. Emotional responses that may be flat.
B. Types of Schizophrenia: paranoid, disorganized, and catatonic.
   1. Paranoid type: have systematized delusions and frequently related auditory hallucinations.

      a. Usually the delusions are of grandeur and persecution including jealousy.

  2. Disorganized type show incoherence, loosening of associations, disorganized behavior, disorganized delusions, fragmentary delusions or hallucinations, and flat or highly inappropriate emotional responses.

  3. Catatonic type show striking impairment in motor activity.

      a. Slowing of activity into a stupor that may suddenly change into an agitated phase.

      b. Waxy flexibility in which the person maintains positions into which he or she has been manipulated by others.

C. Theoretical Views.

  1. Psychological views:

      a. Psychodynamic perspective suggests that the ego is overwhelmed by sexual or aggressive impulses from the id.

         i. The person re treats (regresses) to an early phase of the oral stage.

      b. Learning theorists explain schizophrenia in terms of conditioning and observational learning.

         i. Inner fantasies become more reinforcing than social realities.

      c. Some researchers are interested in the connections between psychosocial stressors and biological factors.

  2. Biological Views:

      a. Schizophrenia appears to be a brain disorder.

      b. Size of the ventricles in the brain.

      c. Activity levels in the brain.

      d. Brain chemistry.

         i. Smaller brains.

         ii. Smaller prefrontal region of the cortex.

         iii. Larger ventricles.

  3. Possible causes:

      a. Heredity.

         i. Chromosome 1.

      b. Complications during pregnancy.

      c. Birth during winter.

      d. Poor maternal nutrition.

      e. Atypical development of the central nervous system.

  4. The Dopamine theory of schizophrenia suggests that people with schizophrenia overutilize dopamine.

      a. They may have larger numbers of dopamine receptors.

  5. The multifactorial model suggests that genetic factors create a predisposition toward schizophrenia. Then other factors contribute to the cause of the disorder.

D. CONTROVERSY IN PSYCHOLOGY: Should we ban the insanity plea?

  1. The issue is competence to stand trial.

2. M'Naghten rule states that the accused did not understand what they were doing at the time of the act, did not realize it was wrong, or was succumbing to an irresistible impulse.
3. Although the public estimates that the insanity defense is used in about 37% of felony cases, it is actually raised in only 1%.
   a. People found not guilty by reason of insanity are institutionalized for indefinite terms.

IX. Personality Disorders

A. Personality disorders are characterized by enduring patterns of behavior that are inflexible, and maladaptive. These behaviors typically impair social or personal functioning and are a source of distress to the individual or to other people.
B. Types of Personality Disorders include: paranoid, schizotypal, schizoid, antisocial, and avoidant.
   1. Paranoid personality disorder is a tendency to interpret other people's behavior as threatening or demeaning.
      a. Mistrustful of others.
   2. Schizotypal personality disorder is characterized by peculiarities of thought, perception, or behavior such as excessive fantasy and suspiciousness, feelings of being unreal, or odd usage of words.
   3. Schizoid personality is defined by indifference to relationships and flat emotional response.
      a. People with this disorder are loners.
   4. Antisocial personality disorder is characterized by persistently violating the rights of others and being in conflict with the law.
      a. Individuals often show superficial charm.
      b. They lack guilt or anxiety about their misdeeds.
      c. They fail to learn from punishment.
      d. They fail to form meaningful bonds with other people.
      e. Women are more likely than men to have anxiety and depressive disorders. Men are more likely to have antisocial personality disorder.
   5. Avoidant personality disorder individuals are generally unwilling to enter a relationship without some assurance of acceptance because they fear rejection and criticism.
      a. They do have some feelings of warmth toward other people unlike the schizoid personality disorder.
C. Theoretical Views.
   1. Psychodynamic model suggests that there are problems in the Oedipus complex. The superego does not develop.
   2. Learning theorists suggest that childhood experiences can contribute to maladaptive ways of relating to others in adulthood.
   3. Personality traits are to some degree heritable.
   4. There is some evidence that those with antisocial personality disorder have less gray matter in the prefrontal cortex of the brain.

X. LIFE CONNECTIONS: Understanding and Preventing Suicide.

A. About 30,000 people each year take their lives in the U.S.
B. Risk Factors in Suicide:
  1. Linked to feelings of depression and hopelessness.
  2. Highly achieving.
  3. Rigid perfectionists.
  4. Set impossibly high expectations for themselves.
  5. Compare themselves negatively with others.
  6. Suicidal Adolescents experience four psychological problems:
    a. Confusion about self.
    b. Impulsiveness.
    c. Emotional instability.
    d. Interpersonal problems.
  7. Suicide attempts are more common following stressful life events.
    a. Exit events are events that entail a loss of social support.
      i. Death of a parent or friend.
      ii. Divorce.
  8. People who consider suicide are less capable of solving problems.
  9. Suicide tends to run in families.
C. Myths about Suicide.
  1. Most people who commit suicide give warnings about their intentions, they aren't just seeking attention.
  2. Many people who commit suicide have made prior attempts.
  3. Discussing suicide with a person does not prompt the person to attempt suicide.
  4. Suicidal thinking is not necessarily a sign of psychosis, neurosis, or a personality disorder.
D. Warning Signs of Suicide:
  1. Changes in eating and sleeping patterns.
  2. Difficulty concentrating on school work.
  3. A sharp decline in school performance and attendance.
  4. Loss of interest in previously enjoyed activities.
  5. Giving away prized possessions.
  6. Complaints about physical problems when no medical basis for the problem can be found.
  7. Withdrawal from social relationships.
  8. Personality or mood changes.
  9. Talking or writing about death or dying.
  10. abuse of drugs or alcohol
  11. An attempted suicide.
  12. Availability of a handgun.
  13. A precipitating event such as an argument, a broken romantic relationship, academic difficulties, problems on the job, loss of a friend, or trouble with the law.

14. In the case of adolescents, knowing or hearing about another teenager who has committed suicide (cluster suicides).

15. Threatening to commit suicide.

E. What Can You Do?

    1. Keep talking. Encourage the person to talk.

    2. Be a good listener.

    3. Suggest that something other than suicide might solve the problem.

    4. Emphasize as concretely as possible how the person's suicide would be devastating to you and to other people who care.

    5. Ask how the person intends to commit suicide. Individuals with a concrete plan are at a greater risk.

    6. Suggest that the person go with you to obtain professional help now.

    7. Extract a promise that the person will not commit suicide before seeing you again.

    8. Do not tell people threatening suicide that they are silly or crazy.

XI. FEATURES: DIVERSITY: The Case of Women and Depression.

A. Women are about two times more likely to be diagnosed with depression than men.

    1. Low levels of estrogen have been suggested as a reason.

        a. Hormonal changes, menstrual cycle, and childbirth may contribute to depression in women.

    2. Men are less likely than women to admit to depression.

    3. Women are more likely to ruminate about stresses.

    4. A panel convened by the APA attributed most of the gender difference to the greater stresses placed on women.

        a. Multiple demands including:

            i. Demands of childbearing.

            ii. Child rearing.

            iii. Financial support of the family.

    5. Women are more likely to have experienced physical and sexual abuse, poverty, single parenthood, and sexism.

    6. Women are more likely to help other people which heaps additional caregiving burdens on themselves.

XII. FEATURES: DIVERSITY: Ethnicity, Gender, and Suicide.

A. Suicide is the third leading cause of death among young people aged 15 to 24.

B. Suicide is more common among college students than among people of the same age who do not attend college.

C. Although teenage suicides loom large in the media spotlight, older people are actually more likely to commit suicide.

D. Ethnicity:

    1. 17% of Native Americans has attempted suicide.

    2. African Americans are least likely to attempt suicide (6.5%).

    3. European Americans at 8%.

4. Latino Americans are at 1 in 8.

E.   Gender:

1. About three times as many females as males attempt suicide; but about five times as many males succeed.

   a. Males are more likely to shoot or hang themselves while females are more likely to use drugs and overdose.

Chapter Thirteen Outline

I. **What is Therapy? The Search for a "Sweat Oblivious Antidote".**
   A. Psychotherapy: a systematic interaction between a therapist and a client that:
      1. Applies psychological principles to affect the client's thoughts, feelings, or behavior in order to;
         a. Help the client overcome psychological disorders,
         b. Adjust to problems in living,
         c. Or develop as an individual.
   B. The History of Therapies.
      1. Treatments often reflected demonological thinking.
      2. Asylums built for warehousing not treatment.
         a. Bedlam derives from St. Mary's of Bethlehem the London asylum.
      3. Humanitarian reform began in:
         a. Paris with Philippe Pinel at the La Bicetre hospital.
         b. England with William Tuke.
         c. America with Dorothea Dix.
      4. Mental Hospitals: gradually began replacing asylums.
         a. In the mid 1950s more than a million people resided in facilities.
      5. The Community Mental Health Movement: attempt to maintain new patients as outpatients and to serve patients who have been released from mental hospitals.

II. **Psychodynamic Therapies: Digging Deep Within.**
   A. Based on the thinking of Freud.
      1. Assume that psychological disorders reflect early childhood experiences and internal conflicts.
   B. Traditional Psychoanalysis: "Where Id Was, There Shall Ego Be".
      1. Psychoanalysis can extend for months, even years.
         a. The aim is to provide insight into the conflicts that are the cause of the person's problems.
         b. Catharsis is a spilling forth of repressed conflicts and guilt.
      2. Free Association.
         a. Hypnosis allowed clients to focus on repressed conflicts.
         b. Free association: the client is made comfortable and asked to talk about anything that comes to mind.
      3. Resistance: clients may not talk about threatening ideas. These ideas are repressed.
      4. Interpretation: the process of showing the client how revealed ideas illustrate deep seated feelings and conflicts.
      5. Transference: clients respond to the therapist with the attitudes and feelings they have toward other people in their lives.

        a.   Often clients reenact their childhood conflicts.
     6. Dream Analysis.
        a.   Freud believed that dreams were the royal road to the
             unconscious.
             i.   Dreams are determined by unconscious processes as well as
                   the events of the day.
             ii.   Unconscious impulses are expressed in dreams as a form of
                   wish fulfillment.
        b.   Perceived dream content is called the manifest content.
        c.   The hidden or symbolic content is called the latent content.
   C. Modern Psychodynamic Approaches.
     1. The modern approach is:
        a.   Briefer and less intense.
        b.   Focus on revealing unconscious material.
        c.   Client and therapist usually sit face to face rather than having the
             client lie on a couch.
        d.   The therapist is usually directive.
        e.   Usually more focus on the ego and less emphasis on the Id.
             i.   Sometimes referred to as ego analysis.

III. Humanistic-Existential Therapies: Strengthening the Self.
   A. The focus is on quality of the client's subjective, conscious experience.
     1. Focus on the here and now.
   B. Client-Centered Therapy: Removing Roadblocks to Self Actualization.
     1. Client centered therapy is intended to help people get in touch with
         their genuine feelings and pursue their own interests, regardless of
         other peo ple's wishes.
     2. Clients are free to make choices and control our destinies.
     3. Psychological problems arise from roadblocks placed in the path of
         self-actualization.
     4. Client centered therapy is non-directive and focuses on helping the
         person feel whole. To achieve this the therapist has the following
         qualities:
        a.   Unconditional positive regard.
        b.   Empathetic understanding.
        c.   Genuiness.
   C. Gestalt Therapy: Getting It Together.
     1. Gestalt therapy was originated by Fritz Perls.
     2. The approach assumes that people disown parts of themselves and don
         social masks.
     3. The goal is to integrate conflicting parts of their personality.
     4. Gestalt therapy is highly directive.
     5. Gestalt exercises include:
        a.   The dialogue.
        b.   I take responsibility.
        c.   Playing the projection.

IV. Behavior Therapy: Adjustment Is What You Do.

A. Behavior therapy (behavior modification) focus is on what people do.
   1. &n bsp; Applies the principles of learning to directly promote desired behavioral change.
      a. The principles of conditioning and observational learning.
B. Fear-Reduction Methods.
   1. Systematic desensitization is a method for reducing phobic responses.
      a. The client learns to handle increasingly disturbing stimuli while anxiety is being counterconditioned.
         i. Counterconditioning: a response that is incompatible with anxiety is made to appear under conditions that usually elicit anxiety.
   2. And What If a (Virtual) Spider Sat Down Besides Her?
      a. Clients perceive themselves to be in the fearful setting although they are safe.
   3. Modeling relies on observational learning. Clients model individuals dealing with the feared object.
C. Aversive Conditioning.
   1. Controversial procedure in which painful or aversive stimuli are paired with unwanted impulses.
      a. The effectiveness of this approach is uncertain.
D. Operant Conditioning Procedures.
   1. We tend to repeat behavior that is reinforced.
   2. Behavior that is not reinforced tends to become extinguished.
   3. The Token Economy.
      a. Patients must use tokens to purchase things they like.
      b. Tokens are reinforcements for productive activities.
   4. Successive Approximations.
      a. Successive approximations is often used to help clients build good habits.
   5. Social Skills Training.
      a. Employ self monitoring, coaching, modeling, role playing, behavioral rehearsal and feedback.
   6. Biofeedback Training.
      a. Help clients become more aware of, and gain control over, various bodily functions.
E. Self Control Methods.
   1. Functional Analysis of Behavior.
      a. Functional analysis of problem behaviors which helps determine stimuli that trigger behaviors and reinforcers that maintain them.
      b. Clients are taught to manipulate the antecedents and consequences of their behavior.

V. Cognitive Therapies: Adjustment Is What You Think (and Do).

A. Cognitive therapy focuses on changing the beliefs, attitudes and automatic types of thinking that create and compound their client's problems.
   1. Heighten insight into current cognitions.
   2. Appraisals of unfortunate events can heighten our discomfort and impair our coping ability.
B. Cognitive Therapy: Correcting Cognitive Errors.
   1. Cognitive Triad:
      a. Expect the worst of themselves.
      b. Expect the worst of the world at large.
      c. Expect the worst of the future.
   2. Therapists need to challenge beliefs that are not supported by evidence.
      a. Clients need to become personal scientists and challenge beliefs that are not supported by evidence.
      b. Cognitive errors contribute to client's miseries by:
         i. Clients selectively perceive.
         ii. Clients overgeneralize.
         iii. Clients magnify.
         iv. Clients engage in absolutist thinking.
C. Rational Emotive Behavior Therapy: Overcoming "Musts" and "Shoulds".
   1. Rational emotive therapy focuses on beliefs about events as well as the events.
      a. Many harbor irrational beliefs.
         i. The irrational belief that we must have the love and approval of people who are important to us.
         ii. The irrational belief that we must prove ourselves to be thoroughly competent, adequate, and achieving.
      b. The methods are directive and active.
         i. Ellis suggested that we need less misery, less blaming and more action.

VI. Group Therapies.
   A. Advantages to group therapies:
      1. It is economical.
      2. Provides more information and life experience for clients to draw on.
      3. Appropriate behavior receives group support.
      4. Affiliating with people with similar problems is reassuring.
      5. Group members provide hope for other members.
      6. Many clients practice social skills in a relatively non-threatening atmosphere.
   B. Encounter Groups.
      1. Encounter groups are intended to promote personal growth not treat serious psychological disorders.
         a. The goal is sought through intense confrontations (encounters).
   C. Couple Therapy.

1. Intended to enhance their relationships by improving their communication skills and helping them manage conflict.
   a. Corrects power imbalances.
D. Family Therapy.
   1. Family therapy is a form of group therapy.
      a. Family interaction is studied and modified to enhance the growth of individual family members and the family unit as a whole.
E. CONTROVERSY IN PSYCHOLOGY: Does psychotherapy work?
   1. ; In 1952 Hans Eysenck published a review of psychotherapy research and determined that the rate of improvement among people in psychotherapy was no greater than the rate of spontaneous remission.
   2. Meta-analysis (statistical averaging) is now used and shows that psychotherapy is effective.
F. Problems in Conducting Research on Psychotherapy.
   1. Problems in Running Experiments on Psychotherapy.
      a. The ideal method for evaluating treatment is the experiment.
         i. Experiments in therapy are difficult to arrange and control.
         ii. Is it ethical to leave clients in the control condition?
         iii. Difficult to have blind and double blind studies.
   2. Problems in Measuring Outcomes of Therapy.
      a. Cannot directly measure some qualities (self actualization, insight, etc.)
   3. Are Clinical Judgments Valid?
      a. Many clinicians believe that important clinical questions cannot be answered through research.
      b. Therapists have a stake in believing their clients benefit from treatment.
         i. They are not unbiased judges.
   4. Does Therapy Help Because of the Method or Because of "Nonspecific Factors"?
      a. Nonspecific factors are other factors besides therapy that may contribute to recovery. They may include:
         i. The client's relationsh ip with the therapist.
         ii. Clients present themselves in a positive light.
   5. What is the Experimental Treatment in Psychotherapy Outcome Studies?
      a. It is difficult to specify just what is happening in the therapeutic session.
G. Analysis of the Effectiveness of Therapy.
   1. Smith and Glass found that:
      a. Psychodynamic and client-centered are most effective with well educated, verbal, strongly motivated clients.
      b. Gestalt therapy wasn't as effective.
   2. Shadish found that:
      a. Psychotherapy is generally effective.
      b. The more therapy the better.

     c.   Therapy is more effective when the outcome measures reflect the treatment.
    3.   It is not enough to ask which type of therapy is most effective. We must ask which type is most effective for a particular problem and a particular patient.

VII.   Biological Therapies.

    A.   Biological therapies apply what is known of people's biological structures and processes to the amelioration of psychological disorders.

    B.   Drug Therapy: In search of the Magic Pill?

        1.   Antianxiety drugs.

            a.   Valium is usuall y prescribed for patients who complain of generalized anxiety or panic attacks.

            b.   Depresses activity of the central nervous system.

                i.   This, in turn, decreases sympathetic activity and the feeling of nervousness and tension.

            c.   Side effects.

                i.   Sedation is the most common side effect.

                ii.   When use is stopped, clients may experience anxiety rebound.

                iii.   Can induce physical dependence.

        2.   Antipsychotic Drugs.

            a.   Antipsychotic drugs reduce agitation, delusions, and hallucinations.

                i.   Clozaril acts by blocking dopamine receptors in the brain.

        3.   Antidepressants.

            a.   Antidepressants are used to help clients with eating disorders, panic attacks, obsessive-compulsive disorders and social phobia.

            b.   May stem from problems in the regulation of noradrenaline and serotonin.

                i.   Antidepressants work by increasing levels of neurotransmitters.

            c.   Monoamine oxidase (MAO) inhibitors block the activity of an enzyme that breaks down noradrenaline and serotonin.

            d.   Tricyclic antidepressants prevent the reuptake of noradrenaline and serotonin.

            e.   Serotonin-reuptake inhibitors (Prozac) block the reuptake of serotonin.

            f.   Usually takes weeks to build up to therapeutic levels.

        4.   Lithium.

            a.   Lithium is used to flatten out cycles of manic behavior and depression.

            b.   Affects the functioning of neurotransmitters, including glutamate.

            c.   Side effects include:

                i.   Hand tremors.

                ii.   Memory impairment.

                iii.   Excessive thirst.

iv. Urination.
C. Electroconvulsive Therapy.
  1. Used mainly for people with major depression who do not respond to antidepressants.
  2. Electrodes are attached to the temples and an electrical current strong enough to produce a convulsion is induced.
D. CONTROVERSY IN PSYCHOLOGY: Should health professionals use electroconvulsive therapy?
  1. Side effects of ECT include:
    a. Memory problems.
      i. Though the effects may be temporary.
E. Psychosurgery.
  1. Prefrontal lobotomy: a picklike instrument severs the nerve pathways that link the prefrontal lobes of the brain to the thalamus.
    a. Egas Moniz b rought the procedure to the U.S. in the 1930s.
    b. Side effects:
      i. Hyperactivity.
      ii. Distractibility.
      iii. Impaired learning ability.
      iv. Overeating.
      v. Apathy.
      vi. Withdrawal.
      vii. Epileptic-type seizures.
      viii. Reduced creativity.
      ix. Death.
    c. This method has been largely discontinued in the U.S.
F. Does Biological Therapy Work?
  1. Drug therapy has helped many people with severe psychological disorders.
  2. The combination of cognitive therapy and antidepressants is superior to either treatment alone with chronically depressed people.
    a. No chemical can show a person how to change an idea or solve an interpersonal problem.

VIII. LIFE CONNECTIONS: Alleviating Depression (Getting Out Of The Dumps).
A. To reverse the characteristics of depression try:
  1. Engaging in pleasant events.
  2. Thinking rationally.
  3. Exercising.
  4. Asserting yourself.
  5. Talk to your instructor.
  6. Visit the college counseling center.
B. Engaging in Pleasant Events.
  1. There is a relationship between our moods and what we do.
  2. One may be able to use pleasant events to lift mood purposefully.

C. Rational Thinking.
  1. People tend to:
     a. Internalize blame.
     b. See problems as stable and global.
     c. Catastrophize problems.
     d. Minimize accomplishment.
D. Exercising.
  1. Exercise is the opposite of inactivity that is often seen in depression.
E. Engaging in Assertive Behavior.
  1. Nonassertive behavior patterns are linked to feelings of depression.
  2. Learning to express feelings and relate to others has been shown to alleviate feelings of depression.
  3. Assertive behaviors incl ude:
     a. Expression of ones genuine feelings.
     b. Standing up for legitimate rights.
     c. Refusing unreasonable requests.

IX. A CLOSER LOOK: Diversity: Ethnicity, Gender, and Psychotherapy.
  A. People from ethnic minorities are less likely than European Americans to seek therapy. The reasons why include:
     1. Unawareness that therapy would help.
     2. Lack of information about the availability of services.
     3. Distrust of professionals.
     4. Language barriers.
     5. Reluctance to open up about personal matters.
     6. Cultural inclinations toward other approaches.
     7. Negative experiences with professional authority figures.
  B. Psychotherapy and Ethnic Minority Groups.
     1. Clinicians need to be sensitive to culture.
        a. They need to develop multicultural competence.
           i. African Americans may need help to cope with the effects of prejudice and discrimination. African Americans often assume that people should manage their own problems and are suspicious of therapists.
           ii. Asian Americans tend to stigmatize people with psychological disorders. The Asian tradition is to practice restra int in public and prefer to receive concrete advice.
           iii. Latino and Latin Americans value the interdependency in the family. Therapists need to use methods that are consistent with the client's values.
           iv. Native Americans feel a loss of cultural identity and social disorganization. Therapy should focus on strengthening cultural identity, pride and cohesion.
  C. Feminist Psychotherapy.
     1. Feminism challenges the validity of stereotypical gender roles and traditional male dominance.

2. Psychological problems develop as a result of women being treated as second class citizens.

Chapter Fourteen Outline

I. **Social Psychology: Individuals Among Others.**
   A. The ways in which the environment influences behavior and mental processes.
      1. Social psychology studies the nature and causes of behavior and mental processes in social situations.
   B. Topics covered in social psychology include: attitudes, conformity, persuasion, social perception, interpersonal attraction, social influence, group conformity, and obedience.

II. **Attitudes-"The Good, the Bad, and the Ugly".**
   A. Attitudes are comprised of:
      1. Cognitive evaluations.
      2. Feelings.
      3. Behavioral tendencies.
      4. Attitudes are behavioral and cognitive tendencies that are expressed by evaluating particular people, places, or things with favor or disfavor.
      5. Attitudes are learned, and they affect behavior.
         a. Attitudes can change, but not easily.
   B. The A-B Problem: Do We Do As We Think?
      1. The definition of attitude implies that our behavior is consistent with our cognitions.
         a. The links between attitudes (A) and behaviors (B) tend to be weak to moderate.
      2. A number of factors influenc e the likelihood what we can predict behavior from attitudes:
         a. Specificity: We can better predict specific behavior from specific attitudes than from global attitudes.
         b. Strength of attitudes.
         c. Vested interest.
         d. Accessibility: brought easily to mind.
            i. Attitudes with a strong emotional impact are more accessible.
   C. Origins of Attitudes.
      1. Attitudes are learned or derived from cognitive processes.
      2. Conditioning may play a role in acquiring attitudes.
      3. Attitudes can be acquired by observing others.
      4. Cognitive Appraisal.
         a. People evaluate information and form or change attitudes, including stereotypes, on the basis of new information.
         b. Initial attitudes act as cognitive anchors.
         c. We judge new ideas in terms of how much they deviate from out existing attitudes.
            i. Accepting larger deviations requires more information processing.

D. Changing Attitudes Through Persuasion.
 1. The elaboration likelihood model describes the ways in which people respond to persuasive messages.
    a. The first (central) r oute inspires thoughtful considerations of arguments and evidence.
    b. The second (peripheral) route associates objects with positive or negative cues.
    c. The three peripheral factors are:
       i. The messenger.
       ii. The context of the message.
       iii. The audience.
 2. The Persuasive Message: Say What? Say How? Say How Often?
    a. Research suggests that familiarity breeds content, not contempt.
       i. The more complex the stimuli, the more likely it is that frequent exposure will have favorable effects.
    b. Forewarning creates a kind of psychological immunity.
    c. Product claims that admit their product's weak points in addition to highlighting its strength are most believable.
    d. Fear appeal seems to work.
       i. Fear appeals are most effective when the audience believes that the risks are serious and the audience members can change their behavior to avert the risks.
       ii. Audiences also tend to believe arguments that appear to run counter to the vested interests of the communicator.
 3. The Persuasive Communicator: Whom Do You Trust?
    a. Persuasive communicators are characterized by expertise, trustworthiness, attractiveness, or similarity to their audience.
    b. Selective avoidance and selec tive exposure.
       i. People tend to seek communicators whose outlook coincides with their own.
 4. The Context of the Message: "Get "Em in a Good Mood".
    a. When we are in a good mood, we apparently are less likely to evaluate the situation carefully.
    b. Agreement and praise are more effective ways to encourage others to embrace your views.
 5. The Persuaded Audience.
    a. People with high self-esteem and low social anxiety are more likely to resist social pressure.
 6. The Foot-in-the-Door Technique.
    a. Research suggests that people who accede to small requests become more amenable to larger ones for a variety of reasons including:
       i. Conformity.
       ii. Self-perception as the kind of people who help in this way.

III. Social Perception: Looking Out, Looking Within.

A. Factors that contribute to social perception include:
   1. Primacy and recency effects.
   2. Attribution theory.
   3. Body language.
B. Primacy and Recency Effects: The Importance of First Impressions.
   1. First impressions are important.

      a. First impressions are examples of the primacy effect.

      b. People tend to infer traits from behaviors.
      c. Fading memories allowed more recent information to take precedence (recency effect).
C. Attribution Theory: You're Free, but I'm Caught in the Middle?
   1. An attribution is an assumption about why people do things.
   2. The process by which we make inferences about the motives and traits of others through observation of their behavior is the attribution process.
   3. Dispositional and Situational Attributions.
      a. Dispositional attributions ascribe a person's behavior to internal factors such as personality traits and free will.
      b. Situational attributions attribute a person's actions to external factors such as social influence or socialization.
   4. The Fundamental Attribution Error.
      a. In cultures that view the self as independent, people tend to attribute other people's behavior primarily to internal factors such as personality traits, attitudes, and free will.
         i. This bias in the attribution process is known as the fundamental attribution error.
         ii. People tend to focus on the behavior of others rather than on the circumstances surrounding their behavior.
   5. The Actor-Observer Effect.
      a. Actor-observer effect: The tendency to attribute other people's behavior to dispositional factors and our own behavior to situational influences.
   6. The Self-serving Bias.
      a. Self-serving bias: people are likely to ascribe their successes to internal, dispositional factors but their failures to external, situational influences.
      b. There are exceptions to the self-serving bias:
         i. When we work in groups we tend to take credit for the group's success but to pin the blame for failure on someone else.
         ii. Depressed people are more likely to ascribe their failures to internal factors, even when external factors are mostly to blame.
         iii. Gender bias: Men are more likely to interpret a woman's smile or friendliness toward a man as flirting.

7. Factors Contributing to the Attribution Process include: consensus, consistency, and distinctiveness.
   a. When consensus is low, we are likely to attribute behavior to dispositional factors.
   b. When consistency is high, behavior is often attributed to dispositional factors.
   c. If a person acts similarly in different situations, distinctiveness is low and we are likely to attribute their behavior to dispositional factors.
D. Body Language: The Body Speaks.
   1. Body language is nonverbal language; it refers to the meanings we infer from the ways in which people carry themselves and the gestures they make.
   2. Touching: Putting the Arm on People (Literally).
      a. Women are more likely than men to touch other people when they are interacting with them.
      b. When touching suggest greater intimacy than is desired, it can be seen as negative.
      c. Touching was considered positive when it was appropriate to the situation and did not appear to be condescending.
         i. It was seen as negative when it was controlling, unnecessary, or overly intimate.
   3. Gazing and Staring: The Eyes Have It.
      a. When other people look us squarely in the eye we may assume that they are being assertive or open with us.
      b. Avoidance of eye contact may suggest deception or depression.
      c. A hard stare is interpreted as a provocation or a sign of anger.

IV. **Interpersonal Attraction: On Liking and Loving.**
   A. Factors that contribute to attraction are physical appearance, similarity, and reciprocity.
   B. Physical Appearance: How Important Is Looking Good?
      1. Many aspects of beauty appear to be cross-cultural.
         a. In one study, men found attractive the following qualities:
            i. Large eyes.
            ii. High cheekbones.
            iii. Narrow jaws.
         b. In a study on what women find attractive the researchers discovered that tallness was an asset.
      2. Preferences for body weight and shape may be more culturally determined.
      3. "Prett y Is as Pretty Does?"
         a. Both men and women are perceived as more attractive when they are smiling.
         b. Women tend to prefer men who are outgoing, self-assertive, and self-confident.

    c.   Men tend to respond negatively to women who show self-assertion and social dominance.

C. The Matching Hypothesis: Do "Opposites Attract" or Do "Birds of a Feather Flock Together"?

    1. The matching hypothesis: people tend to date people who are similar to themselves in physical attractiveness.

        a.   One motive for this seems to be fear of rejection by more attractive people.

    2. Research findings show that:

        a.   Nearly 94% of single European American men have European American women as partners.

        b.   About 82% of African American men have African American women as partners.

        c.   About 83% of the women and men in the study chose partners within five years of their own age and of the same or a similar religion.

D. Reciprocity: If You Like Me, You Must Have Excellent Judgment.

    1. Reciprocity is a powerful determinant of attraction.

        a.   We tend to return feelings of admiration.

        b.   We tend to be more open, warm and helpful when we are interacting with strangers who seem to like us.

E. Love: Doing What Comes…Culturally?

    1. The Love Triangle.

        a.   Triangular model of love proposed by Sterberg includes three components: intimacy, passion, and commitment.

           i.   Intimacy refers to a couple's closeness, to their mutual concern and sharing of feelings and resources.

           ii. Passion refers to romance and sexual feelings.

           iii. Commitment means deciding to enhance and maintain the relationship.

           iv. Passion is the most crucial in short-term relationships.

           v.   Intimacy and commitment are more important in enduring relationships.

    2. The ideal form of love combines all three and is called consummate love.

    3. Romantic love is characterized by passion and intimacy.

        a.   Passion involves fascination, sexual craving, and the desire for exclusiveness.

        b.   Intimacy involves caring-championing the interests of the loved one, even if it entails sacrificing one's own.

    4. Men are generally more reluctant than women to make commitments in their romantic relationships.

        a.   The affective shift hypothesis suggests that

           i.   Women tend to experience a greater feeling of love and commitment-a positive affective shift-after first time sex than men do.

  ii. As a group, men are more likely than women to be interested in short-term relationships and multiple sex partners.

  iii. Men with high numbers of sex partners tend to experience a negative affective shift following first-time sex. This motives them to end the relationship.

  iv. Men with fewer sex partners and more of an interest in developing long-term relationships also tend to experience the positive affective shift after first-time sex.

  v.

V. Social Influence: Are You an Individual or One of the Crowd?

 A. Social influence focuses on the ways in which people alter the thoughts, feelings and behaviors of others.

 B. Obedience to Authority: Does Might Make Right?

  1. The Milgram Studies: Shocking Stuff at Yale.

   a. Subjects in the study were designated as the "teacher" and delivered shocks to the "learners" (there really were no shocks).

    i. The study was designed to determine if the teachers would comply with the requests of the scientist.

   b. Results indicate that of the 40 men in the project 65% complied with the scientist throughout the study.

  2. Why Did People in the Milgram Study Obey the Experimenters?

   a. Socialization: people are taught from a young age to obey authority figures.

   b. Lack of social comparison.

   c. Perception of legitimate authority.

   d. The foot-in-the-door technique.

   e. Inaccessibility of values.

   f. Buffers in the experiment.

 C. Conformity: Do Many Make Right?

  1. We are said to conform when we change our behavior in order to adhere to social norms.

   a. Social norms are widely accepted expectations concerning social behavior.

  2. Seven Line Judges Can't Be Wrong: The Asch Study.

   a. One subject and the rest are confederates. Does the subject conform to the group though they are obviously wrong?

   b. 75% agreed with the majority's wrong answer at least once.

  3. Factors That Influence Conformity:

   a. Belonging to a collectivist rather than an individualist society.

   b. The desire to be liked by other members of the group.

   c. Low self-esteem.

   d. Social shyness.

   e. Lack of familiarity with the task.

VI. Group Behavior.

A. Social Facilitation: Monkey See, Monkey Do Faster?
   1. Social facilitation is the effects on performance that result from the presence of others.
      a. The presence of others increases our levels of arousal and motivation.
         i. At high levels of arousal our performance of simple tasks is facilitated.
         ii. Our performance of complex responses may be impaired.
      b. Evaluation apprehension: Our performance before a group is affected not only by the presence of others but also by concern that they are evaluating us.
      c. Social loafing: impaired performance because of the group.
      d. Diffusion of responsibility: each person may feel less obligated to help because others are present.
B. Group Decision Making: Is a Camel a Horse Made by a Committee?
   1. Social decision schemes are rules that govern much of group decision making. Examples include:
      a. The majority wins scheme.
      b. The truth wins scheme.
      c. The two-thirds majority scheme.
      d. The first-shift rule.
C. Polarization and the "Risky Shift".
   1. Polarization: is the group effect of taking an extreme position.
   2. Groups tend to take greater risks than those their members would take as individuals.
      a. Explanations for this include:
         i. Diffusion of responsibility.
         ii. Self-serving bias.
D. Groupthink.
   1. Groupthink: members tend to be more influenced by group cohesiveness and a dynamic leader than by the realities of the situation.
      a. Groupthink is usually fueled by a dynamic group leader.
      b. Threat heightens the cohesiveness of the group and is a source of stress.
         i. Under stress, group members tend not to consider all their options carefully.
      c. Contributions to groupthink flaws include:
         i. Feelings of invulnerability.
         ii. The group's belief in its rightness.
         iii. Discrediting of information contrary to the group's decision.
         iv. Pressures on group members to conform.
         v. Stereotyping of members of the out-group.
E. Mob Behavior and Deindividuation: The "Beast With Many Heads".
   1. The Lynching of Arthur Stevens.

        a.   Arthur Stevens was an African American who was tortured and murdered by a mob in 1930s.

    2. Deindividuation is a state of reduced self-awareness and lowered concern for social evaluation.

        a.   Many factors lead to deindividuation including:

            i.   Anonymity.

            ii.   Diffusion of responsibility.

            iii.   Arousal due to noise and crowding.

            iv.   Focus on emerging group norms rather than on one's own values.

            v.   Under these conditions crowd members behave more aggressively than they would as individuals.

  F.   Altruism and the Bystander Effect: Some Watch While Others Die.

    1. Altruism is selfless concern for the welfare of others.

    2. Story of Kitty Genovese. (38 by-standers allowed Kitty do die).

    3. The Helper: Who Helps?

        a.   Many factors contribute to helping behavior:

            i.   Observers are more likely to help when they are in a good mood.

            ii.   People who are empathic are more likely to help people in need.

            iii.   Bystanders may not help unless they believe that an emergency exists.

            iv.   Observers must assume the responsibility to act.

            v.   Observers must know what to do.

            vi.   Observers are more likely to help people they know.

            vii. Observers are more likely to help people who are similar to themselves.

    4. The Victim: Who Is Helped?

        a.   Traditional gender roles persist strongly in the South.

        b.   Attractive and unaccompanied women are most likely to be helped by men.

VII.   LIFE CONNECTIONS: ; Understanding and Combating Prejudice.

  A. Prejudice is an attitude toward a group that leads people to evaluate members of that group negatively-even though they have never met them.

    1. Cognitively, prejudice is linked to expectations that members of the target group will behave poorly.

    2. Emotionally, prejudice is associated with negative feelings such as fear, dislike, or hatred.

    3. Behaviorally, prejudice is connected with avoidance, aggression and discrimination.

    4. Discrimination: negative behavior that results from prejudice.

  B. Stereotypes: are prejudices about certain groups that lead people to view members of those groups in a biased fashion.

    1. Some stereotypes are positive rather than negative.

        a.   Attractiveness is positively correlated with popularity, social skills, and sexual experience.

        b.   Attractive people are more likely to be judged innocent of crimes in mock jury experiments.

            i.   When they are found guilty they are given less severe sentences.

C. Sources of Prejudice include:

    1. Dissimilarity.

    2. Social conflict.

    3. Social learning.

    4. Information processing.

    5. Social categorization.

D. Combati ng Prejudice.

    1. Encourage intergroup contact and cooperation.

    2. Present examples of admired individuals within groups that are often stigmatized.

    3. Attack discriminatory behavior.

    4. Hold discussion forums.

    5. Examine your own beliefs.

To view the Study Plan:

1. Under Step 2...Study Plan, click **Personalized Study Plan** or click one of the topics listed under Pre-Test results.

To view a list of all sections and their associated assets:

1. Under Step 2...Study Plan, click **All Chapter Content**.

Step 3—Taking the Post-Test

The Post-Test is an evaluation of what you have learned since working through the Study Plan. You can take the Post-Test as many times as you want.

To take the Post-Test:

1. Under Step 3...Post-Test, click **Take a Post-Test** or click the **Post-Test** button in the center of the page.
2. To close the test before finishing it, click **Save & Exit**.
3. To end the test, click **Show Results**.
4. Use the **Back** and **Next** buttons, or select a specific question from the drop-down menu to view feedback for each question.

Note: To return to your Post-Test results from another page, under Step 3...Post-Test, click **View Results**.

Step 4—Working Through the Revised Study Plan

After you finish the Post-Test, your Revised Study Plan is ready to view. You can work through the Revised Study Plan in the same way as the original Study Plan. The Revised Study Plan is updated each time that you take the Post-Test.

To view the Revised Study Plan:

1. Under Step 3...Post-Test, click **Revised Study Plan** or click one of the topics listed under Post-Test Results.

Enrolling in an Instructor's Course

If your instructor sets up a *Study course, your instructor can enroll you in the course or send you a course access code so that you can self-enroll.

To self-enroll using a course access code:

1. After you log in, click **Enter Course Access Code** in the left menu. The Course Access Code Entry page opens.
2. Type the course access code in the **Access Code** field, and then click **Submit**. You will receive a message indicating that you have been successfully enrolled.
3. Click **DONE** to access the syllabus for your course.

Taking an Assignment

Note: You must be enrolled in an instructor's course before you can take an assignment.

To take an assignment:

1. After you log in, click **My Assignments** in the left menu.
2. To take an assignment, click the **Take** button for that assignment.
3. Read the instructions on the screen, and then click **START**.
4. When you have completed the assignment, click **END ASSIGNMENT**.

Thomson Wadsworth *Study Products Student Quick Start Guide

Registering and Logging In

Your First Visit to a *Study Product

1. Go to the Web site specified on the access code card.
2. Click the **REGISTER** button. The Find Your School page opens.
3. Click your state in the School Location list, type the name of your school in the School Name box, and then click **Search**. In the list of schools that appears on the right, click the name of your school. The First Time User Registration page opens.
4. Type the access code from the access code card, type your e-mail address, re-type your e-mail address, and then click **Submit**.
5. Create a new password, re-type your password, and then click **Submit**.
6. Fill out the registration form, and then click **Register and Enter iLrn**.

Second and Later Visits

1. Go to the Web site specified on the access code card.
2. Click the **LOGIN** button.
3. Type your login ID (the e-mail address you entered when you registered) and password, and then click **LOGIN**.

Accessing Chapter Content

After you log in, the Table of Contents for your text opens.

Note: If the iLrn logo is displayed instead of the Table of Contents, click **Courseware** in the left menu, and then click the cover of your textbook to display its Table of Contents.

To access chapter content:

1. Click the name of the chapter or select the chapter from the Select a Chapter... drop-down menu.

Step 1—Taking the Pre-Test

You must take the Pre-Test before you can see your Study Plan. The results of the Pre-Test determine your Study Plan.

To take the Pre-Test:

1. Under Step 1...Pre-Test, click **Take a Pre-Test** or click the **Pre-Test** button in the center of the page.
2. To close the test before finishing it, click **Save & Exit**.
3. To end the test, click **Show Results**. The Pre-Test results are displayed.
4. Use the **Back** and **Next** buttons, or select a specific question from the drop-down menu to view feedback for each question.

Note: To return to your Pre-Test results from another page, under Step 1...Pre-Test, click **View Results**.

Step 2—Working Through the Study Plan

After you finish the Pre-Test, your Study Plan is ready to view. The Study Plan shows which sections in the chapter that you need to study. Links to assets such as Web sites, online videos, and pages in the textbook are listed under each section. Check marks show which items you have viewed.